THE OXFORD COMPANION TO
SCOTTISH HISTORY

THE OXFORD
COMPANION TO
SCOTTISH
HISTORY

EDITED BY
MICHAEL LYNCH

OXFORD
UNIVERSITY PRESS

OXFORD

UNIVERSITY PRESS

Great Clarendon Street, Oxford OX2 6DP

Oxford University Press is a department of the University of Oxford.
It furthers the University's objective of excellence in research, scholarship,
and education by publishing worldwide in
Oxford   New York

Athens Auckland Bangkok Bogotá Buenos Aires Calcutta
Cape Town Chennai Dar es Salaam Delhi Florence Hong Kong Istanbul
Karachi Kuala Lumpur Madrid Melbourne Mexico City Mumbai
Nairobi Paris São Paulo Singapore Taipei Tokyo Toronto Warsaw
with associated companies in Berlin Ibadan
Oxford is a registered trade mark of Oxford University Press
in the UK and in certain other countries

Published in the United States
by Oxford University Press Inc., New York

Oxford University Press 2001
Database right Oxford University Press (maker)
First published 2001

British Library Cataloguing in Publication Data
Data available

Library of Congress Cataloging in Publication Data
Data available

ISBN 0–19–211696–7

1 3 5 7 9 10 8 6 4 2

Typeset in Dante MT
by Alliance Phototypesetters, Pondicherry, India
Printed in Great Britain by
Biddles Ltd,
Guildford and King's Lynn

Contents

Preface

THE *Companion to Scottish History* was first mooted some seven years ago. It seemed an obvious gap to fill, a highly desirable volume to put in the hands of the large, potential audience interested in all aspects of Scottish history but also a huge challenge. Although I had recently written a sizeable one-volume history of Scotland, I quickly came to the conclusion that the proposed *Companion* represented a different kind of opportunity. The aim of presenting a coherent and reasonably complete view of Scotland's history, in all its aspects, within a single volume had become more possible with the remarkable advance of knowledge over the course of the past generation but also more forbidding in terms of what it should cover. History as a discipline—what it covers as well as the various prisms through which it views the past—has moved on at an ever-accelerating pace. Wide-ranging and searching discussions were held over the course of almost two years to establish both an agenda of what the volume should encompass and a strategy of how to tackle the agreed content. They involved a dozen people, representing three generations of Scottish historians; they ranged chronologically from the early medieval period to the 20th century and in interests from 'mainstream' history to art, archaeology, ethnology, Gaelic culture and language, Highland history, and business history. Out of this group came eight section editors, who drew up detailed plans, based on seventeen sections, which are described in the Note to the Reader and are also reflected in the Guide to Further Reading.

The fact that these discussions took place in the mid-1990s, at a point in Scotland's history where the political future remained uncertain yet when there was also emerging what was recognized, both inside and furth of Scotland, as a cultural renaissance— described by some as a second Scottish Enlightenment—inevitably made its mark on the shape of the *Companion*. The shape and approach of similar Companions, on both British and Irish history, had an influence, but not a decisive one. A Scottish Companion, it was felt, should reflect a distinctively Scottish agenda and try to meet Scottish needs. This was, however, not a 'little Scotlander' agenda: Scotland's relations with its immediate neighbours, from Scandinavia in the north, to Ireland in the west, as well as England, France, and the Low Countries, featured prominently in the planning of the volume.

It is a common feature of those who happen to live in the midst of complex change to hold the view that they are living at a unique moment in their country's history. The *Companion* does not necessarily dispute that view. But its editors were also aware of the dangers of short-termism and conscious of the fact that only selected portions of Scottish history—usually drawn from the 18th and 19th centuries—were still being taught in the nation's schools. These were some of the reasons why it was agreed that it would be highly desirable for the volume to draw together the important forces, factors, and themes which had shaped Scotland over the course of many centuries—such as climate, famine and disease, geology and topography, living conditions, and settlement, as well as the more conventional themes such as kingly power, nobility, government, and politics. With housing, for example, the Highland black house, the urban single-end tenement, and the modern tower block feature alongside the palace and tower house.

With many of these themes, it was impossible to find one individual to write about them with any authority over a long span of time. The answer to this dilemma, which proved to be a fundamental device in the planning of the *Companion*, was the 'chain' entry—a piece on a particular theme or topic written by anything up to half a dozen authors. Not surprisingly, one of the first themes to be agreed upon was national identity, a recurrent interest of commentators throughout the 1990s. Other examples of chain entries are the economy, kingship, historians, and religious life, where successive authors tackle different periods in turn. In the case of culture, a team of authors drawn from different disciplines, including art, architecture, literature, music, and philosophy, consider different periods of Scotland's complex but complementary cultural history. With the four chains involving rural and urban society and rural and urban settlement, it was planned that different kinds of historians looked at different aspects of rural or urban life in complementary ways.

The *Companion*, as a result, tries to cover a very wide range of what might be understood as representing Scotland's history. An early and calculated decision was taken not to follow the example of some similar reference works, both on history and other subjects, which tried to guarantee that a volume would emerge by keeping to a relatively small team of authors. Every author approached was an expert in the field that he or she was asked to write about. Authors were not asked to extend themselves into unfamiliar territory for the greater good of the *Companion*. One inevitable consequence of this decision was more work for the section editors, in keeping in touch with so many authors. But there is a more important result. With over 180 authors, drawn from a variety of disciplines, the *Companion* has deliberately tried to reach those parts of the Scottish past which no single-authored volume could aspire to, however wide-ranging the interests of its author. The size of this assembly of historians, three times as many in number as in any other similar work previously attempted in Scottish history, represents an unrivalled pool of expertise. In no other single place, it might well be claimed, have so many written so much about Scotland's past.

What did that past consist of? There are a series of possible answers in this volume to that question—some obvious and some less so. Much of Scotland's history has been conditioned by its landscape and archaeologists and historical geographers are prominent amongst the contributors. Equally, a great deal of Scottish history has had to do with the impact and absorption of various foreign influences, ranging from Scoto-Irish and Scandinavian settlers and raiders before 1000, or Anglo-Norman and Flemish immigrants in the 12th and 13th centuries onwards: experts in architecture, the languages of Scotland, place names, and rural and urban settlement offer different perspectives on these themes. Scots have been immigrants, migrants, and emigrants for centuries. Almost a tenth of the volume is taken up with these themes, including the outflow of Scots to different parts of the globe, from Russia to South America and South Africa as well as the more familiar story of the Scottish diaspora in Australia, Canada, or New Zealand. Particular attention, it was agreed, should also be given to one of the least well-known centuries in Scotland's history—the 20th.

The *Companion* has not aspired to be a historical dictionary or to achieve a complete comprehensiveness in terms of individuals it covers. There are enough 'Great Scotsmen' volumes already. Even so, many prominent historical figures who do not have their own entry will be found, via the Index, in other entries. Both James I and Sir Walter Scott, for example, appear in more than twenty entries and Marie of Guise features in ten. The *Companion*, however, has sought to place the emphasis on the people of Scotland, as distinct from dictionary-style entries on personalities or institutions. It considers the people in the pews as well as clerics or religious denominations. It tries to explain the forces and factors which affected people's lives, including climate, housing, living standards, and famine and disease. Even so, the important topics and the great issues are all to be found, including the Wars of Independence, the Reformation, the Wars of the Covenant, the Union of 1707, Jacobitism, the Clearances of the Highlands and Islands, and Labour, Unionist, and nationalist politics in the 20th century.

The *Companion*, it was agreed, should aim to be authoritative but approachable, and at times to try to surprise as well as to inform. The origin of the phrase 'steamin' drunk' will be found within its pages, as will the discovery that it was recognized in the Highlands fully three centuries ago that nursing mothers should abstain from alcohol. Scottish history is never far away from human tragedies, but some are less well known than they should be. One such episode is the crisis of the 1690s, when something like 13 per cent of the Scottish population died of famine, with terrible consequences for fertility which lasted for a generation or more. Another is the estimate that perhaps one in five Scottish males went abroad to find work as mercenaries in foreign armies in both the early 17th and the 18th centuries.

History is a broader church than it used to be. A twofold challenge faced by the editors was to reveal how historical interpretations have fluctuated over time and to highlight how much historians' minds have changed as to what they thought important to consider. No attempt was made by the editors to suggest a party line or to conflate the different opinions of authors in chain entries into any agreed stance on what are often controversial issues. Authorship of the chain on national identity, for example, was deliberately chosen so as to highlight conflicting opinions. Historians have a reputation of being something of the awkward squad, and Scottish historians are no different. They are amongst the opinionated of commentators. Readers, it is hoped, will enjoy their opinions and differences of opinion and feel free, as a result, to make up their own minds.

The very fact that opinion about the past is continually changing is testimony to its importance. In few decades has this been more so than in the 1990s. This volume is fortunate to appear at a time when, with a new Scottish parliament having recently come into being, it is widely recognized that history has obviously affected the course of the future. Yet some of the historical understanding which underpinned political developments in recent times may well turn out to be myth. Forecasts of the death of Unionism now appear to have been premature and it has its own entry, alongside Labourism and nationalism. With due caution, the *Companion* chose to cover amongst its entries both Robert Bruce (Robert I) and William Wallace, as well as the Stone of Scone—not least because each of them has figured prominently in the politics of the 1990s and a political mythology of the past. Yet, as the entries make clear, rival cults of Bruce and Wallace have vied with each other for centuries. The dialogue between past and present, in this debate as in many others, will go on. It is hoped that the *Companion*, a reflection of the thoughts of a very wide range of Scotland's historical community, will be one of the first and most obvious places to go to in order to discover more about its history.

MICHAEL LYNCH

Acknowledgements

I N a work as large and wide-ranging as this, there are bound to be many debts of gratitude. At an early stage in its planning, John MacCaffrey, Donald Meek, and Tony Slaven contributed an immense amount, both in terms of their time, generously given, and their expertise. Equally, I owe a great deal to the sustained efforts of the eight Section Editors, who have been unstinting in the help, in planning and execution, which they have given. At a crucial, late stage, I owe much to Ian Campbell for his advice and encouragement. The shape of the volume and its organization was the result of many hours of debate and negotiation. It is genuinely a collective enterprise.

The contributors are the most important asset in such a volume. There are many. Each deserves thanks, not only for having agreed to have taken part in the *Companion* but also for fitting readily into its plans and format and for helping with the compilation of the Guide to Further Reading. It is hoped that they will be pleased with the overall results of their collective efforts.

It is only fitting that a large part of my thanks should go to the staff of the Reference Division of Oxford University Press. First, I wish to extend my heartfelt thanks to Michael Cox, whose idea this volume first was. I owe a very considerable debt of gratitude to Pam Coote, Wendy Tuckey, Alison Jones, Joanna Harris, Rowena Anketell, and Peter Gibbs for having seen this volume through to publication and, perhaps even more, for their patience. Not least, I owe to all of them an apology for its tardiness as well as thanks for their having kept faith in it.

Such a project needs organizers. I have been particularly fortunate in having been able to rely on John Brady and Doris Williamson, who over a considerable period of time were the mainspring of the editorial team and kept me in touch with what I should be doing. Without them, there would be no *Companion*. My last and greatest set of thanks go to them.

MICHAEL LYNCH

Edinburgh
January 2001

List of Editors and Contributors

GENERAL EDITOR

MICHAEL LYNCH, Professor of Scottish History, University of Edinburgh, is an authority on the early modern period.

SECTION EDITORS

DAUVIT BROUN, Lecturer in Scottish History, University of Glasgow, is an authority on the pre-1200 period.

EWEN CAMERON, Senior Lecturer in Scottish History, University of Edinburgh, is an authority on the Highlands, particularly in the modern period.

RICHARD FINLAY, Senior Lecturer in History, University of Strathclyde, is an authority on the modern period.

JOAN MACDONALD, a graduate of the Department of Celtic, University of Edinburgh, is an authority on Gaelic.

NORMAN MACDOUGALL, Senior Lecturer in Scottish History, University of St Andrews, is an authority on the medieval period.

MARGARET MACKAY, Director of the School of Scottish Studies, University of Edinburgh, is an authority on ethnology and the Scots abroad.

DUNCAN MACMILLAN, Professor of Fine Art, University of Edinburgh, is an authority on art and cultural history.

GEOFFREY STELL, Royal Commission on Ancient and Historic Monuments of Scotland, is an authority on material culture and vernacular building.

CONTRIBUTORS

RJA   Robert Ackroyd, a graduate of the Department of Scottish History, University of Edinburgh

DA   David W. Allan, Lecturer in Scottish History, University of St Andrews

MA   Michael Anderson, Professor of Economic History, University of Edinburgh

RDA   Robert D. Anderson, Professor of Modern History, University of Edinburgh

CNA   Neil Ascherson, journalist and commentator on Scottish affairs

BA   Bernard Aspinwall, Research Fellow, University of Strathclyde

CB   Crispin Bates, Senior Lecturer in Commonwealth History, University of Edinburgh

JRB   Jamie Reid Baxter, historian and promoter of performances and recordings of Scottish music

DWB   David W. Bebbington, Professor of History, University of Stirling

MB   Mary Beith, freelance writer and researcher specializing in Highland and Gaelic traditional medicines, everyday life, and culture

MBe   Margaret Bennett, freelance writer and researcher, Edinburgh

PB   Peter Bilsborough, Acting Director of Sport, University of Stirling

SB   Steve Boardman, Lecturer in Scottish History, University of Edinburgh

KRB   Kenneth Bogle, a graduate of the Department of History, University of Edinburgh

JMB   Joseph M. Bradley, Lecturer in Sports Studies, University of Stirling

AB   Alexander Broadie, Professor of Philosophy, University of Glasgow

JB   Jeanette M. Brock, Lecturer in History, University of Strathclyde

TB   Tom Brooking, Associate Professor of History, University of Otago, New Zealand.

TBr   Terry Brotherstone, Senior Lecturer in History, University of Aberdeen

DB   Dauvit Broun, Lecturer in Scottish History, University of Glasgow

IGB   Ian G. Brown, Principal Curator of Manuscripts, National Library of Scotland, Edinburgh

MBr   Michael Brown, Lecturer in History, University of St Andrews

SJB   Stewart J. Brown, Professor of Ecclesiastical History, University of Edinburgh

YB   Yvonne Brown, Ph.D. student, Glasgow Caledonian University

DBr   David Bruce, photo-historian, Helensburgh

CBur   Charles Burnett, Ross Herald of Arms and Curator of Duff House

JAB   John A. Burnett, Arkleton Centre for Rural Development Research, University of Aberdeen

JBur   John Burnett, Curator of Health and Recreation, Department of Social and Technological History, National Museums of Scotland

JBut   John Butt, Professor Emeritus of History, University of Strathclyde

ACa   Alan Cameron, Archivist, Bank of Scotland

EAC   Ewen Cameron, Senior Lecturer in Scottish History, University of Edinburgh

EC   Ewan N. Campbell, Lecturer in Archaeology, University of Glasgow

IC   Ian Campbell, Professor of English Literature, University of Edinburgh

KC   Kerry Cardell, retired Lecturer in the School of Literary and Communication Studies, Deakin University, Geelong, Victoria, Australia, currently undertaking freelance research and writing

MC   Martin Carver, Professor of Archaeology, University of York

HC   Hugh Cheape, Curator of Scottish Modern History and Applied Arts, National Museums of Scotland

AC   A. C. Cheyne, Professor Emeritus of Ecclesiastical History, University of Edinburgh

TC   Thomas Clancy, Lecturer in Celtic, University of Glasgow

JRC   James R. Coull, Professor of Geography, University of Aberdeen

RCC   Cairns Craig, Professor of Scottish Literature, University of Edinburgh

BEC   Barbara Crawford, Senior Lecturer in Medieval History, University of St Andrews

CC   Cliff Cumming, Research Fellow, Faculty of Arts, Deakin University, Geelong, Victoria, Australia

GRD   George Dalgleish, Curator of Scottish Decorative Arts, History and Applied Art Department, National Museums of Scotland

JEAD   Jane Dawson, Senior Lecturer in History and Theology of the Reformation, University of Edinburgh

EPD   E. Patricia Dennison, Director of the Centre for Scottish Urban History, University of Edinburgh

MD   Mark Dilworth OSB, former Curator, Scottish Catholic Archives, Edinburgh

HMD   Helen M. Dingwall, Lecturer in History, University of Stirling

DDi   David Ditchburn, Lecturer in History, University of Aberdeen

PJD   Piers Dixon, Field Manager, Archaeological Field Survey, Royal Commission on the Ancient and Historical Monuments of Scotland

STD   Stephen Driscoll, Senior Lecturer in Archaeology, University of Glasgow

PD   Paul Dukes, Director of the Centre for Russian, East and Central European Studies, Aberdeen

DD   Douglas Duncan, formerly Professor of English, McMaster University, Hamilton, Ontario, Canada

AJD   Alasdair Durie, formerly Senior Lecturer in Economic History, University of Glasgow

JD   John Durkan, Senior Research Fellow in Scottish History, University of Glasgow

CE   Carol Edington, a graduate of the Department of Scottish History, University of St Andrews

ODE   Owen Dudley Edwards, Reader in American History, University of Edinburgh

List of Editors and Contributors

RF   Richard Fawcett, Principal Inspector of Ancient Monuments, Historic Scotland

AF   Alexander Fenton, Director of the European Ethnological Research Centre, Edinburgh

WF   William Ferguson, formerly Reader in Scottish History, University of Edinburgh

RJF   Richard Finlay, Senior Lecturer in History, University of Strathclyde

IF   Ian Fisher, Architectural Investigator, Royal Commission on the Ancient and Historical Monuments of Scotland

JF   Janet Foggie, a graduate of the Department of Scottish History, University of Edinburgh

KF   Katherine Forsyth, Lecturer in Celtic, University of Glasgow

WHF   W. Hamish Fraser, Professor of Modern History, University of Strathclyde

MRGF   Michael Fry, Fellow in the Centre for Research in Scottish History, University of Strathclyde

EMF   Edward M. Furgol, Curator, United States Navy Museum, Washington DC

JGe   Jane George, a graduate of the School of Scottish Studies, University of Edinburgh

WG   William Gillies, Professor of Celtic, University of Edinburgh

MG   Miles Glendinning, Manager, Threatened Buildings Survey, Royal Commission on the Ancient and Historical Monuments of Scotland

JG   Julian Goodare, Lecturer in Scottish History, University of Edinburgh

AG   Anne Gordon, author

LG   Laurence Gourievidis, Lecturer in English, Université de Savoie, France

SG   Simon Green, Architectural Investigator, Royal Commission on the Ancient and Historical Monuments of Scotland

EFG   Elaine F. Greig, Curator, the Writers' Museum, Edinburgh

WSH   W. Hanson, Professor of Archaeology, University of Glasgow

MDH   Marjorie D. Harper, Lecturer in History, University of Aberdeen

RH   Robert Harris, Senior Lecturer in History, University of Dundee

TvanH   Theo van Heijnsbergen, Lecturer in Scottish Literature, University of Glasgow

DMH   Diana M. Henderson, Research Director of the Scots at War Trust and a serving soldier

JH   John Higgitt, Senior Lecturer in Medieval Art, University of Edinburgh

AH   Alison Hiley, Freelance teacher and researcher, Edinburgh

PH   Peter Hill, former Director of the Whithorn Trust

NMMcQH   Nicholas Holmes, Curator, Numismatics, National Museums of Scotland

DH   David Horsburgh, Department of Celtic, University of Aberdeen

JRH   John R. Hume, formerly Principal Inspector of Monuments, Historic Scotland

IGCH   Ian G. C. Hutchison, Senior Lecturer in History, University of Stirling

RDSJ   R. D. S. Jack, Professor of English Literature, University of Edinburgh

FJ   Fiona Jamieson, Landscape historian and consultant

LJ   Lynn Jamieson, Reader in Sociology, University of Edinburgh

GJ   Grant Jarvie, Professor of Sports Studies, University of Stirling

APJ   Andrew Jennings, a graduate of the Department of Scottish History, University of Edinburgh

MJ   Mark Jones, Director, National Museums of Scotland

CCK   Colin Kidd, Senior Lecturer in Scottish History, University of Glasgow

CHL   Clive Lee, Professor of Historical Economics, University of Aberdeen

IL   Ian Levitt, Professor of Scottish History, University of Central Lancashire

MLo   Mark Loughlin, Housemaster of Weekites, Charterhouse

EL   Emily Lyle, Honorary Fellow, School of Scottish Studies, University of Edinburgh

ML   Michael Lynch, Professor of Scottish History, University of Edinburgh

JMac   James Macaulay formerly Senior Lecturer in Architectural History, Mackintosh School of Architecture, Glasgow

JMcC   John McCaffrey, Research Fellow, Department of Scottish History, University of Glasgow

DMcC David McCrone, Professor of Sociology, University of Edinburgh

ARM Alan R. MacDonald, Lecturer in History, University of Dundee

AAMacD Alasdair A. MacDonald, Professor of English Literature, University of Groningen

CMMM Catriona M. M. MacDonald, Lecturer in History, Glasgow Caledonian University

JMacD Joan MacDonald, a graduate of the Department of Celtic, University of Edinburgh

NATM Norman Macdougall, Senior Lecturer in Scottish History, University of St Andrews

WMcD Bill McDowell, a graduate of the Department of Scottish History, University of Edinburgh

CAMcG Christine McGladdery, a graduate of the Department of Scottish History, University of St Andrews

MMacG Martin MacGregor, Lecturer in Scottish History, University of Glasgow

JMacI John MacInnes, formerly Senior Lecturer in Ethnology, University of Edinburgh

JAM James Mackay, author and biographer

MAM Margaret Mackay, Senior Lecturer, School of Scottish Studies, University of Edinburgh

CAMcK Charles McKean, Professor of Scottish Architectural History, University of Dundee

AMacKe Aonghus MacKechnie, Historic Buildings Inspector, Historic Scotland, Edinburgh

AMacK Andrew Mackillop, Lecturer in History, University of Aberdeen

MLM Marianne McLean, Senior Policy Analyst, National Archives of Canada

HDMacL Hugh Dan MacLennan, an authority on shinty

MM Morag MacLeod, Senior Lecturer in the School of Scottish Studies, University of Edinburgh

DM Duncan Macmillan, Professor of Fine Art, University of Edinburgh

AMac Alan Macquarrie, Research Associate, Research Centre in Scottish History, University of Strathclyde

HLM Hector L. MacQueen, Professor of Scots Law, University of Edinburgh

AMa Alastair Mann, Research Fellow, Scottish Parliament Project, University of St Andrews

GMa Gilbert Markus OP, a Dominican Friar and Honorary Research Fellow in the Department of Celtic, University of Glasgow

RAM Roger A. Mason, Reader in Scottish History, University of St Andrews

IMa Irene Maver, Lecturer in Scottish History, University of Glasgow

DCM Deborah Mays, Principal Inspector, Head of Listing, Historic Scotland

DEM Donald Meek, Professor of Celtic, University of Aberdeen

JM James Mitchell, Professor of Politics, University of Strathclyde

DMo David Moody, Libraries Officer, East Lothian Council

CDM C. D. Morris, Professor of Archaeology, University of Glasgow

AM Alex Morrison, Senior Research Fellow in the Department of Archaeology, University of Glasgow

IM Ian Morrison, Endowment Fellow in Geography, University of Edinburgh

MMo Michael Moss, Archivist, University of Glasgow

GM Graeme Morton, Lecturer in Economic and Social History, University of Edinburgh

MMu Margaret Munro, a graduate of the Department of Scottish History, University of Edinburgh

RWM R. W. Munro, Edinburgh, an independent author and journalist

AJM Alex Murdoch, Senior Lecturer in Scottish History, University of Edinburgh

SM Steve Murdoch, Research Institute of Irish and Scottish Studies, University of Aberdeen

DMM Douglas M. Murray, Principal of Trinity College and Senior Lecturer in Ecclesiastical History, University of Glasgow

SN Stana Nenadic, Senior Lecturer in Economic and Social History, University of Edinburgh

CNO'D C. N. O'Dochartaigh, Professor of Celtic, University of Glasgow

List of Editors and Contributors

MKO Miles K. Ogelthorpe, Manager of Industrial Survey, Royal Commission on the Ancient and Historical Monuments of Scotland

IAO Ian Olson, retired medical practitioner with a long-standing interest in Scottish traditional culture and history

RO Richard Oram, Honorary Lecturer in History, University of Aberdeen

LP Lindsay Paterson, Professor of Educational Policy, University of Edinburgh

PLP Peter L. Payne, Professor Emeritus of Economic History, University of Aberdeen

RNP Roy N. Pedersen, independent writer and lecturer

NP Nicholas Phillipson, Reader in History, University of Edinburgh

NHR Norman H. Reid, Keeper of Manuscripts and Muniments, University of St Andrews Library

AR Anna Ritchie, Edinburgh, an independent archaeological consultant and authority on early Scotland

HMJR Marie Robinson, editor-in-chief of the *Concise Scots Dictionary*

RR Richard Rodger, Professor of Urban History, University of Leicester

ACR Andrew C. Ross, Honorary Fellow in Ecclesiastical History, University of Edinburgh

JMS Jennifer Scarce, Honorary Fellow in Islamic and Middle Eastern Studies, University of Edinburgh

WDHS W. D. H. Sellar, Honorary Fellow in Scots Law, University of Edinburgh

JS John Shaw, Reader, School of Scottish Studies, University of Edinburgh

ASi Alan Simpson, formerly Senior Curator, National Museums of Scotland

ATS Anne T. Simpson, Aberdeen

GGS Grant G. Simpson, Honorary Reader in Scottish History, University of Aberdeen

AS Andrew Skinner, Professor Emeritus, Dept of Political Economy, University of Glasgow

BS Brian Smith, Archivist, Shetland Islands Council

DS David Smith, a sheriff and an authority on curling

JSo Joanna Soden, Assistant Librarian, Royal Scottish Academy

GS Gavin Sprott, Keeper, Department of Social and Technological History, National Museums of Scotland

GPS Geoffrey P. Stell, Head of Architecture, Royal Commission on the Ancient and Historical Monuments of Scotland

JCS Jeffrey C. Stone, Honorary Research Fellow, Department of Geography, University of Aberdeen

NEAT Naomi Tarrant, Curator of Costume and Textiles, National Museums of Scotland

JT Jim Tate, Head of Conservation and Analytical Research, National Museums of Scotland

ST Simon Taylor, Scottish Studies Institute, University of St Andrews

ET Elaine Thomson, Lecturer in Marketing, Napier University, Edinburgh

WT William Thomson, Reader in Contemporary History, Glasgow Caledonian University

RET R. E. Tyson, Reader in Economic History, University of Aberdeen

MW Michael Wade, Sub-Editor, Sports Department, *The Scotsman*

BW Bruce Walker, Senior Lecturer, School of Architecture, University of Dundee

GW Graham Walker, Reader in Politics, Queen's University of Belfast

JWa John Walker, Professor Emeritus, Department of Spanish and Italian, Queen's University, Kingston, Ontario, Canada.

FW Fiona Watson, Senior Lecturer in History, University of Stirling

CAW Christopher A. Whatley, Professor of Scottish History, University of Dundee

IDW Ian D. Whyte, Professor of Historical Geography, University of Lancaster

AWi Andy Wightman, freelance writer and researcher, Edinburgh

CWJW Charles Withers, Professor of Geography, University of Edinburgh

DJW Donald Withrington, formerly Senior Lecturer in History, University of Aberdeen

AW   Alex Woolf, Lecturer in Celtic and Early Scottish History and Culture, University of Edinburgh

JW   Jenny Wormald, Fellow of St Hilda's College, Oxford

DW   D. Worthington, Ph.D. student, University of Aberdeen

LY   Louise Yeoman, Curator, Manuscripts Division, National Library of Scotland, Edinburgh

AY   Alan Young, Senior Lecturer, University College of Ripon and York St John

JY   John Young, Lecturer in History, University of Strathclyde

Classified Contents

Classified Contents

Classified Contents

Classified Contents

List of Abbreviations

b.	born
BBC	British Broadcasting Corporation
CBI	Confederation of British Industry
cm	centimetre(s)
COSLA	Convention of Scottish Local Authorities
CSD	*The Concise Scots Dictionary*, ed. M. Robinson (Aberdeen, 1985)
d.	died
DOST	*A Dictionary of the Older Scottish Tongue*, 12 vols. (Edinburgh, 1931–)
EEC	European Economic Community
EIC	East India Company
EMU	European Monetary Union
ENSA	Entertainments National Services Association
FC	Football Club
fl.	floruit
HQ	headquarters
HMSO	Her Majesty's Stationery Office
ILP	Independent Labour Party
kg	kilogramme
km	kilometre(s)
lit.	literally
m	metre(s)
MSP	Member of Scottish Parliament (since 1999)
MS(S)	manuscript(s)
NAS	National Archives of Scotland (formerly SRO)
NAVSR	National Association for the Vindication of Scottish Rights
NGS	National Gallery of Scotland, Edinburgh
NLS	National Library of Scotland, Edinburgh
NSA	*New Statistical Account* (Edinburgh, 1845)
OSA	*Old Statistical Account* (Edinburgh, 1791–9)
pl.	plural
PRO	Public Record Office, London
r.	reigned
RCAHMS	Royal Commission on the Ancient and Historical Monuments of Scotland
SDD	Scottish Development Department
SED	Scottish (formerly Scotch) Education Department
SFA	Scottish Football Association
SHRA	Scottish Home Rule Association
SND	*The Scottish National Dictionary*, 10 vols. (Edinburgh, 1931–76)
SNH	Scottish Natural Heritage
SNP	Scottish National Party
SNPG	Scottish National Portrait Gallery, Edinburgh
SRO	Scottish Record Office (see NAS)
SRU	Scottish Rugby Union
SSHA	Scottish Special Housing Association
SSPCK	Scottish Society for the Propagation of Christian Knowledge
STV	Scottish Television
STUC	Scottish Trades Union Congress
UK	United Kingdom
USA	United States of America
V & A	Victoria and Albert Museum, London

Note to the Reader

THE organizing principle of the volume is as an alphabetical list of headwords. They include personal and family names, events, places and place names, institutions, bodies, and movements as well as modern terms which reflect the thinking and debates of historians. Amongst the latter are kingship, regional identities, and rural settlement.

The reader may take any one of four routes to find information: by headword; through the structural, thematic spine of the volume which is revealed in the Classified Contents; by cross-references within headword entries; or via the Index.

There are over 500 headwords. Both the Classified Contents and the Guide to Further Reading show that the headword entries have been planned within a framework of seventeen broad areas or themes: events; biographies; politics and power; government and administration; economic life; social life; religious life; families (such as the Douglases) and peoples (such as the Picts); demography; physical environment (including climate and geology), settlement, and material culture; places; the Highlands and Western Isles; culture in its broadest sense; Scottish links with other countries (such as Australia or Russia); ethnography; historians, historical sources, and heritage; and the media and communications. Within economic life, the distinctions made between primary, secondary, and tertiary economies may clarify the approach taken. Likewise within social life, the structure may help locate the existence of headword topics otherwise seemingly as disparate as urban society, schools and schooling, languages, women, dress, and sport.

Within the entries, a term which is asterisked, such as St *Columba or *Canada, indicates that it has its own headword entry. Also, cross-references have been made within an entry to other main entries which may be relevant or of interest. Within the piece on Columba, for example, there are references to St *Adomnán, *church institutions, and *religious life. These have been inserted where they might be of most help to the reader and, generally, only at first mention within the article. One exception to this is within longer, 'chain', multi-authored entries, such as national identity and rural society, which cover a considerable time span. Here, cross-references may be repeated in different periods; with again the guiding principle being that of trying to be of assistance to the reader. The multi-authored entries are generally divided by the following periods: pre-1100; 1100–1500; 1500–1770s; and post-1770s. In the case of the sequence of entries on culture, however, it seemed more appropriate to use a different set of period divisions: after early sections on prehistoric, Picto-Celtic, and medieval, there are several entries covering the period 1460–1660; then 1660–1843; 1843–1914; and post-1914.

Personal names can be something of a trial in Scottish history. Names in 'Mc' and 'Mac' have been treated as if they are spelled 'Mac' and grouped together, both in the Index and as headwords. Difficulties, however, arise in the early period, before surnames came into general usage. At this time, 'A mac B' (distinguished by a lower case 'mac' as in 'Kenneth mac Alpin') meant that A was literally the son of B. Biographical entries from this period are grouped under the Christian name: thus Kenneth mac Alpin appears under 'K' not

'Mac'. The spelling of names from this early period, when Gaelic or other languages were predominant, is a matter of some controversy. Up to *c.*1100, personal names are generally given in the Gaelic form with exceptions for people more generally known under the Anglicized version; one such example is Macbeth (Mac Bethad mac Findláig).

In the case of families, such as the Campbells, the Index refers to 'Campbells' rather than to 'Argyll, Archibald Campbell, fourth earl of', so that all Campbells can sit conveniently, if not always happily, together. In this case, however, there is also a cross-reference in the Index at 'Argyll, dukes / earls of', to 'Campbell'. In other cases, the guiding principle in the Index is what is thought to be appropriate. It would be unhelpful to have given 'Thomson, William' for Lord Kelvin. In cases where there may have been doubt, such as Henry Dundas, first Viscount Melville, a cross-reference is provided in the Index under 'Melville'. Place names have usually been given in their modernized form, although the fact of two local government reorganizations within the last fifteen years can often complicate matters. Here, pre-1975 usages which are readily understandable and have survived for centuries, such as Aberdeenshire, are generally preferred to the inventions of modern politicians.

Generally, the headword list and the Index are mutually exclusive. James VI, for example, is a headword and does not feature in the Index. The cross-references within the article on this king should take the reader to other entries of interest. One exception to this general rule lies with significant places, such as major towns or areas, such as Edinburgh, Glasgow, or Orkney. Here, because of the potential diversity of other topics associated with these places, they feature both amongst the headwords and in the Index, where they are featured in small capitals in order to distinguish them from other entries.

An attempt has been made to give a brief overview of events in the Chronology and an explanation of terms which may be unfamiliar is given in the Glossary. A reference to 1235 × 1253 indicates that the exact date is unknown but will be within this span of years. All pre-1707 references to the £ is to the £ Scots rather than to sterling. The exchange rate fluctuated considerably over time: in the 1390s it was approximately 1 : 3, by 1560 it was 1 : 4.5, and by 1603 it was 1 : 12, where it remained throughout the 17th century. After 1707, however, references are to the £ sterling.

Entries are signed with initials, which can be identified from the List of Editors and Contributors. In the case of composite entries, two sets of initials are given, usually reflecting the sequence of the piece. Within multi-authored chain articles, each section is ascribed by initials of its author.

Aberdeen: 1. to 1750; 2. since 1750.

1. to 1750

The modern city of Aberdeen has as its nucleus two medieval burghs: Old Aberdeen, the small settlement beside the Don, dominated by St Machar's cathedral; and New Aberdeen, the commercial burgh concentrated on the Dee. The history of the site of the modern town, however, goes back much further. Evidence of flint-knapping on the banks of the Dee in the mesolithic period (*c.*6500–4000 BC) suggests some sort of settlement; and the finds of Bronze Age flint arrowheads imply that the site was inhabited *c.*1700–1500 BC, but the exact nature of this Bronze Age human activity is uncertain. By the time of the Roman occupation of Britain (see NORTHERN ENGLAND AND SOUTHERN SCOTLAND: ROMAN OCCUPATION), there was a settlement known to them as Devana; and this may possibly have been on the site of Aberdeen. A good case can certainly be made for accepting as Aberdeen the Apardion mentioned in the *Heimskringla Saga*—this medieval township was attacked by the Norwegian King Eystein in or about 1153.

By this time, it is known from documentary evidence that Aberdeen was already a well-established trading burgh. As early as the reign of Alexander I (1107–24), it was one of only three trading centres cited as being north of the Forth, the other two being Perth and Inverkeithing. This gave Aberdeen a strong potential to dominate trade in the northern parts; an asset reinforced by a *c.*1180 grant by William I 'the Lion' (1165–1214) to his burgesses at Aberdeen, Moray, and north of the Mounth that they should enjoy their free Hanse as they did in the time of *David I (1124–53)—a specific reference to the existence of settlements of foreign and native traders and an established trade in the first half of the 12th century. Moreover, by 1136, the bishop of Aberdeen was the recipient of an important concession: the grant of the tithes of all the ships coming to Aberdeen—not only a clear indication of royal favour, but also confirmation that the haven of Aberdeen was well known to, and well frequented by, both ships and merchants. The granting of burghal status in the reign of David I set the formal seal on the potential commercial success of the town. He issued at least one charter from Aberdeen; Malcolm IV (1153–65) is known to have entertained the Norseman Sweyn Asleifson in the town; and William I, after losing control of Roxburgh, Berwick, and Edinburgh, held his larger courts at Aberdeen, as well as at Stirling and Perth. By the 12th century, Aberdeen was clearly a town of sufficient stature to house not only the king and his household, but also the magnates and prelates who attended the royal court.

The smaller settlement to the north, Old Aberdeen, was also established by this time. There is a tradition that the first church here, by the River Don, was founded by St Machar, reputedly one of the companions of St *Columba. The dedication to St Machar certainly suggests early religious associations. At the instance of David I, in 1125 × 1130, a new bishopric was established at Old Aberdeen, probably after transference from Mortlach, and soon after this either a new church may have been built or an old church replaced. The establishment of a bishopric and eventually a cathedral chapter created not merely a demand for an ongoing workforce of stonemasons, joiners, and other craftsmen, but also the need for the routine services of food suppliers. The route from Old Aberdeen to the trading settlement at New Aberdeen via the Spital ridge and Gallowgate offered a ready access for traders and a natural outlet for their goods from the more northerly settlement. Although small, a viable community was well established by the time it received formal status as a burgh in 1489.

New Aberdeen consolidated its position as the centre of an important regional trade. With its port on the fringe of a hinterland rich in tradable commodities, such as wool, wool-fells, hides, and fish, it was in a position to exploit not merely local commerce, but also overseas trade. Its burgesses travelled to England and the *Low Countries, importing from them wine, spices, and luxury items, and into the Baltic (see GERMANY, THE BALTIC, AND POLAND: 1) for such commodities as flax, timber, iron, and sometimes grain. Although there is little archaeological material that can be construed as direct evidence of trade, a flavour of European and wider contacts is present from the 13th century onwards in a range of imported pottery and a few exotic objects such as a piece of silk and a spindle whorl of elephant ivory. Although Aberdeen served as an entrepôt for much of the north-east and its export trade and salmon and dried fish became renowned, its wealth did not rely solely on the success of its merchants; by the late Middle Ages there had emerged a small but significant group of craftsmen capable of challenging in wealth the dominant merchant group. By the period 1535–94, based on an average of burgh taxation, Aberdeen ranked as the third town in the country, following Edinburgh and Dundee.

The wealth of the burgh was reflected in the townscape (see URBAN SETTLEMENT: 1), with the focal point the market area, which became concentrated on the broad Castlegate, with its tolbooth, built early in the 15th century. The castle that once dominated the town is last documented in 1308. The other imposing architectural features of the town were the main ecclesiastical establishments: the church of St Nicholas, one of the most splendid Scottish medieval parish churches, which benefited from the generosity and good works of wealthy burgesses, the Carmelite and Trinitarian friaries in the Green, the Dominican friary on Schoolhill, and the Cistercian friary on Broadgate. By contrast, the majority of houses of the townspeople were small, timber structures with thatched roofs (see HOUSING: 2; URBAN SOCIETY: 1). Fire was, in consequence, as in other burghs, a constant hazard. In spite of this, the replacement of stone for wood and slate and tiles for thatch was a slow process. There was indeed a stone house in the town by the early 14th century, one of the earliest in Scotland, and recent archaeological evidence has suggested that a number of other stone buildings also soon existed; but as late as 1448 a house in Exchequer Row, just off Castlegate, was described as a 'sclate house', thus implying that slates were not the norm. A prestigious house on the south side of Castlegate, Menzies of Pitfoddel's Lodging, was replaced in stone as late as 1529 and the Earl Marischal's town house, further east, built c.1540, was probably the first stone structure on the site. The earliest part of Provost Skene's house, in Guest Row—a three-storey wing—probably also dates from this time.

Old Aberdeen likewise consisted basically of simple timber houses, mostly lining the single street leading northwards to the cathedral and chanonry. These dominated the little townscape, along with, after the commencement of building in 1500, the impressive accommodation attached to King's College, at the south end of the burgh. The founding of a university (see UNIVERSITIES: 1) by Bishop William Elphinstone added considerably to the prestige of the small community as well as to its population. In 1636, it was estimated that there were 832 inhabitants, which was swelled to around 900, with 50 to 100 personnel at the university. New Aberdeen, by contrast, it is thought, had a population of between 4,000 and 5,000 by the early 16th century.

The *Reformation crisis was to have an inevitable effect on the townscape and people of both burghs. Although the arrival of the Protestant mob from Angus and the Mearns early in 1560 was met with an extremely ambivalent reaction, ultimately, life, particularly for Old Aberdeen, was to be profoundly different. Its status as a burgh of barony dependent on a bishop was shaken. Not only did the cathedral and chanonry suffer material deprivation, but the town also felt itself impoverished financially and culturally. Political events in the 17th century would also take their toll: by the turn of the century the great tower of the cathedral had fallen in ruins to join those of the erstwhile bishop's palace. But stone was a valuable and reusable commodity: the decaying manses were converted for lay use or their sites redeployed, for example, for a trades hospital. In 1725, the stones from the Dunbar aisle helped rebuild the south side of the college; and a new tolbooth and school were built early in the century. Much of this has survived into the 20th century.

New Aberdeen was to witness similar transformation. In 1593, George Keith, Earl Marischal, founded the University of Marischal College on the Greyfriars site; two mills operated by the tide were constructed and the town quay extended eastwards in the early 17th century; a slaughterhouse was built in 1631; a craft hospital was founded in 1632; Greyfriars church was refurbished; a new water supply was provided in 1633; a correction house was built three years later (giving Correction Wynd its name); and a new packhouse, where food could be weighed and duties levied, was erected.

In spite of these indications of prosperity, the town functioned, after its refusal to sign the *National Covenant in 1638, as the sparring ring for both Covenanters and Royalists until 1646. Monck's troops arrived in 1651; they erected a bastioned fort on Castle Hill, using stones from St Machar's cathedral and the Bishop's palace at Old Aberdeen. Worse was to follow. Aberdeen's economic situation declined throughout the latter part of the century. The famines (see HEALTH, FAMINE, AND DISEASE: 2) of 1695 and 1699 hit the north-east badly and Aberdeenshire faced starvation on a massive scale. Mortality, infertility, and emigration reduced the population of Aberdeen parish from approximately 7,100 in 1695 to 5,600 in 1700. It would take the town half a century to recover to a population of 10,700.

Only one or two small signs gave indication that improvements lay in the future: the town council bought the lands of Gilcomston, to the west of the town, in 1679—the first indication of a potential westwards expansion; a number of mills were established; in 1730, Robert Gordon's College was founded for the maintenance of boys 'whose parents were in indigent circumstances'; and, significantly, for the urban setting, stone quarries started to be opened: Loanhead in 1730, the first local granite quarry, and Rubislaw in 1741.   EPD

2. since 1750

For two centuries Rubislaw Quarry produced the grey granite from which Aberdeen gets its most striking physical characteristic. Most of what we recognize as typical of the heart of what was New Aberdeen was built in the next 100 years with the elegant Union Street, stretching 1 mile (1.6 km) west from the Castlegate, and the slightly less elegant King Street stretching north.

Union Street was well underway by 1805: a great single span crossed the Den Burn and, by the 1820s, an elegant West End was developing complete with Assembly Hall, the later Music Hall. Gradually over the next half-century the surrounding streets gained their distinctive granite façades thanks to such architects as Archibald Simpson (1790–1847) and John Smith (1781–1832), the city's first official architect. From then on it was westwards through affluent suburbs, most notably Rubislaw Den. King Street was planned, but was slower to develop until a Telford bridge over the River Don in 1830 smoothed the way north. George Street, even less elegant, was embarked on as a new road north-west in 1790. A second crossing of the Den Burn, now with railway lines, came with the development of Rosemount Viaduct in 1883, bringing distinctive granite edifices such as Her Majesty's Theatre and the Central Library. It allowed the development of extensive tenement housing in the north-west.

Aberdeen's early industrial development had focused largely on the woollen textile industry linked to the stocking-making of the hinterland. Papermaking, too, began to flourish, as did shipbuilding (see ECONOMY: 4). The textile industry had largely collapsed by mid-century, with only two major firms remaining, and wooden clipper-ship building was at its short-lived peak. But, over the next few decades, it was the fishing industry for which Aberdeen was most noted. From the end of the 18th century it had become a whaling and trading centre and the harbour was steadily and usually

controversially developed. In the 1870s it became a herring fishing port and, with the coming of steam trawlers in the 1880s, a centre of white fishing, which had largely eclipsed herring fishing by the end of the century. Between the wars the industry faced increased foreign competition, leading to reduced investment in boat building and it never fully recovered from the lack of investment in these years, with gradual decline becoming a catastrophic slide by the 1970s. But generally Aberdeen avoided the worst effects of the economic depression (see ECONOMY: 6) in the inter-war years. A strength of its economy has always been its diversity and that remained a feature in the years after 1945 although it was failing to attract much new industry.

The discovery of oil (see ECONOMY, SECONDARY SECTOR: 3) and gas in the North Sea came in 1965 and by the 1970s Aberdeen was beginning to feel significant effects of this. It required, once again, new harbour developments, to cope with the demands for support ships, and most major oil companies had a presence in the city. It brought airport expansion, particularly for helicopters, and massive office and hotel development sending house prices soaring. At the same time, it may be that the changes in the 1970s and 1980s drove away as many non-oil related jobs, particularly for men, as they created and removed some of the economic diversity on which Aberdeen's stability so long depended.

In the 19th century civic leadership in the city reflected to a great extent economic clout. From the 1790s, the unelected town council was dominated by the textile-manufacturing Hadden family and their business associates. Staunchly Tory in their politics, they survived the 1817 bankruptcy of the council, brought about largely by the failure to find takers for the King Street feus, and, with government help, saw off the demands for burgh reform. When reform (see POLITICAL SYSTEM: 2) did come in 1833, divisions in the elected council largely became between 'improvers' and 'economists'. Vigorous provosts, like Thomas Blaikie (1839–46), pushed through harbour improvements, railway and market developments, and municipalization of the gasworks. The first to get the title *Lord* Provost was Alexander Anderson (1802–87), lawyer and bold financial speculator, whose dynamic period of office (1859–65) saw many city improvements. Anderson was a conservative in politics, but Aberdeen was predominantly a Liberal city (see LIBERALISM) by the second half of the century, with a conservative *Aberdeen Journal* which dated from 1747, more than matched first by James Adam's radical *Aberdeen Journal* and then by William McCombie and William Alexander's *Aberdeen Free*

Adomnán, St

Press (see NEWSPAPERS: 1). Both papers opposed Gladstone's *Irish Home Rule policy in 1886 and Liberals had to look to the weekly *People's Journal* for a radical voice. But it was not until 1922 that the *Journal* and *Free Press* amalgamated.

In national politics Aberdeen, from the time it got its own MP in 1832 until 1885, tended to opt for 'favourite sons', generally of broadly Liberal tendencies. The redistribution of 1885 created two constituencies, a more working-class Aberdeen North, which in the main returned radical members, and a more prosperous Aberdeen South, which returned the Liberal James Bryce until 1908. Aberdeen was never without its more radical elements; it had a lively *Chartist movement in the 1830s and 1840s. In the 1880s, a diverse socialist movement emerged and the trades council, founded in 1868, was at the forefront of campaigns for an eight-hour working day by legislation. Labour candidates began to be returned to the town council, often in association with the powerful local *temperance movement, but increasingly with a more firmly socialist stance. It was in Aberdeen that James Leatham launched Scotland's first socialist paper, the *Workers' Herald*, and local socialists with trades council support put up Henry Champion as a socialist candidate in 1892. At a by-election in North Aberdeen in 1896 the socialist Tom Mann came within 500 votes of his Liberal rival and Labour candidates were regularly brought forward. The extended franchise in the 1918 election changed much and brought the return of Frank Rose, a Labour journalist, for North Aberdeen and a Conservative, F. C. Thomson, for the southern division. Labour and Conservatives continued to divide the two constituencies until the 'National' Government landslide of 1931. But Labour regained Aberdeen North in 1935 and never lost it again. In 1947, Labour gained a majority on the town council. The South fell to Labour only on rare occasions: in 1966 when Donald *Dewar ousted Lady Tweedsmuir, who had held the seat since 1946; and again in 1987 and 1997, by which time housing developments had made the seat much more marginal.

Aberdeen was unique in the 18th and 19th centuries in being able to boast two *universities with King's College in the Old Town and Marischal in the new. 'Fusion' was pushed through in 1860, amid much resentment from those who feared that Marischal would be overshadowed. But Marischal got its new granite edifice in the 1890s and the university began to expand its departments with history established in 1889 and the country's first psychology department in 1897. It continued to draw its students predominantly from the northeast of Scotland and it was its attempt to break out

of this in the 1960s, by going for over-rapid growth, which led to a major financial crisis for the university in the 1980s. It was gradually pulled out of crisis and concentrated most of its activities in Old Aberdeen, leaving Marischal College a largely empty shell for which it is hard to conceive an alternative use.   WHF

Adomnán, St. After St *Columba (Colum Cille) himself, Adomnán was the most important abbot (fl. 679–704) of the monastery of Iona in its early centuries. We know little of his career before he became abbot, though there are some hints that he served in some managerial role in Iona for a time. Certainly the monastery of Raphoe in Co. Donegal acknowledged Adomnán as its founder, and this could well have been before he came to *Iona. He inherited a monastic federation which had suffered some diminution of fortunes following the loss of a direct link to Lindisfarne and Northumbria in the wake of the Synod of Whitby, and Adomnán's 25-year abbacy may be said to have restored something of its prestige.

His most appreciable legacy was undoubtedly the *Vita Sancti Columbae (Life of St Columba)*, composed perhaps largely in the final years of the 690s. It is through this work that we get our best understanding not only of the monastery of Iona during the 6th and 7th centuries, but also of the founding saint himself, as a historical figure and as patron. Without the *Vita Columbae* we would be very much in the dark about many aspects of early medieval life and religion in Ireland and Scotland (see RELIGIOUS LIFE: 1). Adomnán's other major literary composition, *De Locis Sanctis*, was more popular for medieval audiences, and had a long and venerable career as the most detailed early medieval guide to the Holy Land. Recent research has also begun to explore its profound and careful theology.

However, Adomnán was also a skilled diplomat. The first historical act of his abbacy was his journey to Northumbria after the battle of Nechtansmere, the death of Ecgfrith, and the installation of Ecgfrith's brother Aldfrith as Northumbrian king, to free Irish hostages who had been taken by Ecgfrith during his punitive raid on Ireland in 684. The close relationship between Adomnán and Aldfrith should not be understated: traditionally, Aldfrith was Adomnán's student, and Aldfrith may have been on Iona when he was recalled to the kingship of Northumbria. Adomnán gave Aldfrith a copy of *De Locis Sanctis* on a subsequent journey. Bede records that on this second journey, Adomnán became convinced of the correctness of the catholic dating of Easter, but could not persuade his own community to abandon their traditional dating.

This may be so: certainly it was only a little over a decade after Adomnán's death that Iona changed its practice in this matter.

Adomnán's most significant achievement was the establishment in 697 of the Law of the Innocents (Lex Innocentium), often known as the Cáin Adomnáin. This was a law for the protection of women, children, and clerics from violence. Guaranteed by some 40 prominent churchmen and nearly 50 kings in Ireland and Scotland, as well as by a system of penalty-collectors and further heavenly guarantors in the person of important saints and also the elements, the law provides stern punishments for those who inflict violence on noncombatants, especially women. The law covers violence from the verbal to the physical, and considers industrial accidents (exploding kilns) and slander in its remit. An important landmark in law, it undoubtedly did much to enhance the prestige, and latterly the wealth, of the monasteries of Columba and Adomnán. By 727, the law was being renewed by means of a circuit of the relics of Adomnán. Nor may this be said to be Adomnán's only contribution to law: recent studies suggest strongly that his influence is to be found on the *Collectio Canonum Hibernensis*, a text which blends dicta on various ecclesiastical issues together to provide the basic outlines of Christian government; it would later become very influential in Carolingian Europe.   TC

Aedán mac Gabráin, king of Dál Riata (574–?608), laid the foundations of Cenél nGabráin dominance of *Dál Riata in the 7th century. The cornerstone of his success was an alliance with Iona and their Uí Néill kinsmen. St *Adomnán, in his *Life of St Columba* (published probably in 697), described how Aedán was ordained king by St *Columba. If true, this would be among the earliest instances of an overtly Christian ceremony of royal inauguration in Europe. In 575 Aedán and the Uí Néill leader, Aed mac Ainmuirech, formed an alliance at the Convention of Druim Cett against the growing power of the Ulster king, Baetán mac Cairill. In the next decade it was Aedán, not Baetán, whose power was increasing dramatically. In 580 or 581 Aedán mounted an expedition against Orkney; in 582 or 583 he won a battle on the Isle of Man. At some point he turned his attentions towards the east, defeating the Maithi in battle, presumably somewhere in the environs of Stirling, which was in or near the Maithi's territory. Towards the end of his life Aedán faced a new threat from the east: the Bernician king Ethelfrith (d. 616) who was becoming the dominant force in what is now northern England and southern Scotland. Aedán attempted to stem Ethelfrith's expansion,

and led an invading force which was defeated at the battle of Degsastán in 603. Aedán died in ?608, allegedly over 70 years of age, and was succeeded by his son Eochaid Buide (d. 629). Another son, Gartnait, established control over the Isle of Skye. Although the alliance between Cenél nGabráin and Uí Néill suffered a hiatus during the reign of Eochaid Buide's son, Domnall Brecc (629–42), it probably remained a significant feature of Dál Riata politics until the eclipse of Cenél nGabráin power in 697.   DB

Africa. Despite the legendary claim of the Gaels to be descended from the pharaoh's daughter, Scota, Scotland's effective connection with Africa begins in the late 18th century with the renewed excitement over European exploration of the world and the beginning of Protestant missionary activity (see MISSIONS OVERSEAS) reaching out from the British Isles. James Bruce was one of the first to bring Africa to the attention of the British public with his very popular five volumes on Ethiopia. He arrived there in 1769 and stayed for two years during which time he confirmed the source of the Blue Nile. Then followed Mungo Park whose story of his first journey (1795–6) to trace the course of the Niger rapidly went through three editions. His death along with two Scottish companions in a further attempt to trace the source and mouth of the Niger increased the public's interest. Hugh Clapperton's two journeys from Tripoli across the Sahara to Chad and the Nigerian emirates, where he died in 1827, fed into this interest in Africa.

All the publicity stemming from these journeys played a significant role in helping the appeal of the missionary societies formed in the 1790s, particularly when that appeal was coupled with the propaganda of the growing antislavery movement among Evangelical Christians and others. The London Missionary Society (LMS) (1795) was very specific in pointing to the necessity of the British making reparation for the destruction of African societies brought about by the impact of the British-dominated transatlantic slave trade. The Clapham sect, among whose prominent members were the Grants and the Macauleys, sponsored both missionary and the antislavery movements.

All this interest focused almost exclusively on West Africa but it was in South Africa that Scots and Scotland began to forge links that would last effectively and continuously up to after the fall of the apartheid regime in the Republic. This was initiated by the strong Scottish element in the staff of the LMS mission to southern Africa. The leader of the original mission party, which arrived at Cape Town in 1798, was Johannes van der Kemp, a

Netherlander who had graduated in medicine at Edinburgh. In the next party of recruits to arrive at the Cape were John Brownlee and Robert Moffat. These men spent the rest of their extraordinarily long lives in South Africa. Moffat, the translator of the Bible into Setswana, one of the four major languages of southern Africa, was the founder of a dynasty of Moffats deeply involved in the development of southern Africa, while the story of John Brownlee is inseparable from the history of the Xhosa people in the 19th century. George Thom, an Aberdonian who headed the mission briefly from 1812 to 1818, resigned from the mission to become a minister of the Nederduits Gereformeerde Kerk van Suid Afrika. He symbolizes the fundamentally important Scottish contribution to the creation of that church and of a self-conscious Afrikanerdom.

Three Scots—Robert Moffat with his son-in-law David Livingstone and the director of the LMS resident in southern Africa as mission superintendent from 1819 to 1851 John Philip—were the most important missionaries sent by the LMS to Africa. Dr John Philip (his relations in Kirkcaldy were called Philp) came to the Cape with Dr John Campbell (another Scottish director of the LMS) in order to survey the work, suggest reforms, and restore good relations with the colonial authorities. Campbell returned and Philip stayed on to see the reforms implemented. Philip not only brought new life to the work of the LMS, he also became the father figure of South African liberalism, campaigning tirelessly in South Africa and in Britain for equal civil rights 'for all His Majesty's subjects'. Closely involved with his activities were Philip's son-in-law James Fairbairn and his friend Thomas Pringle, both Borderers and Edinburgh graduates who were the key figures in creating a free press in the Cape Colony in the early 1820s. To a degree Philip was successful in his campaigning for legal equality between the races in that from 1828 until 1910 a degree of legal non-racialism was built into the constitution of the Cape Colony; the non-racial franchise of 1851 is a classic example of this. The importance of Philip's role in South African history was made clear when, in 1956, Prime Minister Johannes Strydom was attacking Trevor Huddleston and went on to warn missionaries 'not to do a Philip', a shorthand immediately understood by his audience. The legal non-racialism of the Cape was ended by the creation of the Union of South Africa in 1910.

The Glasgow Missionary Society was an offspring of the same drive that created the LMS and missionaries from that society began work in the Eastern Cape in the 1820s. This mission, greatly daring, began a school at Lovedale in the Thyume Valley in 1843 which rapidly developed into a major educational institution with a high school, a teacher-training institution, a technical school, and a nurse training college. It was non-racial until, at the beginning of the 20th century, action was taken to make it inexpedient for whites to attend. It also became co-educational, among other developments educating the first African women to become fully qualified state-registered nurses. It produced the first true newspaper in an African language in southern Africa and a journal, in English, of critical opinion on social, political, and religious matters. The *South African Outlook* lasted, under various changes of name, to be an outspoken critic of the post-1948 apartheid regime.

William Govan and James Stewart were the institution's two principals during the 19th century; their ideals of equality of education for all had a powerful impact on southern Africa until the pattern of education they had pioneered was ended in the Republic by the coming of 'Bantu Education' in 1954. In the view of many, Lovedale was the womb that produced the African National Congress.

What has received somewhat less attention is the fact that Scotland played an important part in the development of the Dutch Reformed Church (DRC) into the institution that played the key role in creating the identity of the Afrikaner Volk. In 1815, the Afrikaner people had only a very nominal relationship with a church that was desperately short of ministers. The recruitment of George Thom began a tradition of that church finding its ministers from Scotland. The children and grandchildren of the first two cadres of Scottish recruits continued to serve their new church and people as ministers and teachers, returning to Scotland for training. Under their influence, the DRC ceased to have a mere nominal hold on the people. It became a church with a highly committed and very pious membership embracing the vast majority of the people: 'die Boer Kerk'. The Scottish influence did not end with these families but continued since a majority of the newly inspired Afrikaner candidates for the ministry went to the Free Church colleges in Scotland for part of their training until the South African War of 1899–1902. This church, which united Afrikaners across the four territories that came to constitute the Union of South Africa in 1910, gave the Volk a sense of their oneness and of their destiny. Its piety helped define what it was to be an Afrikaner. This church shaped, as David Jacobus Bosch, professor of the history of missions at the University of South Africa, has said, by 'Scottish Pietism' (see RELIGIOUS LIFE: 6), was a ready-made tool to be taken up in the 20th century by the Christian Nationalism of Dr Malan to further ends never envisaged by its 19th-century begetters.

The massive development of gold and diamond mining in southern Africa brought another Scottish connection into being. Among the miners on the Rand, some of the first leaders to try to teach socialist ideals and organize trade unions were Scottish. They played their role in the struggle for miners' rights that tragically became a struggle not just for white miners' rights against the mine companies but also for the elite status of white miners over and against black miners. In the South Africa of the miners' strike of 1922, the socialism brought from Lanarkshire and from South Wales came to be represented by banners that said 'White Workers of the World Unite'.

Between 1840 and 1880, although Scottish Presbyterians began missionary activity in what are now Ghana and Nigeria (1846), Scottish interest and involvement in Africa was dominated by one man: David Livingstone. His astonishing walk across Africa in 1853–6 made headlines across the western world. From the Cape he travelled by ox-wagon then by foot to the Kololo kingdom in what is now Zambia. He then walked with Kololo help and Kololo companions from western Zambia to the Atlantic coast at Loanda, then back again across Africa to the east coast at Quelimane. He made the journey to seek a route by which 'Christianity and Civilisation' could reach central Africa avoiding the white-dominated south. His fame and popularity was dented but not removed by the failure of his government-sponsored Zambesi Expedition. His last wanderings (1866–73) in east-central Africa, during which he was obsessed with ending the terrible destructive force of the Portuguese and Arab slave trade, brought the interest of the British public in Africa to a level not known before.

This level of interest led to a new missionary effort in Africa from Scotland and elsewhere. Tragically it also provided a rationale for the 'Scramble' when, between 1885 and 1895, all of Africa, save Ethiopia, was parcelled out among the European powers. Apologists for this massive imperialist effort constantly asserted at the time that the European powers were taking over Africa in order to bring about Livingstone's dream of Africa transformed by 'Christianity and Civilisation'.

The 'Scramble' saw two Scottish entrepreneurs arrive on the scene. Sir Robert Williams's Tanganyika Concessions developed the copper industry of both Zambia and the Congo while Sir William Mackinnon's Imperial British East Africa Company made possible British control of Uganda and Kenya. Although these were both Scots, their activities did not involve a close African / Scottish connection, except perhaps Mackinnon's support for the Church of Scotland's Gikuyu mission. One product of its schools was Mzee Jomo Kenyatta and it was deeply involved in the 'Emergency' in the Kenya of the 1950s.

More in keeping with Livingstone's actual ideals were the Free Church (it was led by a member of the United Presbyterian Church) and Auld Kirk missions to Malawi that worked in concert from their arrival in 1873 and 1874. The two missions, Livingstonia and Blantyre, worked together with the Glasgow-based African Lakes Company to open up the Zambesi Valley and Malawi to the outside world. These missions went on to create a link between Malawi and Scotland that has been a lively part of the history of both countries for over 120 years.

The story began with the Scots missionaries marshalling Scottish public opinion to pressure the British government into blocking Portugal's claim to the territory. Then the Blantyre mission, in the early 1890s, persuaded Scottish politicians, both Liberal and Tory, to prevent the Colonial Office handing over Malawi to Cecil Rhodes's British South Africa Company which administered what is now Zimbabwe and Zambia. This defeat did not stop the desire of the white south to absorb Malawi. First in the 1920s and then the 1930s, the white leaders of Southern Rhodesia attempted to have Malawi brought into union with the two Rhodesias to form a 'White Dominion'. The Scottish missionaries and the African leaders in Malawi opposed both attempts and persuaded the imperial government to refuse them. In the period 1949–51, however, the old alliance of Scottish missionaries and African churchmen and politicians failed to dissuade the British government from creating the Central African Federation of the two Rhodesias and Nyasaland, as the territories were then called. The people of Malawi never accepted this new relationship and consistently opposed it with Scottish help. An ex-missionary, Kenneth Mackenzie, set up the Scottish Council on African Questions, which became one of the most powerful lobbying groups in the UK from 1955 through the 1960s.

When, in 1959, over 1,000 Malawi leaders were placed in detention without trial, a wave of protest was aroused in Scotland. At the meeting of the General Assembly of the Church of Scotland in May of that year, with Rab Butler, Douglas-Home, and other members of the government in the gallery, a motion condemning British policy in Malawi was passed by an overwhelming majority. Within weeks the Devlin Commission of Enquiry was set up. This was the first step that led rapidly to the end of the Federation and the independence of Malawi and Zambia. The leader of the new Zambian nation was Kenneth Kaunda: the son of a Malawian missionary sent by Livingstonia into what is now north-east Zambia. May 1959 was the last time that a decision of the church's General Assembly has had a major impact on the policy of the British government. Scottish involvement with Malawi did not end then but has continued through the Banda dictatorship, its downfall, and since.

The Scottish missionaries in eastern Nigeria sided with their people in the tragic Biafran war and aroused some Scottish lobbying on Biafra's behalf. Despite this, in the 20th century the connections between Scotland and West Africa, although real, have not had the same widespread impact upon Scottish popular consciousness as the connections with central and southern Africa. Yet it was Scottish travellers in West Africa that first brought Africa to the attention of the public and it was also from West Africa that the majority of African students at Scottish universities came in the 19th century. In particular, a steady trickle of West Africans, sponsored by the colonial authorities, came to Aberdeen, Glasgow, and Edinburgh to study medicine. Sadly, this connection was stopped as a result of the discoveries related to malaria and public health made by Dr William MacGregor and Sir Ronald Ross. Whites could survive more readily in West Africa by 1900 so there was no need to send indigenes for advanced education.

One notable 19th-century student was Tiyo Soga, a young Xhosa alumnus of Lovedale. He trained at Glasgow University and the United Presbyterian Theological College in Edinburgh before returning with a Scottish wife to the mission in the Eastern Cape. Tiyo Soga was the first African graduate ordained to the ministry in southern Africa. Two of his sons also graduated from Scottish universities, one of whom became the first historian of the Xhosa people.

It was not until the 20th century that the trickle of African students entering the Scottish universities became, if not a flood, at least a significant stream. Perhaps the most significant among the many have been H. Kamuzu Banda of Malawi, Kenneth Dike of Nigeria, Julius Nyerere of Tanzania, and Mohamed Forna of Sierra Leone. The Scotland/Africa connection has been such that whereas in many parts of Africa Scotland is simply a name on a map, in others it is *the* other country in popular historical and political consciousness. As Nathan Shamiyarira, later Foreign Minister of Zimbabwe, said to the present author years ago, 'When we complain, who listens? But when Malawians complain, so does Scotland.'   ACR

Alison, Archibald (1792–1867), high Tory who lived long into the era of Liberal hegemony (see EQUIPOISE, AGE OF) in Scotland, distinguishing him-

self in letters and the law. He was born in Shropshire, where his father, an Episcopalian clergyman, had had to go to find a parish. In 1800 the family returned to Edinburgh. Alison was educated there, and called to the Bar in 1814. He was appointed an advocate depute in 1820 but lost his job when the Whigs took office in 1830. He turned to writing, and was a frequent contributor to *Blackwood's Edinburgh Magazine*. He achieved fame with his ten-volume *History of Europe during the French Revolution* (1833–42), the first treatment of the subject in English. It adopted a strongly anti-revolutionary line and, full of foreboding, drew implications for the current situation in Britain, since Alison regarded reform as a slippery slope. Meanwhile, in 1834, he had been appointed sheriff of Lanarkshire. He persecuted the trade unions then becoming active in the west of Scotland (see CHARTISM). His smashing of the weavers' union in the Great Strike of 1837 dealt a lasting blow to the Scottish labour movement, which did not recover decisively till the end of the century. Yet Alison also felt distressed by the callous aspects of contemporary capitalism. His personal political programme of poor relief, diffusion of property, and penal reform foreshadowed the progressive Toryism of Benjamin Disraeli. His brother, William Pulteney Alison, was the pioneer of the reform of public health in Scotland, and from him Archibald had the idea of softening the rigours of the Scots poor law (see LIVING STANDARDS: 4) by his own judgements in court, particularly by extending relief to children of the able-bodied unemployed. Appeals to the Court of Session overturned these judgements, however. His efforts retrieved his popularity and his funeral was attended by 100,000 working people.
        MRGF

Anglo-Scottish relations: 1. 900–1100; 2. 1100–1513; 3. 1513–1603.

1. 900–1100

In the decades around AD 900 kingdoms emerged at either end of Britain that can be regarded as ancestral to the late medieval kingdoms of England and Scotland. In the south the kingdom of Wessex, hitherto confined on the north by the Thames, began to creep northwards. This northward expansion of the west Saxons was sometimes legitimized through the rhetoric of 'liberation', exploiting the conquest of the other English-speaking kingdoms by Danes in the preceding half-century. In the north the Pictish kingdom (see PICTS; KINGSHIP: 1), riven by civil war and Viking occupation, re-emerged transformed into a self-consciously Gaelic polity bearing the name Alba (see KINGSHIP: 2).

Alba also sought to establish a regional hegemony but could hardly use the same kind of legitimizing myth of ethno-linguistic unification (see NATIONAL IDENTITY: 1) that served the west Saxon kings so well. At the start of the 10th century *Gaelic was probably still a minority language within the core of the kingdom and the neighbouring regions spoke British, Anglian, or Norse. Instead the kings of Alba may have utilized the ideology of Christian solidarity in the face of Scandinavian (see SCANDINAVIA: 1) paganism as a binding agent in their relations with the Britons and Angles. The possession of the relics of St *Columba, whose disciples had founded the Bernician church (see CHURCH INSTITUTIONS: 1), may have facilitated such a policy.

As early as 918 *Constantine II, king of Alba (c.900–43), led an army south to Corbridge on the Tyne to help Ealdred, son of Eadwulf, the ruler of Bernicia (913–34) against the Viking king Regnald, grandson of Ivarr. Regnald had for several years been building up a kingdom around the Irish Sea which probably stretched from the Mersey to Galloway and, at this point, was attempting to extend his power east of the Pennines. The battle of Corbridge was bloody but indecisive, resulting in Bernicia being split with the southern portion falling to Regnald and the north, under Albanian protection, being ruled from Bamburgh by Ealdred.

Two years later, in 920, the first recorded contact between the West Saxon dynasty and the kings of Alba took place. Edward of Wessex, who had annexed the midland English kingdom of Mercia the previous winter, came north and met Constantine, Regnald, Ealdred, and Owain, king of Strathclyde. According to the *Anglo-Saxon Chronicle*, the mouthpiece of the west Saxon regime, the northerners all submitted to Edward. Whether some kind of recognition of overlordship took place or not, the main function of the meeting must have been to establish the new boundaries that had emerged following the collapse of Mercia and Northumbria. Not only had Regnald seized a huge coastal strip and some territories east of the Pennines but Ealdred's position at Bamburgh had to be defined. It is also during this period that the kings of Strathclyde, the Clydesdale rump of the old kingdom of *Dumbarton, expanded south to encompass Annandale, Liddesdale, and the Solway Plain. The exact context is unclear but it seems likely that the Men of the Clyde (see BRITONS AND ANGLES) took advantage of the collapse of Bernicia. Whether the local Angles saw them as Christian liberators from the pagan yoke or just another brand of foreign aggressor is a moot point.

A similar meeting took place in 927 when the new west Saxon king, Ethelstan, after annexing York, met the northern kings Constantine, Owain, and Ealdred at Eamont Bridge on the Westmorland-Strathclyde border. Once again the west Saxon ruler was probably ensuring that his right to rule in Yorkshire was recognized by neighbouring kings. Seven years later in 934, Ethelstan and Constantine met again under rather different circumstances. The southern king gathered a huge army, including many of his own bishops and ealdormen as well as a dozen Scandinavian mercenary chieftains, and invaded Alba itself. Constantine retreated to the stronghold of Dunottar (Kincardine) but after a siege was forced to come to terms. The details are not known but he was certainly at Ethelstan's court in Buckingham over the following Christmas where he witnessed a charter using the title *subregulus* (under-king). The exact cause of this conflict is uncertain but the death of Ealdred of Bamburgh in the same year may have been the catalyst. Both Constantine and Ethelstan had an interest in the lordship of Bamburgh and may have supported alternate rivals to the succession. In the event, Ealdred's son Oswulf (934–63) succeeded and proved a loyal client of successive west Saxon kings.

Constantine, eager to win back his honour, entered into league with Ámlaíb, the current ruler of the kingdom founded by Regnald, and invaded Ethelstan's kingdom in 937, apparently aided by Owain of Strathclyde and Idwal of Gwynedd. The allies penetrated deep in England but were ultimately defeated at an unidentified place called Brunnanburh in English and Dún Brunde in Gaelic. Constantine and Ámlaíb escaped with their lives, though Owain may not have done, and Ethelstan's imperium suffered a blow from which it was not to recover.

For the rest of the 10th century the kings of Alba continued to try to exert control of what remained of Bernicia. In the reign of Illulb (or Indulf, 954–62), Edinburgh, and presumably some of Lothian, passed into Scots control. Kenneth II (Cinaed mac Maíl Choluim) (971–95) attended a meeting of kings instigated by Edgar 'the Peaceable' of England at Chester in 973, but this did not stop him continuing warfare in Bernicia and even capturing the son of the lord of Bamburgh. Indeed it was later claimed that Edgar had formally recognized Kenneth's right to Lothian at Chester. No west Saxon king after Ethelstan led armies north of Yorkshire.

Malcolm II (Mael Coluim mac Cinaeda) (1005–34) made at least one attempt to capture Durham (1006) and, together with Owain of Strathclyde, won a major victory against Uhtred of Bamburgh at Carham on the Tweed in 1018. Uhtred was purged by Cnut, the new Danish king of England, and warfare continued between the two countries into the 1020s when a peace agreement setting the border at the Tweed was brokered by Richard, duke of Normandy.

It is unlikely that the kings of Alba were entirely satisfied with this settlement for they continued to claim the lands of the lordship of Bamburgh until at least 1157. In 1066 Harald III Sigurðarsson of Norway (1046–66) came to Scotland and stayed with King Malcolm III 'Canmore' (Mael Coluim mac Donnchada) (1058–93), whose wife was first cousin to his own, and raised support from Orkney (see ORKNEY AND CAITHNESS, EARLDOM OF) and the Isles (see ISLES, KINGDOM OF THE) before making his ill-fated attempt on the English throne. It was to Scotland that the survivors, Harald's son, Olaf, and Malcolm's step-sons, the earls of Orkney, fled overland after the disaster of Stamford Bridge (1066).

After the Norman conquest of England (1066) many Anglo-Saxon nobles also found refuge at Malcolm's court and in 1072 the Scots king took as his second wife a west Saxon princess, *Margaret. This clearly worried William 'the Conqueror' (1066–87) who led an expedition across the Forth and met Malcolm at Abernethy. Malcolm handed over his son Donnchad, as surety, and made some form of submission to William.

On the western side of the island, England and Scotland (and we probably can use these terms now) were still separated by the kingdom of Cumbria or Strathclyde which extended from Penrith to *Govan. The English had periodically ravaged Strathclyde in the 10th century and in 945 Edmund had 'let' it to Malcolm I (Mael Coluim) of Alba. It retained its own kings at least as late as Carham, however, and maybe later. The last days of Strathclyde are entirely lost to us. By the 1070s it was firmly under the control of the Scots kings. In 1092 the southern portion of the old kingdom was seized by William Rufus, who established a potentate of Carlisle which seems to have included Cumberland and eastern Dumfriesshire. Malcolm was forced to attend the English court at Gloucester (August 1093) in order to recognize this annexation. This area was then heavily settled by incomers brought from Lincolnshire and very little trace of British settlement survived.

Following the death of Malcolm III during a raid on Alnwick (1093), succession disputes in Alba allowed the English to intervene, imposing first Duncan II (Donnchad mac Maíl Choluim) in 1094 and then Edgar (1097–1107) in 1097. In later times, these interventions were presented by the English crown as evidence that the kings of Alba held their kingdom as a fief from them (see ANGLO-SCOTTISH RELATIONS: 2). In reality, this way of thinking about territory and lordship was probably alien to both parties at the time.   AW

2. 1100–1513

Scotland's development as a kingdom and a community between the 12th and 15th centuries took place against the background of her relations with England. In the later 15th century, James III of Scotland said that only the English king could make war on him and, in external conflict or contacts, England loomed large in Scotland's medieval experience. The internal structure of Scotland, the boundaries of the realm, her place in Europe, even the survival of Scotland as a political unit, were shaped by the presence of a far more powerful and populous neighbour to the south, whose kings exercised a varying dominance over the British Isles and parts of the Continent. The watershed in medieval Anglo-Scottish relations came in 1296 with the onset of war between the realms. During the two previous centuries the two realms seemed to be drawing closer together, even to the point of plans for dynastic union, but 1296 was followed by warfare and enmity which dominated relations until the 16th century. The beginning of Anglo-Scottish hostility was an event of significance, not merely for a medieval kingdom, but in the long-term development of the British Isles (see INDEPENDENCE, WARS OF).

Though peace and stability were the hallmarks of Anglo-Scottish relations between 1100 and 1296, there were areas of friction between the realms and their rulers. The issue which would have greatest long-term impact was the claim of the Norman and Plantagenet kings of England to have inherited rights to overlordship throughout the island of Britain. As overlords, English kings could press for rights to appoint kings of Scots and interfere in their realm, and in 1095 Edgar of Scotland acknowledged that he held Lothian, if not his crown, from the king of England. However, between 1095 and 1292 only one Scottish king repeated Edgar's submission. In the Treaty of Falaise in 1174 William I 'the Lion' of Scotland recognized that his kingdom was subject to the ultimate authority of Henry II, king of England. As Henry's prisoner, William had little alternative to acceptance of the terms of the treaty, and fifteen years later, in 1189, he paid heavily to be released from them. The kings of Scots were, in general, determined to stress their rejection of the English crown's claim to overlordship.

Between the 1180s and 1280s the issue was never seriously pressed. When seeking to interfere in Scotland in the 1250s, for example, Henry III of England made clear that he was not acting as the Scottish king's superior, while his son, Edward I, did nothing more than register his claim in the first decade of his reign. The answer of Alexander III that 'nobody but God' was his superior in Scotland summed up the stout defence of their rights, and by implication, the rights of their realm, undertaken by Scottish kings. Though they might back the claims of York to authority over the Scottish church and block attempts by kings of Scots to secure the full rite of coronation, in practice English kings dealt with their northern neighbours as equals (see KINGSHIP: 2, 3).

It was not the English crown's claim to overlordship which caused major Anglo-Scottish tensions before 1286 but the Scottish crown's claim to lands in northern England. These claims, based on the desire to annex the southern part of the old Cumbrian kingdom in the west and on inherited rights to Northumberland in the east, led to *David I of Scotland securing the three northern counties of England in 1139 and holding them until his death in 1153. His success had been achieved during a period of civil war in England and when Henry II secured the English throne he quickly forced David's grandsons to surrender these gains. Attempts by William I to recover Northumberland, Cumberland, and Westmorland dominated Anglo-Scottish relations during his long reign and ended in repeated failure. Both William and his son Alexander II tried military and diplomatic means to achieve their territorial goals, but lacked the military or political muscle to secure them permanently.

Tensions eased on both issues during Alexander II's reign. The Treaty of York in 1237 was a compromise. Though English kings would not tolerate the cession of their Northern Marches as a principality to their Scottish neighbour, Henry III promised Alexander major estates within the areas he sought. It was the best deal the king of Scots could hope for. The treaty did not mention overlordship, but since 1124 the possession of English lands by the Scottish crown had circumvented the issue. From David I to Alexander III all kings of Scots willingly paid homage for these lands, recognizing that, though sovereign in Scotland, they remained vassals of the king of England. This spirit of compromise was the key to Anglo-Scottish relations before 1296. Both kings and their leading subjects had much more to lose than gain by major warfare and, throughout the period, most crises between the kings were resolved without bloodshed. From the marriage in 1100 between Henry I of England and Edith, daughter of Malcolm III 'Canmore' (Mael Coluim mac Donnchada) and St *Margaret and sister of three Scottish kings, the two royal dynasties regarded each other as kinsmen. Alexander III, married to an English princess, carried on a twenty-year correspondence with his 'most hearty' brother-in-law, Edward I, emphasizing that Anglo-Scottish relations were guided by the interests of two closely interrelated families. The interest of the royal houses in peace was shared by a *nobility whose lands and family ties likewise spanned both realms and whose rights and inheritances would be threatened by conflict between the realms. Before 1296 English and Scottish realms can largely be regarded as closely linked parts of a French-speaking world, with common cultural and political values. The border between them existed only as a boundary between jurisdictions.

The end of this relatively stable relationship came in the last two decades of the 13th century. Edward I's aggressive pursuit of political mastery over Scotland was the exploitation of the succession crisis which followed the end of the Scottish royal line. However, it was also the revival of the old claim to power in the whole of Britain in a new and more forceful guise. After the death of Margaret 'Maid of Norway' ended the plans for a union between the royal houses of England and Scotland, Edward ruthlessly pressed his right to be overlord of the king of Scots and his realm. Once this had been accepted by the new king, John Balliol, in 1292, Edward I employed his rights to the full and, when faced with resistance, treated Scottish king and community as rebels. In Edward's eyes Scotland passed to him as an estate forfeited by its lord because of his crimes. For the rest of his reign and that of his son, the English government regarded their Scottish enemies as disobedient subjects. This position was used to justify the execution of William *Wallace and *Robert I's brothers amongst others and made any compromise peace with the new Scottish king impossible. Only two decades of military failure altered this perspective. In 1328 Edward III's government recognized Robert I as king of Scots and ended the war. However, this 'shameful peace', as it was regarded by many English, lasted only until 1333. When Edward III launched war with Scotland his claims differed from those of his grandfather. He recognized Edward Balliol, son of John, as king of Scots and claimed to be intervening in a civil war. In return Balliol recognized Edward III as his overlord and ceded southern Scotland to him. The result was a conflict between England and Scotland which lasted without formal peace until 1474.

This state of war shattered most cross-border ties. For many landowners and lesser men, the opening decades of conflict must have had something of the character of a civil war. Families and ecclesiastical institutions which had retained lands in both kingdoms for generations without difficulty now faced a clash of loyalties and the loss of wealth and status. By the later 14th century the Bruce and Stewart kings and those noble families who upheld their cause retained no lands in

Anglo-Scottish relations

England, while Edward Balliol found support from the heirs of Scottish nobles excluded from their lands by the hostility of Robert I. As late as the 1450s the domestic enemies of the Scottish kings found support south of the Border. This Anglo-Scottish border (see BORDERS: 1) had become a barrier between conflicting political hierarchies.

On the ground, though, the frontier between these hierarchies remained a source of conflict. Much of Scotland south of Forth had been ceded to Edward III and the English sought to maintain their hold on these lands and the areas held by their Scottish allies. In the 1330s garrisons were based in burghs and castles as far north as Perth and Dunottar. The recovery of these strongholds and the lands they controlled became one of the main objectives of Scottish governments. By the 1380s only *Berwick, Roxburgh, and a few other Border keeps remained in English hands but these would be retained until the early 1460s despite sporadic Scottish attempts to recover them. Between the 1330s and the 1460s, the Scottish Marches remained divided between the agents and adherents of the two realms and Anglo-Scottish warfare continued to affect the societies of northern England and Scotland south of Forth.

As the 14th century continued, major warfare between England and Scotland became increasingly linked to wider Anglo-French conflict. The Hundred Years War which began in the 1330s defined Scotland's place in Europe as an ally of France and 'the antidote to the English', as Pope Martin V referred to the Scots in 1421. On the Continent, Scotland was seen as a northern counterbalance to England, ready to wage war against her neighbour in alliance with the French. In practice the Scots quickly became wary of major military involvement. David II's invasion of England in 1346 led to crushing defeat at Neville's Cross, and French attempts to encourage the Scots by sending military aid led to English kings leading major invasions of Scotland in 1356 and 1385. Though the strategy to be pursued against England divided Scots, by the 1370s the conflict was recognized by writers and leaders as having a central place in the political life of the kingdom.

Yet the importance of Anglo-Scottish warfare should not obscure continued and inevitable contacts between the two realms. Trade between England and Scotland continued throughout the 14th and 15th centuries. Fish, salmon and herring in particular, seem to have been major exports, while licences to import English grain were frequently received by Scots, perhaps affected by worsening climatic conditions and falling yields of cereals in the later Middle Ages (see ECONOMY: 2). Though much reduced by war, cultural contacts were not completely severed. Some Scots studied in the now rather hostile environments of Oxford and Cambridge, and St Thomas's shrine at Canterbury remained the most popular pilgrimage site for Scottish royalty, nobility, and merchants. Despite the existence of real war between their realms, nobles from England and Scotland shared in the international cult of chivalry, participating in tournaments which, admittedly, often left the participants dead or mortally wounded.

The most significant partaker of such chivalric contacts was David II, son and heir of Robert I. In English captivity between 1346 and 1357, David was attracted by the atmosphere of Edward III's court and became his captor's friend. He returned to Scotland to re-create this chivalric ethos and his personal connections influenced his approach to relations with England. In the 1350s and 1360s David, who was childless, suggested plans to end Anglo-Scottish conflict by accepting Edward or one of his sons as his heir. After 60 years of warfare this plan was unacceptable to most of his subjects, but in the 15th century several of David's Stewart successors would also see an English peace as an attractive prospect. Like David, James I endured a long captivity in England which left him with significant connections in the southern kingdom. He was released in 1424 following his marriage to Joan Beaufort, a cousin of the English king, and throughout his personal reign the English government sought to use their contacts with James to sever Scotland's ties with France, even offering to surrender Berwick and Roxburgh in 1434 in return for an alliance. The English offer was, in itself, an indication that Anglo-Scottish warfare had become less intense and threatening in the early 15th century.

The contacts of David II and James I with English kings and nobles and their desire to re-create the status and power of the English crown in Scotland did not lead to the cessation of Anglo-Scottish rivalries. Both kings ended their reigns at war against England and in alliance with France, while James's son, James II, adopted a consistently bellicose attitude towards his southern neighbour. The attacks which James II launched between 1455 and 1460 marked the most sustained period of fighting in the Marches during the whole century. They ended with the successful siege of Roxburgh in 1460, during which James was killed, and the following year Berwick was surrendered by the Lancastrian party in England, desperate for help against their Yorkist enemies in the Wars of the Roses.

The recovery of the last English-held strongholds and the end of sustained Anglo-French conflict removed factors which had shaped Scotland's relations with England since the 1330s. The possibility of a settled peace with England seemed more attractive to James III than to any of his recent predecessors. In 1474 he concluded a formal peace with the English king, Edward IV, and for the rest of his reign showed a consistent desire to maintain or restore friendly relations with England. The Treaty of Perpetual Peace, agreed between James's son, *James IV, and Henry VII in 1502 and sealed with James's marriage to Henry's daughter Margaret Tudor in 1503, seemed the continuation of a process which would reach its crucial phase in the later 16th century.

However, while the treaties of 1474 and 1502 marked new developments, there remained major obstructions to uniformly peaceful relations between the two kingdoms. Peace with England did not enjoy wide support in Scotland. Fifteenth-century Scots took pride in their ancestors' resistance to English attempts at conquest or control. Works like Blind Harry's anti-English diatribe *The Wallace*, which was written in the 1470s, appealed to Scots to maintain previous attitudes, while the attractions of the French alliance were championed by the group of Scots in the service of the kings of France. Moreover, James III's experience of peace with England was not inspiring. Within six years of the treaty the Scots found themselves at war with the English without hope of French assistance. The war cost the Scots Berwick and James's attempts to renew his pro-English policies contributed to his defeat and death in a civil war in 1488 (see FRANCO-SCOTTISH RELATIONS: 1).

James IV learnt the lessons of his father's reign. Balanced against the treaty of 1502 and his marriage were two renewals of the French alliance in 1492 and 1512. For a king like James IV, who sought a role in Europe, a secure English alliance seemed to limit his prospects. James's war against England in 1496–7 won widespread support for his rule and his decision to repeat this feat in 1513 seems to have been equally popular. War against England had been a measure of kingly ability in Scotland for two centuries. It retained a symbolic significance even after its obvious objectives had lost their value. However, war against the greater power of England had always carried risks. The defeats of William I in 1174 and David II in 1346 had threatened the status of Scotland. James IV's death at Flodden did not, but was a high price for the continuation of the old rivalry.   MBr

3. 1513–1603

The 'perpetual peace' promised by the treaty of 1502 and cemented by the marriage of *James IV and Margaret Tudor lasted barely ten years. The intervening period was marked by growing tension, posturing on both sides, and a naval race, on which more than £100,000 was spent by the Scots. The Scottish king calculatedly named his second male child Arthur and delighted in sitting English ambassadors at a 'round table' like Arthur's. Both gestures aimed to highlight the weakness of the English succession after the death of Henry VII's elder son, Arthur. The result of this growing tension and of the disaster at Flodden itself, in effect, was to restore business as usual. The first half of the 16th century was not marked by a steady progress towards friendlier relations. The voice of John Mair, who in his *History of Greater Britain* (1521) looked forward to a more rational relationship and even union, was one in the wilderness. The history of the nation, reflected in the more conventional *Scotorum Historia* (1527) of his fellow academic Hector Boece, rested on the collective memories and resentments of the Wars of *Independence; its translation into Scots by royal warrant in the 1530s enshrined that version of the past as official (see HISTORIANS: 2). The cold war which had marked so much of relations between the two countries since the 1330s was resumed in the reign of *James V (1513–42).

By the early 1520s, if not before, English policy was attempting to encourage and finance a pro-English party in Scottish politics—a tactic which would be employed for the rest of the century. 'Money is the man in Scotland', as William Cecil later testified. English concerns were manifold and often paranoid. The English succession was weak from the moment Prince Arthur, the future Henry VIII's elder brother, died in 1502. Arguably, it was this simple fact which induced successive generations of English diplomats to invest and squander resources in solving the 'British problem'. Yet the Scottish succession was also weak. It is a salutary exercise to ask of almost every year in Scottish history from 1513 until the mid-1590s who would have succeeded to the throne if the reigning monarch had died (see KINGSHIP: 5–6).

England was also almost traditionally fearful of invasion by a French army from the north (see FRANCO-SCOTTISH RELATIONS: 2). Were *Berwick to fall, generations of armchair generals argued, nothing stood in the way of preventing an invasion force from reaching York. The *Border was a near-constant irritant. The inhabitants of the frontier zone made a living by exploiting the lack of control which both central governments had over their border. The garrison towns of Berwick and Carlisle were embattled and remote outposts of London government. Governors of Berwick were consistently worried by illegal immigrants: it was estimated in the 1580s that almost a third of the population of the Eastern March was made up of Scots squatters. One solution offered, as late as

1588, to stop this human traffic was to build another Hadrian's Wall. When Henry VIII's *Rough Wooing and Protector Somerset's policy of trying to create a pale policed by a chain of forts throughout southern Scotland went disastrously wrong in 1549–50, English strategists were forced into a massive and hugely expensive programme of fortifications at Berwick; it was a stratagem which Elizabeth I was still paying for in the 1570s.

Yet there were not one but two frontiers between Scotland and English possessions. The second lay in Ulster (see IRELAND: 2). The habitual tactic of English promotion of the MacDonald lords of the *Isles continued after the annexation of the lordship by James IV. It reached a crescendo in the early stages of the Rough Wooing, with the pretender Donald Dhu poised to launch a massive amphibious attack on the soft underbelly of the Scottish realm, which of course coincided with Campbell territory in southern Argyll. The prospect ended with Donald's death in 1544. Increasingly, English ambitions of exploiting the short distance across the North Channel between Ulster and the Scottish *Gaidhealtachd* were overtaken by their anxieties about the annual traffic of West Highland mercenaries or redshanks into Ireland (see MERCENARIES IN IRELAND). They complicated Irish clan wars. After 1560, they helped check the progress of the English conquest of Ireland. The curtailment of this regular influx of redshanks and a settlement of the land frontier between the two realms were the two key objectives behind the formal league between England and Scotland concluded in 1586. They were also the main reason why this league was so long delayed.

The *Reformation of 1560 provided a fresh opportunity—and an enormous gamble—for the new Elizabethan regime to solve the multi-layered Scottish problem. It was no accident that the policy of going into Scotland was that of Elizabeth's secretary William Cecil, who had served in the Somerset administration of the late 1540s. For Cecil, there was now a new ingredient in the Scottish theatre of operations: a common Protestantism (see RELIGIOUS LIFE: 3). The new 'amity', as he liked to call it, between England and Scotland was based on a cardinal principle: 'There is no surer ground for amity than that which proceedeth from religion.' A good deal of the events of the next dozen years, which included the personal reign of *Mary, Queen of Scots and the bitter, confusing civil war which followed her removal in 1567, conspired to prove him wrong. Persistently, Scots nobles (see NOBILITY: 3) voted for kinship, self-interest, or loyalty to their Catholic queen rather than for their religion. Bewildered English diplomats found their erstwhile fellow Protestant allies in the Wars of the

*Congregation of 1559–60 on opposing sides in the civil war of 1568–73 and each side appealing to England for support.

The civil war was brought to an end by a deal struck amongst feuding nobles and its last rites were played out with the dispatch of an English artillery squadron which brought the siege of *Edinburgh castle to a close in a four-day bombardment. Yet the 1570s saw a curious relationship develop between England and what some historians have seen as its satellite state. There was no English ambassador in Edinburgh, still less a Scottish diplomatic presence in London. In the crisis of 1584, when radical Scottish ministers fled to London, they were refused the accommodation of a strangers' church. French- or Dutch-speaking fellow Protestants were one thing; English-speaking Scots troublemakers were another. The loyalties of the Calvinist international did not stretch that far. The chief mechanism which developed from the 1570s onwards to control the Scots was not Protestantism but money. Pensions—we might now call them bribes—were granted by the Elizabethan regime to most of the key Scottish nobles as well as to *James VI himself. It is a moot point who was controlling or manipulating whom in this calculated relationship. The annual pension was regularly delayed by the English paymaster until some proof of intent was made. On the other hand, the Scots realized that this was by far the cheapest policy in Scotland which England could get away with and regularly tried to raise what in effect was protection money.

By the 1590s, much of James VI's concerns were directed at securing the elusive English succession. It has sometimes been argued that his mother was obsessed by it. Yet it was James who, in a fit of panic, thinking that he might be shut out, went to the Scottish parliament in 1598 to demand the enormous sum of 100,000 crowns to raise an army for a war of the English succession. Parliament had the good sense to say no. James had himself been baptized—as Charles James (redolent of his uncle Charles IX of France)—in a thoroughly French-inspired Renaissance triumph, at *Stirling castle in 1566. For the baptism of his own first-born son, significantly named Henry (after Henry VIII), James staged an English-style festival at the same venue in 1594. Perhaps nothing indicates more strikingly how far, in terms of its relations with England, the Scotland of James VI was removed from that of his mother or grandfather.   ML

architects, artists, and craftsmen. It has been suggested that architecture is the national art of Scotland, and that its architects and constructors have been its primary artists. Until the full development of the architectural profession in the 19th century, architects tended to be either masons who also designed or rose to become architects, or clients with a knowledge and interest in the subject (see also ARCHITECTURAL STYLES AND FEATURES). Our knowledge of medieval masons remains scanty, with the exception of the outstanding John Morvo, who signed his name on Melrose abbey and is thought to have worked also on Lincluden priory, Glasgow cathedral, and Paisley abbey. In the 16th century, the identification of builders, at least, becomes clearer; particularly prominent were the Mylne family which bred a dynasty of master masons and architects which lasted to the late 18th century; the French family, much involved in Linlithgow, Aberdeen, and perhaps at Stirling in the early 16th century; the Bel family of Aberdeenshire (fl. 1570–1620), responsible for the superstructural reformatting of the great houses of Midmar, Crathes, Craigievar, Castle Fraser, Fyvie, and probably many others; and individuals such as Walter Merlioun (fl. 1490s) who built Holyrood abbey gatehouse and Thomas Leiper (fl. 1580s) who built much at Castle Fraser and most of Tolquhon. The principal craftsmen involved in building, beyond masons and carvers, were painters, of whom there grew to be a considerable number in the 17th century.

Architects in the form of aesthetically knowledgeable aristocrats or lairds emerge in the post of Master of Works Principal. The first was Sir James Hamilton of Finnart (c.1495–1540), who designed much of Linlithgow, the palace at *Stirling, and his own villa of Craignethan, followed, inter alia, by William Schaw of Sauchie (fl. 1580–1600) who may have been responsible for the *James IV chapel in Stirling, and a new royal lodging in Dunfermline. Sir James Murray of Kilbaberton (fl. 1600–34), effectively the Jacobean court architect, designed the Scottish Parliament House, reformatted Holyrood abbey, the palace in *Edinburgh castle, and his own villa of Baberton, inter alia. In Glasgow, John Boyd appears to have been responsible for the splendid 1626 Town House—quite the finest in Scotland of that date—and the 1636 façade to the University.

Fluidity between masons, builders, developers, and architects remained until the 19th century. Occupying a professional role between craftsmen and architects were the master masons/architects William Wallace (d. 1631), who began George Heriot's hospital, and his successor at Heriot's, William Aytoun (d. 1643) who also designed the reworking of Innes House, Moray. Some—like Tobias Bauchop (fl. 1700) responsible for Dumfries town hall—remained predominantly masons, whilst others—like Robert Mylne (1633–1710)—moved from being a mason and builder of Holyroodhouse, to the developer and designer of Mylne's Court and Square.

The principal architect of the later 17th century, presiding over a mini-boom of substantial reconstruction and reformatting of Scottish country houses, was Sir William Bruce (c.1630–1710). Bruce's designs represented a merging of the Scots architectural tradition of plain austerity, proportion, materials, and the continuing fondness for a flamboyant skyline—Dunkeld House and the refitting of Thirlestane castle—with symmetry and a new continental elegance—in his own house of Kinross—and with a classical disposition and orders—as in Holyrood palace. The way he twinned *James V's tower at Holyrood and adapted the existing buildings rather than beginning new ones represented a significant homage to the past. Robert Mylne's son-in-law James Smith (c.1645–1731), who had trained in Rome, returned to Scotland initially as an assistant to Bruce, and became the most significant late 17th-century architect in Scotland. Smith's imagination was European baroque, with a fondness for a design climax in elaborate roofscapes. He designed a number of country houses—including his own at Whitehill (later Newhailes)—and also the complete recasting of Hamilton, Drumlanrig, and Dalkeith palaces.

A number of prominent artists and craftsmen came to the fore in the building boom, particularly the Dutch painter Jacob De Wet, the plasterers George Dunsterfield and John Hulbert, and the Dutch carver Jan van Santvoort—who undertook work at Holyrood, Thirlestane, and Dudhope, Dundee (all effectively for the Maitland family).

The predominant architects of the early 18th century were John Douglas (d. 1778), of whom little is known save a number of country houses such as Archerfield and possibly Touch, and William Adam (1689–1748). Descendant of minor lairds and stonemasons, Adam was a contractor, substantial undertaker, and extensive manufacturer of building materials who dominated the Scottish architectural world until his death in 1748. He designed public buildings such as the Dundee Town House (1732), the Royal Infirmary, Orphan Hospital, and George Watson's School in Edinburgh (1738), but his specialism was great country houses in which he was a master of compact planning. Possibly as a result of guidance from his mentor Sir John *Clerk of Penicuik (1676–1755) with whom he created the baroque country villa of Mavisbank, Midlothian, in 1723, Adam transformed the inherited Scots tradition. He retained a fondness for vertical proportion, the piano nobile remaining at first-floor level, an elaborate skyline of swept roofs and chimney stacks, and powerful massing. The fusion of European baroque with the Scots tradition may be seen in Duff House, Banff (1748). Adam employed his own high-quality masons and stonecarvers, but tended to employ the plasterers Thomas Clayton and Joseph Enzer and the stuccoist Samuel Calderwood to great internal effect as can be seen, for example, at the House of Dun.

In Glasgow, the coachmaker architect Allan Dreghorn (1706–65) designed his own villa, the baroque 1728 St Andrew's church in association with the mason Mungo Naismith, and the Town House (later Tontine Hotel)—possibly the purest piece of classicism in Scotland at the time. The Aberdonian James Gibbs (1682–1754) designed mostly in London, but produced a new church in the nave of St Nicholas, Aberdeen, substantial alterations to the Duke's Lodging, Glasgow, and Balvenie House, Moray. Lesser architects included Gideon Gray of Stirling to whom Touch House is attributed, and George Jaffray (fl. 1788) who designed the Town House of Old Aberdeen.

William Adam was succeeded by his sons: John (1721–92) a pleasantly competent architect in the inherited Scots tradition—see Moffat House, Dumfries House, and Castle Grant; Robert (1728–92)—the outstanding architect of his generation; and James (1732–94) something of a dilettante, largely responsible for the firm's work in Glasgow in the 1780s and 1790s. Having trained in Scotland, and practised with his brother John on Dumfries House and the Royal Exchange in Edinburgh, Robert spent his patrimony in Italy 1754–8, acquiring a Continental sophistication. His principal Scots buildings include romantic castellated houses such as Culzean, Seton, and Dalquharran; compact villas such as Sunnyside, Liberton; great country houses such as Newliston and Mellerstain; and substantial urban interventions in Edinburgh and Glasgow. Such projects included new bridges into Edinburgh, a new university, Register House, and the design of Charlotte Square in 1792; and in Glasgow, many unbuilt proposals for the University and the new town, but built projects include the Royal Infirmary, the Atheneum, the Tron church, the Trades House, and part of Stirling's Square. The Adam family were their own contractors (they took their own Scots craftsmen to London to build their Adelphi development) and designed their own furniture and fabrics.

The period of Improvement caused the construction of some 500 'new towns'—principally rectilinear planned rural settlements—some dozens of which were majestic suburban expansions of towns and cities. Improvement bred architects: James Craig (1739–95) who designed the plan for the New Town of *Edinburgh and not much

else; John Baxter the elder (d. 1770) and junior (d. 1798) who mostly designed country houses— notably Gordon castle, Fochabers; and William Sibbald, one of a number of developer/architects in Edinburgh's New Town. Once the New Town of Edinburgh, no longer a suburb, recast itself as a replacement for the Old Town, and aspired to be the modern Athens, it spawned magnificent Athenian architects. The undisputed master was William Playfair (1790–1857) who designed the National Monument (under Charles Cockerell) and the Observatory, both on Calton Hill; and the Surgeon's Hall, the Royal Scottish Academy, the National Gallery of Scotland. He was run a close second by Thomas Hamilton with the Dugald Stewart Monument, the Burns Monument, Alloway, and the outstanding Royal High School and the Orphan Institution; and tailed by the terrifyingly competent but soulless William Burn (1789–1870) who designed the Scottish National Gallery of Modern Art, Camperdown House, Dundee, a number of churches, and countless country houses.

The profession was undergoing change. A number of sons of builders now aspired to be architects, and sometimes the same person would be treated as a professional for a fee on the same occasion of supplying marble fireplaces, masonwork, or panelling for which he would be paid on piecework as a tradesman. That was the case with the brothers Archibald (1761–1823) and James Elliot (1770–1810)—James designing Taymouth and Archibald supplying the wainscoting. The Elliots also designed Stobo and Loudon castles; and Archibald, after James's death, Waterloo Place in Edinburgh; Robert Reid (1774–1856) moved from being developer to the architect of St George's West church in the New Town, Leith Customs House, and the Bank of Scotland headquarters on the Mound with Richard Crichton (c.1771–1817), and of the recladding of the Parliament Hall of Scotland from 1807. In a career of virtually 50 years, the extraordinarily prolific and eclectic self-taught James Gillespie (later Gillespie Graham, 1776–1855) designed baronial country houses, countless lacy Gothic churches, the Moray Estate in Edinburgh; and Brodick and Ayton castles in baronial—a style he claimed to have invented. In 1840, the profession sought recognition with the foundation of the short-lived Institute of the Architects of Scotland, succeeded by the Architectural Institute of Scotland in 1849.

Although there had always been regional schools of masons, and eventually locally based architects, information about them is only slowly being discovered. By the early 19th century, however, most substantial Scots communities had their own architects. The finest were Archibald Simpson

(1790–1847) and John Smith (1781–1852)—the two architects responsible for transforming *Aberdeen into a neoclassical granite city. In addition to designing Aberdeen's civic monuments, both had an extensive practice in the north-east designing public buildings, villas, and country houses. By contrast, the two Town's Architects of *Dundee— Samuel Bell (1739–1813) and David Neave (1773–1841)—appear almost entirely dependent upon designing the public buildings and suburban villas of the town itself. The surrounding countryside was close enough to Edinburgh for patrons to select the likes of Adam, Gillespie, Graham, and Burn to refit their mansions. The dominant architect in Elgin and Inverness was William Robertson (1786–1841), matched down in Dumfries by the much more prolific Walter Newall (1780–1863) whose villas can be seen throughout the south-west.

*Glasgow had developed into an architectural centre in its own right, led by David Hamilton (1768–1843), the 'father of the profession' in the west of Scotland, who may have worked in the Adam office. Hamilton designed many large and small villas, largely for the Glasgow mercantile aristocracy, his prominent buildings being the Theatre Royal, the Western Club, and the enormous and imposing Hamilton palace—the largest country-house project in north Britain of the time. Glasgow's ambition had been indicated by the invitation to Sir John Soane to design one—possibly two—villas in the expanding west end, and it had nurtured the short-lived career of William Stark (1770–1813) who designed the University's Hunterian Museum, St George's church, and the Justiciary Courts. Under Hamilton's influence, but executed until mid-century by a number of substantial neoclassicists like John Brash (d. 1848), John Baird (1798–1859), John Stephen (c.1807–50), Alexander Kirkland (c.1824–92), Charles Wilson (1810–63), and J. T. Rochead (1814–78)—who could and did design with flair in any style he chose, like an early-day Basil Spence—Glasgow's uphill western expansion developed a gracious homogeneity moving gracefully from purely classical to Italianate Renaissance, providing the context for many individual buildings of considerable distinction.

The arrival of iron technologies provided mid-century architects with new opportunities, and new railways gave them easier access to remote areas. Mid-century Scotland was dominated by Alexander Thomson (1817–75) in Glasgow and his opposite in Edinburgh David Bryce (1803–76). Thomson, nicknamed 'Greek' but largely unclassifiable if not Egyptian, created a unique neoclassical language of almost primitive strongly modelled power and vividly coloured interiors, best seen in the Egyptian Halls, the St Vincent Street church,

and Great Western Terrace. Bryce was more eclectic: neoclassical banks in city centres contrasted with wildly expressive country houses in the baronial manner, of which he was the master. His country architecture—as in Castlemilk or The Glen—was of modern buildings, using the new technologies, clad in the confident new Scottish style using details from *The Baronial and Ecclesiastical Antiquities of Scotland* published in 1852 by R. W. Billings. His masterpiece, Fettes College, was just as flamboyant but slightly less obviously derivative. Similar, less refined, and even more prolifically eclectic was the work of Peddie and Kinnear (founded in 1848 and, in different formations, continuing to the 1990s), and Wardrop and Brown (from 1849).

The fascination with technology was revealed more in Glaswegian commercial buildings: the iron-curtain-walled Gardner's Warehouse in Glasgow (1855) by John Baird, the Ca' d'Oro (1872) by John Honeyman (1831–1914)—otherwise a noted church architect, the Templeton's Carpet Factory (1889) by William Leiper (1839–1916)—otherwise best known for his Clyde Estuarial villas in idiosyncratic Scottish mode, the concrete Lion Chambers (1904–7) by James Salmon (1873–1924), the framed McGeoch's Warehouse (1905) by J. J. Burnet (1857–1938), and the steel-framed, increasingly curtain-walled American-influenced banks (most 1924–34) by James Miller (1860–1940). For all its fascination with developing technology, and the espousal of the iron, then steel, frame, and the elevator, 19th-century Glasgow also provided exceptional opportunities for outstanding figurative sculpture including works by John and William Mossman, Sir George Frampton, Phyllis Archibald, and Albert Hodge.

A further Scottish revival occurred toward the end of the century, influenced by James MacLaren (1853–90)—who, practising from London, designed farm buildings in Fortingall,—but led by Sir Robert Rowand Anderson (1834–1921). Described on his death in June 1921 by A. N. Paterson, president of the Institute of Scottish Architects, as 'The premier architect of Scotland', Anderson was to found the Royal Incorporation of Architects in Scotland in 1916. Arts and Crafts by nature, Anderson was as capable in florid Italianate (the McEwan Hall and adjacent Medical School, Edinburgh) as in old Scots Gothic churches or baronial villas. To counteract the largely Glaswegian tendency to imbibe a French neoclassical training in Paris, he established both a School of Architecture and the National Art Survey—a programme of undertaking measured drawings of Scots historic buildings—equivalent learning for an architect, he said, to anatomy for a doctor.

The revival was widespread. It included Patrick Geddes's (1854–1932) proposed reoccupation of the Old Town of Edinburgh with the construction of Ramsay Garden by S. Henbest Capper (1860–1924). The circle of artists and craftsmen involved in his projects and his magazine *Evergreen* included the painters Phoebe Traquair and William Hole. The principal architect—and influence upon the future—was Sir Robert Lorimer (1864–1929) an Arts and Crafts architect of the Anderson stable, the principal feature of whose buildings was the incorporation of work by the Edinburgh craft designers—carvers, carpenters, stained-glass makers, and ironworkers—exemplified particularly in the Thistle chapel, St Giles, Edinburgh, and the Scottish National War Memorial in *Edinburgh castle. He was the last architect in Scottish history to make a predominant living from large country houses, smaller villas, and restoring older houses—of which Ardkinglas and Formakin, which Lorimer claimed to be 'the purest Scotch I've ever done', are good exemplars. By contrast, Charles Rennie Mackintosh (1868–1928) designed only a small number of buildings, principally in the west of Scotland. Inspired by historic Scots architecture, like Lorimer, he nevertheless abstracted from it to create a new departure: strong heavily modelled, almost cubist, external forms with lavish, spatially complex interiors vividly coloured and patterned in a manner showing Japanese and European influences. These qualities may best be appreciated in the Hill House, Helensburgh, the Glasgow School of Art, and in the restored Willow Tea Rooms.

Twentieth-century architects faced a changed world: the principal client would become the state, with its requirement for subsidized *housing, city centre redevelopment, and social buildings, followed closely by the architecture of an increasing consumerism. Buildings would be constructed more and more cheaply, deploying further technological advances in prefabrication, to the extent that within less than 50 years construction moved from being largely craft-based, with components made or fashioned on site, to the assembly of prefabricated components. One consequence was the marginalization of craft skills that were increasingly restricted to the very rare country house or to churches such as, for example, the Reid Memorial church, Edinburgh, by the Lorimer pupil Leslie Graham Thomson (1896–1974) or the curiously Byzantine churches in Glasgow by Jack Coia (1898–1981).

Between the wars, the most extensive construction was council housing, of which the neo-Scots tenement blocks of Ebenezer MacRae (1881–1951) in Piershill, Edinburgh, were amongst the most distinctive, although the Scots cottage developments by J. A. W. Grant (1885–1959) throughout the country had considerable rural charm. To judge by the numbers of small, white, flat-roofed houses from one end of the country to the other, the Scots nationalized a version of the international style, but almost nobody specialized in it. An unusual cluster in Inverness can be attributed to the office of Carruthers Ballantyne, but the two best examples were No. 6 Dick Place, designed for himself by William Kininmonth (1904–88) in 1933, and Gribloch, by Kininmonth's partner Basil Spence (1907–76) in 1937–8, in association with the client's architect Perry Duncan. Kininmonth and Spence was the most considerable new practice of the period, but would design in whatever mode the client pleased. Spence, as his post-war buildings, particularly Coventry cathedral, were to demonstrate, was fundamentally an Arts and Crafts architect, with a fondness for strong modelling, elaborate skylines, diffused light, and the deployment of craftsmen.

The principal modern practice of the period was Burnet, Tait and Lorne, under the guidance of Thomas Tait (1882–1954). Responsible for the pioneering Kodak House in London's Kingsway, Tait went on to design the Infectious Diseases Hospital in Paisley and St Andrew's House—the principal government building of the period—before taking overall charge for the 1938 Empire Exhibition in Bellahouston Park, and commissioning a number of the new generation of Scots designers to assist him.

The main consequences of the war were an enhanced legacy of urban dereliction, a belief in town replanning, a demand for new social buildings, and greater experience with prefabrication. City and regional plans were coupled with proposals for New Towns, and rate of production took priority over design. In the immediate post-war years, government, local authorities, and state agencies built up considerable architects' departments which, by the 1970s, had become responsible for over half the building output of the country. Within the mass construction boom there remained space for a small number of craft architects—pre-eminently Gillespie Kidd and Coia of Glasgow (d. 1981), Peter Womersley (1923–93), and Rowand Anderson Kininmonth and Paul (particularly 1956–76). Gillespie Kidd and Coia designed predominantly Roman Catholic churches and schools and some University buildings, of which St Peter's Seminary, Cardross, and Robinson College, Cambridge stand out. Although Womersley principally designed jewel-like cubic houses, his monuments are Bernat Klein's Studio near Selkirk and the Borders Regional Council HQ. Rowand Anderson

Kininmonth and Paul designed a few spectacularly geometric buildings with an echo of the Scots inheritance in the Mary Erskine School, Craigsbank church in Corstorphine, and the Scottish Provident Offices in St Andrew Square. The latent 'Scottish' fondness for strong white forms with a picturesque disposition appeared in the work of Wheeler and Sproson (particularly 1952–76) and the houses of Baxter Clark and Paul in the same period.

The dominant firm of mid-century was Robert Matthew Johnston Marshall and Partners, acclaimed for their work at Dundee University, Stirling University, Ninewells Hospital, Dundee, and the Royal Commonwealth Pool, closely challenged by Basil Spence, Glover and Ferguson, who designed the Edinburgh University Library, the Scottish Widows Headquarters, and the Mortonhall Crematorium. The boom was largely over by 1970, to be followed by a rapid growth in tenement repair, reuse, and in architectural conservation. With reuse becoming as important as building new, craft trades were revived and ancient techniques haltingly relearned, with the vaguely negative result of an opposition growing between the reuse of a building and its replacement. In the boom-and-bust rollercoaster of the last twenty years of the century, a new generation of architects fed initially off tenement repair before being commissioned for major new projects. The new 'Glasgow Style' emerged from Elder and Cannon, Page and Park, Simister Monahan, Davis Duncan and McGurn Logan, Duncan and Opfer.

There was a tendency for insecure clients (universities, the Scottish Office, Enterprise Companies, and the like) to commission non-Scottish architects such as Norman Foster, Michael Hopkins, Richard Meier, and Terry Farrell for major projects—an attitude culminating in the refusal to include a solely Scots architectural practice in the competition for the new Scottish parliament which was won by Enric Miralles (see PARLIAMENT HOUSE, EDINBURGH). The two exceptions were the *Royal Museum of Scotland and the Dundee City Arts Centre (DCA). Won in competition by Richard Murphy, the DCA incorporated an older building within a new civic monument, and exemplified a new delight in the use of contemporary materials which was characterizing the new generation of architects. Won in open competition in 1991 by Benson and Forsyth, the Royal Museum of Scotland opened in 1998. The architects chose deliberately to reflect not just its locale in Edinburgh, but also abstractions from Scottish buildings of the past in a building designed to house the Scottish Collections of the Royal Museum. It was a statement that although *regional identity in architecture was now largely a matter of aesthetic choice rather than

local technical necessity, it was still possible to produce a building which—as they had hoped in the 1930s—could be simultaneously modern and identifiably Scottish.   CAMcK

architectural styles and features. With the reign of King *David I (1124–53), Scotland became a part of the western European polity of feudalism. Its most visible symbol was the castle, which was introduced by the new landholding class of Anglo-Normans, many of whom were members of the *royal court. With royal encouragement burghs (see URBAN SETTLEMENT: 1) were founded, the country was divided into dioceses with parishes and Continental monastic orders (see CHURCH INSTITUTIONS: 2) were invited to settle. Tironensians founded Kelso abbey, Roxburghshire, in 1128 which, with its double transepts, reflects contemporary central European planning. Another outstanding Romanesque monument is the Benedictine abbey of Dunfermline, Fife, a royal foundation, completed in 1170, where the massive columns of the surviving nave rank with those in Durham cathedral. As late as the 15th century, the rebuilding of the Cistercian abbey of Melrose, Roxburghshire, with its echelon east end, is derivative of northern English practice. Only the ruined choir and a row of chapels on the south side remain at Melrose where the virtuosity of the architectural ornament is the high point in late medieval Scottish ecclesiastical architecture (see CHURCHES: 1).

Glasgow cathedral is alone among Scotland's greater medieval ecclesiastical edifices in being intact despite the loss of its western towers. The present building was begun in 1233. Uniquely in Scotland, it has a lower church where the early English geometry and spatial complexity is of European importance. Throughout the 13th century there were major building programmes at Elgin cathedral, Morayshire, which has double nave aisles, and at St Andrews cathedral, Fife. Founded in the mid-12th century with fourteen bays in the nave, the latter was comparable in length to Norwich cathedral. In the later Middle Ages, Scotland's architecture became more inward-looking and retrospective. St Machar's cathedral, Aberdeen, has round columns and round-headed windows while its granite western towers with machicolations at the wall heads are cousin germane to the local tower houses.

The tower house was the almost universal dwelling of the landed classes. Drum castle, Aberdeenshire, of the late 13th century is a rectangle with bull-nosed corners. Huntly castle, Aberdeenshire (1452), is the first of the L-plans and Claypotts castle, Angus, begun in 1569, the most spectacular of the Z-plans. The great castles of enclosure, such as Bothwell castle, Lanarkshire, with its mighty donjon, or Kildrummy castle, Aberdeenshire, with D-shaped entrance towers, were royal enterprises of the late 13th century. At the moated Caerlaverock castle, Dumfriesshire, the main accommodation is in the twin-towered gatehouse. Rothesay castle, Bute, also moated, has a circular plan with four towers linked by curtain walls. Royal patronage initiated the precocious Renaissance (see CULTURE: 8) syntax of pilasters and tondos at Falkland palace, Fife, and the ornately sculptured palace block at *Stirling castle, in the reign of King *James V (1513–42) as well as the Chapel Royal, with its classical entrance, in the reign of his grandson, King *James VI, in 1594.

The *Reformation in 1560 and the removal of the royal court to London in 1603 (see UNION OF THE CROWNS) left the landowning class as the major architectural patrons. Tower houses continued to be built and the last to be begun was Leslie castle, Aberdeenshire, in 1661. The castle style reached its apogee with the Bell family of masons working in the half-century after 1575 in the north-east at Crathes castle, Kincardineshire, an L-plan, and Castle Fraser, Aberdeenshire, a Z-plan. Craigievar castle, Aberdeenshire, was the last and the finest, with a finely balanced silhouette and a great hall with a richly plastered vault and a musicians' gallery. Painted tempera decoration was popular and the finest extant ceiling is in Provost Skene's House, Aberdeen, 1626.

In the burghs (see URBAN SOCIETY: 2) the slow improvement in economic wealth is reflected in the larger town houses of merchants and nobles. Good surviving examples are Lamb's House, Leith, and Huntly House, Edinburgh (c.1570), although the Palace, Culross, Fife, a generation later, has symmetrical fenestration. Renaissance detailing occurs tentatively on Mar's Work, Stirling (1570), and more assuredly at Moray House, Edinburgh, and the contemporary Heriot's Hospital, Edinburgh, begun in 1628, where the symmetry and detailing of the arched courtyard indicate a knowledge of Italian forms which appeared also in Glasgow's College (demolished) which was Scotland's largest building enterprise of the mid-17th century.

The *Restoration in 1660 and the gradual incrementation of aristocratic fortunes mark the introduction of the country house, a non-defensive residence which, in plan, elevations, and details, accorded with the canons of classical architecture. Sir William Bruce (c.1630–1710) was the prime mover. As overseer of the royal works in Scotland he was responsible for the new palace of Holyroodhouse, Edinburgh, in 1671–8. The courtyard elevations set over a continuous loggia have the three classical

orders beneath a pediment. Bruce can be credited with fifteen country houses. Dunkeld House and Moncreiffe House, both in Perthshire and both begun c.1676, were hip-roofed with two storeys and an attic over an exposed basement with a tripartite plan divided from front to back. This new type of compact house would have a long run, being favoured by men of lesser fortune. At his own houses, first at Balcaskie, Fife, and then more assuredly at Kinross House, Kinross-shire, Bruce experimented with Palladian layouts of a rectangular block connected by curved screens to pavilions, which were scarcely paralleled in England. Though acknowledged by Deborah Howard as the 'great gentleman architect' of the Restoration period, Bruce may have felt threatened by younger men. Thus his last work, Hopetoun House, West Lothian, begun in 1699, is a new departure with a Greek cross plan copied from the château of Marly while published drawings show unusual convex colonnades. James Smith (c.1645–1731), who had been a mason at Holyroodhouse, also used an Italian and French repertoire at Hamilton palace, Lanarkshire (demolished), whereas the later Dalkeith House, Midlothian (1701), shows a Dutch influence in the stepped plan and the high pediment over Corinthian pilasters. Smith's own house at Newhailes, Midlothian, as well as Raith House, Fife, and Strathleven House, Dunbartonshire, probably the first classical villas in Britain, evoke Smith's stay in Italy.

The range of classicism was extended by William Adam (1689–1748). His remodelling of Hopetoun House after 1721 introduced Anglo-Palladian planning, albeit many of the façade details hark back to Sir John Vanbrugh. Although Adam borrowed heavily from Palladio and current architectural texts and made use of his visits to England, his work has a sturdy independence that overrides the solecisms as at the Drum, where the entire façade has channelled masonry. As mason to the Board of Ordnance, Adam oversaw the erection of Highland fortifications (see BUILDINGS: 4) after the last Jacobite rising, the Forty-Five. Fort George on the Moray Firth is the outstanding monument of military engineering. In the plates engraved for Vitruvius Scoticus, Adam left a record of his achievements which include the demolished Royal Infirmary, Edinburgh, and the town house in Dundee.

William Adam's elder sons, John (1721–92) and Robert (1728–92), continued their father's practice, completing Inveraray castle, the first major neo-Gothic building in Britain. Much later Robert Adam would build, uniquely in Scotland, a series of castles culminating in Culzean castle, Ayrshire, on a dramatic site overlooking the Firth of Clyde and approached by a viaduct as a recollection of Hadrian's Villa which he had sketched on his Grand Tour. He introduced new standards of classicism into public architecture in Edinburgh, at the Register House and the University and in the layout of Charlotte Square, all incomplete at his death.

The penetration of Scotland by architects working in England was rare. Sir William Chambers designed Duddingston House (1763), where neoclassical correctness owed much to the newly published awareness of Greek architecture. Cairness House, Aberdeenshire (1791–7), by James Playfair has Greek detailing in combination with French neoclassical planning. It was in the Regency period that the Greek revival became potent. Good examples are Camperdown House, Dundee (1824), by William Burn and Strathcathro, Angus, by Archibald Simpson (1827). Prominent porticos also adorn the North church, Leith (1814), by William Burn; the Music Hall, Aberdeen (1820), by Archibald Simpson; the *Royal High School, Edinburgh (1825), by Thomas Hamilton; and the Royal Exchange, Glasgow (1827), by David Hamilton, although by then Roman grandiloquence subsumes the purity of Greece. *Edinburgh was stamped as the Athens of the North by W. H. Playfair with the dozen Doric columns of the unfinished National Monument on the Calton Hill and the sombre colonnades of the Royal Scottish Academy.

The first asymmetrical country houses were Tullichewan castle and Balloch castle, both overlooking Loch Lomond and both designed by Robert Lugar (c.1808). Another Englishman, William Wilkins, introduced the Tudor style to Scotland most notably at Dalmeny House, West Lothian (1815). After a notable early flourish at Abbotsford, Roxburghshire—the creation of Sir Walter Scott—the Scots-baronial style was developed by William Burn, as at Milton Lockhart, Lanarkshire (1829), although that was outclassed by the bravura of James Gillespie Graham's Brodick castle on the Isle of Arran (1845).

In architecture the 19th century was Glasgow's. In the three-quarters of a century after 1850 Glasgow's population rose from 500,000 to a peak of 1,250,000. Other cities such as Edinburgh and Aberdeen also had increases but none so spectacularly as Glasgow which contained one-fifth of Scotland's population (see POPULATION PATTERNS: 2). In all the cities (see URBAN SETTLEMENT: 3), however, classicism was dominant, especially the Greek revival, although in England it was a spent force after the 1840s. The Greek revival was reinvigorated in Glasgow by Alexander 'Greek' Thomson (1817–75). Of his four churches, only St Vincent Street is intact and in use (see CHURCHES: 3). On a monumentally scaled basement, an Ionic temple with projecting glazed aisles is flanked by a free-standing tower of idiosyncratic design incorporating Assyrian as well as Egyptian details. The galleried interior is supported on extravagantly barbaric cast-iron columns and illuminated by plate glass set directly into the masonry which is tied by ornamented beams. It was a sign of the times that Thomson had numerous commercial commissions where the façades become ever more complex, as in the stone Egyptian Halls or the cast-iron Buck's Head Building. In domestic work, the Holmwood villa, carefully assimilated with the immediate policies, and the almost planar Great Western Terrace are the outstanding achievements.

Thomson's influence was widespread as in James Sellars's Kelvingrove church and the St Andrew's Halls where the columnar screen recalls Schinkel's Altes Museum in Berlin. After the death of Sellars in 1888, his assistant John Keppie became a partner of John Honeyman, a distinguished ecclesiologist. Charles Rennie Mackintosh joined the firm as an assistant, becoming a partner in 1904 having won the competition for the new Glasgow School of Art in 1895, which, although internationally acclaimed for its art nouveau traits and modernity, owes much to the Arts and Crafts movement. Mackintosh's contemporary and friend was the younger James Salmon. Having trained in France, his output, often corner blocks for a bank with flats above, as at Anderston Cross, combines rich sculptural decoration with plasticity in façade modelling. An earlier exponent of the Arts and Crafts was James MacLaren who had removed to London. In Scotland, the harled and thatched buildings at Fortingall, Perthshire, and the rubble-walled High School extension at Stirling (1888) show a sensitive combination of Scottish and English historical traditions.

Historicism adapted to new uses was attempted by Sir George Gilbert Scott, one of the few English architects to compete successfully in Scotland. St Mary's episcopal cathedral, Edinburgh, has triple spires mass-set on the axis of Melville Street. In Dundee, the Albert Institute (1867) with its mix of Franco-Scottish details was the forerunner of the new buildings for the University of Glasgow, the largest commission in Britain since the building of the Houses of Parliament. Though much criticized, the University's south range, dominated by a tower modelled on Scott's favourite Flemish (see LOW COUNTRIES) civic halls, provides Glasgow with its most distinctive landmark. Other notable educational buildings are Fettes College, Edinburgh (1862), a French Renaissance pile by David Bryce, and Marischal College, Aberdeen (1900), where the architect, A. Marshall Mackenzie, departed from the city's adherence to a neoclassicism in favour of a dizzy array of Gothic spirelets.

The Glasgow architect James Miller was much employed by the Caledonian Railway Company at the Central Station, Glasgow, and at Wemyss Bay station, a half-timbered marine pavilion enclosing a glass and iron loggia curving down to the waiting steamers. There is also fantasy in the Caledonian Mansions, Glasgow—a *fin-de-siècle esprit de jeu* of rotund towers and many gables. A similar mélange occurred at the Charing Cross Mansions by J. J. Burnet who, having returned from an architectural training in Paris, had commenced his career in Glasgow with the galleries of the Fine Art Institute (demolished), an essay which blended Thomson and Beaux Arts motifs. In 1896, Burnet travelled to the USA which resulted in the steel frame and masonry cladding of the Atlantic Chambers and in the McGeoch warehouse, which has an affinity with H. L. Sullivan's output in Chicago. Though the heroic age of country-house building was past, Sir Robert Lorimer had numerous commissions. Though some, such as Rhu-na-Haven, Aberdeenshire, are modest, Ardkinglas, Loch Fyne (1905), is an opulent conflation of older Scottish themes without any loss of the attention to planning and the refinement of detail which are the hallmarks of Lorimer's Arts and Crafts. Helensburgh was much favoured by the Glasgow bourgeoisie, as was William Leiper who moved from baronialism to a lighter derivative of Norman Shaw with red-tiled roofs and white walls. Baillie Scott built the White House and at the top of the town is the Hill House by Mackintosh, which in its poetic imagery is a landmark in British domestic architecture prefacing the 20th century.

The arrival of the modern movement in Scotland, as in the rest of Britain, was slow, sporadic, and often promoted by foreigners. The designer of the North British Diesel Works, Glasgow (1914), was Karl Bernhard who, when in the office of Peter Behrens, had worked on the AEG Turbine Factory, Berlin. The Glasgow derivative has a steel frame infilled with brick and glass. Weir's Administration Building, Glasgow (1915), by the American Albert Kahn, is a reinforced concrete rectangular box of four storeys with large American steel-framed windows. There was an increasingly evident transatlantic influence in commercial buildings. J. J. Burnet's 200 St Vincent Street, Glasgow, is a truncated skyscraper with a grid of small windows set on an arcaded base. Somewhat similar is James Miller's Royal Bank of Scotland, Bothwell Street, Glasgow (1935), where the street façades are contrasting arcades, one being a distyle Ionic porch and the other infilled with glass and metal panels. The highpoint of art deco, however, is the sprawling St

Andrew's House, Edinburgh (1934) (see SCOTTISH OFFICE). As the seat of government, it is embellished with much stone-carved symbolism relieved by the use of glass and metal around the entrance and in the glazed end towers. The architect Thomas S. Tait laid out the Empire Exhibition, Glasgow (1938), as a showcase of art deco, aided by a galaxy of talented young designers including Basil Spence and Jack Coia. Tait's Tower of Empire, a 300-foot (91.4 m) observatory, is still remembered for its futuristic stepped outline. As the exhibition has vanished, the new machine age is best epitomized by the newspaper offices, such as in Albion Street, Glasgow—a smooth sheath of alternating layers of ribbon glazing alternating with black vitriolite, although at the St Cuthbert's store in Edinburgh the transparency of the glazing reveals the cross-framing of the concrete supports.

After the Second World War a priority was to ease urban overcrowding. One solution was to set up new towns. These provided opportunities for innovative practices such as Gillespie Kidd and Coia. Whereas St Anne's, Whitevale Street, Glasgow (1931), was an Italian Renaissance brick basilica, St Paul's, Glenrothes, Fife (1957), is fan-shaped and uses industrial materials. More assertive is St Bride's, East Kilbride (1962), set on high ground with a massive windowless shell keep with a bifurcated campanile to one side. While much of the housing in the new towns is mundane, Seafar 2 in Cumbernauld has a consistency of simple outlines and split levels judiciously integrated with the sloping site and laid out to command the distant views. In the historic towns, programmes of renewal were often driven using designated comprehensive development areas, which meant clearing the site, and multi-storey residential blocks. In Hutchesontown, in Glasgow's Gorbals, there were twenty-storey blocks, by Basil Spence, cradled within gigantic reinforced concrete frames, which have now been demolished, to make way for medium-rise tenemental housing. Although tenemental housing was excoriated after the war, there has been a revival invigorated by the 21st-century tenement competition (1984) for Stratford Street, Maryhill, Glasgow, where a split-level section allows for large rooms with traditional high windows on the convex blockwork façade with its Thomsonian overtones.

The expansion of higher education (see UNIVERSITIES: 2–3) created a demand for halls of residence which are as diverse as the finely scaled and cloistered Pollock Halls for Edinburgh University (1952) and the brutalist power of the splayed Andrew Melville Hall, St Andrews University, by James Stirling. Of the new universities, Stirling has the most spectacular site, at the centre of which is a loch from which the teaching and residential units spread into the parkland.

If much public work is dull, there are highlights such as the Royal Commonwealth Pool, Edinburgh, where differing materials are layered horizontally against a spectacular hilly backdrop. Glasgow has the sophisticated shining elegance of the Scottish Amicable building, St Vincent Street, and the Burrell Gallery (1983) which still has the freshness of a youthful design. Yet at the end of the 20th century the loss of faith in the modern movement, the search for a *national identity, and the reappearance of classical features indicate that in a hundred years the wheel has turned full circle.

JMac

army: 1. to 1600; 2. 1600–1750; 3. Highland regiments 1750–1830; 4. Highland regiments since 1830; 5. Volunteers.

1. to 1600

Perhaps the most distinctive feature of the Scottish army in the medieval and early modern period was its method of recruitment and mobilization. Major Scottish hosts from the early Middle Ages to the 16th century were based on a general call-out of able-bodied males between the ages of 16 and 60 who were liable to serve in the defence of the kingdom, at their own expense, for a period of 40 days. The origins of this so-called 'common army' were ancient, but the system was capable of some adaptation to absorb new military technologies. Over much of the kingdom the common army was mobilized and led on a provincial basis (especially north of the Forth) by territorial earls such as the lords of Carrick, Strathearn, or Lennox, while royal sheriffs and burgh officers were responsible for the turnout of eligible males in their own jurisdictions (see REGIONAL IDENTITIES). Descriptions of royal armies campaigning in England and within Scotland during the 12th and 13th centuries reinforce the nature of the king's host as a composite that was made up of a number of provincial levies. By the later Middle Ages, when the power of many provincial earls had waned, the responsibility for mobilization seems to have been assumed by the dominant regional magnates who led their own affinities to the muster and into battle. From the crown's perspective the major advantage of the common army was that it provided a relatively large infantry force that was armed and provisioned at the expense of the king's subjects rather than the monarch. In times of national emergency or internal rebellion, individual kings did have recourse to paid troops and there were certain full-time professionals, such as crossbowmen and, latterly, artillery gunners, whose skills could not be

maintained in the general levy and who were therefore paid by the crown. On the whole, however, Scottish kings obtained their military forces on the cheap. The major drawback in this situation was that, in the absence of crown payment for service and arms, the host was available only for defensive warfare within Scotland or for short campaigns in northern England. In addition, the level of military preparedness in terms of up-to-date equipment and training could not be guaranteed in a largely amateur force. The chief mechanism for maintaining the readiness of the host was the wapinschawing, where those eligible for military service would be summoned by the local earl, sheriff, or burghal officer to drill and display their weaponry and armour. These assemblies were not always regular or well attended, as despairing parliamentary legislation of the 15th and 16th centuries makes clear.

The Scottish host was overwhelmingly an army of infantrymen, typically with little in the way of body armour except for an iron headpiece, padded jacket, and gloves. The distinctive infantry weapon was the longshafted spear or pike, supplemented in some cases by a sword. The mass of infantry was supported by a small cavalry component, initially drawn from the greater and lesser aristocracy. In the 12th century European-wide advances in the technology and practice of cavalry warfare had encouraged the crown to develop means of raising a trained mounted force. From the reign of *David I (1124–53) onward, a number of men able to support the cost of providing trained mounted troops were given land by charter to be held directly from the crown in return for specified military service in the king's host usually, although not invariably, as heavily armoured cavalrymen, knights, or men-at-arms. For a time this so-called 'feudal' host seems to have been quite distinct from the common army, but by c.1300 the differences in terms of recruitment and mobilization had become blurred. By the 16th century, the main cavalry element in Scottish armies seems to have been derived from the troops of lightly armoured horsemen maintained by *Border lords. Other regional specialisms produced further variations in the make-up of the Scottish host. Selkirk forest, Argyll, and the islands of the Firth of Clyde, for example, seem to have provided large contingents of skilled archers for royal armies (see WARFARE, WEAPONS, AND FORTIFICATIONS: 1).

The Scottish host probably reached the height of its power, expertise, and effectiveness during the sustained campaigns of the Wars of *Independence, although even in this period the Scots' most successful strategy, with the obvious exception of Bannockburn, was to avoid full-scale set-piece confrontations. The success of the Scottish army at

Bannockburn, and that of smaller forces raiding into northern England during the 1320s, must be balanced against the disastrous defeats at Dupplin Moor (1332), Halidon Hill (1333), and Neville's Cross (1346). The warfare of the 14th century undoubtedly built up a military tradition and expertise in Scotland, particularly in the affinities and kindred networks based around great aristocratic lineages, such as the earls of *Douglas, which operated in the militarized border zones in the south of the kingdom. The existence of a large pool of experienced soldiers underlay the creation of the one truly professional full-time Scottish army of the late medieval period, essentially a privately raised force under the command of the earls of Douglas and Buchan, which fought against the English in France for around five years in the pay of the French crown. The expeditionary force was wiped out at the battle of Verneuil in 1424, but the supply of Scottish troops for service on the continent was considered as a possibility in subsequent negotiations between the French and Scottish crowns (see FRANCO-SCOTTISH RELATIONS: 1; NOBILITY: 2). By the 16th century, particularly after the bloody losses to English armies at Flodden (1513) and Pinkie (1547) it was clear that the amateur Scottish levy lacked the training, skills, and equipment to function as an effective force against increasingly professional, state-funded opponents, capable of employing sophisticated battlefield tactics. Scottish monarchs, in particular *James VI, began to experiment with smaller professional forces that were equipped and paid by the crown. Anglo-Scottish friendship (see ANGLO-SCOTTISH RELATIONS: 2–3) after 1560 and the *Union of the Crowns in 1603 undercut the justification that the large militarized affinities of Scottish noblemen were essential for the defence of the kingdom. This development, combined with James VI's unwillingness to allow his aristocratic subjects to maintain a private military capability outwith state control, gradually eroded the social basis that had allowed the mobilization of the Scottish host. By 1600 the system which had been used to defend the kingdom throughout the medieval period was effectively dead. SB

2. 1600–1750

Scottish soldiers constituted one of the most 'successful' export industries during the 17th century and was part of the demographic process of high levels of *migration and a culture of mobility (see EMIGRATION: 1; SCANDINAVIA: 3). The Thirty Years War (1618–48) provided a major outlet for Scottish military participation as mercenaries (see MERCENARIES IN EUROPE) or in service in national levies. Estimates suggest that over 40,000 Scots took part in the conflict. Many of these veterans returned to

Scotland to serve in the Covenanting armed forces against the rule of Charles I. Forces ranging in size from 2,000 to 24,000 men were raised during the Wars of the *Covenant between 1639 and 1651, with shire committees of war providing a formal institutional link for the raising of troops between the Covenanting leadership in Edinburgh and the Scottish localities.

The Royalist *'Restoration' Parliament of 1661 acknowledged that the power of raising and disbanding the armed forces lay solely with the monarch. Legislation of 1663 was designed to create a national militia of 20,000 foot and 2,000 horse and was reiterated in further legislation of 1669. The notorious Highland Host of 1678, consisting of 5,000 Highlanders and 3,000 regular troops, was used as a device for suppressing the operation of conventicles in the south-west as a source of tension between the second generation of *Covenanters and the Scottish state. The 'Killing Times' witnessed regimental reforms as part of the process of suppressing the Covenanters. For example, the Royal Scots Regiments of Dragoons, the 'bluidy dragoons', were in action at Drumclog, Bothwell Brig, and Airds Moss in 1679–80 and they also took part in the suppression of the 1685 Argyll rebellion.

The size of the armed forces in Scotland remained fairly static during James VII's administration of Scotland (1685–8). In contrast to the influx of Catholics to the Irish armed forces, relatively few Catholics managed to secure entry into the Scottish army under James VII's rule and the command structure of the Scottish army remained staunchly Protestant. It has been estimated that 175 commissions were available in the Scottish army but only 67 of these 175 commissions changed between 1685 and 1688. On the eve of the 'Glorious' Revolution, the Scottish army amounted to c.3,000 men in marching regiments, supplemented by a further 268 veterans stationed in places like Edinburgh, Stirling, and Dumbarton castle. The cost of this relatively small force in Scotland to the Scottish Treasury was c.£80,000 per annum. The collapse of James's regime in Scotland was aided by the removal of the Scottish army, numbering 2,946 men, to England in October 1688, thereby leaving only veteran garrison troops in Scotland. The establishment of a pro-Williamite regime in Scotland as part of the 'Glorious' Revolution aided strategic security in the wider struggle of the Nine Years War (1689–97) with Louis XIV's France and also offered additional sources of manpower which William could draw on to fight in major European warfare. As early as 2 July 1689 William of Orange asked the Scottish privy council to recruit soldiers to make up for the shortfall of Scottish troops in the duke of Schomberg's regiment in the Anglo-Dutch Brigade in the service of the United Provinces of the Dutch Republic (see LOW COUNTRIES). Three Scottish regiments of 500 men each, 1,500 in total, had traditionally served in the Brigade by the late 17th century.

Initial Jacobite military victory at the battle of Killiecrankie on 27 July 1689 despite inferior numbers (c.2,000 Jacobite troops compared to 4,000 Whig troops) was neutralized by the death of John Graham of Claverhouse, Viscount Dundee, an effective Jacobite military commander. Jacobite defeats at Dunkeld (21 August 1689) and Cromdale (1 May 1690) complemented by the military defeat of James VII and II in Ireland ended the first phase of *Jacobitism. Levy Acts for the raising of troops were passed in the parliamentary sessions of 1693, 1695, and 1696. The 1693 Levy Act provided for 2,970 foot, whilst the Acts of 1695 and 1696 allowed for the levying of 1,000 men per annum. On 22 January 1701 the Scottish parliament voted by a majority of 108 votes to 94 for the standing forces in Scotland to be continued at a level of 3,000 men. The 1704 Parliamentary Commission for Auditing the Accounts of the Public Funds noted that a sum of £1,744 was due to the burgh of Montrose for the levying of seamen to serve in the English Royal Navy. The potential supply of Scottish manpower to aid English military commitments in an age of European warfare had been a leading theme articulated by English commentators in the pamphlet war over the Union debate in the early 18th century. Scottish regiments served in the War of the Spanish Succession (1702–13), the War of the Austrian Succession (1740–8), and the Seven Years War (1756–63).

It has been estimated that up to 20,000 Scots supported the Jacobite cause at some stage or another in the 1715 rebellion, whilst fewer than 7,000 participated in the Hanoverian forces. In statistical terms, roughly 8 per cent of the adult male population participated in the Jacobite cause in 1715 whereas only 2.5 per cent came out for the Hanoverians. At the battle of Culloden on 17 April 1746 Hanoverian regiments enjoyed superiority in numbers of c.9,000 to 5,000 of their Jacobite adversaries. The pacification of the Highlands in the aftermath of Culloden provided an opportunity for Highland manpower to be employed in the service of the British *Empire. From 1757 onwards Highland regiments were raised for military service in North America in the Seven Years War. Military service became a central feature of Scottish participation in the British Empire.   JY

3. Highland regiments, 1750–1830

In May 1740 the British army's first formal Highland regiment was instituted when the Highland independent companies were united to form the 43rd (later 42nd) Highland Regiment, the 'Black Watch'. This tentative catering to regional distinctiveness by the British army was reinforced in May 1745 when a second regiment was raised by the fourth earl of Loudoun in response to the heavy defeat at Fontenoy. Yet any further expansion in the army's efforts to recruit Highland manpower by offering culturally customized regiments appeared to be blocked permanently by the military and legislative crackdown upon all expressions of *clan militarism in the aftermath of Culloden (see JACOBITISM). Although the development of Highlanders in kilted regiments (see DRESS, HIGHLAND) was later proclaimed as somehow natural and inevitable, the years from 1750 to 1756 show the military was extremely reluctant to create any such units. By late 1756, however, the threat to Britain's imperial interests in North America (see USA), allied with William Pitt the Elder's refusal to pay for additional German mercenaries, forced the duke of Cumberland to accept two new Highland units. The result was the 77th and 78th Highland regiments, commanded by Archibald Montgomery, later eleventh earl of Eglinton, and Simon Fraser of Lovat respectively. The latter regiment, not least because it contained fifteen Frasers amongst its officers, has become the focus of over-sentimentalized and unsustainable arguments that view Highland units as simply state-sponsored clan levies—a perception that has consistently clung to all kilted regiments. The 78th did, however, fight with distinction in 1759 during the battle of the Plains of Abraham, which ensured the fall of Quebec (see CANADA). Montgomery's regiment, meanwhile, was to play a prominent role in the suppression of the Cherokee from 1760, a campaign that, ironically, witnessed Highlanders perpetrating punitive policies of fire-raising and summary execution that had been the hallmark of Cumberland fourteen years earlier.

It is a measure of the performance of these regiments and the subsequent units raised in 1759–61 for deployment in Europe and India (see INDIAN SUBCONTINENT) that, upon the commencement of hostilities in the American colonies in 1775, the crown immediately accepted Simon Fraser of Lovat's offer of a regiment of 2,000 men. While the Seven Years War had demonstrated the potential of Highland manpower, the American War of Independence witnessed a wholly disproportionate reliance upon kilted regiments. In 1778, in an effort to reverse its defeat at Saratoga, the crown raised eleven regiments, six of which were Highland. Both of these conflicts witnessed the entrenching of extremely positive official attitudes towards Highland regiments, a trend mirrored by the emergence, within all sectors of Scottish society, of the perception that such units were the torchbearers of Scotland's culturally important martial tradition (see NATIONAL IDENTITY: 5).

The sea change brought about by Highland regiments within Scottish and, indeed, British attitudes towards Gaeldom is reflected in the fact that the French Revolutionary War from 1793 to 1801 witnessed the apogee of recruitment in the region. No fewer than 30 kilted regiments, mostly home defence battalions, were raised in this period. Although many, if not all, actually contained a large minority or, indeed, majority of non-Gael rank and file, the perception was that the region represented Britain's most productive source of military manpower relative to population. The majority of regular Highland regiments that survived into the Victorian era and the 20th century—the 78th Seaforths; the 79th Cameron Highlanders; the Argyll, Gordon, and Sutherland regiments— emerged in this decade. Thereafter, from 1800 to 1830, these units constituted one of the most potent symbols of Scotland's acceptance of the *Union of 1707, all the more powerful in that they also appeared to demonstrate that such acceptance did not and should not involve the downplaying of Scottish distinctiveness.

Yet for Gaels and their landlords, the period from 1750 to 1830 saw Highland regiments offer the means to far more practical ends. For Jacobite chiefs like Fraser of Lovat and, indeed, Hanoverians like the third duke of Argyll, they provided political rehabilitation and, in a wider sense, the mechanism whereby the region's politically and economically marginalized landed classes could obtain acceptance within Britain's ruling elite. For ordinary Gaels, they represented a double-edged sword. Severe landlord coercion and the likelihood of eviction faced most families if proprietary demands for their sons were not met. That said, military wages and pensions produced income on a scale that has been seriously underestimated, with remittances home often constituting 25–30 per cent of rent. Ultimately, the emergence of Highland regiments parallel, almost exactly, the development of both kelping and sheep farming. Indeed, as specialized regional economies (see ECONOMY OF THE HIGHLANDS AND ISLAND: 2–3), kelp and recruitment rose in the 1750s and collapsed almost simultaneously in the 1810s. As such, Highland regiments, in the period from 1750 to 1830, should not be seen as romantic hangovers from the age of clanship but rather as a manifestation of the Highlands' difficult and traumatic integration to the economy and society of Britain and its empire.

AMacK

4. Highland regiments since 1830

Since 1830 the Highland regiments comprised battalions of the British Regular Army, the Volunteers, the Militia, the Territorial Army, and the New Army of 1914. The battalion numbering system gave way to titles, and the whole has been the subject of considerable reductions by disbandment and amalgamation.

The regiments with a Highland designation or association in 1830 comprised the 42nd or the Royal Highland Regiment, 71st Highland Regiment (Light Infantry), 72nd or the Duke of Albany's Own Highlanders, 78th (Highland) Regiment of Foot (Ross-shire Buffs), 79th Regiment of Foot (or Cameron Highlanders), 90th Perthshire Light Infantry, 92nd (Highland) Regiment of Foot, and the 93rd (Highland) Regiment of Foot. Between 1830 and 1881 a number of regiments regained Highland status or association. They were the 74th (Highland) Regiment (1845), 73rd (Perthshire) Regiment (1862), 75th Stirlingshire Regiment (1862), and the 91st (Argyllshire Highlanders) (1864).

In 1881 a major reorganization took place in the British army. The old numbers were abolished and battalions were grouped together in pairs to form the 1st and 2nd battalions of each named regiment. Recruiting areas were allocated with a depot, which also accommodated the Militia and Volunteer battalions. Those in the Highland area were the Black Watch (Royal Highlanders) 42nd and 73rd—Perth, the Seaforth Highlanders (Ross-shire Buffs, the Duke of Albany's) 72nd and 78th—Fort George, the Queen's Own Cameron Highlanders 79th (one battalion only until 1897)—Cameron Barracks, the Gordon Highlanders 75th and 92nd—Aberdeen, and the Argyll and Sutherland Highlanders (Princess Louise's) 91st and 93rd—Stirling. And the Highland Light Infantry 71st and 74th were based in Glasgow.

At the end of the Second World War the 2nd battalions of each of these regiments were disbanded, amalgamated, or placed in suspended animation. Further amalgamations have followed: the Royal Scots Fusiliers and the Highland Light Infantry formed the Royal Highland Fusiliers (1959), the Seaforth Highlanders and the Queen's Own Cameron Highlanders formed the Queen's Own Highlanders (Seaforth & Camerons) (1961), the Gordon Highlanders and the Queen's Own Highlanders formed the Highlanders (Seaforth, Gordons & Camerons) (1994). The Militia battalions were not revived after the First World War and the Territorial battalions have been considerably reduced.

The Highland battalions have fought in some famous formations, most notably the Highland Brigade in the Crimean War 1854–6 under Sir Colin

Campbell, the 9th Scottish Division in the First World War; and the 15th Scottish Division, 51st Highland Division, and 52nd Lowland Division in both the First and Second World Wars.

In the 19th century the mark of a Highland soldier was both the kilt and tartan trews (see DRESS, HIGHLAND). The kilts were 'made up' with the pleats stitched in and a plaid worn separately. The ostrich feather bonnet became reserved for full dress and gave way to the 'hummel' or knitted humble bonnet, the glengarry, the Tam o'Shanter, and the steel helmet of 1915. In 1881, Lowland Scottish regiments also adopted tartan trews and, as a result, a strong but erroneous opinion grew up that only kilted regiments could be Highland. Throughout the First World War attempts to introduce a khaki kilt or replace the kilt with trousers were fiercely resisted. The last battalion to wear the kilt in battle was the Queen's Own Cameron Highlanders in France in 1940. In combat dress, there is now little to distinguish the Highland soldier from any other.

The Highland regiments made considerable efforts to retain their recruiting base in the Highland area. With falling population numbers this was often neither realistic nor possible, and as British army regiments they always maintained a healthy mix of nationalities and were no less Highland in their character as a result. Highland men and second-generation Highlanders from Lowland towns (see MIGRATION), together with Irish, Welsh, and the large numbers of English who were drafted in during the Second World War, all served the Highland regiments well.

A number of forms of music are known to have existed in the Highland regiments: pipers playing alone and in numbers, pipers and drummers as a pipe band, drummers, buglers, fifers and drummers, and military bandsmen, in what was called the Band of Music. Fifes had all but disappeared by the 1850s, the 91st Argyllshire Highlanders being the last known Highland regiment with a fife and drum band. Pipe bands, with drummers and pipers playing together, developed in the 1860s and there is evidence to suggest that they first began in Highland Volunteer Corps.

The Highland regiments have provided a number of leading composers of pipe music and these include John MacDonald, John A. MacLellan, Donald MacLeod, G. S. McLennan, and William Ross. The world-famous 'army class' for pipe majors, begun in 1910 by military members of the Piobaireachd Society and originally taught by John MacDonald of Inverness, made an important contribution to the preservation of Piobaireachd, the classical music of the Highland bagpipe. The military bands, which had existed in Highland regiments from the earliest days, ceased in the economies of the 1990s.

Highland battalions have served all over the world and have a deserved reputation for their endurance and fighting qualities. Notable events in their history include the 93rd Sutherland Highlanders at Balaclava (1854); the 78th at Lucknow (1857); the Gordon Highlanders at Dargai (1897); the Seaforths and the Camerons at Omdurman (1898), the Highland Division at Magersfontein (1899); the 51st Highland Division at Beaumont Hamel (1916), Saint-Valéry (1940), and El Alamein (1942); the Argylls defence of Singapore (1941) and the occupation of Crater during the Aden crisis (1967); the Camerons at Kohima (1944); the 15th and 51st Divisions at the Rhine crossing (1945); and many others.

Much of this Highland history, along with the memory of the men who made it, is preserved in the regimental museums of the Highland regiments.   DMH

5. Volunteers

A popular Scottish pastime in the second half of the 19th century was the Volunteer Movement. Volunteer corps, under the control of lords lieutenant, were raised as a result of French threats and popular demand in 1859. Initially they were little more than uniformed rifle clubs, although there was a real belief that they would be used for local defence in the event of invasion. The Volunteers of 1859 were entirely distinct from the Volunteers of the Napoleonic period—the Fencibles, the Militia, and the Yeomanry—and comprised Rifle, Engineer, Light Horse, and Mounted Rifle Volunteer Corps.

Membership of the Volunteers had a certain social cachet, for they were exempt from the Militia ballot and the cost of all arms, equipment, ammunition, and expenses were, at the outset, borne by the men themselves. Uniforms were the result of the preferences of the commanding officers who bore much of the operating expenses. The only government requirement on formation was that the corps provide a safe range for firing practice. Many Volunteer corps had excellent bands. The Volunteers were especially popular with tradesmen and professional men in towns and cities in Scotland many of whom were subscribers to the *Temperance movement, facts reflected in the early corps titles of, for example, 27th (Warehousemen) and 82nd (Total Abstainers) Lanarkshire Rifle Volunteer Corps. Over 400 separate corps were raised in Scotland.

These corps were reorganized as Volunteer battalions in the 1860s and linked with Regular Army depots in 1872. They gradually adopted the uniforms of their parent Regular Army regiments after the Army reforms of 1881. In 1908 the Volunteer battalions were converted into Territorial Army battalions. They relinquished their home defence role, became a reserve field force, and fought with distinction in two world wars.   DMH

art, exhibiting. Until the 19th century there was little opportunity in Scotland for artists to exhibit their work. Changes occurred through the actions of artists themselves, through government patronage, and through commercial art dealers.

The Associated Artists was the first artist-led organization. It mounted the 'First Public Exhibition of Paintings in Scotland by Artists' in 1808 at Mr Core's Lyceum in Edinburgh. Others followed and the tempo increased with the first annual exhibition of the (Royal) Scottish Academy of painting, sculpture, and architecture in 1827. Elsewhere, Aberdeen saw its 'First Exhibition of Paintings and Drawings' in 1821, as did Glasgow. The (Royal) Glasgow Institute of the Fine Arts (RGI) was established in 1861. In 1891 the Society of Scottish Artists (SSA) was founded to provide a platform for younger artists. Smaller groups were important in exhibiting contemporary art such as the Society of Eight (1912–33) and the Glasgow Society of Painters and Sculptors (1919–21). A later initiative was the 57 Gallery in Edinburgh, founded as a co-operative for contemporary Scottish artists in 1957. Individuals mounted their own exhibitions. In 1822 Hugh William Williams presented his views of Greece and Italy, and in 1894 James Guthrie assembled recent paintings in his studio at 7 Woodside Place, Glasgow.

Government patronage of the visual arts led to the opening of the National Gallery of Scotland in 1859, and local authority art galleries followed; for example, Dundee (1873), Aberdeen (1885), Glasgow (1901), Kirkcaldy (1925), and Perth (1935). The Edinburgh International Festival was launched in 1947 and art exhibitions have played an important role each year. In addition to the officially sponsored exhibitions such as Cézanne (1954) and Rouault (1966), contemporary Scottish work has been given a platform each year. During the Second World War the Council for the Encouragement of Music and Fine Arts (CEMA) assembled and toured art exhibitions. It was replaced by the Arts Council of Great Britain in 1945, whose Scottish Committee operated from 1947 to 1967 and was reformed into the Scottish Arts Council (SAC). The SAC also ran exhibition venues, such as the Fruitmarket Gallery in Edinburgh from 1975 to 1984, and it had a travelling gallery to serve remote areas. It provided funding for other venues such as Peacock Printmakers in Aberdeen (established in 1974), the Third Eye Centre in Glasgow (founded 1975), and the 369 Gallery in Edinburgh (1978–91). A move to site contemporary sculpture outdoors was made when the Scottish Sculpture Trust placed work at Carrbridge, Inverness-shire in 1978. Other initiatives include the placement of sculpture in Scottish towns, for example Perth, through the Perthshire Public Art Trust, and alongside the M8 between Edinburgh and Glasgow.

Art dealers also created exhibitions. Alexander Reid (1854–1928) introduced French avant-garde art to Scotland when he opened a gallery in the centre of Glasgow in 1889 where he also exhibited the work of the Glasgow School painters. In Edinburgh, Aitken Dott and Son began to exhibit paintings in 1896. Renamed the Scottish Gallery, subsequent exhibitions included William McTaggart (1901) and Samuel John Peploe (1903) and ever since it has promoted, exhibited, and sold the work of living Scottish artists. Other influential dealers in the 20th century include Cyril Gerber in Glasgow, co-founder of the Charing Cross Gallery in 1963 and of the Compass Gallery in 1968, and more recently Tom Wilson of the Open Eye Gallery in Edinburgh.

                                                    JS

art galleries and dealers. The earliest recorded public exhibitions of paintings in Scotland marked the royal entries such as that of Charles I into Edinburgh in 1633. George Jamesone's *Self Portrait with an Easel* (SNPG cl 644) appears to show his studio hung as an art gallery and this may have been common practice. In Boston, Scottish painter John Smibert's studio served as the first art gallery in America and in Edinburgh in May 1778 a list of paintings offered for sale by Alexander Runciman is not only evidence that his studio was indeed a gallery, but is also the first printed catalogue of an exhibition in Scotland. Raeburn's studio in York Place, Edinburgh, certainly served as a gallery for his own collection of his portraits, and also for the exhibitions of the Society of Incorporated Artists in 1809 and several years thereafter. This organization which existed from 1808 to 1813 was the first exhibiting society established in Scotland. It was followed by the (Royal) Institution for the Promotion of the Fine Arts in 1819 which also held exhibitions in Raeburn's studio. In 1826, however, the Institution was housed in a new building on the Mound (now known as the RSA), the first purpose-built, public exhibition gallery in Scotland. In 1826, however, a group of artists seceded from the institution to form the Scottish Academy. Granted its Royal Charter in 1838, its annual exhibition was the main event in the art calendar for much of the century. From 1856 the RSA shared a separate building with the new National Gallery of Scotland, but in 1908 the whole of the building was made over to the National Gallery and the RSA moved back into what had been the premises of the now defunct Royal Institution. There were also a number of other exhibiting societies such as the Royal Glasgow Institute and the Society of Scottish Artists (SSA) and there were local exhibiting societies in Dundee, Aberdeen, and elsewhere. The idea of the *Scottish National Portrait Gallery had been mooted in the late 18th century by the earl of Buchan, but it was not realized till 1885. Its present building was not completed till 1890.

In Glasgow, the McLellan Galleries housed the exhibitions of the Royal Glasgow Institute, but major municipal galleries were also established in Glasgow, Aberdeen, and other Scottish towns and cities in the later 19th and early 20th centuries. In 1842 Aitken Dott was founded in Edinburgh and was certainly exhibiting paintings before building a purpose-built gallery in the 1890s. Similarly in Glasgow, dealers like Alexander Reid also held regular exhibitions of work by contemporary artists. A number of private spaces were also available to smaller organizations like the Edinburgh Group or the Society of Eight. Many of the art institutions had corresponding members overseas whose work was regularly shown in Scotland and from the 1930s the SSA, in particular, regularly showed the work of leading contemporary artists. This pattern remained largely unchanged until the creation of the Scottish National Gallery of Modern Art in 1960 and of the Scottish Arts Council in 1967. The latter helped support a much more diverse gallery system distributed throughout the country which was also complemented by the expansion of the art trade in the 1980s and 1990s.   DM

art, Highland. A widely recognized concept of Highland art is witness to a distinctive visual and aesthetic tradition; powerful, persistent, and conservative in character, it gives the impression of belonging in a continuum embracing everything from prehistoric material culture, to modern styles and the plastic arts. We meet the loosely formulated term 'Celtic art' illustrated by often spectacular and sophisticated examples of cast and beaten metalwork such as torcs, bronze armlets, and brooches. Drawing on classical Graeco-Etruscan and eastern sources, so-called Pictish art (see CULTURE: 2) is in its turn a source of contemporary inspiration with its impressive surviving corpus in stone and metal, using a glossary of decorative motifs and the much-studied but ultimately enigmatic symbols in their remarkably uniform and consistent style. 'Celtic art' may also be a latter-day expression of the Romantic movement (see CULTURE: 12) and part of a Highland and Hebridean *genius loci*, building on Scottish styles of the art nouveau and notions of Highland culture. Highland art

today represents an espousal of real and imagined cultural roots, generally lacking authenticity but undoubtedly inspirational, even providing new impetus to scholarship.

Historically, Highland art is a phenomenon more complex and eclectic than might be imagined, associated with European Romanesque art styles and the late medieval *Gaidhealtachd* of the Highlands and Islands, embracing the period of the lordship of the *Isles until the *Jacobite wars of the 18th century. The lordship of the Isles defines a period from the late 12th century in which a society and its patronage flourished which sustained the arts (although, following the forfeiture of the lordship in 1493, paradoxically perhaps, Highland art continued to flourish in the 16th and 17th centuries, an era of apparently endemic warfare in which the *clans and their territories were formed and defined). Art, its practitioners, and patronage can be more clearly perceived with Somerled (d. 1164), the immensely powerful lord of the Isles, and his successors emerging from Gaelic-Norse stock and exploiting the political and strategic division between the kingdom of Scotland and a Norse overlordship (see SCANDINAVIA: 1). As a powerful and independent 'kingdom' (see ISLES, KINGDOM OF THE) with control of the sea, especially from the late 14th century under John MacDonald (or MacDomhnaill) of Islay, the lordship of the Isles became the focus of Gaelic art and culture in Scotland and with close links in terms of its practices and aesthetics with Gaelic Ireland.

Some sense of background and established traditions may be detected in the craftsmen described as *Oes Dana* 'Men of Art' in the Irish Law Tracts of the 7th and 8th centuries and in the life of the Celtic church of the 6th to 12th centuries; this was a monastic church with an emphasis on learning and community life, with workshops, *scriptoria*, and schools which have left the material evidence of standing crosses and manuscripts such as the Book of Kells (see ADOMNÁN, ST; CHURCH INSTITUTIONS: 1; COLUMBA, ST; IONA; IRELAND; RELIGIOUS LIFE: 1–2). It is appropriate that some of the earliest survivals of Highland art are shrines—the Kilmichael Glassary and Guthrie bell shrines—used to cover and protect earlier hand bells, enhancing the memory of the Scoto-Irish missionary saints whose virtual badge of office seem to have been the hand bell and the *bachall* (pastoral staff). Another famous church relic is the crozier or pastoral staff of St Fillan, known significantly by its familiar Gaelic name of the *Coigreach* 'Traveller'. The relics of the 8th-century missionary saint were kept in Glendochart and assigned to hereditary relic-keepers or 'dewars'. The *Coigreach* was the most celebrated survivor of this group and consists of an early bronze

covering for the crozier head, itself missing, enclosed in a 14th-century silver gilt case.

Probably the same craftsmen successors of the
'Men of Art' also made surviving pieces in metal
such as the 15th-century Dunvegan Cup (made for
an Ulster patron) and jewellery; a considerable
number of simple open ring brooches survive, engraved with geometric patterns and lettering and
sometimes decorated with niello. More elaborate
brooches set with crystals, pearls, and coral seem to
be forms of reliquaries in which a large crystal con-
ceals a cavity and amuletic formulas of names such
as Christ and the Magi protected the wearer. Examples are the Brooches of Glenlyon, Lorne,
Lochbuie, and Ugadale, named because of their association with respective families for generations.
Crystal settings in some instances may have come
from earlier church relics and also found their way
crafted into later silver settings for use as charms.
Too little is known at the moment about the craftsmen who made these objects although some may
have been settled in the vicinities of head-houses
such as Dunvegan, Castle Tioram, Duart, and Inveraray, on lands held rent-free by virtue of their
art. These castles created the context for the arts
and patronage such as was immortalized in the
conventional metaphors of Gaelic song (see SONG,
TRADITIONAL AND FOLK: 2):

> To the dwelling that is not mean,
> Where the roar of the pipes will be
> And again the sound of the harps,
> With the gleam of silver cups,
> Making the wine flow free
> And pouring it into the work of the goldsmith.

Other materials such as bone were worked elaborately by craftsmen and two caskets of whalebone
fitted with locks and bronze mountings are preserved in the collections of the National Museums.
The bone plates which form the box are carved
with panels of interlace in characteristically dense
patterns filling all the surface space. Similar caskets
are shown on contemporary grave-slabs at Craig-
nish, Iona, Kilbrandon, and Keills Knapdale. Other
intricately carved objects of bone were gaming-
table pieces of which many examples have been
found; a 13th-century praise poem to Angus of Islay
described the patrimony from his father Donald:

> To you he left his dwelling-place,
> Yours is each breastplate,
> Yours each treasure
>
> .   .   .   .   .   .
> His tapering swords
>
> .   .   .   .   .   .
> His brown ivory chessmen.

These *fir-tàileasg* (woodcarvings), used in table
games such as backgammon, were commemor-

ated in panegyric poetry and song as a fitting recre-
ational pastime for the warriors of the clan with
their metaphor of battle and the chase. Surviving
woodcarving is best represented by the *clàrsaichean*
(Highland harps) in the national collections, important indicators also of the musical tradition of
Gaelic Scotland. The finest known medieval *clàrsach*, dated to about 1450, is said to have been given
by Queen Mary to Beatrix Gardyn of Banchory and
survived in the family of the Robertsons of Lude.
The wood of the soundbox, forepiller, and harmonic curve is highly decorated with low-relief
carving and the detail was almost certainly highlighted by colours. The second *clàrsach*, known as
the Lamont Harp, has been dated to about 1500.

One of the most striking achievements of Highland art is still visible in the series of sculptured
monuments in the form of effigies and grave-slabs
in churches and churchyards in the west Highlands
and Hebrides. More than 600 are known, dating
mainly from the mid-14th century to about 1560 and
within the territorial ambit of the lordship of the
Isles. They are carved in a rich and intricate decorative style with familiar and symbolic objects set on
fields of Romanesque-style foliage and leaf design
with animals and mythical beasts. The largest
single concentration of carvings is in Iona where
more than 80 have survived. Other former monastic centres also preserve good examples such as a
tall disc-headed cross in Campbeltown carved with
a dense covering of foliage, mythical beasts, and a
crucified Christ which was removed after the *Reformation; the cross commemorates the parson of
Kilkivan in Kintyre. A grave-slab in Oronsay commemorates in a Latin inscription Murchadh Mac-
Duffie of Colonsay who died in 1539. The design of
a deerhunt, galley, and plant scrolls terminating in
mythical beasts is worked round the symbolic
sword (*claidheamh-mór*). Research has identified
four main schools of carving centred on Iona,
which was probably the earliest (the others were at
Oronsay, Kintyre, and Loch Awe), and two families in particular, O Brolchán and O Cuinn, brought
over from Ulster under the lordship of the Isles.
After the forfeiture of the lordship, this work was
carried out by independent carvers who probably
travelled to carry out their commissions.

The stone carvers' art seemed to decline in the
16th century and to have suffered a terminal blow
at the Reformation when crosses and other grave
monuments were discouraged by the Protestant
Church. The decoration of smaller and portable
items seemed to survive and even to flourish, and,
significantly, the market seemed to expand so that
fine brooches and decorated accoutrements such
as weapons (see WARFARE, WEAPONS, AND FORTIFI-
CATIONS: 2) were now acquired by all classes.

Significantly, much of this later art was produced mainly in the eastern Highlands and closer to larger markets. The now archaic Romanesque-style motifs such as interlace, foliage, and beasts were engraved on silver and brass brooches, some of large diameter or, as a contemporary commented, 'as broad as any ordinary pewter plate'. They were used by women to fasten the plaid (*earasaid*) across the chest and remained in fashion into the 18th century.

Typically, any broad, flat surface seemed to invite decoration with patterns of interlace and foliage such as the leather covering of targes (powder horns of flattened cow's horn) and the graceful curving butts of Highland long guns. In the course of the 18th century, the quality of design and craftsmanship seemed to fall away and decorated Highland accoutrements such as pistols, swords, and sporrans began to be made by craftsmen working in a Lowland tradition in burghs on the fringe of the *Gaidhealtachd* such as Inverness and Dumbarton, and market and droving centres such as Crieff and Doune. Within the Highlands, art and craftwork was in the hands of the *luchd-cèirde*—the *cèardan* or 'cairds' who travelled to make their products in the different districts and for clients who could supply the raw materials of their respective crafts. The families who had provided dynasties of craftsmen turned away from their inheritance in the changing world of the late 18th century, and one of the last armourer-blacksmiths of the MacNabs of Dalmally described the making of the traditional dirk with richly carved wooden hilt to a French traveller in the 1780s: 'we never deviate from this form, which is a very good one, being agreeable to the eye, and affording at the same time a solid hold to the hand which uses it. All the weapons of this kind which are made here, or in the neighbouring mountain, are of the same form with these, and that from time immemorial.'   HC

art history and criticism. George Turnbull's *History of Ancient Art* (1740) was the first major text on art by any Scottish author. In spite of its subject it also had specific relevance to contemporary art. It was followed by Allan Ramsay's *Dialogue on Taste* published in 1754, one of the first essays in empirical aesthetics, and by Archibald Alison's widely influential *Essay on Taste* (1790). Alison was a pupil of Thomas Reid whose own writings had wide implications for the visual arts (see CULTURE: 12). Otherwise, early art criticism was largely limited to newspaper notices, but Amédée Pichot comments illuminatingly on Scottish painting in his *Voyages littéraires et historiques en Angleterre et en Ecosse* (1825, also published in English and German.) From 1888 to 1890 the *Scottish Art Review* offered much more

ambitious art criticism than had been seen before. Contemporary pamphlets by Patrick Geddes, John Forbes White, and others show similar aspirations.

The first published history of Scottish art was by Sir George Chalmers in the *Weekly Magazine* in 1772, but the first extensive account was given by Alexander Campbell in his *Journey from Edinburgh through Parts of North Britain* in 1810. Allan Cunningham gives biographies of the principal Scottish artists in his *Lives of the Most Eminent British Painters* (1829–33) and his *Life of Sir David Wilkie RA* (1843) was the first extended biography of any Scottish artist.

In the mid-19th century David Laing collected extensive information on Scottish art, but it was never published and the first major text on the subject was Robert Brydall's *Art in Scotland* (1889). This was followed by James Caw's *Scottish Painting* (1908). A lively book, it was followed in turn, but not displaced, by such publications as John Tonge's *The Arts in Scotland* (1938) which coincided with the landmark exhibition Scottish Art at the Royal Academy that year.

In the 1930s Hugh MacDiarmid, William McCance, and others produced polemical writings which sought to align the visual arts with the Scots Renaissance in literature (see CULTURE: 22, 24). J. D. Fergusson's *Modern Scottish Painting* (1943) was a similar polemic and this trend continued in the 1940s in *Scottish Art and Letters*, a journal on which latterly MacDiarmid and Fergusson collaborated. In the 1950s and 1960s, a revived *Scottish Art Review* provided a mix of scholarly articles and more sober criticism, but the modern historiography of Scottish art really began with Alastair Smart's *Life and Art of Allan Ramsay* (1952) and Ellis Waterhouse's *Painting in Britain* (1953). Thereafter the volume of historical and critical publications began to increase, particularly in the form of exhibition catalogues, both historical and contemporary. David and Francina Irwin's *Scottish Painters at Home and Abroad* (1975) was the first of a number of modern histories of Scottish art, while the present author's *Scottish Art 1460–1990* was the first attempt to locate the achievement of Scottish artists where it belongs, in the broader intellectual history of the country and indeed of Europe.   DM

art trade. Evidence for the import of works of art before the *Reformation is also evidence for the existence of an art trade, but the first identifiable art dealer is John Clerk of Penicuik, a merchant who dealt in pictures in the 1630s and whose inventories even included a work by Rembrandt acquired in Holland and almost certainly from the artist. Generally, however, evidence for the existence of any significant art trade is slight till much later. There were certainly auctions in the later 17th century that included paintings and during the 18th century some artists dealt from time to time, or worked as agents, but because of the popularity of the Grand Tour aristocratic collectors were more inclined to acquire work abroad than through dealers based in Scotland. In Rome Gavin Hamilton, for instance, dealt in significant Old Masters and in antiquities. A little later Andrew Wilson dealt in paintings for collectors like Sir James Erskine of Torrie. With increased prosperity, collecting in one form or another ceased to be the prerogative of the very rich, and so private collecting provided material and customers for auctioneers like Thomas Dowell and later Lyon and Turnbull, who occasionally handled some major sales like that of the collection of Lord Clerk of Eldin in 1833.

The main market for contemporary art was provided by the annual exhibitions of the Royal Scottish Academy (RSA) and other exhibiting societies, but in 1842 Aitken Dott (now the Scottish Gallery) set up as a dealer in artist's supplies and seems very early to have expanded into art dealing. Later the firm established the Scottish Gallery where they showed artists like McTaggart and Peploe. There were also other dealers in both Edinburgh and Glasgow. In the later part of the century, for instance, Alexander Reid, who had worked first in Paris, set up in Glasgow and later in London where, as Reid and Lefevre, the business still continues. Reid handled some very important recent French art as well as providing support for a number of progressive Scottish artists.

The art trade boomed in the 1890s, but crashed in the late 1920s. Even an artist of the standing of F. C. B. Cadell died penniless in 1934 and S. J. Peploe had to turn to teaching at the end of his life. Although contemporary artists continued to sell work, prices were very low and their incomes had to be supported by teaching. In the post-war years artists like Alan Davie enjoyed considerable success, but to do so moved south, while others, like Joan Eardley or Elizabeth Blackadder, though they remained in Scotland, also found their market in London.

In the 1970s, due in part to investment by the Fine Art Society but also to the recovery of Scottish self-confidence, the market in historical Scottish painting began to grow rapidly. This was gradually matched by the development of a new market for contemporary art, but confidence was slow to develop and generally public taste remained conservative so that many more progressive artists still had to look for their markets in the south, or indeed overseas where Scottish artists enjoyed a considerable reputation.   DM

Australia. The earliest Scotland–Australia references, such as those of Revd John Dunmore Lang (Greenock), Sydney's first Presbyterian minister in 1823, were written to encourage 19th-century *emigration from Scotland to Australia, and promoted success stories of individual Scots. General histories of Australia up to the 1950s, however, made little differentiation between English and Scottish emigrants and did not recognize any measurable Scots influence. It was not until the 1960s and 1970s that a Scotland–Australia connection became a feature of Australian historical writing, but the context was a limited one. These studies highlighted the role of Scots capital and successful individuals, the 19th century, and the eastern states, while working-class Scots, 20th-century immigrants, and those in central and western Australia remained less well documented.

It is only the most recent studies, from the 1980s, which, while not denigrating the contribution of Scottish capital or that of individual Scots, devote more attention to the experiences of working-class Scots, and to regional and cultural factors associated with the departure and resettlement of these immigrants. A Scotland–Australia historiography, however, must acknowledge the 'great man' thesis which argues that Scots, as witnessed by a catalogue of prominent individuals, were over-represented among those who contributed to Australia's development.

Leaders in exploration included Captain James Cook, son of a Scottish father, who charted the east coast in 1770, facilitating British settlement in 1788; Thomas Mitchell (Craigend), surveyor-general of New South Wales who explored the Murray–Darling Basin and pushed southward into present-day Victoria in 1836; and Angus McMillan (Skye), who overlanded into the eastern part of that district, later named Gippsland, in 1839. Allan Cunningham, son of a Renfrewshire man, opened a way to the Darling Downs, southern Queensland, in 1827. Captain Patrick Logan (Berwickshire) took over command of the first party of convicts sent to the Moreton Bay area, southern Queensland, in 1825 where his extensive exploration led to closer settlement of that region. John Macdouall Stuart (Dysart) completed the first crossing of the continent from south to north in 1862.

In public affairs, Scots were prominent in the formative decades of the colony's administration. They included three early Governors of NSW, John Hunter (Leith), Lachlan Macquarie (Ulva), and Thomas Makdougal Brisbane (Ayrshire). Macquarie during his term (1810–21) initiated an enlightened policy of social rehabilitation for law-abiding ex-convicts. Penal reformer Captain Alexander Maconochie instituted a humane administration at Norfolk Island convict settlement in the years 1840–4.

Although differences between English and Scottish law initially limited the number of Scots at the Australian bar, the early legislative influence of reforming Scots parliamentarians was significant, especially in the area of popular land reforms. Prior to Federation, Scots were prominent as State premiers and as parliamentarians out of all proportion to their numbers in society, particularly in Victoria and Queensland. The nation's first governor-general and two of its first three prime ministers were Scots.

Although Scots are generally represented as bastions of political conservatism in Australia, there was a distinct vein of Scottish democratic radicalism and, occasionally, republicanism. In the formative years especially, Scots such as J. D. Lang, William Kerr (Galloway), Dr Alexander Thomson (Aberdeen), William Westgarth (Edinburgh), and Patrick Leslie led agitations in their respective colonial districts for the end of transportation and for independence from New South Wales control. Scots radicals contributed significantly, especially in New South Wales, Victoria, and Queensland, to the implementation of responsible government in the 1850s.

In various states, notably Queensland, New South Wales, and Victoria, Scots became influential newspaper proprietors, using their journals to champion political and social causes. Perhaps the most famous of these was David Syme, publisher and editor 1859–1908 of the Melbourne *Age*, which promoted land reform, a democratic legislature, and the protection of local industries.

Scots have been equally prominent in economic development. A major founder of the Australian wool-growing industry, John Macarthur, son of Highland-born Jacobite parents, began breeding merino sheep in 1797 and successfully promoted Australian wools in Britain. Niel Black (Argyll), with Scottish capital backing, established a squatting empire in Victoria's Western District. Fife-born George Russell, one of many Scots who crossed from Van Diemen's Land (later Tasmania) in 1836, developed and managed the extensive Clyde Company properties near Geelong, leaving a fully documented account of a large-scale Scottish pastoral enterprise from the 1830s to the 1870s.

Thomas Elder (Kirkcaldy) followed his brothers from the family merchant and fishing firm to South Australia and used profits from successful copper mining ventures at Wallaroo (commenced in 1859) and Moonta (1861) to sink bores, extend fencing, and develop dry-land farming north of Adelaide. He bred camels to expedite transportation and exploration in the outback. Elder's pastoral empire

exceeded Scotland in area, and with Robert Barr Smith (Renfrewshire), he built the firm Elder Smith into one of the world's largest pastoral agencies.

Among the many other Scots who initiated rural settlements were George Augustus Dalrymple (Aberdeenshire), leader of an expedition to settle Bowen in north Queensland in 1861; the Leslie family, Patrick, George, and Walter, also from Aberdeenshire, pioneers of south-east Queensland; and Captain James Stirling (Lanarkshire) who led the first Swan River Colonisation Company settlers to the Perth (Western Australia) region in 1829, and became first governor of Western Australia in 1831.

Surplus Scottish capital also made its way into Australian secondary and tertiary industries. Robert ('Merchant') Campbell, 'The father of Australian commerce', challenged the trading monopoly of the EIC from 1800 and liberated colonial trade from the control of the local officer corps in NSW. Scottish money and expertise underpinned the formation of several major banks and insurance companies. Founder and first manager of the Commercial Banking Company of Sydney, Leslie Duguid (Aberdeen), for example, had earlier helped found the Bank of Australia. Other major institutions founded by Scottish capital and expertise include the insurance giants National Mutual and the AMP Society.

Shipping, engineering, and steel manufacture all attracted Scottish endeavour. James Burn (Edinburgh) arrived in Queensland in 1862 and developed a shopkeeping business and shipping agency into a giant steamship company which, in partnership with Glasgow-born Robert Philp, became Burns Philp. Pioneers of the steel industry were Melbourne-based brothers Henry and Robert Langlands (Dundee), and Peter Nicol Russell (Kirkcaldy), who established first in Tasmania and then in Sydney. Scots were prominent in Australian mining ventures as investors, owners, and managers. In New South Wales, in 1885, Broken Hill Proprietary Company (BHP) for example, was largely founded on Scottish money and managerial skills.

But what does this roll-call of 'great Scots' mean? Not much, according to most studies. No significant causal link between a general 'Scottishness' and Australia's development can be demonstrated. Scots emigrants generally had but a footnote role in Australia's history, quickly becoming anonymous. Other studies, however, leaning heavily on the 'great Scots' thesis, associate so-called definable Scottish characteristics with advantages and with the disproportionate influence of these characteristics upon Australia's development.

Largely absent from studies up to the 1980s is the wider context of Scottish settlement. Variables such as the presence or absence of convict labour, the effectiveness of initial administrative controls, and the degree of internal as well as external migration make generalizations about overall settlement difficult. Over the whole of the 19th century Scots averaged 13 per cent of emigrants to Australia, but Scottish strength varied from state to state and even from district to district within states, and Scots never represented a homogeneous group within society, being a mixture of Highland and Lowland, capitalist and working class, town and country, and with mixed church affiliations.

Only 5 to 8 per cent of all transportees were Scots, half of these sentenced outwith Scotland (hence the range). Initially, the number of Scottish free settlers remained small. The long voyage and the initial absence of kin networks, as well as the cost, generally made Australia a less attractive destination than *Canada and the *USA. Those free settlers who came were usually people of substance, often with Indian mercantile or direct EIC connections.

Assisted and bounty immigration in the 1830s brought a dramatic change. Over 80 per cent of the 12,000 Scottish immigrants who arrived 1836–46 were working class. The Victorian gold rush in the early 1850s, famine, and perceived overpopulation in the Highlands in the 1840s and 1850s swelled the numbers of working-class immigrants (see HEALTH, FAMINE, AND DISEASE: 3; POPULATION PATTERNS: 2). Between 1852 and 1857 the Highland and Island Emigration Society conveyed almost 5,000 Scots from these distressed regions, mostly to Victoria, South Australia, and Tasmania.

Greater tolerance of family migration was a feature of assisted migration schemes operating in Scotland, partly as a concession necessary to induce Scottish migration. There were few attempts, however, to give land grants to immigrant communities or to preserve locality or even family ties when integrating disembarking immigrants into the labour market. There were thus few heavy concentrations of Scots, especially Highlanders, and most were diffused throughout the country.

Regional studies since 1980 have directed closer attention to the individual experiences of Scots who arrived without capital, demonstrating the extent to which, in this class, modest prosperity was, generally, a feature of the next generation. An upsurge in family genealogical research with a consequent flood of settler histories has stimulated this recent historical research.

Approximately 85 per cent of Scottish immigrants were Presbyterian, and faced the same difficulties as other denominations. Recent work has looked beyond the standard church histories, com-

prising records of individual congregations and ministries, to explore diversity and division within Presbyterianism. Those states with a strong Highland presence saw the development of a considerable number of Gaelic congregations; their struggles to maintain Gaelic ministers and survive the influx of English-speakers have been little charted, though a number of Gaelic churches continued into the 20th century.

Scots religious minorities have also suffered through historical neglect. The Anglican Church, identified as it was with the political 'establishment', provided an ever-present temptation to those Scots 'on the make'. Only some 2 per cent of Scottish immigrants were Roman Catholic (see ROMAN CATHOLIC COMMUNITY) and mostly from the Highlands. One of these, a Gaelic-speaking priest Ranald Rankin (arrived 1855), had assisted his starving Moidart parishioners to sail to Victoria. Unhappy without a Gaelic ministry, they appealed successfully for Rankin to Rome after the bishop of Glasgow had declined to spare him. Second-generation Scot Mary McKillop (1842–1909), founder of a teaching order, the Sisters of St Joseph of the Sacred Heart, is shortly to be canonized Australia's first official saint.

Although a Gaelic journal, *An Teachdaire Gaidhealach*, commenced in Tasmania in 1857, only in the 1990s is interest being shown in the Gaelic culture in Australia generally and in the Gaelic writing (see GAELIC LITERATURE) which flowed from Australia. *Shinty and the variety of *Highland games, as well as the evolution of the various Scottish and *Caledonian societies, are only beginning to gain attention from social historians.

In the last twenty years, regional studies have revealed the ferocity of interracial collisions over land exposing, at times, the ruthless face of Scottish capitalism dispossessing aborigines as it had previously dispossessed Scottish Highlanders. Although many individual Scots, such as Revd James Forbes in Melbourne, wrote feelingly about the plight of aborigines, the kirk in the various states was slow to organize work among them. While the positive contribution towards aborigines of authors like Dame Mary Gilmore (née Campbell) is known, only recently has work begun on regional folk poets and commentators such as James Grassie (ex-Inverness), who sympathetically recorded, sometimes in Ossianic verse, the wars and sufferings of aborigines in western Victoria. Australia's Flying Doctor Service is an outgrowth of the (Presbyterian) Australian Inland Mission's general concern for the social and medical well-being of all outback Australians.

The Scotland–Australia relationship goes much deeper than the well-documented capital and entrepreneurial links. Despite the wealth of surviving letters, official records, newspapers, and periodicals, the experiences of working-class Scots have been inadequately researched and there are few studies of 20th-century Scottish immigrants. 'Gaelic Scotland' in Australia has largely been ignored, and much work remains to be done on the collective processes by which aspects of perceived Scottishness were retained or discarded over time. General histories of Scots in Australia still accentuate notable individuals at the expense of social and regional history, leaving a comprehensive history of Scotland and Australia yet to be written.

KC/CC

Bairds of Gartsherrie, coal-owners, iron-masters, and landowners, were the eight sons of Alexander Baird of Old Monkland, Lanarkshire, a successful farmer who took mineral leases over a wide area. John concentrated on farming like his father, but the other seven, led by William (1796–1864) and James (1802–76), established the greatest coal and iron dynasty of the 19th century (see ECONOMY, SECONDARY SECTOR: 2). They began in 1816 with a small colliery assigned to them by their father, but in 1830 the firm of William Baird & Company, initially with three of the brothers and all the father's mineral leases, was formed. The first furnace at Gartsherrie began production in May 1830, and the firm used the hot-blast process patented by James Beaumont *Neilson (1792–1865) without the inventor's permission. This led to a famous trial in 1843 at the end of which William Baird signed a cheque for £106,000, an indication of the profits made. Expansion followed in Ayrshire via the Eglinton Iron Company (1845), with ironworks at Eglinton, Blair, Muirkirk, Lugar, and Portland. By 1870 the Bairds were the largest pig-iron producers in the world, with 42 furnaces, an annual capacity of 300,000 tons (304,800 tonnes) and an estimated profit of £1,000,000. The brothers provided entrepreneurship without family disputes: every aspect from mineral exploration to marketing was covered by one or other of them. After 1848 they acquired landed estates in seven counties, costing well over £1 million, gradually leaving the firm's management to relatives and concentrating on social advancement; their sons did not enter the business, but went to English public schools and 'Oxbridge' and took membership of London clubs and commissions in exclusive regiments; their daughters married well. William and James became Conservative MPs for Falkirk Burghs. The partners established schools in all the company's villages; they also financed institutes, reading rooms, libraries, and public parks.   JBut

Balliol family. The recorded history of the Balliols extends over eight generations from about 1093 to 1364 when Edward de Balliol, the last representative of the main branch of the family, died.

The first known member of the family, Guy de Balliol, was attracted to the service of William Rufus, and became established in northern England in the late 11th century. However, it was not until almost two centuries later that the family assumed any major significance in Scottish affairs: in November 1292, following what later became known as the *Great Cause, John (II) de Balliol, lord of Barnard castle, and, since the death of his mother, Dervorguilla, in January 1290, lord of Galloway, emerged as the successful competitor in the adjudication by King Edward I of England concerning the vacant throne of Scotland. His successful claim was based on the fact that his mother was the second daughter of Margaret, eldest daughter of Earl David of Huntingdon (d. 1219), brother of William I 'the Lion', king of Scots (d. 1214).

In the 12th century the Balliols had had little or no direct connection with Scotland. The first members of this family who settled in the kingdom, probably around 1200, were Ingram and Henry de Balliol, lords of Urr and Cavers respectively, and uncles of John (I) de Balliol of Barnard Castle who married Dervorguilla of *Galloway in 1233. This marriage, from which the Balliol claim to the Scottish throne initially stemmed, was also a major watershed in the fortunes of the family, given the series of substantial inheritances which fell to Dervorguilla following the deaths of her father, Alan of Galloway (d. 1234); her uncle, Earl John of Huntingdon and Chester (d. 1237); her sister, Christiana (d. 1246); and Earl John's widow, Helen (d. c.1253). By the middle of the 13th century, Balliol estates in England and Scotland were extensive, and Matthew Paris referred to John (I) de Balliol as being 'rich and powerful' and having 'money . . . in abundance'. After his death, his widow founded the Cistercian house near Dumfries known as Sweetheart abbey and erected friaries at Dundee, Dumfries, and Wigtown, as well as a hostel for poor scholars at Oxford, later to be called Balliol College.

By contrast with most of the cross-Channel baronage, the Balliols were also remarkable for the almost unbroken possession of their Continental properties through into the 14th century. Their estates, including the lordship of Bailleul-en-Vimeu, near Abbeville, from which they took their name, lay in the counties of Vimeu and Ponthieu in Lower Picardy, beyond the eastern frontier of the duchy of Normandy, which had been lost to the Capetian kings of France in 1204. In 1279 Ponthieu was inherited by Edward I of England and his consort, Eleanor of Castile, on the death of Eleanor's mother, and thereafter, the Balliol's Picard inheritance became only as secure as Anglo-French relations permitted.

Little is known of King John's early life and career. Born between about 1248 and 1250, possibly in Picardy, he succeeded to the family estates in 1278, following the deaths of his father, John (I) (d. 1268), and his three elder brothers Hugh, Alan, and Alexander. As the youngest son of an especially devout mother, he may well have been destined for a monastic career, having, on his own admission, for a long time attended the schools of Durham, almost certainly the novices' school. He was enthroned as king of Scots at *Scone on 30 November 1292. Balliol family links made themselves manifest almost from the outset. His royal councillors included many trusted associates such as John Comyn of Badenoch who was related to Balliol by marriage (see COMYN FAMILY). Royal officials included kinsmen such as Alexander de Balliol of Cavers, chamberlain or associate-chamberlain since 1287, and his cousin, Hugh de Eure or Iver, executor of his father's will, who served as royal envoy. Links with Picardy also emerged particularly clearly. In 1293, for example, John issued a royal letter of protection in favour of the merchants of Amiens coming to or staying in Scotland, almost certainly promoting their lucrative trade in woad-dye. Also, by the terms of the Franco-Scottish military treaty of 1295–6, part of the money for the dower of the French king's niece, to be married to John's son Edward, was to be raised from Balliol's own private estates in Picardy.

Administratively, John's short reign was distinguished, witnessing a significant assertion of royal authority through *parliament, and a constructive ordinance of 1293 creating three sheriffdoms in the west Highlands: Skye, Lorn, and Kintyre. Politically, however, his reign was dominated by a series of appeals from Scottish courts to those of Edward I of England, the pressure from which eventually led to his downfall.

War with England broke out when Edward's demand that certain Scottish towns and castles be granted as sureties for the answering of appeals was refused. The only battle of this campaign, at Dunbar in April 1296, resulted in a decisive victory for the English under King John's father-in-law, John de Warenne, earl of Surrey. By early July, King John had formally surrendered, and may have been publicly cashiered, possibly even paraded as a penitent, the removal of the royal blazon from his surcoat or tabard giving rise to his nickname of 'Toom Tabard', meaning empty surcoat.

Imprisoned in England until 1299, John was then transferred into papal custody. By 1301 the king of France had established him at 'his castle of Bailleul in Picardy', and the letter containing this news referred to a rumour that Philippe IV might be preparing to send Balliol back to Scotland 'with great strength'. Since 1296, Scots leaders had continued to treat John as their lawful king, and now, with a strong affirmation of French and papal support, the prospect of his restoration, or his son's succession, appeared realistic. However, the defeat of the French army at Courtrai in 1302 ended all possibility of French military support. Although to the end Balliol retained the style of 'king of Scots', after 1304 the likelihood of his restoration was much reduced. He died in Picardy shortly before 4 January 1315, having lived long enough to have learned of the outcome of the battle of Bannockburn in June 1314, and possibly even of the Cambuskenneth Parliament in the following November. (See ANGLO-SCOTTISH RELATIONS: 2; FRANCE; INDEPENDENCE, WARS OF).   GPS

banknotes. Scotland is unusual in that the issue of banknotes in sterling denominations is currently the responsibility of three resident commercial banks: Bank of Scotland (1695) (see DARIEN), Royal Bank of Scotland PLC (1727), and the Clydesdale Bank PLC (1838), rather than the Bank of England (1694). Scotland was not the first country to issue paper money. It had been tried in China during the 14th century, and there were also experiments in Sweden in the generation before 1695. But Scotland was the first country to issue and sustain a successful paper currency on general issue to the public. The process of learning to control note issue was one of the keys to the rapid development of the 'Scotch' banking system during the 18th and early 19th centuries. In Scots law, there is no concept of legal tender in paper money, and all paper in circulation has the status of a promissory note guaranteed by the assets of the issuer. It is noteworthy that for the first 100 years the banknote was not only a medium of exchange like gold and silver, but also a method of providing short-term credit to customers. By 1800 this had disappeared, being replaced by the overdraft and the term loan. The limits of note issue were established by the 1845 Bank Act (the first serious attempt at regulating Scottish banking from Westminster), which allocated an authorized issue of banknotes to each of the then existing eighteen banks of issue, based on their average circulation during the previous twelve months. No new banks of issue could be created thereafter, and since that time, amalgamations, bankruptcies, and mergers have reduced the number to just three in 2001.

The total authorized note issue of 1845 was £3 million sterling. In 1998 the average daily note issue of the three banks stood at £1,718 million sterling. The Royal Bank of Scotland is the major issuer with approximately £870 million in circulation, Bank of Scotland has approximately £500 million on issue, and the Clydesdale £350 million. The difference between the authorized issue and the actual value of banknotes in circulation is balanced by securities deposited or on call to the Bank of England at 24 hours' notice. Each bank issues only its own banknotes, and those of the Bank of England. Until the 1960s the weekly note exchange was a regular feature of branch banking in each of the major towns and cities throughout Scotland. In 2001 the exchange is handled centrally, daily, and the resultant balances settled electronically.

The note exchange started in the 1770s, and was an important part of the 'Scotch' system of banking. Peer-group willingness to admit a new bank to the note exchange, therefore mutually guaranteeing the creditworthiness of a bank's banknote issue, was a vital element in that bank's ability to trade. If a bank had to stop trading, its note issue was honoured by the other banks, thereby providing a public safety net without the need for a government central bank operating as guarantor. This system demonstrated its worth in 1793, when the Bank of England was forced to close its doors—the result of a collapse of confidence due to the onset of the French Revolutionary Wars. The Scottish banks' unregulated note issue in this period is seen as a successful example of a 'free banking' system. It is clear that the two chartered banks, Bank of Scotland and Royal Bank of Scotland, operated under strong political guidance as a lender of last resort for the system with defined spheres of influence. This worked well up to 1815. It fell apart thereafter, partly because political control was loosened, but more fundamentally because it was not capable of dealing with the financial and capital requirements of the second phase of industrialization (see ECONOMY: 4) in the west of Scotland.

Banknote design applies technology and artistry to produce a note, which is attractive to look at and handle, but serves the fundamental purpose of making forgery difficult and expensive. It is this, and the variety of possibilities, which makes Scottish banknotes attractive to the collector. So far as the banks are concerned, any note in public hands is issued and no matter how old or rare to be redeemed at face value.

Since 1918 banknote issue has become a central bank monopoly in most countries. Scotland's (and Northern Ireland's) situation looks anomalous. Most banks buy their notes from the central bank. The attractions of retaining a Scottish note issue are threefold. First, banknotes held in cash machines and branch tills do not count as part of the notes issued to the public. Secondly, the production costs of banknotes are less than the costs of buying Bank of England notes, and thirdly, it brings the bank's name before every member of the Scottish public, in a way which could not be achieved in any other way. Assuming that Britain joins EMU then the future of Scottish banknote issue must be in doubt. Theoretically it can continue, but Scottish banks would be seen to have an unfair competitive advantage, which will not be tolerated by the European Central Bank.   ACa

Barclay, William (1907–78), biblical scholar and communicator. Born in Wick and brought up in Motherwell, the son of a bank manager, he was educated at the universities of Glasgow and Marburg. He was ordained as a minister of the Church of Scotland in 1933 and served for fourteen years at Trinity church in Renfrew. He was appointed lecturer in New Testament at Glasgow in 1947, and was then professor of divinity and biblical criticism in 1963 until his retirement in 1974. He received a DD from Edinburgh University in 1956 and was made CBE in 1969. His primary concern was to communicate the Christian faith to the ordinary person. He saw himself as a 'theological middleman' whose strength lay in an ability to impart the results of biblical scholarship in language which the 'plain man' could understand. His output as an author and journalist was prodigious. He wrote over 70 books, including the popular *Daily Study Bible*, a seventeen-volume series on the New Testament, which has sold well over 3,000,000 copies in English and continues to be in demand. He also published an influential translation of the New Testament. His success as a television broadcaster was phenomenal. He became a well-known figure throughout Scotland with his gravelly voice and Lanarkshire accent. His traditional style of lecturing proved to be immensely popular and exhibited his meticulous preparation, amazing memory, and down-to-earth approach. He combined rather conservative views about the composition of the books of the Bible with more liberal views about the Virgin birth and the miracles of Jesus. Willie Barclay was first and foremost a preacher and a teacher of the Christian faith. He was a kind, generous, and modest man, for whom the call of God, faith in Christ, and the place of prayer were of the utmost importance.   DMM

Beardmore, William, & Co. William Beardmore & Co., owner of the Parkhead Forge in the east end of Glasgow, was established in 1871 when the business was acquired from Robert Napier & Sons, the shipbuilders. Under Sir William Beardmore (1856–1936; Lord Invernairn, 1921–36) the firm expanded rapidly and during the inter-war depression collapsed. In 1879 he began making open hearth steel and added a steel foundry the following year. In 1888 armour plate plant was installed, followed in 1891 by a mill to roll plates for high-pressure boilers. Beardmore acquired Napier's shipyard in 1899 and opened his own naval construction works at Dalmuir on the lower Clyde in 1905. This and other investments left him short of capital and he was forced to sell half his equity to Vickers. This was an unhappy relationship, which came to an end in 1913. On the outbreak of the First World War, Beardmore enthusiastically responded to the emergency, laying down plant to build howitzers, tanks, aeroplanes, airships, and steel. During the early part of the war the company's plant was the focus of industrial unrest over issues of rent increases, dilution of labour, and restrictive practices. There was serious confrontation between Beardmore and David Kirkwood, the leader of the shop stewards, which led to Kirkwood's arrest. Beardmore planned to convert wartime plant for the construction of ships, locomotives, buses, lorries, taxis, aeroplanes and airships. This scheme was ill-conceived. With the collapse in demand for steel, the business was in serious difficulty by 1926. Beardmore was ousted from the business the following year and the Dalmuir yard closed in 1930. Other plant was either liquidated or sold off. The Parkhead Forge continued to operate until the early 1980s—albeit on a much-restricted site. It is now the Forge Shopping Centre—a fitting metaphor for de-industrialization. (See also ECONOMY, SECONDARY SECTOR: 2; ECONOMY: 5.)   MMo

Begg, James (1808–83), prominent member of the Free Church of Scotland and one of Thomas *Chalmers's principal lieutenants at the time of the *Disruption of 1843. Begg came from a Church of Scotland family which had strong associations with the Evangelical or 'Popular Party' within the 18th-century church which had been opposed to the Moderates led by Principal William Robertson (see RELIGIOUS LIFE: 5–6). Begg grew up in an environment which denounced patronage and the right of the state to interfere in matters of church government. In spite of this, Begg remained resolutely opposed to the voluntary principle of church government and believed that the Church of Scotland should remain a 'national' or established church which had the endorsement and support of the state. He held this conviction to the end of his life. Begg was called to the parish church of Liberton in Edinburgh in 1835, where he remained until the Disruption of 1843. Thereafter he moved the short distance to Newington, where he stayed for the last 40 years of his life. Begg was a vociferous campaigner against what he called 'the evils of popery'. His book, *A Handbook of Popery*, was a best-seller in the 1850s and Begg was especially keen to invite former priests into his parish to expose the supposed corruption inherent in Roman Catholicism (see ROMAN CATHOLIC COMMUNITY). Unfortunately for Begg, not all his former priests were genuine and one, after being made an elder, absconded with the parish collection. His obsession with Catholicism led him to press the government for inspections into nunneries. Begg was also a devoted disciple of the ethics of 'Self-Help' and he campaigned among the Edinburgh working class to promote a workers co-operative housing scheme (see RESPECTABLE CULTURE). He was always identified with the 'die-hard' section of the Free Church and remained opposed to innovations such as singing hymns. His stern, unbending approach to worship was supported by the 'Highland Host', a group of Highland fundamentalists, with whom Begg was frequently identified (see RELIGIOUS LIFE: 8). His opposition to the voluntary principle and church disestablishment surfaced in his latter years as he opposed any attempt to unite the Free Church with the United Presbyterian Church.   RJF

Bell, Andrew (1753–1832), educationalist and clergyman. Bell was born in St Andrews, where he studied at the university, taking a particular interest in mathematics and natural philosophy. He emigrated to America in 1774 to work as a private tutor, and moved from there to England to become a Church of England clergyman. In 1787 he went to India (see INDIAN SUBCONTINENT), and his educational interests expanded when he became head of an orphanage in Madras (a post he combined with being chaplain at Fort St George). Having to teach large numbers of boys with only a few unenthusiastic assistant teachers to help, he devised the system known as Monitorial: pupils were taught not only the subjects of the curriculum but also how to teach these to younger children. Bell believed that this was educationally effective and encouraged a sense of responsibility.

He returned to England in 1798, and set about promoting his Madras System throughout Britain (while holding a series of church appointments culminating in being made a dean of Westminster abbey in 1819). Eventually over 13,000 schools in Britain had adopted the system, although this was also due to the similar ideas developed independently by Joseph Lancaster some years after Bell.

Bell founded the Madras College school in St Andrews, based on his system, and left money for similar foundations in Edinburgh, Leith, Glasgow, Aberdeen, and Inverness. To promote the study of this and other educational methods, the trustees of his will donated part of the money he left to found chairs of education at Edinburgh and St Andrews universities in 1876, the oldest chairs of education in Britain. Although the Monitorial system became unfashionable with the rise of fully trained teachers in the late 19th century, the idea that the independence of learners can be enhanced through their teaching their peers became commonly accepted from the 1980s onwards.   LP

Berwick, once Scotland's most prosperous burgh, was finally lost to England in 1482. Based on a peninsular site between the River Tweed and the sea, the settlement was of obvious strategic and commercial importance. It had been a burgh for almost two centuries by the outbreak of the wars with England in 1296 and was unusual among Scottish burghs (see URBAN SOCIETY: 1) in having a provost, burgesses, and common seal by 1212. Its economic hinterland was rich wool- and grain-producing Teviotdale, returning customs dues of £2,190 in 1286. By 1253 the burgh had agreed an annual fee of 500 merks with Alexander III (1249–86), marking its further independence from direct royal control. Its importance in northern European trade was marked by the colonies of Flemings (see LOW COUNTRIES) and Germans (see GERMANY, THE BALTIC, AND POLAND: 1) who each had their halls within the burgh.

Positioned on the border between England and Scotland, the outbreak of war between these two countries placed Berwick on the front line and its history was profoundly affected by it. In the first actions of the war the burgh defied the large English army brought across the Border by Edward I on 30 March 1296. Needless to say, that army easily broke through the timber palisade that constituted the town's defences and the castle soon submitted. The burgesses, who were too lowly to be saved by the conventions of medieval warfare (see WARFARE, WEAPONS, AND FORTIFICATIONS: 1), were killed in their thousands, the Flemings having perished in their Red Hall during the attack itself.

Despite this onslaught, Edward I had high expectations for the town. After all, the English government of Scotland resided in the castle and it was necessary, in the first instance, to upgrade its defences. However, the Scottish treasurer, Hugh Cressingham, deemed building in stone unnecessary in the interests of economy.

Edward also wished to indulge in a town-planning exercise for the burgh and ordered a number of English experts to convene to advise him. Having killed many of the original inhabitants, it was necessary to attract English settlers to the burgh, although the outbreak of revolt in Scotland by 1297 soon put an end to the experiment. In the following years, building works concentrated on strengthening the defences against Scottish attack and a small standing army of up to 60 men-at-arms and 1,000 foot soldiers was usually resident in the town. However, strong walls were no defence against lack of payment and in September 1301 there was nearly a mutiny among the foot soldiers.

By 1302, however, Berwick seems to have been in a relatively peaceful state and the English burgesses in the town lobbied the king for a new constitution, which was duly granted on 4 August. This revived many of Berwick's previous privileges, including the right to a twice-weekly market on Mondays and Fridays and an annual fair from 3 May to 24 June. The royal officers in the town were ordered not to interfere with the burgesses' administration of their own affairs.

Berwick remained largely unaffected by the war (see INDEPENDENCE, WARS OF), largely because of its proximity to the English border, until 2 April 1318 when *Robert I finally managed to wrest this last piece of Scotland from English control. The town remained in Scottish hands until Edward III entered the war formally in 1333, having been granted much of southern Scotland by his puppet king, Edward *Balliol, son of King John. A Scottish relieving force under the Scottish guardian, Archibald Douglas, was defeated at Halidon Hill on 19 July, and Berwick was once more in English hands. It was not, in fact, restored to Scottish control until it was ceded to James III (1460–88) by the Lancastrian side in the English Wars of the Roses in April 1461. However, James's reign was also to see the final handover of Berwick to England during the crisis of 1482, when the king's brother, Alexander, duke of Albany, led an English force into Scotland and James's nobles refused to fight for him. The town remains in England, though the sheriffdom is still in Scotland.

The wars with England can have done little to enhance Berwick's trading potential—the colonies of foreign merchants certainly disappeared—but we must be careful not to exaggerate their effect. In the long term, the slump in the wool trade at which Berwick and its hinterland excelled surely had a much greater effect. However, the burgh's appropriation to England from the 1330s onwards did permit the rise of *Edinburgh to an unparalleled position of pre-eminence within Scotland's economy, due to the lack of competition in south-eastern Scotland. One of the original four burghs of Scotland, Berwick's final loss to the Scottish crown in 1482 must be considered more potential than actual, given that its final transfer took place with little or no protest.   FW

Birsay. The Brough of Birsay, a tidal island, is one of the best-known archaeological sites in Orkney, projecting out into the Atlantic at the north-west corner of Birsay Bay. Its name derives from the Old Norse *borg* (fortress or stronghold), which is likely to refer to the natural defensive qualities of an island difficult of access. In the 19th century, Sir Henry Dryden cleared out remains of a chapel, and considerable clearance and excavation took place to lay the site out for the general public after the site came into the care of the Secretary of State for Scotland in 1934. This work was curtailed with the outbreak of war, but work resumed in the 1950s and 1960s, followed by later campaigns on a large scale from 1974 until 1982, taking in both the laid-out area and areas to the south and the 'Peerie Brough'.

Impressive buildings were found to the north of the chapel, and an extensive churchyard with both Norse and earlier burials to the south and east of the chapel. A Pictish stone with three warriors depicted was a notable find. Earlier structural elements uncovered below the chapel and around the churchyard have been claimed as Celtic. However, it can now be argued that these may be dated to the Christian Norse period.

There has been much discussion of the significance of the entries in the *Orkneyinga Saga* concerning the 'minster dedicated to Christ' established by Thorfinn at Birsay. Some scholars take the view that the buildings mentioned in the saga can be identified with structures excavated on the Brough. Others see these structures as 12th century (rather than 11th), monastic in character, and favour a location for the 'minster' in the village area. In 1982, excavations took place in advance of restoration of the parish church of St Magnus. Structural elements uncovered below the present church have been accorded a probable 12th-century date, and it is suggested that the present building was preceded by a pre-Reformation church of some sophistication. However, the dating accorded to the remains does not enable firm associations with the historical data, and so it cannot yet be claimed that the 'minster' was originally located in the village. Norse Christianity clearly focused upon Birsay (see SCANDINAVIA: 1), but once the cathedral was built in Kirkwall in 1148 × 1165, the focus of secular and ecclesiastical power shifted away.

The earlier excavations on the Brough uncovered buildings of the Viking period to the north and west of the churchyard, together with a complex of structures from the Pictish and late Norse periods to the east. The complex of buildings to the east has been shown to come from four major periods: an initial Pictish phase, followed by three Viking and late Norse phases. Only the last relates to the laid-out, standing buildings. In the north, west, and south, there is particularly clear evidence for multi-phase activity, with the replacement and reorientation of buildings in the Viking period, as well as clear evidence for many more buildings dating to these four periods, and across a far wider area than recognized formerly. There is a rich artefactual assemblage from both Pictish and Viking periods.

Within the village area, there are now clear indications that building foundations have been discovered below modern houses and that further structures from the Viking and late Norse periods remain to be discovered. The place name 'Tuftaback' (bank or slope of house sites) might well be equated with the area to the south of the Burn of Boardhouse. Here, Viking and late Norse buildings and middens of some complexity have been uncovered on top of a mound site with archaeological deposits going back into prehistory, and a second mound site exists below an adjacent modern building, extending down to the river bank.

Beyond the village to the south, and at the south end of the Links, is Saevar Howe, another multi-period mound site, examined both in the 19th century and more recently. Pictish buildings here were apparently built on top of a prehistoric site, then superseded by Viking dwellings. On top was the remains of a Christian Norse cemetery probably from the 10th or 11th century—although not recognized as such at the time.

Cemeteries, from both the Roman Iron Age / Pictish and Viking periods have also now been recognized from the area between the village and the Brough to the north (the Point of Buckquoy). The earlier burials are marked by cist graves below mounds of sand and stone cairns, without accompanying grave goods, and the later ones by burials either in cists or simply dug into the contemporary ground-surface, but accompanied by grave goods recognizably Viking in form and date. Fragmentary Viking settlement remains, with accompanying rich midden deposits, and several characteristic Pictish-period cellular and figure-of-eight shaped dwellings, have also been excavated. One Pictish farmstead was succeeded by a Viking-period farmstead and burial. It has also been suggested that the evidence from this latter site points to some degree of co-existence by the two groups of *Picts and Vikings. Even earlier, the area was clearly of significance in the earlier Iron Age (structural evidence) and the Bronze Age (midden deposits).

Clearly, from the above account, it can be seen that there is much archaeological material to support the conclusion, derived from written sources, that Birsay was a centre of political and ecclesiastical power during the Viking and late Norse periods, and also now evidence to support an importance in the preceding Pictish period, together with an imperfectly understood role in prehistoric Orkney. CDM

bookselling pre-dated and was a more important engine for culture and literacy than Scotland's small domestic printing press (see PRINTING AND PUBLISHING). By the late medieval period, manuscript and imported printed books were sold from stalls in the burgh fairs, the traditional markets for paper, and 'stationers'' stalls at the universities. However, it is only from the 1590s that a clear network of 'permanent' bookshops had taken root, mainly in Edinburgh, but also in other burghs like Perth (c.1587), Glasgow (c.1599), St Andrews (c.1599), and Aberdeen (c.1613). Of course, from the early modern period many printers and bookbinders were also booksellers.

During the 17th century bookselling spread to other provincial centres, especially from the late 1650s, and specialists appeared mainly in Edinburgh such as Andrew Wilson (fl. 1634–54) and John Vallange (fl. 1678–1712), school and law book specialists respectively. The 18th century was characterized by long, family bookselling dynasties like James Chalmers and son in Aberdeen (fl. 1736–1810) and the still surviving John Smith and Son of Glasgow, founded in 1751 and perhaps the world's oldest continuously trading bookseller. In Enlightenment *Edinburgh the most famous booksellers were Allan Ramsay (fl. 1718–40), the poet and editor, and William Creech (fl. 1771–1815), publisher of Burns, whose office became the focus for literary society. Meanwhile in the streets cheap ballads, chapbooks, and news-sheets were distributed by the many chapmen and 'running-stationers'.

Most of the greatest booksellers of the 19th century were also the renowned publishers and printers of Edinburgh such as Archibald Constable (1774–1827) and William Blackwood (1776–1834). However, new mass market demands for printed matter enticed the Edinburgh bookseller John Menzies (1808–79) to move into the wholesale trade in the 1830s, offering newspapers and stationery as well as books, and in 1857 to join the railway-station bookstall trade in direct competition with W. H. Smith of England. John Menzies's distribution network and periodical sales left it unable to respond to the paperback revolution from the 1930s. Ironically, Menzies bookshops are now under W. H. Smith, yet a small number of independent booksellers with branches of UK bookshop chains still minister effectively to the needs of Scottish readers.
AMa

Borders: 1. to 1603. 2. since 1603.

1. to 1603

The notion of a fixed border with England was a comparatively late medieval development. The 10th century saw progressive Scottish expansion south-eastwards into former Northumbrian territory in Lothian and the Tweed basin, matched by a readvance of Strathclyde into the Solway region in the south-west. Victory over the Northumbrians at Carham in 1018 confirmed Scottish control of the region between the Forth and the Tweed, but, while subsequent events established the Tweed as the southern limit of expansion, 11th- and 12th-century rulers harboured ambitions to push that frontier further into Northumbria. The contemporary growth of English royal authority north of the Humber, however, represented by earls based on York, checked Scottish ambitions. In the west, annexation of Strathclyde after 1018 brought Scottish influence to the Solway, and later to Carlisle, held down to 1093.

The extension of Norman royal power north of the Humber brought a contraction of the area under Scottish domination in the 1090s. This retrenchment was exaggerated by creation of a substantial apanage in the southern Uplands for the future *David I, where he established the power base from which he governed Scotland after his accession in 1124. This territory's centrality to David's power was reinforced in the 1130s by seizure of Cumberland, Westmorland, and Northumbria north of the Tees, and their integration into his kingdom. Secure under David's rule, this extended zone, and Tweeddale in particular, emerged as the economic heart of his domain, where the crown enjoyed unquestioned regional supremacy founded upon the creation of a dependent 'feudal' colonial aristocracy and reinforced by the foundation of a string of royal monasteries and burghs.

Loss of control over the northern English counties in 1157 and the establishment of a new frontier on the Tweed–Solway line did not end the prosperity of this southern zone and its place as the hub of royal power in Scotland. Scottish kings down to 1237 sought restoration of their extended domain, but warfare with England to this end after 1173 underscored the exposure of this economically vital region. In the more stable environment of the late 13th century, buoyed by expanding domestic and foreign markets, the eastern border territory and in particular its chief outlet at *Berwick, reached new levels of prosperity founded largely on the wool trade. Although generated by general economic expansion (see ECONOMY: 2), continuation of this prosperity and stability depended largely on the maintenance of good relations with England. The collapse of that relationship after 1296 had disastrous consequences for what had become the Borders.

After the failure of their attempts at the total conquest of Scotland in the early stages of the Wars of *Independence, recognition of the economic potential of this zone saw English effort in the period down to 1314 concentrated on maintenance of their grip over it. Restoration of Scottish control, however, did not lead to a re-establishment of the status quo ante, reflected in the permanent shift northwards of the centres of royal power and in the failure of Berwick to regain its mercantile domination. The former resulted in the substitution of the regional primacy of the crown through delegation of that role to military deputies, in particular to the *Douglas family. The erosion of crown authority accelerated with the renewal of warfare with England in 1333. When peace was restored in 1357, with the English still in possession of Berwick, Roxburgh, and Annandale, the Douglases had established domination over the political life of the region, underscored by their near-monopoly over the wardenships of the Marches, the offices created by the crown to formalize the role of their lieutenants in the Borders.

The maintenance of peace down to 1384 and resumption of trade with England permitted a brief economic revival, reflected in the wool-based wealth of the Douglas earls. The revival occurred against the backdrop of continued militarization of Borders' society, already entrenched in the 'unofficial' warfare through which the Scots eroded the English-held salients, To maintain leadership of this militarized culture, the Douglases pressed for a renewal of hostilities in 1384. After 1424 the crown sought to resume that leadership for itself, thus undermining the loyalty of Douglas vassals, as was revealed in 1455 when the lords of the Middle March followed the Scotts of Buceleuch into crown service against their former patrons. In the aftermath of the destruction of Douglas power, families such as the Scotts, the Humes in the East March, and Maxwells in the West, were entrusted with the defence of the Marches.

Intermittent warfare after 1384 brought final collapse to the old economic patterns of the region. This was symbolized by the decline of Roxburgh, reduced to little more than a garrison post before its recapture and destruction by the Scots in 1460. Likewise Berwick, shorn of its shire hinterland, continued to decline in population and prosperity. New centres emerged, principally Hawick, whose market was buoyed on the proceeds of raids into England. By the early 16th century, reiving contributed significantly to the wealth of the region's great families, whose heads were entrenched in the power structure as March wardens and sheriffs. Reliance on such men for the defence of the Border saw little concerted action to curb the disorder and feuding generated by rivalries for the control of office or territorial dominance. Indeed, direct royal intervention such as *James V's campaign in 1530 was ultimately self-defeating, serving only to alienate the Border lords.

By the mid-16th century, disorder in the Borders was perceived by government as being as much of a problem as the turbulent Highlands. While the militarized Borders' kindreds were valuable for the defence of the realm and as providers of military muscle in factional warfare, such unstable forces were anathema to a monarchy and government which was extending its sphere and scope of effective operation. Punitive ayres were aimed at curbing reiving and cross-border feuding which threatened to undermine the developing good relations with England. The Borders, nevertheless, still offered a refuge for the crown's enemies in the 1590s, but increasing co-operation with the authorities in the English Marches ensured more effective policing. Even before *James VI crossed the Tweed to assume the crown of England in 1603, the Borders were well on their way to becoming the peaceable 'Middle Shires' of the Jacobean monarchy (see ANGLO-SCOTTISH RELATIONS: 3).   RO

2. since 1603

Already by 1603, the Borders had been largely transformed from a lawless frontier zone to the more peaceful Middle Shires of the new kingdom. Indeed, from 1625 onwards, it was considered safe enough to leave the city gates of Carlisle open at nights. A decisive battle was fought at Philiphaugh near Selkirk on 13 September 1645, when the Royalist army of the Marquis of Montrose was defeated by the army of David Leslie. The general chaos of war in the 1640s (see COVENANT, WARS OF THE), including plague (see HEALTH, FAMINE, AND DISEASE: 2) and poor harvests, temporarily returned the Borders to reiving times, whilst between 1660 and 1688 religious intolerance led to the persecution of local Presbyterians (see COVENANTERS).

Agricultural changes were limited until c.1760, but by the 1790s enclosure was largely complete on the low-lying lands of the Merse and Teviotdale. Progress was slower on the upland parishes of Roxburghshire, as more generally in Selkirkshire and Peeblesshire. The Borders played no significant part in the heavy industrial development of central Scotland. From the late 18th century, the principal manufacturing industry of the Borders was textiles, in particular hosiery and tweed, and in later times, high-quality knitwear and cashmere. In 1771, John Hardy, a general and spirit merchant, introduced four knitting 'frames' into Hawick and began to manufacture full hose (stockings) of linen and coarse worsted. Production rapidly expanded in the early 19th century and by the mid-1830s Robert Chambers could describe Hawick as 'a sort of Glasgow in miniature'. The textile industry also developed in Peebles, Walkerburn, Innerleithen, Galashiels, Selkirk, and Jedburgh, all of which were conveniently situated on the banks of fast-flowing rivers.

The shift of the population away from the countryside, plus the influx of many migrant workers, including some Irish, created overcrowding and unsanitary conditions in the towns (see URBAN SOCIETY: 4), and there were several major cholera epidemics (see HEALTH, FAMINE, AND DISEASE: 3) in the 1830s and 1840s.

Much of the early textile industry was organized in small 'shop' units, which allowed an independent artisan culture to flourish. Pre-industrial work habits, such as irregular working hours, survived relatively late in the Borders, and this may partly account for the continuation of the local Common Ridings. There are signs of Radical activity from the 1790s onwards, whilst the passage of the 1832 Reform Bill (see POLITICAL SYSTEM: 2) was widely celebrated in the Border burghs. The first Chartist co-operative store in Scotland was opened in Hawick in November 1839. A new railway ('The Waverley Line') (see TRANSPORT AND COMMUNICATIONS: 2) was constructed between 1847 and 1862, which linked Edinburgh and Carlisle through the Borders, and created new opportunities for exports as well as providing cheap coal for steam-powered machinery. The textile trade was vulnerable to trade fluctuations, and went through several severe depressions, especially in the late 1890s, which was also a period of high *migration away from the Borders.

Like other regions of Scotland, the Borders suffered heavy losses in the First World War, notably at Gallipoli. One action by the King's Own Scottish Borderers on 12 July 1915 became known as a 'second Flodden'. In the later 20th century, attempts have been made to diversify the local economy into forestry, electronics, precision tool-making, and plastics manufacture. Inevitably, tourism has become a major employer, although the Borders has attracted visitors since the heyday of Sir Walter Scott, who built his Gothic fantasy home at Abbotsford by the River Tweed. The Borders is now a popular retirement location, despite the closure of the local railway line in 1969. Many incomers settle from other parts of Britain, seeking a higher quality of life, but there is an ongoing loss of young people, who drift away in search of work and educational opportunities.   KRB

British Empire. The Scottish role in the British Empire was a source of great pride for many Scots in the period from the late 18th century to the mid-20th century. Since the late 18th century when Henry *Dundas controlled the activities of the EIC and used his position to promote the activities of his fellow countrymen in the Asian subcontinent, many Scots, including Lord Rosebery, believed that Scotland was a 'race of Empire Builders'. By the late 19th century the Union with England was called the Imperial Partnership and *Glasgow as 'second city of the Empire' was a fitting testament to all that Scotland had contributed to British imperial expansion.

The Empire was important to Scots in two ways. First, there were the activities of Scots in the Empire itself in the fields of exploration, missionary work (see MISSIONS OVERSEAS), colonial government, military service, and emigration. The Empire was also an important market for Scottish investment and exports. Secondly, there was the impact of such imperial activities on domestic society and its effect on perceptions of Scottish *national identity.

While activities in the imperial adventure in the 18th century were confined to the governing elite, by the early 19th century a larger number of avenues were opening to a greater number of Scots. The Empire was very important because the opportunities it afforded could be utilized by both the 'old' governing elite of the aristocracy and the new commercial middle class. Aristocrats (see NOBILITY: 4) found a new role as imperial administrators; between 1850 and 1939 almost a third of all colonial governor-generals were Scottish. Military service (see ARMY: 4) in the Empire was another source of aristocratic employment, especially for the sons who were not the direct heirs. The new middle class could make their fortune in the Empire, which gave rise to one of the most pervasive of all 19th-century myths: the Enterprising Scot. Teachers, clergymen, engineers, doctors, lawyers, and scientists, produced in great abundance by the Scottish *universities, were all forced to find employment outside Scotland, and the Empire helped absorb excess Scottish professional capacity.

The growth of communications from the mid-19th century onwards facilitated this development. Transcontinental travel was safer, cheaper, and quicker, and the growth of advertising and the rise of the popular press meant that images of successful émigré Scots were consumed in great abundance by the population at home. *Emigration to the Empire, as well as providing employment opportunities for frustrated Scots, also contributed to the notion of Scotland as an imperial nation. Rather than hold up emigration as symptomatic of poor social and economic opportunities at home, widespread Scottish emigration was celebrated as evidence of the virility and expansiveness of the Scottish race. The fact that Scottish émigré communities were usually adorned in tartan, formed *Caledonian societies and *Burns clubs, and raised statues to William *Wallace did much to reinforce the stereotypical images of the Scots at home.

For many Scots in the 19th and 20th centuries, David Livingstone was the embodiment of Scottish virtue. Livingstone was at once an imperial hero who was both an explorer and missionary, and a Scottish 'lad o' pairts' who had risen from humble origins through dedication and hard work to eminence in society. He was a source of inspiration for many Scottish missionaries and, in spite of intense rivalries at home, the Free Church, the Established Church, and the United Presbyterian Church were able to cooperate in overseas missions (see AFRICA). In Scotland, missionary endeavour was highlighted by fund-raising campaigns in which the 'magic lantern' was used to show slides of strange and exotic people and places. Part of the reason that missionary endeavours were so enthusiastically supported in Scotland in the 19th century can perhaps be explained by the fact that most local churches had their own individual missionary who would keep in touch with the congregation and for whom the Scottish community would also raise funds. In this way, local churches felt that they were personally contributing to the imperial mission.

*Regional identities were also important in military recruitment as most Scottish regiments were locally recruited. Scottish military prowess was a great source of pride in the period before the First World War and the activities of the Scottish regiments were enthusiastically reported in the local press which could highlight the activities of local regiments. As with missionaries, the regional loyalty was an important aspect of Scottish and British identity. For those Scots unable to take part in the military activities of the imperial mission, there was always the Volunteer (see ARMY: 5) movement. This was the 19th-century equivalent of the Territorial Army and it allowed frustrated bank clerks, shopkeepers, insurance agents, and others to fulfil their imperial fantasies in weekend exercises and parades. The growth of the popular press (see NEWSPAPERS: 1) was an important factor in the transmission of imperial values and ideas. Scots were able to read in newspapers and magazines about the imperial endeavours of their countrymen. Juvenile literature also had a heavy imperial theme

and much was devoted to the inculcation of values which were deemed essential for the maintenance of the Empire. Missionaries such as David Livingstone, Robert Moffat, Mary Slessor, and Mungo Park were cited as examples for youngsters to follow. The Boys' Brigade, founded in Glasgow in 1883, was an organization which intended to imbue Scottish boys with the spirit of Christianity and imperialism.

Exhibitions such as the 1911 Glasgow Exhibition and the 1938 Empire Exhibition were used to show Scots the contribution that they had made to the Empire. Cigarette cards and other ephemera often had an imperial theme. In Scotland in the period from 1850 to 1950, it would be hard to avoid coming into contact with some aspect of Scottish popular imperialism. The First World War knocked off some of the sheen of Scotland's imperial identity because of the subsequent economic collapse (see ECONOMY: 6). Emigration dried up in the 1930s and imperial markets were not as important. After 1945 as the Empire collapsed and Britain's world role shrank, so too did the opportunities for Scottish participation on the global stage.   RJF

Britons and Angles. Roman rule in Britain ended in 409 when the native aristocracy of the British provinces rose up against the administration of the usurper Constantine who had led the British garrison overseas in an attempt to make himself emperor. Whether the action of the Britons was motivated by nationalist or loyalist sympathies is not clear but the result, de facto independence, was ensured by the chaos and military disasters which the Romans faced on the Continent. Within Britain the expulsion of Constantine's officials led to local governments, tribal and cantonal, taking the full burden of responsibility for administration. In Scotland the disappearance of Roman imperium revealed a divide on the ground that might seem to contradict the impression gained from the archaeological record. Whilst Roman civilization appears to have stopped short at Hadrian's Wall, the fact that the cultural divide between the barbarian *Picts and the Christian and 'Roman' Britons lay on the Forth indicates that the inhabitants of southern Scotland had regarded themselves as integrated within the Empire even if they lacked the material trappings of their aspirations (see NORTHERN ENGLAND AND SOUTHERN SCOTLAND; ROMAN OCCUPATION).

Historical sources for this period are meagre and generally unhelpful. We can postulate that a number of kingdoms (see KINGSHIP: 1) arose in the north of Britain, some of which are directly named and others of which can be inferred. The most enduring British kingdom in Scotland was that based around

*Dumbarton Rock or Al Clut. This kingdom probably covered most of the modern counties of Dunbartonshire and Renfrewshire and perhaps extended further afield as well. To the south of Dumbarton lay the kingdom of Aeron, roughly equivalent in extent to modern Ayrshire and probably ruled from the fortress of Dundonald. Lying around Castle Rock, *Stirling, was the kingdom of Manaw whose name is preserved in modern Clackmannan and Slamannan. To the east lay Gododdin whose centre was probably the rock on which *Edinburgh castle now stands. To the south and south-west there were probably other kingdoms, one in Nithsdale, perhaps, based around Tynron Doon and one in *Galloway and perhaps further east in the southern Uplands. The names of these kingdoms, however, do not survive.

Two other kingdoms that emerged in this region deserve mention. The first is the kingdom usually referred to as Rheged in the secondary literature. In the later Middle Ages this kingdom, clearly one of the most powerful amongst the north British, was believed to have lain around Carlisle and it is often located there or in Galloway by modern scholars. A good argument could be made, however, that in fact it lay further to the south, in the central Pennines, and was represented in later times by the boundaries of the archdeaconry of Ripon as they stood c.1100.

The last significant kingdom in the north was Bernicia. Although the name of this kingdom is British, apparently meaning 'of the pass(es)', by the end of the 6th century its people, or the dominant portion thereof, spoke a Germanic rather than a Celtic or Romance language (see LANGUAGES OF SCOTLAND: PRE-1100). The kingdom seems to have originated around Hadrian's Wall, perhaps just the eastern end, but not necessarily. In the mid-6th century their king, Ida, moved north and captured the rocky citadel of Bamburgh, about 12 miles (20 km) south of *Berwick, and this was to become their chief stronghold. Although they are always counted amongst the Anglo-Saxons, the archaeology of the Bernicians does not display many of the features typically associated with the pagan English further south. Burials accompanied by weapons, or in the case of women brooches, are rare. Cremation, the dominant rite in Anglian England, seems unknown. Also, like their British neighbours the Bernician kings seem to have ruled from fortified hilltops, such as Bamburgh (Northumberland), Dunbar (Lothian), and the Mote of Mark (Kirkcudbright), a practice alien to the other Anglo-Saxons. Their Anglo-Saxon character seems to be predicated largely upon their Germanic language and upon the assertion of their own propagandist, the historian and computician Bede (d. 735). Whether they truly shared an origin with the Angles of middle England or were perhaps descended from Germanic troops stationed on the frontier during the Roman period remains to be seen.

Whatever their origin, by the end of the 6th century the Bernicians were the most successful and aggressive people in the region. The earliest narrative account is contained in a 9th-century Cambro-Latin account of how a number of British kings besieged Theodric, king of Bernicia on the island of *Lindisfarne. The British kings were Rhydderch, known from other sources to be king of Dumbarton; Urien, king of 'Rheged'; and two kings, Morgant and Gwallog, whose realms are not known. Urien is said to have been their leader, and the most successful, but on the brink of victory he was murdered at the instigation of Morgant out of jealousy. Theodric probably reigned in the 570s, which allows us to date the death of Urien to that decade.

The British tradition seemed to revel in accounts of failed attempts to stem Bernician expansion. This topos is best represented in the collection of verses known as Y Gododdin. This work (or works) is preserved in a late 13th-century manuscript from Wales. The verses purport to be the elegies of a large number of warriors who died fighting the Bernicians in the years around AD 600. Scholars hotly debate the extent to which these verses are genuine products of the 6th or 7th century. All admit that some corruption and augmentation have occurred during their transmission, but some would argue that few, if any, of the elegies are genuinely pre-11th century. It is also widely inferred that the warriors named were all slain in a single battle at a place called Catraeth, identified as somewhere on the Swale (Yorkshire), perhaps Catterick or Richmond, though this is not explicitly stated in the texts. Edinburgh appears to be named as the royal centre from which the warriors set out but there is little other substantive information about date or political scenario. If Catraeth was on the Swale, and if the enemy were the Bernicians, then the expedition, in which some of the warriors were said to be engaged, is likely to have taken place after AD 604. This can be inferred from the fact that the Swale lay in the Anglian kingdom of Deira which was conquered by the Bernicians in that year under their king Ethelfrith, grandson of Ida. One scholar, John Koch, in The Gododdin of Aneirin (1997), has recently suggested, however, that the Anglo-British slant to the conflict at Catraeth is the result of accretions to the corpus. He suggests, instead, that the victor at Catraeth was Urien, whose praise poetry, if genuine, locates Catraeth in his territory. This would put this battle in the 570s or earlier.

Whether he was the victor of Catraeth or not, Ethelfrith is said by Bede to have conquered much territory from the Britons. Whether this was north-wards into Gododdin territory in Lothian or west-wards into Dumfriesshire we are not told. Bede, our best source for the period, was remarkably un-informative about the Britons. He believed that through their failure to live up to their Christian ideals, and particularly in their failure to proselyt-ize the Anglo-Saxons, they had forfeited their right to the sovereignty of Britain. To his mind, influ-enced by the writings of the 6th-century British monastic reformer Gildas, the Anglo-Saxons had been sent by God as a scourge to the Britons. As the Britons were doomed as a nation it was not neces-sary for Bede to deal with the specifics of their his-tory and he was satisfied simply to recount their progressive loss of territory to the *gens Anglorum*.

The Irish chronicles recount a siege of Edin-burgh in 638 and this has generally been taken as the extinction of Gododdin at the hands of Ethel-frith's son Oswald. Oswald had spent his youth in exile amongst the Gaels and on becoming king he had invited *Iona to send a bishop for the Berni-cians. From this time on Bernicia maintained very close links with the Gaelic world on a cultural and religious level. *Monuments to Bernician Christi-anity can be seen throughout the region, notably at Ruthwell (Dumfriesshire) and Abercorn (Lothian).

By the 670s the Bernicians had captured all the lands of the northern Britons, including the major ecclesiastical site of *Whithorn. In 685, however, they overstretched themselves and were defeated by the Pictish king, Bridei, son of Beli, at Dun-nichen Moss (Nechtansmere) in Angus. Following this defeat the Britons of Dumbarton and Aeron re-asserted their independence. In 750 Eadberht of Bernicia reconquered the plain of Kyle. This ex-pedition followed immediately upon the death of Teudubr of Dumbarton, and this may indicate that Dumbarton had held sway over Aeron in the pre-ceding period.

The territories of Bernicia in Scotland were probably bounded on the north-west by the two river Avons, in West Lothian and in Lanarkshire, for the succeeding century. The Britons were con-fined to Dunbartonshire, north Lanarkshire, and Renfrewshire. This stability came to an end in the third quarter of the 9th century when a Viking army led by the brothers Ivarr and Halfdan ap-peared in the region. Halfdan severed Deira from Bernicia in the late 860s and in 870 Dumbarton was destroyed by Ivarr and his ally Olafr.   AW

Bruce, Robert. See ROBERT I.

Buchanan-Smith, Alick. Alick Buchanan-Smith (1932–91) came from a family of Scottish Tories with a strong sense of *noblesse oblige*. He was not a nat-ural rebel but increasingly found himself in oppos-ition to his own party towards the end of his life. He was never, in Margaret Thatcher's terms, 'one of us'. Born in 1932, son of Lord Balerno, he was edu-cated at Edinburgh Academy, Glenalmond, and Cambridge and Edinburgh universities. He was a junior Scottish Office Minister during Ted Heath's premiership (1970–4). He came to prominence in the 1970s when he was Shadow *Scottish Secretary under Mrs Thatcher. As well as being a supporter of devolution, which he remained throughout his life, he was on the left of the party. When Mrs Thatcher decided that the party should oppose the second reading of the Scotland and Wales Bill, the Labour government's ill-fated first devolution pro-posals, Buchanan-Smith resigned from the Conser-vative front bench along with Malcolm Rifkind. Rifkind later recanted and accepted Mrs Thatcher's hard-line opposition to devolution but Buchanan-Smith never did, though after 1979 he could see little to be gained from arguing his corner on that issue especially when he found himself at odds with the leadership on so many other matters. His abil-ities and tact were such that Mrs Thatcher felt obliged to offer him ministerial office but it was only after the Conservatives had suffered a serious setback in Scotland in 1987 that she asked him to accept a position at the *Scottish Office which he refused, preferring to sit on the backbenches and able to speak out without the fetters of ministerial office. As a Minister of State at the Ministry of Agri-culture, Fisheries, and Food (1979–83) and then at the Energy Department (1983–7), he proved invalu-able with his ability to master complex briefs. His doubts about the general direction of government policy meant that he never made it to the cabinet. Illness robbed him of the opportunity to make a mark on his return to the backbenches. His had been an old-style Scottish Conservatism (see UNIONISM) rooted in a strong sense of Scottishness, compassion, consensus, and moderate state inter-vention.   JM

building materials and techniques. The com-monly held concept that traditional Scottish build-ings, of all sizes and all ages, were constructed using load-bearing stone walls in conjunction with thatched or slated roofs, is completely erroneous. The misconception stems from an exceptional period of activity which started in the more pros-perous districts in the late 18th century before spreading through the rest of the country during the 19th century. Before and after that exceptional period, the situation was quite different and in many respects was inferior to most other European countries since most Scottish peasants were ten-ants rather that owner-occupiers of their own prop-erty (see RURAL SOCIETY; RURAL SETTLEMENT).

building materials and techniques

The confusion is further compounded by the existence of specific areas of the country where a local phenomenon such as an easily quarried flagstone, close to the surface of the ground or exposed round the seashore, resulted in a long tradition of stone-built structures, which in the rest of the country would have been built in timber (see GEOLOGY AND LANDSCAPE). These structures, ranging from burial tombs to dwellings and dating back to about 3,500 BC, appear to support the theory that the Scots have always built in stone. The truth is quite different and even in Orkney where the flagstone is particularly accessible and easy to quarry using the simplest of tools, and where some of the most outstanding stone structures survive, the ordinary houses and farm buildings were still largely constructed of turf at the beginning of the 19th century.

It is intended to deal with the range of building materials used in Scotland under three main headings: structure, walling, and roofing. This should illustrate the wide range of materials used and the former diversity in traditional building techniques.

Structure

Timber Timber appears to have been the predominant structural material in the early medieval period. The Venerable Bede (AD 673–735) in his *Ecclesiastical History* describes three main types of timber structure: block work or log construction, stave work or mast construction, and Scottish work referring to the type of timber construction introduced into Scotland and the North of England by the Scots from Ireland. This has been claimed in the past to be a form of half-timbering but is more likely to be the cruck-frame combined with a basketwork lining, described in the 18th century as 'creel houses'. Half-timbering appears to follow at a later date, probably as a result of increasing demands on the stock of available timber. Half-timbering can be linked to butt-purlin roof construction and the butt-purlin roof survived the initial move to the use of load-bearing masonry walls, although by the first years of the 19th century it had given way to the close-couple roof. Timber frames became lighter in the 19th century and moved from the use of native hardwoods to imported softwoods, initially from the Baltic and later from Canada. This trend continues to the present day in the ubiquitous timber-framed kithouse, usually disguised to look like a masonry structure.

Load-Bearing Masonry Load-bearing masonry and mudwall construction gradually replaces half-timbering in upper-class structures starting with the churches and abbeys of the great ecclesiastical foundations and gradually moving through the royal castles and palaces to the castles and tower houses of the lesser *nobility and from there to the

houses of the professional classes. By the 19th century all new urban housing (see URBAN SETTLEMENT: 1–2) employed this technique. In the majority of instances, masonry in Scotland is built using clay mortar and lime pointing. Lime and clay harls and plasters can also be applied to both masonry and mudwall construction. Brick is also found from the mid-17th century onwards. In poorer quality buildings turf and alternating stone and turf are used in place of conventional masonry. Drystone is occasionally used for housing but pointed externally and internally with a clay mortar. Drystone is also used as facing to mudwall or turf walls, particularly in the Hebrides. Mass concrete is used from the late 1820s and when technical books are produced on the subject in the 1870s it is mainly Scottish examples that are quoted. No-fines concrete dating from the 1870s has been found along the western seaboard of the Highlands. Breeze-blocks made from engine ashes were widely used after the Second World War but these gave way to concrete block and reconstructed masonry block as steam engines disappeared and the post-war restrictions on building materials were lifted in the 1950s.

Structural Frames The early structural frameworks have been mentioned under timber. The first major change away from traditional timber construction occurred in the 18th century when cast-iron columns and wrought- or cast-iron beams began to replace timber. Highly sophisticated cast-iron structures were developed for bridges, mill buildings, and department stores. This happened throughout the 19th century, particularly in *Glasgow where some of the early cast-iron-framed department stores formed the models for the first Chicago skyscrapers. By the end of the 19th century cast iron had been largely superseded by steel-frame construction. This was originally exposed but later structures were encased in concrete to protect the steelwork from fire. An alternative to steel frame encased in concrete was reinforced concrete and ferro-concrete, both of which appeared in the early years of the 20th century.

Early forms of laminated timber have been recorded in 19th-century contexts but the material did not gain widespread acceptance until the 1960s when improved adhesives and new methods of construction, combined with a recognition of its fire-resisting qualities and insulative properties, resulted in its widespread use in constructing sports halls, commercial garages, storerooms, and other buildings demanding large uninterrupted floor areas.

Prefabrication It is worth noting that Glasgow and, to a lesser extent, Edinburgh were both centres for the production of early prefabricated buildings.

These were primarily aimed at providing accommodation in the expanding colonies but they also filled a gap in the home market by providing houses and other buildings for those parts of the Highlands and Islands (see ECONOMY OF THE HIGHLANDS AND ISLANDS: 1) where there was no established construction industry. Many Scottish families moved from turf-walled houses to corrugated-iron prefabricated houses in the mid- to late 19th century and only moved to masonry-walled houses in the early to mid-20th century.

Roof Coverings

Thatch The predominant roofing material in Scotland from the prehistoric period to about 1900 was thatch. This does not mean that there was a single material covering all roofs in the country but rather that roofs were covered with a range of vegetable materials from seaweeds, straight-stemmed plants such as bracken, dock, iris, reeds, rushes, natural grasses, and cultivated cereals to woody plants such as broom, juniper, and heather. This list is not exhaustive and the final choice was dependent on site location, degree of exposure, roof pitch, local farming practice, local economy, number of helpers available, and many other factors. The final choice is not always easy to understand in relation to present-day criteria but the range of thatching materials, methods of application, anchoring devices, and so on, was limitless. Gradually, as construction firms began to replace volunteer labour, the range of thatches reduced but even then there was an extremely wide choice available. Thatch types, surviving into the 20th century, have been studied and guidance has been provided for repair and renewal. Many Scottish thatches required periodic resurfacing to ensure their continued performance. This resulted in a stratified accumulation and by introducing archaeological techniques to the roof covering it has proved possible to identify changes in the husbandry of the thatching materials over successive decades.

Skailie Skailie appears to be a generic term for any scale-like roofing material. It is taken to include shingles, grey slate (thinly split flagstone), and tile (glazed plain tile). All have a long history of being used as roof coverings, but the lack of archaeological evidence, on sites where documentary sources suggest large quantities of skailie were used, suggests that the skailie purchased prior to the 17th century must have been predominantly shingles, since they deteriorate in the ground.

Shingles Traditional shingles were cleft radially from clear, knot-free timber, known to contain natural oils. The core of the heartwood was discarded as was the sapwood, leaving that part of the timber that was least likely to warp or shake. Before the invention of saws, and during the medieval period when by tradition wood was not sawn, the timber was split in long lengths from which a number of individual shingles were cut. This was probably the most prestigious roofing material in use in the Dark and Middle Ages and images of shingles appear on early stone monuments such as the hog-backed tombstones, early Christian cross-slabs (see MONUMENTS: 1), *illuminated manuscripts, and the copes of buttresses on high-status churches.

Slates Little distinction is made between grey slate and blue slate in early documentation other than when the source of the material or the port of dispatch is given. The usual sources are the flagstone-producing areas and this is supported by the archaeological evidence since grey slate is commonly found from the early 17th century onwards whilst blue slate is extremely uncommon before the 18th century. This is not surprising since Scottish blue slate is notoriously difficult to split and even at the height of its production could not compete for price with imports from Wales.

Tile Roofing tiles are known in Britain from Roman times but do not appear to survive the Roman withdrawal. They reappear in Scotland in the late medieval period in the form of glazed plain tiles. These have been excavated in King Edward Street, *Perth, and on the Isle of May, Fife. These sites emerged from a preliminary investigation but there are many references in a forthcoming volume of *DOST* although the types of tile are not stipulated.

Pantile appears to date from the 1720s when William Adam (1689–1748) is claimed to have introduced its manufacture into Scotland. A similar date is claimed in England and there is no evidence to support the theory that it was ever imported from the Low Countries. Pantile held a similar position in 19th-century public opinion to that held by corrugated asbestos in the 20th century. It was a material considered ideal for roofing kilns and smiddies where ventilation and fire proofing were major considerations. It was also used for outhouses, sheds, and farmsteadings, but not houses. There was a major row when it was first used for housing in Ellice Street, Cellardyke, Fife, in the 1850s and the protests in the press continued for several months. It is interesting to note that, in the change from thatch to slate or pantile, slate was adopted in those burghs which were prosperous and pantile in those that were depressed, although this holds good only in counties like Fife where there was no indigenous material available.

Sheet Materials Sheet materials such as copper and lead may have been used on prestigious buildings from an early date but this requires further investigation. St Andrews cathedral, Fife, the richest ecclesiastical foundation in Scotland at the time of the Reformation, is shown on an early seal as being thatched and on a later seal as being covered in skailie.

Paper roofs made from sheathing paper dipped in tar and applied in three overlapping layers in a similar way to three-ply bituminous felt are known from the 16th century.

Milled iron sheets were available by the end of the 18th century and the material was exported from Britain to *Russia where it was used on important buildings in Moscow and St Petersburg. Nineteenth-century survivals of this type of roof are known in England but have yet to be fully investigated in Scotland. The Torosay Castle Farm Steading on Mull is roofed with a particular form of this technique where the sheets run lengthwise up the roof being attached to the rafters on either side and dished in the intervening space. This particular technique appears in manufacturers' catalogues as early as the 1830s although this steading could be considerably later.

Sheet iron and later sheet steel were corrugated by a variety of processes and sold under the generic name of corrugated iron from the 1820s onwards. Corrugated iron more than any other material ensured Scotland's position in the forefront of heavy-engineering production (see ECONOMY: 4) since its comparatively light weight combined with its structural strength along the lines of the corrugations made it the ideal material to enclose large workspaces under which the other industries could develop.

Walls

Load-Bearing The most common forms of load-bearing walls have been dealt with under structure. It should be noted that early masonry is often extremely well cut, tightly jointed, and beautifully finished usually in the form of ashlar work. This is the result of its association with only the richest of clients. When the whole country turned to masonry construction in the early years of the 19th century the traditionally trained high-class masons continued to work on high-class structures but there were insufficient trained masons available to take on the additional burden. Unskilled operators took up masonry construction to build the thousands of new farm buildings required. In many areas the work produced was crude and badly finished and with age has taken on a mantle of antiquity that is quite unwarranted. Standards of workmanship gradually improved through the rest of the 19th century and by the early years of the 20th century the standard of workmanship was similar in both camps.

Non-Load-Bearing: External Scottish work, as described earlier, can be used as an armature to support turf or peat external walls or can be thatched.

Half-timbering can be infilled with masonry, brick, or mudwall. The mudwall is applied to an armature normally formed of stake and rice, that is wattle; timber rails; or rope. Both the wattle and the timber-rail armatures cause cracking of the panel as it dries and shrinks whereas the rope armature allows the panel to shrink as a mass leaving a gap between the top and side rails of the frame which can be calked at a later date.

Timber-framed structures can also be clad with boarding, shingles, slates, tiles, and corrugated iron. The range of cladding types and methods of application is very wide and deserves further study.

Metal structures are suitable for cladding with the same range of materials but are normally associated with sheet iron, buckled plate, or corrugated iron. The corrugations were formed in a range of pitches; that is, the distance from crown to crown or trough to trough. These pitches varied from 1 to 9 inches (2.5 cm to 22.9 cm) and the depth from crown to trough was usually one-third the pitch, although some deeper corrugations were made by specific companies.

Reinforced concrete and steel-framed structures are often infilled with less expensive materials such as clay brick, composition brick, concrete block, timber or metal framing, and insulation panels. Externally these structures may be clad with thin facings of stone, slate, or various types of prefabricated panels in a wide range of finishes.

Glass Glass is known from Roman times but window glass is restricted to the highest classes of building until the 18th century when it is eventually introduced into tenant farmers' dwellings. Before that, window openings in the majority of houses are described as being open or shuttered.

This is an extremely brief and in places superficial survey of an extremely complex subject. The generalizations accepted in the past must now be reinvestigated in the light of recent discoveries and planning officers must be informed of the pre-19th-century situation if Scottish architecture is not to be strangled by an unrealistic and unsustainable image of the past. BW

buildings: 1. civic and administrative; 2. educational; 3. industrial and commercial; 4. defensive and military.

1. civic and administrative

From medieval times the buildings erected by burghs for their councils and courts proclaimed civic pride and local identity. Situated in or near the market area and often on prominent island sites, their steeples still dominate many historic town centres.

Royal burghs obtained much of their income from market tolls and customs, and the buildings used to collect these were known as *tollonea* or, in Scots, *tolbuiths*. Already at *Berwick in the late 13th century the *tolbotha* housed meetings of the head courts, and the name came to identify buildings used for burgh administration. During the 17th century 'tolbooth' came to be synonymous with 'prison', and classical architectural styles in the 18th century were accompanied by the increasing use of 'town house'.

About 70 royal burghs were recognized in the late 18th century, and over 50 of these preserve civic buildings pre-dating the Municipal Reform Act of 1833. The provision made in burghs of barony and regality varied with the relationship to their superior, but the most complete surviving tolbooths of the 16th century, at Canongate and Musselburgh, were in burghs of regality.

No tolbooth of medieval date survives, but from 1325 onwards royal charters granted land to several burghs for building or enlarging a *tolloneum* or *pretorium* (courthouse). Among these is the 1393 charter to *Aberdeen of a plot whose dimensions were unchanged until 1867. The site in the market place of *Edinburgh, granted in 1386, was occupied until 1817 by the most celebrated of Scottish tolbooths, Scott's 'Heart of Midlothian'. Its 15th-century east wing, decorated with Gothic niches, housed the Scottish parliaments (see PARLIAMENT: 1–2) and royal courts until accommodation was contrived in the adjacent church of St Giles in 1562. This followed a threat to remove the courts to St Andrews because of the building's dangerous condition. Thereafter it became a prison and place of execution. The earliest surviving tolbooths, from the second half of the 16th century, include massive steeples at Crail and Dysart.

An Act of Parliament in 1597 obliged royal burghs to accept county as well as local prisoners, and to provide 'sufficient and sure jailles and warde-houses . . . upon the charges of the burgh'. This royal frugality ensured that for over two centuries civic pomp was to be mixed with penal squalor. The obligation, with that of head (county) burghs to accommodate sheriff courts, led to the rebuilding or extension of many tolbooths. A five-storeyed wardhouse was added at Edinburgh in 1610, while at Aberdeen (1616–30) the east end was heightened into a massive tower with prison cells above an arcaded vestibule and the courthouse. The most remarkable tolbooth of the 17th century was the five-storeyed Scots Renaissance building (1626–7) whose slender crown-steeple survives at Glasgow Cross. Admired by English travellers, it provided an exceptional number of halls, courtrooms, and offices, as well as prison cells. The Renaissance style was also employed at Linlithgow (1668–70).

The beginning of the 18th century is marked by town houses in simple Renaissance style but with steeples of traditional type, at *Stirling (Sir William Bruce, 1703–5) and Dumfries (1705–8). The rich documentation for Dumfries shows the town council's search for building materials and its efforts to execute the design by the Liverpool 'masterbuilder' John Moffat (d. 1708), before a contract was made with the mason Tobias Bachup. The contemporary steeple at Tain, however, remained in the tower-house tradition. Purer classical styles were seen in William Adam's town house at Sanquhar (1735–9) and his 1731 design for the great town house of *Dundee (demolished 1932). At *Glasgow in 1736–40, a five-bay 'town hall' was built in Palladian style above an arcaded piazza adjoining the tolbooth, and in 1758–60 it was doubled in length to house an assembly room. A richly furnished 'Great Room' for civic functions was created on the top floor of Aberdeen town house in the 1750s, where in 1773 Dr Johnson was made a burgess. The provision of rooms for balls, assemblies, and charity concerts attracted the subscriptions of burgesses and neighbouring gentry, and elegant town houses with assembly rooms remain at Montrose (1762–4) and Haddington (1788). Trades incorporations and Masonic lodges also contributed to new buildings and gained meeting rights, as at Old Aberdeen (1788–9).

Extensive rebuilding took place in the first third of the 19th century, with increasing division of functions. The benefits of sharing costs and facilities led to a number of joint Town and County Buildings, seen at their most elaborate at Ayr (Robert Wallace, 1818–22). This period produced some of Scotland's most impressive classical civic buildings, including the dominating town steeples of Ayr (Thomas Hamilton, 1828–30), Haddington (James Gillespie Graham, 1830–1), and Port Glasgow (David Hamilton, 1813–16).

The period following the Municipal Reform Act in 1833 saw stricter financial control and little new building in the older burghs, except for further improvements to prisons. Subject to national inspection from 1835, these came under county boards from 1839 and many were built to improved standards on new sites, although cell blocks were added to existing civic buildings at Cromarty and Nairn. The erection of sheriff courthouses by central government in the middle decades of the century restored to many burghs full control of their own buildings. The creation of new parliamentary and police burghs saw the construction of town houses, often in the national baronial style, in small towns such as Portobello (1877). Elsewhere increasing numbers of professional staff and more elaborate committee structures demanded new accommodation. At Aberdeen the historic town house was replaced, except for the wardhouse tower, by the granite-faced County and Municipal Buildings (Peddie and Kinnear, 1867–74). The commercial prosperity of Glasgow was symbolized by the monumental Municipal Buildings (William Young, 1883–8). Edinburgh's council remained in the former Royal Exchange (John Adam, 1753–61) which it had occupied since 1811 and to which successive additions were made. In the second half of the 19th century new town halls provided venues for Evangelical and other public meetings and concerts.

The most important functions of civic buildings were to house council meetings, elections, and burgh or sheriff courts, and to serve as prisons. In larger burghs, the council chamber and courtroom were separate apartments and both might be embellished with moralistic inscriptions, royal and burgh armorials, and the arms or portraits of magistrates and benefactors. Particular attention was lavished on the council table and magistrates' bench, and meetings were held with due formality. In contrast, prisoners awaiting trial and debtors were held in overcrowded, squalid conditions which were deplored by reformers from the late 18th century onwards. Special provision was often made for 'prisoners of note and distinction', and the venality of the gaolers at Edinburgh Tolbooth ensured that it had 'no power of retention over people of quality'. Gaolbreaks were frequent (although penalties levied by the crown led to new building at Wick in 1826), and prisoners were often manacled for security or confined in a cage. Until 1839 condemned prisoners were chained to the gad, an iron floor-bar which survives in Aberdeen wardhouse and is described by Scott in *Guy Mannering*. Notable prisoners in the late 17th century included Quakers at Aberdeen and Edinburgh, and *Covenanters at Dumfries, both of whom made converts among fellow-prisoners. At Stonehaven in 1748 Episcopalian clergymen conducted worship and baptisms through the bars of their prison window. Numerous Jacobites were imprisoned, and a party of them were released from Leith Tolbooth in 1715 when their comrades seized the port. Tolbooths were attacked at Lauder in 1598, when the earl of Home removed and killed a bailie in pursuit of a local feud, and at Edinburgh in 1736 when Captain John Porteous was removed and executed by a mob. Capital and lesser punishments were often inflicted at tolbooths or mercat crosses, and jougs (iron collars) are attached to several buildings.

The town council of Kirkcudbright in 1642 recorded 'the necessitie of ane steiple and bel house

to keip their knok [clock] and bel, quhilk is ane speciall ornament belanging to every burgh', and steeples or bellcots are prominent features of many Scottish civic buildings. A burgh bell was in use at Berwick in 1284, and Scotland preserves a fine series of bells, hung in the tolbooth steeple or that of a nearby church. They were used not only to signal council meetings and market hours but also for the nightly curfew, a custom still observed at Montrose and Selkirk. The few bells of medieval date are of ecclesiastical origin, and as with church bells there is a shift from imports, mainly from the *Low Countries, to the use of native and English bells in the 18th century. Several burghs had carillons of Continental type and the 'musick bells' at Glasgow (1730s, recast 1881) and Stirling (1729) are still in working order. Clocks, which survive from the 16th century, show a similar increase in local manufacture.

Until the 19th century little space was provided for burgh officials. At Aberdeen a timber extension of 1597 housed the town clerk's offices and charterroom. Greater security was achieved at Glasgow in 1628 by an iron-lined record room, and stone-vaulted document stores remain at Aberdeen and Montrose. Standard weights and measures were commonly kept in the tolbooth, although Edinburgh and Aberdeen had separate weigh-houses, and linear measures (see WEIGHTS AND MEASURES) were often chained to the building or, as at Dumfries, built into an external wall-face. Storage was provided for burgh property ranging from armour at Aberdeen to fire engines at Kilbarchan and Linlithgow, and the equipment of town criers, drummers, pipers, and the town guard.

Other public and private uses brought in revenue or avoided expenditure on separate buildings. Burgh schools were often accommodated in town houses and might influence their design, as at Falkland in 1801 (see SCHOOLS AND SCHOOLING: 2). Dancing classes became popular in the late 18th century, and public reading rooms and libraries were a feature of the early 19th century.

As in Continental countries, the ground storeys of tolbooths often included open space for market traders or exchanges for merchants, best preserved at Montrose. The renting of booths or shops brought a regular income to many burghs, since their central locations were highly valued. Those below Dundee Town House included a bank, which in 1788 was broken into through the floor of the guildry room.

Individual buildings were used for many other purposes including 'strolling companys of show and playactors' at North Berwick in the 1770s and 'gentlemen of the theatre' at Old Aberdeen in 1834. A unique feature at Montrose is a burial vault, formed in 1819 when the town house was extended over part of the churchyard and used for interments until about 1850. It houses the table tomb of town clerk William Speid (d. 1774), bearing his professional emblem, an ink-pot and quill. (See also LOCAL GOVERNMENT, TO 1707; URBAN SOCIETY; URBAN SETTLEMENT).   IF

2. educational

Buildings provide many clues to the distinctive history of Scottish education, but despite Scotland's early educational lead (see SCHOOLS AND SCHOOLING: 1–2; UNIVERSITIES: 1–2) nearly all those which survive date from after 1800. Of the ancient universities, only Aberdeen and St Andrews retain buildings recalling their 15th-century origins, notably the chapel at King's College, Aberdeen. Both Glasgow (founded in 1451) and Edinburgh (1582) entirely replaced their buildings in the 19th century. Universities apart, the most characteristically Scottish types are rural parish schools and the urban burgh schools of the 19th century. The late 19th and 20th centuries saw a great expansion of education of all types, especially after the Education (Scotland) Act of 1872 which began the modern state system, but the architectural models adopted differed less than in earlier years from the British norm.

The Act of 1696 which became the charter of the parish schools required the heritors to pay for a 'commodious house for a school'. Early schools had little to distinguish them externally, but the late 18th and early 19th centuries saw large-scale rebuilding, reflecting the new wealth created by improved agriculture. Schools usually had a single large schoolroom, holding up to 70–80 children, with the schoolmaster's house built alongside in the same style. The results were often picturesque, especially where schools were built by landlords as part of an estate village. In the 19th century, the original parish schools were supplemented by several additional types, including Free Church schools and schools for girls, but after 1872 elected school boards took over responsibility. Smaller schools were closed down, but the old parish school usually survived, with extension and adaptation. New construction after 1872 was most vigorous in industrializing parishes and in the Highlands and Islands (see SCHOOLS AND SCHOOLING: 3), where the existing schools were mostly small and inadequate. It was only in the later 20th century, with rural depopulation, a declining demand for agricultural labour, and improved *transport and communications, that extensive closure of rural schools began, though many survive as private houses.

The parish school consisted of one room because it was taught by a single teacher, and at first this was equally true of urban schools. The Act of 1696 did not apply in burghs, and elementary education was mostly left to private enterprise until the growing social problems of the industrial age led to the intervention of the churches, charitable bodies, and (at first only through subsidies to voluntary effort) the state. Where schools were purpose-built, they consisted of a hall-like structure, with one or two smaller classrooms for teaching infants or girls, but with no teacher's house. Few such buildings survive in the cities. Only wealthy endowed bodies could afford to erect impressive buildings: examples are the 'Dr Bell's' schools for the poor (classical at Inverness, Gothic at Leith), or the free schools built by the Heriot's Trust in Edinburgh. Schools gradually became more elaborate as the teaching staff increased (at first in the form of adolescent pupil-teachers) and as the state insisted on higher pedagogic and hygienic standards. But it was not until the school boards took control that the type of school now thought typically Victorian became standardized.

The large number of these built between the 1870s and 1914 remain a familiar feature of the townscape (see URBAN SETTLEMENT: 3). Where space permitted, they had one or two storeys, but on central sites, where schools were often designed for over 1,000 children, they rose to three or four, and their plainness matched the surrounding tenements. Classes of 60 or more remained normal: Charles Rennie Mackintosh's Scotland Street school in Glasgow (1906; today a Museum of Education), though architecturally novel, was quite orthodox in providing for 1,250 children in 21 classrooms. Apart from school boards, the only significant builders were now the Episcopal and Roman Catholic churches, whose schools—usually built adjoining the church—received separate state funding until the Education Act of 1918 brought them into the public sector.

Between the two wars, school building was mainly associated with suburban expansion. Space was less constricted, styles were simplified, and there were a few modernist experiments. Much greater changes took place after 1945. Movement from city centres to housing schemes and new towns required large building programmes, though no distinctively Scottish building type emerged. In general, primary schools became more cheerful and humane; new ones were low and flexible in plan, and the older schools, with smaller rolls and classes, were adapted to new child-centred methods.

Scots who made their fortune and wished to benefit their native town and perpetuate their memory in stone could follow the example of George Heriot, whose hospital at Edinburgh, begun in 1628, was an influential architectural and educational model. Hospitals gave free education to deserving children (180 boys in the case of Heriot's) who boarded in the institution. Heriot's and Robert Gordon's at Aberdeen, designed in the 1730s by William Adam, are the only early examples which survive, others in Edinburgh having lost their original buildings. The hospital model remained popular with 19th-century benefactors, whose lavish legacies paid for some spectacular buildings. Edinburgh had the largest selection, including John Watson's (today the National Gallery of Modern Art), Donaldson's, and Daniel Stewart's; even Fettes, eventually developed as an English-style public school with residential houses around David Bryce's central building, was originally conceived as a hospital. Another 19th-century example was Morgan's at Dundee. By the 1870s, however, educational reformers disapproved of hospitals as a wasteful use of resources, and nearly all were turned into large day schools.

Endowed institutions were one ancestor of the modern secondary school, but much more widespread was the burgh school run by the town council. All towns of any size had these schools, and they multiplied in the 18th century as extra teachers were appointed to teach modern and commercial subjects. Where buildings of that era survive in other uses (as at Annan, Stirling, or the *Royal High School, Edinburgh of 1777), they are substantial but plain, not differing much from other town houses. From about 1790, however, towns began to combine their schools and install them in a single imposing building, often renamed the academy, and partly financed by a public subscription or a legacy. The result of this expansion and rebuilding, which continued until the 1870s, is a body of handsome architecture testifying to the strong civic sense in Scottish towns (see URBAN SOCIETY: 3) as well as to burgeoning middle-class educational demand.

At first, a classical style was universal. Small schools might form a single mass, with a spire or other central feature, but for larger ones the favoured pattern was a building with a central pediment, low wings, and end pavilions. Since Scottish burgh schools were secular and non-residential, they did not need the dining halls and chapels found in English public schools of the period. Schools were often intended as a key feature in the townscape. Dundee High School of 1832–4 is a good example, but the grandest was Thomas Hamilton's Edinburgh High School (1825–9), rebuilt on a new site by the town council to outshine the 'proprietary' (privately financed) Edinburgh Academy, built by William Burn in 1824. Perth and Montrose Academies are other fine examples of the classical style, while William Playfair's Dollar Academy of 1818 was unusual in being built in a rural parish because of a large endowment. In later years Gothic, Tudor, or Jacobean styles also became popular (for example, Burn's Madras Academy at St Andrews, 1832–4), though the fully fledged Scottish baronial style arrived only in the 1860s. Aberdeen Grammar School of 1864 was an example, significant also in moving from the town centre to a new west-end site.

In 1872 most secondary schools were transferred to the school boards, and schools built or rebuilt by them often resembled the standard elementary model. Since secondary education was still confined to a minority of children, the demand for new schools was limited, and extensions or annexes were usually enough to keep the older ones up to date. It was only after 1945, with the introduction first of 'secondary education for all', then of comprehensive schooling, that most of the older schools finally abandoned their historic buildings, leaving them to find new uses as flats, council offices, or hotels. Their replacements have seldom had the same impact on the urban scene.

The early universities were small, enclosed institutions with teaching and lodging accommodation in quadrangles or ranges, and Glasgow was rebuilt on this pattern in the 1630s. Though there were no dining halls as at Oxford or Cambridge, the universities remained residential until the early 18th century, but with their successful expansion in the age of the Enlightenment (see CULTURE: 11) students came to live at home or in private lodgings. By 1789, when Robert Adam began the rebuilding of Edinburgh (not completed, by Playfair, until the 1840s), the essential requirement was for a set of large lecture rooms, along with a library, laboratories, and museums. At Glasgow the same needs were met by ad hoc additions, until the university moved to George Gilbert Scott's building at Gilmorehill in 1870. This included, like the old college, a set of professors' houses. All the universities grew between 1870 and 1914, and demand for new buildings arose from the growth of science and medicine, from a new taste for ceremony, and from new forms of social and 'corporate' life for students: the complex at Edinburgh, which includes the medical school of 1884, the McEwan Hall for graduations (1888–97), and the students' union of 1887–8, neatly expresses these three tendencies, as does the massive rebuilding in granite of Marischal College, Aberdeen, around 1900. But the Scottish universities remained essentially non-residential, and halls of residence were mostly a post-1945 development.

By 1914 technical colleges had also made their architectural mark, as had specialized institutions like Glasgow School of Art, where the first phase of Mackintosh's building was completed in 1899. The inter-war years saw only modest expansion of higher education, but a new building boom came in the 1960s and 1970s, when student numbers increased three- or fourfold. Heriot-Watt, promoted from technical college to university status, moved from Edinburgh to an out-of-town campus, but other universities chose to expand on their existing sites, requiring controversial demolitions and high-rise building. Of the mass of university buildings which now dominate certain city quarters, the libraries are usually the most architecturally distinguished. RDA

3. industrial and commercial

The number and variety of industrial buildings constructed in Scotland since the late 18th century is enormous but certain generalizations can usefully be made. Though there are overlaps between categories, the majority of industrial buildings can be divided into four different groups: the single-storey shed, the engine shop, the multi-storey mill, and the purpose-built building for a particular industrial process. In three of these, the building provides primarily an envelope for the protection of workers and machinery. In some instances, these shells also include services such as heating, lighting, water or steam supplies, and systems of power distribution attached to the building. In the fourth category, the building itself is used in an industrial process. Within an industrial complex, buildings of more than one type may well be, and frequently were, integrated and the buildings which dominate a site physically may not necessarily be dominant in functional terms.

The simplest, in constructional terms—and often also in architectural expression—of the three categories of buildings used primarily as shelter, is the shed. Simple sheds have been built since time immemorial for craft purposes and are still being constructed. Buildings such as blacksmiths' shops, joiners' shops, and small loom shops were constructed of stone, wood, and slate in the manner of domestic buildings, and in some instances materials like clay, pantiles, and later corrugated iron were used as local variants. These sheds, which were generally modest in scale, could be extended to cover larger areas, either longitudinally or transversely, or both. Such extensions posed little technical difficulty. Sheds of this enlarged type were first built in numbers in the 1840s, initially, mainly for weaving. By that time cast iron (see ECONOMY, SECONDARY SECTOR: 2) as a constructional material was fairly well advanced, and the intermediate supports were generally of cast iron, although not always. Sometimes timber was used.

In industries like light-iron founding and cotton weaving, the scale of these buildings remained consistent with that of their predecessors, but in linen and jute weaving and particularly where fancy cloths were made using jacquard looms, both the span between supports and the height of the building tended to increase. This type of building, with glazing on the north side of the roof slopes, was much more generally adaptable, and during the first half of the 20th century, and indeed well into its second half, buildings of this type were used for a wide range of manufacturing purposes.

In the earlier examples of the second type, the so-called weaving-shed type of construction, power was generally transmitted by belts from horizontal shafts powered by a central steam engine or engines, but after electric power became available at the turn of the century individual electric motor drive became standard, and so the need for power transmission through the building was eliminated (see PUBLIC UTILITIES). Buildings of this type were also extensively used in the whisky industry for housing maturing stocks of whisky in barrel. The single-storey shed could be adapted to other purposes by introducing specific features. For example, in shipbuilding yards, open-sided single-storey sheds were commonly used to house plate-working machines and other shipyard crafts such as coppersmiths. As machine sizes increased it became necessary to introduce lifting equipment into buildings and to house ever larger machines during the assembly stage. This resulted during the middle of the 19th century in the development of the engine shop. In such buildings, brick or stone walls were commonly integrated with a system of internal supports intended to carry, not only the weight of the roof, but also the overhead cranes necessary to move heavy components. Cast-iron stanchions became a standard method of supporting both crane rails and roof during the 1860s and 1870s, and remained so until steel became available in suitable sections during the 1890s. By using systems of 'patent glazing' much higher levels of natural lighting could be incorporated into such buildings, and many acres of these large engine-shop-type buildings were constructed to house, not only final assembly of components, but also their machining and operations such as heavy-iron founding.

With iron- and steel-framed buildings, it was not necessary to have load-bearing walls. Thin skins of brick or corrugated steel were common. Various firms specializing in the construction of such buildings grew up in the west of Scotland, notably Sir William Arrol & Co., the Arrol Bridge and Roof Company, and P. & W. McLellan. Where heat-producing processes were used in such buildings, both of the low single-storey and high single-storey type, it was not uncommon to integrate some form of roof ventilator. In some of the earlier engineering works, louvred roof ventilators running along the ridge of the building were a prominent feature. Later on, such ventilation could be incorporated in a less immediately obvious way.

The third type of industrial building common in Scotland was the multi-storey or mill building. Its antecedents lie in Scottish domestic building of an earlier age, and more immediately in corn mills, sugar refineries, and the larger whisky distilleries. In their developed form, multi-storey mills can be most immediately linked to Richard Arkwright's early English cotton mills of the 1770s where central water wheels were used to drive machines on a number of floors. Between about 1780 and 1890 buildings of this type were constructed in their hundreds to house cotton, flax, jute, and wool spinning. Buildings of this type were also used for weaving and for the warehousing of a range of products, including grain, both in sack and in bulk, and whisky, wine, and tobacco. The materials of construction changed over time and with location. The early multi-storey mills had masonry, or occasionally brick walls, timber or cast-iron uprights, timber beams, joists, and floors. Within a very few years, flat brick arches came into use to support floors and were incorporated in a minority of mills and warehouse buildings constructed right up to the 1880s. Brick arches gave both a measure of fire resistance and greater rigidity to the building. By the 1880s brick, either all red or polychrome, had become a common walling material, and mass concrete and hollow tiles were to be found in a minority of such buildings.

The plan form of multi-storey buildings also changed over time. In the early mills the span between walls was limited by the length of wooden beams available, but in later mills multiple rows of columns were introduced. The greater thickness of such buildings required larger windows and a greater height between floors. At roof level, pitched roofs were supplanted by ridge and furrow roofs often with north light glazing. Multi-storey buildings continued to be constructed in the interwar and post-war period but by that time they generally had reinforced concrete or steel frames with thin brick skins supported by the framing.

The final type of industrial building discussed here is defined by its participation in the process. The range of such structures is enormous and only a few examples can be highlighted. Buildings with louvres, generally timber, in the upper floors were common, at least from the early 19th century. They were used in tanneries for drying hides at the end of the tanning process, and in breweries and distilleries for directing a current of air across the open cast-iron tanks used for cooling malt liquor before fermentation. Temperature and humidity control was also a function of a range of kilns of which those used in drying grain before milling or malt were the most conspicuous with their roof ventilators. The pyramidal ventilators of malting kilns and some of the larger grain mill kilns were, and remain, prominent landscape features and the whisky-malting kiln is now a trademark of the industry. The internal arrangement of these buildings was to have a fire in a constricted area at the base, then a metal or brick fan to allow the hot gases to expand and cool to some extent before passing through a perforated floor and a layer of drying grain. The moist gas was drawn through the ventilator. In bleach works and calico printing works, cloth was dried in stoves. These were generally windowless and often multi-storey buildings which were essentially simple heated spaces. In linoleum mills, the mixture of cork and linseed oil which formed the coating of the linoleum required time to dry and this was done by hanging the cloth in festoons in tall rooms, which were externally expressed in the tall windows of the ground floor of some linoleum mills. Heat also played a part in the firebrick industry where moulding shops with heated floors were generally used to dry goods before firing in a kiln. In malting, traditionally the moist grain was spread on a floor and allowed to germinate before being dried in a kiln as mentioned above. It was desirable to exclude light from these spaces as much as possible and so windows with shutters were commonly provided and the headroom between floors was often limited. Such floor maltings, with kilns adjoining, are a very distinctive building type.

Other built structures with a process purpose included chimney stalks, lime kilns, and blast furnaces. Coke ovens could also be considered to fall within that category. The design of these various types of process-based building showed constructional trends similar to those in other types of industrial building with brick becoming commoner in the later 19th century, and with metal and concrete framing being introduced in appropriate places. The fire risk inherent in kiln and drying stove operation encouraged the use of fire-resistant materials such as iron and steel.

The aesthetics of industrial buildings were seldom complex, but there was often some effort made to achieve architectural effect. Classical or Renaissance features such as symmetry, rustication, the use of columns and pilasters, architraved openings, pediments, urns, and Venetian or thermal windows all feature in many buildings. There were some buildings with Gothic, and some with Egyptian, features. From about 1860 the use of red and white brick, often with some Venetian influence, was common, especially in the west of Scotland. However unadorned they might be, Scottish industrial buildings were, until well after the Second World War, generally well-proportioned, decent buildings, making a valuable contribution to the places in which they were set. This intrinsic, often simple, aesthetic quality has been recognized by officially listing the best of the survivors, and in many cases, by subsequent conversion to new uses. The finest are of international importance: numbers one and three mills at New Lanark, the Bell Mill at Stanley, Leiper's Templeton's Carpet Factory in Glasgow and former Linthouse Engine Work now at Irvine, and the Fairfield Engine Works in Govan are just a few examples. These are not dark satanic mills, but thoughtful buildings reflecting worthwhile uses and the ingenuity and skill of those who commissioned, designed, and built them.   JRH

4. defensive and military

Fortification is a theme which runs through much of Scotland's building history from the earliest times. Such fortifications have mainly been of private or communal origin and local in scope; they have also been surprisingly inconsistent, Scotland, for instance, possessing the least evidence of town defences of any of the countries of the British Isles.

From the beginnings of the Wars of *Independence in the late 13th century, however, notions of an overall defensive strategy on a regional, if not a national, basis were probably always in the minds of Scots rulers and their advisers. But it was not until the last quarter of the 15th century that the construction or garrisoning of strategically linked strong points began to be clearly recorded, a period when, coincidentally, gunpowder artillery was also becoming a more potent threat. In 1476, for example, a revocation of grants made during the minority of King James III acknowledged that certain castles were 'the keys to the kingdom' and should revert to the crown. And in 1481, faced once again with the prospect of war with England, the Scots parliament announced the king's intention of repairing the royal castles of Dunbar and Lochmaben, charging the Lords of Parliament to follow suit so that all strongholds near the Border and on the sea coast, such as St Andrews, Aberdeen, Tantallon, Hume, Douglas, Hailes, Haddington, and especially Hermitage, 'that is in maist danger', might be kept and defended. Each lord was enjoined to supply sufficient artillery, munitions, men, and victuals for his own defence, and to alter and repair his fortifications where necessary.

The problem of coastal defence, especially the intermittent threat to commerce and property in the Forth estuary, likewise became more pressing in the late 15th and early 16th centuries. Thus, the construction of private strongholds such as

Inchgarvie—built on an island in the estuary specifically to resist marauding pirates—was actively encouraged and promoted by the crown. The resulting network of littoral defence included such major structures as the one-time royal castle of Ravenscraig, Fife.

In the aftermath of Flodden (1513) (see JAMES IV), the threat posed by English land and maritime forces in this same region led to the building of the earliest scientifically engineered artillery fortifications in Scotland. The first of these, a blockhouse built to reinforce the defences of the medieval castle of Dunbar, was completed in 1523 and was followed, especially during and after the so-called *Rough Wooing in the 1540s, by other coastal fortresses which also incorporated the new Italianate style of bastioned design. They were strategically located at places such as Eyemouth, Inchkeith, and Blackness, the last a late medieval riverside castle adapted massively for use with and against artillery, as indeed *Edinburgh castle was after the experience of the siege of 1573.

In order to protect their main lines of communication, the English military forces themselves erected a series of small forts in the mid-16th century, the best preserved of which is at Dunglass. A century later, in the 1650s, Scotland experienced a much more intensive and widespread programme of fortress-building at the hands of Cromwellian military engineers. In order to nullify any rebellion in support of the Royalist cause, they extended Commonwealth military control westwards and northwards beyond the Highland line with five major citadels at Leith, Ayr, Perth, Inverlochy, and Inverness linked to a series of no fewer than twenty lesser fortifications.

Attempts to secure military control of the Highlands through a system of fortifications were resumed after 1688, following the flight of King James VII and II and the succession of William of Orange in 1688. Strengthening the fortifications at each end of the Great Glen was a major feature of the Williamite wars in the 1690s; Inverlochy became Fort William, while at Inverness, in preference to the Cromwellian citadel which had been slighted in 1661, the new works were focused on the medieval castle site in the middle of the town. Key Lowland strongholds such as *Stirling, Dumbarton, and Edinburgh were also developed during this period.

The Hanoverian Succession and the first *Jacobite rebellion of 1715 led to the implementation of yet more schemes for the military policing of the Highlands: first, in 1718–19 with four defensible garrison-posts (Inversnaid, Ruthven, Bernera, and Kiliwhimen); and then, following a report of 1724 prepared by General Wade, with two new forts, one at Inverness (the first Fort George) and one near Kiliwhimen Barracks (Fort Augustus), all to be linked by what became a celebrated network of military roads through the Highlands (see TRANSPORT AND COMMUNICATIONS: 3). None of the forts and garrison-posts exercised much influence over the course of the Jacobite uprising in 1745–6, but in the construction of the second Fort George at Ardersier (1748–69), close to the decisive battlefield of Culloden, the Hanoverian government went to considerable trouble and expense to establish a base for a significant military presence—two infantry battalions of 1,600 men and an artillery unit—in the heart of the Highlands. Fort George remains one of the outstanding artillery fortifications in Europe.

From the last quarter of the 18th century onwards, military and defence works in Scotland were once again trained against external threats, rather than on an enemy within. A number of coastal batteries were built as protection against American and French commerce raiders, and three Martello towers were erected by the Board of Ordnance in Scotland, one at Leith Harbour and two in Orkney guarding Longhope Sound, all three dating from the very last years of the Napoleonic Wars.

A Victorian coastal defence programme led eventually (in the 1880s) to improvements in Scottish coast defences, especially around the Forth, where Edinburgh was potentially vulnerable to seaborne bombardment. But by the turn of the 20th century the dramatic rise in German sea power brought Scotland—which lay much closer to Germany than the Royal Navy's traditional bases in southern England—to the very forefront of British naval strategy. Naval bases were established at Rosyth in the Forth and Invergordon in the Cromarty Firth, while Scapa Flow in Orkney, which still retains much evidence of a considerable wartime military presence, became the Royal Navy's principal fleet anchorage in both world wars. During the Cold War era it was the Clyde estuary that assumed the greatest strategic importance, Faslane and Holy Loch (until 1992) serving as bases for British and American submarines respectively, armed with nuclear missiles. Today, Faslane still remains at the core of Britain's nuclear deterrent programme.   GPS

Burghead. The fortified headland of Burghead is the most impressive of all the coastal promontory forts which are such a distinctive feature of the archaeology of the north-east. Built on a massive scale achieved at few other late Iron Age or early medieval fortifications, its size and its unique sculptured stones place it in an elite category of regionally important centres alongside Traprain Law, *Edinburgh castle, and *Dumbarton.

Three outer ramparts swept across the promontory and enclosed two inner wards, which in total occupied an area of nearly 12.4 acres (5 hectares). The outer ramparts were substantially destroyed when the fishing harbour and planned town were constructed in the early 19th century, but the innermost ramparts still stand an impressive 9.8 feet (3 m) high. Just outwith the headland enclosure, there is a subterranean well which is reached by a flight of rock-cut stairs. Springs and wells are a common feature of Scottish hill forts, but such an elaborate arrangement is without parallel. The well is believed to be contemporary with the fortification.

The 19th-century demolition work brought to light a series of as many as 30 stone panels bearing a finely incised image of a bull. These are amongst the most fluent examples of Pictish animal art (see PICTS; CULTURE: 2). Most have been lost (built into the quay), but six examples are preserved in various museums including the *Royal Museum of Scotland and the British Museum. It has been suggested that they were erected as a frieze set into the ramparts. Limited archaeological investigations in the 19th century revealed that the earthen and stone ramparts were timber-framed. This method of construction is characteristic of the vitrified forts of northern Scotland and is described in Gaul by Caesar. Calibrated radiocarbon dates from what are presumed to be structural timbers cluster between AD 400 and 600, while material below the ramparts has been dated to AD 220–300. The sculpture can be dated to the 5th century or later.

Burghead's Pictish name does not survive, and it appears to have been abandoned as a political or religious centre before the documentary horizon of the 12th century. The scale and elaboration indicate that Burghead was a major Pictish power centre. Its hinterland includes the Laich of *Moray, some of the richest agricultural land in this part of Scotland, while its strategic coastal position allows it to dominate the eastern Moray Firth.

There was an important church at the site in the early Middle Ages, but prior to this Burghead probably served as centre of pre-Christian religious activity (see RELIGIOUS LIFE: 1) as suggested by the well and bull carvings. This sacred dimension is underscored by the survival to this day of a burning of the Clavie every New Year (os), a ceremony which may reflect pre-Christian fire purification rituals.
                                                    STD

Burns clubs are societies devoted to the life and work of Robert Burns. The earliest meeting of devotees of Burns took place in the summer of 1801, only five years after the poet's death. Nine gentlemen of Ayr, friends and admirers of Burns, held a dinner in the poet's birthplace (then a tavern). Haggis formed a part of the fare and Burns's *Address to a Haggis* was recited. The Revd Hamilton Paul delivered the toast to the 'Immortal Memory' of Burns in verses of his own composition. Thus was established the essential form of the Burns supper. Before breaking up, the company resolved to celebrate the birthday of Burns the following January. Out of these informal gatherings the Alloway Club developed, later dinners being held at the King's Arms, Ayr, in midsummer. This early club ceased to exist in 1819 and was not revived until 1908.

The Greenock Burns Club owed its genesis to a much older body called the Greenock Ayrshire Society, which appears to have held Burns suppers from 1802 and by 1811 had metamorphosed into the Greenock Burns Club. Greenock have had a continuous existence down to the present day, whereas the rival Paisley Burns Club (1805) was in abeyance from 1836 till 1874.

The Kilmarnock Burns Club first met at the Angel Inn (formerly Begbie's Tavern) in January 1808, but was dormant from 1814 to 1841. The Dunfermline United Burns Club (1812) likewise had a lengthy period of suspended animation, being revived in 1870. Though a relative latecomer, the Dumfries Burns Club (1820) has flourished ever since its foundation. It arose out of the campaign (1813–19) to erect a mausoleum over the poet's grave.

By 1810 Burns suppers were being held on an ad hoc basis in many parts of the country. The first in England was held at Oxford in 1806 and Burns Night celebrations were taking place in London by 1810. The idea spread to India in 1812, and thereafter to *Canada, the *USA and the *Australian colonies.

The Burns movement received enormous stimulus from the celebrations of the centenary of the poet's birth in January 1859; out of the many hundreds of dinners and concerts around the world developed some of the oldest clubs in existence today. Nothing was done to bring them together until February 1885, when Burnsians met in London for the unveiling of the monument in the Thames Embankment Gardens. A meeting in Kilmarnock on 17 July formally instituted the Burns Federation, with its international headquarters in the town where the poet's works first saw the light of day in printed form.

In its inaugural year the Federation had ten members: eight clubs in Scotland and two in England. A further 23 joined in 1886, including ten in Scotland, six in England, one in Ireland, two each in Australia and the USA, and one each in Canada and *New Zealand. Progress was slow in the early years, but the launch of the *Burns Chronicle* in September 1891 gave the Federation fresh impetus and in the run-up to the centenary of the poet's death in 1896 it grew dramatically.

By 1925 the number of affiliated clubs had grown to 350, at which level it has remained remarkably constant ever since, although many of the older clubs have disappeared and new ones continually take their place. Annual conferences were confined to Kilmarnock until 1894 when Glasgow was the venue. In 1907 it went south of the Border for the first time, to Sunderland. By the 1930s, the custom of holding the conference alternately in Scotland and England was well established. Since 1978, when London, Ontario, was the venue, the conference has taken place in Canada or the USA on several occasions. The current number of members affiliated to active clubs worldwide is estimated at 80,000.   JAM

Caledonian societies are gatherings of Scottish emigrants and exiles which act as the focus for the perpetuation and the celebration of specific aspects of Scottish national character. The most notable Caledonian society was that of London, instituted in 1837 'to promote good fellowship and brother-hood, and to combine efforts for benevolent and national objects connected with Scotland, and to preserve the picturesque garb of "Old Gaul" '. Clause 9 of its original constitution precluded attendance at dinner without adornment of the kilt. Within the term Caledonian society is included St Andrews societies and *Burns clubs, Gaelic associ-ations, Highland associations, Celtic associations, and Bruce and Wallace associations. These soci-eties are to be found in all parts of the world where Scots have emigrated, particularly since 1750 and from the Highlands, but not exclusively so (see EMI-GRATION: 3–4). Celebrating the centenary of the birth of Robert Burns in 1859, there were, for ex-ample, 61 suppers held in the *USA, 48 in the Col-onies, and one in Copenhagen. Concurrent with the revitalization of the *clan societies within Scot-land in the mid-1880s, and the political issue of Home Rule at that time, a surge in Caledonian soci-eties was witnessed. The Gaelic Society of *New Zealand (instituted 1881) started out with 500 appli-cants for membership by descendants of High-landers who possessed a desire to improve their knowledge of the Gaelic language; its membership was soon to split by the newly formed Celtic Soci-ety. St Andrews Clubs contributed much to coun-try dancing and the consumption of whisky in Japan in the 1870s; the publication exploits of the Caledonian Society of Toronto in 1900, it was claimed, were only right and proper because Scot-land had produced more bards than any other na-tion. The Ballarat Caledonian Society in *Australia unveiled the then only statue of *Wallace outside Scotland in 1889 (a special train brought Mel-bourne's most prominent Scottish worthies, dressed in tartan, to the unveiling ceremony).

Many have noticed that the Scots abroad have enjoyed a profile much greater than their actual numbers: 'America would have been a poor show if not for the Scotch' is the well-known saying of the industrialist and philanthropist Andrew Car-negie. It has been argued by Christopher Harvie that the flourish of Caledonian societies in the 1880s allowed the emigrant Scots' communities to dispense with their British imperial identities at a time of its greatest unpopularity. The numeral strength of the Scots diaspora, exaggerated to 10 or 20 million, could strengthen the question why Scots did not govern at home, and why *emigra-tion was 'forced' in the first place. Yet the phenom-enon of expatriate nationalists continues to sit uneasily with those who remain behind. Caledon-ian societies have sustained a sense of Scottishness abroad, and helped financially a number of na-tional causes and campaigns at home including, re-cently, the new *Royal Museum of Scotland. Yet they perpetuate a history of Scotland too often locked in to a romantic and Highland-dominated past which ignores the socio-economic hardship which prompted so many to seek a life elsewhere.

GM

calendar and seasonal customs. The Old Style (OS) or Julian twelve-month calendar dates to the time of Julius Caesar (46 BC), who reformed the ten-month Roman calendar. It was based on the esti-mation that a solar year was 365 days long. By the time of Pope Gregory XIII, however, the spring equinox, 21 March, was observed to have 'moved' back to 11 March, due to the cumulative effect of the oversimplistic calculation. In 1582 the Gregor-ian calendar was introduced, based on 356.2422 days, solving the problem by dropping the extra days that year, and ever afterwards adding one extra day every four years, to be observed as leap years. It was not until 1752, however, that the British government officially adopted the Gregor-ian calendar as a modus operandi for the entire country.

Regardless of legislation, the New Style (NS) cal-endar made no impression on certain seasonal cus-toms that had been established on the previous calendar. For example, some parts of Shetland cel-ebrate Christmas on 6 January (Aald Christmas Day), and in Burghead, 'the Broch' in Morayshire, New Year's Eve is celebrated on 11 January.

Furthermore, as the first custom of the Scottish New Year straddles the last day of the old and the first of the new, a catalogue of Scottish calendar customs would sit uneasily on the current calendar, 1 January to 31 December. In Scotland, as in other Celtic regions, therefore, calendar customs can be understood only in the context of the ancient Celtic calendar, which mirrors the cycle of the seasons and of life—planting to harvest, birth to death, rebirth and renewal. This calendar not only underlies many national and domestic customs but is virtually superimposed on the established Gregorian calendar.

Quarter Days
The Celtic year was divided into two halves: the dormant, dark winter half, and the vibrant, bright summer half, then divided again producing four quarter days that marked the seasons. As darkness was believed to precede light, so the year began with the dark half at *Samhainn*, the eve of 1 November, that is, 31 October, commonly known as Hallowe'en. The second quarter day, 1 February (OS or 13th NS), was dedicated to Brigit, the Celtic goddess of the Spring, then, from about the 6th century onwards, to St Bride whose feast day, *Latha Féill' Brighde*, is traditionally regarded as the first day of spring. There is no evidence that *Imbolc*, the equivalent term in Old Irish, was ever part of Scottish Gaelic. The third quarter day, 1 May (OS, or 13th NS) Beltane, *Bealltainn (Latha buidhe bealltainn)*, marked the beginning of summer, and the fourth, 1 August (or 12th OS) Lammas, *Latha Lunasdal*, heralded the start of the harvesting season.

In accordance with the policy of the early Christian church, festive days were retained and invested with a new significance on the Christian calendar (see CHURCH INSTITUTIONS: 1). Thus, Hallowe'en appears as 'All Saints' Day', 1 November, with 2 November, 'All Souls' Day' remembering the souls of the departed. St Bride's Day extends to 2 February, observed as Candlemas, commemorating the Feast of the Purification of the Virgin Mary. Close to Beltane, a day dedicated to the 'Invention of the Holy Cross' was fixed on 3 May, and Lammas, formerly connected to the Celtic goddess Lugh, was transplanted into the church calendar as Loaf Mass Day, the day when the first fruit of harvest, a loaf of bread, was given to the priest. The requirements of the church need not conflict with the ancient spirituality of the Celtic calendar or vice versa. Both systems have coexisted for fifteen centuries, with prayers of supplication offered at every stage of the traditional customs.

On the first day of every quarter *(a h-uile latha ceann ràithe)* animals, land, crops, people, and abodes had to be *sained* (protected from evil), especially against witches, fairies and other-world beings believed to be abroad on these nights. Lighting a bonfire, carrying firebrands around an area or subject, tying sprigs of rowan (the sacred tree) or holly over doorposts and lintels of house, barn, byre, or stable, were all common practices, as was sprinkling the threshold (point of entry) with salt or urine to ward off evil.

Dressing in disguise, masking or face-blackening at Hallowe'en, activities known as 'guising', are rooted in a belief that returning spirits or malevolent powers might recognize the living and harm them. Thus, food was left as an offering, and people ventured out only if they could not be recognized. The Hallowe'en bonfire was believed to burn witches.

On Beltane eve it was common to light two fires and drive the cattle between them for *saining*. A special bannock was prepared, divided by the number of people attending, then, before putting the pieces in a bag, one was charred. Everyone chose one, then the person with the blackened segment jumped across the embers of the dying fire for good luck. At dawn everyone arose to welcome the sun and to wash in the May dew, thought to have been the holy water of the Druids, but, according to oral tradition, believed to assure beauty. The widespread May dew custom outlasted the Beltane fire which died out in the 19th century, though 1988 saw the revival of it in Edinburgh. Since then, the Beltane Fire Festival is held annually on Calton Hill, and combines tradition with theatre. It is presided over by the May Queen, a Green Man, several Red and Blue Men, and many drummers and dancing maidens. In 1988 approximately 300 people attended, in 1994 over 3,000, and by 1999 it attracted over 10,000 people.

The observation of Candlemas is mainly church-based, notably in the Scottish Episcopal and Catholic churches, which hold candlelit services that have long outlasted most of the secular festivities. One of the most common, cockfighting, is now illegal, though village ball games, such as the Borders' Ba' (see BORDERS), continue to be played on a date calculated from the Candlemas new moon and closely associated with Shrovetide rather than quarter days.

Lammas was an annual fair day in most parts of Scotland. By the end of the 20th century only a few remained, such as the Lammas fairs at St Andrews and Kirkcaldy. The most ancient Lammas ritual to survive is in South Queensferry where, on the first Friday in August, the Burryman walks the marches of the town. Clad from head to foot in burrs, a hat of roses on his head, a Scottish flag about his middle, and a staff in each hand, he slowly walks the route accompanied by two officials, led by a bell-ringer and chanting children who collect money (for luck).

The Christmas Season

Until at least the 1970s it was common to hear people say: 'Christmas is hardly celebrated in Scotland, but New Year is the big day'. Before the *Reformation, however, Scots celebrated in a similar manner to other European countries, notably France. The season extended over the Twelve Days of Christmas, and in the Northern Isles Yule lasted twice as long. Kirk session records from the late 16th century abound with examples of cases where individuals were fined for breaking the rule against celebrating Christmas. For example, in 1673 the St Andrews kirk session dealt with several cases, and in 1674 one individual who did not comply was threatened with the stool of repentance, fined 45 s. (a little over £2) and made to promise that he would never again keep Yule but would work 'as upon any other day'.

As with the Celtic New Year (and now Hallowe'en), masking, dressing-up, and house-visiting were common. In the Lowlands troupes of boys with faces blackened and clothes inside-out would perform a play, commonly called 'Galoshins', with the theme of good triumphing over evil. Afterwards they collected money and were given food and drink. In Orkney and Shetland Yule guisers went house-visiting, dressed in straw costumes, and in Gaelic Scotland groups of adolescent boys or young adults, faces blackened with soot or burnt cork, went from house to house after dark, led by one with a sheepskin tied around his shoulders, leather-side out. They would recite the *rann challuinn* (rhyme) outside the door, knock loudly, then enter. The leader then put a stick wound with sheep's wool in the fire, and, followed by the boys, circled the fire as the incense-like odour pervaded the room. In response to the *rann*, they would be offered food and drink, and the group would entertain the household with songs and music before moving on. Similarly from the north-east to Perthshire, New Year guising was common till after the Second World War. The opening song, 'Rise up guid wife and shak yer feathers', made a modest request for food and drink, then the guisers 'did a turn' to entertain the household.

Families exchanged small gifts, such as hand-knitted socks or a home-made purse or basket, though it was more common to give at New Year than at Christmas. Houses were decorated with greenery around doors and lintels, believed, as on quarter days, to keep away evil. During the reign of Queen Victoria the Christmas tree, borrowed from Prince Albert's German tradition, replaced the greenery. The childhood custom of hanging up stockings on Christmas Eve became popular in the 20th century, though the contents (usually an apple, an orange, sweets, nuts, and a small toy) remained very modest until after the Second World War. By the 1960s and 1970s most families had adopted what might now be regarded as a more Americanized attitude to the festive season. Most homes have lavishly decorated trees, tables groaning with food, and gift-giving on a hugely commercialized scale. At the end of the 20th century, house decoration extended to exterior porches, gardens, and trees illuminated with decorative lights.

Seasonal greetings cards date from the mid-19th century, with New Year preferred to Christmas till the 1920s and electronic-mail greetings supplementing the multi-million pound card industry by the late 1990s. The steady escalation of consumerism has been reflected in a decline of church attendance, though churches are still packed on Christmas Eve where services are held by most denominations, except the Free Church and the Free Presbyterian Church as there is no scriptural evidence that Christ was born on 25 December. Both of these churches, however, hold a New Year's Day service.

Since New Year's Eve is the most celebrated event on the Scottish calendar, preparation has always been important. Cleaning the house for New Year's Eve was, and still is, widely practised, popularly with the aim of beginning the year in the best possible condition. When fires were the sole source of heat, they had to be kept lit and food and drink prepared for the customary hospitality. Both Christmas and New Year were days for special meals, traditionally locally produced foods, such as domestic or wild meat or fowl. Roast turkey was virtually unknown until the second half of the 20th century when overeating also became the expectation of the season.

As midnight approaches, every family and community follows age-old traditions, which vary from place to place. For some, it is essential to be at home with family 'for the bells', the stroke of midnight, while for others it is the market cross, the village square, or traditional gathering place. The 1990s saw the creation of street parties in the towns and cities, with Edinburgh boasting the biggest New Year party in the world. No matter what the scale of the celebration, as midnight chimes everyone in the country raises a glass (traditionally whisky or port-wine), and exchanges New Year greetings and a kiss. Afterwards the custom of going first-footing can last until dawn with people visiting neighbours, sharing a dram, food, songs, music, and, in some places, dances. The preferred 'first foot' to visit a neighbour is traditionally male and dark-haired—the notion was that a blonde-haired one might be from *na Lochlanaich* who invaded long ago.

New Year's Day games have a long history, in particular community ball games. In the Highlands, and anciently on the Meadows in Edinburgh, there was a special *shinty match for as many men and boys as wanted to play. The game began to the tune of the pipes, and it could go on for hours. In the 20th century the traditional football matches on New Year's Day in Glasgow and Edinburgh, the 'local derbies', drew huge attendances to watch Rangers–Celtic and Hearts–Hibs kick off the year.

Just as fire was a vital part of ancient customs, so it has continued to be the central focus of several New Year celebrations. Arguably the oldest in Scotland is the Burning of the Clavie in *Burghead on Old New Year's Eve, 11 January. It is led by the Clavie King who begins the route carrying a huge barrel fuelled with tar and wooden staves. A team of men, all 'Brochers', take turns to complete the circuit, ending on the top of Drurie Hill where the blazing barrel is placed on a stand, and finally bursts into flames. The charred remains are gathered up by locals who take pieces home to ensure the year's luck. Other fire festivals held on Hogmanay (NS) include the Flambeaux at Comrie, which begins on the stroke of midnight. A pipe band leads six men carrying spectacular flaming poles round the village, anciently 'the marches'. At the end of the set route, the flambeaux are ceremoniously thrown into the river. At Stonehaven the burning objects are fireballs attached to the end of a rope and carried through the streets by a team of men who swing them above their heads. The concluding fire festival of the season of Yule is in the Shetland Islands, and is held on the last Tuesday of January. 'Up-Helly-Aa', based on the ancient tar-barrel festival, began in Lerwick in 1881, seven years after the earlier fire festival was banned. It now takes place in several communities and has evolved into a spectacular event, led by the Guiser Jarl and his men, all bearded and dressed as Vikings with winged helmets, carrying shields, followed by a procession of 'squads' of men dressed according to chosen themes. In 1982 there were 49 squads, with over 1,000 guisers in all. The climax of the Lerwick procession is the burning of a Viking galley in the harbour. All the fire festivals are followed by a night of merrymaking, in homes, halls, and hotels.

Movable Calendar Customs

The Easter season does not fall on a fixed date but is based on the Jewish lunar calendar. Neither Scot nor Gael needs the official church calendar to find out when it begins as people accustomed to observing the moon followed the traditional sayings: 'First come Candlemass, Syne the new mune; The neist Tyseday eftir that is Fastern E'en' (First Candlemas, then the new moon; the next Tuesday after that is the eve of the fast, that is Shrove Tuesday). Or, in Gaelic Scotland, *Chiad Di-màirt de'n t-solus Earraich* (The first Tuesday of the Spring Light, i.e. after the new moon which follows the vernal equinox). Shrove Tuesday is the day before Ash Wednesday, which marks the start of Lent, 40 days of austerity, observed by Scottish Episcopal and Catholic churches, though largely ignored by Protestant ones.

Throughout the Christian world there are traditions of sports, festivals, and carnivals on Shrove Tuesday but apart from the Borders' Ba', few survive in Scotland. Though illegal since the 19th century, the most popular sport was once cock-fighting, with the schoolmaster taking the bets for the day.

Lent is observed as a religious season, during which devoted Catholics and Scottish Episcopalians give up certain normal 'luxuries' such as eating meat. Fish, almost a luxury by the late 20th century, was traditionally eaten, and in the Outer Hebrides seal and cormorant were also permitted in the diet.

The season lasts for six weeks, punctuated by special days and culminating in Easter Sunday. The fifth Sunday, Palm Sunday, marks the beginning of Holy Week observed in both Protestant and Catholic churches. Some, such as Old St Paul's Episcopal church in Edinburgh, hold a Palm Sunday procession carrying palms through the adjacent streets. Maundy Thursday is observed on the ecclesiastical calendar, to commemorate the day when Christ washed the feet of his disciples. A custom dating back to the Middle Ages is still practised, usually in an English cathedral, by the Queen, who gives Maundy money to men and women, traditionally from the poorest people, one coin for each year of her age. In the Hebrides, Maundy Thursday was also known as *Là Brochain Mhòire* ('the day of the Big Porridge'), when produce from the land— usually porridge—was poured into the sea while reciting a prayer for seaweed to fertilize the land.

The next day is Good Friday, more aptly named in Gaelic *Di-haoine na Ceusa* (Crucifixion Friday). Until the late 19th century there was a strong belief that no iron spade or plough should be put in the ground, and that the band should be removed from the spinning wheel so it could not be used to bind Christ's hands and feet.

Easter Sunday, marking the end of Lent, celebrates Christ's resurrection and is traditionally a day of large church attendances. In some places it is also the day for Easter egg-rolling (though others wait till Monday) to commemorate the rolling of the stone from Christ's tomb. Traditionally the eggs were hard-boiled in onion skins or tea to decorate them, and taken to a local hillside. Chocolate eggs became popular in the 20th century and, in keeping with other commercial pressures, a new fashion (borrowed from America, along with the Easter bunny) encouraged parents to hide store-bought varieties for children.

The ecclesiastical calendar notes that Pentecost falls on the seventh Sunday of the Easter season, and is known as Whitsunday. In Scotland, however, 'Whitsunday' is a fixed term day, 25 May (os), referred to as 'flitting day' because the year's house-lease runs from that date. Farming communities hired labourers on that day and also six months later at Martinmas, 11 November. Both dates are also established on the Scottish legal calendar.

The Scottish year is punctuated by innumerable customs, many of which have a local significance while remaining unknown outside of their immediate domain. The Scottish Tourist Board keeps an account of all such customs and should be consulted for annual dates. Few are celebrated on a national scale, notably St Andrew's Day, 30 November, which is dedicated to the patron saint of Scotland. Since the *Union of the Crowns (1603) it became better known as an expatriate celebration with processions held through the streets of London. From the late 19th to the mid-20th century it was better celebrated by the Scots overseas than those at home, though, since the 1980s, the rise of nationalism (SEE NATIONAL IDENTITY: 6) has been reflected in a widespread celebration of St Andrew's Day (or Night). Special dinners—now styled on Burns-supper haggis rather than the traditional wild game, sheep's head, or codfish—are held, with speeches paying tribute to the patron saint, and whisky dispensed to toast all things Scottish. The nation has now become the focus of celebration.   MBe

Campbell, Alexander (1796–1870), joiner, co-operator, Owenite socialist missionary, and journalist. Born in Kintyre, in 1825 he joined Abram Combe's co-operative community at Orbiston near Motherwell. On its collapse in 1828, Campbell was gaoled for its debts, but after his release he returned to Glasgow and launched the Glasgow Co-operative Society. He was probably the first to propose that co-operative dividends be paid on the basis of purchases. He was no a believer in the ideas of Robert *Owen that co-operation was an alternative to capitalism and that, through it, society could be transformed. Campbell believed that it was necessary to convert the emerging trade unions and, throughout the 1830s, he was secretary of various Glasgow trades' committees. He contributed to working-class *newspapers and in 1834

was again imprisoned for publishing the unstamped *Tradesman*. At the same time, he was an active supporter of the campaign for parliamentary reform, including votes for *women, although he never believed that the franchise itself was likely to be enough to change society.

Between 1838 and 1842 he was a full-time missionary for the Owenite movement, based in Birmingham and then in Stockport. He and his family joined the Concordium, a commune in Richmond, before setting up a progressive school in High Wycombe. During the 1840s in London he was involved in many of the attempts to link *Chartism and socialism in a new social democratic organization and he was an active opponent of free trade. Returning to Scotland in 1856 he became a reporter on the *Glasgow Sentinel* and editor in 1863. He played a major part in the formation of Glasgow Trades Council and of the second Glasgow Co-operative Society in 1858, was secretary of the campaign for repeal of the Master and Servant Acts in 1864, and spoke in favour of working-class MPs in 1868.   WHF

Campbell family: 1. 1200–1500; 2. 1500–c.1750.

1. 1200–1500

Between 1200 and 1500 the Campbells emerged as one of the most powerful families in Gaelic-speaking Scotland, dominant in Argyll and capable of wielding a wider influence and authority in the Hebrides and the western Highlands. Just as striking was the role of successive Campbell chiefs, from around the middle of the 15th century onward, as prominent figures in the politics of the Scottish kingdom as a whole and as councillors and officeholders at the royal Stewart court.

The ultimate origin of the Campbell kindred remains obscure. Men bearing the surname 'Campbell', probably derived from the Gaelic byname 'twisted mouth', began to appear on record around the middle of the 13th century and by 1300 members of the family were active in a number of lordships clustered around the Firth of Clyde. The head of the family seems to have enjoyed strong links to the Stewart lords who dominated that region. The distribution of early Campbells around Loch Long and the Lennox may give some credence to the claim advanced in the family's own medieval genealogies that the kindred was of Brythonic descent.

In the 14th century the Campbells experienced a rapid growth in their regional territorial power and influence. The expansion of Campbell interests is usually explained by the loyalty of Sir Niall Campbell (d. c.1315) to the cause of Robert Bruce in the civil and dynastic wars initiated by Bruce's seizure of the throne in 1306. Niall's service to the king secured a number of territorial gains for his family and kinsmen at the expense of those opposed to King *Robert I in the central and western Highlands. In particular, the defeat and exile of the Macdougall lords of Argyll, who were kinsmen and allies of Bruce's main dynastic rival, John *Balliol, are seen to have opened the way for the establishment of the Campbell ascendancy in Argyll.

Although clearly significant, the importance of Niall's relationship with Robert I for the long-term development of Campbell lordship has probably been exaggerated. After the king's death in 1329 many of the most important gains made by the Campbell family were lost in the turmoil of David II's minority. The foundations of the family's rise to territorial greatness in the 15th century were in fact laid by Niall's grandson, Gill-easbuig (d. 1385 × 1387). In the course of a long career Gill-easbuig spearheaded a dramatic expansion of Campbell lordship in mid-Argyll, Cowal, and the Firth of Clyde. In many instances these territorial advances arose from Gill-easbuig's friendly relations with the overlord of Cowal, Robert the Steward, who became king as Robert II in 1371.

In May 1382 the regional status of the Campbell chief and his family was confirmed when Robert II granted Gill-easbuig and his heirs, already established as sheriffs of Argyll, a heritable royal lieutenancy in mid-Argyll, embracing the entire area between the lordships of Lorn and Knapdale. Although the royal lieutenancy and the close personal relationship between Gill-easbuig and Robert II might suggest that the Campbells were little more than royal agents in the west, it is likely that the family itself saw the grant merely as recognition of its rise to the leadership of the provincial society of Argyll. Indeed, by 1395 Gill-easbuig's son and successor, Cailean, was openly using the style 'lord of Argyll', a title which was not a royal creation and had previously been used by the Macdougall lords as an assertion of their autonomous provincial overlordship.

The Campbells' association with figures at the heart of royal government continued after Robert II's death with the marriage of Cailean's son Donnchadh to the daughter of Robert, duke of Albany (d. 1420), governor of the kingdom between 1406 and 1420. The personal reign of James I (1424–37), however, saw that king launch a great political assault on the Albany Stewarts and their allies in the west. Although Donnchadh escaped the fate of his Albany kinsmen, who were either executed or exiled, the king and his agents undercut the Campbell lord's authority inside Argyll. After James I's assassination in 1437, Donnchadh made a determined effort to prevent any future royal intervention inside Argyll by becoming more directly involved in the politics of the *royal court and also by presenting Campbell lordship in Argyll as a natural defence for royal interests in the region.

The Campbell concern with assuming an active role in royal government to defend and enhance their regional power was most obvious in the career of Donnchadh's grandson and successor, Cailean, first earl of Argyll (d. 1493). Cailean was a councillor and an active royal administrator for both James III (1460–88) and *James IV (1488–1513), serving as Master of the King's Household from c.1464 before eventually attaining the highest secular office in the land, the chancellorship, in 1483. Cailean's influence at the royal court helped the Campbells in a number of territorial disputes, most strikingly perhaps contributing to Earl Cailean's acquisition of the lordship of Lorn in 1469. Gill-easbuig, second earl of Argyll, also claimed a place in central government, becoming Master of the King's Household for James IV in 1495. The Campbell presence at the royal court, and particularly the family's support for crown action against the MacDonald lordship of the *Isles in the second half of the 15th century, has contributed to a view that the Campbell earls were increasingly out of step with the Gaelic culture and the political and social values of their Argyll heartland. However, it is clear that the earls continued to patronize the full range of Gaelic learned orders, poets, genealogists, and medics and to claim for themselves a leading role in the wider Gaelic world. Indeed, following on the forfeiture of the MacDonald lordship of the Isles in 1493 the Campbell lords may well have viewed themselves as the natural successors to the Clan Donald in terms of the leadership of the Gaels of the Hebrides and the western highlands (see HIGHLANDS AND ISLANDS: GENERAL). The Campbell lordship thus remained one of the most significant bastions of Gaelic learning and culture in late medieval and early modern Scotland.   SB

2. 1500–c.1750

The Campbell family was the most successful noble kin-group in early modern Scotland, led by their chiefs, the earls and later dukes of Argyll. The Campbells were able to combine the attributes of a Highland clan with those of a Lowland surname and were the only powerful kin-group to operate effectively in both the Gaelic and Scots-speaking worlds. One ingredient of this success was the solid and unchallenged power base established in the Campbell heartland of Argyll and the western Highlands (see HIGHLANDS AND ISLANDS: GENERAL). Throughout the period the clan consolidated its grip over the region and also continued to expand into other parts of Scotland, particularly Ayrshire, Angus, Breadalbane, and Moray. By the 17th and

18th centuries family members were increasingly found among the business and professional communities in Edinburgh, Glasgow, and other burghs. This gave the Campbells a country-wide network of connections within most significant national organizations.

The *clan possessed one asset which eluded all their major rivals, though these might be more numerous and dispose of greater landed power. The Campbells' unity and cohesion ensured that the clan's combined strength was greater than the sum of its considerable parts. That unity periodically came under severe strain, as in 1592 when the murder of John Campbell, third laird of Cawdor, revealed deep rifts or during the power struggle between the earls of Argyll and Breadalbane in the late 17th century, but it was never destroyed. Throughout the early modern period the house of Argyll could usually rely upon the support of the whole of Clan Campbell. This huge reservoir of strength enabled successive leaders of the house of Argyll to play a major role within national politics. When that strength was combined with the political talent and ambition of men such as the marquess of Argyll or the second duke of Argyll, Campbell power could dominate the whole country. The potential for the clan chief to play a decisive role in national politics was always present. Throughout the 16th and 17th centuries, the earls of Argyll retained an independent military capability, being able to raise a powerful army from their own followers. By the 18th century that capacity had been integrated into the British *army through regiments such as the famous Black Watch, recruited in Campbell territory, and through a seemingly inexhaustible supply of officers drawn from the clan (see WARFARE, WEAPONS, AND FORTIFICATIONS: 3).

A vital ingredient in this success was the family's ability to employ the authority and resources of the Scottish crown to further its own aims. In return for access to power and influence the Campbells were almost always loyal to the government of the day. This relationship was at its closest and most celebrated after the *Union of 1707 when the second duke, assisted by his brother the earl of Islay, became the 'uncrowned king of Scotland' through his tight control over the country's politics and monopoly of its patronage. When Campbell chiefs did oppose the monarchs they usually picked the winning side, as in 1559–60 during the *Reformation crisis. Even when there was a spectacular failure, such as the ninth earl's disastrous rebellion of 1685, the long-term damage to Clan Campbell was minimal. To have successive chiefs executed for treason, the marquess of Argyll in 1661 and his son the ninth earl in 1685, might have blighted the fortunes of a noble house. However, the ninth earl's

son restored the family's political influence and in 1701 was created the first duke of Argyll whilst his own son entered the British peerage as duke of Greenwich in 1719 and became the most powerful Scot within British politics (see GOVERNMENT AFTER THE UNION).

The Campbells' deep political involvement was matched by their close and enduring support for the Church of Scotland. The fourth and fifth earls had been Scotland's most important early supporters of Protestantism and their role had been decisive in the crisis of 1559–60. In particular, the Reformation would have struggled to establish itself throughout the western Highlands without the clan's backing. In the mid-17th century Campbell support for the Covenanting movement was of crucial significance in a national context but proved divisive within the Highlands. After the 1688–90 Revolution and the Hanoverian succession of 1714 the clan's consistent support for Presbyterianism and for the Protestant succession made the Campbells the champions of the Whig cause.

Within the Highlands the successful and ruthless expansion of Clan Campbell from the beginning of the 17th century was conducted at the expense of their neighbours and created a pool of resentment among those who had been dispossessed. This was utilized by the MacDonalds to create a coalition of anti-Campbell clans who supported Alasdair MacColla in his ferocious campaigning through Argyll in 1644–5. Anti-Campbell feeling became inextricably linked to the Jacobite cause, especially after such events as the notorious massacre of *Glencoe. By the 18th century Clan Campbell were the main agents for the Whig government and for the repression which followed the Forty-Five rebellion. In many historical accounts the Campbells have been portrayed as the enemy of Highland life and Gaelic culture. This charge is primarily based upon the romanticized interpretation of Highland history produced in the 19th and 20th centuries. The Campbells were the most successful Highland clan because they became part of the wider political system, first within Scotland and then within Great Britain. By the middle of the 18th century their chief, the duke of Argyll, was the most powerful Scottish politician within the British Isles. The rebuilding in the grand manner of the duke's seat at Inveraray castle provided a visible demonstration of the success which had been achieved by the Campbell family.   JEAD

Canada and Scotland have been linked for more than 200 years by the people who left both Highlands and Lowlands for the northern half of North America. Scottish emigrants and their descendants (see EMIGRATION: 3–4) gave Scots a knowledge of and common inheritance with Canadians and created communities in North America which were influenced, at times substantially, by Scottish character and culture. If, as Isobel Lindsay has argued, 'migration is a mainstream and not a deviant tradition' in Scotland, then Canada is where the result of this activity is most clearly observed.

What was perhaps the defining moment of Canadian history—the conquest of the French colony by Britain with the resulting duality of Canadian national identity—was also the moment at which the continuous involvement of Scots with Canada began. It was Fraser's Highlanders who found a way up the cliffs of Quebec in 1759 and made possible Wolfe's defeat of French forces there (see ARMY: 3). Over the next 200 years, 1,000,000 Scots emigrated to Canada, and by 1961 some 2,000,000 people of Scottish origin could be found in Canada. Except for years of depression, Canada was the most popular destination of Scottish emigrants and, in the 20th century, perhaps as many as three out of every eight Scottish emigrants came to Canada. By 1971 there was one person of Scottish origin for every person of Irish and every two people of English origin in Canada.

Between 1770 and 1815, 15,000 Scots emigrated to British North America, an average of 330 yearly. That yearly average jumped to 4,100 people annually between 1815 and 1857, when over 150,000 Scots (40 per cent of those who left Scotland) arrived in Canada. Over the next 44 years, Canada's poorer economic prospects for emigrants were reflected both in the small decline in actual arrivals (112,000 in these years) and in the much greater decrease in the percentage (13 per cent) of Scottish emigrants whom Canada attracted. But when the Canadian west opened and the economy boomed in the early 20th century, Scottish emigration to Canada skyrocketed to 276,000 arrivals between 1903 and 1913, representing 48 per cent of all overseas emigration from Scotland.

This pattern of heavy emigration in good times continued on through the 20th century, although improvements in transportation made it easier for some emigrants to return to Scotland. Between 1921 and 1930 138,000 Scots entered Canada, an average of 17,000 yearly, but the following fifteen years of depression and war saw the number tumble to one-tenth of that average. Post-war prosperity saw Scottish migration to Canada soar once again, with an average of 10,000 emigrants yearly (over 60 per cent of total departures) between 1946 and 1960, and an average of 7,600 annually (50 per cent of total departures) through the 1960s. Even in the closing decades of the 20th century, 240 years after it first began, emigration to Canada remains an unquestioned part of the Scottish experience and references to it are embedded in popular music and fiction: Runrig's Cutter spends the winter in Ontario and in *The Crow Road* the hero's girlfriend leaves him for a job in Canada.

Like the *USA, Canada has represented an opportunity to obtain land or to exercise a trade, a skill, or a profession for those who could not find such opportunities in Scotland. What distinguished Canada from the USA was not simply the enduring British connection but, more significantly, a sense that Canada was in part a Scottish community. Such a perception originated in the substantial impact which Scots had on the first 75 years of British North American colonial development and was reinforced by the waves of Scottish emigrants who arrived in the 20th century.

The impact of Gaelic-speaking (see GAELIC LANGUAGE) Scots on early Canada is clearest since Highland emigrants both travelled in large groups and formed emigrant chains with the intention of settling together in selected Canadian destinations. Particular Canadian townships or even counties were populated by people from adjacent Highland parishes. Thus people from Lewis went to Megantic, Quebec; emigrants from Glengarry, Knoydart, and Glenelg went to Glengarry, Ontario; and others from Beauly, Kilmorack, Kirkhill, Urquhart, and Loch Broom went to Pictou, Nova Scotia. The majority of Highland emigrants consisted of families: the newly married, parents with young children, and parents with completed families. In addition, these families travelled or settled with the families of their brothers, sisters, and cousins. Even assisted emigrants often followed this pattern of settling with those who were assisted by the same landlord or with earlier emigrants from their home parish. In districts where interest in emigration was high and tenants were able to pay transatlantic fares, many small local kin groups (*cloinne*) completely re-established themselves in Canada. Canadian Highland settlements therefore represented a substantial transference of Gaelic clan society (see CLANS OF THE HIGHLANDS AND ISLANDS: 2) to America.

Crucial for the evolution of these Canadian Gaelic communities was the nature and purpose of the Highlanders' departure from Scotland. A large number, but not all, of the emigrants chose to come to Canada, having decided it represented the best option for their families. While most Highlanders believed that they had been betrayed by their traditional leaders and that emigration was a choice forced on them by this betrayal, it was nonetheless most often the people who actively organized their own emigration to Canada, at times in spite of concerted landlord opposition. The principal purpose behind this migration was the protection of Highland communities, whose social and economic foundations were seriously threatened by landlord-supported change (see LANDOWNERSHIP IN THE HIGHLANDS AND ISLANDS). How open the Highlanders were to economic change is an issue of some debate in scholarly writing. J. M. Bumsted contends that the pre-1815 emigrations were conservative reactions to change, and in spite of landlords offering reasonable economic prospects to tenants. Marianne Maclean has argued that the tenants emigrated both to preserve traditional communities and to escape or avoid economic impoverishment. Regardless of the extent of economic rationalism as a motivation for emigration, it is clear that the Highlanders successfully populated Gaelic townships in which most families owned their farms. The result was a significant sense of achievement among the Highlanders, as well as a commitment to their new home, both in the local and in the national sense.

The Lowland Scottish impact on the Canadian colonies differed in intensity from that of the Highlanders but it was equally significant. Lowlanders too were drawn to Canada through complex networks of kin and friends which facilitated their departure abroad and provided support in their new lives, whether in rural or urban communities. The difference between the two groups was one of degree: the density of emigration from Lowland districts tended to be lower and the propensity for settling together in extended kin groups was not as strong. Many Lowland Scots found in Canada the land which agricultural improvement made more difficult to obtain in Scotland. In the early 19th century, people from the *Borders, eastern and western Lowlands, and the north-east acquired land in all parts of Ontario (with notable concentrations in Lanark county, about Toronto and Guelph), in Richmond and Megantic counties in Quebec, up the St John River and along the Gulf shore of New Brunswick, and scattered across Nova Scotia. In the early 20th century, substantial lowland settlements emerged on the prairies, including Minnedosa and Russell, Manitoba; Moffat, Saskatchewan; and Carstairs and Banff, Alberta. While transplanted kin networks were not as complex as among the Gaels, Ted Cowan, then professor of Scottish history at Guelph, Ontario, has argued that Scots often felt that in emigrating 'they were returning home' since in Canada they were 'joining a community of compatriots whose language, customs and values they understood'.

But beside the powerful attraction of land to a broad cross-section of the Scottish population, Scots were drawn by the economic opportunities offered by the villages and cities of the developing Canadian colonies. Immediately behind Wolfe's Highland soldiers were Scottish merchants. Regular transportation links were established between the Clyde and Quebec by 1764, with New Brunswick in the same year, and with Nova Scotia by 1768; eleven Glasgow area firms were engaged in the Quebec trade by 1770, only seven years after the cession of the province to the British. To the rapidly growing Scottish economy (see ECONOMY: 4) and particularly to its manufacturing sector, Canada was an attractive prospect. The new colony had been cut off from its French suppliers and offered the possibility of a ready market for Scottish goods and services.

Scottish firms sent out younger brothers, sons, or partners to act as their agents in Canada. One such was Christopher Scott, sent in 1799 by his Glasgow shipbuilding family to St John where he played a leading role in the expansion of that industry and of trade in New Brunswick. Across British North America, Scots merchants created social and business networks linked by blood and marriage. Robert Hamilton and Thomas Clark of Dumfriesshire dominated trade at Niagara; John Mure joined his Ayrshire uncle John Porteous in the import–export trade in Quebec and Montreal; and John Black of Aberdeenshire brought a brother and two cousins to expand his business enterprises first in St John and then in Halifax. Men such as these developed the timber trade, exported potash, furs, and wheat, served as wholesale importers, and built a commercial infrastructure, particularly banks (see ECONOMY, TERTIARY SECTOR: 2), throughout the Canadian colonies. In the years 1770–1825, British North America was close to a Scottish commercial preserve.

The Scottish influence on Canadian economic development was not limited to the early colonial years, but continued through the period of industrialization. In mid-19th-century Montreal, then the pre-eminent Canadian business centre, Scots dominated commercial activity, including dry goods, shipping, and the organization of company ventures. What is perhaps more striking is the fact that in the 1880s, when Scots formed one-sixth of the Canadian population, one-third of the industrial elite were of Scottish origin, outnumbering the combined total of English and Irish origin. Scottish success in industry was derived from two factors: the first was the transfer of technology from the more sophisticated Scottish industrial economy to the more primitive Canadian and the second was the traditional practice of providing some form of training for those sons who would not inherit. In Canada, Horatio Alger was most apt to be a Scottish farmer's son, born on either side of the Atlantic and apprenticed to a trade in his early teens. Scottish success was repeated in the following generation, fuelled by the provision of training and by intense ethnic loyalty. To Scots, Canada represented opportunities not just for individuals but also for companies to use skills nurtured in the more mature Scottish economy for advantages they could not find at home.

The underlying characteristic of Scottish involvement in Canada is one of 'enracinement' in British North America. Such a putting down of roots is evident in the case of the new Highland communities in places such as Arisaig, Nova Scotia, or McIntyre's Corners in Grey County, Ontario. Where there was significant group settlement, Highlanders were able, according to Margaret Mackay, 'to reproduce and foster the community characteristics that were most important' to a Gaelic people: a shared language, mutual aid, hospitality, the church, and the wide circle of family and friends in which everyone was more or less related. The Gaelic cultural tradition flourished with songs and satire written to describe Canadian experiences, and customs adapted to the physical conditions found in their new homes. Highland reverence for place was transferred to Canada, and within two generations each community had Gaelic names and stories for recognizable physical features within its bounds. New loyalties developed too as MacDonnells, MacMillans, and MacLeods all became Glengarry men and identification with a *baile* became loyalty to a common island origin. To succeeding generations, it was the Canadian Gaelic communities that were their homes. Just as 19th-century tombstones in Glengarry County proudly recorded that the men and women buried there were natives of Inverness-shire, Scotland, so 20th-century tombstones in Macdonald, Manitoba, boast of origins in Glengarry County, Ontario.

In the longer term, Canadian Gaelic communities faced some of the same difficulties as their Scottish counterparts in maintaining a minority language. Because modern economic and social development originated in urban centres, Gaelic became identified with backwardness and poverty. Depending on the degree of isolation, particularly from the Anglicizing force of the public educational system, Canadian Highlanders largely ceased teaching the *Gaelic language to their children, in Ontario in the 1880s and in Cape Breton in the 1930s. To a large extent, those Gaels successful in the mainstream were isolated from their geographic and cultural origins, and the transition generation passed on only a narrow band of the traditions developed by the Gaels in Canada. Later generations adopted as badges of cultural identity certain of the invented or adapted traditions of the pipe band, the kilt (see DRESS, HIGHLAND), and

Highland dancing. Within the Gaelic settlements in Canada, the fiddling tradition and step dancing were one element of Gaelic culture which survived the period of Anglicization. In Cape Breton classical Scottish fiddle music is still the centre of community life as people of all ages listen, discuss, and dance to it in village halls across the island. The art of step dancing, too, remained well known in Cape Breton and skilled practitioners such as Willie Fraser and Mary Janet MacDonald have reintroduced it in Scotland (see MUSIC, HIGHLAND).

Taking root in the Canadian land and its emerging society was the experience of Lowland emigrants too. St Andrews Societies, the Presbyterian Church, and the Sons of Scotland were some of the organizations that served as ethnic anchors while Scots contributed more broadly to Canadian society. As in Scotland, Highland and Lowland Canadians were keen to create *clan societies, some based on Scottish identities but others derived from Canadian allegiances: there were Glengarry associations in Montreal, Ottawa, and Winnipeg, and Cape Breton clubs in Halifax and Boston. As symbols of Canada emerged in the 20th century, it is striking how often Scottish or more particularly Highland traditions were adopted by English-speaking Canadians for their new country. The clearest evidence of this is in the growth of the number of Scottish regiments in the Canadian infantry in the early 20th century. Kilted regiments were a drawing card for Canadians, and a roll call of the eighteen Canadian Scottish regiments reads like a settlement map of Scots in Canada and its major cities. With the exception of two Irish regiments, the phenomenon of ethnic military units has been uniquely Scottish in Canada but such regiments attracted Canadians of all ethnic backgrounds. To new immigrants Highland surnames are so ubiquitous that a name beginning with Mac is a Canadian not an immigrant name.

The result of the long relationship between Scotland and Canada is a remarkable resonance between the two countries. For Scots arriving in Canada, whether in the late 20th century or any time earlier, there have always been families, friends, and communities to join where Scottish accents and traditions have been valued. Canadian society, while now truly multicultural in composition, shows myriad Scottish–Canadian influences whether in politics, business, education, religion, or the arts. In a very real sense, Canada is the country many Scots could not have at home. For the Scottish *Gaidhealtachd* in particular, which lost so many of its people to Canada, part of the Scottish Gaelic tradition is now Canadian.

As revealing are Canadian attitudes to Scotland. Canadians first arrived in Scotland in large numbers as members of the armed forces during the First and Second World Wars. To Canadian military authorities in 1914–18, it was a standing joke that Canadian servicemen given a week's leave always asked for a railway warrant to Edinburgh, Glasgow, or even Inverness. During both wars, regardless of national origin, Canadian airmen and soldiers felt more warmly received in Scotland than in England. To these servicemen and to the thousands of tourists who now arrive in Scotland annually from Canada, it has been easy to feel at home in Scotland. The tremendous human investment which Scots made generation after generation in Canada has created a sense of kinship which resonates across the distance which separates the two countries.   MLM

Caustantín mac Aeda. See CONSTANTINE II.

Caustantín mac Cinaeda. See CONSTANTINE I.

Caustantín son of Fergus (Uurgust), king of Picts (fl. 789–820). Although debate has been locked over the ethnic identity of Caustantín, neither side is in doubt of his importance. Until recently seen as a descendant of the royal line of *Dál Riata who took over the *Pictish kingship, recent scholarship has argued that he was instead a Pictish king, perhaps descended from the *Ungus (Onuist), son of Uurgust who reigned so successfully 729–61, and who achieved some measure of dominance over Dál Riata. Whatever the case, Caustantín's son seems to have been inserted into the kingship of Dál Riata, perhaps in 811, and Caustantín's brother, son, and nephew all succeeded him in the Pictish kingship: a stable dynasty which lasted some 50 years, until the disastrous defeat by Vikings in 839. Important here is that for much of this period we can be fairly confident that Dál Riata and Pictland were under the same overlordship, and Caustantín's reign has been seen by some as a foreshadowing of the political developments of the later 9th century. Caustantín's name is inscribed on the Dupplin Cross as 'Custantin filius Fircus[sa]', and that monument is a witness to his power and prestige, standing as it probably did within or near the royal palace of *Forteviot. Caustantín has been linked within another prestigious monument, the St Andrews sarcophagus, either as patron or subject.

This Pictish king was known and perhaps commemorated in a contemporary martyrology in Ireland, the *Martyrology of Tallaght*. Since this is a text emanating from one of the main *céli Dé* monasteries, dedicated to ecclesiastical reform, this is suggestive of Caustantín's possible involvement in such reform, as is the tradition that he founded Dunkeld. It may be that he worked alongside the abbot of *Iona, *Diarmait, foster-son of Daigre (fl.

814–39) in instituting some measure of church reform in Pictland.   TC

central Europe. A visitor to Vienna today is likely to hear passers-by talking not only in German, but Hungarian, Czech, Slovak, Polish, and many of the south Slavic languages. However, the lands which these and many more linguistic groups inhabit occupy a *Mitteleuropa* that is difficult to define. For the purposes of this survey, 'central Europe' will include only the successor states of the lands that comprised the dominions of the Habsburg monarchy from 1526 to 1918.

Although Scots could be found in central Europe and central Europeans in Scotland much earlier, the relationship seems to have been most significant in the 17th and 18th centuries. Nevertheless, several more recent examples spring to mind, not all of them related to the tragedies of modern warfare. When Lajos Kossuth visited Glasgow after the 1848 revolutions, he was apparently welcomed 'amidst deafening cheers and the waving of handkerchiefs'. Conversely, a Scot, Adam Clark was employed by Count István Széchenyi to supervise the construction of the famous 'Chain Bridge' over the Danube in 1849, this being the first permanent crossing point between the cities of Buda and Pest. Further south and much later, Sir Fitzroy Maclean was leader of the British military mission to Tito's partisans and subsequent friend of the Yugoslav leader. In Prague, Edwin Muir, the Orkney-born poet and translator of Kafka, was simultaneously a director of the British Council.

The two-way nature of the relationship is also reflected in its historiography. T. A. Fischer's 1902 publication *The Scots in Germany* covered not only soldiers but also merchants, scholars, and ecclesiastical figures and as its title implies went well beyond the geographical boundaries of the area covered here. Scottish historians such as John Malcolm Bulloch added much to our understanding of these relations in the first half of the last century. Also influential were the efforts of R. W. Seton-Watson, who published his first book *The Future of Austria-Hungary* in 1902 under the pseudonym 'Scotus Viator'. More recently, the many publications of the Czech historian Jozef V. Polišensky have brought the attention of many to the role of the Scots in Bohemia. Other than that though, current research depends largely for secondary sources on scattered references with the exception of the military sphere, in which the history of the Scots in imperial service was covered in an ambitious 1971 University of Vienna thesis by Ernst Schmidhofer.

It is clear though that the Scots had become familiar figures in all the eastern regions of the Holy Roman Empire and beyond, from the 8th century, when Scoti priests, of Irish or Scottish background, were undertaking missionary work. There was a *Schottenabtei* in Vienna in medieval times to which they must have arrived not only from the west but from neighbouring Poland and Lithuania, numerically the most significant destinations for Scottish emigration until 1707. The Scots established themselves not only in the Baltic ports there but also much further south from where many were drawn to the neighbouring region of Silesia (see GERMANY, THE BALTIC, AND POLAND).

The year 1433 witnessed the burning for heresy of a Silesian, Pavel Kravar, in St Andrews. However, the relationship was not always so hostile. Fischer recorded details of a trial at Breslau (Wroclaw, Poland) towards the end of the 15th century involving a group of Scottish refugees who reported that 'distress and wars drove us out of Scotland'. It is not clear if this is the same group of pilgrims who in 1470, returning from Rome to Danzig (Gdansk), were tried for 'unlawful vagabondage'. The town authorities reported that this latter group included a Lorentz Green from Edinburgh, who 'had no shoes, and has been ill for three quarters of a year' yet had 'found countrymen here and a friend at Brünn [who] has advised him to move to this place'. Another of them, 'Reichart of Wicke, Kathnes', had spent 'four years in the service of the queen of Hungary'. Much later in 1533, the town issued an edict against 'pedlars, Scots, gypsies' and others. By this time though, the map of central Europe had changed considerably, since Louis II Jagiellon, the last independent king of both the Bohemian crown lands and Hungary, had been killed fighting the Turks at Mohács in 1526. Only then did the Bohemian kingdom (which consisted of the province of Bohemia itself, Moravia, the two Lusatias, and Silesia), along with a small chunk of north-west Hungary, come under Austrian Habsburg control. Nevertheless, Scottish emigrants continued to arrive (see EMIGRATION: 1). A student at the Jesuit seminary in Braunsberg from 1582, an Andrew Jack, was recorded as having been 'sent to Vienna to continue his studies'. James Grant tells us that simultaneously, a John Paterson was an imperial physician, who lived at Eperies (Prešov, Slovakia). Another Scot, Peter Green, taught philosophy at the University of Graz and then at Olmütz (Olomouc, Czech Republic) in 1612.

Besides, there was one Scottish family in the early modern period which claimed links dating back much further. Indeed, the Leslie family still traces its origins to the arrival of a noble in Scotland in 1067 in the train of St *Margaret, the future wife of Malcolm III 'Canmore' (Mael Coluim mac Donnchada). The Hungarian-born queen is said to have employed a Bartolf or Bartholomew, to escort her on horseback, hence the family motto 'Grip Fast'. Tradition has it that he was knighted and bestowed with the land now associated with the Leslies in Fife and the north-east. However, evidence from the 17th century suggests that this tale may be apocryphal.

One motivation for many of the Scots who served in the Thirty Years War from 1618 was the fate of Elizabeth Stewart, the Scottish-born daughter of *James VI and wife of the German Elector Palatine, Frederick V. In 1619, the Bohemian estates deposed the Habsburg king and placed Frederick and Elizabeth on the throne. The couple briefly took up residence in the Hrǎdany palace in Prague, but were forced to flee the city following imperialist victory at the White Mountain in November 1620. Many Scots served against the emperor there, including Sir Andrew Gray and Colonel John Seton.

Nevertheless, some Scottish officers fought for the Habsburg cause too. One of them was Walter Leslie (1606–67). In 1632 he was given command of a thousand imperialist dragoons at the border garrison of Eger in Bohemia (Cheb, Czech Republic), where he was based until 1634. In February that year he and the garrison's commander, a fellow Scot named John Gordon, both became deeply implicated in the events surrounding the assassination of the imperialist generalissimo Wallenstein. After arriving in Vienna with the news, Leslie was awarded the post of imperial chamberlain and given the command of two regiments. His main reward, however, came in the form of the confiscated property of one of Wallenstein's last remaining cronies, the castle at Neustadt (Nové Mesto-nad-Metují, Czech Republic). Gordon received property elsewhere in Bohemia (see MERCENARIES IN EUROPE).

Leslie's acquisition of the title of count of the Holy Roman Empire three years later was made in response to a letter he had sent to the emperor claiming his 600-year family connection with the Habsburg lands. He later married Anna Franziska von Dietrichstein, daughter of a leading Bohemian noble and, by 1650, he had become a field marshal and general on the so-called 'Croatian–Slavonian military frontier'. Five years later, and still childless, an entail was drawn up specifying that all his property and possessions should fall on his death to his young nephew James Leslie. James arrived from Scotland the same year. By this time, Walter Leslie had acquired properties in Prague, Varazdin, and Graz, although the next year he sold the Prague property and bought the ancient castle of Oberpettau (Ptuj, Slovenia) with the profits.

Meanwhile, the Ottomans were occupying lands just a few miles to the south-east. The imperialists were eventually to defeat them in battle at St Gotthard (Szentgotthárd, Hungary) in 1664. Subsequently, James and another Aberdeenshire nephew, Francis Hay of Delgaty, accompanied the count on his last, lavish embassy to Constantinople to ratify the peace treaty. On returning to Vienna in early 1666, Leslie was to see James marry a princess of the Liechtenstein family in a ceremony attended by the Emperor Leopold I. However, on 3 March 1667 he died and was buried in the *Schottenkirche* in Vienna.

James Leslie soon acquired the so-called 'Leslie-hof' in Graz. His military and diplomatic abilities at the head of his own 'Leslie regiment' also led to him being appointed a field marshal, in which capacity he served during the defence of Vienna in 1683. He obtained gold and silver brocade and jewelled Turkish armoury following his involvement in several battles in Croatia–Slavonia and Hungary including the recapture of the lower town of Buda in 1684, and some of these prizes were sent back to Scotland. Meanwhile, other Leslies had come over from Scotland including James's brother, William Aloysius, a Jesuit. After a period as canon at Breslau he wrote a family genealogy, the *Laurus Leslaeana*, which was published in Graz in 1692. Another was William Leslie of Warthill, who travelled on a number of diplomatic missions for Emperor Joseph I, the acclaim for which led to him being appointed in 1716 as bishop of Waitzen (Vács, Hungary) and then, two years later, prince-bishop of Laybach (Ljubljana, Slovenia). He died there in 1727. Indeed, the Leslie's central European branch continued until 1802 when the fifth count, Anthony Leslie died.

This family provide just one example of historical links between Scotland and central Europe in the post-Reformation period. Many other Scots served in armies in central Europe during this period, as is evident from an account of the 'Bergschotten' in the Vienna Gazette of 1762. An example of Scottish–Austrian political links in the latter half of the 18th century is that of the two Sir Robert Keiths, father and son, from Kincardineshire and successive British ambassadors in Vienna. Finally, connections can also be found in the field of music (see CULTURE: 15). By 1799, Haydn had set arrangements for around 100 Scottish melodies while Beethoven too expressed a liking for Scottish airs, arranging nearly 50 between 1815 and 1818. DW

Chalmers, Thomas (1780–1847), political economist, theologian, and minister of the Church of Scotland, best known for his role in the Scottish *Disruption of 1843. Educated at St Andrews and Edinburgh universities, Chalmers became minister of the rural parish of Kilmany in Fife in 1803, but neglected his pastoral duties while he pursued, unsuccessfully, a university appointment. Then in 1810–11, following a prolonged illness, he was converted to an Evangelical piety, and soon established a reputation as a fiery preacher. In 1815, he was translated to a crowded parish in the industrializing city of *Glasgow. Distressed by the poverty in Glasgow, he became convinced that the main cause of urban deprivation was the breakdown of community, which he sought to restore by reviving the traditional parish system in the city. In 1823, he left the parish ministry for an academic career, becoming first professor of moral philosophy at St Andrews University and then, after 1828, professor of divinity at Edinburgh University. Leader of the Evangelical party (see RELIGIOUS LIFE: 6) in the Church of Scotland after 1831, he worked to revive the parish system on a national level, seeking to transform Scotland into a 'godly commonwealth' of close-knit parish communities. Between 1834 and 1841, he led a national church extension campaign, which erected over 220 new churches in Scotland. However, by the later 1830s his efforts to revive the established church were overshadowed by a bitter dispute between church and state over lay patronage in the appointment of parish ministers. At the Disruption of 1843, Chalmers led over a third of the clergy and perhaps half the lay membership out of the Church of Scotland, in protest against what he perceived as undue state interference in church affairs. They formed the Free Church, and Chalmers devoted his last years to building the new denomination and serving as principal of the Free Church College. SJB

chambers of commerce have played an important role in the economic development of modern Scotland. All major cities and most large towns formed chambers of commerce in the 18th and 19th centuries to give the business community a forum in which common interests could be identified and strategies pursued. The two most significant chambers were those of *Edinburgh and *Glasgow. Chambers were particularly interested in the development of town and city strategies with reference to how these would effect business dealings. For most of the 19th century, business leaders were prominent in their own right within local government mainly because ratable business premises entitled them to vote along with their residential vote. Chambers were also important in communicating the view of the business community to local MPs. This was especially important in the 19th century as powers of local government were insufficiently developed and major urban projects such as harbour extensions or river deepening required parliamentary consent. It comes as no surprise, for example, to find that the chambers of commerce in both Glasgow and *Dundee were prominent in promoting port developments which would improve local business. Chambers of commerce were also active in the debate about reform of local government and in Glasgow in the 1880s plans to extend the municipal powers of the authority were given approval by many business leaders. Chambers were also active in sending representations to Westminster and various resolutions were passed from the Scottish business community with regard to aspects of government policy. For example, the issue of tariff reform in the early 20th century was resolutely opposed by the Glasgow chamber which feared that orders would be lost in heavy engineering and shipbuilding (see ECONOMY, SECONDARY SECTOR: 2). Chambers also strongly disapproved of *Irish Home Rule and several were prominent in urging imperial expansion as a source of new markets (see BRITISH EMPIRE). After the First World War, the political complexion of the chambers in Scotland were more closely identified with the Conservative Party, although this did not stop both Edinburgh and Glasgow chambers from criticizing aspects of government policy in the 1930s which seemed to harm Scottish economic interests. Glasgow was particularly prominent in urging the national government to help subsidize the shipbuilding industry (see GOVERNMENT AND ADMINISTRATION). With the advent of larger business organizations such as the Federation of British Industries, the Economic Committee, and the *Scottish Council (Development and Industry) and specific industrial concerns such as the Engineers Employers Union, Scottish business had better and more powerful outlets to express their concerns. Such groups had more influence with government and could formulate more specific recommendations than the local chambers. As such, organizations became more powerful in an increasingly rationalized economy so the influence of the chambers declined, although they remained an important social function for local business communities and a forum for the expression of specific local economic issues.   RJF

Chartism The term 'Chartism' is used to describe the campaign for political reform which became focused on the 'People's Charter', issued by the London Working Men's Association in June 1838. The demands for manhood suffrage, vote by ballot, annual parliaments, payment of MPs, equal electoral districts, and the abolition of property qualification for membership of the Commons had been around for decades. They form the background to the Reform Act of 1832. While that Act transformed the Scottish political scene, demands for extension of

the franchise to include the working class continued. A visit to Glasgow by Daniel O'Connell in September 1835 brought a working-class demonstration calling for 'household suffrage, triennial parliaments and vote by ballot'. In December 1836, a Radical Association of the West of Scotland was formed to campaign for universal suffrage, annual parliaments, and the ballot, and to organize a visit to Scotland by the radical campaigner Feargus O'Connor. A year later a meeting of both working-class and middle-class radicals had before it resolutions for an extension of the suffrage and the ballot, but the Ayrshire middle-class journalist Dr John Taylor moved an amendment calling for universal suffrage and this was carried.

Contact with Birmingham activists who had launched the campaign for a national petition for the 'Charter' came soon afterwards and old middle-class reformers and new artisan campaigners started to broaden the campaign. A meeting in April 1838 is usually taken as the start of Chartism in *Glasgow, and a Universal Suffrage Association was formed in July 1838. An Aberdeen Working Men's Association emerged at the same time. Various *newspapers began to appear aimed at the movement, the *True Scotsman*, the *Scottish Patriot*, the *Chartist Circular*, and the *Scots Times*. There was a demand from some that physical force as a means of achieving the Charter be unequivocally rejected. The leaders of this approach were Evangelical Christians like Abram Duncan and John Fraser and the Revd Patrick Brewster from Paisley (see RELIGIOUS LIFE: 6). They were looking for some Whig grandee to provide moderate leadership for the campaign. Resolutions on these lines, passed at a rally on Edinburgh's Calton Hill in December 1838, split the movement, with Taylor leading the attack on behalf of the more class-confrontational position being taken by O'Connor's *Northern Star*. The support of the Birmingham Chartist Convention for a month-long general strike unleashed further deep fissures within the movement. Most of the petty-bourgeois leaders, like James Moir in Glasgow and John Mitchell in Aberdeen, saw the proposals as an encouragement to a harsh reaction by the authorities.

Over the next three years there were endless debates on strategy and tactics. There was a strong moral reform element pushed by the *Scottish Patriot* which advocated total abstinence (see TEMPERANCE). The *Chartist Circular*, with a claimed circulation of 22,000 at its peak, blamed 'Old Corruption' and aristocratic rule and called for the productive classes to unite against them. Yet others developed a more class-conscious line and took every opportunity to intervene in middle-class meetings and push through resolutions in favour of the Charter.

A Northern Democratic Association split from the Universal Suffrage Association at the end of 1839 and declared itself willing to consider the use of force against 'the shackles of the government and of the capitalist'. Relations between different groups were often acrimonious and a constant stream of visitors from the south battled for influence. Nonetheless, by 1840–1 Chartism in Scotland, albeit divided, was undoubtedly vigorous. Meetings and organizations flourished, with more than 100 Chartist associations stretching from Elgin to Hawick; organized trades joined in demonstrations; candidates stood in elections for police commissions; at least twenty female Chartist associations appeared (see WOMEN: 3); and Anti-Corn-Law League meetings were hijacked.

The three years between 1839 and 1841 also saw the emergence of what was, in some ways, the most vital part of Scottish Chartism, the Chartist churches. At least 29 have been identified and most emerged as a reaction to the hostility of clergy to Chartism and their often unsympathetic role in the distribution of poor relief. But they were also a search for community and fellowship among working-class families in an increasingly harsh and uncertain world. A high proportion of Chartists seemed to have been from craft occupations which were increasingly under threat from changing work patterns and mechanization. During these years the Chartist movement became a focus for a variety of working-class activities involving self-education through evening classes, Sunday schools, and day schools, total abstinence, co-operative production and retailing, and exclusive dealing, all of which involved at least some rejection of middle-class-dominated cultural institutions (see RESPECTABLE CULTURE) and ideology.

By 1842, with widespread unemployment, the more militant aspects of Chartism seemed to have run their course. It allowed a number of sympathetic middle-class supporters to gain leadership again through the Complete Suffrage Association, formed in 1842 by Joseph Sturge, to re-create a union of middle- and working-class reformers. The debates unleashed by the *Disruption of the Church of Scotland, with the attack on patronage, allowed the landed aristocracy to be once again firmly identified as the enemy and the exploiter, and facilitated the reassertion of middle-class leadership. The Chartist press in Scotland collapsed and, although some effort was made by Chartists to provide leadership for the unemployed and support for the strikes, they met with little response.

Over the next few years, reform activity was firmly in the hands of a middle-class leadership campaigning for corn law repeal, poor law reform (see LIVING STANDARDS: 4), and church reform. The occasional visit to Scotland by O'Connor or others could arouse enthusiasm and controversy, but there was limited support for O'Connor's land plan. With corn law repeal achieved in 1846, there was an attempt to extend the campaign to other areas of 'aristocratic privilege' and former prominent Chartists could join with parliamentary radicals like Joseph Hume in pressing for further reforms. There were none of the mass arrests and lengthy imprisonments which broke the movement in England. Most leading Chartists now saw the route to reform as coming through constitutional methods in collaboration with middle-class *Liberalism.   WHF

childbirth and infancy. Pre-Christian evidence records the testing of female urine on wheat or spelt to confirm diagnosis of pregnancy; modern pregnancy testing, also using urine, was not developed until the 1920s. Until the late 17th century, the management of pregnancy and childbirth depended upon the traditional knowledge of women, handed down through countless generations.

Care during childbirth was entirely in the hands of the 'granny-woman', 'howdie', or bean ghlùin (lit. 'knee woman') who acquired her midwifery skills from older women. While pregnancy and childbirth were regarded as a series of natural processes, there was a keen awareness of the perils involved. Thus every precaution was taken to ensure safe delivery, although those in attendance were less familiar with the importance of cleanliness and the dangers of germs than they were with the threat of supernatural influences. Fairy belief, once common all over Scotland and beyond, was especially significant in cases of confinement. People feared that an unprotected mother or baby might be stolen by fairies seeking a lactating mother for their children or a new baby to pay a 'teind' to hell. In place of the stolen human, fairies were said to leave a 'changeling' and, regardless of more formal religious faiths, there are many accounts of this happening, including one witnessed by Martin Luther in 1541. To protect mother and baby, therefore, the midwife placed a piece of iron near the confinement bed, an open bible near the mother, and made sure that neither would be left alone until after the mother was churched and the baby christened.

Newborn babies were bathed in salted water, as salt was regarded as having protective powers, and the baby was given three tastes of the water. Then, depending on gender, the baby was immediately wrapped in her father's shirt or his mother's chemise. Among the travelling people it was common to bathe the newborn in the nearest running stream, an instant baptism which not only cleansed the skin but induced the first gasp and cry of the baby who was then warmly wrapped and placed at the mother's breast. The afterbirth was then buried by the howdie, who usually stayed with the new mother for several days to help with domestic duties as well as care of the mother and baby. For her services, the midwife was given a modest fee if the family could afford it, or she was paid in kind, for example with home-grown produce, while the very poorest were exempt from any obligation.

Early in the 17th century, influenced by the work of William Harvey (1578–1657), 'father of British midwifery', university medical schools (see MEDICINE AND THE ORIGINS OF THE MEDICAL PROFESSION) and hospitals began to teach midwifery. From then on, the natural process of childbirth was regarded as a medical condition to be managed by man-midwives or medical doctors. In 1739 an Edinburgh doctor, William Buchan, published his popular book *Domestic Medicine* (reprinted over 150 times), which included a section on pregnancy and childbirth. While he strongly favoured professional medical attention, he also aimed to make better medical education accessible to the general public. Buchan's advice to traditional midwives attending a difficult labour was to call a 'skilful surgeon or man-midwife'. For severe problems, such as threatened miscarriage, he recommended bloodletting, 'at least half a pound from the arm', a common treatment for a wide range of ailments until the late 19th century. Buchan's recommended cure for infertility (an 'affliction of the affluent') was a *diet of milk and vegetables.

The first professor of midwifery was appointed at Edinburgh University in 1781, though the teaching of obstetrics was not established there till 1825. The first lying-in hospital, set up for the treatment of women in labour, as well as the teaching of obstetrics, was established by Glasgow University in 1792. Traditional midwives continued to practise and, although criticized by the medical profession for their lack of training, they were sometimes called upon to assist the doctor on a house visit. Only families who could afford it engaged the services of the all-male medical profession, while poor women with complicated pregnancies needing medical treatment could use the services of a lying-in hospital, which provided free treatment and cheap medicine to the sick poor. Some admitted only married women presenting proof of marriage, while others would admit the unmarried for a first pregnancy only. Lying-in patients were used in treatment demonstrations and instruction of student doctors.

Until the 20th century, breastfeeding was universal and in cases where the mother could not lactate, was too ill to breastfeed, or had died, a neighbouring woman with plenty of milk would wet-nurse. It was common in the cities for wealthy women to employ a wet-nurse who received higher pay than other domestic servants. In his *Description of the Western Isles* (*c.*1695), Martin Martin noted that nursing mothers refrained from drinking alcohol (nearly three centuries before medical science discovered foetal alcohol syndrome) and they drank the broth of boiled limpets and periwinkles to improve lactation. If a mother lost her milk entirely the broth and fat of boiled limpets was fed to the infant.

The care of newborn babies and infants was influenced by traditional practices, medical advice, or a combination of both. In the Lowlands, the unnatural custom of binding newborn babies may have originated with midwives trying to emulate the surgeon's skill at bandaging. Though it was discouraged by doctors of the 18th century, it persisted until after the Second World War. Attention to diet, rest, and exercise was encouraged to promote good health, while the common ailments of infancy were treated by a range of traditional home remedies. Specialized paediatric care developed with the establishment of hospitals such as the Edinburgh Hospital for Sick Children (1860). Registration of live births in Scotland dates back to 1855 and registration of stillbirths to 1939.

The passing of the Midwives Act of 1902 required all midwives to pass an examination for certification by the Central Midwives' Board. After 1910 uncertificated women were not allowed to practise and it was the responsibility of county councils to supervise each district. The National Health Service Act of 1946 (1947 in Scotland) divided responsibility for maternity care between hospital authorities providing beds, antenatal and postnatal care, domiciliary consultation, and emergency obstetric services, and local authorities providing domiciliary midwifery service, health visitors, and home help.

In the mid-1950s, Professor Ian Donald at Glasgow University developed the technique of using ultrasound in obstetrics to identify foetal abnormalities and to monitor the unborn baby. By the late 1970s it had become the common method of foetal surveillance in modern maternity hospitals.

Social and spiritual aspects in the care of mothers and the newborn have generally been the concern of the family and the clergy. In the 20th century it has undergone many changes that not only reflect modern society but also mirror developments in health care. Today we have reference books of names in both Gaelic and Scots, though, for centuries, it was widely considered bad luck to speak aloud the name of a new baby before baptism. This notion is based on a fear that the fairies could use the name for malevolent purposes and is probably the basis for the strong tradition, especially in the Highlands (see HIGHLANDS AND ISLANDS: GENERAL), of naming children after a close relative. Decisions such as 'he will be called after his paternal grandfather' were clearly understood without enunciating the name.

At the same time, new mothers remained at home and neighbours would not visit her house until after she was 'churched'. The Roman Catholic Church held a special churching service till the 1930s and, although the Church of Scotland did not have a special order of service, churching was expected of all new mothers. Ministers of the late 19th century record that a woman's first Sunday in church after childbirth was marked by prayers of thanksgiving for her safe delivery. Churching of women, which dates to Levitical Law, is no longer practised by either denomination.

The custom of 'hanselling the baby' always involved a piece of silver, usually a coin, offered without comment to the new baby. A token of well-wishing from adult to child, it dates to an era when silver was believed to avert the evil eye. Standard practice until the 1950s, it is becoming increasingly rare.

Infant baptism, generally (though not always) performed in church, is still common to all denominations except the Baptist Church. While the usual age ranges from 3 to 12 months, if a baby is sickly Roman Catholic parents may call the priest (or, in an emergency, any adult) to baptize within hours of the birth. Godparents are chosen to stand by the parents and support them in their vows, and though the custom of choosing close friends or relatives for this role is similar in both the Roman Catholic Church and Protestant churches, the Church of Scotland favours the term 'supporter'. The importance of the ceremony is also reflected in the custom of dressing the baby in elaborate christening robes and a delicately hand-knitted shawl, often handed down from one generation to the next.

On leaving the church, it was customary in Lowland Scotland for the baby's father to offer a 'christening piece' to the first child he met who was of the opposite sex to the new baby. Usually a sandwich, made of two slices of bread or two biscuits with butter or jam along with a silver coin, the 'piece' was always offered in a paper bag until plastic took over. Christenings, sometimes referred to as the first public rite of passage, were celebrated by the family, usually at home, where all drank a toast to the parents and baby, and shared a modest meal which included a christening cake. If the baby was the first child of the marriage, the cake was usually the top layer of the parents' wedding cake, care-

fully wrapped and preserved for this special occasion, As the 20th century drew to a close, the sharp decline in churchgoing was reflected in fewer christening ceremonies and even in the gradual rejection of traditional robes in favour of baby's best outfit. The trend in the 1990s was for parents to send out invitation cards to a christening, then, after the ceremony, to hold the christening party in a restaurant or hotel where the catering was taken over by professionals. (See also CHILDREN; CULTURE: 16, 19, 23; ROMAN CATHOLIC COMMUNITY; WOMEN).

MBe

children are and have been regarded very differently in different contexts. It is possible, for example, to find religious teachings, the teachings of experts of their time and place, that regard children as inherently wicked—hence, needing to be civilized by discipline—as innocents needing protection from the evils of the world; and as morally neutral, inexperienced, malleable human material that must be shaped into good lives (see RELIGIOUS LIFE). Most contemporary societies have a set of social practices and beliefs that clearly sets aside a differentiated period of childhood in opposition to adulthood. There is considerable variation in how children are regarded as different from adults or deficient in adultness, and the boundary of childhood is variously expressed by their exclusion from certain 'adult' activities and confinement in age-specific socializing and educational activities.

The relational otherness of children, however defined, is used to justify their relative lack of power, subjection to adult authority, and denial of adult privileges often matched by a degree of diminished responsibility and freedom from adult duties. Calls in recent decades for children's rights have not yet radically modified the power of adults over children or given children a strong voice in how they are governed. Many societies also recognize a transitional phase of adolescence or youth between childhood and adulthood. In Britain, many of the boundaries were drawn legislatively in the late 19th century. This was the time of the establishment of compulsory education (see SCHOOLS AND SCHOOLING: 4) and the laying down of age-specific restrictions on access to employment and a whole set of other activities, such as purchasing alcohol (see TEMPERANCE) and tobacco or placing bets. Neither childhood nor youth necessarily straightforwardly correspond to individual or typical physical maturation. Nor do histories of childhood simply follow the state of expert knowledge in a society concerning child development, although dominant claims of expert knowledge have often played a very important role in the construction of childhood. A growing body of historical work is piecing together ever more complex pictures of patterned variation across time and place. The evidence includes depictions of children, material artefacts of childhood, and diverse writings about and for children (see also CHILDBIRTH AND INFANCY).

Philippe Ariès's work *L'Enfant et la vie familial sous l'ancien régime*, first published in 1960 and subsequently translated as *Centuries of Childhood*, is positioned as the classic that much subsequent work disputes or augments. Ariès argued that, after a brief period of indulgence in infancy, French medieval parents and adults were unsentimental about the young, treating them more or less like little adults from the age of about 7. Hence beyond 7 there was no childhood in the sense of a protected socially segregated existence shielded from aspects of the adult world. Shift in religious and pedagogical ideas about children and their education did not translate into a more elaborate childhood until the 17th or 18th century and then only for the more privileged sectors of society—first the sons and then the daughters of the highest rank—trickling down much later for the majority.

Much work has been devoted since to debating where and when a concept of childhood could be said to exist. It is possible, for example, that sentimentality over children developed earlier in China than it did in Europe. Historians of medieval Europe since Ariès have argued that a notion of childhood did exist, at least in some parts of Europe, albeit that the meaning of childhood was very far removed from the dominant ideas of centuries proximate to our own. For example, there were no shared assumptions of the possibility of having an effect, good or bad, on the child's future character as an adult. The experiences of children were not regarded as of any great relevance to their unfolding character. At the same time, European scholars have contested whether children were less loved in the past. This is an issue that is difficult to unpack as efforts at measuring love are undermined by the fact that the very meaning of love, like the meaning of childhood, changes.

The experience of being a child has varied enormously across time and place, and continues to do so. For example, in Britain at the beginning of the 20th century, class (see SOCIAL CLASS) differences in the experience of childhood were still extreme. The child of a middle-class family was brought up in a house with at least one servant and in a wealthy upper-class household children slept in a nursery tended by a nanny. Their childhood world had childhood games, toys, books, parties, sports, and hobbies and was largely adult-supervised. Both boys and girls in such families would continue to be educated into their teens, perhaps followed by college or university, although upper-class young women were not expected to work. Meanwhile, a working-class child had very few childhood props. They had no nursery but were probably sharing a bed with several siblings in a two-roomed house. Their childhood world consisted of playing on the street when they were not working or otherwise required. In cities and the countryside alike, a whole host of chores were delegated to children, including foraging for fuel and travelling distances to fetch cheap food as well as home-based tasks. Children and particularly daughters were typically expected to do certain routine household cleaning tasks (cleaning cutlery, brasses, shoes, blackleading the grate, scrubbing worktops and floors) and in large families, older children, and particularly daughters, were often given younger siblings to look after. Working-class children had no choice but to leave school aged 14 and could expect to be in employment more or less on the following working day. Many were involved in paid employment while still at school, through part-time, Saturday, and holiday jobs. This was not about earning pocket money but about contributing to the family household. Any money earned was handed over 'to the house'.

The majority of both the wealthy and the poor, nevertheless, shared some attitudes to children that have since been eclipsed by a quite different set of dominant understandings. *Family households were not typically child-centred at the beginning of the 20th century. The adage that 'children should be seen and not heard' still held sway in many households. Distance and deference were more normal than cuddles and shows of affection between mother and child and even more so, between father and child. This was not regarded as a matter of neglect or perversity but a normal happy childhood. A good working-class mother ensured the physical well-being of her children by devoting all her energy to trying to keep a clean orderly house in which they were well fed and a good working-class father put in long hours in paid employment in order to bring home a wage packet. Neither had much time for personal leisure or playing with children. Upper-class and middle-class mothers who were neither driven by a constant burden of toil nor in paid work, nevertheless typically devoted their energies somewhere other than entertaining their children which was often left to servants. This was extreme in many upper-class households, as young children lived separately in a nursery with a nanny and might only be brought to the drawing room for an hour a day to see their parents and older children were often sent to boarding schools (see WOMEN: 3).

Dominant ideas of good motherhood did not yet require playing with and enjoying the child.

Christianity, conversion to

The demise of class deference and respect for traditional forms of authority, the demise of domestic service, the views of psychologists and medical experts on the psychological needs of children, greater affluence, smaller families, shorter working hours in paid employment, and a lighter burden of domestic work all contributed to a shift in attitudes to children in Britain. After the Second World War, both mothers and fathers seemed to want closer and more friend-like relationships with their children. Experts emphasized mothers' responsibilities for the psychological well-being of children and playing with and psychologically stimulating children became part of good mothering. Feminist authors have called for childcare to be an activity shared more equally between the sexes and at the beginning of the 21st century there are expert calls for more involved and emotionally engaged fathers.

Historically, childhood has often been a very different experience for boys and girls. Early 21st-century props of childhood are highly gendered—from Barbie dolls to computer games. Systematic differences in how adults respond to children by gender persist even in societies that pride themselves on gender equality. Class differences in the experience of childhood also persist. Even in wealthy nations, differences in life chances, including the chance of survival to adulthood, continue to differentiate poor from rich. For example, in Britain, childhood deaths from car accidents follow a clear and marked class gradient. Nevertheless, inequalities in childhood are less visible in wealthy nations like Britain in the early 21st century than they were a century before. However, differences remain stark between the wealthy and the poorer nations of the world. While the children of wealthy nations are increasingly imprisoned in family households by parents who fear the real risks posed by the car and less common but highly emotive risks of dangerous strangers, children in poor countries continue to work for family households, sometimes in unregulated and dangerous trades. And many countries contain many thousands of children surviving without family or childhood due to death and catastrophic disruptions in their life.   LJ

Christianity, conversion to. Names such as Ninian, St *Columba, and Kentigern may spring to mind when we think of Scotland's conversion, the names of bishops or monks, but these men were not church-founders. They first appear in places where churches had already been established, not by missionaries but by a gradual diffusion which is now invisible to the historical eye.

Officials of the northern Roman empire brought Christian ideas to southern Scotland (see NORTH-ERN ENGLAND AND SOUTHERN SCOTLAND: ROMAN OCCUPATION). Sailors and traders carried the Gospel along with their Mediterranean pottery. Local rulers perhaps sought to enhance their prestige by adopting the latest trend in European culture, which was now Christianity. Marriages, slave-trading, and conquests also provided pathways for the spread of Christian ideas.

With such a haphazard diffusion of faith, we must reject a picture of conversion in which large numbers of pagans suddenly opened their hearts to Jesus, rejecting their wicked pagan past. The process of conversion was one in which people began to adhere in some way to Christ and his church, and then gradually worked out how to re-express their culture in these terms. There was considerable stitching together of old ways and new faith, and much pre-Christian culture was woven into the new Christian framework. The old ways could be seen as a natural way of knowing the God who was now known by revelation (see Acts 17: 22–3f, and Romans 1: 19–2: 16).

The Britons

There was certainly a church among the Britons of southern Scotland by the 5th century. In *Whithorn a carved stone erected in the 5th century proclaims 'Te Dominum laudamus' and a stone of slightly later date in Kirkmadrine commemorates *sacerdotes* (probably bishops). The dedication of Whithorn's Candida Casa to St Martin of Tours may suggest a Gaulish influence. As Bishop Ninian probably arrived in Whithorn in the first half of the 6th century—the often-mentioned date of 397 is entirely spurious—he was obviously sent not to announce the Gospel to a pagan south-west, but to govern a church which already existed there.

Further east, in the territory south of the Forth, British burials suggesting sub-Roman Christianity appear in the 5th century. A poem composed there in the 6th century shows how well established Christianity was by then: Gododdin warriors confessed their sins and received communion before being slaughtered at Catraeth.

In the Strathclyde area, Kentigern is known as the first bishop, but even his Life does not claim that he brought the faith to that region. The wicked Coroticus was probably ruler at *Dumbarton when he was condemned by St Patrick in the 5th century, and he had already embraced Christianity long before Kentigern's time. Patrick protests that Christians in Coroticus' retinue were accepting gifts from him which had been obtained by oppression and murder.

The Picts

According to Bede, Ninian brought Christianity to the southern *Picts, but we may question the claim. By Bede's time Whithorn was under English control, and his claim that Ninian had evangelized the Picts can be read as a political ploy, a way of persuading the Pictish church that they owed allegiance to Ninian's successor—who happened to be an English bishop. In fact there is evidence of pre-Ninianic Christianity in Pictland. Patrick's letter condemning Coroticus also mentions 'apostate Picts', implying that some Picts were already Christian by the mid-5th century, even if he thought they behaved in unchristian ways.

In the 6th-century poem *Y Gododdin*, Pictish warriors join the Britons in the attack on Catraeth, and they appear to have shared their faith as well as their fate. The Northumbrian English left their mark on the early Pictish church too, sending a bishop who attempted to govern it from Abercorn for a few short years in the 7th century, and again in the early 8th century by guiding King *Nechtan's church reforms.

The Picts also received Christian culture from the Gaels of *Dál Riata. Conquests and intermarriage, as well as missionary endeavours by Gaelic-speaking clergy, were probably a factor from the 6th century onwards. A poem written c.600 on the death of Columba suggests that he had preached successfully to 'the fierce ones on the Tay', while St *Adomnán mentions his contacts with northern Picts—though, significantly, claiming little in the way of evangelical success. During the 7th century, however, *Iona established many churches among the Picts, and by 697 a bishop Curetán seems to have held office among northern Picts (see CULTURE: 2).

Gaels

In spite of legends that Columba brought the Gospel to Dál Riata, it is unlikely. Scottish Dál Riata was the eastern part of a political and cultural unity whose western part was in *Ireland. It is unlikely that these Gaels, sharing a single language and culture across a narrow stretch of sea, differed in religion. Columba brought his monks to an already-Christian Dál Riata and was presumably given the island of Iona by a Christian king. This is why St Adomnán, his biographer, describes him not as a missionary but as an ascetic monk. Of course Iona monks, together with monks of non-Columban monasteries, did much to consolidate the church's presence and trained clergy to provide pastoral care in Dál Riata and beyond. But the Christian faith had gone to Scotland before Columba. The names of the men and women who first spoke the Gospel on these shores remain unknown. (See also CHURCH INSTITUTIONS: 1; MONUMENTS: 1; RELIGIOUS LIFE: 1). GMa

church institutions: 1. early medieval; 2. medieval; 3. post-Reformation; 4. Presbyterian Church and factions, 1649–1690; 5. Presbyterian Church and denominations, post-1690; 6. Highlands.

1. early medieval

Past historiography concerning the church in early medieval Scotland has readily identified it as 'monastic' and 'Celtic': both these terms are now seen as problematic, as our understanding of the early medieval church has become more complex. Previous dichotomies drawn between monastic and episcopal tendencies now seem simplistic, in light of the dominance of the monastic ideal throughout the early medieval church in Europe, and the frequency with which we find bishops who were also monks and monastic founders—one may cite Martin of Tours and Pope Gregory 'the Great' in this regard. Increasingly, also, scholars have come to recognize the importance of pastoral care in the church, and its relevance both for structures of authority and for the ecclesiastical landscape at the local level. It is impossible now to generalize about the nature or structure of the early medieval church in Scotland, but we may point to some broad observable tendencies.

Our first encounter with Christianity in Scotland, on inscribed stones in the south and south-west, testifies to a church in which bishops, priests, and perhaps deacons played a role. Despite the tradition of a monastery of 5th-century date at *Whithorn, there is little archaeological evidence of such a development at the site before the 6th century, which is in keeping with developments further south in Britain, and in Ireland. The Northumbrian church, which included much of southern Scotland from the middle of the 7th century and for several centuries thereafter, was ruled by territorial bishops, one of whose sees was in the monastery of Whithorn, another in *Lindisfarne. That Lindisfarne's bishops came initially from *Iona suggests that, peculiar as the priestly authority of the abbots of Iona may have been, they recognized the need for bishops in those areas in which their clerics acted as missionaries. The role of bishops in the Gaelic church, and later the church of Alba, is nowhere clear. That they existed is demonstrable, but their jurisdiction is more problematic. Bishop Cellach, swearing a binding contract between church and king in 906 at Scone, appears to be acting in the role of a chief-bishop of Alba, and such a term is used to designate Tuathal mac Artguis, *primepscop Fortrenn* (chief-bishop of Fortriu) and abbot of Dunkeld, who died in 865: at this period Fortriu was frequently synonymous with the Pictish kingdom as a whole. By the 11th century it is clear that there was a chief-bishop in Alba, who seems to have been usually situated in *St Andrews. Whether the other bishops who appear in the 12th century are new creations, or represent continuity, is a matter of some controversy. It is, however, debatable that other areas of Scotland had bishops by this period: the Isles, Orkney (from c.1050), and Cumbria.

There were numerous important monasteries in early medieval Scotland: Iona, Lismore, Applecross, Kingarth in the west; Abernethy, Rosemarkie, St Andrews, Dunkeld in the east; in the south Whithorn, Hoddom, Melrose, Coldingham. Archaeology continues to reveal further important unnamed early centres, such as at Portmohomack (see TARBAT) and the Brough of *Birsay. The nature of the monasticism in these centres is still overshadowed by our relatively intimate knowledge of 7th-century Iona, but the development of hereditary abbacies, such as at Dunkeld, and the concept of abbatial property encapsulated in the term *apdaine* and found in place names such as Appin of Dull, suggest that the monastic ideal became mixed with economic and secular concerns here, as it did elsewhere. At some point in the 9th or 10th century the reformed ideals of the *céli Dé* were introduced into Scotland, and by the 12th century these monks could be found both as subunits within larger monasteries, as at St Andrews or Abernethy, and in their own, presumably more recent, foundations, as at Loch Leven or Monymusk. However, the hereditary nature of the positions of the *céli Dé* in at least St Andrews suggests that here too, monastic ideals had not always been preserved, and the 12th century began the process of monastic reform once again.

It has been recognized that the many small churches which must have been in existence by around 800 at least are testimony, not to the dominance of monasticism, but to a precocious network of local provision of pastoral care. That such churches may often have been staffed from, and had close relationships with, the larger monasteries should not lead us to think of these small churches as necessarily monastic. We should also leave open the strong possibility of 'private' chapels, endowed by local nobility and perhaps staffed largely by clerics from important local kindreds. Research on areas such as Strathspey and Perthshire has suggested that the roots of the 12th-century parish lie in the early Middle Ages, and that if anything there were more churches and chapels in the earlier period. In the east, these observations make much sense of the clearly close relationship between the secular *nobility and the church to which the Pictish 'Class II' sculpture, with scenes of aristocratic pursuits such as hunting on one side of the stone and the Christian image of the cross on the other, and 'Class III' stones, which have more unambiguously Christian scenes, bear witness.

It is one further aspect of secular involvement with the church which gives a striking tone to Scottish developments: the role of kings as patrons and decision-makers. One may contrast in this regard the dominance of the clergy in the Gaelic church, as represented by St *Columba's ordination of *Aedán mac Gabráin as king of *Dál Riata, as against the role of the Northumbrian kings, in establishing bishoprics and deciding ecclesiastical policy at synods like that at Whitby in 664. This more pro-active royal role may be found in Pictland as well, in the decision of *Nechtan, son of Derile, king c.710–29, to change his churches' practice as regards Easter and the tonsure. The Gaelic takeover of Pictland did not change this involvement, and *Kenneth mac Alpín's installation of St Columba's relics in Dunkeld, and the contract of Bishop Cellach and *Constantine II at Scone in 906 seems to indicate some sort of kingly prerogative in the church. This royal involvement in the church laid the groundwork for the ecclesiastical reforms of the 12th century, led, as they were, by the sons of Malcolm III 'Canmore' (Mael Coluim mac Donnchada) and St *Margaret.   TC

2. medieval

The organization of the medieval church in Scotland came out of the codifying and structural changes of the 12th century. The supremacy of the rule was demonstrated by the rapid success of reforming orders such as the Cluniacs, founded in Paisley and Renfrew, and the Cistercians, who founded six out the final total of eleven houses in the 12th century. Similar to the reforms of Cîteaux were those at Tiron and five houses of the Tironensians were founded in the south and east of Scotland in the same century. The international, universal nature of the church was emphasized within Scotland by the arrival of these orders and King *David I, accredited with much of the impetus for reform, undoubtedly had an international perspective concerning his national church.

The dioceses were already set out by this period and the sees, from the reign of David I, became increasingly subject to royal appointment. The bishops used their diocesan revenues to establish and build stone *churches and entrench their position. These reforms were mainly carried out by monastic bishops, and the rule of the enclosed order became the administrative force of the secular church as the bishops pushed forward reform.

The changes reform brought were not always welcomed. In 1144, at St Andrews, a chapter of Augustinian canons was established in order to supersede the resident culdees. The plan for peaceful transition failed and at the end of the century the two orders cohabited uncomfortably side by side on the one site. Another injured party by the end of the century was the archbishop of York. The struggle for primacy over the Scottish church was a complex four-sided war of words between York, Canterbury, St Andrews, and the papacy. It was, paradoxically, the bullish policies of Henry II towards the papacy which lost the English archbishops their claims and yet St Andrews failed to achieve primacy either. In 1176 the pope forbade the Scottish church to obey York and in 1192 this position was confirmed by the bull 'Cum universi' which opened a direct relationship between the papacy and the Scottish church, giving the clerical estate the metaphorical role of 'special daughter' (see ANGLO-SCOTTISH RELATIONS: 2).

The coming of the friars gave an explosive start to the 13th century as Franciscan and Dominican institutions began to spring up in Scotland's towns. Equally the new status of the Scottish church brought about Britain's first Dominican bishop, Clement of Dunblane, who was nominated by three bishops with papal commission while the king and earl of Strathearn argued about patronage. Only *Whithorn remained outside royal control in the south, keeping allegiance to York in defiance of 1192. In the north-west, Sodor and the Isles were under the jurisdiction of Trondheim in Norway, following the political territorial boundaries (see SCANDINAVIA: 1).

If the 12th century was the age of the monastery the 13th was the age of the cathedral, not only in the great architectural improvements which gave the buildings new splendour but also in the development of chapters. By 1165, four dioceses had archdeacons to assist the bishop. By 1300, all the Scottish sees had hierarchical chapters which claimed the right to elect their bishop. This did not, of course, end royal involvement in appointments but it did mean that the diocese had become a significant power base in the church. The bishops were further strengthened in 1225 when Pope Honorius III allowed provincial chapters to be held in Scotland under his direct authority. This was following the decree of the fourth Lateran Council of 1215, at which four Scottish bishops attended, commanding annual provincial councils. Of course, the reality was certainly not annual meetings but the importance of being recognized as an independent province was not lost on the Scottish churchmen.

Added to this was the impact of the *Crusades, first preached in the late 12th century but to become the obsession of the monarchs of the 13th. The international co-operation of the Crusades was encouraged by the preaching of the friars and the zeal of kings to outshine their rivals. Money was required and taxes were raised upon the church's income. In Scotland there was predictably

resistance to these taxes but by the 1270s there was eventual capitulation. More grievance was caused, however, on the death of Alexander III and with the addition of Scotland's crusading taxes to Edward I's war chest.

Throughout the troubled years of the Wars of *Independence the ecclesiastical position of Scotland's clerics cannot be easily summarized. It is fair to say that the majority maintained the most patriotic line possible in each given situation. A majority of the prelates backed John *Balliol in refusing to do homage to Edward I in 1296 and yet by 1306 a majority was behind Bruce's claim to kingship, despite his excommunication from Rome. In the period 1319–28, there was an interdict on worship in Scotland and particularly on the Eucharist, yet this was broken by clergy loyal to *Robert I. The national church was asserting its independence yet, as soon as it could be sought, approval from the international church was desirable (see NATIONAL IDENTITY: 2).

The universal church was not without its challenges. In 1378, in the Great Schism, Scotland followed her ally France (see FRANCO-SCOTTISH RELATIONS: 1) in giving allegiance to Avignon. Not to lose the benefits which such easy access to the papacy had brought, the Scots remained loyal to the antipope Benedict XIII to the last, and did not participate in the Council of Constance. When, of necessity, governor Albany finally accepted Martin V in 1418 the Scottish conciliarists had their first significant victory. The Council of Basle saw far more Scottish representation, most notably in the person of Thomas Livingston, abbot of Dundrennan. The election of the antipope in 1439 began the Second Schism which lasted until 1449. Again Scotland sided with the antipope and the confusion which subsequently arose over benefices given to different claimants in different papal courts took many years to resolve.

The great religious foundations of the 15th century were the *universities, all founded by bishops and placed in the centre of their sees: St Andrews (1413), Glasgow (1451), and Aberdeen (1495). Before this the Scots had travelled abroad for further education, before the conflict with England to Oxford and Cambridge, and then mainly to Paris, but also to Orléans, Avignon, Louvain, and Cologne. Foreign study was expensive but it did not stop with the foundations in Scotland, rather further degrees were sought abroad, building on the Scottish Master of Arts (see NORTHERN EUROPE: MONKS AND SCHOLARS).

The long rule of the Stewart dynasty (see KINGSHIP: 5) led to a cohesion between church and state in Scottish society which did not need to be forced and the history of co-operation with the papacy also had its dividends. In the reign of James III, Sodor and the Isles came under Scottish episcopal oversight and several religious orders founded Scottish provinces: the geographical unit which is now modern Scotland was being formed. Of course, the system could break down, as was seen in the personality clash between Patrick Graham and James III which led to the foundation of the archbishopric of St Andrews in troubled circumstances in 1472. Under the more stable hand of William Scheves, the primacy came again into harmony with royal wishes and remained so until the archbishopric of Glasgow was erected in the 1490s.

By the beginning of the 16th century the Scottish church was confident, buoyant, and secure in its own tradition. The placing of 70 Scottish saints in Elphinstone's *Aberdeen Breviary* was not an act of insularity, for they were given their place in the communion of European saints, but an expression of the confidence of Scottish identity (see RELIGIOUS LIFE: 2). Thus the church in the era of the Renaissance was at once Scottish and universal.   JF

3. post-Reformation
The Scottish *Reformation saw the disappearance of a range of ecclesiastical institutions and their replacement with a new system, based on a graded series of courts. At the bottom were kirk sessions: parochial courts corresponding to the consistory of Calvin's Geneva. They were the first reformed institutions to appear, one being established in *St Andrews and another in *Dundee in 1559. From 1560, sessions spread across Scotland and, by 1600, most Lowland parishes, and many in the Highlands (see RELIGIOUS LIFE: 8), had one, consisting of the minister, elders, and deacons. The minister moderated the weekly meetings, which were largely taken up with the moral life of parishioners. The elders participated in this work and in the overseeing of education (see SCHOOLS AND SCHOOLING: 1). The deacons, along with the rest of the session, were responsible for poor relief (see LIVING STANDARDS: 4). Elders and deacons were initially elected annually but, by the 17th century, the posts were generally held for life, with congregational consent rather than election required for new office-bearers chosen by the session.

Presbyteries, in many ways the essential courts of the Church, were relative latecomers, emerging largely by accident. *The Second Book of Discipline* (1578) recommended the replacement of kirk sessions with a court for three or four parishes. Instead, sessions persisted and the 'exercise', a regular meeting of ministers from ten to twenty parishes for discussion of doctrine, became the presbytery. The first thirteen were established in 1581 and they

gained legislative recognition in 1592. Numbers rose to over 50 by 1606 and over 60 by 1637. Meetings were weekly in some places, fortnightly in others, and sometimes monthly in winter. They consisted of ministers and elders but, between 1586 and 1637, only the clergy attended, with elders returning thereafter. Presbyteries heard appeals from kirk sessions, delegated commissioners to general assemblies, examined candidates for the ministry, visited parishes, and approved schoolmasters. While episcopacy prevailed (c.1606–38 and 1660–89), some of these powers were shared with bishops.

In the 1560s, synods began to meet as the courts of superintendents and commissioners, the Church's regional overseers. Some covered medieval dioceses (see CHURCH INSTITUTIONS: 2), such as *Galloway, but most disregarded the old diocesan structure. With the emergence of presbyteries, many of which crossed diocesan boundaries, this break with the past was re-emphasized, although the reassertion of episcopacy after c.1606 meant the loss of this tidiness for a time. Although they originally consisted of ministers, elders, and deacons, only ministers attended from the later 1580s until the 1640s, when the laity returned. Synods met twice a year and heard appeals and oversaw and co-ordinated the work of the presbyteries within their bounds.

The General Assembly, the national court of the Church, came into being in 1560. In the 1560s, it was an assembly 'of this haill realme'. As well as ministers, a significant proportion of attenders were nobles, lairds, and burgesses. By the 1580s, with the Reformation more firmly established, the politically powerful were less inclined to attend and assemblies became more purely ecclesiastical, in line with recommendations of the *Second Book of Discipline*. Presbyteries became the principal agents of delegation and lairds and burgesses attended in an ecclesiastical capacity, as elders. The nobility returned from 1606 onwards, as *James VI drafted in votes for his ecclesiastical policies, and they continued to attend after 1638 when, once more, the Assembly became highly politicized during the Covenanting revolution.

General assemblies initially met at least once a year. Before 1603, in only three years was there no assembly but only six more met before 1638 (in 1606, 1608, 1610, 1616, 1617, and 1618). The Covenanting revolution (see COVENANT, WARS OF THE) saw the return of annual assemblies. Cromwell prevented them from meeting after 1653 and they were not restored until 1690, ecclesiastical government under Charles II and James VII being conducted by the bishops under the crown. General assemblies were the church's executive and legislature, deciding how it should be governed, appointing committees and individuals for particular tasks, and overseeing the work of the lower courts of the church. They also advised and admonished the state regarding the conduct of government and petitioned *parliament and the privy council on particular issues, although under episcopacy this critical tendency was greatly curtailed.

Courts of High Commission were established by James VI in 1610. At first there was one under each archbishop (St Andrews and Glasgow) but, in 1615, they were united. The court consisted of the archbishops and bishops, along with some ministers and laymen. It had supreme jurisdiction over all ecclesiastical cases, dealing with Catholic and Protestant nonconformity, disobedient clergy, and cases of moral discipline passed up from the lower courts of the church. It was abolished, along with episcopacy, in 1638 (see RELIGIOUS LIFE: 3).   ARM

4. Presbyterian Church and factions, 1649–1690

After the collapse of the Royalist cause, the radicals in the Church and their allies seized power. In January 1649, a sympathetic parliament passed the Act of Classes which in effect barred most Royalists from office. By removing political opponents in this way, the Act opened the way for the implementation of a radical church agenda: patronage was abolished, power over poor relief was handed to kirk sessions (see CHURCH INSTITUTIONS: 3), and nobles could be and were forced to do penance before church courts.

When Charles I was executed on 30 January 1649 and the monarchy abolished, there was outrage in Scotland, followed by immediate proclamation of the new king. On 23 July 1650 after prolonged negotiations, Charles II, perhaps the greatest enemy of the Covenants (see COVENANT, WARS OF THE), was brought home as the sworn head of the Covenanted state. Cromwell invaded Scotland in reply. The catastrophic defeat of the Scots army at Dunbar on 9 September 1650 turned crisis into disaster. The Committee of Estates now turned to the 1650 Commission of the General Assembly with a set of public resolutions: asking whether the Act of Classes could be repealed, so that they could recruit widely against Cromwell. The Commission agreed, splitting the church. They were opposed by a party later to be known as the Protesters who prescribed very different remedies. They adhered to the Act, believing that Scotland's problems were caused by too much association with the ungodly and not too little. To avert disaster, they demanded both personal repentance from the king and national repentance from everyone else. They had increasing—and correct—misgivings about Charles's commitment to the Covenants.

The Commission and its allies, known as the Resolutioners, soon found that their practical inclusive policy was not enough to stop Cromwell. Under the ensuing English occupation the schism continued, with both parties holding rival church courts and sending rival delegations to seek recognition and favours from Cromwell. Attempts to end the division failed and the *Restoration of Charles II found the Church of Scotland still split. Still smarting from the humiliations forced upon him in 1650, Charles's new government embarked on a purge: executing leading Protesters and exiling others abroad. In the face of restored Episcopacy, and the ejections which followed, however, the old divisions were rapidly forgotten.

The solidarity amongst the outed Presbyterian clergy was dented by the introduction of Indulgences in 1669, 1672, and 1679 which allowed ministers to hold regular charges conditionally, rather than having to lead perilous lives as illegal conventiclers. Not all ministers accepted Indulgences but co-operation of indulged and non-indulged Presbyterians was the rule and not the exception. The revocation of the fulsome 1679 Indulgence drove this well-organized dissenting church underground. One small faction supported by the exiles in the Netherlands refused to co-operate with this mainstream of dissent. This group, sometimes known as the Cameronians (later the United Societies), was famed for its armed conventicles and uncompromising commitment to the Covenants. Having declared war on the state, they became the target of intense government violence in 1685—a period known as the 'Killing Times', but they remained a very small schism within a schism (see COVENANTERS).

The granting of freedom of worship to other Presbyterians in 1687 saw the re-emergence of the mainstream dissenters. This majority group formed the basis of the re-established Church of Scotland at the Revolution of 1688–9. The re-established Presbyterian Church jettisoned the Covenants, choosing instead to base itself on the Westminster standards of 1647. In consequence, the United Societies stayed out, later forming their own denomination: the Reformed Presbyterian Church.   LY

5. Presbyterian Church and denominations, post-1690

After the Covenanting struggles of the 17th century, Presbyterianism was established by parliament as part of the Revolution Settlement of 1690, and the Westminster Confession of Faith was recognized as the public and avowed confession of the church. The *Union of 1707 with England also secured the Presbyterian worship, government, and discipline of the church. The more extreme *Covenanters, the followers of Richard Cameron, stayed out of the Church of Scotland and in 1743 formed the Reformed Presbyterian Church, the majority of whom would later join the Free Church in 1876.

The reintroduction of patronage in 1712, which had been abolished in 1690, restored the right of the lay patron to nominate the local parish minister. The Patronage Act was seen as a clear breach of the Treaty of Union and the General Assembly called annually for its repeal until 1784. Dissatisfaction with the operation of patronage, and the call for the popular election of ministers, led Ebenezer Erskine and three other Evangelical ministers to form the Associate Presbytery in 1733. Division took place in 1747, however, over the taking of the Burgess Oath which had been imposed following the *Jacobite rebellion of 1745, and the church split into the Associate (Burgher) Synod and the General Associate (Anti-Burgher) Synod. The Burghers in 1799, and the Anti-Burghers in 1806, each divided into 'New Licht' and 'Auld Licht' bodies over the role of the civil magistrate in religion. The two New Light bodies rejected anything in the Westminster Confession which taught persecuting and intolerant principles in religion and came together to form the United Secession Church in 1820.

Another denomination which had come to adopt voluntary views of church–state relations was the Relief Church, formed in 1761 following the deposition of Thomas Gillespie for his opposition to patronage. The Relief Church was noted for its emphasis on evangelism and its policy of admitting members of other churches to the Lord's Supper. This more liberal outlook was continued in the United Presbyterian Church, formed by the union of the United Secession and Relief churches in 1847. The Auld Licht Burghers returned to the Church of Scotland in 1839. The majority of the Auld Licht Anti-Burghers joined the Free Church in 1852, while a minority continued as the Original Secession Church until 1956.

In the Established Church the ascendancy of the Moderates (see RELIGIOUS LIFE: 5) led to an increasing acceptance of patronage. When the Evangelicals (see RELIGIOUS LIFE: 6), led by Thomas *Chalmers, gained a majority in the Assembly in 1834 they sought to modify its operation by passing the Veto Act, whereby the patron's choice of minister could be rejected by the congregation. In addition, the Chapels Act gave full ecclesiastical status to church extension congregations. Both Acts were challenged in the civil courts and declared to be illegal. For the Evangelicals the issue became one of spiritual independence, the ability of the church to carry out its work free from interference by the state, and this was affirmed in the Claim of Right of 1842. The government was approached but, when attempts at compromise failed, about a third of the ministers left the Church of Scotland at the *Disruption in 1843 to form the Free Church of Scotland.

The Free Church at first held to the establishment principle and sought to set up a parallel organization to that of the Established Church throughout the country. The majority in the Assembly, however, came to adopt Voluntaryism and, along with the United Presbyterian Church, sought the disestablishment of the church. The Free Church also followed the United Presbyterian Church in passing a Declaratory Act which modified the church's adherence to the Westminster Confession. Discussions on union, which had previously been unsuccessful, were resumed and the United Free Church of Scotland was formed in 1900 with half a million members. A largely Highland minority continued as the Free Church (the 'Wee Frees') (see CHURCH INSTITUTIONS: 6). They saw themselves as the true successors of the Disruption (see RELIGIOUS LIFE: 8), since the majority had departed from both the establishment principle and a strict adherence to the Confession of Faith, and they claimed the entire property and assets of the former Free Church. Their case was upheld by the House of Lords in 1904 and an Act of Parliament was required before the property could be distributed equitably between the two churches. The Free Presbyterian Church had previously been formed in 1893 by a smaller Highland group opposed to any relaxation in the doctrinal stance of the Free Church. The Free Presbyterian Church has more recently experienced division when the Associated Presbyterian Churches, favouring a more open outlook, came into being in 1989 following the case of Lord MacKay of Clashfern who had attended a Roman Catholic funeral service.

The decision of the House of Lords in the Free Church Case led the United Free Church to restate its position in an 'Act anent Spiritual Independence' in 1906. Reunion with the Church of Scotland, whose jurisdiction was recognized by the state, now seemed an attractive possibility. Patronage had been abolished in 1874 and the Church of Scotland no longer insisted on establishment as a prerequisite for discussions. Union took place in 1929 following the passing of two parliamentary measures. The Church of Scotland Act of 1921 recognized the Articles Declaratory of the Constitution of the Church of Scotland in Matters Spiritual. According to the Articles, the church is free to determine all matters of doctrine, worship, government, and discipline, and it has a national role as a Christian church. The church would no longer be 'established', but neither was it 'disestablished'; it was said to be both national and free. An Act in 1925 made over the property and endowments of the church to its exclusive use. After 1929 a minority committed to voluntary principles remained in being as the United Free Church. The Church of Scotland became the largest Presbyterian church, its membership reaching a peak in 1956 but declining since then to just over three-quarters of a million members in 1997.   DMM

6. Highlands

Though Highland religion is often regarded as an indigenous growth, the Scottish Highlands and Islands (here restricted to the Hebrides) have imported their main expressions of the Christian faith. From at least the time of St *Columba, who came to *Iona from *Ireland in c.563, the region has hosted all the principal Christian alignments of Ireland and Britain. Throughout the Middle Ages, the Highlands and Islands were Roman Catholic, though later Protestants have detected enduring traces of pagan cults. After the *Reformation, the stage was set for the creation of a potent Presbyterian presence (see RELIGIOUS LIFE: 8) in the region, and for the displacement of Roman Catholicism. This was achieved gradually by political, pedagogic, and discriminatory methods. After 1690, the established Church of Scotland became the dominant force in the heart of the Highlands, while Roman Catholicism (see ROMAN CATHOLIC COMMUNITY) was gradually confined to the eastern and western edges of the Highland mainland. Catholicism was also preserved in some of the Hebrides, chiefly Barra and South Uist, and the Small Isles (Rum, Eigg, Muck, and Canna). Episcopacy, which was once strong in the region in the 17th century, was also displaced, but it survived in Perthshire, Inverness-shire, and mainland Argyllshire (see EPISCOPALIAN COMMUNITY). This remains the broad picture.

In certain parts of the mainland (notably the eastern and southern edges of the Highlands, where the *Gaelic language was weakening) and in the Inner Hebrides, small, dissenting Protestant bodies (see PROTESTANT SECTS AND DISESTABLISHMENT), mainly Independents (also commonly known as Congregationalists) and Baptists, appeared from the end of the 18th century. Their emergence reflected dissatisfaction with the preaching and pastoral provision of the established church, and they carried much influence in their own localities during the 19th century. Most had, however, disappeared by 1900, particularly from the mainland, but Baptist churches dating from a vigorous wave of itinerant evangelism in the early 19th century are still to be found in the Inner Hebridean islands of Tiree, Islay, Mull, and Colonsay. This evidence

alone would suggest that the sea-girt communities of the Highlands and Islands are apparently better able than the mainland to preserve the more conservative forms of evangelical expression.

Congregational and Baptist churches are each independent, and form autonomous units, usually linked together in local and/or national groupings or associations, such as the Baptist Union of Scotland. Theological or other difficulties are thus contained within the individual congregations to which they are relevant, and seldom cause strife of national significance. The Presbyterian churches exert local power through their presbyteries, operating within their own districts, but they are more closely regulated by a hierarchy of church courts. Yet, while answerable ultimately to the synods and general assemblies of the churches, the presbyteries have considerable power at ground level, so to speak. This is certainly true of the presbyteries of the Free Church of Scotland and the Free Presbyterian Church. The Highland presbyteries are known for their distinctiveness, and the wider Scottish denominations are often reminded forcefully of the existence, and distinctive perspectives, of their Highland parishes. When theological or other controversies arise, there is a marked tendency for the Highland wings of the Presbyterian churches to be on the conservative side, and to be very vocal in making their views known. Perhaps it would be nearer the mark to say that the island churches are on the conservative side, while the mainland churches tend to become less and less conservative as one moves south. Recent tensions within the Free Church indicate that there are certain aspects of modern church life which some of its members and ministers do not wish to countenance. On these matters, there is often something of a north–south divide.

As the presence of dissenting bodies indicates, the larger Highland churches have not been spared from dissension and secession, and in this they reflect wider patterns. The first serious secession from the Church of Scotland came in 1733 with the creation of the First Secession Church by Ralph and Ebenezer Erskine, but this had relatively little impact in the Highlands, as did the founding in 1761 of the Relief Church, which established only a couple of congregations in the Highlands. The *Disruption of 1843, when the Free Church of Scotland was formed, was the first of the schisms within the established church to affect the Highlands seriously. The Free Church, which rejected patronage and parted company with the Church of Scotland on this issue, attracted massive Highland support. The Evangelical principles of the Free Church, rooted in purity of worship and doctrine and regulated by the Westminster Confession of Faith (1647), were attractive to the Highland area which had already been strongly influenced by Evangelicalism (see RELIGIOUS LIFE: 6) from the beginning of the 19th century.

The concept of a pure church, braced by subordinate standards, appealed strongly to contemporary Highlanders. Why this should have been so is not clear; it may be that a church with a strong sense of purpose and a very firm adherence to biblical authority provided stability in the midst of the far-reaching changes which were occurring in Highland society—through improvement (see ECONOMY OF THE HIGHLANDS AND ISLANDS: 3), *clearance, and *emigration—in the preceding 70 years. Loyalty to purity of worship and doctrine became an identifying mark of Highland Presbyterians, but it also became a fruitful source of secession.

The peace of the Free Church was disturbed twice by the beginning of the 20th century, first by a secession and then (paradoxically) by a union. In 1893, the Free Presbyterian Church of Scotland was created by a couple of ministers in Highland charges who disagreed with the Free Church's position on the Westminster Confession of Faith. Through the passing of its Declaratory Act (1892), the Free Church was seen as being disloyal to the Confession, and undermining its authority. In 1900, a substantial proportion of the ministers of the Free Church—those who were broadly in support of the Declaratory Act—left it to join with the United Presbyterians to form the United Free Church of Scotland. A remnant of the original Free Church continued as the Free Church (Continuing), and repealed the Declaratory Act, thus asserting its loyalty to the Westminster Confession. This body, which became the 20th-century Free Church of Scotland, is sometimes known as 'the Wee Frees'.

The complexity of church life in the Highlands and Islands is well illustrated by the denominational profile of the island of Lewis. While sometimes dubbed 'the last stronghold of the Gospel', it has never been a haven of ecclesiastical uniformity. The island has accommodated all, and nurtured several, of the foundations, fragments, and fissures of Scottish Presbyterianism throughout the centuries: the Church of Scotland, the Free Church of Scotland, the Free Presbyterian Church of Scotland, the United Free Church, 'relief' congregations of the Free Church, and most recently the Free Church (Continuing). Stornoway, the main port and 'capital' of Lewis, accommodates all these bodies, as well as Roman Catholic and Episcopal congregations, in addition to the recently arrived Church of Jesus Christ of the Latter Day Saints (Mormons).

In Lewis, as elsewhere in the Highlands, the various disputes which created the post-1890 Presbyterian bodies generated considerable heat when they occurred. For most of the 20th century, however, a 'cold peace' has been maintained between the various groups, while natural decay has simplified the ecclesiastical landscape, thus removing some earlier sources and symbols of strife. The United Free Church has gradually disappeared from the Highlands, partly as a result of reunion with the Church of Scotland in 1929. The other bodies remain, with some variation in their distribution. The Church of Scotland is found throughout the region; the Free Church has a following in most areas, notably in Lewis, but it is weakest in the Inner Hebrides and Argyll, where Congregationalists and Baptists had won a significant part of the Evangelical constituency before 1843. The Free Presbyterians are represented in Lewis, but are stronger in Skye, Harris, and North Uist.

The decline of the Presbyterian presence in the Highlands and Islands has been ongoing, in numerical terms, since the middle of the 19th century, but its strength as a single cohesive force has waned as well. Presbyterians have lost control of several domains of influence, particularly in the 20th century. Since 1872, education has been within the remit of the local authorities and national agencies. The loss of their educational responsibilities also seriously affected the churches' role as significant publishers of *Gaelic literature. Now, they publish Gaelic books only very occasionally. Similarly, the churches have lost influence in the area of social welfare. The usual pattern nowadays is for individual denominations to maintain eventide homes for older members but their role in social welfare is otherwise relatively slight. Here, as in education, responsibility has passed to secular authorities, with occasional clerical or ecclesiastical input.

Where the Presbyterian churches do retain their influence to a certain extent is in the field of moral guardianship. The churches are very active in inculcating moral values consistent with their understanding of the Bible. They also do their utmost to preserve sabbath observance and, in Lewis and Harris in particular, they offer strong opposition to the possibility of Sunday sailings by the ferries of Caledonian MacBrayne. Likewise, they will oppose the Sunday opening of hotels and public houses, and will go to the expense of hiring QCs to support their case. The granting and extension of licences for the sale of strong drink are often opposed by the churches. Issues of national significance are sometimes raised by the more conservative bodies, often in order to rebuke secularizing tendencies.

In this respect, the Presbyterian churches still see themselves as having a duty to keep society clean (see TEMPERANCE). The great Evangelical thrusts into the Highlands in the course of the 18th and 19th centuries cast the churches in the roles of purifiers of what was perceived to be an impure society. The fact that they adhered to the establishment principle gave them the authority to police wider society, and to place restraints on people who might not be churchgoers themselves. Nowadays, the churches might be described as the negative conscience of society, reacting against trends which they do not like, rather than taking positive action. Having lost their earlier roles as powerful institutions, they have not replaced them with structures which might help to reassert their principles sensitively in terms of contemporary society. No Highland church of any denomination has produced a blueprint for linguistic, social, or political development within the region.

In political matters, the churches have, on the whole, been less than enthusiastic participants. It is probably true to say that the Highland wings of the churches are fairly conservative in their public voice, though their ministers and members represent a varied cross-section of political opinion. It could still be claimed, nevertheless, that the churches encourage political quietism and loyalty to the establishment, including the British crown. Ministers of the various churches have served in recent years as councillors on local councils, as have priests. The first convener of the Western Isles Islands Council, the Revd Donald MacAulay, was a Church of Scotland minister. It is, however, clear that, for members of the more conservative Presbyterian bodies, public service of this kind is not without its hazards. The Free Presbyterian Church, for instance, has been uneasy with the actions of some of its ministers who have served on local councils, and at least one has been the subject of censure, for asking a Roman Catholic priest to pray at a council meeting. This censure was one of the factors which added to the tension which resulted in the creation of the Associated Presbyterian Churches in 1989. The difficulty is that involvement in secular affairs exposes ministers and members of the churches to contamination by the world.

The most recent disputes in the churches have had a very serious impact on the Highlands and Islands. In 1989, the Free Presbyterian Church of Scotland was rocked by a high-profile controversy triggered by the attendance of one of its most prominent members, Lord Mackay of Clashfern, the Lord Chancellor, at a Roman Catholic Requiem Mass. This fracas brought to a head tensions which had been simmering for several years within the church, and it resulted in another secession, whose members formed the Associated Presbyterian Churches (APC). These churches continue to exist in a very uneasy relationship with the Free

Presbyterians, the tension being caused mainly by claims and counter-claims to manses and church buildings. The strength of the APCs appears to be diminishing in the process. Liberty from the shackles of Free Presbyterian synodical jurisdiction was fundamental to the APC's position, but the quest for freedom has not stopped there, and the group has had great difficulty in establishing a lasting identity. Three of its most progressive and influential ministers had moved to the Church of Scotland by September 2000. A considerable number of members, who were crucial to the emergence of the APC, have also sought emancipation from traditional APC styles of worship and have moved to other churches, sometimes within Evangelical independency in a non-Gaelic context.

In the mid-1990s the Free Church of Scotland also entered a period of great tension caused partly by the clash between conservatives and modernizers. This struggle found its focus in another high-profile leader, Professor Donald MacLeod, a native of Lewis and currently principal of the Free Church College, who was cleared by an Edinburgh sheriff of alleged sexual assault in 1996. The argument of the defence, that MacLeod was the victim of a conspiracy within his own denomination, was upheld by the sheriff. This left a number of unanswered questions which are periodically contested by those out of sympathy with the verdict. As MacLeod is perceived by some within the Free Church as its chief modernizer and liberalizer, the more conservative elements have tended to rally round the anti-MacLeod banner. Opposing groups, Free Concern and the Free Church Defence Association, emerged within the church, though Free Concern had disbanded by 1997. Eventually, in January 2000, pending the disciplining of some 30 ministers, a dissenting minority group seceded and have named themselves 'the Free Church of Scotland (Continuing)'. This group is, in effect, a reconstituted version of the Free Church Defence Association. The APCs are found predominantly on the Scottish mainland, where they have some fifteen congregations, compared with three in the Outer Hebrides. The Free Church (Continuing) is well represented in Lewis, but its strongest and most cohesive body of support (as distinct from 'splits') appears to lie in Skye. Of the most recent secessions, it appears to be the one with the best prospects for long-term survival.

As the traditional Highland churches have fragmented in the later 20th century, other smaller bodies have continued to come into the region. To some degree, these bodies are repeating the patterns characteristic of Baptists and Congregationalists who penetrated the Highlands and Islands in the early 19th century, in the sense that they are 'plugging gaps' in pastoral provision, but it must be noted that, in the case of the Baptists at least, the impetus is not based on the old-style missionary endeavour that planted the first generation of churches before 1850 (see MISSIONS AT HOME). Over the past 25 years, the Highlands have received an incoming population, with Lowland and non-Highland cultural perspectives. Retirement, disenchantment with previous roles beyond the Highlands, job availability, and a range of personal factors, have brought several 'new' Baptists (and others) to the region. The Baptist church at Alness gained much initial support from families attracted to the area by the Invergordon smelter (see ECONOMY, SECONDARY SECTOR: 3). Newcomers to the Highland churches do not fit easily into the predominantly Presbyterian structures of their areas, and this has been a stimulus to missionary activity by nonconformists. In addition, most newcomers are unlikely to be sympathetic to the churches' position on contemporary life and culture (see HIGHLANDS AND ISLANDS: COMMUNITY LIFE); they generally find the older worship styles, with their conservative theological and cultural legacy, too staid and too obviously out of tune with patterns known in the areas which they have left.

During the last decade or so, new Evangelical groups, some of which are associated with wider Scottish and British networks of various kinds, have arrived in the mainland Highlands and the Inner Hebrides. Small independent churches and congregations associated with the Apostolic Fellowship are to be found in Portree (Skye), Kyle, and Glenelg, and in Stornoway, Tain, Nairn, and Newtonmore. A small Baptist venture, unrelated to earlier Baptist work in Skye, is under way in Bracadale, and is led by a couple who are formally connected with the Baptist Union of Great Britain (rather than the Baptist Union of Scotland). A new Baptist church in Dingwall gained affiliation with the Baptist Union of Scotland in September 2000.

It is unlikely that the new groups will recruit many older Gaelic-speakers, since the latter will be aware of significant cultural differences and may be uneasy in the close and informal environment which these groups encourage. Their main recruits are likely to be people, probably incomers in the first instance, who, like the leaders themselves, have been unable to find a place within existing Presbyterian structures. Nevertheless, the groups will aim to evangelize their localities, in the face of what they will probably regard as neglect by the Presbyterian churches and traditional or out-of-date religiosity. Their general perception of existing religious patterns will be of an old-fashioned, and largely lifeless, loyalty to outmoded practices. While some of these groups may be inclined to en-

courage the pentecostal gift of tongues, they are very unlikely to have any deep interest in the indigenous Gaelic tongue. Gaelic too will be regarded as a thing of the past, irrelevant to the faith.

Despite their earlier Gaelic affiliations, new Baptists have similar attitudes to the language. The older Baptist congregations of the Inner Hebrides had lost their Gaelic preaching capacity by 1965, and had to move to English-only ministries. Having done so, they found it extremely difficult to identify and maintain forms of ministry which are well suited to the multicultural profile of present-day Highland society. In Baptist churches which have been to some extent revitalized by an incoming group (as in Mull and more recently Tiree), the earlier membership, which may be residually Gaelic-speaking, has found it difficult to make adjustments to new worship styles derived from Spring Harvest and other mainstream British Evangelical jamborees. Guitars jangling in small island chapels, overhead projectors, and more obviously participatory forms of worship, sometimes led by young men and women in casual clothes who are determined to make the congregation learn a constantly changing set of choruses off the wall, do not appeal to the older membership. Contrasts with earlier, more deferential worship patterns are inevitably drawn, and renewal is often contrasted with the idealized revivals which these churches had experienced in an earlier day. This reaction is not, however, peculiar to older Baptist members, nor is it restricted to churches. The mounting of local, mildly charismatic celebrations, such as 'Skye Alive', in the Highland areas has been greeted with a range of views, from the welcome of younger people and incomers to the condemnation and dismissal of the more conservative Presbyterians.

DEM

churches: 1. to 1560; 2. 1560–1843; 3. 1843–1929.

1. to 1560

By the late Middle Ages the Scottish church (see CHURCH INSTITUTIONS: 2) was well equipped with buildings for its 1,100 or so parishes, 13 dioceses, 130 religious houses, and unknown numbers of chapels. Though many of them have been destroyed or survive only as fragments, enough remain to demonstrate that high-quality ecclesiastical architecture had been provided throughout the country.

Written and archaeological evidence suggest most of the earliest churches were of timber. Nevertheless, Bede's description in his *Ecclesiastical History* of St Ninian's church at *Whithorn may indicate a lime-rendered masonry structure there in the 5th century, and it has been suggested that the Irish-inspired stone beehive cells on Eileach an

Naoimh in the Garvellachs are linked with the 6th-century mission of St Brendan. Other pointers to early stone architecture include King *Nechtan's request of 710 to St Ceolfrith of Monkwearmouth for masons to demonstrate how to build in the Roman manner, and a finely carved arch may have been part of a 9th-century church at the Pictish royal centre of *Forteviot. By the 11th century, stone building was more readily achievable, and impressive survivors are round towers of Irish type at Abernethy and Brechin and the base of a square tower at Restenneth.

The revitalization of the European church in the late 11th and 12th centuries had a massive impact within Scotland. St *Margaret, wife of Malcolm III 'Canmore' (Mael Coluim mac Donnchada), introduced a first community of Benedictine monks at Dunfermline around 1070. But it was during the reigns of three of Margaret's sons that most was achieved, and especially under the leadership of *David I (1124–53). Bishops' dioceses were revived and augmented, the establishment of a nationwide network of parishes was encouraged, and large numbers of houses for monks, canons, and the military orders were founded. All this created a massive demand for buildings, and masons had to be imported to design them. David's personal links with England meant that most masons working for him were brought from there, establishing a pattern for a continuing fruitful exchange of architectural ideas between Lowland Scotland and England throughout the 12th and 13th centuries. Amongst the major surviving churches started during David's reign are the nave of Dunfermline abbey, for which a master mason was probably brought from Durham cathedral, and the choir of Jedburgh abbey, whose designer possibly came from Romsey abbey (in Hampshire). The unusual double-cross plan of Kelso was perhaps inspired by examples in eastern England such as Bury and Peterborough.

In the excavated remains of David's Melrose abbey, we see the beginnings of a close interest in the northern English buildings of the Cistercian order. Some of the architectural solutions which that order introduced from its original home in eastern France were to be an important factor for general architectural developments well into the 13th century. They are reflected in several details of the magnificent cathedral priory church started soon after 1160 at *St Andrews and the continuing impact of both St Andrews and northern England is evident in several churches of the later decades of the 12th century, of which Jedburgh abbey's nave, Dundrennan abbey's transepts, and Arbroath abbey church are the finest. It is in these buildings that the transition from Romanesque to Gothic architecture is seen.

In the 12th century it had generally been the monasteries which were at the forefront of church renewal. But during the 13th century many of the bishops set about rebuilding their cathedrals on a scale to reflect their growing authority. The results of cathedral building campaigns started in the earlier decades of the century are seen at Brechin, Dornoch, Dunblane, Dunkeld (choir), Elgin, Fortrose, Glasgow, and Whithorn (choir). Many of these were buildings of high architectural quality, though often not of great scale. The most ambitious campaign was at Glasgow, which was given an extended eastern limb for the choir of the cathedral clergy and the shrine of St Kentigern; this was elevated above a crypt of quite extraordinary spatial subtlety for Kentigern's tomb and a Lady chapel.

While the cathedrals were becoming more architecturally prominent, however, new parish churches were tending to be less ambitious. Several 12th-century churches had been carefully planned to reflect their division of functions, with a chancel at the east end for the priest (occasionally with a semicircular apse for the main altar) and a distinct nave for the layfolk (sometimes with a bell tower at its west end) (see RELIGIOUS LIFE: 2). The most complete example of this type is at Dalmeny. But from the 13th century increasing numbers of churches were of simple rectangular plan, with only a timber screen separating the two parts, as at Abdie. This greater simplicity was perhaps partly because many parishes were being impoverished by the diversion of their endowments to the religious houses and cathedrals, though it was probably also a matter of taste.

The outbreak of the long Wars of *Independence with England in the late 13th century greatly reduced the opportunities for church building over much of the following century. When a new momentum for building gathered strength in the last quarter of the century, patrons and masons increasingly chose to look elsewhere than England for inspiration. The main sources for new ideas were to be *France, which was Scotland's chief political ally against England, and the *Low Countries, with which close trading links were created. From an inscription at Melrose, we know that a Paris-born mason called John Morow was responsible for introducing elegant design details from France in the early 15th century into operations at Melrose and Paisley abbeys, at Glasgow and St Andrews cathedrals, and at Lincluden collegiate church. French masons were probably also behind the overall designs of St Salvator's college chapel at St Andrews and Trinity collegiate church in Edinburgh, among much else. The first documented cases of the employment of Netherlandish craftsmen come with the importation of church furnishings, such as the stalls ordered from Cornelius de Aeltre of Bruges for Melrose abbey. But in fact Netherlandish architecture must have been an inspiration in Scotland from as early as the rebuilding of the nave of Old Aberdeen's St Machar's cathedral in the late 14th century. Nevertheless, in seeking fresh architectural stimuli Scottish masons did not adopt imported ideas wholesale; rather, they modified them to meet Scottish tastes and needs, progressively developing an approach to design which also looked to well-established solutions.

While the monasteries and cathedrals remained important sponsors of architecture, and the urban mission of the friars may even have increased their popularity, the later Middle Ages saw yet another shift in patronage. At a period when religion was becoming an increasingly personal matter, it was more attractive for benefactors to patronize their local churches, where they themselves worshipped and made provision for prayers to be offered for their souls. Among the finest architectural products of the 15th and 16th centuries were the parish churches of some of the wealthier burghs. Several were rebuilt on a grand scale and to a more or less unified design, including those at *Aberdeen, Dundee, *Edinburgh, Haddington, Linlithgow, *Perth, *St Andrews, and *Stirling (see URBAN SOCIETY: 1–2). Of equal architectural quality, albeit of smaller scale, were a number of rural churches which were partly rebuilt when collegiate bodies of priests were founded within them by a local landowner. Among these are Biggar, Crichton, Dalkeith, Dunglass, Foulis Easter, Lincluden, Roslin, and Seton. It is perhaps in these latter churches, designed as the setting for a perpetual sequence of prayers for the salvation of their founders, that we come closest to the spirit of the late medieval church.   RF

2. 1560–1843

The *Reformation in Scotland was not a sudden cataclysmic event as so often described but a gradual process where many existing kirks were cleansed of their popery and adapted for the new faith. The First Book of Discipline of 1560 stated that reformed worship required 'a bell to convocate the people together, a pulpit, a basin for baptism and a table for the ministration of the Lord's Supper' (see RELIGIOUS LIFE: 3). This could easily be catered for in the simple rectangular kirks found throughout Scotland, which were not often elaborated with towers or chancels. Many apparently later churches still retain within their walls part of their medieval predecessors. The suitability of existing buildings meant that there was surprisingly little new church building in the late 16th and 17th centuries.

The structure of the reformed church, as outlined in The Second Book of Discipline of 1578, was crucial to understanding this new body. It was based on the parity of ministers and founded on a series of courts; the kirk session, the presbytery, the synod, and the General Assembly (see CHURCH INSTITUTIONS: 3). The church is the minister and his congregation, not the building they occupy. This is in stark contrast to the episcopal structure which relied on the authority of the bishops, archbishops, and ultimately the crown, where the church building was seen as a tangible expression of faith. The equality created within the Presbyterian Church has ironically contributed to its inordinate number of secessions. The Church of Scotland itself was not until 1690 firmly established along Presbyterian lines, as a reaction to the overt Catholicism of James VII.

The medieval rectangular churches were often extended by the addition of a wing or aisle often paid for by the local landowner to accommodate a family burial vault with a private family pew or loft above, often with retiring rooms (see DEATH AND BURIAL). One of the finest examples is East parish church at Cromarty, which is a T-plan church of medieval origins, retaining its two lairds' lofts and a paupers' loft all dating from the 18th century. Abercorn church is more complex with three separate families all maintaining separate burial vaults within the 12th-century church. The Hopes of Hopetoun rebuilt the chancel as a family loft and vault with palatial retiring room added by Sir William Bruce to the side outdoing the earlier aisle of the Dayells of the Binns. More often a single aisle was added, resulting in a T-plan building which gave the congregation the optimum opportunity to see and hear the minister.

During the 17th century a number of notable new churches were built including the magnificent St Columba's parish church in Burntisland completed in 1600. This was the first centrally planned church in the country ideal for reformed worship. The great hall church of Greyfriars, Edinburgh, completed in 1620, adapts a medieval form of building beloved of preaching friars to reformed worship. It was used for the signing of the *National Covenant in 1638 and later divided into two churches, only being reunited into one in 1938. The Canongate church of 1691 by James Smith, also in Edinburgh, adopted a cruciform plan which is interesting as James VII's parish church could easily be adapted for Catholic worship.

As the century progressed the classical style was regarded as the only polite style especially for city churches. The work of Archibald Simpson at St Giles, Elgin, of 1825–8 is one of the best examples of the Greek revival in Scotland. It is a worthy successor to the 18th-century churches. Fine examples of this include James Gibbs's remodelling of West St

Nicholas Aberdeen of 1741, St Andrews by the Green by Alan Dreghorn of 1739–56 in Glasgow, and William Burns's North Leith parish church of 1813–16. Architects broke away from the rigidity of rectangular plans, producing interesting spaces including the circular church of Kilarrow at Bowmore on Islay of 1767 and a number of octagonal churches including Kelso of 1771–3 and Gannochy at Dalmally of 1811.

Heritors Gothic was a peculiarly delicate form of Gothic which developed during this period using the style decoratively rather than archaeologically. The prettiness of the style found favour with numerous lairds who were often the principal heritor, as at East Saltoun parish church built in 1805. During the 19th century a more antiquarian approach was used, taking elements from English and European examples. James Playfair records looking at Westminster abbey to gain inspiration for his church at Farnell in Angus which was completed in 1806. As the century progressed, the Gothic became the dominant style for all denominations under such masters as Gillespie Graham at his Roman Catholic cathedrals in Edinburgh and Glasgow and William Burn at St John's Episcopal, Princes Street, Edinburgh.

The Episcopal Church (see EPISCOPALIAN COMMUNITY) received emancipation in 1790 but it was not until the Catholic Emancipation Act of 1829 that Roman Catholicism (see ROMAN CATHOLIC COMMUNITY) was accorded legality. Both these faiths followed the general move to the Gothic.

In the early 19th century the practice of taking Holy Communion seated around a designated table was abolished. Examples of these communion tables can be seen at Croik church in the Highlands and an ingenious demountable one at Durisdeer church, Dumfriesshire. These were an important element of reformed worship. They are still remembered in the white clothes laid over the pews on communion Sundays. The removal of these large tables meant that the congregation no longer had to move about the church (see RELIGIOUS LIFE: 8). Seating could be fixed and only an area around the pulpit left open. A good example of such an arrangement is found at Tibbermore church near Perth.

In 1823 the Act 'for building additional places of worship in the Highlands and Islands' was passed. This provided funds for the erection of churches and manses of standard designs under the direction of Thomas Telford at 40 different sites in the Highlands and Islands. Good surviving examples of these parliamentary churches are found on *Iona and in Acharacle, complete with adjacent manses. These simple rectangular or T-plan designs formed a useful source for the design of numerous churches erected during the following 50 years.

In 1828 the General Assembly of the Church of Scotland set up a committee 'To enquire into the adequacy of church accommodation'. This was due to the appalling condition of many churches and it promoted the erection of a number of new churches especially in urban areas. Dr Thomas *Chalmers was the chairman of this committee, becoming the moderator in 1832. SG

3. 1843–1929

In the space of 74 years the Church of Scotland ripped itself in two, created a massive church building boom, and then reunified with the Free Church, creating a tremendous problem with redundant churches. In parallel, a number of other smaller seceding congregations were amalgamating and splitting, all giving Scotland its amazing and dazzling array of 19th-century churches.

On 18 May 1843 at the General Assembly of the Church of Scotland what has become known as the *Disruption occurred. Thomas *Chalmers led 190 clergy out to form the Free Church. Eventually 474 ministers out of a total of 1,203 joined the new church. They believed that congregations should have the ability to choose their own ministers rather than it being the responsibility of the local laird or heritor. By 1845 they had built 500 new churches. After the Disruption the Free Church congregations had very little money and relatively modest buildings were erected. As the century progressed, however, more flamboyant buildings were built to establish the importance of the church. These most often were created in the towns where there were larger wealthier congregations. Two potent symbols of the new church were William Playfair's New College of 1845–50 on the Mound, Edinburgh, and Charles Wilson's Trinity College, Glasgow. Frederick Pilkington with his exuberant form of Gothic created a series of unique churches including the Barclay-Bruntsfield church of 1862–4 in Edinburgh and the Trinity church of 1863 in Irvine. He not only created fabulously modelled exteriors but also interestingly shaped interiors all focused on the pulpit and the word.

As the century progressed, all denominations favoured the Gothic style and this continued up until the Second World War. However, there are notable exceptions, particularly the architect Alexander 'Greek' Thomson and his work for the United Presbyterian Church. This seceding sect had become very wealthy and created some of the major monuments of 19th-century architecture in Scotland. These included three designed by Thomson, although only the St Vincent Street church of 1858–9 survives—a building recognized to be of truly international importance. His unique vision of the classical form created a magnificent fanfare and celebration of the United Presbyterian faith. The church was not, however, averse to the Gothic, commissioning William Leiper to build Dowanhill church, 1865–6, in a High French Gothic style without and a galleried preaching space within. Both Thomson and Leiper worked with the talented designer Daniel Cottier on the exuberant interior decoration. Other magnificent temples to faith include the Coats Memorial Baptist church by Hippolyte Blanc of 1894. This cathedral-scaled space is surmounted by that ultimate symbol of the Scottish kirk, a crown steeple.

The Oxford Movement of the 1830s in England had a surprisingly long-lasting effect on church design in Scotland. It promoted the use of the Gothic over all, epitomized in the work of A. W. N. Pugin. This High Anglican movement sought to re-establish medieval precedents of worship and architectural design. Two English architects, William Butterfield and George Bodley, working for the Episcopalian Church, produced the finest examples in Scotland of this doctrine at the cathedral of the Isles, Cumbrae, of 1849 and St Salvators, Dundee, of 1865–75. But the influence was widespread in the Church of Scotland. This was most clearly expressed in 1886 with the foundation of the Aberdeen, later Scottish, Ecclesiological Society by James Cooper. He sought to enhance, beautify, and sanctify Presbyterian worship moving the Communion table into an apse or chancel-like space often surrounded by elders' chairs. Rowand Anderson's Govan parish church of 1883–8 celebrates Presbyterian worship through the beauty of the building. This was a radical shift in approach since prior to this the minister and his congregation were perceived as the church, and the building as a mere shelter. Unfortunately for the architecture, this belief remains in certain circles. Towards the end of the century, many churches were reordered from a centralized plan focused on the pulpit to an alternative long axis in which a sort of chancel area was created with the pulpit, communion table, font, and elders' chairs. This often necessitated the removal of at least one gallery. Churches that resisted this move are the exception rather than the norm.

The other radical alteration to design of churches was in 1865 with the foundation of the Church Service Society which led a year later to the admittance of organs in Church of Scotland worship. The introduction of such large instruments often presented problems. The obvious location was on the, often blank, wall behind the pulpit. The building of an apse-like space resulted in a suitably Gothic external appearance but could appear more like a concert hall than a church.

Between 1845 and 1852 R. W. Billings published a series of detailed drawings of Scottish medieval ecclesiastical architecture. These prompted architects to look more closely at Scottish versions of the Gothic rather than looking to the Continent and by the turn of the century Scots Gothic was the accepted norm. Exponents such as John J. Burnet, Ninian Comper, Reginald Fairlie, and Peter MacGregor Chalmers produced a masterly collection of buildings as at St Molio's, Shiskine, Arran, of 1889, St Margaret's, Braemar, of 1899, Our Lady of the Assumption and St Meddan, Troon, of 1909, and at Linton parish church of 1912. The cataclysm of the First World War produced one of the last flowerings of this style, the Scottish National War Memorial at Edinburgh castle by Sir Robert Lorimer of 1924–7, but little other church building.

The 1925 Church of Scotland (Property and Endowment) Act transferred the parish church from the heritors to a new body: the General Trustees. The maintenance of the buildings became the responsibility of the congregation. With the later amalgamation of churches, the church with the least maintenance problems and the most car parking is usually the one chosen rather than the most historically or architecturally important.

In 1929 the Church of Scotland and the majority of the Free Church reunited giving the church new strength and purpose but creating a tremendous problem of what to with redundant churches. In the period following the Disruption, the church in its many forms created some of Scotland's most striking buildings and adorned our towns and cities with a wonderful array of towers and steeples.

SG

Cinead mac Ailpín. See KENNETH MAC ALPIN.

clan societies are comparatively modern institutions, unlike the way of life whose memory they seek to cherish. Gone are the days when most of the bearers of a clan surname were found in one region or district, united for mutual protection, and owing allegiance to their chief. Now, with the scattering of the clans, any 'clannit' person who still feels the bond of kinship (real or fancied), or looks to a chief as head of a worldwide family, is likely to find others similarly inclined in what the heralds see as a 'corporate clansman'.

The earliest clan societies were founded primarily for benevolent, charitable, and educational purposes. The Buchanan Society appeared in 1725, and four more had made a start by 1822, when the extravaganza of George IV's visit to Scotland added only one, the Clan Gregor Society. Glasgow's international exhibition of 1888 saw the Clan Mackay Society (1806) reconstituted, and in the next decade came the biggest increase ever, coinciding with awakened interest in *Gaelic and the problems of crofting areas. In a spate of periodicals and books focusing on the genealogical and social history of the clans, the Mackays led the way, Macleans sponsored a collection of clan music, and Lamonts printed papers on their clan tartan. Most clan society magazines instruct and inform their readers, as well as recording their own activities.

A cluster of new and revived societies around 1951 was mainly due to the Gathering of the Clans in Edinburgh, part of Scotland's share in the government-sponsored Festival of Britain. The Council of Clan Societies which promoted this event brought them together, even the most inward-looking. The idea of a 'tented field' where a score or so of clans pitched their marquees facing each other in a great square has spread, so that a round of *Highland games is now a regular feature of clan society life in the USA.

Some important clan relics have been preserved. The white banner of the Mackays has long been exhibited in Edinburgh; the Macphersons opened the first clan museum in Badenoch in 1952, and others have followed. Some clan chiefs still own part of their lands and welcome those who wish to hold gatherings, but it is difficult for others to establish a clan centre in the old territory. Castle Menzies near Aberfeidy was acquired by the Menzies Clan Society in 1957, and with government aid full restoration began in 1972; the Clan Donald have a centre at Armadale in Skye.

Feelings of kinship breed a healthy interest in genealogy, but for busy office-bearers, generally unpaid, this can be embarrassing. The 'roots' industry took off in the 1970s, and computers have hurried the pace. Some enquiries are of purely personal interest, but others may provide clues to the structure and history of a clan.

There were clans in the *Borders as well as the Highlands, but their descendants have been slower to join the clan society movement. The Clan Armstrong Trust, founded in 1978, believe in a culture beyond sheep stealing, burning, and feuds, and have set an example in making their own history known.

Advanced technology has made the world a smaller place, with easier and faster travel and communication. It is tempting to let clanship become absorbed in the tourist industry, and the remedy lies with those most in touch with current thought and understanding of the past.   RWM

clans of the Highlands and Islands: 1. to 1609; 2. 1610 onwards.

1. to 1609

The clan was the most obvious manifestation of the centrality of kinship to the organization and ethos of society in Gaelic Scotland. This was a key legacy inherited by the medieval Scottish kingdom (see KINGSHIP: 1) from its Gaelic prototype. The concept was adopted with alacrity both by the Norse on the western seaboard, giving rise to kindreds of ultimately Norse (see SCANDINAVIA: 1) origin such as the MacLeods, and by the 'new Scots' of Anglo-French origin in the 12th and 13th centuries, giving rise to kindreds such as the Chisholms. Its pervasiveness within Gaelic Scotland down to 1609 is demonstrated by the existence not only of territorial kindreds such as the *Campbells, but also of professional kindreds such as the MacMhuirichs, pursuing a particular discipline, such as poetry (see LITERATURE, GAELIC) on a hereditary basis.

An almost mystical aura surrounds the word 'clan', deriving from Gaelic *clann*, but in fact it takes its place within a chronological sequence of terms used to describe a kindred within the Gaelic world of Scotland and *Ireland down to the 17th century, each term enjoying an apparent shelf-life of 400 or 500 years. *Clann* was preceded in the sequence by *cenel*, and by the 16th century was being replaced by *cinneadh*. The primary meaning of *clann* is not 'kindred', but 'children', and the secondary technical meaning of 'kindred' which it developed between the 11th or 12th and the 16th centuries has been completely lost in modern Scottish *Gaelic. Although *clann* was the most common term meaning 'kindred' within this period, variants such as *siol* and *sliochd* were also in use.

Clann in the sense of kindred was one of three elements in the new naming system coming into being in Scotland from perhaps as early as the 11th century: the clan name consisting of *clann* followed by the forename of the eponym of the kindred (for example, Clann Domhnaill, 'the kindred of Donald'); the style, applied to the chief of the kindred (for example, MacDomhnaill, 'MacDonald'); and the surname, identical to and deriving from the style, and which was applied generally to all who claimed descent from the eponym. The common assertions that the surname was in origin a patronymic, and that fixed surnames were a relatively late innovation within Gaelic Scotland, are both false. Surnames began life at the very highest levels of society in Scotland, as a means of identifying members of a ruling lineage, and were in common use for this purpose by the 14th century. Through time, and as that lineage expanded, the surname was inexorably carried down to lower social levels.

Strictly defined, a clan was a biological phenomenon, a patrilineal descent group deriving from a common ancestor or eponym. The dynamo at its core was its ruling lineage or family, from which the eponym's successors as chiefs were normally drawn. As the ruling family grew, collateral lines were established, and the clan expanded. *Clann* might also be used in a wider and looser sense to embrace individuals and groups who were affiliated to the kindred, although not of the blood; these might include dependants and clients, such as small kin groups which were not viable in their own right, or lineages which performed specific functions on behalf of the kindred, such as castle-keepers.

In the right conditions, new clans could be spawned with remarkable speed. It would appear that within two generations of the lifetime of the eponym, his name could have given rise to a new clan name, style, and surname. Fundamental to the process were Gaelic Scotland's relaxed attitude to marital and sexual matters, which permitted rapid multiplication rates; and rapid territorial expansion by the 'parent' kindred, perhaps aided by the existence of a vacuum of power within the area concerned, or by a sudden or unforeseen event which affected the stability of its ruling lineage. The descendants of Somhairle or Somerled were known collectively for a time as Clann Shomhairle, but Somhairle's sudden death in 1164, coupled with the sheer extent of his territorial gains made on the western seaboard at the expense of the Norse, probably explain why Clann Shomhairle swiftly divided into three kindreds: Clann Dubhghaill (the Macdougalls), Clann Domhnaill (the MacDonalds), and Clann Ruairi (the MacRuairies). In this case, the nature of the birthing process meant that the original 'parent' kindred effectively ceased to be, but this did not always happen. The MacDonalds, *Campbells, Macleans, and MacGregors are examples of clans which underwent profound expansion in the later Middle Ages, resulting in the creation of numerous subdivisions. These 'mini-kindreds' possessed particular identities as evinced by their own 'clan' name, subchief's style, and subsidiary surname, while tensions and differences might well exist among them. Nevertheless, they remained unmistakably parts of the parent kindred, which retained a capacity for collective action. Continuity and stability within the ruling lineage may well have been the crucial factor here.

Clearly, at the hub of this society was an expansionist dynamic from which vital consequences flowed. As the ruling family of a clan grew over generations, earlier lineages within it which failed to achieve viability in their own right would tend to be replaced by newer lineages, and thus decline in social status. This phenomenon of 'expansion from the top downwards' was vitally important in spreading aristocratic values and practices, such as the use of the surname, across society. The physical expansion of a kindred would obviously have consequences for those in its path. A military solution

entailing the decimation of one party was possible, but it seems to have been more common for the lesser kindreds to have been either physically displaced (witness the MacKinnons shifting the centre of their operations to Skye in the face of Maclean expansion in Mull), or socially displaced, assuming a position subordinate to the more powerful kindred within the social hierarchy. Sometimes the chief of the resident kindred, or the resident landlord, would be forced to accept members of the expanding kindred as his tenants, his superiority in tenurial terms masking the fact that his status had been compromised.

Territorial encroachment by a more powerful neighbour was one circumstance which could create a relationship of clientship between kindreds. Other causes were possible, a common theme being the exploitation of a vulnerability or discontinuity within the ruling lineage of a kindred. Clientship would typically revolve around the rendering of exactions and services in return for protection, but could also be expressed through specific mechanisms. The key issue was the extent to which the overchief compromised the autonomy of the ruling family of the client kindred, for example by interfering in the election of the client kindred's new chief. In the most extreme cases, the ruling family of the client kindred might find itself bypassed and redundant.

Through territorial expansion achieved by means such as sheer kin power, the use of military clients, and the acquisition of feudal rights and jurisdictions, regional lordships could be created. The outstanding example was of course the lordship of the *Isles in the era when its headship was monopolized by the chiefs of the Clan Donald in the 14th and 15th centuries, but the same era saw the Campbells achieve a stranglehold over Argyll and Breadalbane, and the beginnings of the MacKenzie hegemony in the north which would ultimately embrace Ross and Lewis. The clearest evidence for the hierarchical arrangement of kindreds within such lordships, presumably corresponding to different degrees of clientship, is provided by the Council of the Isles, comprising the heads of numerous vassal kindreds, divided into several grades, which advised the lord of the Isles.

The phenomenon of kin expansion was a major reason for the extraordinary complexity of the interaction between landholding, loyalty, and jurisdiction existing in Gaelic Scotland by the later 16th century. The patterns which each of these three phenomena imposed upon the landscape (see GEOLOGY AND LANDSCAPE) were not congruent. Within this society, possession of land was not determined purely, or even primarily, by written legal right under Scots law (see LAW AND LAWYERS:

1), but by sheer kin power which could very rapidly thereafter acquire what to the kin-based society was the ultimate legitimacy of hereditary status. At its simplest, this could mean that a landlord was unable to command the loyalty of his tenants; but there was almost infinite scope for more convoluted permutations, both on the 'feudal' and 'kin-based' sides of the equation, and in the interaction of the two. Practical compromises could be worked out, such as the coexistence of both primogeniture and the kin-based system in determining the succession to the chiefship of kindreds such as the MacLeods of Dunvegan by the 16th century. But the lack of congruence in the patterns of landholding, loyalty, and jurisdiction posed particular problems for the increasingly centralist Scottish state under *James VI (1567–1625). James's quest to ensure the answerability of his Gaelic-speaking subjects found its fullest expression in the Statutes of Iona of 1609, which were revised and toughened in 1616. They aimed to pull the roof in on Gaelic society in the Isles by undermining the economic and social pillars upon which the authority of the ruling grades rested, and by refocusing southwards their lifestyles and loyalties.   MMacG

2. 1610 onwards

Within Scottish history clanship and kinship tend to be very closely identified, indeed, often seen as one and the same. Yet it is far more accurate to say that one, kinship, formed a component part of a wider social system, namely, clanship. That the word clan is derived from the Gaelic *clann* (children) underlines kinship's central place within clanship as a whole. Its importance cannot be better exemplified than by the way each clan was conceptualized as a *siol*; that is, as the seed, or direct blood descendants, of a powerful and prestigious founder whose historic exploits and status justified and confirmed the position of each clan group. Thus, for example, the MacLeods of Dunvegan were distinguished from the MacLeods of Lewis in that the former saw themselves as *siol Tormod* (the seed of Norman) and the latter as *siol Torquil* (the seed of Torquil). Yet the belief that every member of an entire clan was the direct kin of such a founder was not the exclusive or even predominant mechanism for expressing the organizing principle of kinship.

Of equal importance with this collective sense of kinship was the person of the chief and his immediate family. Thus it was that each chief's patronymic was that of the original clan founder: hence the head of the *Campbells of Argyll was known as *MacCailein Mor* (the son of big Colin). It is important to stress that, at the start of the 17th century at least, any potential incompatibility between a col-

lective sense of kinship and this notion of the *ceann-cinnidh* (chief) was more apparent than real. At this time, the chief was still seen in many respects as the trustee, or protector, of his clans' *duthchas*; that is, their heritage, or more specifically, their prescriptive access to and possession of certain, specific lands. Traditionally, this notion of *duthchas* has been taken to mean that the clan, because they were all either distantly or closely related kin, somehow held the land in common—that a clan's territory did not belong to the chief but rather to the *siol* as a whole. Yet care is needed when making such an argument. First, the notion of a clan all being related to each other did not necessarily find tangible, day-to-day expression on the ground: indeed, in a sense, kinship worked against this notion of a common collective descent. Instead, the use of patronymics—that is stressing one's father, grandfather, etc.—was as likely as the notion of calling oneself by a collective clan name. Second, concepts of kinship served more as a broad, overarching theme rather than a specific claim to actual descent, or to specific farms or lands. Thus, bonds of manrent and bonds of friendship tied obviously non-related kin groups into a wider military, political, and land/food resource sharing alliance of clanship. The small sept of the MacMartins of Letterfinlay who, for example, were allied closely with the Camerons of Locheil, might conceive of themselves as distinct within their own lands, but also saw themselves as Camerons if operating elsewhere outside Lochaber.

These forms of local association reveal that, while clearly central, kinship was but one element within what was a multifaceted form of social organization. For example, while the concept of *duthchas* might well entrench a belief in a collective right to the resources of the land, the crown envisaged the chief as the sole owner of his territories—his *oighreach*—a function that simultaneously made him accountable for those populations that lived upon it. Thus, in the early 17th century, the crown reissued charters of ownership to chiefs in an effort to imbue elites with a sense of legal responsibility (see HIGHLANDS AND ISLANDS AND CENTRAL GOVERNMENT: 2). In other words, while the traditional perception is that clanship perpetrated violence and disorder, in an official sense it was seen as an organizing mechanism for local legal arrangements. It was in fact clan gentry acting as arbitration panels that often thrashed out issues of property theft and compensation in the localities: indeed, it was precisely because it actively sought to co-opt the legal authority of the gentry that the Commission for Securing the Peace, instituted in 1682, was so successful. In a more extreme form, commissions of fire and sword were simply orders from the privy council sanctioning the use of one clan to carry out de facto policing upon another. Part of the problem with clanship's historical image is that it is the official view from the centre, from Edinburgh and London, which has predominated. Of course it was certainly the case that during the 16th century clanship could spawn significant levels of violence. However, from the early years of the 17th century, two central features of clan violence are worthy of note. First, incidents of large-scale feud were in steep decline, largely because the military aspects of clanship had suffered considerable erosion. Indeed, the last private feud fought occurred in 1688, and was fought between the MacDonalds of Keppoch and the Mackintoshes over lands in the Braes of Lochaber. Similarly a survey from 1705 of the Grant estate in Eastern Inverness-shire reveals that of over 600 men (a mere 12 per cent) were armed with a sword and a gun (see WARFARE, WEAPONS, AND FORTIFICATIONS: 3). A second important dimension to clan violence was that, increasingly, it occurred because the political centre was willing to back one side or the other. True, the campaigns of Alasdair MacColla against the Campbells of Argyll in the mid-1640s were in some fundamental respects a traditional feud legitimized by Scottish national politics. However, as the century wore on, clans simply would not commit themselves to violence without the crown's official sanction. Thus, Lachlan Mackintosh, chief of Clan Chattan, only moved against Keppoch in 1688 because the crown was prepared, not only to recognize the validity of his claim, but also to actively intervene on his behalf by supplying troops to augment his levies.

Ultimately, however, it was nothing as dramatic as military violence, either between different clans or by the crown, which led to the demise of kinship and clanship. Instead, clanship was in a sense hollowed out by processes whereby commercial productivity and profitability replaced kinship as the means of organizing relations between Highland elites and their clansmen. The same criteria now also governed the leasing of land to clansmen, even if they were of the same kindred. The early decades of the 17th century had witnessed a growth in black cattle droving from the region. The devastation of the Wars of the *Covenant and the indebtedness that it had spawned ensured the *Restoration period witnessed sustained development in this economic activity. Subsequent profits ensured that the concept of *duthchas* was undermined in practice, if not yet in appearance, by the tendency for clan chiefs to mortgage clan lands in return for credit. These wadset arrangements bestowed on the creditor effective property rights until the original loan was repaid. However, kinship and commercialism should not be seen as automatically incompatible. As specialists in the droving trade, for example, most of the new wadsetters were in fact clan gentry and kinsmen of the chief. Likewise, even as late as the 1770s, the fact that MacLeod of Dunvegan managed his debt in such a way as to ensure that his main creditors were kinsmen, rather than banking institutions, was a vital component in staving off the family's bankruptcy.

Nonetheless the decades from the 1660s to the early 1700s also witnessed more fundamental alterations in clan society. Tacks, or leases, which had once run for up to 90 years or even several lifetimes, were now restricted by chiefs to a period of nineteen years or less. In effect, the chief no longer saw land less in terms of *duthchas*, as resource for the maintenance of his kinsman—real and fictive—but rather in terms of his *oighreach*—his territory or property. The result was that the social and economic position of the tacksman was undermined—above all as chiefs sought to access the differential between what subtenants paid to their tacksmen and what the latter then paid to their chief. That these leading tenants had formed the vital link between the chief and the mass of his clan, as well as providing much of the managerial and agricultural expertise that had marshalled and dispensed food resources on the ground, was now increasingly irrelevant.

In 1737 the second duke of Argyll sanctioned a general assault on the tenurial privileges of the tacksman. This development signalled the cumulative triumph of commercial concerns over kinship almost a decade before Culloden, the event that is usually, if erroneously, accredited with destroying clanship in the region. Thus, while emphasis has traditionally focused on high-profile state legislation such as the 1747 Heritable Jurisdictions Act and the law against bagpipes and tartan (see DRESS, HIGHLAND) the more destructive policies were in fact introduced by the chiefs, and usually modelled on the Argyll estate changes. Within twenty years of Culloden, intensifying rental increase and tenurial reorganization witnessed ever-increasing levels of *emigration by both tacksmen and ordinary tenantry. That many erstwhile chiefs, especially north of the Great Glen, sought to retain their departing clansmen has often been seen as evidence of residual clannish sentiment. The truth behind such apparent paternalism, however, is a striking indication of just how meaningless concepts of kinship and clanship had become. Landlords (see LANDOWNERSHIP IN THE HIGHLANDS AND ISLANDS) now sought to retain their tenantry, not because they were an expression of the collective power and prestige of the *siol*, but rather because, for a while at least, human labour remained as profitable as either cattle or sheep.   AMacK

Clearances of the Highlands and Islands.
The Highland Clearances are one of the most evocative and symbolic but least understood episodes of Scottish history. The evocation and symbolism have perhaps contributed to the lack of perspective on the events themselves. Our view of the Clearances is heavily informed by 19th-century accounts of the events in question and these have been taken up in 20th-century cultural forms, notably a series of important Scottish novels which have the Clearances as their central theme (see CULTURE: 25).

The process of commercialization in *rural society was one of the major themes in European history in the period between 1500 and the mid-19th century. The results were similar in many locations: the enclosure of common land, the infringement of traditional rights, and the movement of population (see POPULATION PATTERNS). Thus, the larger historical forces behind the Clearances were not unique to Scotland. This does not mean, however, that the Clearances themselves were not distinctive. There were four particular elements of the Highland Scottish experience which proved so. The first is that the events took place in an extremely concentrated period. Although commercialization can be detected in Highland society from the late 17th century (see ECONOMY OF THE HIGHLANDS AND ISLANDS: 1), the process which we know as the Clearances was largely concentrated in the period between 1770 and 1860. Secondly, the process was unregulated, largely unfettered by legal inhibitions; in other societies, notably Denmark, changes in landownership and use were governed by statute. Thirdly, the landowner (see LANDOWNERSHIP IN THE HIGHLANDS AND ISLANDS) in Scotland had enormous power to do what he willed with his land. In particular, in Highland society where formal leases for small tenants were rare, landowners could evict and relocate people without any legal impediment. Finally, there was a lack of economic opportunity for the evicted and, where economic opportunities did exist, they were, as in the case of kelp or fishing, mostly controlled by the landowner.

The first problem with the process which we have come to know as the Clearances is placing a chronology on events. There are Clearances which are well known, such as the frighteningly well-organized events on the Sutherland estate in the 1810s or the violent events in Skye and North Uist in the 1850s. The process as a whole, however, is not confined to this short period. Many historians have pointed out that the first large-scale reorganization of a Highland estate came in the 1730s when John, second duke of Argyll, introduced a strong element of commercialism into the allocation of tacks on his estates in Mull, Morvern, and Tiree. This was held to have seriously weakened the military strength of the most important Whig clan in the Highlands for no obvious economic benefit and the third duke put the policy into rapid reverse after his succession in 1743. The search for the origins of the Clearances could, however, go much earlier than this. Traditional clanship (see CLANS OF THE HIGHLANDS AND ISLANDS: 1) was not characterized by stability: movements and relocations of people by clan chiefs were common. These events were localized and intermittent, however, and did not represent the wholesale and large-scale assault on traditional values by the forces of commercialization which characterized the period between 1780 and 1886.

If one defines the Clearances as a concerted and managed reorganization of estates which had as one of its consequences the removal of people from traditional townships to new forms of living in new localities, then one can identify an important acceleration of events in the 1770s and 1780s. These events came, not in the traditional areas associated with the Clearances in the popular mind such as Sutherland or the Hebrides, but in the central Highlands and in particular along the Great Glen. On the estates of the duke of Gordon and of Alexander MacDonnell of Glengarry in particular, wholesale Clearances resulted from the introduction of sheep and from the requirement for men for military service during the American (see USA) War of Independence. This was also a period of substantial *emigration from the Highlands as, perhaps in protest or perhaps as a direct material result of tenurial changes, large groups of Highlanders led by tacksmen left for North America (see CANADA). In the 1790s, as the process of clearance wore on and became more closely associated with the creation of labour-intensive crofting communities, landlord opposition to emigration deepened. In an attempt to retain people who were now seen as a vital resource for industries such as kelp and military employment, landlords conducted a vociferous lobby of government in favour of the limitation of emigration through the regulation of the passenger trade. This bore fruit with the Passenger Vessel Act of 1803, which had the effect of pushing the price of a transatlantic passage beyond the price of most Highlanders.

The key phase of the Highland Clearances was now ready to begin. The best-known example of the kind of events which went on in this period are the Sutherland Clearances carried out between c.1811 and c.1821 and involving the relocation of around 6,000–10,000 people to coastal crofting communities where the allocation of land was deliberately insufficient for subsistence, thereby coercing the population into the landlords' labour force for the exploitation of kelp and fish. The lands from which the people were evicted in Strathnaver and the Strath of Kildonan were turned over to very large-scale sheep-farming operations. It is crucial to understand that the crofting communities are the product of this phase of the Highland Clearances and not a survival of pre-clearance forms of social organization.

Many of the most powerful symbols of the Highland Clearances come from this aspect of the process: the burning of houses, which resulted in the trial and acquittal of Patrick Sellar in 1815, for example. Two contrasting, but equally powerful, 20th-century comments on the Clearances, Iain Crichton Smith's *Consider the Lillies* (1968) and Neil M. Gunn's *Butchers' Broom* (1934), are based on the Sutherland Clearances. The continuing symbolic power of these events can also be seen from the controversy which has surrounded the statue of the first duke of Sutherland atop Ben Bragghie (see MONUMENTS: 2). The Sutherland Clearances, however, are not a very representative example of the process as a whole. They were exceptional in a variety of ways. The sheer scale of the events lies at the heart of their distinctiveness. Few landowners held such power over such a large swathe of territory, or had the material resources to conduct such a vast project of social engineering affecting such a large number of people. Further, they came at a time when the motivations for such an operation were at their peak. This particular window of opportunity for landlords was closing rapidly in the years of peace after 1815 when the industries upon which clearance, and the resultant communities, were based went into rapid decline.

This economic transformation brought a new and vicious cycle of clearance into operation. The people of the crofting communities now represented an incubus for landowners. In all the areas where the crofting community had been established as a potential kelp labour force, landlords sought to rid themselves of a 'redundant' population. This brought the process of clearance sweeping through the Hebrides, especially in Skye, Lewis, the Uists, and Barra in the 1820s and 1830s. Smaller-scale events predicated upon the continuing profitability of sheep farming occurred in the central Highlands, in Inverness-shire, Ross-shire, and Sutherland. The second phase of the Clearances was most evident during and immediately after the potato famine of the 1840s and 1850s. The economic base of many of the crofting communities which had been created by the first phase of clearance was thoroughly eroded and, with poor law reform (see LIVING STANDARDS: 4) in the air, many landowners took the opportunity to expel large numbers of population. The relationship between clearance and emigration was closest in this phase of the process, and large numbers of emigrants were assisted by landowners and the Highlands and Islands Emigration Society. The focus of emigration shifted in this period to the *Australian colonies. The link between clearance and emigration was highly coercive and great bitterness was occasioned by evictions such as those at Borreraig and Suishnish in Skye in 1853 or at Sollas in North Uist in 1849.

Although large-scale evictions were rare after c.1860 this does not mean that coercion by landowners was at an end. On many estates the threat of eviction was a powerful coercive tool for the intimidation of tenantry who did not acquire security of tenure until the Crofters Holdings (Scotland) Act of 1886. By the 1880s, the Clearances were part of the political debate in Scotland as land reform became an increasingly important issue. The political impact of the Clearances was wider than this as they contributed to the strong current of anti-landlordism which permeated the ideologies of both Liberal (see LIBERALISM) and Labour (see LABOURISM) politics in Scotland in the late 19th and early 20th centuries. The publication of Alexander MacKenzie's *History of the Highland Clearances* in 1883 and the evidence given to the Napier Commission in the same year had a massive public impact. Gaelic poetry (see GAELIC LITERATURE) had increasingly sought to deal critically with the Clearances from the 1860s, with denunciations of landlords and the Clearances by poets such as William Livingstone, John Smith, and Mary Macpherson. The Clearances also formed an important motif in Scottish painting in the late 19th century, most notably, perhaps, in William McTaggart's powerful picture *The Sailing of the Emigrant Ship* (1895).   EAC

Clerk, John, of Penicuik (1676–1755), lawyer and virtuoso, Scotland's leading arbiter of taste and patron of the arts in the first half of the 18th century. He was the central figure of a family distinguished over several generations for its cultural and scientific tradition. For his grandfather, a merchant and art-dealer in Paris, luxury trade had developed into connoisseurship for its own sake, and he established himself as a country gentleman surrounded by pictures, books, and works of art. Clerk's father (created a baronet in 1679) was keenly interested in both architecture (see ARCHITECTURAL STYLES AND FEATURES) and mining technology. Upon these foundations Clerk was to build a distinguished reputation for antiquarian learning, knowledge, and enlightened patronage of all the arts and sciences, and for practical ability in architecture, landscape gardening, forestry, agricultural improvement, and coal mining. He, in turn, passed on these tastes and talents to subsequent generations of the main and cadet branches of the family. James, third baronet, was a gentleman amateur architect of distinction and an art patron of note. Clerk's seventh son, John Clerk of Eldin, was famous as the inventor of the naval tactics of the age of Nelson, but was eminent also as artist, etcher, and geologist. Eldin's son John, great advocate and judge, formed one of the finest collections of his day. James Clerk-Maxwell, a collateral descendant, is a towering figure of 19th-century science.

Educated at Glasgow and Leiden, Clerk made a highly important Grand Tour (1697–9) during which the tastes of a lifetime in art, architecture, and the classical world were formed. Music and antiquities, which (as he said) had become his passions in Holland (see LOW COUNTRIES), secured for him social and cultural success in the courts of Germany and imperial Vienna, and in the great cities of Italy. In Rome he became a pupil of Arcangelo Corelli and attained proficiency on harpsichord and violin (see CULTURE: 15). His compositions show him to have possessed a genuine talent which sadly he was never to develop fully in later life due to a profound inhibition which led him to shelter behind the mask of gentleman and judge: he considered composition and public performance beneath his dignity. Clerk was certainly diffident, but it is also true that the pattern of his life is one of failure to achieve, in a number of fields, quite all that might have been expected of a man whose early career showed so much promise.

Clerk was called to the Scottish Bar in 1700. An advantageous first marriage to a cousin of the duke of Queensberry brought him to the notice of the most influential men of the immediate pre-Union period. He sat for Whithorn in the last Scottish parliament, and served subsequently in the first parliament of Great Britain. The Treaty of *Union of 1707, for which he was one of the commissioners with responsibility for negotiating the financial clauses, was the cornerstone of his political faith, and he remained committed to a future for Scotland within the wider British Empire. He took arms for the Hanoverian cause in 1715; and in 1745, too old to fight, buried the manuscript of his long-pondered and much-revised Latin history of the Union, full of anti-*Jacobite sentiment, and retired to England.

Rewarded in 1708 with the lucrative and relatively undemanding office of a baron of the Court of Exchequer, Clerk—who might have risen high in politics and the law—devoted himself to his many interests. He travelled widely throughout Britain; his journals are full of valuable social, economic, and cultural comment, and he was one of the great observers of his age. As an antiquary he enjoyed

considerable prestige, forming the most important Scottish private collection of Roman sculptured stones and artefacts. On archaeological matters he wrote much—his correspondence is extensive and wide-ranging—though he published little. In architecture and gardening he is a significant figure both as amateur practitioner and much-consulted adviser. With William Adam he designed the influential villa of Mavisbank at Loanhead. Among literary friendships that with Allan Ramsay was particularly close: Clerk was himself something of a poet (in Augustan blank verse) and song-writer. With his interest in the world of Rome he idealized a life of cultivated ease on the pattern of the ancients. To call him the Lord Burlington of Scotland is to approach some way to an understanding of his cultural position (see also CULTURE: 12).   IGB

climate. Direct evidence for the broad patterns of the Scottish climate is hard to come by. Meteorological observations recorded directly by scientific instruments became abundant for Scotland only during the 19th century. For most of Scottish history, indirect evidence has to be used in attempts to reconstruct the complex variations of former climates. It is not easy to interpret such 'proxy data sources' reliably. For example, because of the masking effect of the day-to-day variability characteristic of Scotland's weather, gradual but eventually significant trends could be imperceptible to the generations living through them, and thus elude documentary records. On the other hand, well-documented developments, such as changes in land use (see RURAL SETTLEMENT; RURAL SOCIETY), or in the upland limits of arable (see ECONOMY: PRIMARY SECTOR: 1–2), may reflect changes in social, economic, or political perceptions, as much as climatic factors.

Approaches through the natural sciences have their own problems. Climate is just one among many variables which can influence plant and animal distributions. *Migration rates, competition, and local differences in habitat, as well as the direct and indirect impact of people and their animals, can all complicate the interpretation even of uncontaminated data samples. Furthermore, different lifeforms respond to climatic changes at different rates. Insects can react very rapidly, whereas there may be a considerable timelag in tree-line variations, say. Rates of response are difficult to calibrate, since even with the same species, they can differ according to whether the climate is ameliorating or deteriorating. Brief climatic variations, perhaps of considerable human importance, may not show up at all.

The difficulty of interpreting even dramatic proxy data is illustrated by one of the most striking landscape changes apparent in the Scottish pre-historic record: the demise of pine forest in Caithness 4,000 years ago. Researchers variously argue for soil podzolization, acid rain from Icelandic volcanic eruptions, and human activity, as alternatives to simple climatic deterioration.

Secure conclusions can seldom be inferred from the evidence available at any single location. The complexity of Scotland's geography and history, however, allow comparisons of contrasting regions, which can highlight common sequences that would be difficult to explain other than as reflections of climatic change. Moreover, when dealing with meteorological processes it is legitimate to consider the physics of 'the world weather machine' as a whole. Through application of very powerful computer systems to atmospheric modelling, there is now broad agreement that a coherent pattern of climatic changes is gradually becoming apparent worldwide. The narrative which follows is founded on more than local data. However, with so many levels of uncertainty, it must be regarded as provisional. More detail is offered in the later centuries, because of the patterns of data availability and of reader interest.

In terms of the widely accepted view that variation in the earth's orbit and axis relative to the sun has a major role as a 'Pacemaker of the Ice Ages', our current period is best regarded as an interglacial—an intermission between the glaciations which have been recurring throughout the 2,500,000 years of the Quaternary Ice Age. The extent to which anthropogenic global warming might interfere with the return to glacial conditions scheduled by astronomical theory is of particular interest for Scots, since it has been calculated that a drop in mean annual temperature of just 1–3 °C could result in the reglaciation of Scotland.

The last occasion when glaciers did push into the Scottish Lowlands was the Loch Lomond Stadial. This episode lasted only about 1,000 years, but it is widely recognized across the northern hemisphere, often called the Younger Dryas Stadial after its indicator plant species. In geological perspective, it was very recent indeed, ending c.8000 BC in radiocarbon terms, with widespread indications around the globe of rapid warming (see GEOLOGY AND LANDSCAPE). The reafforestation of Scotland began, and there is soon evidence of mesolithic hunting and gathering communities.

In Britain, the period of maximum warmth in the Climatic Optimum of the present interglacial appears to have been between about 5000 and 3000 BC, with temperatures 1–3 °C higher than at present during the neolithic, when agriculture was becoming established. The earlier part of the Optimum, classed Boreal in pollen terms, was dryer than the succeeding Atlantic phase: perhaps 90 per cent and 110 per cent of present-day precipitation averages respectively. From around 4500 BC, there is evidence of widespread growth of ombrogenous blanket peat, but interpretation of this and changes in forest cover as indicators of climatic change becomes progressively more difficult because of deliberate and inadvertent effects of early farming communities. It seems probable, however, that there was then a general deterioration in climate in northern temperate lands.

A relatively warm intermission seems likely between 1100 and 800 BC, before the onset of a notably cooler and wetter phase c.500 BC. There is not yet evidence that this affected the whole country, but in some areas its impact on the landscape was probably enhanced by increasing population pressure, and iron technology. Cases can be made for a remission towards warmer and drier summers during the Roman occupation of Scotland (see NORTHERN ENGLAND AND SOUTHERN SCOTLAND: ROMAN OCCUPATION), up to about AD 400, followed by a more disturbed phase with significant glacier advances in Scandinavia and the Alps. Between AD c.700/900 and 1300, however, evidence for warming is sufficiently widespread for this to be known internationally as the Little Climatic Optimum. This is the period of the Viking settlements in Greenland, and of viticulture in southern England. In many parts of Britain, crops were grown to higher altitudes than for some time previously or since; Kelso abbey had a grange at c.1,000 feet (300 m) with over 247 acres (100 hectares) of tillage.

Although there was an earlier downturn in temperature in Greenland and Iceland, and a marked increase in storminess during the 13th century did affect Scotland and other North Sea lands, it was not until the opening two decades of the 14th century that a quite abrupt deterioration affected Europe. Around the period of the battle of Bannockburn, the growing season shortened, probably by most of a month, and the frequency of harvest failures increased. The Little Ice Age was underway worldwide, and though there were intermissions it can be said to have continued right into Victorian times.

Much of the 15th century was characterized by wretched summers and frequent cold winters. Only the 1690s seem to have had so many severe winter spells within a single decade as the 1430s (see HEALTH, FAMINE, AND DISEASE: 1–2). It was not until the start of the 16th century that there was a major remission. This affected much of the world, and Scotland may have enjoyed temperatures approaching those of the 1920s or 1930s. But this did not last. As in much of Europe, the winter of 1564–5 exceeded in length and harshness any winter since the 1430s. By the 1580s, in several summers the seas between Iceland and Greenland were impassable because of sea ice. The enhanced North Atlantic thermal gradient gave gales in Scotland and Ireland's latitude which exceeded most of the worst 20th-century storms, with dire results for the retreating Spanish Armada in 1588.

In the opening decade of the 17th century there may have been a brief remission, for there was surplus grain to export, to the profit of Edinburgh merchants. By the early 1620s, however, much of Scotland was again suffering from recurrent harvest failures. This seems consistent with the decline of the Faroese cod fishery from c.1615—the cod is a useful indicator of sea temperatures (see NATURAL HISTORY).

The final third of the 17th century is now widely agreed to have been the harshest phase of the Little Ice Age for much of the world, with the coldest regimes of the last 10,000 years. In Scotland, the onset was marked by serious blizzards in 1670 and 1674, with heavy losses of sheep. Cold summers inhibited crop growth, and clusters of years with harvest failures brought disaster to subsistence farmers by forcing them to eat their seed corn, leaving nothing to plant for later years. Between 1693 and 1700, the harvests failed in seven years out of eight in many upland areas. This may have been a greater disaster in some places than the Black Death (see RURAL SOCIETY: 2–3). Certainly there was famine in Norway too, and Finland may have lost a third of its population. A factor contributing to the climatic disasters of this decade may have been the massive eruptions of Hekla in Iceland (1693) and Serua (also 1693) and Aboina (1694) in Indonesia, the pollution of the atmosphere by these volcanoes filtering the sunlight.

Soon after 1700, there was a rapid shift to warmer conditions. This characterized much of the first four decades of the 18th century, though some cold snaps hit Scotland, as in 1708–9, 1716, 1724, 1739–42. The 1740s tended to be both warm and dry, but during the 1750s there was a notable increase in rainfall; and in the decades that followed, cooler summers reduced evaporation so that crops sometimes rotted in the fields. The 1780s were especially bad for Scottish farmers (and Rabbie Burns's Mouse), and again the unusually heavy volcanic pollution of the stratosphere, particularly in 1783, may have contributed to this.

Although the trend towards higher temperatures was resumed between 1800 and 1808, it was interrupted by cold spells in the early 1820s, the 1840s, and the 1890s. Indeed, the winter of 1879 was as severe as those in the 1690s. However, since Edwardian times it has been clear that the Little Ice Age is over. Between 1920 and 1940 warming was

rapid. After that there was a pause, with some cooling, but a rapid rise in world temperatures became apparent again in the mid-1970s.

As suggested above, Scots have a particular interest in the possibility of human-generated global warming giving a reprieve from another glaciation. The perspective given by the problems of attempting to understand the complexities of past climatic changes is a warning against jumping to simplistic conclusions. We do now have access to comprehensive direct instrumental measurements of meteorological data. Yet understanding does not come easily, even of current events. Thus, in the latter half of the 20th century there has been a curious change in the pattern of climatic variability. Although overall variability has been rather lower than in previous decades of the century, embedded within this has been a notable increase in the occurrence of extreme seasons: droughts, deluges, severe frosts, and heatwaves. Such extremes, perhaps more than any underlying trend towards a warmer or colder climate, seem likely to confront the new Scottish parliament, now charged with managing the country's complex infrastructure and economy, with immediate planning problems as Scotland heads into the next millennium.

It was amidst 'derk and drublie dayis' of the Little Ice Age that William Dunbar, James IV's court poet, wrote: 'Here nocht abidis, here standis no thing stable . . . | So does this warld transitory go'. But half a millennium later, it still seems that the only safe conclusion regarding climate is the paradox that 'change is the norm'. IM

Cockburn, Henry. A literary and reforming lawyer, Cockburn (1779–1854) was born and educated in Edinburgh. Though a nephew of the Tory manager of Scotland, Henry *Dundas, he joined the group of junior Whigs associated with the foundation of the *Edinburgh Review* in 1802. Called to the Bar in 1800, he became an advocate-depute in 1806 through his connection with the Dundases but gave up the post in 1810, preferring to forget that he had ever accepted it. He returned to the courts, and made his name as an advocate for the defence, often in association with Francis *Jeffrey, in the criminal prosecutions of radicals during the social disturbances which broke out after the end of the Napoleonic Wars (see FRENCH REVOLUTION, AGE OF THE). This was also the period when agitation for political reforms in Scotland started up in earnest. Cockburn won prominence as a speaker and pamphleteer for the Whigs. He was especially concerned with the allegedly irresponsible position of the Lord Advocate, on which he wrote a notoriously intemperate article in the *Edinburgh Review* in 1823. He was rewarded with the post of solicitor-general when the Whigs came to power in 1830. He became a principal draftsman of the Scottish Reform Bill, passed after numerous vicissitudes in 1832. The fact that in many counties of Scotland it made next to no difference to electoral malpractice may well have been due to Cockburn's silly contempt for feudal law. He went on the bench in 1834, and was twice elected rector of Glasgow University. But he is best remembered for the literary production of his late years, a *Life of Lord Jeffrey* (1852), a *Journal* (published posthumously, 1874), and above all the charming *Memorials of his Time* (1856), lamenting 'the last purely Scotch age' which he had joined with some glee in bringing to an end. MRGF

coinage can be seen as a reflection of the political, economic, and cultural status of Scotland during various periods of its history. Hoards and individual finds from Scottish soil indicate that, at various times between the 1st and 11th centuries AD, coins of the Romans (see NORTHERN ENGLAND AND SOUTHERN SCOTLAND: ROMAN OCCUPATION), Northumbrians, Vikings, and Anglo-Saxons were in circulation, but in each case their use was restricted geographically and/or socially.

*David I (1124–53) was the first Scottish king to issue his own coins, after his capture in 1136 of the town of Carlisle, where a mint had been striking for King Stephen of England. Until 1280 silver pennies, or sterlings, were the only coins struck, these sometimes being cut into halves and quarters to provide smaller sums of money. Alexander III (1249–86) then ordered the minting of round halfpennies and farthings.

David II (1329–71) experimented unsuccessfully with a gold coinage. He was also responsible for the issue of Scotland's first silver coins of higher value than a penny—groats (worth fourpence) and half-groats—but his latest coins were of lighter weight than previous issues. This was the first step in a series which led to the progressive devaluation of the Scots coinage in comparison to that of England, and probably resulted in part from a shortage of silver bullion caused by the large ransom paid for David's release from captivity in England in 1351.

Under Robert III (1390–1406) the striking of gold coins recommenced, this time with greater success, the 'lions' bearing the image of St Andrew on his cross—the first use of the saltire on a Scottish coin. Robert's pennies and halfpennies were made from metal comprising two parts silver to one part alloy, and bullion supply problems were exacerbated by the payment of another ransom to secure the release of James I from English captivity in 1424. Pennies of the first four Jameses of the Stewart dynasty (see KINGSHIP: 5) are of highly debased sil-

ver, or billon, and in the second half of the 15th century higher value coins were also struck in this alloy, owing to the ever-increasing price of silver. Coins of pure copper were struck for the first time then, and these have generally been seen as a reflection of the parlous state of the Scottish economy, but it is by no means certain that the policy of issuing debased, low-denomination coins was not chosen by the Scottish kings rather than forced on them.

Until the later 15th century, only stylized representations of royal busts had appeared on coins, but two issues of James III (1460–88) bore the first attempts at genuine portraits. A three-quarter facing bust on an issue of base silver groats struck from about 1471 is of no great artistic merit, but these coins are also important as the first to bear thistles as a heraldic emblem. James's last issue of groats (1484–9) bears a realistic portrait which is similar to those which appear elsewhere, for instance on the Trinity College church altar panels, and which has been described as the earliest Renaissance-style coin portrait outside Italy. These groats can be seen as the precursors of the great flowering of Renaissance (see CULTURE: 4, 8) numismatic art which is evident on the gold and silver coins of *James V, *Mary, Queen of Scots, and *James VI. These bore not only a variety of royal portraits, but also reverse designs of political and religious significance, particularly those of James VI.

By this time all Scottish coins were minted in Edinburgh, but in earlier times mints had existed in many different places. In the 12th and early 13th centuries, Border strongholds such as Roxburgh and *Berwick had housed mints, as had some, like Carlisle and Bamburgh, which are now in England. For Alexander III's first great recoinage in 1250 no fewer than sixteen mints briefly operated at the same time, to enable old coins to be handed in and exchanged for new ones. In the later Middle Ages the main mints were at Berwick, Edinburgh, Perth, and Aberdeen, but coins were also issued from royal residences in places such as Stirling and Linlithgow in the 15th century, possibly from a travelling mint accompanying the royal progress. The last coins known to have been struck other than at Edinburgh were a small issue of billon bawbees (sixpences) of Mary from Stirling in 1544.

After the *Union of the Crowns in 1603, Scottish gold and silver coins closely resembled those of England, but by this time the ratio of value had reached 12 : 1, so that a Scottish twelve-shilling piece was of the same size and weight as an English shilling. Under Charles II (1651–85) silver coins were issued in fractions and multiples of the merk (13s. 4d. Scots). The terms of the Act of *Union of 1707 provided for a standard coinage for the whole of Great Britain, with the mint at Edinburgh to continue in operation, but silver coins of Queen Anne, dated 1707–9, proved to be the last ever minted there. Since then all coins used in Scotland have been manufactured at the British Royal Mint or, occasionally in the early 19th century, at private mints in England. NMMcQH

Columba, St (Colum Cille), abbot of Iona, c.521–97. Colum Cille, whose name means 'dove of the church', was born around 521 or 522 into the powerful family of the Uí Néill, whose multi-part dynasty remained overlords of much of the north of Ireland throughout the early Middle Ages. He was the son of Feidlimid, grandson of Conall Gulban, who was the eponym of the Cenél Conaill kindred whose main territory was Co. Donegal. Despite his royal ancestry, he seems to have been destined for the church from early on, as he was fostered with a priest. He studied with various masters in both Leinster and the north, and as deacon with Bishop Uinniau either at Clonard or Moville. In 561, a battle fought between his own Cenél Conaill and their southern relatives involved the churchman in some act of partisanship, and he was subsequently excommunicated at a synod, a verdict which was later reversed. Nonetheless, subsequent to this, in 563, he left Ireland for the west coast of Scotland, in 'pilgrimage for the love of Christ'.

There he established a series of monasteries, Hinba, Mag Luinge on Tiree, and others, with *Iona as the mother house. As far as we can judge, the component houses of this monastic archipelago had different functions: Hinba was partly for anchorites, those well skilled in monastic discipline who wished to move further up the ladder of perfection; Mag Luinge was partly for lay penitents. Iona itself would appear to have been large and bustling by the end of Colum Cille's life, with major buildings, agricultural compounds, and scriptoria, as well as church and dormitories. During his life at least one monastery back in Ireland was also established, that of Durrow, and Derry may have been founded by him as well. Colum Cille thus became head of a monastic federation, or *familia*, which would last through the Middle Ages, with subsequent abbots of Iona, and, much later, Kells and then Derry, taking the title *comarba Coluim Chille* (heir / successor of Colum Cille). Most of these abbots continued to be drawn from Colum Cille's own kindred, the Cenél Conaill.

Part of the *familia*'s success may be due to Colum Cille's royal connections—for part of his abbacy, his cousins ruled the Uí Néill—but much of it must result from personal charisma. His *Life*, written by his relative and successor St *Adomnán,

presents Colum Cille as a stern negotiator with kings, ordaining the king of *Dál Riata, *Aedán mac Gabráin, only after heavenly pressure, and facing down the wizards of the Pictish king, Bridei, son of Mailcon. Some of these depicted relationships may reflect those of later decades, when Iona had indeed achieved virtual ecclesiastical mastery over Dál Riata and Pictland. That Iona, not consistently headed by a bishop, had authority over the monasteries and bishops of the Gaelic and Pictish parts of Scotland was noted by Bede, but Iona should not be seen as typical in this regard of the Gaelic or 'Celtic' church—certainly Bede did not think it was. Rather, its authority must have arisen from its productivity of the clerics who converted and ministered to these regions. It was certainly not the only monastery working in such a vein—we may note the likes of Lismore and Kingarth, and later Applecross—but it was certainly the most prominent.

Columba's cult as a saint was actively fostered by his community in the century after his death, with poetry written in his praise, and collection of traditions about his holiness, which resulted in the now lost *Liber de Virtutibus Sancti Columbae* of Cumméne Find in the mid-7th century, and finally Adomnán's *Vita Sancti Columbae* at the end of the century. The latter gives a good impression of the cult in its early decades, with both criminals and kings turning to Columba in times of need. Most importantly, Oswald, king of Northumbria who had been raised in exile partly on or near Iona, seems to have regarded Colum Cille as a patron, and it was to Iona he turned for churchmen to help him re-Christianize his kingdom. Much later, in the 9th century, the Gaelic dynasty who took over Pictland espoused Colum Cille as their patron. *Kenneth mac Alpin's establishment of Colum Cille's shrine at Dunkeld is significant, as is the later use of the name Mael Coluim ('servant of Columba') in the royal dynasty. Although other saints grew in importance in the 12th century, Colum Cille remained a potent Scottish saint, with a new Augustinian house at Inchcolm established then, and later, Colum Cille's relic-shrine, the *Breccbennach* or Monymusk reliquary, was carried before the victorious Scottish army at Bannockburn. In recent decades, Colum Cille has become something of an ecumenical saint, uniting both Catholic and Protestant in respect for him as an 'apostle of Scotland', and forming a means of dialogue and co-operation between Scotland and Ireland on issues such as religion, heritage, and Gaelic enterprise. TC

Colum Cille. See COLUMBA, ST.

Colville, David (1813–98), founder of Scotland's greatest steel dynasty. In the late 1840s, Colville moved to Glasgow with the objective of becoming a provisions seller. The upsurge in Scottish industrial production at that time, however, convinced him that more money could be made in the iron industry (see ECONOMY, SECONDARY SECTOR: 2). The increasing use of the 'hot blast' meant that the abundant supplies of coal and blackband ironstone in the west of Scotland could be utilized to produce iron cheaply (see NEILSON, JAMES BEAUMONT). In 1861 Colville went into partnership with Thomas Gray who owned an iron foundry at Coatbridge. Together they built the Clifton Ironworks near Glasgow and were producing 600 tons (610 tonnes) of malleable iron after the first year of business. The partnership did not last, however, and in 1872 Colville sold out to Gray in order to set up his own company with his two sons. The new operation, based in Dalzell near Motherwell, was soon a success and Colville began to manufacture steel in 1881. This development was spurred on by its increasing use in shipbuilding. Steel was more tensile and elastic than iron and Clyde shipyards were prominent in pioneering its use. By 1889 the plant at Dalzell had almost doubled in size, with additions such as a new strip mill, as orders came pouring in from the shipbuilding industry. In 1895 the business was taken over by his sons and by that time Colvilles had become the dominating force in the Scottish steel industry.   RJF

Comyn family, the most powerful noble family in 13th-century Scotland. The Comyns have long been associated in Scottish tradition with the role of over-mighty subjects, involved in the kidnapping of young king Alexander III in 1257, and as traitors, betraying William *Wallace at the battle of Falkirk (1298) and Robert Bruce (see ROBERT I) to Edward I in 1306. It should be remembered, however, that the makers of this tradition were pro-Bruce and pro-Wallace writers of the 14th and 15th centuries (see HISTORIANS: 1). The Comyns were rivals and opponents of both these heroes of Scottish tradition.

The first member of the Comyn family to make an impact on Scotland was William Comyn, chancellor to *David I by c.1136. Like many individuals introduced into David's household, Comyn was from a family of Continental origin and had served his apprenticeship in the English chancery of Henry I in the 1120s. Further royal patronage from David I, Earl Henry, and William I 'the Lion' ensured that the Comyns established a firm territorial base in southern (Peeblesshire and Roxburghshire) and central Scotland (Kirkintilloch) by 1200 through William's nephew Richard (d. 1179) and Richard's son William (d. 1233). The family's further rise onto the political stage came through their

success as 'troubleshooters' for a Scottish monarchy anxious to define its authority in the north and south-west during the first three decades of the 13th century. Thus William Comyn (d. 1233) became justiciar of Scotia (north of Forth), the premier administrative office in the kingdom, in c.1205, and then through marriage earl of Buchan in c.1212, the first earl of Continental origin in Scotland. William's son Walter (d. 1258) became hereditary lord of the strategically important northern lordships of Badenoch and Lochaber by 1230, and gained the family's second earldom, the earldom of Menteith, again through marriage c.1234. Early signs of Comyn patronage in their two earldoms were the Cistercian abbey of Deer (1219) in Buchan and the Augustinian priory of Inchmahome in Menteith, (1238). Alexander II also involved Earl Walter in the pacification of *Galloway in 1235.

By the 1240s the Comyns had virtual viceregal power across northern Scotland and had emerged as a formidable political grouping consisting of three branches: Buchan, Badenoch, and Kilbride. As a family they controlled three earldoms directly (including Angus before 1242) and through marriage connections three further earldoms (Mar, Ross, and, before 1242, Atholl). In the political crises of the 1240s and 1250s Comyn power in Scotland was tested by the internal opposition of the Bissets and Durwards and by external interference from Henry III. Though the Comyns were forced to swear an oath of good behaviour to Henry III in 1244, the English king recognized Comyn leadership of the Scottish political community in 1251 when, as father-in-law to the young Alexander III, he returned them to power during the minority period. It was only when Henry supported a Durward-inspired takeover of Scottish government in 1255 that the Comyns resorted to kidnapping the young Alexander III in 1257.

Rather than suffering political eclipse when Alexander III's minority ended, the Comyns and their allies dominated public offices at the centre and in the provinces between 1260 and 1286. It is a remarkable testimony to the family's role as pillars of the Scottish monarchy that the Comyns of Buchan were justiciars of Scotia for no fewer than 66 out of the 100 years between 1205 and 1304. The Comyns also controlled the majority of ecclesiastical offices, especially the bishopric of St Andrews, in the second half of the 13th century. Further marriage alliances extended the Comyn sphere of influence to the earldoms of Strathearn, Dunbar, and Angus and linked the family with the *Balliols, Macdougalls of Argyll, Morays, Umphravilles, and Mowbrays. The Comyns controlled key lines of communication across Scotland, especially the north, through their castles of Ruthven, Blair

Atholl, Lochindorb, Inverlochy, Dundarg, Cairn-bulg, Rattray, Slains, Kingedward, and Balvenie (in the north) and Dalswinton, Bedrule, Scraesburgh, Kirkintilloch, and Cruggleton (in the south).

Anyone who sought influence in Scotland following Alexander III's death in 1286 needed to seek accommodation with the Comyns. The Comyns continued to dominate political offices through the guardianship period, 1286 to 1290, and then again during John Balliol's kingship, 1292 to 1296. The Bruce family sought, unsuccessfully, to overthrow the Comyn-led government by force in 1286, then by legal means when they set their long-held claim to the throne against the claim of John Balliol, the brother-in-law of John Comyn of Badenoch in the *Great Cause (1291-2). Edward I sought to support and control the Comyns as a means to exert his own overlordship over Scotland in the period 1289 to 1296. All three branches of the Comyn family held land in England, fulfilled their obligations to the English king from this, and in times of peace as well as in political crises looked to the English king for support. Edward I sought to exploit this, neglecting to acknowledge that the Comyns, in alliance with Alexander III, led a sophisticated political community in Scotland which sought to preserve Scottish independence. The Comyns were responsible for clear, self-conscious expressions of national independence in the terms of the Treaty of Birgham negotiated with Edward I in 1290 (see NATIONAL IDENTITY: 2). It was the Comyns, not the Bruces, who led Scotland into war with England in 1296 after Edward had broken these terms. Following their military defeat in 1296, and their imprisonment in England (1296-7), the Comyns' acceptance as leaders on their return and after *Wallace's defeat at Falkirk (1298) casts doubt on contemporary accusations of betrayal. The Comyn-negotiated surrender to Edward I in 1304, and their refusal to support Robert Bruce's attempts to revive Scottish kingship led to the infamous murder of John Comyn of Badenoch, the senior (or Red) Comyn branch, in the Greyfriars church, Dumfries, on 10 February 1306. Comyn resistance to *Robert I, now king, but lacking in popular support until 1307, continued in Scotland until 1308 when Bruce destroyed the Comyns' northern bases. The family was then reliant on English support. The battle of Bannockburn (1314) ended a century of Comyn influence on Scottish history (see ANGLO-SCOTTISH RELATIONS: 2; FRANCE; INDEPENDENCE, WARS OF).

AY

Congregation, Wars of the. Wars of the Congregation is the rather misleading term for the struggle of the Protestant 'Lords of the Congregation of Christ' against the established church and the queen regent, Mary of Guise. Triggered in May 1559 by the riot of the 'rascal multitude' inflamed by a sermon of John *Knox against 'idolatry', the wars were in fact a series of minor skirmishes without a single pitched battle. More altarpieces and stained glass windows were broken (see ICONOCLASM) than either heads or limbs over the course of the next fourteen months. The Congregation was led by dissident nobles, prominent among whom was the half-brother of *Mary, Queen of Scots, the Augustinian prior of St Andrews, Lord James. But their ranks included trimmers and even Catholics such as the fourth earl of Huntly as well as convinced Protestants. Despite Knox and despite appearances, which convinced an appalled Archbishop Mathew Parker that the people were the 'orderers of things' in Scotland, the leaders of the revolt were forced to admit to their erstwhile English allies in the summer of 1559 that it was difficult to 'persuade a multitude to revolt against established authority'. The army was hardly a revolutionary *jacquerie*. It was a makeshift, poorly trained force, made up of the kinship networks of the rebel lords, with pressed men and mercenaries as well as volunteers; all of them had a habit of melting away, especially after the promised funds from England failed to materialize in the autumn of 1559. Money, as William Cecil wryly explained, was indeed 'the man in Scotland'. Without it, the Congregation found it impossible to stage a conclusive victory against the 3,000 or 4,000 trained professionals, many of them Scots, who made up the royal *army. Neither side, however, had access to what might have been the decisive firepower of the royal artillery, held in a kind of cautious neutrality in *Edinburgh castle by its keeper, Lord Erskine, a convinced Protestant whose commitment to the religious cause fell short of outright rebellion. In the course of the revolt, the Congregation's aims changed, in their bid to find respectability and wider support. The battle, in the propaganda of the Congregation, became a struggle against the 'thralldom of strangers', which was one of the pretexts for the dismissal of the queen regent in October 1559. The stalemate was not broken by English military intervention (see ANGLO-SCOTTISH RELATIONS: 3). Admiral Winter's pre-emptive strike in January 1560 on the port of Leith, seen as the linchpin of the French occupying force, proved abortive. And the English army dispatched north in April 1560, as soon as the campaigning season started, laid siege but repeatedly failed to storm Leith's *traice italienne* fortifications. In the event, it was largely the unexpected accident of the death probably by stomach cancer of Mary of Guise in June 1560 which settled matters. Within little more than three weeks, the Treaty of Edinburgh was concluded, both foreign armies agreed to withdraw, and the stage was left vacant—for an unlikely Protestant victory and the enshrinement of a religious settlement in the so-called *'Reformation' Parliament, which met illegally in August 1560, a mere five weeks after the treaty was concluded.   ML

Constantine I (Caustantín mac Cinaeda), king of *Picts 862–76, son of *Kenneth mac Alpin. He succeeded his uncle, Domnall, in April 862, and was killed by Vikings in 876. In his reign southern Pictland endured repeated and unprecedented devastation by Vikings. In the mid-860s the country was plundered and hostages taken; in 871 large numbers of Picts, along with Britons and Angles, were taken as slaves to Ireland; in 875 the Vikings inflicted a massive defeat against the Picts at Dollar, and for a year occupied the lowlands of southern Pictland. After the Vikings killed Constantine his brother Aed briefly succeeded him, but the Viking menace continued and forced St *Columba's relics, which had been housed at Dunkeld by Kenneth mac Alpin in 849, to be evacuated to Ireland. Constantine and his brother Aed were the last kings of the Picts, and the Picts disappear from record in the aftermath of the devastation suffered in 875–8. Constantine was probably of Gaelic royal stock, and promoted close ties with the most powerful king in *Ireland, Aed Findliath (862–79), who married Constantine's sister. Nevertheless, Constantine's most enduring (and least recognized) legacy is the idea that Pictland was a single kingdom, stretching from Caithness to Fife. This idea was promoted for the first time in the longer list of Pictish kings (a text known as *Series Longior* or king-list 'P'), written in his reign. Before this time there may have been individual kings, such as *Ungus, son of Uurgust, who exercised a personal overlordship over lesser Pictish kings (and non-Pictish kings, too). But no one, it seems, imagined that Pictland was a single kingdom. The most powerful kingdom would have been Fortriu (southern Pictland). A kingdom of all Pictland never became a reality, but it has captured the imagination of historians ever since.   DB

Constantine II (Caustantín mac Aeda). The last of *Kenneth mac Alpin's grandsons, Constantine (b. before 879, d. 952, r. c.900–43) succeeded his cousin Donald II (Domnall mac Caustantín) in 900 and reigned as king of Alba for more than 40 years before taking the monastic habit at St Andrews for the last decade of his life. His reign can be divided into two main phases. In his early years he fought against the Viking dynasty of the Uí Ímair (in 904, 918, and 927) often in alliance with the English rulers of Bamburgh. From 934, however, his conflicts were mainly with the expanding power of Wessex, from 937, at least, in alliance with the Uí

Ímair king, Amlaíb mac Gofraid (Olaf Gothfrithsson, 934–41). The two rulers, with Owain of Strathclyde, led a massive invasion of southern Britain in that year which was stopped only with great cost at Brunnanburh. The breakdown in relations with the English probably resulted from a disputed succession to the lordship of Bamburgh on the death of Constantine's ally Ealdred. Constantine's regime was self-consciously sacerdotal. In the campaigns of 904 and 918 the crozier of St *Columba (the *Cathbuaid*) was carried before his army and in 906 he undertook a public ceremony at *Scone, along with Bishop Cellach, swearing to uphold the rights and customs of the Gaelic church. In his last years at *St Andrews he became abbot of the *céli Dé* community there. His ally Amlaíb was also said to have been his son-in-law and one of his sons bore an apparently Norse name (Illulb, king of Alba 954–62) which may indicate that he himself had a Norse wife. It may well be the case that the transformation of Pictavia into Albania and the promotion of Gaelic identity over *Pictish identity was largely a product of this long reign (see NATIONAL IDENTITY: 1). Constantine was succeeded by his second cousin.   AW

corporate state and Scottish politics. Corporatism may be briefly defined as the involvement of government, business, and organized labour in a joint endeavour to develop a concerted approach to economic and social issues. It seemed to exert a particularly potent appeal in Scotland between the 1930s and the 1970s. This in part arose because the economic and social problems afflicting Scotland were especially acute (see ECONOMY: 6).

Businessmen had been interested from the First World War in looking to the state to assist in creating an orderly framework within which industry might cope with the dire pressures posed by the inter-war depression. William Weir, a major engineering employer, was very active in urging government action to promote economic well-being. Others prominent between the wars included Sir James *Lithgow, the shipbuilder, and Lord Bilsland, a director of several public companies. The STUC became a decisive force in the corporatist build-up. Under the direction of William Elger, general secretary from 1921 to 1946, the STUC joined business interests in a number of agencies promoting the case for state action to assist the growth of both the Scottish economy and employment—for example, the National Advisory Council for Juvenile Employment.

The trend to corporatism was stiffened in the 1930s as strenuous efforts were made to put the Scottish economy on a profitable and stable basis. Businessmen pushed for government-supported schemes to rationalize the basic industries such as shipbuilding and coal mining. Within the *Scottish Office, there were sympathetic responses. Walter *Elliot, the most dynamic inter-war Scottish Secretary, had pursued corporatist techniques when Minister of Agriculture, and he adopted a similar stance on Scottish affairs.

Elliot's approach was maintained by Thomas *Johnston, Scottish Secretary from 1941 to 1945. He set up a committee composed of former holders of his office to advise on the future development of the Scottish economy. Even if the committee's plans were not very realistic, the bipartisan approach, straddling all sides of industry and politics, had been established for the post-1945 era.

For some 30 to 35 years after 1945, a strongly corporatist strategy was espoused in Scotland, irrespective of which party held power. Part of the reason was the distinctive position adopted by both the Scottish CBI and STUC. On the whole, there were closer relations between these two bodies than their British parents. Both were more flexible on ideology and frequently combined to advocate action on Scottish needs. The forum for corporatist discussions was the *Scottish Council (Development and Industry). Established in the 1930s by Lithgow and like-minded businessmen, it operated as both a lobby for Scottish economic interests and an economic research centre. Businessmen and trade unionists met together on the Council to hammer out policy objectives and organized lobbies of government to press the case for economic development in Scotland. Its influence on government economic policy grew steadily after 1945, until it was effectively eclipsed by the *Scottish Development Agency (SDA) in the 1970s.

One of the most significant high-tide moments in corporatism came with the publication of the Toothill Report in 1961. Toothill, a company director, and his committee, which included trade unionists, were commissioned by the Scottish Council (Development and Industry) to recommend how the economy of Scotland should evolve. The Scottish Office was intimately associated with the report: one of the committee's joint secretaries was seconded from St Andrew's House. The report advocated a more vigorous, closely focused strategy for growth which broke decisively with existing nostrums. The government was already moving in that direction, and Toothill underlined the broad agreement on the way forward. The cabinet decision to site a steel strip mill at Ravenscraig in the late 1950s began this, and the state's direction of two new car production plants into Scotland in the early 1960s continued the trend. Both labour and capital endorsed the Conservative government's interventionist programme.

Under Labour between 1964 and 1970, corporatism was even more central. The forming of development agencies, with trade union and industry representatives sitting on the boards, was a key feature of the period. The STUC, not unnaturally, enjoyed very close relations with Labour ministers, and their advice was regularly solicited on a range of policy concerns. In 1973, the STUC had nominated trade unionists to around 1,500 seats on public agencies. But the views of businessmen were also sounded out, and frequently backed if deemed feasible. The *Highlands and Islands Development Board was the most important achievement of the corporatist trend in this decade. A bid to establish a Scottish Economic Planning Council was less successful. It comprised businessmen, trade unionists, local government representatives, and civil servants, and was chaired by the Scottish Secretary. It collapsed in the aftermath of the deteriorating economic situation in the later 1960s.

In the 1970s there was little diminution in the corporatist process. Under the Wilson and Callaghan ministries of 1974–9, a battery of state agencies emerged, thronged with representatives of both labour and management, often with local authorities also involved. Scotland acquired its own version of bodies like the Health & Safety Executive and the Manpower Services Commission. The creation of the *SDA in 1975 was the apogee of corporatism in Scotland. Although responsible to the Scottish Secretary, who appointed the chairman and depute chair, it operated autonomously from day-to-day ministerial control as a public body. It was acclaimed by all sides, management and unions alike, as a significant advance in tackling Scotland's economic difficulties.

During the 1980s, however, the corporatist movement was excluded from influence with the new government. Market forces were reinstated as the ruling factor, state agencies were dismantled, emasculated, or ignored. The STUC was no longer able to bend the ear of ministers and officials in St Andrew's House. The Scottish CBI fared no better. The Development Agencies had their functions reduced and narrowed, and eventually were renamed as 'Scottish Enterprise'. The STUC's stance grew ever more oppositional as unemployment followed widespread factory closures in the 1980s, while business interests were pulled, not always enthusiastically, into supporting the line being pursued by a Conservative government. The era of corporatism was effectively over by the later 1980s, and showed no sign of being reinstated subsequently.   IGCH

courtship and marriage patterns in Scotland have varied widely depending on social class, religion, and region. Details before the 17th century rely on the literature of the time, especially the ballads. Land inheritance or family titles account for instances of arranged marriages between certain families, and there is evidence of *children as young as 12 being married.

Till the late Victorian era, middle-class couples courted under the watchful eye of chaperones, working-class couples were controlled by the strict rules of employers, and the patterns of rural couples varied widely between farming, crofting, and fishing areas. Marriage within *social class prevailed until the 1950s when statistics show that a man was seven times more likely to marry a woman of lower social status than the other way around. Religious boundaries dictating choice of marriage partners did not begin to break down till after the 1960s. Parental disapproval of prospective partners often forbade further contact and there was virtually no hope of marriage unless the couple eloped.

In the Highlands and Islands (see HIGHLANDS AND ISLANDS: COMMUNITY LIFE), when the relationship advanced to a certain stage (ideally the young man had 'honourable intentions'), it was widely accepted that the couple would follow the custom of bundling—that is, spending the night lying together in bed, either fully clothed but separated by an ingenious blanket and/or bolster arrangement, or with the girl tied (by her mother) into a large stocking-like garment reaching her armpits and tied across her upper body. In most instances, chastity was expected and observed. Statistics of illegitimacy in the late 1800s indicate a lower rate where bundling prevailed than elsewhere—for example, the Isle of Lewis records less than 2 per cent, compared to 16 per cent in another area which forbade it.

In some areas (such as Orkney), where land inheritance was an important factor in choice of partner, it was desirable that a man should be certain his wife could produce a son and heir. It was quite common, therefore, for the couple to marry after the first son was born. Under Scottish law (though not English law) subsequent marriage legitimized children.

From the 17th century, bundling was denounced by clergy preaching disapproval and publicly shaming the guilty. Nevertheless, it survived until well into the 20th century when rural thatched houses, built only on ground level, gave way to two-storeyed houses, and the cinemas and dance halls in towns gave couples of the twenties and thirties greater freedom to spend time together.

After a couple had decided to marry, betrothal, the pledge of marriage, was expected by family and community. Although customs varied widely according to social class and locality, throughout the country a suitor was expected to ask his sweetheart's father for her hand in marriage. The widespread tradition of giving of a ring as a token of betrothal (a precursor to modern engagement rings), is said to derive from a Roman custom, with the ring symbolizing fidelity. In Gaelic Scotland, however, a betrothal was celebrated with a *Reiteach*, common practice until after the Second World War, with a few isolated instances recorded in the 1980s. The groom and his closest friend, the 'best man', would visit the prospective bride's house, where they would engage the girl's father in a witty dialogue, traditionally based on symbolic references and double entendre. If permission to marry was granted, the father was given a bottle of whisky to toast the couple, who were presented with a *cuach-phòsda* (marriage cup), the traditional symbol of betrothal. Sharing this cup signified their pledge that, from the day they were united in marriage, they would drink from the cup of life together. The wedding ceremony usually took place within a few weeks.

Scots law (1999) recognizes two kinds of marriage: religious, performed by a celebrant authorized under the Marriage (Scotland) Act 1977, and civil, solemnized by an authorized registrar. Both require publication of notice (a safeguard against bigamy) and two witnesses. Couples must be over 16, not related in a way that prevents marriage, not of the same sex, and must be capable of understanding the ceremony. A third type, irregular marriage, is recognized by custom and repute of cohabitation, and dates back to 'handfasting', common all over Scotland till the 18th century. This ceremony took place on a quarter day, the Lammas Fair being most popular. Before two witnesses, the couple joined hands (sometimes across running water) and declared their intention to handfast. If the union proved successful, then a 'year and a day' later couples would exchange marriage vows before a clergyman. Eventually wiped out by the church, the custom dates to an era when remote communities had only one or two visits a year from an abbey or church. Rules governing handfast marriages provided for the care of children born to such a alliance, with the responsibility placed on the father until such time as the mother married.

While marriage laws remain consistent, there are as many variations in weddings as there are in social status, economic standing, and personality of individuals involved. Paradoxically, books of formal etiquette advise standard rules for all weddings, beginning with the preparation, which, in the 1990s, took over a year. Until the First World War, guests were personally invited by the bride and her 'best maid' just a few weeks, or even days, before the wedding. Printed stationery giving much longer notice became established as the norm by the 1950s, and has become increasingly formalized by computer technology.

Scottish marriage statistics from 1861 to 1980 show that, until 1970, May was consistently the least popular month for marriages. While the attitude reflects the old saying 'Marry in May and you'll rue the day', the custom may date to ancient Roman customs. Some areas also favour one day of the week over another though there is no national preference. In a few places (for example, Shetland) marriage had to begin with the new moon.

Until the late 19th century, where land and title were important to the marriage parties a contract of marriage was drawn up and signed prior to the wedding. Though the custom has virtually died out, the 1980s and 1990s produced a few revivals in the form of prenuptial agreements. Older contracts usually involved the payment of a dowry by the bride's father to the groom. While the rich agreed upon fortunes and material goods, folk of modest means offered 'mairriage gere' or 'mairriage gude' (15th and 16th centuries), a 'tocher' or a 'portion' (16th to 19th centuries), usually paid in cows, sheep, and goats.

By the 20th century, the dowry was becoming obsolete, though preparation still included the 'plenisin'. Brides were (and some still are) encouraged to keep a 'bottom drawer' to prepare for marriage. The intention was not only to equip the future home but also to show the groom's family her values of industry, economic sense, and skill in handicrafts.

Etiquette books have never succeeded in influencing the high-spirited pre-wedding customs that have characterized Scottish weddings for centuries. Friends of the couple hold a celebration, traditionally a night or two before the wedding, which many couples try to avoid because of its humiliating consequences. Most, though not all, are single-sex events, popularly known as the feet-washing, blackening, bottling, bottlin', hen-night, stag-party, or pay-off. Some involve dressing up in colourful, hilarious, or ridiculous attire, or stripping the groom naked to 'tar [treacle, oil] and feather' him, and all include drinking as a main activity. Good fun is the order of the night, though licence is taken over definition and some have ended in injury and offence. Many incorporate ancient symbols of silver and salt as the bride carries a chamber pot filled with salt into which passers-by press a coin, sometimes in exchange for a kiss.

The wedding trousseau ('mairriage braws'), chosen by the bride and her mother in the 20th century, were once bought by the groom who would take pride in buying his bride's wedding outfit. As it would usually be kept for 'best dress' afterwards,

practical colours were common, apart from green, regarded as bad luck (or the colour of the fairies), and black, signifying mourning. While veils are an ancient symbol of the bride's submission to her husband, the wearing of a white or ivory wedding dress is comparatively recent.

Fashions for the groom's wedding clothes have changed just as much as the bride's, especially in the Lowlands where, in the 1980s and 1990s, the kilt became the order of the day, even for men who had never worn one in their lives. Members of the wedding party usually wear or carry flowers, usually one white carnation for the groom and red for his attendants, while the bride and her bridesmaids carry bouquets or posies of their choice. Many, however, avoid colours regarded as bad luck or suggesting death, especially red and white flowers together without the inclusion of another colour.

Wedding rings have also undergone changes in fashion for, although a gold band is the recognized symbol of today, during the 15th, 16th, and 17th centuries gold rings with two clasped hands were common. Until the 17th century 'spousing rings' were worn on the right hand and, although they remained part of the wedding ceremony in the Catholic Church, during the Reformation period no rings were exchanged at weddings. Eventually, during the reign of Charles I, the custom was re-established with the left hand as standard throughout Britain, apart from St Kilda where wedding rings were not part of the ceremony even in the 20th century.

As it is considered unlucky for couples to see one another the night before the wedding, the groom usually spends the night with his best man and the bride with her bridesmaid or sisters. Religious marriage ceremonies were commonly held in the manse or church for a modest fee (one guinea (£1.05) in the 1940s) or outdoors. Since the 1950s, most are solemnized in a church, chapel, or, if civil, in a registry office.

Although wedding presents are usually brought to the reception nowadays (apart from items too big to carry), it was customary to deliver the present to the bride's parents' house a few days before the wedding. Today's lavish presents bear no resemblance to typical gifts from the past, and, till after the Second World War, wedding presents were often a contribution to the wedding feast. In rural Scotland, gifts such as oatmeal, butter, whisky, dried fish, salted mutton, pieces of stoneware, or small household items were frequently given, while the most common gift of all was a hen for the feast. Then, a few nights before the wedding, the bride, her mother, sisters, and female friends got together to pluck and prepare them and to prepare the entire bridal feast. The hard work was made light by the hilarity and banter among the women—thus the origin of the 'hen-party' of the late 20th century.

Although commercial bakers have mostly taken over the baking of wedding cakes, it was generally done by one of the women, who gave it as a gift. Tradition dictated it had to be as rich a fruit cake as they could afford, and decorated with icing and symbols of good luck, such as five or six small ornamental silver horseshoes and white heather. After the ceremonial cutting of the cake, it was the custom to give these ornaments, known as 'favours', to selected female guests at the wedding. At the close of the 20th century this custom seemed to have all but disappeared, with the widespread takeover of commercially produced 'favours' which reflect the Italian tradition of giving sugared almonds to all female guests.

Showering the bridal couple with confetti is a more modern version of throwing rice or other grain, symbols of fertility in many cultures. The ecological conscience of the early 21st century now discourages this practice as does the beadle who had to sweep up. Another much-observed Scottish custom is the 'poor-oot' or 'scatter' which takes place on leaving the church (or manse). When the bride and groom emerge from the church, he throws a handful of coins from his pocket, and youngsters waiting outside scramble for them. Less common are 'racin', 'ropin', and 'playing the marriage ba', all of which involve competing for a reward of money, whisky, and/or a kiss from the bride.

In small or rural communities, bridal processions from the ceremony to the reception were nearly always on foot, with piper or fiddler leading the procession. The chosen venue was often a barn, cleared out and swept for the night, or a community hall rented from church, Masonic order, or local co-operative. Tables are laid out following accepted formalities, with the top table for bride, groom, and wedding party. The meal or 'feast' is followed by speeches and toasts from the bride's father, the best man, and the groom. Once over, the tables are cleared away for the dance which traditionally begins with the bride and groom dancing the first dance together and may last till the early hours of the next morning. Fiddles and bagpipes supplied the music of the past while dance bands now take over that role.

From the early 1600s to 1970 couples with very little money would hold a Penny Wedding, inviting friends and family to contribute to the cost. The ceremony usually took place on a Thursday, and, depending on the contributions, celebrations could last until the following Sunday when the wedding party attended a special church service where the bride was 'kirked'.

Before the days of easy transport and accessibility to hotels, a bridal couple would usually spent the wedding night in the bride's parents' home. At her official 'beddin', the bride was undressed for bed by her attendants who, midst mirth and laughter, would combine modesty with seductiveness. Once in bed, the bride flung her stocking among her friends, all eager to catch it, for the girl who succeeded would be the next to be married. In modern times, this custom is reflected in throwing the bouquet among the unmarried female guests, and, at some weddings, the garter among the unmarried males.

Honeymoons were not a standard expectation of earlier centuries and, compared to the early 21st century, were very modest. If the couple could afford to do so, townsfolk would simply spend two or three days' holiday in the country, and country folk a few days in the town. Afterwards, many couples began married life in the home of parents and it was customary for the groom to carry his bride over the threshold as his first gesture of commitment to protecting his wife from all harm. The custom dates to an era when the threshold was considered to be the place where evil spirits might lurk, though it was eventually adopted by wedding photographers as an attractive pose for a picture.

Wedding photographs, an important consideration since the late 19th century, not only retain personal memories but record trends in customs and fashions. As the 20th century closed, video recording was becoming standard at weddings in Scotland. Although modern weddings still reflect traditional Scottish customs, there is increasing pressure to conform to the dictates of market-driven bridal consultancies determined to homogenize weddings throughout Britain, which, according to the *Sunday Telegraph*, March 1999, cost an average of £11,000. (See also CALENDAR AND SEASONAL CUSTOMS; FAMILY; WOMEN.)   MBe

Covenant, Wars of the. The Wars of the Covenant, which lasted from 1639 until 1651, had their origins in the conflict between Charles I, king of Scotland since 1625 although not crowned as such in Edinburgh until 1633, and the emergence of the Scottish Covenanting movement as a national movement of opposition. Constitutional disaffection had emerged due to the subordination of parliament to the royal prerogative and the stifling of dissent from the political nation. Religious disaffection had emerged through a fear of Anglicization of the Church of Scotland through the reform programme of William Laud, Archbishop of Canterbury, the introduction of the Book of Common Prayer without the consent of the General

Assembly, and the employment of clerics in the offices of the Scottish state, thus breaching the separate spheres of church and state in Scottish Presbyterianism. Economic grievances were based mainly on the Revocation Scheme, which was perceived as an attack on the vested interests of the Scottish landed elites.

By 1638 an organizational structure had emerged, based on the Tables (nobles, lairds, burgesses, and ministers), with leadership invested in the fifth table, the executive table. The Tables had been involved in the organization of petitions and supplications against the Prayer Book from the Scottish localities. Covenanting ideology was incorporated in the 1638 *National Covenant, which included a demand for 'free' general assemblies and parliaments. The 1638 Glasgow Assembly proceeded to abolish episcopacy in Scotland, which then required constitutional sanction by *parliament. In military terms, the Covenanting armed forces were composed of many Scottish veterans of European warfare (such as in the Danish and Swedish armies), who had constituted one of the most successful Scottish export industries in the 1620s and 1630s. Swedish military influences were particularly important. Over a twelve-year period from 1639 to 1651 the Covenanters raised over twelve armies and one of the main devices used at the local level for recruitment was that of shire committees for war. These were appointed by parliament and contained the local MPs for the shire as well as other local landed dignitaries.

Charles I's determination to defeat his 'rebel' Scottish subjects resulted in a military confrontation between Covenanting armed forces and Charles's newly raised troops at Kelso in June 1639. This First Bishops' War resulted in stalemate and the 1639 Pacification of Berwick allowed for a parliament and general assembly to be held in Scotland. The 1639 General Assembly at Edinburgh ratified the abolition of episcopacy. By the time parliament convened on 31 August a radical political and constitutional agenda had been prepared by the Covenanters and John Stewart, earl of Traquair, King's Commissioner, was forced to prorogue the session in the face of this constitutional attack. The parliamentary sessions of 1640–1 enacted this constitutional agenda and the royal prerogative in Scotland was weakened whilst the powers of the Scottish parliament increased.

Charles I was forced to call a parliament in England, which had not met since 1629, in order to raise money to fight against the Covenanters in the Second Bishops' War of 1640. This then offered a forum in which English grievances could be raised against Charles I as king of England. Charles was defeated by a Covenanting armed force of around 18,000 troops in the Second Bishops' War at the battle of Newburn on 28 August 1640. The Scottish constitutional settlement of 1640–1 also provided a constitutional model for the English 'Long' Parliament to draw on. Charles was forced to come to Scotland in August 1641 personally to experience a reduction in his monarchical powers. Whilst in Edinburgh the Ulster rebellion broke out in October 1641 and, with the subsequent descent of England into civil war in 1642, the Scottish Covenanting movement became involved militarily in both England and *Ireland.

In terms of the Ulster crisis, the Covenanters had agreed with the English parliament to send 10,000 men to Ulster to crush the Irish rebels who had massacred their Protestant brethren. In fact over 11,371 men and officers had been sent to Ulster by the autumn of 1642. Scottish forces had their base in Carrickfergus and north-east Ulster was occupied. Scottish forces suffered a major defeat by Owen Roe O'Neill and the Irish Confederates at Benburb on 5 June 1646, although part of the force remained in Ulster until 1648 before it was withdrawn to help in the Royalist Engager invasion of England.

Rival appeals for Covenanting military aid came in 1642–3 from both the English Parliamentarians and the Royalists under Charles I in the aftermath of the inconclusive battle of Edgehill in England, such was the reputation of the Covenanting armed forces. The administration of Scotland was under Covenanting control through parliamentary interval committees established after the end of the 1641 parliament. In May 1643 these committees secured the calling of a convention of estates (similar to a parliament but with restricted powers) to arrange Covenanting intervention in the English Civil War. The upshot was the Solemn League and Covenant. Covenanting military aid was secured via the Treaty of Military Assistance, whilst the Solemn League and Covenant had an ideological price for military support. Presbyterianism was to be duly established in both England and Ireland.

Covenanting military forces crossed the border in two phases in January and June 1644. The January invasion force consisted of 18,000 foot, 3,000 horse, and 500–600 dragoons. The second force of June 1644 consisted of roughly 7,000–8,000 men. The coordination of military strategy was to be based on a new Anglo-Scottish structure for the war, namely the Committee for Both Kingdoms, although it remained an English committee in reality. Covenanting armed forces aided a Parliamentarian victory over the Royalists at the battle of Marston Moor, near York, on 2 July 1644.

The combination of a radical constitutional and political agenda, as pursued by the radical core of the movement, and Covenanting military involvement in the English Civil War on the side of the English Parliament resulted in a civil war within Scotland. Tension and splits within the movement had been evident as early in 1640, with the articulation of the Cumbernauld Bond, a conservative Covenanting reaction to the radical political agenda which was ultimately enacted in the Scottish Constitutional Settlement of 1640-1. James Graham, fifth earl and first marquis of Montrose, inflicted a series of military defeats of Covenanting forces (including victories at Tippermuir, Inverlochy, Auldearn, Alford, and Kilsyth) over a two-year period in 1644-5, thus destroying the reputation of the military prowess of the Covenanters. The civil war in Scotland was effectively ended by Montrose's defeat at Philiphaugh on 13 September 1645. Fining of rebels and the confiscation of estates were incorporated in the Act of Classes of 8 January 1646.

Wider developments in British politics resulted in the withdrawal of Covenanting armed forces from English soil in 1647 in return for the payment of arrears of pay due to the Covenanters by the English parliament (which amounted to £4.8 million Scots). This emanated from a growing tension in Anglo-Scottish relations over the jurisdiction of the king on English soil, with the English parliament claiming sole jurisdiction over Charles I despite the fact that he was also king of Scots. The emergence of the New Model Army in England as an effective fighting force had reduced the need for Covenanting troops, whose reputation had been diminished by its lacklustre performance in the First English Civil War (1642-6).

The abandonment of Charles I to the English parliament had important political repercussions in Scotland, with a conservative Covenanting and Royalist reaction to defend the king. Its focal point was based on Charles's trusted adviser at the outset of the 'troubles', James, third marquis and first duke of Hamilton. The Engagement Treaty was agreed with the king on 26 December 1647 and the 1648 Scottish parliament, the 'Engagement' Parliament, contained a majority of MPs who wanted to defend the king, although a smaller element of radical diehards was also present. In the summer of 1648 a force of 14,000-15,000 troops entered England to defend the king. This invasion, known as the 'Engagement', was disastrous and resulted in defeat at the hands of Oliver Cromwell at the battle of Preston on 3 September 1648. Not only was this disastrous for the king's cause on a British basis, but it also resulted in a putsch of radical *Covenanters and an armed attack on Edinburgh known as the Whiggamore raid. Emanating primarily from the Covenanting heartlands of the south-west and initially backed by Oliver Cromwell, a radical political

regime was established in Edinburgh. Politically exclusive in outlook, and staffed solely by those who had been vetted by the regime's leadership, the 1649 Scottish parliament and the Commission of the Kirk of the General Assembly of the Church of Scotland sought to create a Covenanted godly state in Scotland. Social and moral legislation was enacted against sins such as fornication and drunkenness, whilst 1649 was one of the major peaks of the *witch-hunt in Scotland. 'New men' came into Scottish politics and anti-aristocratic legislation was also enacted, especially concerning the traditional rights of the nobility over patronage.

The execution of Charles I as king of England in January 1649 by a minority of the English political nation was crucial to the continuation of the Wars of the Covenant. The Scots had not been consulted over the execution. The response of this radical regime was immediate when news of Charles's execution reached Edinburgh. The prince of Wales was proclaimed as Charles II, king of Great Britain, France, and Ireland, on 5 February 1649, although he would be required to be a Covenanted king of three Covenanted kingdoms with Presbyterianism established in both England and Ireland. The terms and conditions of Charles's admission to the office of monarchy were laid down in the Act anent the Securing of Religion and Peace of the Kingdom of 7 February 1649. The resurrection of monarchy on a British basis ensured that there would be a further Anglo-Scottish conflict following the abolition of monarchy in England. The final stage of the Wars of the Covenant in 1650-1 was essentially a clash between two godly Protestant nations for supremacy in the eyes of the Lord.

Cromwell's subjugation of *Ireland in 1649 ensured that his military resources could be more directly focused on Scotland. Cromwell's invading army of 16,000 troops crossed the border on 22 July 1650 in the aftermath of Montrose's abortive rebellion and defeat in the Orkneys at Carbisdale on 27 April 1650 (Montrose was ultimately executed on 21 May 1650). The ability to resist a Cromwellian advance was fundamentally weakened by three factors. First, the drive for social and moral purity as part of the godly state was extended into the military sphere. Only the godly were deemed worthy of military service and the ungodly were to be purged from the armed forces. Driven primarily by the religious zealots in the church, committees for purging the army were set up by the Scottish parliament as part and parcel of the process of the extermination of sin from the land and national purification. Military purging became particularly prevalent in the aftermath of the battle of Dunbar on 3 September 1650, which was perceived to be a reflection of God's wrath on the ungodly. Fourteen thousand men were lost at Dunbar (with 4,000 killed and 10,000 captured), despite the fact that the Covenanters had a superior strategic position and superior numbers (20,000 to Cromwell's 11,000). Cromwellian victory at Dunbar led to the occupation of south-east Scotland, whilst victory at Hamilton on 1 December effectively led to the occupation of the south-west.

The second weakening factor to Cromwellian advance was based on political factionalism and the exclusive political nature of the radical regime. Royalists and Engagers were excluded from military service as well as political participation. A patriotic political accommodation slowly emerged in 1650–1, in consultation with the church, but only in the face of intense ideological division—the third weakening factor hindering unity. Royalists in the north-east of Scotland issued the Northern Band and Oath of Engagement calling for national unity to defend the kingdom, whilst Covenanting hardliners in the south-west, as articulated in the Western Remonstrance, refused to acknowledge Charles II as king because he was ungodly. Charles II was eventually crowned as king of Great Britain and Ireland at *Scone on 1 January 1651, but was subjected to a humiliating sermon by Robert Douglas, moderator of the General Assembly, on the sins of his father and grandfather and the need for a fuller 'reformation' of the land (which was to include the royal family).

In military terms, the 'Public Resolutions', issued by the Commission of the Kirk on 14 December 1650, allowed former Engagers into the armed forces. A Committee for Managing the Affairs of the Army was formed on 28 March 1651 to allow Royalists, still excluded from participation in public office under the 1649 Act of Classes, access to the policy-making process for military affairs. The Acts of Classes of 1646 and 1649 were not finally repealed until June 1651. Reconciliation came too late, however, and by the summer of 1651 the Cromwellian penetration into Scotland was well underway with a further victory at Inverkeithing on 20 July and the occupation of Perth on 2 August. The Wars of the Covenant ended with military defeat at the battle of Worcester on 3 September 1651, with Charles II having invaded England to secure the support of English Royalists to his cause. Royalist forces were routed by superior numbers and Charles II fled into exile. Many of the captured Scots were never to see their homeland again and Scotland was subjected to a military and administrative occupation. The outbreak of the Covenanting revolution in Scotland had turned full circle and resulted in a military conquest of Scotland. (See also ARMY: 2; CHURCH INSTITUTIONS: 4; IRELAND: 2; WARFARE, WEAPONS, AND FORTIFICATIONS: 4). JY

Covenanters was the popular term for those who resisted the Restoration church settlement in Scotland. The *Restoration regime in Scotland, which came to power in 1660–2, abolished the Covenants (see NATIONAL COVENANT AND SOLEMN LEAGUE AND COVENANT) and all legislation enacted by Covenanting governments, whilst re-establishing crown control of the Church of Scotland; however, the issues of doctrine and worship which formed a key part of the original Covenanting movement did not resurface. The struggle now focused fully on the extent to which the crown could exert its supremacy in church matters. One way of resisting this new settlement was to proclaim adherence to and to reswear the Covenants, but in fact, the resistance took a variety of forms and ended up by jettisoning the commitment to the Covenants altogether.

The initial phase of the struggle was precipitated by the Acts of Parliament of 27 May and 11 June 1662 which reinstated episcopacy and patronage. As a result, all ministers who had been ordained and called after 1649 had to seek presentation from the lay patron and the relevant diocesan bishop. This was followed in October by an Act of Council which punished nonconforming ministers with ejection and banished them from residing in their former charges. The scale of the exodus provoked, especially in Fife and the south-west, caused an instant crisis: as many as 270 ministers left their charges. They were hard to replace. The Act did not eject ministers called before 1649, thus ensuring that an influential Presbyterian 'passive resistance' remained in an outwardly Episcopalian church. Some ministers resisting the new settlement were within the church, some were outside it, and the most radical few had already, even at this early stage, taken refuge in the Netherlands from whence would issue a steady stream of inflammatory literature and missionaries over the years to come.

The outed ministers almost immediately began to hold illegal conventicles. Many of them defied the terms of the Act and continued to minister to their old parishioners. The government soon acted against this. The repression which followed, particularly in the west, led to the abortive Pentland rising of 1669, which was crushed at the battle of Rullion Green. The bloodshed and executions involved led to a change of policy under the duke of Lauderdale, who resorted to the tactic of Indulgences, in both 1669 and 1672. These were a limited toleration of Presbyterian worship under what were supposed to be strictly controlled conditions. Lauderdale's aim was to make the efforts of the Presbyterian clergy ineffectual by confining them in out-of-the-way parishes where they would have nothing to do but preach to the converted. Contrary to the duke's intention, the Presbyterians used the Indulgences successfully to organize a church within the church which pursued a broad range of resistance strategies.

In the west, indulged and non-indulged Presbyterian ministers co-operated, forming presbyteries, coordinating preaching, and licensing probationers. In the east, preachers such as John Welsh swooped into episcopally controlled areas such as Fife, to hold large-scale armed conventicles. They could not offer an alternative church structure there, because there were no indulged ministers to provide a base for these tactics, but they could and did provide a powerful show of resistance. This was the pattern for the 1670s, and it is at this point that an extremist group, later to call itself the United Societies but better known as the Cameronians, began to emerge.

A group of extremists were responsible for the assassination of Archbishop Sharp in 1678. They fled to join radical co-religionists in the west and were involved in initiating the failed Bothwell Bridge rising of 1679. The government tried again the pattern of savage repression followed by Indulgence, only for the new Indulgence to be revoked as the political situation became destabilized by worries over the succession of the Catholic James, duke of York (later James VII and II). In this disturbed situation, the government became ever more vigorous in pressing conformity: a policy which was to culminate in the frenzy of concentrated violence known as the 'Killing Times' in which almost 100 individuals, nearly all belonging to the radical Cameronian party, were summarily executed over a short period of months in 1685. The martyrology and mythology of the 'Killing Times' has often dominated the historiography of this entire period, despite the fact that it was a short-lived aberration affecting only the adherents of one tiny Presbyterian faction.

Eventually a policy of indulgence also prevailed under James, allowing the 'alternative' indulged Presbyterian Church to re-emerge, whilst the Cameronian radicals were all but extirpated. With the Revolution of 1688–9, this 'alternative church' was able to re-emerge as the established Church of Scotland, basing itself not on the Covenants but on the Westminster standards of 1647. The tiny Cameronian remnant protested bitterly against this settlement and went on to form its own denomination: the Reformed Presbyterian Church. (See also CHURCH INSTITUTIONS: 3–4; PROTESTANT SECTS AND DISESTABLISHMENT; RELIGIOUS LIFE: 4).   LY

Craig, John (1874–1957), leading Scottish industrialist whose business expertise resulted in him holding a large number of company directorships in the first half of the 20th century. In many ways,

Craig was emblematic of the large degree of interconnectedness which ran through Scottish industry in the inter-war era. He started out in the steel industry and became a leading light in Colvilles (see COLVILLE, DAVID). His reputation as an efficient administrator and company leader led to directorships with Harland and Wolff, the Belfast shipbuilding firm, the Lanarkshire Steel Company, and the Steel Company of Scotland. In the inter-war period he was a leading light in the Scottish industrial community and was prominent in offering advice to the government on how to rectify the structural imbalance in the Scottish economy, although like the majority of his peers, he preferred to pursue a 'wait and see' policy in the hope that things would pick up, rather than a programme of industrial diversification (see ECONOMIC POLICY: 4). As a man of wide-ranging business experience, Craig was appointed governor of the Bank of Scotland after the Second World War.   RJF

Craik, Sir Henry (1846–1927), educational administrator and Unionist politician. Craik was born in Glasgow, where he studied at the university and then at Balliol College, Oxford. After working as an examiner with the Committee of the (Privy) Council on Education, he was appointed in 1885 as the secretary of the newly established Scotch Education Department (see SCOTTISH OFFICE), the government department responsible for Scottish education (see SCHOOLS AND SCHOOLING: 4). He held the post until 1904, and laid the basis for Scottish school education until the present day. His first achievement was to end so-called payment by results, by which teachers in elementary schools were paid according to the results of their pupils in tests set by the schools inspectorate. This had been controversial in Scotland, and Craik shared the general Scottish view that teachers should be accorded as much professional autonomy as was consistent with a general governmental oversight of standards. Believing also in the value of a broad liberal education for all, he abolished fees in elementary schools and promoted the study in elementary and secondary schools of subjects beyond the core of reading, writing, and arithmetic; in particular, he was a proponent of physical education. He firmly believed in the value of secondary education, and sought to extend it and to raise its status by a new Leaving Certificate in 1888 (the main component of which, the Higher Grade, lasted unchanged in principle until the end of the 20th century). He broadened the social basis of secondary education by inaugurating Higher Grade schools and Supplementary Courses in elementary schools.

He was a *Unionist MP from 1906 until his death, speaking frequently on educational matters, and promoting the involvement of the state in education. He wrote prolifically on educational and literary topics. Although responsible for much of the distinctiveness of 20th-century Scottish education, he was also a firm opponent of Scottish Home Rule. LP

Crusades. 'You might have seen crowds of Scots, a people savage at home but unwarlike elsewhere, descend from their marshy lands, with bare legs, shaggy cloaks, their purse hanging from their shoulders; their copious arms seemed ridiculous to us, but they offered their faith and devotion as aid.' Thus one Picard writer described the impact of the summons of the First Crusade in 1095. The pope's intention in summoning Christendom to fight for the liberation of Jerusalem had been to recruit Frankish knights, but the papal appeal had wider repercussions, causing 'other peoples, not only from the mainland but from the isles of the sea and the dwellers in the furthest ocean' to set out for the Holy Land. Among them was Lagmann, king of *Man and the Isles.

Although French knights formed the mainstay of most crusader armies, participants from many other western nations took part as well. Prominent in the work of spreading news and recruiting were the Knights Templars and Hospitallers, who had several houses or 'preceptories' in Scotland, at Temple, Torphichen, and Maryculter. Hugh de Paiens, first Grand Master of the Temple, visited Scotland in 1128.

The presence of Scots was not always appreciated by their companions in arms. A Scottish contingent sailed in 1147 with a fleet of Normans, Germans, Flemings, and Englishmen, and assisted the king of Portugal at the siege of Lisbon while en route for Palestine. One commander, faced with a threat of desertion by English knights, made a rousing speech praising the steadfast loyalty of the Normans and Germans, then commented: 'Who would deny that the Scots are barbarians? Yet while in our company they have never broken the rules of loyalty and friendship.' The English remained with the army until Lisbon fell.

Even the saintly King Louis IX of France, who encountered Scots during his great Crusade of 1248–54, was not impressed by them. Within a few years of his return to France, he was exhorting his son to win the love of his people, 'for I would prefer that a Scot should come from Scotland and govern the people well and faithfully, than that you should be seen to govern them badly' (see FRANCO-SCOTTISH RELATIONS: 1).

For those Scots who made the journey, however, it was the adventure of a lifetime. A group of Orcadian crusaders boasted of their journey to Jerusalem in 1150 in runic graffiti cut into the walls of Maes Howe. A group of Gaelic-speaking crusaders from both sides of the Irish Sea preserved in verse a record of their anxieties, homesickness, and pride as they joined the Crusade against Damietta in Egypt in 1218–21. Among them was Muiredhach Ó Dálaigh, who became known as 'Scottish Murray' and was the ancestor of the famous bardic family of Mac Mhuirich.

A later writer commented of the Egyptian Crusade: 'A great multitude throughout the whole of Scotland . . . took the cross; few of them, however, were from among the rich and powerful of the kingdom.' One who was 'rich and powerful' was Saher de Quincy, lord of Leuchars and Tranent in Scotland and earl of Winchester in England, who died in the crusader camp at Damietta in November 1219. His father Robert de Quincy had been with Richard 'Cœur de Lion' on the Third Crusade (1190–3). It was probably Robert who founded a hospital of canons of the Church of Bethlehem at St Germains near Tranent in East Lothian.

The Scottish contingent which joined the first Crusade of Louis IX in 1248 was led by Earl Patrick of Dunbar, whose death at Marseilles was noted by writers in the Holy Land. Before his departure, his wife had founded a hospital of Trinitarian brothers 'for the Redemption of Captives of the Infidel' at Dunbar. A number of Scottish knights were in his company, and continued the journey to Palestine after his death.

The last of the great Crusades was the second journey of Louis IX in 1270. A separate English contingent on this expedition was led by Lord Edward, the future Edward I, and there were Scots among Lord Edward's company as well as in the retinue of the king of France. Louis's army met disaster when their assault on Tunis had to be abandoned because of disease ravaging their camp. Among the dead was the leader of the Scottish force, David, earl of Atholl. The Scots were thereafter led by Adam, earl of Carrick, who died at Acre the following year. Present with him in Palestine in 1271–2 were Robert Bruce of Annandale 'the Competitor' and his son Robert Bruce (later earl of Carrick). Soon after the younger Robert's return in 1273, he travelled to Carrick to visit Countess Marjorie, Earl Adam's widow. Marjorie allegedly compelled Robert to go with her to Turnberry castle, where she imprisoned him until he would consent to become her new husband.

Even after the loss of the Holy Land, the call to unite Christendom to fight for the recovery of Jerusalem continued to echo. While King *Robert I lay dying in 1329 he decreed that his heart should be carried on Crusade against God's enemies and buried at the Holy Sepulchre. The first part of his wish was fulfilled when Sir James Douglas died fighting against the Moors at the siege of Teba de Hardales in Spain in August 1330; but the second part was not, for the king's embalmed heart was brought back and buried in Melrose abbey. Scots knights were present at the storming of Alexandria in 1365, and a few Scots are later recorded fighting against the Moors in Spain and elsewhere in the Mediterranean, most notably with the Knights Hospitallers of Rhodes (for example, Sir Colin Campbell of Glenorchy, d. 1480). Many Scots who wished to go on campaigns for Christendom in the later Middle Ages joined the forces of the Teutonic Knights fighting against heathen Lithuania, but a combination of the conversion of Lithuania to Christianity and the defeat of the Teutonic Knights at Tannenberg in 1410 effectively ended the Northern Crusade.

The appeal of Jerusalem and the concept of Christian unity for its recovery persisted for centuries after any realistic possibility had passed. Even as Erasmus was condemning Christian warfare against the Turks, King *James IV was vainly appealing to the monarchs of Europe to set aside their ambitions and unite in the face of the Turkish threat. His failure led him to defeat and death at Flodden in 1513; rumours persisted after the battle that he had survived, badly wounded, and had gone to live as a hermit in the Holy Land.   AMac

culture: 1. prehistoric Scotland; 2. Picto-Celtic; 3. medieval; 4. Renaissance and Reformation (1460–1660): general; 5. Renaissance and Reformation (1460–1660): philosophy; 6. Renaissance and Reformation (1460–1660): language and literature; 7. Renaissance and Reformation (1460–1660): literature; 8. Renaissance and Reformation (1460–1660): art; 9. Renaissance and Reformation: poetry, to 1603; 10. Renaissance and Reformation (1460–1660): music; 11. Enlightenment (1660–1843): general (including philosophy); 12. Enlightenment (1660–1843): art; 13. Enlightenment (1660–1843): language and literature; 14. Enlightenment (1660–1843): the novel; 15. Enlightenment (1660–1843): music; 16. Enlightenment (1660–1843): medicine; 17. age of industry (1843–1914): general; 18. age of industry (1843–1914): art; 19. age of industry (1843–1914): medicine; 20. age of industry (1843–1914): literature; 21. modern times (1914–1990s): general; 22. modern times (1914–1990s): art; 23. modern times (1914–1990s): medicine and medical achievements; 24. modern times (1914–1990s): literature; 25. modern times (1914–1990s): the novel.

1. prehistoric Scotland

Prehistoric Scotland spans some eight millennia prior to the emergence of historic kingdoms in the 6th century AD. Without written sources, dating relies upon scientific methods such as radiocarbon analysis and dendrochronology, and the emphasis is on economic resources and changing modes of land-use rather than on artefact typologies.

There is no conclusive evidence for human colonization before the end of the last ice age, and the earliest known mesolithic campsite was Kinloch c.7000 BC. This was a mobile lifestyle based on seasonal hunting, fishing, and gathering wild foodstuffs, and camp sites tend to be coastal or in river valleys. The toolkit was characterized by flint microliths, which were set into bone or wooden handles. During the fourth millennium BC, this way of life was gradually transformed into a farming economy. Cattle, sheep, goats, and pigs were bred and barley and wheat were grown on permanent farms. Substantial houses and barns were built in stone, as at Skara Brae, or in wood, as at Balbridie, and monumental burial tombs were created for the ancestors. Other innovations were pottery and polished stone axes, both of which demonstrate cultural contacts over wide areas of Britain. The material record affords glimpses of belief and ritual and, from the early third millennium, overtly ceremonial monuments were built in the form of earthwork circles (henges), circles of timber posts, and circles and linear settings of standing stones.

The next major innovation, in the late third millennium, was *metalwork, initially in copper and gold and soon followed by copper alloyed with tin (bronze). Alongside was a new type of pottery (beakers), probably introduced by a small-scale immigration of settlers from western Europe. Funeral rites changed from communal burial in tombs to individual burial with personal gravegoods in stone cists. Bronze was used for axes, daggers, and jewellery, and later for spearheads, swords, and vessels. From the mid-first millennium BC, bronze was complemented by the use of iron for tools and weapons.

A combination of climatic deterioration (see CLIMATE), population pressure, and shortage of fertile farmland led to the adoption of fortifications from about the 9th century BC. Hilltops were fortified with timber stockades, earthen ramparts, and stone walls, within which lived communities from a few families to hundreds of people. In the north and west, stone-built roundhouses evolved by the 2nd century BC into massively walled small forts (duns) and towers (brochs). Society had become Celtic (see CULTURE: 2) in character, speaking a Celtic language (see GAELIC LANGUAGE) and using a European art style for prestigious jewellery and feasting equipment. The wheel had been in use throughout the first millennium BC.

Most of Scotland was little affected by the Roman military presence in the 1st–3rd centuries

AD, although Roman goods were widespread through trade, loot, or gifts. Supplying food to the Roman army may account for the large underground storehouses (souterrains) of Angus and Perthshire in the 1st and 2nd centuries. Large quantities of late Roman silver were in circulation either as political bribes or as loot, and much was melted down and reused by the *Picts (see NORTHERN ENGLAND AND SOUTHERN SCOTLAND: ROMAN OCCUPATION). AR

2. Picto-Celtic

Picto-Celtic describes the artefacts, architecture, and burials of the inhabitants of Scotland between the 3rd and the 9th centuries AD. *Picts, Britons, and Gaels shared the same basic material culture, reflecting their common Celtic ancestry. Their lifestyle centred around a mixed farming economy and a social hierarchy of which the upper echelons are better known than the lower. This is text-aided archaeology, but historical dates have increasingly been complemented by scientific dates, as greater precision has made radiocarbon dating a more useful tool.

Several forts mentioned in historical records have been proven by excavation (for example *Dunadd, *Dundurn, Dunollie). Isolated rocky hills and stacks were favoured locations, as were coastal promontories, defended by ramparts of stone or earth, sometimes strengthened by a timber framework. Dunadd has an upper citadel where the chieftain's hall is likely to have been situated and lower walled terraces for housing, workshops, barns, and stables. The largest fort was *Burghead, a coastal promontory on the Moray Firth, where an inner citadel and lower enclosure were fortified not only by a timber-framed wall but also by a series of ramparts and ditches cutting off the landward approach.

Such high-status sites provide evidence of trading networks and fine *metalwork. Sherds of distinctive pottery and glass imply the importation of wine and olive oil from France in the 6th and 7th centuries, for which furs and slaves were probably exchanged. Jewellers created brooches and dress-pins for their wealthy patrons, and silver was used by the Picts both for jewellery and tableware. Scholars remain divided over the massive silver chains found both north and south of the Forth: were they Pictish or British royal regalia?

These were centres of population in a landscape peopled mostly by small farming communities. Here the buildings show a mixture of rectilinear and curvilinear plans and the use of stone or timber according to available materials. Cattle, sheep, and pigs were bred, and depictions of horses on sculpture are witness to their importance for transport

and the hunting activities beloved of the aristocracy. Barley, wheat, oats, and rye were grown; wild boar and deer were hunted; and the sea was exploited for fish, shellfish, seals, and whales. Burials were inhumations in long cists, over which the Picts built round or square mounds.

Unique to the Picts were symbol stones. From the mid-6th century, stones were incised with a system of graphic symbols that was uniform throughout Pictland. It included abstract symbols, together with realistic depictions of artefacts such as mirrors and combs and of birds and animals such as the goose, horse, and serpent. Symbol stones are thought to have acted as personal memorials, boundary markers, and kinship memorials. With the adoption of Christianity (see RELIGIOUS LIFE: 1) in Pictland by the early 8th century, Christian symbols were added to the sculptor's repertoire (see MONUMENTS: 1). On cross-slabs, the cross and figural scenes from the Bible were carved in relief, along with Pictish symbols and hunting scenes. The earliest symbol stones were around the Moray Firth, whereas the earliest of these cross-slabs appeared in Strathmore. AR

3. medieval

In the 1560s, the Edinburgh lawyer George Bannatyne began compiling a manuscript collection of Scotland's surviving poetry. Probably intended for a middle-class and professional literary circle in the capital, the *Bannatyne Manuscript* is one of the very few links which we have with Scotland's medieval literary heritage. It contains the surviving copy of a number of poems by even the most celebrated of the makars, such as Robert Henryson and William Dunbar (see CULTURE: 9). And one of Dunbar's poems lists a number of poets whose names are otherwise totally unknown. We should probably not be surprised by the paucity of the medieval inheritance. The problem of 'survivalism' persisted into the 16th century, even after the setting-up of Scotland's first printing press in 1507 (see PRINTING AND PUBLISHING). Only twenty works printed in Scotland survive for the period between then and 1540. Manuscripts must have been more vulnerable still. The work of Robert Carver, musician, composer, and Augustinian canon of Scone, has survived only by accident and often in unintended fragments, including a single choirbook now known as the *Carver Choirbook* (see MUSIC, ECCLESIASTICAL). 'Musick fyne' has been a notable rediscovery of the 20th century.

Whereas the cultural legacy of the *Picts still survives in the form of standing stones or other striking, physical artefacts such as the St Andrews sarcophagus (see MONUMENTS: 1) in the landscape, the medieval world we have lost is much more difficult to recapture. There are, in textbooks on medieval Scotland, conspicuously few pages or even index entries devoted to culture. The recent preoccupation of many medieval historians has been with issues of lordship, power, and politics; the *nobility had power, patronage, a near-monopoly of violence, few scruples, and no souls. It is little wonder that, as a result, after the *Reformation, when more records become available to give a more complete picture, the noble acquires piety, a conscience, and a fear of death, and is transformed into the 'godly magistrate'. Yet that impression is almost certainly a distortion of a more complex picture. It has been noticed only recently how nobles, when elevated to the new status of 'Lords of Parliament' in the 1450s, demonstrated their enhanced status by the founding of collegiate churches, such as those at Crichton, Rosslyn, and Kilmaurs. Religious patronage was almost certainly expanding down through the layers of both rural and urban establishments in the later Middle Ages and this was, in turn, a reflection of new patterns of piety amongst the laity (see RELIGIOUS LIFE: 2).

It remains true, nonetheless, that much culture—and especially most literature—was centred in the royal court and was the product of churchmen. *Schools and schooling, ranging from the urban song schools to the 'great schools' or *universities, first founded in Scotland in the 15th century, were run by clerics. They were both the guardians and the manufacturers of the archive of national memories (see NATIONAL IDENTITY: 1–3). Almost invariably, what literary work, poetic as well as in chronicle form, survives from the 14th or 15th centuries was written by ecclesiastics. The exceptions are so few that the more prominent are worth noting. The *Kingis Quair* was the work of an ambitious king, James I. *The Wallace*, a work which heavily influenced the errors and infelicities in the film *Braveheart*, was written by 'Henry the Minstrel', otherwise known as Blind Harry. New developments in the 15th century, most notably the founding of a dozen houses of the reformed Observant Franciscan order of friars, reinforced rather than slackened the grip of the clergy on court and other culture. A good deal of the literature of the Passion, which swamped devotions in the later 15th century, was Observant Franciscan in impulse. One notable work was the *Contemplacioun of Synnaris* (c.1497), a Lenten observance written by William of Touris, who was probably a laird's son, for *James IV.

What remains largely unknown (except in specific instances such as the *Contemplacioun*) is not authorship or artistic patronage but the audience. By the 1560s, as we have seen, a literary circle had

extended downwards to the professional and merchant classes. It is uncertain how far it extended beyond the new Lords of Parliament a century before that. But one notable example is suggestive. In 1451, St Giles's in Edinburgh was elevated to collegiate status. A prominent local landowning family, the Prestons of Craigmillar, somehow managed to acquire a precious relic—the armbone of St Giles, almost certainly a secondary relic—from Bruges, Scotland's old *staple port in the *Low Countries. From this, there developed a civic cult, with its high point in the annual procession on the feast day of the saint (1 September), with the precious relic paraded through the burgh. The old concept of the burgh as a *corpus christianum* had new life breathed into it. And the traditional concept of a hierarchy, underpinned by the Great Chain of Being, was reinforced by the procession of the burgh's worthies, headed by the local lord, through the streets of the town. New saints' cults were almost certainly reaching a new and wider audience in the 15th century.

Almost all the surviving literary works of the pre-1500 period were, in one sense, in the genre of 'mirror of princes' literature: they included, in the period of the Stewart dynasty (see KINGSHIP: 5) up to the death of James II, the celebrated *The Brus* (1375) by John Barbour, cast as a heroic romance; the anonymous and less well-known pieces *Buik of Alexander* (c.1438), a Latin text known in translation as *Buke of Gud Consaill* (c.1455–60), and Richard Holland's *The Buke of the Howlat* (c.1448). This might in turn suggest the centrality of the *royal court as a cultural dynamic. Yet the effect of two changes of dynasty, with the successive failures of the Canmore and Bruce dynasties (see KINGSHIP: 3–4), and the remarkable habit of Stewart monarchs of dying young and leaving long minorities after them must have had an unsettling impact on the culture of the royal court. Some of these few surviving works, however, are known to have been commissioned by, or dedicated to, nobles or even small landowners. The massive *Scotichronicon*, by Walter Bower, recently published in a a definitive edition, was dedicated to the laird of Rosyth and *The Buke of the Howlat* acknowledged the Black *Douglas family as its patron.

In sharp contrast to England, the 'stripping of altars' was wholesale in Scotland in and after the *Reformation (see ICONOCLASM). As a result, very little evidence of late medieval worship or civic ceremony exists: only two medieval altarpieces survive, the most celebrated being in the parish church of Foulis Easter in Angus. The incorporation of urban craft guilds took place in the half-century after 1475. On incorporation, each craft founded an altar dedicated to its patron saint, such as St Crispin for the skinners or St Eloi for the metalworkers. The cult of these craft and other saints, which was a notable feature of late medieval *urban society, has all but disappeared from view. Only two craft banners remain intact: one is the banner of the incorporation of glovers of *Perth, saved from destruction because it was at the menders on the day of the Protestant riot orchestrated by John *Knox; the other is the incomplete so-called Fetternear Banner (now in the *Royal Museum of Scotland), which belonged to the prestigious Edinburgh merchant guild and survived by being hidden in the obscure backwater of Fetternear. Very few churches survive in anything like their medieval form. Most monasteries probably suffered from neglect rather than calculated destruction after 1560 because, as at Melrose, only part of the large abbey complex was put to use—a central part of the nave, pressed into service as the parish church for the small population of the town (see CHURCHES: 1). Others, however, such as the great Charterhouse and the friaries at Perth, were subjected to calculated destruction, both of the structure and of the contents including library and archives. Those in Perth were reduced to the ground within 24 hours of an inflammatory sermon by Knox. It is in remoter places, such as the Isle of Inchcolm in the Forth estuary, where robbing stone was more difficult, that most of the best-preserved ecclesiastical buildings survive in something like their original structure.

Some of the losses undoubtedly were the result of calculated iconoclasm by Protestant reformers in and after the Reformation. In 1560, one of the first actions of the new General Assembly was to order the dismantling, stone by stone, of the royal chapel at Restalrig, just outside Edinburgh, which had been the centre of the new chivalric order of St Andrew, founded by James III partly in imitation of the Order of the Golden Fleece of the dukes of Burgundy, also dedicated to Andrew. There are hints, too, in some post-Reformation records such as the register of Stirling presbytery, of a systematic and sustained campaign of the burning of Mass books, psalters, and books of hours as well as statues and relics during the 1560s and 1570s.

With little evidence to go on, it becomes necessary to work harder later sources, such as the *Banntayne Miscellany*, a treasure trove of vernacular poetry in the *Scots language. In the same way, the *Aberdeen Breviary* (1509–10), a collection of saints' lives brought together by William Elphinstone, bishop of Aberdeen, can be used as a depository of earlier medieval material. The *Breviary* contained some new, upmarket Continental saints but otherwise its conscious intent seems to be the creation of a national hagiography: national saints such as Ninian (see WHITHORN), *Columba, and

*Margaret feature in it, but there was also an attempt to include a sprinkling of saints from every one of Scotland's dioceses, as well as some obscure local saints. The chronicler Hector Boece, appointed as the first rector of Elphinstone's new University of Aberdeen, recounts in his *Vitae* of the bishops of Aberdeen how Elphinstone 'sought out in many places' the legends of the saints included in the *Breviary*. Not all have been identified because some do not survive elsewhere but it is clear that Elphinstone culled sources ranging in period from at least the 12th century to the later 15th. One obvious example of any early source is Turgot's early 12th-century hagiography of St Margaret, who experienced a remarkable revival in the reigns of James III and *James IV, no doubt helped by the fact that two successive pious queens of Scots— Margaret of Denmark and Margaret Tudor— shared her name.

The great national chronicles of Scotland written between the 1380s and the 1440s, most notably by John of Fordun and Walter Bower (see HISTORIANS: 1) also included substantial earlier and otherwise unique material. Fordun's chronicle, for example, recycled a life of St Kentigern compiled for Bishop Herbert of Glasgow (1147–64). Bower appropriated a number of earlier Irish saints' lives on the slender basis that they were 'Scoti', many belonging to the period before 650 (see IRELAND: 2). And other foreign legends and cults, both English and Continental, were similarly raided and domesticated for native use.

It was the 12th century, the period of the new, Continental religious orders and a reorganization of dioceses and parishes (see CHURCH INSTITUTIONS: 2), which was, perversely, the high point of *vitae* and other hagiography of early Celtic and other early native saints. Foundation legends for religious centres, both new and old (such as *St Andrews, *Glasgow, and Dunkeld), were embellished or invented. The 15th century, which saw a range of new contacts between the Scottish church and parts of the Continent, most notably the Low Countries, *France, and *Germany, witnessed another revival of old, native saints alongside new, fashionable Continental cults.

Typically, in culture, both religious and secular, new and old admixed and imported material was customized and given a Scots face. It is a well-known and repeated phenomenon in Scots architecture (see ARCHITECTS, ARTISTS, AND CRAFTSMEN). One early and important example is how 'palace' came to have a different meaning from its former strict meaning of *palatium* or great hall—a phenomenon probably first seen in Scotland with James I's audacious reconstruction of the palace of Linlithgow, an elaborate statement of royal power which scorned serious defences. Two non-architectural examples must suffice. The 15th century saw the revival of St Andrew as a royal saint. In a sense, this was part of a widespread revival of interest in native saints' cults. Ninian, Kentigern, and Columba all had new altars dedicated to them in both cathedrals and the new collegiate churches founded in the period. But Andrew was also a chivalric saint, who chimed in with the preoccupation of both kings and nobles with the cult of honour. The Order of the Golden Fleece, founded by Philip 'the Good', duke of Burgundy, had Andrew as its patron saint. So had James III's Order of St Andrew, founded 50 years later. And in secular literature, one of the most 'popular' works of the period seems to have been *Greysteil*, the translation into vigorous vernacular Scots of a French chivalric romance. Remarkably, it was still popular, to judge from booksellers' inventories, more than a century later in post-Reformation Scotland.

Written culture, and especially vernacular Scots, came to predominate during the 15th century, becoming the language of government. Yet its sources are fragile in volume. Little that is tangible survives to hint at either the interests or the wider impact of the royal court much before the reign of Robert II (1371–90), although it is safe to assume that much of its preoccupations would have lain in history, romance, and chivalry. It has been claimed that the *Romance of Fergus* by Guillaume le Clerc (William the Clerk), a pastiche of the Grail legend written in French, the natural language of the court in the reign of William I 'the Lion' (1165–1214), but put into a Scottish setting in *Galloway, is a sign of a cultural revival as well as a unique glimpse into the court life of the period, with William cast in the role of King Arthur. Yet, if so, within considerably less than a century of William's death, French had lost its prominence at court. The interest in romance and chivalry continued, but it was either of a customized variety, such as in the translation of *Greysteil*, or in devising home-grown epic romance, such as *The Brus*, in order to underline the legitimacy of the Stewart dynasty.

It is in oral culture, and especially that of the *Gaidhealtachd*, that it is more easy to be confident of a long process of cultural enrichment throughout the medieval period. Successive dynasties of the so-called 'learned orders' ensured the survival over generations of traditions of medical expertise (the family of Macbeth, later Beaton), piping (the Mac-Crimmons and others) (see MUSIC, HIGHLAND), harping (including the family of Mac an Bhreatnaigh, later Galbraith, in Gigha and Kintyre and the McMaschenachs, later MacShannons, who served the lord of the *Isles), and tale-telling (see ORAL TRADITION; SONG, TRADITIONAL AND FOLK: 2). It is

here that the best glimpse of the cultural legacy of the past is to be found. There still survived in the court of James IV the office of King's Harper, which can be traced back some seven centuries or more. It was probably for this reason that George Buchanan, a man of Lennox, in composing his *History of Scotland* (1582) assumed that the part of Scotland most in touch with its past was Gaelic society. Like the eleventh earl of Buchan, who felt impelled in 1781 to found the Society of Antiquaries of Scotland (out of which emerged the National Museum of Antiquities), in order to preserve what remained of a past which was by then fast slipping out of the memory, Buchanan, his contemporary George Bannatyne, and antiquarians who followed them by collecting what was left of earlier manuscripts and libraries helped to give us a glimpse today of the medieval world which we have largely lost.

ML

4. Renaissance and Reformation (1460–1660): general

Although remote from the main centres of European civilization, late medieval Scotland was by no means isolated from them. The Scottish kingdom had long maintained extensive trading and diplomatic links across the North Sea with the Baltic states (see GERMANY, THE BALTIC AND POLAND: 1), the *Low Countries, and *France, while the Scottish church (see CHURCH INSTITUTIONS: 2) was fully integrated with the legal and administrative structures, as well as the common Latin culture, that bound western Christendom together. Moreover, despite the foundation of three *universities in the 15th century (St Andrews 1411, Glasgow 1451, and Aberdeen 1495), Scots continued to seek further education in the intellectual centres of Europe. From Cologne to Bologna, but above all at Paris and Orléans, Scottish students and masters participated to the full in the learned world of contemporary Europe. If Scotland was fully integrated with the culture of Christendom, however, it was also fully exposed to the novel modes of thought that in the course of the 16th century were to tear Christendom apart. No less than the rest of Europe, Scotland was to be transformed by the combined impact of the Renaissance and Reformation.

Renaissance influences first become apparent at the *royal court. Fashion-conscious monarchs such as *James IV and *James V spent lavishly on equipping the Stewart dynasty with the trappings of Renaissance *kingship. An extensive building programme at royal palaces such as *Stirling created the appropriate architectural settings (see ARCHITECTS, ARTISTS, AND CRAFTSMEN) for the display of kingly magnificence, while the development of a chivalric cult of honour allowed for the self-conscious display of royal power. The spectacular tournaments staged by James IV in 1507 and 1508 betray strong Burgundian influence, but it was French models that subsequently came to predominate. France also inspired the symbolism that best encapsulated the Stewarts' aspirations as Renaissance monarchs. In the last *coinage of his reign (c.1485), James III was portrayed wearing an arched 'imperial' crown in what has been described as possibly the earliest Renaissance coin portrait to be minted outside Italy. Traditionally worn only by the Holy Roman Emperor, the arched or closed crown symbolized the complete territorial and jurisdictional sovereignty now being claimed by the monarchies of Renaissance Europe. By the beginning of the 16th century, when Bishop Elphinstone embellished the chapel of his new university chapel at Aberdeen with a crown steeple, imperial iconography was being vigorously exploited by the Stewarts to proclaim their status as Renaissance monarchs.

Such self-confidence stemmed in part from the Scottish elite's long exposure to European life and learning. Although more influential than most, Elphinstone was not untypical in using a Continental education as a stepping-stone to advancement in the royal bureaucracy as well as the church. Trained in law at Glasgow, Paris, and Orléans, he became both bishop of Aberdeen and a leading figure in James IV's government. Education abroad also ensured that the Scottish intelligentsia was well aware of the renewed interest in classical literature and learning that lay at the heart of Renaissance humanism. Just as Elphinstone possessed a copy of Lorenzo Valla's *Elegances of the Latin Language* (c.1440), a key text of humanist Latinity, so the Cologne-educated Archibald Whitelaw, royal secretary from 1462 to 1493, amassed a classical library that included a manuscript copy of Cicero's works as well as printed editions of Horace, Lucan, and Sallust. The influence of the printing press (see PRINTING AND PUBLISHING) was only just beginning to make itself felt in Europe, but the ability to mass-produce books was a technological innovation with massive cultural repercussions. Chepman and Myllar's Edinburgh printing press proved short-lived, but Whitelaw's library clearly indicates that Scots had ready access to the printed texts which, whether produced in Paris, Antwerp, or Venice, lay at the heart of the 'new learning' of the Renaissance.

While often rarefied and arcane, such learning also had direct practical application. It was Whitelaw's long tenure of the royal secretaryship that ensured that humanist rhetorical skills were institutionalized in the Scottish chancery just as they were in the chanceries of Europe generally. Among

Whitelaw's successors as royal secretary was the highly accomplished Latinist Partick Paniter, one of a remarkable group of Scots who in the 1490s were fellow students of Erasmus in Paris. Another was Hector Boece, author of the first humanist history of Scotland (see HISTORIANS: 2), the *Scotorum Historia* (Paris, 1527), who served for 30 years as principal of Elphinstone's new university at Aberdeen, establishing it as the main Scottish centre for the dissemination of the 'new learning'. Not all the Scottish universities proved as open as Aberdeen to humanist influences. The dominant figure at St Andrews was John Mair who had also studied in Paris with Erasmus, but who remained deeply sceptical of the humanist movement's championing of rhetoric over dialectic. Mair taught at Paris for 25 years, establishing a European reputation as a logician, philosopher, and theologian before returning to Scotland in 1518 to teach initially at Glasgow and then St Andrews. For all his commitment to traditional scholastic method, however, Mair was not unsympathetic to the humanists' key aim of creating an educated lay elite. Gradually, St Andrews and Glasgow were to follow Aberdeen's example and fashion an arts curriculum that was aimed at serving the laity as well as the clergy.

The emergence of a literate, often highly educated, lay elite was undoubtedly the most significant cultural development of the era. The spread of literacy from the upper *nobility and merchants (see URBAN SOCIETY: 2) to a wider population of lesser landowners and burgesses is reflected in the adoption of the *Scots language as the language of government as well as in the remarkable explosion of vernacular poetry (see CULTURE: 9), written for or by the laity, and best exemplified in the works of the great makars, Henryson, Dunbar, and Douglas. Of these three, only Gavin Douglas was deeply touched by humanism, translating Virgil's *Aeneid* into Scots for his lay patron, Lord Sinclair. Yet many laymen were becoming sufficiently accomplished in the language of learning to read such Latin texts for themselves. By the 1530s, it was common enough for laymen not only to have graduated in arts but also to have gone on to study law, often in France or Italy. Thus Sir James Foulis, the son of an Edinburgh burgess and an accomplished Latin poet, studied law in Paris and Orléans before serving as clerk-register from 1532 until 1549, while from 1526 to 1543 the post of royal secretary was held by Sir Thomas Erskine, a minor landowner who had studied law at Pavia.

These crucial social and cultural developments came to fruition during the personal rule of James V, whose glittering court was characterized by growing tension between an entrenched clerical hierarchy and educated laymen receptive to both

evangelical humanism and emergent Protestantism. The biting anticlerical verse of the king's
lifelong confidant Sir David Lindsay was initially
written for court consumption, but after James V's
death Lindsay reached out to a wider lay audience
in works such as his brilliant *Ane Satyre of the Thrie
Estaitis* (1552). Although later appropriated for Protestantism, Lindsay is best characterized as an Eras-
mian Catholic whose sometimes heterodox views
reflect both the fluidity of contemporary religious
opinion and the educated lay elite's deep dissatisfaction with the established church. The timing
and course of a distinctively Protestant *Reformation was determined primarily by political and
diplomatic circumstances. Yet the deep-seated
anticlericalism of a newly literate laity, fuelled by
access to printed English bibles, provided critical
purchase for the hard-line Protestant convictions
of reformers such as John *Knox.

The Reformation came comparatively late to
Scotland and in the form of a radical Calvinist biblicism. The result was a vision of a godly society,
modelled on Old Testament Israel, in which kirk
and community alike were strictly regulated by the
law of God as revealed in Scripture (see RELIGIOUS
LIFE: 3). The biblical fundamentalism of preachers
such as Knox both inspired the apocalyptic enthusiasm that ensured the success of the new reformed
kirk and legitimized the *iconoclasm that led to the
destruction of much of the material remains of
Scotland's once flourishing medieval and Renaissance culture. It did not, however, happen overnight. The establishment of the reformed kirk, and
the spread of Christian discipline into the localities,
was a slow and painstaking process. Indeed, it
would require the second Reformation of the mid-
17th-century Covenanting (see COVENANT, WARS OF
THE) Revolution to complete it in the Lowlands
and make serious inroads into the Highlands. Nor,
as this suggests, did the Reformation constitute
quite such a break with the past as is sometimes
imagined. The new Israel was often built on old
foundations. The medieval song and grammar
schools (see SCHOOLS AND SCHOOLINGS: 1) provided
the basis on which the reformers' vision of a school
in every parish could be realized, while the medieval universities—supplemented by the foundation of Edinburgh's 'toun college' in 1582-3—were
reformed on lines that combined Calvinist orthodoxy with a classically based arts curriculum that
owed less to Protestantism than to Renaissance humanism.

In fact, Knox's extreme and culturally destructive biblicism represents only one strand of Scotland's Reformation. His successor, Andrew
*Melville, a brilliant academic and former student
at Paris, Poitiers, and Geneva, represents another,
more complex, tradition in which the pursuit of
godliness was tempered by a humanistic concern
with civility. It was Melville rather than Knox who
was befriended by George Buchanan, the greatest
of 16th-century Scottish humanists, who inspired a
tradition of neo-Latin poetry that cut across religious and political divisions and culminated in the
publication in 1637 of the greatest monument to
Scottish humanist Latinity, the *Delitiae poetarum
Scotorum*. Buchanan is best known for his republican politics and for justifying the revolution of the
1560s in ways that inspired reverence among generations of Whig Presbyterians and revulsion among
their Episcopalian (see EPISCOPALIAN COMMUNITY)
and *Jacobite opponents. However, while Buchanan's political ideas proved deeply divisive, not
least during the mid-17th-century Covenanting
crisis, the humanist culture that he represented
was striking deep roots in Scottish society.

A humanist education was by the late 16th century the norm both for Scotland's aristocracy and
for the increasingly self-conscious lairdly class (see
RURAL SOCIETY: 2) that was finding a new role in the
crown's burgeoning bureaucracy. *James VI's attempts to extend law, order, and civility into the
localities resonated with a landed elite as familiar
with the civic values of the classical world as they
were with the Christian morality of the reformed
kirk. As Lowland society began to demilitarize (see
WARFARE, WEAPONS, AND FORTIFICATIONS: 2), so the
elite began to extend and embellish their stark but
defensible tower houses or to abandon them altogether in favour of more luxurious country
dwellings (see HOUSING: 1). Whereas earlier in the
century it was the crown that had taken the lead in
architectural innovation, it was now a fashion-
conscious elite that was investing heavily in remodelling their town houses and rural retreats in
ways that combined distinctive Scottish traditions
with novel Renaissance features. At the royal court,
as in the localities, continuity through the Reformation is as evident as discontinuity. Traditions of
public pageantry were maintained through the
elaborate spectacles modelled on French Renaissance fêtes that accompanied the baptism of both
James in 1566 and his first son in 1594. Moreover,
James VI's own literary interests ensured that vernacular verse continued to be strongly represented
at the royal court, where the leader of the king's
Castalian Band of poets was the Catholic Alexander Montgomerie. Yet, despite such continuities,
there clearly were ways in which the Reformation
did in the long term profoundly change the cultural
landscape. Gradually, Scottish culture was reorien-
tated away from *France towards Continental centres of Protestantism in Germany and the Calvinist
Netherlands, Leiden replacing Paris as the mecca

for Scottish students abroad. At the same time, culturally as well as politically, Scotland was drawn into an English orbit. England's burgeoning print culture dwarfed the small Scottish book market and, particularly after the *Union of the Crowns in 1603, squeezed the life out of the vibrant vernacular Scots poetry and prose of the 16th century. In many respects, union made participation in an English-speaking, British-orientated culture inescapable. Despite the union, however, Scottish intellectual life retained its distinctiveness, shaped by the creative tension between humanism and Calvinism, civility and godliness, that marked the cultural life of the country throughout the 17th century and beyond.   RAM

5. Renaissance and Reformation (1460–1660): philosophy

By 1460 Scotland had already produced a number of notable philosophers and one, John Duns Scotus (1266–1308), who ranks among the greatest of the philosophers of any age and any country. It is demonstrable that he cast a long shadow across the philosophy in Scotland for the subsequent two and a half centuries. He certainly had a significant effect on John Ireland (c.1440–95), who attended the University of St Andrews in the 1450s before going to the University of Paris where he rose rapidly, becoming rector of the university in 1469. Ireland was a nominalist thinker, for he held that whereas the members of a species, say the species of whale or of worm, are in the natural world, the species itself does not consist simply of the members but is instead an idea in the mind which can be applied equally to everything that is in the species. Those who opposed this doctrine, and who held instead that the species, no less than its individual members, exists in the natural world, were called realists. In 1474 Louis XI formally approved the teaching of realist philosophy, of which Scotus was an exponent, at the University of Paris, and banned the teaching of nominalism. Ireland was a member of the deputation that sought from the king a revocation of the ban, but it remained in force for seven years.

Ireland's two most significant works were his Commentary on the Sentences of Peter Lombard and his Meroure of Wyssdome. The first of these is a massive work of theology based upon the most important theological text of the Middle Ages, though only the last two of the four books of Ireland's Commentary survive. The sole extant manuscript is in Aberdeen University Library. The second work is the first ever philosophy book published in the vernacular language of Scotland (see SCOTS LANGUAGE). It contains valuable ideas on such topics as the freedom of the will and the problems raised for our freedom by the fact that God has foreknowledge of all human acts. The work, which was finished in 1490, was written for *James IV and is partly advice on the duties of *kingship. The advice to the king is based upon a theological premiss concerning the nature of God's governance of the world for divine governance should be used as a model for creaturely governance.

While Ireland was teaching at the University of Paris James Liddell of Aberdeen joined the student body there. In 1495, the year of the founding of a university in his home town, Liddell became the first-ever Scot to have a book of his printed in his own lifetime. The book is On Concepts and Signs, and is an investigation of the natural signs and conventional symbols by which we experience the world and communicate our experiences to others.

A number of the Scots who would shortly be arriving in Paris to attend classes there duly published books on this same subject. Of that new influx of Scottish students the central figure was John Mair (or Major) (c.1467–1550) from Gleghornie near Haddington, who rose to become professor of theology at Paris. In 1518 he returned to Glasgow to be principal of the university, before transferring to St Andrews University and thence back to Paris. In 1531 he returned to St Andrews, becoming provost of St Salvator's College, and he remained in that post till his death. He was a colleague of Erasmus in Paris—they lived in the same house—and his lectures there were attended by Loyola, Vitoria, Buchanan, Rabelais, Calvin, and Vives. At St Andrews he tutored John *Knox. He was an eclectic thinker, influenced at different points by Aquinas, Scotus, and William Ockham, though he retained to the end a special affection for Scotus, and was by no means as single-mindedly nominalist as some have thought him to be. He wrote within all the major areas of philosophy, such as ethics, philosophy of mind, and perception theory, and he was in addition one of the great logicians of the late Middle Ages. His many books on logic are extant and in some he develops in detail solutions to logic problems which were thought to be unsolvable until the new mathematical logic came onto the scene at the end of the last century. Mair's formidable logic powers, and his need to find a rational justification for things, inform all his writings, including his History of Greater Britain, a piece of historiography (see HISTORIANS: I) far ahead of its time in respect of the critical acumen displayed by the author.

He gathered around him a brilliant galaxy, the circle of John Mair, who collectively and separately dominated the Scottish university scene before the Reformation. One was the Dundonian Hector Boece (c.1465–1536), whose Exposition of Certain

Terms is a wonderfully clear and incisive account of the science of logic. Boece was the first principal of the newly founded King's College, Aberdeen. Others among Mair's Scottish circle were George Lokert (*c*.1485–1547), a brilliant logician who was rector of St Andrews University and, for the last thirteen years of his life, dean of Glasgow; Robert Galbraith (*c*.1483–1544), senator of the College of Justice in Edinburgh and author of *Four-part Work on Oppositions, Conversions, Hypothetical and Modal Propositions* (1510), one of the great works of medieval logic; and William Manderston (*c*.1485–1552), graduate of Glasgow, rector of St Andrews University and author of two authoritative treatises, one on logic and one on moral philosophy. Gilbert Crab (*c*.1482–1522) of Aberdeen and David Cranston (*c*.1479–1512) of the Glasgow diocese were also prolific members of Mair's circle.

The writings of these men form a major contribution to the Scottish philosophical tradition, and nothing of the same quality was produced till the Enlightenment some two centuries later. But in the intervening period there was a good deal of philosophy written. Two major changes took place. First the humanist revolution reached Scotland, with its emphasis on the classical languages of Latin, Greek, and Hebrew, and an attendant interest in the great classical texts, including the Old and the New Testaments in the original languages. As a result of this, Scottish philosophers were for the first time able to read Plato, Aristotle, and other major Greek thinkers in the original. Secondly, and relatedly, there was a close study of those same classical authors, not as seen through the distorting lens of medieval Latin translations and the surrounding medieval Latin commentaries, but instead in the original versions. John Mair knew some Greek, probably very little, but by the end of the 16th century Robert Rollock, first principal of Edinburgh University, was dictating the original Greek texts of Aristotle to his students.

With the arrival of humanism there came also a revised view of the task of the logician. Short, clear, simple expositions were called for, and among the earliest such works were *A Compendium of Dialectic* (1540, 2nd edn. 1545) by William Cranston, a friend of Mair's who followed Mair as provost of St Salvator's, and the *Method of Dialectic* (1544), written by Patrick Tod in the Ciceronian style adopted by many humanist philosophers. Cranston's successor at St Salvator's was John Rutherford of Jedburgh (d. 1577) whose one work on logic, *Four Books of Commentaries on the Art of Reasoning* (1557, 2nd edn. 1577), pays close attention to the original texts of Aristotle and displays little or no knowledge of the major advances in logic made by John Mair and his circle. Other Scots writing on logic at this period

include John Dempster and William Davidson, both of Aberdeen, and Robert Balfour (d. *c*.1625) of Tarrie in Angus.

One Scot of particular interest is Florence Wilson whose first work was *A Theological Commentary* (1539), a devotional work in the style of a litany, which contains many humanist touches, such as the reference to God as the highest Jupiter and as ruler of immense Olympus. Nevertheless the God about whom he philosophizes is undoubtedly the Christian God, as also is the God of Wilson's second book *A Dialogue on the Tranquility of the Mind* (1543), which contains a deep philosophical discussion on the notion of a mind at peace with itself.

In the three decades after the death of Robert Balfour in 1625 very little philosophy of note was published by Scots. The universities were, however, fully alive to what was happening on the European continent, and the latest ideas were being taught and digested in Scotland. René Descartes in particular was quickly taken up into the lecture courses alongside the writings of the Greek and Roman philosophers. But one has a sense that the country was biding its time. After the immense achievements of Mair and his circle things went comparatively quiet until the even more astonishing philosophical achievements of the Scottish Enlightenment.   AB

6. Renaissance and Reformation (1460–1660): language and literature

The history of early Scottish literature is closely linked to the issue of language (see SCOTS LANGUAGE). While this entry is primarily concerned with the rise and fall of Middle Scots, attention has to be paid to Gaelic, Latin, and English as well. Thus, although John Barbour's *The Brus*, composed in the late 1370s, provides a late start to most literary histories, texts in Latin (such as the hymns of St *Columba) and Gaelic, such as *Y Gododdin* (see GAELIC LITERATURE), survive from as early as the 6th century. Barbour's work itself demonstrates a secure mastery of Romance traditions, which suggests that early medieval texts in Northumbrian English existed before Malcolm Canmore and *David I ousted *Gaelic as the national language within their realms and Scots began to distinguish itself as a separate dialect.

The supposed loss of so much material has to be viewed in the context of a mainly aural tradition. It is no coincidence that practically all the manuscript texts surviving between 1370 and 1470 are lengthy narrative poems with ambitious topics. The church regarded the Scottish *Legends of the Saints* as worthy of copying. Martial romances and allegorical accounts of the nation's past were also favoured. Barbour's poem is succeeded in the 1420s by James I's

Kingis Quair; by Robert Holland's *Buke of the Howlat* 30 years later; and by Blind Harry's *The Wallace* in the 1470s. As the authors of these poems were all learned men, they accept Aristotle's view that poetry is an essentially practical discipline, justified by its effects in persuading people to good action. The campaigns of Bruce and Wallace, James I's love for Johanne Beaufort, and the role played by the *Douglas family in Scottish history are, therefore, founded on accurate evidence, drawn from chronicles and empirical evidence.

What distinguishes poetry from history, however, is its potentiality for dealing with ideas across a wider range of fanciful speculation. To guarantee that the broader questions of freedom and justice may clearly emerge from this evidence, mythic and divine patternings of history are also drawn in, while extreme moral contrasts at the level of characterization produce clarity of moral guidance at the expense of psychological subtlety. To turn the young William *Wallace into a cross between Christ and Hugh of Lincoln or delete from the historical record all evidence of Robert Bruce's (see ROBERT I) support for Edward I may be a lie when measured against 'the truth of chronicles' but in poetry's pragmatically persuasive realm, it is the higher lie against 'sentence' or topic which has to be avoided, as Blind Harry notes. James uses a Boethean, allegoric structure to achieve the same end, while Holland employs a microcosmic-macrocosmic structure working outwards from the Douglas escutcheon to questions of order in empire and church.

Despite their skills, these early makars or word-builders had been limited by the relatively crude state of Early Scots. It is not until the late 15th century that Middle Scots developed into the subtle instrument of expression which modern Scottish poets envy. Nor is it coincidental that the four finest writers of the medieval and Renaissance belong to that period: Robert Henryson (*c*.1450–*c*.1505), William Dunbar (*c*.1460–*c*.1513), Gavin Douglas (*c*.1475–1522), and Sir David Lindsay (*c*.1486–1555). The development of the 'treasure-house' of words was a conscious aim in the Middle Scots period. Gavin Douglas in his *Eneados* admits that he translated Virgil's epic into Scots as part of a patriotic linguistic agenda. To provide vernacular renderings of any Latin work is a test; to do so for the *Aeneid* necessarily extends the vernacular by means of coinages and borrowings. Douglas is the first Scot to argue for the development of the Scots tongue on political rather than artistic grounds.

If Douglas provides the linguistic theory, Robert Henryson and William Dunbar add, respectively, the argumentative subtlety and the lyrical virtuosity, so difficult to attain in Early Scots. Henryson

was a schoolteacher in Dunfermline and his major poems reflect that occupation. His *Orpheus, Testament of Cresseid*, and *Morall Fabillis* are overtly designed to test his audience's ability to relate storyline to moral message. The narrative configures our moral or spiritual expectations in one way, but the lesson drawn may be quite different, forcing us to examine any surface oddities which signed another, 'hidden' sense. As a good teacher, Henryson varies both the form of the test and his chosen area(s) of moral application. Social commentary here competes with philosophical, Christian, and metaphysical lessons. Of his thirteen *Morall Fabillis*, 'The Two Mice', 'The Sheep and the Dog', and 'The Lion and the Mouse' are the most obviously political in intent. The rivalry between town and country mouse is adapted to mirror the growth of the Scottish burgh. The innocent sheep's vain appeal for justice satirizes both civil and consistorial practice. The lion's unlikely reliance on the weaker animal becomes veiled advice to James III that the common people become part of the political equation.

William Dunbar is the most virtuosic of the makars. As a poet at the *royal court of *James IV, he was paid to prove the range of his stylistic skills. His vision of Scotland is therefore, at times, officially eulogistic. In commissioned lyrics, such as 'To Aberdein', he can scarcely celebrate a royal entry in other than ecstatic terms. His best work, however, combines lyrical and satiric modes, the two elements coming together in a vast variety of forms and tones. The forthcoming wedding between James and the young Margaret Tudor in *The Thrissill and the Rois*, for example, is celebrated within a formal allegorical framework but includes caustic warnings to the king against philandering. In the more conversational Middle Style, he can give advice to merchants ('The Merchants of Edinburgh') or lament the passing of his poetic predecessors ('The Lament for the Makaris'). The light satiric sketches of 'Dancing in the Quenis Chalmer' coexist with bawdy farce in 'The Sowtar and the Tailyouris War'. But the most bitter Low Style attacks are reserved for those foreigners and scientists in 'The Fenyeit Freir of Tungland' mould, who deflect fame and money away from home-born artists like Dunbar himself!

In the middle years of the 16th century, when Sir David Lindsay was writing, the Protestant *Reformation had begun. His best-known work is the political morality play *Ane Satyre of the Thrie Estaitis*. This was composed towards the end of his artistic career. But its democratic appeal and major attack on the clergy are consistent with views he had expressed much earlier. Indeed, when John the Commonweil enters from among the audience to join the cast on the Cupar stage in 1552, he is fulfilling a promise 'he' made much earlier in *The Dreme*. Only when political reforms are initiated would he return. When one fictive character, King Humanitie, promises this, he exits from the early allegory to inhabit the later drama.

The Middle Scots makars set qualitatively high standards. In no other period do most critics agree that Scottish literature was superior to English. Alexander Scott (?1520–1582/3) and Alexander Montgomerie (c.1550–98) did continue the traditions of courtly lyric in Scots but, within the narrative of most histories of Scottish literature, they are seen as lesser talents. This is probably a fair judgement. The associated suggestion that their Anglicized Scots is, itself, unpatriotic is less securely based. It is important to address this question, as the process of Anglicization continued and this sense of 'un-Scottishness' results in the poets and prose-writers of the 17th century getting a worse press from their modern compatriots than from anyone else. This is largely because the early 20th-century movement which, in a sense, created the discipline called Scottish literature had a clear political agenda. The idea of Scottishness as embodied by its most brilliant advocate, Hugh MacDiarmid, was left-wing, nationalistic (even Anglophobic), atheistic, and communistic. It was the fate of the Scottish Renaissance to meet none of these criteria (see also CULTURE: 9).

If one approaches the Renaissance period on its own terms, a rather different picture emerges. Outside forces—notably the translation of the Bible into English and the Anglicizing effect of printing (see PRINTING AND PUBLISHING)—were largely responsible for the thinning of Middle Scots. Various attempts were made to counter this tendency in its earlier stages. The Bannatyne and Maitland anthologies of the late 1560s, which preserve the writings of the Middle Scots makars, derive from this climate, as do *James VI's Reulis and Cautelis of 1584.

It is true that the Calvinist Reformation was inimical to imagery and popular theatre. This meant that while England was enjoying the golden age of Shakespeare, the only Scots play to survive between Lindsay and the *Union of the Crowns is the anonymous farce *Philotus*. But this was also the period when Latin literature in Scotland was boosted by the European status of George Buchanan (1506–82) and by his dramas, notably *Jephthes* and *Baptistes*. A varied programme of court entertainments (see ROYAL COURT: 2) also existed, while broadsheet verses translated the actual drama of religious confrontation to a wider audience. Even the beginning of fictive prose in Scots may be assigned to this period. *The Pretended Conference*, attributed to Thomas Maitland (1522–c.1572) for

example, presents an imagined plot against Mary, Queen of Scots, via witty parodies of the voices of leading Protestants, including *Knox.

In his *Reulis and Cautelis*, James advised court poets to highlight those elements within the Scots language which distinguished it from English. Rhetorical effects, verse structures, and the sources of literary borrowing were also discussed so as to maximize the difference between this Scottish Renaissance and its English counterpart. The young king even advanced on a formulated programme of translation to boost the ailing vernacular. The writings of Montgomerie, Stewart of Baldynneis (1550–1605), and William Fowler (1560–1612) are, therefore, part of an energetic performance culture. But that same culture is learned, artificial, and unhealthily divorced from popular verse, such as the ballad. The fact that this tradition flourished particularly well in the 16th and 17th centuries may in part be due to this negative sense of populist isolation.

Essentially, however, any form of language was valued against the practical persuasive criteria, which defined the poetic discipline. The most subtly useful form of language would be preferred on rhetorical grounds rather than advocated on nationalist ones, if and when a choice had to be made. That choice was even easier in a land whose linguistic heritage was polymathic anyway and where the English origins of Scots had been enthusiastically acknowledged by the earlier makars. The case is well argued in the 1630s by William Alexander (1567–1640) in his critical essay *Anacrisis*. There, he sees language as a means towards an imaginative end, which transcends the particular and the political.

This helps to explain why James, the staunch advocate of Scots, could, with no sense of inconsistency, anticipate his British rule by advising Scottish poets to Anglicize their writing. In addition, the favoured modes of the day—sonnet, madrigal, pastoral, and prose romance—all belonged to artificial traditions, shared by poets throughout western Europe. This made it easy for the finest Scottish poets of the period—Robert Ayton (1569–1638) and William Drummond (1585–1649)—to forge poetic alliances with their English counterparts—Ayton with Jonson's school of wit and Drummond with Drayton.

Governed as they are by the rules of art and allegory, many 17th-century poems do not reveal their meaning easily and this is as true of their political content as of all else. Drummond's *Moeliades* and *Forth Feasting* offer respectively a lament on the death of Prince Henry and a poignant rebuke to James for preferring London to Scotland. The first, however, is a stylized classical elegy, anticipating

Milton's *Lycidas*, while the satirical content of the second is indirectly conveyed within a formal, pastoral celebration of the monarch's return. Thomas Urquhart (1611–60) presents a powerful case for Scottish heroism in *The Jewel* but does so by outdoing parodically that most euphuistic of all prose forms, the euphuistic romance. George Mackenzie (1636–97) uses the same broad form in *Aretina*, but his direct comments on Scotland's role in British history are confined to Book 3 and conveyed in dark, allegorical fashion.

More direct political expressions do exist. They are, however, mostly Unionist in sentiment and composed in Latin, having been diverted to that language by one of James's 'Reulis'. Within the massive volumes of the *Delitiae Poetarum Scotorum* (1637) the Scottish Stewart dynasty (see KINGSHIP: 7), enriched by years of peace under its wise and pious king, descends to lead its war-torn neighbours into a new golden age. In vernacular terms, the accommodation of 'Scottis' with 'Inglis' signs this political harmony. Anglicization is further justified as the best practical means of persuading this new audience.   RDSJ

7. Renaissance and Reformation (1460–1660): literature

Scots literature provides its own variations on the European paradigms of Renaissance and Reformation. In this period, vernacular literatures throughout western Europe developed a new self-confidence through translations and by absorbing humanist culture and Petrarchan poetry. In Scotland, however, after an impressive start this process was temporarily disrupted and ultimately annulled by the joint forces of history and religious conflict. A late 15th-century flowering of vernacular literature, stimulated by humanist incentives through figures such as William Elphinstone (1431–1514), chancellor of James III, and royal secretaries such as Archibald Whitelaw (c.1425–98) and Patrick Paniter (c.1470–1519), was cut short by the battle of Flodden (1513). This was followed by an era of development rather than progression during which literary expression was increasingly dominated by Reformation issues. In the 1580s *James VI tried to reactivate literature, propagating translation and original poetry to bring Scots literature in line again with European developments. However, in the long term the absence of a dramatic tradition and, after 1603, a *royal court, made this revival evaporate in the 17th century.

Before Flodden, then, Scots writing had humanist rather than Petrarchist features: its literary persona began to explore the potential of human individuality to balance physical, moral, and intellectual faculties in search for new values but did not

primarily use amatory metaphors to do so. A spiritual instead of aesthetic renaissance was what concerned the key poets; assimilating classical and medieval texts, they created images of a reborn Christian self in a secularized world, developing metaphors of self-rule rather than self-expression.

The *Morall Fabillis* by Robert Henryson (c.1450–c.1505) offered moralized fiction as a means towards spiritual revitalization, while his *Testament of Cresseid* linked an interpretation of a Chaucerian model and material from Boccaccio to the Christian humanist command to 'know thyself': Cresseid achieves self-knowledge in this world, not the next. In *The Palis of Honour* (c.1501), Gavin Douglas (c.1475–1522) emphasized the value of poetry as a speculative and regenerative medium by reconceptualizing moral qualities in terms of honour, reconciling private responsibility with public career. These poems show a willingness to experiment with the capacity of fiction to equivocate and with the narrator-persona's reliability as a moral guide: this fiction is also about fiction, constantly searching for voices of literary authority. The lyrical voice of William Dunbar (c.1460–c.1513) alternated between court jester and preacher, always stressing not personal value but that of his writing. Such layering of meaning through fictional play required a sophisticated audience.

Douglas's *Eneados* (1513, printed 1553) revealed a Renaissance interest in epic. The first full-length translation of Virgil's *Aeneid* in Britain, Douglas's own prologues to Virgil's books also provided the first humanist literary criticism in Scots, proclaiming Scots a national literary medium and merging classical (religious, pastoral) concepts with late medieval ones.

After Flodden, literary progress (including the spread of printing (see PRINTING AND PUBLISHING)) was temporarily halted. The major poet in this period is David Lindsay (c.1486–1555), his lively concern for commonweal leadership reflecting secular humanism with popular, reformist features. After *James V's death in 1542, Reformist plain style increasingly asserted itself, as in the satirical verse of Robert Sempill (fl. 1530–95) and *The Gude and Godlie Ballatis*, including Protestantized versions of secular lyrics (1565). In contrast, from within the constraints of courtly conventions and public performance, Alexander Scott (?1520–1582/3) and Alexander Montgomerie (c.1550–98) modulated lyric voices into those of putatively authentic selves. Montgomerie's achievement underlay James VI's *Reulis and Cautelis to be obseruit and eschewit in Scottis Poesie* (1584), a truly Renaissance document outlining how translation (c.1585: Ariosto's *Orlando Furioso* by John Stewart of Baldynneis (c.1539–c.1606); 1587: Petrarch's *Trionfi* by William Fowler

(1560–1612)), imitation, and invention helped create modern Scots poetry. Courtiers rather than clerics now explored the permutations of sexual love in Petrarchan sonnets and sonnet sequences (Fowler, *The Tarantula of Love*; Sir William Alexander, first earl of Stirling (*c*.1567–1640), *Aurora* (1604)), invoking classical literature by styling themselves 'Castalians'.

After 1603, these poets (including Robert Ayton (1570–1638)) followed James VI to England, and works like *Amorose Songes, Sonets and Elegies* (1606), a sonnet sequence addressed to eight women by Alexander Craig, 'Scoto-Britane' (*c*.1567–1627), reflected the fragmentation of literary convention but also that of a Scots literary identity (see NATIONAL IDENTITY: 3). Only William Drummond of Hawthornden (1585–1649) remained in Scotland, developing a creative intertextuality with foreign Renaissance writers. A positive aspect was the emergence of the first named women poets: *Ane Godlie Dreame* (1603) by Elizabeth Melville (fl. 1585–1630) is a popular religious dream allegory, while Anna Hume's adaptation of Petrarch (*Triumphs of Love: Chastitie: Death*, 1644) shows vernacular literature is still absorbing Renaissance material.

While socio-religious developments indeed disastrously affected drama, the traditional claim that there are hardly any dramatic texts in Older Scots (George Buchanan's plays are in Latin) is based on restrictive definitions of performance: a significant 21st-century discovery will be the performance aspect of much early Scots verse. The one extant pre-Reformation play, David Lindsay's *Ane Satyre of the Thrie Estaitis* (performed 1552, 1554), is carefully constructed from stanzaic verse; the anonymous 'The Maner of the Crying of ane Play' (*ante* 1568) and *Philotus* (printed 1603, written ?1560s), a Renaissance comedy after Roman example, are instances of stanzaic direct speech, meant to be performed. This different conception of verse and drama is confirmed, in reverse, by William Alexander's *Monarchicke Tragedies* (1603–7), 'Tragicall Poemes' never meant to be performed on stage (see also CULTURE: 9).

Vernacular prose differed from poetry in quantity (most prose authors preferred Latin) and kind (most is translation and practical) but followed a similar trajectory. Amid mainly didactic texts (Asloan Manuscript, *c*.1520), *The Meroure of Wyssdome* (*c*.1490) by John Ireland (*c*.1440–95), confessor to Louis XI and lecturer at the Sorbonne, stands out, a didactic work written in a Latinate expository style for the young *James IV. Under James V, the major 'Renaissance' advance was in translation from Latin combined with historiography. John Bellenden (*c*.1495–1547/8) translated Hector Boece's *Scotorum Historia* (1531) and Livy's *History of*

Rome (1533) on royal demand. His Latinate style mixed with energetic Scots culminated in *The Complaynt of Scotland* (written 1548/9, printed Paris 1550), attributed to Robert Wedderburn (*c*.1510–53), which framed political comment in aureate pastoral. In contrast, this period also saw the first 'Protestant' prose. Murdoch Nisbet's manuscript transcription of Wycliffe's New Testament into Scots (*c*.1520) apparently did not circulate, but tracts by John Gau (*c*.1495–*c*.1553; *The Richt Vay to the Kingdome of Heuine*, Malmö, 1533, a translation from Danish) and Henry Balnevis (*c*.1512–79; *On Justification*, 1548, printed 1568) established the plain, direct style that characterizes Reformist writing (see RELIGIOUS LIFE: 2–3).

In the subsequent period, *Reformation events inspired historiographical texts, in which this Latinate (John Lesley, *c*.1527–96) versus plain-style Reformist (Robert Lindsay of Pitscottie, *c*.1532–80?) dichotomy prevails (see HISTORIANS: 2). John *Knox (*c*.1513–72) used a preacher's rhetorical acumen to present his version of events as fact in *The Historie of the Reformatioun in Scotland*. His Anglicized texts highlighted the fact that post-Reformation Scots writing relied for centuries on an English bible and was thus imbued with English idiom. This is very marked in the powerful *sermons of the earlier 17th century.

Literary Scots prose was enriched by Fowler's translation of Machiavelli's *Il principe*, essays by James VI and Drummond, and Alexander's literary-critical treatise *Anacrisis* (*c*.1634). These texts linked rhetoric, ethics, and aesthetics in ways that prepared the conventions of a novelistic prose style. In a class of his own stands Thomas Urquhart of Cromartie (*c*.1611–60), who adapted Rabelais's *Gargantua and Pantagruel* (first two books printed 1653, third 1693), adding to the vitality of his Renaissance original with copious 'Scots Gothic', while his 'Admirable' Crichton in *The Jewel* (1652) provided a Quixotic self-portrait.

There is one prose category that is almost always forgotten: what the ballads are to poetry, proverbs are to prose. Collections such as 'Scottish Proverbs' by David Fergusson (*c*.1523–98) prove that, orally at least, Scots prose was very much alive.   T vanH

8. Renaissance and Reformation (1460–1660): art

Scotland was part of the Renaissance in northern Europe. James III, *James IV, and *James V and their great courtiers commissioned high-quality work from *France and Flanders (see LOW COUNTRIES). The St Salvator's mace, for instance, was made for Bishop Kennedy of St Andrews in 1460 by a Paris goldsmith, Jean Mayelle, who may have been a Scot. The *Trinity College Altarpiece* (HM the

Queen, NGS) was painted by Hugo van der Goes for James III in Bruges (see STAPLE PORTS) in the late 1470s. But art was not only imported. The rood-screen in the church of Foulis Easter, the work of an unknown painter in the late 15th century, was painted on the spot. James III's groat designed by his 'sinkar' (master of the mint) with the king's portrait in three-quarter view is recognized as the first use of this device in a coin or medal outside Italy (see COINAGE).

Nothing comparable survives in Scotland, but the altarpiece made for the Scottish community in Elsinore no doubt reflects the kind of art that a Scottish congregation might expect. The most important surviving work from the reign of James IV is, however, an illuminated manuscript, the Hours of James IV and Margaret Tudor, by Simon Bening, James's wedding present to his queen in 1503 (Österreichische Nationalbibliothek, no. 1897). Illuminated manuscripts were also produced in Scotland and Sir Thomas Galbraith, a clerk of the Chapel Royal, wrote and illuminated the treaty documents relating to James's marriage (PRO E/ 39/81) which are therefore the earliest works surviving by a named Scottish artist. Though we do not know the names of the artists, contemporary sculpture has a distinctive style seen in the carved, wooden heads made for James V's great hall of *Stirling castle, in other woodcarving, and also in stone sculpture. Mary of Guise, too, had artists at her court and her daughter, *Mary, Queen of Scots, clearly understood the power of imagery. She is recorded in a number of paintings from her lifetime, for example, Mary Queen of Scots and Henry Darnley (c.1565, National Trust, Hardwick Hall).

In the reign of *James VI it is for the first time possible to identify known artists with significant surviving works, the fierce portrait of Regent Morton attributed to Arnold Bronkhorst, for example, and the portrait of James himself by Adrian Vanson. Adam de Colone, who may have been Vanson's son, also produced some fine portraits though he worked only briefly in Scotland.

The painters also produced pageants, particularly the royal entries like that of James and his queen into Edinburgh in 1590 (see ROYAL COURT: 2), and were skilled in *heraldry. This kind of work is linked to the fashion for painted ceilings which was a distinctive Scottish form of decoration between c.1560 and c.1640. These ceilings together with the evidence for the use of colour on the outside of buildings suggest that *Reformation Scotland was by no means a drab place. The vividly sculpted tombstones of the period also testify to the skill of the masons and to the emergence of a society in which individual pride and independence were no longer the sole prerogative of the rich.

The first native artist for whom we can establish a distinct personality, however, was George Jamesone. Trained in decorative painting in Aberdeen, he became a national figure. He was, for instance, brought to Edinburgh to orchestrate the decoration of the city for King Charles I's entry in 1633. Jamesone's art is low-key, but it does not lack subtlety. It is seen at its best in a gentle, half-length portrait like that of Mary Erskine (1626, SNPG). Jamesone also painted several self-portraits. The best is his Self-Portrait with an Easel (c.1644, SNPG). It is both self-assured and introspective in a way that speaks to us directly of the complex self-awareness of the emerging Scottish professional class. With the Wars of the *Covenant many artists went overseas. William Gouw Fergusson (1632/3– after 1695), for example, became well known as a still-life painter in the Netherlands, but foreign artists like Jacob de Wet and John Medina also settled in Scotland.   DM

9. Renaissance and Reformation: poetry to 1603

The history of poetry in Scots up to 1603 presents a process of incrementation in which new influences were continually assimilated into a vernacular tradition which already contained literary influences from abroad and from within Scotland itself, where it rubbed shoulders with Latin, Gaelic, English, and French texts. This leads to an exceptionally dynamic 15th-century corpus, used by 16th-century poets to evolve a distinct national literature.

Within this complex process of independence and assimilation, there are two main literary traditions. The Brus (c.1375) by John Barbour (c.1320–95), the earliest extant Scots poem, represents the older of the two. Its combination of epic, chronicle, and romance reflects European-wide chivalric modes of writing. Andrew of Wyntoun (c.1355–c.1420) continued Barbour's poetic quest for nationhood (see HISTORIANS: 1) in The Orygynale Cronykil of Scotland (c.1406) using The Brus's metrical format— octosyllabic couplets—which the contemporaneous anonymous Legends of the Saints applies to hagiography. The oldest datable Scots romance, The Buik of Alexander (1438), translated from French, also uses it.

The other tradition is more typically courtly and lyrical rather than epic. It favoured allegory and dream vision to exploit the imaginative and expressive potential of fiction and replaced couplets by stanzas, prioritizing rhyme over alliteration. The Kingis Quair (c.1424, attributed to James I) is the first and major poem in this tradition. Its investigation of the nature of love overlays Boethian and Chaucerian stimuli with a lively, personalized engagement with intellectual concepts which characterizes this tradition.

In both cases Scots poetry emerged relatively late, but also preserved an identity of its own. Subsequent 15th-century poems oscillated between these two traditions as well as between native and imported influences, yielding hybrid texts that ingeniously combine genres and styles. *The Buke of the Howlat* (c.1448) by Richard Holland (fl. 1430–82) revives the alliterative bob-and-wheel stanza but also uses Chaucerian motifs and an intricate structure in a pointed engagement with crown–magnate politics (see KINGSHIP: 5; NOBILITY: 2). *The Wallace* (c.1477) by Blind Harry (fl. 1470–92) mythologized a national founder-hero in decasyllabic couplets mixed with stanzaic, lyrical verse.

Such crossovers also characterize late 15th-century anonymous texts: *Rauf Coilyear* combines motifs and forms of oral literature with parodies of Quixotic chivalry. Serious romances, usually based on French sources, still use the bob-and-wheel (*Golagros and Gawane*) which the peasant-brawl poem *Christis Kirk on the Grene* adapts for popular festive verse. *The Freiris of Berwik* is a tightly constructed *fabliau* set in a Scots urban milieu, while *The Thre Prestis of Peblis* (c.1490) provides an elaborately framed didactic narrative incorporating both Continental and English material.

During the stable reign of *James IV (1488–1513), the enrichment of poetry by mixing high and low, Scots and non-Scots, culminated in an intensification of 15th-century experiments such as the juxtapositioning of conflicting styles and of narrative frame versus body. This required the audience to resolve these conflicts. In the process, the relationship between text, author, persona, and audience is constantly redefined; here, the persona's petitionary, satirical, devotional, and moral-didactic stances prefigure the modern, self-referential author. Relatively unobstructed literary interaction between cultural and intellectual currents leads to vibrant poetry; its textual impulse is often late medieval and clerical with humanist tendencies, generating a Scots authorial persona with a wide range of reference. Thus, Robert Henryson (c.1450–c.1505) imaginatively reworks medieval and classical sources such as Chaucer's *Troilus and Criseyde* (in *The Testament of Cresseid*), Aesop (in *The Morall Fabillis*), and the Orpheus myth (in *Orpheus and Eurydice*). The satires, lyrics, dream visions, and invectives of William Dunbar (c.1460–c.1513) establish the vernacular as a flexible vehicle for poetry of any kind. In *The Palis of Honour* (c.1501), Gavin Douglas (c.1475–1522), a cleric like Dunbar, picks up metapoetic aspects of *The Kingis Quair* but also injects humanist and classical sources into Scots, as he does in his translation of Virgil's *Aeneid* (*Eneados*, 1513), adding prologues to Virgil's books that display the versatility of Scots poetry.

After Flodden the reign of *James V (1513–42) produced verse usually impressive in width rather than depth. David Lindsay (c.1486–1555) is its outstanding literary figure, writing energetic narratives, satires, elegy, and a romance as well as the only extant pre-Reformation play in Scots, *Ane Satyre of the Thrie Estaitis* (performed 1552, 1554), which uses verse to excellent dramatic effect.

From c.1555 to c.1580 politico-religious struggles overshadowed cultural expression, while the reformed kirk generally discouraged poetry other than devotional. Nevertheless, Sir Richard Maitland of Lethington (1496–1586) produced meditative and satirical poems in Dunbar's style; John Rolland (fl. 1530–75) published framed and allegorical narratives in Douglas's mode; Alexander Hume (c.1556–1609), courtier turned minister, left a small body of verse including nature poetry and epistolary satire; polemical verse thrived. Meanwhile, more directly court-related circles developed the short lyric, often set to music. In this genre Alexander Scott (?1520–82/3) prepared the way for the so-called Castalian poets who in the 1580s were part of *James VI's attempt to revive Scots poetry. Translating key Renaissance texts, they continued to write lyrics in a native vein while their sonnets and short sonnet sequences provide typically Scots variations on initially predominantly French patterns, with a characteristically wide range of reference and a penchant for parodic experiment. Thus, they used sonnets for invective, nature description, and burlesque as well as love. Chief of these poets was Alexander Montgomerie (c.1550–98), whose best lyrics have an exquisite balance of lightness and depth. Others include John Stewart of Baldynneis (1550–1605) and William Fowler (1560–1612). Their example inspired later court poets such as Sir William Alexander, first earl of Stirling (c.1567–1640), Alexander Craig (c.1567–1627), and Robert Ayton (1570–1638) to provide alluring, idiosyncratic inflections of Renaissance literary paradigms. Outwith immediate royal influence, however, a distrust of cultural catholicity drove a wedge between European and native literature. Soon after the court's move to London in 1603, Scots poetry dissolved into its English equivalent at James's court while allowed to develop only specific aspects of its own resources at home, becoming local or occasional. What, however, this absence of court poetry did was to allow the oral ballad to become one of the richest strands of Scots literature.
T vanH

10. Renaissance and Reformation (1460–1660): music

The scanty extant remains of pre-Reformation Scottish music, sacred (see MUSIC, ECCLESIASTICAL) and secular, indicate the existence of a flourishing musical culture similar to that of any other small Renaissance kingdom. But Scotland's composers, unlike its poets, were not to have a George Bannatyne to collect and copy a huge and representative sample of what had been written before 1560 (see CULTURE: 3). For the post-Reformation period, the part-books of Thomas Wode (d. 1592), vicar of St Andrews, and its invaluable 'song-book' continuation by unknown hands, did save just such a sample, although it is important to note that it is an arbitrary one, its limitations dictated by Wode's physical location and lack of social status or connections. If the pre-Reformation losses are incalculable, those for the latter period can also be shown to be considerable, thanks to the fragmentary survival of other sets of part-books. The very late arrival of music *printing in Scotland undoubtedly contributed to the scale of the losses. Much of the extant manuscript material has now been made available in the published editions of Kenneth Elliott, in particular, which are essential to any serious study of the full range of the music of the entire era, ecclesiastical and secular, vocal and instrumental.

The baleful impact of the *Reformation on the musical profession, and, indeed, on potential patrons, meant that the country failed to participate in the growth of secular concert and theatre music in 17th-century Europe. Thomas Wode himself wrote in the 1570s that 'music sall pereishe in this land alutterlie', explaining that men acquired a science and craft in order to live by it. Since there was no living to be made out of being a trained musician in Scotland, music 'perforce man die'. Inevitably, then, the finest monuments of Scottish music are the surviving large-scale works written for the liturgy of the Roman Catholic Church (see CHURCH INSTITUTIONS: 2). The main repository for what survives in this field is the Carver Choirbook, a large manuscript volume so denominated because it contains five Masses and two motets by the Augustinian canon of Scone Robert Carver (1485–c.1568). It also contains music by English composers, a Magnificat by the Scottish-surnamed Nesbet also found in the Eton Choirbook, the Mass 'L'Homme armé' by the great Burgundian (see LOW COUNTRIES) master Guillaume Dufay, and a number of fine anonymous works, the earliest in an international style similar to Burgundian music of the 1480s or earlier, and the latest a dizzying tour de force of variation technique, almost certainly Scottish in origin. The earliest Mass settings may possibly hint at the kind of music sung in great establishments during the reign of James III (see RELIGIOUS LIFE: 2).

While it is dangerous in the extreme to extrapolate any general principles from one random survival, the Carver Choirbook would seem to indicate that, in music as in literature (see CULTURE: 4, 6, 7, 9), Scotland was open to both insular and Continental developments. What is beyond dispute is that in Robert Carver the country possessed an individual genius comparable with his contemporaries Henryson, Dunbar, and Douglas in terms of range, depth of feeling, richness of expression, and originality. Carver's music is often strikingly rhythmical and dance-like; but there is also a distinctly mystical streak, unusual in Scottish art, but fully in keeping with Augustinian teaching on the role of music in lifting the mind to the contemplation of the Infinite Godhead (see CULTURE: 5). This is heard above all in Carver's settings of the latter parts of the Mass, and above all in the final 'pacem' of the Agnus Dei of his large-scale festal Masses for four, five, and ten voices. The equally impressive 'pacem' of his six-part Mass is jubilant and military, which would seem to link it with *James IV's crusading ambitions, like the 'L'Homme armé' Mass and the ten-part 'Dum sacrum mysterium' in honour of St Michael the Archangel. Carver's most overtly impressive work is his staggering motet 'O bone Jesu', for nineteen voices, which again creates an ocean of sound conducive to mystical contemplation. Two further anonymous Masses of high quality, for three and six voices respectively, have been attributed to Carver on stylistic grounds.

To date, very few solid biographical facts have been established about Carver. Even his exact date of birth is still in dispute, despite the fact he himself appended some ambiguous dating information to two of his compositions. Carver's use of the alias 'vel Arnot' in some of his early music has led to an unfortunate attempt to identify him with a noncleric of that name, a burgess and bailie of Stirling, and to speculations that he was actually a member of the Chapel Royal in *Stirling castle. It is more likely that he remained in his abbey, although his music is certainly on a regal scale and may well have been intended for the chapel, which was closely linked with Scone. Carver had a clerical uncle in *Aberdeen, became a monk at a young age, and was still at Scone in August 1568. The loss of most of the abbey's records means that we cannot follow his career in any detail, thus fuelling speculation. Equally scanty are the details we possess about the other two names to which we can attach outstanding polyphony, Robert Johnson and David Peebles. Since the former, according to Thomas Wode, was a priest 'delatit for heresy' who fled to England in the 1530s, more of his work has survived than anyone else's, although it is impossible to say with certainty how much of his Latin church music may have been composed in

Scotland. Johnson inhabits an entirely different sound world from Carver, as does David Peebles, an Augustinian like Carver, based at the cathedral priory of *St Andrews. Described by Wode as 'ane of the finest composers in all this land', Peebles's sole surviving pre-Reformation composition is the serene and luminous Pentecost motet 'Si quis diligit me' (c.1530). It is a masterpiece, apparently known to and even sung by *James V. In the early 1560s, Peebles was commissioned by the then prior James Stewart, illegitimate son of James V and future Regent Moray, to harmonize the 105 tunes of the new metrical psalter. After much prodding by Thomas Wode, he completed the task, and the results are uniformly excellent. Wode also recorded a dramatic polyphonic setting of a Latin version of Psalm 3 made in 1576, and this work indicates that however little polyphony was being sung anywhere in Scotland, Peebles had somehow kept very up-to-date with musical developments.

A fine polyphonist known from a single work, dated to the 1550s, is Patrick Douglas, who appears to have been a prebendary of St Giles's in Edinburgh; he remained a Catholic and died on the Continent, while another composer associated with the same pre-Reformation collegiate church is John Fethie, whose surviving works are relatively simple settings of vernacular religious texts. The fatal long-term impact of the Reformation on Scottish art music was mitigated for some years by the existence of musicians like Fethie, trained under the old dispensation. Some of these are only names to which no music can be attached, but the Augustinian Andro Blackhall, of Holyrood abbey, became a successful and prominent Protestant minister. None of his Latin polyphony is extant, but his vernacular works testify to his skill. He appears to have enjoyed close links with the *royal court of the young *James VI, and three fine vernacular psalm settings for five voices, preserved by Thomas Wode, appear to have been commissioned by the earl of Morton in the years 1569, 1573, and 1579. They show that Blackhall was aware of developments in England. As for the other extant music of the Reformed church (see CHURCH INSTITUTIONS: 3), the strictures placed on composition were very severe, but the psalm-tune harmonizations of Peebles, Andro Kemp, John Buchan, and John Angus all have a marked personality of their own (see RELIGIOUS LIFE: 3).

No popular music, such as vernacular carols, seems to have survived from the pre-Reformation period, other than one or two tunes associated with the militantly anti-Roman Catholic Gude and Godlie Ballatis, first published in a collected edition in 1565. These tunes are those of the popular songs adapted by the compilers of the 'Ballatis' for religious ends. The richness of Scotland's secular music is indicated by the famous list of songs and dances in The Complaynt of Scotland (1549) and, as with church music, the fragmentary remains are often of very high quality. Many of the surviving poems of the period 1460 to 1600 are clearly songs, but their music has perished.

For the late 15th century, only the anonymous, jubilant, and inventive 'Pleugh Sang' survives, and very little can confidently be assigned to the court of James IV, although he was apparently constantly accompanied by music. A notable discovery has been the melody of the epic romance Graysteill, which is known to have been performed by two musicians for the king. French influence (see FRANCE: THE 'AULD ALLIANCE') is clear in the equally exiguous survivals from the flourishing court of James V, his widow Mary of Guise, and *Mary, Queen of Scots, which include part-songs of rare beauty. Since Mary's second husband, Lord Darnley, brought a family of Yorkshire musicians with him to Edinburgh, we may assume a strong presence of English song and dance. These musicians, the Hudsons, survived to thrive at the court of James VI, although no extant music actually bears their name.

Most of our evidence for secular art music comes from the time of James VI, notably after the advent of French influence in the shape of Esmé Stewart. There are fine four-part settings, in chanson-style, of some twenty poems by the dazzling court laureate Alexander Montgomerie, composer(s) unknown, barring one setting made by Andro Blackhall. A solitary masterpiece for viols, 'My Lord of March pavane', survives with an attribution to James Lauder, while a number of very impressive keyboard compositions bear the name of William Kinloch. Both these men appear to have been long-term supporters of Mary, Queen of Scots, and Kinloch may have been involved in Anglo-Scottish recusant circles. Some instrumental music by John Blak of Aberdeen survives, revealing a talent of a high order, as does the keyboard music attributed to Duncan Burnett after the turn of the 17th century. Thomas Wode copied several fine anonymous pavanes and galliards into his collection; the dance repertoire of Scottish instrumentalists appears to have been as international as everywhere else in Europe, while dance tunes marked 'Scottish' turn up in mainland collections.

Thomas Wode's song-appendix, completed well into the 17th century, and the Aberdeen Songs and Fancies publication of c.1660 indicate a major presence of English material and, at the same time, a strong attachment to often very old Scottish song material (see SONG, TRADITIONAL AND FOLK: 1). A slightly different attachment to the past seems also to be reflected in the various Scottish lute manuscripts, the earliest dated *c.*1620 and the latest 1700. The vast repertory includes English and Continental music, and hundreds of ravishingly lovely Scottish pieces. Many of these are of a distinctly Celtic cast (see MUSIC, HIGHLAND), indicating that whatever Lowland racism claimed to think of the Gaels (see HIGHLANDS AND ISLANDS AND CENTRAL GOVERNMENT: 1–2), their music was appreciated in the aristocratic households where these books were compiled. It is an irony of history that these beautiful lute pieces are, ultimately, the seedbed from which the bogus tartanry of Ossian and Walter Scott would emerge to create a wildly misleading picture of Scotland's cultural heritage in the minds of non-Scots and Scots alike.   JRB

11. Enlightenment (1660–1843): general (including philosophy)

The period bounded by the *Restoration of Charles II and the *Disruption in the Church of Scotland was one of immense achievement across a wide range of cultural activities. Giving some sense of order, however, as well as doing much to help explain the principal dynamics, are two overarching themes: Anglicization and Enlightenment.

The process of convergence with England provided a familiar constant throughout this period in Scottish history and had applications across many different cultural fields—at some times gathering pace, at others making rather slower progress. Meanwhile, even as specialist studies agree that the Scottish Enlightenment, which placed several aspects of the nation's culture in the international forefront, peaked between the 1740s and the 1790s, it has become common practice to identify its first glimmerings in the later 17th century and to regard its last moments as occurring sometime around the death of Sir Walter Scott in 1832.

The challenges posed by Anglicization in post-Restoration Scotland were manifold for a people sharing both a monarch and a similar language with the English. Not least, late 17th-century Scots, like the historian James Craufurd, lamented the lack of cultural patronage since the *Union of the Crowns: 'That which beyond all other things has set us so far back in learning', he claimed in *The History of the House of Este* in 1681, 'is our having no more the great incitements which a Court residing among us would afford.' Many Scots' work thus exhibited an unresolved tension between a perceived need to conform to Anglicized literary norms and the patriotic instinct to preserve and promote native traditions. After 1700, these problems crystallized in the publishing and authorship of James Watson and, above all, Allan Ramsay. Both men

wished to preserve vernacular poetry from extinction: Ramsay's collection *The Ever Green* (1724) was the outstanding result, interspersing originals with his own compositions—even though he was careful to claim that 'Their Images are native, and their Landskips domestick; copied from those Fields and Meadows we every Day Behold'.

Ramsay's pastoral drama *The Gentle Shepherd* (1725), one of the 18th century's most enduringly popular literary works, balanced vernacular language (see SCOTS LANGUAGE) and Lowland Scots settings with moral sentiments which clearly reflected the increasing influence of English models, especially the periodical press led by Joseph Addison's *Spectator* (1711–12). The success of the latter, which promised its readers 'such sound and wholesom Sentiments, as shall have a good Effect on their Conversation', was emblematic of the urgent refashioning of Scottish culture which accelerated following the *Union of 1707. Addison's emphasis on politeness and sociable interaction, aimed at the 'wearing out of Ignorance, Passion, and Prejudice' in a country previously beset by political dissension and religious conflict, defined Scotland's literary and intellectual agenda for much of the 18th century. It encouraged forms of cultural expression in keeping with English styles, helped nurture the growth of bourgeois civility, and provided a key component of what would soon mature as the Scottish Enlightenment.

Balancing these trends towards convergence, however, were other crucial cultural patterns which still clearly differentiated Scotland from England. Above all, the exemption of Scots law (see LAW AND LAWYERS: 2), education (see SCHOOLS AND SCHOOLING: 2), and the church (see CHURCH INSTITUTIONS: 5) from the assimilationist provisions of the Union ensured that Scottish culture would continue to be replenished from powerful national institutions. Viscount Stair's *Institutions of the Law of Scotland* (1681) definitively set Scots law within the rational framework of European natural jurisprudence. Sir George Mackenzie of Rosehaugh's studies of the criminal law, as well as his miscellaneous philosophical essays and conspicuous part in the foundation of the Advocates' Library (see LIBRARIES), Edinburgh's principal research resource, were other beacons of cultural light in late Stuart Scotland.

Education was simultaneously being strengthened as a characteristic Scottish institution in the immediate pre-Union period. An Act of 1696 reinforced the old Reformation principle of parish-based elementary education, a system which helped bring literacy, numeracy, and the catechism within reach of most Lowland Scots over the next 100 years. *University reform also underscored

Scotland's historic commitment to a rigorous, philosophically based intellectual grounding for young men of promise. From around 1700, the five Scottish institutions gradually abolished 'regenting' and introduced subject-specialist professorships. They also sought to incorporate the latest foreign ideas (notably Newton's science and Pufendorf's moral philosophy) into the curriculum, with teachers like Gershom Carmichael at Glasgow and David Gregory and Sir Robert Sibbald at Edinburgh among the leading innovators.

Not least in response to the Union of 1707, which stimulated a sense of national renewal as it also posed new threats to *national identity, Scottish culture had within a generation of the Treaty begun to develop in unanticipated ways. Religious change was a key factor in both diversification and widening participation. For where the early 18th-century Church of Scotland was preoccupied with doctrinal squabbling over relations with the state, a different mood had emerged by the 1740s, characterized by the rise of the Moderate party (see RELIGIOUS LIFE: 5). Committed to religious toleration and to a more relaxed attitude towards secular interests, the clerical leaders of the established church now emerged as protectors and promoters of intellectual and literary activities and, in persons like the historian and academic William Robertson (see HISTORIANS: 3), the literary critic and sermonizer Hugh Blair, the diarist Alexander 'Jupiter' Carlyle, and the playwright John Home, important participants in the Scottish Enlightenment.

Partly because of pre-Union developments, key achievements in Enlightenment culture lay in the disciplines of law and science. Scotland's legal practitioners included such eminent minds as Lord Kames, who explored the social construction of the law; Lord Hailes, a political historian and antiquarian; and Lord Monboddo, an early anthropologist. Science, meanwhile, was gilded by the presence of the brilliant Colin Maclaurin, who interpreted Newton's complex findings for an entranced 18th-century readership; by the chemists William Cullen and Joseph Black; by numerous path-breaking medical professors (see MEDICINE AND THE ORIGINS OF THE MEDICAL PROFESSION; CULTURE: 16) at Edinburgh and Glasgow; and by the pioneering geologist James Hutton, whose Theory of the Earth (1788), claiming that 'the greater part of our land, if not the whole, [has] been produced by operations natural to this globe', shattered previous assumptions about the formation of the planet.

Philosophy, still at the core of the university curriculum, was a central aspect of Enlightenment culture and lay behind many other developments. Francis Hutcheson, Carmichael's star pupil and Glasgow's great pedagogue, produced numerous works before 1750 which argued influentially for the existence of a 'moral sense' in human nature. David Hume's Treatise of Human Nature (1739–40), with its denial of everything (including the 'moral sense') which could not be proved either by reason or by empirical evidence, was the most provoking but also most misunderstood publication of the age. Thomas Reid and James Beattie from Aberdeen both ventured ripostes to Hume's caustic scepticism. Dugald Stewart, an Edinburgh professor of towering contemporary reputation, conveyed their 'common-sense' doctrines to a wider public.

Historical writing fully justified Hume's aphorism that his was 'the historical age' and Scotland 'the historical nation'. Hume's own History of England (1754–62), advancing what he described as 'moderate opinions', taught Hanoverian Britons how their precious liberties had really come about and how vulnerable they remained to the depradations of political parties and ideological bigots. But his fellow Scots also supplied many other educational studies of the past. Robertson's History of Scotland (1759), for example, promoted the progressive modern causes to which he was committed: it chastised religious extremism by all groups, cleansed the sullied reputation of Mary, Queen of Scots, and showed how Scotland had benefited from the Union. His other studies, on America and 16th-century Europe, were among the age's best-selling works.

Allied to history but drawing also upon the interests of the legal philosophers, some Scots achieved international celebrity for deductions about the essentially social origins of key human phenomena. Adam Smith (see ECONOMIC POLICY: 2) in The Wealth of Nations (1776) showed how property had emerged and how specialization, the famous 'division of labour', lay behind modern economic advances. Adam Ferguson's History of Civil Society (1767) revealed the development of art, government, marriage, and other institutions in different historical contexts, arguing persuasively that human society progresses by degrees: 'Not only the individual advances from infancy to manhood', he insisted, 'but the species itself from rudeness to civilization.'

Creative literature was also central to Scottish culture in this period. James Thomson's pastoral cycle The Seasons (1726–30) was typical of the more Anglicized work, achieving immense contemporary success. Henry Mackenzie's The Man of Feeling (1771) was superficially similar in language and won wide admiration, though in fact it explored the sentimental emotions in a way indebted to the Scottish philosophers who were among the author's friends. This affinity was also clearly seen in the moral essays which he contributed as editor of the *Mirror* (1779–80) and the *Lounger* (1785–7), in which he stressed in Addisonian fashion the essentially sociable nature of humankind.

Some Scots, however, were less obviously imitative of English culture. James MacPherson's Ossianic translations, despite doubts as to their authenticity, retailed a seductive image of ancient Celtic warrior society in which the outlines of a viable and distinctive Scottish identity could be clearly discerned by his contemporaries. Replete also with sufficient sentimentalism and politeness to attract a wide public, MacPherson's work was rapturously reviewed by Blair (who praised its 'tenderness and sublimity' and testified that it 'breathed a most ferocious spirit') and duly became an international cause célèbre. Robert Fergusson with his boisterous vernacular poetry, Robert Burns with his own passionate Scots lyrics, and the searing Gaelic verse of Alexander MacDonald (see GAELIC LITERATURE), the *Jacobite poet of Moidart who railed against 'The boar who's called King George, | son of the German sow', all stood outside the modes, language, and assumptions of English literature as zealously promoted by Blair and his colleagues. Accordingly, they largely escaped the attentions of Enlightened *Edinburgh and Europe.

Artistic life also blossomed amid general 18th-century prosperity and the growing belief that learning and aesthetic appreciation yielded moral and intellectual improvement. From William Aikman in the age of Ramsay and Thomson (who were his friends) to Ramsay's son and namesake in the age of Hume (this painter and philosopher were also favourite associates), Scottish portraiture was emerging to wider notice. By the time of Henry Raeburn, whose close friends included Reid and Stewart, the connections between art and philosophy had been cemented: painters shared with other Scottish intellectuals a fascination with the mechanisms of visual perception and with the manner in which the human mind apprehends the external world.

Not coincidentally, Hutton's friend and companion on his field trips was John Clerk of Eldin, subsequently one of Scotland's greatest landscape painters. Robert Adam (see ARCHITECTS, ARTISTS, AND CRAFTSMEN), a companion of Hume and Smith, completed architectural commissions at Hopetoun House and Culzean castle, which pushed neoclassicism to its conceptual limits. Sir John *Clerk of Penicuik, landed proprietor, designer of his own residence at Mavisbank, and an accomplished musician and composer after the fashion of his teacher Corelli, was also an intimate of the elder Ramsay.

A peculiar social environment underpinned these ties between art, philosophy, and scholarship, with academics, lawyers, landowners, doctors, clergy, merchants, and other educated people, sometimes women as well as men, students as well as mature adults, meeting to discuss and debate issues of public, literary, or intellectual interest. In the towns especially, many cultural institutions emerged. The Select Society of Edinburgh (1754–64), founded by the younger Ramsay, Hume, and Kames, provided a focus for many of the capital's finest minds. Other clubs like the Philosophical Society (later the Royal Society of Edinburgh), the Aberdeen Philosophical Society, and both the Literary Society and Political Economy Society in Glasgow, supplied a venue for polite exchange and gregarious interaction. Burns's Crochallan Fencibles and Edinburgh's Cape Club to which men as diverse as Raeburn and Fergusson belonged were also convivial institutions which in taverns and oyster-cellars permitted Scots to explore the practical possibilities of Addison's seductive philosophy of sociability.

Historians remain uncertain where exactly to draw the line between the educated culture of the Enlightenment and the popular culture of the rest of the Scottish people. After all, the vital context of sociability experienced in clubs and societies seems to have spread relatively widely across urban society in particular. Nevertheless, popular culture also had distinctive characteristics. Partly, it was defined by belief: whilst 18th-century philosophers and painters doubted the dogmatic claims of the theologians, herdsmen on Raasay or labourers in Berwickshire were more likely still to believe in the efficacy of curative magic, the accuracy of 'second-sight' (precognition of events), and the existence of fairies. Social distinctions in culture may also have been experiential. It was unlikely, for example, that members of the elite would be found participating actively in urban riots on the king's birthday or in Evangelical religious phenomena such as the Cambuslang 'revival' of 1742 or the anti-Catholic rioting of the late 1770s.

In the decades after 1800 various developments, including once again accelerating Anglicization, gradually unravelled the tightly bound fabric of the Enlightenment, producing an unmistakable sense that Scottish culture had taken on a new direction. Ironically, it was also now at its most influential on the international stage. Sir Walter Scott's Romantic ballads, and especially the extraordinary series of historical novels beginning with *Waverley* (1814) and continuing on through such best-sellers as *Heart of Midlothian* and *Rob Roy* (both 1818), attracted unprecedented attention and were eagerly mimicked and translated overseas. So too was 'the

Scotch philosophy' at its formidable height, the works of Ferguson, Reid, and Stewart in particular proving integral to early 19th-century German, French, and American university education.

Pessimistic cultural commentary, however, had emerged with a vengeance by the end of the Napoleonic Wars. Much of this was the result of an increasingly politically polarized intellectual and literary scene, epitomized by the Whiggish *Edinburgh Review* (1802–1929) and the Tory-inclined *Blackwood's Edinburgh Magazine* (1817–1980). Whig intellectuals like Henry Cockburn and Francis Jeffrey seemed to advocate a reformism which was tantamount to further Anglicization: Scott's son-in-law and biographer John Gibson Lockhart bitterly satirized this manifesto in *Peter's Letters to his Kinsfolk* (1819). Whig critics like Robert Mudie equally mocked the stultifying values of academic Toryism. Other commentators, like Thomas Carlyle, himself soon to abandon Edinburgh for London, also bemoaned the materialist philosophy and lack of moral vigour at the heart of modern culture, in part the consequence of Enlightenment thought: 'Practically speaking', he complained in the *Edinburgh Review* in 1829, 'our creed is Fatalism . . . free in hand and foot, we are shackled in heart and soul.'

In the following years, the ten-year civil war in the national church and a growing sense that, following the Reform Act of 1832, Scotland was becoming, as Scott scathingly put it, 'an inferior species of Northumberland', signalled conclusively that the age of Enlightenment was over.   DA

12. Enlightenment (1660–1843): art

The Scottish Enlightenment and especially the ideas of Hume and Reid were central to the evolution of modern art and so Scottish artists played a precocious role in its early history. An important preliminary was the change in status of artists from craft to profession. The success of the portrait painter Sir John de Medina (1659–1710) who came to Scotland in 1693 and was the last person to be knighted before the *Union of 1707 reflected the beginning of this change. Native artists followed and William Aikman, who was a pupil of Medina, John Smibert, who eventually settled in America, and John Alexander all studied in Italy. In Edinburgh in 1729 the decorative painter James Norie and others established Scotland's first art institution, the Academy of St Luke. Aikman was an important model for Allan Ramsay's early style and in spite of their Italian experience, all these painters looked back to the empirical character of Dutch painting. The Union depressed patronage, however. Aikman and Smibert left Scotland and Ramsay followed them. He was nevertheless central to the development of Scottish art. Like his friend Hume, he combined a

commitment to perceived truth with a profound sense of humanity and he is at his best when most informal, as in his portrait of his second wife, Margaret Lindsay, or of Martha, countess of Elgin (1766, Private Collection, Scotland).

Links between painting and the other branches of Scottish thought are numerous. Gavin Hamilton's *Death of Lucretia* (1767), for example, is an essay in moral sentiment. In his series of pictures from the *Iliad* begun in 1759 Hamilton also explored the idea pioneered by Thomas Blackwell in his *Essay on the Life, Times and Writings of Homer* (London, 1735) that Homer was a primitive poet. Hamilton settled in Rome and young painters of many nationalities gathered round there, including the Runciman brothers John and Alexander, John Brown, Anne Forbes, and David Allan.

Alexander Runciman's *Hall of Ossian*, painted in 1772 for Sir James Clerk of Penicuik, combined Hamilton's inspiration with the more radical primitivism represented by Ossian and for the first time in modern art, spontaneity and freedom from convention were presented as the objectives of painting. This parallels the contemporary revival of vernacular poetry and music as do David Allan's Scottish genre pictures, his illustrations to Allan Ramsay's *Gentle Shepherd*, and his illustrations of Burns's songs for George Thomson.

In 1693 John Slezer began the history of modern landscape in Scotland with his *Theatrum Scotiae*, a set of topographical prints of the principal towns and houses of the country (see MAPS AND MAP-MAKING; URBAN SETTLEMENT: 1). James Norie practised a style of decorative landscape that was developed by Charles Steuart, Alexander Runciman, Jacob More, and Alexander Nasmyth—all linked by the apprentice system to the Norie firm—into an independent art. It was Nasmyth, a close friend of Robert Burns, who really established the iconography of Scottish landscape, however. Nasmyth was widely influential on painters of the younger generation: his own son Patrick, John Knox, David Roberts, Hugh William Williams, Andrew Wilson, and others. His paintings represent a stable, harmonious world in marked contrast to the more subjective approach developed by John Thomson of Duddingston who was temperamentally closer to his friend Walter Scott and whose influence is still seen in the work of Horatio McCulloch and the painters of the mid-19th century. In contrast to Nasmyth's work, the etchings of historic buildings by John Clerk of Eldin reflect the interests of the antiquarian, yet the drawings that he did for James Hutton's *Theory of the Earth* record collaboration between artist and scientist.

Portrait painting remained central to Scottish art. Henry Raeburn trained originally as a goldsmith, but was encouraged to paint by David Deuchar. He retained Allan Ramsay's respect for the individual, not only in such forceful but sympathetic portraits as Baillie William Galloway or Mrs James Campbell, but also notably in his portraits in the grand manner such as Sir John and Lady Clerk of Penicuik (1792, National Gallery of Ireland).

Raeburn cultivated an informal and intuitive approach to painting. His portrait of the fiddle player Neil Gow, for instance, suggests an analogy between his own painting and the simple, intuitive strength of Gow's playing. Such qualities closely parallel the theory of perception of Thomas Reid and it is perhaps because of Reid's subsequent influence in France that it is possible to see a real analogy between Raeburn's painting and impressionism. Raeburn's principal contemporaries were the pastelist Archibald Skirving and George Watson, as well as miniature painters like Andrew Robertson and John Bogie and portrait sculptors like William Gowans (fl. c.1770), Robert Burn (fl. 1790–1816), and James Tassie (1735–99) who produced remarkable portrait medallions using vitreous paste. Other sculptors were Laurence MacDonald (1799–1878) and Thomas Campbell (1790–1858). Both spent long periods in Rome and worked in an elegant neoclassical manner derived from Canova.

Raeburn's younger contemporary and friend David Wilkie was the most influential of all Scottish painters. He settled in London, but he took his principal inspiration from the Scots poets, especially Burns, and shaped the future course of Scottish art. He also had close links with developments in philosophical thought, especially through his contact with Charles Bell whose *Anatomy of Expression* (1806) was an important stage in the evolution of his ideas on the physiology of the brain and nervous system. There is a direct link, partly through Bell, between Wilkie and Géricault and the early history of psychiatric medicine in France. Wilkie's *Distraining for Rent* (1815, NGS) and *Penny Wedding* (1818, HM the Queen) also provide a commentary on contemporary social change and the human cost of the agricultural and industrial revolutions. They are closely paralleled by John Galt in his novels, though in his approach to history in painting Wilkie was closer to Walter Scott whose inspiration is clearly seen in *John Knox Preaching before the Lords of Congregation*. Wilkie's *Chelsea Pensioners Reading the Dispatch of Waterloo* (1822, V & A, Apsley House) was hugely successful and even more radical, however. In it, a major historical event is seen through the eyes of ordinary people. This approach to the psychological interpretation of history was widely influential in France with painters like Delacroix and Bonington. Wilkie's

earlier style of genre painting was also widely imitated in his lifetime by artists like Alexander Fraser sen., John Burnet, and Walter Geikie. Geikie's etchings and drawings are of particular interest because of the unaffected way that they record the lives and circumstances of ordinary people, but in subsequent generations this degenerated into the 'Kailyard' imagery of painters like Tom Faed and Erskine Nicol. Later, Wilkie imitated the breadth of handling of Rubens, Rembrandt, and Velasquez in a way that influenced painters in the next generation such as John 'Spanish' Phillip and Robert Scott Lauder. Wilkie died two years before the *Disruption, but the themes of such pictures as *Knox Preaching* and his late masterpiece *The Cotter's Saturday Night* (1837, Glasgow Art Galleries) gave expression to the ideas at the centre of the developing religious crisis in Scotland. DM

13. Enlightenment (1660–1843): language and literature

If the Bannatyne and Maitland anthologies, which had self-consciously compiled a 'treasure house' of Middle Scots literature, reminded Scots of their distinctive literary heritage before the Union of the Crowns, so the parliamentary *Union of 1707 was anticipated by George Watson's *Choice Collection*. While the continued existence of writing in Latin, Gaelic, Scots, and English was confirmed in this anthology, the increasing dominance of English was the major, defensive motivation for publication (see PRINTING AND PUBLISHING). It follows from this that the phrase 'Vernacular revival', as applied to the early 18th-century movement initiated by Allan Ramsay (1684–1758), consolidated by Robert Fergusson (1750–74), and immortalized by Robert Burns (1759–96) is, strictly speaking, a misnomer. What Ramsay initiated was a return to the polymathic breadth threatened by the weakening of the Scots line within the admixture. That his first printed poem, 'To the Memory of Archibald Pitcairne M.D.', is an undisguised statement of Scottish nationalist sentiment, written in English about a Latin poet, encapsulates the situation neatly.

Neither Ramsay nor Fergusson negated the value of English and Latin in order to advance Scots and Scottishness. Instead they united decorous and political approaches to language while bridging the gap between courtly and popular traditions, which had been allowed to grow. This allowed the continuation of the strong Scottish line in European pastoral and Georgic literature within a modally and linguistically broadened context. Barbour, Dunbar, and Lindsay would surely have applauded both the English of Fergusson's 'Damon to his Friends' and its Scottish parodic counterpart 'On Seeing a Butterfly in the Street'. Drummond and (particularly) Ayton would have welcomed Ramsay's *The Gentle Shepherd* as a continuation in justifiably heavier Scots, for new persuasive purposes, within a new political climate.   RDSJ

14. Enlightenment (1660–1843): the novel

Faced with the challenge to write about their country and its character, above all its changing character, novelists of what we like to call 'the age of Scott' rose magnificently to that challenge. It was, of course, the age of Sir Walter Scott if one measures it by sales, by worldwide popularity, by translation and adaptation, song and opera, painting and costume, and by the extraordinary attraction Scott exerted on the imagination of people all over the world. Whether during the war years when Europe was blocked to the normal tourist, or afterwards when *Edinburgh, 'the Athens of the North', played host to the hordes who came to see the city of Scott's imagination, Scott in his poetry and prose fiction created a picture whose impact was, and is, powerful. That he altered and amended was to be expected: the royal visit of George IV in 1822 is widely recognized as (in the true sense) a charade orchestrated by Scott, with scant regard to historical detail, a pageant of tartan (see DRESS, HIGHLAND) and picturesque which succeeded marvellously in making a royal occasion great. When the regalia of Scotland were rediscovered, when the currency had to be defended against proposals to merge it with England's, when Scotland needed a great public figure of world stature to represent its culture and its interests, Scott was the obvious choice, before his ruin in 1826, and even afterwards when he was painfully trying to write off his colossal debts.

But what Scotland did he write about? In his poetry, he dwelt on the ancient, the ruined, the vanishing—the Border abbeys, the vanishing minstrels, the great families and their martial traditions. In his fiction he ranged far and wide in his imagination, to the East, to continental Europe, to England, to Scotland and above all to Edinburgh. The Porteous Riots of *The Heart of Mid-Lothian*, the march of the *Jacobite forces through the Royal Park to Holyrood, the splendid evocation of the regular stagecoach's departure for Fife from the old Tron church in the High Street, the atmosphere of the new bourgeois squares (see URBAN SETTLEMENT: 2) to which Alan Fairford's father removes in *Redgauntlet* from the pestilential air of the Old Town: Scott wrote about these with the familiarity of one who had lived his adult life there, and who walked its streets day and night. When his imagination required him to go to the Highlands (in *Rob Roy* or *Waverley*), to the south-west (in *Redgauntlet*), or merely to the *Borders he knew in-

timately (in *Waverley* again), Scott had the peculiar ability to charm the Scottish reader with recognized scenery, and the non-Scot with a landscape (see GEOLOGY AND LANDSCAPE) which fixed in the world's imagination a picture of a country of Highland beauty and civic grandeur (*Glasgow or Edinburgh), of lingering history (see HISTORIANS: 3; HISTORICAL CLUBS AND SOCIETIES) wherever the novelist turned, of national pride and passion below the surface of confident Enlightened North British-ness (see NATIONAL IDENTITY: 4), of Jacobite rebellions either re-created or remembered, a dangerous edge to a land of beauty.

What unites the impact of Scott to that of his distinguished contemporaries Galt and Hogg is a curious double vision the historian will recognize and respond to. Scott the historian used the freedom of the creative writer to reshape the events of Scottish history, and to populate these re-creations with living copies of real personages, intermixed with totally fictitious characters. The Reuben Butler who is caught up in the Porteous riots ministers to the last moments of a totally historical Porteous, even though he is Scott's creation; his future wife Jeanie Deans is indebted for her sister Effie's pardon to a historical duke of Argyll and Queen Caroline even though Jeanie is purely Scott's invention—though an invention based on the true story of Helen Walker of Irongray whose walk to London was the initial spur to Scott's imagination. The pattern is repeated endlessly. Alan Fairford grows up a student lawyer only yards from where Scott himself suffered the same boredom and mixed motives in George Square. Edward Waverley pays homage to a real Prince Charles Edward Stuart in Holyrood, even though in *Redgauntlet* Alan Fairford meets the same Charles Edward on a purely invented visit in the 1760s which Charles never made in reality—though the idea of his furtive landing on the Solway shore to lead another rising makes for great fiction. Whether reinvigorating in the imagination the Wars of the *Covenant of *Old Mortality* or the Highland society of *Rob Roy*, Scott had no compunction in mixing fact and fiction, and living the tale through an invented character (the 'Scott hero') who lives, survives, travels, experiences—and has to have explained to him (usually him, though Jeanie Deans is a splendid exception)—this mysterious Scotland through which he travels, passing on to the majority of his readers an introduction to Scotland past and some idea of Scotland in Scott's own present.

For all three novelists—Scott, Galt, and Hogg—this is the crossing point which animates their fiction, fiction published in the memory of real European war, and almost living memory of the *French Revolution, fiction published when both

British society and Scottish society was in ferment to the extent that (as Scott memorably wrote in the last chapter of *Waverley*) 'there is no European nation which, within the course of half a century or a little more, has undergone so complete a change as this kingdom of Scotland'.

That change was still evident, if anything accelerating, in the 1810s when Scott rose to fame as novelist, and in the 1820s when Hogg and Galt published their most famous work. In *Annals of the Parish*, Galt's best-known (but not always best understood) work, a country minister spends 50 years in a parish far from the cities and the industrial upheaval (see RURAL SOCIETY: 4; URBAN SOCIETY: 3), keeping his annals, his diary of events which he writes up in his retirement, in a style very obviously indebted to the OSA and the interest it bred in parish affairs. Which years? The years 1760 to 1810—Galt's masterly choice (very like Scott's similar choice) covering years just within living recollection, but not quite contemporary, years when the seeds of present society are being sown, but their fruition still not quite accomplished. Galt's country minister is a masterpiece: conservative, timid, not very clever, well intentioned and honest in his ministry, but desperately unwilling and badly equipped to face up to the changes which are the background to his 50 years' ministry. The industrial revolution comes (see ECONOMY: 4), the parish expands with mills and weaving folk, the church empties, the old landowners lose their pre-eminence and the new rich take their place, centralized education and state services replace the old kirk session mechanisms—Galt's minister wants nothing to do with them. He likes to live (in his own masterly phrase) in 'the lee of the dyke'. When he retires, his church will need a strong hand to bring it back to life after 50 years of slumber, but Galt's criticism of a static ministry is tempered by an affectionate realization that here, too, was something valuable in preserving what was good about a vanishing Scotland. The minister who keeps the *Annals* (like his fellow-minister in *The Ayrshire Legatees* and the eponymous *Provost*) does not so much tell us about himself as let details slip by accident. The reader, irresistibly, is drawn into the story, piecing together what the minister does not see or will not tell, realizing the change that is going on all around. For the minister, 1789 is a year of blessed quiet, when nothing happened in the parish. But a year later, a bookshop opens in his parish, and the working lads crowd in to see the London paper and read the news. Scotland is changing: Galt found an irresistible way of showing the change, like Scott equally attractive to those familiar with Scottish country life, and those who could imagine it only from afar.

And what of Hogg? All but forgotten a few decades ago, Hogg is now enjoying the long-overdue compliment of a multi-volume critical edition, incredibly the first ever. While he is known now, and rightly admired, for his extraordinary *Confessions* (which appeared in the same year as *Redgauntlet*) he is being revealed in this new edition as a multi-faceted talent, in his own lifetime widely admired as a poet, ballad collector, short-story writer, magazine editor, and novelist. His fiction includes masterpieces of historical writing (the *Three Perils of Man* deserves to be far better known than it is) but for most people the main attraction is the re-creation of Scottish grim, Presbyterian life (see RELIGIOUS LIFE: 6) satirized in *The Confessions*, a tale of Satanic possession and abuse which is now very widely reprinted and read.

What perhaps is only slowly being realized is that Hogg is satirizing many of the religious with which he populates the pages of his *Confessions*, late 17th-century extreme Calvinists, heretical believers in extraordinary (and unscriptural) notions that they alone would go to Heaven, 'justified', while the world's masses would tumble to hell regardless (as Holy Willie would have said) of any good or ill they had done in their own lifetimes. The idea is absurd, as Hogg's contemporaries would have seen at once, though perhaps in our own time people may take a little longer to see through the absurdity of the religious nonsense Hogg's extremists spout, and the Devil-figure Gil-Martin gleefully echoes and encourages.

The *Confessions* is much more than that; among other things, it is an extraordinary recreation of Old Town *Edinburgh, its wynds and its High Street, Arthur's Seat at dawn, and the appalling ghostly presence which seems likely to push George Colwan to his death from the Salisbury Crags. Even more astonishing for the production in 1824 of someone regarded patronizingly at the time as a simple shepherd, the *Confessions* is a near-modernist masterpiece of storytelling through multiple narrators, no one version quite the 'truth' and nothing but the truth, and at the heart of the confusion and arrogance and terror the shadowy presence of an enigmatic Devil-figure who alone knows what is going on and will not tell.

Of course Scotland had more to boast of than the famous three names here listed: Scott's son-in-law Lockhart and his study of religious guilt and carnal desire in *Adam Blair*, the fiction of John Wilson ('Christopher North') and a little later John Stuart Blackie, of David Macbeth Moir and a little later William Edmonston Aytoun. In the Whig *Edinburgh Review* and later the Tory *Blackwood's Edinburgh Magazine* Scotland had two immensely influential periodicals (see NEWSPAPERS: 1), influencing literary taste but also carrying a multitude of factual articles on, among other things, Scotland, past and present. The press began to aspire to something recognizably modern at this time, as *transport and communications made the distribution of the printed word more practicable—a point picked up by Galt in his *Annals*, where the London paper becomes the preferred source of political news and comment, not the local pulpit.

Scotland was changing, changing. When Scott wrote the last chapter of *Waverley* in 1814 it was visibly true: when he wrote the last chapter of *Redgauntlet* in 1824, he made it describe the realization in Redgauntlet's own mind that there would never again be a Jacobite rising, that those days were finished, that a new society was coming which had no time, or wish, for the restoration of the old Scotland, whatever pride there might be in that vanished country and its institutions. ' "Then, gentlemen", said Redgauntlet, clasping his hands together as the words burst from him, "the cause is lost for ever!" ' An imaginary scene, an imaginary character, but an illustration of Scott at the peak of his powers as a historical novelist, catching the pivotal moment of change, irrevocable, regrettable, welcome. Ahead, a recognizable modern Scotland of relative peace and prosperity; behind, a glorious history. In the pages of fiction it was possible to see both, and above all to see the moment—the moment when change became irresistible, and Scotland moved forward.

IC

15. Enlightenment (1660–1843): music

The cataclysmic effect of the *Reformation's removal of the main reason for training musicians and composers, namely to supply the demand for liturgical music (see MUSIC, ECCLESIASTICAL), meant that Scotland has had a very slim tradition of 'European art music' right through to the 20th century. In virtually every country in western Europe, secular music in an Italian-inspired international idiom came into its own in the 17th century. For Scots, however, music came to mean their own 'native airs'—what would today be described as traditional music (see SONG: TRADITIONAL AND FOLK), which flourished uninterrupted by the Reformation, despite all the church's sporadic efforts to discourage it. The great body of superlative, quasi-improvisatory Scottish lute compositions recorded in the various 17th-century lutebooks belong to this tradition, as do the equally artistic fiddle compositions of Neil and Nathaniel Gow, to name but two, in the later 18th century, or the many sets of anonymous fiddle variations on folk tunes which are one of the glories of Scottish culture.

The native air had a major impact on 18th-century Scottish concert music, but the relationship between the two was an uneasy one, as the musicologist David Johnson has brilliantly shown. The poet Alan Ramsay patriotically attacked the Italianizing trend of the concerts of the Edinburgh Musical Society, founded in 1728 as successor to the St Cecilia's Society of 1695. Like Burns after him, Ramsay wrote new words to folk tunes, and new poems in the style of folk songs. But he also wrote artful and highly polished texts for the upper-class concerts of European music mounted by the Society, including a whole cantata in Scots for Lorenzo Bocchi. His ballad opera *The Gentle Shepherd*, however, takes John Gay's approach in *The Beggar's Opera*, setting composed texts to existing and popular tunes though, unlike Gay, the result is douce to say the least. In a country whose Reformation had entirely deprived it of a living tradition of religious art (see ICONOCLASM) capable of fostering intellectual aesthetic sensitivity, the stupendous richness of Scotland's 'native airs' was ultimately to prove fatal to attempts to develop a school of 'classical' composition. What Scots did produce in the way of baroque, galant, and rococo music is often distinctively Scottish, even when not based on pre-existent Scots airs; but this attempt to woo those who saw those airs as embodying the essence of all that was best in their country failed.

There is nothing specifically Scottish about the music of the singer John Abel, from Aberdeen, who joined the English Chapel Royal in 1679, nor about most of the handful of very fine Italianate compositions written—mostly abroad—by the young Sir John *Clerk of Penicuik. These include no fewer than five cantatas for soprano and instruments, the longest of them, 'Odo di mesto intorno', was composed in Rome to celebrate the marriage of the duke of Bedford. Clerk was studying at the time with Pasquini and with Arcangelo Corelli, the most renowned composer of his day, who did his pupil the signal honour of leading the players at the performance. Another, 'Leo Scotiae irritatus', celebrates Scotland's colonial venture in *Darien. It sets a text by Clerk's fellow student at Leiden (see LOW COUNTRIES), the celebrated physician Nikolaas Boerhave, and the work is very stirring even in its present incomplete form. A gifted composer, whose works are deeply rewarding, Clerk appears to have stopped writing music on his return to Scotland. He nevertheless remained interested in music all his life, being a leading figure in the Edinburgh Musical Society. This body attracted international figures to Edinburgh: some came, performed, and went; some, like Francesco Barsanti, remained a few years; and some, like Johann Schetky, stayed. Schetky's fondness for the air of

Edinburgh, however, did not lead him to emulate Barsanti (or indeed Gemminiani) in his fondness for the Scots native air in his compositions.

While the highly attractive music of William McGibbon (1690–1756) often leans heavily on Corelli, and the fine sonatas of his contemporary James Foulis are equally international in idiom, the sonatas of Alexander Munro (published in Paris in 1732) and of Charles MacLean (fl. 1737), and, above all, the vast output of James Oswald (1710–69) are all imbued with the spirit of Scots song and dance, thus making it quite distinctive in the cosmopolitan 'Euro-sound' world of its time. This remains true of much of the music Oswald composed in London after his move there in 1741.

Edinburgh taste was conservative (Corelli remained beloved throughout the century) and nationalistic (the Musical Society's very lengthy concerts featured many Scots songs). The Society's success was such that it built its own oval concert hall, St Cecilia's, in 1762, as part of the general 'improvement' of the city fostered by the Society's long-serving secretary, six times Lord Provost George Drummond—the father of *Edinburgh's New Town. By 1775, Edinburgh was a fully functioning, if minor European musical centre, with resident composers both native and foreign, and a body of professional performers.

The works of Thomas Alexander Erskine, sixth earl of Kellie (1732–89), are thoroughly international in idiom. Like Clerk, he studied abroad with one of the leading avant-garde figures of the day—in this case, Johann Stamitz in Mannheim. The earl, known as 'Fiddler Tam', was a great drinker and bon viveur, and much of his music is lost thanks to his own insouciant carelessness. The surviving chamber music and symphonies reveal a very talented creative mind. In the age of Ossian and the French Revolutionary Wars, the modest but lovely blooms of Scotland's classical flowering withered and died. Largely restricted to Edinburgh, this music ultimately failed to find enough appreciation to sustain it even in the capital. A mind and ear as acute as those of Robert Burns proved deaf to the European concert music of the Edinburgh Musical Society. Of the improvised decorations added to the psalm tunes sung by his cottar's family on a Saturday night, he wrote 'compar'd with these, Italian trills are tame'. Burns's prestige damned concert music to failure in 19th-century Scotland, for all his energies in the last years of his life were poured into his massive contribution to Johnson's six-volume Scots Musical Museum. Burns's great work undoubtedly saved the native culture, music no less than language (see SCOTS LANGUAGE), of Lowland Scotland, which his admired Robert Fergusson had seen as being threatened by mainland

European musical cosmopolitanism in the 1770s, when he wrote his Elegy on the Death of Scottish Music. But the triumph of the native air consigned the music of McGibbon, Maclean, Kelly, and the rest to oblivion. The delightful creations of Scotland's 18th-century composers failed, in the end, to overcome the suspicion which Scotland continues to lavish on so many of her own intellectual and artistic prophets to this day. The Edinburgh Musical Society gave its last concert in 1798. It was wound up in 1801, its beautiful concert hall sold off to become a Baptist kirk. St Cecilia's became the Grand Lodge of Scotland in 1809, two years after General Sir John Reid left his considerable fortune to found a chair of music at Edinburgh University. It took nearly four decades of struggle and effort before the University actually did so. And Scotland itself was to have no full-time professional symphony orchestra until 1951.   JRB

16. Enlightenment (1660–1843): medicine

The medical faculty of the University of Edinburgh, founded in 1726, dominated the professional practice of medicine (see MEDICINE AND THE ORIGINS OF THE MEDICAL PROFESSION) in Scotland, drawing in talent from elsewhere, particularly Glasgow. In the second half of the 18th century it was the leading medical school in the English-speaking world; yet at that time formally trained medical men treated no more than a tenth of the Scottish people (see HEALTH, FAMINE, AND DISEASE: 3).

Since antiquity, medicine had had an international dimension. Peter Lowe, who founded the Faculty of Physicians and Surgeons in Glasgow in 1599, spent 30 years as a military surgeon in France. The leading figures in Edinburgh at the end of the 17th century were Robert Sibbald and Archibald Pitcairne, who had both studied in Paris, and Pitcairne was professor at Leiden in 1692–3 (see FRANCE: THE 'AULD ALLIANCE'; LOW COUNTRIES). Several of their colleagues had been at Continental medical schools such as Montpellier and Padua.

The stimulus to found a medical school at Edinburgh came from John Monro, a surgeon, and George Drummond, Lord Provost. They realized that Leiden's medical students brought wealth to the town, and used this as a model for repairing that part of *Edinburgh's fortunes which had been lost after the *Union of 1707 when the aristocracy moved their social focus to London. Edinburgh followed the Leiden programme of excellence in teaching, the observation of clinical cases, and the construction of the facilities needed to support medical education. The botanic garden, established in 1676, was encouraged. From 1720 the professor of anatomy was John Monro's son Alexander primus: he had been apprenticed to his father before studying in Paris and Leiden. He was a fine teacher, and had an anatomical theatre built to the east of the College. In 1726 he was joined by four more young Scots who had taken their MDs in various parts of Europe: John Rutherford (Rheims), Andrew St Clair (Angers), Andrew Plummer (Leiden), and John Innes (Padua). Alexander Monro's son, Alexander *secundus*, who succeeded him in the chair of anatomy 1766–7, was the most original of the Monro dynasty, writing particularly on delicate structures: the nerves, brain, and lymphatic system. Alexander *tertius* shared the chair with him from 1797 to 1819, and continued alone until 1846.

An area on the south side of the city developed with the medical institutions within a compass of a few hundred yards—the College, Infirmary (1729), Surgeons' Hall—and there too were the houses where extramural lecturers taught medicine. This remarkable concentration remained until the Infirmary moved to a new site at the end of the 19th century.

*Glasgow, too, had a distinguished, though smaller, medical school. There, William Cullen (1710–90) built his reputation as a teacher and systematizer of knowledge: the great chemist Joseph Black was his pupil and successor. Both men migrated to Edinburgh, in search of larger classes and fees. At *Aberdeen, King's College had a mediciner or professor of medicine from its foundation in 1494. Medicine there was taught largely as part of the arts course until about 1750; medical teaching grew slowly in the following century.

Many of the most able Scots surgeons and physicians settled in London. Most took their medical knowledge to a larger field for practitioners, though one or two sought its literary opportunities. The ill-tempered John Armstrong (*c.*1709–79), born in Liddesdale, had a hostile bedside manner but found success with *The Art of Preserving Health* (1744) in blank verse. Tobias Smollett, once an apprentice surgeon in Glasgow, also had more success as a writer than as a medical man, and edited the three volumes of the *Treatise on the Theory and Practice of Midwifery* (1752–64) by William Smellie. Smellie had developed his skill as an obstetrician in Lanark, but spent the years 1738–59 in London, teaching and working as a man-midwife. He improved both the design and the deployment of obstetrical forceps and is probably the single most important figure in the history of obstetrics: when 'Jupiter' Carlyle dined with eight Scots medical men in London in 1758, he heard William Hunter toast, 'May no English nobleman venture out of the world without a Scottish physician, as I am sure there are none who venture in.' Born at East Kilbride, Hunter attained great wealth, and trained one of the greatest of medical scientists, his brother John, whose relent-

less curiosity brought him to make discoveries over an enormously wide range, but especially in comparative anatomy.

James Lind (1716–94), born in Edinburgh, became a naval surgeon before returning to take his MD in 1748. His *Treatise upon the Scurvy* (1753) suggested prevention of scurvy at sea by the use of lime juice. Lind was appointed physician at the Royal Hospital at Haslar, near Portsmouth, but was unable to enforce the use of his method. One of the most important contributions of Edinburgh medicine was the use of quantitative methods. Sir Gilbert Blane, who came from Ayrshire and was Physician to the Fleet from 1780, studied disease by using his position to collect statistics; among other studies, he used numbers to show that Lind was right.

John Gregory (1725–73), professor of the practice of physic at Edinburgh, wrote *Lectures on the Duties and Qualifications of a Physician* (1773), the first restatement of medical ethics since ancient times. He deployed the idea of moral sentiments which had been developed by Hutcheson, Hume, and Smith. He argued that medicine was an art rather than a trade because the sympathy which the physician felt for his patient meant that their relationship was not purely commercial. His ideas were developed into the standard 19th-century view of medical ethics by the Edinburgh-trained Thomas Percival (1740–1804) of Manchester.

Most 18th-century practitioners lived in the cities and towns (see URBAN SOCIETY: 3), where there was a sufficient demand for them, though the number of country doctors did increase towards the end of the century. In 1780 there were still only two doctors and a surgeon in the burgh of *Perth. Gentlemen in the country could enjoy the services of urban physicians by describing symptoms in a letter and receiving advice and a prescription in return. Ordinary folk depended on neighbours, collective knowledge, and the occasional wise woman (see TRADITIONAL HEALING). In the 17th century, the Faculty of Physicians and Surgeons of Glasgow had not attempted to force irregular practitioners out of medicine if they had useful skills, but rather to find out what they were capable of doing and then to license them to act within their capabilities. Thus in 1666 John Logan, a smith in the Gorbals, was permitted to continue cauterizing. Gardeners were also allowed a limited medical role because of their knowledge of herbs. People also sought to conserve their health by visiting once-holy wells, on the Celtic quarter days, especially Beltane, and by ritual, particularly at New Year (see CALENDAR AND SEASONAL CUSTOM).

Slowly, the numbers of doctors increased and formal medicine became accessible to more of the people. The Royal Public Dispensary (1776) was the first institution of its kind in Scotland: supported by charity, it gave those of modest means access to professional medical advice. The man behind it was Andrew Duncan (1744–1828), professor of the Institutes in Medicine from 1789 to 1819, shaper of institutions, and organizer of sociable dining clubs. Shocked by Robert Fergusson's death in the Edinburgh Bedlam in 1774, he campaigned until the Royal Asylum (now the Royal Edinburgh Hospital) opened in 1813. He encouraged the young Royal Medical Society, which promoted discussion among its student members. A few of his students died poor and far from home, and Duncan had them buried in Buccleuch burying ground, where a cluster of little headstones surrounds his own.

Disease was generally believed, both by doctors and the people, to be caused by the environment and by habits of living: fevers caused by sleeping in damp shielings, or rheumatism by drinking whisky (see TEMPERANCE) and wearing linen rather than wool next to the skin. The possibilities of medical intervention in disease were thus limited.

The major advance in the health of the people was the reduction of smallpox, particularly in childhood, by vaccination. Its possibilities had been demonstrated in the 1720s. Vaccination reached the most remote areas—folk in Durness in Sutherland were vaccinated about 1760—long before Edward Jenner, a pupil of John Hunter, conclusively demonstrated its effectiveness in 1796. Some lairds and ministers saw vaccination as a social duty, and the minister's pastoral role enabled him to overcome hostility: 'the people have more confidence in their minister than in any other', maintained the minister of Golspie in his contribution to the OSA.

Throughout the period, anatomy dominated medical training: in the absence of a supply of cadavers, the anatomists made delicate preparations of structures by injecting the arteries with wax or mercury. As teaching expanded, this was not enough, and the 'resurrection men' set to exhume newly buried bodies. In 1829 occurred the case of Burke and Hare, who increased the supply of corpses by murder; and three years later the Anatomy Act made the bodies of unknown paupers legally available for dissection (see IMMIGRATION, IRISH). JBur

17. age of industry (1843–1914): general

A truism among students of Scottish culture avers that the society over which Victoria reigned was marked by a lamentable decline from the glories of the Enlightenment and the days when *Edinburgh could be described as 'a Hotbed of Genius' (see CULTURE: 11). With the 1830s and 1840s (so opinion has it), we enter the age of the epigoni, when there is less intellectual brilliance and mediocrity and

conventionality dominate the scene. Burns had been dead for several decades; the great Sir Walter died in 1832; Carlyle finally migrated to London in 1834; there was no painter equal to Raeburn (d. 1823), no historian as accomplished as William Robertson (see HISTORIANS: 3), no philosopher fit to hold a candle to Hume; and of course the *Disruption of 1843, by shattering the unity of the national church, weakened one of the principal unifying forces in Scottish society, with all the damage to morale and even a sense of *national identity which that entailed. Music-making was at a fairly low ebb; of world-class art there was little, at least until the closing decades of the century; much of the literature was crudely demotic, culminating in the 'Kailyard' writers of the 1880s and 1890s, so popular in their time and so often ridiculed in ours; and most modern commentators deplore what they see as a society vitiated by an oppressive Calvinist theology (which, incidentally, they seldom clearly define), a strange blend of sentimentalism and indifference to the parlous condition of the 'lower orders', and a suffocatingly puritanical conventionality. Fortunately for the Victorians, however, that picture is by no means a complete one, as certain counterbalancing, if not contradictory, aspects of the scene will show.

At the very outset, it should perhaps be remembered that the period between the fall of Napoleon and the First World War saw Scotland confronting changes greater and more all-encompassing than any since the fall of Rome and the barbarian invasions. Industry was dramatically eroding the age-old predominance of agriculture in the life of the people. Cities like *Glasgow and *Dundee—not to mention smaller places (see URBAN SETTLEMENT: 3; URBAN SOCIETY: 3)—were experiencing a phenomenal population increase (see POPULATION PATTERNS: 2) and consequent multiplication of problems in health, *housing, and social control (see LIVING STANDARDS: 3; HEALTH, FAMINE, AND DISEASE: 3). The gulf between the Gaelic-speaking Highlands (see ECONOMY OF THE HIGHLANDS AND ISLANDS: 3), themselves undergoing a parallel transformation, and the rest of the country was becoming ever wider. And in partial response to all these challenges the political life of the nation underwent its own revolution when the Great Reform Act of 1832 began Britain's long march to universal suffrage (see POLITICAL SYSTEM: 2), arousing high hopes among all who longed for a truly democratic form of government and deep fears among many others. In the midst of such cataclysmic events it is hardly surprising that literature and the arts suffered something of an eclipse.

Even in literature, while the superiority of the immediately preceding period is generally recognized, and no one of the calibre of Galt or Hogg (not to mention Scott) adorns the scene, good things are to be found. Four writers in particular merit attention, though none of them is in the front rank: Hugh Miller (1802–56), John Brown (1810–82), Margaret Oliphant (1828–97), and George Macdonald (1824–1905). Miller, brilliant if flawed, was not only a formidable journalist and polemicist, as his editorship of the Free Church's influential weekly the *Witness* amply demonstrated. His autobiography, *My Schools and Schoolmasters*, is a classic description of Highland life (and much more) in the opening decades of the century, while *The Old Red Sandstone* displays his outstanding ability as a geologist. His prose style at its best puts him on a level with the masters of the language. John Brown's best work, though not free of sentimentality, has a memorable charm. Indeed, it would be difficult not to respond favourably to his perceptive understanding of the human (and the canine!) mind and his moving evocations of Secession piety (see RELIGIOUS LIFE: 6; PROTESTANT SECTS AND DISESTABLISHMENT). If Margaret Oliphant had not been obliged to support her many dependants by a flood of 'pot-boilers', her reputation might have stood higher today. Her *Chronicles of Carlingford* can stand beside Trollope's Barsetshire novels; her lives of Edward Irving and Principal Tulloch remain valuable studies; and there is much to appreciate in her autobiography and in her history of Blackwood's, the publishing house (see PRINTING AND PUBLISHING). As for George Macdonald, his standing is probably higher today than for many years, partly because of his passionate theological liberalism, partly because of the atmospheric picture of Scottish provincial life contained in his best novels, and partly because of the enthusiasm which his 'romances' have aroused in modern scholars like C. S. Lewis and J. R. R. Tolkien. Scottish literature had greater things to come, particularly from the pens of Stevenson and George Douglas Brown, but even to mention these four is to suggest that their country was not the literary wasteland that some critics declare it to have been during the high Victorian period.

By international standards, the story of music in Victorian Scotland is hardly remarkable, yet even in the early decades of the century there were signs of life. The ancient tradition of ballad-singing (not least in the bothy ballads of Aberdeenshire) and work-songs (industrial or fishing) survived and even flourished (see SONG, TRADITIONAL AND FOLK)—helped later, perhaps, by the vogue of the *music hall. Clarsach, fiddle, and bagpipe maintained their popularity among the common people, particularly in the Highlands and the north-east (home of that redoubtable fiddler Scott Skinner). The Prot-

estant reformers had excluded all music except psalm-singing from church services, and no composer of real note appeared between Robert Carver in the early 16th century and such lesser lights as Alexander Campbell MacKenzie (1847–1935) and Hamish MacCunn (1868–1916) in the late 19th century. But the existence of a sympathetic audience had been indicated by the welcome given to both Mendelssohn and Chopin in the 1840s, and much energy was profitably expended on the study and collection of Gaelic melodies by scholars like Father Allan Macdonald (1859–1905) and the more controversial Marjorie Kennedy-Fisher (1859–1905). From the 1860s, the Church Service Society helped greatly to raise musical standards in worship, particularly by encouraging the return of organs. (The first instrument appeared in Glasgow in 1860.) About the same time, psalmody was enriched by the introduction of hymns: the Relief Church published a book as early as 1794, and was followed by the United Presbyterians in 1852, the Auld Kirk in 1870, and the conservative Free Church in 1882. By that time, the tide of musical interest was rising fast. The Glasgow Athenaeum was founded in 1870, the Scottish Orchestra in 1893, and among performers of distinction should be mentioned the pianist Frederic Lamond, the singers Mary Garden and Joseph Hislop, and the mannered but impressive Hugh Roberton, conductor of the Glasgow Orpheus Choir. The first Gaelic Mod (a festival of literature and music) took place at Oban in 1892 (see MUSIC, HIGHLAND; MOD, THE ROYAL NATIONAL). And when the magisterial Donald Tovey was called to Edinburgh University's chair of music in 1914, Scotland definitely re-entered the mainstream of music worldwide.

The signs of a resurgence in literature and music were even more evident in the realm of the visual arts. In painting, strikingly fresh attitudes, as well as vast differences from the preceding age in both subject matter and style, began to appear. Men like Alexander Nasmyth and the highly influential David Wilkie (d. 1841) had inspired a concentration on religious and historical themes, many of them indebted either to the Bible or to such writers as Scott and Galt. There also prevailed a great delight in sentimental genre painting which may betray a longing—understandable in an age of helter-skelter change—for the idyllic rural past, more imagined than real (see REGIONAL IDENTITIES). Though old habits died hard, however, a transformation began to take place with Robert Scott Lauder, who taught in Edinburgh's Drawing Academy from 1852 to 1861. His greatest pupils, George Paul Chalmers (1833–78), William Quiller Orchardson (1832–1910), John Pettie (1839–93), and (above all) William McTaggart (1835–1910), reworked the themes beloved of their predecessors but with a passion for colour and a sense of atmosphere suggestive of French impressionism. Less storytelling and dark interior scenes, more fresh depiction of open-air subjects as in Constable and Turner, characterized their work. But it was in the 1880s and 1890s that the old artistic establishment finally gave way to the excitingly innovative approach of the self-styled 'Glasgow Boys', George Henry (1858– 1943), James Guthrie (1859–1930), Edward Hornel (1864–1933), John Lavery (1856–1941), and others, whose bright colours and adventurous techniques appear again, slightly later, in the work of the 'Scottish Colourists', Samuel Peploe (1871–1935), Leslie Hunter (1877–1931), John Duncan Fergusson (1874– 1961), and Francis Cadell (1883–1937). A more exuberant, less introverted mood prevailed as the 19th century yielded to the 20th, and Scotland—particularly the Clydeside of men like Charles Rennie Mackintosh (1868–1928), architect, designer, and leading exponent of art nouveau in this country—luxuriated in the affluence and self-confidence of its boom years.

Despite all that, Victorian Scotland could hardly claim an outstanding place on the international scene for its music, literature, or art. The case is very different in the realms of pure science, technology, and medicine, where its pre-eminence cannot be challenged. Of the great names deserving mention—all notable either for the conscious application of their discoveries to useful ends or for the very practical effect which their discoveries would eventually have—James Clerk Maxwell (1829–79), Lord Kelvin (1824–1907), James Young Simpson (1811–70), Joseph, Lord Lister (1827–1912), and William Macewen (1848–1924) stand supreme. Educated in Edinburgh and Cambridge, Clerk Maxwell became professor of natural philosophy at Marischal College, Aberdeen, when only 25, and in later life he taught for a time in King's College, London; but his greatest work was done in the newly founded Cavendish Laboratory at Cambridge, where he became the University's first professor of experimental physics. His researches into electricity and magnetism laid the foundations of modern physics and paved the way for the equally astounding achievements of Einstein and Planck. As for Kelvin, it is impossible to give an adequate summary of his incredibly productive (and profitable) career. A brilliant graduate of Glasgow and Cambridge, the Belfast-born William Thomson (he was raised to the peerage in 1892) made Clydeside his home, and in over 50 years as Glasgow University's professor of natural philosophy he contributed more than anyone to the fame of his alma mater and the scientific and technological achievements of his adopted country. A captivat-

ing teacher, indefatigable researcher in many fields from thermodynamics to wireless telegraphy and marine engineering, inventor, and entrepreneur, he bestrode the contemporary world like a colossus, and merits recognition as the most distinguished citizen of Scotland in his time.

Between them, James Young Simpson, Joseph, Lord Lister, and William Macewen—three of the greatest figures in the history of medicine (see CULTURE: 19)—exceeded all others as diminishers of the pains and hazards of life, both in childbirth and in the course of major operations. Simpson (who was professor of midwifery in Edinburgh from 1840 to 1870) introduced the use of chloroform during surgery, greatly advanced the science of gynaecology, and championed the cause of hospital reform. Lister (professor of surgery in Glasgow from 1860 to 1869, and of clinical surgery in Edinburgh from 1869 to 1877) and Macewen (professor of surgery in Glasgow from 1892) pioneered antiseptic and aseptic surgery respectively; Macewen was also one of the pioneers of neurosurgery. Though Lister spent half of his life in England, Macewen remained faithful to Glasgow and Simpson to Edinburgh: all three kept the reputation of Scotland's medical schools as high as in the great days of the Enlightenment.

No survey of Scottish life between Disruption and Great War would be complete without reference to the vital subjects of education and religion. Tradition has it that education was more democratic north than south of the Border. Recent authorities have questioned this, but it may well be that even the widespread belief that primary, secondary, and university education were more open than elsewhere to the 'lad o' pairts' had its own beneficial effects (see SCHOOLS AND SCHOOLING: 2–4; UNIVERSITIES: 2). Certainly Scotland had more in common with the most efficient and thrusting aspects of Continental education than with England's somewhat elitist system. At any rate, a new era dawned with the Education Act of 1872. Schooling to the age of 14 was made compulsory; the state took over the great diversity of institutions previously existing (see GOVERNMENT AND ADMINISTRATION: 2); more rigorous standards were imposed; teaching became a properly trained, efficiently supervised, state-controlled profession; and the ever-increasing number of *women teachers effected a gradual revolution in atmosphere and discipline. The age also saw a recovery of vitality in Scotland's ancient universities, with the great Acts of 1858 and 1889 improving efficiency, loosening the stranglehold of the professoriate over bodies which were after all the servants of the community, and attracting to their chairs some of the leading scholars and teachers: philosophers like the brothers Caird (John, 1828–98, and Edward, 1835–1908), classicists like John Burnet (1863–1928) and Gilbert Murray (1866–1957), and authorities on English literature like David Masson (1822–1907), George Saintsbury (1845–1933), and Andrew Bradley (1851–1935).

Finally, religion. In the secularized climate of today, it is difficult to realize the extent to which Victorian society was deeply imbued, one might almost say saturated, with religious influences, yet it was so. Steeples dominated the landscape (see CHURCHES: 3), and clergymen like Norman Mac-Leod of Glasgow Barony (1812–72), Dean Ramsay (1793–1872), John Cairns the United Presbyterian leader (1818–92), Bishop Henry Grey Graham (1842–1906), and Alexander Whyte of Free St George's, Edinburgh (1836–1921), were household names. In the schools, minister and presbytery, priest and bishop exercised very considerable power, after 1872 as before. In the universities, the Faculty of Divinity could still claim to be *primus inter pares*, incidentally providing several great principals like John Caird, Robert Story (1835–1907), and George Adam Smith (1856–1935). No doubt the old certainties were becoming eroded in some quarters; but it is noteworthy how many intellectual leaders, including such outstanding scientists as Clerk Maxwell, Kelvin, and J. Y. Simpson, were not just nominal but outspoken Christians. Ever since Thomas *Chalmers, the alienation of the 'labouring' classes from organized religion had been a matter of concern; but it was increasingly recognized that environmental factors were more responsible for this than individual delinquency. Churchmen, particularly in Glasgow, were in the forefront of practical campaigns for social betterment (see RESPECTABLE CULTURE; TEMPERANCE). As late as the very end of the century, religious organizations still surpassed secular ones in the number of working folk and their children who belonged to them (see MISSIONS AT HOME). Social services were becoming increasingly professionalized, yet the churches continued to take a major part in them; and while the very notion of a religious 'establishment' had long been under fierce attack it nevertheless survived, if in a modified form (see CHURCH INSTITUTIONS: 5).

Perhaps more momentous than anything so far mentioned, a theological revolution took place in Scottish Presbyterianism between 1860 and 1914. The historical approach to Holy Scripture was pioneered by A. B. Davidson (1831–1902) and William Robertson Smith (1846–94), both ministers of the conservative Free Church: they had many followers. The teaching of John MacLeod Campbell (1800–72) helped to modify the harshness of traditional Calvinism; and all the major Presbyterian denominations began to distance themselves from what were now considered to be the more questionable statements of the 17th-century Westminster Divines.

Early in our period, Charles Dickens declared that 'the world is, in all great essentials, better, gentler, more forbearing, and more hopeful as it rolls'. Looking back, we are almost inclined to agree—until we remember how it all ended on 4 August 1914.   AC

18. age of industry (1843–1914): art

The end of the 18th century saw a rapid increase in the number of artists working in Scotland and to represent their interests the Scottish Academy was established in 1826, becoming the Royal Scottish Academy (RSA) twelve years later. Prosperity was the key to this expansion and artists like Tom Faed or Joseph Noel Paton pursued successful careers providing the new public with the sentimental art that it wanted. Scott's romantic vision of Scotland also dominated the landscape painting of Horatio McCulloch and younger painters like Alexander Fraser jun. and Sam Bough. In the mid-century, however, painters like George Harvey, David Scott, Thomas Duncan, Robert Scott Lauder, and William Dyce worked to maintain the standards of seriousness of the older generation. Dyce's *Pegwell Bay, a Recollection of October 5th 1858* (Tate Gallery), for example, is a profound reflection on the struggle to maintain faith in the face of scientific progress. The *Disruption dominated the mid-century and in partnership with Robert Adamson, D. O. Hill, the Academy's first secretary, was inspired by it to turn to *photography to record the principal actors in the drama. The resulting Calotype portraits were among the first and finest art photographs.

In the 1850s, Scott Lauder passed on Wilkie's influence, including his belief in the importance of drawing, to his pupils, an important group in both England and Scotland. W. Q. Orchardson and John Pettie were the two most prominent in the south. Close friends, they developed a kind of narrative genre which in Orchardson's hands, in *Mariage de Convenance: After* (1888, Aberdeen Art Gallery) for example, became a sophisticated and subtly understated commentary on contemporary life.

William McTaggart and George Paul Chalmers were the leaders of this group in the north. Chalmers's unfinished painting *The Legend* (1864–79, NGS) is one of the finest paintings of the time. McTaggart concentrated increasingly on landscape, developing a style of great expressive freedom. This has links to contemporary Dutch painting, but also to Constable and Turner, and pictures like *The Storm* or *The Sailing of the Emigrant Ship* (both 1892, NGS) (see EMIGRATION: 3–4) belong in the tradition of the grand, romantic landscape. McTaggart was a

Highlander and the latter picture is a tragic commentary on the destruction of the Highland way of life in the *Clearances, but its force depends, not on sentimental narrative as in Tom Faed's *The Last of the Clan*, but on the dramatic fragmentation of the means of representation itself. As such, it is profoundly modern.

A distinctive Glasgow point of view emerged in the 1880s with the Glasgow Boys. The group included James Guthrie, W. Y. MacGregor, E. A. Walton, James Paterson, and others. Pictures such as Guthrie's *The Hind's Daughter* (1884) and W. Y. MacGregor's *The Vegetable Stall* (1884) eschew narrative in favour of a bold and matter-of-fact approach, bringing the radical immediacy of recent Continental painting into British art. Although identified with Glasgow, they also had close links to painters in the east, especially to Arthur Melville, one of the most original painters of the period, especially in watercolour.

The ideas of the Arts and Crafts movement were also influential in Scotland, reflecting the increasing awareness of artists of the social changes of the 19th century and the need to respond to them. The leading Scottish spokesman in this was Patrick Geddes. He promoted the idea of art as essential to the public good. Geddes also championed the equality of the sexes and in Edinburgh his ideas found a leading interpreter in Phoebe Traquair, one of the first major women artists of the period, as well as in John Duncan, Robert Burns, and others. Phoebe Traquair's mural paintings in the St Mary's Song School (1889–92) and in the Catholic apostolic church, Edinburgh, are among the most distinguished of their kind.

In Glasgow this view of the decorative, social function of painting is reflected in the work of the younger Glasgow Boys such as George Henry and E. A. Hornel. They followed the example of Arthur Melville to adopt a more formal, flatter style linked to contemporary, Continental symbolism. The most radical works of the period, however, were the watercolours of Charles Rennie Mackintosh and the Macdonald sisters, Frances and Margaret. The two latter were prominent among the women artists who were beginning to take advantage of the new opportunities offered them by art education, especially at Glasgow School under its enlightened principal, Frances Newbery.   DM

19. age of industry (1843–1914): medicine

Victorian medicine (see also HEALTH, FAMINE, AND DISEASE: 3) is characterized not only by a rapid expansion of medical knowledge, but also by a significant increase in medicine's ability to cure disease and a vast improvement in surgical practice. Particularly after 1870, medicine began to benefit from advances in other sciences, especially bacteriology.

Surgery was revolutionized by the development of general anaesthesia and of antiseptic methods: in each of these, crucial work was done in Scotland. The use of an anaesthetic gas, ether, was pioneered in America in 1846: in *Edinburgh, James Young Simpson (1811–70) followed this lead and then discovered that chloroform was more effective. The surgeon no longer had to operate with great speed. Simpson was a larger-than-life character, with an enormous head and extrovert personality; the procession which followed his coffin to Warriston cemetery stretched across the city, the largest Scottish cortège ever. Simpson also found time for intellectual interests outside medicine: he was a leader in the then amateur study of prehistory, and president of the Society of Antiquaries of Scotland.

Joseph Lister (1827–1912), London-born, Edinburgh-trained, and Regius professor at *Glasgow, became concerned about the very high death rate among surgical patients in the Glasgow Royal Infirmary: they survived surgery but died after the surgical wound became infected. Lister reasoned that the cause was the presence of micro-organisms in the air and on the surgeon's hands. He therefore, from about 1867, operated in a spray of carbolic acid and used chemically treated dressings and sutures. His method was adopted by the French army in 1870 and used successfully in the Franco-Prussian War. By the end of the century, his technique of attempting to kill bacteria had been replaced by the aseptic method in which every instrument and dressing was sterilized before use: it was pioneered in Germany and Glasgow, where Sir William Macewen (1848–1924) had the reputation of being 'the man who put doctors into white coats'.

In the first half of the 19th century the Edinburgh medical school still had a European reputation: Alexander Munro *tertius*, for example, was a fine anatomist if a poor lecturer. He was succeeded by younger men with new ideas, such as John Hughes Bennett, who adopted from France the use of the microscope in anatomy, and John Goodsir. At St Andrews, where there had been a chair of medicine since 1722, but little teaching, the subject sprang into prominence in 1840 with the appointment of the brilliant anatomist John Reid. There was still a degree of public hostility to the godlessness of anatomizing the human body; much was made of Reid's supposed recantation of atheism on his deathbed in 1849. A medical school was formed at *Aberdeen in 1860, following the creation of the University from the two independent colleges.

The teaching of *medicine in Scotland remained largely in the hands of Scots throughout the 19th century. The first Englishman to hold a Scottish medical chair was Bennett at Edinburgh in 1848; he was an Edinburgh graduate. The first professor who had no prior connection with Scotland was Thomas Laycock in 1855. In the second half of the 19th century, the Scots medical schools still had a European reputation, but so had dozens of others.

The teaching at Edinburgh University was complemented by a large extramural school. Medical lecturers had taught in their own homes before the establishment of the university medical faculty, and the number teaching independently of the University grew in the latter part of the 18th century. Sometimes they worked in partnerships and occasionally in larger associations. The extramural lecturers had the freedom to teach novel courses which reflected the rapid increase in medical specialization: A. W. P. Pinkerton on tropical medicine from 1858, Argyll Robertson on the diseases of the eye from 1863, Arthur Gamgee on histology in 1870, and several others. In 1857–65, James Warburton Begbie offered courses in the history of medicine.

A steady flow of men of ability left for London. Robert Knox was a brilliant comparative anatomist before his associations with the 'resurrection men' who exhumed newly buried corpses made him notorious. William Sharpey, extramural lecturer in the new subject of physiology, went to a chair at the new University College, London, in 1836. Robert Lister, denied the Edinburgh chair of surgery, took his amazing dexterity to a more rewarding environment. Lister, after seventeen years in Scotland, left for his native London in 1877. Where Edinburgh had been the intellectual centre of British medicine in the 18th century, and London the locus for profitably deploying medical skills, by Victoria's reign London was the British capital in both senses. Edinburgh was a small city replete with medical teachers and personal tensions: 'they were giants in those days, but they were very quarrelsome giants', said Sir William Tenant Gairdner, trained in Edinburgh but professor in Glasgow.

At the end of the 19th century there was a great variety of knowledge and approach among medical practitioners, for it was a time when medical knowledge was changing and rapidly expanding. General practitioners varied from the recently qualified, who knew a significant quantity of the new scientific medicine, to the elderly and unaware, who did not. In the *Lays of the College* (1886) 'The Fine Old School Practitioner' was described by a progressive Edinburgh doctor: 'He knew not Spray producers, Aspirators, Ecraseurs, | Nor haemadynomometers, nor taking Temperatures'. In the teaching hospitals were specialists who could stand with any in the world. Nearby, in dispensaries, their newly qualified pupils gained ex-

perience from their patients. Particularly in the country, folk medicine continued (see TRADITIONAL HEALING), and if the doctor was distant, another educated individual such as the minister or teacher might offer an opinion. The smith, a figure of power who by common repute had the skills of bone-setting, was believed to be able to cure rickets by passing his tools round a child's legs. He lost his medical power not because he was confronted by doctors' scientific knowledge; he was simply displaced as the number of qualified medical men increased. Quacks were no longer exotic figures at the annual fair, but the advertisers of patent medicines such as Dr J. Collis Browne and Dr De Jongh. There was also a small number of women practitioners.

The medical education of *women in Scotland began with Sophia Jex-Blake. She arrived in Edinburgh in 1869 and enrolled at the University, but the hostility of some of the professoriate, of male students, and of the managers of the Infirmary made it impossible for her, and six who joined her, to progress far. The opposition was partly due to misogyny, and partly to the belief that the female student should not be exposed to anatomy: 'For delvin' in a corpses's wame | was neither sweet nor womanly' (*Lays of the College*). Jex-Blake took a degree in Switzerland and her qualification to practise in Ireland, returning to Edinburgh in 1878. By founding her own medical school, and with the help of sympathetic male teachers, she was able to advance slowly the medical training of women. Until the First World War, however, the number of women doctors was small, and they often worked in unprofitable areas which did not appeal to male doctors, such as paediatrics and dietetics.

Medical architecture illustrated social developments (see PUBLIC UTILITIES). The hospital before the middle of the 19th century was a plain block which might have been taken for a mill, but an increasing desire for fresh air in the wards led to high ceilings and to tall, dominating buildings. The surgeon had become a figure of high status, and the towers and spires of the Victorian hospital showed medical confidence. The rural asylum looked from the outside like a country house: it was a place for doctors as well as patients.

As medical knowledge grew, it affected more aspects of life and public policy. In recruiting soldiers for the Boer War, it was found that young men from the cities and industrial areas were small and unfit (see LIVING STANDARDS: 3): how could the nation be defended? The cause was identified as poor *diet in childhood, and milk was promoted as the key to healthy babies and national security. At the same time, however, bacteriologists were beginning to understand that milk was an effective medium for communicating disease: the bacteria of a dozen fevers could thrive in it, and be delivered to the consumer. The Public Health Department of a city like Glasgow had to take action in the countryside, pressing for clean byres, clean hands for milking, and the rigorous sterilization of equipment. By 1925 dirty milk was rare, though it was still an important carrier of tuberculosis.

Medical services in the Highlands and Islands were still woefully inadequate. In 1910, after scarlet fever was spread from Glenquoich to Invergarry by a postboy, the Medical Officer of Health for Inverness-shire summarized the problems in observing that it could hardly be expected that people would send 25 or 50 miles (40 or 80 km) for a doctor when their children were ill from a disease which might not turn out to be infectious, for the expense was great even for one visit from the doctor. It was becoming clear that if medical services were to reach all the people, they would have to be funded publicly.   JBur

20. age of industry (1843–1914): literature

The Victorian period has often been discounted as insignificant in Scottish writing, undermined by the emigration of Scottish writers to London and by the success of 'Kailyard' literature produced by émigrés such as J. M. Barrie (1860–1937), 'Ian MacLaren' or John Watson (1850–1907), and S. R. Crockett (1859–1914) in the 1880s and 1890s and which represented Scotland in a nostalgic, rural fashion. As such, the failure to record the furore of 19th-century industrialization (see ECONOMY: 4, 5) is seen as the sign of a communal 'loss of nerve' on the part of Scottish culture. Yet this is also the period in which Scottish writers dominated the intellectual landscape of Victorian Britain: the Mills in philosophy in politics, Ruskin in aesthetics, Thomas Carlyle (1795–1881) in social analysis and historical writing (see CULTURE: 17), and, at the end of the century, William Robertson Smith (1846–94) and J. G. Frazer (1854–1941) in the new science of social anthropology. The ninth edition of the *Encyclopedia Britannica* (1875–89), which sought to present all of human knowledge as shaped by evolutionary theory, stands as the monument to the intellectual energy of Scotland in this period, a dynamic stemming from the *Disruption of 1843 and the crisis of Christian commitment that it produced (see RELIGIOUS LIFE: 7). As James Thomson (1834–82) was to put in one of the most powerful of Victorian poems of religious despair, *The City of Dreadful Night* (1874), all were to be afflicted by the sense

> That all the oracles are dumb or cheat,
> Because they have no secret to express:
> That none can pierce the vast black veil uncertain
> Because there is no light beyond the curtain.

Under the tutelage of Free Church minister and publisher William Robertson Nicoll (1851–1923), the Kailyard writers sought to recapture a past not yet dominated by that 'vast black veil uncertain'. The central role accorded to Kailyard, however, disguises the fact that Scottish writers were influential in the development of new genres aimed at the emergent mass reading publics of the modern world. Thus the creation by Conan Doyle (1859–1930) of the archetypal detective in the Sherlock Holmes stories and the development by John Buchan (1875–1914) of the modern thriller in *The Thirty-Nine Steps* (1915) both have deep roots in the culture of 19th-century Scotland.

If 18th-century Scottish thought had been dominated by the question of the nature of man in society (see CULTURE: 11, 14), the 19th century was marked by questions about the nature of man before or beyond or outside society. The vast compendium of savage myth by J. G. Frazer (1854–1941), *The Golden Bough*, rewritten several times between the 1890s and 1930s, summarized the sense that society is 'a thin crust stretched over a vast abyss of the irrational'. That awareness was to drive Scottish writers from documenting the social world to exploration of what lay beyond it in the primitive, the supernatural, and the unconscious. Such explorations required the invention or elaboration of new modes of writing. As early as 1858, George MacDonald (1824–1905) was exploring in *Phantastes* the possibilities of a 'faery story for men and women' that would chart the spiritual significance of the unconscious. Almost all modern fantasy literature can be traced back to *Phantastes* and to the later *Lilith* (1895), as well as to MacDonald's children's tales, *At the Back of the North Wind* (1871), *The Princess and the Goblin* (1872), and *The Princess and the Curdie* (1888). MacDonald also wrote 'realistic' novels of the Victorian world, but it is his exploration of alternative worlds and alternative states of consciousness that are symptomatic of Scottish culture in this period.

Though much more acknowledged now for the depiction of women's experience in her realist fiction, the same can be said of Margaret Oliphant (1828–97), who published over 100 best-selling novels, many of them studies of manners set both in Scotland (*The Minister's Wife*, 1886; *Kirsteen*, 1890) and in England (*The Chronicles of Carlingford*, 1861–76). Her most powerful work, however, is in her supernatural tales, such as *A Beleaguered City* (1880) and *The Library Window* (1895), which explore the limits of the material world of her realist fiction.

The development of the fantasy novel and the supernatural tale were to culminate in the most influential of Scottish fictions of this period, one malign—*Dr Jekyll and Mr Hyde* (1886) of Robert

Louis Stevenson (1850–94)—and the other (apparently) benign—*Peter Pan* (1906) of J. M. Barrie (1860–1937). In both, the psychological consequences of modernity are plumbed in ways which challenged the ability of realistic fiction or naturalistic theatre to document the important consequences of an industrial, imperial society (see URBAN SOCIETY: 5). Even the most powerful literary invention of the earlier 19th century, the historical novel, was subject to the same transformation. In works such as Robert Louis Stevenson's *Kidnapped* (1885), John Buchan's *John Burnett of Barns* (1898), or *Flemington* (1911) by Violet Jacob (1863–1946), the historical novel is transformed from an exploration of the historical past as a social reality into a symbolic or allegoric tale, charting the universal workings of the unconscious rather than social conditions. The most important achievement of this period, Stevenson's *The Master of Ballantrae* (1888), challenges the limits of historical fiction by driving its characters out into the American wilderness to confront a world where imperialism encounters the sources of its power in the very forces of 'savagery' it seeks to outlaw or subdue.

Because of the critical value given to realism in British literature in the late 19th century, and because of its challenge to the Kailyard tradition, *The House with the Green Shutters* (1901) by George Douglas Brown (1869–1902) is often seen as a key text of the period, overturning 19th-century nostalgia with 20th-century realism (see CULTURE: 24). But Brown's novel, with its insistent use of Scots, is also a product of the enduring tradition of fiction-writing in Scots that was sustained from the 1840s by serialized novels in the *newspapers and journals. In the work of David Pae, Latto, and William Alexander, Scots was the medium not only of dialogue—as it had been for Scott and Galt (see CULTURE: 14)—but of the narrative voice itself. The particular combination of the oral and the written in a Scottish context, including the development of typographic styles for the rendition of regional Scots speech—as in William Alexander's *John Gibb of Gushetneuk* (1871)—can be seen as one of the seminal elements of the period, undermining the dominance of standardized, written English. In poetry, too, the gradual revival of Scots in the work of Stevenson, and of the poets of the north-east (see REGIONAL IDENTITIES: 2), such as Charles Murray (1864–1941) and Violet Jacob (1864–1941), was to cement the key role of the *Scots language in the maintenance of an independent Scottish literature.

RCC

21. modern times (1914–1990s): general

Scottish culture in the modern era has been dominated by two principal themes. The first is an endur-

ing effort to carve out a distinctive Scottish culture (more often than not to make it different from England) and the second is the impact and influence of global cultural trends which have been absorbed and modified within a Scottish frame of reference. These two themes are very much inter-linked and both have helped to give Scotland a distinctive cultural identity (see NATIONAL IDENTITY: 6). Indeed, it may be argued that in the endeavour to be different from the English, many Scottish artists have actively sought out continental European influences as a means of extenuating their distinctiveness within the British Isles. Also, it may be suggested that the desire to jump into the European mainstream was not a little fuelled by a sense of cultural inferiority. The so-called 'Scottish Cringe' (a phrase first devised by the historian Owen Dudley Edwards) in which many figures of cultural authority express an excessive deprecation of things Scottish has been another marked feature of Scottish cultural identity in the modern period.

In the inter-war era, cultural polemicists reacted against the romantic and backward-looking stereotypical representations of Scotland which was known as the 'Kailyard' (see CULTURE: 17). The maudlin, sentimental depiction of Scots and Scotland as an essentially rural and coothy society in which virtue and salvation was to be found within the village (see RURAL SOCIETY: 4; URBAN SOCIETY: 4) rather than the industrial heartland, was one that struck a chord not only within Scotland itself, but also in the wider global community. Such representations were denounced, not only for the false picture they painted, but also because they provided an ineffective vehicle to tackle the real artistic issues of the day. The demand for realism and that art should be politically charged meant that culture had to be directed towards addressing the real social issues of the day such as poverty, poor housing, and deprivation (see LIVING STANDARDS: 3). Kailyardism was seen as escapist, unreal, and irrelevant to the majority.

Relating this to our second theme, the attack on the Kailyard was also inspired, assisted, and influenced by the growth of modernism, which was an international movement that sought to extend artistic boundaries and adapt culture to the new political realities of the day. The shock of global war, the emergence of new political ideologies in the form of socialism and communism, the rise of feminism, the growth of democracy, and a reaction to the cultural norms of the 19th century were essential components in this movement. As in other societies, Scottish artists sought to readapt or recreate culture to reflect, accommodate, and promote the widespread social, economic, and political changes which had followed in the wake of the First World War. As in other parts of the world, Scotland was convulsed by the experience of global war and many of the key protagonists of modernism had their artistic sensibilities shaken to the core by their experience of war and the ensuing turmoil which followed in its wake.

The Scottish 'renaissance' of the inter-war period found its locus in a group of writers centred around Hugh MacDiarmid (C. M. Grieve), Lewis Grassic Gibbon (Leslie Mitchell), Neil Gunn, Edwin Muir, and others. Gaelic culture also experienced a cultural reinvigoration in the form of the poetry of Sorley Maclean and subsequently Ian Crichton Smith (see GAELIC LITERATURE). For cultural commentators and literary critics, the renaissance marks one of the high water periods of Scottish artistic creativity. Its vitality contrasts with the sterility of the Kailyard, its style and form moved Scotland closer to the European mainstream, and finally it halted the widespread notion that Scottish culture was incapable of rising above the provincial.

The Scottish renaissance is a somewhat amorphous term which bands together writers, poets, sculptors, and composers, all of whom were new and different but otherwise lacked an overall cohesion. In many ways, a sense of crisis permeated the renaissance in that all knew that something was wrong and that the artistic status quo had to be overturned, yet there was no agreement as to what should replace it. For some it was anarchy, for others a new order, and, probably for most, it signified uncertainty. Although MacDiarmid would claim that the renaissance was a project designed to invigorate Scottish culture and free it from the shackles of the British past, not all the artists associated with the movement shared his aspirations. Indeed, MacDiarmid's own political and artistic agenda suffered from violent swings of direction ranging from nationalism to communism and from the promotion of a new *Scots language to a belief in *Gaelic as the universal tongue of Scotland. Although the movement has been identified with nationalism, in reality it was politically inchoate. Gibbon was a utopian Marxist with a deep aversion to Scottish nationalism, while Edwin Muir encouraged the wrath of MacDiarmid for his claim that Scots as a language lacked the necessary sophistication for higher intellectual thought. Also, the movement contained a variety of different literary forms. The experimental and modernist approach was not to be found in all authors with some such as Neil Gunn using fairly conventional literary techniques.

The main achievement of the renaissance was to leave a cultural legacy which has become more appreciated after its demise. The poetry of MacDiarmid laid the basis of a new and dynamic form of poetic expression and expanded the themes tackled by the Scottish artist. The debates engendered during the renaissance have become the focal point of much cultural discussion ever since and the artistic output has been recognized to be of such considerable merit as to deserve the claim that this was a high point in Scottish cultural achievement. Yet, this was not how it was seen by contemporary society and much of the dynamic of the renaissance has to be understood in the context that it was a backlash against a conservative and unyielding artistic environment. Throughout the inter-war period there was a profound sense of cultural depression which mirrored the economic climate (see ECONOMY: 6). Writers such as George Malcolm Thomson and Andrew Dewar Gibb told of a different Scotland, one whose artistic high points had passed, and it was held as conventional wisdom that no Scottish poet would ever come near the towering height of Robert Burns. Indeed, much of Scottish culture at this time was concerned to bury its head in the past and the claims of the renaissance were treated with derision.

This cultural pessimism was pervasive in Scottish society. While renaissance critics sought to turn social chaos to advantage and to a large extent revelled in the opportunities this created to make things anew, conventional wisdom held that it was the end of Scottish culture. It was believed by the pessimists that economic decay would bring Scottish culture, as they knew and understood it, to an end. In many ways, their interpretation of the renaissance was that it was symptomatic of a general cultural malaise and, indeed, their criticisms were similar to those being voiced elsewhere in Europe against 'decadent modernism'. In spite of this, much of the cultural mainstream managed to do quite well in the inter-war period. Conventional literature in the guise of Compton MacKenzie and John Buchan continued to sell well and, if we add Neil Gunn—although in ideals rather than part of the renaissance technique—modern Scottish fiction had a sizeable audience. Music was well served by Hugh Roberton and the Orpheus choir which helped to bring classical music to a wider audience and the theatre was well served by James Bridie. Painting, likewise, was in a healthy state and able to build on the foundations of the Glasgow Boys. So, all in all, Scotland in the inter-war period was not the cultural desert that many of its critics claimed.

The best efforts of the renaissance continued throughout the Second World War and into the 1950s with writers such as Robert Gairloch, Sidney Goodsir Smith, and Norman McCaig contributing much, although the prevailing ideological and political climate militated against the maintenance of a distinctive Scottish culture. For many, the obsession with a Scottish identity was a backward step into romantic nationalism which had no place in the modern technological world. Whereas internationalism was used as a means to bolster a distinctive Scottish identity in the inter-war period, in the post-war era it was used as a means to smother it. The appearance of the International Edinburgh Festival in 1947 was remarkable in its career both for the quality of the performances it attracted to Scotland and the paucity of Scottish material that it sponsored. The prevailing ideas at the time stipulated that the worse cultural sin of all was to be parochial. In part, this was shaped by the fact that 'Kailyardism' still attracted a considerable audience. *Dr Finlay's Casebook* was a popular television programme which adhered to the coothy qualities of rural Scotland. *The White Heather Club* was another celebration of all that the renaissance idealists despised with its celebration of tartanism (see DRESS, HIGHLAND) and Highland flings. The fact that so many Scots tuned in to watch them shows that the cultural gurus were out of kilter with the wishes of the population and helps explain why the Communist Hugh MacDiarmid was an out-and-out elitist.

Coinciding neatly with the appearance of political nationalism in the mid-1960s, Scottish culture began to develop deeper and more hardy roots. Although literature and poetry were in the vanguard of Scottish culture, newer and more accessible forms of artistic expression were becoming available. The growth of folk music and a deeper interest in the popular culture of Scotland pioneered by Hamish Henderson and his colleagues in the School of Scottish Studies at Edinburgh University helped to bring a more democratic edge to Scottish culture. Folk groups (see SONG, TRADITIONAL AND FOLK: 1) like the Corries and the McCallums introduced it to a larger audience. Broadcast devolution in the late 1960s helped to remove the shackles of received pronunciation on the television (see RADIO AND TELEVISION) and provided an avenue for local talent to get an airing which would not be deemed suitable for a mainstream British audience. The televising of Neil Munro's *Para Handy*, for example, brought it to a larger audience than was possible with the book. Indeed, television has been one of the most important ways of communicating a distinctive Scottish identity in the latter part of the 20th century as more and more Scots rejected the Kailyard in favour of more realistic and gritty portrayals of Scottish life. Indeed, in the 1970s, television was largely responsible for transforming the stereotypical image of the Scot as a coothy, Highland crooner into a hard-drinking, swearing football hooligan.

The failure of the devolution referendum in 1979 (see POLITICAL SYSTEM: 3) has often been presented by cultural commentators as an important turning point in the nation's artistic development. Shorn of the opportunity to use politics as an avenue for expressions of *national identity, it is said that this frustration was channelled into artistic development. Certainly in most forms, the period of the 1980s seems to have witnessed a flowering of Scottish culture which arguably matches the quality of the renaissance of the 1920s. In literature, the novels of William MacIlvaney and Carl Macdougall portrayed the gritty realities of ordinary life, while Alastair Gray demonstrated one of the most fertile imaginations of the modern era which, whether by design or accident, arguably took Scotland into the postmodern era. If Gray did not, then the novels and writings of Irving Welsh and James Kelman certainly did. Devoid of moral certainty and truth, the depiction of the 'underclass' (see SOCIAL CLASS) of Scottish society was popular with a new generation of younger readers. *Women have been making a bigger impact on Scottish culture since the 1980s. Stalwarts such as Jessie Kesson, Muriel Spark, and Naomi Mitchison, were complemented with a newer generation of writers, with Liz Lochead, A. L. Kennedy, and Janice Gallway among the better known. However, one of the main features of Scottish culture in the 20th century is the fact that it has been male-dominated, arguably to a greater extent than most modern societies.

The explosion of Scottish culture in the 1980s has been assisted by a growing public awareness of the importance of maintaining a distinctive national, cultural identity. The teaching of Scottish literature and history in the schools and universities has increased towards the end of the 20th century and has been instrumental in militating the 'Scottish Cringe' and has helped to promote a greater sense of cultural confidence. For many commentators, the 'reawakened' sense of cultural identity has been an important factor in mobilizing support for a Scottish *parliament. One feature of the post-industrial and postmodern age has been the growth in the 'heritage industry' (see HERITAGE CENTRES) in which culture has become a commercial commodity. Selling Scottish culture for foreign and domestic tourist consumption has raised important issues of cultural ownership and a major source of criticism has been the reappearance of a new form of Kailyardism which sentimentalizes the past and dumbs down culture into accessible sound bites for mass consumption. Also, the fact that so much Scottish culture is in the hands of government-appointed quangos such as the Scottish Tourist

Board, the Scottish Arts Council, and Historic Scotland raises important issues of accountability and democratic ownership. Another source of concern is the influence of the international mass media which is beyond government control and has immense power to shape cultural aspirations.

Yet, for all these concerns, there is a sense of cultural confidence in modern Scotland which operates in tandem with the global culture of the mass market. It is worth remembering that more people read Scottish novelists, listen to Scottish music, attend Scottish plays, purchase Scottish paintings, and watch Scottish broadcasts than at any other time in history.   RJF

22. modern times (1914–1990s): art
In the 20th century maintaining their connections with the wider world reinforced the identity of Scottish art. J. D. Fergusson's painting *Les Eus* (Hunterian Museum, Glasgow University), for example, painted in Paris *c*.1912, is one of the most ambitious British paintings of its time. It reflects his links with Matisse and Picasso, but as a utopian vision it also reflects a long Scottish tradition. Fergusson and his friend S. J. Peploe, together with F. C. B. Cadell and Leslie Hunter, subsequently became known as the Scottish Colourists and provided an important example to the younger generation of a free and adventurous kind of painting. Several international dealers, such as Alexander Reid, who were established during the boom in the art market in the late 19th century supported these painters. By the end of the First World War, however, artists had to maintain themselves by teaching. William Johnstone, William Gillies, and many others all taught throughout their lives.

Fergusson was much influenced by Patrick Geddes and Muirhead Bone's prints and drawings also reflect the commentaries of Geddes on the state of contemporary cities and the threat of the divergence between the human and technical sciences, a prophecy terribly fulfilled in the conflict of the First World War. The tragedy of the war also produced in the National War Memorial the fullest expression of the social and collaborative ideal of art. It was designed by Robert Lorimer with a team of artists and craftsmen including the sculptors Pilkington Jackson (1887–1973), Alice Meredith Williams (*c*.1870–1934), Alexander Carrick (1882–1966), and Phyllis Bone (1894–1972); the stained-glass artist Douglas Strachan; and the woodcarvers Alexander Clow (1861–1946) and his brother William (dates not known).

One of the most original painters in the 1920s and 1930s was James Cowie. His *Falling Leaves* (1934, Aberdeen Art Gallery) is a complex, poetic study of the transition from child to adult and can be compared to Lewis Grassic Gibbon's contemporary novel *Sunset Song*. In his later work Cowie created some of his most remarkable pictures under the influence of surrealism. A similar duality between symbolism and modernism is seen in the work of his contemporary, Eric Robertson, the leading figure in the Edinburgh Group. Cecile Walton and Dorothy Johnstone were also distinguished members of this group.

In the early 1920s, William McCance produced some dramatic interpretations of the machine aesthetic and in alliance with Hugh MacDiarmid attempted to formulate an equivalent frame of reference for painting to that provided by Scots renaissance for the poets. It was William Johnstone, however, who gave the most convincing expression to this ambition in his major painting *A Point in Time* (1929–33) which evokes the dynamic interaction of the present with the immemorial, through the artist's own identification with the landscape of the Borders.

Much less ideological were William Gillies, William McTaggart, William Wilson, John Maxwell, and others who evolved a style that became identified with Edinburgh. Influenced by French painting and by the English painters of the St Ives school, it reached real poetry, especially in the landscapes of Gillies. In Glasgow, however, a different influence was at work through the presence there of J. D. Fergusson. Fergusson founded the New Scottish Group, including painters like Donald Bain and Millie Frood and later Tom MacDonald and Bet Low. The most important Glasgow painter was Joan Eardley, however. Her pictures of Glasgow children combine social realist purpose with a real sense of individual dignity. Her later seascapes draw on the example of contemporary American, abstract-expressionist painting, but also reflect the long tradition of Romantic landscape painting.

The Second World War disrupted exchanges with the Continent, but these were resumed immediately afterwards. In Paris, William Gear worked alongside Asger Jorn, Karel Appel, and other members of the Cobra group. Inspired by what he learnt in Paris too in the late 1940s, Eduardo Paolozzi attacked the narrow definition of fine art to argue that art must embrace all imagery, the perception that later gave birth to pop art. Paolozzi developed from the art of collage a metaphor for the experience of modern life. In his later work he invoked the classical tradition to restate human values for contemporary society. In the 1950s and 1960s, working in parallel to Paolozzi, Alan Davie explored spontaneous, informal abstraction inspired by contemporary American art, but also through Johnstone by the ideas of

Jung. Johnstone's own later work is also free and spontaneous and yet still inspired by landscape.

In the 1960s Ian Hamilton Finlay began his most ambitious undertaking, his garden at Little Sparta. It is a metaphor in itself, created as it is on the edge of the tree line. It combines wit and irony, art, poetry, and nature in a way that is typical of his art. Also in the early 1960s, John Bellany was one of a group that led a return to figurative art. He was directly influenced by MacDiarmid and he was in turn an important influence on his own contemporaries. The admiration for German art that Bellany shared with Sandy Moffat has, for instance, been echoed by a good many of the younger generation. Will Maclean has also continued the traditions of the Scots renaissance and has made fishing and the sea a source of rich, poetic metaphors.

One of the most significant developments of the post-war decades was the advent of direct state patronage through the Scottish Arts Council formed in 1964 and the subsequent increase in the number of small galleries. This broke the near monopoly of the exhibiting societies and so encouraged experiment. Sculptors like Hew Lorimer and Eric Shilski had, for instance, remained loyal to older traditions of carving or modelling, but in the 1970s, encouraged by this new source of support, younger sculptors like Jake Harvey, Doug Cocker, Ainslie Yule, and Gavin Scobie began to explore the language of constructed, modernist sculpture. Painters like John Houston, Elizabeth Blackadder, David McLure, and David Michie, and also younger artists like Duncan Shanks and Barbara Rae, however, all developed directly from the tradition established by Gillies, Maxwell, Redpath, and Eardley, though artists like Mark Boyle, Bruce McLean, and several minimalists like Kenneth Dingwall and Alan Johnston reacted against this tradition.

In Glasgow in the 1980s, a group of artists led by Steven Campbell pioneered a more radical approach to figurative painting. Campbell achieved international recognition and in his work especially some of the deeper insecurities of the late 20th century are given expression in a way that is paralleled in contemporary literature. In the 1990s other young Scottish artists like Douglas Girdon and Christine Borland followed them to achieve international reputations and generally in the 1990s and later, *film, video, *photography, and installation were the chosen form of expression of most of the younger generation in keeping with the dramatic changes in forms of visual communication that characterized the era. Calum Colvin, for instance, developed a very original form of photographic collage, but traditional forms of painting and sculpture also continued to be practised with distinction by younger painters like Callum Innes

as well as by the older generation keeping alive a long and distinguished tradition. DM

23. modern times (1914–1990s): medicine and medical achievements

Throughout the 20th century great changes occurred in medicine in Scotland. The development of drugs for eliminating disease and combating infection, and the emergence of new technologies to aid diagnosis and cure, meant that changes in medical knowledge and practice were more rapid and profound than at any other period in history. In addition, a restructuring of the administration of health care in the early part of the century, and again from 1948, allowed the techniques of modern medicine to be brought within reach of the whole of Scotland for the first time.

By 1914, the infectious diseases which had dominated the health of the nation for centuries were already declining. Tuberculosis was the most tenacious, lingering on well into the 1950s. The arrival of successful streptomycin-based drug treatment from 1948, however, cured all but the most advanced cases, rendering unnecessary the sanatorium treatment pioneered by Scotsman Dr (later Sir) Robert Philip in the 1910s. With the discovery of vitamins in 1920, diseases associated with poor diet and malnutrition also diminished. Complaints such as rickets (vitamin D deficiency) and pellagra (vitamin B deficiency) had been almost exclusively confined to the working classes and, in Scotland, nutritionists led by Aberdeen's John Boyd Orr clearly demonstrated the link between poverty and disease. In 1936 Boyd Orr published his controversial report *Food, Health and Income*, claiming that one-third of the population was underfed. These findings were reluctantly accepted by the government, and the food policy adopted during the Second World War was based on the principles established by Boyd Orr and his colleagues. Carrying on the Scottish tradition of medical research in nutrition and diet into the second half of the century, Glaswegian Sir Alexander Todd (1907–97) won the Nobel Prize in 1957 for his research into vitamins B1 and E. His efforts led to vitamins being synthesized for commercial uses, which transformed the field of human nutrition worldwide. It is perhaps incongruous that two of the 20th century's leading researchers in diet and nutrition should come from the country which gave the world such coronary horrors as the deep-fried battered Mars Bar. Indeed, despite Scotland's reputation for research in this field—the Rowett Institute, founded in 1913 with Boyd Orr as its first director, remains an internationally renowned centre for research into nutrition and health—the diet of the Scots continues to be a subject of dismay amongst medical professionals. An advertising campaign by the Health Education Board for Scotland (HEBS) in early 2000 indicated that many Scots do not eat a balanced diet. The consumption of excessive amounts of sugar, fat, and salt, combined with the nation's passion for cigarette smoking and reluctance to engage in sustained exercise, have led to the health of the Scots being amongst the worst in Europe. Indeed, by the mid-1970s Scotland had earned the dubious distinction of having the highest rate of lung cancer in the world, whilst the incidence of cancer of the colon and of heart attacks, strokes, and coronary heart disease remains amongst the highest in Europe. Medical science has ensured that the Scots certainly live longer than their ancestors, but whether their lives are healthier is a question still open for debate.

By 1914, the administration of medical services in Scotland were developing into the institutions we recognize today. A National Health Insurance scheme was implemented in 1911, which enabled working men and women to gain health care as and when they needed it through regular monthly payments. In addition to this, by 1918 the Highlands and Islands Medical Service (HIMS) was up and running, providing health care to communities in these remote areas. The scheme extended to the inhabitants of such far-flung places as St Kilda, and by 1935 an air ambulance was ferrying patients from the Western Isles to and from the hospitals of Glasgow. Meanwhile, advances in medical techniques of diagnosis and cure within the voluntary hospitals, and a consequent decline in the treatment of private patients in their own homes, resulted in ever-growing pressure on hospital facilities. In 1948 the National Health Service (NHS) was established, optimistically promising free 'cradle to grave' health care for all. Its establishment did much to even out administrative differences between medical provision in Scotland and the rest of the UK. However, Scotland had a distinct head start in the quality of medical treatment available under the new health service. During the Second World War, Scotland had benefited from the establishment of the Emergency Medical Service (EMS), which had involved the construction of military hospitals. These were transferred to the new NHS in 1948. Furthermore, specialisms, such as anaesthetics, radiology, and pathology, were encouraged by the EMS, as were brain surgery (pioneered by Norman Dott at the Edinburgh Royal Infirmary) and plastic surgery, both little developed before 1939. Under the auspices of the EMS the Burns Unit at Glasgow Royal Infirmary became a world leader in the scientific study of shock and tissue transplantation. The Second World War had also seen the setting-up of the first blood bank in Scotland, at the Edinburgh Royal Infirmary, in 1939. By the 1950s the blood transfusion unit in Edinburgh was one of the best in the world.

*Women doctors also benefited from the establishment of the NHS. General practitioners were to form the front ranks of the NHS and there was an increasing need for them from 1948. Prior to the Second World War women's entry to the medical profession had been slow, but steady. Dr Gertrude Herzfeld had become the first woman member of the Royal College of Surgeons of Edinburgh in 1916. From the 1950s and 1960s, however, women began to enter medicine in Scotland in ever-increasing numbers, and by 2001 more women than men were applying for places at Scotland's great medical schools. However, despite their growing numbers within medicine in Scotland, especially as general practitioners, women doctors remain in the minority within hospital medicine and within medical research.

By the 1920s, with the days of the lone pioneering scientist all but over, Scottish medical scientists collaborated in international efforts in the battle against disease and in the development of modern medicine. Penicillin, which was developed into antibiotics in the late 1930s, was discovered by accident in 1928 by a Scotsman, Alexander Fleming (1881–1955). Fleming was a notoriously messy scientist and often left bits of decomposing food lying around in his laboratory for weeks. He would then discover interesting things growing on them. In this way, so legend has it, he came across an unusual mould—penicillin—growing in one of his unwashed culture dishes. Although recognizing its antibacterial properties, Fleming did not fully realize penicillin's medical importance until collaboration with chemists Howard Florey and Ernst Chain in the late 1930s and early 1940s. Fleming was awarded the Nobel Prize in 1945 for his work in this field, along with Florey and Chain, who developed penicillin's commercial production.

John James MacLeod (1876–1935), a Scottish physiologist, was co-winner of the Nobel Prize for medicine in 1923 for his contribution to the discovery of insulin; whilst Sir James Whyte Black (1924–) shared the Nobel Prize with two American biochemists for his development of beta blockers in 1988. Technological medical instruments were also developed in Scotland. Ian Donald (1910–87), professor of Obstetrics and Gynaecology at Glasgow, adapted ultrasound, a technique developed in shipyards for checking the quality of welding, for use in revealing the difference between a foetus and a tumour in the womb. Its use has since become a standard part of obstetric practice. In the late 1970s Professor John Mallard, from Aberdeen, developed the first clinically useful Magnetic

Resonance Imaging Scanner, which detected and defined tumours.

More recently, medical science in Scotland has moved into the realms of what would have been considered science fiction twenty years ago. The cloning of Dolly the sheep at the Roslin Institute, near Edinburgh, in 1998 for some represented a gross manipulation of nature and a travesty of medical ethics. Recent years have seen a growing wariness towards scientific medicine, and a great increase in popularity of alternative forms of medical treatment. Non-medical therapies such as herbalism and homeopathy are on the increase in Scotland at the beginning of the 21st century, whilst eastern therapies, such as Chinese herbalism and acupuncture, are also growing in popularity, and are now often used as complementary therapies to western medicine with some, such as acupuncture, being practised by Scottish GPs.

Medicine in Scotland since 1914 has seen the elimination of many diseases, but is also now battling against new ones. Although we live longer, the incidence of cancers in Scotland, especially lung cancer, breast cancer, and colo-rectal cancer, are growing, although earlier diagnosis and ever-improving methods of treatment do much to improve chances of recovery. Furthermore, since its emergence in the early 1980s the HIV virus has defied the efforts of medical research. In Scotland, as elsewhere, its cure and elimination has become one of the greatest concerns of medical science at the beginning of the 21st century. ET

24. modern times (1914–1990s): literature

Perceptions of Scottish literature in the 20th century have been significantly shaped by the nature and the achievements of the Scottish Renaissance movement of the 1920s, led by Hugh MacDiarmid, pseudonym of Christopher Murray Grieve (1892–1978). The Renaissance sought to redeem Scotland from what was believed to be a long period of cultural decline, dating at least from the death of Burns (see CULTURE: 13) and going as far back, perhaps as the *Reformation. The antidote to this cultural malaise was to be the rebirth of the nation's native languages, *Scots and *Gaelic, and the creation of a modern culture which would reverse the effects of the Anglicization which had dominated Scottish life since the removal to London of the *royal court of *James VI in 1603. MacDiarmid's early poetry was written in 'synthetic Scots', adopting words and idioms from any region and from any period of Scottish writing. It culminated in the epic achievement of *A Drunk Man Looks at the Thistle* (1926), which heroically sought to encompass modern Scottish experience in a new national language and in a poetic style which was informed

by the most radical elements of modernist practice. MacDiarmid's experiments led directly to some of the major achievements of 20th-century Scottish literature in the Scots poetry of Sidney Goodsir Smith (1915–75; *Under the Eildon Tree*, 1948; *Figs and Thistles*, 1959) and Robert Garioch (Robert Garioch Sutherland, 1909–81; *Collected Poems*, 1977) and the Gaelic work of Sorley MacLean (1911–96; *Poems for Eimhir*, 1943; *From Wood to Ridge: Collected Poems*, 1989).

For MacDiarmid, even figures such as Burns, the national poet, and the country's most internationally successful writer, Walter Scott, had betrayed the true potentialities of the nation and replaced it with a culture of frauds and fakes which could be overcome only by a return to the makars, the late medieval Scots poets (see CULTURE: 6, 9) whose language was uncorrupted by Reformation. For Scottish writers the issue of which language to use, and what the cultural and political implications of that choice might be, dominated the cultural landscape from the First to the Second World Wars (see CULTURE: 21). The issue was especially potent in the theatre: James Bridie (Osborne Henry Mavor, 1888–1951), in works such as *The Anatomist* (1930) and *Mr Bolfry* (1943), adopted the 'Anglicized' language of middle-class Scotland while the plays of working-class writers, from Joe Corrie (1894–1968; *In Time o' Strife*, 1926) to Ena Lamont Stewart (1912– ; *Men Should Weep*, 1947), exploited the potentialities of industrial and urban vernacular. Others, like Robert McLellan (1907–85), in plays such as *Jamie the Saxt* (1937), used Scots to supply Scotland with theatrical representations of its past which that past had, itself, failed to provide.

Commitment to the centrality of Scots to any modern Scottish literature was to lead to a rancorous debate between MacDiarmid and the outstanding English-language poet and critic of the era, Edwin Muir (1887–1959). Originally an ally in the Renaissance cause, Muir came to believe that Scots was of no value in helping a writer deal with the modern world and his own poetry, maturing slowly from the 1930s to the 1950s and achieving international status with *The Labyrinth* (1948) and *One Foot in Eden* (1956), adopted English as its medium. Muir's lead was to be followed by many of the major Scottish poets from the 1950s to the 1990s, including Norman MacCaig (1910–96; *Collected Poems*, 1985), Iain Crichton Smith (1928–98; *Collected Poems*, 1992) and George Mackay Brown (1921–96; *Selected Poems*, 1954–83, 1991). Each maintained a distinctive regionalism but wrote in an English which was internationally accessible.

By the 1960s, the changing nature of the English language itself, which MacDiarmid had celebrated in his late poem, *In Memoriam James Joyce* (1955), was reshaping the relationship between standard English and the vernacular. In the work of Edwin Morgan (1920– ; *Collected Poems*, 1990), Ian Hamilton Finlay (1925–), Tom Leonard (1944– ; *Intimate Voices*, 1984) and Liz Lochhead (1947– ; *Dreaming Frankenstein*, 1984; *Bagpipe Muzak*, 1991), a recognition of the vitality of American English justified a celebration of the local voice—of a Scots that was not the synthetic construction of poets but the authentic speech of urban Scotland. That revitalized sense of the Scots tongue, asserting itself against the banality of international English, found expression most vividly on the stage. Successful historical dramas, such as Stewart Conn's *The Burning* (1971) and Hector MacMillan's *The Rising* (1973), and workplace drama, such as Bill Bryden's *Willie Rough* (1972) and Roddy McMillan's *The Bevellers* (1973), paved the way for a new, politically committed form of community theatre that was inaugurated by the 7:84 Company, with their production of John McGrath's *The Cheviot, the Stag and the Black, Black Oil* (1973). Despite its socialist intent, McGrath's plays, such as *The Game's a Bogey* (1974), focused the energy of a resurgent nationalism (see NATIONALISM; NATIONAL IDENTITY: 6) in Scotland in the 1970s and formed the model for later companies such as Wildcat and Tag, and for the stylized forms that would be exploited by C. P. Taylor's *Walter* (1977), John Byrne's *The Slab Boys* (1977), Liz Lochhead's *Mary Queen of Scots Got Her Head Chopped Off* (1987), Sue Glover's *Bondagers* (1991), and Chris Hannan's *Shining Souls* (1996).

In the aftermath of the failed referendum on devolution of 1979 (see PARLIAMENT: 4; POLITICAL SYSTEM: 3), many anticipated a cultural wasteland. Instead, writing flourished in the vacuum left by the politicians. Edwin Morgan's *Sonnets from Scotland* (1981) and Douglas Dunn's *St Kilda's Parliament* (1981) pointed the way towards a reimagining of the potentialities of Scotland that was also a reintegration of the potentialities of Scotland's various languages, including, in Dunn's case, the reincorporation of modern English poetic tradition, as defined by Philip Larkin, with whom he had studied in Hull, back into a Scottish framework. The pluralism of Morgan and Dunn set the tenor of the last years of the century, which saw writers such as Aonghas MacNeacail and Meg Bateman working effectively in Gaelic (see GAELIC LITERATURE); Sheena Blackhall, Raymond Vettese, Robert Alan Jamieson, Robert Crawford, and W. N. Herbert working powerfully in Scots; and Jackie Kay, Kathleen Jamie, Don Paterson, and Angela McSeveney in various versions of English. The linguistic purities sought by an earlier generation gave way to an acceptance that Scots spoke a mixed language,

whose very vitality was precisely in its flexibility, in its ability to combine high seriousness with vulgar comedy.

The explosion of Scottish writing in the last two decades of the 20th century has often been described as another Renaissance. It took place, however, in a very different cultural and economic framework. The Scottish Arts Council (SAC) provided the underpinning for the Scottish magazines, such as *Lines Review, Chapman, New Edinburgh Review, Cencrastus*, which provided outlets for poetry; it also provided the infrastructure for the theatres, despite the much-debated failure to establish a National Theatre. Without the SAC, the small, independent Scottish publishing industry would not have been able to provide many of the writers with their first book publication and projects such as the *Canongate Classics* would not have been able to make available a wide range of Scottish literature, both classical and modern. Instead of the sense of isolation from the national past which characterized the Renaissance of the 1920s and 1930s, the writers of the end of the 20th century worked in an multi-layered and receptive environment. In it, Scottish literature had gained full recognition within university Arts faculties, in which many of the poets worked as writers-in-residence. It had been acknowledged in the school curriculum. The history of Scottish literature was being explored and analysed, whether in one-volume narratives such as Roderick Watson's *The Literature of Scotland* (1984) or multi-author collections such as the Aberdeen University Press's *History of Scottish Literature* (1987–9). The achievements of Scottish writing were acknowledged in major anthologies such as Douglas Dunn's *The Faber Book of 20th-Century Scottish Poetry* (1992) or Tom Scott's *The Penguin Book of Scottish Verse* (1970), replaced by Robert Crawford and Mick Imlah's compilation of the same title in 2000. By the end of the 20th century, Scottish writing had acquired the institutions of a national literature to match the aspiration towards nationhood that had been the theme of much of the literature of the century.   RCC

25. modern times (1914–1990s): the novel

There is a special relationship between poetry and *national identity, and the Scottish Renaissance movement of the 1920s and 1930s made poetry—especially poetry in the 'synthetic' *Scots of 'Hugh MacDiarmid' (C. M. Grieve, 1892–1978) or in Gaelic (see GAELIC LITERATURE)—the test of its revitalization of the nation's culture. Nonetheless, it was the novel that was to contribute some of the most significant developments of 20th-century Scottish literature (see CULTURE: 24). Many of the aspirations of the Renaissance had already informed the work of older writers such as John Buchan (1875–1940), not only in his poetry but in editorial work such as his anthology of poetry in Scots, *The Northern Muse* (1926). Already famous, by 1918, for thrillers such as *The Thirty-Nine Steps* (1915), Buchan was to make major contributions to the Scottish novel in the inter-war period with *Witchwood* (1926), a historical novel set in 17th-century Scotland, and the posthumously published *Sick Heart River* (1941), a study of psychological breakdown set in the frozen wastes of *Canada (of which Buchan had become governor-general in 1936). Buchan's work forms a link between the period of the modern Renaissance and the tradition of Scott and Stevenson, as do the works of Eric Linklater (1899–1974), whose ironic picaresque of the United States during prohibition, *Juan in America* (1931), revealed a talent for comic absurdity which was to focus on the Renaissance movement itself in *Magnus Merryman* (1934) and on the nature of modern war in *Private Angelo* (1946). It was, however, in *A Scots Quair* (1932–43) of 'Lewis Grassic Gibbon' or Leslie Mitchell (1901–35) that the principles of MacDiarmid's Renaissance were to be fulfilled in the novel. In its merging of the Aberdeenshire dialect (see REGIONAL IDENTITIES: 2) of its characters with the narrative voice of the novel and its dramatization of the changes in language as characters move from country (see RURAL SOCIETY: 4) to town to city (see ABERDEEN: 2), Grassic Gibbon's trilogy (*Sunset Song*, 1932; *Cloud Howe*, 1933; *Grey Granite*, 1934) dispelled the notion that Scottish novels could not engage with the modern world and that they always had to be split between the dialect speech of the characters and the Standard English voice of the narrator.

Grassic Gibbon was MacDiarmid's co-author of the polemical *Scottish Scene, or the Intelligent Man's Guide to Albyn* (1934), but his novels also owed as much to earlier experiments in the Scottish novel as to MacDiarmid's theories. In particular, *Sunset Song* is indebted to *The Quarry Wood* (1928) of Nan Shepherd (1893–1981). In Grassic Gibbon's novel, the central female character chooses to stay on the farm and resist the path towards social advancement through education; in Nan Shepherd's she goes to university but discovers that her true values lie in a return to her native village. Shepherd's novel combined a subtle narrative technique with a use of dialect that was to foreshadow many of the developments of later Scottish fiction: her novel of Scotland in the aftermath of the First World War, *The Weatherhouse* (1930), is probably the most subtly wrought work by any Scottish novelist of the century.

Shepherd was one of a large number of women writers whose work contributed enormously to the Renaissance even though they were rarely given any credit as contributors to it. *Open the Door!* (1920) and *The Camomile* (1922) by Catherine Carswell (1879–1946) were clarions to the awakening of new feminine consciousness which was to be explored further by Willa Muir (1890–1970) in *Imagined Corners* (1931) and *Mrs Ritchie* (1933). Naomi Mitchison (1897–1999) was the most prolific of these women writers, contributing works that ranged from narratives of the ancient world—such *The Corn King and the Spring Queen* (1931)—to Scottish historical novels such as *The Bull Calves* (1947) which, written in the aftermath of the Second World War, reflects on the post-war condition by comparison with events in the aftermath of the 1745 rebellion (see JACOBITISM).

The centrality of the novel was affirmed in the 1930s as leadership of the Renaissance movement passed from MacDiarmid (by then living in isolation in Shetland) to Neil Gunn (1891–1973), whose novels, rooted in traditional Highland communities (see HIGHLANDS AND ISLANDS: GENERAL), explore by insistent changes of genre alternative possibilities for the renewal of Celtic culture. From historical novel (*Butchers Broom*, 1934) through meditative quest (*Highland River*, 1937) to epic (*Silver Darlings*, 1941) and allegoric fable (*The Green Isle of the Great Deep*, 1944), Gunn searched for the ways in which alternative Scotlands be constructed by various narrative forms.

In the work of the writers of the 1920s and 1930s, Scotland produced a distinctive modernism—one which explored the ways in which the storytelling traditions of an oral culture (see ORAL HISTORY; ORAL TRADITION) could be contained within the narrative medium of modern industrial society. The novel, more than poetry, however, was affected by the Second World War, which silenced many established writers and delayed the careers of younger ones. In particular, the two most important writers of the post-war period, Robin Jenkins (1912–) and Muriel Spark (1918–), were both in their late thirties before their first novels appeared in the 1950s. Very different in tone, their novels are linked by a deep scepticism about the relativistic values of modern society and by narrative techniques which juxtapose a surface realism with powerful symbolic or allegoric narrative structures. Jenkins's major novels—such as *The Conegatherers* (1955), *The Changeling* (1958), *Fergus Lamont* (1978), and *Just Duffy* (1988)—focus on the dilemmas of working-class characters in a world without spiritual consolation for their impoverished material conditions. They combine a bleak realism with a sense of an alternative world of magic and myth always just beyond reach. The survival of magic and myth is a theme that Spark, a convert to

Roman Catholicism, explores in her brief and satiric novels of modern social life. In *The Ballad of Peckham Rye* (1960) and *The Prime of Miss Jean Brodie* (1961)—her only explicitly Scottish novels—or *The Hothouse by the East River* (1972) and *Symposium* (1991), she reveals with a rich and sophisticated wit the inability of modern philosophies to explain or justify the human condition. The combination of surface realism and allusive playfulness that characterize Spark's fiction is also typical of Allan Massie (1938–), despite the fact that he often focuses on serious, historical subjects, drawn sometimes from 20th-century European experience (*A Question of Loyalties*, 1989; *The Sins of the Father*, 1991) and sometimes from the ancient world (*Augustus*, 1986; *Tiberius*, 1991). Massie's novels combine an existential sense of history as lived experience with an equal awareness of the fictionality of all history. In this respect, his novel about Walter Scott, *The Ragged Lion* (1994), is a significant reflection on the debt that all Scottish fiction owes to the historical framing of Scott's novels.

Despite the achievements of Spark and Massie, Scottish fiction from the mid-century onwards found itself characterized increasingly by its working-class content, since only the working classes were seen to have retained a distinctively Scottish identity (see ROUGH CULTURE; SOCIAL CLASS). From *The Shipbuilders* (1935) of George Blake (1893–1961) and *Major Operation* (1936) and *The Land of the Leal* (1939) of James Barke (1905–58), the effort of novelists to grasp the life of the industrial working classes dominated the sense of what a particularly *Scottish* fiction ought to offer. From the 1940s to the 1960s, works such as *Fernibrae* (1947) by J. F. Hendry (1912–86), *The Dear Green Place* (1966) of Archie Hind (1928–), *A Green Tree in Gedde* (1965) by Allan Sharp (1934–), *Mr Alfred MA* (1972) by George Friel (1910–75), and *Docherty* (1975) by William McIlvanney (1936–), developed particular modes of approaching this material, usually by focusing on working-class artists or intellectuals struggling to escape the consequences of their class position.

The theme was to culminate in 1981 in *Lanark*, an epic novel by Alasdair Gray (1934–) that combines realist and fantasy narratives, encrusted with self-conscious allusions to earlier Scottish fiction, and, like so many of its predecessors, concerned with the destruction of the imagination in modern industrial Scotland. Despite their working-class content, these novels assumed nonetheless the linguistic centrality of the English language to the presentation of Scottish experience. The role of Scots, however, was reinvented in the 1980s by James Kelman (1946–), whose *Bus Conductor Hines* (1984) and *A Disaffection* (1989) adopted the speaking language of working-class, urban Scotland

(see URBAN SOCIETY: 5) as the medium of their narrative. Kelman's creation of a hybrid language, at once ornately literary and vernacular, was to have as powerful an influence on Scottish writing in the last two decades of the century as MacDiarmid's notions of a revitalization of Scots had had in the 1920s. Kelman's narrative style—the written presentation of the consciousness of a dialect-speaking character—was to be taken up by many other writers, and produce a notable international success in *Trainspotting* (1993) by Irvine Welsh (1958–). Kelman's linguistic influence was to be matched by Alasdair Gray's formal experiments, both narrative and typographic. Gray's *1982 Janinie* (1984) adopts the form of Hugh MacDiarmid's *A Drunk Man Looks at the Thistle* to explore Scotland's place in international capitalism and, at the same time, parody the literature of pornography, while *Poor Things* (1992) explores the capitalist and imperialist origins of modern Scotland through an inverted version of Mary Shelley's *Frankenstein*.

The work of Gray and Kelman was to be prologue to a huge outpouring of Scottish fiction in the 1980s and 1990s as writers sought to dramatize the radical shifts in the identity of a nation struggling towards the political rebirth which was eventually achieved in 1997 (see PARLIAMENT: 4; POLITICAL SYSTEM: 3). Novelists such as Janice Galloway (1956– ; *The Trick is to Keep Breathing*, 1990; *Foreign Parts*, 1994), A. L Kennedy (1965– ; *Looking for the Possible Dance*, 1993; *So I am Glad*, 1995), Iain Banks (1954– ; *The Crow Road*, 1992; *Complicity*, 1993), Candia McWilliam (1955– ; *Debatable Land*, 1994), Frank Kuppner (1951– ; *Something Very Like Murder*, 1994), Andrew O'Hagan (1968– ; *Our Fathers*, 1999), brought an experimentalism and self-confidence to their fiction which was often a counterbalance to their bleak view of a Scotland trapped in political limbo. And just as, at the turn of the 19th century, Scotland had produced some of the most effective writers of new genres for a mass reading public in Conan Doyle's Sherlock Holmes stories or John Buchan's thrillers, so at the turn of the 20th century writers such as Ian Rankin (1960–) in the detective novel, Iain M. Banks (a carefully disguised pseudonym for Iain Banks) in science fiction, and J. K. Rowling (1965–) in children's fantasy, carried the themes and styles of Scottish fiction to a mass international audience.   RCC

curling. 'To Curle on the Ice, does greatly please, Being a Manly Scotish Exercise', wrote the Peeblesshire physician Alexander Penicuik in 1715, proclaiming for the first time in print the Scottishness of the game, for Scottish it certainly is. Lowland Scotland was the country of its birth and development. References from the 16th to the late 18th century vouch its widespread popularity, from Paisley in 1541, to Perth in 1620, to Clackmannanshire in 1664, to Midlothian in 1671 and 1673, to West Lothian in 1685, and to Dumfriesshire in 1694. From the last quarter of the 18th century the progress of the game can be glimpsed in surviving minute-books (such as Cupar Angus and Kettins, Perthshire, 1772; Sanquhar, Dumfriesshire, 1774; Wanlockhead, Dumfriesshire, 1777; Leadhills, Lanarkshire, 1784; Douglas, Lanarkshire, 1792; Duddingston, Midlothian, 1795; Sorn, Ayrshire, 1795; Blairgowrie, Perthshire, 1796), in newspaper reports, and in general literature, such as the *Statistical Account of Scotland*. The OSA of the 1790s contains five references; the NSA of the 1840s twenty-seven.

Curling is a game of the winter, played on ice, by teams, or rinks, of curlers, who throw stones from one end of the playing surface, also called the rink, to a point, or tee, surrounded by a large circle scored into the ice, at the other. The game was played on frozen lochs, rivers, and artificially created ponds or dams. The advantage of the last was that fewer days of frost created ice sufficient to bear the curlers and their stones. Until the 1850s rinks varied in size from four, each throwing two stones, to seven, eight, or nine, each of whom threw a single stone. The establishment of a national governing body, the Grand Caledonian Curling Club in 1838, which promoted the 4×2 game, meant that that form prevailed. The Grand Club, one of the earliest national sporting bodies in the UK, soon gained royal patronage and in 1843 became the Royal Caledonian Curling Club. It encouraged local and national competitions; the Grand Match, between the North and South of Scotland, involved between 2,000 and 3,000 curlers.

The earliest form of stone was a flattish disc with a groove on one side for the fingers, and a hole on the other for the thumb. By mid-18th century, handles of iron or wood were fixed to the top surface of smooth stones, often of remarkable weight, (some weighed as much as 112 lb (50.8 kg)), won from the beds of rivers. By the late 18th century, the advantages of predictability which arose from circularity of stones began to be appreciated, as the angle of rebound of one stone from another could be predicted, and by the 1820s circular stones of lighter weight (35–45 lb (15.9–20.4 kg)) had prevailed, and the game had changed from a course trial of brute strength to a game of scientific skill.

Until the explosion in popularity of *golf and *football in the later 19th century curling was *the* Scottish game; it involved whole communities and all classes of society and its egalitarianism was constantly vaunted (see RESPECTABLE CULTURE). In 1838, 42 curling clubs joined the Royal Caledonian Curling Club (RCCC). By the end of the century, there were over 600. Whereas there were only 58 golf clubs in the whole of the UK in 1869, there were 414 clubs affiliated to the RCCC, and many more which never troubled to join the mother club. Since the opening of the first indoor ice rink in Glasgow in 1907 the game has more and more come to be played on indoor rinks, of which there are presently 29 in Scotland, catering for between 20,000 and 30,000 curlers. The game was spread by Scots to the colder parts of the world and is now played in 25 countries, and was a medal sport at the Winter Olympic Games in 1998.   DS

D

Dál Riata, kingdom of. Dál Riata is the name of
the Gaelic overkingdom which, in the late 6th and
early 7th century, encompassed roughly the modern counties of Argyll in Scotland and Antrim in
Ireland. In Argyll it consisted initially of three kingdoms: Cenél Loairn (kindred of Loarn) in north
and mid-Argyll, Cenél nOengusa (kindred of Oengus) based on Islay, and Cenél nGabráin (kindred of
Gabrán) based in Kintyre. By the end of the 7th century a fourth kingdom, Cenél Comgaill (kindred of
Comgall), had emerged, based in eastern Argyll.
Lorn and Cowal, districts of Argyll, take their name
from Cenél Loairn and Cenél Comgaill respectively.

Dál Riata is one of the best documented corners
of early medieval Europe north of the Alps. A
chronicle was written on *Iona from the early 7th
century, and partially survives up to 740. Dál Riata
is also the setting for many episodes in St *Adomnán's Life of Columba, published probably in 697 (see
COLUMBA, ST). The most remarkable document
from this rich period in Dál Riata's history is a survey of the military and fiscal potential of Dál Riata's
kingdoms, which has been dated to the mid-7th
century. This survey survives in a damaged state
only as part of a late 10th-century text known as
Senchus Fer nAlban ('History of the Scots', so-called
because of the predominantly genealogical character of the text as a whole). This period of Dál
Riata's past is also greatly illuminated by the wealth
of archaeological evidence revealed at *Dunadd.
As a result of these varied and rich resources historians and archaeologists have been able to reconstruct more about the politics, society, and
economy of Dál Riata than about any other part of
Scotland before the 12th century.

The picture elicited from these sources is of an
overkingdom dominated by Cenél nGabráin until
the end of the 7th century, when Cenél Loairn
kings became more than equal rivals. The origins
of Cenél nGabráin predominance was enshrined in
the figure of Fergus Mór, son of Erc, who it was
said moved the kingship of Dál Riata from Antrim
to Argyll around the year 500. The most powerful
king in this period was *Aedán mac Gabráin, ordained by *Columba himself in 574, whose activi-

ties stretched from northern Ireland to Orkney,
and into Pictland and Northumbria. The abbots of
Iona and his Uí Néill kinsmen, the rising force in
Irish politics, were important allies of Cenél nGabráin, although not consistently so: Domnall Brecc
(629–42) fought the king of Uí Néill at the battle of
Mag Rath (Moira) in 637. Domnall Brecc's disastrous record while king (four battles, four defeats)
left Dál Riata so weak that it, along with the *Picts,
succumbed to Northumbrian overlordship. This
continued until the Picts destroyed the Northumbrian army at Dunnichen / Nechtansmere in 685. It
is possible that Cenél nGabráin maintained their
supremacy in Dál Riata because of Northumbrian
backing, in much the same way as their ascendancy
had gained strength from Uí Néill support.

The military and fiscal survey embedded in
Senchus Fer nAlban appears to have been written at
the behest of a Cenél nGabráin overking who
needed to identify what resources he could muster
to fulfil his obligations to a Northumbrian overlord. It suggests that each of the three major divisions of Dál Riata could raise about 700 fighting
men who would serve on sea as well as land. The
sea was the most efficient way to travel between
the coasts and islands of Dál Riata. Its strategic significance is underlined by the fact that the first sea
battle recorded in Britain took place in 719 between
Cenél Loairn and Cenél nGabráin. The survey also
points to a society based on the relationship of
landholding kindreds to their lords. The bond between lord and follower is graphically illustrated
by the discovery of moulds for the manufacture of
brooches at Dunadd. Decorated brooches made
from precious metal were potent symbols of high
status; presumably the lord of Dunadd (who may
often have been the overking of Dál Riata himself)
bestowed these brooches on his most favoured
clients as a sanction of their status. The significant
quantity of imports from France and beyond also
suggests that the lord of Dunadd had plentiful supplies of raw material to export in return, such as
hides from the regular supplies of cattle he would
have received as tribute.

The rich sources for Dál Riata in its heyday can,
however, conceal and distort as well as reveal. The

Darien

claim in *Senchus Fer nAlban* that Cenél Loairn and Cenél nOengusa were descended from brothers of Fergus Mór has been exposed as a 10th-century fabrication. It used to be generally accepted that Fergus founded the kingship of Dál Riata in Scotland, and that Scottish Dál Riata was in origin an Irish colony. A cogent case has been made, however, for regarding Argyll as part of the Gaelic world from a much earlier date. There are problems even for the period *c.*620–740 when there is a relative abundance of information. Part of the problem is that too much of this information is from Iona, which had a close link with Cenél nGabráin. Adomnán, abbot of Iona, was keen to promote the ideal of an ordained king, and to emphasize the abbot's role as kingmaker in Dál Riata. It is possible, therefore, that the dominance of Cenél nGabráin was not as solid in reality as Adomnán or the Iona Chronicle would have us believe. There must also be some doubt about the status of Cenél Loairn as simply a subordinate local kingdom. In the survey embedded in *Senchus Fer nAlban*, Cenél Loairn alone comprises other kin groups who might represent local kingdoms. Dunadd itself, as well as Iona, would seem normally to have been in the territory of Cenél Loairn. Perhaps Dunadd only became a Cenél Loairn stronghold, however, during their ascendancy (697–736).

The abundance of sources dries up dramatically after 740. From then on information is not only meagre, but also contradictory and ambiguous. There has been a tendency to read back from the alleged takeover of the Picts by *Kenneth mac Alpin and consequent 'union' of Picts and Dál Riata (see NATIONAL IDENTITY: 1). The alternative is to read forwards from the dramatic events preceding 740, when the Pictish king, *Ungus (Onuist), son of Uurgust (729–61), defeated and captured the king of Dál Riata, took Dunadd, and finally smashed Dál Riata. The most recent reinterpretation of the obscure century between 740 and 840 is that Dál Riata ceased to exist as a separate kingdom. The last 'king of Dál Riata' mentioned in contemporary sources died in 792, just when the Vikings had begun to dominate the seaways in the west which were the lifeblood of Dál Riata. Subsequent kings appear to have been subordinate to Pictish kings. Kenneth mac Alpin, who was probably of Cenél nGabráin royal stock, ushered in a new era: the end not of the Picts, but of the kingdom of Dál Riata. His power base was in the east, where he may have been joined by Cenél Comgaill in Strathearn and Cenél nOengusa in Angus. Where the kingdom of Dál Riata had once been there eventually emerged the kingdom of the *Isles. **DB**

Darien, an ambitious venture to found a trading colony in the Isthmus of Panama, was the brain-child of William Paterson (1658–1719). He was born at Skipmyre in Dumfriesshire but largely brought up in England, and later lived intermittently in the West Indies and the continent of Europe before settling in London where he became a noted projector and financier. He was a keen supporter of the 'Glorious' Revolution, which he hoped would open up an era of increased commercial enterprise. To this end he helped to set up the Bank of England in 1694 and advocated numerous projects. He first hit upon his Darien Scheme in 1684, basing it on information he garnered in the West Indies. As his scheme matured he tried unsuccessfully to win backers for it on the Continent, but his opportunity seemed to have come with the establishment in 1695 of the Company of Scotland Trading to Africa and the Indies. In helping to promote this venture he was closely associated with Andrew *Fletcher of Saltoun and, indeed, Paterson was largely responsible for the favoured status granted to the Company by an Act of the Scottish Parliament.

At first, however, to Paterson's disappointment, the Company of Scotland was not committed to the Darien Scheme, and the title sometimes given to it of 'the Darien Company' is a misnomer. Originally the Company aimed at securing English as well as Scottish investment, though control was to remain in Scotland. Many merchant interests in England resented being excluded from the lucrative African and Indian trades by the great English chartered companies. The necessary subscriptions were raised in England and Scotland, but the fledgling Bank of Scotland (see ECONOMY, TERTIARY SECTOR: 1) remained aloof and hostile, fearful that the Company of Scotland would become a rival banking interest. The English EIC, however, caused such a storm of protest that the English parliament forced English interests to withdraw their investments in the Company of Scotland. A similar hostile reception was encountered in Holland, and in desperation Paterson and others were sent to Hamburg to solicit support. Thwarted by the intervention of King William's representative there, Sir Paul Rycaut, the Company of Scotland then took up Paterson's Darien Scheme in a spirit of all or nothing. Paterson himself sailed with the first expedition to Central America in 1698, but he had little real influence over the colonists whose lack of experience caused many problems.

The scheme itself was not quite as wild as it is usually made out to be. The aim was to set up a colony, New Caledonia, on the Isthmus of Darien, now known as the Isthmus of Panama. New Caledonia was to be a free port which hopefully would become a rich emporium commanding the trade of two great oceans. The idea was to link the Caribbean (or North Sea) with the Pacific (or South Sea) by carrying goods over the narrow isthmus. In theory this was a brilliant idea which, if realized, would have generated a great trade, cutting out as it would the long stormy voyage round Cape Horn. Darien, it was hoped, would become a vast emporium to the enrichment of impoverished Scotland. But the Company had failed to take into account the difficulties involved. Of these Spain, then in a very enfeebled state, was not the greatest, except in an indirect way through the needs of King William's diplomacy. More formidable than the opposition of Spain was the intractable terrain of Darien, its rugged mountains and steamy rainforests, and, perhaps deadliest of all, a pestilential climate. The Darien Scheme, too, overtaxed Scotland's strength, although a rich sea power like England, already experienced in colonization and world trade, might possibly have succeeded in realizing Paterson's dream. But English participation, or even support for the Scots, was ruled out by the needs of King William's diplomacy which sought to prevent Louis XIV from acquiring the entire Spanish inheritance on the death of Charles II of Spain who had no immediate heir. To ravage part of Spain's colonial empire whilst striving to secure Spain's agreement to a partition treaty was clearly not practicable. Thus England was hostile to the Company of Scotland's Darien venture. Three expeditions in all were sent from Scotland. Spanish resistance on land was feeble, and on 15 February 1700 the Spaniards were defeated at Toubacanti by Captain Campbell of Fonab. But lack of sea power doomed the enterprise. A superior Spanish fleet blockaded New Caledonia and by April 1700 fever and lack of provisions forced the Scots to capitulate.

The fate of New Caledonia and the collapse of the Company of Scotland had profound repercussions. Not only was Scotland's economic situation worsened by the loss of much of its liquidity, but a constitutional conflict also arose between the Scottish and English parliaments which involved economic grievances as well as the succession, and in the end this conflict led to the parliamentary *Union of 1707.

But the Darien Scheme was not a swindle. Paterson lost a considerable sum in the venture as well as his wife and child. He was, in fact, obsessed by his scheme and the idea of free trade. His views on finance, too, were sound for his time, as was evidenced in 1705 by his successful opposition to John Law's proposal for a paper currency in Scotland not tied to specie. And his dream of connecting the Atlantic and Pacific Oceans continued to rouse interest. He believed that a canal was feasible; and this was finally achieved, after prolonged and difficult labour, with the opening of the Panama Canal in 1913.   WF

David I (*c.*1080–1153) stands as the prime architect of the dynamic Scottish monarchy of the 12th and 13th centuries. His long and eventful reign witnessed a period of crown-driven change in the political structure, social organization, and culture of the kingdom. This saw the protection of royal authority into regions remote from its traditional territorial base, the radical reform of the church, and rapid economic development driven forward by the introduction of aristocratic and burgess colonists. A reputation for personal piety, reflected in his generosity to the church, and a devotion to justice is largely a posthumous development, and must be tempered by his parallel portrayal as an aggressive warlord and ruthless operator driven by ambition.

As the youngest child of Malcolm III 'Canmore' (Mael Coluim mac Donnchada) by his second wife, St *Margaret, Scotland held few prospects for David. The flight of his family to England after the death of their parents in 1093 opened new horizons to him, and he remained there to receive a Norman-style education after his brothers' triumphant return to Scotland in 1097. His sister's marriage to Henry I in 1100 secured the talented David advancement as one of the 'new men' upon whom Henry founded his government. Loyal service brought its reward, with the gift of marriage in 1114 to Matilda, daughter of Waltheof, earl of Northumbria, the widow of Simon de Senlis, earl of Northampton. Matilda brought David the earldom of Huntingdon, claims to her ancestral lands in Northumbria, and a reservoir of wealth and manpower with which to further his ambitions in Scotland.

There, the death in 1107 of the childless Edgar brought his remaining brother, Alexander I, to the throne. David's new significance as Alexander's heir was marked by the cession to him of Strathclyde, Tweeddale, and Teviotdale, which he ruled as 'prince of the Cumbrian region'. Here, he introduced English and Continental techniques of secular and ecclesiastical government to consolidate his grip on a region which became his principal power base following his accession to the Scottish throne in 1124. Here, too, he initiated the process of ecclesiastical reform which is one of the hallmarks of his reign, commencing with the appointment of his reformist chaplain, John, to the bishopric of Glasgow, and the introduction of a colony of Tironensian monks to Selkirk. After 1124, it was in the region south of the Forth that the bulk of his ecclesiastical patronage took place, with the Cistercians and Augustinian orders in particular enjoying royal favour. Possibly from before 1124, his policy of monastic foundation was paralleled by his creation of 'feudal' lordships for friends and dependants from his English lands, such as the Morvilles and Bruces, who came to form the new elite of government around David as king.

David's accession to the throne was not uncontested within Scotland, with opposition rallying around Alexander I's bastard son, Malcolm. Although David's superior resources quickly overcame this first challenge, he continued to face hostility from important elements within the Gaelic nobility of Scotland, particularly in *Moray and Ross. The defeat in 1130 of a rising in support of Malcolm, led by Angus, earl of Moray, and the capture in 1134 of Malcolm mac Heth, claimant to Ross, provided David with the opportunity to impose royal authority in the north. This was achieved through the forging of personal bonds with the native rulers of Atholl, Sutherland, and Caithness; a colonial plantation in the Moray coastal plain based on a string of royal castles and burghs stretching from *Aberdeen to Inverness; and the reorganization or foundation of bishoprics in Aberdeen, Moray, Ross, and Caithness. Within the heartland of his kingdom, however, David worked closely in alliance with the traditional forces of lordship, such as the earls of Fife, encouraging, but not forcing, their acceptance of the innovations which he was introducing. By 1136, David had achieved an unprecedented degree of power within mainland Scotland.

The internal stability of his kingdom gave David free rein to intervene in the developing civil war in England. After initially accepting the accession of King Stephen, in 1136 he determined to realize his wife's ancestral claims to Northumbria by aligning with his niece, Matilda, Henry I's designated successor, invading northern England and occupying Cumbria and Northumbria. Stephen sought to come to terms, confirming David's possession of Carlisle and agreeing to address the claims of Henry, David's son by Countess Matilda, to the earldom of Northumbria. On the failure of this settlement in 1137, David resumed his conquest of the northern counties of England and, despite the defeat of his army at Northallerton in 1138, consolidated his hold. To win peace, Stephen recognized David's conquests and granted Northumbria to Henry. Despite the renewal of warfare in 1141, David retained control of this territory and proceeded to integrate it firmly into an expanded kingdom. Ambitions for further expansion to embrace York were thwarted in 1149. In the same year he sought to safeguard his acquisitions when he extracted oaths from the future king, Henry II, that he would honour the status quo. The measure of the integration of these territories into his kingdom can be gauged by the prominence of Carlisle as the regular seat of David's government after 1138—

indeed, it was there that he died in May 1153—and, or so it seemed at first, by the maintenance of Scottish control over Northumbria after the death in 1152 of his son, Earl Henry, who left as his heirs three young boys, the eldest just 12 years old.

David's conquests added substantially to the resources of the Scottish crown. In particular, the silver output from mines at Alston near Carlisle underwrote his programme of monastic foundation, which otherwise entailed the alienation of substantial crown resources, and provided the bullion with which he began to mint Scotland's first native *coinage. The period after 1136 witnessed an acceleration in the development of burghs (see URBAN SOCIETY: 1; URBAN SETTLEMENT: 1) with trade further stimulated by the new coinage in circulation. Coupled with his rapid development of the mechanisms of local revenue-gathering and administration, this economic growth provided a firm foundation for the new-style monarchy of the 12th century (see ECONOMY: 2). Much, however, depended on the powerful personality of the king, and the weaknesses in David's legacy were swiftly exposed following his death. Without a mature adult to succeed him, inroads were made into the extended sphere of royal authority in the north and west, and within four years Cumbria and Northumbria had been prised from Scottish control, opening nearly a century of vain struggle for their restoration. Although territorial aggrandizement had proven transitory, the social, cultural, and economic revolution which he initiated was to endure. (see also ANGLO-SCOTTISH RELATIONS: 2; CHURCH INSTITUTIONS: 2; KINGSHIP: 3; NOBILITY: 2; RELIGIOUS LIFE: 2). RO

death and burial. Early burials are a matter for archaeologists. Within documented history, it is clear that burials for the well-to-do were matters of ceremony in the Middle Ages. And the increase in the number of collegiate churches in the century after 1450 was closely associated with the growing practice of votive Masses being said for the souls of the dead so as to reduce the time spent by them in purgatory (see RELIGIOUS LIFE: 2).

After the *Reformation of 1560 Protestant reformers wanted to sweep away everything 'popish' and therefore forbade any form of religious services at burials. The *First Book of Discipline* (1560–1) stated that it was 'judged best' that there should be no singing, reading, nor sermons at burials but that the dead should be carried to burial 'with some honest company of the kirk . . . and committed to the grave' without further ado (see RELIGIOUS LIFE: 3). However, some freedom was apparent in the phrase, 'This we remit to the judgment of particular kirks, with the advice of the ministers', and John

*Knox himself preached at the funeral of the Regent Moray in 1570. Many people liked funeral sermons and so a loophole was also left in the *Book of Common Order*, sometimes known as 'Knox's Liturgy', which was confirmed by the General Assembly in 1562.

The political and religious position swung to and fro during the 16th and 17th centuries, and following the restoring of bishops by *James VI, there was a revival of burial services. In 1633 parliament ordered that surplices should be worn for celebrating the Lord's Supper, baptism, and burials, in effect ranking burial with the Sacraments. During this period there might be a graveside homily on death, a prayer, or a funeral hymn and impressive funerals were held for important dignitaries. After the signing of the *National Covenant in 1638 burial services went out of favour again. In 1645 the *Directory of Public Worship* stated that 'when any person departeth this life, let the body, upon the day of burial, be decently attended from the house to the place appointed for publick burial, and there immediately interred without any ceremony'. Such strictures, however, were not applied to food, which was always offered to those who attended burials and gradually grace was said before and thanks given afterwards. This might be done by a layman but if a minister were present, he did so; from this grew prayer, which was the thin edge of the wedge and, with Scripture reading added, it ultimately became the service over the dead which is familiar today.

Both before and after the Reformation, immediately a death occurred all windows and doors were opened to let the spirit escape and the clock was stopped and not restarted until the burial was over. Everything was draped in white (or in black in great houses) and in the 18th century, iron, cheese, a plate of salt, and earth were placed upon the chest of the corpse. Ordinary people had simple grave clothes but an Act of Parliament in 1686 indicated that these could include lace, silk, wool, hair, and gold and silver materials.

The reformers' attitude to burial denied people the comfort of burying a loved one with some little ceremonial and they clung to such ritual as they could (see CALENDAR AND SEASONAL CUSTOMS). Incense was occasionally still used at burials as late as the early 18th century. Tolling of church bells was officially forbidden but went on and indeed became permitted when a charge was made that could raise money for the poor. The mort bell, a metal handbell akin to the Roman Catholic passing bell, was hired from kirk sessions to be rung by the bell-ringer to announce a death and it could also be used to lead the funeral procession. Its hire—about a merk for adults and half a merk for a child—was divided between church and beadle. Burial letters were introduced in the mid-17th century and became increasingly common in the 18th and 19th centuries. A form of this old type of intimation still occurred in the 1920s in Comrie, Perthshire, where the street cleaner knocked on doors, and in Lilliesleaf, Roxburghshire, where the lamplighter did the same thing into the 1930s.

The bell-ringer's invitation to the funeral was taken to include the lykewake, the watch over the dead for the two or three nights before burial. The better off the household the longer the lykewake, while family members were summoned, perhaps from afar. The corpse lay in a box bed or a bed in the best room and there was meant to be quiet, appropriate conversation, and Bible readings. But food and drink were always available and there could be music too, probably originally meant, as with bells, to drive away evil spirits. There could even be dancing, also a part of early worship and believed to counteract evil. Unfortunately, the combination of all these could lead to drunkenness and very unseemly behaviour (see ROUGH CULTURE).

The final part of the lykewake was the kisting or coffining of the corpse which became commercially important in the late 17th century, when the linen industry needed support. The Act anent Burying in Scots Linen of 1686 required the shroud to be of plain linen or harden, prepared and spun in Scotland, and this had to be verified by two reputable people and ultimately often by the parish minister. The kisting ceremony itself, without the reference to linen, was common in Caithness until the 1920s and occurred occasionally elsewhere until 1940. In some fishing communities, almost within living memory, if a mother died in childbirth leaving a living child, the baby was baptized 'over the coffin', father and minister standing on either side of it, prior to leaving for the burial.

Those attending on the day of a funeral were always given a series of 'services': combinations of food and drink in a special order, usually including bread, shortbread, cheese, and ale, with perhaps cake, sherry, whisky, or rum. It was a matter of honour for the departed to intoxicate the living and many families were beggared for a year or more after funerals. The poor gathered to share in the largesse, which could include cash at large funerals but ultimately ministers and landowners managed to persuade heads of families to agree that they would limit what they offered so as to avoid abuses. The introduction of hearses in the 18th century helped with this as it reduced the need for large numbers of bearers for the coffin.

Before departure, the coffin was covered with a mortcloth, a fringed pall usually made of velvet.

Dewar, Donald Campbell

Originally designed to cover an uncoffined corpse, it came to be regarded as an indispensable feature of all funerals. It was in use from at least the 15th century onwards and was encouraged by a proclamation of the privy council in 1684 forbidding elaborate coffins. Mortcloths were usually owned by kirk sessions, burghs, and craft guilds, cost about £12 to provide and were hired out for some 6s. or 7s., an important source of income for the poor and, in Edinburgh, for education. Their use gradually died out although one was laid over a coffin at the entrance to a churchyard about 1906.

When covered, the coffin was 'lifted' and carried on men's shoulders to burial. A procession formed up outside the house, two by two, with a leader in charge who called out at intervals the word 'Relief' when some six or eight men immediately slipped in to take their turn as bearers. They might have to dig the grave when they got to their destination. In the Highlands, as the procession went along, women cried the coronach (impromptu verses and phrases in honour of the departed). A BBC radio programme in December 1982 gave one beautiful example although Captain Burt, writing in the 18th century, described it as a 'hideous howl or Ho-bo-bo-bo-boo'. Crying the coronach has now died out, although it is said to have been heard in the Western Isles as late as 1965.

Many people wished to be buried in family graves, possibly at a considerable distance, hence the long routes to be found especially in the west Highlands, known as coffin roads, and large-scale maps show 'resting cairns' where the coffin was placed during refreshment halts. When Lady MacKenzie of Gairloch died in childbirth in Wester Ross in the late 19th century, her corpse was carried shoulder high some 70 miles (112 km) to Beauly. Repeated burials in a family plot could lead to humpy graves as yet another went on top of earlier ones, something seen at places like Murlaggan in west Inverness-shire.

The funerals of the nobility and important townspeople featured elaborate processions with baton men, saulies (hired mourners), and mutes (funeral attendants). House and church were draped in black with 'tears' painted on and looking like tadpoles or fat commas, something that may be seen on the Bolton hearse in the *Royal Museum of Scotland in Edinburgh. While ordinary people just wore their best for funerals, others donned black for specified lengths of time, and many women were seldom out of it.

For many years the poor were buried as best might be but in 1563 the General Assembly ordered every parish to have a bier for carrying them to burial—a reusable 'common coffin' with a hinged base which allowed the body to be dropped into the grave and the coffin retrieved. Everyone wanted a 'decent burial' but for paupers this fell to kirk sessions, craft guilds, or burgh councils to finance. A little ale and bread was often allowed, in addition to a coffin or perhaps just a winding sheet, but that was largely to encourage people to come and then act as bearers. A custom slipped into practice in the mid-18th century—the law is silent on it—whereby those seeking admission to the paupers' roll were required to bequeath all their effects to the kirk session to pay for their maintenance in life and for their funeral expenses, with any surplus going to the poor.

Inadequate lykewakes for the poor could result in their bodies being stolen by body-snatchers before burial. Many churchyards have evidence of the efforts made to foil these people, including watch towers and mort safes. In Edinburgh in 1694, it was decreed that the bodies of foundlings and those who died in the Correction House might go for dissection, as did those of murderers.

There are few pre-17th-century memorials in churchyards because those who could afford such things were buried inside the church. In some places, everyone was, so that corpses might be barely covered by the earthen floor and bones might well protrude. Before the Reformation the churchyard was public open space, ideal for archery practice and wapinschawings when men showed that they were ready to take to the field. Fairs and markets were also held in churchyards; some still have market crosses within them. Churchyards could provide sanctuary and act as meeting places for craft guilds, for bleaching linen and drying hides. They were also used for punishment; church towers could be used as prisons and jougs (iron neck collars) may still be found near church doors. Once burials were moved out into the churchyards, stones appeared but very few inscriptions are in Gaelic as Gaelic-speakers tended to be the poorest and in any event Gaelic was politically unpopular after the Forty-Five. Bare open space may well indicate 'cholera ground' where the dead were tipped into communal graves in the outbreaks of 1832 and 1849.

In the 18th and 19th centuries Benefit and Friendly Societies developed to give financial help in sickness and for funerals. The passing of the Registration of Births, Deaths and Marriages (Scotland) Act of 1855 put death registration on a proper footing and these developments, along with hospital deaths and cremation, have greatly changed death and burial customs in Scotland. AG

Dewar, Donald Campbell (1937–2000). Born as the only child of middle-class parents in Glasgow, Donald Dewar had a sheltered but fairly lonely upbringing. He joined the Labour Party in 1956 and after quickly abandoning the idea of studying history in favour of law at Glasgow University, he showed himself as a talented debater by becoming president of the Union in 1961–2. He was already recognized as a prominent and talented member of a generation at the University which included his lifelong friend and future leader of the Labour Party, John Smith. He unsuccessfully contested the seat of Aberdeen South in 1964, at the age of 25, but became the first Labour MP ever to hold the seat in 1966. The concern for social deprivation which marked his career was sharpened during the 1970s, when he became a children's reporter in Lanarkshire after losing his seat in 1970. An early supporter of devolution, when it was deeply unfashionable in Labour Party circles, he himself identified J. P. *Mackintosh as one of the formative influences on his thinking. He returned to Westminster in 1978 after winning a by-election at Garscadden, which he represented for the rest of his life, though it was later renamed Anniesland after boundary changes.

He spent much of the long and increasingly bleak years of the Conservative Party's domination of politics after 1979 in the thankless role of Shadow Secretary of State for Scotland. After Labour's sweeping general election victory in 1997, he was appointed Secretary of State for Scotland and charged with shepherding the Scotland Bill, which he claimed to be the 'most far-reaching programme of constitutional reform this country has seen for over a century', through Westminster. His stature and the widespread respect in which he was held in political circles allowed him to construct a coalition involving both Liberals and the SNP which secured a resounding 'yes' vote in the referendum of 1997 on the double issue of a Scottish parliament with tax-raising powers.

Although Scots were represented in large numbers in the government of Prime Minister Tony Blair, Dewar was the only prominent Labour politician to stand for the new Scottish *parliament. As leader of the majority party in the new parliament, he became Scotland's first First Minister. The high point of his career, the opening of the parliament in May 1999, was marked by a speech which revealed the intensity of his commitment to the cause of Home Rule as well as much of an intensely private man. His simple words, 'Today there is a new voice in the land, the voice of a democratic parliament. A voice to shape Scotland, a voice for the future', reflected his widely acknowledged status as 'father of the nation'. His transparent integrity and refusal to accept the blandishments of New Labour 'spin doctors' made him stand out in politics. If one side of him was his deep concern for the lives of ordinary people, which encouraged his constituents to refer to him simply as 'oor Donald', the other was the breadth of his interests in art, architecture history, and theatre. His premature death in October 2000, only fifteen months after the opening of the parliament, left a nation in mourning and a gap both in Scottish politics and the Labour Party in Scotland which proved hard to fill.　　　ML

Diarmait, foster-son of Daigre, abbot of Iona (fl. 814–31), was heir of St *Columba and head of the Columban federation of monasteries at a crucial period in its history. In the decades before he became abbot, *Iona was subject to numerous Viking raids, the most severe in 806 when 68 monks were killed. Between 807 and 814, a new monastery was built on formal royal land at Kells, and the then abbot seems to have retired there on its completion. Nonetheless, Iona continued to be the hub of the federation for most of the 9th century, and Diarmait is recorded on numerous journeys between Scotland and Ireland, usually accompanied by the relics of St Columba. During Diarmait's abbacy, one of the most famous attacks on Iona occurred, in 825, when Blathmac mac Flainn was martyred refusing to reveal the whereabouts of St Columba's shrine. This event was subsequently commemorated in poetry by Walahfrid Strabo, a monk of the monastery of Reichenau, on Lake Constance. We last hear of Diarmait in 831: no obit is recorded for him. He must have died before 849, when the next abbot, Indrechtach, is recorded as bearing the relics of St Columba from Scotland to Ireland.

We also know that Diarmait was involved with the reforming churchmen known as the *céli Dé*, probably both before and after becoming abbot. He appears in some of their literature as a figure of authority, and hence he is a plausible candidate as the conduit through which *céli Dé* ideals were introduced into Scotland. Through the *céli Dé* material we get a clearer idea of the monastic regime under Diarmait, and the way in which an abbot might abide by received tradition, or innovate if circumstances warranted. These texts bear witness to the existence of a Rule of St Columba, but whether this was a written text or simply tradition we cannot say.　　　TC

diet. The diet of the Scots can be divided into four phases up to 1800, by which time all the ingredients of the later forms of diet were in place: prehistoric, medieval to the early 17th century, the 1650s to around the 1760s, and the later 18th century. There are, of course, overlaps, but each period has defining characteristics.

The first and, in part the second, period is distinguished by the largely non-documentary nature of the evidence. Pollen analysis of soil samples from or under prehistoric sites provides evidence for early cereal cultivation. Impressions of cereal grains on prehistoric pottery and finds of charred grain in prehistoric structures may indicate the practice of drying prior to grinding. In later times, even into the 19th century, means of drying grain on a small scale have been recorded that could well have been used in antiquity. Threshed ears of grain could be dried in a pot over the fire, or if still on the stalk they could lie on a net slung over the fire. A common method, in Ireland as in Scotland, was to 'graddan' the grain: it was taken a bunch at a time and the ears set on fire. At a suitable moment the fire was dashed out with a stick and the hot ears made to fall on to a collector on the ground. Threshed grain could be stored in underground pits, showing that there were on occasion temporary surpluses, which had to be hidden from marauders but could also be used for trade. Above ground, receptacles of coiled straw for grain storage, known as recently as the early 20th century in Caithness and in Ireland, may again provide evidence of prehistoric practices, though we cannot be sure, since, like the above-mentioned small-scale drying techniques, they leave no evidence on the ground. The likelihood is that cereal grains were mainly eaten in the form of gruels.

Stock-keeping also played a role in the domestic economy. Cows provided milk, one of the by-products of which was 'bog butter'. There have been numerous finds, often containing cow hairs, mostly in wooden troughs or containers. The apparent depositing of often quite substantial amounts in peat may point to some level of trading, or at least to a requirement for preserving the butter for an extended period.

Cereals and milk products appear to have been two of the major prehistoric food resources, along with the flesh of domesticated animals, game and wildfowl, and fish. Wild plants and berries and fruits would have supplemented the diet. Excavated plant and animal remains, the analysis of faecal matter, and the worn state of surviving teeth, show that the diet was tough and fibrous.

In many cases, seasonality was a mark of food availability during the centuries before the advent of refrigeration and canning. Spring hunger was a recurring feature of life. To judge by the practices of later times, the tubers of 'arnuts' (*Bunium flexuosum*) would have been relished, as well as edible forms of goosefoot (*Chenopodeia*), the leaves of wild sorrel, the roots of silverweed, wild skirret and wild liquorice, watercress, and other plants. Shore-hugging fish like coalfish, and whelks, mussels, limpets, and other shellfish would have helped to fill the blank hungry period of spring, and other times of scarcity or famine.

The second period may be taken to coincide with the beginnings of Scotland's towns (see URBAN SOCIETY: 1), which, if defined as communities with special privileges conferred by king or overlord, means the early 12th century. The phenomenon, at least in Lowland Scotland, indicates very clearly that living conditions were changing. The bulk of the food consumed in these developing towns would have come from the rural hinterland and stock was also kept in and around the houses, but foodstuffs and wine from further afield played an increasing role as trading contacts widened. Excavations in midden deposits in medieval Scottish towns, notably Perth and Aberdeen, have produced the bones of cattle, sheep and goats, pigs, chickens, geese and sometimes wild birds, cod and salmon. There were oysters and mussels. The seeds of wheat, oats, and barley point to the use of porridge, bread, and ale. Turnip seed was found, as well as pease and beans, nuts and berries of various kinds, and exotics like figs and grapes. Cabbage and kail were on the menu, and the spinach-like plant fat hen. Spices such as pepper and coriander helped to disguise the taste of fading meat for the better-off, and Perth merchants were already trading in wine with Bordeaux before 1246.

Cooking methods were largely confined to boiling meat and gruels in pottery vessels over open fires, bread was baked in small clay ovens, and no doubt there was occasional spit roasting. The food was eaten mainly from wooden bowls or platters, or directly from the containers in which it was cooked, and the use of the fingers was normal, or chunks or slices of bread could have served as holders for other forms of food. The cuts on the bases of wooden containers show that they could be inverted and used as cutting boards, no doubt for meat. There were knives, and spoons for the moister gruels, but no forks. It is likely that chunks of meat were boiled along with cereal-based gruels, in a way that has been widespread in Europe, in the form of the so-called 'one-pot dishes'.

The pattern for the diet of the countryside is more inferential. For example, John Barbour's *The Brus*, the writing of which began in 1372, says that 'James of Douglas' bought food for the ladies of the court around Aberdeen—venison, pike and salmon, trout and small fish from the rivers. In the following century, Walter Bower tells in his *Scotichronicon* how, during the wars of the Scots and *Picts against the Britons, the country dwellers were exposed to plundering and pillage. Those who escaped lived in remote corners, eating grass roots, fruit, and the leaves and bark of trees, with acorns and wild honey found in tree trunks and amongst reeds, and the milk of any animal they might happen to have. Such evidence reflects the twin patterns of settled adequacy and of emergency situations or of life in the remoter and wilder places.

The plague years following 1349 (see HEALTH, FAMINE, AND DISEASE: 1) probably had an appreciable effect on diet for a good century and a half afterwards. It is thought that the high mortality (see LIVING STANDARDS: 1), rate led to a shift in lord and tenant relationships, expressed in reduced rents and enlarged holdings, with less emphasis on the meat-producing pastoral economy and more on the growing of oats and barley. The thesis needs to be tested, but it is certainly true that at later dates the great mass of the people were consumers of cereals and of vegetable and dairy products rather than of meat.

The bulk of the evidence for diet, however, comes from the towns, and in this context it is instructive to consider the custumar's accounts which form part of the *Exchequer Rolls* of Scotland. The rights and privileges of the burghs provided the revenues for the crown and, as international trade expanded, especially in the 15th and 16th centuries, these depended very much on customs charged on exports. The leading product was sheep's wool, woollen cloth and wool-fells, followed by the skins, fells, or hides of adult sheep, cattle, and other animals. The inevitable question is what happened to the meat?

Though townsfolk kept their own animals, most of the exported wool and hides came from the rural districts. Much of the slaughtering of animals was done by fleshers in the burgh shambles, where the meat was also displayed for sale, as a jealously guarded right. 'Outintownes burgesses' could slaughter within the town if they paid their dues, but were not allowed to break their meat up into smaller portions. They had to present the carcass whole for inspection, and it is not at all clear that the meat was actually sold by the individual cut. The better-off may well have bought beasts whole for cutting up—fleshers would prepare cuts from carcasses in the homes of individual families—hence the need for the 'elcrooks' or flesh hooks that figure prominently in their inventories of goods.

Flesh in bulk was a prestige item for the elite. It may also have been easier to inspect for disease whole- or part-carcasses than cut-up portions. But numerous regulations about substandard meat imply that it was far from uncommon, and when ordinary townsfolk ate meat they could afford, its quality may have been very poor indeed. It is likely too that offal and otherwise waste parts of animals were much used in the form of sausage types. 'Haggis' and 'puddings', recorded from the 16th century, were made of the stomach or part of the entrails of an animal stuffed with oatmeal, suet, and inferior meat or offal, and in 1636 Aberdeen even had a female 'puddinwricht'. Sausages, called 'sasis', 'sauses', or 'sawster', recorded from the late 16th century, and 'rodykyns' (the fourth stomach of a ruminant) and white sausages, presumably something like mealy puddings, were known in the royal households of *James IV and *James V in the early 1500s. 'Panches', the viscera or entrails of animals used as food, or tripe, were also common, sometimes mentioned along with the heads and feet of animals. Mostly, these products were not seen as the food of the elite; but, though widely consumed, neither were they the food of the poorest since they required preparation and involved an intention to keep them for at least a little time.

Meat was likely to have been reasonably plentiful in the towns and immediate surroundings, with different forms and qualities serving the different social groupings. But for most folk, the twin staples of the urban diet were bread and ale. The prices and weights of bread were carefully controlled by burgh regulations. Wheat bread was the commonest bread grain in the towns and for the higher classes; it was a prestige dietary element, though itself divided into specific qualities according to the degree of refining. The whiter the flour, the greater the prestige.

Though the burgh bread assizes relate to standard loaves, they appear to say little about other bakery items, smaller in size and more like present-day baps or buns or rolls. Being smaller and cheaper and seemingly outside regulation, the town bakers may well have got their profit from them by selling to a wider social range, and to inns and alehouses. In private households in towns and in the countryside the standard 'bread' form was the flat bannock of beremeal, peasemeal, or oatmeal, baked over an open fire on a flat iron girdle, or on an openwork brander. Flour 'baiks' were also made in both town and country, as well as flour 'scones', from the 16th century at least. These items reinforce the fact that Scotland lies in the flat (unleavened) bread zone of Europe, and that baking ovens were rare except in town bakeries and in big houses and monastic buildings.

Ale brewed from barley was also treated as a kind of food. There were brewhouses at bigger establishments, but otherwise the work was carried out in the kitchen. This domestic background may explain why in later medieval times most of the brewers in *Aberdeen were *women. Though evidently drunk in large quantities, it does not follow that ale had a bad effect, for much of it was not strong. It served, amongst other things, as a substitute for milk when that was scarce, to wash down porridge.

The third phase, starting from around the mid-17th century, is characterized by innovations: the spread of sugar, and the adoption of hot drinks, one facilitating the other. The earlier world was more a savoury world and a spiced world, but not a sweet world. Honey was well known as a sweetener, though its function was equally medicinal and for seasoning. Cane sugar spread widely between the 15th and 18th centuries, though it was not until the later 19th century, with the cheaper beet sugar, that it really reached all social levels, accompanying the wide adoption of tea, and the domestic making of jams and jellies, sponges and biscuits, and the like.

Hot chocolate, referenced in Scotland from 1667, was essentially a drink for the upper-class ladies, at breakfast, as a nightcap, and as a pre-dinner drink. The third duke of Hamilton's duchess was fond of it. There were also drinking-chocolate shops in the towns. But the use of chocolate seems to have been on the wane by the mid-18th century, having been superseded by tea and to a lesser extent by coffee.

Coffee reached Scotland soon after 1650, both in the homes of the upper classes (who had their own sources of supply), and in coffee houses, which reached a wider, but still middle-class professional, audience. Coffee did not spread to the wider social classes in Scotland or England, as it did in many other countries of Europe. But for a time it seems to have taken a lead over tea, which was being used from the 1670s—at first as a kind of *medicine. The evidence indicates that the way of making this hot beverage was still being learned only in the early 1700s.

These hot drinks involved a veritable revolution in kitchen and table equipment—pots, boxes, mills and roasters, milk jugs, cups, tea and coffee tables—which, taken together, amount to the three-dimensional expression after the 1650s of an altogether more sophisticated view of the world and symbolize rising *living standards. Thereafter, they continued to spread through the social scale, and, especially in the case of tea, became a general element in the daily diet, though not before the latter half of the 19th century.

The fourth phase that completes the story down to 1800 was marked by the widespread adoption of green crops in the fields. Some green crops—pease and beans, cabbage and kail—had long been established and were regularly eaten in the form of bread made at least in part of the flour of pulses, or of porridge, or in gruels and broths. No house was complete without its kailyard, a primary source for vitamin C when fruit, vegetables, and salads were little eaten as regular elements in meals.

The main new crops were the potato and turnip, both of which had been known since the 17th century in the gardens of big houses, and which then spread in the following half-century to the kitchen gardens of farms and to the farmers' fields. In some areas of the Highlands and Islands (see HIGHLANDS AND ISLANDS: GENERAL) the potato became the major food item after the 1740s, and for the century after that it ruled supreme until the potato blight struck in the 1840s. It was also widely eaten elsewhere in Scotland, though forming a less major part of the diet, except possibly for poorer folk both in town and country, for whom it also was a godsend. The turnip also became an item of domestic consumption, mashed and as an element in broths, but its main influence on the diet was because it permitted the overwintering of farm stock, so improving the resources in meat and milk products and making them available over longer periods of the year.

By 1800, all the ingredients of the later forms of diet were in place. There was, however, much regional—and seasonal—variation in availability, and great differences across the social spectrum. Eighteenth-century travellers who stayed at the houses of the elite in the Highland areas were entertained well, with meat, fish and fowl, broth and often wheaten bread, syllabubs and tarts, butter, orange marmalade and currant jelly, washed down with claret, porter, and punch, or tea, chocolate, or coffee. And all this at a time when tenants and farmworkers were surviving on potatoes, milk, and milk products, and on dishes made from oat- or barley-meal, with only occasional tastes of salt meat and fish.   AF

Disruption, the. In May 1843, the established Church of Scotland was broken up, as over a third of the clergy and nearly half the laity left to form the Free Church. This was a watershed in the history of modern Scotland. Before 1843, the established church had been widely perceived as the religious expression of the Scottish nation and the guardian of the nation's faith. Through its parish system and hierarchy of church courts, it had exercised considerable control over popular education, poor relief, and public morals. Following the Disruption of 1843, however, the Church of Scotland became a minority establishment, its moral force greatly diminished and its authority over education and poor relief weakened.

The Disruption was the culmination of a prolonged dispute within the Church of Scotland over patronage, or the right of patrons to present candidates for the parish ministry. Patronage had emerged in the medieval church, as the founders of parish churches, generally lairds or nobles, had been rewarded with the right to present the priests who would officiate in those churches. This right was vested in the founder's family and passed from generation to generation. At the *Reformation, the reformers sought to abolish patronage and empower parishioners to select their own ministers. The lairds and nobles, however, with the support of the crown, continued to claim their patronage rights, and lay patronage survived in the reformed church. Patronage was, however, a source of contention, supported by the crown and landowners, despised by zealous Presbyterians and *Covenanters. In 1690, with the Presbyterians now dominant in the established church, the Scottish parliament had abolished patronage, replacing it with a system of election of ministers by kirk sessions and heritors in the parish. Then in 1712, despite guarantees made at the *Union of 1707 to preserve Scotland's religious settlement, and against the strenuous protests of the Church of Scotland, the new British parliament restored lay patronage within it.

For the next decade, patrons were reluctant to exercise their right to present ministers to vacant parish livings. In the 1720s, however, they began asserting their right, and the church courts were forced to acquiesce. According to the law, the patron could present only a candidate licensed to preach by a presbytery. Moreover, the majority of male heads of family in the parish were to signify their acceptance of the candidate by signing a 'Call', before the local presbytery could settle the minister in the parish church. However, it soon became clear that the civil authorities expected the church courts to settle patrons' candidates regardless of the Call. Parishioners, however, viewed the Call as a fundamental right of a free Christian people. From the 1730s onwards, parishioners often rioted against the settlement of patrons' candidates, with confrontations between troops and parishioners resulting in injuries and deaths. As blood was spilt, the patronage issue assumed an increasing importance in the popular imagination. Opponents of patronage believed they were carrying on the struggle of the Covenanters and claiming the rights won for them at the Reformation. They viewed patronage as a form of privilege and hierarchy, a corruption of Christ's church (see CHURCH INSTITUTIONS: 5).

Not all within the church, however, were prepared to condone violent resistance to patronage. While the majority within it opposed patronage, few desired to see a revival of the unrest of the Covenanting era. One section of ministers and elders within the church, referred to as 'Moderates' (see RELIGIOUS LIFE: 5), argued that the church courts had no choice but to enforce the law of patronage and discountenance the popular resistance. Such accommodating attitudes gained the Moderates' support among Scotland's landowners and political managers, and this in turn brought them advancement and growing influence within the church.

In 1733, four devoutly orthodox, anti-patronage ministers, led by the brothers Ebenezer and Ralph Erskine, seceded from the Church of Scotland, in protest against both patronage and the spread of Moderatism within the church. Others, who shared their hatred of patronage, their strict Calvinist orthodoxy, and their puritanical piety, soon joined them. The Secession Church maintained the same Presbyterian organization, Calvinist doctrine, and liturgy as the Church of Scotland, and perceived itself to be the true church, purified of patronage and moderatism. The Secession Church itself split in 1747, following a dispute over whether or not Christians should take the 'Burgess Oath' required of all local officials by the 'uncovenanted' state in the aftermath of the *Jacobite rising of 1745. Despite the split, the two branches of the Secession continued to grow, with individuals and entire congregations leaving what they viewed as a corrupted established church. In 1752, the patronage controversy led to the formation of still another Presbyterian sect. In that year, the General Assembly of the Church of Scotland, under Moderate influence, deposed Thomas Gillespie from the ministry for refusing to participate in the ordination of an unpopular patron's candidate. Gillespie's congregation followed him out of the church, but they elected not to join one of the puritanical Secession churches. They were joined by others who, though alienated by patronage and Moderatism in the establishment, also felt no affinity with the strict piety of the Seceders, and in 1761, they formed the Relief Church. By 1766, it was estimated that the Secession and Relief churches had over 100,000 adherents, representing nearly 10 per cent of Scotland's population.

Within the Church of Scotland, meanwhile, Moderatism was strengthened by these secessions of the most zealous opponents of patronage, as well as by its association with the new intellectual mood of the Scottish Enlightenment (see CULTURE: 11). In 1784, the General Assembly of the church ceased making an annual petition to parliament for the abolition of patronage. Following the outbreak of the *French Revolution in 1789, the Moderate dominance in the church was further ensured by the widespread suspicion of all forms of popular expression.

This situation began to change, however, in 1815, with the end of the Napoleonic Wars. A new group of Evangelical clergy, influenced by the larger Protestant Evangelical awakening in the North Atlantic world, began exercising leadership within the established Church of Scotland. Including such men as Stevenson Magill, Andrew

Thompson, and Thomas *Chalmers, they empha-sized direct, conversionist preaching, an emotional piety, and a zealous pastoral ministry. They were particularly committed to strengthening the church's parish system in the rapidly expanding urban districts and to carrying on aggressive *mis-sions at home among the industrial working classes. They sought to make the church more popular. In the mid-1820s, the Evangelicals (see RE-LIGIOUS LIFE: 6) revived the anti-patronage move-ment within the church. They were encouraged in their efforts for a more popular church by the par-liamentary Reform Act of 1832. In 1834, the Evan-gelicals convinced the General Assembly to pass an act of church law aimed at limiting the worst ef-fects of patronage and restoring a form of the popu-lar Call in the appointment of ministers. This was the Veto Act. It enabled a majority of male heads of family in a parish to veto a patron's presentee to a parish vacancy, if they sincerely believed that the patron's candidate would not be an effective minis-ter in that parish.

With the Veto Act, many believed the long-standing patronage dispute was finally resolved and the church could concentrate on restoring its influence among the Scottish people. During the next five years, the Church of Scotland was re-vived. Voluntary contributions for church work in-creased fourteen-fold between 1834 and 1839. The church embarked on an ambitious programme of church and school building (see SCHOOLS AND SCHOOLING: 2), adding over 200 new parish churches (see CHURCHES: 2). It greatly expanded its *missions overseas. The Veto Act seemed to work effect-ively. Of 150 presentations between 1834 and 1839, only ten were vetoed. There were hopes that the more popular established church would attract the Presbyterian seceders back into the fold, restoring the unity of the national church and strengthening its control over poor relief, education, and public morals. Such leaders as Thomas Chalmers began speaking of Scotland becoming at last the godly commonwealth envisaged by the 16th-century re-formers.

But this was not to be. For in the later 1830s a conflict emerged over the Veto Act, which brought the church into bitter confrontation with the state. The conflict began when Robert Young, who had been presented to the parish living at Auchterarder but then rejected under the terms of the church's Veto Act, appealed against his veto to the civil courts. The case eventually came before the Court of Session, Scotland's highest civil court, which in 1838 decided that the Veto Act was an illegal in-fringement on the civil rights of patrons and pat-rons' candidates. The church appealed against the ruling to the House of Lords, but in 1839 the Lords

upheld the Court of Session and pronounced the veto illegal. The Court of Session began instructing the presbyteries to ordain vetoed patrons' candi-dates, on threat of fines and imprisonment. The Evangelical majority in the church, however, re-fused to set the Veto Act aside. For them, the Court of Session had no right to 'intrude' unpopular patrons' candidates on parishioners; such actions were threats to the spiritual independence of the church. The General Assembly instructed the pres-byteries not to ordain vetoed patrons' candidates, and appealed to parliament for legislation that would legalize the veto. But a parliament domi-nated by Anglican landowners had little sympathy for Presbyterian anti-patronage feeling, and de-clined to pass the desired legislation. As the civil courts increased the pressure on the church to withdraw the Veto Act, the Evangelical majority in the church responded with a 'Claim of Right', a new covenant, insisting on the church's independ-ence in spiritual matters, including the appoint-ment and ordination of ministers. Finally, in May 1843, the anti-patronage Evangelicals withdrew from the established church and founded the Free Church of Scotland.

The Free Church inspired considerable popular support. In rural districts, especially the Highlands (see RELIGIOUS LIFE: 8), Free Church adherents ex-perienced persecution at the hand of landowners, who viewed the new church as a challenge to the traditional social order. But the new church sur-vived the ordeal, and within five years had created a national territorial structure, with over 700 churches, over 500 primary schools, a college, and an active home and foreign mission. It emerged as the most dynamic denomination in Victorian Scot-land. The established church, meanwhile, was reduced to a minority establishment, with the ad-herence of only about a third of Scotland's church-going population. Its social influence waned. With the Scottish Poor Law Act of 1845, the established church lost most of its control over poor relief (see LIVING STANDARDS: 4) and with the Scottish Educa-tion Act of 1872 it gave up much of its authority over popular education. The Disruption was in one sense a tragedy, breaking up the unity of the na-tional church. But in their rejection of aristocratic and crown patronage, the outgoing clergy and laity also contributed to the development of a more pluralistic, more liberal, and more democratic Scotland.   SJB

Douglas family: 1. to 1455; 2. since 1455.

1. to 1455

The foundations for the rise to prominence of the Black Douglas family arose out of the support and service given by James Douglas, known as 'the good Sir James', to Robert Bruce (see ROBERT 1) before and after he attained the Scottish crown. His exploits, particularly in cross-border warfare, earned Douglas lands and lordships in the Border region, the description of Black Douglas arising from his dark colouring and ruthlessness in battle. Following the death of James Douglas in Spain in 1330 while conveying the heart of Robert I to the Holy Land, the Black Douglases adopted the symbol of a red heart on the family crest, probably in the late 1340s.

Prowess in the years of warfare which followed won Archibald Douglas, half-brother of the good Sir James, the guardianship of the kingdom, but he was killed in battle at Halidon Hill in 1333 along with his nephew, William, lord of Douglas. The mantle of Douglas power was assumed by William, lord of Liddesdale, who embarked on a career where self-aggrandizement played a large part although, as before, the invaluable service performed by the Douglases in resisting English claims and engaging actively in military campaigning prevented David II from outright opposition to their pre-eminence in the Middle March. The return from exile in France of Archibald's son, William, lord of Douglas, challenged Liddesdale's position, and the latter was killed in 1353. William became first earl of Douglas and established his position by defending the kingdom in the south and building up his network of followers. When he died in 1384, he was succeeded as a matter of course by his son, James, second earl of Douglas, although his death at the battle of Otterburn in 1388 opened the way for arguably the real founder of subsequent Black Douglas power (see ANGLO-SCOTTISH RELATIONS: 2).

In 1369, David II confirmed Archibald 'the Grim', so called because of his 'terrible countenance in warfare', in the lands of eastern Galloway between the Nith and the Cree. Following the death of James, second earl of Douglas, leaving no legitimate heirs, the terms of a tailzie, dated 26 May 1342, came into effect, allowing Archibald, the illegitimate son of the good Sir James, to succeed as third earl of Douglas, inheriting the entailed Douglas estates of Douglasdale, Lauderdale, Eskdale, and the forest of Selkirk. It was at this stage that the Douglas family was split into two main branches. As inheritor of the Black Douglas tradition, Archibald's descendants were known as the Black Douglases, whereas the Douglases of Angus became known as the Red Douglases. Margaret Stewart, countess of Angus, had been the mistress of William, first earl of Douglas, and borne him a son, George Douglas, to whom she resigned her earldom of Angus on 9 April 1389. The castle of Tantallon was the major stronghold of Red Douglas power, but it was the Black Douglases who emerged triumphant from the struggle to secure the chief Douglas lands and titles.

A steady increase of Black Douglas power and influence followed, with the important resignation in February 1372 by Thomas Fleming, grandson and heir of the first earl of Wigtown, of the lands and rights of his earldom to the earl of Douglas in exchange for £500 sterling. The lands of *Galloway, which had been split in 1235, were reunited with this grant to Douglas, confirmed by royal charter in 1372, although there is no evidence of a formal grant of the title, and the Black Douglases did not use it until at least 1406. The prestigious marriage of Archibald, third earl of Douglas, to Joanna Murray brought him possession of the lordship and castle of Bothwell in Lanarkshire, where he founded a collegiate church. The entailed Douglas lands and title made Archibald the most powerful magnate south of the Forth, and he emphasized his impressive power base in Galloway by constructing the major stronghold of Threave, in addition to securing the marriage of his daughter Marjorie to David, earl of Carrick and, from 1398, first duke of Rothesay, the eldest son of Robert III.

Archibald 'the Grim' died at Bothwell at Christmas 1400 and the earldom of Douglas was inherited by his son, also called Archibald. Intense military campaigning was the hallmark of the fourth earl's career, although he met with little success, being captured by the English at Homildon hill in September 1402, then again in 1403 at Shrewsbury, having taken part in Percy's rebellion against Henry IV. It was not until 1407 that Douglas returned to Scotland, by which time Robert III had died, shortly after learning of the capture at sea by the English in March 1406 of his son, James, while on his way to France. Douglas found an interim government in place, offering wide scope for political exploitation and acquisition by a magnate with such strong territorial and kinship ties.

Douglas held the earldom of Wigtown, the lordships of Galloway, Annandale, Eskdale, and other Dumfriesshire lands, the lordship of Bothwell in Lanarkshire, the lordship of Ettrick forest in the Middle March, and lands extracted from the earldom of March in the south-east. The Black Douglases held unrivalled power in the south of Scotland, controlling all three March wardenships following the disgrace of their main rivals, the earls of March, in 1400. These wardenships carried with them special military and judicial powers and, by 1420, Douglas was using the title 'Great Guardian of the Marches of Scotland' (see BORDERS: 1). He was also connected with the religious foundations of Coldingham, Dryburgh, and Melrose, and, in Edinburgh, he held the keepership of the castle and was 'principal protector' of Holyrood abbey.

Douglas family

Certain areas of Douglas influence came under considerable pressure prior to the return of James I, especially when the new earl of March succeeded in 1420 and William, earl of Angus, attained his majority, as both men opposed Black Douglas ambition. Douglas took part in negotiations for the king's release, aided by the fact that he was married to James I's sister, Margaret, and he also pursued Continental ambitions which led, in 1423, to active military service in *France. During his absence, Douglas left his eldest son, Archibald, in control of the bulk of his Scottish affairs, although the administration of the earldom of Wigtown and the lordship of Galloway were left in the hands of the king's sister Margaret, countess of Douglas, and his brother James.

An important adviser to the younger Archibald Douglas in his new position of responsibility was his uncle, James Douglas of Balvenie, known as James 'the Gross' because he was extremely fat. He had been one of the closest advisers to his brother, the fourth earl of Douglas, with the Banffshire estates of Balvenie in north-eastern Scotland forming part of his landed power, while the lands and castle of Abercorn in West Lothian and estates in Strathaven and Stonehouse in north-west Lanarkshire formed the other. Balvenie married Beatrice Sinclair, sister of William, earl of Orkney, further expanding the family's influential political ties, and the Douglas influence on the king's council ensured the protection of their interests, especially with the fourth earl of Douglas having been newly created duke of Touraine by the French king in recognition of his military service in France. The exclusion and undermining of such influence as remained to the Albany Stewarts occupied James I after his return until the momentous news reached Scotland that, on 17 August 1424, the Scottish army had been all but destroyed at Verneuil in Perche, the earls of Douglas and Buchan being among the dead. At a stroke, the main Douglas insurance policy was gone, and although James I launched no overt attack on them, he did take steps to ensure that the more personal offices and local influences belonging to the fourth earl of Douglas were not assumed by his son (see FRANCO-SCOTTISH RELATIONS: I).

In the face of James I's determination to assert his personal authority, the political influence of Archibald, fifth earl of Douglas, was greatly reduced. He continued to hold the wardenship of the West March, although the wardenships of the Middle and East Marches had been lost to the earls of March and Angus respectively. Douglas's position at court, where he continued to serve as councillor and military retainer, owed more to his royal connections than his position as a powerful independent southern magnate. It was not until after the assassination of James I in 1437 that Douglas was brought back to court as lieutenant-general during the minority of James II, a position he held by virtue of being the king's nearest male relative, and he was also one of the few adult heads of a Scottish magnate family in 1437. Douglas did not hold office for long, as he fell victim to an outbreak of plague (see HEALTH, FAMINE, AND DISEASE: I) in June 1439, leaving an heir, William, who was only 15 years old.

A dramatic shift in the Black Douglas power base took place on 24 November 1440 at the infamous 'Black Dinner', when the young sixth earl and his brother David were invited to dinner at *Edinburgh castle by William, Lord Crichton, who was chancellor and keeper of the castle. After dinner, the boys were seized, along with their close adherent Malcolm Fleming of Biggar and Cumbernauld, and Earl William and his brother were executed on the grounds of treason. The course of events point to the involvement of the boys' great-uncle, James Douglas of Balvenie, who had acquired the title earl of Avondale at the start of the minority, as no treason charges survive, and no sentence of forfeiture was passed, allowing a large proportion of lands and titles which formed the entailed Douglas estates passing to James as seventh earl of Douglas. In order to recover the lordships of Galloway and Bothwell, Douglas arranged the marriage of his son, William, with the sister of the sixth earl, Margaret, known to later chroniclers as the 'Fair Maid of Galloway'. The seventh earl's ambitions extended to securing the earldom of Moray for his third son, Archibald, and he attempted, unsuccessfully, to exploit the schism within the church to have his second son, James, provided to the bishopric of Aberdeen.

William, eighth earl of Douglas, succeeded his father in March 1443, rapidly assuming a very active role in government. His brothers, Archibald and Hugh, were earls of Moray and Ormond respectively, and his youngest brother, John, appeared in parliament as Lord Balvenie. Archibald's twin brother, James, was held to be the elder and was therefore styled 'Master of Douglas' as heir to William. Such pre-eminence as the Douglases achieved during the minority was challenged upon James II's assumption of personal rule, and the king moved against Douglas interests in the winter of 1450–1, while Douglas was absent on a pilgrimage to Rome on the occasion of the papal jubilee. Facing financial difficulties in securing sufficient provision for his new queen under the terms of their marriage settlement, James II seized the earldom of Wigtown, although this alarmed the Scottish nobility to the extent that the king was persuaded to come to terms with Douglas on his return and confirm him in his lands and possessions in the parliament held in June 1451. He was not, however, persuaded to return Wigtown until October.

Douglas's unexpected vulnerability in the face of royal hostility led him to seek allies, but in making a bond with the earls of Crawford and Ross, both of whom had proved troublesome to the crown, he was unlikely to allay royal suspicions, and the summons to attend the king at *Stirling castle in February 1452 worried Douglas sufficiently for him to demand a safe conduct before agreeing to attend. On the second day of talks, heated argument, apparently concerning the bond, led James II to stab the earl of Douglas, aided by his attendants to the extent that the murdered earl's body was said to have had 26 wounds. The king reacted quickly to placate Douglas adherents and allay the fears of the political community, and it was not until March that the new ninth earl of Douglas organized a show of defiance by bringing a force of 600 men to *Stirling to renounce his allegiance and sack the town. James II secured exoneration for the murder of Douglas in the parliament held in June, but his indiscriminate raids carried out in the south of Scotland in July lost him much support, and he was compelled to come to terms with the ninth earl on 28 August. Further pressure brought about the bond of manrent between the king and Douglas in January 1453 which appeared to restore Douglas's position, but these were effectively exercises to buy time while each side prepared for the ultimate showdown.

The final onslaught against the Black Douglases was launched at the beginning of March 1455, with the king attacking the castle of Inveravon and ravaging Douglas lands in Avondale, after which he undertook personal supervision of the artillery bombardment of Abercorn. Douglas did not appear to defend it, and, following its destruction, and the routing of the Douglases at Arkinholm on 1 May by a party of southern lairds—during which encounter Archibald, earl of Moray, was killed and Hugh, earl of Ormond, was wounded, captured, and subsequently executed—parliament proceeded with the formal forfeiture of the family in June. James, ninth earl of Douglas, fled to England with his mother and youngest brother, John, Lord Balvenie (see KINGSHIP: 3–4; NOBILITY: 2).

CAMcG

2. since 1455

After the destruction of the Black Douglases' sprawling power in 1452–5, leadership of the many men who called themselves Douglas passed to the junior branch of the family, the Red Douglases, since 1397 earls of Angus. Their scattered lands lay more on the *Borders than in Angus itself. Until 1492 they were based in the strategic Hermitage castle, thereafter in the formidable fortress of Tantallon.

The fifth earl, Archibald (c.1452–1514), was prominent in the aristocratic opposition to James III, intriguing with England and participating in the seizure of unpopular royal favourites in 1482. Under *James IV he became chancellor (1493–7). His younger son, Gavin (c.1475–1522), bishop of Dunkeld, was a learned poet who translated Virgil's *Aeneid* into Scots (1512–13) (see SCOTS LANGUAGE).

The sixth earl, Archibald (c.1489–1557), married James IV's widow, Margaret Tudor, in 1514, but their joint bid for power failed—as did their marriage. In 1526, though, Angus gained custody of the young *James V and launched a *coup d'état*, grabbing the chancellorship and distributing other offices to his kinsmen, notably his brother Sir George. All attempts to shake the Douglas monopoly of power failed until James escaped in 1528. Even then it proved difficult to dislodge Angus and his followers from Scotland; they were exiled, but not destroyed as the king wished. After James's death the Douglases bounced back. Angus briefly returned from England (1543) to assume leadership of a pro-English faction in Scottish politics—a position which his family retained for half a century.

The Douglases' leader after 1557 was James, fourth earl of Morton (1516–81), chancellor from 1563 and regent of Scotland in 1572–8. His territorial power rested on his guardianship of the young eighth earl of Angus. His ascendancy marked a second high point for the family—more firmly rooted since 1560 in the Anglo-Scottish 'amity' that accompanied the *Reformation. Even in his difficulties (he was exiled after participating in Riccio's murder in 1566) he could count on English support. His execution in 1581 for Darnley's murder was politically motivated, although he was probably guilty as charged. Archibald, eighth earl of Angus (c.1555–88), inherited Morton's Protestant and Anglophile stance but died young (see ANGLO-SCOTTISH RELATIONS: 3).

One of the eighth earl's associates was David Hume of Godscroft, who later produced a literary monument to the family, *History of the Houses of Douglas and Angus* (1644), presenting the Douglases as patriotic bulwarks against royal tyranny. Possibly using oral tradition, Godscroft fashioned the heroic legend of the fifth earl of Angus as 'Bell-the-Cat', taking the lead in challenging the overbearing James III, while his son Archibald (brother of the poet Gavin) gained the chivalric nickname 'Greysteel'.

But the Angus earls celebrated by Godscroft were in decline. After 1591 the tenth earl's

Catholicism led to exclusion from patronage. Though they attained a marquisate (of Douglas, 1633) and even a dukedom (1703), they were no longer politically significant. Their titles became extinct through failure of direct heirs in 1761, whereupon succession to their property was contested in the headline-hitting 'Douglas Cause' (1762–9). John Home's play *Douglas* (1756), a medieval melodrama without historical characters, also maintained the family name's prominence.

During the 17th century, effective leadership of the family gradually passed to the Douglases of Drumlanrig, a Dumfriesshire family descended from the Black Douglases. They climbed steadily, becoming earls of Queensberry (1633), then marquises (1682) and dukes (1684). James, the second duke (1662–1711), was the most prominent Scottish politician of the 1690s and 1700s. His manoeuvres contributed to the *Union of 1707, and he was royal commissioner to the last Scottish parliament in 1706–7. Charles, the third duke (1698–1778), interested himself in agricultural improvement, linen, and canals (see ECONOMY: 4). In 1769 he was a moving spirit and leading investor in a large new bank: Douglas, Heron, and Company, known as the 'Ayr Bank'. The bank's aggressive trading led to a collapse in 1772 that echoed throughout Britain, leaving Queensberry with debts that took decades to repay (see ECONOMY, TERTIARY SECTOR: 2). Landed power had become subordinate to money.　　JG

dress and body ornament have been used by all societies to create identity. Clothes are used, amongst other reasons, to show adherence to a particular way of life, or membership of a group, to mark out friend from foe, or to show solidarity with a cause. What and how a person wears clothes can give anyone they meet important information, which helps in determining their response to each other.

There is very little visual, material, or documentary evidence for clothing worn in Scotland for the period before 1500 so that it is difficult to determine exactly what Scots wore. We can only speculate that they followed general European trends. The evidence from the Highland areas is even sparser. Misinterpretation of what evidence there is has occurred in the past because of a desire to see a long tradition to later elements of dress.

For the majority of people living in Scotland throughout history what they wear has depended on what they can afford rather than on what they might wish to wear. Cloth and leather for clothing have always been expensive in terms of raw materials and production, making garments items of great monetary worth. Reuse of cloth and leather until only small scraps are left has been a constant of the economy.

Wool and linen, together with leather and fur, were the main elements used for clothing in the medieval period. Finds from other northern European cultures have shown that cloth weaving could be very sophisticated, particularly the various twill weaves which were used. Twill is a weave which can provide very tightly woven cloth capable of shedding water and being windproof, factors which must have been appreciated in Scotland. Fulled and felted cloths were also used. Linen has left few traces in the archaeological record but some of Bronze Age date has been found suggesting that it was in regular use by this period in Scotland.

Dyeing cloth was expensive so that early clothing probably depended on different naturally coloured fleeces for contrasting stripes and checks. Herringbone twill weaves also created liveliness in fabrics by the play of light on the different directions of the weave. Where dyed cloth was used it was probably reserved for the wealthy. However, small areas of colour could be added by elaborate braids, sometimes including beaten gold, or by embroidery.

Garments are rare survivors and all have come from archaeological excavations or chance finds until the 17th century. The occasional shoe or traces of fabric impressions in the corrosion of a metal object such as a brooch are the most usual, but these give little idea of the cut or colour of the clothing. The Orkney hood is an impressive survivor, finely made and obviously a high status piece. Its shape is reminiscent of the hooded capes used by the Iron Age inhabitants of Britain and Europe in the early centuries AD.

The thorough destruction of churches and monasteries in the 16th century (see REFORMATION) has meant that Scotland lacks any relics and church vestments, nor are there many *illuminated manuscripts or sculptured tombs (see MONUMENTS: 1). In other countries relics and vestments have shown the reuse of precious silk from Byzantium and the east, indicating how widespread trade was at this period. Relics have also preserved more ordinary clothing, such as St Louis's tunic, which help to show the cut and construction of medieval garments. Only a few tombs have been opened in Scotland, including that of *Robert I, where scraps of fabric have been found. But excavations in Perth and other urban sites have shown that Scotland imported fine materials in the medieval period although again these give us no idea of the styling of clothes.

Trends and fashions in the rest of Europe influenced dress in medieval Scotland. These were brought to Scotland by travellers and by Scots who travelled abroad. The clergy and the lay *nobility were very much part of the wider Christian world and travelled quite extensively, bringing back new fabrics and fashions, as well as different habits. Marriage to foreign-born royalty and diplomatic gifts also brought new ideas to the Scottish *royal court, so that Scotland was not isolated from the dress trends of the rest of Europe during this period.

Clothing remained relatively unchanged for long periods; fashion as we know it today was not a feature of medieval life. Sometime in the 14th century the change from chain mail to plate armour (see WARFARE, WEAPONS, AND FORTIFICATIONS: 1) appears to have been the catalyst for the new fashion of tight, body-fitting clothes for men which also affected women's dress. From this period onwards clothing changed more quickly and there was a sense of change for change's sake, the lead being taken by different countries depending on their importance or influence at the time.

New fabrics also affected clothing styles. Europe gradually managed to create elaborate silks and velvets which imitated or rivalled the silks imported from the east, whilst the northern Europeans developed new woollen cloths that were more pliable, draping better and creating more elegant clothes. Woollen cloth of all qualities was used by the less wealthy, but usually in fairly drab colours. Some was made in Scotland but fine cloth had to be imported, as the home industry was not able to produce it.

One new fabric that benefited the less wealthy was knitting. Hand-knitting is believed to have come to Europe from the east via Spain. By the late 15th century bonnetmakers were established in Scotland, knitting bonnets in imitation of the velvet ones worn by the wealthy. These later became the blue bonnet. Hand-knitting became a major industry in Scotland with stockings, caps, underwaistcoats, and sleeves all being made for home consumption and export. Later, hand frames were introduced and then machines, creating the modern knitwear industry in the Borders. In the 19th century, hand-knitting became a major component of the Shetland economy which produced the delicate lace shawls and brightly patterned sweaters, gloves, stockings, and caps, mainly for export.

The 15th century saw the development of the very short tight doublet for men that ended at the waist. To cover the lower half of the body the cloth leg coverings, known as hose, were extended up and joined together to form something similar to a pair of tights. These are the ancestor of the Highland trews (see DRESS, HIGHLAND) which were also footed hose cut on the bias of the fabric.

From the 16th century onwards there is more evidence for the kind of clothing worn in Scotland. Inventories and other documentary evidence indicate the names of garments, their colours, fabrics, and the numbers owned by different groups, but visual evidence is confined to the wealthy who could afford portraits, a new medium which was becoming increasingly popular throughout Europe. Increasing wealth allowed more people to have a wider variety of garments. This also led to complaints about extravagance, particularly aimed by men at women.

One garment that is found in documents from the 16th and 17th centuries is the plaid, which was worn by working- and lower-middle-class men and by women of all classes, except the very wealthy, in all parts of the country. It could be up to 16 feet (5 m) long and made of two widths of fabric, but was not necessarily of tartan. It was worn as an outer garment instead of a cloak. Some women apparently used the lack of a plaid as an excuse for not attending kirk, so it must have been seen as a necessary garment for respectability.

Related to the plaid was the shawl, a fashion that developed in the late 18th century when Indian shawls were imported into Europe. By the 1790s, Edinburgh, together with Norwich, was imitating these articles. Edinburgh shawls are not as well known as those from Paisley but the products were of high quality. Paisley developed an extensive industry in both woven and printed shawls of all qualities, and the town's name became synonymous with the Indian-derived pattern usually found on these garments.

By the 17th century there are various accessories that survive, mostly gloves, shoes, parts of embroidered bodices, and purses. From these it is possible to get some idea of the richness of clothing. Also for the first time some idea of ordinary men's dress is available. From several bogs in the more remote areas have come the clothing remains from bodies that appear to have been accidentally buried. These all probably belong to the end of the century but, because they are not of very fashionable clothing, are difficult to date precisely. The cloth used for these garments is all of coarsely woven drab wool, often heavily patched.

Of the three main finds, that from Gunnister, Shetland, has the most garments, with shirt, wide-legged breeches, long coat, short coat over it, knitted cap, gloves, and stockings, with another cap and purse, also knitted. The man from Barrock, near Wick, had a hip-length coat with full skirts and a pair of knee breeches. Under these he wore another coat and breeches of similar style and cloth. His clothing was completed by cloth stockings, a bonnet, and a plaid of plain fabric, about 8.2 feet (2.5 m) long by 4.9 feet (1.5 m) and made of two widths of material. Both these men had coins dating from the 1690s. These were years of great hardship throughout Scotland and this might account for the very patched clothes. On Lewis a young man who might have been a murdered student was found on Arnish Moor. He wore a jacket, a knee-length shirt, an undershirt, cloth stockings, a knitted bonnet, and a small bag. This dress conforms to later 18th-century descriptions of poor Highlanders' clothing. None of the bodies had any trace of linen garments but the acid peat does not preserve linen or leather.

Nothing comparable has been found for women's dress. However, if the men's clothing is any indicator, women must have had equally coarse cloth for their dresses. One article of clothing that was commented upon by contemporary visitors was the white pinner, a kind of head covering which resembled a napkin pinned to their head. The Henwife of Castle Grant in her portrait by Richard Waitt, dated 1726 but showing a very old-fashioned style, appears to have a triangular folded cloth pinned to an undercap, with long hanging ends which may be a pinner. White linen and later cotton caps, often called a mutch, remained very important for married women until the late 19th century, being a sign of their status.

By the 18th century much more survives in the way of actual garments. Most are from the wealthier middle ranges of society but there are virtually none from the wealthiest. Their clothes tended to be handed on to servants as part of their perks of office, a system that had a long history and extended from the king downwards. Again the clothes of the poor have not survived because clothing was still expensive and every scrap of cloth precious. The greater number of portraits and the new interest in drawing scenes of contemporary Scottish life help to fill in some gaps. There were also more travellers' accounts, starting with Martin Martin's description of the Western Isles in the late 17th century, which allow a better impression of dress for all levels and areas. As the authors usually note aspects that are different to the norm it is necessary to know the general trends of fashionable dress to understand the comments.

How fashions were disseminated becomes clearer from the 17th century onwards. Once the king moved to London in 1603 there were many letters sent from friends and relations in Scotland to friends in the city requesting news on the latest fashions, and giving commissions to buy fabric. Exactly how the correspondent in Scotland managed to interpret the information from their source in London, often a husband, is a puzzle as some of the fashions must have been difficult to describe. However, in the later 17th century a few actual fashion plates appear for the first time from Paris. Later there were plates in pocketbooks showing actual dresses, but at the end of the 18th century hand-coloured fashion plates were produced. These plates were part of new magazines for women and continued throughout the 19th century until photographs replaced them in the 20th century. The magazines also regularly reported on the fashions in Paris which was seen as the leader in this area.

If possible, people had clothes made for them to their own measurements. Plenty of small country tailors in Scotland earned a living travelling to homes to work, where they made new garments, but their main business was altering or repairing clothes. Undergarments were made by women at home, often of linen spun from their own flax and woven by a local weaver. Women in the countryside probably made their own dresses although there were plenty of dressmakers in towns. Shoes were made by souters, and most villages had at least one, for repairing shoes was constantly necessary, but until the present century many country women would wear shoes only in towns or on Sundays.

Ready-made clothes have been available for much longer than many people imagine. Most towns probably had some clothes that could be bought made up from early in the medieval period. However, it was expensive to stock items on spec so they were probably things which were in constant need, such as linen undergarments, stockings, caps, and shoes. In ports there was the possibility of travellers needing items urgently, especially if they had lost clothes or had them stolen. Second-hand clothes were also readily available, a source which lost its importance only for a brief period in the 1960s and 1970s.

There is no tradition of folk dress in Scotland similar to that found in most of the rest of Europe where clothing was deliberately developed as an expression of national culture. In Scotland the development of Highland dress cannot be compared to folk dress, although it is seen in a similar light by some commentators. However, unlike folk dress there was no difference from area to area in the style. Lowlanders saw the dress of Highlanders as outlandish because it did not conform to their idea of what was proper. Similarly, Highlanders resented having to wear Lowland dress in the late 18th century after their own was banned. More distinctive perhaps is the occupational dress that certain groups developed, such as the fishwives of Newhaven, whose dress distinguished them from the rest of their community throughout the 19th century, and the bondagers of East Lothian in the years from about 1880 to 1930. NEAT

dress, Highland. A distinctive style of dress and selection of garments with large tartan plaid and close-fitting breeches became the hallmark of Highland society at least from the 16th century onward, and earned a widespread, sometimes fearsome reputation in the 17th and 18th centuries, to be proscribed by law throughout Scotland in the wake of the last *Jacobite war of 1745–6. Coming under the enthusiastic gaze of European Romanticism, warmed to a new fervour by the literary discoveries of James 'Ossian' Macpherson, Highland dress was then adopted in an attenuated form, mainly through the medium of late 18th- and early 19th-century military uniform (see ARMY: 3), as national costume for Lowlanders and Highlanders alike, being designed and customized even by those whose fathers and grandfathers had held it in dread and contempt. The royal seal of enthusiastic approval and a new line in castle tartan interiors fed an international tartan mania through Queen Victoria's long reign; this was triggered initially by George IV's espousal of Highland dress during his celebrated visit to Scotland in 1822 when parties of Highlanders gathered in Edinburgh under the command of their respective chieftains. But one onlooker, James Smart of Dunearn, also spoke for many when he carped at the new image and commented: 'Sir Walter [Scott] has ridiculously made us appear to be a nation of Highlanders, and the bagpipe and the tartan are the order of the day' (see NATIONAL IDENTITY: 5).

The colour and design of Highland dress as much as its form has given it its cachet in modern times, using typically patterned cloth described as 'tartan' in which yarn is woven in sequences of colour in warp and weft to produce stripes and regular and regulated checks described as 'setts'. The decorative technique is simple and must originally have been achieved with naturally coloured wool of early breeds of domesticated sheep, separated out and spun into different coloured yarns which, when woven, would achieve muted checks. The principle is recalled in the tradition of the so-called 'Shepherd's Plaid' or 'maud' which in the 19th century was absorbed along with other pre-existing setts by a creative and vigorous wool textile weaving industry into its rapidly expanding lists of tartans to be associated with specific families and clans (see CLAN SOCIETIES), both Lowland and Highland. Boosted by an insatiable market and the researches between about 1815 and 1845 of the Highland Society of London, James Logan and the self-styled Sobieski Stuarts, manufacturers such as Wilsons of Bannockburn, began to differentiate and label the ever-increasing selection of setts as separate clan tartans. Highland dress and tartan rapidly became therefore an indicator of belonging both to the larger entity of nation and to the smaller community of kin and *clans. In that era of

a new and excitable historical consciousness, the origins of tartan were described in such dubious oeuvres as the *Vestiarium Scoticum* of 1842 as the immutable badge of clanship whereas the reality was simpler and more intelligible, that tartan and its use of colour and pattern was no more or less than a form of Highland fashion and conspicuous consumption.

Highland dress derived from forms of mantle or cloak in medieval dress, then not obviously differentiated by nation or culture in Europe. The mantle was more common in northern and western regions, where it supplied an ideal and often extravagant protective overdress which sparse material evidence suggests was made in a twill weave to give colour and pattern and a tight weatherly finish. Two contemporary descriptions suggest a local style emerging with a strong note of a fashion consciousness in the *Gaidhealtachd*. In his *History of Scotland* of 1578, Bishop John Lesley wrote: 'All, both nobles and common people, wore mantles of one sort, except that the nobles preferred those of several colours.' George Buchanan, himself a Highlander by descent, described in 1582 how 'they delight in mottled clothes especially that have long stripes of sundry colours; they love chiefly purple and blue'. Fashion in the Highlands dictated that the mantle evolved into the lighter but longer and highly coloured plaid, novel but still in a universal tradition of the untailored garment such as the toga, sari, or clerical habit; artfully arranged round the body, this was a versatile dress and distinction and effect were added by quantity and quality of cloth, colour, and style of wear. Though remote from the metropolitan centres, Highlanders were perfectly well informed and this conspicuous style of Highland dress belonged to a new heightened European dress sense of the late Renaissance.

Trade brought goods as well as ideas into the Highlands and Islands and contemporary Gaelic song (see SONG, TRADITIONAL AND FOLK: 2) makes it clear that luxury fabrics and dyestuffs were eagerly acquired. Madder from Rotterdam and Hamburg and later cochineal from Central America gave expensive but exciting and colourfast shades of red and it is no coincidence that panegyric poetry in Gaelic consistently characterizes tartan or *breacan* in terms of bright scarlets and flaming reds. John Michael Wright's portrait of Lord Mungo Murray of about 1685 is one of several examples of the figure and outfit idealized in Gaelic song in which good personal dress sense, love of colour, appreciation of finely woven textiles, and attention to detail become self-evident in Highland dress which in turn confers nobility and dignity.

The Highlander in plaid and kilt had by the 18th century become equated with continuing loyalty to the Stuart dynasty in exile, a concept exploited by Prince Charles Edward Stuart in 1745 when he landed in the west Highlands and raised an emphatically tartan army. Response was swift and catastrophic for Highland life and culture, and the Disarming Act of 1747, while outlawing it, neatly defined Highland dress as 'Plaid, Philabeg or little kilt, Trews, Shoulder Belts, or any part whatever of what peculiarly belongs to the Highland Garb'. Prohibition failed to eradicate Highland dress and Boswell's description of Allan MacDonald of Kingsborough in 1773 hints at the persistence of the imperative of taste and fashion in adversity: 'He was quite the figure of a gallant Highlander. . . . He had his tartan plaid thrown about him, a large blue bonnet with a knot of black ribbon like a cockade, a brown short coat of a kind of duffle, a tartan vest with gold buttons and gold buttonholes, a bluish filibeg, and tartan hose.' (See also CALEDONIAN SOCIETIES; MOD, ROYAL NATIONAL; HIGHLAND GAMES).

HC

Dumbarton, 'fort of the Britons', was the political centre of the British kingdom based in Strathclyde as well as being the Clyde's principal port until the end of the Middle Ages. Several 7th-century British kings are explicitly identified as kings of Clyde Rock, Alcluith, in contemporary Gaelic and Welsh sources. The fortifications of Dumbarton occupy a twin-peaked volcanic plug that towers 243 feet (74 m) above the north bank of the river. The Rock stands at the upper navigable reach of the Clyde (prior to dredging) at the mouth of the River Leven. This highly strategic position allowed Dumbarton to control traffic into the central Clyde valley and to Loch Lomond and the Lennox.

Scant traces of the early medieval defences were revealed by Leslie Alcock's excavations, but the interior layout—hall, accommodation, and outbuildings—remains completely unknown. All evidence of early medieval buildings and most of the fortifications seem to underlie or to have been swept away by successive modern military works, which continued until the Second World War. The exceptional character of early medieval Dumbarton is revealed by fragments of imported pottery and glass. This includes Mediterranean amphorae, E-ware vessels from around Bordeaux, and German glassware, indirect evidence of a long-term taste for wine. Other significant finds include a metalworking crucible, a small balance weight, and a Viking sword pommel. The majority of the finds date from the 5th to 9th centuries and this narrow range is reinforced by calibrated radiocarbon dates for structures which fall between AD 450 and 850. The site also produced Roman Samian pottery as well as Romano-British pottery, which suggests that Dumbarton's commercial foundations may have begun as the supply base for the western end of the Antonine Wall. Two examples of early medieval sculpture, 10th-century recumbent cross-slabs in the *Govan tradition, are in the castle but presumably came from the chapel dedicated to St Patrick, which formerly stood near the castle.

Dumbarton was certainly one of the major landmarks of early medieval Scotland. It features in both Adomnán's *Vita Columbae* and Bede's *Ecclesiastical History*, while a 7th-century tradition places Coroticus, who is addressed in a letter from St Patrick, at Dumbarton. The demise of Dumbarton can be dated to AD 870, when it was sacked and destroyed by a large force of Dublin Vikings following a four-month siege. After its collapse the centre of power seems to have shifted upstream to *Govan. This shift notwithstanding, Dumbarton retained its strategic significance and remained a royal castle until the modern era. Nevertheless Dumbarton drops out of the historical record until the 13th century, when a royal burgh was established at a site about 0.6 mile (1 km) up the River Leven from the Clyde (see URBAN SETTLEMENT: 1).

STD

Dunadd is one of the most important early medieval sites in Scotland, both in terms of its historical associations with the first Scottish kings and the impressive archaeological remains. The site itself is a stone-built fort which sits on a craggy double-summitted hillock on the floodplain of the River Add. The surrounding landscape contains the densest concentration of prehistoric funerary and ritual monuments in western Scotland. Although the only direct historical references to the site consist of two laconic entries in the Irish Annals, it is widely regarded as the inauguration place of the kings of *Dál Riata, and therefore the predecessor of *Scone before the takeover of Pictland by the Scots in the 9th century.

The first reference, in the *Annals of Ulster* for the year 683, merely records the siege of Dunadd. The second, for 736, records the seizure of the site by *Ungus (Onuist), son of Uurgust, king of the Picts, during a campaign which devastated Dál Riata and resulted in the capture of two sons of the Dalriadan king. These records show that the site was important in strategic military terms, and was perhaps associated with Dalriadan royalty, but it is the unique set of carvings on the summit of the hill which have led to the suggestion that this was a royal site. These consist of a rock-cut footprint and basin, an outlined boar in a style similar to those on Pictish symbol stones (see PICTS), a natural rock chair formation, and an ogham inscription. Rock-cut footprints, basins, and chairs are known from 17th-century accounts to have been used for the inauguration of Irish kings, and there is little doubt that was the function of the Dunadd footprint. The ogham inscription, long thought to be unintelligible Pictish, has recently been shown to be written in Old Irish.

Interesting as these inscriptions and historical references are, it is the archaeology of the site which confirms its royal status. Recent excavations have elucidated the history of the site, and have provided a wealth of finds paralleled at this period only on a few other important royal sites in Ireland such as Lagore, Meath and Clogher, Tyrone. The fort itself had its origins as a small summit fort or dun in the late first millennium BC, was reoccupied in the 5th or 6th centuries AD, and received additional defences around the 7th and 9th centuries. The stone walls, up to 9.8 feet (3 m) thick, enclose a series of natural terraces with abundant evidence of metalworking workshops which produced large numbers of fine brooches. Gold, silver, bronze, lead, and iron were worked, along with glass, jet, and other materials. The form and decoration of the metalwork show that the site was a major crossroads of artistic styles, combining Anglo-Saxon, Pictish, British, and Irish elements. Dunadd was thus a key site in the development of the Insular art style exemplified by the great illustrated manuscripts such as the Books of Kells. Some moulds for brooches are early examples of the large ornate type which reached an apogee with the Hunterston and Tara brooches, a type previously considered to have originated in Ireland. These brooches were used by the aristocracy as status symbols, and the Dunadd evidence suggests that the king controlled their production and distribution (see KINGSHIP: 1). The finds also revealed a wide variety of trading and diplomatic contacts. There was pottery and glass from Merovingian Gaul, glass and minerals from the Mediterranean, metalwork from England and Ireland, as well as metals and other materials from other areas of western Britain (see CULTURE: 2).

The site fell into disuse after the 9th or 10th century, but appears to have kept its royal associations and was used sporadically, the last reference being in 1506 when the earl of Argyll chose the site to issue an important proclamation from King *James IV to the chiefs on the future governance of the lordship of the *Isles.   EC

Dundas, Henry (1742–1811), the dominant Scottish politician of his age, as well as a British and imperial statesman. Born into a legal family and educated in Edinburgh, he was called to the Bar in 1763. He became solicitor-general in 1766 and Lord Advocate in 1775, after election as MP for Midlothian. In parliament he supported Lord North, but

established himself as a power-broker. In the crisis at the end of the War of American Independence he helped to bring to office William Pitt 'the Younger', with whom he would serve eighteen years. He now dispensed Scottish patronage (see POLITICAL SYSTEM: 1). He built up control of the parliamentary representation, which by 1796 covered 43 of the 45 MPs and nearly all the 16 peers from Scotland. This grip extended to national institutions. Meanwhile he was also Pitt's right-hand man in London, as Treasurer of the Navy but more especially in taking charge from 1784 of the Board of Control for India (see INDIAN SUBCONTINENT), of which he became president in 1793. In 1791 he was made Home Secretary and in 1794 Secretary of State for War, planning and executing the containment of Revolutionary France. He opposed expeditions in Europe and advocated a long-term maritime strategy of expanding the *British Empire and overcoming the French by economic strength. He resigned with Pitt in 1801 on the issue of Catholic emancipation in an Ireland newly brought into union with Great Britain, but came back in 1804 as First Lord of the Admiralty, having been created Viscount Melville in 1802. By prompt reforms he restored British naval supremacy, confirmed for the rest of the French wars by the battle of Trafalgar. A report had meanwhile found evidence of his misuse of funds while Treasurer of the Navy. In the last impeachment of a British minister, he was acquitted in June 1806. Pitt's recent death excluded any chance of a comeback.

                                                    MRGF

Dundas, Robert. The only son of Henry *Dundas, Robert (1771–1851) stepped into but never quite filled the paternal shoes as political manager of Scotland. Born and educated in Edinburgh, he then went on a Grand Tour. He entered parliament in 1794, at first merely serving as private secretary to his father. He took over as MP for Midlothian, a seat controlled by his family, in 1801. He gained no senior office till the fall of the Ministry of All the Talents in 1806. The Tories, in their struggle to regain control of government, badly needed Scottish support, and to secure it appointed the junior Dundas to the presidency of the Board of Control of India earlier held by the senior one. Dundas later briefly served as Chief Secretary for Ireland and then, after succeeding as Viscount Melville in 1811, assumed another of his father's former offices, First Lord of the Admiralty. He served at this post for fifteen years, winning approval by his conciliatory nature from both his political chiefs and from the admirals. He succeeded both in maintaining British maritime supremacy while the wars with France lasted and in running down the Royal Navy without loss of security afterwards. He had meanwhile also assumed control of his father's political machine in Scotland, but he had no burning interest in elections and allowed it to decay somewhat. It still held a clear majority of Scottish seats by the time crisis overtook the Tory party at the resignation of Lord Liverpool in 1827, as rampant factionalism at Westminster heralded the collapse from within of the old regime. Melville muddled his stance and was not reappointed by George Canning. He went back to the Admiralty in 1828–30 but was unable to restore his former power. The half-century during which his family had ruled Scotland then ended.   MRGF

Dundee: 1. to 1650; 2. since 1650

1. to 1650

Dundee was an east-coast port of major importance in the medieval Scottish economy. It was raised to burghal status in the reign of William I (1163–1214) and was subsequently placed under the superiority of the king's brother, David, earl of Huntingdon. All the evidence, however, suggests that it functioned as a township, and probably a market, as early as the 11th century; and was, by 1173 × 1178, considered as a town of some note, since Hadgillin was referred to as being situated in 'Dundeeshire'.

Little of the historic medieval burgh now remains standing, the great west tower of the parish church of St Mary, much destroyed both at and after the *Reformation, and Gardyne's House being notable exceptions and the erstwhile garden of the defunct Greyfriars (Franciscans), later a burial ground, creating a quiet oasis in the heart of the modern city. The core of Dundee, however, largely focuses on the medieval town plan (see URBAN SETTLEMENT: 1)—a linear development by necessity, with the Tay to the south and dolerite ridges and swampy land to the north preventing expansion in these directions. The medieval Marketgait is still the High Street; Flukergait became called the Nethergate; Seagait, Murraygait, and Cowgait are visible in the modern street alignments and street names. The Overgait and Wellgait have disappeared under modern shopping malls.

Lining these medieval streets, in a herringbone pattern, were the burgage plots of the inhabitants. Here, the burgesses built their homes on the frontages and sited workshops, wells, middens, gardens, and animals in the backlands to the rear. It is estimated that in the late 15th century there were approximately 6,800 people within the town walls, a figure that was to rise to about 11,200 by 1645, placing Dundee probably second in size only to Edinburgh. The town walls were, in fact, merely small

wooden fencing until the latter half of the 16th century, when the burgh invested heavily in both labour and finance to surround itself on the landward side with stone walls, thus making itself one of the most defensible towns of the realm. Its vulnerability had been shown in English invasions (see ROUGH WOOING) in 1547–50. Punctuating the wall were a number of town gates or ports, one of which (now called the Wishart Arch, although this may date to the mid-17th century) still survives.

The town's two churches—St Clement's, the older, which stood on the south side of Marketgait, approximately on the site of the present City Square, and St Mary's—were the dominant features on the townscape. Numerous chapels, probably four medieval hospitals, one of which was supported by the Trinitarians, and the houses of the Dominicans, Franciscans, and Grey Sisters added to the religious atmosphere and contrasted architecturally with the modestness of many Dundee homes.

Some dwellings, however, were substantial, housing as they did nobility and wealthier merchants and craftsmen. Until sometime in the early 14th century and taken alternately by both the English and the Scots in the Wars of *Independence, there was a castle, sited on Castle Hill, a dolerite exposure, now largely blasted away, although St Paul's Episcopal church still clings to a tiny remnant. The survival of several later dwellings until at least the 19th century has permitted not only an appreciation of their architectural merit but also a reflection of the medieval burgh's prosperity. One of the most notable was Strathmartine's Lodging, the home of the earls of Strathmartine. A three-storeyed stone building with a semi-octagonal entrance tower, it stood in the Vault at the rear of St Clement's churchyard and its position is marked today by a plaque in City Square. Built between c.1608 and 1616, it survived until the 1930s. Close by was Provost Pearson's mansion. Constructed between 1562 and 1640 at the Greenmarket on land reclaimed from the river, this was an impressive square building with round towers on three corners and an unusually sophisticated example of an arcaded building. Whitehall Mansion, sometimes called 'the Palace', probably as the building bore the arms of Charles II, stood further west. Its massive vaulted cellars and elaborately carved stonework were all indicative of its grandeur. Increased wealth and the relative peace of the later 16th century also encouraged the extension or establishment of country seats outwith the town boundaries, but nearby and with strong associations with the burgh. Dudhope castle, the home of the Scrymgeour family, once the constables of Dundee, still stands. Claypotts castle and Mains, or Fintry, castle are both outstanding examples of 'fortified' houses (see ARCHITECTS, ARTISTS, AND CRAFTSMEN). The only surviving example of a medieval stone house within the town itself is Gardyne's House, situated in a close once called Gray's Close, between 70 and 73 High Street. The western frontage of this five-storeyed tower block, built between c.1560 and 1600, is a fine example of quality building.

Much of the town's wealth emanated from the secular landmarks of the town: the market place (the nucleus of the town); the tolbooth, where the town weights were kept, council and court meetings were held, and the town gaol was housed; and the harbour, which the townspeople fought hard to retain from silting. Dundee emerged as a strong trading centre early in its history. In 1199, an agreement was entered into between King John of England and the burgesses of Earl David of Huntingdon that their merchants should have the right to trade free of toll or custom in all English ports except London; eight years later the ships of Dundee were specifically granted the protection of King John. One of the important factors in the emergence of the town as a wealthy market, entrepôt, and port was the agricultural potential of the fertile northern hinterland, with which Dundee had ready links through the gaps in the Sidlaw Hills. But concessions from the crown were an equally vital factor. While *Robert I's (1306–29) charter of 1327 reveals Dundee to be an already well-established trading port, further privileges were granted: it prohibited anyone within the sheriffdom of Forfar except burgesses of Dundee to buy wool or skins, two of the staple commodities of the Scottish economy; insisted that, in the same sheriffdom, foreign merchants might trade with only Dundee burgesses; and demanded that all goods brought to the shire be offered first for sale at Dundee. This demarcation of a large, fertile hinterland including very rich monasteries held potential not only for the economic growth of the burgh, but also for trading conflicts with others— Brechin, Forfar, and Montrose—and Dundee's desire to control the River Tay brought in a further protagonist—*Perth; much of Dundee's medieval history is dominated by the town's defence of its trading rights.

The burgh's main early medieval exports of wool, sheepskins, and, to a lesser extent, hides reflected its significant interaction with its rural hinterland and by the mid-14th century Dundee was recognized, along with *Edinburgh, *Aberdeen, and Perth, as one of the 'four great towns of Scotland'. By the 16th century, however, it had emerged to rank second in importance only to Edinburgh. An analysis of tax assessments and customs revenue derived from exports in the period

from 1460 to 1599 not only highlights this, but also raises a further significant factor: the burgh's economic health was not solely dependent on traditional overseas trade; by then Dundee had diversified into the successful manufacture, finishing, and export of coarse cloth. This diversification brought with it a transformation in the structure of burgh society. By the middle of the 16th century, Dundee had nine incorporated crafts—the bakers, shoemakers, glovers, tailors, bonnetmakers, fleshers, hammermen, weavers, and dyers—and by the following century the United Trades—the masons, wrights, and slaters—were also to gain incorporation. Dundee was to enter the 17th century not only as the second burgh of the realm, but also with an urban aristocracy that embraced both merchants and craftsmen.   EPD

2. since 1650

Dundee's relative decline in the 17th century was hastened by its sacking by the New Model Army in 1651. If slowly at first, it appears that considerable restorative work was carried out to the extent that after a visit around 1725 Daniel Defoe could describe Dundee as 'one of the best trading towns in Scotland . . . populous, full of stately houses, and large handsome streets' (*A Tour through the Whole Island of Great Britain*, 1724–6). Throughout most of the 18th century the burgh continued to function mainly as a regional and mercantile centre. Except for handloom weavers and some bonnetmaking, most industrial processes were carried on in the hinterland until the 1790s. Merchants consolidated their position in the linen trade, often through links with London and, indirectly, the West Indian market for coarser grades of linen cloth. Indicating a degree of civic confidence and ambition as the burgh began to exploit the benefits of state support (through export bounties) and empire markets was the town council's decision in 1731 to commission William Adam to design a new town house.

In a series of waves of capital investment (1790s, c.1818–22, c.1828–36, and early 1850s), Dundee became Scotland's chief producer of linen. By 1826, the burgh had overtaken Hull to become Britain's largest flax importer. Although Dundee's ascendancy to c.1850 was largely based on linen, it was the manufacture of jute (commencing in the 1830s) with which the city became most closely associated, ultimately creating a precariously unbalanced economy. Jute also skewed its social life to the extent that Dundee could justifiably be described as 'a large manufacturing centre of physically retarded children, overworked women and demoralized men'. Infant mortality rates (see POPULATION PATTERNS: 1) in the late 19th century were the highest in Scotland, while many of the

Dundee

*children who survived infancy were physically underdeveloped. Many thousands were employed as 'half-timers' in the mills (see ECONOMY, SECONDARY SECTOR: 1). Typically, males were turned out when they reached 18 and were due to be paid adult rates. Fifty per cent of those who presented themselves to the army recruiting office in Dundee in 1914 were considered unfit for military service; adult death rates, too, were above the urban norm.

Historians have tended to focus on the social costs of mass production of a low-value, coarse cloth which, by the 1880s and 1890s, was beginning to face stiff competition from overseas. Migrants (see MIGRATION) from the Angus countryside, complemented in the 1840s by a surge in Irish *immigration, had poured into Dundee during the earlier periods of growth and prosperity but by the later 1870s the labour market was overstocked. Jute and linen workers, two-thirds of whom were female, earned amongst the lowest rates in textiles in the UK. Partly as a consequence, *housing was poor and overcrowding rife. In 1911 almost 70 per cent of the city's housing was either one- or two-roomed dwellings, a higher proportion even than Glasgow.

Less attention has been paid to the factors which lay behind the town's emergence as 'Juteopolis', or to the fact that Dundee also boasted small but significant shipbuilding and engineering industries. Along with whaling, these employed some 7,000 men and boys in 1901. The city's deserved reputation for 'Jute, Jam, and Journalism' notwithstanding, printing and publishing employed fewer people at the end of the Victorian period than did Glasgow, Edinburgh, or Aberdeen, and while food, drink, and tobacco were the chief employers of female labour outside jute (and domestic service), hundreds rather than thousands were involved. Fronting the Tay estuary, Dundee had locational advantages denied to inland rivals such as Leeds. It was well placed to carry on importing flax from the Baltic (see GERMANY, THE BALTIC AND POLAND: 2) (and from 1863, jute brought directly from Calcutta), and to bring in by sea burgeoning quantities of coal from Newcastle and the Forth. That Dundee was also active in the whaling trade was a fortunate coincidence in that whale oil was needed to soften jute fibres during batching. The advantage was seized by the city's manufacturers, amongst whose attributes were tenacity, stealthy observation, and a preparedness to adapt their main rivals' techniques. More striking was the achievement of the burgh's merchants who between 1780 and 1850 managed to overcome difficulties encountered in selling cloth in northern Europe by establishing direct trading links with the *USA and *Canada. Between 1805 and 1850 the number of Dundee-owned vessels rose spectacularly from 138 to 339.

Business success and easier profits from wartime production, when linen and jute substituted for cotton (most notably during the American Civil War, when Dundee boomed but Lancashire struggled), were heralded in massive mill and factory building and extensions which were embellished with Italianate or Gothic flourishes, as well as in civic amenities such as public parks. That on the wooded Balgay Hill, a 'People's Park' purchased by the town council in 1869, was described by one commentator as 'our local Lebanon'. Like their counterparts in other great industrial and commercial centres, Dundee's business elite engaged in art collection and the patronage of young artists such as the landscape painter William McTaggart.

Dundee was distinctive. It was Scotland's premier working-class city; its middle class was proportionately smaller than Glasgow's, Edinburgh's, or Aberdeen's, and less affluent (see SOCIAL CLASS). It had the highest proportion of married *women workers in Scotland (23.4 per cent in 1911). Yet this should not obscure from view those features which Dundee shared with the rest of urban Victorian Scotland. Scottish towns have been described as 'places of order' (see RESPECTABLE CULTURE). Levels of drunkenness and disorder on Saturday nights were high (see ROUGH CULTURE) but not outstandingly so and, with the exception of squalid and overcrowded ghettoes such as the Scouringburn and the Overgate, Dundee was relatively peaceable during the mid-Victorian years, with the queen's birthday night being the only regular occasion for large-scale disturbance. Troops had been garrisoned in Dundee from 1837 and the *Chartist rising of 1842 had looked fearsome at first, causing the authorities to swear in over 700 additional special constables, but a distinctive working-class voice in the subsequent three decades was hard to distinguish in a city 'steeped with *Liberalism'. Civic pride was much in evidence, read and heard in a vigorous stream of popular poetry of which William McGonagall was only a somewhat eccentric product, and seen in the turning out of a massive crowd—estimated at 70,000—for the opening of Baxter Park in 1863. Dundee's female mill and factory workers were noisy and boisterous, and more capable of acting collectively, on their own terms, than an earlier generation of labour historians realized, but their politics—the suffrage (see POLITICAL SYSTEM: 2) question apart—were those of the mainstream.

The 20th century was a period of readjustment, with the central theme being the undulating pattern of decline of the textile industry. Wars, with their demand for cheap coarse cloth for sandbags and other wartime necessities, continued to provide short-term relief. After the end of the First

World War, however, the depth and severity of Dundee's plight as a 'one industry town' was vividly exposed as former markets were closed, either through tariffs or Indian competitors (see INDIAN SUBCONTINENT). Amalgamation and rationalization, along with the Second World War and jute control, helped to prop up jute and from the 1960s diversification into polypropylene has enabled some older firms to survive and even flourish. Since the 1970s, however, manufacturing in Dundee has declined sharply while the service sector has flourished, backed by a marketing strategy which has announced Dundee as the 'City of Discovery'. That Dundee has undergone a remarkable process of transition to a 'post-industrial' city is underlined by the fact that higher education, provided principally by the Universities of Dundee and Abertay, was in the later 1990s one of the city's biggest single employers.   CAW

Dundurn. Standing at the western end of Strathearn, this Pictish fortification occupies a strategically important crag. It overlooks the main land route from southern Pictland via Strathfillan through the mountains to Argyll. The fort towers 197 feet (60 m) above the constricted valley bottom and genuinely can be said to command movement into Strathearn.

Dundurn consists of a sequence of ramparts which utilize the natural topography to define tiered terraces covering most of the hill. The summit was crowned by a massive drystone dwelling. Similar hill forts characterized by a summit dwelling surrounded by subsidiary enclosures, known as 'nuclear forts', exist at other early medieval power centres, such as *Dunadd and Moncreiffe Hill. The massive scale of the fortifications is revealed by the extensive spreads of rubble and scree from the collapsed ramparts. In some cases the terrace ramparts must have approached 33 feet (10 m) in height. Its overall size of 6.2 acres (2.5 hectares) is twice as large as Dunadd, although when one allows for the steep slopes they have comparable usable space.

Excavations conducted by Leslie Alcock revealed structural details, including timber building components, and a wide range of evidence relating to the domestic and political economy. The building on the summit was poorly preserved, but quantities of nails show that large timber elements were incorporated in this largely drystone-built fortification. On the first terrace below the summit, waterlogged deposits preserved organic materials including building elements such as a wickerwork wall panel and worked timbers, leather artefacts including a shoe, and the remains of a range of domesticated and wild plants and animals. The excavations produced a small number of high-quality

finds. These included imported Continental pottery from Bordeaux (E-ware) and the Rhine, evidence of a trade in wine, and imported glassware. Dundurn also yielded evidence for the production of high-quality metalwork. Amongst the finds were crucible and mould fragments and an exceptionally fine glass-boss, with both Pictish and Irish parallels. The shoe was the most striking find. It was fashioned from a single piece of leather in the Irish manner, but its all-over punch decoration is unique. The dates assigned to the artefacts on stylistic grounds span the 6th to the 9th century, which corresponds well with the scientific and historical evidence. The most precise date is provided by a large structural timber from what may have been the original phase of construction: AD 578–683. Conventional radiocarbon dates when calibrated fall into the period AD 500–950.

Dundurn is almost unique amongst Pictish sites in having more than a single historical citation. In 683, the *Annals of Ulster* note that it was besieged along with Dunadd. The linking of the two events is frequently interpreted as evidence of an escalating conflict between the *Picts and Scots, but there is no further historical evidence for this. The second event is the death there of the Pictish king, Giric, son of Dungal, in AD 889. Evidence of extensive burning may relate to this event, which to judge from the finds appears to mark the end of the fort's use.

Just below the summit is a hollow in the rock, known as St Fillan's well, a few hundred metres away is a small circular churchyard, also dedicated to St Fillan. These associations suggest that the hinterland of Dundurn may have included the narrow glens (Strathfillian) leading to Argyll as well as western Strathearn.   STD

Dunlop, James & Co., proprietors of the Clyde Ironworks and the Calderbank steelworks. The Clyde Ironworks at Tollcross in the east end of Glasgow was established in 1786 by William Cadell junior of the Carron Company to relieve pressure on that company's works. Within ten years the Clyde Ironworks had five blast furnaces in operation and from 1798–9 almost the entire production was devoted to casting cannon. The works was purchased in 1810 by Colin Dunlop, MP (1779–1837). In the 1820s James Beaumont *Neilson conducted his famous 'hot blast' experiments at the Clyde Ironworks, demonstrating that three times as much iron could be produced for the same amount of fuel if hot air rather than cold air was used in the furnaces. On Colin Dunlop's death, the works was inherited by his nephew, James Dunlop of Tollcross (1811–93). The business was registered as a limited company and in 1886 was acquired by the

Dunlop, James & Co.

Glasgow firm of coalmasters James Watson & Co., whose partners had just sold the Clydebank shipyard to John Browns. At the turn of the century, they purchased the Calderbank Steel and Coal Co. in the Monklands and in 1900 a new company James Dunlop & Co. (1900) Ltd was registered to control both this works and the Clyde Ironworks. Until the end of the First World War the business prospered. In 1920 as part of the scramble to control steel supplies, Lithgows Ltd., the Lower Clyde shipbuilders, took a controlling interest in the company. Lithgows only bought steel from Dunlops, however, if no cheaper sources could be found by their brokers. At the same time they resisted any proposals to merge Scottish steel interests, unless their yards' supplies were secured. In 1930 Sir James *Lithgow came to an understanding to merge Dunlops with David *Colville & Sons (owned by Harland & Wolff, the shipbuilders) to form a new company, Colvilles Ltd. In return, Lithgow agreed that Colvilles would meet all his steel requirements. Subsequently, improvements were made at the Clyde Ironworks to make it one of the most efficient plants in the UK. MMo

East Asia. The involvement of Scots in East Asia was one of their most remarkable overseas ventures. Trade between Europe and China, pioneered by the Portuguese in the late 15th century, was to offer new fields to adventurous Scots. Their role in the China trade began modestly. The Portuguese had progressed from seasonal visits to Canton to negotiation of a permanent base at Macau in 1556. They operated a complex trade pattern importing porcelains, silks, spices, and drugs from China to Lisbon and then on to Europe, picking up Indian cottons from Goa and Malacca, while exporting such novelties as metalware, cut glass, and mirrors to the Far East. They were so successful that, until the opening of the Suez Canal in 1869, their China route was the main link between Europe and the Far East.

Inevitably the rival trading powers of England and Holland wished to enter this lucrative trade. In 1579 Sir Francis Drake became the first Englishman to reach the South China Seas, where he traded for 6 tons (6.1 tonnes) of cloves in the Molucca Islands. He also captured a Spanish treasure galleon *Cacafugo* in the Pacific and transferred 26 tons (26.4 tonnes) of gold, gems, and some pieces of the Chinese blue and white export porcelain to his ship the *Golden Hynd*. English and Dutch trade efforts continued in this sporadic manner during the 16th century, concentrating on the most profitable goods of spices, silks, and drugs while collecting valuable information about local conditions and shipping. Here, the records of voyages gathered by British sailors who had also joined the crews of Portuguese and Dutch ships provide evidence of a Scottish presence. Michael Carmichael, for example, sailed from Lisbon in 1579, stopped at Macau, and then spent 30 years in Portuguese government service in Goa.

From the 17th century, European trading activities were organized by companies of merchant adventurers who sponsored voyages to the Indian Ocean and the China Seas with varying degrees of success or failure, depending on the amount and security of the original investment, the profits realized on return, and such wilful factors as storms and pirates. The charter of 1600 to the Governor and Merchants of the London Company trading into the East Indies introduced a venture which eventually developed into the Honourable East India Company (EIC), a mighty organization promoting British trade and influence throughout India and the Far East. The EIC's first direct venture to China took place in 1635 dispatching the merchant ship *London* to trade for spices, drugs, silks, and porcelain but on landing at Macau the crew found the Portuguese and Chinese hostile. Eventually, however, the EIC from the security of their bases in India—Madras, Bombay, and Calcutta founded respectively in 1639, 1661, and 1691—were able to undermine the Dutch who had monopolized the trade in tea and porcelain from the 1630s. The Chinese Emperor Kangxi (1662–1722) had in 1685 also made available to foreigners the port of Canton where the EIC's ship *Macclesfield* was able to trade in 1699.

From then onwards a trade steadily developed in which British wool, tin, lead, and silver was exported for tea, spices, silks, porcelains, and luxury goods such as wallpaper, ivory and lacquer objects, and painted fans. Independent Scottish efforts to gain a share of the lucrative China trade were short-lived. In 1618, Sir James Cunningham received a patent from *James VI to found a Scottish East India Company but this was revoked later in the same year through lack of proper support. Thereafter, the Scots took service with the English and indeed other nations' companies.

Their chance came in the 18th century through employment with the Honourable EIC in India and China. Overseas staff were answerable to the Board of Directors in London, who required a steady sale of cargoes from India and China which would yield good dividends to the EIC's shareholders. By 1715 the EIC was established in Canton where it became the dominant foreign power in the China trade. The Co Hong, a syndicate of local Chinese merchants, regulated access to goods and services. From 1729, foreign trading companies were confined to their factories or hongs consisting of business offices, warehouses, and living quarters for staff and servants, which were located on a narrow strip of land outside the walls of Canton along the waterfront of the Pearl River. Employees could stay only during the winter trading season from September to March. They then went home or moved down to Macau to await the next season.

The president and a council of supercargoes, officials responsible for the handling and selling of the cargo of each ship, administered the 60–70 EIC staff at Canton. Employees also included inspectors of teas, accountants, surgeons, clerks, and servants. There was much competition at home for these overseas postings which offered career opportunities and financial incentives to the younger sons of landed families. Here the Scots played an important role as much for political as economic reasons because the supporters of Prince Charles Edward Stuart (see JACOBITISM) had to find employment away from Scotland after his defeat at Culloden in 1746. The career of James Drummond (1767–1851), grandson of William Drummond, fourth Viscount Strathallan who was killed at Culloden, well illustrates both his own success and the EIC's administrative structure. He arrived in Canton in 1787 and by 1792 was one of the two senior writers to the Select Committee of the President and the three senior supercargoes. By 1793 he was promoted to supercargo and set up his own commission agency. Commission was legal and consisted of two elements: a percentage of the profits of the cargo of a merchant ship for captains, supercargoes, and crew according to rank and service and an allocation of space for private orders of luxury goods negotiated by each officer.

The China trade offered both risk and enormous profits. Voyages were costly and long, involving a round trip of three years including shore leave for the crew. An East Indiaman merchant ship embarked from Blackwall on the Thames and sailed for the China Seas often calling at Bombay, Madras, and Calcutta to pick up more cargo. On arrival, the ship sailed up the Pearl River to Whampoa Island for unloading. It was then the responsibility of supercargoes such as James Drummond to negotiate the best price and buy goods for the return journey. Once home, this cargo was sold at the EIC's auction rooms in London. Although the traditional range of Chinese goods continued to be imported, tea dominated the trade since there was great demand for it as a fashionable drink in Europe. The Chinese required silver as payment for tea but, as metal reserves dwindled, the British resorted to their monopoly of Indian opium to make up the shortfall. From the first imports of Bengal opium in 1782, a complex network of contacts between the EIC and independent British and Chinese traders developed whereby cargoes of opium were exchanged for cash which then financed the purchase of tea.

Inevitably such operations required long residence abroad for EIC staff. Here, James Drummond settled easily into the routine of EIC life, commuting between Canton and Macau where his house and garden were much admired. Apart from his commercial activities, he developed a keen interest in local botany, collecting examples of about 200 forest trees in Manila. He was president of the Select Committee from 1801 to 1807, when he returned to Scotland where his titles and honours were restored to him in 1824 as eighth Viscount Strathallan. Material evidence of his career in China has survived in the handsome dinner service of blue and white porcelain which he brought home in 1807 and in personal mementos.

A fellow Scot, Colin Campbell of Moray, went to China in foreign service. After a career as a financier and stockbroker in London, he had to flee to Ostend in 1723 when the investment scandal of the 'South Sea Bubble' burst. He joined the Ostend East India Company and made a fortune trading in India, which he invested in the Swedish East India Company when he was invited to join its board in 1731 as one of the three founding directors. He accompanied the EIC's first voyage to China as a supercargo from 1732 to 1733. The Scottish link offered an alternative route for Chinese exports, especially of porcelain, to Scotland as many pieces were commissioned through the Swedish EIC until it ceased trading in 1803.

Scottish participation in the China trade changed during the 19th century as adjustments to the EIC's charter since 1793 recognized private traders who were employed to import the Indian opium required as a currency substitute of tea, silk, and porcelain. Two Scots—William Jardine (1784–1843) of Lochmaben, Dumfriesshire, who had joined the Company's ship Brunswick in 1802 as an assistant surgeon and James Matheson (1796–1878) of Lairg, Sutherlandshire, who had embarked on a business career in India and China—went into partnership as private traders and in 1832 founded Jardine, Matheson and Company, which was to develop into the dominant commercial enterprise of the Far East. They both transported opium from Calcutta in their fast clipper ships and explored the coasts around Canton in search of further trading opportunities. After vigorous campaigns for free trade at home supported by William Jardine and the Glasgow merchant Kirkman Finlay, an Act of Parliament of 1833 ended the EIC's monopoly and appointed another Scot, Lord Napier, as the first trade commissioner. By 1839, about 57 private companies operated freely in Canton and the first settlements in Hong Kong Island are recorded including those of Jardine and Matheson. The First China War (1839–42) opened Shanghai and other ports to foreign trade and ceded Hong Kong, which officially became a British Crown Colony in 1842. After the Second China War (1856–60), embassies were opened in Peking (Beijing), Tientsin and Hankow became Treaty Ports, while the Kowloon Peninsula was sold to the British consul at Canton. The leasing of the New Territories in 1898 completed Hong Kong's links with mainland China.

Jardine and Matheson, already securely based in Hong Kong, soon extended their trade interests by opening offices in the Treaty Ports, especially in Shanghai which became the most thriving commercial settlement on the south China coast. They continued to trade in tea and silk but the China tea monopoly was challenged by the crops exported from the plantations of Ceylon (Sri Lanka) and India. Even the most famous and swift tea clipper of the China trade, the *Cutty Sark*, launched in 1869 from Scott and Linton's shipyard at Dumbarton on the Clyde was too late and ended her days transporting mixed cargoes to Florida and South America. Exports of Chinese porcelain dwindled in the face of competition from the cheaper products of English and European ceramic factories. As trade necessarily diversified into industrial and technical services, Jardine and Matheson, together with the Hong Kong Shanghai Banking Corporation founded in 1865, developed China's railways.

Change brought increasingly varied Scottish residents to China. Apart from administrators, diplomats, soldiers, and trading company employees, there were the engineers, missionaries, doctors, teachers, and explorers whose work took them into China beyond the world of the Treaty Ports. These included the missionary and EIC interpreter Robert Morrison (1782–1834), who wrote a grammar of Chinese and the first English-Chinese dictionary, and the gardener Robert Fortune (1812–80), whose published accounts of his plant collecting journeys are full of information about Chinese rural life and customs.

By the end of the 19th century, the transformation of a monopoly into a dynamic structure of free enterprise seemed complete. Foreign trade enclaves flourished despite the quarrels between the Chinese warlords of the early 20th century. Jardine and Matheson established their head office in Shanghai in 1912, supervised branch offices elsewhere in China and Manchuria, and along with other foreign companies invested in capital projects. The results of the Second World War, however, changed British relations with the Far East. Jardine and Matheson returned to Shanghai, which again prospered as the largest port in China. After China passed to Communist control in 1949, foreign companies and banks along with many Chinese migrated to Hong Kong. From the 1960s,

Jardine and Matheson shared in the transformation of the islands whose potential they had realized in the 1830s into a dynamic centre of manufacturing, trade, and finance. JMS

economic policy: 1. economics and the Union; 2. Adam Smith; 3. laissez-faire; 4. government intervention.

1. economics and the Union

Overseas trade (see ECONOMY: 3) was of increasing importance to Scotland in the 17th century. The home market was small, relatively poor, and badly integrated and thus export markets were vital for expansion. Scottish manufactures (see ECONOMY, SECONDARY SECTOR: 1) were few and generally of a low quality and luxury goods had to be imported, as did crucial raw materials such as flax and Norwegian timber. The failure of the ambitious *Darien Scheme by March 1700 revealed how vulnerable Scotland was in an age of rampant mercantilism. Tariffs abroad further squeezed the Scottish economy. By the end of the 17th century England had become Scotland's single largest trading partner, but by the Alien Act of 1705 had threatened to block Scotland's trade to the south. Economic issues therefore were a matter of much concern to those Scots responsible for negotiating the *Union of 1707. For one proponent of union with England, trade was where the 'hony lies' (Hamilton MSS, NAS). A 'union of traid' with England had been a long-standing Scottish aspiration. The Fourth Article, which created a free-trade area within the British Isles and England's overseas possessions, was passed with the support even of two dozen consistent opponents of Union. Recognition of the potential damage which could result as English goods flowed into Scotland, however, led to breaches in the principle of equal taxation. Accordingly, there was a protectionist tinge to some of the fifteen Articles of Union which dealt with economic matters, with pressure groups on behalf of industries such as salt and coal obtaining preferential tax treatment, as too did some individuals. Even so, the Union was not a guarantee of economic success; it provided opportunities but also presented risks.

The short-term economic impact of the Union still has be to fully researched, and care should be taken not to confuse the effects of the Union with pre-existing trends or wartime dislocation. *Jacobite propagandists were prone to blame the Union for all Scotland's ills. The impression is of mixed outcomes, with finer woollens and linen cloth suffering, the former from English competition, the latter from duties imposed by the British parliament between 1711 and 1717. Yet coastal trade seems to have increased and the export of grain (see

ECONOMY, PRIMARY SECTOR: 1) soared, while interest in the cross-border traffic in black cattle grew. Such was the impact of expansion that serious localized riots occurred, amongst the inhabitants of some east coast burghs (see URBAN SOCIETY: 3) and dispossessed cottagers in Galloway (see RURAL SOCIETY: 4) in 1720 and 1724–5 respectively. Opposition to raised malt taxes imposed by Westminster produced widespread rioting in 1725. Competition had positive effects in some quarters, as in the west of Scotland for example, where the linen industry diversified into new branches of manufacture.

It is in the medium term that the benefits of the Union were most obviously realized. The buoyant London market and unrestricted cross-border routes allowed black cattle numbers to rise from a figure of 30,000–37,000 in 1723 to 62,500 by 1770. Their price, too, doubled. *Glasgow, the Clyde ports, and the west central region of Scotland reaped the rewards of the spectacularly successful re-export trade in tobacco from America (see USA). Output of linen, Scotland's staple, rose strongly, assisted by the state in the form of export bounties and, to a lesser degree, by the work of the Board of Trustees for Manufactures (established in 1727). By 1770, at least three-quarters of the value of Scottish textile exports was derived from linen; the industry was the largest employer of labour outside agriculture, with at least 15,000 weavers at mid-century, and perhaps 180,000 female spinners (see WOMEN AND SOCIETY: 2), although many of them were part-time. The English market took a sizeable proportion of output, while coarse linen such as 'Osnaburgs' went in growing quantities to the West Indies. Modern scholarship would emphasize the significance of indigenous factors in these successes and the extent to which the Scottish political and social elite made the Union work for them.

How far Scotland benefited from Union in the long run is open to debate. While some historians have argued that Union provided one of the conditions for Scotland's industrial revolution (see ECONOMY: 4) others have adduced evidence which complicates the issue, such as the fact that Ireland's linen industry was larger than Scotland's in the 18th century without incorporating union. Protection for Scots under the Navigation Acts disintegrated after 1783 and the formation of an independent USA—precisely the time when Scotland's textile-led and ultimately coal-fuelled industrial revolution got under way. There is little doubt, however, that the 19th-century Scottish 'Victorian miracle' owed much to the advantages of being part of the *British Empire, which itself of course was aided by Scottish efforts in the form of soldiers, capital, and enterprise. With relative economic decline in

Scotland for much of the 20th century and massive structural readjustment as a consequence, the Union has seemed less important and of less advantage to Scotland. There are economic historians, however, who have argued strongly that in the latter half of the 20th century net transfer payments have been very much to Scotland's advantage. With the referendum on devolution in 1998 resulting in a vote in favour of a Scottish *parliament with modest tax-varying powers, after almost 300 years Scots will again have some direct control over taxation levels.   CAW

2. Adam Smith

The celebration to mark the 50th anniversary of the publication of the *Wealth of Nations* (1776) by Adam Smith (1723–90) showed wide and continuing acceptance of the doctrine of economic liberty. It was a point which had already been emphasized some 30 years before by Dugald Stewart, academic entrepreneur and professor of moral philosophy in the University of Edinburgh, in his lectures on political economy. In 1876, at a dinner held by the Political Economy Club to mark the centenary of the book, one speaker identified free trade as the most important consequence of the work done by 'this simple Glasgow professor'. It was also predicted that 'there will be what may be called a large negative development of Political Economy tending to produce an important beneficial effect; and that is, such a development of Political Economy as will reduce the functions of government within a smaller and smaller compass'. It is hardly surprising that a contemporary leader in *The Times* could claim that the period 'is not yet distant when the supremacy of Adam Smith's teaching shall surpass his largest hopes'. Nor is the late George Stigler's famous claim, uttered on the occasion of the 1976 Conference, lightly to be dismissed: 'Adam Smith is alive and well and living in Chicago.'

Yet it is important to recall that the agenda for economic action by governments was largely determined by Smith's choice of the problem to be addressed. He was not, for example, concerned (as Sir James Steuart had been) to analyse or to consider the socio-economic problems which are likely to be involved in the transition from a primitive version of the exchange economy to the relatively elaborate capital-using system which actually attracted his attention. Nor was Smith concerned with the problems of regional imbalance or underdeveloped economies generally, not to mention the rich country/poor country theses introduced by his friend David Hume. Moreover, Smith's views on economic adjustments were relatively long run—a position which allowed him to discount certain areas of concern. As J. A. Schumpeter once remarked of the German economist von Justi, 'He was much more concerned than A. Smith with the practical problem of government action in the short run vicissitudes of his time and country.'

This was not Smith's position. Yet even given this, the list of government functions is quite impressive, serving to remind the modern reader of two important points. First, Smith's list of recommended policies was longer than some popular assessments suggest. Smith emphatically did not think in terms of 'anarchy plus the constable', to use Carlyle's phrase. As Jacob Viner has observed, in a classic article, 'Adam Smith and Laissez-Faire' (1927): 'Adam Smith was not a doctrinaire advocate of laissez-faire. He saw a wide and elastic range of activity for government, and he was prepared to extend it even further if government, by improving its standard of competence, honesty, and public spirit, showed itself entitled to wider responsibilities.' Second, it is important to recall the need to distinguish between the principles which Smith used in justifying intervention (which may be of universal validity) and the specific agenda which he offered and which may reflect his arguably limited understanding of the situation which he actually confronted at the time of writing.

The principles which justify intervention are wide-ranging in their implications. On Smith's argument, the state should regulate activity to compensate for the imperfect knowledge of individuals; it is the state which must continuously scrutinize the relevance of particular laws and institutions; the state which has a duty to regulate and control the activities of individuals which might otherwise prove damaging to the interest of society at large. It is the state which must make adequate provision for public works and services, including education (see SCHOOLS AND SCHOOLING: 2), in cases where the profit motive is likely to prove inadequate.

In dealing with public works, Smith illustrated the problem of market failure. His preference was undoubtedly for a competitive environment, so structured as to ensure efficiency. Where competitive forces work effectively, his position suggests that there will be no need for further (external) scrutiny. But where the market for public services either fails or operates only partially, as a result of a perceived inability to introduce or to sustain the arrangements needed to ensure efficient delivery, Smith's argument may be interpreted to suggest the need for steps to be taken, which could involve the introduction of other control mechanisms. If any public service cannot be rendered capable of self-regulation, the implication would seem to be that the 'wisdom of Parliament' would have to be deployed in setting up 'proper courts of inspection' for 'controlling their conduct'.

If the key principle is that intervention is a function of market failure in terms both of the provision and the organizations of a public service, then it is little wonder that A. L. Macfie could remark that under certain conditions the strategies which can be culled from the *Wealth of Nations* could be interpreted to 'suggest a formidable state autocracy; a socialist spread of controls that would make some modern socialists eyes pop'.

Points such as these remind us of E. R. A. Seligman's warning to readers of his 1910 edition of the *Wealth of Nations*: that they should avoid 'absolutism' and respect the point that recent 'investigation has emphasised the principles of relativity'. It is not appropriate uncritically to translate Smith's policy prescriptions from his selective understanding of his own time to the 20th century—and moreover it is quite inconsistent with Smith's own teaching. Smith's work was marked by relativity of perspective—dominant features of the treatment of scientific knowledge in the essay on *Astronomy* and of the analysis of rules of behaviour in the *Ethics*. AS

3. laissez-faire

The term 'laissez-faire' is used to describe a doctrine which argues that economy and society operate best when there is the minimum of interference by the state. Although he himself did not use the Physiocrats' term laissez-faire, Adam Smith (1723–90) believed that for nature to operate best 'it requires no more than to leave her alone'. Government's role was to ensure 'peace, easy taxes, and a tolerable administration of justice'. His ideas were absorbed by a group of young Edinburgh Whigs who began to translate these broad principles for a wider political audience. In the *Edinburgh Review* founded in 1802, Francis Horner, Francis Jeffrey, Henry Brougham, and others wrote extensively on economics. A political philosophy of laissez-faire took shape. Government was seen as potentially autocratic, possibly corrupt, and generally inefficient and, therefore, its powers to interfere in any aspect of people's lives should be kept to a minimum. It was a useful theoretical back-up to the general demands for political reform and opposition to specific government regulation.

There were many opportunities for propagating these ideas as political economy entered what was to become its classical age. The Scottish journalist David Buchanan (1779–1848) published the first complete edition of Smith's work in 1814; Ricardo's work came into the public domain between 1810 and 1821. Smith had written in the *Wealth of Nations* and *Theory of Moral Sentiments* that 'the invisible hand' and 'moral sentiments' would ensure that laissez-faire did not result in rapacious anarchy. The newer political economists argued that economic growth would come from the unfettered play of market forces and that the pursuit of individual self-interest was the best route to human happiness. Competitive behaviour, they argued, would lead to the greater common good. The editor of the *Scotsman* newspaper from 1817 to 1821, John Ramsay McCulloch (1789–1864), was a prolific popularizer of these ideas for the next 40 years. Another protagonist was James Mill (1773–1836), the son of an Angus shoemaker and another product of Edinburgh University. Mill's *Elements of Political Economy* (1821), interpreting Ricardo's views with a clarity that Ricardo's own works lacked, reiterated the importance of free trade and the sweeping away of vested interests which acted as a barrier to economic development. In parliament, Mill's school contemporary Joseph Hume (1777–1855) kept up a relentless assault on government expenditure and government intervention, using the argument of no interference with labour to justify repeal of the Combination Laws in 1824.

Additional support for the doctrine came from Christian Evangelicals, on moral rather than economic grounds. The Revd Thomas *Chalmers regularly pronounced on economic policy, broadly on the lines that government intervention would undermine both self-help and community responsibility. Evangelicals (see RELIGIOUS LIFE: 6) saw the operation of the free market as likely to strengthen Christian characteristics. It made them wary of even limited factory legislation. As Chalmers told the factory reformer Richard Oastler, 'if Free Trade be right, the Ten Hours' Bill is wrong'. This kind of argument was powerful support for those Scottish factory owners who were adamantly opposed to any regulation. McCulloch, on the other hand, while arguing in the *Edinburgh Review* in 1825 that 'the less the textile trade is tampered with the better', declared that it was 'absurd' to contend that children were free agents and should equally be expected to operate within a free market economy. T. B. Macaulay's famous speech in support of the 1846 Ten Hours' Bill took a similar line.

By the 1830s and 1840s a great deal of the effort of those who had been influenced by the ideas of laissez-faire became concentrated on the campaign for repeal of the Corn Laws, although probably most of those in the Anti-Corn Law League were concerned exclusively with achieving free trade and did not necessarily have a wider programme. However, in the new weekly *The Economist*, another Scotsman, James Wilson (1805–60), editor from 1843 to 1859, propounded a doctrinaire ideology of laissez-faire. It provided the ammunition for a handful of the more extreme liberal radicals to argue that any state intervention would aggravate rather than ameliorate any problem. By the 1840s and 1850s governments clearly were intervening in all kinds of areas, and bureaucracy and regulation were spreading. None the less, there were still many who argued that any intervention in the market by government, trade unions, or charitable effort was against the law of nature and only the unhindered operation of the laws of supply and demand would ensure the advance of both the individual and society.

A case can be made that Scots played a particularly powerful role in spreading the ideology of laissez-faire, and it may be that Calvinism produced a fatalism that all was God's will and that spiritual salvation had always to precede material improvement. But it is perfectly possible to find Scots who argued against such doctrines with equal fervour. Set against the *Edinburgh Review* was *Blackwood's Edinburgh Magazine* arguing that government had a responsibility to take care of the deserving poor and that the process of the market would undermine the political and social order. The strongest denunciations of the 'dismal science' and of 'paralytic radicalism' were to come from Thomas Carlyle, and even Samuel Smiles, the best-known proponent of self-help, denounced in *Thrift* (1875) a philosophy which asserted that nothing could be done. While Charles Loch and the members of the Charity Organisation Society kept Chalmers's ideas alive well into the 20th century, many Scots from the 1870s embraced the idealist philosophy with its emphasis on the need for the state to create the conditions for positive freedom.

In understanding the significance of laissez-faire in the 19th century, it is always necessary to distinguish between the carefully qualified and elaborated arguments of the classical economists, all of whom recognized an often substantial role for government, and the way in which these arguments were translated into simplistic clichés. The effect of laissez-faire ideology on government policy was limited at any time. But a presumption in favour of non-intervention as the best solution had always to be overcome. WHF

4. government intervention

Prior to the 20th century, government economic policy was comprised primarily of strategies relating to international trade. Thus the acquisition of colonies, free trade, protectionism, and imperial preference all represented policies that were as important for foreign-policy objectives as for their effects on the economy. It was not until the 20th century that economic policy, in the form of direct intervention into the workings of the economy, became a significant and familiar phenomenon. This form of intervention grew in conjunction with rising direct taxation and increased public expenditure as government assumed responsibility for the delivery of services such as education (see SCHOOLS AND SCHOOLING: 4), welfare, and public transport (TRANSPORT AND COMMUNICATIONS: 2). These developments, in turn, led to the creation of a variety of institutions designed to deliver and control public policy.

The earliest encroachment of the state came as central government imposed upon local agencies the responsibility for delivering services and granted them authority to levy taxation to cover the costs of provision. In the Victorian period this process expanded and was increasingly supplemented by financial transfers from central government to local authorities. In the 20th century the process grew considerably as the state undertook responsibility for welfare provision (see LIVING STANDARDS: 3), previously devolved to parochial boards, and for a greatly extended state system of health and education. Direct taxation, in the form of income tax, paid for an increasingly large part of this provision. Since the levels of taxation and expenditure were determined on a UK scale, the system was beneficial for Scotland throughout the 20th century. Relatively low personal incomes, compared to the UK average, meant that Scots paid less in direct taxation than did citizens in other regions. But the policy of maintaining equity of expenditure meant that Scotland received from the Exchequer more income from transfer payments than was paid in tax, approximately £5 received for every £4 paid by the later decades of the 20th century.

Direct intervention by the state for specific economic-policy purposes has been a 20th-century phenomenon. Scotland, as part of the UK, was treated in the same way as other regions in respect of macroeconomic issues such as monetary policy or free trade. Policy intervention was most significant for Scotland in the form of regional and industrial policy. The problem of relatively high levels of unemployment, concentrated into particular localities, emerged in the 1920s and remained a problem that appeared periodically for the rest of the century (see ECONOMY: 6). The phenomenon was associated very largely with structural change and the decline of hitherto prosperous industries (see ECONOMY, SECONDARY SECTOR: 2). Parts of Scotland felt the full force of this transition as the shipyards of the Clyde and the closely related manufacturers of iron and steel, engineering companies, and coal-mining enterprises, found essential export markets increasingly difficult to sustain. State intervention, initially in the 1930s, sought to identify special areas that needed aid to generate employment. One of the earliest special areas was established in the west of Scotland, and included North Lanarkshire and Clydeside although not Glasgow. This form of intervention increased greatly after the Second World War, and was especially prominent in the 1960s and 1970s (see CORPORATE STATE AND SCOTTISH POLITICS). The principal aim was to move industry from areas of full employment to areas of industrial decline in order to provide work for those who had become unemployed. Characteristic of this was the transfer of motor-vehicle production from the West Midlands to Linwood near Paisley. In the short term there was a gain of employment, although the jobs created in Scotland were never as numerous as those that were being lost. Furthermore, the motor industry, facing intensive competition even in the British market, never settled either in Scotland or in Merseyside, the other principal area chosen for relocation. By the 1980s, changed policy preferences and a different administration led to the abandonment of attempts to transfer work to unemployment black spots. The new focus was placed on providing opportunities for private-sector initiatives, and especially to helping small businesses. This new policy did not enjoy much success in Scotland.

Perhaps the most important, and relatively unique, feature of policy intervention in Scotland was manifest in the creation of an organizational structure. The *Scottish Office began operation in 1885 although it did not open an office in Edinburgh until 1935. But in the latter half of the 20th century it exercised an increasingly important influence on economic policy in Scotland and formed a highly effective conduit to lobby for Scottish interests in Westminster and Whitehall. Many of the most influential economic agencies in Scotland were established and controlled by the Scottish Office. For example, both the Scottish Special Housing Association and the corporations of new towns such as East Kilbride and Cumbernauld were used in the 1950s to implement the policy of relocating families from Glasgow slums, and in face of opposition from Glasgow City Council. Similarly the formation of the *Highlands and Islands Development Board in 1965 was designed to stem outward *migration from the region and to effect economic regeneration in the rural north. The transition to more competitive solutions in the last quarter of the century was marked by the introduction of the *Scottish Development Agency in 1975, and its free-market persona, Scottish Enterprise, into which it was transformed in 1991. Both institutions were designed to attract inward investment and employment to Scotland and, by the 1990s, to improve the competitive environment.

The Scottish Office became extremely adept at special pleading for funds and used its knowledge of civil service structures to enhance its effectiveness. When the allocation of central funds to Scotland became formula-driven, in 1978, Scotland's share of 10 per cent was markedly higher than the 8 per cent that might have been expected on a per capita basis. Scotland was undoubtedly a beneficiary from the economic intervention of government in the 20th century, enjoying both a net transfer of gains through expenditure in excess of taxation, and a substantial measure of independent action through the Scottish Office and its agencies.

CHL

economy: 1. to 1100; 2. 1100–1500; 3. 1500–1770s; 4. 1770–1850: the age of industrialization; 5. 1850–1918: the mature economy; 6. 1918–present: economic dislocation / de-industrialization.

1. to 1100

The economy of Scotland in the period before 1100 was, in some respects, relatively undeveloped compared to that of neighbouring European states. *Coinage, essential to a market economy, was not issued during this period, and the first, formal establishment of towns and markets (see URBAN SETTLEMENT: 1) was not until the 12th century. In contrast, both coinage and market towns were established by the 8th century in Anglo-Saxon England. In general terms, Scotland had a rural, subsistence economy for most of the first millennium. Most people lived on the produce of the land (see RURAL SETTLEMENT: 1; RURAL SOCIETY: 1), with whatever surplus there was going to support an aristocratic, and later religious, elite who would often redistribute the surplus to their clients either by gifts or in ritualized feasting. Necessities which were not locally available could be obtained by barter, and tributes were paid in kind with agricultural produce. Some exotic goods were available to the aristocracy through plunder, gift exchange, or long-distance trade. Coins were sometimes obtained in these transactions, and hoards of Roman, Anglo-Saxon, and Norse coins have occasionally been found. The failure to develop a monetary economy is one of the major puzzles of this period, especially as there are now archaeological indications that the economy of Scotland was at least as advanced as that of England in the 7th century (see NORTHERN ENGLAND AND SOUTHERN SCOTLAND: ROMAN OCCUPATION). The existence of a civil survey of households in 7th-century *Dál Riata and of tax collectors in 8th-century Pictland (see PICTS) also seems to show the beginnings of a sophisticated administrative structure.

The nature of the rural economy can be reconstructed from the analysis of food remains and tools from archaeological sites and the records of pollen from waterlogged deposits. In most areas of Scotland the basis of the rural economy was probably little different from that of the 17th century, before Improvement. There was a mixed agriculture of cultivated crops and animal husbandry, varied to suit the climate and soil conditions. The main crop from prehistoric times was barley, supplemented in the first millennium by oats. Wheat was a minor crop, perhaps because it needed drier conditions to thrive, and was confined to the southeast. Flax, for the production of linen, became important in the Norse period. Cattle were the main domesticated animals, but sheep and pigs were widely reared. The contribution of wild resources varied from place to place. Marine resources were exploited in coastal and island areas, with fish, seals, and whales being important contributors to the *diet. Deep-sea fishing has recently been shown to have been on almost an industrial scale in late Norse Caithness and Orkney. The hunting of wild deer was an important social event in aristocratic circles, but does not seem to have been a major supplier of food. Horse, dogs, and cats were domesticated, as were geese and fowl.

Craft production was generally a small-scale and part-time activity, but there is evidence for more specialist craftworkers associated with aristocratic and monastic sites from the 7th century onwards. Pottery was used only in the Western and Northern Isles at this period; in other areas wooden, metal, and leather vessels were being utilized. Where pottery was used it was produced locally, probably within a household or settlement, and handbuilt rather than wheelthrown. Ironworking was an essential requirement for tools and fittings such as nails, and most sites produce some evidence of smithing debris. In contrast, fine *metalwork in copper alloy, silver, and gold reached heights of perfection in the 8th and 9th centuries equal to anywhere in Europe. Wooden items are rarely preserved except in the waterlogged conditions of crannogs, but lathe-turned bowls, troughs, and ladles have been found and were presumably ubiquitous. Many buildings may have been constructed of wattle as in contemporary *Ireland. Wattle techniques were also used for the frames of leather-covered boats, currachs, which were large seagoing vessels capable of holding a dozen or more people. Leatherworking was an important craft given the dominance of cattle in the agricultural economy. Goods manufactured included shoes, jackets, and satchels, some of which were highly decorated with tooled ornament. Woven woollen and leather garments were supplemented in the Norse period by linen clothing. Stone was utilized for utilitarian items such as millstones and querns, as well as for inscribed and decorated items. From the 7th and 8th centuries a series of stone memorials and crosses (see MONUMENTS: 1) displaying a great command of stoneworking were erected throughout Scotland. Stone could be transported considerable distances, for example stone for some of the 8th-century *Iona crosses was brought from Loch Sween in Argyll, almost 62 miles (100 km) away (see CULTURE: 2). Deposits of steatite, suitable for carving soapstone bowls and other items, were exploited in Shetland, particularly in the Norse period. Although we have no surviving evidence for mining, copper, iron, and lead were probably all extracted.

Although many tools and structures show little development from Iron Age predecessors, there were advances in the level of technology, some of which are associated with the advent of monasticism. Water-driven horizontal mills were introduced from Ireland in the 7th or 8th centuries, surviving till recent times in the Northern Isles. The circular wooden or drystone-walled buildings of the Iron Age were gradually replaced by rectilinear structures, probably under the influence of early churches and chapels. Although these religious buildings were originally built of wood, by at least the 11th century a few important sites had stone *churches built of mortared ashlar stonework.

In chronological terms, the first signs of a more developed economy appear in the 6th century, when western areas were part of a trading network which brought exotic goods such as wine, olive oil, and fine red tableware from the eastern Mediterranean. In the 7th century this network shifted focus to western France, and the goods imported included glass drinking vessels and pottery containing rare goods such as spices, dyestuffs, and probably exotic foodstuffs. The major Scottish sites involved in this trade were secular power centres such as *Dunadd and *Dumbarton Rock, while smaller quantities of goods were redistributed to client sites of lesser status. Even important ecclesiastic sites such as Iona were supplied from Dunadd, and rare minerals from the Mediterranean used in *illuminated manuscripts such as the Book of Durrow were found at Dunadd (see RELIGIOUS LIFE: 1). These secular power centres have large quantities of debris from the manufacture of personal jewellery. Brooches in particular appear to have become the main method of expressing rank and identity, and are often very elaborate and made of silver or gold. Royal control of trade and of the means of expressing rank suggest an intensification of the social hierarchy, coupled to increased wealth of the aristocracy (see NOBILITY: 1). By the 8th century the wealth of the church was also increasing and was expressed in the elaborate carved crosses and religious metalwork. The onset of the Viking incursions disrupted this pattern of trade, and the power centres it supported. New trading patterns were established by the Norse (see SCANDINAVIA; ORKNEY AND CAITHNESS, EARLDOM OF) linking Ireland, Scotland, and northern Europe, and although towns were established in Ireland, none appeared in Scotland (see URBAN SOCIETY: 1). The new power centres of the kingdom of Alba were undefended and lack the signs of economic control shown in the earlier western centres, but were closely allied to important symbolic ecclesiastic centres such as Dunkeld and *St Andrews.   EC

2. 1100–1500

At the beginning of the 12th century, Scotland's economy was still very rudimentary and underdeveloped. Throughout much of the country it may have operated at or close to subsistence level, with little in the way of surplus produced for trade, and few established commercial centres through which trade could flow (see RURAL SOCIETY: 2). Commercial development was hampered by the absence of a native *coinage, although foreign, mainly English or Dublin, silver pennies circulated around the early market centres, such as *Whithorn, where there was a thriving commercial and manufacturing community in the 11th century, or the pre-burghal communities recognizable at locations such as *Berwick, *Edinburgh, *Stirling, or *Perth. Such silver was the product of a limited foreign traffic, with an already well-established export trade in bulk produce, such as hides and skins, set against the import of low-bulk, high-value luxuries. Coinage, however, seems to have been valued chiefly as bullion and most trade would have been conducted through barter. Certainly, in the absence of coin, the rents and revenues of crown (see KINGSHIP), church, and *nobility would have been received in kind, mainly in the form of agricultural produce. With no preservatives available other than salt, and with no developed transport infrastructure, most of such produce had to be consumed locally (see REGIONAL IDENTITIES).

This position had changed significantly by the mid-12th century, as the effects of the so-called 'Davidian Revolution' made themselves felt. The reign of *David I (1124–53) was pivotal in many ways in the development of medieval Scotland, but the economic initiatives that he set in motion had a particularly profound and long-lasting impact. The two principal developments were the establishment of a native silver coinage and the creation of commercially and jurisdictionally privileged communities through the grant of burgh status (see URBAN SOCIETY: 1; URBAN SETTLEMENT: 1). The burghs received local monopolies over trade and their markets became the chief conduits of commercial activity in the kingdom. Economic colonists were encouraged to settle in the new burghs, bringing with them particular mercantile, manufacturing, and craft skills and, through links with their homelands, stimulating foreign trade. Coinage further stimulated trade and, as the crown was able to convert more of its revenues in kind into payments in coin, had the knock-on consequence of aiding both the development of the royal administration and the general social state of the kingdom. For example, the great programme of ecclesiastical building works (see CHURCHES: 1) in David's reign was floated on the back of the new silver coinage.

Trade through the burghs was still chiefly in the form of bulk produce. Alongside hides and skins, wool and wool-fells, much in demand by the Flemish cloth industry, gained in importance. The increasing flow of wool has been linked traditionally to the 12th- and early 13th-century development of commercial sheep farming on monastic estates, but this must be placed alongside evidence for the active involvement in this trade of the secular nobility and peasantry in general. By the 14th century, estimates suggest that in excess of 50 per cent of the wool output was owned by the peasantry. The 12th and 13th centuries also saw a developing export trade in cured fish, mainly salmon and herring, to the major urban centres of the *Low Countries. Against this growth in exports, Scotland was a net importer not only of grain, primarily wheat from East Anglia and *Ireland, but also of fine finished goods, especially cloth and metalwork, and exotic luxury items.

This burgeoning trade in the 13th century stimulated a rapid expansion of the moneyed economy, with a steady increase in the volume of silver in circulation during the reign of Alexander III. This coincided with a period of population expansion (see POPULATION PATTERNS: 1), which forced up both prices and rents. Landlord incomes were high and relatively stable, which can be seen reflected in major aristocratic building projects, such as Bothwell, Kildrummy, or Caerlaverock castles, or ecclesiastical works, such as Glasgow and Elgin cathedrals. An abundance of labour forced down wages, and enabled landlords to employ a labour force rather than enforce their seignurial rights over the peasantry.

These trends were thrown into reverse by c.1300, largely through a combination of commercial dislocation through *warfare with England (see ANGLO-SCOTS RELATIONS: 2) and the onset of deterioration of the *climate at the end of the 13th century. The plague (see HEALTH, FAMINE, AND DISEASE: 1) of 1349 triggered a sharp fall in population, which

established the economic trend towards lower prices and rents, but higher wages. The freeing up of European capital in the post-plague period produced a boom in the Scottish economy that commenced in the late 1350s and lasted into the early 1380s. Demand for wool, leather, and hides soared, with a peak of c.1,500 tons (1,524 tonnes) of wool reached in 1372 and some 1,450 tons (1,473 tonnes) of hides in 1381. This established Scotland as one of the principal exporters of wool in Europe, second only to England in the volume of exports. By the 1380s, however, a slump in trade, part of a Europe-wide recession, had begun, and through the 15th century wool exports averaged around a quarter of the levels attained in the 1370s. This decline was in part offset by the development of a trade in coarse woollen cloth, which stimulated the domestic industry, but this amounted to only around one-third to one-fifth of the lost wool revenues.

A number of factors compounded the effects of the recession on the Scottish economy in the 15th century. Chief amongst these was Scotland's slide into a long-term balance-of-payments deficit with its principal overseas partners. This saw a net drain of bullion from the kingdom, part of a Europe-wide crisis in silver supply, recognized in successive 15th-century acts of parliament that attempted to prevent the export of silver and require merchants to bring back a proportion of their proceeds from overseas trade in coin. The drop in bullion levels had been triggered by a series of substantial cash outlays, commencing with *Robert I's contribution for the peace with England and culminating with David II's ransom payments down to 1377. This must have significantly reduced the volume of coin in circulation, a problem offset in part through manipulation of the coinage. The weight of coins fell by 20 per cent before 1350 and by a further 15 per cent in 1367. This was followed by a series of devaluations that commenced in the 1390s and saw the Scots' currency by 1470 contain one-sixth of the silver content of the 1350s. A fresh low was reached in 1480 with James III's heavily debased 'black money', the issue of which provoked a political crisis in 1482.

The most visible consequence of the currency crisis in the later 14th and 15th centuries was the inexorable rise in prices. By the 1450s, the prices of some basic food commodities, such as oatmeal (see DIET), had doubled or trebled. Imports may have risen even more sharply in price. Wages rose, too, which bore heavily on landlord incomes and was only redressed in part by steadily higher valuations of land and rent increases of up to 40 per cent by the mid-15th century. Coupled with the steady contraction of the economy from the later 14th century, the inflationary regime of the 15th century fuelled existing pressures within Scottish political society and contributed significantly to the tensions in crown–magnate relations evident from the 1430s to 1480s. RO

3. 1500–1770s

In 1500 Scotland's economy was still essentially medieval, based on the export of the primary products of agriculture, fishing, and mining (see ECONOMY, PRIMARY SECTOR: 1, 4, 3) along with a limited range of low-grade manufactures. In return, Scotland imported a wide range of goods and luxury items as well as some basic raw materials like iron and timber. In the 16th and much of the 17th centuries, while European horizons were expanding, Scotland's trading patterns remained stubbornly conservative, centred around the North Sea, using tried and tested routes and markets. In the early 16th century Scotland's trading *staple moved to Veere. It remained important as a framework for regulating commerce with the *Low Countries, one of Scotland's major trading partners, throughout the 16th and early 17th centuries, though its significance declined thereafter. From a low level in 1500, trade expanded in the 1530s, slumped during the English invasions of the 1540s (see ROUGH WOOING), then grew more steadily in the later 16th century to reach a peak during the 1620s and early 1630s.

The economy did not expand fast enough to cope with population increase (see POPULATION PATTERNS: 1), however, and unemployment and vagrancy became a problem in the later 16th century. The late 16th and early 17th centuries saw considerable expansion of industry, admittedly from a very low baseline, in sectors such as coal and lead mining, salt making, and iron smelting. Although salmon provided an important source of income in many areas, the exploitation of Scotland's rich coastal fisheries lagged due to lack of investment. Scottish fishermen were small-scale operators and could not compete with the highly capitalized Dutch.

Peace and political stability under *James VI was probably the most significant contribution of a king whose interest in, and grasp of, economic affairs was limited. Official encouragement of industry relied on the granting of monopolies to individuals; most were short-lived and of little consequence. The *Union of the Crowns of 1603 did not mark a watershed in economic relations between Scotland and England though the pacification of the Borders encouraged a shift to more commercial livestock production in this region. James's aim of promoting a full economic union between the two countries foundered on mutual suspicion and mistrust. Charles I aimed at a closer integration of the English and Scottish economies, with equal lack of success. Again the Scots viewed proposals, such as one for a common fisheries scheme, with distrust.

Recent research suggests that the scale and impact of economic growth in the early 17th century was greater than has sometimes been appreciated. *Edinburgh accumulated an increasing share of Scottish overseas trade until it had a virtual monopoly in many key commodities and in the early 17th century more and more trade came into the hands of a small elite of Edinburgh's 'merchant princes'. Their profits were diversified into a range of industrial activities, including coal mining and salt production, as well as into agricultural improvement, urban property, and moneylending.

The economic boom was ending by the late 1630s but the outbreak of the Wars of the *Covenant brought two decades of difficulty which created an economic disaster of major proportions, the full effects of which have yet to be assessed by historians. Towns (see URBAN SOCIETY: 2) were hit by rapidly rising taxation, forced loans, quartering, and direct military action as well as a severe plague (see HEALTH, FAMINE, AND DISEASE: 2) epidemic in the mid-1640s. The drafting into the *army of up to 6 per cent of the male population at any time must also have had a major impact on agriculture. Under the Cromwellian occupation the economy was stable but impoverished with a heavy tax burden.

Economic recovery after the *Restoration was slow and did not restore prosperity to the levels reached in the 1630s. The 1670s were a good decade but the 1680s were poorer for the economy as Scotland's trading partners, notably France, adopted more mercantilist policies, erecting higher tariff barriers. Scotland's merchants remained small-scale operators. Overseas trade was vital to Scotland but Scottish trade was less important to her main trading partners. Scotland's first transatlantic ventures date from the 1680s, showing that merchants were nevertheless prepared to try new ideas. Some of these, however, like the disastrous *Darien Scheme, were ill-judged. Efforts were made in the late 17th century to encourage the Scottish economy by promoting a wide range of manufactures and passing legislation encouraging agricultural improvement but success was limited.

Trade with England, notably in linen and cattle, expanded so that by the early 18th century England may have been taking half the value of Scotland's exports. The Revolution of 1688–9 marked the start of a period of increasing difficulty for the Scottish economy. War with France led to a loss of French markets and by the early years of the 18th century deteriorating Anglo-Scottish relations were threatening to disrupt the existing union. The importance of economic issues to the *Union of 1707 has been hotly debated by historians. The English government pushed for an incorporating union for purely political objectives, but Scottish commissioners may well have been significantly influenced by the lure of economic prosperity in agreeing to England's terms. The Treaty of Union emphasized economic matters, made a number of concessions to special interest groups in Scotland, and was, overall, fair or even generous. Nevertheless, the overnight economic miracle expected by Scottish optimists failed to materialize and there was considerable short-term disillusion with the Union. Its short-term impact on the Scottish economy was marginal but in the longer term, by offering unhindered access to English and colonial markets, it was a basic influence behind economic growth by providing a more favourable setting within which indigenous skills could develop (see GOVERNMENT AFTER THE UNION).

The Union was important for Scottish economic development but was not decisive on its own. The origins of many 18th-century economic developments, such as agricultural improvement (see RURAL SOCIETY: 3–4) lay in the 17th century, obscured by the crises after 1688 which precipitated the Union. The Union offered a new framework for Scottish economic development but no guarantees of success. Scotland could easily have become an economic dependency of England, a mere source of raw materials and cheap labour, had it not been for indigenous drive and enterprise. Economic growth in Scotland during the first half of the 18th century was very slow. The linen industry (see ECONOMY, SECONDARY SECTOR: 1) was the clearest success story with output nearly trebling between 1728 and the mid-1750s. The cattle trade with England also expanded significantly, from around 30,000 a year in the early 18th century to perhaps 80,000 in the 1750s but progress in some sectors such as coal mining may have been underestimated. The tobacco (see USA) trade was an area of major growth, the profits of which provided spin-off into industry and agricultural improvements. Imports of tobacco grew sluggishly immediately after 1707 but official figures are probably misleading due to large-scale smuggling. Economic growth began to accelerate more markedly during the 1750s and 1760s. By the 1770s, with agricultural improvement well underway in the central Lowlands, a rapidly expanding industrial base, and a greatly increased volume of trade with England and British colonies, the Scottish economy had made remarkable progress in modernization and was poised to enter the industrial revolution in step with, rather than at the coat-tails of, England.

IDW

4. 1770–1850: the age of industrialization

While many English historians have questioned the notion of an industrial revolution, given that the economic transformation south of the Border was a long-drawn-out affair, the speed of urbanization and industrialization in Scotland during this time has meant that the concept still has some validity. In this period, Scotland was transformed from a predominantly agrarian and *rural society (see also RURAL SETTLEMENT: 4) to one which was increasingly urban (see URBAN SETTLEMENT: 2; URBAN SOCIETY: 3) and industrial.

There are four factors which can be identified as critical to the success of Scottish industrialization: cheap and abundant labour resources; natural resources such as coal, blackband ironstone, and water power; new technology such as the steam engine; and markets to sell industrial products. A number of other factors can be identified as important precursors to the process of industrialization. The development of *transport was important in opening up markets. Canal building gathered pace in the late 18th century, as did road construction, and the Scottish coastline meant that there were few parts of Scotland which were not within easy reach of sea transportation. This was especially true of the central belt which was the nation's economic dynamo. Banking (see ECONOMY, TERTIARY SECTOR: 2) was remarkably well developed and the widespread use of credit facilities enabled rapid business growth. Finally, ideas which were conducive to economic development, most of which had their roots in the 18th-century Enlightenment (see CULTURE: 11), were widespread in Scottish society.

The period after 1760 witnessed a fundamental transformation of the rural economy as estates became enclosed and commercially reorganized to maximize output and profit. Agricultural transformation (see ECONOMY, PRIMARY SECTOR: 2) was crucial in removing an economic bottleneck as improved production of foodstuffs (see DIET) enabled the growth of urbanization because the expanding cities and towns were important sources of labour and valuable markets. The rationalization of agriculture was also important in releasing labour for industry. In explaining Scottish industrialization it is important to remember that it is the coming together of a number of these various factors which explains the process rather than any one single factor. For example, it is common to think of industrialization as dependent on new technology, but in actual fact, most technology was primitive, if non-existent, and the bulk of Scottish industrial production was labour-intensive with much of it dependent on the muscle power of *women and *children. For example, Scottish coal was dug out by the father and carried to the surface by his wife and children.

A conventional chronological account of the Scottish economy in this period might categorize the first part up to c.1830 as the age of cotton and the latter part as the age of iron and coal. The cotton industry was able to expand largely due to the fact that it was able to build on the success of the Scottish linen industry (see ECONOMY, SECONDARY SECTOR: 1). A skilled and plentiful workforce, a lack of competition, new technology such as the water frame, the mule, water power and steam power, and an abundance of raw cotton, were the main factors which promoted the growth of cotton. The first mill was opened in Penicuik in 1778 and by 1795 the number had risen to 39. By 1839, with the advent of steam-power looms which enabled mills to be sighted away from water, the number had risen to 192. Although figures for output are not available for the industry, its rapid expansion can be demonstrated by citing the figures for the importation of raw cotton. These rose from 430,000 lb (195,044 kg) in the period 1781–6 to 7,190,000 lb (3,261,312 kg) in the period 1799–1804. After the Napoleonic Wars (see FRENCH REVOLUTION, AGE OF THE), the industry began to suffer setbacks. The European depression, the rise of foreign competition, and changing fashions created much hardship. In addition to these problems, there was a problem of overproduction. Power looms which greatly increased efficiency meant that there were too many mills chasing too few orders. The impact of the American Civil War disrupted supplies of raw cotton in the 1860s and brought to an end the industry's dominance of the Scottish economy.

Just as cotton was going into decline, the iron and coal industries began to take off, which was due to fortuitous circumstances and ameliorated any adverse effects the decline of cotton could have had on the Scottish economy. The invention of *Neilson's 'hot blast' in 1832 meant that the native blackband ironstone could be smelted with ordinary coal (see ECONOMY, PRIMARY SECTOR: 3). This was a geological boon for Scottish iron production. Coal and iron grew hand in hand, although coal was given extra opportunities for expansion as a result of the growth of the domestic market due to urbanization. The percentage of Scots living in towns or cities over 5,000 people expanded from 21 per cent in 1801 to 27.5 per cent in 1821, 32.7 per cent in 1841, and 35.9 per cent in 1851. Urban centres provided a ready market for coal, as well as a magnet for cheap labour as migrants (see MIGRATION) and immigrants (see IMMIGRANTS, IRISH) flocked to the towns in search of work. Easy access to water transport was an important factor in the expansion of coal as it could be moved cheaply and efficiently along the coast. By 1828, almost 500,000 tons (508,000 tonnes) were shipped from Scottish ports. Scottish iron (pig-iron) was of basic quality and like cotton it was produced in bulk largely for export. Scottish ironmasters preferred to produce basic malleable iron which would be finished off once it had reached its final destination. The growth of iron can be seen in the following figures. In 1830 Scotland produced 37,000 tons (37,592 tonnes) (5 per cent of UK production) which rose to 700,000 tons (711,200 tonnes) (25 per cent of UK production) in 1849.

The very reasons for the success of the Scottish economy in this generalist phase were also the reasons for its undoing. Dependence on cheap labour, low-grade technology, and an absence of competition meant that this growth could not continue and indeed, as other countries began to industrialize and build up their own basic industries, so the Scottish economy began to become more specialized as a way of protecting itself from foreign competition. RJF

5. 1850–1918: the mature economy

This period of Scottish economic development can be characterized as the age of specialization. As the basic industries of cotton, coal, and iron faced increasing foreign competition, the Scottish economy took refuge in specialized industries which could not be easily emulated by other countries. The west-central belt was known as the 'workshop of empire' as the area produced heavy engineering, steel, railway locomotives and, most important of all, ships. By the eve of the First World War the Scottish economy was centred around shipbuilding and its ancillary industries of steel and marine engineering (see ECONOMY, SECONDARY SECTOR: 2). In 1913–14, the Clyde launched 18 per cent of the world's new ships and was bigger than either the German or American shipbuilding industry. Another feature of the Scottish economy during this time was regional specialization as different parts of the country produced their own particular products. While the heavy industries dominated in the west-central belt, Jute was important in Dundee, the Borders specialized in textiles, Edinburgh concentrated on finance, and the north-east became renowned for specialist agricultural production. Extensive railway construction (see TRANSPORT AND COMMUNICATIONS: 2) from the 1840s onwards was important because it not only created a unified Scottish economy in the sense that products from different regions could be easily sold in different parts of the country, it also linked the nation with the economy of the UK. Railways made the Union a tangible economic entity.

While the Scottish economy took on a more specialized hue in this period one important feature remained the same; namely, it was dependent on low wages. Scottish economic well-being was reliant, as before, on exports. While basic industries such as coal, iron, and cotton were vulnerable to foreign competition, shipbuilding, marine technology, and heavy engineering were able effectively to compete in the international market by producing high-quality specialized products which could not be produced as cheaply abroad. In shipbuilding, for example, there was a pool of cheap, highly specialized labour, a technological expertise in design, and a willingness to produce to highly specific requirements. The sobriquet 'Clydebuilt' was a testament to the high degree of specifications and quality craftsmanship which customers could call upon in placing orders with the shipbuilding industry.

Yet, this overwhelming reliance on heavy industry had a number of significant effects on Scottish economic development. First, it meant that shipbuilding became the base of the Scottish economy which supported an increasing number of ancillary industries. Scottish steel was a good example of this. Although the Scots had moved into steel at an early stage and had pioneered a number of important developments, the industry was not able to match the economy of scale of either German, English, or American production and its lack of competitiveness was compensated by the fact that the shipbuilding industry placed large bulk orders. In turn, coal and iron were also dependent on a vibrant steel industry. Marine technology and other aspects of heavy engineering were likewise thirled to shipbuilding as an important source of orders. Various crafts such as joinery, plumbing, and interior decorating were part of the chain of dependency on shipbuilding. It is worth remembering that the building of ships was largely done through subcontracting to many small firms. Secondly, this overdependence on heavy industry meant that the health of the Scottish economy was dependent on international trade and exports.

One effect of this reliance on overseas sales was that low wages were the critical factor in ensuring Scottish economic competitiveness. Low wages had a significant impact on Scottish society. They were a major factor in maintaining poor *housing (see also LIVING STANDARDS: 3; URBAN SETTLEMENT: 3) and they also hindered the development of a vibrant domestic market for consumer durables which would have helped to promote economic diversification. Indeed, the problem of low wages and poor domestic purchasing power was exacerbated by the reliance on the export trade as this was prone to cyclical downturns which led to sporadic short-term unemployment. Also, as foreign competition increased, manufacturers resorted to keeping wages low to maintain competitiveness

which in turn reinforced poor domestic purchasing power and increased dependence on exports. It was a vicious circle which the Scottish economy found impossible to break. Exports were also critical for the expansion of the coal industry (see ECONOMY, PRIMARY SECTOR: 3). The development of new mines in Fife was dependent on the growing markets of Eastern Europe and, again, low wages were the critical factor in maintaining competitiveness.

While there is a common perception that this period was one of Scottish industrial might, the reality was that the Scottish economy was in a precarious position which already was showing signs of fundamental weakness. First, it was dependent on the international trade for capital investment goods which meant that any downturn in world markets would mean that the Scottish economy would be one of the first to feel the effects. Although there were signs of economic diversification before the First World War, for example in motor car production and electrical engineering, they were not sufficiently developed to compensate for overdependence on heavy industry. Secondly, the Scottish economy was reliant on a narrow range of customers for a narrow range of goods. Ships, steam locomotives, and engineering plant were not everyday products. Indeed, the global economic trend was for mass production and greater standardization. Ironically, the Scottish economy derived a great part of its income from designing and producing the heavy engineering machinery which made mass production goods. Thirdly, the Scottish economy was to some extent being propped up in the period before the First World War by government orders for warships, which were stimulated by the Anglo-German naval race. The failing health of the economy at this time can be shown by the fact that many of these ships were being constructed at a loss. The impact of the war pushed the Scottish economy into heavy industry overdrive and when it was all over, the collapse in international trade, the freeze on government orders for warships, the loss of former markets in the Far East and Europe, and a mood of global economic pessimism all combined to bring the heavy industries to their knees (see ECONOMY: 6).   RJF

6. 1918–present: economic dislocation/ de-industrialization

The demands of the First World War and its aftermath resulted in Scotland being even more committed to coal mining, iron and steel manufacture, shipbuilding and marine engineering, constructional engineering, and carpets and textiles, particularly jute. These industries were all subject to cyclical instability and heavily dependent on external markets (see ECONOMY: 5). With the exception of carpets and jute—which were to experience their own peculiar difficulties—these activities were, moreover, so closely related that falling orders for the products of one were transmitted to the others. When to these characteristics are added the potential problems attendant upon linkages in ownership and management, the vulnerability of much of Scottish industry to adverse movements in the pattern of world trade is apparent.

During the war, the equivalent of some 30 per cent of the world's merchant fleet had been lost and it was in the belief of a replacement boom that the Clyde's shipbuilding capacity was greatly expanded in the post-war years; but so too was the berthage installed elsewhere in the world. Yet, contrary to expectations, international trade failed to grow and during much of the inter-war period the capacity of the world fleet was greater than was needed to transport the volume of goods carried by sea. The consequence was the collapse of freight rates and a steep diminution in the orders for new ships. This meant that the shipbuilders' demand for steel plates and sections, and for the pumps, ventilating equipment, and other heavy machinery that were the typical products of Scotland's engineering firms, was choked off and, in turn, so were their own demands for coal. At every stage, workers lost their jobs and much of their purchasing power, so widening the circle of those affected. To this malign sequence the term 'regional multiplier' has been applied, and in Scotland its ravages were particularly severe, unemployment reaching nearly 30 per cent in 1932.

At first, it was believed that the cycle would eventually be reversed; that prosperity, similarly transmissible, would return. It was this belief—totally misplaced in coal, cotton, and jute, which were already in terminal decline—that partially explains the sluggish movement of unemployed resources into other fields of activity. But there were other factors that contributed to the slowness of structural change. Foremost of these was the deficiency of demand for services and consumer durables stemming from the relatively low level of Scottish incomes. Almost 8 per cent below the British average in 1924, thereafter—certainly until 1938—the position worsened, especially in the west of Scotland. With few of the new growth industries; with well-paid professional occupations in banking (see ECONOMY, TERTIARY SECTOR: 2), commerce, government (see SCOTTISH OFFICE), and education (see SCHOOLS AND SCHOOLING: 4; UNIVERSITIES: 2), largely confined to the Edinburgh area; and with crushing levels of unemployment, the Scottish economy stagnated for two decades, wait-

ing—like Mr Micawber—for something to turn up, but too traumatized to seek its own salvation.

Eventually, in the late 1930s, something did turn up: the prospect of European war. Rearmament, five years of global conflict, and post-war reconstruction stimulated the heavy industries and preserved the unbalanced structure of the Scottish economy. Nationalization, trade-union power, and the political desirability of maintaining full employment gave it a further lease of life, so that when change did come it seemed to do so with startling rapidity (see GOVERNMENT AND ADMINISTRATION: 3). Employment in coal, iron and steel, shipbuilding and marine engineering plunged from 200,000 in 1955 to but a quarter of this figure in 1980. Ten years later, these basic industries had all but disappeared along with swaths of related engineering activities. From contributing over 30 per cent of GDP in 1963, manufacturing's share of GDP had fallen to a little under 22 per cent by 1988. The Scottish economy was experiencing de-industrialization. Indeed, had it not been for the explosive growth of electronics, the share of manufacturing in GDP would have been even lower.

With such a decline, the structure of the economy had to alter, if only because the decimation of the traditional industries automatically raised the relative contribution to GDP of other activities. In Scotland, however, the service sector grew not simply as the passive beneficiary of decline elsewhere but because it had developed its own momentum. Employing less than half of the labour force in 1960, the number employed in distribution, hotels and catering, *transport and communications, public administration and defence, and education and health, had risen to almost 60 per cent of total employment by the late 1970s, when the services' share of Scotland's GDP was about 54 per cent in comparison to manufacturing's 28 per cent). Thereafter, the most dynamic subsector was financial and business services which grew so rapidly that by the end of the 1980s it was contributing 15 per cent of Scotland's GDP, and employing no fewer than 220,000 persons or 11 per cent of the total labour force. This dynamism reflected a positive response to the deregularization of the economy instigated by the Thatcher governments, the opportunities offered by the coming of oil, and the increased use of business and financial consultants by manufacturing enterprises grappling with fierce competitive pressures.

By the 1990s the economic structure of Scotland had come to reflect that of the UK as a whole. The long-desired transformation had been achieved: electronics and high technology has usurped metal bushing; highly remunerated financial services supplanted ill-paid jobs in distribution; and real incomes in Scotland finally equalled, even sur-passed, the national average. Yet anxieties remain. Firms once locally owned and controlled have be-come dependent for their survival not on their own productivity and profitability but on the value of their contribution to the strategy of powerful multinational companies. The pace of technical change is breathtaking. The new industries (even the 'new' services) are highly capital-intensive and require ever larger investment for the creation of each new job. Only constant adaption to change, dependent upon rising expenditures on research and development, will ensure Scotland retains its place in the global economy.   PLP

economy of the Highlands and Islands: 1. to 1700; 2. 1700–1800; 3. since 1800.

1. to 1700

Before the 18th century the economy of the High-lands and Islands suffered from various forms of marginality. The Highland environment (see GEOL-OGY AND LANDSCAPE) was not well suited to cereal production, due to a moist, maritime *climate and poor soils. During the relatively cool and wet con-ditions of the 16th and 17th centuries, crop failures and consequent famines were probably more fre-quent in this region than elsewhere in Britain. Nevertheless, the resource base within the High-lands varied from district to district. Areas such as Islay, Tiree, Caithness, or Orkney, which were rel-atively fertile, exported grain to districts which were less well endowed.

The Highlands and Islands were also marginal in terms of their location within the British Isles. The difference in language (see GAELIC LANGUAGE), cul-ture, and social structure between the Highlands and the Lowlands engendered mutual distrust and suspicion which made the Highland Line perhaps the sharpest cultural and economic barrier in Britain. Despite this, the inhabitants of the High-lands were forced, by the limitations of their envir-onment, to trade with the Lowlands, selling cattle and horses at a string of market centres close to the Highland boundary and buying in return meal and manufactures which they could not produce for themselves. Timber from Highland pine forests was floated down rivers like the Dee, Spey, and Tay to Lowland towns. Contacts between the Western Isles and *Ireland, or between Shetland and Norway (see SCANDINAVIA), were at least as sig-nificant as links with the Lowlands.

During the 17th century, Highland chiefs were drawn increasingly into national politics and the economic orientation of the region was redirected towards greater contact with the south as the region became more firmly linked with the de-mands of Lowland and English markets. Although the Highlands contained few burghs, virtually none of which were truly urban, increasing com-mercialization of the economy during the 17th cen-tury was marked by an increase in the number of authorized market centres, especially in districts adjoining the Lowlands.

The Highland agricultural economy was a mixed one with most farmers having both cattle and sheep, as well as cultivating small plots for cereals—usually oats and bere (barley) though with some rye in sandy machair areas. Population (see POPULATION PATTERNS: 1) seems to have grown from the 16th century, encouraging an expansion of cultivation into more marginal areas—upslope and on to valley bottom land. An intensification of cultivation also occurred in many areas with a switch from plough to hand tillage with spade and cas chrom or foot plough. Hand cultivation in ridged 'lazy beds' also allowed the exploitation of tiny plots on steep slopes which could never have been worked with ploughs. Holdings were gener-ally small, measured in terms of arable acreage, be-coming even smaller as population levels rose. Rough hill grazings, however, were extensive in many areas, being exploited by the use of summer shielings.

Within individual clans (see CLANS OF THE HIGH-LANDS AND ISLANDS), large blocks of land were sub-let by the chiefs to the clan gentry or tacksmen who sublet them in turn, for higher rents, to ordinary farmers, often working a farm jointly. Below these tenants was a large class of cottars and scallags, some with smallholdings, others with only grazing rights. Access to at least some land spread far down the social scale.

Fishing (see ECONOMY, PRIMARY SECTOR: 4) was not a very significant element in the economy, being conducted close inshore from open boats while the deeper water fisheries were exploited by boats from the Firth of Clyde and Holland. Only in Shetland, where there was a long-established sea-faring tradition, was fishing more of a full-time, more heavily capitalized occupation.

The Highland cattle trade developed markedly during the 16th and 17th centuries. Animals were being driven from Argyll to Lowland burghs in the later 16th century. In the later 17th century droving to England, especially for the London market, ex-panded. By the end of the century, animals were bring driven from as far away as Skye through the Highlands to be sold to English buyers at market centres such as Crieff before making another long journey to the pastures of East Anglia, where they were fattened before their last walk to the slaugh-terhouses at Smithfield. The cattle trade was in-strumental in encouraging a move towards a money economy in the later 17th century which provided a valuable source of income for Highland landowners but it did not involve significant structural change or improvement within the rural economy, though by 1700 there was a move on some estates towards establishing large, specialist cattle ranches.

By the end of the 17th century, Highlanders had started to leave the Highlands and Islands on both a temporary and permanent basis (see MIGRATION). Seasonal workers came south to help with the Lowland harvest as a way of generating further cash income but Highlanders were also settling permanently in the larger Lowland towns (see also ECONOMY: 3; RURAL SOCIETY: 3). IDW

2. 1700–1800

In 1700 the Highland economy was characterized by two distinct though by no means incompatible sectors. The majority of economic endeavour centred upon arable subsistence, the basis of which was the nucleated settlement of the *baile* and the sustained use of infield and outfield resources. Alongside this local activity, however, was a sophisticated pastoral economy that entailed the annual and increasing sale of thousands of black cattle to urban markets in England. Between 1700 and 1800 these parallel economies came into increasing opposition as proprietors placed ever more emphasis upon the production of cattle and, later, sheep, at the expense of the *bailtean* strategies for arable cropping. The triumph of commercialized pastoralism and the *Clearances that followed have, in the past, been attributed to the defeat of *Jacobitism in 1746. As early as 1700, however, the region was already subject to influences that stimulated the commercialization of landed resources. The decay in military clanship (see CLANS OF THE HIGHLANDS AND ISLANDS: 2), for instance, was clearly underway by the turn of the century, notwithstanding the masking effects of Jacobite risings. Decline in large-scale conflict, if not necessarily in reiving-inspired violence, allowed chiefs to re-evaluate features of their estate management, most notably the allocation of estate resources to close kin for the purposes of military security. Thus, in apparently secure areas of the Argyll estate, tacksmen had been phased out as early as the 1710s. Such restructuring, along with the post-1660 policy of the Argyll and Breadalbane families of shortening tacks from 99 to 19 years, marked the steady commercialization of social relations. Such estate management strategies enabled these *Campbell proprietors, along with other elites whose estates were closest to the pull of southern markets, to profit from the increasing value of Highland black cattle in the decades after the *Union of 1707. The primary symptom of these

underlying changes was rental increase. Even on the fringes of the Argyll estate, in areas like Mull, Tiree, and Movern, competition between Campbell tacksmen and Maclean or Cameron kindreds, when allied with increasing cattle sales, saw rents increase from £688 in 1703 to £1,300 60 years later. Crucially, however, the first half-century of change occurred within the traditional framework of the *baile* economy, with most areas experiencing little or no real disruption. More generally, the decades from the Union until 1750 also witnessed a diversification in the economic activity of both Whig and Jacobite clans, a development that belies the region's reputation as a primitive commercial backwater. Lead mining, slate quarrying, timber cutting, wool spinning, linen weaving (see ECONOMY: 3; RURAL SOCIETY: 4), and even small-scale experiments in the harvesting of kelp for use as an alkali agent in the chemical industry were all evident by the 1740s.

These developments reinforce the argument that Culloden was incidental to the long-term economic development of the region. By the 1750s, however, the scale and pace of change had intensified. Initially, this took the form of ever-increasing emphasis on cattle production. As the market value of cattle and then sheep was enhanced so landlords used tack regulations to expand the amount of outfield left under pasture. The result was twofold: from 1750 to 1800 rents generally increased by 300–700 per cent across the region. Meanwhile, the traditional cropping regimes that constituted the aim objective of lower tenants were phased out. This situation was compounded from the 1760s to the early 1800s as ever-larger amounts of crucial hill grazing in Argyll, Highland Perthshire, and central eastern Inverness-shire were attached to consolidated pastoral farms that maintained, almost exclusively, large herds or flocks of cattle and sheep. The result was the redundancy of tenant populations and their steady if undramatic *migration to Scotland's growing urban centres or, alternatively, their *emigration to the colonies of North America (see CANADA; USA). This new economic regime ensured that, by 1801, the eastern, southern, and central Highlands were a region of net population decrease (see POPULATION PATTERNS).

Yet the depopulating effects of cattle and sheep did not apply over the entire region. Indeed, a prominent feature of Highland economic development from 1700 to 1800 was that it divided the region into two general sub-zones. Broadly, pastoralism came to predominate to the east and south of the Great Glen: in the north-west, however, an entirely different economy emerged, producing, in turn, a radically different pattern of settlement and population density. In this latter area the new economy was generally labour-intensive. On estates in Mull, Tiree, Skye, and the Outer Hebrides, land settlement and labour practices were increasingly geared towards fishing and, most importantly, the collection, drying, and burning of kelp. As Britain's chemical industry lost access to alternatives, such as Spanish barilla, so Highland kelp increased steadily in value. In the 1770s production totalled 2,000 tons (2,032 tonnes); by the early 1800s it had reached circa 7,000 tons (7,112 tonnes), employing a seasonal workforce of between 25,000 and 40,000 people. In order to retain the required labour the *bailtean* were deliberately subdivided into ever-smaller holdings called crofts.

This new form of settlement was, essentially, a symptom of the region's own form of strictly limited industrialization. However, the crofting system was designed to ensure that agrarian activity could not sustain the communities in question, forcing them to shift, instead, into kelping. Yet the industry was strictly seasonal and in no way compensated for this lack of agricultural viability. This, in turn, stimulated other ancillary economic activities; namely, weaving, distilling, military employment, and seasonal *migration which aimed, in effect, to prop up increasingly congested communities specializing in the core commercial strategies of fishing or kelping. Outwardly, by 1800, the north-west appeared as something of a success story, with an expanded population that seemed to stand in marked contrast to the depopulated central, southern, and eastern Highlands. Yet within two decades of 1800, a rapid decline in market demand for Highland kelp, when allied with a collapse in the support activities of military employment, distilling, and, to a lesser extent, fishing, revealed how the region had developed as an overly specialized and vulnerable economic region.   AMacK

3. since 1800

The economy of the Highlands since 1800 is superficially distinctive in a Scottish context; an apparently underdeveloped rural economy attached to one of the most heavily industrialized and urbanized economies in Europe. Examination of the Highland economy, however, reveals that economic change is closely linked to that of Scotland as a whole (see ECONOMY: 4–6). Arguably, the links between the Highlands and the Lowlands were most evident in the crofting communities of the west coast and the islands, despite the spatial distinction between the two regions. The creation of the crofting communities in the late 18th and 19th centuries resulted in a society which had insufficient landed resources for subsistence and was compelled to

rely on secondary sources of employment for survival. Initially, this was provided by the kelp and fishing industries and by military employment. As these sources of income became less reliable, the importance of temporary *migration increased, thus linking the crofting economy with that of the fishing economy of the east coast of Scotland or the east coast of *Ireland, the agricultural economy of Lowland Scotland or the industrial economy of central Scotland. The periodic crises which have struck the crofting economy, as in the 1840s or the 1930s, have been exacerbated by wider failures of the industrial economy which has thrown the Highland population (see POPULATION PATTERNS: 2) back onto the meagre resources of the land.

The period between the end of the Napoleonic Wars and the failure of the potato crop in 1846 was a crucial one for the Highland economy. This period saw a dramatic change in the basis of the economy: the industries for which the crofting communities had been created to provide labour were in severe decline. Military employment was clearly affected by the end of the war but so was the highly labour-intensive kelp industry, which was now exposed to competition from Spain. This led to a severe fall in the price of the commodity which had brought such massive profits to Highland landowners (see LANDOWNERSHIP IN THE HIGHLANDS AND ISLANDS) such as, among others, the MacKenzies of Seaforth in Lewis, Clanranald in the Uists, and the duke of Argyll in Mull. The impact on the Highland population was even more severe: the crofting communities had been deliberately kept short of land in order to coerce them into the landowners' labour force; now they were flung back on the resources of their smallholdings. This, in turn, with its high food value and high yield from a small acreage, encouraged dependence on the potato. The potato had proved to be a dependable crop and reliance on it had been rational when it was combined with earnings from such as the kelp industry. Partial failures of the potato crop in 1816 and 1836–7, however, signified the vulnerability of a community completely dependent on it. This period also saw an increasing amount of land devoted to commercial sheep farming and a series of large-scale *Clearances in order to create space for sheep. These clearances were of a new type; they can be characterized as expulsive, in contrast to the experiments in social engineering and relocation of population, which characterized clearances prior to c.1820.

The extreme vulnerability created by the combination of these factors was clearly demonstrated by the massive failure of the potato crop in the years from 1846 to 1855. Agrarian crisis was evident across northern Europe in this period, most obviously in

Ireland, but also in Flanders and in the Netherlands. There was more to the crisis in Highland Scotland, however, than rotten potatoes. A conjunction of an almost complete failure of the potato crop, a dramatic fall in the price of black cattle (still the major export earner of the Highland economy) and a slump in the Lowland industrial economy, which reduced the prospects of earnings from temporary migration, brought the Scottish Highlands to the brink of a mortality crisis such as was unfolding in Ireland. Several features prevented such a disaster from occurring in the Highlands. A famine relief operation funded by philanthropic contributions and the proximity of the Scottish Highlands to the industrial economy of Lowland Scotland were both important. The Highland famine was also on a much more manageable scale than the tragedy in Ireland, which resulted in massive mortality and extensive emigration. The landlord class in the Highlands had been bolstered by an influx of new men of wealth in the generation before the famine. These men were in a much better position to support the population than their less wealthy Irish counterparts. The crisis in Scotland was also notable for its longevity, with partial failures of the potato crop continuing until the mid-1850s.

The period from the mid-1850s to the early 1880s has been variously interpreted by historians. A optimistic outlook on this period would emphasize the recovery from the famine conditions of the 1840s, the fact that the economy did not revert to potato dependence, and the revival of the market for temporary migration which increased the circulation of money in the region and facilitated the growing practice of the purchase of foodstuffs (see DIET). This assessment emphasizes that the outbreak of protest in the early 1880s was as a result of a revolution of rising expectations which was dashed by the return of economic and social crisis at the beginning of that decade. A more pessimistic view of the period would emphasize the continuation of landlord coercion in many areas, especially the intrusive control of subdivision on some estates. In other areas, where subdivision was not controlled to the same extent, congestion was the result. Although there was no return to the worst conditions of the late 1840s and early 1850s, there were some very bad years, the worst coming in 1863.

A further feature of this post-famine period was the growing importance of commercialized sport to the Highland economy. This was predicated on the declining profitability of the sheep-farming industry, which itself had had such a profound impact on the Highland economy. The economic effect of deer forests were minimal; as befits such a highly exclusive form of land use, they created very little demand for labour and those who availed themselves of the pleasures of deerstalking did little to stimulate the retail trade in the Highlands.

The early 1880s saw a return to crisis in the Highlands. The decade began with severe storms which wrecked fishing gear and destroyed crops. A major reorganization of the fishing industry in 1884 worked to the disadvantage of the crofter fisherman, who was now exposed to the falling prices which characterized the period. Modest recovery was evident in the 1890s, as the crofting community benefited from the tenurial protection provided by the Crofters' Holdings (Scotland) Act of 1886 and the rent reductions awarded by the Crofters' Commission established by the Act. The economic depression of the Edwardian period produced a new cycle of agrarian protest as the market for temporary migration was once again disrupted. The Highlands suffered along with the rest of the country in the severe economic fluctuations of the early 1920s. The immediate post-war boom was immediately followed by a severe depression which severely handicapped the new crofting settlements that had been established during the period of high prices in the two years after the war.

The next great watershed in the economic history of the Highlands came at the end of the 1920s, as the world economy went into severe depression. This had a number of peculiar effects in the Highlands. The extremely high levels of *emigration which had characterized the 1920s in Scotland as a whole were brought to an end as the traditional destinations for Highland emigrants began to close their doors as their own economies went into recession. In the 1930s, many people of Highland origin returned to the region as levels of unemployment climbed in the Lowland industrial economy. The result, exacerbated by the creation of a large number of very small holdings by the post-war land settlement operation, was a crisis of similar structure to that of the 1840s, although of much reduced intensity, with the Highland population thrown back onto the resources of the land. This crisis produced new thinking on the Highland problem, which emphasized the need to develop the economy of the region rather than further changes to land tenure. The application of this new thinking was delayed by the onset of the Second World War.

One key event during the war was the establishment of the North of Scotland Hydro Electric Board (NSHEB) in 1943. In the pre-war period, hydroelectric schemes had been limited to private ventures in connection with the aluminium industry at Foyers and Kinlochleven. Attempts to develop hydro-power for domestic electricity consumption were scuppered by an unlikely lobby composed of landowning and coal interests. The government's embrace of the development of hydro electricity, and the NSHEB's determination that the bulk of its output should go to domestic consumers at a flat rate regardless of the cost of distribution, had a major impact on the Highlands. Many people regarded this as a waste of money which could have been put to better use. Nevertheless, the transformation of the living conditions (see LIVING STANDARDS: 3) of many Highlanders through the provision of a domestic electricity supply had an untold impact on the tourist industry as it now became possible for crofters to take paying guests. Partly under the influence of this development, the tourist industry (see ECONOMY, TERTIARY SECTOR: 3) moved from an elite to a mass basis over the course of the post-war period. Many governments came to see this industry as a panacea for the Highlands.

Crofting came to be seen in the post-war period as part of the problem of the Highlands rather than the solution. It was regarded as a system which perpetuated the underutilization of land. The thrust of attempts to put the Highland economy on a firmer basis focused on manufacturing industry rather than agriculture. In the 1940s and 1950s, there were few successes in attracting industry to the Highlands, even to the regions scheduled as Development Areas under the various post-war regional policy statutes. The Dounreay Experimental Reactor brought major changes to the economy of Caithness and Sutherland in the 1950s. Further large-scale projects, such as a pulp mill at Fort William and an aluminium smelter at Invergordon, provided short-term boosts in the 1960s, but in the long term they induced a vulnerability reminiscent, in some ways, of the early 19th century.

Contemporary impressions of the health of the Highland economy have been countered by the recent award of Objective One funding from the European Union under a scheme designed to apply to its very poorest regions. The principal area of continuity in the period since 1800 has been the continuation of a crofting region in the north-west and Hebridean region of the Highlands which is dependent on the meagre resources of limited land, bolstered by earnings from other forms of employment. Although the diversity of these areas of employment has changed, that basic structure has not.

EAC

economy, primary sector: 1. agriculture, to 1770s; 2. agriculture, 1770s onwards; 3. mining and quarrying; 4. fishing.

1. agriculture, to 1770s

Early prehistoric field systems consisting of small plots of improved ground surrounded by simple stone boundaries have been discovered under peat in Shetland or in association with cairnfields, piles of stones created by land clearance, on the mainland. Cultivation ridges and terraces have been identified in association with some Iron Age forts in southern Scotland while traces of the boundaries of late prehistoric field systems have been discovered by aerial survey underlying more modern field patterns in some Lowland areas. This suggests that late prehistoric Scotland was already quite densely exploited for agriculture (see RURAL SOCIETY: 1).

From late medieval times, arable farming in Scotland was organized on an infield-outfield system, a variant of the open-field agriculture practised widely throughout Europe. The distinction between infield and outfield developed from simpler infield-only medieval systems. Open-field farming may have been introduced with feudalism, replacing earlier systems based on small, enclosed fields which had continued from prehistoric times. The infield, on the best soils, was relatively small in extent but received most of the manure. It was intensively cropped with bere (a form of barley), oats and sometimes wheat, rye, and legumes. The more extensive outfields, producing only oats, received manure from the overnight folding of cattle in summer and were regularly rested to restore their fertility. In fertile areas, the extent of infield was relatively great but in more marginal locations only outfield cultivation might be used. As well as manure, seaweed was applied to the land in coastal areas and urban refuse around the larger burghs. Crop yields were fairly low; a return of three times the quantity of seed sown was regarded as an acceptable minimum though infields sometimes produced returns of four, five, or six to one. Arable land was frequently held in shares, with holdings fragmented into intermingled strips and parcels under a system known as runrig. Land in runrig was sometimes allocated to tenants using a regular system of sunwise division resembling Scandinavian *solskifte*. A team of eight oxen, pulling a heavy plough, and ploughing the soil ridge and furrow, was normal.

In the west Highlands population growth (see POPULATION PATTERNS: 1) from the late 16th century encouraged a shift from ploughing to more intensive cultivation using foot ploughs and spades with lazy beds. Although there was an emphasis on arable farming in the eastern Lowlands, all communities produced some grain for basic subsistence. Cattle and sheep were kept on most farms; goats in parts of the Highlands. The eastern *Borders had a focus on sheep farming going back to medieval monastic times but developing further and becoming more commercialized after the *Union of the Crowns in 1603. Galloway concentrated on cattle rearing. The western Lowlands had a degree of specialization in dairying by the end of the 17th century. In the Highlands, cattle provided the main saleable commodity but arable land was essential for sustaining the local population. In the medieval Lowlands, and the Highlands into the late 18th century, cattle were driven to summer pastures, or shielings, among the hills and mountains to make use of the upland pastures for the few weeks when they were at their best.

During the 17th century, arable farming in the Lowlands expanded with population growth, particularly around the major towns, especially *Edinburgh. The Lothians and other parts of central Scotland saw the use of liming and improved rotations developing. In the later 17th century, the demands of the English market for beef led to landowners in Galloway constructing large parks for fattening cattle and sometimes cross-breeding them with larger Irish animals. Enclosure of land on estate policies and home farms began in the later 17th century on a small scale, continuing into the 18th century. As well as cattle parks, new rotations were tried, new crops including sown grass introduced, and large-scale planting of trees undertaken on some estates. The crop failures and famines (see CLIMATE; HEALTH, FAMINE, AND DISEASE: 2) of the 1690s brought home to many the inefficiency of Scottish farming. Acts passed by the Scottish parliament in 1695 for the removal of runrig and the division of commonties, common pastures under joint or multiple ownership, were far-sighted but were not fully utilized for many decades (see RURAL SETTLEMENT: 3). The Highlands also experienced a major expansion of the cattle trade in the late 17th and early 18th centuries. The spread of the potato helped accommodate a growing population in an area whose arable resources were generally limited.

In the first half of the 18th century the pace of change was slow and there was little modification of the basic infield-outfield system. Nevertheless, landowners were increasingly aware of better English farming practices, and became more keen to emulate them. Enclosure began to spread to tenanted farms in some areas such as East Lothian but only on a few estates. Early improvers such as Sir Archibald Grant of Monymusk were in a minority and some, like John Cockburn of Ormiston, overreached themselves and went bankrupt. More important in the long term were organizational changes, originating in the 17th century and continuing in the 18th, such as the granting of longer written leases to tenants, the commutation of rents in kind to money, and the reduction of farms in multiple tenancy with the gradual amalgamation of holdings. Rising prices, increased prosperity, and the spread of the ethos of Improvement throughout landed society encouraged the start of full-scale improvement on many estates from the 1760s. The hallmarks of this included full-scale enclosure, the abolition of infield-outfield, the use of balanced rotations incorporating root crops and sown grasses, the expansion of the improved area, and the consolidation and enlargement of further holdings with the emergence of a class of capitalist farmers. Such innovations would become widespread as the agricultural revolution swept through Scotland in the last quarter of the 18th century.   IDW

2. agriculture, 1770s onwards

The agricultural revolution was in effect the industrialization of farming. As a revolution it took a remarkably long time to come to maturity, because agriculture proved difficult to mechanize. Thus many old pre-industrial farming techniques and skills survived in a modified form until the spread of tractor and combine harvester after the Second World War. That is not how it would have struck people in the 1770s. In what was still an overwhelmingly rural country the primary source of livelihood—the land—was being totally reorganized (see RURAL SOCIETY: 5).

At the heart of this lay a drastic change in the way the land was used. With traditional old-style farming, cultivation was concentrated on the best workable land. Beyond lay the commonty or common pasture, in appearance not unlike the rough hill grazing of today. The intensively worked spots of arable were but islands in the much larger commonty. Although the emphasis differed, the system was common to both Lowlands and Highlands. It worked for a thin population living in communities remote from one another, and was heavily dependent on having natural resources such as grazing, peat, and timber that would regenerate faster than they were depleted. By the end of the 17th century population (see POPULATION PATTERNS: 1) expansion was destroying this balance.

The alternative of improvement abandoned the old fixed zones of cultivation and pasture, replacing that with a vast increase in cultivation but at a greatly reduced intensity, with new rotations that included the sowing of fodder crops such as grass, potatoes, and turnips (see DIET). This meant unpicking and reassembling a whole landscape and its patterns of settlement (see RURAL SETTLEMENT: 4). A majority of heritors or landowners of a parish had to agree to proceed, because common assets such as the grazing might have to be apportioned. The process had an all-or-nothing character to it that left no room for a minority of traditionalists to obstruct change. The old-style farming would not just fade but vanish over two or three seasons.

By the 1770s considerable improvement had taken place throughout East Lothian and Midlothian, Berwickshire, and the southern part of Fife was sweeping west into the western central Lowlands, and north of the Tay. By the turn of the century, only parts of Galloway, Buchan, and Easter Ross had large areas 'unimproved'. This was when the Lowland landscape we recognize today was largely created. With grazing integrated with the arable, there would be livestock next to standing crops, hence the field boundaries of hedge, dyke, and eventually barbed wire.

The physical character of improvement was driven by the need to get a good crop of sown grass. This was impossible on the sour, ill-drained, and weed-ridden soil of the old-style farming. Lime and drainage were the improvers' two great weapons in lowering the acidity of the ground and releasing its nutrients. Whether burnt locally or near the sources of both stone and coal as at Charleston in west Fife, this alone required a whole new *transport system. Hitherto cattle and sheep had been the principal item of trade, and good roads were not necessary for them to travel. Improvement stimulated the creation of numerous turnpike trusts, and these provide an interesting index to its progress. Between 1760 and 1790 a new transport system was created throughout most of the Lowlands. The principal users were the improved two-wheeled horse-drawn box carts.

The first generation of improvement was done with existing tools, but as transport improved and the soil became more easily worked, technological developments followed. Ploughs got lighter, with James Small's revolutionary curved cast-iron mould-board (1763) spreading from the south-east into the rest of Scotland in the 1770s. Andrew Meikle's threshing mill (1788) removed a serious bottleneck in processing, and Patrick Bell produced the world's first successful reaping machine (1828). At the same time, his rival James Smith turned from reaping machines to improving subsoil drainage. Hitherto the land was laid out in rigs or ridges averaging about 15 feet broad (4.6 m), shedding water into a drain set into the soil between it and the next rig. But often the surface water would not penetrate to the drain. Smith devised a method of ploughing that broke up the subsoil barrier without disrupting the topsoil. This signalled the improvement of hitherto low-lying unworkable carselands, the final advance of improvement in the Lowlands, and the even field surface we see today.

The *Union of 1707 had provided the development capital and settled economy that had made improvement possible. Improvement also created two Scotlands. Although the Lowland model

spread to some areas of the Highlands and Islands—parts of the east coast glens, Speyside, Kintyre, Islay for example—most parts adapted the old system to an expanded cattle trade, with beasts from the shielings of the north-west finding their way through Yorkshire and East Anglian dealers to the markets of the South. From the middle of the century some lairds in the central Highlands began to let the hill grazings separately. It was a short step to the *Clearances of the Highlands and Islands.

The Highland Clearances were the application of the industrializing mentality to an already fragile economy and environment that backfired. The masterful zeal that history has applauded in the Lowlands furnished a demonology for popular memory in the Highlands. The law invested landowners (see LANDOWNERSHIP IN THE HIGHLANDS AND ISLANDS) with the astonishing power to turn out whole populations, and some did, replacing the old small farms with large and economically staffed sheep-runs and sometimes a considerable investment in infrastructure. The primary clearances moved people from the better to the poorer land, often on the coasts, where they had to carve out new crofts (a Lowland word) or smallholdings. Secondary clearance, as an fhearann (off the land), followed when the kelp business failed after the Napoleonic Wars and the dreadful potato famines struck from 1845. The coming of na Caoraich Móra (the big sheep) established the first of a series of Highland monocultures. Deer and forestry would follow.   GS

3. mining and quarrying

That Scotland was fortuitously and richly endowed geologically (see GEOLOGY AND LANDSCAPE) has been of profound importance in shaping the economy and society of modern Scotland. Precious metals such as gold or silver were found, but invariably in small quantities which were quickly worked out, as in the case of Sir John Erskine's silver mines at Alva in the early 18th century. Mining—of lead and coal for example—has been documented as taking place in the 13th century, and almost certainly began much earlier. Coal, the most important of the underground deposits, was to be found in five main coal-bearing districts across the central belt of Scotland, with smaller fields at Canonbie and Sanquhar. Minor outcrops at Brora in Sutherland and on Kintyre were mined off and on during the 18th and 19th centuries; coal has also been worked on Arran and sought on Islay, Skye, and in other more distant parts of Scotland.

The much-used coal output figures for c.1700 produced by Nef in 1930 are probably exaggerated. Reduced to a more realistic 200,000 tons (203,200 tonnes), Scotland's share of British production can be guesstimated at some 8 per cent, rising to 10 per cent in 1830, and almost 15 per cent by 1913. Growth in the 18th century was probably faster than has normally been assumed. More or less elastic supplies of coal which could be easily transported to virtually all parts of Lowland Scotland were crucial for industrialization (see ECONOMY: 4) and the remarkably rapid rate of urban growth (see POPULATION PATTERNS; URBAN SETTLEMENT: 2) which accompanied it in the later 1700s and early 1800s. Coal output almost doubled between the period 1830–4 and 1845–9, and continued to grow thereafter until it peaked at just over 42 million tons (42,672,000 tonnes) at the outbreak of the First World War.

Iron ore had been mined and smelted in Scotland for centuries but until the 18th century Scotland's principal advantage was the availability of vast quantities of cheap wood to which English and Welsh ore could be transported for smelting. Indigenous supplies of iron ore were first exploited on a large scale with the establishment of Carron Ironworks in 1759, the first in Scotland to smelt with coke. The discovery by David Mushet in 1801 of blackband ironstone (see NEILSON, JAMES BEAUMONT), which was found in vast quantities in Lanarkshire and Ayrshire, was one of the principal reasons for the surge in Scottish iron (see ECONOMY, SECONDARY SECTOR: 2) production after around 1830, following Neilson's invention of the hot blast in 1828. Iron was one of the links in a chain which was to include steel (see ECONOMY: 5), engineering, and shipbuilding (collectively Scotland's largest employers of male labour at the beginning of the 20th century), which made west central Scotland one of the leading workshops of the Victorian world. Ore output peaked in the 1870s, however, and dwindled after 1918 (during the First World War it had even been mined on the Hebridean island of Raasay). Pig-iron production peaked in the decade before 1914; with its decline, one of the principal foundations of Scotland's industrial empire crumbled. The much smaller and only locally significant lead mining industry probably enjoyed its longest run of prosperity between c.1740 and 1810, although there were periodic upturns thereafter, notably in 1914, but it had virtually died out by 1928.

Scotland's quarries were said by David Bremner, the Scottish industrial commentator of the 1860s, to 'contribute largely to the wealth of the country, and afford employment to a great number of persons' (*Industries of Scotland* (1869)). Granite was rather different from coal in that it had no other rival in Britain. Granite quarrying in and around Aberdeen was well established by 1800; machinery to dress and polish the stone which was introduced in the 1830s and the laying of local rail lines in the

following decades heralded a new era of expansion. While local use for the stone continued throughout, by the end of the 19th century some 70,000 tons (71,120 tonnes) of granite were being exported, mainly to the USA. Kirkcudbright, too, supplied granite as building and paving stone, which was also sent to England and even Russia and South America, while red granite was worked on Mull. Other building stone—'freestone'—of variable quality and appearance, was quarried throughout Scotland and mostly used in the home market. Regional specialization occurred in the production of paving stones, extensive quarries for which were found in Angus and Caithness; stone from both was exported worldwide. Extensive deposits of slate, used for roofing from the 17th century at least, were quarried on Easdale island and at Ballachulish, both in Argyll.

The numbers employed in mines and quarries varied over time and according to what was being mined or quarried—132,096 is the figure given for 1907, which is not much less than the number of textile workers. During the 1840s, the increase in coal miners in Scotland was 8.7 per cent per annum, the fastest of all the British coal-producing regions. The parishes of Old and New Monkland (Airdrie and Coatbridge) experienced over 100 per cent increase in their population in ten years. The degree of industrial concentration in coal in Scotland in 1913 was higher than elsewhere in the UK; the Fife Coal Company, for example, accounted for half of Fife's coal output, while many of the mining communities of Lanarkshire and Ayrshire were dominated by the great iron companies.   CAW

4. fishing

Fishing was important in Scotland in contributing to the food supply from the earliest known prehistoric settlement, and also in the commerce of the country from at least medieval times. This is related to the abundance of the resource in both salt and fresh water (see also NATURAL HISTORY); and the relative importance tended to be greater in the less fertile parts of the country, particularly the Highlands and Islands.

The importance of fish in the archaeological record is especially well shown by the coastal shell mounds of the mesolithic period, the biggest of which contain millions of shells. There was a sustained importance throughout the historical timespan of salt-water species at the coast, and freshwater species inland; and both feature in the earliest descriptions of the country and of its parts. While there is record of a number of freshwater species, including trout, pike, and eels, by far the most prominent species in the rivers was the anadromous salmon, which came back to the rivers to spawn after its marine phase. The fisheries for salmon were a crown prerogative, and in the early national records it features more conspicuously than any other fish species. Salmon spawned in all rivers of any size, and were most prominent in the bigger eastward-flowing rivers like the Tweed and Dee. The salmon fisheries in the medieval period were given out to religious houses and royal burghs; and several of the latter, like *Berwick and *Aberdeen, were conveniently at the mouth of major salmon rivers. The main fishing was by net and coble in the estuaries. Salmon were an important diet item and, cured in barrels, were also an important trade and export item. After the Reformation the salmon fisheries passed into lay hands, and in the 19th century there was a big growth in coastal netting prior to the salmon entering the rivers. From the late 18th century, improving market contacts, especially with London, saw fresh salmon become a high-value luxury product.

Herring from medieval times was the species of sea fish which featured most in records and in trade. Up to about the 17th century it was largely limited to inshore fisheries with small open boats with nets in the Firths of Forth and Clyde, although it was realized that the Dutch with their decked 'busses' had built up a major open sea fishery in the North Sea. There were various initiatives to develop a buss fishery in the Dutch manner: this involved carrying supplies of barrels and salt and curing the herring aboard. Part of the intention was to build up a fishery in the Minches where the Dutch were little active, and eventually in the second half of the 18th century some success was achieved with the help of tonnage bounties paid by the government to help fit out busses that were nearly all based on the Clyde. The profitability of these ventures, however, was always questionable, and there were always proponents of the rival method of bringing the catches to shore for curing, which was feasible in Scotland as the herring could generally be caught within a few miles of the coast: this could be done at much lower cost.

In the late 18th century, barrel bounties were introduced for herring satisfactorily cured, and under the Fishery Board these were increased after 1809. The bounties were linked to a government system of inspection and quality control; and the engagement system developed whereby the curers gave the fishermen a guaranteed season's price. Together, these proved a much more effective stimulus, and the open boat inshore fishery developed on a big scale in Caithness from the late 18th century. It continued to expand after all bounties were phased out in 1830, and spread to many other places, especially to the Aberdeenshire ports of Peterhead and Fraserburgh on the east coast. As

well as the home market, the main early outlet for Scottish herring was in Ireland, but by the mid-19th century they were dominating the main market on the north European plain.

The fishery was originally largely restricted to the east coast in the period from mid-July to mid-September; but success led to investment in bigger and (ultimately) decked boats, and it was possible to use these for an extended period by moving to bases where herring were available at other seasons. From the mid-19th century this led to fishing in the Hebrides in May and June; the 1860s saw the beginning of participation in the main English herring fishery at East Anglia in autumn, and from the 1880s the fishery at Shetland developed on a big scale. The increase in the size of boats culminated at the turn of the century in the advent of the steam-powered herring drifter, and by the peak years before the First World War the output of the Scottish fishery alone was around 2 million barrels. The inter-war period of readjustment was particularly painful in the herring fishery, with the disorganization of the main markets in Germany (with its great balance of payment and inflation problems) and in Russia (where the revolution was followed by civil war). There was a downward trend in production, and after the Second World War the herring fishery shrank further to a minor affair as the main cured market dwindled with improving living standards, while the new main (but low value) outlet of fish meal was dominated by Norway and Denmark. From the 1970s mackerel became the main pelagic species fished.

Although early white fisheries are less recorded than herring fisheries, throughout history they were a more steady source of fish supply at the coast, and also are recorded from medieval times in trade. By the 17th century there was an increasing number of fishing villages around the coasts of the Lowland part of the country; their main function was line fishing for white fish, among which the haddock was particularly important. Originally, much of the marketing was at the local level by fishwives, but increasingly part of the catch was cured for longer-distance trade. Specialized fishing settlements developed to a very limited extent in the Highlands and Islands, where most fishing into modern times has been done by crofter-fishermen (see LANDOWNERSHIP IN THE HIGHLANDS AND IS-LANDS). From the 18th century in the Shetland Islands, the *haaf* or half-net fishery for cod and ling for export developed, which made the regional economy of the islands the most fishing-dependent in Britain; it was organized by the landlords on the controversial 'Shetland method' by which participation in fishing was a condition for tenure of house and land.

The line fisheries reached their peak in the 19th century, mainly in catering to an expanding national market in fresh fish reached by improving communications. In the longer term, and especially from 1880 in Scotland, this market was to be dominated by the more productive method of trawling by steam-powered boats which could pull the heavy trawl. This resulted in landings being concentrated at auction markets at much fewer points, especially in Aberdeen, while exploitation intensified and spread outward to include grounds as far afield as Faroe and Iceland. The inter-war problems of the white fisheries, for which the main outlet was the home market, were less severe than those of the herring fisheries, and in this period an increasing number of erstwhile herring fishermen took to white fishing with the seine-net gear which had been copied from Denmark, and which could be worked with less engine power than the trawl. This was to continue to expand during and after the Second World War and in the 1960s and 1970s became the most important fishery of the country.

After the Second World War, the 'inshore' fleet of drifters and seiners, together with the coal-burning steam trawlers, were replaced by more economic diesel vessels with the help of government grant-and-loan schemes. The trawler fleet met increasing difficulties with the extension of national fishing limits in the 1970s and was greatly reduced, while the 'inshore' fleet diversified with the use of the light and pair trawls; and part of its effort went into supplying the expanding modern market for shellfish, especially scallops. Increasing efficiency in fishing methods had produced a crisis of conservation by the 1970s, and the entry into the EEC in 1972 entailed that these be tackled through catch limits and national quotas under the Common Fisheries Policy. Since the 1970s the innovation of commercial salmon farming has added a major new component to Scottish fish production.
JRC

economy, secondary sector: 1. industry, to 1770s; 2. heavy industry, 1770s onwards; 3. new industries.

1. industry, to 1770s

As an exporter of unprocessed raw materials and an importer of manufactures, medieval Scotland was deficient in industries. Down to the 17th century Scottish burghs (see URBAN SOCIETY: 1–2) functioned more as finishing centres for goods such as cloth produced in the surrounding rural areas rather than as major focuses of industrial production. In the later 16th and early 17th centuries there was a significant expansion of coal mining (see ECONOMY, PRIMARY SECTOR: 3) and salt making, especially around the Firth of Forth. In the early 17th century,

improved technology from England and Flanders allowed the construction of deeper coal mines, such as Sir George Bruce's mine at Culross which extended nearly 1 mile (1.6 km) under the Firth of Forth. The dross from the coal mines was used to fire strings of salt pans, while the burning of limestone to produce lime for agriculture also expanded significantly. Lead mining at Leadhills also developed at this period but much of the ore was exported unsmelted. Iron working was done on a widespread, small-scale basis but by 1610 Sir George Hay had set up a charcoal-fired blast furnace beside Loch Maree, the forerunner of several later Highland smelters.

Industries such as these were still relatively small-scale ventures, mostly undertaken by estate proprietors as adjuncts to their income from agriculture. Textile manufacture (see ECONOMY: 3) concentrated on the production of coarse cloth. Attempts in the early 17th century to bring in Flemish weavers to teach the Scots how to manufacture new higher-grade fabrics were unsuccessful, though legislation in 1641 encouraged the setting up of one or two fine woollen manufactories. The production of coarse woollen plaiding developed on a large scale in the north-east, exported via Aberdeen. In the later 17th century, the authorities made further attempts to encourage home manufactures in order to cut down the cost of expensive imports. A number of manufactories were set up, especially for fine woollens, with some protection from outside competition. Other enterprises included the manufacture of paper, glass, gunpowder, porcelain, and the refining of sugar. Most of the manufactories were located around *Edinburgh and *Glasgow; and their merchants provided much of the capital to finance them. Despite tax incentives and protection from imports, most of these enterprises were fairly short-lived and were vulnerable to even slight shifts in the market. Fine woollen manufactures like the one at New Mills, outside Haddington, did not long survive the opening up of competition from English producers which occurred with the *Union of 1707. On a more positive note, linen manufacture expanded greatly in the later 17th century with c.650,000 ells being sent to London each year by 1700, total exports to England being between 1.2 and 1.8 million ells. Exports of coal and salt were hit by rising tariffs in the late 17th century and Scottish production was geared increasingly to the needs of the home market. Nevertheless, coal output may have stood at around 225,000 tons (228,600 tonnes) a year in the late 17th century.

The Union encouraged those Scottish industries such as linen which complemented rather than competed with the English economy. Glasgow's flourishing tobacco trade encouraged the output of linen and other manufactures in west central Scotland as return cargoes for the American plantations. Access to English and colonial markets after 1707 encouraged linen production, which doubled every 20–5 years. Much of the output was of coarse cloth but by the 1740s production of finer linen was growing rapidly. As linen weaving became increasingly a full-time occupation rather than a part-time adjunct to agriculture, the organization of the industry became more complex, and a growing number of stages in the manufacturing process became mechanized. By the 1740s, the size of firms in the textile industries was increasing steadily with true factories beginning to appear, heralding the late 18th-century development of mechanization in the cotton industry. The first large-scale cotton mill was established at Rothesay in 1779.

Coal mining also expanded steadily during the first half of the 18th century, with production reaching at least 700,000 tons (711,200 tonnes) a year by 1750. Although the first Newcomen steam engine was set up at a Scottish colliery in 1719, water power remained the most important power source for large-scale industry. Under the pressure of mounting demand from an increasing urban population and the growth of fuel-consuming industries, the annual output of Scottish coal rose between 1775 and 1830 from an estimated 1 to 3 million tons (1,016,000 to 3,048,000 tonnes). This expansion was made possible by improvements in mine practice and the supercession of the landed proprietor by profit-seeking, leaseholding partnerships, and joint-stock companies, the members of which were frequently active in ironmaking.

Iron smelting grew more slowly. Blast furnaces in the Highlands, at places like Bonawe, were set up by English ironmasters using local charcoal and imported English ore. The Carron Ironworks (1759) near Falkirk marked the shift to large-scale integrated production, using carboniferous ironstone for smelting the iron ore. By the later 18th century, the works was producing ten times as much iron a year as any charcoal-fired blast furnace and was consuming as much coal as the entire city of Edinburgh. Although it remained the only plant of its kind for many years, it presaged the coming of the industrial revolution (see ECONOMY: 4) and was a wonder in its day.   IDW

2. heavy industry, 1770s onwards

Despite the establishment of several major ironworks at the close of the 18th century, thereafter the industry stagnated. In 1830 production was less than 40,000 tons (40,640 tonnes); yet by 1860 it reached almost 1 million tons (1,016,000 tonnes), an increase explained by the rapid adoption of *Neil-

son's hot blast, devised in 1828. This technique so reduced fuel inputs that by the late 1830s Scotland had become the lowest cost iron-producing region in Britain. Huge profits accrued to the leading firms in the industry (the *Bairds of Gartsherrie, William Dixon & Co., and Merry & Cunninghame) from exporting their pig-iron. Few made any sustained attempt to process their iron further. Instead, they integrated backwards, investing ever more heavily in coal, and leaving the exploitation of the Bessemer and Siemens processes, which made possible the manufacture of cheap steel, to newcomers such as the Steel Company of Scotland, William Beardmore & Co., and David *Colville & Sons. By 1885, Scottish steel production was roughly 20 per cent of total British output and already the fortunes of the steel melters had become inextricably bound up with the well-being of the shipbuilding industry, the source of their major demand. On the eve of the First World War, the Scottish iron and steel industry was unintegrated and locationally dispersed: the economies offered by the continuous flow of molten metal from the blast furnace into the steel melting furnace (hot metalworking) were impossible to attain.

Initially, the close connections of Scotland's heavy industries brought great prosperity. Coal, iron and steel, and engineering all benefited enormously as Scottish shipbuilding was transformed by the adoption of the steam engine for marine propulsion and iron, and later steel, replaced wood in hull construction. From insignificance at the end of the Napoleonic Wars, within 60 years the Clyde (see GLASGOW) was launching more iron ships than the rest of the world put together. The technical and economic advantages of using mild steel in ship construction and water tube boilers were swiftly appreciated and rapidly adopted, and the power output of the reciprocating steam engine was pushed to its technical limits. Yet by 1900 this most successful of Scottish industries, on whose buoyancy the entire economy had come to depend, had developed serious weaknesses: it was dominated by small-scale family firms utilizing labour-intensive techniques, the majority of which had become dangerously reliant on either a limited range of commercial customers or, like John Brown's and Fairfield's, on fulfilling the needs of the Admiralty. Even more alarmingly, an increasing proportion of the contracts undertaken by the shipbuilders were incurring losses (see ECONOMY: 5).

By 1913, the apparent prosperity of the Scottish heavy industries obscured numerous fundamental weaknesses. These were exacerbated by the First World War and cruelly exposed in its aftermath, when shipbuilding suffered from chronic overcapacity, bringing down the Scottish steel and engineering industries and adding greatly to the difficulties of coal. The ensuing depression was so profound and far-reaching that it seemed to defy both comprehension and remedial action. The shipbuilders were almost completely paralysed. Colvilles' ultimately successful efforts to gain financial control of the Scottish steel industry failed to reorganize its productive capacity to attain the maximum economies of scale. In coal mining, the efforts of the more progressive owners to in-stall cost-reducing mechanical equipment and to improve marketing arrangements were largely nullified by the implacable realities of geology and the low selling prices of their major grades of coal.

If the required radical reconstruction of the heavy industries was not delivered by the midwife of acute depression, the ensuing period of rearma-ment, war, and reconstruction under state owner-ship, was similarly barren of long-term benefit. Well-meaning politicians were instrumental in giv-ing priority to full employment and ignoring the underlying realities of a coal industry grappling with exhausted mineral resources (see ECONOMY, PRIMARY SECTOR: 3); an iron and steel industry un-able to compete with newer, fully integrated works on tidewater sites; and a fragmented shipbuilding industry, sadly deficient in modern managerial techniques, operating in cramped esturine loca-tions totally unsuitable for the construction of new bulk carriers or elephantine oil tankers. Despite rationalization, Scottish pits proved incapable of covering their costs, and there was no alternative to closure. The days of steel-making in Scotland were numbered by Colvilles' rejection of a plan to build a fully integrated works on the Clyde, first mooted in 1929; the fatal consequences of this omission were hastened by a government decision to force the company to erect a hugely expensive but underutilized steel strip mill at Ravenscraig and the contemporary collapse of Scottish shipbuild-ing. Despite the continuous injection of public funds, one by one the famous yards closed. Even the labour force, initially prepared to 'work in' and suffer every deprivation short of abandoning age-old ideas of demarcation, finally accepted the in-evitable and participated in a massive rush for redundancy (see ECONOMY: 6).

The heavy industries, once constituting the very sinews of the Scottish economy and employing a substantial share of the nation's total labour force, have now gone. And if past errors of judgement— so easy to see in retrospect—accelerated their dis-appearance, their role was slight compared with the exhaustion of mineral resources, the pace and nature of technical change, and inexorable market forces which have undermined the comparative advantages which, fleetingly, Scottish entrepre-neurs had so avidly seized. PLP

3. new industries
The 'new industries' are those which resulted from the major innovations of the late 19th and early 20th centuries. They comprise the manufacture of motor vehicles, aircraft, cycles, and rubber tyres and mechanicals; electrical machinery and house-hold appliances; radios and electronic equipment; synthetic fibres; scientific instruments, cameras, and office equipment; and certain non-ferrous met-als, such as aluminium. Firms making such prod-ucts were established in Scotland before the First World War. Indeed, a handful of them were among the foremost of their kind: Argyll, Arrol Johnston, and Albion in motor vehicles; Beard-more in aero-engines; the North British Rubber Co. in rubber mechanicals and tyres; Mavor & Coulson in heavy electrical machinery; Kelvin & White in optical and electrical instruments; and the British Aluminium Co. But their contribution to an increasingly diverse economy was far outweighed by Scottish extreme specialization in the heavy in-dustries (see ECONOMY, SECONDARY SECTOR: 2). Moreover, such activities became less rather than more significant. Of the 50 or so companies estab-lished to make motor cars in Scotland before 1914, virtually all rapidly disappeared, the victims of poor management, inadequate capital, and lack of vision; and the sole post-war survivor, Arrol John-ston, controlled by Sir William Beardmore, suc-cumbed with Beardmore's collapse in 1929, along with that company's interests in the manufacture of aero-engines, aircraft, and airships.

Thus it was that by 1924 the contribution of the new industries to the value of total net output in Scotland was but 8 per cent, or scarcely more than one half of the comparable figure for the UK. This proportion failed to increase between the wars. Many explanations have been put forward. On the supply side, these have included an inability to ob-tain raw materials, semi-finished goods, and elec-tricity at low cost and a scarcity of appropriately skilled labour; and, on the demand side, difficulties in marketing the product and the persistently low level of real incomes in Scotland.

By 1950, the inadequacy of indigenous private enterprise was finally recognized: outsiders had to be induced to establish branch factories and, if that failed, the state itself must take action (see ECON-OMY: 6). In the event, the efforts of the industrial es-tate companies and a vigorous campaign by the *Scottish Council (Development and Industry) to attract companies from the USA were remarkably successful. At last, the new industries began to ar-rive on a significant scale: Scottish needs coincided with the post-war desire of American corporations to expand overseas and plants were established by Euclid, Caterpiller, Goodyear, Monsanto, Honeywell Controls, National Cash Register, IBM, and Burroughs.

Meanwhile, the government was being urged to locate a strip mill in Scotland, its proponents believing that in its absence the expansion of those industries dependent upon thin steel sheet would be retarded. This argument was highly persuasive, especially when allied to the hope of re-establishing the car industry in Scotland. Finally, the government, fearful of the political consequences of rising unemployment, forced a reluctant Colvilles to build a strip mill and then induced an equally reluctant Lord Rootes to establish a car plant at Linwood. It was a disaster. Existing on the periphery of the traditional networks of the motor industry, making just one untried model, and owned by a relatively small producer bedevilled by poor industrial relations and desperately short of working capital, Linwood passed into the hands of the Chrysler Corporation in 1967. Chrysler, in turn, sold out to Peugeot-Citroën in 1979, which with indecent haste closed the works in 1981. A similar failure attended the major initiative at Invergordon, where British Aluminium were encouraged to build an aluminium smelter by the promise of low fuel costs which was never fulfilled.

Even the possibilities of developing new industries implicit in the coming of North Sea oil in 1969 have been realized only to a disappointingly limited degree, largely because the opportunity for indigenous industrial enterprise was more apparent than real and more transitory than structural change demands. Many American firms established branch plant but the government's insistence on the rapid exploitation of the UK's offshore oil and gas reserves gave native enterprise little real chance of disrupting the long-established relationships that had been built up by the major oil companies with their specialized suppliers of patent-protected, high technology instruments and gadgets. Few Scottish firms proved sufficiently perspicacious or able to emulate the Wood Group's strategy of buying in the necessary expertise and engaging in joint ventures with companies already possessing the technical know-how. Instead, the great majority contented themselves with providing mere 'rope and dope' and promptly collapsed in the oil price crisis of 1985-7. The survivors constitute an important addition to Scotland's new industries, but their economic weight poorly reflects the early hopes engendered by the North Sea oil bonanza.

The new industry that has fulfilled its high expectations has been electronics, the importance of which has grown strongly since the late 1940s. Within 50 years companies engaged in the manufacture of industrial products, information systems (including computers), defence-related products, avionics, and electronic components employed 45,000 and contributed over 40 per cent of Scotland's manufactured exports. The major American firms had been followed by the Japanese: NEC, Mitsubishi, Oki, JVC, and Terasaki, drawn by generous financial incentives, the blandishments of Locate in Scotland, the ready availability of custom-built factories for immediate occupation, and—increasingly—by the magnetism of those very economies of concentration that had so painfully eluded the government-inspired prestige projects. Although reference to the cluster of electronics firms as 'Silicon Glen' has become less ironic, it can still be argued that the prospects for self-sustaining, internally generated growth of the Scottish electronics industry are unpromising. This is because, of all the world's electronic centres, Scotland is strongest in areas of limited importance to long-term competitiveness. There is an urgent need to reduce Scotland's concentration on hardware by promoting indigenous capability in original product design and development as well as software.

Whereas the staple industries were largely the product of resilient native family firms, the new industries have been brought to Scotland by giant multinationals, ever ready to move their operations when opportunities for even greater profits are available elsewhere. Already, many of the post-war successes have gone: Goodyear's factory at Drumchapel, the Caterpillar plant at Uddingston and the Timex factory at Dundee are notable examples, but there have been many more, and Hyundai, gravely weakened by financial crisis in Asia, did not even arrive. The new industries are not simply new; they are footloose, and without continuous cost-reduction and adaptation to technical change they wither and die. These industries, now dangerously dominant in Scotland's manufacturing economy, are alarmingly fragile.   PLP

economy, tertiary sector: 1. commerce and early banking, to 1770s; 2. commerce and banking, 1770s onwards; 3. the tourist industry.

1. commerce and early banking, to 1770s

The 17th century was not a golden age for Scottish commerce. The opportunities which seemed to be offered by the *Union of Crowns in 1603 remained unfulfilled. Despite a number of developments after 1670 Scotland remained dependent upon a subsistence rural economy. The most prominent manufactured exports in 1704 were coarse linens and woollen goods which represented 21 per cent of the estimated value of all exports; 80 per cent of the remainder was agricultural products, the most important of which was black cattle. Before 1707, the Scots merchant was a general dealer providing credit facilities, buying and selling produce, and working in a *coinage which was one of the most debased and unreliable in Europe. No gold coins were issued by the Edinburgh Mint after 1638. A theoretical exchange rate of 12 : 1 between the £1 sterling and the £1 Scots was set in 1603, but political circumstances and comparative fineness of silver in the respective coins meant that the actual rate fluctuated between 8 : 1 and 14 : 1. Throughout the 17th century there was a consistent balance of payments deficit, which had to be met by exporting silver coin or bullion. One practical result of this was that only a minority of coins in circulation between 1680 and 1707 were in Scots denominations. Merchants had to be able to perform instant, multi-currency conversions. Charitable bequests normally specify both the sum of money and the coin in which they were to be paid.

In the 1690s with more settled conditions, the Scottish parliament began to consider ways of developing and supporting the Scots economy. In 1695 a trading company was established (see DARIEN), as was Scotland's first joint-stock bank, Bank of Scotland. The latter was given a monopoly on banking business for a period of 21 years, its shareholders were granted limited liability in their shareholding, and it opened for trade in February 1696 with a working capital of £10,000 sterling (£120,000 Scots). It issued paper money (see BANK-NOTES), made loans, and operated on the exchange systems in Amsterdam and London. It was designed to support trade not government. Loans to government agents were made on the same basis as any other commercial loan. After the *Union of 1707 it supervised the reminting of the Scots silver coinage into sterling denominations.

The generation after 1707 saw Scotland struggling with depression—the immediate impact of monetary union with an economically powerful neighbour. Out of the collapse of the Darien Company a second bank was created in 1727: the Royal Bank of Scotland. Each bank had powerful political supporters and until the 1740s attempted to put the other out of business. After 1745 a modus vivendi was reached as the focus of Scottish trade and development moved from the east to the west coast and the Atlantic trade. In 1746 the two banks were joined by the British Linen Company designed as a linen development corporation for Scotland, but one which in a very short time was actively involved in banking operations.

The gradual recovery of domestic industry and agriculture was overshadowed by the rapid growth of the West India and Virginia trade from Glasgow and the Clyde ports. To support this a number of partnership banks were founded by Glasgow merchants in the 1750s: the Ship Bank in 1749, the Arms Bank in 1750, and the Thistle Bank in 1761. In addition a number of private bankers also emerged in Edinburgh and Glasgow. The competition resulted in a bank war between the old and new banks which only gradually subsided after the 1765 Bank Act. The same period saw banks being established in the major towns of Scotland, usually with six to ten partners and varying in the occupations of their principal customers. The most aggressive of these was the Ayr Bank, founded in 1769, which was backed by two dukes, two earls, and many prominent landowners of the south-west. It aimed to replace the note circulation of all other banks with its own, and therefore provided very widespread credit particularly to landowners. It closed its doors through over-trading in 1772 with liabilities of £1.2 m (£70 m at 2000 figures). A general banking collapse was only just avoided, but most of the shareholders went bankrupt, one of whom, the duke of Buccleuch, was still paying off his portion of the debt from his estates in the 1840s. It is estimated that 40 per cent of land in the south-west changed ownership, as a result, during the next twenty years. The danger to the Scottish economy, banking system, and political structure led directly to a more structured banking system in which Bank of Scotland and Royal Bank of Scotland operating under the guidance of the government became lenders of last resort for the system.   ACa

2. commerce and banking, 1770s onwards

Between the collapse of the Ayr Bank in 1772 and the end of the Napoleonic Wars there were few fundamental changes in Scottish banking. The situation was dominated by the political and social structures created to support the government by Henry, first Viscount Melville and the two Edinburgh banks, Bank of Scotland and the Royal Bank of Scotland. Their influence extended over the rest of the banking system in Glasgow and the other provincial towns. At least part of the reason was the collapse of the trade with the American colonies in the 1780s (see USA), and the reduced importance of the Glasgow partnership banks. The 'Scotch' system showed its worth first in 1793 and then in 1797 when the Bank of England was forced to suspend payment in gold and issue paper money. The first hint of challenge came with the foundation of the Commercial Bank of Scotland in 1810, backed by Whig interests.

After 1815, the system of banking and political control faded rapidly under the pressure of the second phase of industrialization, which was of particular importance in Glasgow and the Clyde towns, but also extended to Aberdeen, Dundee, and many of the smaller inland towns. The decline of agricultural prosperity severely affected the ability of local and private bankers to continue, and during the 1820s and 1830s they gradually gave up business or were merged into the new joint-stock banks which were founded in Glasgow and to a lesser extent in Edinburgh. By 1850 there were eighteen banks, all of which had the right of *banknote issue under the 1845 Bank Act. The collapse of the Western Bank of Scotland in 1857 and more seriously the City of Glasgow Bank in 1878, coupled with an 'agreement' by the Scottish banks to keep out of the English market, led to 100 years of banking conservatism which only began to change in the 1960s. In 1945 there were eight note-issuing banks and the savings banks, which merged during the 1970s to become the Trustee Savings Bank (now Lloyds TSB). A series of amalgamations in the 1950s and 1960s meant that from 1971 there were just three note-issuing banks. The catalyst for change was the advent of North Sea oil, and the 1971 Competition and Credit Act. The Scottish banks met competition and, although smaller, managed to become more efficient than their larger English-based competitors. The year 1999 saw the Royal Bank of Scotland and Bank of Scotland in competition for a hostile takeover of Natwest, a London clearing bank twice the size of either. The winner was the Royal Bank, a result which left its rival, the Bank of Scotland, itself vulnerable to a takeover.

The life insurance business in Scotland began in the 1830s. This and its concomitants of fund management remain a vital part of Scotland's financial business. Standard Life, now the biggest life company in Europe, was founded in 1825, to be closely followed by a number of others such as Scottish Amicable, Scottish Provident, and Scottish Widows. In general insurance General Accident of Perth grew to become the third largest composite insurance company in Britain, with agents in every part of the world.

Natural concomitants of these moves were the development of institutes to train, examine, and certify professional competence. The Scottish Institute of Accountants dates from 1853, the Institute of Bankers from 1875, and Actuaries from 1848 (becoming the Faculty of Actuaries in 1856). The combination of training, experience, and restricted opportunities in Scotland was one reason why the Scottish accountant or banker was a stock figure in every one of the English-speaking colonies or dominions before 1914 (see SCOTTISH LINKS). It was the personal and even family contact that this represented that made overseas investment so easy and certain.

Underneath the bankers and insurance companies there was a layer of organizations dedicated to the investment of savings generated in Scotland which could be more profitably invested overseas. This was of particular importance between 1870 and 1914, when funds were being generated far faster than the local economy could absorb. These organizations varied in scope from a single restricted purpose, for example the settlement of Otago province in *New Zealand or the Scottish Indian Coffee Company (see INDIAN SUBCONTINENT), to general investment companies which attempted to achieve a spread of investment in a wide variety of places and schemes. These were particularly prominent in Aberdeen and Dundee. The most prominent was Robert Fleming's Scottish American Investment Trust (now Robert Fleming PLC), and William J. Menzies Scottish American Investment Company Ltd. So successful were these companies that in 1893 the Texas legislature passed an act forbidding foreigners from acquiring any more land or water rights in the *USA. Throughout the 1920s to 1980s Investment Companies and Fund Managers continued to expand, among them Baillie Gifford and Co., and Ivory and Syme.

In 2001, financial services in all its forms, investment management, insurance, banking, accountancy, and the dependent businesses of law and call centres, probably represent the most significant employment sector in the Scottish economy. Many of the businesses are no longer exclusively Scottish-owned, but Edinburgh with Glasgow is now reckoned to be the fourth financial centre in Europe, and to have developed sufficient critical mass to be self-sustaining in the medium-term future.   ACa

3. the tourist industry

By the late 19th century tourism had become the lifeblood of many Scottish communities, both coastal and inland, just as much as coal or steel dominated others. There were mass resorts such as Rothesay or Portobello; elite professional retreats such as Elie and North Berwick; and decorous spas at Strathpeffer and Moffat. Many were to benefit from this stream of tourists, whether travelling by tram or by train, steamer, bicycle, coach, car and bus, or on foot (see TRANSPORT AND COMMUNICATIONS: 2). The beneficiaries included tradesmen, innkeepers, hoteliers, lodging housekeepers, even crofters. There was a celebrated case in 1914 between Arran crofters and their landlord, who wished to put up their rents on the basis of their summer takings. The growth of tourism in Scotland was of major significance to its economy.

What factors led to the growth of Scotland as a tourist destination? Since the later 18th century, interest in Scotland had been growing, fed by the passion for picturesque scenery. The outbreak of war in 1793 turned attention north to a tour in Scotland rather than the Continent, and persuaded Scots themselves to explore their own country. Thomas Handyside Baxter of Dundee undertook a jaunt to the Highlands in August 1811 and was astonished at Taymouth castle by how much there was to see 'where I always thought there was nothing but poverty and Barrenness'. Sir Walter Scott's *Lady of the Lake* (1810), for example, drew many to the Trossachs. Arguably Scott (see CULTURE: 14) was the single most important promoter of tourism—as one foreign visitor remarked 'truly Scotland is Scott-land'—but there were other cultural contributors: Ossian, Burns, Barrie, and in the 20th century *Braveheart*. Transport changes were important; particularly the coming of the steamships which opened up access to the Western Isles, notably Iona and Staffa. The railways did much to cash in on the holiday trade, running excursions and building large hotels, as at Cruden Bay and Gleneagles. There was the appeal of Scotland as a sporting playground. For the rich, there was grouse shooting and deerstalking; the heaviest traffic on the Highland Railway was always on the eve of the Glorious Twelfth. Others enjoyed the fishing: the German visitor Theodore Fontane in the 1850s remarked on the thousands of English sportsmen coming to the Highlands for a 'fishing campaign'. And by the end of the 19th century no Scottish resort was without its *golf course or bowling green. The cult of Balmoralism (see NATIONAL IDENTITY: 5), playing on the romance of tartan and heather, promoted Scotland and shaped its image. The work of travel agencies such as Thomas Cook's was also significant. Starting in 1846, he was in Scotland two or three times a year with his Tartan Tours for the next twenty years: his signature, along with those in his parties, is regularly to be found in the visitors' books at Abbotsford, which was a key draw for many tourists, particularly North Americans.

Working-class participation also grew. In some places, the appearance of the rowdy day tripper or weekender caused friction. They were less inclined to observe the decorous conventions of single-sex bathing: select resorts had either separate beaches or, as at North Berwick, different times of the day for men. Sabbath-breaking provoked unhappiness and what further aggravated tension was drinking, especially after the passing of the Forbes-MacKenzie Act in 1855 which created the bona fide traveller. Steamboat proprietors were quick to exploit this by running Sunday sailings down the Clyde, denounced by critics as floating shebeens—hence the Glasgow patois of 'steaming' for 'drunk' (see RESPECTABLE CULTURE; ROUGH CULTURE). By contrast,

there were the spas such as Moffat and Strathpeffer, and Hydropathic hotels, usually firmly devoted to *temperance, as at Crieff and Dunblane (but not at Peebles) where respectable society went for rest and a tonic rather than a cure.

The First World War dislocated tourism, though not as severely as the Second when whole areas were out of bounds to visitors, and the beaches covered with defences against invasion. In both wars many large hotels such as Craiglockhart Hydro were requisitioned either for military or medical purposes. But even before the Armistice in 1918, domestic tourism had revived, thanks to the wartime wages of the working classes. Patterns of tourism began to change in the inter-war years. Hoteliers complained that the car enabled people to tour rather than stay any length of time. Motorbus and charabanc tours began to cut into railway profits. The severest effects were to be felt after the Second World War in the late 1960s with the arrival of cheap package airtours to destinations where sun was guaranteed, and some resorts suffered despite the creation of the government-funded Scottish Tourist Board in 1969. The opening of Glasgow Airport in 1991 to direct transatlantic flights also proved a two-edged sword, with increasing numbers of Scots taking holidays in North America. Yet tourism remains a major source of earnings in the Scottish economy, second only to oil.   AJD

Edinburgh: 1. to 1650; 2. 1650–1750; 1750 onwards.

1. to 1650

The castle rock of Edinburgh has been occupied for the better part of some 3,000 years and it seems more than likely that some kind of outline settlement clustered in its shadow well before the first documentary evidence of 1124 × 1127, which refers to a church of the community or burgh of Edinburgh. The new urban parish, of St Giles, was carved out of the larger parish of St Cuthbert, which may date to the 9th century and embraced it like a horseshoe. It seems equally likely that there had been some settlement in the area occupied by the neighbouring burgh of the Canongate, to the east, before the foundation of the abbey of Holyrood in 1128. Edinburgh otherwise provides the most enigmatic early history of all the major Scottish burghs. By 1334, with the loss of Scotland's major port of *Berwick to the English, Edinburgh was on its way to becoming the foremost of what Bruges (see STAPLE PORTS) termed 'the four great towns of Scotland'. In 1329, *Robert I granted it feuferm status, allowing it to collect its own petty customs. In 1364, David II granted a piece of ground to the west of the old tron (weigh beam) for the building of a new one, on the way up to *Edinburgh castle. This was probably close to the West Port, at the head of what is now the Lawnmarket, for it was here that in later royal entries up to and including the reign of *James VI the monarch was greeted with the gift of the keys of the burgh. In 1386, Robert II granted another piece of ground which seems to have been for the building of a tolbooth, which remained until it was replaced by a larger building in 1561. The construction of a wall, halfway down the steep slope between the High Street and the Cowgate, first mentioned in 1330, was probably begun in the reign of James II (see KINGSHIP: 5), although only fragments of it have been found. The spreading of the town over the King's Wall accelerated as the 15th century went on. Following the defeat at Flodden in 1513, invasion scares prompted the beginning of a new wall along the south side. Although it was called the Flodden Wall, it was not completed until 1558.

Edinburgh was built on an eccentric site and access between what were in effect an older upper town and a growing lower town, straddling the line of the Cowgate and Grassmarket, was difficult. In between lay a slope which was in places as steep as 1 in 5. The result was that the main gates lay at either end of the High Street and as late as 1477, all of its fifteen markets were arranged along that street. To the north lay the Nor' Loch, which increasingly became a dumping ground for waste from the burgh's industries. A water supply was difficult the further up the slope from east to west one went. It was no accident that most of the trades which required a plentiful supply of water, such as dyeing, lay to the east end of the town, where wells did not have to be so deep. It was not until the 1670s that a piped water supply, from Comiston Springs, was devised. The stratigraphy of the site also made building difficult. Most houses were of only one or two storeys until the late 16th century. The six-storey tenement in the Lawnmarket known as Gladstone's Land, symbol of a new, wealthy bourgeoisie in the capital, was built in 1600. Yet building on such a scale into the hard volcanic rock was formidably expensive. Thomas Gledstanes lived on the top floor of the building named after him in 1635. He paid £240 a year in rent. On the south side of the Grassmarket, in Edinburgh's poor quarter, where most stables were located and where butchering of animals was carried out until put out to the satellite town of Dalkeith in the 1670s, rent levels were less than £10 (see URBAN SETTLEMENT: 1).

Edinburgh's success and growth rested on two developments: its growing domination of the export trade following the loss of Berwick and its status as a capital from the reign of James III onwards. In the 1320s, Edinburgh enjoyed 21 per cent of the wool trade; by the 1370s it was 32 per cent, by

the 1440s 47 per cent, and over 90 per cent by the 1590s. The 15th century saw it steadily accumulate a greater share of other sectors of overseas trade, including skins and hides. By 1500, it paid 60 per cent of all customs revenue. Its port of Leith became a warehouse for much of Scotland's exports and imports. This was the basis of wealth and influence enjoyed by Edinburgh's merchants, who numbered some 400 by the 1580s. But real wealth was confined to the top quarter who were members of the merchant guildry and traded overseas (see ECONOMY: 2).

In 1474, the skinner craft became an incorporated guild. Over the next 50 years, another thirteen crafts followed suit. The largest and wealthiest were the hammermen, tailors, and bakers; the meanest and poorest the weavers, bonnetmakers, and candlemakers, who were pushed to the edge of the town. The story of the century after 1570 was one of the gradual flight of the poorest to the suburbs, to escape taxation and to effect lower costs of production. It was in Dalry, along the Water of Leith, that a new kind of 'manufactory', often dye works or primitive paper mills, first began to spring up, from 1610 onwards. Within the burgh itself, a craft aristocracy, largely comprised of prestige trades such as tailors, goldsmiths, and surgeons (see MEDICINE AND THE ORIGINS OF THE MEDICAL PROFESSION), was emerging, reflecting the changing demands of what was by now a capital city. Its symbols were Tailors Hall in the Cowgate, built c.1625, and Heriot's Hospital, built by George Heriot, a goldsmith who achieved spectacular wealth as a moneylender; his clients included *James VI and Anne of Denmark.

The original parish church of St Giles was extended over the course of the centuries. In 1387, five new chapels were added in the south nave, probably as a result of damage caused by the English attack on the town of 1385. It is the first traceable example of endowments by individual burgesses or lairds. Further work was undertaken in the mid-15th century but it was after the conferring of collegiate status on St Giles in 1468–9, which gave it an establishment of a provost and fourteen prebendaries, that the most dramatic expansion of the interior took place. By the *Reformation of 1560, more than 40 altars, aisles, and pillars, each dedicated to a different saint, had been founded or rededicated. The layout reflected a society governed by hierarchy and status. The Holy Blood altar, a cult imported from Bruges, belonged to the merchant guild and occupied a prestigious side chapel on the north side. Each of the burgh's fourteen craft guilds had its own altar and chaplain, located in order of seniority, in the nave. Here and in the religious processions which must have wound their way through the town almost every week of the liturgical year, the urban hierarchy was played out in the most visible fashion (see RELIGIOUS LIFE: 2–3).

The effect of the Reformation on St Giles was dramatic. Its complex layout did not suit reformed worship since nowhere within the piecemeal additions of a collegiate church could a pulpit be erected which enjoyed a clear line of sight. The solution was drastic. St Giles was divided into three separate congregations and internal walls built to separate them. The burgh's fourth quarter was sent to worship in the separate Trinity collegiate church, where Waverley Station now stands. John *Knox, Edinburgh's first minister, presumably had to scuttle from one congregation to another to preach. Things became easier only in the late 1570s, when Edinburgh had four ministers rather than one.

The growing population pressures (see POPULATION PATTERNS: 1) forced Edinburgh's ministry to rethink provision. The presbytery commissioned the first Edinburgh census in 1592. It found 8,000 adults, divided almost equally north and south of the High Street. Its solution was eight model parishes, each with its own church. It settled for four and as a result Greyfriars church was begun in 1602 and the Tron church in 1636. A fourth church, for the north-west quarter, depicted on Rothiemay's well-known map of 1647, was never built because of lack of funds. But in 1633, at the insistence of Charles I, St Giles was turned into a cathedral, worthy of a capital city, and the internal walls taken down.

There are also parts of the economy which records seldom reach. Merchants and craftsmen burgesses, who enjoyed the freedom of the burgh, never comprised more than 30 per cent of adult males. The rest were journeymen, day labourers, or apprentices, whose real wage rates were falling amidst the pressure of the 16th and early 17th centuries, which saw sharply rising population, price inflation, and the beginnings of Edinburgh's later disgrace, of chronic overcrowding. Another group often unnoticed were single *women or widows, who probably comprised one household in five. The more fortunate of them, burgess wives and widows, found employment as brewers, where they enjoyed an artificially created monopoly; there were 288 of them in 1530—a brewer for every 40 inhabitants. But the burgh authorities were increasingly nervous of female domestic servants who tried to make a living for themselves by setting up in business, usually selling food or drink. The town council feared masterless women even more than masterless men (see URBAN SOCIETY: 2).

The economy of the burgh was steadily changing, as Edinburgh acquired the attributes of a capital. The centralization of the law courts, begun with the erection of the Court of Session in 1532, brought increasing numbers of suitors and criminals as well as lawyers. The growth of the legal profession was the most spectacular development of the 16th and 17th centuries; by the 1690s lawyers had more accumulated wealth than all the burgh's merchants and craftsmen combined. The more frequent holding of *parliament, General Assembly (see CHURCH INSTITUTIONS: 2–3), and the Convention of *Royal Burghs brought prosperity, tension, and violence to the capital. The *royal court was increasingly in residence at the palace of Holyrood, especially after it was rebuilt in the reigns of *James IV and *James V. Yet it was in the reign of James VI, from 1579 onwards, when the court came to spend most of its time at Holyrood, that the full effects of royal residence came to be felt, although because the palace of Holyroodhouse could not accommodate all the royal household, courtiers, their retinues and many nobles lived in relatively modest dwellings within the burgh proper. Conspicuous consumption, as a result, went hand in hand with a conspicuous culture of violence. Feuding nobles and lairds restaged their disputes in the burgh's streets and gun battles were not uncommon. It should not be thought that burgesses were shrinking violets. An Edinburgh Protestant murder gang cut down the Dominican friar John Black on the same night in 1566 as David Rizzio, servant of *Mary, Queen of Scots, was stabbed at Holyrood by its aristocratic counterparts.

A burgess born in 1550 would have little difficulty navigating his way around his town in 1650. Buildings had expanded upwards in the meantime, in order to accommodate a population which had almost doubled, but the town was still largely contained within its medieval bounds. The most spectacular change was the building of *Parliament House, begun in 1633, at ruinous expense largely borne by the town itself. It was the symbol of a new kind of capital, no longer dependent on a royal court. Its fortunes were by now largely bound up with its alternative role, as the centre of government of a new kind of state, busier and more intrusive than ever before. Most roads by now led to Edinburgh.   ML

2. 1650–1750

The century from 1650 to 1750 was of considerable importance in the development of Edinburgh as the intellectual and professional capital of Scotland, as well as continuing the process of urbanization which confirmed it as unique within the Scottish burgh network. The period saw significant developments in the areas of institutions and professions, although Edinburgh retained an important economic role, despite the rise of *Glasgow.

Edinburgh

Comparison of taxation records from the 1630s and the 1690s reveals a significant change in occupational distribution. By 1694, professionals outnumbered merchants, and Edinburgh was clearly no longer a typical merchant-craft town. There were over 200 legal professionals, from advocates to ordinary lawyers (see LAW AND LAWYERS), together with 24 surgeons and 33 physicians to cater for the legal and medical health of the population (see MEDICINE AND THE ORIGINS OF THE MEDICAL PROFESSION). These professionals generally paid tax at the highest level, indicating a change in the balance of wealth among the population also. Edinburgh boasted a wide range of occupations, from aleseller to executioner, including specialized and ceremonial occupations not found elsewhere. No other burgh boasted a royal trumpeter or Keeper of the Signet. Edinburgh was becoming highly urbanized in terms of the availability of professional services, a broad spectrum of wealth, an even broader spectrum of occupations, and a significant number of middle-range households in terms of all of these parameters. The sex ratio was biased towards females, with around 70 men : 100 women in the central parishes. In the much more rurally configured peripheral parishes the ratio was much closer to parity. The preponderance of *women is explained in part by the large number (over 5,000) of domestic servants. Of the 27 residents in the household of Viscount Tarbet, for example, 23 were servants of various sorts, from wet-nurse to gardener.

Towards the end of the century some of the professional groups were beginning to consolidate and become professionally, economically, and politically important. In 1681, a golden year for the professions, the enthusiastic patronage of the duke of York helped to bring about the establishment of the Royal College of Physicians and also the Advocates' Library. In this year also appeared Stair's *Institutions of the Laws of Scotland*, a milestone in the exposition of Scots law.

Major steps in medical education came in the first quarter of the 18th century, with the foundation of the medical school at the Town's College in 1726, followed by the first infirmary which opened its doors in 1729. This helped to consolidate Edinburgh as a centre of medical excellence, and the rest of the 18th century would confirm the capital as a world leader in that field.

The town was also still a major player in overseas trade, through the port of Leith, and in the 1690s over 20 per cent of the inhabitants were engaged in a variety of manufacturing occupations, although these were by now becoming more concentrated in the peripheral parishes. Some of the items manufactured reflected Edinburgh's status as a wealthy, cosmopolitan, professional town.

The luxury trades of gold- and silver-smithing and wigmaking were flourishing, the latter stimulated by the needs of the growing legal profession as well as by the influence of London fashions. The quaich maker, jeweller, and fencing master would have found it difficult to make a living elsewhere.

Despite intellectual and institutional advances, Edinburgh remained a crowded, dirty, and insanitary place (see URBAN SETTLEMENT: 1). The many-storeyed, ramshackle tenements housed families from all social ranks under the same roof. Classical architecture would be a feature of the New Town, and most of the tenements remained as they had long been, though Gladstone's Land in the Lawnmarket is the best surviving example of a tenement owned by a wealthy merchant and embellished in the early 17th century. Some attempts were made to raise the standard of buildings, supervised by the Dean of Guild and his officials. The slaughter of beasts within the tenements was banned, and legislation to enforce the use of stone was brought in after a particularly devastating fire in 1700. Mylne's Square, built opposite the Tron Church in the 1680s by Robert Mylne, entrepreneur royal mason, and Mylne's Court, in the Lawnmarket dating from 1690, provided more spacious accommodation for those who could afford it. Mylne's Court survives as a hall of residence for students of Edinburgh University.

A new church was built in the Canongate in the 1650s, and Heriot's Hospital was a grand architectural confirmation of the generous charitable bequest to the town from 'Jinglin Geordie' (goldsmith George Heriot), but perhaps the most important construction in the 17th century was the new *Parliament House, finished in 1639, at a cost of £11,600. This was the seat of Scottish government until 1707, and its great hall was of suitably grand dimensions. The century bridging two crucial centuries in Scottish history was important to the development of Edinburgh in its many aspects, and laid the foundations for the New Town and the intellectual fame of the Enlightenment (see CULTURE: 11). HMD

3. 1750 onwards

After 1750, Edinburgh was never likely to become the capital of an independent country; nor could it continue to mark time, as it had for the previous 50 years. It had, instead, to forge itself a new role within Britain, with the particular advantage of retaining two capital city functions—headquarters of the Scottish law and of the Scottish church—which lent it a status much greater than that of just another provincial city. Moreover, the departure of the aristocracy, the politicians, and the placemen to London created a vacuum in the capital's elite which was filled by people with aptitude, but with a social background which in any other society—save, perhaps, that emerging in North America—would have prevented them from reaching such a position of eminence: wigmaker (Allan Ramsay), ploughman (Thomas Ruddiman), shopkeeper (William Smellie), and unemployed (Robert Fergusson)—to say nothing of the law lords, professors, ministers, architects, economists, and historians who comprised so much of the Enlightenment glitterati. It was the Enlightenment (see CULTURE: 11) that lent Edinburgh so much of its international renown in the mid–late 18th century, and formed the foundation of its early 19th role as the Athens-substitute during the Napoleonic Wars.

Its industrial boom of the early 17th century had quite faded, its residual primary industries—save international shipping (primarily Baltic) from Leith—being those needed to feed the church and the law: namely printing (later publishing) and brewing. It never lost its pre-eminence as Scotland's leading intellectual centre, and the percentage of its inhabitants who were professional was rarely less than double its nearest rival. Indeed, in 1828, the total number of lawyers in Edinburgh approximately equalled the combined strengths of all other professions. What was extraordinary was how the professional influence of lawyers and the clergy came to create Edinburgh's most distinctive physical character.

In 1751, a survey disclosed widespread dilapidation within the Old Town, leading to the publication of *Proposals for carrying out certain Works* in 1752. These proposals envisaged some new public buildings and new bridges joining the city, on its ridge, to the lands north and south. The main proposal was to construct an aristocratic suburb on lands to the north, for people 'of a certain rank and fortune only', by which it hoped to attract the aristocrats back from London. It was planned as a suburb, rather than as a replacement for the Old Town, leaving all the city's social and economic functions behind on the High Street. There were to be no shops, no places of entertainment, and no professionals. Probably deliberately, it contained no place of public congregation.

North Bridge began in 1763, and in 1766 a competition for the design of a new town on the far side was won by the architect James Craig. His initial concept of terraced houses laid out in the form of a Union Jack was modified into sensible rectangularity: a grid of streets focused upon two squares, one to the east, the other to the west. Despite the prohibition on places of entertainment, the first building to be completed in the New Town was the Theatre Royal. Within ten years, houses facing Princes Street had become shops. The aristocrats never really returned from London, and the occupiers of the New Town, carefully graded according to status, were generally those of the Scots elite: minor lairds, dowagers, and copious quantities of professional people. Support services were crammed into the narrow Thistle and Rose Streets, and the servants into the lanes behind. The plan was ideal for a socially segregated suburb, but entirely inappropriate to a commercial city; there were no suitable shopping streets, for example—they were either single-sided, or too short, or too wide.

At some point in the very late 18th century, Edinburgh's physical similarity to Athens was noticed, and the artist Hugh 'Grecian' Williams painted it to prove it. The city's role developed thereafter into that of 'Modern Athens'—much to the amusement of Londoners who mocked the pretension. However, it gave the New Town an opportunity to ennoble itself beyond a few streets of decent Craigleith-stone houses (with tenement flats in the cross streets disguised to look like terraced houses). However, since the territory of the New Town was largely built-up, the symbolic monuments needed to mark its elevation to 'a splendid and magnificent city' had to be built around its perimeter: on Calton Hill or upon the earthen Mound that had emerged across the Nor' Loch site to enable Lawnmarket tailors to satisfy their clients across the marsh. Beginning with the erection of a portion of the Temple of Minerva Parthenon upon Calton Hill as an example to others, the New Town's elevation to city status was confirmed by the construction of the Observatory, the *Royal High School, two classic Attic monuments on Calton Hill to Robert Burns and to Dugald Stewart, and the Royal Scottish Academy and the National Gallery of Scotland on the Mound. Spared the drastic surgery implied by some of the more manic plans to open a southward avenue from the Mound by Alexander Nasmyth and others, the Old Town had nevertheless been profoundly altered by the rebuilding of its Renaissance university by Robert Adam, from 1789, and the construction of the bridges which ruptured the wind-enclosed High Street.

It took the Old Town barely 50 years to die. David Hume left Riddle's Court in the Lawnmarket for St David's Street in 1769, and Robert Chambers claimed that the last person of quality to live in the High Street—Governor Fergusson of Pitfour—departed in 1817. For the remainder of the 19th century, those who lived in the Old Town were those who had no choice. Lower professionals, tradesmen, and craftsmen followed the middle classes out to suburbs in repeated waves, and skilled workers constructed themselves five separate colonies of houses on marginal suburban land. When the scandal of the Burke and Hare murders erupted in the West Port, however, Walter Scott returned—in a carriage—to the streets that he had walked as a student, filled with horror and remorse that, had people like him remained in the Old Town, perhaps it might not have sunk so low. It was the Old Town that bore the brunt of the cholera outbreak (see HEALTH, FAMINE, AND DISEASE: 3) in 1832, and in the Cowgate that Dr Thomas Guthrie founded his mission to the poor. As Robert Louis Stevenson observed, if you stood on George IV Bridge and looked down on the miseries teeming in the Cowgate, you would look from one class to another in a twinkling of an eye. That same contrast was observed by Nathaniel Willis as between the Old and New Towns, the latter 'thinly populated and by the well-dressed only'. It was well painted by Nasmyth: a new town of Attic repose contrasted with an old town of romantic savagery.

The cynosure of the first New Town was Charlotte Square, designed at the behest of the Lord Provost by Robert Adam in 1792, one of the most coherent and elegant squares of fashionable terraced houses to be found in the country. A second new town was begun downhill, from 1801, a third round the east of Calton Hill in the 1820s, a fourth from 1821 on the earl of Moray's land designed by James Gillespie Graham, and a fifth to the west, focused upon Melville Street. For almost 70 years, Edinburgh developed neoclassical suburbs, always with minor variations or improvements, but essentially within the classical architectural language (see ARCHITECTS, ARTISTS, AND CRAFTSMEN). Behind the regularity, however, the city was being tamed.

Edinburgh's role as the modern Athens, crowned by the visit of George IV in 1822, ushered in a 19th century where it became one of the principal *tourist destinations of Europe. The Enlightenment had left the capital with a legacy of intellectual achievement and a legacy of clubs, of which perhaps the Aesthetic Club most kept its spirit alive. Edinburgh became the evidential capital of the Scottish professions—the surgeons, the physicians, the lawyers, and after 1840 the architects—each eventually with its own headquarters, library, and museum. It was also reflected in the number of bookshops, and in literary magazines, the most notable being the slightly radical *Edinburgh Review* and the staunchly reactionary *Blackwoods Edinburgh Magazine*. Publishing was to be a particular feature of Edinburgh life, with the works of Robert and William Chambers (largely antiquarian), A & C Black, Nelson's, and eventually Oliver and Boyd. Equally, Edinburgh's growing role as the centre of Scottish banking (see ECONOMY, TERTIARY SECTOR: 2) and thereafter of a burgeoning insurance industry, provided the capital with some of its

most notable architectural monuments as both headquarters and important branches of the Royal Bank, the Bank, the Commercial Bank, and the British Linen Bank adorned city streets.

Edinburgh was becoming douce, class-segregated, and greatly ordered in its proceedings. Its finest memorialist, Henry, Lord Cockburn, felt that by the 1840s, he was living in sublunary days, and enjoyed recollections of an altogether more vivid period 50 years earlier. Princes Street became the most fashionable street of the capital, adorned with handsome Victorian department stores, several of which catered particularly for the needs of the diaspora of Scots building the *Empire. The city capitalized on its 18th-century reputation for boarding schools by adding what contemporaries scornfully derided as 'pauper palaces' out in the suburbs—the grandiose educational establishments of John Watson's, Donaldson's Hospital, Daniel Stewart's, and Fettes College—to supplement the already imposing Royal High School and Edinburgh Academy. Not that it was without excitements—the greatest of which was the *Disruption of the Church of Scotland in 1843, when a procession of almost two-thirds of the General Assembly walked out and marched down to Tanfield to establish the Free Church. by the end of the century, the social highlight of the year was beginning to be the two General Assemblies:—of the Church and of the Free Church of Scotland.

The development of the Leith Docks (a contributory reason for the city's bankruptcy in 1833), and the arrival of both the Union Canal (begun in 1818) and the railways in 1836 brought Edinburgh into the industrial age (see TRANSPORT AND COMMUNICATIONS: 2). Industry, and the tenements of the workers servicing it, clustered into the unbuilt segments of Edinburgh surrounding these new communications—Fountainbridge and Dalry to the West, Leith to the north, and St Leonard's to the southeast.

For the most part, modernization avoided both old and new towns until the epidemics of cholera and typhus and further evidence of structural dilapidation in the Old Town made action unavoidable. Lord Provost William Chambers inaugurated the cleansing of closes, the widening of streets (usually by the demolition of one side), and the creation of two new streets: Cockburn Street (named after Henry), linking the High Street to Waverley Station, and Chambers Street parallel to the High Street to the south. Chambers Street was to become an educational boulevard, with the Industrial Museum built alongside the University in 1861, the James Watt Institute, eventually various other buildings for the University, and finally the *Royal Museum of Scotland in 1998.

In parallel, suburban villa expansion continued to the south (Grange) and west (Merchiston) and to the south-east (Newington) and south-west (Morningside), calling down upon them Robert Louis Stevenson's plea to Edinburgh citizens to rise up and make the night hideous with arson.

Nineteenth-century Edinburgh could be perceived as a professional, minister- and lawyer-dominated tourist trap with literary ambition, its industries and workers safely out of sight, spreading out in even further concentric rings as its core became increasingly rotten. Uniquely, the quality of the New Town meant that it retained its cachet. The first to challenge the pattern was Sir Patrick Geddes (see CULTURE: 18). Geddes, central to the fin-de-siècle revival in art, applied art, crafts, publishing, and architecture, had a vision of the revival of the Old Town through the University. He envisaged the Lawnmarket as a university street comparable to the High in Oxford, repaired ancient buildings with 'conservative surgery' for use by students or by the University, and undertook the construction of flats at Ramsay Garden for occupation by the professoriate. It was the first proposal for the middle or professional classes to move back into the Old Town for over 100 years. Partially successful, Geddes abandoned his proposal half-complete; but he had already used Edinburgh as the primary case study in his pioneering study of cities in evolution.

If Edinburgh seemed as though it had swollen in the 19th century, it exploded between the wars, vast agricultural acreages and their related villages and hamlets being overwhelmed by either bungalow development, or by new council house estates, as the city decanted more of its poor to allow rebuilding at the core. Roadhouses, pubs, garages, suburban super cinemas, shopping parades, and relief churches surged out into the country along all the principal arterial routes (see URBAN SETTLEMENT: 4). They represented a new age of consumerism and—to some extent—democratization, for the emancipated bungalow and car owner no longer sought to emulate the lifestyle and habits of those of the New Town. Edinburgh—particularly Rose Street pubs—was also a focus of the Scottish literary renaissance (see CULTURE: 24), but it seemed inert to the literary nationalists who had congregated instead in Glasgow, and where the Saltire Society first flourished. There being a distinct impression that Edinburgh's glory lay in the past, Lord Bute commissioned Robert Hurd to rescue and restore both Acheson House in the Canongate and Lamb's House in Leith—continuing the pioneering work of Geddes, and presaging the conservation of the city that was to emerge after the Second World War.

The 20th century ended with Edinburgh undergoing rapid change, but it had begun slowly. The post-war years, governed by the 1949 Abercrombie Plan, were characterized by proposals for an outer bypass and inner ring roads. Leith went into decline as a port, and substantial demolition followed. The New Town began to decay until the 1972 establishment of the Edinburgh New Town Conservation Committee, and more population was decanted from the Old Town until it had declined to a near terminal 2,000 in 1959. The High Street was zoned for offices, but sites remained derelict. The arrival of the Edinburgh Festival in 1947 had a rejuvenating impact on the city as a whole, but principally upon the New Town, where it was based. The growth of the Fringe, however, provided a new use for a host of unused or derelict buildings in the Old Town. The University, turning its back on Geddes's vision, sought to create a campus around George Square which it planned to demolish in its entirety and to line the Meadows with a row of high-rise towers. Lawyers prospered, ministers lost their commanding position, and the financial sector filled the gap. The principal physical changes at the centre were the restoration of the Canongate from 1947 under Robert Hurd, and creeping dereliction in former industrial lands, disused railway lands, and along the lines of the proposed inner motorways. There was substantial physical expansion of, principally, council estates to the south and north, and of bungalows to the west.

Over 30 years of relative stagnation—save for the Festival—were ended by a change of council in 1984 and the subsequent release and building of the multiple derelict sites and railway land—coincident with the construction of the bypass some 40 years after it had been first planned. The financial sector rose to being the fourth largest in Europe, rendering much of it liable to takeover from outside Scotland, and great high Victorian banking headquarters were transformed into pubs. Edinburgh began to rebuild itself with sites much larger than the first New Town, but without applying a comparable strategy or quality. Changing commercial practices led many professional and financial sector firms to abandon the New Town for purpose-built premises, some at the West End, and some out by the bypass. Much of the capital's economy has followed in dispersing to the 'edge cities' and the waves of largely indifferent houses that now lap up against it. Without either spotting or being able to control the dispersal of the city's economy, the Council focused instead upon the construction of a new east–west string of monuments comprising a Conference Centre, Festival Theatre, and the Dynamic Earth 'geological experience' ending in the Scottish Parliament Building by the palace of Holyrood. Meanwhile, peripheral housing estates, isolated, largely out of sight, and too far from the centre for their inhabitants to enjoy city centre amenities, earned an awesome reputation for social deprivation, drug abuse, and Aids.

Pioneering restoration of houses in the Old Town began in the 1980s, since when its population has risen by over 500 per cent. There is now little space left to build upon. Edinburgh has thus developed the paradox that, contrary to most other cities in the world, a number of its inhabitants commute outwards to work. The High Street has been rejuvenated as a commercial thoroughfare, and both Festival and Fringe have moved their headquarters there. The arrival of the Scottish *parliament in the Canongate will not only complete the resurrection of the Old Town as the heart of the capital, but return to it some of the sense of purpose that it lost in 1707.   CAMcK

Edinburgh castle. The volcanic rock on which Edinburgh castle stands has been occupied by man since at least the Bronze Age. There is an early, enigmatic reference to it in a poem of AD c.600, when it was occupied as the northernmost stronghold of the Gododdin whose power extended from the Tees to the Forth. Its first fully documented use as a royal castle belongs to the reign of Malcolm III 'Canmore' (Mael Coluim mac Donnchada) (1057–93). It has been argued that the oldest surviving building on the Castle Rock, the so-called St Margaret's chapel, probably belongs to the reign of *David I (1124–53), son of Malcolm and St *Margaret. So much has been dismantled, destroyed, or reconstructed that little of any substance survives from before the reign of *James IV (1488–1513), in whose reign the Great Hall was probably completed. The remnants of an earlier set of royal apartments, an L-shaped block known as David's Tower and dating from the reign of David II (1329–71), now lie entombed within the massive Half Moon Battery, constructed after the siege of 1573. By James IV's reign, the castle was an artillery park as well as a royal residence, housing the crown's impressive collection of bombards such as Mons Meg and other guns. Although there seems to have been an intention to construct a palace precinct within the castle, as at *Stirling, the increasing use of the more comfortable palace of Holyroodhouse, just 1 mile (1.6 km) away, gave different roles to the castle, which became a repository for the national archives, a residence for officers of state, and a prison as well as a fortress and arsenal.

Despite its formidable appearance, the castle has been far from being an invulnerable fortress and much of its history has been taken up with ineffectual attempts to make it so. It surrendered to Edward I of England after a three-day siege in 1296 (see INDEPENDENCE, WARS OF), fell to a surprise attack by Thomas Randolph, nephew of *Robert I in 1314, and the supporters of *Mary, Queen of Scots surrendered after a four-day bombardment from English guns lent to the king's party in 1573. The extensive fortifications built after 1573, including an extensive Spur encompassing most of the present-day Esplanade, gave the castle a better defence against artillery; sieges during the Wars of the *Covenant in 1640 and by Cromwell in 1650 lasted much longer. From that point onwards, the stronghold changed its function from a fortress to a military barracks and, on occasion, a prisoner-of-war camp, as in the *Jacobite rising of 1745–6, the Seven Years War (1757–63), the American War of Independence, and the Napoleonic Wars.

The 19th century brought new roles and a novel status for the castle. For centuries, it has alternately defended and threatened the burgh of *Edinburgh, laid out to its east along the crag and tail of the volcanic outcrop. The building of a New Town and the draining of the foul-smelling Nor' Loch which separated it from the Castle Rock gave the castle a new, iconic status, worthy of the 'Athens of the North'. The rediscovery in 1818 of the Honours of Scotland allowed Sir Walter Scott to make them one of the centrepieces of the ceremonial visit to Edinburgh of George IV in 1822. Mons Meg, the Burgundian mortar given as a wedding present to James II, which had been taken to the Tower of London in 1754, was returned in 1829, after prolonged lobbying by Sir Walter Scott and the Society of Antiquaries. St Margaret's chapel was rescued from its role as an artillery magazine in 1845; the rediscovery—or invention—of a shrine to Scotland's only royal saint, even if it could never have been one at which she worshipped, was a significant moment in the re-creation of Scotland in the Victorian age (see NATIONAL IDENTITY: 5). The construction of a massive Scottish National War Memorial, begun in 1924 at the highest point on the Rock, was a further moment of real symbolic importance, recognizing the disproportionate contribution that Scots had made in the First World War. Its very name underlined a *national identity that was both British and Scottish, unionist and nationalist at one and the same time. The return of the Stone of *Scone, a Dark Age inauguration stone, 700 years after it was pillaged by Edward I in 1296, reflected a last attempt by the Conservative Party (see UNIONISM) in the 20th century to pose as 'tartan Tories' and to recover that dual identity. After a flurry of 'consultation', it was placed, somewhat incongruously, next to the 16th-century regalia housed in the castle; it was the first meeting in history of two very different sets of symbols of Scottish identity. However bizarre the rendezvous, it seemed appropriate that the venue should be Edinburgh castle, itself another symbol of Scotland, home of the *Edinburgh Military Tattoo, the photogenic subject of countless millions of postcards and tins of shortbread, and the most popular tourist destination in Scotland. ML

Edinburgh, civic monuments. As befits a capital city, Edinburgh is well provided with civic monuments. Given the fourteen sieges it had to endure, the Old Town begins naturally with its once vividly harled castle, the *castellum puellarum*, high on its volcanic rock at the west end of the High Street (see EDINBURGH CASTLE). Apart from the 12th-century St Margaret's chapel, its principal buildings surround the upper or Crown Square, comprising the late 15th-century Great Hall, the largely 16th-century palace reworked in 1617 by the royal architect Sir James Murray of Kilbaberton, and Sir Robert Lorimer's Scottish National War Memorial of 1924. The city's church, St Giles', at the centre of the Market Place, was begun by the early 12th century and was richly endowed with civic and craft altars. Its magnificent 1500 crown spire is a key feature of the Edinburgh skyline, but the rest of its exterior was neutered by William Burn in 1829. It has an atmospheric interior with excellent tombs and the outstanding 1910 Thistle chapel by Lorimer. The re-created Mercat Cross stands alongside. Immediately to its south is the 1632-9 *Parliament House of Scotland, also by Murray, cruelly refaced in Adam-classical by Robert Reid from 1807, but retaining within its glorious timber roof built by John Scott, with its gilded knops. Opposite is the 1752 Royal Exchange (now city chambers), designed by John and Robert Adam as a trading floor for the capital's merchants; they rejected it and preferred trading in the open in the High Street. It takes the European form of a U-plan hotel with a screen wall to the street and the principal rooms upon the first floor. Just downhill is the 1647 Tron church by John Mylne, the second new parish church to be built in the capital. Although gutted, foreshortened when South Bridge was driven through, and capped by a later 1824 tower after its earlier one had burnt off, it remains impressive with its splendid oak roof, and, in its details, is reminiscent of the contemporary palace at Heidelberg. The stately University, facing North Bridge, was begun by Robert Adam in 1789 to replace the double-courtyard Renaissance university, and was completed by William Playfair from 1819, whose Upper Library is the finest neoclassical space in Scotland. In the eastern suburbs, where the Canongate used to be, lie the Canongate

Tolbooth, 1591, and Holyroodhouse, which became the premier royal palace in Scotland in the early 16th century. Developed from the cloisters of the abbey of Holyrood, the tall, north-western tower was constructed in 1529, and the remainder fashionably reformatted in homage by Sir William Bruce in 1672 to produce an enormous, classically correct hôtel on a regal scale. On the lands to the south lie the Royal Museum, begun by Captain Francis Fowke as the Industrial Museum in 1861, and its adjacent competition-winning *Royal Museum of Scotland by Benson and Forsyth, completed 1998. Nearby, on George IV Bridge, are the National Library of Scotland, a blind stone box with sculpture by Hew Lorimer designed in 1934 by Reginald Fairlie, but not completed for another 20 years, and, facing it, the vigorously French Central Library, designed in 1887-90 by George Washington Browne in very attractive florid clothing. To the west lies the Greyfriars' church, begun 1602 and probably incorporating earlier work and the adjacent George Heriot's Hospital, a quadrangular charity school with ogee-roofed stairtowers in the advanced Danish mode of the time, begun by William Wallace in 1628, and completed by William Aytoun probably under the guidance of the royal architect Sir James Murray of Kilbaberton.

Civic monuments in the New Town lie around its periphery, since they were mostly added after the first New Town was completed. The sophisticated Register House, facing North Bridge, was designed by Robert Adam in 1774 to house the nation's records, its top-lit domed rotunda displaying the influence of Adam's four years in Italy. In 1787, the Assembly Rooms was built by John Henderson as an austere cube, later extended to each side, given a pedimented portico, and then a huge Music Hall with a coffered ceiling added to the rear, 1843, by David Bryce. Of the many churches in the New Town, the most striking are the elliptical, steepled St Andrew's church, George Street, 1782, by Major Andrew Frazer; St George's West (now West Register House), a stodgy, domed Adam imitation, 1814, by Robert Reid, which closes the western vista down George Street, and is now gutted within; and 1828 St Stephen's church, a stupendous triangular church by William Playfair facing up Howe Street, cleverly using the sloping site to enter at gallery level.

The two great temples on the Mound—the Royal Scottish Academy and the National Gallery of Scotland—are the principal contributors to Edinburgh's 19th-century status as the 'Athens of the North'. Designed by William Playfair in 1822 (extended 1831) and 1854 respectively, the former betrays its original use as a government building by powerful Doric porticos and colonnades, whereas the latter confirms its artistic pretensions by delicate Ionic porticos, and an enfilade of red-clad toplit octagons behind blank ionic pilastered walls. Standing nearby, in total contrast, is the Scott Monument, a spacecraft composed of openwork stone details from Melrose abbey, completed in 1846 to designs by the antiquarian architect/carpenter George Meikle Kemp. The Melville Monument—the 135 feet (41 m) high glorification of Henry Dundas, Viscount Melville, designed by William Burn in 1823—is a suitable antidote.

The neoclassical Valhalla of Calton Hill, however, is the focus: the twelve columns of the National Monument designed in 1817 by Charles Cockerell with the young William Playfair, and Playfair's adjacent Observatory, 1818, based upon the tower of the winds; two superb circular cenotaphs—one to Dugald Stewart, 1831, by Playfair, the other to Robert Burns, 1830, by Thomas Hamilton—and, most dignified of all, Hamilton's 1829 *Royal High School. Nearby, lining the edge of Calton Hill is St Andrew's House, headquarters of the *Scottish Office designed in 1934 by Thomas Tait. To the north lie two prominent, classical 'pauper palaces' converted into civic buildings: the Scottish National Gallery of Modern Art, designed as John Watson's School in 1825, and, across Belford Road, its Annexe, designed in 1833 by Thomas Hamilton as the Orphan Institution.

The late 19th century added monumental buildings, predominantly on the west and south, including the McEwan Hall, and adjacent Medical School, both designed by Sir Robert Rowand Anderson in confidently florid Italian in 1888. In 1910, the floridly baroque concert hall, Usher Hall in Lothian Road, was designed by Stockdale Harrison. On Blackford Hill, to the south, the powerful Royal Observatory, with its twin metal cylinders sitting on florid red stone plinths, was designed in 1892 by W. W. Robertson.

Late 20th-century civic monuments—apart from the plethora of sophisticated swimming pools/leisure centres in the suburbs—have been the Royal Commonwealth Pool, 1967, designed by Robert Matthew, Johnson Marshall & Partners, a composition of austere, glistening horizontal planes offset against Arthur's Seat; the Conference Centre, an unsubtle and overscaled rotunda designed by the Terry Farrell Partnership in 1994; the curved glazed Festival Theatre, reusing an old cinema auditorium, 1993, by the Law and Dunbar Nasmith Partnership; and Dynamic Earth, designed by Michael Hopkins, and opened in 1999, of which all you can see is the fabric canopy, retaining walls and amphitheatre, the remainder being a wholly enclosed 'experience' within. More than a year after the formal opening of the Scottish *parliament in July 1999, the precise form, designers, and cost of the building remain uncertain.   CAMcK

Edinburgh Military Tattoo. Staged annually on the spectacular setting of the Esplanade, or old parade ground, of *Edinburgh castle, the Tattoo is one of the popular events of Edinburgh International Festival. The colourful displays are built around the simple military ceremony of 'Tattoo' or 'Taptoo', beaten out by the drummers as a signal for the ale taps to be turned off and for the roll to be called prior to the setting of the watch and lights out.

The first Festival Tattoo was performed on the Esplanade in 1948. There was no fixed seating and the early performances, which also took place in Princes Street Gardens, were lit by car headlights and wartime searchlights. The first performers were the 7th Hussars, the 1st Battalion the Royal Scots, and 1st Battalion the Queen's Own Cameron Highlanders. The programme was simple but effective: military band music, a trumpet fanfare, pipes and drums (see MUSIC, HIGHLAND), a thirtytwosome reel, an 'automatic' drill display, and Highland dancing, followed by the sunset ceremony. Although nearly all of the soldiers were still in khaki, the performances were an instant success, particularly with overseas visitors.

By Coronation Year, 1953, the seal was set on the success story: 27 performances, tri-service participation, an international cast, and a worldwide reputation. The seating was still, however, makeshift, and a lively trade was carried on hiring cushions for the hard benches. The performances have always been held in the open air and, notwithstanding the rigours of a Scottish summer, no performance has ever been cancelled. The introduction of television coverage served only to enhance the reputation of Edinburgh Military Tattoo, and now thousands of videos and recordings are sold each year.

Overseas performers come from many countries including Norway, Italy, the Netherlands, Germany, Oman, the USA, and the Commonwealth. To organize such an event, on an arena that slopes 14 feet (4.3 m) from top to bottom, requires considerable skill, and the Production Team has included Alasdair Maclean, the first producer, Jack Sanderson, Sandy Storm, Leslie Dow, David Murray, and Michael Parker. The performers have to work hard and are frequently wet and often tired, but there can be no greater thrill on a clear cool Edinburgh evening than to see the massed Pipes and Drums spill from the Castle Gate on to the historic Esplanade, playing some of the most evocative music man has yet devised.   DMH

elites in modern Scotland. In the 19th century, the landowning class, and more particularly the aristocratic portion, operated as a Scottish elite both on the British stage and within Scotland itself. They were well represented in parliament. By the 19th century the great majority of Scottish peers sat in the Lords. The bestowal of post-1707 (see UNION OF 1707) British peerage titles bypassed the restriction imposed in the Treaty of Union that only sixteen of their number be chosen to go to Westminster. Thus the duke of Atholl also bore the British title Lord Strange. Even after the 1832 Reform Act, landowners found Commons' seats with little difficulty, mostly winning them through deference rather than outright corruption and bribery. Scottish peers often held ministerial office in the 19th century—indeed Lords Aberdeen and Rosebery were prime ministers—and in the absence of a Scottish minister before 1885, accordingly were very significant. By contrast, virtually no Scot who was not a landowner held a government post before the 1900s. It is noteworthy that in the first twenty years of the *Scottish Office, five of the seven *Scottish Secretaries were peers, one other being a mere baronet.

The aristocracy (see NOBILITY: 4) also integrated Scotland into the British state by holding top positions in symbolic areas which were a source of pride to many Scots (see BRITISH EMPIRE). The contribution of Scottish regiments (see ARMY: 4) of the British army was a prominent factor shaping a sense of the importance of Scotland within the Union in this period. The very names of many regiments emphasized aristocratic involvement; for example, the Gordon and Seaforth Highlanders. Moreover, the officer class was overwhelmingly drawn from the upper landed class, Lord Panmure's exploits in India during the Mutiny and General Gordon at Khartoum being outstanding instances. Scottish peers also played prominent roles as imperial governors and viceroys—Lords Elgin and Aberdeen in *Canada, Linlithgow in *Australia, and Minto in India (see INDIAN SUBCONTINENT).

Within Scotland, landowners were appointed to many public bodies, notably government boards of supervision: Lord Polwarth presided over the Prison Board for nigh on twenty years. They routinely held honorific positions in national charitable and voluntary associations; for example, occupying the top rungs of the Masonic movement. Again, one of their number was usually the monarch's representative at the General Assembly of the Church of Scotland.

On the whole before about 1900 the business elite was less prominent at national level. Businessmen's influence was stronger within local communities, where they dominated *urban society. They ran municipal government: the lord provosts of the main cities were invariably drawn from their ranks. They also took a leading role in the myriad voluntary societies which catered for the social, cultural, and religious needs of the towns (see RESPECTABLE CULTURE). The prevailing influence of the Coates and Clark families in Paisley is a good example of this. Some of the business elite entered parliament, reflecting the esteem they enjoyed in their locality. However, they rarely made much impact at Westminster: most were well into middle age before being elected, and few were effective debaters.

From the turn of the century, and accelerating after the First World War, the profile of the elite shifted dramatically. The position of the landowning class became less secure. Under mounting financial pressure, many sold off all or part of their estates, so weakening rural deference, and moved away—one marquess of Breadalbane ended up in a Brighton bedsit. Salvation, economic and social, for the landowning order was more and more sought through closer identification with the business elite, who were themselves in the later 19th century increasingly buying rural estates; for example, Sir Charles *Tennant of the great Glasgow chemical concern bought a large estate in Peeblesshire. Marriages between landed and business families, previously infrequent, became commonplace. This process was reinforced by the emergence of a complex set of interlocking multiple directorates which embraced the major business families in Scotland, plus a smattering of landowners. Thus in 1937–8, 23 per cent of the directors of the biggest Scottish companies held 45 per cent of the directorships; 14 per cent of these multiple directors were titled, with Lord Elphinstone holding seats on sixteen boards.

The changing nature of this elite can be gauged politically: Scottish secretaries appointed since 1922 by the Tories and their coalition allies did include several representatives of the traditional landowning class (Lord Novar, Sir John Gilmour, James Stuart, Gordon Campbell), but increasingly the businessman-cum-landowner element prevailed (Colville, MacLay, Noble, Younger).

The influence of landowners in local government dwindled, too—partly because their numbers were thinned by economic factors. But the local government reforms of 1929 and 1973 meant the advent of the 'professional' councillor and a shift in power to council officials, so doubly challenging the old deferential pattern.

It is possible that within professions, elites successfully perpetuated their position, most especially in law (see LAW AND LAWYERS: 2), where a considerable number of judges and leading advocates continued to come from the same families across the generations; for example, Hope, Clyde, Cameron. But local urban business elites were systematically eroded as the 20th century progressed.

227

Economic influence dwindled steadily. The problems of traditional industries broke many firms (see ECONOMY, SECONDARY SECTOR: 2), others were taken over by larger British-wide concerns, and nationalization after 1945 destroyed many local elites. The new post-1945 private-sector employers tended increasingly to be multinational enterprises, whose managers usually stayed on a short-term basis in Scotland and rarely developed any involvement with the surviving local business elite. The power in urban local government of the business class effectively ended in the 1930s and 1940s, as Labour (see LABOURISM) finally mobilized working-class electors in order to seize power in the municipal chambers. The rise of state welfare provision removed the role of the civic elite as sponsors of charitable projects. The National Health Service, for example, took hospital funding out of the local fund-raisers and placed it on a secure, centrally determined footing. The professionalization of social work similarly reduced the scope for voluntary work with the deprived. Appointments to new national quangos and new local bodies like health boards operated on different criteria, such as professional interest and political balance, rather than social standing. IGCH

Elliot, Walter (1888–1958), progressive Conservative politician and innovative Scottish Secretary of State. He was born into a minor Lanarkshire landowning family. Educated at Glasgow Academy and Glasgow University, he qualified in medicine. An active member of the student political community, Elliot immediately entered politics after war service, where he won the Military Cross. He sat in parliament more or less continuously from 1918 until his death.

Elliot's ministerial career between the wars was very successful. After holding junior Scottish Office posts in the 1920s, he was Minister for Agriculture, 1931–6; Scottish Secretary, 1936–8; and Minister for Health, 1938–40. In the 1930s he was frequently tipped as a future prime minister. But his identification with the policy of appeasement meant that Churchill systematically refused to offer him a job. From 1940 until his death he remained on the backbenches.

Elliot was an immensely articulate, highly progressive Tory. He consistently advocated active state interventionism in the spheres of both economic and social policy. At agriculture, he initiated a state-directed policy of price-fixing and production quotas to rescue farming from the acute depression of the early 1930s. At the *Scottish Office, his drive to tackle the social deprivation of the country was impressive. As a junior minister he pioneered the distribution of free milk in city

schools. When Scottish Secretary, he grew impatient with the tardiness of local authorities in building houses (see HOUSING: 3), and set up the Scottish Special Housing Association, both to stimulate action in areas of greatest need and to encourage experimentation in construction and design. He stressed to the Treasury and Whitehall the urgent need for greater state activity to counter Scotland's economic and social problems.

Elliot was the most forward-looking and imaginative 20th-century Conservative Scottish minister. He came from outside the party's two traditional recruitment areas, being neither a landed grandee nor a businessman. His medical background may have spurred him to radical thinking about solving social problems. IGCH

emigration: 1. to Europe, to 1750; 2. to Ireland, to 1750; 3. from the Highlands and Islands, post-1750; 4. post-1750 (excluding the Highlands).

1. to Europe, to 1750

Education, trade, and warfare encouraged Scottish travel abroad; population pressure on limited land resources and crop failures (notably 1622–3 and the 1690s), famine, and dearth also encouraged emigration. *France, the *Low Countries, the Baltic (see GERMANY, THE BALTIC, AND POLAND: 1), and *Scandinavia were already prime destinations by 1600.

The rise in economic importance of Holland and Zeeland led to the establishment of Veere as the Scottish *staple port in the Netherlands in 1540. A Scottish community quickly grew up around this staple. A resident Scottish factor, known as the Conservator of Scottish Privileges, was appointed to oversee Scottish activities. During the late 17th century Rotterdam replaced Veere as the centre for Scottish activities in the Low Countries. The United Provinces proved attractive to Scottish settlement not only because of long-established trade, but also because of similar legal systems (see LAW AND LAWYERS: 1) and the profession of Calvinism. Some Scots and their families set up as 'hoteliers' in the larger Dutch and French towns where they provided lodging for fellow Scottish merchants and travellers.

Recruitment also played a factor in Scottish emigration. The Eighty Years War (1568–1648) in the Netherlands, the Thirty Years War (1618–48), and the War of the Spanish Succession (1701–13) attracted large numbers of Scots (see MERCENARIES IN EUROPE). Recruits for the Low Countries came mainly from the Lowlands around the Forth and arrived at ports in South Holland and Zeeland. Subsequently some Scottish troops settled, took up trade as weavers, tailors, or mariners, and married Dutch women. Dutch widows of Scottish soldiers sometimes requested commissions for their half-Scottish sons from the States General. The Scots were already well established in Poland but the 17th and early 18th centuries also witnessed a steady increase in Scottish settlement in *Russia. Scots in Russian military service are noticeable from the time of the War for Smolensk (1632–4) and rose to prominence under Peter 'the Great' (1689–1725). General Patrick Gordon of Auchintoul (1635–99) is among the better-known Scots resident in Russia at this period. Relations with the native populations were, overall, quite friendly, and most Scots were absorbed over two or three generations.

For a time the Church of Scotland played an important role in maintaining the identity of Scottish communities abroad. The Scots were permitted a Scots preacher at Gdansk in 1577. The Scots church at Veere was regularly provided with ministers from Scotland. In 1647 the moderator of the General Assembly addressed a letter to all Scottish communities resident in Germany and Poland (see GERMANY, THE BALTIC, AND POLAND: 2) asking them not to neglect the Presbyterian confession of faith. In 1668 the elector of Brandenburg permitted the Scots of Königsberg to worship publicly and privately after their own form of religion. In the 1690s contributions were still being sent to the Scottish community at Königsberg to allow them to build a church. However, the union of the English and Scottish congregations in 1707, and the decline of immigration, led eventually to their being absorbed into the German population. Similarly, the kirk session of Veere noted in 1718 that children in the Scottish community were being lost to Dutch-speaking schools.

Many Scots went abroad to study, became teachers, and stayed in their host countries. Between 1582 and 1642 the names of 79 Scots appear in the Album of the University of Leiden. Some Scots were well known: Walter Donaldson (c.1570–1630) became principal of the Academy at Sedan while Arthur Johnston (c.1587–1641), who taught at Heidelberg, Sedan, and La Rochelle, was a noted Latin poet contributing to literature on the Thirty Years War. The influential evangelist John Durie (1596–1680) also travelled around Europe preaching the cause of Protestant unity. Scottish Catholic exiles attended the *Scots colleges at Douai (after 1600), Madrid (from 1613), Paris (after 1569), and Rome (from 1600). Some returned to preach in Scotland but many others stayed as students, teachers, and benefice-holders in France, Germany, the Low Countries, and Spain (see MEDITERRANEAN LANDS IN THE MIDDLE AGES).   DH

2. to Ireland, to 1750

Migration between Scotland and *Ireland predates history, maritime civilization making Ulster and Scotland probably closer neighbours than Ulster and Munster. Whether or not St Patrick's unknown Romanized birthplace was in our Scotland, his *Confessio* graphically depicts the life of the many slaves kidnapped by Irish pirates from north as well as south Britain. His later missionary career (5th century) also symbolizes saintly traffic, building up after Ulster's St *Columba established *Iona as missionary centre (6th century) whence students, scholars, and other agents came to Ireland temporarily and sometimes permanently. Irish conquerors of Pictland (see PICTS) would also have despatched agents homeward to consolidate kinship links, trading, and warrior recruitment.

Norman penetration of Ireland brought land grants to descendants of Fergus, lord of *Galloway, Duncan FitzGilbert of Carrick receiving the Antrim Glens from King John of England for sending him the wife and son of the rebellious William de Braose (John starved them to death in Windsor castle), while Alan of Galloway and his brother Thomas of Atholl (cousins of John via Fergus's marriage to a bastard of Henry I) gained coastlands from the Glens to Lough Foyle for mercenary services. Thomas's castle at Coleraine was destroyed in 1223 by de Braose's ally de Lacy aided by King Aed O'Neill of Tír Eoghan, and his son Patrick's murder in 1242 at Haddington was ascribed to their cousin John Bisset who fled to Ulster. Such judicious migration was followed from about 1275 to 1425 by the regular practice of Scots mercenary enlistment in Irish service (see MERCENARIES IN IRELAND), becoming known as *gallóglaigh* (gallowglasses) and initially deriving from the Hebrides after Norse power had been broken at Largs. O'Donnell of Tír Conaill rewarded the MacSweenys with land in the Rosses, at Creeslough, Fanad, and Slieve League. O'Neill established the MacDonnells as a formidable fighting force at Ballygawley, notably against O'Donnell. The invasion by Edward Bruce (1315–18) (see KINGSHIP: 4) brought Ulster further mercenary settlers, for example MacRorys, and others then or later, including Mac-Cabes, Macdougalls, MacSheehys, and MacQuillans. Fifteenth-century absorption of the Isles under royal control brought extensive MacDonnell settlement in the Glens of Antrim, partly through a marriage in 1399 to Margery Bisset, and in English and Irish eyes these MacDonnells seem to have preserved a Scottish identity much more than their precursors now established in west and central Ulster.

England's Nine Years' War against O'Neill and O'Donnell (1594–1603) ended just after *James VI's accession to England's throne, whence plantation then was directed to populate Ulster under the most drastic such scheme in Irish history. Massive populations embracing all ranks were settled, 8,000 Scots by 1625, 10,000 by 1640. Lanark, Renfrew, and Stirling shires, and the *Borders were heavily depleted, many in evicted tenants, many from families bereft by forest clearance, most being radical Calvinists. The indigenous Catholic insurgents of 1641 were initially less Scotophobe than Anglophobe but many Scots were among those massacred when the Scottish parliament landed 2,500 troops under Robert Monro in aid of their endangered emigrants (1642): they promoted the Solemn League and Covenant, captured Belfast, but were defeated by the Catholic (and Spanish) general Owen Roe O'Neill at Benburb (1646), thus eliminating a Scottish stake in the Cromwellian solution to Ireland (1649) (see COVENANT, WARS OF THE). Scots Covenanting Presbyterian refugees from the restored Stuarts (1679–88) made a small but influential addition to Ulster Protestantism (see COVENANTERS). ODE

3. from the Highlands and Islands, post-1750

Having first attracted sustained public and government attention in the second half of the 18th century, Highland emigration has since then consistently generated more documentation, debate, and denunciation than any other aspect of the Scottish emigrant experience. Pejorative images of *Clearances and involuntary exile have impeded dispassionate analysis of a phenomenon which has been integral to the region's demographic history (see POPULATION PATTERNS: 2) for more than two centuries, and commentators' preoccupation with expulsive influences has stimulated a persistently negative historiography of a Highland diaspora which has often owed as much to persuasion as persecution.

Eighteenth-century Highland emigrants were simultaneously driven away by economic, social, and demographic dislocation resulting from rising rents and agricultural restructuring (see ECONOMY OF HIGHLANDS AND ISLANDS: 2), and enticed across the Atlantic by the offer of abundant freehold land, the ready availability of passages and money to pay for them, and the assurances of earlier emigrants and agents that conditions and prospects in North America were the opposite of those which were creating hardship, disgruntlement, and apprehension at home. Chain migration and the liberal land policies of Scots-born governor Gabriel Johnston ensured that North Carolina (see USA) became a favourite resort of Highland emigrants for almost half a century before the American Revolution, the resort of agricultural entrepreneurs and exiled *Jacobites alike. When after 1746 Highland militarism was harnessed to the ends of the *British Empire, military service became the harbinger of

emigration, through the allocation of colonial land grants, primarily in the northern colonies, to veterans of Highland regiments (see ARMY: 4) who had served in two American wars. Tacksmen, whose status had been particularly adversely affected by the erosion of traditional clanship (see CLANS OF THE HIGHLANDS AND ISLANDS: 2), were prominent officer-colonizers, dispensing information about colonial opportunities and often recruiting fellow-clansmen in order to establish prefabricated transatlantic Highland communities unchallenged by government and commercially minded chieftains.

The community-based penchant for emigration which in the 1770s saw entire Highland neighbourhoods embark on single ships, sometimes with significant amounts of specie, aroused the alarm of landlords (see LANDOWNERSHIP IN THE HIGHLANDS AND ISLANDS) and government, as well as the curiosity of travellers like James Boswell. Legislative attempts to stem a haemorrhage which was perceived by mercantilists as economically and militarily damaging were largely ineffective, and most of the 27,000 Scots estimated to have emigrated between 1763 and 1815 were probably Highlanders. Although after 1783 the British government, recognizing the vulnerability of its redefined American frontier, began to endorse proprietary soldier settlement in strategic parts of *Canada, emigration remained anathema to the Highland hierarchy until the early 19th century, and the ill-conceived Passenger Act of 1803, masquerading as a piece of humanitarian legislation, was passed at the behest of the vociferous Highland Society lobby, which aimed to impede emigration by making it prohibitively expensive.

The landlord-driven emigration which epitomized the demographic history of the 19th-century Highlands and signified such a complete reversal of earlier attitudes was primarily the result of long-term economic downturn in the region, reinforced by professional agency activity and well-publicized overseas opportunities. After landlord solidarity had been eroded by Lord Selkirk's persuasive writings and colonization schemes, the impact of post-war recession and recurring subsistence crises after 1815 finally transformed their mercantilist antagonism against the expatriation of the cream of the Highland population into an active Malthusian approbation of emigration as a safety valve; this, they anticipated, would relieve them of the redundant and expensive demographic legacy of their flawed estate development plans. As systematic census-taking alerted proprietors to chronic—and increasing—congestion, poverty, and land-hunger, they began to encourage and even subsidize emigration, often replacing people with sheep and later deer, the only profitable commodities in the Highlands' marginal economy. While proprietorial attempts to secure state assistance in implementing emigration schemes procured several government investigations, little tangible assistance was forthcoming in a climate of laissez-faire economics (see HIGHLANDS AND ISLANDS AND CENTRAL GOVERNMENT: 4), which discouraged official involvement on the grounds of both expense and expediency. Despite the unambiguous assertion of the 1841 Select Committee that extensive state-aided emigration was an essential preliminary to effective relief measures for the Highlands in the aftermath of the 1830s famine, it was only following the more devastating famine a decade later that the government responded, and even then the Emigration Advances Act of 1851 simply allowed landlords to borrow public money to assist tenants who wished to emigrate.

In the absence of state funding, impecunious Highlanders were assisted to emigrate by a variety of organizations and individuals. In 1837 the extension to Scotland of a scheme which used money from Australian land sales to assist the passages of eligible emigrants came at a fortuitous time for the famine-stricken west Highlands, and by 1840 about 5,200 Scots, mainly Highlanders, had gone to New South Wales (see AUSTRALIA) under the bounty programme. Although the selecting agents' emphasis on elite recruitment provoked some conflict with destitution relief committees, the scheme was administered flexibly, regulations often being relaxed to permit elderly or unemployable relatives to accompany eligible emigrants on specially chartered ships, and Highland emigration continued to be based on the extended family and community. Australia re-emerged between 1852 and 1858, when the short-lived Highland and Island Emigration Society—constituted in the wake of the famine to give loans to landlords and tenants—expedited the relocation of almost 5,000 'surplus' Highlanders in New South Wales. Throughout the 19th century, however, Canada remained the preferred destination of Highland emigrants, including several thousand whose transatlantic passages were funded by landlords who had become convinced that emigration was the only alternative to tenant congestion and starvation, as well as proprietorial bankruptcy. The *Scotsman* of 25 August 1849 claimed that the previous decade had seen 20,000 Highlanders emigrate to Canada, a tally which increased in the early 1850s, as Outer Hebridean proprietors especially responded to persistent famine with intensified emigration programmes.

Although changing perceptions of clearance and emigration by both landlords and tenants means that the precise relationship between these two demographic phenomena remains ambiguous, it was in the mid-19th century that the negative concept of enforced exile became firmly embedded in the psyche of emigrants and commentators alike. Canada's chief immigration agent was scathing in his condemnation of the deliberately inadequate provision made by some landlords who, having chosen Canada for its proximity and cheap access, despatched maximum numbers of emigrants at minimum cost and expected his department to foot the bill for onward travel from port of landing. But greater opprobrium was heaped on infamous evictors, particularly John Gordon of Cluny, for the brutal recruitment techniques allegedly used in rounding up emigrants from his southern Hebridean estates. As numerous instances of unwilling exile were publicized by bards, politicians, and journalists, notably Alexander MacKenzie, Highland emigration—in all eras and circumstances—was presented as an uninterrupted tragedy of savage, comprehensive clearance, and any concept of voluntary relocation was expunged from the popular and public mind.

By the 1880s, when the government began to acknowledge and respond to swelling Highland discontent, crofting opinion was firmly set against any further removals. Grasping the unprecedented opportunity of the Napier Commission to express their grievances, assisted by radical land reformers, and emboldened by the support of the Gaelic literary movement (see GAELIC LITERATURE), crofters inveighed publicly against the injustice of earlier emigration, and urged the commissioners to tackle the Highlands' ongoing demographic problems by redistributing land rather than expelling people. The commissioners, however, thought enlargement of holdings could best be achieved in conjunction with state-aided emigration of the more impecunious; this recommendation caused the government to take uncharacteristic action in 1888, when it advanced £10,000 towards the settlement of 465 northern Hebrideans on Canadian prairie homesteads. This unprecedented experiment in state-directed colonization, beset by financial and administrative difficulties, failed to inspire crofters' confidence that relocation overseas, however constituted, was the answer to congestion and persistent poverty, and for more than three further decades the government retained, but did not further utilize, the emigration option. Only in the mid-1920s, after the Empire Settlement Act had made provision for Westminster to share the cost of imperial colonization ventures with dominion governments and approved societies, was there a temporary upsurge of emigration, particularly from the Outer Hebrides, until the onset of depression on both sides of the Atlantic ensured a return to the persistent and predictable pattern of Highland antagonism to emigration.

Indiscriminate demonization of Highland emigration can create a misleading one-dimensional image of an enforced diaspora in which landlords consistently expelled an unwilling tenantry over almost two centuries, obscuring important changes in the attitudes of all concerned. While government and proprietorial mercantilism gave way to a mixture of Malthusian and imperialist concerns in the 19th century, by 1900 imperial colonizers were competing with eugenicists and land reformers who wished to keep the Highlander at home. The emigrants themselves were characterized by variety rather than uniformity of background, motives, and experiences. Rarely completely passive victims of famine and clearance, even if they concurred in the fashioning of such an image in order to legitimize and disclaim responsibility for their radical actions, they participated actively in a complex, controversial, and dynamic demographic phenomenon which was itself part of a wider Scottish, British, and European mosaic.   MDH

4. post-1750, excluding Highlands

Although the long-standing inclination of Scots to seek advancement or refuge overseas was enhanced and given a clear transatlantic focus by the parliamentary *Union of 1707, only after 1750 did rising numbers of emigrants attract sustained government, press, and public attention. Despite periodic prohibitions and wartime disruption to shipping, it has been estimated from patchy statistics that around 27,000 Scots emigrated to North America between 1763 and 1815, while in the century before the First World War more comprehensive records reveal that approximately 1,900,000 emigrants left Scotland for non-European locations. Forty-four per cent went to the *USA, 28 per cent to *Canada, and 25 per cent to *Australia or *New Zealand, in a relentless, well-publicized, and frequently controversial exodus which had profound demographic and psychological implications for donor and destination countries alike, even if Scots contributed only 8 per cent to 19th-century emigration from the British Isles. Between the wars, when a combination of assertive British imperialism and restrictive American legislation turned emigrants' attention primarily to Canada, Scottish participation increased to 22 per cent, and the 1920s remains the only intercensal period when Scotland's population loss has exceeded the natural demographic increase.

The emigration debate was shaped primarily by differing perceptions of the emigrants' economic, social, and sometimes political value. While 18th-century mercantilists feared the damaging repercussions of losing military and economic manpower, particularly to the rebellious American colonies, 19th-century Malthusians argued—primarily in the 1820s and 1870s—that state-assisted emigration could be a vital safety valve in tackling domestic unemployment, poverty, and potential disaffection. But while the government abandoned its mercantilist opposition to emigration after 1783, and between 1815 and 1823 gave limited assistance to impecunious Scots and Irish to settle in Canada, its priority was to avoid positive intervention, so the repeated pleas of 22,000 impoverished weavers from the west central Lowlands for state-aided emigration generally fell on deaf ears. Meanwhile—despite colonial complaints of disparities between demand and supply—concern was frequently expressed at the calibre of Scottish emigrants, both the handpicked recruits to organized colonization schemes and the vast numbers of provident unassisted emigrants, who invested their savings in land or employment abroad.

Unlike Highlanders, Lowland emigrants were often more interested in carving out successful individual careers than in transplanting a communal lifestyle overseas. Their quest for economic and social betterment has not only shaped the volume and direction of Scottish emigration, it has also created a lasting image of the Scot abroad as the essence of shrewd, clannish, and often disproportionately successful business or farming practice. In the 18th century, some ambitious young urban artisans felt their goal could best be attained through indenture, which was practised mainly in the thirteen colonies, and offered recruits a free passage, both skilled and unskilled work at good wages, and assured accommodation for the five or seven years of the indenture. Others sojourned rather than settled, particularly in unhealthy or hostile locations such as the Caribbean, India (see INDIAN SUBCONTINENT), or the Arctic, intending ultimately to return home with the fruits of their labours as tropical planters and factors, military and administrative officers, fur traders, and explorers. Episodic emigration and temporary contract labour became more widespread as transportation improved and industrial opportunities expanded, particularly in the USA, although Scottish miners, granite cutters, and civil engineers were also prominent in South Africa (see AFRICA) and the Antipodes. Scots entrepreneurs pioneered Australia's pastoral industry and eastern Canada's lumber trade, with timber ships also providing cheap and ready emigrant passages from a wide range of Scottish ports until the mid-1850s, and in the second half of the 19th century Scots investors—notably Alexander Mitchell, Donald Smith, and George Stephen—masterminded transcontinental railway construction in both the USA and Canada.

Overwhelmingly, however, emigrant interest for almost two centuries focused on farming opportunities, simultaneously stimulated and reflected by an unremitting barrage of information and advice in lectures, guidebooks, press articles, specialist journals, and published and private correspondence. Rural Lowlanders in particular were lured overseas by prospects of independence and security through landownership, at the same time as the steady commercialization of agriculture—involving the eradication of smallholdings and swingeing rent increases—was frustrating the domestic landholding ambitions of small tenant farmers and farm labourers alike. A growing army of professional and amateur agents penetrated even the remotest districts to deliver lectures and arrange passages, land settlement, or employment, sometimes orchestrating quite sophisticated colonization schemes for 'industrious' agriculturists. Canada particularly poured large sums of money into promoting settlement of the prairies after Confederation, with resident government agents stationed at Glasgow from 1880 and Aberdeen from 1907, supervising the recruitment activities of itinerant representatives of the dominion and provincial governments and railway companies, and trying to counteract American and Antipodean competition. Australian recruitment campaigns, which had begun with the appointment of Charles Boyter as selecting agent for the New South Wales bounty scheme in the 1830s, continued into the era of self-government, as state and commonwealth agents included Scottish venues in their British tours, while men such as John McGlashan, secretary of the Otago Association, and pioneer Aberdeen emigrant James Adam were particularly successful in enticing Scots to Dunedin in the mid-19th century.

Bodies like the Otago Association, or the Inchinnan Company of Renfrewshire farmers seven decades earlier, aimed to encourage relatively affluent agriculturists to go to New Zealand and New England respectively. Most emigration societies, however, were charitable institutions which assisted unemployed artisans, single *women, and destitute *children, particularly between 1870 and 1930, the government's consistent refusal to undertake any major programme of state-aided emigration guaranteeing a continuing role for philanthropists. William Quarrier, like his English contemporary Thomas Barnardo, sponsored juvenile emigration as part of a wider programme of rescue work among disadvantaged children, sending almost 7,000 children from his Orphan Homes of Scotland in Renfrewshire to Canada between 1872 and 1933, in a scheme which predated the ultimately much larger Barnardo exodus. The Aberdeen

Ladies' Union (1883–1914) was one of a number of societies which promoted the emigration of domestic servants in the hope of redressing the imbalance of the sexes in Britain and the colonies, as well as offering recruits better prospects than were available at home, although far more such women emigrated independently through booking agencies than under the auspices of specialist societies. The Salvation Army, which claimed by 1914 to be the world's largest emigration agency, was active in Scotland both before and after the war, being joined after 1922 by several other Christian organizations which capitalized on the shared funding facilities of the Empire Settlement Act to co-sponsor the relocation of unemployed men and youths from the depressed central belt in rural occupations across Canada and Australia.

While agents and societies offered emigrants a modicum of assistance and aftercare, they were no substitute for the personal encouragement of pioneer colonizers, particularly when this was reinforced—as it frequently was—by the provision of a remittance, prepaid ticket, farm, or job to family or friends in Scotland. But the family- and community-based patronage networks which have consistently underpinned Scottish emigration were crucial not only in stimulating steady secondary movement and helping the new arrivals to establish economic roots, but also in providing both formal and informal mechanisms through which rootless and vulnerable emigrants could reconstitute their Scottish identity overseas. Otago was explicitly promoted as a well-ordered Scottish Presbyterian colony, enshrining values allegedly superior to those of convict-blighted Australia, while Canada's enduring popularity was due not only to relative proximity and abundant virgin land, but also to its well-attested tradition of Scottish settlement, similarly preserved through careful attention to two crucial pillars of Scottish identity (see NATIONAL IDENTITY), education and religion, and repeated assurances about the social advantages of settling amongst compatriots in a Christian country. Since the 1770s clergymen of all denominations had periodically accompanied emigrant parties overseas, and in the 19th century the Scottish churches became increasingly responsive to the spiritual needs of their growing flocks overseas. Nor were secular ethnic symbols neglected by emigrants, but while *Burns clubs and sporting and piping associations were usually purely social in function, St Andrew's and *Caledonian societies often fulfilled a charitable purpose as well, offering practical succour to emigrants in distress.

That not all emigrants prospered is demonstrated in statistics of shipping casualties, evidence of fraudulent agency activity, and the pessimistic accounts of those who found that the harsh realities of pioneer life did not match their high expectations. Judicial decree, moral or financial misdemeanour, and penury all played a part in ensuring that a proportion of emigrants did not leave voluntarily, although hardships were encountered by virtually all exiles in every era, whatever their origins, destinations, and motives. For many, however, modest ambition was rewarded by modest success, an experience reflected in the recent historiography of Scottish emigration, which has moved away from simply denouncing the expulsion of the destitute or celebrating the achievements of the highly successful or infamous to a more penetrating examination of the multifarious influences which have shaped a complex, persistent, nationwide exodus.   MDH

Episcopalian community. The Scottish Episcopal Church, which was to become a province of the worldwide Anglican communion, originated in the refusal of a substantial section of the Church of Scotland to accept the re-establishment of Presbyterianism in 1690. The Scottish bishops remained loyal to the house of Stuart, retaining the allegiance of many northern clergy and laity, especially in Aberdeenshire. Those who were willing to break with the Stuarts were granted toleration under an Act of 1712 so long as the clergy had received English or Irish ordination and the congregations used the Book of Common Prayer of the Church of England. Most of the clergy accepting these terms, who were said to have 'qualified' under the Act, served places of worship in the south. The first qualified congregation in Glasgow, set up in 1750–1, included a number of merchants and later manufacturers. After the *Jacobite rising of 1745, however, the non-qualified clergy were prohibited from officiating to any congregation consisting of more than five members beyond a single household. Episcopalianism survived in parts of the north through the services of lay catechists; and in other parts, such as Caithness, it withered away entirely. Worship was at this time not dissimilar to the Presbyterian style, with four communions a year as the norm. Yet there were a number of special and cherished usages including the epiclesis, or invocation of the Holy Spirit to consecrate the elements in the eucharist, a practice shared with Eastern Orthodoxy. Under the penal laws the Episcopal community gradually emerged with a distinct identity.

The death of Charles Edward Stuart in 1788 allowed the non-qualified clergy to submit to the Hanoverian dynasty with a clear conscience. In the same year John Skinner, who had been bishop of Aberdeen from 1782, was chosen primus, or presiding bishop, by his colleagues. Under Skinner's leadership the church obtained the abolition of the penal laws in 1792 and went on, in 1804, at a convocation in Laurencekirk, to adopt the Thirty-Nine Articles of the Church of England and invite the qualified congregations to reunite with it. Most did so, though a few remained separate long into the 19th century. The tradition of using the English Prayer Book in the former qualified congregations made it easier for a number of Evangelical clergy to take up posts within the church. In 1843, however, their most prominent figure, David Drummond, seceded to form a separate English Episcopal congregation in Edinburgh and, although several other similar causes arose, the Evangelical party was virtually extinguished within the church.

The great resource of Episcopalianism was its strength among landed proprietors. As the steady consolidation of the British elite proceeded, the Episcopal Church, with its similarities to the Church of England, attracted an increasing proportion of Scottish landowners. In 1843 it was estimated that 86 per cent of Scottish peers were Episcopalians. From 1838 landed wealth was tapped through the Scottish Episcopal Church Society, which was founded to support poor congregations, help candidates for the ministry, relieve elderly clergy, and promote popular education. From 1847 there existed Trinity College, Glenalmond, to train candidates for ordination (a purpose that faded) and educate the sons of the elite along public school lines (which flourished). Church building became widespread, culminating in the consecration of St Mary's—later a cathedral—in Edinburgh in 1879. Between 1838 and 1858 the number of churches increased from 73 to 150 and the number of clergy from 78 to 163 (see CHURCHES: 3). By 1872 there were about 100 Episcopal schools (see SCHOOLS AND SCHOOLING: 2). After much debate, the leading laity whose generosity had made possible this transformation were given a formal role on the Representative Church Council, which in 1876 assumed responsibility for central financial affairs. At the same time the church was being stirred by the Oxford Movement. A. P. Forbes, bishop of Brechin from 1847, was the first disciple of the movement to reach the episcopate anywhere. A sermon of his on the real presence in the eucharist roused much opposition in 1857 and led to his censure by the other bishops. The ritualism taken up by others influenced by the Oxford Movement, especially at Perth, was stoutly resisted by Bishop Charles Wordsworth of St Andrews, who also championed the use of the English Prayer Book. Many southern congregations were substantially English in composition; and, in 1856, when 87 of the church's clergy were men who had received

Scottish ordination, fully 69 had been ordained in England. From 1864 Scottish clergy were eligible for office in the Church of England. The Episcopal Church as a whole never warranted the common soubriquet of 'the English Church', but it is clear why the term arose.

By 1900 worship in the Episcopal Church normally included monthly or weekly eucharists, surpliced choirs, and musical services. These sustained the appeal of the church, which reached its peak of adherents around 1921, when the Glasgow diocese alone had 55,816. Some urban congregations reached a remarkable size, most notably St Mary Magdalene's in Dundee with around 5,000, but the traditional rural strength decayed, especially in Aberdeenshire and Argyll. Relations with Presbyterianism had mellowed, and intermittently from 1932 to the 1960s there were formal but ultimately fruitless talks aiming for union between Anglicans and Presbyterians north and south of the Border. Meanwhile the Episcopal Church played a significant part in social welfare, supporting, for instance, the Aberlour orphanage on Speyside, and in *missions overseas, maintaining links inaugurated in the 1870s with the dioceses of St John's in the Transkei in South *Africa and of Nagpur in central India. It also nourished a fine tradition of historical scholarship. By 1947 Scottish Episcopalianism embraced 405 churches, 316 clergy, and 55,270 communicant members. Thereafter it was to weaken further, including in its traditional bastion in the north-east, and by 1994 its greatest strengths were to be found in the Borders and Edinburgh. In that year a survey of the churchmanship of its congregations showed that nearly half described themselves as Broad or Liberal, a quarter as Catholic, and the rest as Evangelical, Reformed, or Low Church. Charismatic renewal, especially in Edinburgh, had disproportionately affected the denomination. Increasingly the future seemed to lie in ecumenical co-operation and perhaps in merger (see RELIGIOUS LIFE: 7).   DWB

Equipoise, age of. This term is used to signify a generation of political and social calm in mid-Victorian Britain. In his book *The Age of Equipoise* (1964), W. L. Burns identified the period c.1852–c.1867 as the relevant years. Political stability followed the ebbing away of *Chartism and the repeal of the Corn Laws (1846) and a lull during the years between the breakthrough 1832 Reform Act and the pressure for further widening of the franchise in 1868. The nationalist revolutions had come and gone in Europe (1848–9) with little political impact upon the proceedings of parliament. The relation between the various social classes in this mid-Victorian period has been characterized as one

of deference and imbued with notions of respectability (see RESPECTABLE CULTURE), despite the promptings of Karl Marx. The Great Exhibition of 1851 stunned both its critics and its organizers, by the ease and evident peace that the different social classes could simultaneously enjoy as they visited the exhibition in their tens of thousands. The period is characterized as one of acceptance of a hierarchical social order.

Yet the political stability that marked the political system in England, where there were few issues to differentiate between the Whigs and the Conservatives, was much less apparent within Scotland. Conservative support (see UNIONISM) in Scotland had been decimated in 1832, and throughout the mid-Victorian period what controversy there was tended to be within the Liberal Party (see LIBERALISM). The issue of religion was at the heart of almost all of these disputes. It not only impacted on parliamentary political debate, but reached many other elements of culture and society too. The criticism which came from the Voluntarists of state religion continued apace in Scotland as it did in England. But in 1843, following a decade of dispute over the right of appointment, the Evangelicals led by Thomas *Chalmers seceded from the Established Church of Scotland and formed the Free Church of Scotland. What was increasingly regarded as the uneasy relationship between the state and the church, of which the *Disruption was the most dramatic manifestation, was seen in terms of education (see SCHOOLS AND SCHOOLING: 2), poor relief (see LIVING STANDARDS: 4), and politics. The debate over the provision of effective primary education was theologically based: if schooling was not to be entirely secular, then whose religion was to be taught and of what religion should the teachers be? Disputes of this kind delayed reform until the Education Act of 1872. The system of poor relief had been updated in 1845, but it remained organizationally in the hands of the parishes and therefore the Church of Scotland. The Disruption fractured this structure when 40 per cent of ministers followed Chalmers out of the General Assembly. Partial compensation, however, came from a range of voluntary and other philanthropic organizations established by the Free Church, often duplicating the efforts of the church they had left, which deepened this area of provision for the poor and needy.

In Edinburgh, the state–religion controversy was rife throughout the first half of the century over the local taxation which was levied to fund the stipends of the Church of Scotland's ministers. This tax, the Annuity Tax, highlighted the inconsistencies of arrangements workable only for a single-religion nation. The state funding of religion was also the key to a further major issue of dispute, May-nooth, the Catholic seminary school in Ireland. If financing the Church of Scotland was deemed controversial enough by so many sections of Protestant Scotland, public funding for the training of Catholic priests (see ROMAN CATHOLIC COMMUNITY) was deemed to be doubly objectionable. Thus the Disruption in 1843 and the fervour over Maynooth resulted in the 1847 and 1852 general elections being dominated by the Voluntarists' agenda. They brought religion into the parliamentary political process in a way not seen before and split the Liberal Party in ways which caused the sorts of ructions the Conservatives and Whigs had failed to ignite.

The belief that political and social stability reigned in the mid-Victorian years in Britain was advanced by the absence of a revolutionary nationalist agenda. This was in sharp contrast to events in Poland, Hungary, and Italy. In the House of Commons, Chartism was regarded as the more pressing concern, and that had receded by the 1850s. With nationality (see NATIONALISM; NATIONAL IDENTITY: 5), as with religion, Scotland lacked the balance and apparent social cohesion of England. The importance of the short-lived NAVSR (1852–6) was as a channel through which the rhetoric of national identity could be directed to the Scottish and English press and periodicals rather than as an organization of numbers. Its leadership was not of the first order, but it took representation from up to 50 town and burgh councils in Scotland. It focused on heraldic issues and returns on public expenditure from the Exchequer as its campaigning themes and it demanded that Scotland receive a fair return from the Union. Its objective was equality with England in the Union, for a better-working Union, not Scottish independence. Its version of self-government was based around municipal and county government.

In the thesis of W. L. Burns, the relationship between central and local government was one of balance despite constant flux. Yet this axis was too great a source of tension not to cause disagreement, especially in Scotland. Politicians and their civil servants in London were increasingly aware that social intervention was necessary in the towns and cities to improve conditions and reduce the urban death rate (see POPULATION PATTERNS: 2). Local politicians resented outsiders and state functionaries telling them how to run their urban affairs and forcing them to spend money and to increase their rate of taxation (or debt) to pay for it. An important reason for municipal support for the mid-century nationalists in Scotland was to promote local government over the perceived generalisms and mediocrity of central intervention lacking special knowledge of the localities. When England was in equipoise, Scotland remained in search of its balance.   GM

family. There have been dramatic changes in family life over time including interesting shifts in the course of the last few decades. Debate continues about how to interpret the overall consequences of these trends. Some commentators focus exclusively on the apparent increase in fragility of family relationships indicated by rising divorce. But there is also strong evidence of the continued importance of family relationships to most people, despite much greater choice and variation in how personal life is conducted. Some commentators present change as a positive shift to a more democratic personal life in which people negotiate their relationships on a nearer equal footing. These changes reflect changes in the physical, social, and economic conditions of an advanced industrial or post-industrial society as well as changes in attitude. Indeed, attitude change is typically bound up with more structural changes in how people live. However, this entry concentrates on documenting changes in behaviour and attitudes rather than exploring the underlying causes.

A number of European societies share a similar set of visible tends in patterns of family living, including change in the age and manner in which people enter marriage or marriage-like relationships (see also COURTSHIP AND MARRIAGE). In Britain, over the 1980s the popularity of marriage seemed to decline from its all-time peak in the 1960s and 1970s. In both Scotland and England and Wales, the average (mean) age of first marriage has climbed to between 29 and 30 for men and between 27 and 28 for *women. This is higher than the previous peak in the decades around 1911–20 when people married in Scotland on average almost a year later than in England and Wales, at age 26 for spinsters and age 28 for bachelors. The numbers marrying have not continued to fall but stabilized in the 1990s. During this same period, there was a significant increase in the number of couples living together without being married. Most couples marrying today have lived together before marriage and some cohabiting couples never marry. By the 1990s, about a third of unmarried young people in their late twenties were living with a partner in Britain, although the proportion is about 10 per

cent lower in Scotland. This is a pattern that is set to continue in the 21st century.

Living as a couple without marriage is also very common among divorcees and changes in the patterns of breakdown of partnership are as noticeable as shifts in partnership formation. As in many other countries, the divorce rate in Britain rose dramatically between the 1960s and the early 1990s. It has remained slightly lower in Scotland than in England and Wales but still following the same general trend. Divorce rates may now have stabilized in Britain, with no rising trend since the mid-1990s. Current research suggests that when couples live together rather than marry, their relationship is just as likely or even more likely to break down than a marriage. It is estimated that one of four children are affected by the separation of their parents before their sixteenth birthday and that about one in three marriages end in divorce. Family disruption, however, is not new. At the beginning of the 20th century significant proportions of children still experienced the death of a parent before they were 16, an event which is now much more unusual.

Family size has fallen across the century and by the 1990s the average family size was between one and two children, and below the number that would mean maintaining a stable population. In the 1970s, relatively young ages of marriage meant earlier childbirth for many women (see CHILDBIRTH AND INFANCY). By the end of the 20th century, the most popular age for having *children was in the late twenties but there were more women giving birth in their early thirties than in their early twenties. Later marriage, and more people living together who are not married, is associated with more births outside marriage. In England and Wales and in Scotland, nearly 40 per cent of all births are now outside marriage. However, the majority are jointly registered by parents living at the same address—70 per cent in Scotland and 60 per cent in England and Wales. About 10 per cent of births are to mothers who are not living with partners.

While households made up of couples remain the most common household type, by the last decade of the 20th century in Britain, family households consisting of a couple with dependent children were outnumbered by couples with no children. Couples with no children have either never had children or are in the 'empty nest' phase. Smaller family size means more couples in the 'empty nest' stage and delayed childbirth means an associated increase in both temporary and permanent childlessness. Although remaining the most common household type, couple households have declined in numbers as other types of households have grown.

The number of people living alone has grown to a quarter of all households. Since the 1960s there has been an increase in single young people living in independent households, particularly in the cities. This is a practice that varies across Europe, with leaving the parental home before entering a partnership being very common in some countries and still very unusual in a minority. In most European countries, the proportion of elderly people living alone has also increased. The common combination of longer life and low birth rates mean that elderly people form a growing proportion of many populations. Elderly women are the most likely to be living alone as they are more likely to outlive their partner than men and, in Britain, they are also somewhat less likely than men to remarry when widowed or divorced. Lone parent families have also increased since the 1950s, to 10 per cent of all households in Britain, largely as a consequence of the rising divorce rate.

One other important change concerns the interaction between men's and women's family relationships and their engagement in paid employment. While for generations some married women have been engaged in paid employment, the norm at the turn of the 20th century was for women to withdraw from paid work on marriage. Indeed, in Britain some employers barred married women from work. This is no longer the case and has changed gradually since the Second World War, along with the beliefs about 'women's place' that made marriage bars possible and legal. In the majority of couple households below retirement age, both men and women are in paid employment, although many more women work part-time than men. While women's greater involvement in paid work has resulted in some men doing more housework, research shows that many women continue to carry more responsibility for housework and childcare than their partner.

While such structural changes cannot be disputed, there is debate about changes in the meaning of 'family', in how people feel about family obligations and what people typically want from their personal lives. It is clear that some ideas about

the rights and duties of particular family members that were still common at the beginning of the 20th century no longer have popular support.

Few people now emphasize the authority of a husband over a wife or his role as 'master of the house'. In the 20th century, feminist campaigning exposed and attacked assumptions about women's lesser worth than men and highlighted how financial dependence on men often disadvantages women. However, the increase in women's participation in paid work after marriage and childbearing is probably more to do with economic changes than feminism. Shifts in the balance of jobs available and the costs of maintaining the prevailing *living standards mean that many couples find ways of both having jobs because they feel they need two wages. The notion that marriage should be a partnership of equals gained strength in the latter half of the 20th century. Surveys of attitudes clearly demonstrate increased support for gender equality in paid work, in housework, and in childcare among both men and women, but with higher support for equality expressed by women. The evidence of behaviour rather than beliefs shows that many couples who believe in equality nevertheless let a situation develop in which women put in more hours of work for the household and carry a stronger sense of responsibility for children than men.

Parents' attitudes to their children have also changed dramatically. At the beginning of the 20th century, the adage 'children should be seen and not heard' was still seriously enforced in many homes. In most households, children were unequivocally at the service of adults and any 'talking back' was 'cheek'. Many mothers and fathers were rather distant from and above their children. They did not see playing with children or doing things with them as a priority and much of childhood play took place outside in the streets or fields. In the second half of the 20th century, parents told researchers that they wanted to be emotionally close to their children and were less concerned about deference; parents as bosses had mutated into parents as pals. By the turn of the 21st century, many younger children have little access to a world of play that is beyond family and adult supervision, since they are increasingly housebound by the domination of streets by cars, parental fears about urban risks, and new home-based technologies of entertainment.

Some commentators argue that the high incidence of divorce and the attractions of cohabitation are because people expect more from their partnership now than before. Above all, people want to feel they are still in love and loved. The marriage certificate, once seen primarily as a 'till death us do part' affirmation, is seen as insignificant in comparison to this feeling of having a high-quality relationship and hence people are less prepared to stay in a relationship that does not match this ideal. Studies suggest that men and women sometimes have different understandings of what makes a good relationship, with women seeking more emotional intimacy, and that a sense of carrying unequal burdens of work in or for the relationship can undermine 'that loving feeling'. When relationships with children end, the children usually lose their father from their family home. It takes considerable effort on behalf of a non-resident father to maintain a good relationship with his children.

One way of looking at the change in attitudes to family life is to say that having a particular family position—mother, father, husband, wife, son, daughter—no longer means living up to a standard set of expectations and obligations but negotiating good relationships with the rest of the family. Studies of people's attitudes and ideals reveal that most men and women value family relationships very highly. Studies also show that people continue to have a strong sense of obligation to help family members although this is not seen as an absolute rule but a matter that has to be negotiated.

A personal life in which people learn to give and take in negotiation with others fits well with the ideals of democracy. Clearly some commentators fear that the balance in the family has shifted too much towards personal goals and away from commitment and obligation and traditional ways of doing things. However, the traditions that have clearly been abandoned include some that were authoritarian rather than democratic. The evidence suggests that people continue to want long-lasting and stable relationships, even if they sometimes fail in the attempt. People's apparent desires for more equal and perhaps democratic relationships than in the past are not fully realized in practice. Gender inequalities in employment are still imported into the home and many couples see the woman's job as secondary to the man's. Opportunities for paid employment remain rather different for men and women with many jobs still being seen as more suitable to one or other sex. Women's average earnings remain lower than men's, many women do not earn enough to easily support themselves and their children, and divorce often leaves women in poverty.   LJ

film, Scotland on. The history of cinema in Scotland (as opposed to Scottish cinema) is as old as the history of cinema itself. The earliest of Thomas Edison's peep-show pictures (initially shown in American nickelodeons) were demonstrated in Edinburgh on Christmas Eve 1894. Almost a year later, the Lumière Brothers gave what is believed to have been the world's first public moving picture show in Paris. The first moving pictures shown in Edinburgh made their debut in a theatre, on 13 April 1896. Within weeks an entrepreneur put cinematograph on the road, showing films in Brechin, Montrose, Aberdeen, Macduff, Elgin, and other places. While the Scots were enthralled by the cinematograph, in the same spring Edison introduced American audiences to his Vitascope.

Most of what was shown in Scotland's hastily converted buildings were either British, French, or American one-reel productions: newsreels, *music hall acts, comedies. Aberdeen's first permanent cinema, the Gaiety, opened in 1908; the first specially built cinema opened in *Glasgow a year later.

Glasgow-based film-makers, aping American successes, delighted audiences with Scotland's first three-reel dramatic adaptation, *Rob Roy*, in 1911. A Scots actor took the title role in the drama shot in a 'studio' (actually a converted tram shed) at Rouken Glen, Glasgow. No prints now survive of this first 'major motion picture' produced in Scotland, which probably capitalized on images still used today: anti-English (or 'establishment'), kilted Highland hero in misty romantic landscape. The move to more sophisticated and longer productions was seen, however, as a way to attract a middle-class audience into the cinema. The Ace Film Producing Company proudly announced the opening of their new studio in Thornliebank, Glasgow, in October 1919. They advertised the opening of a school for 'cinema aspirants to train for cinema acting' and produced one five-reeler, *The Harp King*, before going bankrupt.

The First World War was to shift the balance of film-making in favour of the USA and principally Hollywood. By its end Hollywood's domination of the industry was complete. Although Scotland had some history of feature film production, its few studios never grew to the size of Ealing or Pinewood, and certainly not of the Hollywood behemoths, such as Fox, MGM, Paramount, and Warner Brothers.

For much of the 20th century the images of Scotland as portrayed on screen were largely determined by Hollywood or designed to please an international market. Despite this American domination, cinema remained a popular art form in Scotland and people continued to make movies in and about Scotland.

Between the wars, cinemas were built in large numbers in Scotland. Dundee with a population of under 200,000 had as many as 28 cinemas; Aberdeen, of a similar size, boasted 19 cinemas in 1939.

Local cinema was dominated by a number of families: the Pooles in Edinburgh, the Donalds in Aberdeen, and the Greens of Glasgow, who spread their cinema empire as far as Edinburgh and Dundee, backed productions in Scotland and invested in Hollywood's United Artists Corporation. Glaswegians of a certain age will remember courting in some of George Singleton's chain of cinemas.

The Edinburgh Film Guild, established in 1930, converted the News Cinema to the Edinburgh Film Theatre in the late 1960s. Before that members of the Guild helped to establish the world's longest running film festival, the Edinburgh Film Festival, founded in 1947. Although television made inroads into cinema attendance in the 1950s and 1960s, the habit has not vanished. Largely, however, the great cinema palaces have given way to chains, multiplexes, and film theatres which provide access to non-mainstream films.

Scots-born movie actors who became well-known idols include Alistair Sim, Jack Buchanan, Deborah Kerr, David Niven, and Sean Connery. Some, like David MacCallum and Gordon Jackson, had their screen careers enhanced by television roles.

Gordon Jackson had a role in one of the great achievements of British cinema: Alexander Mackendrick's 1949 *Whisky Galore* (released in the USA as *Tight Little Island*). The simple story of a merchant ship with a cargo of whisky running aground off a Hebridean island at the height of wartime restrictions is a compelling study of attitudes towards authority, the meaning and functioning of a small community, and how that community deals with incomers. Like Universal Television's 1990s cult hit *Northern Exposure*, *Whisky Galore* observed with humour and percipience a group of remote inhabitants who are far more acute than outsiders would give them credit for!

The Scottish film world produced two individuals of genius: father of the documentary film John Grierson (1898–1972) and Norman MacLaren (1914–87), an animator who did much successful work for the National Film Board of Canada. Before his tragically early death in 1991, the Newcraighall film-maker Bill Douglas gave audiences his soul in the stunning trilogy *My Childhood* (1972), *My Ain Folk* (1973), and *My Way Home* (1978). In the 1980s Bill Forsyth secured an international reputation with *Gregory's Girl* and *Local Hero*. He left Scotland and went to work in the USA.

Scots-born screenwriters have included Oscar-winning Neil Paterson and former chairman of Macallan, Alan Scott, whose creative writing talents shaped the 1973 thriller *Don't Look Now*. Malcolm A. Irvine, a Glasgow-based entrepreneur,

speaking in 1946 produced a comment that would have been as familiar to the early pioneers in the 1890s as to film-makers, writers, and actors today: 'At the moment we find it impossible to produce feature films in Scotland in their entirety, having neither the personnel nor the equipment for large-scale productions.'

What makes a good film? A captivating story (with some kind of resonance), good actors, and money. *Braveheart*, the inspirational story of Scots hero William *Wallace, and *Rob Roy* (in its fourth incarnation as a film), both made in the mid-1990s with Hollywood actors in the lead, were made with American money, for international audiences.

Scottish images tend to be the familiar ones: the Jacobite hero, the lovable rogue, the kilted Highlander, the hardbitten working man (who likes a good dram), the faithful matron, the tight-fisted Scot are all sentimental 'Scottish' themes, together with Anglophobia, romanticism, pawky humour, and strong personal values, most brilliantly brought into play in Walt Disney's 1960 production *Kidnapped*.

The frothy American-financed fantasy *Loch Ness* (1996) was released in the same year as *Trainspotting*, a 'real' study of heroin addiction in contemporary Edinburgh. And while tourists did not flock to see the council estates of Pilton and Muirhouse, they did in great number discover all over again Highland landscapes. Stirling Council was especially successful in playing the *Braveheart* card and the success of 1997's *Mrs Brown* aided tourism in Royal Deeside. *Carla's Song* and *My Name is Joe* and *The Ratcatcher* were all 1990s films which demonstrated that Scottish-based film-makers and actors are capable of dealing with international issues and timeless values.

Public funding of all aspects of film-making has improved. Scotland's first unified film agency, Scottish Screen, was established in 1997. Plans are underway to create Scotland's first major studio. The Scottish Film Council has been operating for 60 years: its activities include an archive, screenings, and funding of films. The Scottish Film Production Fund provides funding for short films. Local authorities have supported film houses in their areas. There has been a welcome growth in film studies at several of Scotland's universities and colleges. Overall, there is much confidence and a sense of direction in the industry as a whole.

The term 'Scottish cinema' is problematic. There has been a reluctance over recent decades to take the subject seriously. Is it a question of films made by Scottish directors, featuring Scottish actors, or simply films shot in Scotland? What about those films financed with Scottish capital? Written by Scots-born or Scots-based writers? For much of its history, Scotland may have been obsessed with defining itself in terms of being 'not English' (see NATIONAL IDENTITY). It remains a matter of debate whether there is yet a 'Scottish cinema'.   ATS

Fletcher, Andrew, of Saltoun (1655–1716). Scottish patriot, anti-Union politician, and author, Fletcher was tutored by Gilbert Burnet, later bishop of Salisbury. An East Lothian shire commissioner, he opposed the authoritarian *Restoration regime, went into exile in 1681, was outlawed as a fugitive rebel in 1684, and in 1686 was sentenced to death *in absentia* for his part in the Monmouth rebellion in 1685. He returned with William of Orange in 1688 but because of delay in lifting his forfeiture could not be elected to the Convention of Estates of 1689. He gave his support, however, to the opposition's demands for radical reform of the government of Scotland, demands that were only partly met.

He also strove to improve his country's economy which had been badly affected by the English Navigation Acts of 1660 and 1663. Thus he helped to initiate the Company of Scotland which was set up in 1695 in an attempt to dynamize Scottish trade. The failure in 1700 of the Company's attempt to implement William Paterson's *Darien Scheme raised a great outcry in Scotland, and Fletcher, who two years earlier had published *Two Discourses* lamenting the ill condition of his country, was confirmed in his belief that Scotland's plight, like the Darien failure, was attributable to the adverse effects of the *Union of the Crowns.

The problem of the succession suggested a way to resolve those difficulties: if Scottish grievances were not redressed, then, on the death of Queen Anne without an heir of her body, Scotland and England might go their separate ways. A half-hearted attempt at union collapsed in 1702–3, whereupon the Scots *parliament in 1703 refused to accept the Hanoverian succession (already adopted, somewhat presumptuously, by England in 1701), or even to discuss the succession until Scottish grievances against English hegemony, exercised through the power of the crown, were redressed. Fletcher dominated the session of 1703 with a series of brilliant speeches and the help of his 'Young Cubs', the youthful earls of Haddington, Montrose, and Rothes. But thereafter his parliamentary influence waned. After bitter debate a treaty for an incorporating union (see UNION OF 1707) was agreed, and despite determined opposition from Fletcher and his remaining allies it was, with the help of some adroit bribery, accepted by the Scottish parliament on 16 January 1707, had a rapid passage through the English parliament, and

became operative on 1 May 1707. Thus was 'Great Britain' transformed from a diplomatic concept into a constitutional reality.

Fletcher was never reconciled to the Union, which he regarded as fatal for Scotland. He was arrested in the French invasion (see JACOBITISM) scare of 1708 but released without charge, for his hostility to the exiled Stuarts had not diminished. A lifelong opponent of divine right kingship, he was an advocate of constitutional limited monarchy. Brought up as an Episcopalian (see EPISCOPALIAN COMMUNITY) though he was, his interests were markedly secular and in many ways he anticipated the attitudes of the Enlightenment (see CULTURE: 11). Political science and not theology, he felt, should dictate politics. An accomplished writer, he was one of the first Scots to master the English language and his pithy writings have preserved his ideas. The unusual purity of his motives in an age of corrupt self-seeking has also kept his memory green. A confirmed bachelor, he was in time succeeded by his nephew, Andrew Fletcher of Milton, who, ironically, as Lord Milton, helped the third duke of Argyll to 'manage' (see GOVERNMENT AFTER THE UNION) Scotland—that is, to run a system based on the kind of corrupt practices that Andrew Fletcher of Saltoun had abominated.   WF

football has its origins in Scotland in the pre-industrial era when rival villagers would compete to see which team (there was no limit on the number of players) could kick a bundle of rags into the opposition's town. Needless to say, it was a conflict which often involved considerable injury. Professional football can be dated in Scotland from 1873 when the Scottish Football Association was founded. The game was largely confined to working-class communities and teams tended to reflect specific features of the locality. For example, Celtic FC was founded by Brother Walfrid in 1888 as a healthy form of recreation for young Glasgow Catholic men. The team was to act as a magnet for Catholic (see ROMAN CATHOLIC COMMUNITY) loyalties in Glasgow. Similarly, Rangers FC was founded in 1872 by a group of young men from Gareloch, but when the club moved to Ibrox in 1899 it drew most of its support from the skilled, Protestant, working class of the traditional heavy industries (see ECONOMY, SECONDARY SECTOR: 2). It was the ability of the sport to draw large audiences, however, which led to its commercialization and professionalization in the 1890s. A Scottish league was established in 1890 and paid professionals were legalized in 1893. Increasing audiences meant that football was a profitable concern and in 1896, 25,000 fans turned up to watch Celtic play Rangers. In the same year, Celtic's turnover was £10,142 while

Rangers raked in £14,076 in 1908. Football was a working-class passion and pundits soon acquired highly specialized knowledge of the game which was reinforced by comment in *newspapers. It also started a Scottish tradition of reading newspapers from the back page forwards.

Such passions often turned to violence and sectarian tensions accompanied games between rival Protestant and Catholic teams in Dundee, Edinburgh, and Glasgow. Assaults on referees were not uncommon and disputed penalties could lead to a pitch invasion or a hail of missiles, rivets being a common weapon at Ibrox. Football was also important in fostering a distinctive *national identity. The fact that Scotland had its own league and that there were international games against the 'auld enemy' did much to promote a national dimension in Scottish football. In 1902, for example, 102,000 spectators turned up to cheer on the national team against England, in spite of efforts to price rougher elements out of the crowd (see ROUGH CULTURE). With the impact of commercialization, success tended to gravitate towards those clubs which could call on a mass following.

The inter-war years have been described as the golden age of Scottish football. It provided spectators with a welcome distraction from the torment of the Depression and it offered talented working-class youth the prospect of fame, money, and escape from the dreary realities of ordinary life. Scottish football prowess was demonstrated by the fact that the nation won twelve out of the twenty internationals against England. In spite of this outward success, many players were attracted south by the richer pickings of the English football league and sectarianism remained an endemic problem, especially in Glasgow where levels of violence scaled new heights. War and full employment maintained the popularity of the beautiful game and it arguably reached its zenith in the early 1950s. Thereafter, the impact of television began to affect its attendance. The 1960s witnessed a high point with Celtic being the first British team to win the European Cup in 1967. Their triumph was shortly followed by Rangers winning the European Cup Winners Cup, although the occasion was marred by crowd trouble. Internationally, Scottish football has been a great disappointment in the post-war years and reached its nadir in the 1978 World Cup. On the positive side, the behaviour of football fans abroad in the 1980s and 1990s has done much to improve the image of the nation.

The further commercialization of the sport in the 1980s has had three significant effects. The first has been the internationalization of the game as the importation of foreign players reached new heights. Money and the ability to buy new talent was the critical factor in Rangers' dominance of the game in the 1980s and 1990s. Secondly, commercial considerations and the search for the best players have meant that teams are more ethnically mixed and sectarian divisions, in the teams, if not the crowds, have disappeared. Thirdly, rising season ticket prices has meant that the social composition of the crowd has become more middle class. RJF

Forteviot. Little remains of Forteviot, the palace of the Pictish kings of Fortriu, where *Kenneth mac Alpin died in AD 858. However, there is an important body of sculpture associated with Forteviot and aerial photographic evidence, which reveals aspects of the settlement layout and its landscape setting.

The tiny village of Forteviot is located in the heart of Strathearn. The palace formerly stood on Haly Hill on the west side of the village overlooking the Water of May. The hill and palace were largely washed away in the 17th century and the only surviving fragment of the palace is a sculpted arch recovered from the stream bed of the May. This arch is the most accomplished piece of Pictish architectural sculpture in existence. Presumably derived from the palace chapel, the arch bears the representations of four classically attired figures flanking a cross and sporting typically flamboyant Pictish-style moustaches. The arch indicates that at least part of the palace complex was of stone. To the east of the modern village are cropmarks of a cemetery containing Pictish square barrows as well as east–west oriented graves. This appears to mark the eastern extent of the settlement. There is no indication that the palace was enclosed by large-scale, defensive ramparts.

In addition to the arch, three fragments of high-quality early medieval sculpture survive in the church. In recent times the spectacular Dupplin Cross stood a few miles away, but a 19th-century account suggests it may have stood in the Forteviot churchyard. There are stylistic traits which link the cross to the arch and a worn inscription appears to refer to the Pictish king, *Caustantin, son of Fergus (Uurgust) (d. 820).

Historical evidence indicates that Forteviot was a major royal estate from Pictish times to the 12th century. The St Andrews foundation legend places the residence of King 'Hungus' (*Uungus (Onuist) I or II), at Forteviot. Both Kenneth mac Alpin and his brother are mentioned at the palace (palacium) of Forteviot. Fifteenth-century poetic tradition suggests that Malcolm III 'Canmore' (Mael Coluim mac Donnchada) resided at Forteviot. Malcolm IV issued a charter from there (1162 × 1164) as did William I (1165 × 1171). Thereafter it drops off the royal circuit, but it remained a royal thanage.

Aerial photography has revealed the presence of a remarkable set of cropmarks less than 0.6 mile (1 km) south of Forteviot. Before modern agriculture, these neolithic ritual monuments would have been prominent features in the landscape. The presence of Pictish-type barrows among the ancient prehistoric monuments indicates that these were recognized by the *Picts. It appears that part of the appeal of Forteviot for Pictish rulers may have been its ancient landscape setting.   STD

France: the 'Auld Alliance'. The French connection, often whimsically known as the 'Auld Alliance', was an intermittent phenomenon but in the three centuries or so after 1296, it operated in four main areas: warriors, women, writers, and wine. Let us take the last first. Although 16th-century Scots, high-born and low-, did not disdain beer or whisky as their alcoholic medium, wine far outshone either. There was not an Edinburgh tavern which did not sell it, nor a noble household which did not stock it. The afternoon (many Scots, like their English colleagues, drank first thing in the morn to bedtime) of 18 March 1286 saw Alexander III quaff 'the blood-red wine of Gascony' (for which the supplier petitioned for years for payment) in Edinburgh castle before he took horse and rode off the cliffs at Kinghorn and into the swirling mists of history. In 1539 alone, John Barton, a noted Scottish wholesaler and carrier, delivered to Cardinal Beaton no fewer than 110 casks of Bordeaux. Measurements are the bane of all economic historians for the late medieval period, but if a French wine cask-tun contained 252 gallons (equivalent to 1,500 bottles) this amounted to something like 165,000 bottles of claret. If early modern wine bottles had the same units of inebriation as modern ones (seven), Beaton's haul comes to something like 1,555,000 units of alcohol. Beaton's household was, of course, huge and wine can be stored for many years. No doubt, it was still an enormous cellar, into which his murderers dipped freely in 1546–7, and its remnants were 'liberated' by the French adventurers who recaptured St Andrews castle in August 1547.

So important was the wine trade (although sherry from Spain (17 per cent alcoholic content) and the new drink of the 16th century, brandy (85 per cent), along with other spin-off products, should not be forgotten) that a large number of Scots found themselves involved in the trade, either as producers or as pirates. Benefiting from various exemptions from customs dues, Bordeaux was home to a lively colony of Scots entrepreneurs acting as warehousemen, retailers, and factors. But many Scots also settled permanently in Guyenne, establishing their own vineyards, enjoying rights of denizenship (the right, for example, to make wills for their French possessions) and high profits. When *James VI tried in 1604 to push through Anglo-Scottish joint citizenship, English MPs complained bitterly about what they saw as unfair competition. The English wine trade was, of course, prodigious and thus was fair game whenever the two countries were at war, and even when they were not. In 1543, during the formal truce after Solway Moss, Scots masquerading as Frenchmen captured on the high seas Henry VIII's entire wine fleet for that year: the sixteen vessels were immediately resold in Scotland, although not at Edinburgh because an English ambassador had just arrived there. Instead the loot was transported to Aberdeen where John Dudley (the future duke of Northumberland), ever a man for the main chance, ensured that one of his agents in Scotland made a bulk purchase which he forwarded to his king that summer.

Temporary colonies of Scots could also be found at 'the schules to lere thare veruis and science', being educated at French universities. The future Cardinal Beaton first studied at Orléans in 1519. His later ecclesiastical rival, Gavin Dunbar, could be found at Angers and Paris. Bishop John Lesley, confidant of *Mary, Queen of Scots and historical apologist for her, studied law for four years at Poitiers, then became a doctor of decreets at Paris before returning to his alma mater, Aberdeen. John Mair (or Major) studied at Paris and then taught there after 1505 and during 1525–31. Perhaps the most famous of all Scots academics, George Buchanan, lived and worked in France so long he was virtually a native. Many of the works of such scholars were first published in France and indeed French presses filled their libraries, including those of Hector Boece and Duncan Liddell, with key texts. Of the more than 1,300 surviving books in Scottish pre-Reformation libraries, fully 711 were printed in France: principally at Paris, Rouen, Lyons, and Caen.

France supplied more than books, however, although it is apt to recall that at least one of the partners of Chepman and Myllar, founders of the first Scottish printing press (see PRINTING AND PUBLISHING), first learned their craft there. The connection created a cultural atmosphere, amounting almost to an osmosis, between the two. One can capture this in numerous artefacts, both concrete and ephemeral. *James V's bombastic building programme encapsulated French mannerist and Renaissance motifs, ranging from the elaborate fountain in the courtyard of Linlithgow palace to the handsome ornamental buttresses at Falkland or the outrageous palace block at Stirling (see ARCHITECTS, ARTISTS, AND CRAFTSMEN). Scottish mints hammered Roman profile portraits of kings of Scots much earlier than English ones. Monarchs bought much of their finery from France: riding cloaks, silver spurs, velvet, gowns, embroidery, lace, and even sweet peas. How much did French cuisine infiltrate onto Scots palettes? Certain many French terms for food did: 'gigot' for shoulder of lamb; 'petticoatails' from *petites gratelles* (shortbread). 'Ashet' comes from *assiette*; 'tassie' from *tasse*. The humble haggis supposedly derives from *hâché* and even Hogmanay, some argue, may be French in origin. 'Loo' supposedly has its origin in the morning warning of many Edinburgh wives emptying chamber pots out of their tenement windows: 'gardez l'eau'. The point to grasp is how many of these French terms are not Norman, but post-date the Conquest (see SCOTS LANGUAGE).

From at least the reign of *James IV onwards, much of the culture, architecture, and iconography of the *royal court was taken from France. Nowhere was this more striking than in the parties, celebrations, or triumphs of the court. Perhaps the most elaborate public spectacle staged in early modern Scotland was the baptismal fête for the future James VI at *Stirling in 1566. Before an audience of British and European notables, Mary, Queen of Scots, orchestrated a deliciously fabulous display: massive fireworks, an ornate castle assaulted by blackamoors, Turks and wild 'Highland men', three days of feastings and masques: all lifted from France.

The point to appreciate is that these mutual awarenesses emerged from the hard rock of war and defence (see FRANCO-SCOTTISH RELATIONS: 1). Both medieval France and Scotland were threatened by Plantagenet aggression and acquisitiveness, notably by Edward I and Edward III. England thus had emerged as the auld enemy to both (see ANGLO-SCOTTISH RELATIONS: 2; INDEPENDENCE, WARS OF). Beginning with the Franco-Scottish mutual defensive pact concluded with King John *Balliol in 1295–6, the Auld Alliance was renewed and upgraded over the subsequent 260 years: in 1326, 1334, 1359, 1371, 1383, 1391, 1408, 1448, 1484, 1492, 1515, 1517, 1543, 1548, and 1558; only one French king and no Scottish monarch failed to ratify the alliance during that period. France and Scotland thus became something of a mini-NATO and, although co-ordinated campaigns did not always materialize (there was, for example, no French help at the time of Bannockburn), the two did cohere in all sorts of ways, such as Scotland following the popes to Avignon. France did not have to send armies to Scotland or invade England; its mere existence was a distraction for English warmakers. This constantly distracted attempts by Henry VIII, for example, to conquer Scotland, as happened in 1513–14 and

1544–5. As an ally, when France made peace with England, Scotland usually (although not always as completely as the Scots would have liked) was 'comprehended'. When France allied with other powers, such as Denmark, again Scotland was often included.

Mutual war-making, however, did occur, quite often with stunning results (see WARFARE, WEAPONS, AND FORTIFICATIONS). French armed forces were landed in Scotland to fight against the English in 1346 and 1385. A large army of Scots mercenaries was sent to France in 1419 and gained what some would claim was the war-winning victory of Baugé in 1421 (see MERCENARIES IN EUROPE). Scots often perished in the cause of France, however, as at Verneuil in 1424, Flodden in 1513, and in Picardy in 1557. French troops also could be found in Scotland in 1523, 1545, and 1547, when they recaptured St Andrews castle from the assassins of Cardinal Beaton. The most audacious campaign, however, was during 1548–50, when French armadas transported two armies which enabled the Scots to emerge victorious from Somerset's *Rough Wooing. Scotland thus came to figure in French warlore; both the celebrated Froissart and Rabelais enlivened their works with tales from Scottish wars against England.

An alliance is a friendship, a confederation. In this dynastic age, such treaties are often sealed by marriage (and by offspring). The second wives of Alexander II and Alexander III were French. Margaret Stewart (daughter of James I) married a dauphin, but then died young which also happened to François I's favourite daughter, Madeleine of Valois, wife to James V. James, of course, then immediately again married into France by his celebrated union with Mary of Guise, mother to Mary, Queen of Scots. Thus came to pass the apogee of the Auld Alliance: Mary's betrothal (1548) and subsequent marriage (1558) to the Dauphin François, who then became king of Scotland before they became king and queen of France in 1559.

The point to appreciate about Mary, and indeed her father, James V, within the confines of French foreign policy is their nearness to the English succession. For centuries, French genealogists had argued that William 'the Conqueror' was both a bastard and a usurper, the Saxon throne properly devolving upon St *Margaret, wife to Malcolm III of Scotland. When Henry VII overthrew Richard III at Bosworth (employing a Scots contingent in his victory), the English throne was again devolved upon a usurper. Did not James IV trace his lineage back to Joan Beaufort, eldest daughter of Edward III and wife to James I? The marriage of the Thistle and the Rose of 1503 between James IV and Margaret Tudor was thus one of the greatest blunders the Tudors made in their hungry quest for legitimacy. By that union, James V was sometimes only one heartbeat away from the English throne, as in the years 1513–16. When Elizabeth I became queen, the awkward fact that she was a bastard meant that Mary should have succeeded, as her son did when Elizabeth finally died. The Scottish marriage into the French royal house was thus another manifestation of Scotland being a back door into England and for a time dangled before a bemused Europe the spectre of a French empire conjoining all four kingdoms: France, Scotland, England, and Ireland, not to mention Wales.

As part of this empire building, French troops were stationed in Scotland throughout the 1550s and French military engineers refashioned Scottish fortifications to safeguard the country against their mutual auld enemy (see BUILDINGS: 4). Perhaps the most engaging lump of building materials is the artillery blockhouse at Dunbar, the earliest such structure in the British Isles, the blueprint for which was sketched by the duke of Albany in one of his visits to Rome as regent for James V. Even more stunning was the massive *traice italienne* fortification at Leith (1548–58), now long eradicated. But shadows of French constructions can still be seen at the spur of Stirling castle (probably 1548) and at Eyemouth (1557–8). Had not France so threatened England then, Elizabeth probably would not have assisted the Lords of the Congregation (see CONGREGATION, WARS OF THE) and Protestant Scotland would have been stillborn: a most ironic spin-off of the Auld Alliance indeed.

In June 1560, the Treaty of Edinburgh, concluded between England and France, brought the Auld Alliance to an end, though only when viewed with the enormous benefit of hindsight. For the unexpected death of François II in December 1560 brought back to Scotland a French dowager queen and a Guise-designed solution to Scotland's wars of religion: a religious standstill until times were better, Trent had decided upon a Catholic strategy, and Mary, Queen of Scots, was able to consolidate her position. Her court was unmistakably French in both accent and culture. Each of the celebrated four 'Marys', ladies-in-waiting of the queen, was the product of a marriage between a French nobleman and a Scottish noble. And as for the queen herself, it is worth remembering that Mary's first letter in English was not written (and then atrociously) until 1568 and that her last one was in French, in which she probably thought and dreamed. It was only the deposing of Queen Mary and the messy civil war which followed that brought the French connection as such to a close and, by implication, ended the threat of a revival of the Auld Alliance. A new 'amity', with England, took its place.   MM

Franco-Scottish relations: 1. to 1513; 2. 1513–1560.

1. to 1513

Between the 14th and 16th centuries Scotland's most important connection with the outside world was the link with *France. This 'Auld Alliance', a military and political contract with the French crown, was maintained by all Scottish kings from *Robert I to *Mary, Queen of Scots. The alliance defined Scotland's place in European politics as much as her hostility to England and strengthened Franco-Scottish ties in other fields—cultural, social, and economic (see FRANCE)—which reached their peak in the early 16th century.

The alliance began in the sporadic contacts between Scotland's kings and the French monarchy from the late 12th century onwards. As with the later connection, these contacts stemmed from the rivalry between the French kings and their vassals, the Plantagenet kings of England. In 1174 and 1215 Scottish and French kings both supported rebellions against the Plantagenets, but the first indication of direct diplomacy came in the 1240s when the English feared the conclusion of a Franco-Scottish alliance against them. No such alliance was finalized and during the 13th century Scotland's rulers remained closer to England, but these events acted as a precedent when Anglo-Scottish conflict spilled into the Wars of *Independence. Faced with Edward I's aggressive overlordship, the Scots looked to Edward's enemy Philippe IV of France for help. The Franco-Scottish agreement of October 1295, regarded as the origin of the Auld Alliance, planned a combined attack against England. The alliance failed in this grand plan. It failed even to protect the Scots from defeat in 1296. However, the indirect significance of the French link remained. The Anglo-French war lasted to 1303, draining Edward I's resources, giving refuge to Scottish exiles, and inducing the fear of French intervention in Scotland. The end of this war precipitated the crisis of Scotland's struggle and from 1309 *Robert I showed his own anxiety to renew the French connection. This reached fruition in 1326 with a treaty of mutual military support agreed at Corbeil near Paris, the basis of later agreements.

The Scots' experience between 1295 and 1326 would prove typical of the alliance. Large-scale, joint campaigns against England rarely worked. The value of the alliance was as the source of diplomatic support, a safe refuge, and a military threat which distracted Scotland's enemy. These benefits were to prove vital to Scotland in the 1330s when the Bruce cause seemed about to collapse in the face of fresh military defeats. In this crisis Philippe VI of France gave refuge to the young Scottish king, David II, refused to conclude agreements on other issues with the English unless the Scots were included in talks, and finally threatened intervention in the north. The Scottish war contributed to the drift towards Anglo-French conflict in the late 1330s, a conflict which drew Edward III of England's attention towards the Continent. The war between French and English monarchies which continued sporadically until the 1450s set the character of western European politics and diplomacy.

Scotland became one of the theatres of this rivalry and the alliance with France worked within the context of these wider conflicts. Its value to the participants is suggested by its renewal by Scottish kings in 1371, 1391, 1428, and 1448. The alliance released the Scots from the fear of isolation and conquest. The 1330s marked the end of sustained English attempts to secure lordship over Scotland and the diversion of English resources to the Continent gradually allowed the Scots to recover the *Borders from their English garrisons. As the Scots were included in any Anglo-French peace talks, they were free to secure these gains. However, this increased security was not without its price. In return, the Scots were obliged to aid their ally in war and David II returned from France in 1341 with a strong sense of this obligation. In 1346 he led an invasion of northern England in response to Edward III's victory at Crécy. David's efforts to help his ally ended in his own defeat and capture at Neville's Cross. Hopes for even more ambitious Franco-Scottish co-operation were hatched in the mid-1380s. In a repeat of the 1295 plan, a French invasion of southern England was to be combined with a Scots attack in the north. While the Scots appreciated the large financial subsidy distributed by the French, they met the arrival of an expedition to France with hostility. The Scots resented French attitudes to warfare and their expectations of Scottish support. The French found Scotland barbaric, its *nobility overcautious, and its people, their allies, violently resentful of their presence. When the southern invasion failed to materialize, the French went home to the relief of both sets of allies.

In the 14th century the alliance worked best on a smaller scale. A small French force in Scotland in 1339 had achieved more than the later expedition and during the 1350s, 1380s, and 1400s small bands of French knights served under Scottish leaders in conflict on the Borders. With even greater long-term significance Scots also served the French king in Continental warfare. David II had appeared in a French army in 1340, while in 1356 William, earl of Douglas, who like David had grown up in France, fought at the battle of Poitiers. Douglas was knighted by the French king before the battle, though his presence did nothing to prevent the

defeat inflicted by the English. Douglas's example set a trend. A number of other nobles followed his lead during subsequent decades and their presence may have encouraged French perceptions of Scotland as a valuable recruiting ground.

Such perceptions had clearly developed by the time Anglo-French conflict reached new heights in the early 15th century. When in 1419 the dauphin (later Charles VII) needed help to prevent the conquest of France by Henry V of England, he turned to Scotland. Charles approached the Scots for direct military assistance. Between 1419 and 1424 a series of Scottish armies, each numbering several thousand men, would be sent to France. Though meeting numerous defeats, the Scots scored the first major victory over the English at Baugé in 1421 and played a crucial part in slowing the English advance. In return Charles rewarded the Scots lavishly, giving them money and making the leading Scots figures of major importance in France. John Stewart, earl of Buchan, became constable of France, while in return for his support in 1424 Archibald, earl of Douglas, was given the duchy of Touraine. This royal favour and the Scots' indiscriminate plundering earned them unpopularity and French feelings were mixed when the Scots army was destroyed and Buchan and Douglas killed at the battle of Verneuil in 1424. Verneuil was not the end of the story of Scots' involvement in France. Smaller companies of Scots continued to serve Charles VII and from them he recruited a personal bodyguard. This Garde Écossaise, numbering 100 or 120 Scots archers, was raised in 1425 and remained in existence until the French Revolution. By the last years of Charles's reign they controlled access to the king, once more a source of resentment, but their loyalty on the battlefield was vital for Louis XI's survival at the battle of Montlhery in 1465 and that of Charles VIII at Fornovo in 1495.

The attractions of mercenary service drew Scots to France in steady numbers and by the mid-15th century there existed a number of Franco-Scottish noble houses. The best known of these was the cadet branch of the Stewarts of Darnley which held the lordship of Aubigny in Berri, which provided a dynasty of soldiers and diplomats for the French crown. Such families succeeded men like Buchan and the Douglas earls as a natural link between Scotland and France and several Stewarts of Aubigny were employed by the French as ambassadors to their original homeland in the 15th and 16th centuries (see NOBILITY: 2–3).

For these Franco-Scottish families and for many other Scots, the link with France assumed a special significance in the 14th and 15th centuries. The wars with England severed Scotland's earlier access to the heartlands of European society and culture.

The special relationship with France assumed its place as Scotland's main link with the wider world. This shift was clearest in education. Before 1300 Scots students seeking *university education had gone in greatest numbers to Oxford and Cambridge. When politics made their presence in England more difficult, they looked to French institutions. Paris, always the chief northern university, became the principal focus for Scottish students, while others travelled to Avignon and, more especially, Orléans, where a Scots 'nation' or association was established by 1336. Though the divisions caused in the church by the Great Papal Schism of 1378 to 1418 created difficulties for Scottish students in France, which led to the foundation of St Andrews University, Scots continued to seek education in French universities, and Orléans in particular remained a centre of Scottish education. For such Scots the French church was a possible source of advancement. In the 1420s Orléans received a Scottish bishop, John Kirkmichael, while the promotion of another Scot, Andrew Forman, to the archbishopric of Bourges in 1512, was a reward for his brokering of a renewed Franco-Scottish alliance. Such contacts left their mark in Scotland. A French architect, John Morrow, was responsible for rebuilding Melrose abbey in the French style in the early 15th century and may also have built or added to other Scottish churches and castles. In economic terms, the *Low Countries remained the principal market for Scottish merchants. However, France also became a major trading partner. Scottish merchants were settled in French towns, and the Scots' taste for French wine fuelled a regular import trade from the Loire to the west coast ports of Scotland.

By the 15th century, Scots from many different parts of society saw France as an attractive field for their talents and a model to be copied, a land of rich rewards, at the heart of Europe and, usually, open to them as allies. Such Franco-Scottish connections grew out of the increasingly significant political alliance. By the 1420s the breaking of this alliance assumed a major place in English diplomacy. The release of the Scottish king, James I, who had grown up in English captivity, was designed to end direct Scottish aid to France. English hopes were dashed when James renewed the French alliance in 1428 and promised to send a fresh army to help Charles VII, still fighting a war of survival. In return for his support, James was promised the French county of Saintonge and his daughter, Margaret, would marry the Dauphin Louis, the heir to the French throne. Though no new Scots army was sent, in 1436 the Scottish and French royal dynasties were linked by marriage. For the first time since the 13th century the Scottish crown had made a Conti-

nental match and over the next fifteen years it opened a wide range of new connections. However, in the short term, the marriage prefaced a return to Scotland's traditional role in Anglo-French conflict. The Scottish siege of Roxburgh in 1436, part of a co-ordinated offensive, was a failure and James I's murder the next year ended active Scottish involvement in the war for a decade.

Military failure ushered in a period of closer diplomatic contact. In the 1440s the sisters of the young king, James II, and of the Dauphiness Margaret were involved in a series of betrothals and marriages with the European princely houses of Brittany, Savoy, and Austria. This process concluded in 1449 with the marriage of James II himself to Mary of Gueldres, niece of the powerful duke of Burgundy. These alliances were all brokered with the support of Charles VII. James II's minority governments handed over their king's sisters to the French, indicating their place within Charles's orbit. The renewal of the Auld Alliance and other alliances with Brittany and Burgundy in 1448 confirmed this connection. However, internal conflicts prevented Scottish involvement in the decisive French successes of the early 1450s and, despite maintaining close contacts with Charles VII, James II waged war against England without active French support after 1455.

The place of the Franco-Scottish alliance was changing. The victory of Charles VII and the Scottish recovery of Roxburgh and *Berwick by 1461 had ended the main reasons for military co-operation. In this environment Scottish governments were increasingly attracted by the prospect of peace with England and in the 1460s short periods of truce became a cessation of hostilities designed to last until 1519. In these circumstances the French king, Louis XI, had to work harder to keep Scottish support. Louis tempted the young James III with the prospect of lands in Brittany, but his efforts simply encouraged James's appetite for Continental possessions which saw him fruitlessly raise family claims elsewhere. James III also put considerable faith in peace with England. The conclusion of a formal Anglo-Scottish treaty in 1474 left France isolated in the face of English invasion the next year. It also broke the Scots' own insurance against isolation in an increasingly unstable international situation. The English attack on France ended in negotiated peace and the English turned their attentions towards Scotland. Louis had no intention of helping a former ally which had deserted him. Between 1479 and 1483 Scotland was forced to face English aggression without French support for the first time since the 1300s. The loss of Berwick and internal crisis caused by the conflict encouraged James III to renew the French alliance in 1484 but he remained drawn to the prospect of a final peace with England until his death at the hands of his own subjects in 1488 (see ANGLO-SCOTTISH RELATIONS: 2).

The reign of James III marked a transition in Scotland's foreign relations. The French alliance no longer had automatic priority but could be balanced by a link with England, while the emergence of new powers, like Spain, in European diplomacy added potential suitors for Scotland's support. The new king, *James IV, recognized these changes. When set on war against England in the 1490s, James looked for alliances with Spain and the Holy Roman Empire rather than France. Like his father, he also saw the advantages of peace with England. However, the connection with France remained natural and desirable for James IV. His council had renewed the link in 1492 and, though James refused French requests for a fresh treaty for several years, his unofficial bonds with France remained strong. Franco-Scottish nobles and churchmen encouraged the connection, while Louis XII of France subsidized James's fleet as a weapon to allow Scottish intervention in European warfare. When James renewed the alliance in 1512, it signalled his readiness to play this role on France's side. For all his planning and caution, like many of his predecessors, James IV found that involvement in such grand alliances carried dangers. His death and the defeat of his French-trained army at Flodden in 1513 was a military, not a diplomatic, failure, but the next half-century would see increased significance attached to the question of Scotland's conflicting links with France and England (see WARFARE, WEAPONS, AND FORTIFICATIONS: 2). MBr

2. 1513–1560

The minority of *James V (1513–42) can be seen as a tug of war, sometimes literally so, for possession of the young king between competing factions at the *royal court. On the face of it, this factionalism mirrored the conflicting links of Scotland with France and England after Flodden. The regent, Albany (son of James III's brother, Alexander, and potential heir to the throne), had been raised in France; the queen dowager, Margaret Tudor, was English. Yet events and motives were more complicated than this might imply. The return of Stewart émigrés from France—from Albany in 1515 to Esmé Stuart in 1579—tended to have an unsettling effect on court politics, where newly arrived power-brokers were seen either as a threat or an opportunity. Albany was appointed governor and given custody of the infant James V by the king's council, but his appointment was a fixed-term one and conditional; he, in effect, was on probation. The fact that he was able in 1521 to renegotiate the Auld Alliance in the form of the Treaty of Rouen,

securing both French pensions and seeming added security for the realm, strengthened his position. His construction of a sophisticated military blockhouse at the strategic strong point of Dunbar in 1523 may have symbolized the revival of an active military alliance with France, which had been in abeyance since the reign of James II. That was the prospect which lay behind plans for a joint Franco-Scottish invasion force in the same year, when 9,000 French troops were dispatched to Scotland. Much is sometimes made of the 'Flodden complex' and the apparent reluctance of the Scottish nobility to engage in invasions of England after 1513; the main reason that Scottish nobles were reluctant to invade England in 1523 was that the French expeditionary force had arrived only in October, too late in the year for a viable campaign. By 1525, however, following the French defeat at Pavia, François I's need for an active Scottish theatre of war had passed: peace rather than war with England was his priority. The episode was typical of the 'stop-go' nature of the Auld Alliance.

As for Queen Margaret, her relations with her brother, Henry VIII, were equivocal at best and sometimes stormy, partly because she refused to play the role expected of her, as the chief agent of English policy in Scotland. That role fell instead to her second husband, the earl of Angus, who along with the extensive *Douglas kin network took upon himself the mantle of head of a pro-English party, in itself something of a new phenomenon in Scottish court politics (see ANGLO-SCOTTISH RELATIONS: 3). The cause of the English faction, however, was not helped by the long, acrimonious, and very public separation between him and Margaret, which eventually resulted in a divorce in 1526. The escape of the young king from the hands of the *Douglases in 1528, together with the continuing fear of James V of another Douglas coup, naturally provoked an increasing hostility between Scotland and England. Yet it did not automatically induce a closer alliance with France. It was to Charles V, Holy Roman Emperor, rather than to François I that James voiced his private thoughts about the 'madness' of the English heretic king. The marriage of James to Madeleine, daughter of the French king, in 1537 was a curious affair. She was not the bride intended by François, and her death after a mere two months in the Scottish climate virtually nullified any prospective gains by both parties to the marriage treaty. The impact made by her replacement, the widow Mary of Guise, took time to have effect. She was on probation: her coronation was delayed until after she had produced a male heir—James had learned the lesson of Henry VIII's marriages. Ironically, the infant prince and another son both died in 1541. Ever dutiful, Mary produced another child to order, just over twelve months later. Unfortunately it was a girl, the future *Mary, Queen of Scots.

The death of James V, the consequent crisis in 1543, and the *Rough Wooing which followed did not provoke active French intervention. That did not come until after the invasion by Protector Somerset in 1547 with the largest English expeditionary army since 1314, the defeat at Pinkie, and the establishment of a network of sophisticated forts in the winter of 1547–8. In 1548, the Treaty of Haddington brought France into the war, provided a safe refuge for the young queen in the bosom of Henri II's own family, and arranged a future marriage for her. The French used the same up-to-date military tactics as the English, with highly sophisticated forts set up in key strong points such as Inchkeith and Eyemouth (see WARFARE, WEAPONS, AND FORTIFICATIONS: 2)—but outspent them. Almost a tenth of the revenue of the French crown was devoted to the Scottish campaign in 1549–50. That, combined with crisis at home, induced the English to sue for peace by 1550. The treaty even settled the centuries-old question of the Debatable Lands on the Border; a typically French, rational solution was devised—a straight-line frontier, marked by the building of Scots Dyke.

With Queen Mary in France, a marriage arranged between her and the Dauphin François, full reciprocal citizenship of both realms offered to major Scottish nobles, Mary of Guise in power as regent from 1554 onwards, and a garrison of some 700 French troops manning the key strong points in the realm, the Auld Alliance had reached a new level of integration. Yet in that lay the seeds of its downfall. A certain resentment of French officials in Mary's administration was coupled with growing uneasiness about the 'example of Brittany'—an independent duchy annexed to the French crown in 1532 some 40 years after a marriage alliance. The fact that François was duke of Brittany—a French equivalent of the sop of the title of 'prince of Wales' conferred on the first-born of English kings— served only to underline these fears. The treaty which guaranteed the marriage of Mary and François in 1558 had within it the most widely leaked secret clause in Scottish history—the promise of the crown matrimonial to her husband should Mary die. The scene was set for the propaganda of the Lords of the Congregation (see CONGREGATION, WARS OF THE): by the middle of 1559 they had virtually dropped the notion of their revolt as a crusade against idolatry; it was by then portrayed as a campaign against the 'thralldom of strangers', a pretext used to depose the queen regent herself.

Yet the problem with history, as with politics, often is 'events'. The series of accidents in 1560, which included the death of Mary of Guise in June 1560 and the death of François six months later, probably gave the victory of the Congregation, the Treaty of Edinburgh which removed French troops from Scotland, and the subsequent, very Protestant 'amity' with England far too much of an air of inevitability. The real root of the crisis which brought about both the end of the Auld Alliance and the fortuitous triumph of the Scottish Protestant lords was ironic indeed. In June 1559, Henri II, architect of the new-style Auld Alliance which saw Scotland as part of a vast Valois empire, was accidentally killed in a tournament. The man who killed him was one of his own royal guard—the Garde Écossaise.   ML

French Revolution, age of the. The ideas associated with American independence from Britain undoubtedly had an impact on a growing number of people in Scotland after 1775. Yet it was the exciting events of what is now called the French Revolution which really marked a turning point in Scottish history from 1789, but particularly after 1792, with the failure of constitutional monarchy in France and the beginning of more radical experiments of republican government. It is also true that the major impact of the ideas associated with the French Revolution on the people of Scotland arrived via the medium of a pamphlet written by an Englishman, Tom Paine's *Rights of Man*, which also appeared in 1792. After 1793 it became an act of treason to be in possession of a copy in Britain, and if reports of a Gaelic language translation circulating in the Highlands were an exaggeration, certainly all over Scotland working people became interested in reading or hearing others read Paine's thoughts on the fundamental rights of all men. By contrast, there is little evidence of significant circulation of Mary Wollstonecraft's *Vindication of the Rights of Women* in Scotland.

The major reaction in Britain to the rapid acceleration of events in 1792 and 1793 was to split those who were dissatisfied with the status quo into those who sought reform within an Anglophone tradition and consequently distanced themselves from the French experiment, and those who literally did see events in France as marking a rebirth on Enlightened terms of human society in Europe and the world. The first major tremor experienced in Scotland indicating that events in France reported in the press were affecting sizeable numbers of the population of Scotland were the King's Birthday riots in Edinburgh in June 1792, when there was a major breakdown in public order and an attack on the residence of Henry *Dundas in George Square (Dundas was absent at the time). Later in the autumn, following the defeat by the French army of invading Austrian and Prussian troops, there were major demonstrations of public discontent with the established order all over Scotland: the erection of liberty poles, the wearing of the red cap of liberty, public rioting, and the burning in effigy of the leading Scottish politician Henry Dundas. He was convinced, writing to London from Scotland, that collapse of public order was imminent, and many moderate reformers began to accept that the middle ground in politics had disappeared and that their only option was to support established authority. With the execution of the French king in January 1793, the declaration of war by Britain on France in February 1793, and what were perceived as French attacks on religion, popular unrest in Scotland subsided and the government began to move against activists.

It is a curious feature of Scottish reaction to events in France that politically what was under debate were British, French, and universal constitutional issues that evoked a very localized and distinctly Scottish response. Popular unrest in Scotland did not focus on the British king or the British prime minister; rather, it was overwhelmingly directed at Henry Dundas, the Scottish politician who had become such a key member of the British government after 1784. By 1792, he was holding national office as Home Secretary for all of Britain, but he continued to be closely identified with Scotland, and certainly in Scotland it was he, not King George III or prime minister William Pitt, who personified the status quo. When Scottish reformers organized to direct public discontent towards reform rather than public disorder in July 1792, they formed a Scottish Association of the Friends of the People. By November 1793, in an attempt to head off government repression, they hosted a British National Convention of the Friends of the People attended by English delegates who, like the Scottish leaders of the meeting, found themselves arrested, subject to trial by the Scottish courts and to transportation to Australia by their authority.

Scotland became notorious during the years of the French Revolution for the severity with which it dealt with those of its citizens who after 1793 continued to question the basis of its constitution. Its Court of Justiciary, headed by the notorious Robert MacQueen, Lord Braxfield, used the lack of safeguards of individual liberty in Scots law to proceed to a series of extraordinary decisions in which men whose objectives were obviously constitutional reform rather than revolution, such as Thomas *Muir and Thomas Fyshe Palmer, were sentenced to the penal colony of Botany Bay in *Australia. Survivors like Muir became radicalized by the experience but most, like Palmer, in effect were sentenced to death. By 1794 Robert Watt, a government spy who became sympathetic to the radical ideas he heard at political meetings, was executed after his arrest for conspiracy to attempt to kidnap the whole of the Court of Justiciary and seize Edinburgh castle. Henry Dundas's nephew Robert Dundas acted as Lord Advocate during these years and his actions and those of the Scottish bench in the crisis years of 1797 and 1798 gave Scotland a reputation within Britain and beyond as the prototype for government attempts to subvert the traditional liberties of the subject in England and the kind of repression throughout Europe which would follow the final triumph of the coalition ranged against France.

As the nature of what was the French Revolution changed and became first a military dictatorship under Napoleon Bonaparte and then the doppelgänger of the *ancien régime* as the Napoleonic Empire, so the idea of France as the champion of popular liberty receded ever further in Scotland, and the nation's contribution to the war effort became more significant. Yet with the final defeat of Napoleon and the experience of acute post-war depression, radical ideas resurfaced almost immediately and in peacetime government repression inevitably appeared heavy-handed. With the restoration of the Bourbon monarchy in France, reformers and radicals could no longer look to foreign example, but the idea of Scots working men being denied their rights as Britons by a selfish and overpowerful Scottish landowning elite gained ground steadily. With the failure of radical action to evoke anything more than renewed repression and executions after the 'Radical War' of 1820, a strong radical reforming movement allied with Whig dissent within the political system began the movement that eventually achieved a degree of constitutional reform in 1832.   AJM

G

Gaelic dictionaries. Scottish Gaelic lexicography originated in the early days of linguistic and ethnological enquiry in the British Isles and in the context of pressure to make the Scriptures accessible in the vernacular. Thus the Revd Robert Kirk (1644–92), whose *Vocabulary* (published posthumously in 1702) is the earliest we have, also published a Gaelic edition of the Psalms (1684), a Scottish edition of the Irish Bible (1690), and the folkloristic *Secret Commonwealth of Elves, Faunes and Fairies* (1691). Scientific motives predominated with the Oxford Welsh polymath Edward Lhuyd (1660–1709), whose Celtic linguistic collections (1697–1701) aimed to determine how these languages were related to one another. Religious and political motives lay behind Alexander MacDonald's *Vocabulary* (1741), which was essentially a product of the SSPCK's recognition that Gaelic literacy (see GAELIC LANGUAGE) could be used to further the civilizing and Anglicizing of the Gaels.

Although external interest in *Gaelic literature increased in the later 18th century, and gave rise to various schemes to investigate the language, Gaelic lexicography came into its own only later, between 1825 and 1850. By then the form of written Gaelic had stabilized due to the presence of a modern Gaelic Bible, and the range of published literature was gradually expanding (see RELIGIOUS LIFE: 8). The heat of the controversy generated by James MacPherson's *The Poems of Ossian* (1773) had given way to a more scholarly interest in the literature, and the rise of philology was bringing a more scientific curiosity about the language itself. The most noteworthy publications of this period were Robert Armstrong's *Gaelic Dictionary* (1825), the Highland Society's *Dictionarium Scoto-Celticum* (1828), and MacLeod and Dewar's *Dictionary of the Gaelic Language* (1830). Between them, these volumes demonstrated that a serious tradition of lexicography had been established. Thus they mirrored contemporary lexicographical advances in providing illustrative examples, indicating provenance ('biblical', 'literary', 'Ossianic', 'provincial', and so forth), and providing etymologies. Additionally, they had developed traits relating to the special circumstances of Gaelic. Thus they tended,

especially in their English-Gaelic sections, to supply definitions and explanations rather than lexical equivalents. This was because, in addition to answering linguistic questions, these works were aimed in the process at improving the Gaelic literacy and English comprehension of Gaelic speakers.

In the later 19th century, Highland revival was mirrored by a growth of confidence in the worth of the Gaelic language. There were advances in the scholarly study of Gaelic, and Celtic became established as a university-level subject. While the scholars laboured to interpret the texts, the principal lexicographical monument to this period was Edward Dwelly's *Illustrated Gaelic-English Dictionary* (1902–11). Dwelly was a London-based learner of Gaelic, and his dictionary—which he compiled, set, and printed single-handedly—was a work of synthesis, containing all recorded meanings of all words that figured in earlier dictionaries or word lists. Dwelly saw this compendium of the knowledge of the 18th and 19th centuries as an interim measure, pending the scholarly editions and analyses that would necessarily precede a scientific Gaelic dictionary.

The present century has seen an explosion of literature in, and scholarship on, Gaelic. The centre of gravity of Gaelic speaking has moved away from the Argyllshire and Perthshire heartlands to which the makers of the earlier dictionaries belonged. Social change, technological advances, and new modes of communication have imported loanwords and neologisms into the language, brought colloquialisms and dialectal forms to the fore, and stimulated semantic developments in the existing lexicon. The numbers of Gaelic learners and the seriousness of their intentions have increased beyond measure. All these developments have implications for the language that need to be reflected in Gaelic dictionaries. Malcolm MacLennan's *Gaelic Dictionary* (1925) aimed to purge some of the dross contained in earlier dictionaries and to redress some Hebridean omissions. More recently, Sabhal Mór Ostaig has published in *An Stòr-dàta Briathrachais Gàidhlig* (1993) the technical terms and other contemporary vocabulary used by various public agencies and departments. In Richard Cox's *Brìgh nam Facal* (1991) we have the first Gaelic-to-Gaelic dictionary for Gaelic-speaking children. Many touristic and popular works have appeared.

Nevertheless, Dwelly remains the standard reference work, despite its reproduction of mistakes and ghost-words from earlier dictionaries, and the difficulty of working with its unanalysed multiple definitions. The current lack of an authoritative historical dictionary bears witness to the painfully small numbers of trained Gaelic linguists and lexicographers in salaried positions throughout the 20th century. The *Historical Dictionary of Scottish Gaelic* which is currently being prepared within the University of Glasgow, will in due course, it is hoped, redress the balance. At that moment, Gaelic lexicography will really have come of age.   WG

Gaelic language. The early history of Gaelic demonstrates a pattern of language interrelations and consequent cross-language borrowings which repeats itself throughout the history of the language. Just as the *Scots language can be seen as an adaptation of Anglo-Saxon, with a close relationship with northern English, so Gaelic can be taken as a linguistic adaptation and readjustment of Irish, with a large number of features shared with Ulster Irish. Essentially it was the multilingual environment of Scotland which contributed much to each of these as they developed in their new land. For Gaelic, the languages of Latin, Pictish, Norse, French, Scots, and finally English (see LANGUAGES OF SCOTLAND, PRE-1100), have each left their traces.

The widest geographic spread of Gaelic can be dated to around the middle of the 12th century, and included *Galloway for some centuries after this date, although in that area it died out by the 14th or 15th centuries. However, in the 12th century the language had already become the regional, as well as social and political, norm over most of Scotland north of the Forth–Clyde region, to where it had spread from the *Dal Riáta area. Excluded were the Northern Isles where Norse (see ORKNEY AND CAITHNESS, EARLDOM OF) had established itself to create a monoglot area. Scots had by this date had all but created its own zone south of the Forth–Clyde valleys. Norse also had become socially and politically merged with Gaelic over wide areas of the northern and western mainland (see SCANDINAVIA: 1). In the Western Isles it had helped to create a Gaelic-Norse bilingual society which lasted possibly until the 13th century and where the influence of Norse on Gaelic represents a major example of external influence on the latter. After several centuries of the two languages living closely together, much of the seafaring terminology in Gaelic is borrowed from Norse, with words such as *acair* (anchor), *bàta* (boat), *birlinn* (galley),

and *trosg* (cod fish) testifying to the connection, as well as some elements from the vocabulary of the house and household such as *tobht* (ruin), *gàrradh*, (stone fence), *margadh* (market), and *nàbaidh* (neighbour). In addition, Norse has provided many *place-name elements, densest in the Western Isles, less so in mainland areas, and items such as *bàgh* (bay), *nes* (cape, ness), *tolm* (hill), and *tolm* (holm) can be found. The historical development of most Norse place names in a Gaelic environment involve the loss of original syllables and of various word-internal consonants as Gaelic passed through its linguistic history from the earliest period. As an example we can compare Norse *bolstaðr* in a place name like Kirkabister in Shetland which shows the final *-ster* retained in a Norse monoglot area, where this same element has been modified greatly in Gaelic–Norse districts to give, for instance, Leurbost and other names in *-bost*.

We can assume that the expansion of Scots from the 12th century started with its domination over the originally Gaelic-speaking upper classes north of the Forth–Clyde line, and eventually finished, through several centuries of Scots-Gaelic bilingualism, by replacing the Gaelic language in the wider community. At first, this Scots expansion was a slow process and Gaelic words were borrowed into Scots, but the increasing weakness of Gaelic led to the reverse of this, with more and more Scots words being taken into the language. Examples are *truinnsear* (plate, trencher), *fabhd* (fault), *cuidheall* (wheel), words which are well established in northwestern and southern dialects. In the Gaelic–Scots border districts there are occasional instances where a Scots borrowing has replaced a native word, for example *saidh* (hay, from Scots) is found in some dialects of eastern Gaelic where western dialects have retained the word *feur* (hay, grass).

By the beginning of the 17th century we can identify what is now described as the *Gaidhealtachd* or area of the Highlands over which Gaelic was dominant. Although this is originally a language term, from *Gaidheal* (Gaelic speaker), it came to be understood more and more as a geographical description, representing the Highlands and Western Isles (see HIGHLANDS AND ISLANDS: GENERAL). From around the 15th century there is evidence of increasing hostility of mainstream Scots society towards the Gaels (see HIGHLANDS AND ISLANDS AND CENTRAL GOVERNMENT: 1), and this appears to have been reciprocated, with degrees of social tetchiness which at times broke into fighting between groups in both societies. Eventually this intergroup suspicion spread into the realm of linguistic conflict and the weakening of Gaelic linguistic identity began.

Gaelic society over the whole of the period down to the 16th century shared broadly a common culture with that of medieval *Ireland, and the language of both areas consisted of a series of dialects. Neighbouring dialects were closely related linguistically but those at the north and south of the range would not have been mutually intelligible. The shared language of the two societies is called Common Gaelic, and represents the written norms of the literate upper classes of both societies over roughly 400 years. Within this class there was constant coming and going between Scotland and Ireland of members of the medical families, the lawyers and judges, and especially the court poets. We can assume that these temporary visitors had evolved a spoken language to enable them to communicate, though we have no evidence of what this might have sounded like. Equally, a standard spoken language never developed in either Gaelic or Irish and both areas show a strongly developed dialectal particularism down to the present. All speakers use their own local dialectal forms, not only of pronunciation but also of parts of the language systems, vocabulary, morphology, and syntax.

From the 17th century the history of the Gaelic world has been one of demographic decline coupled with increasing cultural shrinkage, including language loss. It would be incorrect to blame any single event for this and a number of factors have contributed to the catastrophic decline over the past 300 years, leading from a situation where a majority of the population of the *Gaidhealtachd* area consisted of Gaelic monoglots, to one where there are no monoglots remaining. Those who speak the language now are all bilinguals whose knowledge of English is much wider than their abilities in Gaelic, and many Gaelic speakers have moved away from the Highlands to live in urban environments (see MIGRATION). Moreover, the remaining population in the native area is demographically unbalanced, with a preponderance of the older generation and decreasing evidence of renewal by children. One effect of this reduction is that the range of dialectal variation in the language has decreased over the past half-century as the mainland dialects disappeared first, followed by those of the islands, and leaving now only the Outer Hebrides as the heartland of the language, with a total Gaelic-speaking population of around 30,000, representing around 80 per cent of their population.

The opening up of the *Gaidhealtachd* to the new economic order (see ECONOMY OF HIGHLANDS AND ISLANDS: 2) which followed the defeat of the last *Jacobite rising in 1745-6 was one of the main contributory factors, though not the only one. Even before this, the Highland border zones had supplied seasonal workers for the farms of the Lowlands, and this movement soon extended to include all parts of the Highlands. Although such work was temporary and workers returned to their home areas for the winter, the rise of the industrial revolution in the *Glasgow and *Dundee areas in particular attracted workers to urban life and to more settled lives. All work outside the Highlands demanded a knowledge of English, but the increased socialization of those who had lived only in a rural economy and who moved to the more open and diverse social structures provided by the cities and towns, sounded the death knell of the language. Gaelic never managed to establish well-structured ghetto areas within cities (see URBAN SOCIETY: 3), areas which might have served the social, religious, and linguistic needs as well as the economic needs of the emigrants.

The economic and social pressures on the Gaels, both push and pull, led almost inevitably to decline. We can interpret the linguistic effects on the Gaels as arising from the notion of *emigration and of the cultural adjustments required for this. The fact that in part this emigration was forced—as through the period of the *Clearances in the Highlands and Islands in particular—and in part voluntary, had the same ultimate outcome, of language death. Such death could result either by families moving out of the area or remaining within it but turning towards English across several generations, from monoglot Gaelic speakers through several generations of bilinguals to monoglot English speakers. Effectively, this represented a form of internal emigration from Gaelic, and Professor Derick Thomson, writer and scholar and a close observer of the society, suggests that native Gaelic speakers will survive only for another 50 to 80 years, or two to three generations. The only temporary reversal of this trend appeared when a number of Gaels in the late 19th century settled as a rural group in Cape Breton, Nova Scotia, where they did maintain the language for several generations, unlike those who had settled in urban areas, either at home or abroad (mainly *Canada, *USA, *Australia, and *New Zealand). However, even here the linguistic decline has continued at roughly the same rate as in the *Gaidhealtachd*. Language loss in the heartland has been a leitmotif of the past three centuries as we have seen the disappearance of a critical mass in a Gaelic-speaking population which could be regarded as socially self-sustaining in community terms.

Schooling and literacy in Gaelic were slow to emerge in the 18th and 19th centuries, and funded over most of this period by the SSPCK and its successors. This was driven by a need to provide Presbyterians with the ability to read the Scriptures (see RELIGIOUS LIFE: 8), and little attention was paid in the education to the linguistic needs of the Gaels.

Gaelic language

The first Gaelic Bible appeared in 1801, having taken just over 30 years to complete, and this formed the major reading matter for the Highland church schools. It was also accepted that the main function of these schools was to teach English, including the ability to read it, but they did succeed in developing a basic reading ability in Gaelic. This emphasis on English affected Gaelic in a similar way to Scots and continued long after the introduction of publicly funded free schooling in the late 19th century. Gaelic was discouraged at school and parents also identified the importance of an ability in English with the economic fate of their children. It was only in the 1970s that the local authority of the Western Isles (later called Comhairle nan Eilean (Islands Council)) opted for a policy of encouraging Gaelic bilingualism through the school curriculum, and the last 30 years have offered signs of a more active public support for the language. Gaelic language radio programmes had existed on BBC Scotland (see RADIO AND TELEVISION: 1) since the 1930s, and public funding is now provided for Comataidh Craolaidh na Gàidhlig (the Gaelic Broadcasting Committee) in addition to that provided for the BBC. This Committee supports all aspects of television and radio broadcasts, including the training of staff. Gaelic never had the resources, either financial or personnel, to develop the range of reading materials demanded by a public becoming increasingly aware of those available for English, and the language suffered accordingly. Gaelic literacy continues down to the present to be associated with education and schooling, and no fully accepted orthography has been established.

One aspect of Highland culture which has survived better than the Gaelic language is that carried by music and song (see SONG, TRADITIONAL AND FOLK: 2), and while the latter does require some aspects of language to sustain it, the former does not and it is likely that it will remain long after other parts of the culture have disappeared. Even here of course it will have to compete for the 'ear-time' resources of its listeners as it comes more and more into the wider world of mass communications. Both Scots and Gaelic are also going to have to compete for financial resources within the new Scottish *parliament and the future relationship of the two languages will be one which will require constant public attention, and political and social influence and lobbying. In this regard Gaelic has some advantages over Scots, but both will remain strongly under the pressures from Standard English, whether from reading or from listening to and watching the electronic media.

The internal language history of Gaelic follows many of the developments of Common Gaelic and demonstrates the process of emergence of a language from a series of dialects shared with Irish. For instance, word stress in Gaelic falls on the first syllable and perhaps linked with this, originally long vowels in the second syllable of disyllabic words have been shortened. Such words mainly involve the vowels /a: o: i:/ in diminutive suffixes and all three in Gaelic have become short [a], as indicated in the spelling: *bradan* (salmon), *uinneag* (window), *cipean* (peg). Original short vowels in such syllables are weakened to the neutral vowel or schwa, but this distinction has been lost in the form of Gaelic spelling system which was developed in the 18th century, so that the very common plural termination *-an* from such a schwa is no longer distinguished from the *-an* of the diminutive: *lochan* (small loch, or lochs).

Gaelic has grammatical gender, unlike Scots or English, with two genders, masculine and feminine, similar to other major European languages. Code-switching, or the regular switching between Gaelic and English sentences within conversations, is a feature of modern spoken Gaelic—much as it is also found between Scots and Scottish English.

From the 17th century English started to assume increasing social and political importance and it becomes more usual to find Gaelic borrowings from it rather than Scots. The widespread social disruptions of the Gaelic world in the 17th and 18th centuries, with their military operations between English- (or Scots-) speaking armies and Gaelic-speaking ones, give rise to many loans into Gaelic, such as *diùc* (duke), *marasgal* (marshal), *batail* (battle), *gunna* (gun) (see ARMY: 2; MERCENARIES IN IRELAND; WARFARE, WEAPONS, AND FORTIFICATIONS: 3).

Instances of naturalization from English (Scots) sources are suggested by all the words illustrated in the previous paragraph. The last of these with a monosyllable with a short vowel ending in a single consonant ('gun') is adopted with the addition of a final syllable in a neutral vowel and this is widespread, though by no means an absolute rule, in similar English words: *còta* (coat), *clòca* (cloak), *geata* (gate), and *tunna* (tun, barrel). Counter-examples, with monosyllables in Gaelic, are becoming more and more common as English loans are adopted for items of new terminology: *lof* (loaf), *tin*, *tram*, and *bus*, though *trèana* and *trèan* (train) are both found.

As part of the process of word-borrowing, we have to consider the extent to which there has been various degrees of naturalization of loans, with phonetic adjustments towards native norms. The early period of Gaelic–Norse bilingualism lasted so long and was so widespread, that the Gaelic sound system was affected. The best example of this is the process of phonetic preaspiration where a voiceless stop in word intervocalic or final position is marked by a brief aspiration or h-sound before the stop, a sound which can often appear in a number of environments as a full voiceless glottal fricative, particularly before a /k/. This feature is one which spread to the hybrid language which emerged over the last 300 years as Gaelic society moved away from Gaelic. This was Highland English, a language which represents another transition from a bilingual to a monolingual society similar to that of the Norse areas around the turn of the previous millennium.   CNÓD

Gaelic literature. The monasteries of the Celtic church (see CHURCH INSTITUTIONS: 1) had a major role to play in the production of Gaelic literature until they went into decline in the 12th century. At this point there was a restructuring within Scottish and Irish Gaelic literary circles, in which conditions of secular artistic patronage were regularized and a supra-dialectal literary language, classical Gaelic (see GAELIC LANGUAGE), emerged which was common to both countries (see IRELAND: 1). The largest body of literature extant which uses this language is the corpus of classical Gaelic verse, composed by the *file* (classical poet), a member of a literary elite who enjoyed a high status at the courts of individual chiefs. Classical Gaelic verse, syllabic in form and largely panegyric in content, continued to be composed in Scotland after it had died out in Ireland. Niall MacMhuirich, the last fully competent practitioner of the MacMhuirich dynasty, poets to the lords of the *Isles and later to the MacDonalds of Clanranald, was still working in the first quarter of the 18th century. The *file* held his position and received his rewards for making poetry for the chief. His output was of a public and official nature and his job combined the roles of poet, chronicler, counsellor, and sometimes diplomat. His training, which some reports hold to be as long as seven years, equipped him with the necessary compositional skill, appropriate phrasing, and references to craft verse for a range of occasions important to the life of the ruling elite (see CLANS OF THE HIGHLANDS AND ISLANDS: 1) and to the wider community, laying heavy emphasis on the continuance of social and artistic tradition. Occasionally, such poets would produce verse of a religious or humorous nature, or romantic verse in the *amour courtois* style. The conservatism of the *file* ensured that classical poetry changed little in either form or content over 500 years until its demise in the 17th and early 18th centuries when chiefs lost interest in patronizing the Gaelic arts.

As the voice of the *file* became less prominent during the course of the 17th century, the work of another type of poet became more significant in the public life of Gaelic society. These poets used stressed, as opposed to syllabic, metre and worked in the vernacular, which had been developing along its own lines during the time when the classical language had remained static. However, the vernacular poets had much in common with their classical counterparts in terms of role, attitudes, and the store of multifaceted images upon which they drew to convey their message. Panegyric imagery, both classical and vernacular, is based on a rich collection of metaphors, drawn mainly from the natural world, together with a range of stereotyped settings in which the subject is pictured; they combine to give an image of the chiefly ideal. At one level, any panegyric can be viewed as an exercise in flattery and such works were seized upon by contemporary non-Gaelic speaking commentators as evidence of the sycophancy of the professional Gaelic poet. However, the repeated attribution of the same qualities—physical beauty, courage, wisdom, good bloodline, generosity, and nobility—suggests the reinforcement of ideals in leadership, rather than reference to particular individual traits. The vernacular panegyrist Màiri Nighean Alasdair Ruaidh (Mary MacLeod *c*.1615– 1707) of Harris, is often seen as a bridge between the classical and vernacular traditions, as her court-style panegyrics combine classical imagery with stressed metre.

Formal court poetry, both classical and vernacular, had run its course by the mid-18th century but many panegyric attitudes and images remained in Gaelic literature despite the increasing influence of non-Gaelic cultures. The 18th century is noted as one of innovation in Gaelic literature, a feature apparent in the poetry of Mac Mhaighstir Alasdair (Alexander MacDonald), Donnchadh Bàn Mac an t-Saoir (Duncan MacIntyre), Rob Donn Mackay, and Uilleam Ros (William Ross). Mac Mhaighstir Alasdair (*c*.1695–*c*.1770), who had connections with Uist and Ardnamurchan, was the most prominent Gaelic literary figure of the period. He was both an innovator and a traditionalist, with an interest in emerging Lowland literature (see CULTURE: 13) including James Thomson's *Seasons* which inspired Mac Mhaighstir Alasdair's own nature poetry, a type new to Gaelic literature because of its concentration on nature without reference to human concerns. His interest in older literature, such as the descriptive runs in traditional tales, is reflected in his major poem *Clanranald's Galley*. Mac Mhaighstir Alasdair was also a political commentator, using his verse to further his *Jacobite sympathies and his desire to see the Gaelic language restored to prominence.

Donnchadh Bàn of Glen Orchy (1724–1812) also composed seasonal verse but he is best known for his hunting songs, and for his nature poetry, such as *Moladh Beinn Dòbhrain* which celebrates the mountain and the deer living there. He was one of the first Gaelic poets to comment on the depopulation caused by intensive sheep farming. Rob Donn (1715–78) from Sutherland had a keen eye for social observation and his commentaries made for biting and witty satire. His elegies are innovative in their emphasis on greater personal reflection and on spiritual rather than temporal values, always guided by the morality of his own time rather than by the traditional ideal. Uilleam Ros from Skye is best known for his passionate love poetry, especially that about Marion Ross from Stornoway with whom he had a brief affair, although he also wrote satires and humorous verse.

The 19th century was marked by *emigration of Gaels to the New World (see CANADA; USA) or south to the Lowlands (see MIGRATION) in search of work, and with them they took their language, literature, and customs, resulting in a severe weakening of Gaelic language and culture, with concomitant effects on the nature of literature produced. A significant body of religious verse of an Evangelical nature was composed, inspired by religious revivalism (see RELIGIOUS LIFE: 6, 8), sometimes distinguished by a passion and drama lacking in the secular literature of the time which was dominated by the theme of homeland, a subject to inspire homesickness in the émigré and to give comfort to the dispossessed and the destitute.

The use of poetry as personal or community therapy has a long tradition in Gaeldom, and never had comfort been so much sought as during the dark years of the *Clearances of the Highlands and Islands. However, poets tended to couch their hopes and fears in terms of clichés, usually to represent a bygone age of plenty and security, seldom addressing the real problems of the time or offering any solutions for the future. Little 19th-century poetry is distinguished by intellectual vision or by arresting imagery. The exceptions stand out because of their rarity: Uilleam Mac Dhun Lèibhe's angry protest against the Islay clearances in *Fios Thun a' Bhàrd* and Bard Iarsiadair's analysis and condemnation of the policies and the individuals responsible for the problems faced by Gaels, in his long, emotional poem *Spiorad a' Charthannais*. The best known of all the poets of the age was Màiri Mhòr nan Òran (1821–98) from Skye, much of whose work embodies the spirit of *land agitation and reform in the 1870s and 1880s. Her verse has been criticized for lack of intellectual weight, but her skilful evocation of place and mood, coupled with lyricism and a host of memorable tunes, has ensured that she is still one of Gaeldom's best-loved poets and songmakers.

Twentieth-century Gaelic literature has been dominated by the work of the poet Sorley Maclean, who caused a revolution in poetic composition in the Scottish Gaelic world when his collection *Dàin do Eimhir* (Poems to Eimhir) was published in 1943. Experiments in freer verse had been conducted before but never had form and content appeared so startlingly different, and a new generation of poets was inspired to produce *nua-bhardachd* (modern poetry) which saw an increasing departure from the regular stress patterns and rhyme schemes of traditional verse and drew upon a wide range of new influences. Sorley Maclean (1911–96) was born in Raasay, Skye, and grew up surrounded by Gaelic traditional music and song which were to influence his later work. His other influences include 17th-century metaphysical poets, 1930s English poetry, and symbolism, the last seen clearly in two of his best-known poems, *Hallaig* and *Coilltean Ratharsair*. His work centres on themes related to his left-wing and Scottish nationalist politics, his love of certain women, anti-landlordism, and some anti-clericalism.

The generation following Maclean includes Lewis-born poets Derick Thomson (b. 1921) and Iain Crichton Smith (1928–98). Thomson's poetry highlights the problems of bilingualism and biculturalism, as well as his relationship to his native Lewis and the fate of the Gaelic language. He is interested in homeland, exile, and Scottish *nationalism and his feelings on the outlook for the Gaelic language are bleak. Iain Crichton Smith's work also includes the theme of exile as well as philosophical, social, and psychological concerns. Younger poets have come on the scene since Thomson and Smith. Many have experimented with form, and much of the verse covers a wide variety of subject matter, some personal, some political, some observational. Most poets cover the essential problems of Gaeldom to a greater or lesser degree: marginalization, cultural and linguistic decay, and exile.

Distinct from the output of 'modern' poets is the ongoing work of the so-called *baird baile* (community poets), who, for the most part, produce work which is oral, localized, and does not have much currency outside the particular community due to a reliance on local characters and specific events. There are exceptions, for instance Donald MacIntyre, the Paisley Bard, a native of South Uist and Murdo MacFarlane, the Melbost Bard, from Lewis; Donald MacIntyre displays his concern for social justice while MacFarlane writes exile poetry and songs about the morality of war.

Running alongside the major genres of Gaelic poetry there has always been an oral song (see SONG, TRADITIONAL AND FOLK: 2) tradition containing a vast array of love songs, laments, humorous songs, poetic debates, poems of complaint, lullabies, songs of the supernatural, and work songs, the best known of which today are the strongly rhythmical *òrain luaidh*, once sung by teams of women when waulking tweed. This corpus displays distinct metrical forms such as rhyming paragraphs, incremental repetition and split line stanzas; refrains of meaningless vocables are common in work songs.

Until the 19th century, Scottish Gaelic prose figured mostly in the form of the oral tradition featuring Gaelic versions of international tales and the exploits of legendary Irish heroes such as Cu Chulainn and Fionn Mac Cumhaill. The tales were later more popular in the form of narrative poems known as Fenian ballads, which were sung in parts of the Highlands into the 19th and occasionally the 20th century. Those were the genuine sources upon which James MacPherson of infamous Ossian renown based his fabricated ancient Gaelic epics, arousing great controversy but also indirectly stimulating the work of Gaelic literature collectors.

The mid-19th century saw the appearance of different prose publications and the Gaelic-speaking Highlands supported periodicals containing a host of different kinds of reading matter. The most influential writer of this period was Norman MacLeod, or Caraid nan Gàidheal. His impressive range of subject matter demonstrates the twin aims of evangelical instruction and the development of a flexible prose style. A brief flurry of Gaelic novels appeared in 1910–20 but the form has never achieved significance, whereas the short story has increasingly become a feature of 20th-century Gaelic literature, greatly influenced by the advent in 1956 of the quarterly *Gairm*, arguably the most influential 20th-century publication in Gaelic Scotland. *Gairm* features a wide range of articles including translations from other European languages, short stories, serial novels, poetry, current affairs, and reviews. The major short-story writer of the 20th century was Iain Crichton Smith, who combined intellectualism with a simplicity of style, producing a deceptively rich and cerebral literary form. Smith was also influential in the development of Gaelic drama, which has been encouraged by the advent of Gaelic drama companies in the 1970s and 1990s, and by increased coverage on television and radio.   JMacD

Gallacher, William (Willie) (1881–1965), Communist leader. Gallacher's political and cultural formation occurred within the orbit of the skilled and politically conscious element of the Clydeside working class, reacting in a variety of modes against the extended social misery and deprivation

of the late Victorian era—in a society renowned for its hard-drinking practices he remained all his life a rigid teetotaller (see TEMPERANCE).

Large-scale industrial unrest among the Clydeside engineering trades during the 1914–18 War and immediate post-war years assumed political and even at times revolutionary (see 'RED CLYDESIDE') overtones. Gallacher emerged a leader on the Clyde Workers' Committee and was associated with John Maclean's anti-war agitation.

The establishment of the Communist International following the Russian Revolution represented a crossroads for the British left. Gallacher's principal historical role was as one of the main influences guiding and prodding British revolutionaries towards adhesion to the Soviet-dominated Comintern. In doing so he rejected the revolutionary Scottish nationalism now advocated by Maclean on the model of James Connolly, becoming thereby Maclean's fierce opponent.

As the Comintern and its component parties evolved towards Stalinism, Gallacher was publicly among the most zealous in the Communist Party leadership pursuing this course; however he vehemently (though not openly) dissented from the Comintern instruction in 1939 to oppose the anti-Hitler war. In 1935 he was elected as MP for the mining constituency of West Fife, working assiduously on behalf of his constituents until defeated in 1950, mainly due to the intense atmosphere of the Cold War. He appears to have been distressed by the extent of Stalin's criminality revealed in 1956, though not otherwise shaken in his convictions. By the closing years of his life he had come to be regarded in the nature of a left-wing icon, and his funeral in Paisley attracted enormous crowds.   WT

Galloway, origins of. Galloway, a peninsula situated in one sense at the south-west margin of the emerging Scottish kingdom, was in another perspective one of the centres of trade and communications in the Irish Sea province. Like Scotland, it takes its name from that of a people, in this case from a group of mixed ethnicity: the Gall Gaidheil ('Scandinavian Gaels'). Galloway comes from the Gaelic dative plural i nGall Gaidhealaib ('amongst the Gall Gaidheil') (see SCANDINAVIA: 1).

The Gall Gaidheil are a nebulous people, occurring very infrequently in the annals. But one thing seems clear; originally they do not seem to have had anything to do with Galloway. According to the *Annals of Ulster*, they were fighting in *Ireland in 856 and 857, under their leader Caittil Find (Ketill 'the Fair'), against both Irish protagonists and the Scandinavians of Dublin. However, the Hebrides, rather than Galloway, appears to be the area where the ethno-genesis of this mixed Gaelic,

Scandinavian people took place. Caittil Find can be identified with Ketill 'Flatnose', whom Icelandic tradition names as a ruler of the Hebrides in the generation prior to the settlement of Iceland which began c.875. Two notes added, at some later date, to the *Felire Oengusso Céli De*, an Irish versified calendar of saints written c.800, firmly place the Gall Gaidheil within the Inner Hebrides. The first claims that St Donnan of Eigg established his monastery amongst the Gall Gaidheil, and the second says that St Blaan was bishop of Kingarth among the Gall Gaidheil. Kingarth is on Bute. Culturally, little is known about the 9th-century Gall Gaidheil, except that since Gaidheil is primarily a linguistic term, it suggests the dominant language of this unusual ethnic group was Gaelic (see GAELIC LANGUAGE). They also appear to have been identifiably Christian. In the 856 annal reference, it is the Scandinavians, against whom they are fighting, who are described as *gennti* (heathens).

At the time of the first appearance of the Gall Gaidheil, Galloway does not seem to have been part of the Gaelic-speaking world. Rather, the predominant cultural affiliation of the area appears to have been British and Anglian. The early British kingdom of Rheged had been overrun by the Angles of Northumbria and, by 731, *Whithorn had become the seat of an Anglian bishopric. This line of bishops continued for a century until the 830s when a certain Heathored became the last on record. However, when 300 years later, a new bishop was recorded in a papal letter of 1128, an intervening period of Gaelicization had apparently taken place, because the bishop bore a Gaelic name Gilla Aldan, as did Fergus, the contemporary lord of Galloway.

The first record of Gall Gaidheil being used with reference to Galloway is in 1034, when the obit of *Suibne mac Cinaedha rí Gallgaidhel* ('king of the Gall Gaidheil') is reported in the *Annals of Ulster*. This title never appears to have been used of a lord of Argyll or the Hebrides. However, it is used in the *Annals of Ulster* of later lords of Galloway. It is applied to Rolant mac Uchtraigh who died in 1199 and his son and successor Ailin who died in 1234, implying *rí Gallgaidhel* was the contemporary Gaelic title for the Galwegian lord.

How had this Gaelicization come about, and how did the name of a mixed 9th-century people become attached to a previously British/Anglian territory? The simplest answer is a population movement, a migration of Gaelic-speaking Gall Gaidheil from the Inner Hebrides at some point prior to 1034. The situation would be analogous to that of the Scoti sailing from Ireland to Pictland, which they eventually came to dominate. The lack of a historical record of the Gall Gaidheil arrival in

Galloway is not a great problem; there is a similar lack of historical information for the Scandinavian takeover of *Man and for their settlement in northwest England. In the latter cases, the Scandinavian settlement can be deduced by the existence of Scandinavian *place names. For the Gall Gaidheil settlement in Galloway we need look no further than the thousands of Gaelic place names.   APJ

gardening and landscapes. Shaped by topography (see GEOLOGY AND LANDSCAPE) and *climate, tempered by horticultural skill, and infused with a deep sense of history and *national identity, Scotland's gardens and designed landscapes have their own distinctive character.

Medieval gardens or 'yards' were strictly formal, enclosed by defensive walls. Commissioned by secular or religious authority, they followed a European tradition of herb garden, kitchen garden, and orchard, with the hunting park an adjunct for more vigorous leisure pursuits. By the late 16th century, Timothy Pont's remarkable *maps highlight gardens of some stature associated with abbeys, castles, and noble houses, such as Castle Menzies, Perthshire, and Paisley abbey, Renfrewshire.

The Stewart dynasty (see KINGSHIP: 5) placed Scotland on the cutting edge of European cultural developments. Pitscottie described James III as 'delighting more in music and policie [pleasure grounds] and building' than he did in the government of his realm. Formal gardens achieve considerable sophistication by the reigns of *James IV and *James V, with the importation of French gardeners at Stirling in 1501 and at Holyrood in 1536. Royal gardens survive in a simplified or modified form at *Stirling, the palaces of Linlithgow, Falkland, and Holyroodhouse. The impressive King's Knot below Stirling castle remains something of an enigma, but Falkland palace, Fife, has the only surviving example of a *jeu quarre* royal tennis court (1539–41), of world heritage importance. Holyrood Park, Edinburgh, is the most complete of the hunting parks still attached to a royal residence.

Hilly terrain suited a tradition of terraced gardening which coexisted alongside the more conventional walled enclosures of the 16th and 17th century, such as Castle Campbell, Clackmannanshire, Culross palace, and Aberdour castle in Fife. Little can yet be said about how these now 'archaeological' gardens mirrored those of Renaissance Italy (see CULTURE: 4; MEDITERRANEAN LANDS IN THE MIDDLE AGES) and to what extent they incorporated the Scots' own proud aesthetic.

By the early 17th century, noblemen's gardens around the traditional tower house could comprise more than a simple walled enclosure. Sir David Lindsay's enlightenment is exhibited at Edzell castle, Angus, where the garden walls (1604) have Italian Renaissance detailing enriched with planetary deities and other emblematic masonry panels derived from German sources. Pinkie House, Musselburgh (c.1613), is a *studia humanitatis*, 'a sophisticated expression of the Renaissance villa and garden as an intellectual and moral sanctuary'. The 17th century saw the proliferation of the distinctive and sophisticated Scottish sundial as a characteristic of Scottish gardens unmatched elsewhere.

The first gardening book by John Reid, the *Scots Gard'ner* (1683), borrowed heavily from John Evelyn's translation (1658) of *Le Jardinier françois* by Nicolas de Bonnefons (1651), but was geared to Scottish conditions. Though this volume was published late by European standards, Scots were well travelled and had access to mainstream European gardening literature and ideas from an early date. The Grand Tour was underway by 1680, when Lord Drumlanrig and his brother William, with the earl of Traquair, visited Versailles, Saint-Germains, Saint-Cloud, Sceaux, Maison, Fontainebleau, Vaux (Vaux-le-Vicomte), and Chantilly—properties which were either famous for their gardens or their waterworks.

Founded in 1670, the Edinburgh Botanic Garden brought together the collections (beyond everyday plants) of two notable Scots physicians, Robert Sibbald and Andrew Balfour. The former had studied at Leiden (see LOW COUNTRIES), while Balfour's interest in botany had been awakened by visiting Robert Morison's garden at Blois belonging to the duc d'Orléans. Morison, a refugee Scot, went on to become the first professor of botany at Oxford.

By the end of the 17th century, enclosing garden walls were being lowered and the countryside was drawn into the garden. Sir William Bruce (c.1630–1710), King's Surveyor and Master of Works from 1671, brought Scotland to the forefront of late 17th-century garden developments. First at Balcaskie and then Kinross, Fife, Bruce united house, gardens, and landscape around an axial vista focused respectively on the Bass Rock and Loch Leven castle. The grandeur of conception is imbued with cultural memory but equally anticipates Stephen Switzer's *Ichnographia Rustica* (1718). Bruce's mantle was taken up by Alexander Edward (1651–1708) who continued the expansive Baroque landscape tradition at Hamilton palace, Lanarkshire, and Kinnaird castle, Angus, and elsewhere, but it was the earl of Mar at Alloa, Clackmannanshire, who created the most ambitious of the Versailles-inspired gardens, described by John Macky in 1723 as 'the largest and the finest . . . of any in Britain'. Sadly, only fragments of this survive. Contemporaneously, the second duke of Queensberry (1662–1712) aggressively reworked an early ter-raced garden at Drumlanrig castle, Dumfriesshire, incorporating the Douglas family crest into the parterre design. Between 1722 and before his death in 1747, Field Marshall, second earl of Stair undertook a massive, militaristic earthwork garden at Castle Kennedy, Wigtownshire.

The expense of maintaining 'Frenchified' gardens led to a sea change as the pace of agricultural improvement (see ECONOMY, PRIMARY SECTOR: 1) after the *Union of 1707 demanded a less authoritarian formal landscape style. Sir John *Clerk of Penicuik (1676–1755), the leading antiquarian and arbiter of taste, consulted the 'genius of the place', reflecting the ideas of Alexander Pope. Clerk's didactic poem 'The Country Seat', written in 1727, is exemplified by his Virgilian landscapes-cum-*fermes ornées* at Mavisbank and Penicuik, Midlothian. Clerk's influence touched his associate and friend, the architect William Adam (1649–1748), a formalist who nevertheless laid down that the 'rising and falling of the ground are to be humoured and make the greatest beautys in gardens'.

From the 1740s onwards, formality loosened to be replaced by a parkland landscape of irregular belts and clumps, in a more naturalistic informal style. Pupils of 'Capability' Brown, Robert Robinson, and Thomas White senior and junior, skilfully captured the market north of the Border. Between 1770 and 1819, the Whites were involved at some 70 estates in Scotland, from Buchanan, Stirlingshire; Cullen, Banffshire; and Glamis and Scone, Perthshire. Meanwhile, contemporaries such as James Justice, author of *The Scots Gardiner's Director* (1754), raised Scottish gardening to new heights through instructions to 'gardiners who make a kitchen garden and the culture of flowers their business . . . particularly adapted to the climate of Scotland'. Horticultural proficiency in the management of greenhouse, hot walls, planting, and training fruit trees led to a strong demand for Scots gardeners south of the Border.

The later 18th century (see CULTURE: 11) saw a response to the tame, spiritless beauty of this imported English landscape style. The growth of Picturesque taste and Ossianic Romanticism, a development of the native appreciation of 'gardens in the wild', represents an early Scottish trend compared with elsewhere. The Hermitage at Dunkeld, and the Falls of Acharn, Kenmore, Perthshire, epitomize the idea of concealment, surprise, and the dramatic revelation of natural scenery which had such a profound influence on English, Welsh, and foreign tourists who came north before and after the Napoleonic Wars. The spectacular and sublime Falls of Clyde, Lanarkshire, were regularly visited and painted by artists from the middle of the 18th century.

geology and landscape

Humphrey Repton, through his sons, was involved with only one landscape in Scotland at Valleyfield, Fife, but his writings were influential in the return of the formal garden close to the house. Sir Walter Scott (1771–1832) grievously lamented the sweeping away of the old, indigenous formal gardens and talked of the propriety of retaining every shred connected with history or antiquity. The reaction to the English 'natural' style of gardening was taken up by both Scott and John Claudius Loudon (1783–1843). Loudon, a Scot by birth, worked in a variety of styles and was the most prolific gardening author of the 19th century in Britain. Both men as writers and practitioners had a profound impact on early 19th-century gardens and landscapes at home and abroad.

The Scottish Victorian and Edwardian garden was one of contrast and diversification (see CULTURE: 17). By 1850, ambitious formal gardens had been re-created at Drummond castle, Perthshire; Dunrobin, Sutherland; and Drumlanrig, Dumfriesshire, often involving a partnership of leading architects (see ARCHITECTS, ARTISTS, AND CRAFTSMEN), landscape designers, and head gardeners. Sir Charles Barry, William Burn, Lewis and George Kennedy, William Sawrey Gilpin, William Andrews Nesfield, Charles M'Intosh, Donald Beaton, and John Caie are amongst notable Scotsmen and Englishmen who practised their craft or exerted a strong influence in the Victorian era. The resultant eclectic mix of the formal, gardenesque, and picturesque from the 1840s is evident at Dalkeith, Midlothian (less so today), and Drumlanrig, Dumfriesshire. From these places, where they worked under the management of the head gardeners and leading authors M'Intosh, and David and William Thomson, young trainee gardeners went on to take up major positions in Britain and overseas, as for away as *Australia. By the end of the century, the creative writings of Robinson and Jekyll, and those of Miss Frances Hope, Edinburgh, stimulated the revival of the intimate 17th-century Scots mixed flower and kitchen garden 'plaisance'. Robert Lorimer (1864–1929) was a leading exponent at Kellie castle and Earlshall, Fife.

The mid-19th century saw the inception of public parks. Notable designers include Sir Joseph Paxton in the 1850s and 1860s at Kelvingrove Park and Queen's Park, Glasgow; Baxter Park, Dundee; and the Public Park, Dunfermline. James Whitton (1850–1925), director of Glasgow parks, took a leading role in the rapid progress of later urban parks. William W. Pettigrew became parks director in Manchester, publishing a pioneering book on public park management in 1937. John McLaren (1846–1943), an émigré Scot and parks superintendent in San Francisco, was involved with the layout of the 494-acre (200-hectare) Golden Gate Park.

In the early 1850s, the introduction of the Himalayan rhododendrons and their subsequent hybrids broke the stranglehold of the Victorian bedding schemes, while the finds of the Scotsmen David Douglas and John Jeffrey in the north-west USA revolutionized ornamental and commercial conifer planting, transforming arboreta and the native woodland landscape. The mild climate and soils of the west coast of Scotland facilitated the creation of specialist plantsmen's gardens at Crarae, Arduaine and Younger Botanic Garden, Argyllshire, and Inverewe and Logan Botanic Garden, Sutherland and Wigtownshire respectively. In association with the Royal Botanic Garden, Edinburgh, these gardens provide arguably the richest collection of north American and Sino-Himalayan species in the northern hemisphere. The intrepid Scot George Forrest continued the Scottish plant hunting tradition into the 20th century, undertaking seven expeditions to western China between 1904 and 1932, yielding more than 30,000 botanical specimens and introducing over 300 new species of rhododendron alone. Other notable collectors were Euan Cox (1893–1977) and George Sheriff (1898–1967).

Scottish gardens of the 20th century echo the modern movement in architecture, harking back to more traditional designs or incorporating new creative influences. Little Sparta, a garden of international significance, has been created by the artist Ian Hamilton Finlay, and contains references to classical themes of the 18th century. The architect and critic Charles Jencks and his late wife Maggie Keswick incorporated ancient oriental traditions and modern chaos theory into their highly significant and still developing post-modern garden at Portrack, Dumfriesshire.

With over half the world's conifers reported to be threatened in their native habitats, the Royal Botanic Garden, Edinburgh, is currently engaged in a major programme to establish endangered conifers from temperate climates in cultivation in Scotland. The Younger Botanic Garden, Argyllshire, and several private estates lead the way in this recent development. The processes of gardening and landscaping continue to exert an ever-changing impact on the Scottish landscape.   FJ

geology and landscape. The tradition of focusing on implications for the country's people, when considering the evolution of Scottish landscapes, is one rooted close to the emergence of the discipline of geology. This is very evident in Archibald Geikie's *The Scenery of Scotland, viewed in connection with its Physical Geology*, of 1865. By the turn of the century, however, he was finding over-enthusiastic environmentalists amusing. Sir Archie caricatured the calumny that denizens of Caithness are of dubious mental calibre as an example of geological determinism: 'so flat is the landscape on the horizontally bedded Caithness flagstones that friends would sight each other from afar. By the time they met, their grins of greeting would have become disturbingly fixed'. It was, however, only simplistic attitudes which he was lampooning. From his decades of fieldwork, Geikie remained convinced that the varied landscapes of Scotland had very different problems and potentials. And more than that, from his long life embracing both the industrializing of the Lowlands and the *Clearances of the Highlands and Islands, he was very aware that the possibilities of the physical environment are perceived and evaluated at different times in quite different ways by different people.

We can agree with him that Scotland is not an isotropic plane, so the aim here is to identify some basic factors in the equation of interaction between people and whatever environment they inherited from those who had gone before them. 'Inherited' is a key word. It is not as if each generation starts with a hitherto unmodified natural world, a clean slate which can be viewed afresh: rather it is a palimpsest, with the inherited landscape bearing the legacies of previous generations, constructive and destructive.

Although we have sure knowledge of humans in Scotland only within the last 10,000 years, some of the options open to them (and indeed to us in the future) have been conditioned by geological events spread over more than 2,500 million years, and involving some of the oldest rocks now visible anywhere on the surface of the planet. Paradoxically, however, it is only in the last thousandth of this time span that glaciations have sculpted the bedrock into the particular landscape forms which have been the stage for human activity.

In the layout of Scotland, the main belts of rock are bounded by major south-west/north-east fault lines, with the Midland Valley lying between the Highland Boundary Fault and the Southern Upland Fault. Furthest to the north-west lie the oldest rocks, the Lewisian of the Outer Hebrides and north-west mainland. Metamorphosed from sediments by heat and pressure into a tough grey crystalline rock, then scoured by glaciation, these have never offered a favourable basis for agriculture. The Torridonian sandstone of the north-west coastlands and Islay, formed about 1,000 million years ago by erosion of the Lewisian material, offers only marginally better potential.

Between 600 and 400 million years ago, the drifting of the continents opened and closed the Iapetus Ocean. The Dalradian rocks of the southern Highlands record the opening. Its closing deformed the Dalradian and Moine rocks, and was marked by the intrusion of the granites of Rannoch Moor and the Cairngorms. The closing also brought together England and Scotland for the first time, the suture coinciding remarkably with the current political boundary—a point surprisingly missed in the Devolution debate.

From 400 to around 350 million years ago, as part of the supercontinent Pangaea, Scotland lay near the equator. Desert sands accumulated under the tropical sun, forming the Old Red Sandstone which can now be seen mainly in eastern Scotland, from the Merse via Strathmore and the Moray Firth and Caithness to Orkney. It has offered considerable advantages to farmers (see RURAL SETTLEMENT; RURAL SOCIETY), ancient, medieval, and modern. Its generally horizontal bedding produces fields with conveniently gentle gradients, but without waterlogging because of its sandiness. Old Red Sandstone soils are doubly advantageous, because unlike wetter ones they warm up earlier in the spring, increasing the growing season. This is particularly important in places like Orkney.

There have always been drainage problems on the relatively impermeable glacial tills and clay soils associated with many of the other rocks of the Midland Valley and of low-lying areas of the southern Uplands and eastern Highlands. Some of these clay soils derive from calcareous rocks, but the benefit of this for reducing soil acidity is offset by their tendency to waterlog. The acidic rocks which preponderate in so much of Scotland give soils typically low on plant nutrients.

Sometimes Scotland is represented as if cardinal characteristics may be summarized in terms of 'north' and 'south'. As an alternative, when reflecting on both Scottish archaeology and history, it seems worth considering the degree of geological and landscape differentiation between 'east' and 'west'. The Old Red Sandstone's easterly distribution is a case in point. Because of geological structure and erosional history, there are striking differences between Scotland's west- and east-coast landscapes. Much of the west rises abruptly from the sea to substantial mountains, which cause heavy orographic rainfall. East of the mountains, gentler slopes grade into broad low-lying coastal plains. With the precipitation mainly coming in from the Atlantic, the east is in a rain shadow, with less cloudy skies letting in more insolation. The way that the oceanic heat sink of the Atlantic upwind holds down summer temperatures in the west sets serious limits for crop growth there, compared to the warmer growing season of the more continental climate where the east faces the shallow North Sea. The benefits for farmers have therefore been multiplied by the way that Scotland's geological evolution has fortuitously placed the advantageous Old Red Sandstone landscapes on the eastern side of the country. From prehistory to the present day, Orkney in the north has offered more scope for prosperous agriculture than Kintyre far to the south.

The Old and New Red Sandstones have left major legacies in Scotland's historic townscapes (see URBAN SETTLEMENT) as well as landscapes, not least in marking the Victorian and Edwardian prosperity of settlements ranging in scale from Dunbar to Glasgow.

By about 350 million years ago, the Midland Valley was forming, a rift valley down-faulted by movements on the Southern Upland and Highland Boundary Faults. There had already been volcanic activity in the area, and new volcanoes erupted. The tougher of the volcanic rocks were later able to resist the erosive power of the glaciers, leaving the landscape of the Scottish 'Lowlands' a distinctly hilly one. Some of these glacially sculpted volcanic features are as large as the Ochil and Pentland hills; others, though much smaller, have been of considerable historical importance, such as the crag and tail formations on which *Edinburgh and *Stirling are set with their castles; Arthur's Seat, also in Edinburgh; the Isle of May in the Forth estuary; and even tiny Inchgarvie (the crucial islet steppingstone for the Victorian Forth Rail Bridge). The volcanoes were erupting into warm seas, for between c.350 and 250 million years ago Scotland's climate was similar to that of the Caribbean today. Remains of algae and forest plants accumulated, forming the oil shales and coal (see ECONOMY, PRIMARY SECTOR: 3) beds which have been the basis of so much of Scotland's economic history.

By about 250 million years ago, the continuing continental drift was stretching the area, and the Minch and North Sea basins began to grow. The Atlantic Ocean, however, did not start to open up until very much later: less than 60 million years ago, after the dinosaurs had come and gone. The spreading of the ocean (sometimes by 32 miles (20 km) per million years) caused tension cracks in the crust. Lavas poured out, their fluidity due to low silica content. Layer after layer of basic basalts covered large areas in Scotland, sometimes with features such as Macleod's Tables. In Mull the magma turned acidic (silica-rich), lost its fluidity, and the ensuing explosion left its mark on today's scenery. Large cone volcanoes also developed, and their eroded roots add character to the landscapes of St Kilda, Arran, Ardnamurchan, Rhum, and Skye.

The importance of glaciation for shaping the landscape involves deposition as well as erosion,

and also effects the levels of land and sea. Glaciations are relatively rare in the planet's history, and the current Quaternary Ice Age has occupied little more than two and a half million years, a very short period in geological terms. It has not, however, been a simple event. In this time there have probably been over twenty major glaciations, separated by interglacial phases longer and sometimes warmer than the Holocene period in which we now live. Though sometimes referred to as the 'Postglacial', the neutral term 'Holocene' (meaning merely 'same as the present') is to be preferred, since it seems likely that we are in an interglacial phase, heading for another glacial unless global warming intervenes. So far, the Holocene has lasted for slightly over 10,000 years in terms of conventional 'radiocarbon years'; these bear a complex relationship to calendar years, but are still widely—and often loosely—quoted in the literature.

During the multiple glaciations, Scotland has been repeatedly buried in major ice sheets, some coalescing with those of Scandinavia. The erosive power of the ice often gouged out the zones of shattered rock along the fault lines of much earlier eras, producing some of the most spectacular features of the Scottish landscape. The Great Glen is one of these, bisecting the Highlands from Fort William to Inverness along the line of a tear fault comparable to the San Andreas fault of Los Angeles. The ice dug deep. Loch Ness, one of the line of long lochs now filling the basins which it excavated, is one and a half times deeper than the seas covering much of the continental shelf on which Scotland stands. By linking the Great Glen lochs, Telford (see TRANSPORT AND COMMUNICATIONS: 3) formed the Caledonian Canal.

Many other glacially excavated lines of geological weakness offered natural routeways. Water routes were created not only along freshwater lochs but as seaways between offshore islands or penetrating far inland, whether up east- or west-coast estuaries, or via the long sea-lochs of the fiord coast of the western Highlands. On land, glacially excavated valleys have also provided routes of historical importance: from prehistory through medieval times, and from drove roads and 18th-century military roads to the railway network of the Victorians. The south-west/north-east Caledonian Trend characteristic of Scotland's geology has produced landscapes favouring movement on that orientation, rather than across the grain of the terrain. Particular historical interest thus often attaches to places where this grain has been breached, offering cross-country routes. Some of these were created where subsidiary fault lines occurring at right angles to the main south-west/north-east trend were picked out by the ice. Other breaches may reflect pre-glacial river patterns.

Argyll offers an illustration of the possibility of considering interplay between geology's landscape legacies and human decision-making. As elsewhere, the Caledonian Trend provides potential routes running south-west/north-east, on land and by freshwater lochs and sea-lochs. At Crinan, however, this trend is crossed by a transverse fault, and the Crinan plain has ready access, not only to the seaways to the west leading to the Scottish islands and Ireland, but also to the Clyde estuary to the east with all its ramifying sea-lochs. The Crinan Canal was constructed across the isthmus to exploit this. In the Crinan plain itself, at the centre of this strategic node, rises the rock knob of *Dunadd, with its evidence of fortification. This has obvious tactical potential for control of the intersecting routeways. Visually, it is a striking feature, and its role as the formal centre for the Scoti of *Dál Riata has led to speculation that they may have perceived it as having a symbolic as well as a functional role in the landscape.

Glacial erosion has been stressed, but glacial deposition was also of major importance in creating the landscapes with which the inhabitants of Scotland have interacted. These include areas of drumlins: streamlined hillocks, notable in *Galloway and also integral to the pattern of *Glasgow's development. Often ice-laid boulder clays form heavy and intractable soils, but fluvioglacial sands and gravels, laid by glacial melt water in spreads or terraces, have proved of considerable human value by providing lighter soils, well drained areas for settlements, and salt-free building sand.

Glaciation affects the relative levels of land and sea. The weight of ice sheets depresses the earth's crust, and isostatic recovery continues long after the ice has gone. During glaciations, world ocean level is lower because of the amount of water locked up in the ice sheets on land. Lower ocean levels still prevailed after the local Scottish ice had gone, because of the later persistence of ice in areas further poleward. There was thus a complex interaction. Ocean level was irregularly restored as the climate varied, while Scotland deformed differentially, with most uplift where ice-loading had been greatest. Some coastlines are fringed by uplifted rock-cut platforms backed by fossil clifflines (sometimes compound products of many glaciations). These offered sites which have given many Scottish fishing (see ECONOMY, PRIMARY SECTOR: 4) settlements their characteristic linear form—not least in the East Neuk of Fife. Holocene raised beach deposits have also been of agricultural value, particularly on the western coast of the Highlands and in the Hebrides. There, the Atlantic climate and bed-

rock geology sets a premium on well-drained land close to sea level, especially where calcareous shell-sand raised beaches or sea sands blown onshore (for example in the machair lands) offset soil acidity.

The Holocene level changes also involved the deposition of muds in estuaries and inlets, and their subsequent uplift above present tide level. These carse clays have figured in both negative and positive ways in the historical development of routeways, settlements, agriculture, and industry, particularly along the Tay, Forth, Solway, and Clyde. Down the centuries, peat was cleared from the carses to bring great areas into agriculture, then in the 19th century major docks were excavated.

The carselands are just one example of the way that archaeological and palynological research, place names, and documentary records all indicate that our forebears had an astute appreciation of the potential of Scottish landscapes. As Archibald Geikie realized, they assessed the possibilities of the country's richly varied geology in different ways at different periods, in terms of their own technologies and social/economic and political circumstances. One must also respect their empirical understanding of geological processes, well before the emergence of geology as a formal academic discipline, during Geikie's lifetime. Sir Daniel Wilson, the Victorian antiquarian and anthropologist, found that the folk around Lochar Moss by the Solway had an ancient rhyme: 'First a Moss, Then a Sea, Now a Moss, And ever will be.' We cannot better that today, as an account of the Holocene stratigraphy there.   IM

Germany, the Baltic, and Poland: 1. to 1600; 2. since 1600.

1. to 1600
The Baltic region—known to the Scots as Eastland—became increasingly important to Scottish trade from the late 13th century when north German merchants were already visiting Scotland. In 1297 Sir William *Wallace and Sir Andrew de Moray informed the communities of Hamburg and Lübeck that Scotland was free from English power and ready to resume trade. *Robert I (1306–29) granted commercial rights to both German and *Low Countries traders. Indeed, during the Scottish Wars of *Independence north German merchants supplied the Scots with arms and other supplies.

Hamburg, Wismar, Rostock, Stralsund, and Colberg were all involved in Scottish trade and by 1500 this network included Gdansk, Königsberg and Riga, Revel and Narva. From the 1380s, when the Danish Sound was opened to shipping, Scots began to trade directly with Baltic countries: flax, hemp, and grain—and Swedish iron via Gdansk—

were imported by Scottish merchants. Scottish exports consisted principally of wool, animal skins, fish, and, by the late 16th century, coal and salt. As early as 1329 German merchants were exporting herring from Scania to Scotland and by 1500 merchants from Bremen and Hamburg were visiting Shetland in search of fishings; the first Scot known to be involved in this trade is Finlay Usher who was active in Scania in 1381. However, by the early 16th century, Scottish home merchants rarely made more than one Baltic trip in a year as appears from the port books of Leith (1510–13).

Scottish merchants increasingly settled in large numbers in Prussia. About 1380 Scots founded the suburb of Danzig (Gdansk) later known as Alt-Schottland while a Scottish factor was appointed to look after the interests of Scots resident there. The presence of these Scots traders can be detected in other Polish place names such as Nowa Szkocja and Sckotówa. *Emigration to Poland was largely drawn from the east and north-east of Scotland—*Aberdeen, *Dundee, and *Edinburgh—and arrived mainly by sea at the port of Gdansk. Large Scottish communities also existed by the second half of the 16th century in Königsberg, Lublin, Warsaw, Poznań, and Elblag. In Brandenburg, Germany, Scottish settlers and travellers were to be found in equal numbers.

In Poland outside Prussia the Scots tended to lead a more itinerant existence avoiding tax, and undercutting local Polish guilds by selling direct to customers. As early as 1457 Casimir Jagiellonczyk enacted that no Scots be admitted to trade at Gdansk unless they were resident there. General laws enacted by the Polish Seym in 1562 and 1565 also sought to restrict Scottish travelling merchants. Finally in 1600 Sigismund III issued a manifesto which recognized two types of Scot: pedlars and traders. The latter were extended privileges so long as they lived and traded in one location and were subject to taxation.

Scottish diplomatic influence in the Baltic world was exerted principally through the dynastic and political alliance with Denmark-Norway which inevitably drew the Scots into enmity with the Hansa and Sweden (see SCANDINAVIA: 1). James I renewed the treaties of Perth (1266) and Inverness (1312) with Eric of Pomerania in 1426; treaties of 1468–9 were confirmed in 1494 in a new agreement between *James IV and his cousin Hans of Denmark-Norway. As a result many Scots began to settle along the Sound which was the principal route for Scottish enterprise in the Baltic. James IV tried to mediate between Hans of Denmark-Norway in his war with Lübeck and Sweden in 1502 but after the curbing of the Hanse in 1534–6 direct Scottish influence declined until the 17th century.

Scotsmen also became involved in military ventures concerning the Baltic region (see MERCENARIES IN EUROPE). A few Scots served in the Order of the Teutonic Knights in Prussia during the 14th century while one Scot—a notary named Robert of Glenesk—acted in a dispute in 1383 in which Flemings attacked and pillaged Hanseatic merchants of Rostock and Colberg off the coast of Scotland. In 1502 a small naval expedition was sent to assist Hans of Denmark in his troubles with the Hanse and Sweden. In 1562 Eric XIV of Sweden tried to obtain Scots soldiers from Scotland for service against Muscovy. Eventually in 1573 some 4,000 Scots under Colonel Archibald Ruthven arrived in Sweden for service in the *Russian wars. The Scots sailed to Livonia and laid siege to Wesenberg which was held by Russian forces but a quarrel broke out between the Scottish and German mercenaries during which some Scots were slain and others defected to the Russians. Ruthven was subsequently court-martialled by the Swedes. However, in 1591 two units of Scottish cavalry under Henry Lyell and William Ruthven were still in Swedish service in Estonia while other Scots were involved (on both sides) in the Polish struggle to claim the Swedish crown during the 1590s.

Parallel to the diplomatic, military, and trade activities, Scots were also involved in cultural links with the region. Scots appear at German universities beginning in the 15th century: Cologne 1419, Heidelberg 1424, Louvain 1426 (see NORTHERN EUROPE: MONKS AND SCHOLARS). Thomas Liel de Scotia was rector of Cologne in 1502. Of particular significance are the links between Scottish religious reformers and Denmark, Germany, and Prussia. John MacAlpine (known as Machabeus) (d. 1557) fled Scotland for Germany in 1534 before accepting a post in Copenhagen where he assisted in translating the Bible into Danish. The reformer John Gau (d. 1553), a graduate of St Andrews, translated *The Richt Way To The Kingdome of Hevine* from Danish (Malmö 1533). Alexander Alane (or Alesius) (d. 1565) was a noted scholar active at Wittenberg, where he befriended Melanchthon, and was later rector of Leipzig University. The Scottish Catholic exile Ninian Winzet (d. 1592) became abbot of Ratisbon in 1577 and translated the Catechism of the Jesuit Canisius into Scots. John Craig, physician to *James VI, studied at Königsberg in 1564, then Wittenberg and Frankfurt-an-der-Oder in 1573 where he taught logic and mathematics in the 1580s (see MEDICINE AND THE ORIGINS OF THE MEDICAL PROFESSION). The Aberdonian Duncan Liddel went to study at Gdansk in 1579 and then to Frankfurt and Rostock. Liddel is noted as the first to teach both the Ptolemaic and Copernican models of planetary motions in Germany (see CULTURE: 5). The Dundee man John Wedderburn also visited north Germany in the 1540s and, inspired by Lutheran ideas, translated German spiritual songs, psalms, and hymns into the popular Scots version known as *The Gude and Godlie Ballatis.*   DH

2. since 1600

Trade, military service, and cultural links continued to govern Scotland's relations with the Baltic, Poland, and German lands for some time after 1600. The 17th-century Scottish mercantile presence spread right across the northern regions of Prussia, Poland, Pomerania, and Mecklenburg. The flood of *emigration from eastern Scotland to Poland and East Prussia (Baltic States) reached its height between 1610 and 1620. Contemporary reports estimated that 30,000 Scots families were present in Poland at this time; their settlements have been traced to over 420 localities. Most led a precarious existence as settled or itinerant 'cramers' who peddled woollen and linen goods, iron, and tinware; alongside the Dutch, German, and Jews, they benefited from the Polish lack of a middle class and disdain for trade. The Poles saw the Scots as a tax-evading threat and denied them citizen's rights; legal disputes were common, but the Scots, formed into self-governing, clannish brotherhoods and backed by *James VI, held their own through judicious financial support of the nobility and resistance to undesirable further immigration. Gradually, as natural assimilation occurred, Scots reached positions of considerable social standing and wealth, especially in the main entry ports of Danzig (Gdansk) and Königsberg (Kroloewiec, Kaliningrad) and the cities of Krakow and Warsaw.

Meanwhile the Scottish Baltic fleet of small merchant vessels was expanding its trade into the north and west of the region. Grain imports rose during the poor harvests of the 1620s; the hides and skins market saw a boom and collapse; and salt, coal, and fish exports grew (see ECONOMY: 3). By the end of the 18th century, with the growth of Scotland's textile and tobacco industries, demand for herring and tobacco in the Polish hinterland and furthest end of the Baltic allowed Scottish import of Polish and Russian flax. The east coast fisheries trade was to revive in the 1830s as Scots curers gained Baltic trade from the Dutch, but the aim of linking the Clyde with the Baltic through Telford's Caledonian Canal (1822) (see TRANSPORT AND COMMUNICATIONS: 3) was unrealistic: *Glasgow was now Scotland's chief trading centre and faced west. The expanding Austrian and North German Lloyd Companies would buy Clydeside steel ships; and today Scotland imports coal from Poland.

For much of the 17th and 18th centuries the Baltic, Polish, and German territories were a battle-ground. Scottish regiments and mercenaries, recruited at home and on the Continent and often changing allegiance (see MERCENARIES IN EUROPE), were to be found fighting on all sides, many rising to high rank and ennoblement (prime amongst them the *Jacobite James Keith, Prussian field-marshal). Confused by their own loyalties, whether to a Scottish queen of Bohemia, a Hanoverian Protestant British king, or a doomed Catholic dynasty and son of a Polish princess, Scots fought Scots, some 20,000 under the Protestant Gustavus Adolphus alone during the Thirty Years War (1618–48). Later in the century, skilled Scottish infantry were recruited by the king of Poland to fight the Turks. Thereafter, Scottish regiments distinguished themselves in the War of the Austrian Succession and the Seven Years War, while Hanoverian troops quelled Jacobites in the Highlands. Scots served Prussia again in the 1860 wars.

Academic and cultural exchange has been sustained throughout the period. The Jesuit colleges of Braunsberg and Vilnius and the Benedictine *Schottenklöster continued to attract Scots in the early years. Developments in German biblical study (under David Friedrich Strauss) coincided with the *Disruption and ensured an active Protestant theological exchange. By the early 1800s, thanks to Scottish excellence in other disciplines, Edinburgh was a chief attraction on extended European study tours: advances in medicine, welfare, and education were enhanced by both rural and urban architectural grandeur and industrial progress. The landed gentry, especially from Poland and Lithuania, studied Adam Smith's political economy (see ECONOMIC POLICY: 1) and returned home to import both new agricultural methods from Lowland Scotland and farmers and engineers. Evidence of the strength of the literary exchange can be found in the work of Herder, Goethe and Fontane, MacPherson and Scott. The last two caused a sensation on the Continent and effected a vogue for Scottish themes in German and Polish literature and music (see CULTURE: 11). By the mid-19th century, visitors from these lands (from students to royalty) had greatly contributed to the firm establishment of tourism in Scotland (see ECONOMY, TERTIARY SECTOR: 3), which they saw as the land of Ossian, Scott, and Schiller's *Maria Stuart.* In turn, in the Victorian enthusiasm for the Gothic, the Scots were 'discovering' the Rhine. The poet Thomas Campbell had championed the cause of partitioned Poland and Thomas Carlyle that of Frederick 'the Great'. German academic influence was felt throughout Scottish *universities and specialist German studies were instituted in the 1890s. Glasgow University now hosts a leading centre of Polish studies, while a tribute to Polish wartime academic achievement was the Polish School of Medicine at the University of Edinburgh (1941–9).

Immigrants to Scotland in the 19th and 20th centuries, both temporary (such as Polish émigrés after the 1830 insurrection) and permanent residents, have included Estonians, Latvians, Western Ukrainians, and Jews from all over the area concerned. The Lithuanians in industrial Lanarkshire arrived mostly in the 1880s and 1890s and numbered over 5,000 by 1914. The Polish contribution to Scottish society has been considerable since the Polish First Army Corps was organized in Scotland in 1940. Of the 70,000 Polish servicemen involved, 15,000 were still in Scotland in the mid-1950s.

Within the framework of the European Union recent political developments have led to a revival of historical links and to ongoing discussions on devolution issues between Scotland and Germany. Scottish and Bavarian towns have been twinned since the 1950s, with formal commercial links established in 1991, while old ties between such partners as Edinburgh, Cracow, and Vilnius have also been renewed. Meanwhile, with the support of such bodies as the Goethe Institut and the British Council, immigrant communities in all countries remain active through ethnic clubs, associations, and churches.   AH

Glasgow: 1. to 1700; 2. 1700–1820; 3. since 1820.

1. to 1700

The area in which Glasgow has grown up was favoured for human settlement, by its geography and geology, from prehistoric times. Lying in a sheltered howe, after the post-glacial period it would have been heavily wooded and the marshy flats on the banks of the River Clyde could offer food for primitive hunter-gatherers. Neolithic farmers and Bronze Age metallurgists have left evidence of their settlements here. The Glasgow site was also located on potential communication routes both between the east and west and north and south. From the early Middle Ages, at least, it also stood at the lowest fording point of the Clyde, which enhanced its potential as a communications centre and natural focus for trade.

Tradition relates that in the late 6th or early 7th century Kentigern, or Mungo as he is sometimes called, founded a monastery at Glasgow at the same spot where St Ninian had consecrated a cemetery and where St Fergus had been buried by St Kentigern. The monastery at Glasgow, it is argued, subsequently became the seat of a bishopric. None of this can as yet be proved; and, indeed, more convincing arguments for *Govan or Hoddam as early episcopal centres might be proffered. What is significant for the burgh's history is that

the legends were believed in the early 12th century, a re-established bishopric was centred at Glasgow, and a cathedral was built on the traditionally hallowed site.

Later that century, in 1175 × 1178, Bishop Jocelin received a charter from King William I 'the Lion' (1165–1214), granting to him and his successors a burgh in Glasgow. The initial laying-out of the burgh in tofts, or burgage plots, probably commenced soon after, for at some date between 1179 and 1199 the bishop donated to the abbot and convent of Melrose 'that toft in the burgh of Glasgow Ranulf of Hadintun built, in the first building of the burgh'. Exactly where these first burgage plots were laid out is not clear; but certainly by the 13th century, at the latest, geography had determined that the commercial centre of Glasgow was to develop along the Trongate–Gallowgate axis. With the episcopal centre situated in the northern end of the burgh, the medieval town would develop very much as a two-centre settlement.

The northerly, upper nucleus of the burgh, Townhead, became dominated by buildings associated with the bishopric: the bishop's castle, the cathedral, and, by the 15th and 16th centuries, the manses, gardens, and orchards of the canons. This enclave of literacy was augmented in 1451, when a university was erected by a bull of Pope Nicholas V. Approximately 25 years later the Greyfriars were granted a tenement and lands on the west side of High Street, the thoroughfare that linked the two centres. Lesser religious foundations, along with the large endowments of the cathedral and increasing foundation of chaplainries, made Glasgow a successful bishop's burgh and the town benefited economically from visitors and pilgrims. The dignity of the burgh superior was further enhanced when, in 1492, Pope Innocent VIII raised the see of Glasgow to an archbishopric. This, too, had implications for the burgh: the jurisdiction of the episcopal courts was extended and Glasgow's role as a judicial and administrative centre was considerably heightened (see CHURCH INSTITUTIONS: 2).

In other ways, particularly economically, Glasgow functioned only modestly in the medieval period. Although given the right to trade overseas, along with royal and other great ecclesiastical burghs, practical obstacles interceded. Northern *France, the *Low Countries, the Baltic, and England were Scotland's favoured trading partners. England apart, these countries were more readily accessible to the east coast burghs; and Glasgow resorted to transporting goods overland to Linlithgow's port of Blackness, and possibly also to Leith, for export. Even trading contacts with *Ireland, the Isles, and western Scotland met with difficulties. Rivalries with Rutherglen, Renfrew, and

Dumbarton existed; with Dumbarton, which controlled the mouth of the Clyde, these persisted into early modern times. Glasgow came to an agreement with Irvine for it to act, in effect, as Glasgow's seaport, but this too necessitated cartage overland.

An assessment of the occupational structure of Glasgow at the end of the 16th century indicates that the town had a broad manufacturing base, particularly in clothing, textiles, and food processing; and while Glasgow had more maltsters, cordiners, or weavers than *Edinburgh, it had less than half the number of merchants. Significantly, however, Glasgow's contribution of 66 per cent of the upper Clyde taxation share of a customs tax of 1581 is clear indication that, while functioning largely as an inland trading town, Glasgow was increasingly becoming the reception centre through which the region's exports passed. It was this rising prosperity that relied on an agricultural economy (see ECONOMY, PRIMARY SECTOR: 1), on internal trade with its hinterland, and on an increasingly important manufacturing base, allied with an element of external exports, that enabled Glasgow to weather the Reformation crisis and the plagues of 1574 and 1584 (see HEALTH, FAMINE, AND DISEASE: 2), in spite of the departure of many ecclesiastics from the Townhead and a consequent slackening in demand for supplies and services.

The increasing prosperity of Glasgow in the 15th and 16th centuries manifested itself in the burgh morphology. It has been estimated that in c.1400 the population was about 1,500 to 2,000, rising to between 2,500 and 3,000 a century later, increasing to about 4,500 at the time of the Reformation, and to approximately 7,500 by 1600. In spite of these increases, the evidence suggests that the burgh did not expand beyond its traditional bounds, resulting in intense pressure for building space, particularly around the market centre at the Cross, and repletion and infilling is clear, with numerous small vennels leading to back premises. Unlike the prestigious stone-built buildings in the Townhead, many of the homes in the southern centre were little more than hovels of wood. The destruction, according to the *Glasgow Registrum*, of 'four scoir closses all burnt, estimat to about one thousand families' in the Saltmarket, Bridgegate, Trongate, and Gallowgate area in 1652 is witness to both the congestion and the continued use of wood as a building material.

The first half of the 17th century saw Glasgow consolidating its position as the primary commercial centre in western Scotland, acting as a reception centre for the export commodities of mainland Scotland and Ireland. There is evidence that Glasgow was also taking an increasing share of the trade with Scotland's traditional overseas trading partners. From only four ships in the 1620s, the burgh's commercial fleet rose to ten or twelve in the 1650s and 1660s, and to about 30 by the late 1680s. The Clyde, however, was too shallow to permit large boats to reach Glasgow's quay at Broomielaw, and the islands in the river made navigation difficult for even small craft. Glasgow's commercial position remained dependent on its outports: Greenock on the Clyde and Blackness, Bo'ness and Leith on the Forth. It is a comment not only on Glasgow's grave need for adequate harbour facilities, but also on the enlightenment of the town's magistrates and council, that land was purchased in Newark in 1668 in order to construct a new harbour for Glasgow, to be known as Newport (later Port Glasgow).

The credit for overcoming the difficulties of geography and capitalizing on transatlantic trade lay largely with a relatively small group of merchant families. They not only mainly controlled the civic offices, overseas trade, and commercial ventures, but were also the major landowners in and around Glasgow. In a population of about 12,000, only some 400–500 were merchants and, of these, only between 80 and 125 traded overseas. From this small group, a central core with close links of kinship operated merchant partnerships and joint-stock organizations that brought wealth to their own families and to the city as a whole. The growing prosperity was reflected in the urban setting: the college was given a new home in splendid buildings to the east of High Street; a new tolbooth, market cross, merchant hall in Bridgegate, Tron church, and Hutcheson's Hospital were constructed; and wealthy merchant houses of stone adorned the city. But, in the backlands and alleys, the hovels of the ordinary folk remained.

Glasgow's prosperity, however, still largely depended on its manufacturers; but to traditional crafts were now added larger-scale industries, which to some extent reflected the city's growing commercial contacts overseas. In spite of the setbacks of plague in 1645–6, the Wars of the *Covenant, the disruptions after the *Restoration, with the city constantly billeted with troops, Glasgow emerged in the later 17th century as the second wealthiest town in the country.   EPD

2. 1700–1820

The character of Glasgow was transformed in the 18th century. A market town of fewer than 20,000 people became one of the great commercial cities of the British Empire, with a flourishing sea trade with the Americas and an important presence in a number of the major areas of industry that characterized the industrial revolution, yielding a vast rise in population and extremes of wealth and poverty.

Glasgow

In 1700 the city was small and compact, with tenement housing clustered in a few streets around the market cross to the north of the river. The River Clyde was never more than 3 feet (0.9 m) deep and was easily fordable by foot at low tide. Fishermen with small boats and nets caught salmon there. The river banks at Glasgow Green were used for grazing animals and many people kept beehives on their rooftops. Gardens and pastures were all around the city and most families supplemented their incomes from these sources. Industry was mostly craft and workshop-based (see URBAN SOCIETY: 3). It was a neat and pretty town with a distinctly Netherlandish look to it. This character prevailed to about the middle of the century, when rapid city development towards the west and to the south of the river, with the building of a modern grid-patterned 'new town' and the creation of fashionable suburbs, resulted in a physical movement of the rich from the old heart of the city into more spacious tenements and town houses. The centre of business life for the commercial elite moved to the newly created George Square. By the later 18th century, modern factory industry was developing immediately to the east of the old market cross, where housing for the poor was also concentrated. Yet even in the early 19th century, after much change but before industrial pollution had begun to take its toll, Glasgow was admired by visitors. Dorothy Wordsworth in 1803, though unimpressed by the sprawling suburbs, thought the High Street 'picturesque' and was generally struck by an air of prosperous bustle about the place.

The development of Glasgow was founded in commerce and in particular in the ability to exploit opportunities for trade with the American (see USA) and West Indian colonies in plantation commodities such as tobacco, sugar, and cotton. Financial innovations and shipbuilding rose in tandem with this vast and complex international trade. Industrial development was also aided by commercial enterprise, though the fortunate proximity of some of the important raw materials of modern industry, notably coal and iron ore, was also critical. The dominant role of the Merchant House in the burgh set ensured that local policy-making in areas such as river dredging and the building of port facilities, advanced the interests of the trading elite. Initially, Glasgow's merchants were obliged to exploit the satellite ports of Greenock and Port Glasgow to service their ships. But the Clyde was widened and deepened in the second half of the 18th century and by 1800 it was 14 feet (4.3 m) deep at low tide and supported 200 wharves and jetties to accommodate ocean-going ships as well as the many smaller vessels involved in coastal trade.

The rise of the merchant city promoted developments in other areas of communication. In 1750 the overland journey to London took seven days, travelling via Edinburgh and Newcastle. The opening of the Carlisle road in the early 1780s nearly halved the journey time and by the early 19th century, before the railways, improvements in coach services allowed journeys of less than 48 hours. The opening of the Forth and Clyde Canal in 1790 meant that ships could sail from Greenock, via Glasgow to Leith and on to Europe in a few days. These were massive and expensive civil engineering projects, funded by joint-stock companies under the encouragement of the city council (see TRANSPORT AND COMMUNICATIONS: 2).

Changes in the city economy were paralleled by changes in social structure and in status hierarchies. Glasgow was the city of the parvenu businessman, the most famous group being the 'Tobacco Lords', Virginia tobacco merchants and planters, noted for their wealth, opulent styles of living, clannish behaviour—their risky enterprises relied on close family partnerships—and a capacity to manipulate burgh politics. Their dominance in the middle decades of the century ended with American independence in 1776 and they were replaced by an equally powerful cadre of West India merchants trading in sugar and rum and later by the East India merchants and 'nabobs' (see INDIAN SUBCONTINENT). Few men with a manufacturing background could match the wealth and power of the mercantile elite at this time. Business was conducted first at the market cross, with merchants promenading in public in the traditional manner of outdoor urban society. It then moved indoors into the Tontine Coffee Rooms, a commercial facility for men that provided refreshments, newspapers, and meeting spaces for private conversations and leisure.

Many merchants had connections with small-scale landowning. Though the city provided winter accommodation for the landed elite in the first half of the 18th century, the attractions of Edinburgh, along with the changing character of Glasgow, ensured a swift decline in the presence of the gentry. The growth of the population was largely built on rural *migration and with the close proximity to the Highlands it was inevitable that a large Gaelic community had been established in Glasgow by 1800.

Irish *immigration in the early 19th century added another dimension to the labouring population, which had changed its character over the century from a broad spectrum of craft workers to a dominance by unskilled industrial and transport workers. Living standards for the mass of the people advanced with commerce and early industry, but the erosion of community welfare systems such as the church-based poor law (see LIVING STANDARDS: 4), along with the growing volatility of the free market economy, inevitably resulted in greater instability, frequent periods of high unemployment, and increased anxiety among many ordinary workers. Tensions between the rich and poor were particularly intense in the first two decades of the 19th century.

The politics of Glasgow were dominated by Tory interests on the town council, though calls for reform were articulated by an increasingly vocal new middle class with strong Whig inclinations. The rising cost of town government, reflected in rapid increases in the burgh rates, yielded growing calls for more democratic and accountable local government from the 1770s. But despite the criticism, many areas of unreformed local government policy in Glasgow were innovative and successful. Major landowners in west central Scotland, notably the duke of *Hamilton, who relied on Glasgow's port facilities and commodity exchange for the marketing of his coal, exercised considerable patronage influence in the city. At a national level, Glasgow shared a single Member of Parliament with three neighbouring burghs, an anomaly that reflected the small size of the town in earlier times and was not reformed until 1832. As with all the great industrial and commercial cities of recent growth in Britain, the lack of national representation generated resentment among inhabitants but also gave rise to creative responses to government. The Glasgow Chamber of Commerce, which was founded in 1783 and was the first of its type in Britain, was a lobby group for businessmen which made a significant impact at this time.

The Enlightenment (see CULTURE: 11) in Glasgow had a particular flavour that was influenced by the predominantly commercial character of the city. Adam Smith was a professor at the University for many years and his *Wealth of Nations* (1776), with its advocacy of the free market and the civilizing tendencies inherent to urban life, was influenced by his acquaintance with businessmen in the clubs and societies that flourished in the city (see ECONOMIC POLICY: 2). Francis Hutcheson, the moral philosopher and clergyman who made a major contribution to the development of the Moderate party in the Church of Scotland (see RELIGIOUS LIFE: 5), was in Glasgow from 1730. Many innovations in science and technology that were pioneered in the University had direct advantages for the success of local industry in the later 18th century. Other Enlightenment initiatives such as the Foulis Academy—established within the University in 1753 to promote art and design—while important for the early training of several painters of note, including David Allan and producing some of the finest

printed books of the 18th century (see BOOK SELLING), foundered for the want of encouragement among an urban elite with an eye focused on the balance sheets of their sometimes precarious firms. Yet, by the early decades of the 19th century, the intellectual sophistication of the city was apparent and though the new wealth was sometimes derided by contemporaries, Glasgow and its institutions were a force to be recognized in all spheres of culture life.   SN

3. since 1820

Throughout the 1820s the process of industrialization (see ECONOMY: 4) continued briskly in Glasgow, the textile sector making a crucial impact on the city's expansion until mid-century. According to the 1821 Census, the number of inhabitants had increased to 147,043, representing a 33 per cent growth over the previous decade. By 1851, Glasgow had emphatically become Scotland's largest city, with a population of 329,096 (see POPULATION PATTERNS: 2). In the interim, steam-powered factories had multiplied, visibly reflecting economic priorities and altering the urban landscape indelibly.

Control of the textile industry throughout the west of Scotland remained overwhelmingly in the hands of Glasgow-based entrepreneurs, whose activities helped to bolster the city's burgeoning commercial sector. In the 1830s and 1840s a plethora of local joint-stock banks (see ECONOMY, TERTIARY SECTOR: 2) was founded (of which the Clydesdale Bank remains the sole survivor), and Glasgow's Stock Exchange commenced trading in 1844. Textiles were not the sole preserve of investment; coal and iron (see ECONOMY, SECONDARY SECTOR: 2) were perceived as particularly lucrative growth areas, and railways attracted considerable speculative interest. Glasgow's banks became noted for their risk-taking approach, which in the case of the City of Glasgow Bank reached reckless proportions. By 1878 the bank had accumulated a £5 million debt, attributable largely to injudicious lending and highly questionable overseas investment. The bank's inevitable failure that year had a devastating impact on the local economy, provoking a crisis of confidence that irreversibly cut across the climate of mid-century buoyancy.

During the first half of the century, districts like Bridgeton, Calton, and Parkhead (in the east end), together with Anderston (in the west) and Gorbals (to the south), were the prime focus of Glasgow's textile industry, as factory-owners built upon the base already established by the handloom weaving sector. Throughout this period the textile communities attracted a substantial quota of incomers both from the rest of Scotland and from Ireland (see IMMIGRATION, IRISH). In the latter instance, the availability of cheap and regular steamship transport was a significant factor in stimulating immigration (see TRANSPORT AND COMMUNICATIONS: 2), with the result that by 1851 over 18 per cent of the city's inhabitants were Irish-born. While the textile sector afforded employment opportunities, so too did navvying, labouring, and domestic service, although the Irish community was by no means wholly concentrated in unskilled occupations. Their presence was of major social and cultural importance to Glasgow, not least because it altered the city's overwhelming Presbyterian profile, as some two-thirds of the immigrants were Roman Catholic (see ROMAN CATHOLIC COMMUNITY).

Rapid population growth focused attention on the fragmented nature of local government authority in the industrial districts, which did not initially come under the jurisdiction of Glasgow Town Council. Indeed, the preservation of law and order had become a middle-class preoccupation, partly influenced by industrial disruption during the abortive 'Radical War' of 1820 and the violent cotton-spinners' strike of 1837. Accordingly, in 1846 the burgh boundaries more than doubled to cover 5,063 acres (2,295 hectares). The enlarged municipality allowed for co-ordinated policing arrangements and also meant that the problems associated with industrialization could more readily be tackled. During the 1820s fear of social dislocation had been compounded by the city's increasingly blighted condition, as overcrowding, destitution, and disease began to overwhelm the urban infrastructure. In contradiction to its impressive cultural heritage, Glasgow acquired an unenviable reputation for the pestilential conditions of its slum districts, with crude death rates averaging almost 40 per 1,000 living inhabitants by the 1840s, one of the highest figures in the UK. The persistence of respiratory diseases, above all pulmonary tuberculosis (see HEALTH, FAMINE, AND DISEASE: 3), was an indicator of the city's chronic environmental corrosion, and remained cause for official concern well into the 20th century.

The recurring incidence of epidemic diseases from 1818, notoriously cholera and typhus, also posed a public health challenge to the authorities because of their virulence and apparent random choice of victims. By 1850, anxiety about contagion and the deteriorating urban fabric helped to precipitate the flight of wealthy Glaswegians to suburbs on the western and southern periphery of the city. Of course, speculative building and transport improvements had also encouraged middle-class resettlement from the 1820s, with imposing architectural developments in districts like Blythswood and Kelvinside (see ARCHITECTS, ARTISTS, AND CRAFTSMEN). The University's shift in 1870 from the city centre to the salubrious west end was a telling statement about the continuing prestige and allure of the suburbs. Yet while the emergence of outlying middle-class communities proceeded into the next century, the phenomenon initially provoked unease about residential polarization which served to heighten the contrast between the city's wealth and squalor. However, it was not until after the boundary extension of 1846 that direct civic interventionism came to be articulated as the most effective means of rectifying the balance and regenerating the city.

The electoral reforms of the 1830s had politically empowered Glasgow's middle classes, and by mid-century the prevailing allegiance was to *Liberalism, support for Conservatism (see UNIONISM) having plummeted in the wake of the 1843 *Disruption of the Church of Scotland. The established church was in disarray, with over half the worshippers in Glasgow seceding to join the Evangelical Free Church of Scotland. For erstwhile Conservatives, the crucial church-state connection had been shattered, and many threw in their lot with the brand of Glasgow Liberalism that espoused free trade, religious voluntaryism, franchise reform, and social welfare. On the other hand, Liberalism was not a homogeneous ideology; in Glasgow there was a pugnacious and persistent radical tradition that derived inspiration from post-1815 reform struggles and *Chartism. Nevertheless, between 1835 and 1874 Liberals held absolute sway at the parliamentary level, and it was not until after the 1886 Unionist split within the party that an effective opposition emerged. That the Scottish Labour Party (see LABOURISM) was founded in Glasgow in 1888 was also significant; as a focus for disenchanted radicals it was a forerunner to the ILP, which between the 1890s and 1930s became a pivotal influence on the city's working-class politics.

The politico-religious connection during the mid-19th century was reflected by the presence of Evangelicals (see RELIGIOUS LIFE: 6), of a decidedly Liberal paternalist outlook, in the municipal sphere. They believed emphatically in the harmonious integration of society through philanthropic endeavour and the promotion of the public good. In 1859 the inauguration of a pure water supply from Loch Katrine was depicted by the civic leadership as a great municipal boon that would cleanse the city both literally and spiritually. Certainly, it was crucial for banishing the scourge of cholera. The 1866 City Improvement Trust was heralded as a pioneering slum-clearance project, aiming to transform Glasgow's unsavoury heartland by introducing broad thoroughfares and constructing prestigious new buildings. The urban landscape was further embellished by public parks and art galleries from the 1850s; amenities that added substantial assets to the municipal patrimony. They were also intended to instil a sense of pride in the community and represented an early manifestation of the commitment in Glasgow to municipal enterprise, or 'municipal socialism' as it was ambiguously known by the 1900s (see URBAN SETTLEMENT: 3).

Civic priorities from mid-century were firmly fixed on the creation of the 'Greater Glasgow', whereby the boundaries established in 1846 would be significantly extended to allow room for the population to expand. However, the emergence of contiguous semi-autonomous communities (known as police burghs) from the 1850s created serious obstacles, with a prolonged legal struggle to absorb districts such as Govanhill, Hillhead, Maryhill, and Pollokshields. After an assertive civic campaign, the long-standing ambitions for 'Greater Glasgow' became a practical reality with major territorial additions in 1891 and 1912. The latter extension added the shipbuilding communities of Govan and Partick, giving Glasgow a total acreage of 19,183 acres (7,763 hectares). In just over four decades, between 1871 and the outbreak of the First World War, the city more than doubled in population from 477,732 to over a million. The status of being the 'Second City of Empire' in population terms was regarded as wholly positive, certainly by the civic leadership, which relished its responsibility for the welfare of almost a quarter of Scotland's inhabitants. Yet as the 20th century progressed, problems of inner-city overcrowding remained as intractable as ever, and priorities shifted towards the drastic reduction of urban density.

Although Glasgow continued to expand territorially, with acreage almost doubling during the inter-war period, after the Second World War the dispersal of population from the city came to be actively encouraged. Indeed, this was a fundamental component of the Clyde Valley Regional Plan of 1946, which recommended the construction of new towns as part of Glasgow's 'overspill' strategy. City dwellers were consequently directed to fledgling communities like East Kilbride, and from 1951 the million-plus population began to fall precipitately, totalling 681,228 by 1991. As for the older areas, a massive programme of comprehensive development was launched during the 1950s, the creation of peripheral council housing estates such as Castlemilk, Drumchapel, and Easterhouse helping to accommodate the displaced population. Substantial tracts of inner Glasgow were cleared, districts like Gorbals, Springburn, and Townhead losing more than their slum tenements as traditional communities were fragmented. By the 1970s it came to be realized that, for all Glasgow's mod-

ern tower blocks and motorways, alienation and antisocial behaviour had been engendered by the new housing estates. A more sensitive planning approach was adopted, aimed at conserving what was best from the old, particularly through the rehabilitation of existing properties.

Glasgow's developing economy had been vitally important for stimulating demographic growth, although the early success of textiles was not sustained. By the mid-19th century the emphasis was changing, due to the large-scale production of cheap iron in the Lanarkshire hinterland. Heavy industry (see ECONOMY, SECONDARY SECTOR: 2) took over from textiles as the city's economic mainstay, with manufacturing centred on iron-founding, machine tools, locomotives, and (crucially) marine engineering and shipbuilding. The accessibility of raw materials was exploited by the innovative body of Clyde shipbuilders, who had been vastly helped by municipal efforts to widen and deepen the river. The use of steel in shipbuilding further shifted Glasgow's industrial base, as the city became a major centre for production from the 1870s. Immediately prior to the First World War, 100,000 people were estimated to be directly dependent on shipbuilding and related industries for employment. That this was a dangerous concentration of resources became glaringly apparent during the Depression of the 1930s, when some two-thirds of shipbuilding workers were made unemployed. While economic fortunes were temporarily revived by wartime rearmament policies, the heavy industrial base was drastically eroding. By the 1960s Glasgow's shipbuilding was in an irreversible crisis, despite a desperate rearguard action to sustain the industry through massive government subsidies.

Glaswegians experienced considerable social and economic changes during the 1920s and 1930s, which partly reflected global uncertainties after the trauma of the First World War. Not least was a changing political direction, as the Liberalism gave way to sustained electoral support for the Labour Party, both at the parliamentary and municipal level. Economic depression jolted the hitherto unshakeable sense of civic pride, and a starkly negative image emerged, amplified by sensationalist newspaper reporting, of a violent, demoralized, and hard-drinking city. However, image-making had long been important for Glasgow's identity, to counter the corrosive impact of multifarious social problems, and this continued to stand the city in good stead. The 1938 Empire Exhibition was one aesthetically striking manifestation of the need to project the city's commitment to progress and modernization during difficult times.

From the 1980s Glasgow went through a searing process of industrial decline, its manufacturing sector all but obliterated. In an effort to maintain the momentum of urban renewal, initiated during the 1970s, energies were directed towards developing the inner city with the aim of creating a service-based economy. The heritage of culture and architecture was identified as a prize asset, and the surviving Victorian city was transformed into a showcase of what Glasgow had to offer, especially for visitors. Indeed, the economic potential of tourism became crucially important in reshaping the city's much-vaunted image as upbeat, dynamic, and creative. Glasgow as the 1999 European City of Architecture and Design was thus a fitting tribute to the city's post-industrial re-invention, despite the dogged persistence of serious deprivation and unemployment problems. IMa

Glencoe, Massacre of. The Massacre of Glencoe MacDonalds on 13 February 1692 has traditionally been portrayed as an example of the endemic clan feuding traditionally associated with the Scottish Highlands. Yet the underlying factors leading to the massacre actually sprang from a tradition within Scottish government for deploying military violence in the region and, more immediately, from instability at the political centre brought on by the crisis of James VII's deposition in 1689 (see HIGHLANDS AND ISLANDS AND CENTRAL GOVERNMENT: 3). Initially, it appeared as if the first *Jacobite rising would end peacefully. The urgent need to reinforce William's campaign in Flanders and forestall a Jacobite invasion from *Ireland resulted in the government accepting a deal negotiated at Achallader in June 1691 by its representative, John Campbell, first earl of Breadalbane. By providing an honourable indemnity to those Jacobite chiefs who swore an oath of loyalty to William before 1 January 1692, the treaty appeared to be a break from the official use of violence. However, the intense factionalism between leading figures in William's administration undermined the deal. Sir John Dalrymple, the Secretary of State for Scotland, had been intimately involved in the administration of James VII. This left him compromised and anxious to confirm his Williamite credentials. He did this by questioning the trustworthiness of the Campbell earl and by opposing his suggestion that Lochaber jurisdictions be redistributed in order to win the loyalty of certain Jacobite clans. Even prior to the expiry of the 1 January deadline, he was promoting the idea that the MacDonalds of Glengarry be targeted in a campaign of military execution.

Nor were the Jacobites themselves blameless. In an effort to demonstrate his own importance within the Jacobite movement, Alasdair MacDonald of Glengarry failed to inform other chiefs of James's permission to swear the required oath. The

result was that Alasdair MacIain, the chief of the MacDonalds of Glencoe, did not arrive at Inveraray and swear his oath until 5 January. His technical default made him and his clan the ideal candidates for Dalrymple's punitive policy. The MacDonalds were habitual reivers, being implicated in the devastation of Argyll lands in 1685 and in raiding against their neighbours, the Campbells of Glenyon and Breadalbane. Deliberate government misrepresentation of their religious affiliation—they were in fact Episcopalians (see EPISCOPALIAN COMMUNITY) and not Catholics—helped ensure an additional layer of justification. Having received the tacit approval of William, detachments of the Argyll Regiment under Captain Robert Campbell of Glenyon arrived at Glencoe on 1 February. The direct involvement of the *Campbells has of course perpetuated the idea that the massacre was an act of feud. Yet the tenth earl of Argyll played no direct part, while his kinsman Breadalbane had nothing to gain by so dramatically undermining his own policy. As a massacre, Glencoe was in fact noticeably ineffective. Ordered to attack at 5 a.m., two hours before detachments from Fort William were to assist, not only suggests Glenlyon was being prepared as a scapegoat, it also had the effect of allowing many to escape. MacIain and perhaps 40 of his clan were killed, although subsequent deaths from exposure are unclear. In the short term, the massacre strengthened the hand of the Scottish *parliament. Dalrymple was accorded the majority of blame by a parliamentary inquiry in July 1695 and dismissed. Glencoe also restored some credibility to what had been a shambolic Jacobite cause by deepening the pro-Stuart sympathies of certain *clans. However, these initial advantages were outweighed in the long term by the fact that British governments realized they could perpetrate unconstitutional acts of military execution in the region with relative impunity—a fact that was to become all too evident in 1746 (see GOVERNMENT AFTER THE UNION). AMacK

golf. The game of golf has been part of the sporting and social culture of Scotland since the 15th century. There have been many other types of club and ball games recorded throughout history as forerunners of golf. For example, in the Roman Empire, *paganica*, a game played by country folk with a ball and stick, was known and *jeu de mail*, played with a mallet and a wooden ball, developed in France. With no clear documented evidence prior to the 15th century, it is difficult to pinpoint a specific date as to when golf as a recognizable game first made its appearance in Scotland. However, the earliest known written reference to golf appeared in 1457, when parliament declared that 'the futeball and golfe be utterly cryed downe and not to be used'. The ban on golf was imposed because, like *football, it interfered with the practice of archery. At this time these sports were popular and played by a wide range of people, including trades-men and apprentices. Early forms of golf were played on links land: undulating areas of turf, gorse, and heather along the mainly eastern coastal strip of Scotland. The royal seal of approval was set by *James VI, who promoted the game of golf by appointing William Mayne, a bowyer and burgess of Edinburgh, as his clubmaker in 1603. Early fe-male pioneering golfers included *Mary, Queen of Scots, who was reputed to have played 'in the fields beside Seton' a few days after the murder of her husband Darnley in 1567, while the fisher lassies of Musselburgh were recorded in the *Statistical Ac-count of Scotland* as having amusements of a 'mas-culine kind', when they played competitively for prizes in 1810.

The 18th century saw the establishment of golf-ing societies for the elite in Edinburgh and the for-mal organization of the game was established when a regulatory set of Rules, drawn up by the Gentlemen Golfers of Leith in 1744, was adopted by the Society of St Andrews Golfers in 1754. The Royal and Ancient became the governing body for golf with its headquarters in St Andrews. This set the seal for golf to develop as a regulated and or-ganized sport. The Open Championship instituted in 1860 was important in popularizing the game as a spectator sport. For many years golf was the pre-serve of the wealthy, but opportunities for play extended to a wider section of society with the de-velopment of the cheaper 'gutty' ball, which re-placed the expensive leather ball at the end of the 19th century.

The advancement of the game regulated in Scot-land had an effect worldwide, particularly in North America, where many of the early professionals and golf course architects, originating from Scot-land, developed the game from the late 19th cen-tury. At the beginning of the 21st century, Scotland is still considered to be the historical home of golf and has developed as a mecca for golfers from all over the world.   JGe

Gordon family, earls of Huntly. In 1444–5, Sir Alexander Seton of Gordon was created first earl of Huntly, and changed the family name to Gordon; thus was established one of the most powerful and influential magnate families in Scotland (see NOBILITY: 2–3). The Gordons originally came from Berwickshire, but it was in the north-east (see RE-GIONAL IDENTITIES: 2) that they were to become dominant. Seton himself, a major Aberdeenshire laird, was one of those ennobled by James II to fill

the gaps in the peerage created by his predecessor. Another was Colin Campbell, first earl of Argyll. For the next two centuries, Gordons and *Camp-bells would control the north-east and the west respectively, as magnates who straddled the Highland–Lowland divide (see HIGHLANDS AND ISLANDS AND CENTRAL GOVERNMENT: 2), and oper-ated powerfully in each sphere.

There were three main ways for a magnate to achieve and maintain power. The first was in royal service. Here the Gordons undoubtedly scored. As early as 1452, Huntly was prominent in James II's fight with the *Douglases, leading an army against the Douglas ally Crawford at Brechin, where he 'displayed the king's banner . . . and [said] he was his lieutenant', and duly won. It was the beginning of a record of remarkably consistent loyalty to the crown, even if, in the end, it went tragically wrong. George, second marquis of Huntly, supported Charles I, and paid for it with his life in 1649. But only twice did they engage in serious rebellion.

The first, by the fourth earl, was against *Mary, Queen of Scots, in 1562, as a reaction to Mary's grant of the earldom of Moray, which Huntly had briefly held, to her half-brother Lord James Stew-art; it was thus a matter of local power politics, which in this instance ended with Huntly's death at the battle of Corrichie, but was to flare up again be-tween their descendants with the sensational mur-der of Moray by Huntly in 1592. The other was the revolt of the northern earls which rumbled on be-tween 1588 and 1595, when Huntly, Erroll and Angus, the Catholic earls, made overtures to Philip II of Spain, although to no purpose. Yet Huntly, erratic adherent of the old faith, was a noted favourite of *James VI; personal affection and the earl's usefulness in the north outweighed this dis-mal attempt at Counter-Reformation, in the eyes of a king who was himself not averse to infuriating Elizabeth by ruminating about the advantages of friendship with Spain. And major though these episodes were, they were a limited and temporary interruption to the general pattern, from which kings (see KINGSHIP: 5–6) and earls both benefited.

The second way to achieve and maintain power was to establish a network of allies, through the ties of kinship and lordship. The Gordons were an enormous kindred; cadet branches sprawled throughout the north-east, as loyal to the earls as they were to kings, providing a massive basis of support throughout the earls' area of influence. To them were added the lairds who were brought into the earls' affinity through bonds of manrent (alle-giance) in return for the earls' bonds of mainten-ance, and bound to them as though they were their kin; Scottish lordship was certainly conceived of as an extension of kinship. Some were imposed on lairds and *clan chiefs resentful of Gordon power; others were made with those willing to invest in it. Not all therefore simply added to Gordon support. But many families did identify themselves with the earls through their hereditary bonds. It is no accident that one of the two great collections of bonds which survive was that of Gordon, the other being Campbell. It is a testimony to how well the earls of Huntly understood the value of these alliances in underpinning magnate power.

The third way to achieve and maintain power was personality. A weak earl was of no use to the crown, nor would he be helped by a charter chest stuffed with bonds of manrent. Here again the Gordons scored. The rogue elephant who challenged King James and murdered Moray was a man of panache and style. The magnificent and defiantly Catholic panel above the main entrance to Huntly castle, the huge letters of his name which adorn the oriel windows, remain as witness to that; and anyone who could turn his reconciliation (one of several) to the godly minsters of the church into a riotous party in Aberdeen in 1596 surely deserves admiration. His predecessor was the subject of a splendid ghost story, but it is a story which also provides us with a vignette of the successful magnate: playing football with his followers, and listening to and advising them about their disputes and concerns over dinner. They were typical of this line of tough and able men, royal councillors and officers of state, royal lieutenants in the north. The first and only exception was, sadly, the one who supported Charles I, the earl of pomp but little substance. He was the last of the major players in Scottish politics. Like the Campbells, the Gordons got their dukedom at the turn of the 18th century, but the Campbells dominated 18th-century politics (see GOVERNMENT AND ADMINISTRATION: 1). The Gordons never recovered the dazzling prestige and power of their predecessors.   JW

Govan. Govan Old parish church houses Scotland's third largest collections of early medieval sculpture, testimony to its political and religious importance during the 10th and 11th centuries. The church stands on the south bank of the Clyde, opposite the confluence of the Kelvin. The medieval parish was extremely large (6.2 by 3.7 miles (10 by 6 km) of a prime agricultural stretch of the Clyde) and exceptionally ran across the river to embrace the royal estate of Partick. At this point the Clyde is still tidal, but before dredging was easily fordable here. The church sits within a raised, curvilinear enclosure that has protected it from encroachment by the shipyards and tenements.

Forty-seven pieces of early medieval sculpture are known, a total which includes four monumental crosses, five hogback stones, 21 (plus 16 now lost) recumbent slabs decorated with interlace crosses, and a unique monolithic sarcophagus. The number and scale of the monumental crosses (see MONUMENTS: 1) is indicative of a major church, even if three now survive as shafts only. The fourth cross is a sturdy slab, perhaps shaped from a prehistoric standing stone, known as the 'sun stone', from its prominent snake-boss swastika. The hogback stones are the largest known examples of a type of house-shaped gravestone that appeared throughout the areas of Norse settlement in northern England and southern Scotland. The collection of cross-inscribed grave slabs is the largest in Scotland. Although they share various stylistic traits, each cross is unique. The sarcophagus too is covered with interlace decoration interspersed with figurative panels, the most prominent of which is a hunting scene featuring a mounted warrior. This horseman, and those that appear on two other crosses, along with the prevalence of interlace, have invited a general comparison with Pictish sculpture. However, although the quality of the carving is amongst the finest known from Strathclyde, it does not approach the artistic heights of the earlier Pictish work (see CULTURE: 2). The collection can only be dated by art historical comparisons, but is generally believed to run from the late 9th to the end of the 11th centuries.

Small-scale archaeological excavations of the perimeter have shown that the pear shape of the enclosure is ancient and that the elevation of the churchyard is an artefact of the original bank and ditch boundary. The site of the early medieval church has been identified east of the modern church. Excavations have also exposed a road which indicates that the original entrance was from the east and appears to link the church to the Doomster hill.

The meaning of the name is disputed, but may derive from the Brythonic *gwo-*/*go-* ('small') and *ban* ('hill'), presumably a reference to the now demolished Doomster hill. The Doomster hill was *c.*148 feet (*c.*45 m) in diameter and stood *c.*16.4 feet (*c.*5 m) high. It is now demolished, but an 18th-century engraving shows the flat-topped mound, with a wide step halfway up, towering over contemporary cottages. Excavations have located its massive quarry ditch, some 26.2 feet (8 m) wide, but have not investigated the site in detail. Although there is no contemporary evidence, antiquarian tradition suggests that this was a court hill. This interpretation is supported by the stepped form, with parallels at the Tynwald in *Man and at the (also demolished) Thingmote of Viking Dublin (see IRELAND: 1).

The earliest mention of Govan seems to be Symeon of Durham's reference to the presence of the Northumbrian army at Ouania in 756 following an assault on Dumbarton. In the absence of historical evidence relating to the period of Govan's prominence, interpretation of the site's significance rests upon the material remains. Twelfth-century sources indicated that Partick was an estate of the royal house of Strathclyde. Given the abundance of sculpture and the Doomster hill, it suggests that Govan was the political centre of the kingdom in the centuries following the demise of *Dumbarton (sacked in 870) and the rise of *Glasgow cathedral (established 1114 × 1118). The character of the sculpture and the form of the court hill both indicate Norse influence and it is not unreasonable to suppose that there was a significant Scandinavian presence in the court (see SCANDINAVIA: 1).

The first unequivocal historical notice of Govan occurs in *David I's early 12th-century Inquisition for Glasgow cathedral, where it is the first parish enumerated. Govan declined as Glasgow rose in importance; nevertheless, it remained an important parish, whose incumbent played a prominent role in the cathedral chapter and latterly served as principal of Glasgow University.   STD

government after the Union, 1707–c.1750. One of the peculiarities of the *Union of 1707 was that little thought was given to how the new British state would work. As far as Scotland was concerned, what eventually emerged, after 1725, was a system of government and administration subordinated to the politics of management. What coherence it possessed was owing to the dominance in Scottish politics after 1725 of the *Campbell interest and the defeat, if not elimination, of their Whig rivals, the Squadrone. With no strong focus in Scotland for administration, following the abolition of the privy council in 1708, the degree and effectiveness of administration depended on the personality and interests of a small number of legal officers, particularly the Lord Advocate and the Solicitor-General, who reported to the English secretaries of state, and the level of interest and interference from London. The existence of a Scottish secretary of state between 1713 and 1725 and again between 1742 and 1746 reflected battles and divisions in English politics and not an attempt to confer greater control on Scottish administration.

The autonomy of Scotland in the first 50 years of the Union, even after 1725, was heavily qualified. Indeed, even the independence envisaged by the Treaty of Union was breached on several occasions. The main English interest in Scotland remained, as it had been before 1707, security. English ministers expected politicians in Scotland to deliver peace and acquiescence in Hanoverian rule

north of the Border. When this was not forthcoming, these politicians, such as the duke of Roxburghe in 1725, who as Secretary of State for Scotland was seen in London as having been responsible for the outbreak of rioting which greeted the imposition of the Malt Tax, were removed from office and favour.

The major initiative behind Scottish government rested south of the Border. Legislation on Scottish government and affairs—for example, that under which the Board of Trustees for the Improvement of Manufactures and Fisheries was established in 1727—usually had its origins and depended for its passage on decisions taken by English (or British) ministers in London. Scottish representative bodies, such as the Convention of *Royal Burghs or the General Assembly (see CHURCH INSTITUTIONS: 5), were brought under close political control under the skilful ministrations of the earl of Islay, the second duke of Argyll's brother and political manager in Scotland, and Lord Milton, Islay's lieutenant in Scotland from the later 1730s. While the Convention kept a close watch on legislation which affected Scotland, and acted as a lobbying body, it is striking how little Scottish legislation was passed in this period. This reflected the lack of political weight Scotland normally possessed within the Union. English historians have recently sought to demonstrate the representative credentials of the British parliament through examination of its legislative activities. From a Scottish point of view, the story appears much less satisfactory.

The desire for stability also explains more constructive intervention on the part of English ministers after the Union. The setting up of the Board of Trustees was an attempt to make the Union work more effectively. It arose from a concern amongst Walpole and his fellow ministers about the fragility of social and political order north of the Border crystallized by the Malt Tax rioting. Similarly, the abolition of hereditable jurisdictions (see LOCAL GOVERNMENT, TO 1707), the establishment of sheriffs as a crucial element of local government, and the annexation of the forfeited Highland estates, all in the aftermath of the Forty-Five (see JACOBITISM), represented attempts to solve finally the problem of the integration (or lack thereof) of the Highlands (see HIGHLANDS AND ISLANDS AND CENTRAL GOVERNMENT: 4) into the British state after 1707. In an age in which property and property relationships were viewed as sacrosanct, the content and ambition of this legislation is striking and says much about the realities of the relationship between London and Scotland in this period.

Several attempts were made in the years immediately following the Union to provide alternative Scottish-based bodies to administer Scotland and

Scottish affairs, in the form of various commissions. All proved abortive, largely because doing nothing threatened fewer vested interests. There was also recurring and persistent concern about the administration of the Scottish customs and excise. Both were notoriously ineffective; their activities were also vigorously and violently resisted. By 1731 Duncan Forbes, the Lord Advocate, was coming to the conclusion that, under existing law, efforts to find a solution to the problem of collecting customs efficiently would have to be abandoned. Following the collapse of Sir Robert Walpole's excise scheme of 1733, which would have replaced customs on particular goods, wine and tobacco, with bonded warehouses and excises, the issue was to raise its head again in the 1740s but once again without striking results.

Eighteenth-century government rarely threatened the interests of the dominant political classes (see NOBILITY: 4); it was always compromised, if not worse, by the operations of patronage and exigencies of building and nurturing political interests. This was substantially the case in Scotland between 1707 and c.1750. In the face of lengthy periods of indifference on the part of English ministers, and the realities of political power in Scotland and in England, the second and third dukes of Argyll, together with Lord Milton, established some autonomy for government in Scotland. In all important matters, however, the power of decision lay outside Scotland with men who knew little of Scotland and who, usually, wanted to know little.   RH

government and administration: 1. the age of management; 2. the age of individualism; 3. the age of the British state.

1. the age of management

In Ireland, the politics of the early 18th century has been discussed by historians as the age of the 'undertakers'. In Scotland after 1707, discussion of government and administration inevitably becomes associated with 'management', as national politics functioned in a new environment without a Scottish *parliament, or even, after 1708, a privy council sitting in Edinburgh to represent executive royal authority. The classic period of political management in Scotland occurred in the period 1725–41 while Sir Robert Walpole was British prime minister. Walpole, after experiments in reform of the Scottish tax system to answer English allegations of malpractice, responded to Scottish protests by devolving executive authority to the second duke of Argyll and his brother the earl of Islay, the first a soldier and the second trained as a lawyer. Both had been at Eton but both had been brought up as leaders of the *Campbell interest in Scotland, their understanding of Scottish history no doubt whet-

ted by their memories of being taken to Edinburgh as young boys to watch their grandfather's execution for treason against James VII and II in 1685. The office of Secretary of State for Scotland, introduced as a British post in the ministry after 1708, was left unfilled in 1725. Argyll and his brother, whose followers became known as Argathelians, worked through more informal means, although both continued to enjoy the salary of high office, with Argyll pursuing a military career and his brother the office of Lord Justice General, nominal head of the Scottish Court of Justiciary, and Keeper of the Great Seal of Scotland.

Under the authority of one of the wealthiest and most influential aristocratic houses in Scotland, two brilliant lawyers set about constructing a system of government and management in Scotland after 1725 that was based on their absolute conviction that the British Union, the Hanoverian dynasty, and the commercial development (see ECONOMY: 3; ECONOMIC POLICY: 2) made possible by both institutions represented the future for Scotland. These men were Duncan Forbes of Culloden, who became Lord Advocate and whose special province of responsibility was the Highlands and the north of Scotland, and Andrew Fletcher of Saltoun, nephew and namesake of the famous patriot, who became a Lord of Session and later of Justiciary but who used his judicial career as cover for his activity as resident minister in Scotland for the Argathelian interest. Forbes sat as an MP while serving as Lord Advocate until his appointment as Lord President of the Court of Session in 1741. He concentrated on extending the military authority of the crown as General Wade used the Scottish military garrison to extend the road system in the Highlands (see TRANSPORT AND COMMUNICATIONS: 3), and in organizing efficient collection of tax using the military force represented by that garrison to provide security for the tax collection from a recalcitrant population. Milton, as he became known under his judicial title (thus avoiding confusion with the memory of his uncle, opposition gadfly of a previous generation), never went to London as an MP. In fact, on one of his rare visits there in 1738 to appear before the bar of the House of Lords with the other Lords of the Scottish Court of Session, most of the assembled peers complained that his accent was so Scots that they could not understand what he tried to report to them! Instead, Milton became a key mover in the restructuring of the Scottish financial system after 1725, and promoted the expansion of the activity of the state in the economy and in other areas such as church (see RELIGIOUS LIFE: 5) and university patronage. The establishment of the Royal Bank of Scotland in 1727 as a government bank (see ECONOMY, TERTIARY

SECTOR: 1), holding tax revenue until remission to London and extending credit to encourage agricultural improvement, manufactures of textiles, and foreign trade was the economic byproduct of the Argathelian system. The establishment of a government board for the 'encouragement of fisheries and manufactures', with Lord Milton prominent in directing its activities, was the state equivalent of the chartered bank, drawing upon Equivalent funds promised at the time of the Union, released on condition Argathelian management maintained order in Scotland.

The Argathelian system ended with the fall of Sir Robert Walpole's ministry in 1741, preceded in 1737 by a break between the second duke and the ministry. It set a precedent, however, which continued to divide Scots between those who sought government intervention and those who sought to avoid it. Paradoxically, it was the former Islay, after his elder brother's death in 1742 third duke of Argyll, who with Forbes and Milton prevented the worst excesses of state reprisals after the *Jacobite rebellion of 1745, using their surviving influence to convince Walpole's successors that Scottish politicians were necessary for the successful administration of the country. Forbes died in 1747, but Argyll and Milton lived on until 1761 and 1766 respectively, and tried to help Argyll's two nephews the third earl of Bute and James Stuart MacKenzie to carry on the system. Pressure had built up among Scottish landowners for genuine integration, however, and from another perspective, increasing hostility to Scots in London discouraged any Scot from adopting a high political profile, but other relations of the Argyll brothers emerged by the end of the 1760s to act as national spokesmen in the form of their cousin's son Jack, from 1770 fifth duke of Argyll, and their grand-nephew the third duke of Buccleuch, pupil of Adam Smith, who attained his majority in 1767.

Neither Argyll nor Buccleuch wished to pursue a political career in London, but both supported the growing influence of Henry *Dundas, member of a prominent Midlothian legal family which had never really been part of the Argathelian system. Dundas, however, tried to revive aspects of Scottish management amidst the crucible of constitutional crisis beginning with the American War of Independence from 1775. By 1784, Dundas was at the centre of the government of the younger Pitt and, unlike the Campbells, admitted to influence over broad areas of general British and imperial policy rather than being confined to Scottish affairs. The great aristocrats (see NOBILITY: 4) of Scotland who supported his system remained in Scotland to lend their regional authority based on the ownership of land to Dundas's political and administrative influence. Dundas worked himself almost to death in London in the service of Pitt and the war effort against republican France (see FRENCH REVOLUTION, AGE OF THE), eventually encountering political scandal and disgrace which ended his career in 1805 over his administration of the Admiralty.

Management in Scotland continued after 1805, however, as Pitt's successors continued to marshal the British war effort against Napoleon. Dundas's son Robert *Dundas came to occupy a place in the cabinet, usually at the Admiralty, and to advise the ministry on the disposal of government patronage to those who would support it electorally in Scotland. Never as adroit as his father, Robert Dundas continued as part of the Conservative governments of the day after peace in 1815 until he resigned in 1827 over the issue of Roman Catholic Emancipation (see ROMAN CATHOLIC COMMUNITY). He seldom took direct action in Scottish affairs, and increasingly it was the new generation of Scottish Whigs led by Francis Jeffrey who acquired the political initiative in Scotland. They sprang from the same social origins as their Conservative opponents but adopted a more utilitarian approach to law and government. When they at last achieved power in 1832, however, they were unable to bring Scottish issues to the attention of their English colleagues in parliament, in part because they had never devoted any thought as to how to replace the Scottish system of political management once they had abolished it. As a result, Scotland once again in the 19th century found itself not yet assimilated to a British state that had no ideas other than English precedent regarding the manner in which it should be governed.   AJM

2. the age of individualism

For 80 years from 1746, when the *Scottish Secretaryship was abolished, the administration of Scottish affairs was effectively handled by the 'manager' (see DUNDAS, HENRY). In 1828, the Home Secretary was placed 'in charge of' Scotland, and the upshot was a loose rather uncoordinated style of government. The Home Office had a general responsibility for matters touching on public security and challenges to law and order, such as the *Chartist agitation of the 1840s and the crofters' resistance of the 1880s. Otherwise, the responsibility within the government for dealing with mainstream Scottish matters reposed essentially with the Lord Advocate until the institution of the *Scottish Office and a specific Scottish minister in 1885. The Lord Advocate thus had the duty of drafting and bringing forward legislation affecting Scotland. This had a number of drawbacks. First, the Lord Advocate was primarily the government's law officer in

Scotland, and this tended to be the priority adopted by incumbents. This involved leading major prosecutions, advising on judicial appointments, and arrangements of all legal matters. Moreover, as Lord Advocates invariably moved on to the judicial bench—frequently as soon as a vacancy occurred—their engagement with strictly political or governmental matters could be limited.

In addition to their legal functions, the Lord Advocates were expected to handle electoral and broad party administrative issues in Scotland. Neither the Conservatives (see UNIONISM) nor the Liberals (see LIBERALISM) constructed any formal national Scottish party organization until after the Second Reform Act. Scottish Whips were shadowy figures until the advent of W. P. Adam in the later 1870s. In consequence, much of the work of choosing candidates, arranging finance, and so forth fell *faute de mieux* on to the shoulders of the Lord Advocate. John Murray and Andrew Rutherfurd in the later 1830s and 1840s are prime examples of this tendency. The time to handle broader governmental issues was thus reduced sharply.

A final disadvantage was that the Lord Advocate did not occupy a seat in cabinet, so that his power to secure the speedy passage of legislation relating to Scotland was much constricted. As a rule, therefore, Scottish legislation followed upon a similar measure being passed for England. The Scottish Franchise Reform Acts, for example, came after their English counterparts. The Scottish Education Act of 1872 (see SCHOOLS AND SCHOOLING: 4) succeeded the English Act of 1870, yet Scotland had been in clamant need of education legislation for upwards of twenty years. The long-serving Lord Advocate, James Moncrieff, was so angered by the procrastination of his fellow-ministers on this topic that he wrote a bitter protest at the relegation of Scottish needs to the end of the parliamentary session, when time inevitably ran out, leaving the bills stranded. By the 1880s this system was seen as inadequate to deal with the needs of complex modern society, and the campaign for a governmental minister responsible for attending to Scottish interests was launched, culminating in the creation in 1885 of the Scottish Office.

Most of the onus for implementing and overseeing central government policy in Scotland was devolved to various boards, rather than to central government departments—indeed, only the SED, originating after the 1872 Education Act, conformed to the latter pattern of administration. The SED was based in London, while its staff were professional civil servants, and it was directly answerable to a minister.

The boards included the Scottish Poor Law Board (established in 1845), the Scottish Board of Commissioners in Lunacy (1857), the Scottish Prison Commissioners Board (1877), and the Fishery Board (1882). They shared a number of characteristics. First, they were run from Scotland: they had offices in Edinburgh and the staff was located there. Secondly, the administration was not composed of professional civil servants, but contained a mix of experts and placemen appointed through patronage. Thirdly, the members of the boards were overwhelmingly drawn from the Scottish *prominenti*. Thus the first chairman of the Poor Law Board was Sir John MacNeill, a member of a Highland landowning family. Landowners, lord provosts, Edinburgh lawyers, and a smattering of professional experts, plus the occasional businessman, composed these overseers of Scottish administration.

Latterly, an increased bureaucratization became apparent, with the officials gaining a dominant influence over the lay board personnel. Thus, the Poor Law authority saw the emergence of specialists, particularly medical men, as the driving force in policy formulation and implementation. *Housing, health (see HEALTH, FAMINE, AND DISEASE: 3), sanitation, and childcare provision (see CHILDREN) were dealt with by the board's officers, in addition to questions directly relating to the treatment of poverty and the poor. The Public Health Act of 1867 was decisive in extending these environmental responsibilities to the Board.

Nevertheless, central government played a fairly marginal role in Scotland. Local government was left to its own devices in coping with the needs of the country. In urban areas, municipal leaders emerged, often pioneering innovative and forward-looking strategies to tackle the formidable problems spawned by rapid expansion. Poor Law Board officials found it difficult to impose their wishes on burgh councils, who had a hefty dose of municipal *amour propre*. The 1862 Police Act, which facilitated the incorporation of burghs, made central direction harder. The Board did not have a large staff, and its powers were ill-defined. In rural areas, local government structures remained pretty informal and relatively incoherent until the 1890s. The goading of the local county leaders by the various boards was perhaps instrumental in pushing change and reform, whereas cities and towns were probably more self-acting.

Scotland thus experienced a form of self-rule. It was largely left to run its own internal affairs with marginal interference by the central state. Parliamentary scrutiny was, compared to England, limited in scope and occurrence. There were few opportunities for questioning the operations of boards, as no minister was directly answerable to parliament for them. This contrasted markedly with England, where ministerial responsibility was clearly identifiable. Only if scandal or gross mismanagement took place, or if a Scottish case impinged on England in some way, was there much concern shown at Westminster. Even after the creation of the Scottish Office, the boards were left intact and quasi-autonomous for almost 50 years.

IGCH

3. the age of the British state

In 1973, the Royal Commission on the Constitution (Kilbrandon) noted that the state had been transformed over the course of the previous century. The 19th-century 'nightwatchman' state had evolved into a welfare state which reached into the lives of people from the 'cradle to the grave':

The individual a hundred years ago hardly needed to know that the central government existed. His birth, marriage and death would be registered, and he might be conscious of the safeguards for his security provided by the forces of law and order and of imperial defence; but, except for the very limited provisions of the poor law and factory legislation, his welfare and progress were matters for which he alone bore the responsibility . . . Today, however, the individual citizen submits himself to the guidance of the state at all times. His schooling is enforced; his physical well-being can be looked after in a comprehensive health service; he may be helped by government agencies to find and train for a job; he is obliged while in employment to insure against sickness, accident and unemployment; his house may be let to him by a public authority or he may be assisted in its purchase or improvement; he can avail himself of a wide range of government welfare allowances and services; and he draws a state pension in his retirement.

As the Royal Commission noted, this had enormous implications for government and administration and the 'centre'. In the late 19th century, Westminster and Whitehall were both geographically and politically distant from the lives of ordinary Scots. Decisions taken in London were made which affected everyday life, most notably when war was declared or taxes were demanded, but in everyday concerns the state at the centre played a relatively limited part in people's lives. The evolution of the state altered this fundamentally. Parliament, the cabinet, and the Whitehall civil service became more important as matters previously left to the market or to local administration became the prerogative of the central state.

Two models might have been followed in the evolution of the welfare state. The first was a highly centralized one in which government and administration were concentrated in London. The alternative was for London to set the broad parameters of policy, leaving local administration the task of interpreting and implementing these. No standard practice emerged but, typical of British

government, compromises and ad hoc decisions were made. The existence of the *Scottish Office facilitated a degree of Scottish administrative and governmental distinctiveness. Both models were applied, though there appears no obvious rationale for deciding which should apply in any given case.

There were a number of distinguishing Scottish features in the evolution from nightwatchman state to welfare state reflecting the distinctiveness of Scotland: the existence of the Scottish legal system (see LAW AND INSTITUTIONS, GAELIC); its own local administration; issues which affected it more or less than elsewhere; and a strong sense of Scotland's own identity (see NATIONAL IDENTITY: 6). The distinctiveness of Scots law was diluted with the onwards march of the state. New bodies of law emerged which tend to be more uniformly applied across Britain or the UK. Labour law, welfare law, and corporate law often had a Scottish component, including new Scottish institutions, but as often were British with British-wide institutions. However, laws and rules passed at the centre require to be implemented locally. A hallmark of the welfare state is that it has a local focus by virtue of its concern for the lives of individuals, even if grand decisions originate from the centre in the form of legislation. The process of interpreting and implementing the variety of new law passed by the centre was left to intermediate bodies and officials up and down the country. Parliament might decide that all children should receive a full-time education (see SCHOOLS AND SCHOOLING: 4) and then raise the school leaving age, but schools (see BUILDINGS: 2) had to be built and provided for in different localities. Given the multifarious responsibilities taken on by the state, this required an elaborate system of government beyond the centre.

In addition to welfare services, the state increasingly developed interventionist economic policies. By mid-century, central demand management along the lines advocated by Keynes was becoming the new orthodoxy. Allied with this, the Attlee government (1945–51) nationalized key industries, adopting a highly centralized model. Efforts to provide decentralized economic institutions were, for the most part, cosmetic though the *Highlands and Islands Development Board, established in 1965, and the *Scottish Development Agency, established in 1975, were examples of 'regional' economic development bodies.

Each of the four types of policy traditionally—redistributive, distributive, regulatory, and process—has been affected by the changes in the nature of government and administration. Redistributive policies, designed to redistribute wealth between individuals, were pursued through the tax (notably income tax) system and welfare payments including old age pensions, unemployment benefits, and maternity and child allowances. These were applied uniformly across the state with very little scope for Scottish distinctiveness. Distributive policies, those concerned with public expenditure on groups and for particular functions (for example, grants to farmers, to local authorities, for defence), became more significant as the proportion of the country's wealth spent by the state and public bodies increased. These did take account of each Scottish distinctiveness and a Scottish block of public expenditure developed in those areas under the responsibility of the Scottish Office. Regulatory polices, policies involving public control over private activities in the public interest (for example, consumer and environmental protection), have been adopted over an ever-widening scope of activity. Often, these too reflected Scottish distinctiveness. Each of these has affected the process of policy-making. The *Scottish Office and attendant institutions ensured that as far as the process of public policy was concerned there was a distinctive Scottish component to the welfare state.

Towards the end of the 20th century, however, there had been an attempt to 'roll back the state'. Starting as crisis management in response to economic problems in the mid-1970s before being elevated to ideological conviction in 1979 when Margaret Thatcher became prime minister, the aim was to cut public expenditure, lower the burden of personal and other taxation, deregulate, and reduce red tape and bureaucracy. After two decades, the burden of taxation has shifted rather than been reduced, the levels of public expenditure remain high but the pattern of priorities has changed, industries have indeed been privatized but new regulatory regimes have been introduced in their place, and new institutions of (semi-private) government have replaced old public institutions.

The welfare state has changed with the rise of the regulatory state but it remains much more similar to the post-war welfare interventionist state than to the 19th-century nightwatchman state. The description of the state by Lord Kilbrandon (1906–89), chairman of the Royal Commission of the Constitution which produced its report in 1973, would have to be amended 30 years on: 'Today, the individual will be provided for increasingly by a combination of public and private institutions. Her health, pension, housing, and education may be subsidized by the state through tax incentives but increasingly provided by private institutions. Those public institutions which exist will be "strategic" rather than "interventionist"; they will be *ad hoc*, established for a particular purpose rather than *ad omnia*, covering a range of services as in the past.'   JM

Gray, Cardinal Gordon, (1910–93), one of the most important Catholic clergymen in 20th-century Scotland. He was born in the east coast town of Leith. A local education at Holy Cross was followed by training for the priesthood in Surrey. Gray was ordained Fr. Gray in June 1935. After serving as assistant priest at St Andrews, Fife, and Saints Mary and David, Hawick, he became rector of St Mary's Junior Seminary, Blairs, in 1947.

Gordon Gray was the first Roman Catholic priest to graduate from St Andrews University. When he took over the diocese of St Andrews and Edinburgh in 1951 he became the world's youngest archbishop at the age of 40. However, it was his elevation to being the most prominent Catholic churchman in Scotland in 1969 that was significant. Gray became the first resident Scots cardinal since the *Reformation 400 years previously.

Gordon Gray was considered a 'heather priest' whose origins lay with an old Scottish Catholic family from the east of the country. In that sense, it could be said that he was unlike most of his flock, the Catholic Church in Scotland being a largely immigrant one. Considered popular among the small Ukrainian and Polish Catholic immigrant groups he was less open to the Irish *Roman Catholic community of the west-central belt, a community that since the mid-19th century has provided the Catholic Church in Scotland with the vast majority of its congregation and priests (see IRELAND: 3).

Cardinal Gray's humble and pious nature was recognized by most people he came into contact with. He was a champion of ecumenism and was invited to address the General Assembly of the Church of Scotland in 1977, previously an unheard-of occurrence. He held office when John Ogilvie was elevated to sainthood in 1976 and he presided over the visit of Pope John Paul II to Scotland in 1982. Aged 83, Gray died in 1993.   JMB

Great Cause is the name given to the extended court process by which Edward I of England judged between the competitors for the Scottish throne after the death in late September 1290 of Margaret, 'Maid of Norway', the granddaughter and sole heir of King Alexander III. On Alexander's death in 1286, the Scottish governing community had elected six guardians to administer the kingdom and make arrangements for bringing Margaret, daughter of Erik II Magnusson of Norway, to Scotland (see SCANDINAVIA: 1). They had conducted the business thoroughly, making treaties with both Erik and Edward I (who was also Margaret's great-uncle) regarding the security of her coming to Scotland, and arranging a marriage between Margaret and the son of Edward I (the future Edward II) whilst at the same time making elaborate provision for the independence of Scotland.

After Margaret's death, however, there was no direct heir of Alexander III, and it became necessary to examine the descendants of previous kings to establish rightful succession to the throne. It was soon apparent that there was no simple solution to the problem: civil war threatened, and an approach was made to Edward I to help keep the peace. Whether by invitation or interference remains a mystery, but by June 1291 Edward I had achieved recognition by the various competitors as arbitrator of the case, appointed himself as the overlord of Scotland, and had formal possession of the kingdom bestowed upon him. There was undoubtedly an element of coercion in these proceedings: a naval blockade had been imposed on Scottish ports, and Edward I had a sizeable military force in attendance at Norham, on the Anglo-Scottish border, when the Scots were due to attend his court there to answer his claims to overlordship. Nonetheless, it is by no means certain that the Scottish community was averse to Edward's involvement, since the disunity within the governing class would otherwise almost certainly have brought about civil war.

Eventually, thirteen competitors put in claims for the Scottish throne. Most had no chance of success, their claims being founded on illegitimate descent, or on too distant or tangential a connection with the royal house. Only three claimants had substantial cases: John Balliol, lord of Galloway; Robert Bruce 'the Competitor', lord of Annandale; and John Hastings, lord of Abergavenny. All were descended from David, earl of Huntingdon, the younger brother of King William I 'the Lion' (1165–1214), each being the descendant of one of Earl David's three daughters. Balliol was the grandson of the eldest daughter, Bruce the son of the middle one, and Hastings the grandson of the youngest. Balliol claimed that the eldest daughter would have inherited before either of her sisters, thus denying them any right to pass on to their descendants. Bruce contended that he, as a male descendant of the common ancestor, would have inherited before Balliol's mother, who could thus pass on no right to her son. Hastings appealed to English common law, by which daughters would normally divide an inheritance between them, and cited the recent partition of the earldom of Chester as precedent. He claimed not the throne, but a third share of the partible kingdom. A kingdom would not normally be regarded as partible, but Hastings played on the dubious nature of the Scottish kingship (see KINGSHIP: 3)—such as the lack of coronation and unction and the English claims to overlordship—to support his contention that Scotland was not, in fact, a true kingdom.

A fourth competitor was also given some credence. This was Florence, count of Holland, the great-great-grandson of Earl David's sister Ada. On grounds simply of lineage his claim was worthless, but he asserted that Earl David had resigned his own claim to the throne, the right to which would thus pass through Ada to her descendant, Florence. A long adjournment was given to allow Florence time to produce evidence, but none was ever forthcoming, and there are grounds for suspicion that Florence's claim was bogus, encouraged perhaps by Robert Bruce in order to allow him more time to combat the Balliol cause, which may well have appeared prevalent.

The case was tried in strict judicial manner, with a jury of 104 men being chosen to hear and assess the various appeals: 40 chosen by each of the two main competitors, Bruce and Balliol, and a further 24 being appointed by Edward I. The court, however, had the major difficulty that there was no precedent in English, Scots, or indeed any other law, to allow a straightforward conclusion to be reached. The claimants made full use of this fact, and appealed to many different types of law, 'natural law', 'imperial law', 'the law by which kings rule', for example. These were popular medieval juristic concepts, and had the great advantage of being uncodified and open to the interpretation which the competitors imposed on them. Eventually in early June 1292, with little progress made, it was agreed to decide between Bruce and Balliol first, and then judge all the other claims against the victor (see LAW AND LAWYERS: 1).

On 6 November 1292 John Balliol's case was judged to be stronger than Bruce's, and within just over a week the other claims were discounted against his. The final judgement in favour of Balliol was given on 17 November, and in the following weeks the possession of the kingdom was given over to him; he was formally inaugurated by the Scottish community in a traditional ceremony at *Scone on 30 November 1292. His kingship was qualified, however, by the awkward relationship with Edward I: he performed homage for the kingdom before Edward—a formal recognition of the English king's superiority—on 26 December, thus giving reality to John Hastings's defeated contentions about the inferiority of the Scottish kingdom. It was the impossibility of reconciling his subordinate kingship with his royal status that was to prove his downfall, but there is no evidence, despite subsequent popular myth, that there was any contemporary feeling that Balliol's elevation to kingship was unjust or corrupt.

The Great Cause was a defining moment in Scottish history, since it created the relationship between the two kingdoms which was to be the root cause of the war (see INDEPENDENCE, WARS OF) which afflicted them for decades, even centuries, afterwards. It also provided the forum for one of the most remarkable (and meticulously recorded) explorations of political theory in medieval Europe, and can be seen as the backdrop against which to view the extraordinary political, military, and diplomatic events of the following years, which were to be crucially formative in the development of Scotland's national identity (see ANGLO-SCOTTISH RELATIONS: 2; BALLIOL FAMILY).

NHR

Guthrie, Thomas (1803–73), important figure in the Free Church of Scotland. Along with James *Begg, he was one of Thomas *Chalmers's principal lieutenants at the time of the *Disruption in 1843. Guthrie was licensed to preach by the presbytery of Brechin in 1825 but due to poor opportunities at home he decided to study in Paris at the Sorbonne where he specialized in natural philosophy, chemistry, and anatomy. After a short spell as the minister of Arbilot near Arbroath, he moved to the church in Greyfriars, Edinburgh, in 1837. Guthrie soon established a reputation for himself as a gifted and eloquent preacher who delivered sermons to enthusiastic audiences. Henry Cockburn, among others, sang his praises as a man who could communicate and appeal across the class divide of Edinburgh. After the Disruption, Guthrie moved to the Free Church parish of St John's in Edinburgh where he embarked on an ambitious programme to reach out to the working class. Although committed to notions of 'Self-Help', Guthrie was passionate in his belief that more could be done by the state to improve the lot of the working poor. He vigorously campaigned for the establishment of a national system of education because he believed that this would lead to greater social mobility and hence, greater social stability. Guthrie was tireless in his espousal of 'ragged schools' which would educate the poorest elements of society and he spent much time teaching in them and convincing businessmen and politicians that more could be done to promote and fund them (see SCHOOLS AND SCHOOLING: 2). In 1844, Guthrie became a total abstainer and argued that alcoholism was a major factor in social degradation (see TEMPERANCE). He campaigned for the Forbes Mackenzie Act of 1853 which limited the sale of alcohol and restricted the opening hours of pubs. The large number who turned out for his funeral in 1873 was testament to his genuine popularity among the people of Edinburgh.

RJF

Hamilton family. The Hamilton family can trace its origins to the Anglo-Norman period. The earliest record is to Walter, son of Gilbert (or Walter FitzGilbert), who appears on 10 January 1295 as a witness to a charter by James, High Steward of Scotland, to the monks of Paisley. Walter supported *Robert I during the Wars of *Independence and was granted the barony of Cadzow in Lanarkshire. He was knighted before 28 July 1323, when he had a further grant of land, including Kinneil in West Lothian and Larbert in Stirlingshire.

Walter had two sons: David, who succeeded him, and John, from whom the earls of Haddington are descended. This arrangement set the pattern for the future advancement and aggrandizement of the family. While eldest sons inherited the main title and lands, younger sons were established as cadet branches with their own titles and lands. Daughters married either within the family (particularly important in the case of heiresses) or made advantageous marriages with other influential families. Equally well provided for were the many illegitimate children of the family, particularly sons who would not normally have inherited.

On 3 July 1445, the lands of Sir James Hamilton (1415–79) were united by royal charter into a barony of Hamilton, and he was created a hereditary Lord of Parliament with the title Lord Hamilton. He married as his second wife, Princess Mary, daughter of King James II, thus ensuring, by its proximity to the crown, the family's loyal support of the monarchy throughout its history. By the 16th century, the Hamilton family was one of the most influential in Scotland—partly by reason of the first Lord Hamilton's marriage with Princess Mary (by which the Hamiltons were entitled to claim succession to the throne of Scotland next in line to *Mary, Queen of Scots, had she died childless) and partly due to the cohesive nature of the family itself, based upon its vast kinship network, bound by a complicated system of secular and ecclesiastic landholding and office-holding, and strengthened by advantageous marriage alliances with neighbouring noble houses, irrespective of religious differences. Although the main concentration of property lay in Lanarkshire, Ayrshire, and West Lothian, the actual number of estates totalled over 200 and stretched from the island of Arran in the west, to Corse in Aberdeenshire in the east, and as far south as Sanquhar in Dumfriesshire. Hamiltons also held positions at court, shire, and burgh level, and controlled strategic castles.

In the mid-16th century, the highest offices in church and state were held by Hamiltons: James, second earl of Arran and duke of Châtelherault, was regent of Scotland during the minority of Mary, Queen of Scots, and heir presumptive to the crown, while his natural half-brother John was archbishop of St Andrews, primate of the Scottish Catholic Church, and papal legate. In the 17th century, James, second Marquis of Hamilton (1589–1625), was a close friend of King *James VI and I, holding the appointment of Lord High Commissioner to Scotland, while his son James, third Marquis and first Duke of Hamilton (1606–49), was executed in 1649 for his support of Charles I. The first duke of Hamilton was succeeded first by his brother William as second duke, and then by his daughter Anne (1632–1716). She married in 1656, Lord William Douglas, earl of Selkirk, the eldest son of the second marriage of William, marquis of Douglas, their descendants adopting the name Douglas-Hamilton.

The fourth duke, who opposed the *Union of 1707, was created a peer of England in 1711 as first duke of Brandon, in Suffolk. Successive dukes, who held the joint title of Hamilton and Brandon, were distinguished as soldiers and politicians. The family's main residence was at Hamilton palace, begun in 1599 by John, first marquis of Hamilton. The family, however, could not cope with the expenditure and heavy debts of 'Il Magnifico', Alexander, the tenth duke (1767–1852), who enlarged Hamilton palace and built up a splendid collection of paintings, furniture, and objets d'art. In 1882 many important treasures were sold from Hamilton Palace in a seventeen-day sale. The palace continued to be occupied until shortly after the First World War, when, due to its unstable position on top of mineworkings, it was demolished. The only parts of the estate left are Châtelherault—the palatial hunting lodge designed by William Adam for the fifth duke—and the mausoleum built for the tenth duke.

The family seat is now at Lennoxlove in East Lothian, purchased by the fourteenth duke of Hamilton in 1946. The fourteenth duke was chief pilot on the Everest expedition of 1933, making the first flight over Everest; he was also an MP and Lord Steward of the Royal Household to George VI and Queen Elizabeth. The present head of the Hamilton family is Angus, fifteenth duke of Hamilton and twelfth duke of Brandon (b. 1938). He is premier peer of Scotland and Hereditary Keeper of the palace of Holyroodhouse, and, as such, had the honour of conveying the crown of Scotland to the state opening of the new Scottish *parliament on 1 July 1999 (see also NOBILITY).   EFG

Hardie, Keir. James Keir Hardie (1856–1915) was the founding father of the British Labour Party (see LABOURISM). After a childhood of poverty and working as a miner, Hardie turned to political journalism. After his efforts to become a parliamentary candidate for the Liberal Party ended in failure, Hardie decided to stand as an independent 'working man's candidate' in the Mid-Lanark by-election of 1888. Although he lost badly, he was convinced that progress for the working class could be attained only through having working-class MPs who would be able to identify with the interests of their constituents. He played an important role in the founding of the Scottish Labour Party in 1888, although a failure to attract trade-union interest and support meant that he soon left for the more promising pastures in England. He helped to found the ILP in Bradford in 1893 the year after he was elected MP for the constituency of West Ham in London. Although Hardie gravitated towards British politics, he never forgot his Scottish roots and spent a considerable amount of his time promoting the Labour cause north of the Border. Although he described himself as a socialist, Hardie's politics were characterized by a Christian humanism rather than doctrinal Marxism. He campaigned vigorously against alcohol (see TEMPERANCE) and in many of his attitudes he shared a broad sympathy with radical *Liberalism. Class war was anathema to Hardie; instead he believed in the idea of goodwill between all sections of society. He opposed the 'imperialist' war in South Africa (see BRITISH EMPIRE) and was a stalwart supporter of both Scottish Home Rule (see NATIONALISM) and *Irish Home Rule. Unlike many of his Labour contemporaries, Hardie refused to support the war against Germany in 1914. This left him isolated, although it was short-lived because of his death in 1915. The subsequent carnage of the Western Front led subsequent generations of Labour supporters to portray him as a man of great principle.   RJF

health, famine, and disease: 1. to 1500; 2. 1500–1770; 3. since 1770.

1. to 1500

'Life was short, sharp and brutal', it has been claimed of the Middle Ages. There is little in the documentary or archaeological resource that would suggest that this was untrue for the vast majority of people. From conception, existence (see WOMEN: 1) was precarious. Foetal and perinatal skeletons excavated in Linlithgow suggest that some foetal babies were as young as 5 to 7 months (intrauterine); and, even if born alive, they could not, given the lack of modern medical techniques, have survived for long. Whether the perinatal group (7 months intrauterine to 2 months after birth) represent live or stillbirths, they are testament to the potential shortness of medieval life. Indeed, the high proportion of youngsters who died before reaching the age of 18 is further emphasized by the fact that over half of these, in fact, died before the age of 6 and approximately a quarter more before the age of 2. It has been estimated that this high mortality rate amongst *children may most likely be attributed to respiratory infections and gastroenteritis in an age when no antibiotics were available.

Such figures need also to be set against the background of a life that was harsh for all age groups. Standards of hygiene in the home (see HOUSING: 1–2) and working environment were not conducive to excellent health. The intermingling of industrial and agricultural premises with residential, the use of straw for flooring and, in some cases, bedding, and the lack of adequate sanitation and effluence contaminating drinking water brought inevitable problems. There is some evidence that, in towns (see URBAN SOCIETY: 1), the authorities occasionally encouraged a measure of cleanliness, by insisting that refuse should be placed in the sea or rivers, or in middens in the backlands of burgage plots. In reality, however, human and animal waste littered the public streets; fish were gutted; and animals, such as cows, sheep, and goats, were slaughtered on the open thoroughfares. Although much might be removed by scavenging dogs and pigs, the accumulated filth did not disappear. The housing of middens in backlands also exacerbated the inevitable squalor, particularly in towns that were experiencing overcrowding at the market nucleus. Analyses of occupation debris on floor surfaces in Perth suggest that attempts were made by private individuals to counteract contamination within dwellings from the filth outside: interior floors were deliberately raised above the level of the adjacent midden or path to aid drainage and a slight measure of cleanliness. Wattle rafts were placed in latrine areas and, in some homes, closets were furnished with wooden seats; and moss was used as lavatory paper.

The medieval *diet (see also LIVING STANDARDS: 1), although limited in range and susceptible to weather and seasons, was not unhealthy. The most common type of meat eaten, according to remains on urban sites, was beef, although other bone deposits suggest that pig, sheep, deer and goat also featured and most meat was eaten spiced in winter. Chicken and geese were reared, small birds were trapped, and fish formed an important part of the diet. This was supplemented with dairy produce and eggs and a limited range of vegetables: leeks, spring onions, fat hen, kale, cabbage, beans, and mushrooms and other fungi. Berries and nuts were also gathered in season; and exotic vegetables and fruits were available for the fortunate few who could afford to purchase imported goods, such as onions, apples, and spices. But cereals formed the staple of the diet, the main crops being oats, rye, wheat, and barley. These were, however, not necessarily guaranteed. As early as 1154, the *Chronicle of Holyrood* bemoaned 'a very great famine and pestilence among animals'; and in 1256 famine fell upon the country, according to the *Chronicle of Lanercost*, due to 'a great corruption of the air and inundation of rain'. Such disasters were to hit the country, either in its entirety or in pockets, throughout the 14th century and beyond.

A further disaster was to hit the country in the 14th century, perhaps the most feared medieval illness: plague or 'pest'. It first hit Scotland seriously in 1349–50, returning in 1361–2, 1379, 1392, 1401–3, 1430–32, 1439, and 1455. It is not possible to quantify the death rate, but mortality was massive. Plague was technically not one but several diseases, bubonic being the most noted. It is clearly identifiable in medieval town records, being kept virulent by rats and other rodents carrying infected fleas, which passed on the infection by biting the new human host. Scotland may, moreover, have suffered more than other countries from pneumonic plague as a result of climatic conditions (see CLIMATE); cold and rain favoured pneumonic plague, not only as a secondary infection of the bubonic variety, but also as a primary disease which could readily be transported merely by sneezing or coughing.

Other diseases were rife, some endemic and chronic, such as leprosy. This disease was common throughout western Europe, and the necessity for isolation was recognized. Most major towns had their leper house outside the urban precincts, and rules were laid down for minimal contact with the townspeople. Medical knowledge was such, however, that herded with the genuinely afflicted were many suffering from merely disfiguring skin disorders. Other infections and diseases flourished, such as smallpox, tuberculosis, cholera, amoebic dysentery, spina bifida, arthritis, and even gingivitis and caries, which also lessened the quality of life. Medieval people also suffered from the debilitating and nauseous effects of ringworm, and of parasitic worms common to man and his domestic animals, such as trichuris and ascaris. Although populations could become resilient to infection, increasing mobility by the end of the medieval period brought contact with new types of bacteria. One such disease to hit Scotland in epidemic proportions in the last years of the 15th century was syphilis.

Provision for the care of the sick was minimal. Hospitals (see MEDICINE AND THE ORIGINS OF THE MEDICAL PROFESSION) such as that evidenced at Soutra were not the norm and town almshouses or hospitals might house a handful of people, but were not genuinely open to all. An almshouse founded in Peebles in 1464 'for tyl harbry in it pur foulk for saull heile [for to harbour in it poor folk for soul health]' indicates the medieval attitude that spiritual healing was as important, if not more so, as physical, medical attention. Self-help was essential, probably in the form of traditional medication brewed from herbs (see TRADITIONAL HEALING). *Hyosycamus niger* (henbane), which induced sleep and if taken in large quantities narcosis, and *Atropa belladona* (deadly nightshade), a muscle relaxant, were probably cultivated; but other species of plants, such as the opium poppy which might have been used as a sedative, were collected from the wild for their medicinal purposes. Imported fruits, such as figs which could have been used as a purgative, were available to the more fortunate of the population.

In such conditions, life was tough not merely for children, but also for adults. Skeletal remains attest to the harshness of life; and heights of adults may reflect this also. The evidence of various archaeological sites suggests that men's stature averaged about 5 feet 5 inches to 5 feet 7 inches (1.65–1.70 m), compared with women of average height of between 5 feet 1 inch and 5 feet 3 inches (1.55–1.6 m). The women's stature is closer to the modern norm, and may be a reflection that female children may not have been as susceptible to illness as male children. Where women did suffer was in the childbearing years, when with multiple and difficult births and related obstetric problems a female was at her most vulnerable. Indeed, one sample survey of skeletal remains in Aberdeen suggests that as few as one-third of women would survive this critical period of their lives (see POPULATION PATTERNS:

1). Adults who did manage to live to middle or old age probably were those lucky individuals who had developed immunities to the epidemic diseases that were rife, such as cholera or typhoid. Given the harshness of life, it is not surprising that, in medieval times, middle age would be the period of life between approximately the mid- to late thirties; and to reach the age of 45 was truly old. Little wonder that, in the widely adopted classical notion of the seven ages of man, the age of 67 marked 'decrepitude'. EPD

2. 1500–1770

As with most other European nations, Scotland experienced epidemic and endemic disease and famine, and all aspects of society suffered. Epidemics occurred during periods of good harvest as well as bad, but when disease coincided with harvest failures and bad weather, the effects were serious indeed.

Dearth was not just a consequence of harvest failure, but also of population growth (see POPULATION PATTERNS: 1) in an economy which struggled to keep pace. By 1700 there were around a million mouths to feed. Scotland was affected by famine on no fewer than 24 occasions between 1550 and 1600, with serious effects on the people. The fragility of the *economy meant that minor downturns had disproportionate effects, it being claimed that 'a scheaffe of oat straw was sold for fourtie shillings in Edinburgh'. A major famine in the early 1620s, caused by successive crop failures, meant that death rates in some parishes rose by as much as one-third. The so-called 'ill years' of the 1690s caused even more devastation. Seven consecutive years of harvest failures and bad weather (see CLIMATE) had severe consequences and, indeed, this disaster is cited as one of the reasons why Scotland agreed to the parliamentary *Union of 1707. Contemporary accounts may be exaggerated, but there was widespread suffering, and many died on the streets. Vagrants converged on towns whose inhabitants were themselves verging on starvation and reduced to eating nettles in an attempt to survive. Perhaps one-tenth of the Scottish population perished during these years, although some areas fared better than others. *Aberdeen was badly hit because of the downturn in foreign trade, on which the town depended. In all areas, the weakest fared worst, particularly widows, the old, and the very young. After the 'ill years' there were no major periods of dearth, apart from a particularly severe winter in 1739/40, when snow and ice halted many mills, with a consequent shortage of meal. The efforts of the agricultural improvers (see ECONOMY, PRIMARY SECTOR: 1) in the 18th century helped to ensure that the people could be fed even in extreme conditions, despite the continuing population growth.

Diseases which afflicted the Scots in numbers were plague, leprosy, and syphilis. Plague came to Scotland in 1349, perhaps brought in by the Scottish army, which had engaged infected English troops on the border. Around one-third of the population perished in that epidemic. Bubonic plague, transmitted by rat fleas, recurred intermittently until the final outbreak in the mid-1640s, though by 1600 the disease was becoming localized to the towns. It was said that 'this evil led to a strange and unwonted kind of death, in so much that the flesh of the sick was somehow puffed out and swollen, and they dragged out their earthly life for barely two days'. Despite the decimation, Scotland was affected less severely than other countries, perhaps because of a relatively better *diet, or the cold *climate, which affected the spread of bubonic, though not pneumonic, plague. During major outbreaks political and intellectual life were affected. Parliament was forced to relocate and universities closed for the duration. 'Public health' regulations were instituted gradually in the burghs, with increasingly severe punishments for non-compliance, and by 1585 there were strict rules on quarantine and the banning of public gatherings. In the early 1600s plague affected most of Scotland, but nowhere on the scale of previous occurrences. The last major outbreak came in the 1640s. Besides the effects on population and economy, the plague forced town councils to introduce measures both to try to prevent the disease and to deal with large numbers of infected individuals during outbreaks.

Leprosy and syphilis were major endemic diseases. By the early 16th century most towns had a leper house outwith their walls, in which the unfortunate victims of this disfiguring disease were confined. Lepers supported themselves by licensed begging, and were also given unsaleable meat or fish from local markets. Perhaps the most remembered aspects of leprosy are that *Robert I was probably a sufferer and the wooden clappers sounded by lepers venturing outwith the confines of the leper houses. Leprosy survived in Scotland longer than in England, the last victim recorded in 1798.

Syphilis, one disease which survived many centuries of Scottish life, was reputed to have been brought in by foreign adventurers in the retinue of Perkin Warbeck. It had many names, such as 'grandgore' or 'glengore', and was quickly recognized as being sexually transmitted. Once again, a major effect was to stimulate burgh councils to introduce punitive measures to deal with the disease, which was often blamed on 'licht women' and their activities. Unlike leprosy and plague, though, syphilis was not eliminated, and many sufferers were probably killed rather than cured by the standard mercury treatment. Eighteenth-century Scottish doctors were the best in the western world, but they still had limited understanding of diseases and their treatment.   HMD

3. since 1770

The last major episode of general famine afflicted Scotland in 1740. Thereafter, although crops failed in 1756, 1762, 1771, 1782, 1795, 1800, 1812, and 1816, this did not result in deprivation or mortality levels comparable to previous occasions. The links between famine and disease became progressively weaker, so that diseases were attributable to the effects of industrialization (see ECONOMY: 4), urbanization (see URBAN SOCIETY: 5), and social change rather than to natural disaster.

Scotland's last major subsistence crisis was the potato famine. The crop failed in 1772 and 1783, and again in 1816 and 1836, but disaster came with the *phytophthora infestans* which struck in 1846. Originating in the Western Isles, the blight destroyed most of the Scottish potato crop, resulting not only in starvation but also in the spread of scurvy and typhus. The scale of the disaster prompted the government to take relief action, directed by the aptly named Sir Edward Coffin, though reaction rather than prevention of disaster was still the norm. Increasingly, though, the causal links between famine and disease were weakened. Disease was still related to deprivation and environment, but rather differently.

In the later 18th century the most prevalent epidemic disease was still smallpox. Inoculation had been available since the 1720s, but faced considerable opposition on religious grounds, and also because of the compulsion involved. The pioneering work of Edward Jenner replaced inoculation with cowpox vaccination, and the Edinburgh Dispensary commenced a vaccination programme in 1800, but the Scottish Vaccination Act was not passed until 1863. Smallpox continued to be a scourge, but by the 1830s cholera and typhoid were much more problematic. Concurrent endemic diseases such as measles, whooping cough, and scarlet fever also had lethal consequences.

The two major trends which characterize the whole period are the changes in the prevalence and nature of endemic and epidemic disease, and the increasing influence of government and public health legislation. Concern was focused increasingly on the containment and prevention of cholera and typhus, and also on improving sanitation and housing conditions. However, one problem which had to be addressed before sustained progress could be made was that of elucidating the nature of the transmission of disease. The opposing contagion and miasma theories precluded a unified view on measures to deal with urban nuisance and epidemic disease. The first of the major cholera epidemics struck Scotland in 1832, when 50 per cent of those affected died, the toll being particularly heavy in Glasgow. Uncertain as to how best to act, the government established Boards of Health, whose main functions were to deal with epidemics by a policy of isolation and containment, together with practical measures such as ordering the lime-washing of tenement closes. The urban hospitals found it difficult to cope with the influx, and separate fever hospitals were established; in Glasgow a fever hospital and no fewer than five cholera hospitals were required. Further major outbreaks of cholera appeared in 1848 and 1853, while typhus was almost endemic. During the 1853 episode Edinburgh Town Council petitioned the government for a national day of fasting and prayer; the response was that improved sanitation would be a better means of seeking relief, perhaps indicating that some progress was being made.

In the light of epidemic and endemic disease and the mounting problems of urban squalor and deprivation (see DIET), the state became more interventionist both nationally and locally as the 19th century progressed. Surveys were commissioned to assess the problems, and the *Report on the Sanitary Condition of the Labouring Population of Scotland* of 1842 confirmed widespread problems of poverty, disease, and poor sanitation, all of which prevented the workforce from operating at maximum potential, a factor perhaps more important to the empire builders than the conditions themselves. Social deprivation (see LIVING STANDARDS: 2–5) was also associated with immorality and drunkenness (see TEMPERANCE).

The Poor Law (Scotland) Act of 1845 contained provisions for paupers to be provided with basic medical attention, but legislation to deal with these problems was slow to appear, and it was not until 1867 that the Public Health (Scotland) Act was passed. This was, though, the start of real attempts to control and improve the environment, and the process continued through the ensuing century, including the Clean Air Act of 1956, which was aimed at ameliorating the problems of chest conditions caused by urban pollution. Parallel to national legislation, local control lay with the Medical Officers of Health. The first of these, Henry Littlejohn, was appointed in Edinburgh in 1862, and William Gairdner took up a similar post in Glasgow the following year, thus providing a professional medical focus and direction to burgh health regulations. Town councils also took steps, albeit slowly and reluctantly, to provide clean water supplies, the Loch

Katrine scheme for Glasgow being the major example.

By the early 20th century tuberculosis was of prime concern, and the work of Sir Robert Philip in setting up sanitoria and treatment programmes was vital. The advent of antibiotics was crucial, as were the post-Second World War mass x-ray campaigns. Poliomyelitis affected many in the first half of the 20th century but, as with other diseases, the subsequent vaccination programmes have prevented much suffering and disability. At the present time, HIV and AIDS offer a similar challenge to the medical profession in Scotland.

As the 20th century progressed, concern was focused on prevention of disease and the provision of suitable health care for the whole population. The major milestone here was the foundation of the National Health Service (NHS) in 1948. This, combined with the provision of school and maternal medical services, screening programmes for women, the availability of vaccination against measles and other infections, and considerable advances in the scope and technology of medicine, has served to boost the general health of the population (though the NHS is barely able to cope with the Scots' needs for health care). Indeed, Scotland is now in the unenviable position of world leader in rates of heart disease and lung cancer, particularly in the west of the country. The eclipse of the Scottish coal industry and improved workplace health and safety regulation have begun to reduce the incidence of occupationally related respiratory conditions which were almost endemic in industrial areas (see ECONOMY, PRIMARY SECTOR: 3).

Since 1770 the general life expectancy of Scots has improved. The state has become involved directly in the provision and regulation of health care, previously endemic diseases have been eradicated, and Scots lead the world in many areas of the medical profession. Major problems remain, not nowadays the consequence of famine, but of the effects of industrialization and demographic and environmental change. HMD

heraldry, the science of armorial bearings, came to Scotland around the second quarter of the 12th century; at the same time this new system of identification spread through western Europe. The practical advantage of the system was quickly appreciated on the battlefield and in legal transactions where personal heraldic seals could be identified on documents at a time when literacy was the prerogative of the few. The foundation of the system is a set of symbols used by one person at a time which are in turn passed to the heir.

Over the years each European country developed heraldry to suit its own needs and priorities, creating a national style in the process. Scotland required a system which showed status and kinship, and these have led Scottish heraldry to recognition as the purest and best regulated in existence. A basic assumption in Scotland is that all of the same name are related, however distantly. Certain charges, or symbols, on a shield have become associated with one surname and these appear as a common element in the shield design of all who bear that name. Various marks, or borders, around the shield are used to indicate the degree of relationship.

One of three different forms of helmet positioned above the shield give the rank of the armiger, be he a peer, knight, or gentleman. Ladies in right of arms use a shield in the form of a lozenge or an oval but do not normally bear a helmet. The latter is covered with a piece of cloth, called mantling, held in place by a circlet of cloth, or wreath, on which rests a further identifying symbol, the crest. This is the least important element but the term crest is now commonly and erroneously used to describe a coat of arms; that is, shield, helmet, mantling, wreath, and crest. One final element completes an armorial achievement: the motto. In Scotland this usually appears above the crest whereas in England the motto is placed below the shield.

Certain Scots, such as peers, heads of Lowland houses, chiefs of clans, or knights Grand Cross of British orders of chivalry are entitled to supporters. These are human figures, animals, or inanimate objects which are positioned on either side to support a shield. Supporters always stand on a piece of ground described as the compartment. Other elements can appear as part of the armorial achievement: the insignia of an order of chivalry or the symbols of an office such as the crossed batons behind the shield which denote an Officer of Arms (see NOBILITY).

In Scotland, heraldry is regulated by a single official appointed by the sovereign entitled the Lord Lyon King of Arms. He is the judge of all matters armorial, has his own court, and powers granted to him by the Scottish *parliament in 1592 and 1672. To assist him he has six other Officers of Arms, three Heralds and three assistant heralds called Pursuivants, who are all members of the Royal Household in Scotland, members of the Court of the Lord Lyon, and officers of the Order of the Thistle. Originally there were six heralds and six pursuivants but by an Act of Parliament dated 1867 the numbers were reduced to three of each. The old titles remain and are now used in turn by newly appointed officers. Heralds were Rothesay, Albany, Marchmont, Snowdon, Ross, and Islay; the pursuivants were Carrick, Unicorn, Ormonde,

Bute, Dingwall, and Kintyre. The Court of the Lord Lyon is situated in HM New Register House, Edinburgh, where the Lord Lyon is assisted by the Lyon Clerk and Keeper of the Records. Attached to the Lyon office are several herald painters who execute the legal documents granting arms to those who petition the Lord Lyon.

The Lord Lyon grants new armorial bearings 'to virtuous and well deserving persons', be they Scots, individuals who own property in Scotland, or those who can prove descent from a native-born Scot even though they live furth of Scotland. All grants of arms approved since 1672 are recorded in *The Public Register of All Arms and Bearings in Scotland*, which now consists of some 80 volumes.

The Lord Lyon King of Arms and his officers in their distinctive uniform—tabards embroidered with the Royal Arms of the UK as used in Scotland—appear on certain state occasions: these include attendance on the Knights of the Thistle, Her Majesty's Representative the Lord High Commissioner to the General Assembly of the Church of Scotland, the installation of the governor of Edinburgh castle, royal proclamations, state visits to Scotland, and at national state occasions such as the coronation and the opening of Scotland's new *parliament in 1999.   CBur

heritage centres describe a new type of museum which has emerged since the 1970s. The emergence and growth of heritage centres can be linked with a broader movement known as the new 'museology' which aims at integrating new developments in the social and human sciences, modernizing techniques of display and communication, and, in the end, changing the perception of museums. Added to this theoretical trend is an economic one with many new museum ventures no longer wholly financed or controlled by central or local government but relying on independent sources of funding. Heritage centres are, in fact, part of a movement which seeks to popularize museums by mixing education with entertainment, by broadening the form and nature of their role, and by putting communication at the heart of their concern before the collection, preservation, and presentation of objects. A simple defining characteristic of heritage centres is that they have no core collection and a strong storyline takes precedence over object-focused displays; they are, first and foremost, visitor-centred.

The division between heritage centres, visitor centres, or museums is not always clearly marked. Whilst a few are listed in the Scottish Museums' Council's compilation of registered museums and galleries, thus meeting the minimum standards required by the Museums' and Galleries' Commis-

sion in a number of areas, the majority belongs to the visitor attractions sector with some operated on a commercial basis, such as those affiliated to a distillery or food producer.

Herein lies one of the controversial aspects of the heritage vogue: an orientation towards profit and commercial viability. Heritage centres are associated, in some critics' eyes, with largely derogatory connotations such as enterprise, commerce, and tackiness, to the detriment of academic soundness and education: heritage turned into industry. At the start of the controversy is the disturbing figure that by the late 1980s in Britain, 'museums' were being opened at the rate of one every fortnight. The trend in Scotland is even more acute with now over 400 museums, of which at least half have opened since the 1980s. Scotland has the most visitor attractions per head of resident population in the UK. Is Scottish heritage a growth industry then? Heritage centres certainly are an integral part of the highly profitable tourism industry: Scotland's premier growth industry. Whilst their development springs from the need to satisfy visitors' curiosity and fascination for nostalgia and to present the individuality of specific communities or areas, it also stems from the opportunity to tap into new sources of revenue. Beyond the 5 million Scots and British visitors are the numerous descendants of the Scottish diaspora (see SCOTTISH LINKS) and foreign visitors. In 1996, 12 million tourists visited Scotland; 16.5 per cent of them came from overseas, and spent no less than 38 per cent of overall tourist expenditure. As a key component of Scotland's tourism industry, heritage centres increasingly need to have an economic impact, to be viable and generate wealth. Competitiveness and the development of a marketing strategy are now notions with which they have to be familiar. As a result, the customers-cum-audience targeted are crucial to the choice of topics tackled and displays created.

These diverging aims and marketing potential are reflected in the diversity of Scottish heritage centres. They vary greatly in terms of size, shape, type of building, and content. Some seek to present as complete a picture of a community as possible, thereby adopting a holistic, all-inclusive approach which includes social, economic, geographic, and, last but not least, environmental features while, at the same time, endeavouring to present material relevant to the present community and to involve its participation; An Tairbeart Heritage Centre in Argyll is one illustration of this. Others, more specific in content, focus on a fairly recent past and combine historical information with genealogical facilities for visitors of Scottish descent in search of their roots such as *Co Leis Thu?* Genealogy and

Exhibition Centre on the Hebridean island of Harris. Others still reinforce some of the iconic elements—whisky, tartan (see DRESS, HIGHLAND), and *clans—so often bound up with images of Scottishness (see NATIONAL IDENTITY: 6) in the mind of outsiders, not least Hollywood film-makers! To these examples can also be added the many sites devoted to Scotland's industrial heritage which have been opened in the central belt to project Scotland's mining past or its textile tradition; the shale oil industry is presented at Almond Heritage Centre in West Lothian; the industrial development of the west of Scotland can be seen at Summerlee Heritage Park near Coatbridge, while Robert Owen's social and industrial experiments are interpreted at New Lanark which is, incidentally, also a nominated World Heritage Site.

In all, however, interpretation plays a major part. Techniques of presentation depart from the more traditional object-oriented displays and often resort to interactive multimedia and other participatory technology designed for a public used to televisual images and computer information systems. Films or slide shows are frequently commissioned to support and enhance displays and the past is often 'brought to life' through scenes with wax models.

Yet many of those changes do not simply result from the commercialization of museum activity due to new economic pressures imposed by a reduction in state funding. They also strongly demonstrate the new questions which are being faced by the museum profession at large: how to respond to the changing expectations of an ever more demanding and eclectic public, also used to comparative shopping? How to keep on attracting visitors to an increasingly saturated field? How to move away from a 'traditional' vision of museums, as revered authority, synonymous with fossilization, empiricist tradition, and hegemonic viewpoints silencing minority voices, towards a museum which raises questions, disconcerts visitors, and does not preclude alternative views? Heritage centres appear as the testing grounds for new methods and approaches also implemented by more prestigious institutions such as the new *Royal Museum of Scotland, which opened in 1998, where both the latest computer interactive technology on site and the remote computer facilities invite visitors to plan self-initiated visits.   LG

Highland games. The Highland games incorporate feats of strength and agility that were practised throughout Scotland but their formal organization and annual occurrence seems to have taken off after c.1820. The Scottish Highland games have not only been a traditional facet of Scotland's sporting history but they have also evoked and presented to the rest of the world a particular image of Scotland that is closely associated with the traditional organized Highland gatherings such as those founded at Braemar (1817), St Fillans (1819), Lonach (1823), Ballater (1866), Aboyne (1867), Argyllshire (1871), and Cowal (1871). That image is bound up with kilted athletes and dancers, the skirl of the pipes, local and in some cases royal patronage, the distinct subculture of the heavies, and the sense of *bonhomie* (see DRESS, HIGHLAND).

Just as important as the more glamorous Highland games of the contemporary period are many of the less formal, local, Highland games (in both the Highlands and the Lowlands). Writing in 1923 in *Hebridean Memories*, Seaton Gordon wrote that 'the greatest event in the lives of the Uist and Barra crofters takes place in July, when the annual Highland Gathering is held'. Although the great feature of Uist Gathering is the piping, the attraction to the component events of the different Highland games was often secondary to the social function of meeting friends and in this sense the actual contests were more of a spectacle than the *raison d'être* for the games themselves. The atmosphere of these less formal events, such as those at Glenelg and Uist, are as equally traditional as Braemar and Lonach and yet they are a world apart from the more formal, rationalized, commercial Highland games circuit of the late 20th century.

Many of the folk origins of the Highland games of today have a popular history that pre-dates the Victorian period. The alleged point of origin of the Braemar Gathering is often quoted as being an 11th-century hill race to the summit of Craig Choinneach organized by Malcolm Cean-Mor to select the ablest athletes as postal runners for the king. Describing his childhood on Islay in the 1820s and 1830s, the land reformer John Murdoch talked of *shinty, cockfighting, athletic events, and feats of strength as being traditional Highland sports. One of the points of origin of 'Tossing the Caber' lies in the raising of the couples of the traditional Highland croft. The hairst-kirn, or gathering after the harvest had been collected, was often seen as seasonal celebration at which dancing, throwing the putting stone, and hurling the hammer all contributed to joyous celebration of communal loyalty and friendly rivalry. Writing in the 1820s, one writer describes such a hairst-kirn celebration at which a party of Celts amused themselves by their extraordinary feats in putting the stone, hopping, leaping, and running.

Queen Victoria's attachment to Balmoral, Braemar, and Royal Deeside is often quoted as the most single important factor that contributed to the development of the Scottish Highland games.

Indeed, the predominant image of the modern Scottish Highland games is one that, perhaps mistakenly, still owes much to the royal patronage bestowed by Queen Victoria upon the likes of the Braemar Royal Highland Society Gathering and the Gathering of the Lonach Highland and Friendly Society. The stamp of royal approval resulted from Queen Victoria attending the Braemar Gathering in 1848 and contributed to a sense of respectability and royal approval but at the expense of some of the traditional content. The Braemar Gathering had its origin in a Friendly Society that, like the carters with their horse racing, started annual games. As the traditional role of the monarchy declined during the 19th century, royal games became increasingly important. Events such as the Braemar Royal Highland Society Gathering contributed to a growing nucleus activities which helped to define a British, Scottish, and Highland sporting calendar (see SPORT, COMMERCIAL) which also included the Derby (Epsom), Ascot racing week (Gold Cup), and various shooting seasons (see NATIONAL IDENTITY: 5).

The development of the Scottish Highland games also contributed to an émigré culture overseas (see SCOTTISH LINKS). One cannot divorce the development of Highland games overseas from the diverse conditions that gave rise to emigration in the first place. Numerous Scottish societies emerged in order to facilitate the preservation, albeit in a particular form, of Scottish customs, including what the 1903 register of Scottish Societies called national athletic games. Highland games were incorporated into the agenda of Scottish societies such as those formed in Philadelphia (1749), Savannah, Georgia (1750), New York City (1756), Halifax, Nova Scotia (1768), St John, New Brunswick (1798), Albany (1803), Buffalo (1843), New York (1847), Detroit (1849), and San Francisco (1866) (see USA). To strike a more critical note, while the attachment of Queen Victoria to Balmoral and Braemar might have contributed to the popularity of the Highland games throughout Scotland, the policies of the same monarchy, most notably the Emigration Advances Act of 1851, also contributed to the process by which Highland games developed in North America and overseas.

Finally, a period from about 1920 to the present has seen the same Highland games become increasingly professionalized and subject to the standardization of rules imposed by various governing bodies interested in promoting world records and commerce. The Scottish Games Association was founded in 1946 and charged with formally regulating the modern Highland games circuit. Yet, the history of commerce readily shows that law closely follows the introduction of money, the pressures of professionalism, and associated problems such as performance-enhancing drugs. Perhaps this has been the price to pay for the continuing survival of the Highland gatherings and yet it is crucial to recognize that the games are as similar as they are different. A different sense of community, place, and function attached to Highland games may exist in Braemar, Aberdeen, Edinburgh, Airth, Cowal, Lonach, Aboyne, Uist, and Halkirk. They all provide insights into Scottish history and culture.   GJ

Highlands and Islands: general. There are many different ways of seeing the Highlands and Islands: as a distinct geographical area, as a region characterized by marginal land, as part of Scotland with a distinctive linguistic history, or as a cultural construct created by external observers who focused on one or more of these aspects. Nevertheless, the relationship with the rest of Scotland has changed over time and perceptions have changed in a similar way. Perhaps the most important initial point to note is the inappropriate nature of any single term to describe such a diverse region. Their extent has also varied over time. In the medieval period, the boundary between Highland and Lowland spheres of influence intruded much further east and north. The history of the Scottish Highlands has been one of the most contested areas of recent Scottish historiography; an aspect of Scottish history which has received a considerable, some would say disproportionate, amount of scholarly attention in recent years.

The diversity of the region stems from the most basic of physical conditions (see GEOLOGY AND LANDSCAPE). The variety of topography ranges from areas, such as the eastern portions of the island of Harris and the north-west coast of Sutherland, which are characterized by extremely thin soils and an almost complete absence of arable land, to the fertile land on the eastern coastal plain, including the Black Isle, Easter Ross, and parts of eastern Caithness. These are areas which present such a contrast to some western and insular districts that some would question whether they should be included in a region identified with the Highlands and Islands. Between these two extremes lies a central Highland region, which itself contains great diversity: from the fertile river valleys of central Sutherland, such as Strathnaver, to the mountainous regions of central Ross-shire and Inverness-shire, including areas with strong local identities; one historian has called Lochaber 'the Highlands within the Highlands'. The margins of the Highlands contain districts which provide further contrasts: the fertile land on the coast to the north of the town of Inverness has already been mentioned, and has much in common with the coastal fringe of *Moray, but contrasts strongly with upland Banffshire and Aberdeenshire and Highland Perthshire. The county of Argyll contains many of these contrasts in microcosm, from the mountainous land of north Lorn running down to the lower lying conditions on the Kintyre peninsula (see RURAL SETTLEMENT: 5).

The islands which surround the north of Scotland are also thoroughly varied. Orkney and Shetland (see REGIONAL IDENTITIES: 4), sometimes misleadingly grouped together under the title of the 'Northern Isles', could not be more different from each other, the ideal grazing land of the more southerly Orkney islands presenting a marked contrast with the more difficult farming conditions in Shetland. A second island group are the Hebrides comprising Lewis and Harris, two islands divided not by the sea but by mountains: Skye (along with the 'Small Isles' of Muck, Eigg, Rum, and Canna to the south and Raasay and Rona to the west); North Uist, Benbecula, South Uist, and Barra (with Vatersay, Mingulay, and Eriskay). Coll, Tiree, and Mull can be considered together but provide further contrasts, and a final group of islands comprising Islay and Jura and Arran and Bute might be said to have more in common with the Lowlands than the Highlands.

These differing physical conditions have had a marked effect on the social, economic, and political history of the Highlands and Islands, as the entries in this *Companion* demonstrate, but they are not the whole story. If the Highlands were perceived as a barren wilderness by outsiders in the period up to the early 18th century, the change which occurred over the next 100 years owed as much to economics as aesthetics. Towards the end of the 18th century it became clear to progressive thinkers such as Sir John Sinclair of Ulbster, as well as to opportunists such as Alastair MacDonnell of Glengarry, that sheep could be grazed profitably in the Highlands (see ECONOMY OF HIGHLANDS AND ISLANDS: 2). The social transformation which flowed from this realization can be broadly thought of as the *Clearances of the Highlands and Islands. Highland land now had economic potential if the impediments provided by traditional forms of communal agriculture practised by the native inhabitants could be eradicated (see ECONOMY, PRIMARY SECTOR: 1). That this was carried through in favour of an economic system which failed to sustain profitability for more than half a century is not the least of the tragic ironies of the Clearances. The craze for deer shooting which developed in the Victorian and Edwardian periods provided an Indian summer of viability for depopulated Highland estates which only a little more than a century earlier had been thought of as economically unproductive.

The perception of this area as undifferentiated has arisen from the tendency of outsiders to identify a 'Highland line' to be crossed, or the tendency of the government, whether of Scotland or of Britain, to see the region as a problem and attempt to implement blanket solutions which fail to take account of its diversity (see HIGHLANDS AND ISLANDS AND CENTRAL GOVERNMENT). This has been the case, in particular, in the 19th and 20th centuries, since government intervention has become a more important factor in the history of the Highlands and Islands. The creation of the seven Crofting Counties in 1886 is the best example of this tendency: this administrative area included most of Argyll, Inverness, Ross and Cromarty, Sutherland, and Caithness; all of Orkney and Shetland; and none of the fringe areas in Moray, Banff, Aberdeen, or Perth. So, although physical conditions can be seen as one aspect of Highland distinctiveness, this is helpful in a consideration of the region only if diversity is fully taken into account.

Language (see GAELIC LANGUAGE) is a further aspect of the Highlands which helps to define it as a distinctive region. Indeed, this is reflected in nomenclature: one way of identifying the region is to refer to the Gaelic-speaking parts of Scotland as the *Gaidhealtachd*. Since the 14th century this has broadly conformed with the Highlands and Islands, but at earlier dates this covered a much wider area: *place-name evidence suggests a Gaelic influence in most areas of Scotland, with the least influence at the peripheries of Orkney and Shetland and East Lothian. The history of the language has been influenced by the spread of English peoples in the south, Scots in the west, and Norse in the North. Further, from the 13th century Scottish Gaelic began to diverge from Irish Gaelic and develop dialects, although the language remains universally comprehensible to speakers of these dialects. The principal theme in the history of the language from the 17th to the late 20th century has been its retreat to the north and west of the mainland and the Western Islands. The main factors behind this have been the growth of contact with non-Gaelic speaking populations, both in the sense of the intrusion of the latter into the *Gaidhealtachd*, and the *migration—whether temporary or permanent—of Gaels to non-Gaelic speaking areas; the attempts made at certain points in the history of the Scottish Highlands to eradicate the language in the interests of civilization, education (see SCHOOLS AND SCHOOLING), and evangelization (although all these processes sought to use the language as an initial medium of transformation); and finally, due to the interplay between these forces, an insidious self-perception was fostered amongst Gaels that their language was not associated with the forces of modernity or progress. This meant that linguistic self-confidence was low amongst Gaelic speakers in the 18th, 19th, and early 20th centuries, a factor which affected the generational transmission of the language. A counter-current has emerged in recent years, building on the limited footholds which instruction in the language gained in the Scottish education system in the late 19th and early 20th century, and an understandably slow recovery in confidence in the second half of the 20th century. This, nevertheless, continues to run against basic demographic factors, such as the vulnerability induced by the ageing of the native Gaelic-speaking population. The current paradoxical history of the language has been summed up neatly by the Gaelic poet Angus Peter Campbell who has pointed out that, while the death of native speakers continues to exceed the number of children being born into Gaelic-speaking environments, 'The language is dying but at the same time it is being born.' A useful tool in the analysis of the history of the language was provided by the fact that since 1881 the number of Gaelic speakers has been enumerated in the decennial census of Scotland.

In terms of the way the region has been perceived by outsiders, the position has changed markedly over the history of the Highlands and Islands. As Geoffrey Barrow has noted in *The Kingdom of the Scots* (1973), the idea of a clear Highland–Lowland dichotomy predicated upon basic physical conditions 'seems to have left no trace in the reasonably plentiful record of two formative centuries'—the 12th and 13th. Nevertheless, as time passed, although immutable physical conditions did not change, both climate and man-made landscape did. In the process, the economic context in which the Highlands were perceived altered fundamentally and perceptions of the people who lived there changed. Various aspects of the social history of the Highlands attracted attention over the period down to the 19th century. Not least of these was the basic social organization of clanship (see CLANS OF THE HIGHLANDS AND ISLANDS), which was one aspect of life in the Highlands which was 'exported' to the rest of Scotland in the medieval period. By the 16th century, the government in Edinburgh was using the term to describe what it saw as its other 'problem' area: the *Borders. The organization of territory and power on the basis of kinship was the principal aspect of clanship. Modern scholars of clanship have emphasized the fact that it was not a static system prior to its erosion and eradication. In later periods the importance of this form of social organization for military purposes was widely recognized. Although the forces of commercialism were beginning to erode the basis of clanship as early as the late 17th century a

determined effort was made to eradicate the threat which its military potential provided in the aftermath of the Jacobite rebellion of 1745–6.

This did not equate to the disappearance of clanship from perceptions of the Highlands. The ethos of clanship was used by Highland landowners (see LANDOWNERSHIP IN THE HIGHLANDS AND ISLANDS) to recruit men into newly formed regiments of the British *army in the second half of the 18th century. Although the Highland regiments found it difficult to recruit from the north of Scotland in the 19th century, the rhetoric of clanship was given another successful airing for the purposes of recruiting in the early years of the Great War. In the 20th century the legacy of clanship proved to be a powerful vehicle in the mobilization of the large armies of tourists who campaigned in the Highlands (see ECONOMY, TERTIARY SECTOR: 3). The afterlife of clanship is a good example of the way in which aspects of Highland history have been transformed to suit new purposes after they have ceased to exist as meaningful aspects of the social life of the Highland population.

An aspect of Highland life which has proved less amenable to romantic reinterpretation is the distinctive religious history of the region. The interaction of religious life with indigenous culture is one of the most potent forces of cultural change in the Scottish Highlands from the period of St *Columba to the present day (see RELIGIOUS LIFE: 8). The medieval church was one of the first institutions (see CHURCH INSTITUTIONS: 2) to try to impose its system of organization onto the Highlands in the shape of the new parochial system which developed after 1200. Recent scholars have argued that the reformed church had a greater early impact in the Highlands than was for long assumed. Nevertheless, the process of evangelizing the Highlands in the cause of Protestantism was a slow process. Acceleration was evident in the 18th century as the connection between *Jacobitism and Catholicism (see ROMAN CATHOLIC COMMUNITY) and, more importantly, Episcopalianism (see EPISCOPALIAN COMMUNITY) compromised these churches in the eyes of central government. Evangelical Protestant activity (see RELIGIOUS LIFE: 6), most notably in the form of the SSPCK, had been active in the Highlands from the early 18th century but their activities became more important in the second half of that century.

In the 19th century the Highlands were in the forefront of Presbyterian fissiparousness (see PROTESTANT SECTS AND DISESTABLISHMENT). Nowhere did the *Disruption have a greater impact (see CHURCH INSTITUTIONS: 6). The Free Church of Scotland was strong in many areas of the Highlands and confirmed its position with its important role in the distribution of famine relief in the immediate aftermath of the potato failure of 1846. It has been argued, however, that the Highland legacy became less important as the Free Church became dominated by Lowland clerics, such as Robert Rainy, who sought Presbyterian reunion. This fact lay behind the creation of the Free Presbyterian Church in 1893, and the maintenance of a Highland 'Wee Free' Church at the Union of 1900. During the 20th century, and especially its second half, the influence of secularization (see RELIGIOUS LIFE: 7) has been less important in the Highlands than in many other areas of Scotland. Although Presbyterianism capitalized on the social and cultural dislocation of Gaels in the 18th century and soon achieved a dominant position in Highland ecclesiastical life, the situation was not monolithic. Important pockets of Catholicism remain in western Inverness and South Uist and Barra; the Episcopal Church retained a toehold in Northern Argyll and Lochaber, a survival of the Jacobite heritage of the latter area; the Baptist Church has a presence in Argyll, especially on the island of Tiree; and the fishing communities (see ECONOMY, PRIMARY SECTOR: 4) of the eastern Highlands to this day display remnants of a Congregationalist tradition.

The political history of the Highlands is also worthy of note. It might be argued that from the rebellions of the 1540s to the Royalist campaigns of the 1640s to the Jacobite campaigns from 1689 to 1746 and on to the Crofters' Wars of the 1880s (see LAND AGITATION AND REFORM IN THE HIGHLANDS AND ISLANDS) there is a tradition of Highland resistance to authority and central government control. This would be overly simplistic. All the causes espoused in these episodes were local manifestations of grievances which were certainly not confined to the Scottish Highlands. A more interesting long-term trend in the political history of the region has been the growing influence of the government in the Highlands. Scottish monarchs struggled to extend their authority into the Highlands after the forfeiture of the lordship of the *isles and perhaps served only to cause alienation by attempting to control the region through the use of the magnates such as *Campbell earls of Argyll or the *Gordon earls of Huntly. The Campbell influence is well known, but that of the Gordons extended as far west as Lochaber and continued as late as the 19th century. As government grew from the mid-17th century onwards, and acquired a British dimension in the 18th century, intermittent but more determined efforts were made to extend the authority of the state, with many new resources at its disposal, into the Highlands. In 1803, the government, in response to the worries of landowners that the Highlands might become depopulated, tried to stem the flow

of *emigration with the Passenger Vessels Act. In the 19th century the state aspired to, but did not always achieve, non-intervention in society (see ECONOMIC POLICY: 3). The 1840s saw the aloof administration of a famine relief operation and the 1880s saw novel interference in the rights of landowners.

A new level of intervention was reached in the 1920s when the state, in the form of the Board of Agriculture for Scotland, acquired the power not only to acquire, but also to hold, land and did so to a large degree in the Highlands. Economic development and improvement of the Highland infrastructure has also been a long-term concern of organizations such as the Annexed Estates Board in the late 18th century, the Central Board for famine relief in the mid-19th, the Congested Districts Board in the early 20th century, and the *Highlands and Islands Development Board from the mid-1960s to the early 1990s.

Although in all these aspects of its history the Highlands show a certain level of distinctiveness in Scottish terms, the forces which have shaped the region are not totally divergent from those which influenced Scotland as a whole.   EAC

Highlands and Islands, and central government: 1. 1200–1500; 2. 1500–1625; 3. 1625–1800; 4. since 1800.

1. 1200–1500

In 1200 the inhabitants of the Hebrides and many mainland areas of the west coast had few, if any, formal links to the Scottish crown. The Hebrides were theoretically subject to the overlordship of the Norwegian king, while the bishopric of the Isles (or Sodor) was under the ecclesiastical supervision of the archbishop of Trondheim (see SCANDINAVIA: 1). Effective local power lay in the hands of various descendants of the 12th-century nobleman Somerled or Somhairle, who had established himself as the de facto ruler of the Hebrides and Argyll before his death in 1164. By 1200 Somerled's territorial empire had been divided between his sons and grandsons who founded the three kindreds that dominated the political and cultural life of the Hebrides and the west for much of the medieval period; the Macdougalls or MacDubhghaills based in Lorn, Mull, and the Treshnish Isles; the MacDonalds or MacDomhnaills in Islay and Kintyre; and the MacRuairis based in Garmoran. The heads of these three kindreds competed with each other for the status of ruler of the Hebrides, a rank described in Irish chronicles as *Rí Innse Gall* (King of the Hebrides or 'Foreigners' Isles') (see ISLES, KINGDOM OF). The same kindreds also dominated the neighbouring mainland province of Argyll.

In the 13th century the territorial lordships of the major west-coast kindreds and their semi-autonomous political status came under increasing pressure from the Scottish crown and expansionist magnate families that were more firmly part of the aristocratic society centred on the Scottish monarch. The earls of Ross and Strathearn, the *Comyn lords of Badenoch and Lochaber, and the Stewart lords of Cowal and Bute all looked to extend their political and territorial influence further to the west. The steady aristocratic expansion was backed up by occasional major royal expeditions against those in Argyll who refused to acknowledge the superiority of the Scottish crown in the area. Alexander II (1214–49) was personally involved in expeditions in the early 1220s, and his death on the island of Kerrera in Oban Bay in 1249 occurred during another punitive expedition against Argyll lords.

The repeated royal expeditions seem to have persuaded the most powerful of the Hebridean/Argyll lords, Eogan MacDubhghaill, whose interests in Argyll were especially vulnerable to disruption by the Scottish crown, to reach an accommodation with the Scottish government that placed his allegiance to the Norwegian crown for his Hebridean territories under strain. In the reign of Alexander III (1249–86) it became apparent that the Scottish king intended to contest the Norwegian claims to overlordship in the Hebrides proper. Intense Scottish provocation eventually prompted a forceful Norwegian response in the shape of King Haakon IV Haakonsson's descent on the Hebrides and the Firth of Clyde in 1263 in command of a huge war fleet. The Norwegian campaign achieved little before it was dispersed by bad weather and its failure confirmed the inability of the Norwegian crown to protect its 'subjects' in the Hebrides from Scottish aggression. Haakon's successor Magnus VI Haakonsson recognized the reality of the situation and in 1266 he ceded superiority over the Hebrides to Alexander III through the Treaty of Perth. Superiority did not equate with effective control, but for the remainder of the century the crown seems to have made consistent efforts to draw the aristocracy of Argyll and the Hebrides into a closer relationship with the Scottish kingdom and to extend the influence of the royal administration into the newly annexed area.

The dynastic and civil wars that broke out at the end of the 13th century effectively threw this process of expansion and integration into reverse. The prolonged conflict meant that the institutional influence of the Scottish crown in the west receded, along with the power of the families that had spearheaded the advance of royal interests in the 13th century. At the same time as interference from outwith the region became less intense, the internal politics of the Hebrides were transformed by the dramatic decline of the MacDubhghaill and MacRuairi kindreds and the rise to regional dominance of Eoin MacDomhnaill, lord of Islay. From early in the 14th century onward, the MacDomhnaill lordship provided a powerful, expansionist focus for the inhabitants of the Gaelic west. Cadet branches of the Clan Donald (Clann Domhnaill) established themselves in Lochaber and extended the kindred's influence further east through the Great Glen into the area around Inverness. Eoin's son and successor Domhnall successfully pursued a claim to the earldom of Ross so that for much of the 15th century the MacDomhnaill lords were acknowledged as earls of Ross and lords of the *Isles (see also IRELAND: 2; MERCENARIES IN IRELAND).

The rise of MacDomhnaill power in the 14th and early 15th centuries had taken place against a backdrop of politically weak and unassertive kingship (see KINGSHIP: 5), and a profound demographic and economic slump (see ECONOMY: 2) that may have had a disproportionate effect on the vitality of lordships based in the eastern Lowland zone of the kingdom. As the 15th century progressed these conditions changed. From the reign of James I (1406–37) onwards, Stewart kings were aggressive in their projection and protection of royal rights throughout the realm. In this new situation the crown was less tolerant of regional variation in law and social custom and in the willingness of men to respond to the king's command. The monarchy and the Mac-Domhnaill lords clashed repeatedly over control of the earldom of Ross and this issue was a key factor in provoking the final crisis that ended with the forfeiture of the lordship of the Isles to the crown in 1493. The political struggle between the monarchy and the MacDomhnaill lordship served to sharpen the views of some in Lowland society who regarded the Gaelic inhabitants of the Hebrides and the west as inherently lawless, rebellious, and disloyal. After the demise of the ruling and unifying dynasty the political and social structures in the area became more fragmented and turbulent as men fought for regional supremacy. Increasingly, the crown relied on two major regional lords whose power bases lay outwith the Hebrides proper, the *Gordon earl of Huntly and the *Campbell earl of Argyll, to ensure that the very limited ambitions of royal government in the Hebrides and the west were fulfilled. SB

2. 1500–1625

The personal reigns of *James IV (c.1495–1513) and *James VI (1585–1625) saw the most sustained attempts so far by central government to deal with the Highlands and Islands. The aims and methods of these kings held features in common with each other, and with their predecessors. Ongoing concerns were the establishment of legal and economic parity between Highlands and Lowlands. Mechanisms continued to form a spectrum ranging from the coercive to the benevolent. But whereas James IV blended coercion with perception, in James VI's time the attitude and policies of government became increasingly intolerant. This had less to do with any dramatic descent of the Highlands into anarchy than with James VI's personal contempt for his Gaelic-speaking subjects, his belief in the 'wealth of the Isles' which was being denied him, the evolution of Scotland into a nation state (see NATIONAL IDENTITY: 3) with centralist tendencies, that state's ideological rejection of Gaelic Scotland, and the development of a British agenda. James's attempt to form the first British state resulted in Gaelic Scotland, *Ireland, and the Scottish *Borders all becoming parts of one policy, and Gaels joining Borderers and papists in the ranks of anti-British bogeymen.

It took over 50 years before the forfeiture of the lordship of the *Isles in 1493 was made good. Its death no less than its life proclaimed the lordship's cohesiveness, and left a vacuum over much of the Highlands which inevitably engendered instability in the later 16th century, as *clans which aspired to follow in the MacDonalds' footsteps contended for *ceannas nan Gaidheal* ('the headship of the Gael'). Nevertheless, the major 'problem' which Gaelic Scotland presented to the evolving Scottish or British state was not its supposed lawlessness, but its increasing distinctiveness in language, economic and social organization, custom, and, after 1560, religion and education (see REFORMATION).

For government, the key was answerability. The complex interaction of land tenure, kin loyalty, and jurisdiction in the *Gaidhealtachd* that proprietors there (see LANDOWNERSHIP IN THE HIGHLANDS AND ISLANDS) did not necessarily command the loyalty of their tenantry, while a prime responsibility of the clan chiefs who did command that loyalty was to protect their clansmen, not to surrender them to central authority. From a central perspective, the clan, and thus Gaelic society as a whole, could form a hermetically sealed unit, resistant to conformist pressure and difficult to penetrate.

The 'Highland problem' was compounded, not by the total absence of central government, but by its discontinuous, insensitive, and obtrusive presence. Causal factors here were the limited resources possessed by the crown even after 1603, the fluctuating level of priority it accorded to Highland policy, and the three royal minorities during the 16th century. The demise of the lordship of the Isles ended the possibility of any genuinely devolution-

ary solution to the governance of the Highlands, and created more problems than it solved. Crown action could precipitate or exacerbate troubles in the Highlands, whether wittingly or unwittingly. Despite its own periodic misgivings, the crown was unable to avoid reliance upon that most traditional of all Highland policies, the commission of lieutenancy. Commissions granted to the heads of indigenous kindreds like the *Campbells could all too easily provide a cloak for private expansionist ambitions. They risked turning the crown's favoured Highland agents into over-mighty subjects. In the case of the earls of Argyll, the crown was to reap what it had sowed after 1625.

James VI sought to make the Highlands and Islands answerable to God, justice, and himself, and to assimilate them into his new Britain. His efforts involved an extraordinary range of old and new mechanisms, but the impression is that these were deployed haphazardly. When early legislative attempts to unravel the Gordian knot of landholding, loyalty, and jurisdiction proved fruitless, James took a sword to it. If Gaels could not be made answerable, they were to be rooted out or displaced, and substituted by Lowlanders who would be. The most radical manifestations of this programme—the extermination of the MacGregors, and the colonization of Lewis by the 'Fife Adventurers'—were unsuccessful. In Lewis, Kintyre, and Ardnamurchan, the indigenous ruling kindreds were displaced or reduced, but the major beneficiaries were the MacKenzies and Campbells, not Lowlanders. A longer-term but arguably no less hawkish approach to the 'normalization' of the Western Isles was taken by the Statutes of Iona of 1609. Reformed churches, schools, and inns were to be employed as tools of homogenization, and the statute requiring the chiefs to send their eldest offspring to the Lowlands for their education sought to bring the values of the ruling grades into line with those of their southern counterparts (see SCHOOLS AND SCHOOLING: 1). In 1616, knowledge of English was made a precondition of an heir's eligibility to succeed. Parts of this legislation were dead letters, but that on education contributed to a process of 'internal colonization', by steadily converting the ruling grades from obstacles, into vehicles for change.   MMacG

3. 1625–1800

The relationship between the north and west of Scotland and central government over the period from 1625 to 1800 is traditionally envisaged through the notion of a 'Highland problem'. By the accession of Charles I, government policy towards the region had settled into a basic pattern. Expropriation of certain clan lands continued when the

*Campbells of Argyll established property control over the territory of MacIain of Ardnamurchan. In addition, bands of surety designed to induce social responsibility amongst the *clan fine by making them responsible for the actions of their clansmen continued to be exacted by the privy council. Operating alongside this strategy was the crown's on-going favouritism towards certain families, such as the *Gordons of Huntly and MacKenzies of Seaforth. These powerful magnates became, effectively, agents of government policy, and their ability to use this role for private gain is exemplified by the fortunes of the house of Argyll. The 1628 extension of its already formidable rights of legal jurisdiction allowed for the use of official legal sanction in a strategy of territorial expansion that induced severe disorder in the region. Any possibility of stable links emerging between Scotland's political centre and Gaeldom foundered during the years of Covenanting revolution, Scottish civil war (see COVENANT, WARS OF THE) and Cromwellian occupation that spanned 1638–60. The impact of such instability was multifaceted, not least by ensuring the complete integration of the Highlands into the Scottish political world. Archibald Campbell, marquis of Argyll, emerged as the main figure in the Covenanting leadership. The Royalist opposition, meanwhile, led by James Graham, marquis of Montrose, and Alasdair MacColla, found the majority of its military support from those clans who were victims or threatened neighbours of the MacKenzies, Sutherlands, Gordons, and, most obviously, the Campbells of Argyll. By planting new political and ideological fissures within Gaeldom alongside traditional territorial disputes, the civil war period reveals how it was often, in fact, instability at the national level that was responsible for Highland problems supposedly born of indigenous conditions. The main political legacy, however, was that the region became associated with resistance to the military, religious, and fiscal authority of the Scottish state—a reputation for chronic disaffection that was to last until the middle of the 18th century (see GOVERNMENT AFTER THE UNION).

The Restoration regime in Scotland exemplified the tendency for the political centre to manipulate the reality and perception of Highland disorder for its own agenda. Initially, the execution of the first marquis of Argyll in 1661 suggested the crown was preparing to curb Campbell acquisitiveness. However, the protection offered to the ninth earl by John Maitland, first duke of Lauderdale and Secretary of State for Scotland, not only ensured the return of the estate but enabled Argyll to pursue private and public revenue arrears, most notably from Sir John Maclean of Duart. The result was that in 1676 the privy council issued a commission

of fire and sword, and later committed shire militias to the furtherance of Argyll's private war and eventual occupation of Duart's lands in 1679. Aside from exacerbating regional instability, the centre used arrears of cess due from Highland counties to quarter both independent companies and militias. This partly offset costs for the military resources deemed necessary to secure the crown's authoritarian regime and, as in the use of Highland levies in 1678, to intimidate districts of the south-west suspected of religious disaffection. James, duke of York's need for political and military support in the pursuit of his succession did ensure a brief period of government co-operation with the clans. In 1682–4, the Commission for Securing the Peace of the Highlands sought to regularize the role of the fine in the implementation of law and order. Moreover, although never actually implemented, James's willingness to consider the redistribution of feudal superiorities in Lochaber imbued many of the Great Glen clans with a renewed sense of loyalty to the Stuarts, a process that was aided considerably by the second forfeiture of the Argyll estates in 1685.

Such practical considerations, allied to the strong cultural tradition of loyalty engendered by the 1640s, a continuing adherence to Episcopalianism (see EPISCOPALIAN COMMUNITY), and nationalist resentment at the *Union of 1707, help explain the high-profile role of certain Scottish clans within *Jacobitism. In the risings of 1689, 1715, 1719, and 1745, clans formed a majority of the fighting men. Even in the large, almost national rising of 1715, Highlanders still constituted over two-thirds of Jacobite manpower. Given this, the aftermath of the 'Fifteen is perhaps surprising. Leniency on the part of the legal establishment in Scotland and General George Wade's remedial programme of disarming, road building (see TRANSPORT AND COMMUNICATIONS: 3), garrison government, and limited patronage distribution to neutral or wavering Jacobite families appeared to be a non-violent yet effective policy. However, more often than not pre-existing hostile government attitudes to the region were compounded by a sense that the Highlands threatened the constituted nature of the state. This ensured that the aftermath of both the 1689 and 1745 risings entailed a return to the military violence that had, ironically, been used so often by Stuart governments. The major contrast with 17th-century commissions of fire and sword was that, at *Glencoe in 1692, and more obviously after Culloden, unconstitutional military execution was carried out directly by the forces of the crown. Nonetheless, after the punitive strategy of William Augustus, duke of Cumberland, and the Disarming and Heritable Jurisdiction Acts of 1746 and 1747, the government did institute legislation such as the 1752 Annexation Act that sought to address underlying issues of poverty, commercial underdevelopment, and the lack of economic diversity (see ECONOMY OF THE HIGHLANDS AND ISLANDS: ECONOMY: 2). The resultant concern to maintain populations that were felt to be economically valuable was strengthened by the single most important government activity in the region: namely, military recruiting. By 1800 the region was supplying inordinate numbers of men to the British army. Both these military and economic motivations explain the official ban on *emigration in 1775 and again, effectively, in 1803, as well as official approval for employment schemes such as the British Fisheries Society, founded in 1784. Ultimately, the evolution in perceptions of the Highland problem, away from primarily military and political concerns and into economic and commercial issues, resulted in the extreme irony of the British state first militarily persecuting then striving to retain Gaels within the region.   AMacK

4. since 1800

The relationship between central government and the Highlands in the modern period can be divided into three parts. The first lasted from 1800 to the 1880s, the second from the 1880s to 1939, and the third from 1939 to the present day.

In the first period, government concern was sporadic and most obvious during periods of crisis. The wartime crisis of 1800–15 induced intervention to discover the causes of *emigration and limit it by driving up the cost of passages and improving the communications infrastructure (see TRANSPORT AND COMMUNICATIONS: 3) in an effort to eradicate emigration at source. The objective in this period was to support landowners who required human resources for the kelp industry and for military employment. These policies were overturned in the late 1820s, when landowners no longer placed such a high premium on supplies of labour. The famine of the 1840s saw further developments. A famine relief operation was administered by Treasury and Board of Supervision officials in the interest of the maintenance of mid-Victorian shibboleths such as economy, self-reliance, and the avoidance of demoralizing and gratuitous relief (see POLITICAL SYSTEM: 1). The money for the famine relief operation came entirely from a fund raised through philanthropic contributions. An increasingly professional structure was put in place to oversee the operation, although its temporary nature was emphasized by its abolition in 1851, long before the end of the crisis which continued to at least 1855.

In the second period, government began to intervene in a more enduring manner, as can be seen by the establishment of permanent institutions; policy, however, was largely based on the land issue. An important development was the establishment of the *Scottish Office in 1885. The early 1880s provided a bridge between the first and second period. Government attention was attracted by economic and social crisis (see ECONOMY OF THE HIGHLANDS AND ISLANDS: 3) and a breakdown in law and order. A Royal Commission of 1883–4 provided much information and increased the perception within government that the Highlands were a problem apart. The 1886 Crofters Holdings (Scotland) Act was based on an Irish statute of 1881 and began a code of legislation which would comprise Acts of 1897, 1911, and 1919. An increasing number of permanent government institutions were established in this period. They included the Crofters Commission, to oversee tenurial relations in 1886, and a Congested Districts Board, again modelled on an Irish precedent, to attempt a policy of land purchase and economic development, in 1897 (see IRELAND: 3). These two bodies were abolished in 1911 and their roles were taken over by the Board of Agriculture for Scotland and the Scottish Land Court. The overriding concern of government in this period was to oversee tenurial relations and then to extend the amount of land available to crofters. In the 1930s, it became increasingly apparent that these policies had failed to establish a secure economic structure in the Highlands and new approaches were sought.

In the third period, central government has become much larger and more diverse and policy has become much more comprehensive. The crofting system (see LAND AGITATION AND REFORM IN THE HIGHLANDS AND ISLANDS) came to be seen as part of the problem rather than the solution. Attempts to reform it, however, proved difficult due to the loyalty of the population to its structures. The principal development in this period has been the increasing diversity of policy. Institutions such as the North of Scotland Hydro Electric Board (NSHEB), established in 1943, and the *Highlands and Islands Development Board (HIDB), established in 1965, have had a wider concern with the economic development of the region. The latter institution was a singular experiment in regional policy, had begun as a response to the high levels of unemployment in the inter-war period, and was initially applied to the Highlands in 1948 with the definition of part of the Highlands as a Development Area under the Distribution of Industry Act.

A long-standing problem with the government of the Highlands has been that the extremely low value of land in the region has made it difficult for local government to raise sufficient revenue for the delivery of services. The development of crofting as a separate tenurial code in the late 19th century, and the rating concessions given to crofters, threw much of this burden onto landowners (see LAND-OWNERSHIP IN THE HIGHLANDS AND ISLANDS) and the problem was not addressed until the provision of Exchequer equalization grants in the 20th century.

A further theme has been the persistent perception of central government that the Highlands presented different problems from other rural areas. This perception has induced governments since the 1880s to see the Highlands as a special policy area. This began when the provisions of the Crofters Holdings (Scotland) Act of 1886 were confined to the seven counties of Shetland, Orkney, Caithness, Sutherland, Ross and Cromarty, Inverness, and Argyll, and the practice has continued down to the present day. Since the 1880s, governments have continued to establish separate institutions for the administration of the Highlands, the NSHEB and the HIDB being two of the most prominent.

The single theme which connects the relationship between central government and the Highlands over the period since 1800 (and before) has been concern with population levels. Highland population (see POPULATION PATTERNS: 2) peaked in most areas in the 1840s or 1850s and has been falling ever since. In the 1850s, there was a perception that the area was overpopulated and government reports in 1851 and 1884 recommended assisted emigration. Depopulation became the concern in the 20th century and large-scale industrial projects were used to try to counter the drift of population which had become a metaphor for the failure of the region in the eyes of government. In the 1980s, there were signs of population recovery but it is, as yet, unclear whether they are enduring and what the effect on the relationship with central government will be.   EAC

Highlands and Islands: community life. In his book *The Highlands* (1959), Calum Maclean (1915–60) wrote that 'there are two histories of every land and people, the written history that tells what is considered politic to tell and the unwritten history that tells everything'. To gain an understanding of community life in the Gaelic-speaking Highlands and Islands all available sources of evidence must be consulted. The documentary record (see HISTORICAL SOURCES: 1–3), often though not always a product of outsiders or outside interests, is valuably augmented by testimony deriving from within the localities themselves, as Maclean shows in his own study. Family and local histories, orally transmitted, the beliefs and customary practices which marked the calendar year (see CALENDAR AND SEASONAL CUSTOMS) or the agricultural cycle or the fishing season, and that vital source of contemporary viewpoint and values, locally composed *bàrdachd* or songs (see SONG, TRADI.IONAL AND FOLK), offer details and perspectives which fill out the data which can be derived from parish registers, census returns, estate papers, and sources such as the three series of the *Statistical Accounts*. *Newspapers reflecting the interests and activities of a district, and private correspondence and diaries, offer useful evidence too, as do drawings, paintings, and photographs when examined critically and contextualized.

The term 'community' summons up a human and a geographical entity and 'community life' can be said to be the outward manifestation of common or shared practices, skills, and value systems. Communication of all kinds plays an important role: the force of example which teaches the unspoken rules by which a small society is regulated, local speech patterns and usages, nicknames for individuals or communally for the inhabitants of neighbouring places and other naming traditions, local weather lore, and a shared history contribute to a sense of place and identity (see REGIONAL IDENTITIES).

The vast and varied territory which is the Scottish Highlands and Islands (see HIGHLANDS AND ISLANDS: GENERAL) includes villages which have evolved or been planned for specific purposes, burghs—some of long standing—and towns, as well as single-family farms and extensive estates. Each has, and had, its own range of dynamics according to its social structure and resource base. But if there has been one characteristic defining focus of Highland and Island community life it is the *baile*. The word sometimes occurs as an actual element in *place names (such as Balavil, Tree Farm; Balemeanoch, Middle Farm) and in some places, especially when linked to or separated from others by features in the landscape such as rivers or hills, townships were also associated in groups.

As a topographical entity the township (see RURAL SETTLEMENT) was the operative unit for agrarian and pastoral management and it provided the context for human interaction and the marking of rites of passage in the individual's life cycle. In the period before the introduction of crofting, which was pioneered on the Argyll estate in the late 18th and early 19th century (see ECONOMY OF THE HIGHLANDS AND ISLANDS: 2–3), the *baile* or farm might have been in the hands of a resident tacksman (see CLANS OF THE HIGHLANDS AND ISLANDS: 2), one of the Highland gentry holding a tack or lease from his chief (to whom he might be related) and operated by him and his household and servants; or by a non-resident tacksman with sub-tenants working the land; or by an entrepreneurial successor to the tacksmen; or by joint tenants who paid their rent directly to the chief or laird and not to his intermediary (see LANDOWNERSHIP IN THE HIGHLANDS AND ISLANDS).

The joint tenants would work the rigs or strips of arable land (infield), in many places distributing them by lot at regular intervals to ensure over time a fairly equable share in a resource which could vary in quality (see ECONOMY, PRIMARY SECTOR: 1). Beyond was poor land, a reserve for grazing and areas for cutting turf or peat. Further, beyond the head dyke was permanent grazing and the àiridh (shieling area), to which the cattle would be taken in the summer. There they were tended by young women from the townships, milked as required, with cheese and butter being made. In coastal areas the resources of the township might include a shoreline as well, with its wealth of seaware for sharing out as a nutrient for the soil and for the kelp industry, which was in some places managed by the joint tenants and in others organized by the estate itself.

The pre-crofting township was characterized by a nucleated or clustered settlement site, which is readily to be seen on Major General William Roy's Military Survey of Scotland (1747–53) and in estate plans of the 18th and early 19th century (see MAPS AND MAP-MAKING). This configuration of buildings gave way to a dispersed settlement pattern as the crofting landscape began to emerge, with individual lots laid out within the boundaries of the old baile. Even when the structures were abandoned and disappeared with the reuse of their materials (see BUILDING MATERIALS AND TECHNIQUES), the location of the previous centre of neighbourhood life often continued to be recalled in folk memory and in the mental map of the community, referred to as the sean bhaile (old township).

An instructive example of a township surviving from at least the 18th century is to be found at Auchindrain (Achadh an Droighinn, 'the Field of the Thorntree'), the Museum of West Highland Life located near Inveraray in Argyll. Its twenty buildings, a mixture of tenant and cottar dwellings, some with byre under the same roof, barns, stable, cart shed, bull's house, and kiln (see BUILDINGS: 3), provide a unique insight into the layout of a baile from the pre-crofting era which subsequent tenure has not obliterated. Building materials, structures, and techniques varied according to available resources and changing expectations.

Land, even a small stake in it, was highly prized and not everyone had this. Fisher families (see ECONOMY, PRIMARY SECTOR: 4) might live in dwellings near the shore on unproductive land and census returns from 1841 and earlier estate population lists (see POPULATION PATTERNS) show the cottars and craftsmen such as weavers, wheelwrights,

blacksmiths, and others who also made their contribution to the township or township group. Cottars might assist tenants or crofters (to whom they were often in any case related) with harvest work or other tasks in return for a plot of land for potatoes and the grazing of a cow. Individuals who were skilled in the medical knowledge (see TRADITIONAL HEALING) needed for curing human and animal ailments were important in the community, as was the muime or midwife.

The Tiree bard Donald Maclean (An Cubair, 'The Cooper') praised the new design of plough copied by the local smith in a song about the move he and his family made from one end of the island to the other when the township of Balephuil was made into crofts (see CLEARANCES OF THE HIGHLANDS AND ISLANDS). But even with the improved equipment and new crops which were a product of general agricultural development in Scotland (see ECONOMY, PRIMARY SECTOR: 2), work on the land was labour-intensive and until the 1886 Crofters Act there was no security of tenure for crofters.

Support came from the community for the completion of tasks and at times of crisis and celebration. Work was lightened by being shared or exchanged. For example, in order to make the quantities of straw rope required for tying down stacks and securing thatched roofs, neighbours from the township would gather in one house and then another, turn about. The only payment might be a pipe-fill of tobacco and something to eat, but it was considered very bad form to absent oneself from this communal event, which might also provide an occasion for storytelling or song. As for the rope, it was made for practical purposes but balls of it might also be used for feats of strength at harvest time or after.

Much of the community ethos of the Highlands and Islands can be summed up in the formula which was invoked when issuing invitations to a funeral (see DEATH AND BURIAL), a practice once carefully maintained: 'càirdeas is comain is eòlas', which may be translated as 'kinship and reciprocity and friendship'. It was important to know to whom you were related by descent or marriage or connected by ties which implied obligations. The person locally who had such genealogical and community-based knowledge, of other families as well as his or her own, was a needed and valued member of the community. This kind of lore, which includes tales and stories, is known as seanachas, the teller as seanachaidh.

Valued too, sometimes with a hint of apprehension, was the individual with bardic skills. Where once they had had chiefs and the gentry as patrons, by the 19th century the local poets saw their neighbours and peers in this role. It was for them, and about them, that songs were composed which recounted events of local significance, gave praise, or laid blame. To be satirized in a song which might continue on people's lips for generations was severe censure and so the bard played a part in regulating society and in expressing its values, as the works produced in the context of the *land agitations, for example, testify (see GAELIC LITERATURE).

To visit a house where newly composed songs might be heard (literally *céilidh*), or where a popular storyteller resided, was a recreation which contributed to the sustaining and transmitting of the *oral traditions of the community. John Francis Campbell of Islay (1822–85), collector of tales and other traditions, described *céilidh*-house scenes in which men, women, and children were a part and immortalized some of the exponents in his watercolours. Instrumental music and dancing (see MUSIC, HIGHLAND), taught by itinerant dancing-masters, was also enjoyed. A quick wit and verbal dexterity were prized and put into practice at events such as the *rèiteach*, a betrothal ritual which was a necessary preliminary to a marriage. The bridegroom, with the help of a skilled spokesman, would seek to identify a potential bride through a series of oblique remarks and ritualized formulas referring metaphorically to finding something that was missing, such as a plank to finish a boat.

Elizabeth Grant of Rothiemurchus describes the men's and women's dress (see DRESS, HIGHLAND) to be seen at a church service in the eastern Highlands in 1812, with the scent in the air of a birch bud decoction used for washing hair. Wool was spun and woven locally, and women would gather to shrink and strengthen the cloth and raise its nap by rhythmic pounding on a board to the accompaniment of song, fulling or waulking the cloth (*luadhadh*). *Drògaid* (drugget) for skirts, jackets, and aprons was produced with a warp of linen (later cotton) and a weft of dark blue or black wool relieved by stripes using natural dyes, both vivid and subtle, and manufactured dyes as these came to be available. *Photographs by M. E. M. Donaldson (1876–1958) and Werner Kissling (1895–1988) not only show the range of clothing worn by women and men of various ages, including both older and newer styles and materials, but also many features of the way of life in the Highlands and Islands in the early years of the 20th century.

The travelling pedlar and later the mail-order catalogue brought goods to the township which were manufactured elsewhere and as out-migration (see MIGRATION) came to be a factor in township life, there were items of dress and for household use which illustrated connections with other places: the china which came home with young women following the herring as gutters or packers, the 'Baltic bowls' from merchant navy travels, the blouse design which came home at the Glasgow Fair with a female relative in service, or nursing or teaching in the metropolis. Earlier, domestic items like the houses themselves reflected locally available materials, bowls turned from wood or clay vessels if there were such deposits nearby. Horn spoons and heather pot-scrubbers made by the Scottish travellers continued to be purchased.

Before the passage of the 1872 Education (Scotland) Act educational provision was varied. Parish schooling might be available but distant (see SCHOOLS AND SCHOOLING: 3–4). From the 18th century, the SSPCK provided schools in some localities and in the 19th century other charity schools, such as those of the Society for the Support of Gaelic Schools or the Ladies' Association of the Church of Scotland, operated in the Highlands and Islands (see CHURCH INSTITUTIONS: 6). Those with an emphasis on Gaelic (see GAELIC LANGUAGE) might provide a teacher to supply instruction to pupils of all ages for a certain period before being moved on to another district, providing the basis for literacy in both languages. It was thus the case that when *emigration came to figure in the world-view of the township, some emigrants were able to write home and communicate their experiences or those of others. Following the 1872 Act, secondary schooling provision was often at a great distance and necessitated boarding away from home for weeks or a term at a time. This rupture in family life was sometimes a prelude to further educational or work opportunities which took young people away permanently from their communities.

Religious institutions were also central to community life in the Highlands and Islands. Roman Catholic belief and practice (see ROMAN CATHOLIC COMMUNITY) and several forms of Protestant membership and adherence characterized the area: Presbyterian (Church of Scotland, Free Church, Free Presbyterian), Episcopalian, Baptist, and Congregational (see RELIGIOUS LIFE: 8). The Evangelical revival (see RELIGIOUS LIFE: 6) of the late 18th and early 19th centuries ensured a place for lay leadership and family worship led by the head of the household came to be a feature of the home life of many (see RELIGIOUS LIFE: 8). The communities created in areas such as Cape Breton, Nova Scotia, or Ontario (see CANADA) by emigrants from the Highlands and Islands reflected the diversity of religious expression at home. And often, too, ecclesiastical fissures at home were mirrored in the diaspora (see SCOTTISH LINKS).

In recent times, the hall has replaced the *céilidh*-house, although friends and neighbours still call and a good singer or raconteur is still prized. The Féis movement in the Highlands and Islands is providing continuity between the older exponents of the traditions of song, dance, storytelling, and instrumental music and the younger generation. Interest from within and beyond the communities, often from descendants of exiles, has encouraged the creation of local museums, resource centres and history societies, and community web-sites (see ORAL HISTORY; HERITAGE CENTRES). Secondary schooling provision in more localities and better transport means that boarding is no longer the necessity it once was and tertiary provision through electronically linked colleges will revolutionize education in the area. Yet land is still at the heart of many issues, and is still a topic for the bard.　　MAM

Highlands and Islands Development Board.

The Highlands and Islands Development Board (HIDB) was established in a blaze of publicity in 1965. Criticisms that Highland policy lacked the co-ordination that could be provided by an overarching body were long-standing. An authoritative expression of this view came in 1938 from the semi-official Scottish Economic Committee (see SCOTTISH COUNCIL). During the 1950s Highland local authorities and the STUC campaigned for the establishment of such a body.

The establishment of a Highland Development Board was a key pledge of the Labour Party during the election campaign of 1964. The rhetoric which surrounded the establishment of the HIDB led many to expect that it would have wide-ranging powers of compulsory purchase to enable the Highland land question (see LANDOWNERSHIP IN THE HIGHLANDS AND ISLANDS) to be tackled. This did not prove to be the case. The HIDB has proved most effective as a facilitator and manager of economic development in the Highlands. The major change in the Highland economy during the HIDB's era, however, was the impact of the oil industry from the early 1970s, which proved to be beyond its control. Solid progress was made in providing encouragement to the fishing (see ECONOMY, PRIMARY SECTOR: 4) industry. The HIDB has been much criticized for paying too much attention to economic rather than social development. In particular, its early strategy of trying to concentrate growth in particular areas of the eastern Highlands was held to have had a detrimental effect on more remote areas. Further, its reputation was severely damaged in the 1980s when two projects with which it had become associated, the Invergordon aluminium smelter and the Fort William pulp mill, both closed with disastrous consequences for the respective localities (see ECONOMY, SECONDARY SECTOR: 3). The HIDB was not wholly responsible for these failures but they seemed to confirm the impression that it was overly concerned with large unstable projects. Much useful work was done in encouraging diversity in the agricultural activities of the crofting community through the Skye and North West Development Programmes of 1986 and 1988. The HIDB was replaced by Highlands and Island Enterprise in 1991 when the nationwide structure of enterprise companies was established by the Conservative government. Perhaps if the HIDB had been established with a lower profile and more realistic expectations the solid, if small-scale, progress which it was able to make in the 1980s would have ensured a better reputation for a singular experiment in regional policy.　　EAC

historians: 1. 1200–1500; 2. 1500–1700; 3. 1700–1800; 4. 1800–1970; 5. since the 1970s.

1. 1200–1500

On the basis of surviving original manuscripts, Scottish historical writing at the beginning of the 13th century appears to consist of very little (see HISTORICAL SOURCES: 1). Only the chronicle of Melrose abbey remains on contemporary parchment. Commencing as far back as material copied from Bede, its content becomes fuller for most periods within the 13th century and it ends at 1272. It includes much detail about Cistercian events (see CHURCH INSTITUTIONS: 2) and pays considerable attention to appointments and deaths of senior clerics, whether Scottish, English, or Continental. Two prominent topics are the *Crusades and the career of Simon de Montfort. Three abbots may have been authors, or at least influencers, of parts of its text: Adam (1207–13), William (1215–16), and Matthew (1246–61). Overall, it is a Scottish chronicle of quite reasonable quality, but it also has interests well beyond Scotland's borders.

The wars with England (see ANGLO-SCOTTISH RELATIONS: 2; INDEPENDENCE, WARS OF), from 1296 to the end of the Middle Ages, naturally had a powerful effect on Scottish historiography. Nationalistic attitudes became prominent and historians were often concerned with the questions of what the kingdom of Scotland was and where it had come from. The traditional viewpoint on the 14th century has been that it is notable for two pre-eminent historical works, one in vernacular verse and one in Latin prose, both of which happen to have been written in the 1370s, and both of which have Aberdeen connections.

The poetic piece is *The Brus*, by John Barbour, archdeacon of Aberdeen. It is lengthy and vigorous, and bursts on the literary scene as the first surviving work at length written in the language nowadays called Scots (see SCOTS LANGUAGE; CULTURE: 6). It has recently been admirably edited, with translation, by Professor A. A. M. Duncan. He describes it, rightly, 'as a romance-biography, not a chronicle'. It sets out to expound, with frequent concern for chivalry, the career of King *Robert I, adding also much on the exploits of his famous lieutenant and friend Sir James Douglas. There is still some controversy on what the fundamental theme of the poem actually is. Patriotism and national freedom (see NATIONAL IDENTITY: 2) are certainly praised, but emphasis on the valour and probity of heroes who fight to redeem their rights unjustly removed is probably an even more basic element. The question of Barbour's 'truth' is now more fully understood than it once was. Although many of his facts are, or appear to be, sound, he has some errors, for example on dating or the order of events, and his 'truthfulness' has to be judged on a literary rather than a documentary basis. His sources, too, have been more fully investigated: he relied not only on oral evidence, but at times also on pre-existing historical works, such as a major written biography of Douglas.

The Latin chronicle, made about the same time, is the *Chronica Gentis Scotorum* by John of Fordun, probably a chantry priest at Aberdeen cathedral. It is the first attempt at a reasonably comprehensive coverage of the story of the Scots and has of course a much wider canvas than *The Brus*, although sharing its patriotic attitudes. Fordun allegedly travelled as far as England and Ireland in his researches and has a broad range of sources. He uses classical writers, Bede and Geoffrey of Monmouth and at least one synthesizer of the origin-legend which recounts the travels of Scota, daughter of a pharaoh of Egypt, to Ireland and the eventual move of the earliest Scoti from there to Scotland. Fordun often found inconsistencies among his sources and sometimes leaves these unresolved: a benefit, in certain respects, to modern scholarship. His chronicle extends as far as the death of *David I in 1153. A continuation to 1383 has at some point been attached to it and was named by a modern editor *Gesta Annalia*. Recent research strongly suggests that this is not the work of Fordun. It appears to be the compilation of anonymous authors of pre-Fordun date, some perhaps writing in the 13th century. Fordun was probably creating his chronicle between c.1371 and c.1385 and he is not, therefore, in any sense producing contemporary history.

Excavation, however, of the sources behind Barbour and Fordun leads to the conclusion that historical writing was being undertaken in Scotland in the 13th and 14th centuries which has not reached us in its original form, but simply through copyists. The pre-Fordun writings just mentioned, and the presumed biography of James Douglas, are not the only instances of this activity. A late medieval Dunfermline manuscript, recently noted in Madrid, contains texts, perhaps initially compiled about 1250, which centre on the life, miracles, and family of St *Margaret. There are signs here of a historical tradition designed to establish Margaret and Malcolm III 'Canmore' (Mael Coluim mac Donnchada) in the status of Scottish royal dynasty-founders. There are hints that a 'Scota-legend' historical piece lay behind the pleading composed by Baldred Bisset and others for presentation at the papal curia in 1301 in rebuttal of Edward I's claim to sovereignty over Scotland. Dr Broun has pointed to the existence of a 'St Andrews Chronicle', probably written there in or after 1363. Dr Steve Boardman has advanced evidence that an anonymous chronicler at work in the early 1390s covered the period 1324–90 and took a much more sympathetic view of the activities of the Stewart family than is to be found in the *Gesta Annalia*. The outbreak of the English wars, the consequent political upheavals, two changes of dynasty, and the emergence of a significant literature in Scots—all these elements stimulated a variety of Scottish historians in the 14th century.

As that century ended another chronicler was active in the verse tradition of historiography. This was Andrew of Wyntoun, prior of St Serf's, Loch Leven, who wrote the *Orygynal Cronykil of Scotland* which concludes in 1408; the concern with origins is still evident. His work depends greatly on standard earlier sources, including Barbour, but from the 1330s to its conclusion has much that is original, detailed, and direct, especially on the wars.

In spite of Barbour, Fordun, and Wyntoun, Scotland still had no major, comprehensive history at length. The necessary 'blockbuster' was provided in the 1440s by Walter Bower, abbot of Inchcolm, who produced a massive Latin work entitled *Scotichronicon*. He built on and much expanded Fordun: as he proceeds he makes less use of that source, but ranges widely for material, both Scottish and European, including some which does not survive as earlier texts. He is concerned not merely to write a history of Scotland, but also to set that in a wider context and to add theological and moralistic advice to benefit his readers. His work is the magnum opus of Scottish medieval historiography, notable for expansiveness and prolixity but not always for detailed historical percipience. It has recently been superbly edited and translated by Professor D. E. R. Watt and a team of colleagues. The editor rightly emphasizes that the author probably intended his title to mean 'A History Book for Scots' and for the mid-15th century it was magnificently that.

The *Scotichronicon* was so voluminous and so popular that it had distinct effects on habits of history-writing. Many manuscripts of it survive and many people therefore read it; but some found it excessively lengthy and it spawned a series of abridgements. The *Liber Pluscardensis*, written about 1460, is probably the best-known example of this genre; the practice continued into the early 16th century. Bower's work was to some degree a model for later writers such as John Mair and Hector Boece. But its dominance may have discouraged some historians in the later 15th century. From that period only a few short original works survive. The *Auchinleck Chronicle* covers 1437–60 and the Asloan MS carries a chronicle for the years 1420–60. Chronicle evidence is thin for the reign of James II and almost non-existent for that of James III.

Fifteenth-century history therefore consists of a mid-century bang, followed by a whimper. Yet as we assess the position at 1500 we can note that Mair and Boece were then already-established scholars and the birth of the most influential historian of the 16th century, George Buchanan, lay only a little ahead, in 1506. GGS

2. 1500–1700

During the 16th and 17th centuries the powerful force of two European movements was felt in Scottish scholarship. First, the late Renaissance produced a glorious flowering of historical writing in Scotland, particularly during the first three quarters of the 16th century. This was followed by the impact of the religious *Reformation; its profound and contradictory influence continued to be felt by historians into the later 17th.

Renaissance historical writing, of which Machiavelli and Guicciardini were perhaps the most famous Italian exponents and Livy and Tacitus the most prominent ancient models, was preoccupied with the eloquent discussion and explanation of the past in such a way as to instruct and improve the present. To this purpose Scotland produced gifted historians such as John Mair, Hector Boece, his translator John Bellenden, and one of Europe's greatest Renaissance scholars, George Buchanan, whose depictions of Scottish history were turned sharply to the task of influencing moral, social, and political conduct in their own times (see CULTURE: 4).

Mair, based for much of his career in Paris, was a truly innovative scholar. *The History of Greater Britain, as well England as Scotland* (1521) is remarkable, developing a cogent attack on the backward-looking aristocracy of his own country. As its title suggests, Mair's work was also precocious for situating Scottish alongside English history, the intention being to advocate harmony, and ultimately union, between the two neighbouring kingdoms (see ANGLO-SCOTTISH RELATIONS: 3).

Boece, however, was probably more typical of European, as well as Scottish, scholarship in the early 16th century. A work long on rhetorical flourishes and very short on either hard evidence or accuracy, his *History of Scotland* (1527), translated from Latin into Scots by Bellenden in 1536 at the behest of *James V, was to be much more influential in its own day. Its stories of more than 100, largely fictional, Scottish monarchs (see KINGSHIP: 1) were widely credited. Vociferously moralistic in the style of Cicero and the ancient Stoic philosophers, it also expresses a distaste for contemporary political morality which enjoyed considerable currency, urging upon the Scots a cleaner, purer, less self-interested life both in public and private.

George Buchanan's *History of Scotland* (1582) has much in common with Boece's work, though also with its author's earlier *Laws of Kingship* (*De Iure Regni*, 1579), a revolutionary political tract insisting on the justice of regicide in times of tyranny. Buchanan's work continues the practice of writing about Scottish history within the moralistic framework provided by the reigns of mythical kings. It also deprecates contemporary standards in political life. But more significantly, it claims to identify a Scottish tradition of accountable and representative monarchy subject to the popular will. This figment of Buchanan's radical imagination earned the ire of his former pupil *James VI but it long attracted both fame and notoriety for its author.

Contemporary with Buchanan, however, 16th-century Scottish scholarship also registered the impact of the Calvinist revolution of 1560. This victory was itself shored up by the coup of 1567 which brought James to the throne. Buchanan's *History* served as the rhetorical defence of the new, morally upstanding Protestant order, founded on the deposition of James's Catholic mother *Mary, Queen of Scots. In this respect it also became the first of many historical works seeking to justify the country's Protestant Reformation by reference to specifically Scottish traditions of religious spirituality and dissidence in the historical past (see NATIONAL IDENTITY: 3). Naturally this provoked outraged Catholic counterblasts, of which John Lesley's *History of Scotland* (1578), written in Latin and published at Rome, was by far the most competent.

For many in Reformation Scotland history was also intensely self-justifying. Nowhere is this truer than in the case of John *Knox himself. Author of a *History of the Reformation of the Church of Scotland* (published 1587), he developed an analysis of Scottish history in which the battle between Christ and the papal antichrist is the principal theme. God's Providence is seen to be everywhere at work in the history of the Scots: all events lead inexorably on to the Reformation, whose momentous passage Knox charts with a meticulousness born of intimate personal involvement. Less Presbyterian but not much less tendentious is John Spottiswoode's *History of Scotland* (published 1655), the work of James VI's archbishop of St Andrews, providing a more moderate and deferential interpretation of the Scottish past.

Throughout the religious controversies of the 17th century within Scotland's Protestant community, history continued to provide an important arena for party dispute. Episcopalian scholars (see EPISCOPALIAN COMMUNITY) sought to establish the ancient existence of bishops in Scotland whilst Presbyterians tried to demonstrate that they were a late arrival, an illegitimate and popish innovation grafted on to originally Presbyterian structures (see CHURCH INSTITUTIONS: 3). Presbyterians were also concerned to deploy the growing number of persecutions and martyrdoms of the Scottish Calvinists further to glorify their cause. Authors such as David Calderwood and Alexander Shields (see COVENANTERS) did much to convince Scottish Protestants, and especially Presbyterians, that history was indeed on their side.

Yet in certain respects the understandable preoccupations of the post-Reformation period did not entirely erode older, less parochial historical interests. In particular, family history and genealogy (see HISTORICAL SOURCES: 4) continued to display all the rhetorical flair, all the moralistic fervour and educational purpose of Renaissance humanist scholarship as it was still evolving across contemporary Europe. Works such as David Hume of Godscroft's *History of the House of Douglas* (published posthumously, 1644) and Sir Robert Gordon of Gordonstoun's manuscript *Genealogy of the Earls of Sutherland* (eventually published, 1813) offer practical guidance to modern Scottish aristocratic dynasties (see NOBILITY: 3). They contain much sentimental and generally dubious hagiography intended to embellish the family name. But this is frequently punctuated by hard-nosed moral and political instruction culled from a close familiarity with Cicero, Seneca, and, above all, Tacitus.

These different strands of 16th- and 17th-century Scottish scholarship often intertwined, providing a rich historical literature which was comparable with that of many other countries in this period. The extraordinary vigour with which 18th-century Scotsmen explored the past, whether as philosophers, academic historians, or simply as enthusiasts, owed much to the tenaciousness and vision of their forerunners between the late Renaissance and the first glimmerings of Enlightenment.   DA

3. 1700–1800

The 18th century was a chequered era for Scottish historiography. On the one hand, it witnessed a rigorous demolition of antiquarian legends, a mellowing of partisan scholarship, and a series of major developments in historical method associated with the social theorists of the Scottish Enlightenment. Nevertheless, a surfeit of cosmopolitan revisionism, compounded by the fact of the *Union of 1707 and various Anglicizing trends, diminished the significance of the Scottish past for north Britain's self-consciously provincial intelligentsia. Among the leaders of the Enlightenment, David Hume began a *History of Great Britain* (1754) devoted to the 17th century which, as he extended it back into the 16th century, became a *History of England*, while John Millar composed *An Historical View of the English Government* (1787) (see CULTURE: 11).

During the first half of the 18th century an older style of polemical antiquarianism prevailed, which centred on disputed events and institutions in the Scottish past. The vexed Anglo-Scottish wrangles which preceded the Union of 1707 generated a historical debate as to whether the kings of Scotland had ever been the feudal vassals of an imperial English crown. The case for Scotland's historic independence was championed by James Anderson (1662–1728), whose antiquarian endeavours were financially rewarded by the Scots parliament. Within the domestic political arena, Whig historians, such as the Revd George Logan (1678–1755), and upholders of a *Jacobite interpretation of Scottish history who included Patrick Abercromby (1656–1716?), author of the *Martial Atchievements of the Scots Nation* (1711–15), and the publisher-antiquary Thomas Ruddiman (1674–1757), continued to gnaw at a canon of controverted episodes in Scottish constitutional history: the mythical founding of the Scots monarchy in 330 BC, the claims of Bruce and *Balliol to the succession, the legitimacy of Robert III, and, inevitably, the career of *Mary, Queen of Scots. Similarly, apologists for Presbytery, Episcopacy, and Roman Catholicism produced rival histories of the Scottish church, including a monumental Presbyterian version of the late 17th-century persecutions, the Revd Robert Wodrow's *History of the Sufferings of the Church of Scotland* (1721–2). Historians of all stripes used the past instrumentally to justify present positions.

These debates were not totally sterile. Fr. Thomas Innes (1662–1744), a convinced Jacobite based at the *Scots college in Paris, demonstrated that the account of Scotland's Dalriadic (see DÁL RIATA, KINGDOM OF) origins, accepted in rival versions by Whigs and Jacobites alike, was nonsense on stilts: it rested on spurious regnal lists concocted in the late medieval period. Although Innes's work was just as ideologically determined as that of his opponents, his contacts with Jean Mabillon and the Maurist Benedictine pioneers of the new diplomatic scholarship enabled him to erase the traditional legendary contours of Scotland's early centuries. Among later generations of Whiggish antiquaries, Sir David Dalrymple, Lord Hailes (1726–92), maintained this spirit of critical detachment and rigorous source scholarship. Field archaeology, practised by Sir Robert Sibbald (1641–1722), Sir *John Clerk of Penicuik (1676–1755), and Alexander Gordon (1692?–1754?), introduced another strain of evidence into the study of Scottish antiquity.

Independent of these developments, the historically minded moral philosophers and jurists who flourished in the Scottish Enlightenment, among them Henry Home, Lord Kames, Hume, Adam Smith, William Robertson, and John Millar, endowed historiography with a greater theoretical sophistication. Recent research, however, questions the novelty of Enlightenment historiography, emphasizing the continuation of providentialism in the work of Robertson and a wider humanist concern with the moral purpose of history. Nevertheless, there were clear advances. Kames, in his *Historical Law Tracts*, set out a new method of investigating ancient history which came to be known as conjectural history: it was possible to speculate beyond the limit of written sources or in areas where there were gaps, through making 'cautious conjectures' drawn from 'collateral facts'. The comparative method was particularly fruitful, enabling historians to utilize contemporary accounts of primitive non-European societies as a way of imagining the social mores of their own earliest ancestors.

Scotland's conjectural historians also recast the overall shape of universal history. Their stadialist theories suggested that mankind had progressed from the rudeness of the hunter-gatherer state to the modern politeness of commercial society through three or four stages of economic, social, and cultural development. David Hume was a scathing critic of the philosophical errors which dogged traditional historiography, most notably the latent anachronisms which underpinned arguments for prescriptive legitimacy. In some respects, history came to be regarded as the queen of the disciplines: in the curricula of the Scottish *universities every subject, even in the natural sciences, was taught with emphasis upon its historical origins and development. One of the most celebrated examples of theoretical history was Smith's essay on the history of astronomy.

There was also an underside to this catalogue of achievement. The focus was rarely on Scotland itself, but was instead often Continental in scope, if not universal. Moreover, there was a curious disconnection between antiquarian erudition and theoretical history. Furthermore, Robertson produced a critically detached *History of Scotland* (1759), centred on the *Reformation, but also including pointed surveys of medieval and modern Scotland. Robertson exposed the weakness of late medieval Scottish state formation, purveyed an unflattering account of the Scottish Reformation, and highlighted the subjugation of the Scottish commons to an overmighty *nobility. Robertson was not unique in holding such opinions. A chorus of enlightened opinion blamed Scotland's feudal elites for the nation's economic backwardness relative to England.

Yet there were other voices on the Scottish historical scene. Gilbert Stuart (1742–86) was a vociferous and sophisticated critic from a radical Whig standpoint, and his fellow radical, David Steuart Erskine, eleventh earl of Buchan (1742–1829), established the Society of Antiquaries in 1780 as a counterweight to Robertson's influence in university circles. By the late 18th century, new issues were emerging which were to exert a profound influence on 19th-century historiography, including a growing appreciation of artefacts and the emergence of race as a factor in historical interpretation. Both trends were exemplified in the work of John Pinkerton (1758–1826). CCK

4. 1800–1970

As Scotland experienced rapid industrialization and urbanization in the early 19th century, many contemporaries were worried about the survival of Scotland as a distinct nation. Urbanization (see URBAN SOCIETY: 5) and industrialization (see ECONOMY: 4) were putting pressure on the Scottish institutions of law (LAW AND LAWYERS: 2), the church, and education (see SCHOOLS AND SCHOOLING: 2) and most were buckling under the strain of adapting to these new circumstances. In addition to the threat to the traditional institutions, the impact of social and economic change was eroding the distinctiveness of many facets of Scottish society. Factories and urban conurbations were making the physical appearance of Scotland similar to England. Contemporaries such as Sir Walter Scott and Henry Cockburn moaned about the disappearance of a traditional Scottish way of life.

It was in this atmosphere of crisis that many contemporaries set themselves the task of preserving what remained of 'Old Caledonia' before the tide of modernity swept it away for good. The period witnessed a craze for the collection of Scottish historical manuscripts, ballads, and folk tales. With the emphasis on the preservation of the written artefacts of the Scottish past, there was little time for analysis and the period witnessed what had been called by Marinell Ash 'the strange death of Scottish history' (see HISTORICAL CLUBS AND SOCIETIES;

NEWSPAPERS: 1). This era was also the high point of the Romantic movement and for many, the Scottish past could be better understood through the use of imaginative literature rather than traditional scholarly tomes. The 18th century saw the development of an inferiorist interpretation of Scottish history which stressed the nation's lack of historical development compared to England and, as such, the Scottish past was dismissed as irrelevant as a pointer towards progress.

The Romantic era, however, liberated the use of the Scottish past from such constricted Enlightenment notions of the purpose of history. With an emphasis on romance, adventure, and the power of the human spirit, writers such as John Galt, James Hogg, and most famously Sir Walter Scott, could use Scottish history as a device to illustrate such universal themes (SEE CULTURE: 14). While not an accurate nor a scientific rendering of the Scottish past, such tales of fiction were important in imbuing the Scots with a sense of their history. Such romantic notions were important in the 'Highlandization' of Scottish identity (see NATIONAL IDENTITY: 5) as many came to see the desolate Highlands as what Scotland must have been like before the impact of urbanization and industrialization. Sir Walter Scott's tales of *Jacobitism and Queen Victoria's infatuation with the Highlands did much to diffuse the idea of Scotland as a Highland nation. Romanticism was also important in the veneration of William *Wallace in the mid-19th century. The fact that Wallace was a 'commoner' who was betrayed by aristocratic duplicity meant that he was a convenient icon for radical liberals to use against the landowning classes who owed their position to birthright rather than meritocracy. The association of Wallace with freedom and liberty was more to do with laissez-faire ideology (see ECONOMIC POLICY: 3) than the medieval conflict against England.

As might be expected, religion was an important part of Scottish historical consciousness in the mid-19th century. The conflict over the *Disruption was cast back into Scottish religious history as all sides of the Presbyterian divide appealed to the past to show that they were the true heirs to the reformed and Covenanting tradition. The 1840s witnessed a flurry of publications, many of them reprints, relating to the struggle of the 17th-century church. Patrick Fraser Tytler's History of Scotland (1828–43) raised considerable controversy surrounding the role of *Mary, Queen of Scots, and demonstrated that Scottish popular perceptions of the past were more important than scholarship. The very notion that Mary may not have been the demonic figure of Protestant legend was too much for many to stomach. Throughout the 19th century, considerable ink was spilled in popular

histories which promoted the notion of Scotland as a Presbyterian nation. For example, The Famous Scots series devoted six out of 25 biographies of Scottish historical figures to religious leaders. A similar preponderance of Presbyterian heroes emerged in the influential Chambers Biographical Dictionary of Eminent Scotsmen (various editions).

Along with religion, the ethnic origins of Scotland emerged as an issue of historical controversy in the early 19th century, although it did not generate the same degree of enthusiasm as the Disruption and the debate was confined to a rather limited section of society. Historians such as John Pinkerton in his Enquiry into the History of Scotland (1814) put forward the argument that the Scots were Teutonic, rather than Celtic, in origin. The controversy of the *Picts was one that energized some intellectual circles, although evidence of its infiltration into Scottish society can be seen in some of the racist notions which were applied to the Irish (see IMMIGRATION, IRISH). Certainly figures such as the eighth duke of Argyll believed that the influx of Teutonic and Anglo-Saxon blood into early Scotland was a major factor in explaining the differences between the Irish and the Scots. The undiluted Celticism of the former was used to explain a perceived proclivity towards laziness, drunkenness, and violence (see ROUGH CULTURE).

Ireland was also instrumental in reactivating interest in the historical foundations of the *Union of 1707. Indeed, the historian James MacKinnon claimed in the 1890s that most Scots were unaware of the importance of the Union in Scottish history. Whereas 18th-century readings of the Scottish past had claimed that Scotland was a poor and backward nation whose history offered little in the way of signposts towards progress and prosperity, 19th-century interpretations modified this accepted wisdom to demonstrate that the nation's pre-Union past was an essential training ground for the fulfilment of its historic destiny as a partner with England. For many, Scottish economic success in the 19th century was driven by the nation's historical experience of poverty. The backwardness of Scotland meant that the Scots were more determined than the English to acquire riches. The internecine warfare of pre-Union Scotland had produced a martial race whose fighting qualities could be put to good service in the Empire. The religious conflicts of the 17th century had made the Scots resolute people of principle. In short, Scottish history did have important pointers to the future, but it was a future contained within the Union and the imperial partnership with England. A few brave souls such as the Conservative MP Sir Herbert Maxwell went even further and pushed for an assimilationist view of the Scottish past, although this meant claiming that the Scots should have surrendered at the Wars of *Independence because this would have avoided centuries of conflict up to the Union. Not only was this interpretation treated with derision, it was denounced since it was precisely because the Scots had a separate history that the Union and partnership with England was possible.

The historical consensus that a separate Scottish past was a vital precondition for the Union began to collapse after the First World War as new political forces sought to use the Scottish past as a means to vindicate contemporary ideological positions. Socialists, such as Thomas *Johnston and James Barr, paid little attention to the Union and sought to demonstrate that the Scots had always been an egalitarian and democratic people. Johnston's *History of the Scottish Working Class* portrayed the history of Scotland as a conflict between an egalitarian people and a feudal aristocracy. James Barr argued that the *Covenanters were fighting for religious liberty as Scotland was a freedom-loving nation. In short, the activities of the *'Red Clydesiders' were presented as a continuation of a fight for freedom from the yoke of capitalism which began in the days of William Wallace. Unionists challenged this thesis. Freedom and liberty were accepted as important parts of the Scottish tradition, but this was used to promote meritocratic individualism. Official historical thinking, reflected in the school curriculum by authors such as E. M. Barron, still promoted the notion that Scotland's historic destiny was realized only in the Union. In the 1920s, the nationalists (see NATIONALISM) were another faction which entered into competition for the claim to the Scottish past. The nationalist reading of the past borrowed liberally from all sides but was distinguished by its claim that the Union of 1707 was a break from the natural trajectory of Scottish history. Far from being the fulfilment of the nation's historic destiny, the Union was a subversion of that destiny. Nationalist accounts emphasized the corruption surrounding the treaty, although, paradoxically, they made much of Scottish achievement within the Union. The polarization of Scottish history into political camps in the pre-war era did much to fragment the subject. The Depression and surrounding economic turmoil of these years also dealt a blow to national self-confidence which was reflected into the study of the past. Historians such as Elizabeth Haldane produced a social history to prove that Scotland was still a nation because it always had been a nation. The formation of the Saltire Society in 1936 was another indication of contemporary concerns for the future of Scottish culture and history.

The Second World War and the enhanced sense of Britishness this engendered further diluted the importance of the subject, as did new ideological trends. The rise of historical materialism and its intellectual counterweights as a primary means of explaining the past marginalized the subject even further until the growth of Scottish nationalism in the late 1960s.   RJF

5. since the 1970s

The period from the mid-1960s to the present day has witnessed a massive increase in the output of Scottish historical studies. A number of reasons can be advanced to account for this state of affairs, some but not all of which relate to internal changes within the nation. First, the period is contemporaneous with the rise of Scottish political *nationalism and it might be suggested that the growing interest in a separate and distinctive *national identity which accompanied this development, stimulated interest in the Scottish past. History has its agenda largely determined by the interests of contemporary society and as it seemed that British homogeneity was not going to be achieved as many historians and social scientists predicted, then the answer to why Scottish nationalism should suddenly re-emerge might be found by examining the nation's historical development. A good example of using the Scottish past to explain the present was H. J. Hanham's *Scottish Nationalism* (1969). A second factor is the expansion of university provision, which greatly increased the number of academic historians working in Scotland. With an emphasis on the democratization of higher education (see UNIVERSITIES: 3) and a democratization of the subject itself, which expanded the range of historical interests to include the lives of ordinary people, the social history of Scotland was a legitimate study of enquiry. The most influential example of this 'democratization' of the past was T. C. Smout's *A History of the Scottish People 1560–1830* (1969). A third factor was the growth of popular historical publishing which took advantage of the increasing interest in Scottish culture. Popular historians and historical novelists, such as Nigel Tranter, John Prebble, and Antonia Fraser, demonstrated public interest in the subject and may have stimulated some to further and more serious lines of enquiry. Yet, it would be wrong to claim that the historical revolution can be explained only with reference to factors peculiar to Scottish society at that time. Just as important was the wider revolution which effected the study of history outside Scotland. The development of new lines of historical enquiry were instrumental in effecting the way that the Scottish past was studied.

Prior to the mid-1960s, and running through a large part of the historical revolution of this period, many historians were preoccupied with only those things which could be deemed truly Scottish. Medieval and early modern history had traditionally fared better than the modern era as there was no confusion as to what Scotland was in these periods. Indeed, most of the chairs in Scottish history in the post-war era have been filled by scholars who studied Scotland when it was an independent state. Unhindered by the difficulties of studying the stateless nation, Geoffrey Barrow's *Robert the Bruce and the Community of the Realm of Scotland* (1965), which was an internationally acclaimed piece of scholarship, and the prolific output of Gordon Donaldson on the early modern era, inadvertently did much to promote the long-standing idea that Scottish history had come to an end in 1707. Aspects of post-Union history which were regarded as falling within the orbit of British history were removed, leaving a subject which focused on matters of local government, the church, and little else. In short, it was parochial history writ large. The one major exception to this was the work of William Ferguson whose *Scotland since 1698* (1968) managed to work in social and economic developments within a political narrative. Indeed, at this point it is worth pointing out the importance of the Edinburgh four-volume history of Scotland which was published in the 1960s. Ferguson's volume finished off a series in which Archie Duncan, Ranald Nicholson, and Gordon Donaldson provided Scots with a comprehensive and up-to-date account of the nation's past based on modern techniques of historical scholarship.

It was the development of economic history which had the first impact on the professionalization of modern Scottish history and its inclusion within a wider intellectual framework. R. H. Campbell's *Scotland since 1707: The Rise of an Industrial Society* (1965) demonstrated the fundamental importance of economic factors in the nation's historical development. Both Campbell and Smout in separate articles and in the latter's *Scottish Trade on the Eve of the Union* (1963) overturned old-fashioned Whig notions on the primacy of politics by explaining the *Union of 1707 in terms of the importance of economic factors (see ECONOMY). Social history was another boon for modern Scottish history in the 1970s as it enabled scholars to escape from the straitjacket of parochialism and the problems of the stateless nation. In addition to the work of Campbell and Smout, and the many path-breaking articles of Rosalind Mitchell, a new generation of younger scholars set about transforming the understanding of Scotland in the late 1970s and early 1980s. Scottish industry and the workforce was subject to increased scrutiny. Some of the subjects studied included T. M. Devine's *Tobacco Lords* (1976), Norman Murray's *Scottish Handloom Weavers* (1979), Alistair Durie's *The Scottish Linen Industry* (1979), the work of John Butt on the cotton industry, and the major contribution of Smout and Louis Cullen's comparative examination of Scottish and Irish society (1979). The mid-1980s and early 1990s stood witness to a prolific outpouring of research. The Social and Economic History Society of Scotland published a three-volume history which covered the period from 1760 to the present. Tom Devine reinterpreted the highly emotive topic of the *Clearances of the Highlands and Islands in *The Great Highland Famine* (1988) and reassessed the process of modernization in the Lowlands in the *Transformation of Rural Scotland* (1993). Hamish Fraser charted the origins of working-class politics in *Conflict and Class* (1988). Urban history became a subject of serious enquiry with Michael Lynch's pioneering work on *The Early Modern Town in Scotland* (1987) and Helen Dingwall's exhaustive study, *Seventeenth-Century Edinburgh* (1994), while Gordon Jackson, T. M. Devine, Hamish Fraser, and Irene Sweeney collected a team of scholars to provide Glasgow with its most comprehensive history to date.

The aftershock of the devolution fiasco of 1979 may have been a factor in steering scholars away from the politics of modern Scotland into social and economic history. Chris Harvie courageously attempted a historical definition of the political nation in *Scotland and Nationalism* (1977), only to find its contemporary relevance wiped out by the failure of devolution. The importation of social, economic, and comparative history was not confined to the modern era. Early modern scholars made imaginative use of new ideas and adapted them to the Scottish past. Michael Lynch pioneered the social study of religious change in his *Edinburgh and the Reformation* (1981), Jenny Wormald reassessed social relations in *Bonds of Manrent* (1986), Allan Macinnes established the importance of nationalism in *Charles I and the Making of the Covenanting Movement* (1991), and Keith Brown used social anthropology to good effect in his study, *Bloodfeud in Scotland* (1986). With one or two exceptions, the study of politics and ideology was left to medievalist and early modernists. High politics remained the central concern of David Stevenson's numerous studies of Scotland and the Wars of the Covenant. Ted Cowan's *Montrose* (1977) charted the impact of political ideology on a critical figure in the Wars of the *Covenant; Roger Mason in a number of articles began to piece together early modern Scottish ideology by examining notions of history, constitutionalism, and contemporary political theory; and Sandy Grant in *Independence and Nationhood* (1984) and Jenny Wormald in *Court, Kirk and Community* (1981) reassessed the role and nature of government in medieval and early modern Scotland.

The re-emergence of home rule as a serious political issue in the mid-eighties may have been instrumental in turning attention back to politics with the appearance of Iain Hutchison's *Political History of Modern Scotland* (1986), providing the first comprehensive account of how Scottish politics operated within the larger parameter of British politics. The political history of the 18th century had been well served by William Ferguson and Alex Murdoch whose *People Above* (1979) has been supplemented in recent years by works from John Shaw and Ronald Sunter. The romanticism surrounding *Jacobitism was also effectively demolished by a succession of scholarly monographs in the 1980s from Bruce Lenman. The period of the Enlightenment has likewise come into its own with a series of articles from Nicholas Phillipson and Richard Sher's *Church and University in the Scottish Enlightenment* (1985). The theme of education has been an important one in Scottish history and was first effectively tackled by George Davie in his path-breaking *The Democratic Intellect* (1961), but has been partly refuted by R. D. Anderson's *Education and Opportunity in Victorian Scotland* (1983). In recent years there have been a number of attempts to 'gather the picture whole'. Michael Lynch's *Scotland: A New History* (1991), Tom Devine's *Scottish Nation* (1999), and Chris Whatley et al's *Modern Scottish History* (1998) have synthesized the prolific outpouring of research over the last 30 years. Since the early 1990s, a new generation of scholars have added much to our understanding of the Scottish past and it seems likely that their efforts will have as much impact as their forebears.   RJF

historical clubs and societies. The club was and remains an essential component of Scottish civil society. Along with formal institutions like the church and the legal system, clubs and voluntary and philanthropic associations have had a role which has been of great significance to Scottish public life. The club has both preserved and promoted culture and history, and it has acted as a mechanism through which access to elite status has been filtered.

The culture of social and political clubs grew out of the 'coffee-house society' of the 18th century. The Poker Club of 1762, so called because of its intentions of stirring up the government to take 'the desired action' on the Militia issue, was for example instituted into the Edinburgh New Club in 1787. The Edinburgh Select Subscription Library (1800) was a society for a self-limited section of the bourgeoisie. It did not appeal for public subscription, but instead opted to be self-financed by its members in order to maintain exclusivity.

Historical clubs came to prominence in the first part of the 19th century out of a widespread interest amongst intellectuals and those fascinated by literature. A survey of their publications by C. S. Terry (*A Catalogue of the Publications of Scottish Historical and Kindred Clubs and Societies, 1780–1908*, 1909, and the second volume compiled by C. Matheson in 1928) subdivided them into 'pre-Waverley', 'Waverley', and 'post-Waverley' societies. The reference is to the author of *Waverley*, Sir Walter Scott, and his role in the Bannatyne Club (founded in 1823), the template for the historical clubs which followed. An influential thesis of Marinell Ash, *The Strange Death of Scottish History* (1980), saw these societies as the manifestation of renewed interest in the history of Scotland and new confidence in Scottish *national identity. The demise of the Waverley wave of these clubs, in the mid-19th century, is presented as symptomatic of a fragmentation in, and a weakness of, both these features.

Terry identified the Society of Antiquaries as the origin of the historical clubs. It was instituted in 1780 and published its first volume in 1792. The remit of the historical club was to gather information on rare publications. Members would each take turns to compile or edit a piece of work for publication under the auspices of the club. The Society of Antiquaries was followed by the Royal Society of Edinburgh (1783) and the Literary and Antiquarian Society of Perth (1784). In the 1820s and 1830s there was a proliferation of historical and field clubs which, in time, were spread throughout Scotland. The most influential historical club was the Bannatyne Club, which had developed out of the smaller and more circumspect Roxburghe Club. Its inspiration came from Sir Walter Scott and its credentials came from Thomas Thomson and David Laing, with a membership list including Lord Henry Cockburn and Patrick Fraser Tytler. Its aim was to promote scholarship in Scottish history and literature. Like other clubs, social exclusivity was important to its formation and its membership was limited, only later to undergo a controlled expansion.

There was soon the formation of many more historical and bibliographical clubs. In Glasgow, the Maitland Club was formed (1829–88) with a mainly commercial membership but overlapping with the Bannatyne Club. Less successful clubs included the Abbotsford Club (1833–56, although moribund since the 1840s) and the Iona Club. The latter's remit was to publish Gaelic manuscripts and promote Highland culture. Two religious-based publishing societies were established in the same mould—the Wodrow Society (Presbyterian, founded in 1841) and the Spottiswoode Society (Episcopalian, founded in 1843)—but again they had a limited lifespan.

As the mid-century turned, most of these clubs had undergone a period of expansion in their membership before a lingering demise. By 1870, only the Spalding Club (1839), which had started out with an open membership in *Aberdeen, and the Society of Antiquaries had survived. A new generation of historical clubs had begun, soon to be spurred on by the publication of the first report of the Historical Manuscripts Commission in 1870. The Glasgow Archaeological Society (1865), the Grampian Club (1868), the Scottish Burgh Records Society (1868), and the Gaelic Society of Inverness (1871) were some of the newer arrivals. In the 1880s two societies were formed with a remit extending beyond Scotland in the reprinting and publishing of works of literary and historical interest: the Aungervyle Society (1881) and the Clarendon Historical Society (1882).

Interest in document-based Scottish history was to take on new impetus. In 1886 both the Scottish History Society (1886) and a revamped New Spalding Club were created. This, in turn, encouraged the Gaelic Society of Glasgow (1887), the Scottish Clergy Society (1888), the Edinburgh Bibliographical Club (1890), the St Andrews Society (1906), and the Old Edinburgh Club (1908). The majority of these clubs still existed in the 1920s and were joined by the Historical Association of Scotland (1911), the Glasgow Bibliographical Society (1912), and the Scottish Church History Society (1922).

The decline of the Waverley phase in historical clubs may have been the end of an era, but interest in Scottish history and of Gaelic culture continued. The literary cliques of that most famous period, which formed around the friendship and then the memory of Scott, were replaced by a few key institutions such as the Scottish History Society, the Historical Association of Scotland, and the Scottish Text Society (1882), which sustained a professional interest in Scotland's historical past, which Laing, Thomson, and Cosmo Innes had started. Chairs in Scottish history were established in Edinburgh (1901) and Glasgow (1913) Universities. The historical club in the 20th century was still important to leisure and to self-improvement. The New Club continues to act as a filter to membership of Edinburgh's social elites. But the post-Waverley change saw Scottish history carried in the universities and the schools, less dependent on the inspiration of a few literary greats. GM

historical sources: 1. to 1750; 2. 1750–1900; 3. since 1900; 4. genealogical.

1. to 1750

There are many Scotlands in history but the historical sources which survive do not reach all of them or often do so only imperfectly. One reason for this is that many records survive only as transcripts, testimony to the dedication of a few individual scribes, archivists, or antiquarians. Scottish archives have also been subject to huge losses, caused by the depredations of war, carelessness, or bad luck. In 1296, a collection of Scottish records was handed over to Hugh Cressingham, treasurer of Edward I of England; it was presumably transported to London, never to be seen again. Yet the same period produced the English 'Ragman Rolls', now preserved in the PRO in London, which give extensive details of Scots landowners. In 1651, the Cromwellian government of occupation decided to move the records housed for safe keeping by the Covenanting (see COVENANT, WARS OF THE) regime in *Stirling castle to the Tower of London. Some legal records were returned in 1657. The remainder was sent north in two ships in 1660; one, called the *Elizabeth*, foundered with the loss of all its cargo. What is difficult to work out with any precision is what was lost, then or at other times in similar circumstances.

But the habitual Scottish habit of blaming the English goes only so far as an explanation of Scotland's losses (see ANGLO-SCOTTISH RELATIONS). Many records which were known to have existed as late as the 16th century, when they were inventoried, have gone missing since; they include 14th-century rolls of the Great Seal register and 15th-century sheriffs' accounts. As a result, virtually everything from before 1306 in official records has disappeared. In urban archives, too, there are huge and unexplained gaps. The only burgh which has records which pre-date 1400 is *Aberdeen, where the council records begin in 1398, more than 250 years after its foundation. Aberdeen, nevertheless, has a virtually complete run of records through the 15th century, amounting to over 4,000 folio pages, bound in seven volumes. It is unclear why other important burghs, such as *Dundee, *Edinburgh, and *Perth, do not have an equivalent archive. In the case of Edinburgh, what survives before 1550 is largely the result of a transcript made in the late 1570s at the behest of the then town clerk, Alexander Guthrie, a Protestant activist known as 'King' Guthrie to his Catholic enemies, during his last years in post. Even so, the explosion in the 16th century of different kinds of burgh records, including accounts of town treasurer and dean of guild, court books, guild registers, burgh registers of deeds, notarial protocol books recording contracts and property, and much more is so overwhelming that much of it lies unpublished or underworked by urban historians (see URBAN SETTLEMENT: 1; URBAN SOCIETY: 2).

The gaps in printed sources are so vast as to be astounding to English historians, accustomed to intensive archival inventories and extensive publication programmes. There is in Scotland no equivalent of either the History of Parliament or the Victoria County History, set up in 1898 to explore local records and to publish detailed histories of individual counties. Scotland still has no equivalent of English and Welsh county record offices. Partly as a result of the turmoil induced by two Conservative governments' reorganization of local boundaries, in 1975 and 1994, the coverage afforded by local archives is still patchy and distinctly variable in quality. Some local authorities, such as Inverclyde, have no archivists at all. For a country with a distinctive sense of place as part of its identity (see REGIONAL IDENTITIES), it is an extraordinary state of affairs.

The records of Scotland's pre-1707 *parliament are patchy and exist only as an early 19th-century, fairly primitive transcription, detailing legislation since the reign of James I. Some earlier fragments exist, but have not been collated. Other material, which appeared in the first full edition of the Acts of Parliament, printed in 1566, has since disappeared. As a result, knowledge of its workings, which largely rests on an analysis written by R. S. Rait in 1924, is the privilege of a few. The financing of a project in 1996 by the then Secretary of State for Scotland, Mr Michael Forsyth, was part of a campaign by a deeply unpopular Conservative government to put on a tartan face in Scotland, which also included the return of the Stone of *Scone. Its aim, to produce a definitive version of the Acts of Scotland's Parliament, will go some considerable way towards correcting scholarly ignorance but it is difficult to see that it will affect the ordinary Scot by a jot.

If parliament was one symbol of Scotland's identity, the law (see LAW AND LAWYERS: 1) was surely another. The Court of *Session was formally established in 1532. Some material has been published of its proceedings before that point and a few samples from after 1532. Yet the unpublished and largely uncatalogued registers of acts and decreets of what was the central court of private law are so voluminous as to defy analysis. It took two years for an accomplished palaeographer to transcribe the records of the single year of 1600 for her doctoral thesis. Hints of what they contain lie in the 'practicks' books of individual lawyers such as Sir James Balfour of Pittendreich, who extracted cases which they used as precedents. Otherwise, acts and decreets are largely untilled ground, which may make any and all generalizations about the nature of landholding, tenure, and much else unsafe. In 1600, for example, so many cases were found of complaints made by tenants of rack-renting and eviction as to call into question received notions of the underlying stability of *rural society in the period. Instead, the prospect of a society stricken by a combination of the price rise, rising population, and unsympathetic landlords may come into view.

The most voluminous records which survive for the period up to 1400 are the cartularies of religious houses, representatives of a mandarin class which both created written record and was the interpreter of it. Monasteries were better organized than lay landowners and often had an archivist to take care of their charter chest. Since the church owned almost a third of the agricultural land of Scotland, their records provide an almost unique glimpse of medieval rural society. Yet it is also a misleading one because so few secular cartularies exist (see CHURCH INSTITUTIONS: 2).

The problems of interpreting the stigmata of charter evidence are considerable but are also largely technical. The difficulties of using chronicles, by comparison, are manifold. There are only two chronicles which were compiled before 1300: the so-called *Chronicle of Holyrood*, which may not come from Holyrood at all, and the *Chronicle of Melrose*. It is tempting to treat each as a surrogate history of medieval Scotland, which neither is nor was intended to be. The *Chronicle of Melrose* provides a very Cistercian view of both Scotland and the wider world. Similarly, the unprinted 'Roit and Quheil of Tyme', a chronicle written by an Augustinian canon, Adam Abell, which covers parts of Scottish history, such as in the reigns of James I and II, which other sources never reach, gives an answer but it is one which is both opinionated and less than full.

Yet there are other sources which have left an indelible impression which has literally lasted for centuries. The aftermath of the Wars of *Independence produced a historical canon of a Scottish past which has captivated, not to say imprisoned, the Scots psyche and its sense of identity (see HISTORIANS: 1). The period between John Barbour's epic poem *The Brus*, written in the 1370s, and Walter Bower's enormous compilation *Scotichronicon*, completed in the 1440s, devised a history of Scotland which articulated a sense of freedom threatened by the yoke of English oppression. It is small wonder that the entrance to the ground floor exhibition within the new *Royal Museum of Scotland, opened in 1998, has etched on the wall an extract from the Declaration of Arbroath. There is little or no alternative view of a period when, it has been said, the central fact of Scottish history was war with England. In vain, Unionist politicians from the mid-19th century onwards argued that the real achievement of *Robert I was to improve Scotland's bargaining position at the negotiating table in 1706–7. A Scottish national movement (see

NATIONAL IDENTITY: 5)—as distinct from a nationalist party—has since the 1850s been able to draw from the well of historical 'truths' constructed in the late 14th and early 15th centuries. Much of the inaccuracy in Hollywood's *Braveheart* came from the poetic licence enjoyed by Blind Harry when he wrote *The Wallace* as a protest against the pro-English drift of James III's foreign policy. It was no accident that the first known printed editions of both *The Brus* and *The Wallace* were produced during a civil war in 1570–1 by Robert Lekpreuik, printer for the king's party, which was allied with the historic enemy of England and needed to rediscover its patriotic roots.

The Scottish *Reformation produced not one but two narrative histories which have conditioned thinking ever since. John Knox's *History*, an epic account of the struggle between good and evil, with himself in a leading role, has encouraged a view of the Reformation in which, as for Knox, there was 'na middis', whereas in reality it is likely that most Scots sought some kind of consensus or middle way amidst the confusions of competing ideologies. It is from Knox's account, which was in one sense an extended sermon and in another a party pamphlet, that the idea of a 'perfect church' uncontaminated by papist leftovers, emerged. It prepared the way for a history of Scotland written in terms of a long struggle between two kingdoms, church and state (see CHURCH INSTITUTIONS: 3; HISTORIANS: 3), in the reign of *James VI and after. In reality, the church by the 1610s was more Knoxian than Knox himself. By then, for example, kneeling was condemned outright as 'papist', whereas Knox, in his English period, had in 1552 inserted a rubric into the English Prayer Book that did not ban kneeling but explained that it did not imply adoration. As a result, the transition of a Calvinist church of the 1560s into a neo-Calvinist one by the 1610s has eluded much attention (see RELIGIOUS LIFE: 3).

The other key work which emerged from the Reformation period was George Buchanan's *History*, first published in 1582. Written in elegant Latin, this extensive chronicle, which might well be termed the memoirs of an amnesiac, went through edition after edition in printing presses throughout Europe. The Latin court poet of *Mary, Queen of Scots, became the apologist for the overthrow of his queen and he justified the act by countless, apocryphal examples drawn from Scottish pre-history. From Buchanan has come a notion of the historicity of a Scottish democratic 'tradition': the right of the Scottish 'people' to determine their own destinies was influential in the thinking of both the cross-party Constitutional Convention and the General Assembly during the years of Margaret Thatcher's period as prime min-

ister. Scotland, it was argued, had a democratic tradition, which differed from the Westminster tradition of the absolute sovereignty of parliament.

It is an extraordinary example both of the resonance of a historical source across the centuries and of the capacity for it to be misunderstood. Buchanan carefully distinguished between 'populus'—the people who mattered—and 'universus populus', who did not. Even then, he had to make a further distinction, because of a civil war in which the majority of the nobility had taken the wrong side, between those who were right and those who disenfranchised themselves by wilful error. It is a view of politics which would not be out of place in Pinochet's Chile. Yet it has become almost an article of faith in a new Scottish political tradition. In fact, the pre-1707 Scottish *parliament, modern analysis of its workings is beginning to reveal, thought and acted in a very similar way to its counterpart in England, in terms of it possessing an absolute sovereignty. Why else, one might ask, did it think that it could legislate itself out of existence? The views that counted were not those of the people but those who 'represented' them.

The *Lyon in Mourning* was the work of an episcopalian propagandist who, in the immediate aftermath of the collapse of the Jacobite army after Culloden in 1746, assembled a series of atrocity stories. These were skilfully woven into a compelling vision of a calculated, brutal assault on a whole culture, not only of *Jacobitism but also of Highland society. It and other sources have even induced some modern-day historians to talk of genocide. It is a rare example of what was in effect a journalist writing what is sometimes claimed—by journalists—to be the first draft of history. Its success stemmed from the vividness and immediacy of the reporting and the fact that it contained more than a grain of truth within it. Untruths and factual inaccuracies can be challenged. A good half-truth, especially one derived from a near-contemporary source, can run and run.

History is in essence about choice. There are relatively few objective facts in the past. Historical sources confront the historian with alternative pasts for much of the business of history is about the selection or exclusion of evidence. A 16th-century historian is, after 1545, faced with the challenge of an entirely new, printed source telling about the business of government and its view of the world around it. The *Register of the Privy Council* might suggest a different view of the reign of Mary, Queen of Scots, from the standard accounts, since this was the first reign to see the growth of what modern historians sometimes call 'state formation'. By 1600, however, the business of the privy council had increased thirty-fold since 1550 and what has been called by Julian Goodare the 'fitted carpet of the state' had begun to extend to the furthest reaches of the realm, including the western Highlands and the Isles (see HIGHLANDS AND ISLANDS AND CENTRAL GOVERNMENT: 2). A generation ago, many Scottish historians, conservative by instinct, thought of strong central government as a good thing. A Highland lobby of historians, which has survived better, would, by contrast, argue that disruption and instability was usually the product of government intervention rather than its cause. With native or local sources, other than those of a tainted *Campbell provenance, notoriously difficult to find, the sceptic had to turn the evidence of the *Register* on its head and see in it the workings of a government which was obsessed with uniformity and control of the localities and especially those which had, in its own mind, developed the status of being a problem (see KINGSHIP: 6; NOBILITY: 3).

If government record is one of the enormous growth areas of the early modern period, the other main areas of expansion in the sources are surely the creation of a central land registry, in the form of the Register of Sasines, begun in 1617, over 350 years before its counterpart was formed in England and Wales, and the reams of folios which represent the paperwork of the courts of the reformed church. From 1617 onwards, as a direct result, ownership of all heritable property in Scotland can readily be traced. But if the state was dramatically extending its record of Scottish society, so was the 'parish state'. The idea of the emergence of a 'parish state' properly belongs to the 18th century, yet the new rigour of a church which produced records—of the prosaic details of birth, marriage, and burial as well as of sins and human failings—suggests from soon after the Reformation an institution with a mission to chart and shape the entire human condition. Much of that condition—or of the kirk sessions which monitored it—seems to have been obsessed with sex. Over 60 per cent of all session entries, typically, are taken up with it. In France, by contrast, the figure is less than 6 per cent. Yet the duties of a moral guardian went much further. By 1616 the keeping of parish registers recording the rites of passage became a duty laid down by the General Assembly, incumbent on every minister. It was an arrangement which persisted until 1854, when registration of births, marriages, and deaths became the business of the state. Very few have been published and since for many people, especially in the far-flung Scottish diaspora, real history is about the rediscovery of their ancestors, both the professional genealogist and the NAS (formerly the SRO), based in West Register House, which has established a sophisticated and lucrative search procedure, have been the beneficiaries.

Different pasts and different Scotlands can be accessed. The danger, at least from the viewpoint of the professional, whether archivist or historian, is karaoke history, in which prejudice or preconceived agendas become the mother of invention. Oddly, it is more prevalent about periods or topics which have few sources—the cult of William *Wallace is a classic example—or where the evidence is difficult to interpret or even, pre-1700, to read. And it is much more common as a phenomenon in pre-modern history. Few are exercised by debates on the origins of modern-day nationalism and only a handful of dedicated, if voluble, brethren care much about the 'Radical War' of 1820, an abortive protest march by a small band of Glasgow weavers which signally failed to light the blue touch paper of class war despite the overreaction of the authorities. The web sites of the world, instead, are full of fake Scottish history, on subjects ranging from Wallace to the Templars and Roslyn chapel and conspiracy theories of the assassination of a Highland culture (see CLEARANCES OF HIGHLANDS AND ISLANDS) in and after the Forty-Five. In each case, the assumption is that anyone's view of history is as good as anyone else's. It is an argument difficult to combat without a resort to elitism, unless the question is asked, 'What sources support this opinion?'   ML

2. 1750–1900

Which historical sources to value and preserve and how to interpret them have generally been determined throughout the ages by prevailing political orthodoxies. This has been no less true of the Scots than of other nations, particularly for the period after 1750 when the older accounts of Scotland's history, backed up by a wealth of textual evidence, from writers such as Robert Wodrow or Thomas Innes concerned with current religious and political controversies, gave way to the more consciously detached and judicious approach of the Enlightenment thinkers (see HISTORIANS: 4). The latter, viewing such polemics as the embarrassing remnants of a former barbarous age, instead interpreted the past by concentrating on the trends which had brought about the *Union of 1707 with England and, thus, its present triumphs in commerce, freedom, and civility. As the economic benefits of the Union began to materialize, along with the political and social stability provided by the defeat of *Jacobitism at Culloden and the taming of the more independently minded Presbyterians through the recent rise to dominance of the Moderates in the national church (see RELIGIOUS LIFE: 5), such changes became inevitable. Antiquarian contentions over the religious and constitutional conflicts of the 16th and 17th centuries, based on detailed study of the documents, were submerged in a tide which saw the future as coming from England.

The chief exponent of the new view was William Robertson (1721–93). Robertson's place as one of the foremost *historians in 18th-century Europe is undoubted. His *History of Scotland* (1759) was based on an extensive study of the relevant sources (including material provided by the chief Marian apologist, the antiquarian Walter Goodall). A recent series of essays, however (S. J. Brown (ed.), *William Robertson and the Expansion of Empire*, 1997), show, among much else, that his conclusions as to the country's past were influenced by his particular view of the future, so that the evidence was interpreted to prove a premiss in which a country going nowhere under an ungovernable *nobility had at last found salvation in adopting the constitutional traditions of English Whiggism. In general, it could be said that his fellow literati such as David Hume, Adam Smith, and John Millar followed his lead in presenting a similar view of Scotland's history to readers both within and without the country. Such men rightly saw themselves as every bit as patriotic in seeking their country's good as their antiquarian opponents, but they perhaps deluded themselves in thinking that a moderate and considered tone absolved them from any charge that their writings, too, carried a political message.

Despite the incorporating nature of the 1707 Union, Scotland's sharply contrasting regional topographies (see REGIONAL IDENTITIES) and its various racial strands did not fit easily into a norm of progressive parliamentary constitutionalism. Westminster governments had to subcontract their patronage powers to a succession of local Scottish notables to 'manage' the country (with its particular modes of parliamentary representation, administration, and customs) on their behalf (see GOVERNMENT AFTER THE UNION). In addition, interpretations of Scotland's past have tended to change whenever fundamental reappraisals of its future as a distinct society have occurred. As Enlightenment certainties (see CULTURE: 11), therefore, gave way to the revolutionary 1790s and 1800s, the past began to be reconsidered in a new search for stability. The chief influence here was Sir Walter Scott who rekindled interest in the Scottish past for its own sake and sought to put it on a firmer footing by a determined effort to preserve the nation's records. Scott was a Romantic but he was equally a child of the Scottish Enlightenment in his fear of challenge from below. He taught that Scotland's conflicts, whether between feudal factions, *Jacobite and Unionist, or Presbyterian and Episcopalian, should be confronted, not ignored, but be reconciled in a historical view which would demonstrate the folly

of extremism in destroying social order and authority.

Patrick Fraser Tytler, who insisted that historical interpretation should be based on as wide a range of relevant sources considered as judiciously as possible, should also be noted among those seeking to re-create the Scottish past more objectively at this time. His nine-volume *History of Scotland* (1828–43), covering the period from Alexander III to the *Union of the Crowns of 1603, set the tone for Scottish histories written in the 19th century which incorporated both the medieval and the contentious *Reformation periods to provide a picture of a Scotland which had something to contribute to the Union. Men like Scott and Tytler were responsible for the remarkable growth of *historical clubs and societies such as the Bannatyne (1823), the Maitland (1828), and the Spalding (1839), dedicated to making the nation's records accessible and usable. Such output inevitably sparked off other, often contrary, views, based on the growing religious excitement which led to the *Disruption, from historians equally intent on record scholarship like Thomas McCrie, or through publishing clubs like the Presbyterian Wodrow Society (1841) and the Episcopalian Spottiswoode Society (1843).

Other impulses by the 1850s making for a redefinition of what Scotland was (see NATIONAL IDENTITY: 5) and where it had come from were the growing forces of centralism in British life under a reformed parliament, and the way Scottish society had been transformed from what had been quite recently a rural, small town structure to one twisted into new shapes by the inexorable forces of commercial expansion, industrialization, and almost total urbanization (see ECONOMY: 4). The first of these continued to encourage a view of the past in which the benefits of Union were increasingly coupled with a new stress on the particularly valuable Scottish contribution to the making of the *British Empire. At a popular level there was a cult of William *Wallace as a 'British' patriot. The new sense of Scottish self-worth appears in the historical works of scholars such as Cosmo Innes; and by the end of the century James MacKinnon, in his *The Union of England and Scotland* (1896), though convinced of the benefits of that measure, had introduced a new critical view, miles removed from that of the mid-18th-century historians, questioning its longer-term beneficial effects on the institutional and social health of the country. Mid-century *nationalism which sought to preserve the Union by amending it to give greater expression to Scottish sentiment had thus become something of a historical norm by 1900. Few of the writers in the Home Rule camp ever sought separation, though as early as 1848 pamphlets calling for a sub-parliament for

Scotland were being argued for from a historical basis. Throughout the 19th century there was a growth in national *monuments, and a country whose social structure was literally being remade at this time responded readily to the growing vogue for local histories. Tracing the elements and functioning of society from below at a time of profound change is also evident in the lively *Chartist press which existed in Scotland in the 1830s and 1840s, all of which may suggest that popular historical notions of social justice and cohesion were quite deeply embedded and still living in Scottish popular culture. Some of this can be sensed in the writing of the land reformer John Murdoch, and it also surfaces at times in pamphlets and newspaper articles addressed by supporters of *Irish Home Rule to the new Scoto-Irish population coming to form a large part of industrial society in Scotland by the second half of the 19th century (see IMMIGRATION, IRISH). When the Scottish History Society was founded in 1886 its patron, Lord Rosebery, saw it as a vehicle for both the promotion of recent social history and a wider popular knowledge of Scottish history. Thus, when chairs of Scottish history were formally established at Edinburgh and Glasgow universities in 1901 and 1913 respectively, a basis had been created on which the diversity of the Scottish past, warts and all, might be developed, free from the finality of the historical judgement of 1750 that the history of Scotland had to all intents and purposes effectively ended in 1707.

The main collections of Scotland's records reside in the NAS (formerly the SRO) in Register House, the imposing Adam building at the east end of Princes Street. Here, and in its various extensions such as West Register House, are kept the official records of how Scotland has continued to be governed in modern times. After the absorption of the Scottish parliament into that of Great Britain in 1707 and the abolition of the privy council in 1708, administration was carried out under the aegis of what was left of the Scottish Exchequer. To this were added an increasing number of units which eventually developed into a considerable devolved administrative apparatus whose records have continued to grow. For instance, the creation of the Board of Manufactures (see ECONOMY: 3) in 1727 inaugurated a new series of records concerning the development of Scotland's trade and industry. Register House also contains the records of the various bodies such as the Board of Supervision (responsible for the poor law after 1845 and much public health after 1867), or those dealing with the Highlands (such as those of the Crofters' Commission of 1886–1912). In addition to all this there is the great mass of everyday material relating to trade, education, land transfers, the business of the civil and criminal courts, as well as the responses of successive Lord Advocates to public questions. Records of the pre-Union administration and of the law of Scotland are described in the *Guide to the National Archives of Scotland* (1996).

Both the NAS and the NLS (located on George IV Bridge, Edinburgh) house a large collection of private muniments which throw light not only on the high politics of the day but also on the everyday lives of the local communities surrounding the great territorial families of Scotland.

The catalogues of both the NAS and the NLS are now becoming increasingly accessible via the electronic highway. So, too, are the indices of the records of births, marriages, and deaths and of the censuses housed in New Register House under the control of the Registrar General (see HISTORICAL SOURCES: 4). For those unable to visit these national repositories, bodies such as the Burgh Record Society, the Scottish Record Society, and, doyen of them all, the Scottish History Society, have made an increasing number of records available in their publications. In these can be sampled, for instance, the work of kirk sessions, the records of 18th-century town councils, of plans for estate improvement, as well as 19th-century government bodies dealing with social welfare. A starting point to what is thus available in print is D. and W. B. Stevenson, *Scottish Texts and Calendars: An Analytical Guide to Serial Publications* (1987) Another useful guide for the reader would be *Scottish Archives*, the Journal of the Scottish Records Association, especially its volume 4 for 1998. Equally useful as to sources in manuscript and in print in the field of historical geography is I. D. and K. A. Whyte, *Sources for Scottish Historical Geography: An Introductory Guide* (1981). For newspapers see J. P. S. Ferguson, *A Directory of Scottish Newspapers* (1984). For industrial and labour history there is *A Catalogue of some Labour Records in Scotland and some Scots Records outside Scotland*, edited and compiled by I. Macdougall (1978) (see also FURTHER READING).

For the increasing band of local historians (described recently as the essential foot soldiers of much of Scottish history writing), in addition to the materials accessible in both the office of the Registrar General in New Register House and in the NAS, local archives have become increasingly available since the 1960s. In these, genealogical and census material is often available on microfilm or fiche, and some have built up considerable holdings of private muniments to add to their formal administrative records. Essential information on current developments in this field, and on what is available and where, is comprehensively detailed in an invaluable journal, *Scottish Local History*, which has gone from strength to strength since its inception in 1983. There are also a growing number of helpful guides like J. P. S. Ferguson, *Scottish Family Histories* (1986), Cecil Sinclair, *Tracing Your Scottish Ancestors* (HMSO, 1992), and M. Cox, *Exploring Scottish History: A Directory of Resource Centres for Scottish Local and National History in Scotland* (2nd edn., 1999). Finally, G. Donaldson, *The Sources of Scottish History* (Department of Scottish History, University of Edinburgh, 1978), though mainly concerned with the pre-1700 records, does consider the post-1700 period, and in its breadth and depth demonstrates that it is impossible to appreciate the nature of Scotland's modern records without an understanding of the national historical context from which they have grown.

In this period historical orthodoxy focused on the gradual growth and triumph of constitutional principles as represented by the British parliament. In that context, Scotland (and Ireland and Wales, too) was bound to be a non-runner. However, as shown above, the longevity and diversity of its records as well as the continuing debate as to its historiography demonstrate that it does have a history in which its regional, family, and group contexts, its particular locality, government, and distinctive debate over matters of belief and conscience, have to be appreciated the better to understand it.

JMcC

3. since 1900

Historians of the 20th century are amongst the most fortunate of researchers as the expansion of public and private organizations and their administrative development has seen an unparalleled growth in printed and other written material that has been preserved by archives and libraries for future historical use. Scotland is no exception and the following provides a listing of the principal repositories of preserved material and their significance for historical research on Scottish topics.

The NAS at West Register House, Edinburgh, holds the preserved records of the *Scottish Office and its associated departments, boards, and public organizations. The records, of course, relate primarily to the work that flowed from the governments of the period and contain the decisions of Scottish ministers on matters of public policy, minutes of meetings, and correspondence with other ministers, MPs, and public organizations. The records also contain submissions to ministers by senior civil servants on relevant matters of state (such as the Scottish Covenant campaign in the late 1940s on political devolution (see NATIONALISM) and the Conservative government's decision to raise the school leaving age in 1964 (see SCHOOLS AND SCHOOLING: 4)), sometimes as a prelude to the preparation of legislation or the preparation of

paper to be submitted to the cabinet. These are usually coloured blue (as opposed to white for other written material) and historians can usually note the decision of the minister concerned in their own script at the top of the paper. The bulk of the records, however, relates to the development and administration of public policy by civil servants and covers the work of the various departments and boards that dealt with agriculture and fisheries, education, health, criminal justice and the judiciary (including the work of the Lord Advocate), the police, the prison service, the social services, the Highlands and Islands, the Forestry Commission, the public utility boards, road, rail, and air transport, and increasingly after 1945 matters affecting the Scottish economy.

The Scottish Office departments (and their predecessor boards) were normally organized on the basis of various departmental divisions holding separate briefs for the administration of government policy. Thus Division I of the Scottish Home and Health Department from 1944 to 1962 dealt with matters affecting the *Scottish Secretary's statutory duties connected with the 1945 Distribution of Industry Act and certain other functions including constitutional affairs (such as political devolution). Division D of the same department dealt with the administration of Scottish prisons. In the Scottish Department of Health, there were separate divisions that dealt with the provision of public housing, town and country planning, the national health service, and the environmental services. It is normally possible to chart out the preliminary discussion amongst junior civil servants on prospective new legislation, often after consulting relevant Scottish public and other organizations, the internal departmental consideration of the consultations, the preparation of a submission to a minister, the discussion with other UK departments of the impact of the legislation on their work, the preparation of a submission to the cabinet, and, if agreed as a legislative proposal, the passage of the bill through parliament.

At various times the Scottish departments and boards either commissioned or received studies and surveys of Scottish economic and social conditions (see ECONOMY: 6) and these, such as the survey on Scottish unemployment in 1921, provide a valuable source of information in themselves which would otherwise be unavailable. The NAS also holds a set of cabinet and cabinet committee papers (minutes of meetings and memoranda) for the period until 1966 and these provide information on the work of other UK departments, such as the Foreign Office, the Board of Trade, and the Ministry of Labour. The memoranda of the latter two, in particular, can also be read in conjunction with

Scottish Office papers on Scottish economic conditions. A number of private individuals of political or social standing have deposited papers in the NAS but, as yet, these are less extensive than earlier 19th-century collections. Some records have also been deposited that belong to public utilities and other organizations, such as the Coal Board, the electricity boards, and the *Highlands and Islands Development Board and certain local authorities, but in recent years the majority of the latter have been transmitted to their respective local archives. Public records in the NAS are subject to a thirty-year closure period, although this can be reduced on application to the Scottish Executive, which after 1999 replaced the Scottish Office.

The Scottish local authorities hold a responsibility to preserve their papers and records and maintain a local archive service. Such material and records deal primarily with the minutes of meetings of the local authorities (town and county councils) and their predecessors in the early part of the century, such as parish councils and boards of education. However, they also contain more detailed records, such as applications for Poor Relief, which usually provides the most extensive of set of records held locally (see LIVING STANDARDS: 4); records relating to school attendance and pupil achievement; and the incidence of public health and building and other development plans. Records (including letter books) relating to the work of town treasurers, chamberlains, the medical officers of health, and lords provost have also been preserved, although the quantity of material preserved can vary, depending on local retention policy after the reorganization of local authorities in the mid-1970s. An invariably interesting set of material usually held in the archives relates to the annual reports of the medical officers of health, which outline the various measures introduced to contain and reduce the incidence of such previously widespread and deadly diseases as typhoid, tuberculosis, and measles (see HEALTH, FAMINE, AND DISEASE: 3). It is often possible to chart out the impact of public policy as it emerged from the preserved Scottish Office files held in NAS to local discussion and, on occasion vice versa, when local conditions led to demands for a change in government policy. For instance, in the mid-1930s the low level of subsidies available for public *housing projects (see LIVING STANDARDS: 5) led many local authorities, including *Glasgow, to petition the Scottish Secretary to press for an alteration in policy, which was eventually granted after much heated debate with the Treasury in 1938. These archives, like the NAS, are in the most case, extensively catalogued (increasingly by computer) and are usually free to the public. Those records not already in the public domain, such as minutes of council meetings, are also normally liable to a thirty-year closure period.

Scotland is well served by a large number of private archives which hold records and other material relating to family estates (such as at Hopetoun House in West Lothian) and to businesses (such as Salveson's, the shipping firm). The papers in these archives give the historian an opportunity to research topics on non-official Scotland and the more private and business lives of the individuals concerned. However, it is usual that these records are available to the public by agreement with the owners and may involve a charge.

A number of Scottish libraries hold deposited papers of individuals of social and public standing and these are generally open for public consultation. For instance, the NLS holds papers that belonged to several Scottish Secretaries of State, including Walter *Elliot and Arthur *Woodburn, although in these two cases the papers are not particularly extensive. The major public reference libraries also hold and have developed special collections relating to local material. For instance, the Mitchell Library in Glasgow and Edinburgh's George IV Bridge Public Library have both sought to build up a collection of material on charitable organizations and other such community groups which would otherwise be lost. These libraries have similarly sought to obtain books and pamphlets belonging to public and semi-official organizations that are not normally published for sale, or not generally available to the public. Thus the Edinburgh Library contains the publication of the *Scottish Council (Development and Industry), the independent body established after 1945 to publicize and promote the development of Scottish industry. Virtually all the major reference libraries stock the principal national and local *newspapers and other journals. Such material, if used in conjunction with other public records, such as those of the local authority and central government, enables the researcher to establish a fuller perspective on events and public policy. For instance, the implementation of the mass x-ray campaign to combat tuberculosis in the late 1950s can be studied through the Department of Health papers at the NAS which outline the origins of the campaign and its official approval by Scottish ministers. Local archives, for example Glasgow City Archives, provide details on the approval and implementation of the campaign by the City Council (including the publicity given in cinemas and on street posters) and the newspapers, such as the *Glasgow Herald*, report an almost day-to-day account of the campaign as the x-ray machines toured the city over a six-month period.

Finally, a number of universities also hold records and other material of interest to the 20th-century historian. Thus Edinburgh University Library holds a complete set of *Parliamentary Papers* and Hansard as well as back numbers of the principal academic journals that dealt with the development of modern medicine, science, and other professional services. They often contain more dedicated material, such as business history records at Glasgow University, and are linked directly or indirectly to the records of the local National Health authorities and boards. The latter, in particular, can supplement the material held on the health services at the NAS and in local authority archives on public-health provision. These records may be subject to certain closure periods.   IL

4. genealogical

Medieval Scottish monarchs (see KINGSHIP) flattered themselves with a genealogy traced from Gaythelos, son of an ancient Greek king (whence Gael). The *clan chiefs, not to be outdone, had their *sennachies* sing of their descent for over 40 generations from exotic forebears such as ancient tribes described by Ptolemy. Genealogical researchers who feel tempted to follow these examples from the oral tradition would do better to reflect on the harsh truth that they will be extremely unlikely to prove a genuine pedigree from historical sources back more than two centuries from the present. The 18th century is full of men and women, even of the highest rank, whose key dates and numbers of children cannot be exactly established.

The aristocratic muniments that do survive were admirably examined by Sir William Fraser in the last century, and his 50 volumes are a scholarly source for interrelationships of Scots landed families—important for understanding political and economic allegiances. Such was the extended structure of landed society that upwards of 10,000 Scots had recognized titles at the time of the Union. The Lord Lyon's Office (see HERALDRY) supports a court responsible for the matriculation of arms, for which it maintains the Public Register of Genealogies. Included are birthbrieves (setting out the descent and status of individuals) and lineal pedigrees.

Difficulties in undertaking genealogical research stem from the late introduction and poor maintenance of the key records: the registers of birth/baptism, banns/marriages, and deaths/burials. A 14th-century synodal decree enjoined the parish priest to keep death registers, but the Vatican archives show no sign of them. The earliest parish register dates from 1553 following a decision of a general provincial council of the Scottish church. The Church of Scotland inherited the good intentions, but the fact that these were so regularly renewed indicates how ineffective they were.

In the 300 years up to the introduction of civil registers in 1855 a motley bag of records were maintained. Death/burial registers are the most meagre, reflecting the lack of sacramental status for the burial service and the feeling that death was God's business. Religious schisms, illiteracy (there are virtually no records from the Highlands before the 18th century; see SCHOOLS AND SCHOOLING: 2), loss and damage, and the high incidence of irregular marriage (see COURTSHIP AND MARRIAGE) in some parts of the country (marriage too was no sacrament) contribute to the patchy nature of the record. Towards the end of the 18th century confidence in the parish registers begins to grow, but then a tax on registration was introduced (1783–92) and the industrial revolution led to the church losing track of thousands upon thousands of the new urban poor. The Register General for Scotland published a *Detailed List of the Old Parochial Registers of Scotland* in 1872.

The content varies from parish to parish according to the session clerk's fancy—he was usually the schoolmaster. Names of witnesses (usually relatives) to baptisms are a useful source and causes of death tell an interesting story. Though non-Church of Scotland members were encouraged to register in the parish, some churches kept their own records, as did the colourful Border stations for runaway marriages. Most of these alternative registers have been gathered into the General Register Office, and transcripts of many have been published by the Scottish Record Society. Burial sites in royal burghs were usually the responsibility of town councils and registers form part of town council records.

The date 1855 is a key one. After the *Disruption the church's jealously guarded right to control of registration was no longer tenable and civil registration was introduced, nearly 20 years later than in England. The network of local registry offices ensures a comprehensive record of births, marriages, and deaths, remitted to the General Register Office. There should be no problems in obtaining full details of anyone born since that date from a relatively speedy skim through annual indexes for the whole of Scotland, provided they remained in their native country. The genealogical researcher has one compensation for the inadequacy of the historical record, namely that indexes to the records we do have become widely accessible, initially on microfiche but more recently via the Internet and CD-Rom. Most of the former drudgery has been eliminated.

The well-known Mormon microfiche resource, the International Genealogical Index, is based on researches of Mormon Church members of varying reliability, and cannot always be referred back to primary sources. The Internet version, *Family Search*, contains 240 million names worldwide and can be accessed at *www.familysearch.org*. A specifically Scottish enterprise of the Mormon Church, the *Index to the Old Parochial Registers*, contains all the names in the baptismal and marriage (but not the death) registers. The names are arranged by county and microfiche versions are still widely used in libraries across Scotland for initial searching. But probably for not much longer, for the General Register Office has established its own web site *Origins* (*www.origins.net*) allowing instant interrogation of 25 million index entries from 1553 to 1898, spanning both the period of the old parochial registers and part of the new era of civil registration. A project under the aegis of the Scottish Association of Family History Societies is working towards providing an index to the death/burial registers, thus completing the last piece of the pre-1855 jigsaw. The new resource also includes specialized registers such as those of Scottish soldiers abroad and the Adopted Children Register and incorporates a refined searching mechanism that allows variant spellings of the same name to be searched concurrently. The next step being considered is to computerize the registers themselves. There is one disadvantage in using the Internet version compared with the microfiche indexes, that search fees are charged.

An important addendum to parish registers is the evidence from gravestones, which became fashionable from the 17th century. The Scottish Genealogy Society have co-ordinated a major programme to transcribe surviving pre-1855 inscriptions and many of these are published. Its work is supplemented by local initiatives in many areas. Surviving lair and burial ground plans can be useful.

A second major set of demographic records is the decennial census enumeration books, dating from 1841 (see POPULATION PATTERNS: 2). The records are covered by the 100-year confidentiality rule. Every individual's whereabouts is recorded on census night, together with a varying number of details from census to census (sex, employment, relationship to head of household, and so on). Age is given but rounded to the nearest five years in the first census. The 1841 and 1851 censuses are particularly important, being the most complete pre-civil registration source with links back to birth dates from the mid-18th century. Microfiche indexes to the names in the 1881 and 1891 censuses have been produced by the Mormons/General Register Office. The former is available on CD-Rom and the latter is incorporated in the *Origins* website. The enumeration books themselves have been widely distributed on microfilm.

There are a range of other sources of middling value, none of which are demographic in intention. Scotland, with its poverty and concentration of property into few hands, is a land of the nameless. Registers of testaments are useful for establishing dates of death and to confirm relations of the few who had movables to leave—they form part of commissary records in the NAS up to 1823 and thereafter a commissary function within sheriff courts. The boundaries of the Commissariats corresponded to pre-Reformation dioceses (see CHURCH INSTITUTIONS: 2), so the first task is to establish under which court's jurisdiction any individual falls. The Scottish Record Society has published indexes of every testament registered up to 1800. Thereafter there are a variety of indexes available. Consistorial court papers (originally part of Edinburgh Commissary Court) deal with all aspects of divorce and separation.

Heritable property owners included some small feuars and bondholders, so sasine registers, Scotland's priceless record of land transactions, can be useful. Under the quasi-feudal law of the land, heritors were obliged to register their inheritance with the superior through service of heirs or precepts of *clare constat*. Major feus direct from the crown are recorded in another register—the Record of Retours—of which abridgements for the years 1544–1699 have been published as *Inquisitionum ad Capellam Regis Retornatarum Abbreviato*.

Local *newspapers (especially if indexed) are a good source, not only for births, marriages, and deaths columns and obituaries, but also for court reports where the relationship of witnesses to the accused is often indicated. Actual court records are useful for the same reason, though name indexes are scarce. Lists of emigrants (see EMIGRATION: 3–4) are to be found in ship passenger lists and various parliamentary papers and can be supplemented by the data collected by many of the host countries. Taxation records are a patchwork and weighted towards the well-off, at least until the advent of modern valuation rolls listing tenants as well as proprietors. Some Scottish burghs boast good registers of burgesses and of electors and there are many other lists and rolls of ministers, university students, and school pupils to tempt the unwary into unsubstantiated ancestry. DMo

Horne, Sir Robert (1871–1940), son of a Stirlingshire manse, elevated to the peerage in 1937 as first Viscount Horne of Slamannan after what has been described as a meteoric career. Following a politically active undergraduate career at Glasgow University, Horne was called to the Bar in 1896.

Nevertheless, his interest in politics did not remain dormant for long, and in 1908 he was adopted as the *Unionist candidate for Stirlingshire and fought—and lost—that constituency at both the general elections of 1910. Horne again went to the polls in 1918, this time securing the Hillhead division of Glasgow for the Unionists. However, it was his wartime service that was to prove the critical influence guiding his later career. As Deputy Director of Agriculture in the National Service Department, Horne attracted the attention of Sir Eric Geddes, who was instrumental in Horne's appointment as the Assistant Inspector-General of Transportation in 1917. Horne became Director of the Admiralty Labour Department in 1918 and, after a matter of months, became the Third Civil Lord of the Admiralty. Following the declaration of peace, Horne was made Minister of Labour in Lloyd George's coalition government of 1919 and subsequently occupied the position of President of the Board of Trade (1920–1) before being appointed Chancellor of the Exchequer in 1921. Party politics, however, intervened to cut short Horne's period in high office. Like many Scottish Unionist MPs, Horne opposed the dissolution of the Unionist–National Liberal Coalition in 1922 and occupied the backbenches for the rest of his career. In the latter years of his life, however, Horne—by promoting various reforms of the *Scottish Office—was instrumental in guiding the Unionists' response to the rising tide of *nationalist sentiment in Scotland.   CMMM

housing: 1. rural Lowlands, before and after 1770s; 2. urban, to c.1770; 3. urban and suburban, since c.1770; 4. country seat, c.1660–present; 5. the Highlands.

1. rural Lowlands, before and after 1770s

The 1770s mark the substantial beginnings of the agricultural Improvement (see ECONOMY, PRIMARY SECTOR: 2) period in Scotland. More, perhaps, than in any other European country, this phase completely transformed the face of the land, especially in the Lowland areas south and east of the Highland Line. The farmtouns, groups of steadings and houses standing to one side of their jointly worked arable, gradually disappeared. They were replaced by individual farms, each sited on their own piece of ground within a dyked, turf-walled, or hedged enclosure (see RURAL SETTLEMENT: 3). The former communal organization of society was replaced by one with new kinds of relations between farmers and their workers, though in the main the organizational basis was still that of estates, largely composed of tenant farms, and with an estate or 'mains' farm on which innovations in tools, rotations and crops, farming techniques, and housing were most likely to originate. Such innovations included sep-

arate housing for the married farmworkers, as a visible symbol of the increasing social distance between masters and men (see RURAL SOCIETY: 3).

The landscape of modern farming was largely shaped between the 1770s and the 1840s. The changes were so all embracing that they amounted to a revolution, and this was equally true of the new farm buildings that began to proliferate. Often built to the instructions of estate architects, sometimes using pattern books, their frequent siting on new positions meant that almost all traces of the former joint farms were swept away. It is clear from a general survey of surviving rural buildings in Scotland that there was formerly a greater degree of regional variety and a wider range of indigenous features that could distinguish local building types. The outcome of the Improvement period was a levelling out of such variables, basically as a result of estate intervention. The new *buildings that were erected were no longer conditioned by the nature of the indigenous building materials and by a do-it-yourself approach by the tenants, but by the skills of architects and tradesmen, and by the type of farming which they had to subserve.

The major variations can be allocated to the following regional breakdown for the Lowlands: the north-east (Aberdeen, Banff, Caithness, Kincardine, Moray, Nairn, and Orkney), the east (Angus, Clackmannan, Fife, Kinross and Perth), the south-east (Berwick, East Lothian, Midlothian, Peebles, Roxburgh, Selkirk, and West Lothian), and the south-west (Ayr, Bute, Dumfries, Dunbarton, Kirkcudbright, Lanark, Renfrew, Stirling, and Wigtown). Analysis of full-time farm units in these areas shows that stock rearing and feeding predominated in the north-east, cropping in the north-east also and in the east, hill sheep in the south-west and Borders, a combination of these with dairying in the south-west, and areas of horticulture in the south-west and east. These types of farming helped to condition the layout of the steadings and the nature of the individual units within them, for grain processing and storing, stock feeding and housing, milking and milk processing, housing the draught horses and carts, and the like. In terms of the modern concept of organization and method, the new farm buildings, wherever sited and whatever purpose they were serving, were models of efficient practice at a time when horses, water, or wind provided the main power source and machinery was largely restricted to the threshing mill in the barn.

Information about the rural buildings of the earlier period is somewhat nebulous because so little has survived in the Lowlands. It is necessary to use the evidence of travellers to find clues, and also to look to survivals in the north and west for possible indicators of what the homes and steadings were formerly like in the Lowlands. The layout of a joint farm is indicated by, for example, the Argyll township of Auchindrain, near Inveraray, now preserved as a museum. It consists of a number of dwelling houses and outhouses, clustered fairly closely together, each with kailyard and stackyard, and cart tracks running between.

In structural terms, an interesting feature is the form of roofing with wooden couples (now known in the technical literature as crucks), the legs of which come down the walls, originally to ground level. Theoretically, it was possible for the roof to be erected on crucks and then to have the walls filled in with turf, or stone and turf, or clay, or wattle. The tenants arranged for the infilling of the walls, but often the roofing timbers, the most valuable part of the building, were supplied by the laird, and so were known as the 'master's wood', 'master's timbers', or 'great timber'. In this way, the building roles were shared between laird and tenant. Crucks continued to be used for some time, even after modern forms of building with solid stone walls had become normal, with their legs coming part-way down the stonework. They therefore survived as anachronisms, because the walls had become fully load-bearing and A-frame rafters would have been adequate. Crucks or couples were, incidentally, set at understood widths apart, since in earlier sources a house or outbuilding was of a recognized number of 'couple lengths' from one upwards, estimated at 12 feet (3.7 m) in the 15th century, which means that, within limits, the lengths of building units can in some cases be established from the documentary evidence.

At Auchindrain, too, there were examples of hip-ended roofs, instead of gables that ran straight all the way up to the roof-ridge, and these were supported by end crucks. Such a feature, as well as the considerable range of forms of the cruck truss throughout the country, indicates something of the regional variety that has been lost.

Another indicator of such variety is the form of the hearth. The simplest lay in the middle of the floor, with a smoke hole in the roof rather than a chimney. Such fireplaces survived in the Highlands and Islands, for example at 42 Arnol in Lewis, and an example has been identified at Auchindrain. They were certainly to be found in the Lowlands too; for example, three travellers in 1629 slept in a thatched house with a door of wickerwork and a central fire at Langholm in Dumfriesshire. A more developed form had a backstone, which could be either a single flagstone or a short stretch of walling (as in the Carse of Stirling in 1792), sited between the fire and the entrance door.

Perhaps as a marker of improving times, there is a good deal of Lowland evidence for hearths with some form of smoke extraction by means of an overhanging canopy, without any chimney opening in the thickness of the gable wall. One type provides evidence for the existence of central hearths, for it consists simply of an inverted funnel dangling from the roof above the roundabout fireside. The sources relate to the shires of Peebles, Roxburgh, and Selkirk for the early years of the 19th century. An alternative form was a canopy overhanging a gable fireplace, against the wall. This may be seen as a translation into timber or plastered wattle of the stone chimney hoods of castles and mansions, adopted in rural buildings as an 18th-century innovation. The name 'Lothian brace' may indicate its place of development; it had spread to Perthshire, along with this name, by 1771, and the 'hingin lum', as it became known in dialectal speech, was thereafter adopted widely throughout the country, reaching as far as Shetland by the early 1800s. Such fireplaces and hoods were for mainly peat-burning kitchen fires. But since their spread appears to have been accompanied the adoption of chimneys built in the thickness of the gable for best-room fireplaces, the bulk of which had coal-fired grates, there can be no doubt that they symbolize improved housing and improved living conditions throughout the Lowland areas, as the era of the farmtoun wore out and was replaced by the phenomenon of individually standing farmhouses with their steadings and supporting farmworkers' housing (see LIVING STANDARDS: 5).

Though historians have often assumed that the multiple-tenancy farmtoun was the standard form of land use in pre-Improvement times, new research shows that the picture must be modified. A study of the late 17-century poll tax returns reveals that out of 2,145 holdings listed for six counties in the 1690s, 644 were multiple-tenancy and 1,121 were single-tenancy farms. There was a steady increase in the number of single tenancies as the 17th moved into the 18th century, until the singles won a complete victory. But these were probably not acting in the way that mains farms did as focal points for innovation, because in forms of rental, marketing possibilities for produce, level of technical development, and nature of labour supply, they had to conform to the same kinds of restrictions as applied to the multiple-tenancy units. It was the French Revolutionary and Napoleonic Wars of the late 18th and early 19th centuries that really boosted estate finances to a level that allowed them to initiate and promulgate the changes, including a massive rebuilding programme, that shaped the nature of farm buildings as it remained into our own times.

It has been said that the small houses and cottages in the Scottish countryside are relatively young, few antedating about 1750, and this is especially true of the Lowlands. Most farm buildings do not date to before the third quarter of the 18th century, though there may well be traces of older features in the bigger farms of the more prosperous farming areas, and in main farms. Nevertheless, thinking about the layout of farm buildings was going on at high social levels already by the second half of the 17th century, presumably in line with the enabling legislation relating to the enclosure of lands lying runrig and to the division of commonties (Acts were passed in 1661, 1685, and 1695), and also with the publication of treatises on farming practice in the 1690s. Of the latter, the most relevant is that by Lord Belhaven, *The Country-Man's Rudiments; or, An Advice to the Farmers in East Lothian* (1699), in which he advocated a four-sided layout of dwelling house, barns, stable, and byres with the dunghill in the middle of the resulting square. An example of a house and some of the offices on three sides of a square has been noted for Wester Gagie in Angus in 1649. These improvements were clearly based on the thinking of estate owners. The linearity of the 'longhouse', with byre and dwelling under one roof and interconnecting, was carried over into a tendency for small farms to be linear, with house, barn, and byre in a row, but for bigger farms the four- or three-sided layout eventually became the norm, with the dwelling house becoming separated from its steading and the housing for at least the married servants being often at a little remove.

The source of inspiration for the multitude of new farm buildings must surely have been the same as for the lairds' houses, which also have been relatively little studied. These derived in part from the late medieval tower houses, in which the service and living areas were one above the other, for defensive purposes. But there was an increasing move towards horizontal expansion and from the late 17th century medium-sized domestic residences appeared, being occupied by lairds, ministers, merchants, and master-craftsmen, and built usually in symmetrical, rectangular blocks, with courtyards containing the usual farm offices. Their antecedents may be British rather than purely Scottish, and they have a general similarity in architectural form, wherever they are found. In spite of this—which suggests a primary source of origin, such as pattern books—they have all the hallmarks of construction by local craftsmen working to local designers. It is out of this background activity that the designs of farmhouses appear to have come in the great Improvement period of Scottish farming.

AF

2. urban, to c.1770

Houses in medieval and early modern Scottish towns exhibited features that were similar at least in spirit, if not in exact form, to those of the *Low Countries and Tuscany, the twin epicentres of medieval European urban civilization and culture. A number of Scottish town houses, for example, are known to have been of semi-fortified tower-house form, a particularly impressive late 15th-century specimen having served as the solar block of a large town house in Linlithgow, possibly associated with the Knights Hospitallers of nearby Torphichen and perhaps aping in part some of the details of the nearby royal palace.

Towers are also known to have occurred in groups, particularly in the west and south-west of the country. The indications are, though, that most such urban towers were relatively small-scale structures, bearing a closer affinity to the character and grouping of towers in Irish towns (such as the five or so late medieval towers huddled together in the small seaport town of Ardglass in County Down) than to distant and more lofty ancestors in northern Italy.

Timber-framed town houses were the norm across the whole of medieval urban Europe, evidently including Scotland, but by the 16th century timber-fronted building practices had developed here, possibly in response to a relative scarcity of timber and a relative abundance of workable stone. Curiously, however, given the known recorded difficulties of obtaining domestic or foreign supplies of timber, there was a fashionable reversion in the last quarter of the late 16th century to building houses wholly or substantially of timber, especially in *Edinburgh where houses of broad, jettied, and boarded form that would not have been out of place anywhere in northern Europe made a remarkable reappearance (see URBAN SETTLEMENT: 1).

Superficially, by the 17th century Scottish urban houses came to assume a recognizable Flemish or Dutch appearance, usually translated into a Scottish building idiom of stone and harl. Typically, such houses are of four storeys with relatively narrow three- or four-bay frontages, gabled or gableted and crow-stepped, and occasionally incorporating fashionable ground-floor arcades or piazzas. In these ways, there were broad similarities in form and appearance between the pre-industrial housing of Scotland and that of mainland Europe. In Scotland, however, there was a noticeable and precocious development of flatted urban dwellings and multiple ownership, not just multiple occupation, of single town properties, a phenomenon which appears to be less clearly detectable in mainland Europe.

The trend is already discernible in the late medieval period in Scotland. A now-demolished two-storeyed building with forestair in Church Street, Inverkeithing, Fife, for example, was interpreted as a self-contained merchant burgess's house set above vaulted stores and was ascribed to the late 15th century. Similar forestaired types appear in a panoramic view of *St Andrews ascribable to about 1580 but clearly depicting the urban built environment of pre-Reformation times. The existence of a forestair points to several functional variations on the same basic design, including inns and ordinary dwellings above warehouses, stores, or shops. Two-storeyed flatted or 'stacked' cottages of this general arrangement with families living above and below became a distinctive urban house-type, most notably in east central Scotland. Such buildings were marked down by foreign travellers as being distinctively Scottish.

What was especially startling to visitors to Scotland from the later 16th century onwards was the Scottish urban skyscraper, which in the main centres of population rose to four or more storeys in height. Sheer height was not their only special feature. Some were self-contained dwellings in single ownership, others were clearly of multiple occupation and ownership, all above a single solum. Inbuilt structural evidence for original flatting, not just later subdivisions for tenants, can be detected in the disposition of original stairs, including forestairs, and in partitions and doorways. By the late 16th century, the upper floors of the so-called 'John Knox House' in Edinburgh's High Street formed a separate dwelling which was reached by its own newel stair in the front corner of the building. Although later usage makes it difficult to work out the original arrangements, Gladstone's Land in the Lawnmarket, Edinburgh, also conforms to the general pattern; Thomas Gledstanes, the builder, occupied one of its four flats after his acquisition and reconstruction of the property in 1617–20. A detailed Edinburgh tax roll of 1635, which itemizes over 4,800 households and businesses, confirms the pattern in which many buildings in central Edinburgh were subdivided into houses of various sizes, with rooms arranged over one or two floors and providing household accommodation for owner-occupiers and tenants alike. By that date, such mixed arrangements were commonplace, at least in Edinburgh.

Pre-Reformation *Edinburgh was already densely packed with buildings, but the extent to which they were designed and modified to suit divided ownership or tenancy is not clear. However, in notarial instruments recording three-way subdivisions of urban properties in early 16th-century Canongate, the divisions agreed upon by the co-parcenors appear to have been horizontal as well as vertical, much importance being attached to the forebooths and forelofts. To suggest that such flatting resulted simply or even mainly from the pressures of overcrowding within the security of the town's defences is not a sufficient explanation. It does not explain why similar and indeed more intense conditions in English walled towns did not provoke a similar response.

Whether horizontally divided occupation has early roots in Northumberland, where it was already flourishing in the early 18th century, has yet to be established. The wider unanswered question is whether Scots custom and practice, as well as Scots law (see LAW AND LAWYERS: 1), have closer affinities with Continental practice than with England, where 'flying freehold' began to take hold only from about the middle of the 19th century. Unfortunately, preliminary investigations into urban housing in the Low Countries, western Germany, France, and Iberia have revealed surprisingly little early evidence, only later tenanted subdivisions.

But the differences are also clearly evident locally. *Berwick, the leading burgh in Scotland in the 12th and 13th centuries, perhaps demonstrates most clearly of all the ways in which the town, lost finally to the English in 1482, moved away from Scottish urban built forms in terms of its ecclesiastical as well as its social background and architecture. Recent detailed examination has revealed that housing in Berwick, going back to at least 17th-century timber-framed structures, has developed along thoroughly English lines. Its domestic architecture is now quite distinct from Eyemouth a few miles up the coast, where truly Scottish flatted tenements and fisher cottages can still be found. GPS

3. urban and suburban, since c.1770

During the years of revolutionary economic and social modernization dating from the late 18th century, Scotland developed into one of the most urbanized countries in the world (see URBAN SOCIETY: 4). As a result, urban housing became one of the most central and emotive areas of modern Scottish material culture. On the whole, its patterns and ideas have been those of the anglophone or 'Anglo-Saxon' world, but with some elements more closely related to continental Europe.

Chronologically, the subject is divided fundamentally by the 1914–18 war. This brought a complete realignment of social and architectural patterns, symbolized by the 1917 Ballantyne Commission report into working-class housing (see LIVING STANDARDS: 5; URBAN SETTLEMENT: 3). In the period up to 1914, the prevailing system sought to reconcile capitalist laissez-faire provision with ideals of social-spatial order and architectural monumentality, partly inherited from the pre-modern era of landed, aristocratic-led Improvement. Most middle- and working-class housing was provided for rent, through an uncoordinated and fragmented system of small developers and landlords. By comparison to the larger-scale development mechanisms of later industrializing societies such as Germany, the Scottish system became increasingly sclerotic and stress-ridden by 1914. The building process itself, however, was organized in a far more systematized, industrialized, and economical fashion than on the Continent, including the use of standardized components and machinery: the ubiquitous use of fine facing stone on even the humblest new dwellings, by 1900, was a unique achievement of Scottish housing capitalism. Out of this progressive building process, from the late 19th century, a new breed of large-scale builder-developer was beginning to emerge, such as Glasgow's John MacTaggart or Edinburgh's James Steel.

Geographically, the predominant pattern was a loosely structured natural diversity. The general urban housing pattern was a fairly normal European one: apartment or tenement blocks in inner areas, two-storey or one-storey single-family dwellings further out. But this took different forms in different towns and cities, including four-storey blocks with internal staircases in *Edinburgh or *Glasgow, four-storey blocks with external stair and gallery access in *Dundee, and two-storey blocks with upper-floor access by external staircases in some smaller burghs and suburbs—similar to the 'duplex' and 'triplex' blocks of Montreal.

This geographical diversity was offset by a preoccupation with imposed architectural and spatial order—something which was typical of Anglo-Saxon urbanism in general, but which was accentuated by the spatial rationalism of the Scottish Enlightenment (see CULTURE: 11–12) and by the colonial-imperialist ethos of 'planting and planning'. Over the 150 years following the foundation of the Edinburgh New Town in 1766, there was a dual focus on the building of new settlements or suburbs, mainly for the wealthy (with some exceptions, such as the industrial tenement village of New Lanark, from 1785), and the remodelling of the slums of the poor, especially by the City Improvement Trusts of the 1860s onwards.

In the architecture of new housing, this search for order expressed itself in an insistent homogeneity and monumentality. The terrace formula of uniform rows of houses, with sharply cut ashlar masonry, austere openings, and shaved-off rooflines, contrasted strikingly with the individualized, *palazzo*-like tenements of central Europe, with their profuse, stuck-on plaster decoration. The lo-

cation and arrangement of housing was driven, again, by an 'un-Continental' preoccupation with separation and openness. In contrast, for example, to the social mixture of French cities, and their relegation of the poor to the city edges, in Scotland new housing was strictly segregated by *class and driven by an unending centrifugal force. There were small tenement flats for skilled workers, and a choice between large inner-suburban tenements or outer-suburban villas for the middle classes; the unskilled poor were left with old, subdivided houses in town centres. Encouraged by growing municipal regulation, new tenements were laid out in shallow strips around the perimeter of street blocks, to encourage the penetration of light and air, while internally there were strenuous attempts to encourage self-containment and functional subdivision of dwellings—a trend that had begun in the 16th-century royal palaces of the Stewarts, and had now percolated down to skilled manual workers. As in England, the concern for ventilation also encouraged the perpetuation of the system of heating and cooking using open fires (rather than the American and European stoves), with its resulting proliferation of flues and chimney stacks, and the development of a world-leading expertise in plumbing technology; the practice of placing pipework externally, to maximize access for inspection, was unique to these islands.

After 1914, there was a revolution in the organization of housing, but more gradual change in what was built. Fuelled by rent strikes in 1915 and the damning 1917 Ballantyne Report, the government intervened to crush the increasingly stigmatized private-renting landlords, and to substitute a system of social housing, centrally regulated by state experts and driven by mass political pressures for 'output'. State intervention and subsidy was common to the whole of western Europe, but only in Scotland did direct state provision become overwhelmingly dominant. In the late 1940s, public housing accounted for over 90 per cent of all output, and the great machine of command production was dismantled only from the mid-1970s, with a growth in tenurial variety and more individualized production. However, most Scottish public housing was controlled by municipalities, whose individualism and competitiveness preserved some of the pre-1914 diversity, in a more professionally structured form.

The housing that was actually built after 1918 continued, and even accentuated, the older trends. The drive for the self-contained, functionally subdivided dwelling, with internal sanitary facilities, rose to a climax in the council housing crusade, and for the first time embraced the poorest in society, seen in Glasgow's utilitarian concrete tenements between the 1930s and 1950s; the inter-war efforts to sustain private housing in Edinburgh, by contrast, spawned large developments of bungalows. The search for light and air, energized at the turn of the century by the garden city ideology, was radically updated after 1945 by the architectural Modern Movement, with its concepts of freely planned high and low blocks in flowing open space. And the centuries-old Scottish doctrine of planned, colony-like settlement and redevelopment reached its climax in the bold, functionally segregated New Towns built by administrative diktat at East Kilbride (from 1947), Cumbernauld (from 1955), and elsewhere, and in the vast programmes of clearance and redevelopment in Glasgow and other cities in the 1960s and early 1970s.

Eventually, in the 1970s, this great drive to transform and reorder exhausted itself, and its central values of newness and planned progress were repudiated or reversed. For the first time in two centuries, Scottish housing is no longer an arena of revolution, no longer in the forefront of the nation's collective psyche.   MG

4. country seat, c.1660–present

The development of the country seat in Scotland reflects the social, economic, and cultural progress of a nation. A new period of architectural change began with the *Restoration, witnessing the first application of classicism in a building's conception. After 1660, half a century of settled, comparatively landed dominance replaced a time of religious and dynastic concerns. Leading buildings of the previous century, such as Cawdor and Winton, had employed a distinctively Scottish design ethic, one outwith the mainstream of European architecture. The ensuing, evolutionary period looked rather to the comforts and grandeur of contemporary England, but still redolent of national style, as at Hatton castle (1664–75).

Seminal in the change to pure classicism was the rebuilding of Holyrood palace (1671–8), where the intervention of Sir William Bruce in the work of John and Robert Mylne, saw the introduction of court taste to Scotland. Bruce's design for Kinross house (1685–91) brought a further advance, this time in planning, with the introduction of the so-called double-pile plan. At Hopetoun, Bruce produced a thoroughly classical great house, encouraging others to focus on updating their ancestral homes in line with European advances. Working in Bruce's wake, James Smith consolidated the new classical fashion with further exemplars, notably at Melville (1697–1703) and Yester (1699–1728). At Drumlanrig (1675–97), Smith offered a more transitional design, the swansong of the Scottish style, closely modelled on Heriot's

Hospital of 70 years earlier, but nonetheless the first to include corridors integral to the composition. By 1700, medieval trappings, French and Dutch detailing, and traditional Scottish planning were outmoded, and a thirst for classical pretensions was in place among improving landlords.

Palladianism was born in Britain through a Scot, Colen Campbell, who harnessed the aftermath of Inigo Jones and demonstrated its variety in *Vitruvius Britannicus* (1715, 1717, and 1725), inspiring subsequent generations with successful examples. The boom in country-house design from 1720 as the economy expanded enabled Palladianism to have full voice. Its leading protagonist in Scotland was William Adam, who worked with Gibbsian boldness, advancing the restrained classicism of Bruce. Adam's Mavisbank (1723), for Sir John *Clerk of Penicuik, was a watershed, establishing the compact villa as a type of country residence. He captured the new and unprecedented patronage of a burgeoning legal profession in Lord Dundas at Arniston (from 1726). At Duff House (1735–49), he continued the transitional compromise, providing a vertical Scottish castle clothed in Baroque garb. The imaginative success of his designs was shared formally with later generations in *Vitruvius Scoticus* (1810).

William Adam was the last architect of the old tradition. His sons, Robert and James, developed a more archaeologically inspired vein of classicism, notably at Dumfries House (1754–60). This new vein served the booming British economy in the closing years of the century, and flourished in the hands of landowners more confident after the demise of *Jacobitism. The revolution brought by the younger Adams lay particularly in compositional massing, interior planning, and design. Ironically, however, Robert Adam's innovative essays in castellated Gothic and castellated Georgian served to break the overriding hold of classicism by the end of the century. Adam followed the precedent of Roger Morris's Inveraray, a landmark in architectural history as the first full-blown British design in this Gothic style, and popularized it for a wider audience, notably Culzean castle (1777–92), and in more Georgian garb at Wedderburn (1771–5). James Playfair followed suit, producing Melville castle (1786–91), a battlemented, symmetrical house, equally remarkable for its more comfortable, classical interiors. James and Archibald Elliot were key exponents of castellated Gothic, evidenced at Stobo castle (1805–11) and Taymouth (1805). William Atkinson explored the genre widely, most famously at Scone palace (1803–6), while James Gillespie Graham at Duns castle (1818–22) and Sir Robert Smirke at Kinfauns (1820) showed how the idiom could become entrenched.

After the Napoleonic Wars, Scotland's aristocratic patrons were heading a strong post-Improvement agricultural economy (see ECONOMY, PRIMARY SECTOR: 2) and, inspired by Continental and English forms, sought with their *architects to express this wealth in an expanded repertoire of architectural styles. James Playfair had shown that the archaeological propriety of neoclassicism could be stretched to more original design in his French-influenced Cairness (1791–97), fusing Greek, Egyptian, and Roman forms in a bold, eclectic masterpiece. Indeed, the reaction to pure classicism was strong and the Romantic school had a willing audience. The Grecian style, embodied in *Edinburgh's New Town, inspired few country houses; William Burn's Camperdown (1821–8) was the most notable, and Archibald Simpson's Crimonmogate (1825) offered a good example of its use on a smaller scale. By the third decade of the century, Romanticism saw a flirtation with Tudor and Jacobean revivals, picturesque advances on castellated Gothic, flexible in their accommodation of the growing fashion for specialized planning. William Wilkins's Dalmeny (1818–19) launched the Tudor style but William Burn was the master, supplementing them with rational plan forms, as at Blairquhan (1824), and Falkland House (1839–44).

The baronial style, however, was undoubtedly the most prolific style employed in the 19th century, giving voice to patriotic pride. Sir Walter Scott was first to experiment in the language, employing William Atkinson to design Abbotsford (1817–24), though it was Burn again, and even more his sometime partner David Bryce, who popularized the style. Burn, at Tyninghame (1829) and Bryce at the Glen (1854–5), showed how appropriate baronial could be for the design of country houses, and Burn's commission to Robert Billings to produce *Baronial and Ecclesiastical Architecture of Scotland* (1848–52) provided a source book for the style and essential vocabulary.

In literary terms, the broad range of styles available from as early as 1833 was circulated in John Claudius Loudon's *Encyclopaedia of Cottage, Farm and Villa Architecture*. Robert Kerr publicized the vogue for segregation and specialization in *The Gentleman's House: or How to Plan Residences from the Parsonage to the Palace* (1864), at the height of the 1855–75 boom in country-house building. The birth of the architectural press from mid-century furnished clients of prospective commissions with a wealth of information on styles and planning.

The agricultural depression of the mid-1870s and the Glasgow Bank (see ECONOMY, TERTIARY SECTOR: 2) crash of 1878 coincided with the turn in the heyday of the country house. A changing social structure was emerging, bringing new patronage:

nouveau-riche industrialists entered the market. The numeric decline in servants coincided with demand for technological advances from the vacuum cleaner to central heating and electric light. By 1880, the eclecticism of the earlier century was increasingly challenged in a search for more forward-looking, convenient planning and a modern national style. Arts and Crafts design first figured in this attempt at Arisaig (1863–4), where Philip Webb's plain Gothic house demonstrated the benefits of high-quality local craftsmanship and materials. William Lethaby seized the mantle in more directly Scottish flavour at Melsetter, Hoy (1898), for a Birmingham industrialist. Sir Robert Lorimer, the best-known exponent of the style in Scotland, developed a successful formula evidenced at Ardkinglas (1906).

Large-scale essays in country-house design were not, however, absent in these years. Notable are Sir Robert Rowand Anderson's Gothic masterpiece at Mount Stuart (1878–97) for the marquess of Bute, and John Kinross's classical achievement at Manderston (1901–5). Similarly, Skibo (1899–1903) underwent substantial redevelopment by Ross & Macbeth for Andrew Carnegie, the American steel millionaire. Right up until 1914, country-house design retained a place in Scottish architecture, however much diminished. At Aultmore, C. H. B. Quennell designed a neo-Georgian house for the owner of a Moscow department store (1912–14), and James Miller built the substantial Cotswold-style mansion Kildonan (1915–23) for a military figure.

A natural lull followed the period of war: the social revolution was firmly anchored and the impetus to build rural mansions reduced to a negligible level. Nonetheless, Professor and Lady Elliot commissioned a compact, traditional yet modern country house and policy buildings from Sir Basil Spence at Broughton (1936), an evolved castle design inspired by Liberton House. Similarly, John Colville, a steel magnate, asked Spence to create a house both modern and alive with tradition, as realized at Gribloch (1937–9), an adventurous and exceptional use of Modern Movement design for a rural mansion.

After the Second World War, the hold of neo-Georgian on surviving instances of country-house design was complete but the post-war shortage of building materials (particularly reserved from luxury work) caused a delay in activity. David Style reopened the field in refronting Logan House in the 1950s. Basil Hughes took centre place in 1960 with a new house at Snaigow, for the earl of Cadogan. Claude Phillimore ventured north of the Border to remodel Gask in 1964, and Schomberg Scott replaced an earlier house by Burn at Dupplin castle, around 1970. Neo-Georgian work (reconstruction or new build), however, was not the only activity in the post-war field of the country-house market: the restoration and reconstruction of tower houses became a leading preoccupation, reviving a fashion of the late 19th century. Oliver Hill restored Inchdrewer in Banff (1965), for example, and many others ensued. Restored tower houses, or their new-build equivalents by architects such as Ian Begg, are again home to the shooting and fishing weekend, and see the modern country house return to its medieval scale without the feudal baggage. DCM

5. the Highlands

In attempting to reconstruct aspects of settlement and housing in the Highlands there is always a danger of generalizing or oversimplifying a complex situation. On the one hand, there is a commonly held belief that little survives on the ground that dates much before the middle of the 18th century; on the other, there are plans and documents that show names and locations suggesting occupation from at least the medieval period. The overall picture is complicated by the quality of the evidence; the ephemeral nature of building materials at quite late dates in some regions; the retention of archaic building techniques well into the 19th century; and the different local physical environments.

A form obviously closely adapted to the local environment is the Hebridean 'black house', of which good examples still survive at Arnol, on Lewis, on Tiree, and on other islands. The drystone walls were double, the space between inner and outer walls being filled with earth, loose stones, or dry peat, providing insulation against the inevitable gaps in the drystone wall. The thatched roof did not hang over the outer wall, but stopped on the inner wall edge, so that the run-off from the roof ran into the drain provided by the filled gap between inner and outer walls and the absence of overhanging eaves reduced wind resistance. This, along with the hip-ended roof, gave the black house a streamlined appearance, which was the intention in these regions exposed to the Atlantic winds.

The form of dwelling most often seen as typical of the Highlands was the longhouse or byre-dwelling. This, in its later 18th-century form, was a drystone built structure with an interior division into living quarters and space for cattle. The floor was usually of stamped earth and the fireplace in the older versions was in the centre of the floor, with an aperture in the roof to let the smoke out. The walls, being of unmortared stones, would not bear the downthrust weight of the roofing, which was usually supported on wooden cruck couples

springing from floor level or from a slot partway up the drystone wall.

William Marshall, writing about habitations in *A General View of the Agriculture of the Central Highlands of Scotland* in 1794, noted:

At present, the building material is stone; but no cement, as yet, is in use, except in particular cases. The houses and office buildings of ordinary farmers are of dry stone; the dwelling-house being stopt on the inside with loam, to prevent the wind from blowing through the walls; which are seldom more than five or six feet [1.5 m or 1.8 m] high; perhaps without glass in the windows (now more commonly the huts of the cottars; some of them wretched habitations indeed), and doorways so low that even a middle-sized man must stoop, not into the houses only, but into the barn.

In a detailed account of the primitive roof construction, he noted that

The roof is set on with 'couples', or large principal rafters, stept in the walls two or three feet [0.6 m or 0.9 m] above the foundations; generally upon large stones set to receive their feet. Upon these couples, lines of 'pantrees', or purlines are fixed, and, resting on these, rough boughs . . . upon these, 'divot', or thin turf, laid on in the manner of slates; and upon this sod covering, a coat of thatch; composed of straw, rushes, heather or fern

His account is valuable in that it also records the type of housing in use in much earlier times:

Formerly sod huts were the common habitations of the tenantry of the Central Highlands, and they are still in use in the more northern districts. Those huts were built with sods, or thick turf, taken from the pasture lands, and having remained a few years in the capacity of walls, were pulled down and spread over the arable fields as manure

The accounts of travellers, landscape drawings, estate papers and ministers writing in the OSA about the earlier 18th century seem often to be describing houses and other structures made of perishable materials rather than stone walls, and this will obviously affect the forms of surviving evidence the modern fieldworker should expect to find.

Travellers' descriptions may not be completely reliable, especially where the word 'primitive' often covers a complete ignorance of local environmental, economic, and social conditions, but they do indicate a general recognition of the impermanent nature of many buildings before the 19th century. Captain Edward Burt, an English officer with Wade's army in the Highlands in the earlier 18th century, described Highland houses as resembling heaps of dirt. Again, the appearance of buildings of turf or wattle might have suggested dirt heaps to someone more used to stone-built structures. Outsiders might also have described structures that by function were necessarily temporary, such as the bothies used for summer transhumance on the shieling grounds. Some of these may have been assumed to be permanent houses. It might be expected that very little of this could survive as field evidence, but some early structures of turf have endured to recent times. An example is the oval turf house excavated at Macewen's castle, Kilfinan, in Argyllshire, in use c.1500. Substantial remains of this type, however, are infrequent and decayed turf structures must in general be difficult to locate and identify.

Some remains may have been given a greater antiquity than they deserve because of the retention of old building techniques and materials down to recent times. An example of this late survival, but one where the date of final use is known, can be seen at an excavated site at Rosal in Strathnaver, Sutherland, where turf walls on drystone founda-tions, narrow interiors, and roofs supported on cruck couples springing from ground level were in use into the second decade of the 19th century. Donald Sage, minister in the area at the time of the *Clearances of the Highlands and Islands, noted that some of the houses burned down in 1819 had walls built of alternate layers of turf and stone.

The remains visible now in Highland and Hebridean landscapes show remarkable adaptations to what could be a very difficult environment and are perhaps only a last instalment in stone of a much longer history of occupation. Although in some regions and at some periods houses and other buildings may have been impermanent in structure, there is good reason to believe that the existence of the settlements themselves was not temporary.

AM

iconoclasm of the *Reformation has left an indelible mark on Scottish history. The country's medieval churches and abbeys seem to have been as richly endowed with paintings, sculpture, and other furnishings as in any country of similar wealth and population, yet that heritage has almost completely vanished (see CULTURE: 3–4; ILLUMINATED MANUSCRIPTS; RELIGIOUS LIFE: 2). The motives of the iconoclasts were no doubt mixed, but their actions were clearly justified by the Second Commandment which states 'Thou shalt not make unto thee any graven image, or any likeness of any thing that is in heaven above or on the earth beneath or in the water under the earth.' When so much of the drive to reform was the result of access to the Bible and obedience to its tenets in place of those of the priests and bishops, it seemed a clear instruction. It was of course also reinforced by the way in which the furnishing and imagery of the churches represented the wealth and power of the old order. The earliest recorded incident of iconoclasm dates from 1533 in Glasgow. Thereafter the fashion spread with the new ideas till in 1541, during the reign of *James V, an Act was passed against the destruction of images. Nevertheless in 1543 there was a major iconoclastic riot in Dundee. In 1545 George Wishart preached against images, causing more damage, and famously at Perth in 1559 *Knox himself used iconoclasm as a means of uniting his audience in concerted action against Mary of Guise. After the Reformation was established, iconoclasm was systematic. There were, however, other factors. The changes in the form of worship and in ecclesiastical organization (see CHURCH INSTITUTIONS: 3) meant that not only the abbeys and monasteries, but also many churches became redundant and were allowed to fall into disrepair as was the case with St Andrews cathedral. The English invasions of the 1540s (see ROUGH WOOING) were also peculiarly destructive. Reformation iconoclasm was, however, specifically directed at religious art. Responsibility for the parallel loss of much secular art and architecture, as for example Linlithgow and Falkland palaces, cannot be laid at the door of the reformers, but was primarily the consequence of the subsequent removal of king and court to England which took with it the only institution with a vested interest in preserving what is now called heritage.   DM

illuminated manuscripts. 'Illumination', the decoration of manuscripts with coloured pigments and, often, gold, appears typically at the beginnings and divisions of texts in the form of initials, frequently with figures, and in the form of pictures (miniatures). Rich illumination was characteristic of important texts, such as service books, and of wealthy institutional or individual owners. Given the immense destruction of books during the Scottish *Reformation, our knowledge of the illuminated manuscripts of medieval Scotland (see CULTURE: 3) is necessarily very imperfect. In early medieval Britain and *Ireland book production was largely monastic. Books were decorated in the shared Insular or Hiberno-Saxon artistic style (based primarily on a fusion of the decorative traditions of Celtic and Anglo-Saxon *metalwork) and variants of this style were probably employed in the monasteries of the Scottish, Northumbrian, Pictish, and British kingdoms of Scotland (see RELIGIOUS LIFE: 1). The amazingly rich and inventive decoration and calligraphy of the Book of Kells, an 8th-century Gospel book, are probably the work of monks on *Iona. The less sophisticated work in the 9th- or 10th-century Book of Deer came perhaps from the north-east. Illumination in derivatives of the Insular style may have continued into the 12th century in parts of Scotland, but new ecclesiastical contacts established in the time of Malcolm III 'Canmore' (Mael Coluim mac Donnchada) and St *Margaret and their sons, especially *David I, introduced new styles of illumination from England and France. During the 12th and 13th centuries styles Scottish illumination seems to have been similar to that in England. The images of kings in the initial of the Kelso Charter (c.1159) and the rather less distinguished 13th-century Lesmahagow Missal hint at what has been lost. Already in the 13th century some wealthy patrons looked abroad to order fine books of devotion illuminated in the latest Gothic styles. Notable examples are the Iona and the Douce Psalters, probably from

Oxford and Paris respectively, and the northern French bible acquired by Devorguilla *Balliol for her new foundation, Sweetheart abbey. Other illuminated books may have come to Scotland as a result of marriages, like the Murthly Hours, or have been acquired by students (see NORTHERN EUROPE: MONKS AND SCHOLARS) studying abroad. In the later Middle Ages the most common privately owned devotional book amongst the laity was the book of hours and many of these bore devotional images, sometimes including Scottish saints, and rich decoration. The most desirable were imported from Flanders (for example, the Hours of *James IV and Margaret Tudor) or northern France (for example, the Playfair Hours). The 15th-century French Virgil made, apparently, for a Scottish royal couple and Bishop Gavin Dunbar's epistolary (Antwerp 1527) exemplify other types of imported illuminated book. A modest number of surviving books and some documentation bear witness to illuminators working in Scotland during the 15th and 16th centuries. Survivals include the effective, if slightly old-fashioned, historical illustrations in the Cambridge manuscript (1440s) of Walter Bower's *Scotichronicon* (see HISTORIANS: 1); a book of vernacular poetry including works of Chaucer and the *Kingis Quair* written for the Sinclair family shortly after 1488; and the missal, psalter, and hours manuscripts connected with the Arbuthnott family (c.1491). The illumination of the book of hours known as the Lundy Primer is a provincial imitation of Flemish work of c.1500. Documented illuminators include Sir Thomas Galbraith, clerk of the Stirling Chapel Royal, who worked for James IV, and a Cistercian monk (1513) at Culross, a monastery that undertook some commercial book production. It seems that the Scottish market was too small to support professional lay illuminators (see also FRANCE; LOW COUNTRIES).   JH

immigration, Irish. Large-scale migration from Ireland to Scotland expanded rapidly from c.1800 because of declining opportunities in Ireland and growing labour demands from Scottish agriculture and manufacturing. By 1841 the numbers of Irish-born in Scotland had risen to 126,321 (4.8 per cent of the population), concentrated particularly in the burgeoning industrial areas where, with their children born in Scotland, they made up a large proportion of the population in towns like *Glasgow, Greenock, Paisley, and *Dundee (see POPULATION PATTERNS: 2). After the famine of 1846 the numbers of Irish-born jumped dramatically to 207,367 by 1851 (7.2 per cent of the population), remaining at around that figure throughout the 19th century (although as a declining portion of the total Scottish population—4.6 per cent, for instance by 1900)

since when it has fallen steadily, especially since the 1920s with the inter-war decline in the heavy industries.

These Irish and their descendants, therefore, make up a large proportion of present-day Scottish society and have played a significant part in shaping its modern history. Any account of how Scotland has become the sort of society it is today has to take their story into account. Yet, although Irish settlement is a central aspect of what kind of society Scotland was becoming, even today their acceptance has never quite been total and they pose uneasy questions as to what being Scottish means in modern Scotland. It is not unusual in everyday acquaintanceships for people with Irish names and background, especially if, as is generally the case, they are also Roman Catholics (see ROMAN CATHOLIC COMMUNITY), to be regarded as somehow not so indigenous as those with traditional Highland or Lowland surnames, even if their families have been settled here for well over a century—as long a period often as, say, the Norman incomers who fought the Wars of *Independence in the 1290s and early 1300s. It has to be said, however, that this ambivalence also often applies to their own self-perception of how far they fit into Scottish life.

The reasons for this are complex. It is partly due to what the Irish incomers were associated with: the dirty jobs of the industrial revolution, in textile factories, as labourers building canals, docks, and railways, in coal mines and ironworks (see ECONOMY: 4)—in short, with that industrial process which was threatening all the existing landmarks of community, church, and law with which the Scots had identified themselves up to then. In addition, they posed an economic threat in the competition for jobs, although it could be argued that their ready labour speeded the creation of the new jobs needed to employ the growing population of Scots. Most of them, too, had attitudes to British authority, law, and behaviour which disturbed their hosts: defiance of the law was not always regarded as a crime and poverty often forced an acceptance of standards of living and behaviour at odds with Scottish aspirations to respectability and getting on (see HOUSING: 3; LIVING STANDARDS: 3). Above all, most of them were Roman Catholics and maintained a firm attachment to their faith as a security for their nationality and personal dignity in a corrosive and often evil industrial world.

In a society as consciously Protestant as Scotland's, with a reformed tradition quite distinct from that of England, yet also characterized by a deep historical antagonism to Rome, this made for inevitable difficulties in adjustment (see NATIONAL IDENTITY: 5). Although many more Irish went to England, their impact was less concentrated there, accounting for only 3 per cent of the population by 1861 compared with 6.7 per cent in Scotland. Finally, since almost all the Irish migrating to Scotland came from Ulster, a significant minority (at least a quarter) were Protestants who brought their own symbols of identity with them in an aggressive Orangeism which led to much communal disturbance in industrial Scotland over the succeeding centuries. Popular stereotypes grew up which defined the Irish as cheap labour undercutting the natives, in thrall to a superstitious religion dominated by priests, primarily concerned with Irish issues, and whose growing presence forced hard-working, law-abiding Scottish working people to emigrate to better opportunities overseas.

The process of their absorption into Scottish society, however, was more complex than these myths suggest. For one thing, there was a continuous effort made by leading elements in industrial Scotland to encourage them in developing educational and welfare institutions necessary for adjustment to the standards of the host society (see RESPECTABLE CULTURE; TEMPERANCE). Among these should be noted the Glasgow Catholic Schools Society of 1817 and the constant acknowledgement of the good work done by religious orders, especially of nuns among their poor. Nor were they aliens. After the Irish Union of 1800–01 they and the Scots were both part of the same United Kingdom. In many ways, the Irish faced the same problems of how to adjust to the soulless individualism in industrial society as the Scots, and often adopted the same expedients of building up defences in local, voluntary self-help groups such as temperance organizations—the Irish Capuchin Fr. Mathew was a figure respected by Irish and Scots alike—and in charitable ventures. By the later 19th century they had created an impressive structure of schools, parish and welfare groups, newspapers, and political organizations, which provided a vibrant and varied social life. Equally, far from replacing an indigenous Scottish workforce, many of them, too, were also part of that wider flow of labour passing through Britain and across the transatlantic world in search of economic opportunity, with Scotland simply a temporary staging post in which to earn enough to reach their ultimate destination: America (see CANADA; USA).

Also, while communal frictions accompanied their growing presence in Scotland, the wonder is that, given the Scottish cultural context, anti-Irish outbursts were not more common. Comparative perspectives reveal, in fact, that instances of sustained anti-Catholic rioting were often greater in similar industrial areas in England. Curiously, the most virulent signs of opposition did not come until the 20th century when there were prolonged calls, particularly from groups within the Presbyterian churches, for an end to Irish immigration and even repatriation. Much of the resentment behind this reflected the lack of confidence among the governing elite in Scotland caused by the industrial decline of the post-war era; the recent granting of separate provision inside the public educational system to Catholics; and the political turmoils which had seen the emergence of the Irish Free State, the decline of the Liberals (see LIBERALISM), and the emergence of Labour (see LABOURISM), the solid block of Irish settlement in the west of Scotland being seen as helping the latter party's breakthrough.

But permanent settlement in Scotland without abandoning their roots could also create bridges as well as barriers. Even in the early 19th century Irish immigrants had been politically active on issues like Catholic Emancipation and Repeal of the Corn Laws which linked them to reform elements in Scottish life. They also helped to swell the existing numbers of indigenous Scottish Roman Catholics (with whom their relationships also were not always easy). Although the later contribution of Italians, Poles, and Lithuanians must be acknowledged, the great bulk of the nearly half-million Catholics in Scotland by 1900 was due to Irish immigration. Religious and national interests intertwined to weave a strong political fabric. This meant mobilizing their voting strength to protect their educational and social issues in local government. By the 1880s they had come to form an important part of the Liberal equation in Scottish political life and what direction it would take. John Ferguson, a Protestant middle-class publisher from Ulster, who once famously remarked that he never realized he was an Irishman until he came to live in Glasgow, a man in every feature the opposite of the Irish immigrant stereotype, might be regarded as the most remarkable political leader of his community until the emergence of John Wheatley and James Connolly in the early 1900s. Through such men immigrant support for *Irish Home Rule could be combined with social politics. The movement of the Catholic vote towards Labour is often portrayed as occurring at the time of the Great War but already in the 1890s steady links with Labour were being created at a local level especially in the trade-union field. Wheatley's efforts to create a socialist movement within the Irish community was never condemned by the Scottish clerical authorities and indeed was tacitly accepted by them. The new Catholic social thinking represented by *Rerum Novarum* in 1891 had already been anticipated in many ways by the Irish in Scotland, not least in their links with Scottish land reformers through Michael Davitt.

The other factor which helped integrate the Irish into mainstream Scottish life was education. Given the separate nature of Catholic schools both before and after 1918 (see SCHOOLS AND SCHOOLING: 2, 4) this might seem surprising. Yet in other respects, being Irish in Scotland meant that they and their children had to conform and aspire to educational standards which were higher than those they would have experienced in either England or Ireland. The effort to keep up and provide efficient schools eventually forced them into accepting the *Scottish Office's policy in 1918 of a place within the public sector with safeguards as to their religious ethos. The determination to regard this as a basic principle in the 20th century is often seen as anachronistic, especially as school education has developed in ways not foreseen at that time. However, viewed as an acknowledgment of their constitutional right to be regarded as a group with certain values which ought to be respected in modern Scotland, the symbolism becomes more relevant—a sign of equal citizenship after a century of so much religious, and racial, discrimination.

It could be said, too, that as a group they have made a valuable cultural contribution judging by the number of Irish names in art, drama, and music in 20th-century Scotland. Writers like Patrick McGill or William McIlvanney have made incisive critiques of Scottish life (see CULTURE: 25). However, there is truth in the criticism that, as a distinctive group, Irish immigrants and their descendants have failed to realize the richness of their cultural potential by making a more consciously determined effort to become part of the country in which they have found their home. The reasons for this may lie in the very real struggle for daily existence which was the norm for the majority until relatively recently. Living in crowded tenements and trying to keep a good timekeeping record at work, the daily struggle, mainly by women, to maintain a decent family life, was in itself an achievement, but it has been an energy-sapping process.

Since the 1960s there has been an increasing movement, through higher educational opportunities, into a broader life. Perhaps it is too soon yet to judge the results of this. Despite the great increase in graduates from this Irish background, very little focused intellectual debate on issues which affect them seems to have yet emerged. The fields of history and philosophy have been occupied by only a few workers. Despite their undoubted voting influence, especially on the modern Labour Party, leadership positions have been slow to emerge, perhaps because of the social and economic restrictions under which they have laboured for so long. Representation as local councillors was meagre up until the 1940s, and as MPs until the middle 1960s. However, the growing European dimension is reshaping the above perspectives. How to view them will be a measure of the maturity of the Scotland of the 21st century as well as the role played by the descendants of the 19th-century Irish immigrants therein.   JMcC

Independence, Wars of. This is the term usually given to the period of warfare resulting from the attempted subjugation of the Scottish kingdom by its southern neighbour, England, between 1286 and c.1353. It is not meant to imply that Scotland first gained its independence as a result. Despite a largely amicable relationship between the two kingdoms for much of the 13th century, the unexpected death of King Alexander III (1249–86) of Scotland on 18/19 March 1286 provided an opportunity for King Edward I of England to become more involved in Scottish affairs. Alexander's direct heir was his young granddaughter, Margaret, the 'Maid of Norway', although more distant male claimants threatened her peaceful succession. A group of six guardians were chosen from among the elites to govern the country and were generally successful in maintaining order in the meantime. However, Margaret's death on c.26 September 1290 scuppered plans for her marriage to Edward I's heir, Edward of Caernarfon, foreshadowing a union of the crowns of England and Scotland, an eventuality deemed necessary by all sides for the sake of the longer-term peace.

The need to choose a new king ensured a continued reliance on Edward I, who now pressed long-standing English claims of overlordship over Scotland in return for his advice and support. The Scots were in desperate need of a king to prevent the outbreak of civil war and remained unable, because of medieval convention and political division, to choose one for themselves. They thus had little choice but to rely on their neighbour, England, as they had done in times of difficulty in the past.

Between May and June 1291 Edward tried to extract a general admission of his overlordship from the Scottish political community but had to content himself with individual acknowledgements from the thirteen candidates for the throne. However, it was really a choice between two: John Balliol of Barnard castle, lord of Galloway, and Robert Bruce of Annandale, 'the Competitor'. The process whereby Edward's court reached a decision, known as the *Great Cause, was not completed until November 1291; John Balliol was duly crowned king of Scots on 30 November but only after having sworn homage and fealty to Edward I (see BALLIOL FAMILY).

Balliol's reign, while conventional enough in domestic terms, was dogged by Edward's determination to enforce his feudal rights as over-lord. The Scots soon realized that only war could prevent the wholesale erosion of the kingdom's sovereignty and on 23 October 1295 a treaty of mutual aid was agreed with France (see FRANCO-SCOTTISH RELATIONS: I), England's principal enemy. In March 1296 a Scottish force raided south of the Border, closely followed by the invasion of Scotland by a large English army. *Berwick, which was first to defy Edward's authority, was captured on 30 March and many of its inhabitants killed; a Scottish army then met an English force under John de Warenne, earl of Surrey, at Dunbar on 27 April, where it was defeated and many members of the Scottish nobility captured. King John had submitted to Edward by 10 July, was stripped of his kingship, and imprisoned in London; Scotland was then placed under direct English government led by Surrey as royal lieutenant and Hugh Cressingham as treasurer.

Despite initial quiescence prompting Edward to return to the fight with France on 22 August 1297, Scotland was already erupting spontaneously in revolt, even though many of the nobility were in prison in England. By August 1297, this had coalesced behind the combined forces of Andrew Murray the younger of Petty and the unknown figure of William *Wallace, who had led uprisings in the north-east and the south-west respectively. On 11 September 1297 this Scottish army defeated Surrey and Cressingham's force at the battle of Stirling Bridge and subsequently cleared Scotland of all English officials with the exceptions of the garrisons in Berwick and Roxburgh castles. Unfortunately, this defeat also united the English, who had been on the verge of civil war, behind their absent king, an uneasy unity which lasted until Edward's death. The latter returned to Scotland on 1 July 1298, defeating Wallace at Falkirk on 22 July, predominantly through the use of archers against the Scottish pikemen, arranged into schiltroms or hedgehog-like formations. However, this time victory in battle did not bring Scotland to heel and the following years witnessed a slow, painstaking war of attrition between Edward's administration in Scotland and the one operated on behalf of King John. This last was led by a succession of guardians, beginning with Wallace and thereafter usually including John Comyn of Badenoch, leader of Scotland's most politically important family (see COMYN FAMILY).

By 1303, the English could claim control over south-eastern Scotland and an increasingly firm grip over the south-west. Equally, the Scots had been able to govern the north-east of the kingdom without interference and had restricted Edward's authority to the south. However, the war had taken its toll: the English increasingly resisted paying for annual campaigns and many Scots in the south could see that the English king was better than no king at all. After a successful Scottish diplomatic offensive, particularly in Rome, King John had almost returned to Scotland with French backing in 1302, prompting Robert Bruce (see ROBERT I), earl of Carrick, grandson of Robert Bruce 'the Competitor', to submit to Edward I by 16 February 1302. However, the diplomatic situation had turned in England's favour by 20 May 1303, the date of an Anglo-French treaty that excluded the Scots. Given Balliol's continued absence and the fact that an English army was able to cross the Forth into north-east Scotland in June 1303, the Comyn-led Scottish government decided to sue for peace on reasonable terms by 9 February 1304, a sign of comparative success in itself.

The building of the peace, which included the restitution of lands to former Scottish rebels and the capture and execution of the resolutely defiant William Wallace on 23 August 1305, was completed by 15 September 1305. Six months later, on 10 February 1305, Robert Bruce, earl of Carrick, killed John Comyn of Badenoch, who presumably did not support the former's regal pretensions, and seized the Scottish throne. Bruce's actions appalled many Scots who abhorred the violent death of the leader of the Scottish patriotic movement before 1304 and found it difficult to accept a new king while Balliol was still alive. Support for Bruce was therefore extremely limited and by September 1306 he was on the run from combined English and Scottish forces after a series of defeats, including Methven on 19 June and Dalry in July or August. Edward's wrath at such treachery resulted in a flood of executions of Bruce supporters, including noblemen, ironically providing some sympathy for King Robert.

Bruce returned to Scotland with a handful of men in February 1307 and had some military success in the south-west, including the battle of Loudoun Hill on *c*.10 May. However, Edward's death on 7 July 1307, negating Scottish oaths of allegiance to the English crown, proved crucial in bringing him support. England's internal problems, caused partly by the debt incurred by the Scottish wars, meant that no English army crossed the Border till September 1310, to little effect.

With success breeding some success, King Robert turned his attention to defeating his Comyn enemies in the north-east, while Edward Bruce, his brother, and James Douglas targeted the south-west. Using an effective combination of brute force and willingness to compromise, his most implacable enemies had been forced into exile in England by 1309, though many continued to sit on the fence.

Bruce also enjoyed considerable support from the Scottish clergy whose formidable propaganda skills were employed to justify his position as king in the courts of Europe. The first parliament of the reign was held at *St Andrews on 16–17 March 1309.

By 1313, King Robert gave the Scottish nobility a year to decide whether or not to support him. In the meantime, he continued to clear Scotland of garrisons controlled by his enemies, rendering castles unusable, and began a policy of raiding in south-eastern Scotland and northern England. King Edward II had, meantime, re-established a consensus within English politics and was able to summon an army to deal with the threat to the English garrison in that most strategic of castles, *Stirling. Though Bruce left his options open, battle was joined at Bannockburn, near Stirling, on 23–24 June 1314, when detailed preparations, high morale, disciplined leadership, and an element of pre-emption won the day for the Scots. Many Scottish waverers now finally accepted Bruce as king, while Edward II's standing was further diminished, especially in the north of England, now completely defenceless against Scottish attacks.

Bannockburn, however, did not win the war. Though Scotland was effectively free of the enemy, with the exception of Berwick and parts of the Western Isles, Bruce needed Edward to admit Scotland's independence and his rights as king. His policy in subsequent years was directed specifically to force such an admission from the English king. Militarily speaking, the Scots dominated the British Isles in this period through the systematic extortion of blackmail from northern England and the opening-up of a second front in Ireland. Edward Bruce, claiming to be high king of *Ireland, launched his first campaign there in May 1315, partly in order to protect Scotland's west coast from enemy attack and perhaps also to concentrate Edward II's mind on peace. He was killed near Dundalk on 14 October 1318.

To make matters worse, Robert I's desire to recapture Berwick resulted in the threat of excommunication by the pope, who wanted English and Scottish participation in a crusade. The Declaration of Arbroath—supposedly written on 6 April 1320 by the Scottish nobility but in reality expertly drafted by a cleric on their behalf—was intended to justify Scotland's, and King Robert's, fight for independence and succeeded in bringing some improvement in Scoto-papal relations, including the recognition of Bruce's kingship in January 1324. However, within months of the Declaration's dispatch, a number of Scottish nobles were implicated in a plot to assassinate King Robert, probably on behalf of King John's son, Edward Balliol. Despite his considerable military success, Bruce always sat far less securely on the throne than his propaganda or some subsequent accounts would like us to believe.

A thirteen-year truce negotiated on 30 May 1323 presumably seemed the best King Robert could hope for and the birth of his son, David II, on 5 March 1324 also helped to bring a degree of security to Scotland. However, English politics dictated succeeding events. The instability of the regency government for the young Edward III, following the deposition of Edward II on 20 January 1327, brought about peace negotiations that resulted in the Treaty of Edinburgh on 17 March 1328, a categorical admission of Scottish independence. King Robert enjoyed a year of peace before his death on 7 June 1329.

This, however, was not the end of the wars. Edward III who, like most of the English, abhorred this treaty concluded while Bruce was ill, was determined to renew the war. He could not do so openly but instead promoted the interests of the Disinherited, a disparate group of men with only one common interest: they all had claims to lands and/or titles in Scotland which had been laid aside because of Scottish/Bruce success and made apparently irreversible in the 1328 treaty. Although the prime mover initially was Sir Henry Beaumont, who claimed the earldom of Buchan through his wife, Alice Comyn, niece of the last earl, John Comyn, the man with most to gain was Edward Balliol, son of King John. Balliol had been courted in England as early as 1320 but with a minor now on the Scottish throne, preparations were soon underway for a Balliol comeback. All Bruce's loyal lieutenants were dead by 1332, leaving Scotland without strong leadership and the initial invasion, launched in August 1332, met with success. After the defeat of a Scottish force at Dupplin near Perth on 12 August, Balliol was duly made king at *Scone on 24 September; acknowledging the (so-far) covert support of Edward III, he made his gratitude concrete by granting most of southern Scotland to his patron in December.

Balliol's position was far from secure, however, prompting the English king to intervene directly in 1333. The first target was Berwick, restored to Scottish control by Bruce in 1318. The defeat of a Scottish relieving force, led by the guardian, Archibald Douglas, at Halidon Hill on 19 July 1333, saw the town change hands once more. Desperation began to take hold in the Bruce camp, to such an extent that by May 1334 the young King David was in exile in France and the puppet King Edward ruled in southern Scotland at least. Edward III had re-established English control and was proving to be at least as ruthless as his grandfather. He was also developing the techniques—essentially the combination of men-at-arms and archers—which would prove so effective in France.

Once again, however, Scotland managed to find effective leadership in its hour of need, this time in the person of Andrew Murray, son of the Scottish leader at Stirling Bridge in 1297. As guardian, Murray defeated David de Strathbogie, earl of Atholl, a leading member of the Disinherited, at Culblean in Deeside on 30 November 1335 and re-established effective guerrilla tactics to force the invaders back. By 1337, Balliol had an administration in name only and the Disinherited controlled only parts of the south-west. Equally importantly, and despite a series of English campaigns up until 1338, Edward III was now being drawn into a full-blown war with France. Scottish success was crowned by the return of 17-year-old David Bruce in 1341.

But, as with the post-Bannockburn era, the war was not yet officially over and King David felt impelled, partly out of gratitude to France and partly to secure an admission of his kingship from Edward III, to raid the north of England. On one such raid on 17 October 1346, he was captured at Neville's Cross in County Durham. He remained an English prisoner until October 1357, but at least the negotiations that resulted in his release also recognized him as king of Scots, one year after Edward Balliol finally gave up his claims.

The wars had finally staggered to an end, but at some considerable cost, both in economic terms and, more enduringly, in the depth of the bitter enmity that now characterized the relationship between Scotland and England. The *Borders became effectively a war zone for centuries thereafter, even without the excuse provided by sporadic official invasions. The Scots had forged a firm *national identity for themselves out of the crucible of war, while England had refined its already impressive military machine. Equally importantly, the propaganda and myth-making which had played such a vital role in sustaining the war, especially on behalf of King Robert I, became indistinguishable from fact in both official and popular history. It is impossible to deny the importance of the Wars of Independence to Scotland's history (see HISTORIANS: 1), just as it is difficult to envisage how the country might have developed if it had not taken place. However, while the period has provided heroes and villains aplenty, the reality is far more complex. (See also ANGLO-SCOTTISH RELATIONS: 2; ARMY: 1; KINGSHIP: 3–4; WARFARE, WEAPONS, AND FORTIFICATIONS: 1.)   FW

Indian subcontinent. Food, clothing, and many other aspects of Scottish lifestyles have been influenced by the centuries-old relationship between India and Scotland. Many of the clothes that

Scots wear today are not merely based on Indian styles but often, as in the 18th century, they are manufactured in the Indian subcontinent and brought here by the collaborative efforts of Indian and British traders. The very first merchants to do this, in bulk, were members of the EIC, founded in 1601. The EIC based its operations in London, but Scots merchants and seamen played their part, especially following an unsuccessful attempt to set up a rival organization based in Edinburgh in 1695. The Scottish Africa and India Company, as it was called, was founded by Sir William Paterson and raised the enormous sum of £400,000 by public subscription in Scotland. All of this was eventually lost after vigorous lobbying against the company by the EIC in London and an ill-conceived attempt to found a colony at *Darien in the isthmus of Panama, and thereby pioneer a new route to India. When attacked by Spain, King William of Orange refused assistance (fearful of a possible alliance between Spain and France), and the defeated and disease-ridden settlement was subsequently abandoned with the loss of 2,000 lives, fuelling anti-English feeling in Scotland. The Scottish Company itself limped on but was virtually bankrupt by 1706.

Amongst the earliest Scots adventurers in India at the service of the EIC was Alexander Hamilton, who sailed east on the merchant ship *The Shrewsbury* in 1688. Hamilton subsequently published one of the earliest available accounts of life in the British bases at Calcutta, Madras, and Bombay. Amongst the soldiers, Sir Hector Munro was most prominent in the 18th century, commanding a force which defeated the Mughal army in the important battle of Buxar in 1764. In later years Scots came to play a still more important role in the EIC, and in India, when the activities of the EIC were brought under the supervision of parliament. It was Henry *Dundas, Solicitor-General and Lord Advocate under Prime Minister William Pitt and the first Secretary of State for India, who introduced the legislation that made this possible in 1783. Under his patronage growing numbers of Scots became involved in managing the Indian territories in the EIC's service from the 1780s onwards.

The number of Scots who served in India was disproportionate to their numbers. The reasons why so many Scots went to India are complex. Scots regiments were of course always favoured by the British *army, especially when service was needed in difficult conditions and for long periods abroad. The Scottish middle classes also found employment in the empire in large numbers, partly for lack of opportunities at home, but partly also due to the quality of the Scottish educational system, with *universities such as Edinburgh and St Andrews turning out large numbers of talented, adventurous, and highly qualified young graduates each year, for whom Calcutta or Lahore seemed no less remote or appealing a destination than London. The dissenting, radical tradition within Scottish society produced many of the more humane and popular administrators and officials within the *British Empire. The Scots middle classes were also great promoters of missionary work (see MISSIONS OVERSEAS) and of liberal causes, such as the abolition of slavery. Thus the City Fathers of Edinburgh indicated their support for one inveterate Indian campaigner against slavery, the Bengali businessman Dwarkanath Tagore (grandfather of the great Nobel-prize winning Indian patriot Rabindranath Tagore), by awarding him the freedom of the City, a considerable honour in those days (he also had an audience with the queen at Holyrood), when Tagore paid a visit to Edinburgh in 1842.

The names of John Malcolm, Mountstuart Elphinstone (governor of Bombay from 1819 to 1827), and Thomas Munro are among the best-known liberal administrators who shaped the Empire in India in its earliest years, the last developing the important *ryotwari* or peasant-based system of land revenue settlement, beginning in Madras and soon spreading to other parts of India. All were influenced by the Orientalist school who pioneered the study of Indian arts, sciences, and cultures in Britain. One of the more famous Orientalists in Scotland was Sir William Robertson, principal of Edinburgh University from 1762 to 1793, who wrote one of the first serious studies of India in the English language (see HISTORIANS: 3). In it he ranked Indian civilization alongside those of ancient Greece and Egypt and warned against European interference (an idea later on vigorously contested by those whose material interests urged a different point of view). It is no surprise that, in the wake of this tradition, Edinburgh University founded one of the very first centres in the UK for the study of Sanskrit, the ancient Indian language, and soon after the very first Indian Students Association for the benefit of Indian students studying in Scotland. In parallel, the efforts of Alexander Duff, sent as a minister to Calcutta by the Church of Scotland in 1829, helped establish the first western-style universities and colleges, supported by government grant, in Calcutta, Bombay, and Madras.

For the most part, British rule in India in the 19th century was a matter of governance for its own sake, at minimum cost and at maximum profit, but there were still many Scots who contributed to Scottish–Indian relations, some for better, some for worse, and who are remembered to this day—not least the 8 out of the 38 Indian viceroys and governor-generals between 1774 and 1947 who were of Scottish origin. The first of these was Gilbert Elliott, later first earl of Minto, who became governor-general in 1807. He was soon followed by James Ramsay, first marquess of Dalhousie, who was governor-general between 1847 and 1856 in the fateful years leading up to the great Indian uprising of 1857. Sir Colin Campbell, the son of a Glasgow carpenter and hero of the Crimean war, led the army of 20,000 that helped suppress the insurrection. Soon after, the EIC was wound up and India came directly under the control of the British crown. The earl of Dufferin (1884–8) was one of the more successful viceroys, or queen's representatives, in India that followed, governing at a time of relative stability and growth. Both the seventh and ninth earls of Elgin, James and Victor Bruce, subsequently served as viceroy. The last Scot to hold this highest of all public offices was Lord Linlithgow, who as viceroy from 1936 to 1943 played an important role in the transition to Independence. Linlithgow oversaw the cabinet mission of 1942 and the suppression of Mahatma Gandhi's great 'Quit India' campaign in that same year. Most unfortunately, it is said, his inadequate response to the famine in Bengal in 1943 (which cost the lives of some 3 million Indians), fuelled anti-British feeling and added to the climate of resistance that precipitated the final British withdrawal in 1947.

In a more constructive fashion, Scots helped to build railways and canals, worked through town planning and medical provision to improve the quality of life in India's burgeoning cities, and pioneered the development of the tea and coffee plantations. Jardine Matheson was one of the most important tea traders, as well as dealing in banking, insurance, and the supply of opium to the Far East in the early 19th century. Later traders and founders of tea plantations in India and Ceylon (now Sri Lanka) included James Finlay of Glasgow and Thomas *Lipton. Liptons Limited became the world's largest tea company by the end of the 19th century. Both of these firms continue trading to this day. Among the more important Calcutta-based commodity trading firms was Andrew Yule & Co, one of fourteen firms run by Scots in Calcutta by 1813. Also to be mentioned are Patrick Geddes, the architect and botanist; Colonel Richard Baird Smith, the canal builder; and finally the great mill owners from Dundee, such as Thomas Duff & Co., who established Calcutta's jute industry, and made *Dundee and Calcutta the world's principal producers of this indispensable commodity, used in sacking, rope, carpet making, and many other products. Dundee owes its size and prosperity until modern times almost entirely to this one commodity. Likewise, *Glasgow largely owed its prosperity until recent times to the benefits of imperial trade.

Culturally, there is no limit to the contribution that India has made to Scottish life. Echoes of Mughal designs are to be seen in Scottish architecture (see ARCHITECTURAL STYLES AND FEATURES), Indian peppers and spices abound in Scottish foods, and the *Scots language is filled with words, such as pyjama, bungalow, thug, shampoo, juggernaut, and 'peely-wally', all imported from the Indian subcontinent—often by servicemen. Chinaware too, first imported by the EIC, its technique and design then copied by 19th-century British manufacturers, is to be found today in every home. Importantly, hundreds of thousands of Indian troops served the EIC and the British crown as mercenaries, or sepoys, in the British army in India throughout the colonial period, and on the side of the British in Europe and north Africa during the First and Second World Wars. Finally, both before and since Indian independence in 1947, tens of thousands of Muslim, Sikh, and Hindu migrants from the Indian subcontinent contributed, and continue to contribute, disproportionately to the prosperity and cultural diversity of Scotland. It is a relationship which has endured, and whilst at times traumatic, it is something for which future generations will continue to have reasons to be grateful.   CB

Iona, an island off the south-west coast of Mull (Argyll), was the principal monastery of St *Columba (521–97), whose name is preserved in the island's Gaelic name, I Chaluim Chille. An abbey and nunnery established c.1200 remained the principal religious houses of the *Isles until the Reformation.

Iona measures 3.4 miles (5.5 km) by 1.5 miles (2.5 km), and the highest summit, Dùn I, is 330 feet (100 m) high. It is composed of Lewisian gneiss, with Torridonian flagstone along the east shore. Much of the surface is moorland, with steep-sided gullies providing grazing for cattle. The coast combines cliffs or rocks with bays of white shell-sand. This sand created an area of machair on the western Atlantic shore, with abundant seaweed for manure. The *campulus occidentalis* (little western plain) was cultivated by the monks, and Columba's biographer St *Adomnán recorded a procession with relics of the saint to end a drought c.680. Later agriculture favoured the glacial soils of the eastern plain, which has always been the main centre of population.

The view from Dùn I, where Columba came to meditate, encompasses the Argyll mainland and the Hebrides from Islay to Rum. Adomnán depicts a local hierarchy of dependent monasteries, hermitages, and penitential stations, corresponding to the variety of enclosed sites in the area. Columban asceticism, with its search for 'a desert in the ocean', as Adomnán put it, defended the margins of the Christian world against unknown forces of the ocean. The saint is also portrayed meditating at 'a remote place' overlooking Tiree, and on 'the little hill of the angels', a natural mound at Sithean beside the machair.

Columba's landing-place in 563 is traditionally identified as Port na Curaich at the south end, where pebble-cairns suggest ancient pilgrimage. The monastery was on the eastern plain, where the Lochan Mór fed Sruth a'Mhuilinn (the mill stream). The medieval abbey stands at the centre of a 20 acre (8 hectare) enclosure formed by the *vallum monasterii* (rampart of the monastery), preserved on the west as a ditch and earthen bank. Elsewhere, aerial and geophysical survey and excavation reveal overlapping ditches and extensive occupation-deposits. This complexity reflects the expansion of Columba's settlement into one of the greatest Irish monasteries, and subdivision for diverse religious and domestic functions. A ditch north of Reilig Odhráin can be ascribed to the period of Columba's death in 597, since peat began to form early in the following century.

Literary evidence that timber was the normal building material is confirmed by excavated beam-slots and post-holes. Adomnán mentions religious, domestic, craft, and agricultural structures, as well as open areas. During his abbacy (679–704) timber was imported from the mainland for large communal buildings. A circular post-hole structure may have been one of these. The principal church may lie under the medieval abbey, for the space to the west was a liturgical focus marked by 8th-century crosses. It is overlooked by Tòrr an Aba, a rocky outcrop with traces of a cell, perhaps the little hill from which the dying Columba blessed his monastery. A tiny rebuilt chapel beside St John's Cross, resembling the smallest Irish churches, marks the traditional place of Columba's burial, from which his remains were enshrined in the 8th century. The present burial ground, Reilig Odhráin, appears to be a later development, and was probably from the first an aristocratic and royal graveyard, whereas the monks' cemetery lay nearer the church.

Adomnán describes crafts including writing and metalworking, and excavation has revealed 7th-century carpentry, bowl-turning, and leather working. Crucibles, moulds, and glass fragments indicate metal- and glass-working in the 8th century, with one mould bearing a pattern of interlocking circles found in the Book of Kells.

The most prominent survivals of the monastery are the high crosses, part of a collection of over one hundred pre-12th-century carved stones. These epitomize the twin aspects of Columban monasticism: ascetic humility contrasting with spiritual and political power. Over half are pillars and slabs bearing simple linear or outline crosses of types found along the Atlantic coasts of Britain and Ireland. Few are inscribed, for personal commemoration was unimportant. One 7th-century grave-marker, inscribed *Lapis Echodi* (the stone of Echoid), bears an elegant Chi-rho cross. Large recumbent graveslabs with ringed crosses of 8th century or later date are paralleled in major Irish monasteries (see MONUMENTS: 1).

The erection of timber crosses began in Columba's lifetime and large stone ones appear on Iona and Islay in the 8th century. Like the Book of Kells, they probably marked the enshrinement and developing cult of Columba. They used carpentry joints, but rich spiral and snake-and-boss ornaments link them with the manuscript and with masterpieces of 'Irish' metalwork, including shrine fragments from Viking graves. Their figure sculpture shows a range of biblical subjects. The iconic Virgin and Child on three crosses recall the Kells miniature and the hymn to Mary by the Iona monk Cú-chuimne (d. 747). St John's Cross, with double-curved arms like Northumbrian crosses, has the widest span in these islands and may have been the first ringed cross.

Repeated Viking attacks between 795 and 825 led to Iona's replacement by Kells (Co. Meath) and Dunkeld (Perthshire) as head of the Columban monasteries, but the community survived. St Matthew's Cross shows an Adam and Eve scene resembling one on a cross of c.900 at Kells. The island was venerated by Norse Christians, and in 980 Olaf Sihtricsson (Amlaíb Cuarán), king of Dublin, retired there 'in penitence and pilgrimage'. Not long afterwards the runic inscription on a graveslab of Irish type named Fukl and Kali, sons of Olvir.

One of the community's officials in 1164 was the 'head of the hermitage', probably based at Cladh an Dìsirt north of the monastery. St Oran's chapel was built or refurbished at this period, perhaps as a mortuary chapel for the family of Somerled (d. 1164). About 1200 his son Reginald founded the Benedictine abbey of St Columba and an Augustinian nunnery, with his sister Bethoc as prioress. Many of their early inmates were probably Irish, and their architecture shows similar influences. The Romanesque nunnery church is preserved, but this style is seen at the abbey only in the north transept. The eastern limb was extended as a two-level choir in the 13th-century, when the claustral buildings were completed. Major rebuilding was begun c.1450 by a local school of masons who for a century had been creating elaborate crosses, effigies, and graveslabs in a distinctive style. Some of the finest were commissioned by MacKinnon chiefs and clerics, who provided several abbots before that office was granted to the bishop of the Isles in 1499. Both

communities remained active until the *Reformation, although the school of carving ended c.1500 and the effigy of prioress Anna Maclean (d.1543) is by an Oronsay sculptor.

In 1635 Charles I ordered an Exchequer grant for the restoration of the abbey church as cathedral of the Isles. The choir was retained with the transepts as antechapel and the bells were recast in the Netherlands in 1638, the year when the bishops were deposed and work ended. Thereafter the monuments on Iona remained picturesque ruins viewed by increasing numbers of visitors until 1899, when the eighth duke of Argyll transferred them to trustees under obligation to restore the abbey church for worship. This was completed in 1910, and the monastic buildings were restored by George *MacLeod's Iona Community in 1938–65.

IF

Ireland: 1. to 1100; 2. 1100–1650; 3. since 1650.

1. to 1100

It need hardly be stated that Ireland and Scotland had a close relationship in the early Middle Ages, given that it was the conquest of eastern Scotland by a dynasty of Gaels (*Scoti*) which ultimately led to the transfer, in common contemporary usage, of Scotia from meaning Ireland to meaning Scotland. In cultural and linguistic terms, it seems clear that the conquest had produced a situation such that, in the 11th century, the secular and intellectual elite of both regions largely participated in the same language and poetic tastes. That said, we must recognize changes over the centuries in each region, and acknowledge that the relationship between the two was not a constant one.

Recent research has called into question the long-accepted idea that the *Gaelic language and the Gaels came into western Scotland by conquest and settlement. Certainly the archaeological evidence for this is thin, but there is nonetheless some reason to think of political change, if not cultural and linguistic, in the period around 500, the date traditionally assigned to the arrival of Fergus Mór mac Eirc. This origin legend, however, need only imply a reorientation of the polity of *Dál Riata, incorporating as it may have done by the 6th century, territory in Argyll and Antrim. It should be noted, however, that the term Dál Riata is not found until rather later, in reference to Argyll. Nonetheless, by the latter part of the 6th century, Argyll was populated by Gaels, and most of them seem to have acknowledged the overlordship of members of the Cenél nGabráin of Kintyre. This dynasty retained interests in Ireland, as witnessed by Domnall Brecc's disastrous participation in the battle of Mag Rath in 637. And there is strong likelihood, with some later evidence in its support, that this dynasty acknowledged the overlordship of the Uí Néill, at least as far as their Irish territory was concerned. Some indication of the continued operation of such kings, as indeed their Pictish counterparts, may be seen in the fact that kings of both Dál Riata and of the *Picts were signatory to the Law of the Innocents (Lex Innocentium) established by St *Adomnán of Iona in 697.

The main churches in Argyll were certainly in some sense planted and maintained by Irish clergy; if in the secular sphere we may doubt Argyll as an Irish colony, the churches may accurately be described as colonial. The abbots, and many of the other higher offices, of Iona continued to be filled by members of St *Columba's kindred, the Cenél Conaill of Co. Donegal, for much of the early Middle Ages; Applecross, and possibly Lismore, had close and explicit links with Bangor. The many smaller churches throughout Argyll dedicated to Leinster saints may testify to the provision of clergy for Argyll from other centres in Ireland. Certainly the legend of the foundation of Abernethy links that Pictish royal monastery with Kildare. Although *Iona was undoubtedly the centre of training for many Pictish clergy, by the 8th century there is evidence that Ireland was also a destination. St Fergus seems to have been a bishop in Ireland, though of Pictish stock; St Drostan too may have died at Ardbreccan in Co. Meath. In the 9th century, a presumably Pictish bishop in Orkney was able to communicate with the kidnapped teenager Fintan, later the saint of Rheinau, because he had trained in Ireland. This aspect of clerical training in Ireland may be noted in the period after the Gaelic conquest of Pictland, and the creation of Alba: there are signs of connections between eastern Scottish churches and Armagh, and the Life of St Catroe describes his training in Armagh. St Dubthach of Tain died in 1065 as a confessor in Armagh.

That the dynasty of *Kenneth mac Alpin looked to Ireland as support and example is backed up by some amount of evidence. Kenneth's daughter, Mael Muire, married Aed Findliath, king of the northern Uí Néill and of Tara (d. 879), and the marriage alliances among her children make her a 'grandmother of kings': two of her grandsons were Amlaíb Cuarán, king of the Gall (the Foreigners of Dublin, *Man, and the Isles, d. 981), and Congalach Cnogba of Brega (d. 956), who became king of Tara, wresting power from the two-branch cartel of the Cenél nEogáin and the Clann Cholmáin who had held it alternately for centuries. In 906, Kenneth's grandson, *Constantine II, swore with Bishop Cellach at *Scone to uphold law 'in the same way as the Gaels', and it seems likely that Irish practice was intended here. It has been pointed out

that for a century or more two branches of Kenneth's descendants replicate the very effective 'cartel' system which operated in the kingship of Tara. It will not do to overstate the Irish relationship, however: in too many respects, Alba was a product of the Pictish state it overlay.

Of course, we should understand Scotland as the whole of its modern territory, and from the 9th century on Alba and the kingdoms of Ireland were separated by a broad zone which was under Scandinavian political, and in varying degrees also linguistic and cultural, influence (see SCANDINAVIA: 1). The relationship between Ireland and the Gall (Scandinavian) polities established in the Isles and in south-western Scotland was very close, and developments in them were not always matched inside Alba. Amlaíb Cuarán, for instance, based largely in Dublin, fostered the church in Iona during the period 963–81, and died in pilgrimage there. Conversely, the power and ambition of another Scandinavian lord, Sigurd 'the Stout' of Orkney, led to his intervention in Ireland at the battle of Clontarf in 1014. During the 11th and 12th century, the Isles were occasionally ruled from Dublin, occasionally by sons of the kings of Irish kingdoms for whom control of Dublin and its marine hinterland had become paramount.

An example of the Irish sea dimension of Scottish politics may be seen in the figure of Echmarcach mac Ragnaill, a great-grandson of Amlaíb Cuarán, who fitfully controlled Dublin, and the greater Gall hegemony during the 1030s and 1040s. He was, however, a king within Scottish territory, probably of the Rhinns of *Galloway and of some of the *Isles, in 1029 when he submitted to King Cnut alongside Mac Bethad and Mael Coluim mac Cinaeda (Malcolm II). Finally expelled from his main kingship by the king of Leinster in 1052, he died as king of the Rhinns in 1065. He died, however, in the company of Donnchad mac Briain, erstwhile king of Munster, who was probably his brother-in-law, on pilgrimage to Rome.

The relationships between all these regions—Alba, the territories of the Gall, and the kingdoms and cities of Ireland—should make us cautious in accepting too readily English or Continental influence for developments in Scotland. An example is the development of Continental-style bishoprics. The first such to have ruled over Scottish territory may well have been the bishop of Dublin, established sometime after 1028, who will have presumably ruled over some of the western Scottish seaboard. The Orkney bishopric was established after 1048, and it is not too fanciful to see *Macbeth's pilgrimage to Rome in this light, and understand the increasing prestige of the bishop of St Andrews in this context.

Finally, we may note that we owe much of our, still thin, knowledge of Scotland in the early medieval period to Irish annalists, who still found kings and clergy in Scotland worthwhile keeping track of. And relationships—marital, diplomatic, and otherwise—may be heavily concealed by the bulk of what we do not know. Consider what may lie behind the participation of three mormaers from Scotland on the side of Brian Bórama at the battle of Clontarf; or the marriage-alliance which made Mael Coluim mac Cinaeda 'the son of the cow who grazes the bank of the Liffey'; or, most intriguing of all, the gift sent by Edgar, king of Alba, to Muirchertach, king of Munster, in 1105: a camel 'which is an animal of immense size'. TC

2. 1100–1650

The retreat of the Scandinavians from their capitals in Dublin, Waterford, and Cork and from the Isle of *Man had a paradoxical effect (see SCANDINAVIA: 1). In one sense, an Irish Sea province continued, at least until the later 13th century. Native Irish provincial kings inherited the Norse links with Man and with the Western Isles. As late as 1219, Rome considered the archbishop of Dublin to be metropolitan of the bishop of the Isles, although Trondheim also claimed jurisdiction. On the other hand, the vacuum made easier the creation after 1169 of an Anglo-Norman colonial zone which stretched along most of the eastern seaboard from Cork to Ulster. The period after 1185 saw the westward consolidation of the footholds the colony already had in Leinster and Meath. Yet the conquest was far from complete; substantial parts of Ireland, especially in Ulster, remained beyond the colonizers' reach. Both the colonial expansion and its failure fuelled a long-lasting sense of resentment within Gaelic society, which left it, and especially Ulster, open to influence from Scottish Gaeldom. Yet English polity also held Dublin responsible for policing the Irish Sea and its fringes in the Western Isles. As a result, Irish armies were involved in three successive rebellions, in 1211, 1215, and 1235, either in Man or *Galloway, the soft underbelly of the Scottish realm.

The first significant intervention by Scotland in Irish affairs took an unusual form. *Robert I, descendant of 12th-century Anglo-Norman settlers in Scotland but by now a Gaelic warlord, sent an embassy, probably in the winter of 1306–7, to Irish provincial kings. In 1310–11, he threatened an invasion of Man. And in 1315, he sent an expedition to Ulster, led by his brother Edward and Thomas Randolph, his most experienced general. Until Edward's death at Dundalk in 1318, the Bruce regime threatened English control of the Irish colony as a whole and even an invasion of Wales. This bruising

experience left English administrators wary of Scots interference for almost 300 years. As late as the reign of Elizabeth, William Cecil thought of two land frontiers between England and Scotland: the *Borders and Ulster (see ANGLO-SCOTTISH RELATIONS: 3).

The spread of the influence of the MacDonald lords of the *Isles into Ulster in the 1390s, as a result of the marriage of Ian Mor to Margery Bisset, heiress of the Glens of Antrim, complicated the two-way relationship between the adjacent Gaelic worlds. Intermittently through the 15th century, English kings lent support both to Clan Ian Mor (the MacDonnells) and successive lords of the Isles. After the annexation of the lordship by *James IV in 1493, large-scale migration from the Isles to Antrim began to threaten the balance of power in the north. The rivalries of both MacDonalds and *Campbells spilled across the Irish Sea, offering both kings a device to disrupt each other's polity in their Gaelic territories. In 1539, it was rumoured that *James V was about to stage an invasion of Ireland, with MacDonnell support. By the early 1540s, it was Henry VIII who used the pan-MacDonald network to disrupt the Scottish crown's control of the Isles (see ROUGH WOOING). Yet on the whole the English crown reaped more trouble than it sowed: in virtually every year of the 16th century west Highland mercenaries or 'redshanks' (previously known as 'gallowglasses': see MERCENARIES IN IRELAND) travelled to fight in the Irish clan wars and jeopardized English control, especially in the north.

The division of Ireland between two worlds, English and Gaelic, was a gradual process which was not completed until the end of the 16th century. In a variety of ways, the north and west of Ireland became more and more in touch with the pan-Celtic world which stretched across the North Channel to the western Highlands and Isles (see CLANS OF THE HIGHLANDS AND ISLANDS: 1; HIGHLANDS AND ISLANDS AND CENTRAL GOVERNMENT: 2). After the incomplete English 'conquest' of the 13th century, the lowland parts of Ireland, areas of English lordship such as Leinster and Munster, gravitated towards Dublin and London. For some Irish historians, the result was interaction and conflict between pan-Celtic and pan-English civilizations. In the 1530s, before Henry VIII assumed the title of king of Ireland in 1541, the English crown still talked of 'two nations': the 'king's lieges' (the old English or Anglo-Irish lords) and the 'king's Irish enemies' or the 'wild Irish', who made up Gaelic society. For others, these processes were marginal to the consolidation of a community and culture which was largely self-contained and localized: English authority and culture, for them, was not expanding but shrinking, into what by the 1530s was only about a third of Ireland, in the Pale and a vague buffer zone around it. The result was the English attempt, from 1541 onwards, to civilize, Protestantize, and Anglicize the Gaelic Irish. By the 1570s, in the reign of Elizabeth I, it was recognized that the policy had failed and a new conquest took its place.

The process of English disillusionment with Ireland had a clear parallel in Scotland. The change in English opinion was summed up by the tract of Edmund Spenser, poet and humanist, *A View of the State of Ireland* (1596), which condemned the Gaels as a barbarian people, 'altogether stubborn and untamed', and able to understand only force. It was replicated by *James VI in *Basilikon Doron*, which contrasted the inhabitants of the eastern and central Highlands with those of the west and the Isles, who were incapable of 'civilitie'. State formation in both England and Scotland produced a new, hard-line policy towards the enemies of the state in the 'dark corners of the land': the Gaels on either side of the North Channel became a target of royal policy, both before 1603 and after, when James VI and I's 'Great Britain' determined to stop traffic between the two Gaeldoms (see UNION OF THE CROWNS). The Protestant, allegedly Irish, state church was increasingly staffed from 1610 onwards by both English and Scots clergy. Ironically, many of the Scots were forced out in the 1630s by Strafford, returning to Scotland with an extra set of resentments against Charles I's government. British unionists in Ireland became Scots Covenanters.

In the 1640s the 'war of the three kingdoms' (see COVENANT, WARS OF THE) briefly reinvigorated the pan-Celtic connection. The invasion of Ireland by Covenanting armies from 1642 onwards provoked the expedition made by Alasdair MacColla on behalf of the Catholic Confederacy in 1644-5, to link up with the marquis of Montrose. For the Covenanting armies, a string of defeats caused by the 'Highland charge' of the 'worst men in the earth' provoked a real crisis. It was compounded by defeat in Ireland, at Benburb in June 1646. Yet MacColla's expedition and Montrose's campaign were full of paradoxes and tensions. Irish Gaeldom and the *Gaidhealtachd* had been drifting apart for 50 years or more. The new union which followed in the 1650s, of the 'Commonwealth of England, Scotland and Ireland' under Oliver Cromwell, did not even pretend to be a British nation state. It was an avowedly English empire. ML

3. since 1650

Historians of modern Scotland and Ireland are learning to think of their relationship as significant in its own right, rather than simply arising from their English problems. The devolution and independence of Ireland (other than Northern Ireland)

since 1922 had concealed Ireland's much greater Englishness in law. Roman Catholic numerical predominance in Ireland resembles that of Presbyterianism in Scotland in that each only obtained social leadership after long periods of degradation, and each depended far more on doctrinal enforcement by popular local pressure than on such national legal status as each ultimately obtained: their theological mutual opposition did not always prevent their acknowledging common political ground as when many Irish Presbyterians made common cause with their Catholic fellow-countrymen in the late 18th century when both struggled for civil rights denied by the ruling but numerically smaller Episcopalians, or when the future leader of the *Disruption of the Church of Scotland in 1843, Thomas *Chalmers, supported the cause and adopted the methods of Daniel O'Connell's crusade for the admission of Roman Catholics to the Union Parliament at Westminster. Nineteenth-century Scots *migration increased the Protestant workers in the Lagan valley, while Irish Catholics transformed the labour force of urban Scotland (see ECONOMY: 4). It is symptomatic of the new Scotland that its two most eminent modern historians of recent years, Michael Lynch and Thomas Devine, are of Irish Catholic descent, and that Scotland's greatest 20th-century poet, Hugh MacDiarmid, should have sworn greater homage to W. B. Yeats and James Joyce than he would have conceded to any other Anglophone creative writer (see CULTURE: 24).

One of the most important links between Scotland and Ireland from 1650 lay in unrealized fears and hopes. Neither as rulers nor as outcasts did the Stuarts co-ordinate their support within the two kingdoms: indeed Charles II, proclaimed in Scotland after his father's judicial murder, repudiated agreements with the Irish Catholics in Charles I's name, and Montrose's execution in 1650 certainly derived in part from his previous usage of Ulster Catholic forces whom Scots Protestants identified with the insurgent murderers of Scots settlers in Ulster in 1641 (see COVENANT, WARS OF THE). Fears of further massacre in 1688 sent some Scots, especially Presbyterian clergy, back to Scotland, and the Presbyterianization of the Church of Scotland which followed sundered the anti-*Jacobite alliance of Episcopalians and Presbyterians in Ireland once they had seen Williamite victory. Irish Presbyterians suffered under penal legislation in some respects comparable to the degradation of the Roman Catholics, despite their Protestant solidarity during the preceding wars; Episcopalians feared that the Church of Ireland might follow the Church of Scotland in being taken over by the numerically stronger Presbyterians. Meanwhile the

Gaelic-speaking Catholics in both countries composed rallying-songs, laments, dream visions, and prophesies in the Stuart cause, more unanimously in Ireland than in Scotland, whose Hanoverian *Campbells also had their inspirational bards (see SONG, TRADITIONAL AND FOLK: 2). A common Ossianic folklore in western Ulster and Scotland testifies to continued migration of populations in Gaelic areas, but the invention of tradition by modern mythologizers such as H. R. Trevor-Roper to the effect that Scotland became a 'dump' for unwanted Irish-Gaelic poets derives from confusion of 6th-century data with that of the 17th century (and from linguistic ignorance). Ireland's Gaelic leadership driven overseas gainsaid Jacobite attempts in sympathy with the Scottish risings of 1715 and 1745, loud though some Irish Gaelic poets might applaud them. Prince Charles Edward's seven men of Moidart in 1745 included four Irish, two of immediate, one of remote, Gaelic ancestry, but while the Antrim exile MacDonnell among them swayed Scots kinsmen into their support, John William O'Sullivan of Kerry quarrelled bitterly with Scots Protestant Jacobite leaders such as Lord George Murray.

Protestant Ireland opened up a more real link with Scotland from the Dublin Enlightenment of the 1690s whose long shadows influenced the Irish schoolmaster Francis Hutcheson (1694–1746), professor of moral philosophy at Glasgow from 1729, father of the Scottish Enlightenment (see CULTURE: 11). Hutcheson's idea of benevolence as the key to morality and contempt for theological bickering derived from ugly Irish memories, and his *System of Moral Philosophy* (1755) influenced the development of Scots common-sense philosophy. Enlightenment made the four Scottish *universities oases for migrant Irish Presbyterian scholars, many of whom availed themselves of *Edinburgh's new status as the medical capital of the world. Dublin, second city of the 18th-century Empire, remained a natural basis of comparison, and new ways of medical wisdom such as the stethoscope were developed from the interplay of experiment between Paris, Edinburgh, and Dublin. Oliver Goldsmith (1728–74) was probably typical of destitute Irish medical students ultimately fleeing to avoid duns, but he remains Ireland's greatest 18th-century literary export to Scotland, brief though exigencies made his stay. The Irish actor-manager Thomas Sheridan (1719–88), kinsman of the Moidart Gaelic-descended Jacobite, and father of the playwright Richard Brinsley Sheridan, came to Scotland to teach correct pronunciation of English to great approval. But later imports to the Scottish Enlightenment, especially in university circles, imbibed political radicalism, among them the Edinburgh

MDs and future United Irishmen William Drennan (1754–1820) and Thomas Addis Emmet (1764–1827), the latter making an involuntary return as a prisoner to Fort St George in 1799. Links were established between the shadowy United Scotsmen and the Irish body, but Scots sympathizers with the French Revolution avoided the violence which convulsed Ireland in 1798.

The transportation revolution in Scotland imported thousands of Irish labourers (fellow-subjects within the UK after the Irish Act of Union of 1800–01), digging the canals through the central belt and the great glen, and subsequently laying the railways (see TRANSPORT AND COMMUNICATIONS: 2). Brutalized by their work and the contempt in which they were held by the bourgeoisie whose civilization they were building, the 'navvies' lived, drank, and fought apart, often in bitter competition with dispossessed and migrant Highlanders regardless of such common *Gaelic as they might enjoy. Catholicism mushroomed in their wake, especially as their part in the rise of the new Glasgow necessitated rapid recruitment of Irish clergy in addition to the overworked scions of Banffshire recusants (see ROMAN CATHOLIC COMMUNITY). The socialization of ex-navvies (when they did not return to Ireland) brought problems and solutions, few as drastic in either case as those associated with William Burke (1792–1829) and William Hare (fl. 1828), who murdered sixteen Irish and Scots to sell their bodies to the Edinburgh anatomist Robert Knox (1791–1862); Burke was hanged on Hare's evidence, the probability being that Hare's wife Margaret, his intellectual superior, trapped the government into giving them immunity for sixteen murders where it had intended to do so for one. The frighteningly likeable Burke impressed counsel at his trial (Christmastide, 1828) with his successful zeal to save the life of his co-accused mistress, the Scotswoman Helen Macdougall.

Formally less homicidal, the rival immigrant workers from Catholic and Protestant Irish origins later found expression in such football teams as Glasgow Celtic and Rangers, Edinburgh Hibernians and Heart of Midlothian; these became identified with the *Irish Home Rule and Orange *Unionist causes respectively, and clashed with bloodshed, *Glasgow being the most intransigent in mutual enmity. Yet Glasgow never succumbed to sectarian riot outside the sporting world, nor did the heavily Hibernicized *Dundee, but the far less Irish-penetrated Edinburgh would explode briefly in anti-Catholic violence in the 1930s.

The migrants brought folk culture with them, including songs, and the melodies of Robert Burns invaded de-Gaelicizing Ireland to such effect that his picture and his poem 'Sweet Afton' became the brand name of Ireland's most popular 20th-century cigarette. On a more artificial level, the poetry of Sir Walter Scott dominated the attempts of Young Ireland and the *Nation* newspaper to inspire a popular romantic nationalism in the 1840s, and many of their writers also owed heavy modelling fees to the heroic histories streaming from Thomas Carlyle. Scott himself claimed that his career as a novelist was made possible only by the example of Maria Edgeworth (1767–1849), whose novels of Irish rural life based on oral evidence and local traditions mingled realism so effectively with romanticism. Scott made little use of Irish characters (other than the exotic, indeed erotic, Irish hero of *Rokeby*) but John Galt's *Annals of the Parish* (1821) has some neat vignettes on the contemporary Irish migrants in Scotland (see CULTURE: 14). Later in the century Robert Louis Stevenson drew heavily on the Irish mid-18th-century Annesley case for *Kidnapped*, while his Chevalier Burke in *The Master of Ballantrae* is virtually on long lease from the early romances of Charles Lever (1806–72): Stevenson was haunted by the plight of the Curtin family in Kerry in the late 1880s and wanted to sacrifice his life defying the boycott against them, by dwelling with them in their home, but the scheme fell through. His younger fellow-Edinbourgeois Arthur Conan Doyle visited landlord relatives in Ireland during the agrarian strife of 1880 with results in the late Sherlock Holmes story, *The Valley of Fear* (1914), where the terrorist secret society in Pennsylvania owes much to his hostile memories of the Land League of Ireland. Conan Doyle's famous detective and masterly narrator, Holmes and Watson, drew heavily on his Edinburgh medical school teachers and their colleagues, and the astonishing achievement of his Napoleonic short story series around the soldier Gerard, seeing an anti-British war through French eyes, evidently derives from the varying perspectives he obtained as a Scotsman of Irish parents who ultimately settled in England. The 1890s were in any case a time when Irish and Scots writers leagued together in opposition to the parochialism of a domineering but rather bankrupt London metropolitan culture, notably in the crusade of the Scots and Irish theatre critics William Archer and George Bernard Shaw to bring Ibsen and his influence to bear on London theatre, where the first successful example of Ibsenism homegrown on the London stage came from Shaw's fellow-Irishman Oscar Wilde.

The Scots-Canadian Grant Allen in his 'The Celt in English Art' (*Fortnightly Review*, February 1891) saw much of the ascendancy of Parnell as stimulative of the advances of Scots, Irish, and other Celtic Anglophone literatures, and this would be so because Parnell's success in agrarian and Home Rule

movements won both imitators and allies particularly in Scotland. The Crofters' War of the 1880s (see LAND AGITATION AND REFORM IN THE HIGHLANDS AND ISLANDS) began from the Irish infection, and it was for participation in the banned Trafalgar Square demonstration against the imprisonment of the Parnellite agitator and journalist William O'Brien (1852–1928) that the Scots essayist, traveller, historian, and horseman R. B. Cunninghame Graham, MP (later founder of the ILP and the SNP), was imprisoned for six months. Urban labour also responded to lessons of the Irish experience, notably the boycott, and it was initially in Scotland that the Edinburgh-born James Connolly (1868–1916) developed his idea of socialist-leavened nationalism in order to evangelize the Irish workers of the world. Connolly was called to Ireland in 1896 to help organize there, went to the USA 1903–9 where he blossomed as an anarcho-syndicalist, and returned to Ireland as part of the great Larkinite challenge in 1913 to organized capital and labour alike only to end before a firing squad after the final desperate action of leading the Easter Rising of 1916 when his dreams crumbled in a war-torn world: but he maintained a Scottish identity in part through his major essays' publication there, notably in the labour weekly *Forward*.

The new Irish Free State and its successors had little interest in perpetuating Connolly's socialism: the new nationalism was so hostile to maintaining any link with the larger island that Celtic, Hibernians, and the rest of the teams embodying Irish Catholic nationalist feeling were denounced as supporting 'foreign games', i.e. soccer. The Church of Scotland in 1923 marked the new foundation of the Irish Free State by calling for the repatriation of what were now alien Irish Catholics. They had some justification in theory for what would have been a horrific decision in practice: many Irish Catholics in Scotland (and indeed Irish Protestants in Scotland) tended to think of themselves primarily as Irish, secondarily if at all as Scots (see NATIONAL IDENTITY: 6). Many had come as migrants from Ireland, often seasonally from Donegal in processes so heartrendingly described for the years before 1914 by Patrick MacGill in *Children of the Dead End* and, its feminist counterpart, *The Rat-Pit*. Catholic *newspapers in Scotland trumpeted Irish issues, squeezing specifically Scottish news to very small dimensions. Suddenly in 1923 if the Church of Scotland wanted the Irish Catholics out, the Irish Catholics themselves realized they had no place to go but in. A Scottish consciousness began to grow among the Irish.

The Church of Scotland grew ecumenical slowly, but by the time of the papal visit of John Paul II there could be few complaints to be heard about the good nature of the welcome he received from Protestants. Even the leading anti-Catholic evangelist Pastor Jack Glass urged Catholics to leave the Church of Rome but added that, if they would not, they should follow the teaching of the pope faithfully as he was a good man who had no truck with liberalism. The leading political parties went to great lengths to ensure that the horrors of sectarian warfare in Northern Ireland would not boil up in Scotland, and although Orangeism in Scotland still had the extremism and some of the violence of Glasgow Rangers in mid-kick when the Northern Ireland crisis began to erupt, it has become a much gentler movement in recent years. Irish presences in Scotland, Catholic or Protestant, are associated with benignity rather than conflict. Ironically the first Irishman to become a Scottish Roman Catholic bishop since the restoration of the Scottish hierarchy in 1878 did not take office until the 1980s, and the spirit of kindly ecumenism could not have been more happily embodied than in one of the present leaders of Scotland's Catholics, the Antrim-born Archbishop of St Andrews and Edinburgh, Keith Patrick O'Brien.   ODE

Irish Home Rule. was a major issue in Scottish politics in the late 19th and early 20th centuries. The existence of a substantial community of Irish Catholics and their descendants in Scotland in this period, amounting to approximately 15 per cent of the population (see IMMIGRATION, IRISH), contrived to make the issue of Irish Home Rule a factor in Scottish politics. The Irish community had a strong political tradition before the advent of Home Rule in the 1870s. They had been active in the radical agitation of the 1820s, prominent in O'Connell's repeal campaign, and supported *Chartism and trade unionism in the 1840s and 1850s. Hostility from the Irish Protestant Orange community in Scotland and indigenous anti-Catholic prejudice had combined to make the community introspective and reinforced their sense of Irish identity. The role of the Roman Catholic Church (see ROMAN CATHOLIC COMMUNITY) as a central pillar of the community did much to fuse together a religious dimension to national identity.

Irish Home Rule played little part in Scottish politics until Gladstone's conversion in 1886. Before this, the Irish were routinely denounced for receiving special treatment, wasting parliamentary time with their MPs' obstructionist antics, and draining resources from the Exchequer. The tendency towards terrorism and lawlessness in Ireland was contrasted with the Scots' record as model citizens. As Lord Rosebery, Scotland's Liberal Party champion, put it: 'Justice for Ireland means everything, even the payment of the natives' debts . . . Justice

for Scotland means insulting neglect. I leave for Edinburgh tomorrow with the aim of blowing up a prison or shooting a policeman.' The effect of Gladstone's endorsement of Irish Home Rule was to split the Liberal Party (see LIBERALISM) in Scotland with more than a third of the parliamentary party denouncing the policy. It was condemned as a submission to terrorism and a danger to the *British Empire. For some, Gladstone's conversion to Irish Home Rule meant that the same treatment would have to be extended to Scotland. After all, many recounted his words when he opposed Irish claims by stating that if Ireland was to have a parliament so too would the Scots and Welsh. The Scottish Home Rule Association (SHRA) was formed in 1886 to press home this point and stated from the outset that if Ireland was given home rule but not Scotland, then this would put a premium on lawlessness and anarchy. For many, if any nation deserved home rule, it was Scotland and not *Ireland.

Although many anti-Home Rule Liberals were to all intents and purposes the same as their Liberal colleagues, the divisions hardened over time to produce a separate party, the Liberal Unionists, which was more right wing and increasingly co-operated with the Conservative Party (see UNIONISM). The Irish National League and the United Irish League were organizations which sought to mobilize Irish opinion in Scotland behind the campaign for Irish Home Rule, which effectively meant voting for the Liberal Party. Led by Robert Ferguson, an Ulster Protestant, many claims were made about its effectiveness. For example, the *Scotsman* claimed that the Irish vote was a critical factor in determining the outcome of elections in Scotland. Opponents of Irish Home Rule frequently cited the large number of Irish Scots in many west of Scotland constituencies as a critical factor in determining Liberal support, which it was claimed was motivated by self-interest rather than principle. Yet, such claims have to be treated with caution. Although there was electoral reform in 1884, about 40 per cent of adult males in Scotland did not have the vote. These were people in marginal income and employment groups, precisely the same group as the Irish Catholic community. While many may have had the vote, it is equally likely that many did not and as such would be unable to exert much electoral influence. In any case, the United Irish league was hardly going to deny claims about its supposed powerful influence. Also, if we examine those Scottish MPs who consistently supported Irish Home Rule, many came from constituencies in the Highlands and northeast which had no Irish community.

With the collapse of Gladstone's government in 1886 and in spite of a half-hearted effort by Lord

Rosebery in 1894, Irish Home Rule was removed from the political agenda in Scotland by the dominance of Conservative governments which would make no concessions to Irish nationalism. Although the issue was fairly quiet in the period from 1894 to 1906, certain elements in the Conservative Party in Scotland did flirt with the idea that the Orange vote could be mobilized against Liberal Home Rulers. It did not work. The Orange Order, while being resolutely opposed to Irish Home Rule, was a proletarian organization which withstood any attempts by the Conservatives to tame it. Indeed, individual Tories were denounced for being in government when the Scottish Catholic hierarchy was re-established in 1878. Also, the Order's violent and drunken image (see ROUGH CULTURE) would be likely to alienate traditional middle-class supporters. The Conservative Party could not mobilize Orangeism as an effective political movement.

Irish Home Rule bubbled to the surface in the period after 1910 as a minority Liberal government was dependent on Irish nationalist support. The prospect that the Liberals would legislate for Irish Home Rule was such that it united the Liberal Unionists and the Conservative Party to become the Unionist Party in 1912. Despite much of the hysterics which accompanied the prospect of Irish Home Rule—'Eighty Irish Nationalist Votes: the Price of Empire' was how the Glasgow Herald denounced Liberal policy—the fact of the matter is that the Conservatives and Unionists made little headway in the elections of 1910 (twelve and eleven seats respectively), all of which suggests that there was hardly a groundswell of anti-Irish Home Rule sentiment in Scotland. The First World War killed off Irish Home Rule and the Easter Rising in 1916, largely because of the Liberal government's part in its suppression, turned the Irish community away from their traditional political allies. There were 80 Sinn Fein branches in Scotland after the war and the Irish community's disillusionment with the Liberal Party's failure to deliver on Home Rule opened the way for the Labour Party (see LABOURISM) to emerge as the champion of their interests.

RJF

Isles, kingdom of the. The history of the Hebrides (see HIGHLANDS AND ISLANDS: GENERAL) before the 14th century is obscure. Before the Viking Age the islands had been divided between Gaelic-speaking *Dál Riata and, north of Ardnamurchan, a *Pictish-speaking population who had closer links with Orkney (see ORKNEY AND CAITHNESS, EARLDOM OF) than with the Southern Isles. This division survived into the Viking Age, the northern zone becoming thoroughly Scandinavianized and the south remaining broadly Gaelic-speaking, despite significant Norse settlement (see SCANDINAVIA: 1) and complete political domination. The maintenance of this division may suggest that Skye and the Outer Isles fell under the political dominion of Orkney. The southern Hebrides seem, by the early 10th century, to have fallen under the political sway of the Uí Ímair dynasty who claimed descent from the Danish sea-king Ivarr 'the Boneless' (d. 873).

The Uí Ímair dominions were far-flung including Dublin and Waterford in *Ireland as well as *Man, parts of *Galloway and north-west England, and even Yorkshire at times, as well as the southern Hebrides and Kintyre. Their political structure seems to have been similar to that of Gaelic kindreds of the time with different islands and mainland districts having their own leaders, who sometimes used the royal title, whilst one member of the dynasty usually held some kind of superiority. Internecine warfare was rife and in each generation leading members of the family struggled to monopolize the kingship for their own progeny. By 1005 all the competitors were descendants of Amlaíb Cuarán (d. 981), and a century later his great-grandson Gofraid Crobán (d. 1095) had managed to monopolize the kingship for his descendants.

There are some hints that the local rulers in the Isles bore the Norse title lagmaðr law-man, which might indicate that local government in these regions was consensual with 'things' or assemblies of free-farmers operating on each island, but such analysis is highly speculative. The most important district in the Isles part of the Uí Ímair imperium was Islay, the most fertile of the islands. It was from there that Gofraid Crobán launched his bid for the kingship in 1079 and there that he was staying when he finally succumbed to the plague sixteen years later.

The 12th century saw Frankish ideas about government and exploitation spread throughout Europe and Gofraid's youngest son Amlaíb 'the Red' (r. 1114–54) seems to have engaged fully with this phenomenon, inviting reformed monastic orders into his kingdom and developing manorialism. Although Amlaíb was an energetic ruler who conquered the northern Hebrides from the earls of Orkney (c.1130), these more exploitative and stationary forms of rulership led to the monarchy becoming identified more closely with its 'demesne' lands on the Isle of Man. This led to the alienation of outlying areas. Galloway seems to have broken away during Amlaíb's reign and, after his death, the Hebrideans found his son Gofraid's rule unacceptable and turned instead to Somerled mac Gillabrigte, the ruler of Kintyre, Amlaíb's son-in-law, who offered them one of his sons as king. By 1159 Somerled had conquered the Isles but on his death in 1164 Gofraid returned from exile and seized back Man and some of the other islands. From then on the title 'King of the Isles' was used by two lines, one descended from Somerled and the other from Gofraid. By the 13th century, a Vietnam-style conflict had developed in the Isles with Norway and Scotland playing the parts of America and China. Some of the kings of the Isles, like Eogán MacDubgall (r. 1248–1268 × 1275), were able to successfully play off the superpowers against one another, but most found that committing themselves to one or other of the great kings would leave them dangerously exposed when that ruler returned east over mountain or sea. After the withdrawal of the Norwegians, following the Treaty of Perth (1266), Eogán and his son Alexander (d. 1310) temporarily found themselves backed by the Scottish crown in a final push against their Manx-based rivals. Their victory was short-lived, however, for they found themselves supporting the *Balliol cause in the Wars of Succession. Once *Robert I had secured his crown he ousted the MacDubgalls and replaced them with their cousin Aonghus Óg MacDomnaill (Angus Og MacDonald) of Islay who was granted the greater part of their lands though, significantly, without Scottish recognition of the royal title (see HIGHLANDS AND ISLANDS AND CENTRAL GOVERNMENT: 1; CLANS OF THE HIGHLANDS AND ISLANDS: 1).   AW

Isles, lordship of the. In some respects, it is difficult to see successive MacDonald lords of the Isles as Scottish magnates at all. Geographically, their domain covered much of the western seaboard, the Isles, and the Glens of Antrim in Ulster (see IRELAND: 2); their descent was from the 12th-century Gaelic-Norse warlord Somerled; they regarded themselves as kings, as is seen in their occasional use of the titles *Rí Innse Gall* (King of the Hebrides or 'Foreigners' Isles') and *Rí Airir Goídel* (King of Argyll); they conducted their own foreign policy and had their own tradition of election; and the *Gaelic language was spoken from end to end of the vast territories which they ruled.

Yet the territorial ambitions of the MacDonald lords during the 14th and 15th centuries lay principally within the bounds of the kingdom of Scotland. Their rise to pre-eminence in the west was based on timely support for Robert Bruce (*Robert I, 1306–29) on the part of Angus Og MacDonald (Aongus Óg MacDomnaill), followed by judicious changes of allegiance during the long and politically troubled reign of David II (1329–71). As early as 1336, Angus's son John styled himself 'dominus insularum' (lord of the Isles); this was no royal grant, but rather reflected the success of the MacDonalds

of Islay in making themselves the dominant family in the west, at the expense of the Macdougalls and MacRuaris. John MacDonald, the first and most successful of the four lords, gradually acquired a huge Gaelic empire in the western Highlands and Islands—Islay, Jura, Mull, Coll, Tiree, Morvern, and Lochaber; from David II he received a grant of Lewis and Harris (1343); through his marriage to the heiress Amy MacRuari in 1346, he acquired that family's Garmoran lands—Knoydart, Moidart, Uist, Barra, and Rhum. Annulling this MacRuari marriage within four years, 'the good John of Islay' remarried in 1350, this time to Margaret, daughter of Robert the Steward. John MacDonald's foresight in negotiating this union became apparent a generation later when the Steward became king as Robert II and the lord of the Isles received a royal grant of Knapdale and Kintyre (1376).

This vast, sea-girt empire was governed by the lord, assisted by the Council of the Isles, which most often met at the centre of the lordship, the Council Isle of Loch Finlaggan on Islay. The council was made up of 'the royal blood' of Clan Donald—MacDonalds of Dunivaig, Keppoch, Clanranald, and MacIain of Ardnamurchan; the major families—Macleans of Duart and Lochbuie, MacLeod of Dunvegan and Harris, and MacLeod of Lewis; the thanes—MacKinnon, MacQuarrie, MacNeill of Gigha, and MacNeill of Barra; and finally the freeholders—Mackay, MacNicol, MacEachern, and MacMillan. The council's business was wide-ranging, including not only obvious tasks like the regulation of land grants and appointments to lordship offices, but also the inauguration of each new lord of the Isles and—significantly—foreign relations, especially with England (see ANGLO-SCOTTISH RELATIONS: 2).

This last task is a potent reminder of the military power of the lordship and the means by which individual lords sought to extend their territories and influence. The lordship's links with *Ireland provided not only a bolt-hole for its leaders, but also a source of troops—Irish *mercenaries (*galloglaigh* or gallowglasses) in huge numbers. There may have been as many as 10,000 in the army of Donald of the Isles at Harlaw in 1411; and lordship armies were the only magnate forces in Scotland capable of inflicting defeats on the armies of the crown—at Inverlochy (1431), Lagebraad in Ross (1480), and Bloody Bay (1481).

Much ink has been spilled over the vexed question as to whether the lords of the Isles actively sought to become integrated within the Stewart kingdom (see KINGSHIP: 5). However, there could be little fruitful contact between a monarchy whose interests lay primarily in the east and south of Scotland, and whose perception of the

Highlands and Islands was of a barbaric region which required to be 'daunted', and a Gaelic-speaking, Irish-orientated, kin-based lordship whose continuing expansion came more and more to be viewed as a threat by the Stewarts.

A great deal turned on the succession to the earldom of Ross, claimed by Donald, second lord of the Isles, in right of his wife, but conferred by the then governor, Robert Stewart, duke of Albany, on his own son, the earl of Buchan. A bloody but indecisive battle at Harlaw near Inverurie (24 July 1411) marked only a temporary setback to the ambitions of successive lords to acquire the earldom. Following James I's abortive attempt to curb the lordship (1428–31), Alexander MacDonald, the third lord, is found using the title of earl of Ross, and frequently resided at Dingwall, the earldom's centre.

In the event, however, Ross proved an Achilles' heel for the MacDonald lords. Attempts to dominate the earldom not only brought them into open conflict with hostile neighbours—the MacKenzies and successive *Gordon earls of Huntly—and ultimately with the crown, but also weakened MacDonald control within the Isles and on the western seaboard. The succession to the lordship of John MacDonald, fourth lord (1449–1503), further undermined MacDonald credibility. The fourth lord, according to the so-called Sleat *seanchaidh* Hugh MacDonald, in his 17th-century *His-

tory of the MacDonalds*, was a 15-year-old who was to grow into 'a meek, modest man, more fit to be a churchman than to command so many irregular tribes of people'. The so-called Treaty of Westminster-Ardtornish of 1462—whereby the fourth lord and his hawkish cousin Donald Balloch negotiated with Edward IV of England for tripartite division of Scotland with the exiled earl of *Douglas—was used as an excuse by James III to forfeit the earldom of Ross in 1475. John MacDonald's status was reduced to that of lord of parliament, and even Knapdale and Kintyre were forfeited to the crown.

Although crown forfeiture of the lordship of the Isles was delayed until 1493, in many ways 1475–6 marks the end of the lordship as a potent force. There followed what the Book of Clanranald describes as 'a great struggle for power among the Gael', with various leaders—Angus Og, the fourth lord's illegitimate son, his son Donald Dubh, Alexander of Lochalsh, and John Mor of Dunivaig—seeking to restore the MacDonald hegemony in the west. But the ultimate victors were the crown's hard men in the north and west—Alexander Gordon, third earl of Huntly, Archibald *Campbell, second earl of Argyll, and John MacIain of Ardnamurchan; and their dominance was underlined when John MacDonald, long a broken reed rejected by his own people and a crown pensioner for 25 years, died at Dundee in January 1503.   NATM

Jacobitism. Although for ever associated with final and dramatic failure in 1746, Jacobitism nonetheless posed a very real challenge to the Scottish and, later, British state for well over half a century. In 1689, 1715, 1719, and again in 1745–6, Scottish supporters of the exiled Stuarts mounted military operations against the Whig and Hanoverian establishments. In addition, risings were planned but either abandoned or aborted in 1708, 1741, and in 1744. While each campaign had its own distinctive character they also had certain key features in common. The first and last, for example, witnessed initially encouraging victories. In the case of the former it was John Graham, Viscount Dundee's spectacular victory at Killiecrankie near Blair Atholl on 27 July 1689. In the case of the latter it was the rout of Major-General Cope's army at Prestonpans on 21 September 1745 by Charles Edward Stuart's astute commander Lord George Murray—an action that secured, for the only time, a Jacobite occupation of central Scotland.

Nor were the various risings unsustainable, flash-in-the-pan affairs. Despite the death of Dundee at Killiecrankie and defeat at Dunkeld on 21 August 1689, and again at Cromdale in Inverness-shire in the spring of 1690, the first rising did not end until mid-1691, and only then by negotiation at Achallader. In the case of the Fifteen, effective defeat at Sherriffmuir on 13 November nonetheless saw military operations continue until early February 1716. Above all, despite the long retreat from Derby after 4 December 1745, Jacobite forces continued to outmanoeuvre their Hanoverian counterparts, even inflicting a further defeat upon the British army on 17 January 1746 at Falkirk. One final point is worth noting: despite their automatic association with defeat, Jacobite armies actually competed well against the forces of the crown. Only one rising was completely extinguished by a single military action—namely the Nineteen, at the battle of Glenshiel on 10 June 1719. Of course the battle of Culloden, fought on 16 April 1746 by a Jacobite army of around 7,000, has an unshakable reputation as the action that ended any military capability on the part of the Stuarts. Yet this is not in fact the case: indeed, only four days later a regrouped Jaco-

bite army of 5,000 assembled at Ruthven in Badenoch.

Derived from the Latin for James, Jacobitism drew its initial motivation by opposing the 1689 deposition of James VII of Scotland and II of England. Whilst in England, Jacobitism was nearly always a social form of political disaffection, which preferred getting on the wrong side of a claret bottle than a bullet or bayonet, its Scottish counterpart was consistently more threatening. This was because in Scotland the deposition of the Stuarts took a particularly violent form. In England, constitutional niceties were pandered to by the fiction that Mary and William succeeded James who, it was decreed, had chosen to abdicate. In Scotland no such niceties were adhered to. On 4 April 1689 the Convention of Estates in Edinburgh declared James to have forfeited the Scottish crown, a constitutional stance that almost inevitably imbued Scottish Jacobitism with a far greater sense of rectifying the break in dynastic legitimacy. This sense that Scotland had cast aside its longstanding national dynasty was the ideological spine that gave Jacobitism its cohesion and longevity in the face of repeated defeats. Many of the socio-economic travails that afflicted Scotland in the years after the deposition of James, such as the famines of the mid- to late 1690s (see DARIEN), were characterized by Jacobite propagandists as a judgement by God upon a nation that had forsaken his chosen royal family.

Yet other elements of the 1688–9 Revolution in Scotland also helped shape the character of pro-Stuart support north of the Border. Arguably one of the most important was religion. In England, the political nation appealed to William to cross the Channel as a result of fears that, alongside property rights, the Church of England was being fatally compromised by James's policies of religious toleration and Catholicization. Their original hope had been that William would persuade or coerce his father-in-law into calling a parliament that would affirm the position of the Church of England. The events of 1688 were thus legitimized and perceived south of border as a defence of the established church. The reverse was the case in Scotland.

Instead, the power and position of the nation's established form of religious worship, Episcopalianism (see EPISCOPALIAN COMMUNITY), was systematically destroyed by the Scottish *parliament in the aftermath of James's deposition. In other words, as with the constitutional position of the monarch, the religious revolution in Scotland was far more extreme than in England, provoking, in response, a more committed and purposeful strain of Jacobitism. Although in 1695 there were attempts to co-opt Scottish Episcopalians and win their recognition of the Williamite regime, large numbers refused to accept the required oath, thus becoming known as non-jurors.

The influence of Episcopalianism took many forms, not least in delineating the geographic boundaries of Jacobite support outwith the Highlands. Ministers 'rabbled', that is, forcibly ejected from their parishes, often found employment in the households of prominent Episcopalian landed families, above all in the north-east. Through their instruction a new generation of elites that otherwise would have had little personal knowledge of Episcopacy were inculcated with the non-jurors' sense of religious grievance, as well as their belief that the spiritual outrage of 1689–90 could be remedied only by the political act of reinstating James or his successors as the divinely ordained head of the Church in Scotland. The need to separate Protestantism from Jacobitism explains why Whig and Hanoverian propaganda consistently equated support for the Stuarts with Roman Catholicism (see ROMAN CATHOLIC COMMUNITY). The rather less threatening reality was that, even in the Highlands, only one in seven of all Jacobite manpower was in fact Roman Catholic. While clans such as the MacDonalds of Keppoch were indeed Catholic, others with whom Jacobitism was synonymous, such as the Camerons of Locheil, were in fact Protestant and Episcopalian. In the latest analysis of Jacobite support it has been calculated that well over 75 per cent of the manpower mobilized for the Stuarts consisted of Episcopalians—a vitally important feature of the movement that enabled Jacobitism to move beyond what would otherwise have been little more than an insignificant and marginalized clique of disaffected Catholics.

Beyond the twin issues of dynastic legitimacy and Episcopalianism, another vital element that propped up Jacobitism was resentment and opposition to the Act of Union which came into force in May 1707 (see UNION OF 1707). Under its terms Scotland accepted the Hanoverian succession, which was deliberately designed to prevent the return of the Stuarts. Similarly, the articles negotiated between the Scottish and English commissioners would almost certainly never have been accepted by the Scottish parliament had an Act guaranteeing the established status of the Presbyterian Church not been passed earlier. The Union was thus an additional layer of grievance that helped focus and animate Jacobite opposition. However, it also prompted new areas of disaffection. Many sectors of the *economy were, in the short term at least, adversely affected by the articles of Union. East-coast ports feared that more efficient English competition would drive them out of traditional areas of operation, such as timber, coal and, above all, wool. In addition, without the parliament's influence to negotiate what had been annual taxation supplies, many Scots argued that the Union condemned Scotland to a crippling tax regime that could never be renegotiated. In a somewhat transparent ploy the Stuarts proclaimed that, upon their reinstatement, they would recall the Scottish parliament and dissolve the Union. Both the initial declaration at Braemar by John Erskine, eleventh earl of Mar, leader of the Fifteen, and the manifesto of Charles Edward Stuart at Glenfinnan in 1745 stressed how the re-establishment of James VIII, the 'Old Pretender', son of James VII who had died in 1702, would end the Union.

This addition to the original remit of restoring dynastic and religious legitimacy was, in theory, an intelligent strategic commitment on the part of the Jacobite leadership, a deliberate effort to broaden their appeal to political constituencies and commercial interests that otherwise would have opposed them outright. Precisely how successful the stratagem was, however, is debatable. Certainly, there is evidence that for radical Presbyterian Cameronians in the south-west the Union was little more than Anglicanism by the back door—a defence mechanism against the Stuarts that was, if anything, an even greater evil. The result was the supreme irony of elements of the Cameronians preparing in 1708 to back the royal house that had persecuted them during the 1660s to 1680s. What is also clear is that the Fifteen, easily the largest and most threatening of the Jacobite risings, was an expression of a widespread and, to some extent, growing dislike of the Union and its political and economic consequences. As predicted, the years immediately following on from 1707 were indeed a disaster for Scotland. The imposition of an additional tax on brewing in 1713 was seen as an attack on one of the country's core economies, prompting, in part, the very close House of Lords vote on the repeal of the Union. That John Campbell, second duke of Argyll, a central figure in the Scottish side of the Union negotiations, voted for repeal is eloquent testimony to the extent of disillusionment north of the Border. This is exemplified in the person of Mar, who went from one of the most effective parliamentary managers of the pro-Union interest, to the political leader and military commander of what, in the end, amounted to a rising of almost national proportions (see GOVERNMENT AFTER THE UNION, 1707–c.1750).

Nor was support for the Stuarts restricted to an assortment of political, religious and economic groups within Scotland. The campaign to restore the royal house formed a subtext within the diplomatic balance of power in Europe. Most obviously, this was the case with France. Locked in a structural conflict with Britain over spheres of influence in the Low Countries and, increasingly, over colonial trade, France saw in the Stuarts the means of internally destabilizing its enemy. For this reason Louis XIV made the hugely important decision in 1702 to recognize James VIII as king of Great Britain. It also explains why, in 1708, and again in 1744, France was willing to commit substantial naval and military resources to reinforcing domestic Scottish efforts at insurrection. Indeed, after 1715, Scottish Jacobites made any rising on their part contingent upon such French or foreign aid. Thus, in 1719, an opportunistic rising in Wester Ross was made barely credible by the presence of Spanish ships and several hundred regulars.

One last facet of Scottish Jacobitism is worthy of note; namely, the role of the *clans of the Highlands and Islands. As the only Jacobites within Scotland, England, or Ireland that retained any armed capacity, the clans were vital in bestowing the movement with military muscle—a fact that is reflected in the overwhelmingly Highland nature of all Jacobite armies throughout the period from 1689 to 1745. Over 90 per cent of the army that marched to Derby through the late autumn of 1745, for example, was made up of clan levies; likewise, 70 per cent of the 16,000 mobilized by Mar consisted of Highland clansmen. Traditionally, the high-profile role of certain Highland clans has been ascribed to specific key influences. First, during the Wars of the *Covenant certain clans developed a regional form of loyalism and support for the Stuarts: a political culture, essentially, that represented a thread of continuity spanning the century between the campaigns of Montrose of the 1640s and Charles Edward Stuart. Nor was this an abstract, theoretical notion whereby Gaelic concepts of the chief as defender and trustee of clan lands and rights were projected onto the monarch at the national level. Such concepts were important but would arguably have meant little had they not found some practical expression. By curtailing the power of the Argylls, most obviously through the execution of the first marquis and ninth earl, the Stuarts won important allies amongst clans like the Macleans of Duart and Camerons of Locheil who had been exposed to the feudal expansionism of the *Campbells. Yet care is needed when ascribing Highland support for Jacobitism to a simple desire to perpetrate feud against the house of Argyll. In contrast to the actions of MacColla in the mid-1640s, clan levies did not use the cloak of Jacobitism to devastate Campbell estates. Moreover, hostility to the Campbells would hardly explain the Jacobitism of the Campbells of Breadalbane or the Mac-Kenzies of Seaforth in 1715—such powerful clans were beyond the reach even of the house of Argyll.

Clearly, Jacobitism was a complex phenomenon that had its origins in a diverse sequence of events. Yet all this multifaceted support begs the question—why did it fail? Ultimately, many of the features that appeared to make Jacobitism formidable actually operated to undermine it. Not least in this respect was the factor of foreign support. Given that the majority of Scotland's population was profoundly anti-Catholic, the prospect of the Stuarts returning at the head of Catholic French or Spanish troops hardly helped them in the battle for hearts and minds. Moreover, states such as France, Spain, or Sweden were exceptionally inconsistent in their support. While sympathetic in 1719, the Spanish authorities exposed a Jacobite invasion plot in 1741. Above all, France had little to gain by the restoration of the Stuarts. Instead, they were best kept in a perpetual state of possible deployment, to be used only when it suited France. Thus, when facing defeats in 1744, the French mobilized substantial forces; however, after the battle of Fontenoy in May 1745, which put the French on the offensive, they were unwilling to commit troops to what, in effect, amounted to a sideshow.

Another factor that hampered the Jacobites was leadership. While Dundee, Bonnie Prince Charlie, and Lord George Murray were charismatic and daring, other prominent leadership figures like James VII and his son James VIII were cold, unattractive men. Even worse, the Jacobite leadership was incompetent in many instances, most obviously in the case of Mar, who threw away a strategic and numerical advantage both before and after Sherriffmuir. By contrast, Mar's opponent, John Campbell, second duke of Argyll, was an effective and daring soldier. True, this was not the case with William Augustus, duke of Cumberland, a plodding, unimaginative general, but he was at least thorough and consistent in his planning and receptive to his officers' suggestions, something that most definitely could not be said of Charles Edward Stuart. Ultimately, however, the fact is that the Stuarts failed because they appeared to oppose too many of the civic institutions that retained the loyalty of arguably the majority of Scots. Whilst appearing to support the return of a Scottish parliament, their record of hostility to the institution was a matter of recorded fact north of the Border. Indeed, by failing to call a parliament in September 1745 after occupying Edinburgh, Charles simply compounded pre-existing prejudices that equated his family with arbitrary tendencies. Finally, in appearing to oppose the Union settlement which, for all its faults, guaranteed the Presbyterian Church (see CHURCH INSTITUTIONS: 5), Jacobitism set itself against the one national institution which had the local prestige and authority to influence the Lowland communities that had to be won over before a sustainable restoration could be effected.   AMacK

James IV (1473–1513), king of Scots (1488–1513), is widely regarded today as the most successful of the nine Stewart rulers of Scotland. This was also the view of his own contemporaries. The Spanish ambassador to Scotland Don Pedro de Ayala, who knew the young king, praised James to the skies in 1498 for his appearance, his linguistic abilities, his piety, his revenues, and his warlike skills; Sir David Lindsay of the Mount, a young courtier late in the reign, provided the classic description of the king as 'the glory of all princely governing'; and Adam Abell, an Observantine friar of Jedburgh (to whose order James IV had been conspicuously generous), recalled the king as a formidable warrior on foot or horse, and refused to accept that King James had perished in the carnage of Flodden.

Born at Holyrood on 17 March 1473, the eldest of three sons of James III (1452–88) and Margaret of Denmark (1457–86), the future king was given the title of duke of Rothesay in infancy, and was involved in his father's abortive English marriage schemes as a prospective bridegroom from 1474 (when Rothesay was aged 1) to 1487. In his youth, he appears to have been more influenced by his mother, Queen Margaret, than by his father; indeed the queen's contemporary biographer Sabadino suggests that Margaret played a major role in the great Stewart political crisis of 1482, when there appeared a real possibility that James III, imprisoned in Edinburgh castle, might be eliminated and Rothesay succeed as James IV at the age of 9. His succession, however, was deferred for almost six years, during which time he lived at *Stirling castle with his mother (until her death in 1486). Fears for his future—his father may have cut Rothesay's allowance and certainly preferred his younger brother in his projected English marriage alliances of 1487—probably led Rothesay to leave Stirling castle in February 1488 and join a wide spectrum of disaffected nobility, for many of whom James III was no longer acceptable as king. The ensuing four months should be understood as a

Scottish civil war from which Rothesay emerged as the victor at the 'field of Stirling' (11 June 1488, a battle later described as 'Sauchieburn'). There is a grim irony in the fact that the battle was fought on the site of *Robert I's great victory of Bannockburn in 1314; that James III, aware of this, brought Bruce's sword to the field; that neither this talisman nor the royal standard, borne by both armies, saved the king from death after the battle; and that Rothesay was crowned king as James IV at *Scone on the anniversary of Bannockburn (24 June).

Sauchieburn had done little more than replace one governmental faction with another. There followed a long period of readjustment and eventually (but not immediately) reconciliation. Wisely, James IV did not attempt to rule until the substantial political struggles of the first seven years of the reign had worked themselves out. Instead he performed elaborate penances for his role in his father's death—there is contemporary evidence for the existence of the famous iron belt which he is said to have worn each Lent—and bided his time. In the spring of 1495, at the age of 22, he was able to take over the reins of government without resistance or bloodshed.

In some sense, James IV's success lay in avoiding the mistakes made by his father. James III had been a static king, endeavouring to conduct royal business from *Edinburgh; by contrast, James IV was a committed traveller, regularly visiting far-flung areas of his kingdom, driving the justice ayres, reconciling feuds, and on one occasion in 1507 setting a record by riding from Perth to Tain in Easter Ross in two days. Unlike his father, King James wisely avoided attempting to impose regular taxation on *parliament, finding extra income instead through efficient exploitation of feudal casualties—wardships, apprisings, and 'recognition' (repossession of lands which had been improperly alienated)—by acts of revocation, by setting royal lands in feuferm in the last years of the reign, and by screwing money to finance his wars out of a compliant clergy. Trebling royal income as a result of these measures, James IV had no need to rely on the three estates for fiscal purposes. His father had summoned parliaments at least once a year throughout his reign; in eighteen years, James IV called the estates together on only four occasions.

In spite of occasional severity or sharp practice directed against individual magnates, James was a popular ruler who never forgot the services of those who had helped him to power in 1488—Hepburns, Humes, Argyll, Huntly, Angus—and was able to reconcile these men with committed supporters of his father, including Bishop William Elphinstone of Aberdeen, who was keeper of the privy seal for 22 years. He was a generous patron, creating new earldoms in the west for the families of *Hamilton (Arran), Kennedy (Cassillis), and Montgomery (Eglinton), and in the east for the Grahams (Montrose). He was not successful in everything which he attempted; he inherited the problem of a forfeited but rebellious lordship of the *Isles, and never solved it, preferring to leave the 'daunting' of the isles to his ruthless lieutenants Argyll, Huntly, and MacIain of Ardnamurchan. King James, however, was lucky to avoid the sibling rivalry which had undermined his father, as his younger brothers James (duke of Ross and archbishop of St Andrews from 1497) and John (earl of Mar) died in 1504 and 1503 respectively.

Later writers have criticized James IV at length for his foreign policy; but it would be a mistake to see the Flodden disaster as the inevitable result of the king's diplomacy. Like his father, James IV made an alliance with England—the so-called Treaty of Perpetual Peace in 1502—and married Henry VII's daughter Margaret in August 1503. But James reached this position only after considering possible imperial or Spanish alliances, and also after using Perkin Warbeck, pretender to Henry VII's throne, as a front for his invasions of Northumberland in 1496–7. Thus the much-praised 'Union of the Thistle and the Rose' of 1503 was a brittle alliance between two former enemies; and James IV was much more interested in pursuing an unofficial link with Louis XII of *France, who provided the Scottish king with skilled shipwrights, timber, and money to build his navy (including the huge 'Michael', launched in October 1511). Faced with the young Henry VIII's determination to restart the Hundred Years War, James IV renewed the Franco-Scottish alliance in 1512. The English king's grandiose dreams of replacing Louis XII duly foundered; but, on 9 September 1513, after a further successful invasion of Northumberland, James IV was defeated by the earl of Surrey at Flodden. The failure of the Scottish spears and swords in close combat with the English halberd cost the lives of James IV, 1 bishop, 2 abbots, 9 earls, 14 lords of parliament, and thousands of Scottish rank and file. (See also ANGLO-SCOTTISH RELATIONS: FRANCO-SCOTTISH RELATIONS: 1; KINGSHIP: 5; ROYAL COURT: 1).

NATM

James V (1512–42), king of Scots (1513–42), was the fourth, and first surviving, child of *James IV and Margaret Tudor, and was born at Linlithgow on 10 April 1512. (A younger brother Alexander, born in April 1514, died within two years.) The death of James IV at Flodden (9 September 1513) precipitated the infant Prince James into the kingship at the age of only 17 months—or rather, plunged the kingdom into a long and politically fractious minority

during which the principal figures were Margaret, the queen dowager; her new husband Archibald, sixth earl of Angus; James *Hamilton, first earl of Arran; and the young king's great-uncle and governor of Scotland between 1515 and 1524, John Stewart, duke of Albany. Albany gave some direction to government, negotiating the Treaty of Rouen (1517) with France and seeking French financial and military assistance in the face of English threats. However, his final withdrawal from Scotland to France left the young James V effectively a pawn in the hands of the dominant Scottish political players; the most aggressive of these were the Angus Douglases (see DOUGLAS FAMILY: 2), whose head, the sixth earl, was chancellor and whose family clung to power through retaining control of the king's person. Shortly after his sixteenth birthday, James V took control of his kingdom in a botched *coup d'état* (June 1528) which included an abortive siege of Angus's stronghold of Tantallon and the taking by the nobility of a solemn oath to support the king.

The adult James V has been variously characterized, but until recently received a bad press. Not surprisingly, this began with adverse English comments. In 1529 the ambassador Thomas Magnus warned King James against the use of young counsellors, and had the impertinence to cite the fate of James's grandfather as a result; while in 1537 the duke of Norfolk made his celebrated remark that 'so sore a dread king, and so ill-beloved of his subjects was never in that land'. However, as the principal aim of English policy towards Scotland in the 1530s was to destabilize, or acquire some control over, Scottish government, we may take these remarks with a sizeable pinch of salt. More influential on later historians has been the malicious vituperation of the reformer John *Knox, writing in the 1560s; for Knox, it was enough that James V was the father of *Mary, Queen of Scots, and a firm adherent of the French/Catholic axis in Europe. King James's reputation was duly savaged; he was 'ane prestis [priests'] king', acquisitive, a murderer of the nobility, who justly deserted him in 1542. On his deathbed, James—according to Knox—turned his face away from his lords and muttered that the dynasty had come into being through a female—and would end with a female—his newly born daughter Mary, the future queen.

All this is splendid post-*Reformation rhetoric, but bears little relation to the facts of the adult kingship of James V. For relations between king and nobility were generally good. His authority was rapidly accepted, and when in 1530 he warded all the major Border lords, this was simply a sensible precaution; the lords were soon released, and one of the most prominent of them, Robert, Lord

Maxwell, served the crown with distinction throughout the personal rule. Likewise James V's hanging of Johnnie Armstrong, a notorious Liddesdale reiver whose point of view is forcefully put in one of the most famous Border ballads, may be seen as a good example of a resolute Stewart monarch performing one of his primary duties, punishing thieves and reivers. And the notorious execution of Lady Glamis—by burning in public in 1537—needs to be put into the context of her guilt, with treasons stretching back to 1528. There was no royal 'reign of terror' against the *nobility; after all, James was confident enough in their loyalty to appoint four of their number to act as regents while he went off for a nine-month holiday in France in 1536–7. At the other end of the social spectrum, James V had the reputation of being a poor man's king, immortalized in later tales, picked up by Sir Walter Scott, of the king travelling throughout his kingdom in the disguise of the 'Gudeman of Ballengeich'.

This popular image has to be offset by James V's ruthless acquisition of money for the crown. Vast sums were acquired through exploiting sources of casualty income and in screwing money out of the clergy. Following his uncle Henry VIII's break with Rome in 1533–4, James V was in the fortunate position of being able to employ polite blackmail of the pope and the Scottish clergy for his continued adherence to Catholicism and the French alliance. Thus he acquired rich Scottish benefices for some of his bastard sons—of whom he had seven by six different mistresses—exacted a huge tax (£72,000 over four years) from the clergy, and a rather more modest £1,400 a year to support a College of Justice (the Court of *Session) in 1532.

Abroad, King James was one of the most eligible bachelors in Europe. He cheerfully accepted Orders of Chivalry—the Garter from England, St Michael from France, the Golden Fleece from the Empire—and then opted for a French match, finally insisting on Madeleine, daughter of François I, whom James married in the cathedral of Notre-Dame in Paris on New Year's Day 1537. Madeleine's death the same year was swiftly followed by James's second marriage (1538) to Mary of Guise, who was made of sterner stuff and who rapidly provided the king with two sons, James (1540) and Arthur (1541) (both died in infancy), and a daughter Mary in December 1542. The dowries for these two French marriages amounted to a staggering £168,750.

James was not a generous patron; but he spent vast sums enhancing the 'imperial' status of Stewart monarchy. He lavished money on French Renaissance palaces at *Stirling and Falkland; his coinage included the magnificent gold 'bonnet piece' of 1539, bearing a royal portrait on one side and an imperial crown on the other; and he had the Scottish imperial crown itself remodelled in 1540. These outward symbols reflected real royal power; and there were no real signs of a decline in this in the autumn of 1542, when a dour Anglo-Scottish war resulted in victory for the Scots at Hadden Rig and defeat at a sideshow on the Solway (Solway Moss) in November. Preparing to renew the war, James V was overtaken by death, probably from dysentery or cholera, at Falkland on 14 December 1542. (See also ANGLO-SCOTTISH RELATIONS: 3; CULTURE: 4, 7, 9; FRANCE: THE 'AULD ALLIANCE'; FRANCO-SCOTTISH RELATIONS: 2; KINGSHIP: 5; ROYAL COURT: 2).

NATM

James VI (1566–1625), king of Scots (1567–1625), is best known for having succeeded Queen Elizabeth I on the English throne in 1603, thus uniting the English and Scottish crowns. He would himself have regarded this as his greatest achievement, but he deserves to be remembered for several others.

Born in June 1566, James was crowned king at the age of 13 months by an ultra-Protestant (see KNOX, JOHN) faction. Their deposition of his mother *Mary, Queen of Scots, led to civil war. Scotland was governed in his minority by a series of regents, the last of whom, the earl of Morton (regent 1572–8), restored some political stability. But further factional struggles erupted between 1578 and 1585; only when they subsided was James clearly ruling personally. Never having known his parents, possessing few close relations, James nevertheless sensed his dynastic mission keenly. He married Anne of Denmark (1574–1619) in 1589, a diplomatic marriage to strengthen Scottish commercial ties with the Baltic states (see GERMANY, THE BALTIC, AND POLAND: 1). James was never closely attached to her, and deprived her of political influence. Three of their seven children survived infancy: Henry (1594–1612); Elizabeth (1596–1662), who was briefly queen of Bohemia in 1619–20; and Charles (1600–49), who succeeded as king in 1625.

James's emotional attachments were with a succession of male favourites, from his cousin Esmé Stewart, duke of Lennox, in the early 1580s to George Villiers, duke of Buckingham, in his last decade. Unlike some contemporary monarchs, James never delegated all decisions to his favourites; they were chosen for their personal attractions. But the largesse they received, in an age where royal largesse mattered to government, inevitably made them influential at court. In other ways, too, James's *royal court was characteristic. Disliking crowds and formality, he was happiest in small gatherings of male cronies—poets, theologians, or huntsmen—where his bantering sense of humour found free rein. He hunted constantly, pursuing stags obsessively and neglecting business. His poor personal image—weak legs, shambling walk, and slobbering tongue—were possibly due to slight cerebral palsy. His celebrated vanity, a common enough royal failing, may have attracted comment because of his intellectual attainments. He was widely respected as a canny politician, though his choice of ministers was sometimes uninspired. As king of England he found the charismatic Elizabeth a hard act to follow; his reputation as king of Scots stands higher.

He was an unusually intellectual monarch. Tutored by the renowned scholar George Buchanan, he absorbed Buchanan's radical political ideas on a king's accountability to his people—and revolted against them. He became a leading proponent of the 'divine right of kings' whereby kings were answerable to God alone. His two major political works, *The Trew Law of Free Monarchies* (1598) and *Basilikon Doron* (1599), were written with an eye to the English succession; James spent all his personal reign in Scotland positioning himself to succeed Elizabeth. This meant keeping his regime stable, Protestant, and pro-English. The last two aims sometimes conflicted with the first; his mother's imprisonment in England, and then the repercussions of her execution in 1587, were constant embarrassments, and there was a troublesome anti-English faction at court.

One of James's earliest declared intentions was to be a 'universal king': to rule without being beholden to any one faction, and to establish his authority over the *nobility. It was to be his chief concern up to about 1598. He probably did not think he was innovating here; but a state in which noble revolts were impossible would be different from one in which king and leading nobles happened to be friends. James was keen to have nobles as his courtiers and servants, but he determined to terminate their autonomous military power.

John Maitland of Thirlestane (see MAITLAND FAMILY), his chancellor in 1587–95, was his most influential adviser. Legislation (see PARLIAMENT: 2) proliferated as central government was galvanized; parliamentary taxation grew; Maitland masterminded lairds' admission to *parliament in 1587. Nobles' role in the privy council was reduced; the Exchequer—a largely noble-free institution—expanded its powers. Unsurprisingly, some nobles resisted. Factional struggle exploded once more after 1589, as the earl of Huntly (see GORDON FAMILY, EARLS OF HUNTLY), the leading Catholic courtier, intrigued with Spain and tried to supplant Maitland. Many disenchanted nobles held aloof, but the regime ultimately held firm. Huntly's failed rebellion of 1594 was in fact the last regional rebellion

(outside the Highlands) ever to take place in Scotland.

All this time, James had had church support through working with the radical Presbyterians (see MELVILLE, ANDREW). This group had come to dominate the General Assembly of the church (see CHURCH INSTITUTIONS: 3), and had built a popular following in several key towns, including Edinburgh. They did not fit the traditional pattern of politics; what drove them was ideology, not clientage. By 1594, the king's relationship with them was increasingly strained; and after Huntly's surrender, the Presbyterians were unnecessary. The showdown came on 17 December 1596, with a religious riot in Edinburgh; the king fled, leaving the radicals apparently in control of the capital, but the insurrection collapsed without noble backing.

In June 1598, James finally brought a convention of estates to accept that nobles' disputes must be submitted to royal justice—the most significant turning point in his reign, and the culmination of a long process of pressure and negotiation. James himself drafted the 'act anent feuding' that resulted. The convention also abolished the permanent exchequer that had curbed royal spending—a signal that subsidies to the nobility would be increased. Feuding faded away, transforming the role of the nobility; to the extent that they retained their networks of kinsmen and dependants, they would now use them in the peaceful service of the crown.

The only question—admittedly a big one—was whether the royal finances could afford the kind of spending spree that the deal envisaged. James had been sinking into bankruptcy for some time. A carefully planned scheme was proposed to revise tax assessments to tap the country's wealth effectually; but in 1600 a convention of estates rejected it, a major defeat for the government. James, who had argued passionately for the proposal, was publicly humiliated. What had gone wrong? One thing that had not gone wrong was his newly established rapport with the nobility; most nobles backed his scheme, and no court faction opposed it. Instead, it was the shire commissioners and burgesses who destroyed it. The opposition's support came from lesser propertied folk—the 'country' as they were described in 1600—more distanced from the court.

James's main Scottish concern between c.1598 and 1610 was to control the church through reestablishing bishops—which alienated the 'country' further. The crown had to browbeat or gerrymander the General Assembly of the church. Episcopalianism became the mirror image of Presbyterianism: a divisive and confrontational ideology. Meanwhile the Presbyterians agitated in the parishes they still controlled; they lobbied parliament, the one institution where they retained a voice; and they hoped for better times.

The *Union of the Crowns came about in 1603, but did not significantly change the way Scotland was governed. James is often described as an 'absentee' monarch, but he was just five days away by post. The governing institutions—particularly the Scottish parliament and privy council—continued unchanged. James had to take English interests into account, but so he had before 1603. There may even have been less English interference in Scotland after 1603 than before. However, union did solve the fiscal crisis. The cost of the court was removed from the Scottish treasury, and pensions to nobles and courtiers could expand comfortably.

Union also had an impact in the *Borders and Highlands (see HIGHLANDS AND ISLANDS AND CENTRAL GOVERNMENT: 2). In the days of Anglo-Scottish warfare a militarized Border region had been necessary; it was now redundant. The Borders were savagely and effectively subdued by military force. In the Highlands, too, military force cowed the most uncooperative clans.

Between about 1610 and 1617 there were fewer contentious political issues, largely because the government had finished forcing bishops down the throats of local elites. There was a temporary lull in religious innovations, and only one parliament—in 1612—which was contentious, because of taxation. Harmony ceased abruptly in 1617, when James visited his ancient kingdom for the only time since 1603. He unveiled a renewed programme of religious innovations, this time involving more ceremonial worship. The most contentious proposal, affecting every worshipper directly, was that communion should be received kneeling, rather than seated round a table in imitation of the Last Supper (see RELIGIOUS LIFE: 3). In parliament, James was obliged to withdraw a controversial act that would have allowed him to introduce these innovations by royal edict. He then had the proposals placed before the General Assembly—and they were rejected. The king, furious, ordered another assembly, threatening that another rejection would have dire consequences. The assembly, held in Perth in 1618, duly passed the proposals, which became known as the Five Articles of Perth.

Implementation of the Five Articles proved a nightmare. The Presbyterians' years of struggle now paid off, and it became clear that they had solid local support in much of Lowland Scotland. The Articles collapsed in many regions, and the rare successes came at a heavy price: hostile congregations, bitter divisions, and the emergence of an organized resistance network run by Presbyterian diehards. In the parliament of 1621, the Presbyterians rallied, leading to a titanic struggle over both the Five Articles and a new tax scheme. The ratification of the Articles came close to defeat. James's policy was in tatters; it was clear that he had gone too far.

After this, the most significant political event of the last four years of James's reign was the one that did not happen. Defeat did not lead to a change of direction, nor to a compromise with the Presbyterians. James had compromised before: he had sought a broad-based government in the 1590s, trying to keep Huntly at court to wean the pro-Spanish nobility away from revolt. By the 1620s his regime had lost that flexibility.

James died in March 1625, after a long and unusually active reign. Of the issues on which he was personally committed, the one on which he spent most time and effort (certainly while in Scotland) was the uprooting of the blood feud. Many things contributed to his success, but his peace-loving nature was surely one. Perhaps few kings would have been so ready to treat honour and revenge as barbaric.

He was intimately concerned with the church, keenly arguing the finer points of Calvinist theology. Against the Presbyterians he insisted that the Bible provided no direct guidance on many issues of worship and church government, and maintained that these issues should therefore be resolved by the church's supreme governor—who was, of course, himself. His ecclesiastical policy had some success, but it was shallow and short-lived.

In the subjugation of the Highlands and Borders he took frequent interest. He saw them in a broad strategic context that included the colonization of Ulster (see EMIGRATION: 2; IRELAND: 2) in the 1610s, where he encouraged participation by his Scottish subjects. Although comparable colonies in the Highlands failed, James did foster client *clans that increased royal authority. The strategic context for Gaelic Scotland and Ireland was, of course, provided by James's most abiding concern, Anglo-Scottish union, at which he worked hard both before and after 1603. Few of his subjects shared his vision, and the institutional union he sought was rejected, but he found ways of making personal union work.

James is often assessed more favourably than his successor. Charles I's reputation currently stands very low, but he deserves parity of treatment with his father. James, we are told, made sure that he stayed within the limits of what was possible. He talked about absolute monarchy, but acted consensually. Yet the Five Articles were well beyond the limits of the possible, and were introduced with no significant consultation or concern for consensus. As for Charles's unpopular innovations, those who objected to them objected equally to James's.

When Charles's regime capsized, James's bishops, and his Five Articles, and his taxes, all went down with the ship. But the struggles of the 1640s (see COVENANT, WARS OF THE) were not wars between regional magnates like the civil war of James's minority: they were struggles for control of a centralized state administration. James, who boasted that he governed Scotland by pen and not by the sword, could reasonably claim that state as his achievement. (See also ANGLO-SCOTTISH RELATIONS: 3; KINGSHIP: 6). JG

Jeffrey, Francis (1773–1850), a founder of the *Edinburgh Review* in 1802 and its editor until 1829. Though born into a Tory legal household in Edinburgh, he early adhered to Whig principles. This was a formula for failure at the Scots bar (see LAW AND LAWYERS: 2) of the 1790s and he had to turn to literature. The plan for the *Review* was conceived with his friends Henry Brougham, Francis Horner, and the Revd Sydney Smith at his flat in Buccleuch Place. It became a huge success, with a wide readership all over Britain and abroad. It stands in many respects as the ancestor of modern higher journalism: clever, probing, and irreverent. Jeffrey's literary criticism was among its strengths, though also the one of least lasting value. Upholding the literary authority of the past, he condemned the poetic spirit of William Wordsworth, Samuel Taylor Coleridge, and Robert Southey, reserving special venom for their unconventional and inelegant diction, obsessions with their Romantic selves, and introduction of characters from the lower orders. He invented the term 'Lake School', intended to be disparaging. Posterity has found these judgements pallid and prissy. On the other hand, he did admire the work of Lord Byron and John Keats. Despite his strong personal preferences, Jeffrey maintained a critical balance in the *Review* as a whole. He never earned enough from it to support himself, but his fame as editor did eventually bring him more lucrative practice at the bar, especially in defence of radicals amid the upheavals following the end of the Napoleonic Wars. The political liberalism about which he had thus far been discreet then turned overt. In 1830 he became Lord Advocate in the Whig government and was elected to parliament. He piloted the Scottish Reform Bill through in 1832 but never enjoyed politics, and went on the bench in 1834. MRGF

Johnston, Thomas. Tom Johnston (1881–1965) as a politician and journalist was one of the key figures of 20th-century Scottish history. He was born and raised in Kirkintilloch, Dunbartonshire, the son of a small businessman. He received a solid schooling and subsequently found employment as a clerk. By this time, he had become attracted to the politics of the Fabian Society and the ILP (see LABOURISM), and in 1903 stood for a local election on the latter's platform. This marked the beginning of Johnston's political career, but in parallel he made his mark as a journalist. While still in his twenties he inherited a printing press and founded a weekly paper, the *Forward*, which rapidly became the leading socialist organ in Scotland. Johnston's reputation as an incisive propagandist for the labour movement rests on writings such as his attack on the Scottish aristocracy, *Our Scots Noble Families* (1909), and his substantial study *The History of the Working Classes in Scotland* (1920).

Johnston opposed the Great War and had to endure a government shutdown of *Forward* for a period in 1916. He first entered parliament in 1922 and became a strong ally of the Labour Party leader, Ramsay MacDonald. In the latter's minority government (1929–31), Johnston held the offices of Under-Secretary for Scotland and Lord Privy Seal (entailing cabinet membership). The fall of the government over the financial crisis of 1931 resulted in Johnston losing his seat and concentrating on writing until 1934, when he returned to the House of Commons. The mid-1930s found him engaged in attempts to prevent the drift to another war, and in schemes for greater autonomy for Scotland. In 1939 the imminence of war persuaded him to become a Regional Commissioner for civil defence, and in February 1941 he agreed to Prime Minister Churchill's request to become Secretary of State for Scotland (see CORPORATE STATE AND SCOTTISH POLITICS) in the wartime coalition. It was an opportunity that the pragmatic yet visionary Johnston exploited to the full: his achievements in creating the North of Scotland Hydro-Electric Board and bringing war work to Scotland have ensured his reputation as probably the greatest *Scottish Secretary to date. Johnston proved adept at harnessing the expertise of his colleagues to his objectives, promoting a sense of national unity, and conducting his own public relations. Johnston retired from politics in 1945 but continued to be active in his own creations such as the Hydro-Electric board and the Scottish Tourist Board (see also ECONOMIC POLICY: 4). GW

Justiciary, High Court of. The High Court of Justiciary is today Scotland's principal criminal court, with exclusive jurisdiction to try the 'pleas of the crown' (murder, robbery, rape, treason, and fire-raising). In addition, since 1926 it has served as the appeal court in criminal matters from all courts of criminal jurisdiction in Scotland (including the High Court as a trial court), following the miscarriage of justice in the Oscar Slater case. In contrast

Justiciary, High Court of

with the Court of *Session, there is no further appeal to the House of Lords.

The origins of the court lie in the medieval justiciary (see LAW AND LAWYERS: 1). From the 12th century on, royal officers known as justiciars or justices toured parts of the country, holding courts in both civil and criminal matters. Early in the 16th century such circuits ceased and the justiciarships were consolidated in one office, that of the Lord Justice General, which became a sinecure until the Lord President of the Court of Session was appointed as the permanent holder ex officio in 1830. In the 16th century a Justice Court for criminal matters sat in Edinburgh, with justice deputes presiding. They also held courts by commission in the localities. In 1672 the office of justice depute was abolished and the High Court of Justiciary established, to sit in Edinburgh and also to go on circuit. The court consisted of the Lord Justice General, the Lord Justice Clerk, and five Lords of Session. Circuits were not fully re-established until the 18th century, but remain a modern characteristic of the court, trials usually being held in the region where the offence was committed. From 1887 all the judges of the Court of Session have also been Lords Commissioners of Justiciary.   HLM

K

Kenneth mac Alpin (Cinaed mac Ailpín), king of the *Picts from sometime in the 840s to 858. Very little is known for sure about him, except that he established Dunkeld as the principal church in southern Pictland in 849, and that he died of cancer at the palace of *Forteviot in February 858 and was succeeded as king of the Picts by his brother Domnall (858–62) and then his sons *Constantine I (862–76) and Aed (876–8). A century after his death he was portrayed as destroyer of the Picts and founder of the kingdom of Alba. Although Kenneth obviously did not destroy the Picts, many historians have accepted that he may have been a king of *Dál Riata who took over or conquered the Picts, and thereby 'united' the Gaelic Dál Riata with Pictland. There is no compelling evidence that such a 'united kingdom' existed. Moreover, the idea that Kenneth conquered the Picts is likely to be a politically inspired fiction designed to consolidate the achievement of Kenneth's descendants (see KINGSHIP: 3) who, by the 950s, had monopolized the kingship (see KINGSHIP: 2). Far from being a conqueror of the Picts, it appears that Kenneth, and particularly his son Constantine, were committed to promoting Pictish identity, which did not 'disappear' until 900 (see NATIONAL IDENTITY: 1). At the same time he may have been of Dál Riata royal stock, although the evidence for this is not universally accepted. Perhaps we should compare Kenneth's situation with that of *David I, who used both his English and Gaelic ancestry to sanction his royal authority and gain prestige. Kenneth, who saw no contradiction in being both a Pictish king and a royal Gael, could be seen in a similar vein, although such duality is clearer in the reign of his son, Constantine. DB

kingship: 1. early medieval; 2. 900–1100; 3. Canmore dynasty; 4. Bruce dynasty; 5. Stewart dynasty, to James V; 6. Stewart dynasty, Mary, Queen of Scots, to James VI; 7. absentee monarchy, 1603–1707.

1. early medieval
The most vivid remains of early medieval kingship are the forts which still dominate their surrounding countryside, such as *Dunadd in mid-Argyll, *Dundurn in upper Strathearn, *Edinburgh, and *Stirling. Some forts stand guard over stretches of sea, like *Burghead looking across the Moray Firth, or Dumbarton on the inner Firth of Clyde. These were fixed points in a violent political world where a king could win and lose a huge realm in the fortunes of war. Both *Aedán mac Gabráin of *Dál Riata and the Pictish king, *Ungus (Onuist), son of Uurgust, became masters of much of what is now Scotland, but could not sustain their conquests. A king's power depended vitally on his warband, a collection of ambitious young men and hardened champions drawn to a king's service by the prospect of plenty. In exchange for the enjoyment of mead, meat, and imported luxuries provided liberally by the king, these warriors were expected to fight to the death as they vied with other warbands for control over territories. A successful king would attract more warriors, which would make it possible to conquer more territory which could be exploited to sustain a greater warband.

Not all kings were mighty war-leaders. *Ireland is the only society in this period which is documented in detail. There local kings (*ríg túaithe*) are a prominent feature in the law tracts of the 7th and early 8th centuries. The authority of these kings rested partly on a ceremonial function to protect the fertility of their locality and the well-being of its landholding families and churches. Their status was also partly determined by the number of clients who gave them food-renders and manpower in return for cattle. A king's claim to office was also underpinned by his position as head of a high-ranking kindred. Some mighty war-leaders were probably local kings who attracted a powerful warband which enabled them to dominate other local kingdoms, extracting tribute from their kings. These overkings (*ruiri*) might, in turn, owe tribute to a king of overkings (*rí ruirech*).

It is impossible to know to what extent such local kingdoms were the norm in early medieval Ireland, let alone in Scotland where so little information survives from this period. Certainly some larger kingdoms began to maintain some continuity in the early Middle Ages. Dál Riata is a well-documented example of what appears to be an overkingdom centred on Dunadd in which control was regularly exercised by one local kingdom over others.

The most significant of the larger kingdoms was probably Fortriu, which may have stretched from Strathearn to the Mearns, a considerable territory controlling most of the fertile land in the east midlands. Kings of Fortriu appear in contemporary record from the late 7th to the early 9th centuries, and some (such as *Ungus (Onuist), son of Uurgust) extended their power well beyond these bounds. Fife, Atholl, and the area around Stirling and Clackmannan may have been local kingdoms which regularly fell under the shadow of Fortriu. Fortriu itself, however, may not have functioned as a group of local kingdoms in the early Middle Ages; it was the territory of the Verturiones, a powerful tribe mentioned in a Roman source in the mid-4th century. The Verturiones are the only 'Pictish' tribe known to have maintained their identity beyond the 6th century. Perhaps this was because a king of Fortriu was established in the sub-Roman period. If this was so, then the kingdom's enduring cohesion would suggest that local kingdoms, if they existed within Fortriu, may have effectively been absorbed early on. Fortriu in due course formed the core of what became the kingdom of Alba (Scotland) in the 10th century (see NATIONAL IDENTITY: 1). The only evidence for concentrations of wealth fostered within a larger-scale political structure before 900 is the clusters of Class II stones particularly in Fortriu and Easter Ross (see MONUMENTS: 1). DB

2. 900–1100

The history of a kingdom of Scotland can be said to begin in 900 when the Gaelic term for Scotland, 'Alba', is first recorded as the kingdom's name. The kingdom was probably simply Pictland in a new guise (minus the areas in the north under Norse rule). But the new name, Alba, also signified a fundamental change in kingship. For the first time, the kingship was kept exclusively in the grip of a single family for more than two generations. This had never been achieved by Pictish kings, partly because of resistance from other families with recent royal ancestors who did not wish to be permanently excluded from the kingship, and partly because of the tendency for ruling families to dissolve into rival branches. The secret of the success of the descendants of *Kenneth mac Alpin after 900 was that a power-sharing arrangement kept the two branches of the family from fighting each other for the kingship. The deal was that the kingship would rotate between the descendants of Kenneth's sons, *Constantine I (d. 876) and Aed (d. 878). This arrangement was modelled on the highly successful rotation between two branches of the Uí Néill,

the dominant dynasty in *Ireland, with whom the descendants of Kenneth mac Alpin had close contacts. Credit for establishing such a rotating kingship in Scotland should go to *Constantine II, who succeeded his cousin Donald II (Domnall mac Custantin) in 900 and resigned the kingship after more than 40 years to Donald's son, Malcolm I (Mael Coluim), who after his death was succeeded by Constantine's son, Illulb (Indulf). This new form of succession meant that descent in the male line from Kenneth mac Alpin became the lynchpin in defining the kingship. Moreover, through Kenneth's Gaelic male pedigree, the kingship was identified explicitly as a Gaelic institution.

The solidarity between the two branches of the family broke down in 965, and the descendants of Aed (d. 878) were finally excluded after 997. The family's monopoly of power came to an end after the reign of Malcolm II (Mael Coluim mac Cinaeda) (1005–34). A new breed of king came to the fore, one whose kingship was acquired by power and opportunism rather than pedigree. The first was Duncan I (Donnchad ua Maíl Choluim), son of Crínán, abbot of Dunkeld, who after six years was killed by *Macbeth. Both were descended from Kenneth mac Alpin through their mothers, and not in the male line. The last descendants of Kenneth mac Alpin in the male line were Meic Duib (MacDuffs), who were excluded from the kingship and instead provided the chief official at royal inaugurations. The next family to assert a monopoly of the kingship was the descendants of Malcolm III 'Canmore' (Mael Coluim mac Donnchada) (see KINGSHIP: 3) and St *Margaret in the 12th century.

Kings of Alba did not control all of Scotland in this period. The west and south-west were at most only occasionally under their overlordship. In the 11th century they had established control over the south-east, but they lost power over *Moray. Unlike earlier kings, whose power was focused on hilltop strongholds, the kings of Alba's most conspicuous residences were associated with churches adorned with sculpture, such as *St Andrews, Dunkeld, Meigle, and Brechin. Otherwise they concentrated on touring from one local centre to another where they and their court would hold sumptuous feasts to consume the produce collected as tribute by officials (known as thanes). Many regions were controlled by semi-independent lords, called mormaers. Mormaers may have existed before 900, but it was probably after 900 that the great regional lordships of the Middle Ages first took shape, many of which remain as regional identities today: Buchan, Mar, the Mearns, Angus, Gowrie, Fife, Atholl, Strathearn, Menteith, and the Lennox. Churches (see RELIGIOUS LIFE: 1), thanes, and mormaers together formed a structure of power which provided the stability for the kingdom to endure. It was on these foundations that the kingdom of Scotland was built.   DB

3. Canmore dynasty

This is the name given to the line of kings of Scotland descended from Malcolm III 'Canmore' (Mael Coluim mac Donnchada) (1057–93) and his wife St *Margaret, sister of Edgar Atheling. Malcolm, who succeeded *Macbeth to the Scottish throne, was the first of a dynasty which, in the course of the ensuing two centuries, spanned the reigns of ten kings. Following Malcolm himself, first his brother Donald III (Domnall Bán) (1093–4, 1094–7), and his son by his first marriage, Duncan II (briefly, 1094), succeeded him. This was a period which saw convulsions within the kingdom: Macbeth, Donald III, and Duncan II all ended their reigns violently. In the following decades, however, the succession became more peaceful. Donald III having been ousted, with English help, by Malcolm's eldest son by his marriage to Margaret, Edgar (1097–1107), all the ensuing kings succeeded without apparent dissent. Edgar was succeeded by his younger brother, Alexander I (1107–24). Both died childless, and it was not until the death of the third brother, *David I (1124–53), that the system of lineal descent known as primogeniture became clearly apparent in the Scottish monarchy. David's own son (Henry, earl of Huntingdon) predeceased his father, who was therefore succeeded by Henry's son Malcolm IV (1153–65). His younger brother, William I 'the Lion', succeeded the childless Malcolm in 1165, from whom the succession passed in direct father-to-son succession through Alexander II (1214–49) and Alexander III (1249–86). All of Alexander III's children predeceased him, however, and the premature death in 1290 of his only surviving heir, his granddaughter Margaret, 'Maid of Norway', precipitated the dynastic crisis which led to the *Great Cause and eventually the Wars of *Independence and the assumption of power by the dynasty of Bruce (see *ROBERT I), followed by that of Stewart (see KINGSHIP: 4–6).

The last effective attempt to enforce the traditional Celtic succession system was made by Donald III, Malcolm III's brother, who seized the throne twice in opposition to Malcolm's sons. But, despite further last-ditch attempts to claim their fading right by a collateral line of the royal house in the north of the country in the early 13th century (the quelling of which rebellions gave William I 'the Lion' the chance to extend his authority in the northern parts of the kingdom), the pattern of succession was thereafter lineal. This was symptomatic of a changing pattern of social and political

organization within Scotland, which became strongly influenced by the Anglo-Norman system of rule, based on landholding and allegiance. The land of the kingdom being held by grant from the crown in return for military service, coupled with the increasing influence of the secular Roman-style church (see CHURCH INSTITUTIONS: 2) (the bishops of which were royal appointments, albeit that they required papal confirmation) and the gradual supplanting of the old Celtic monasteries by the major religious houses of Europe (again holding land through royal grant), all had the effect of leading the country towards increasingly centralized government, in the hands of a powerful royal line (see RELIGIOUS LIFE: 2). Added to this, with the strengthening of fiscal control of the country through a system of taxation and trading privileges based on the 'burghs' (see URBAN SETTLEMENT: 1) founded by successive kings, the kingdom saw quite radical change, particularly during the 12th century.

The character of the reigns of the 13th century was one primarily of consolidation. Although hardly the 'golden age' which later historians have painted it, the 13th century was nonetheless probably fairly prosperous (see ECONOMY: 2). Further extension of the centralization which had been initiated by previous kings was pursued by Alexander II and Alexander III, particularly in relation to the western areas of the mainland and the Isles. For centuries there had been a strong Scandinavian (see SCANDINAVIA: 1) influence in this area, and the kings or lords of the *Isles were generally ambivalent about any allegiance owed to either the crown of Norway or of Scotland. Both Alexander II and III came into conflict with the Norwegian monarchy over the Isles; Alexander II, indeed, died on an expedition to make good his claims to the islands in 1249. In 1263, following Scottish raids in the area, Haakon IV Haakonsson of Norway led a fleet to reassert Norwegian authority, but after a skirmish with a Scottish royal force near Largs, the fleet retired northwards, and Haakon died in Orkney. Three years later, in 1266, his successor Magnus VI Haakonsson formally ceded the Western Isles to Scotland, by the Treaty of Perth.

If the kings of the Canmore dynasty were successful in establishing their house as the undisputed royal dynasty of Scotland, and in achieving an unprecedented level of centralized control over the kingdom, their area of least success must be seen in the issue of *Anglo-Scottish relations. Although the relations between the two countries, particularly in the 13th century, were for the most part cordial, the influence exerted over the Scottish kingdom by the more powerful monarchy to the south was a recurring feature. The English crown had been instrumental in establishing Malcolm III,

Duncan II, and Edgar on the throne of Scotland, and there was no doubt that it harboured ambitions to make real a claim to overlordship over Scotland. One of the low points of the Canmore dynasty came in 1174, when William, captured in battle against the English, was imprisoned and forced to offer homage for his kingdom to Henry II. In 1189, when the English kingdom was weak following Henry's death, the overlordship was formally surrendered, but the episode was to herald a long-standing argument over the status of the Scottish monarchy. There were regular statements and rebuttals of the English claim to overlordship, and the ability of the English crown to interfere in the internal affairs of Scotland was well exemplified by the actions of Henry III during the troubled minority of Alexander III. The fact that many of the nobles to whom the Scottish kings had granted land in their bid to gain control already held estates in England, meant that much of the Scottish *nobility by the end of the 13th century owed joint allegiance to both crowns. This was to prove a major cause of conflict in the early 14th century, and undoubtedly fanned the warfare which eventually saw the relationship between the two kingdoms become better defined (see INDEPENDENCE, WARS OF).

That said, however, the two centuries during which the Canmore dynasty held sway over Scotland saw major developments within the kingdom, which, by the time of Alexander III's untimely death in 1286, demonstrated a political maturity and sense of developing *national identity which were to be vital elements in the kingdom's survival through the long decades of warfare which followed.   NHR

4. Bruce dynasty

The Bruce dynasty consisted of only two kings, *Robert I (1306–29) and his son David II (1329–71), yet the importance of the family in the history of the medieval kingdom is profound. Although now thoroughly identified with the preservation of the independent Scottish kingdom in the era of dynastic, civil, and international warfare known as the Wars of *Independence, the dynastic interests of the Bruce family and the cause of the Scottish kingdom were not always convergent.

Robert I's accession to the throne in March 1306 was hardly conventional. His inauguration at *Scone revived a personal kingship that had been in abeyance since 1296, when the previous monarch, John Balliol, had been forced to abdicate by the English king Edward I. In the intervening years Edward had struggled to impose his authority on the northern kingdom through military force. However, Robert I's attempt to re-establish Scot-

tish kingship was not guaranteed universal support from those Scots who opposed Edward. Many men regarded the deposed John Balliol as their legitimate king and viewed Bruce's seizure of the crown in 1306 as an act of blatant illegality. The contesting Bruce and Balliol claims to the throne (both families were descended from David, earl of Huntingdon, the younger brother of King William I 'the Lion' (1165–1214)) had been a live political issue since the unhappy demise of Alexander III (1249–86) and his direct heirs in the period 1286–91, and the Bruces had never been reconciled to the triumph of the *Balliol claim in 1292. The pro-Balliol opposition to Robert's kingship was made more intense by the events preceding Bruce's inauguration, for in February 1306 Robert had been involved in the killing of John *Comyn, lord of Badenoch, a leading member of the most powerful magnate family in the kingdom.

From 1306 onwards, Robert I was engaged in two distinct but interlinked struggles: a civil war against Balliol supporters and the kinsmen of John Comyn, and a wider campaign against English control of the Scottish kingdom. Initially the cause of the Bruce dynasty looked hopeless, and a succession of military reverses in the summer of 1306 saw the king become a political refugee in the Hebrides and perhaps Ireland. Bruce returned to Scotland in 1307 and his prospects of success improved dramatically with the death of Edward I in July of that year. With the driving force behind English claims in the northern kingdom removed, Bruce was able to fight and win a ruthless war against his Scottish enemies. At the same time, English forces in Scotland were placed on the defensive by an unglamorous but highly effective guerrilla war against isolated garrisons and vulnerable supply routes. Robert I's triumph at Bannockburn in July 1314 was an unusual example of the king committing his forces to a pitched battle.

Despite the success at Bannockburn Robert's kingship and the future of his dynasty were not secure. Many Scottish noblemen (see NOBILITY: 2) remained sympathetic to the Balliol cause, the English crown refused to recognize either Bruce as king or the independent status of the Scottish kingdom, and the succession after Robert I was unclear. Bruce's sole remaining brother and designated heir, Edward, died fighting in *Ireland in 1318 leaving the infant Robert the Steward (the future Robert II), the son of the king's daughter Marjorie, as heir to the throne. Before the end of his reign in 1329 Robert I had provided partial solutions to all these problems. In 1324 Robert was blessed with a male heir, the future David II, to continue the dynasty. Consistent military pressure on the north of England and a political crisis in the English government produced a formal, although as it turned out temporary, recognition of the Bruce dynasty and its hold on the Scottish throne in the Treaty of Edinburgh-Northampton, which also made provision for the marriage of David Bruce to the sister of the future Edward III.

In reality, however, the settlement depended entirely on the personal authority and prestige of Robert I. After the king's death in 1329 the Bruce dynasty was once more engaged in a battle for political and military survival in the face of open war (see WARFARE, WEAPONS, AND FORTIFICATIONS: 1) with dynastic rivals and/or the English crown. In the wake of Robert's death the son of John Balliol, Edward, revived his family's claim to the throne, and Balliol's cause soon received the military and political backing of the English king Edward III. Armies fighting in the name of the infant David II experienced major reverses at the hands of Balliol and the forces of the English king, and in 1334 the young king was forced into exile in *France.

Although the dynasty seemed about to collapse, resistance to the Balliol regime and its English backers was maintained in David's absence by a number of men, including Robert the Steward, the king's nephew and nearest heir. Increasingly, David seemed to regard the Steward as a dangerous internal rival for leadership of the Bruce/ Stewart cause and the relationship between the two men remained poor for the remainder of the king's life. By 1341 the Balliol/English threat had receded sufficiently for David to return to his kingdom. In a bid to persuade the English crown to abandon its support for Balliol David readopted his father's policy of raiding in northern England. The strategy backfired when the king was captured by the English at the battle of Neville's Cross, near Durham, in 1346. In the king's absence the Steward acted as guardian and steadily increased his influence in the kingdom. The captive king became increasingly desperate to win his release, and began to support plans to amend the Scottish succession by naming the English king or one of his sons as heir-apparent to the Scottish throne if David himself should remain childless. The plans were consistently rejected by Scottish parliaments both before and after David's release, for the payment of a heavy ransom, in 1357.

Despite David's release the king proved incapable of producing an heir of his own, notwithstanding several romantic dalliances and two marriages. His rather unexpected death in February 1371 handed the throne to his nephew and rival Robert the Steward, the first Stewart king of Scotland. The legend of the Bruce dynasty remained potent, however, for despite his personal hostility to David, Robert the Steward wished to portray himself as

the true heir to his heroic grandfather's kingship. Portrayals of Robert I thus remained uniformly positive despite the change of dynasty, enshrining the first Bruce king as an iconographic figure for late medieval Scots.   SB

5. Stewart dynasty, to James V

The Stewart dynasty was founded by Robert the Steward, who succeeded to the throne in 1371 as Robert II following the death of his uncle by marriage, David II (1329–71), the last of the Bruce kings (see KINGSHIP: 4). The Steward's mother was Marjorie Bruce, daughter of Robert I (1306–29), after whom the younger Robert was named. The descendants of Robert II would dominate the government of the Scottish kingdom for the remainder of the medieval period.

When Robert II came to the throne he was already 54 years of age and brought with him the massive territorial resources he had acquired during a long and successful baronial career. Robert's accession also provided the kingdom with an extensive new royal family in the form of his thirteen legitimate and nine illegitimate children. These two factors allowed Robert to establish a low-key style of governance that made limited financial demands on the kingdom and generally worked with and through established aristocratic leaders and power structures in the localities. The fact that the king had at least five legitimate sons ensured that the succession problems that had dogged and weakened the Bruce dynasty were not replicated after 1371. In 1373 the succession to the crown was formally limited to the male heirs of Robert II's five sons in order of seniority. The king also used his family to extend his influence in a pragmatic sense by establishing his adult sons as important members of the royal administration and as major regional magnates (see NOBILITY: 2), often wielding extensive delegated royal powers. The king's third son, Alexander, earl of Buchan and lord of Badenoch, for example, became lieutenant of the king for a huge area to the north and west of Inverness. The king's daughters, meanwhile, were married to prominent regional and local aristocrats who were thereby bound to the new royal dynasty. The marriage network of the royal family embraced the most important and powerful figures in the kingdom, men such as John, lord of the *Isles, and the heir to the earl of Douglas. This was particularly important given the long-term entrenchment of the authority of these great regional lords during the disturbed conditions of the early 14th century. The Clan Donald and Douglas lordships, and others, had been built by militarily powerful figures often with little or no reference to the legitimizing authority of the crown. In that sense

Robert's style of kingship recognized that Scotland had in many ways become a more regionalized kingdom in the course of the 14th century. Buoyed by the resources of his own extensive patrimony and an upturn in customs revenue, the king was also able to dispense considerable patronage in the form of pensions and annuities to his own sons and other great magnates. Robert's rule was based on this wide and informal network of kinship, marriage alliance, and mutual self-interest. It was a style of government that laid little stress on the formal rights and privileges of kingship.

It was also a style of government that did not transfer smoothly or easily to Robert II's successor, John, earl of Carrick, who became king as Robert III in 1390. Even before 1390 Carrick had been made aware of the difficulties of controlling a political system in which he was surrounded by ambitious quasi-royal Stewart kinsmen and powerful regional lords with an established and accepted role in the governance of the kingdom. In the 1380s the consensus underpinning Robert II's rule had gradually unravelled and a series of palace coups saw first the king displaced from the full exercise of power by Carrick, who became lieutenant of the realm in 1384, and then Carrick himself removed from the lieutenancy in favour of his younger brother Robert, earl of Fife, later duke of Albany, in 1388. The ambitions of Albany and the earls of Douglas dominated the unhappy reign of Robert III (1390–1406) and almost brought the senior line of the Stewart dynasty to an end. Hamstrung by ill health, Robert III was unable to assert his control over royal government and for most of the reign the exercise of justice and warfare lay in the hands of lieutenants and guardians, most notably Albany. The weakness of royal line was cruelly exposed in the fate of Robert III's sons. The king's eldest son and heir David, duke of Rothesay, died in suspicious circumstances in March 1402 in the custody of his uncle Albany. In 1406, the ailing King Robert was so concerned that his remaining son, James, might be placed in the guardianship of his uncle Albany after his own death that he attempted to send the young prince to the French court. Unfortunately James's vessel was intercepted by English pirates and the heir to the throne became a prisoner of Henry IV of England. The king died shortly after hearing news of his son's capture. James would remain a prisoner in England for the next eighteen years. In Scotland, Albany became governor of the realm and, when he died in 1420, his son Murdoch succeeded him in the office.

The release of James I from English captivity in April 1424 heralded the arrival of a new style of vigorous and aggressive kingship in which the rights of the crown were ruthlessly enforced. The king initiated a sustained campaign to reclaim control of crown resources and the functions of royal government from the major magnate houses, such as the Albany Stewarts and the *Douglas earls, that had established a substantial role in the governance of the realm during the governorships and lieutenancies of the previous four decades. There may have been a degree of personal vendetta in the king's treatment of his Albany Stewart kinsmen. The fate of David, duke of Rothesay, had not been forgotten, and the emergence of a popular cult based around Rothesay's miracle-working tomb at Lindores abbey may have been encouraged by the king to embarrass the Albany Stewarts and to focus loyalty and reverence on the Stewart line represented by David and his younger brother. In the year after his return James engineered the trial and execution of the principal members of the Albany Stewart family, including his cousin, Duke Murdoch. The earldoms of Fife, Menteith, and Lennox were forfeited by the Albanys and their supporters and annexed to the royal patrimony. The increase in royal revenue was consolidated by the king's reclamation of customs revenues that had been granted out to members of the nobility in the form of pensions and annuities. The king also made repeated, and increasingly contentious, attempts to persuade the *parliament that he should be allowed a general tax to help pay for his English ransom. There was deep and justifiable suspicion that any money raised from the king's subjects would be diverted to pay for an increasingly lavish royal lifestyle. The king's rebuilding of Linlithgow as a sumptuous unfortified residence was an expression of the king's ambition, power, and confidence. In political terms, however, James's rule continued to be based on the intimidation and terrorization of real or potential opponents. Complaints about the king's 'tyranny' began to circulate in the last two years of the reign. A final political and financial crisis precipitated by the failure of a crown-led siege of the English garrison in Roxburgh castle ended with James's assassination in February 1437. The conspirators were headed by the king's uncle Walter, earl of Atholl, who may have hoped to claim the guardianship of King James's young heir, also James, in aftermath of the assassination. In the event Walter was defeated by a coalition of men fighting in the name of James I's widow, Queen Joan, and her infant son. Earl Walter was executed for his role in the king's death and his earldoms of Atholl and Strathearn were added to the royal patrimony. Despite the nature of his death and the fragility of his authority, James I had, by 1437, broken many of the restrictions on the exercise of royal power inherent in the settlement of the kingdom established by his grandfather Robert II.

The dominant political theme of the reign of James II (1437–60) was the struggle between the king and the Black Douglas family which ended in the military and political defeat and exile of the Douglas earls and a further enhancement of royal resources and prestige. The long and turbulent minority of James II had seen the rise of the Douglas family to an unprecedented level of political and territorial influence within the kingdom. By 1449, when James II reached his majority, the Douglases held three earldoms, claimed a fourth, and wielded great power in and around the royal court. The relationship between the young king and William, eighth earl of Douglas, quickly deteriorated and the dispute climaxed when the king personally led a fatal attack on Douglas while he and the earl discussed their problems in *Stirling castle in February 1452. A prolonged military and political struggle with the Douglas family over three years culminated in the forfeiture and permanent exile of Earl William's brother and successor, James, and the deaths of Earl James's brothers, the Douglas earls of Moray and Ormond. The forfeited estates of the Douglas earls were added to the crown lands, adding £2,000 in rents to the royal coffers. The stable ordinary income from the crown lands now far outstripped the resources of any other noble family, while the demise of the Douglas earls removed one of the few centres of chivalric display and ceremonial magnificence that could remotely rival the *royal court. At the same time as the Stewart kings were acting as regional lords over a larger and larger area the Stewart dynasty was, in other ways, distancing itself from the rest of the nobility. Where Robert II and Robert III had married their sons and daughters into Scottish families, the royal family of the 15th century sought their marriage partners amongst the monarchical elite of western Europe.

The growing power of the Stewart kings and their never-ending quest for the resources needed to sustain an increasingly expensive royal lifestyle created political tensions and problems that were most obvious in the reign of James II's son and successor, James III (1460–88). James seems to have been intent on the promotion of royal power as a laudable principle in itself, often with little apparent care for the practical repercussions of his actions. James's adoption of the closed imperial crown in royal iconography, his concentration of government in *Edinburgh, his preference for clerical and bureaucratic rather than noble counsel, all seem to point to an attempt to develop a style of governance normally associated with the historically more centralized and bureaucratically developed French and English crowns. If this were the case, James's ambitions proved ill-suited to the political and social realities of a Scottish kingdom in which the goodwill of the regional and local aristocracy remained essential for the successful exercise of government. James III's kingship was blighted by poor relations with his brothers and other kinsmen, persistent complaints that the exercise of royal justice was lax and chiefly concerned with raising money for the crown, vocal disapproval of the king's dalliance with a pro-English foreign policy, and deep discontent with his attempts to raise money through taxation and a disastrously unpopular debasement of the coinage in 1479–80. The simmering discontent produced two major political crises in which other members of the royal dynasty sought to sideline the king. In 1482 the king was briefly captured and imprisoned by a number of major noblemen who may have intended to appoint James's brother, Alexander, duke of Albany, as lieutenant general of the kingdom. The attempt failed, but James's reign was brought to a premature end by a second rebellion in 1488, this time nominally led by the king's own son Prince James (James IV), which ended with the monarch's death in open battle against an army of his own subjects at Sauchieburn in June 1488.

Despite its inauspicious beginnings, the reign of *James IV (1488–1513) is usually reckoned to have been highly successful. The king maintained good relations with his nobility, successfully presenting himself as the natural social leader of the kingdom's martial, chivalric class. James IV's development of the royal court as a glittering and attractive venue for pageants, tournaments, and spectacles was combined with a dynamic approach to the provision of 'good lordship' to his subjects. One of the most itinerant of Scottish kings, James IV's personal intervention into local and regional affairs suppressed disorder at source and had the effect of encouraging a growth in the scope, jurisdiction, formal organization, and popularity of the crown's central courts. Unlike his father, James IV managed to increase royal income and expenditure without creating massive political unrest. The more systematic exploitation of royal lands and the crown's rights as a feudal superior did arouse localized opposition or alienate individual landowners, but discontent was largely confined to marginal areas and groups that could never threaten the king directly. The king also supported royal spending by manipulating vacancies in bishoprics and other ecclesiastical offices to siphon off church revenues, by imposing direct taxes on the clergy, or by appointing dependent members of his own immediate family to high office in the church. The relatively huge sums spent by James IV on the building of warships, the development of an extensive artillery train, and the purchase of armour seem to have been regarded as a reasonable investment in the kingdom's defences, while the expenditure on courtly pageantry and chivalric spectacles involved and embraced many of the most important and influential aristocrats in the kingdom. The personal popularity of the monarch and the glamour of James IV's 'Renaissance' court remained intact at the time of the king's death, along with a great swathe of Scottish noblemen, at the disastrous battle of Flodden in September 1513.

The techniques employed by James IV were to be developed further by his son and heir *James V (1513–42) after the latter had assumed control of the governance of the realm, following a long and fractious minority, in 1528. The basic problem for the crown remained that of finding sufficient income to pay for the spiralling costs of a 'Renaissance' monarch. The prestigious building projects supported by James V at *Stirling, Falkland, and Linlithgow, for example, involved substantial expenditure. The ordinary income of the crown was increased by a small rise in customs revenues, and a more substantial increase in the profits from royal lands as a result of extensive feuing. The bulk of disposable royal income, however, came from the dowries granted over to the king through his French marriages and, more particularly, his increasingly ruthless exploitation of the resources of the church through taxation, the retention of revenues during episcopal vacancies, and the shameless appointment of royal bastards to senior ecclesiastical offices. The centralization, professionalization, and gradual secularization of justice and administration that had been a feature of late 15th-century Stewart kingship also continued apace, most notably through the foundation of the College of Justice (or Court of *Session) in 1532.

Despite the sometimes gloomy estimation of James V's rule, there was no indication of significant unrest during his personal reign, and the crown remained solvent to the time of the king's death in 1542. The real problem lay elsewhere, in the crisis provoked by the unexpected death of not one but two male infant heirs, James and Arthur, in 1541. The infant Princess Mary, born a few days before James V's death, had only bastard siblings. Should she die, as had the young Maid of Norway some 250 years before to bring to an end the Canmore dynasty (see GREAT CAUSE), a similar succession struggle was likely to result, this time between rival magnates from *Hamilton and Lennox Stewart families.   SB

6. Stewart dynasty, Mary, Queen of Scots, to James VI

After 1542, the Stewart line faced a number of new challenges. The reign of *Mary, Queen of Scots

(1542–67), was the sixth in a row in which a minor had succeeded to the throne. Yet there was also a vital difference. *James V's two infant sons, James and Arthur, had died within a week of each other in 1541. So 1542 was the first time since the founding of the dynasty in 1371 that a king had died without a male heir. James V's infant daughter, Mary, entered uncharted territory in political terms, but she was bolstered by the prestige of her descent and by the royal establishment and traditions of deference and service that had been created and cultivated by her ancestors over a century and a half. The queen dowager, Mary of Guise, had barely five years' experience of her kingdom and her position had not been confirmed until after she gave birth to a male heir; it was only then that she was crowned, in 1540. The difficult years of the 1540s, which saw the *Rough Wooing, war, and English invasion nevertheless also witnessed a steady consolidation of her position, at the expense of the hapless governor, the earl of Arran.

The 1540s were about not one royal wooing but two. The failure of Henry VIII's attempts to secure both his northern frontier and a dynastic marriage between Mary and his son, the later Edward VI (1547–53), opened the door for the Valois dynasty at the expense of the Tudors. The price of the removal of the child queen to *France for safe keeping in 1548 was another marriage treaty, with the Dauphin François, son of Henri II. The link between the Stewart dynasty and the French royal house, which had lapsed after the premature death of Madeleine, James V's first wife, was renewed. Their marriage at Notre-Dame in Paris in 1558 brought, for Henri II, the glittering prospect of a foothold in the British Isles and a claim to the crowns of England and Ireland as well as the crown matrimonial should Mary die. For many Scots nobles, the prospect was worrying: the example of Brittany, which had been annexed to the French crown in the 1530s, some 50 years after another dynastic match, played on many minds in the *Reformation crisis and the Wars of the *Congregation of 1559–60.

The fact that Scotland avoided becoming a French colony defied the expectations of many and was the result of a series of unexpected events, most notably three deaths: that of Henri II in a jousting accident in mid-1559; of the regent Mary of Guise, stricken with dropsy, in the summer of 1560; and of the new king, François II, of a brain abscess in December 1560. Mary Stewart, reigning queen of France, became a dowager queen virtually obliged to return to her own realm in August 1561 to reclaim her inheritance in the aftermath of the unprecedented circumstances of a Protestant revolt, which affected not to be a rebellion against her authority. The bargain was struck between Mary and her half-brother, Lord James, later earl of Moray, on behalf of the Lords of the Congregation. Once home, Mary found herself surrounded by illegitimate half-brothers, the produce of the prolific James V. In another sense, she was isolated, at least until her marriage in 1565 to a Lennox Stewart cousin, Darnley. The marriage quickly produced a male heir, baptized Charles James in a glittering Renaissance fête at Stirling, which proclaimed the divinity of the Stewart line, guarantor of peace and prosperity in troubled times. The complex events of the next seven months, which saw the mysterious murder of Darnley, Mary's unpopular marriage to Bothwell, her forced abdication, and the coronation of her infant son as *James VI, provoked a bitter civil war (1568–73) between 'king's men' and 'queen's men' but not a threat to the Stewart succession.

James VI's reign, once the rivals in the civil war had fought themselves to a standstill, otherwise followed a familiar pattern—of a long minority followed by a rapid consolidation of royal power. The early 1580s also saw a return of the sprawling, extended Stewart family to positions of influence, in both the *royal court and government. Like many royal families, the Stewarts had their black sheep and a fair amount of James's reign was spent hauling into line or punishing errant kin, including the ambitious Francis Stewart, earl of Bothwell, who fled into exile in 1595, or Patrick Stewart, earl of Orkney, who was executed in 1615 after a record of over twenty years of misdemeanours.

In one important respect James was remarkably slow to attend to his royal duty: the quest for a wife and an heir. Candidates were considered and spurned for much of the 1580s. By 1589, when James was 23, there was a distinct shortage of Protestant princesses of a suitable age and James was forced to choose between what his chancellor Maitland saw as the 'wise, staid woman', the 28-year-old Catherine of Navarre, and the 'child', Anne of Denmark. After a week's deliberation in his chamber, James chose the 14-year-old. By the second half of the 1590s, there was, for the first time for over a century, a large royal family: seven children were born, although only three survived beyond infancy. A number were, to the dismay and fury of their mother, fostered out amongst rival nobles to help keep court factionalism in check.

The spiralling costs of the royal household and court forced James, like Stewart monarchs before him, into an increasingly desperate search for new sources of income to avoid bankruptcy. Taxation at unprecedented levels and debasement of the coinage overtook income from royal lands as the crown's main money-spinner. The exodus to London of the royal Stewarts after James succeeded to the English throne in 1603 brought some relief and new sources of income for the king, but tax demands made of his Scottish subjects steadily increased throughout the rest of his reign. In England, a pointedly patriotic and chivalric cult grew up around the figure of James's eldest son and heir, Prince Henry, calculatedly named after Queen Elizabeth's father, Henry VIII. His premature death in 1610 vested the succession in his younger brother, Charles, who did not enjoy the same lionization. Born in Dunfermline in 1600 but wholly English in upbringing, the next king of Scots did not visit his northern kingdom until 1633.   ML

7. absentee monarchy, 1603–1707

In his speech to the Star Chamber in 1616, *James VI and I echoed Christ's words, 'My sheep hear my voice'; his own people, he claimed, 'most willingly hear of the voice of me, their own Shepherd and King'. He did not explain how his Scottish subjects, faced since 1603 with absentee kingship, would be able to hear that voice; and it fell more sweetly on English than Scottish ears when he cited the prophecy of his ancestor Henry VII that 'the lesser Kingdom . . . would follow the greater'. He was dodging a problem which had become a commonplace in early modern Europe, with the emergence of composite monarchies, of which the Spanish *monarchia* was the greatest but not the only example. Multiple kingdoms and personal kingship did not sit well together.

James's preferred solution at the beginning of his composite kingship was a closer union than the mere personal uniting of the crowns: the single kingdom of Great Britain (see UNION OF THE CROWNS). By the time of his Star Chamber speech, that policy was visibly dead, or at least comatose; apart from an incorporating union under Cromwell in the 1650s, it would take another century to unite the kingdoms. But he never tried to apply to Scotland another possible method of rule, the 'king of all and king of each' which was the Spanish model and also that used in *Ireland, whereby the crown emphasized its kingship of individual kingdoms through use of regents or deputies. Careful use of ritual, such as the full funeral service performed over the effigy of Charles V in each of his territories, did ameliorate the tensions of Spanish absentee kingship, but the revolts of the Netherlands in the 16th century and of the Catalonians in the 17th show its limitations; and in 1607 James's Scottish subjects emphatically opposed the imposition of a deputy, explicitly citing Ireland but no doubt with the Spanish practice also in their minds.

Moreover, effigies were hardly a substitute for the living ruler. Charles V probably gained from his ferociously peripatetic kingship, compared to the intense reluctance of his successors to leave Castile. But that also could be a double-edged weapon. James, famously, promised to return to his ancient kingdom every three years, but came back only once, in 1617. Charles I doubled the record, visiting Scotland in 1633 and 1641. He might have been better to stay away. Arriving eight years late for his Scottish coronation in 1633 and demonstrating, when he did, how Anglicized he was, did nothing to enhance his prestige among his northern subjects; and his return in 1641, after he had used his English subjects to make war twice on his Scottish ones, and been defeated in both (see COVENANT, WARS OF THE), meant that he came rather as a suppliant than as a ruler. But at least James and Charles adopted a style of kingship which showed some awareness of the need for personal presence in Scotland.

In the second half of the 17th century, this changed completely. Charles II did come to Scotland after his father's execution, on the very practical grounds that the Scots, unlike the English, were prepared to recognize him as king. But he refused to be crowned only as king of Scotland and thereby break the union; and such commitment to his Scottish kingdom as he had was undoubtedly undermined by the horrors of being a covenanted king, a role all too brutally imposed on him in his travesty of a coronation in 1651. The effect was to ensure that after the *Restoration, he never returned. His successor James VII and II did spend time in Scotland, as James, duke of York, but that was more in order to keep him out of England while the Exclusion Crisis—which sought to remove this Catholic from the succession—raged rather than from any real interest in Scotland as a kingdom rivalling England in importance. His Dutch supplanter, William III, was even less interested. And while Anne made much of the fact that she was a Stuart, she made it very clear that the Stuarts were now the English, rather than Scottish—or British—royal house. Why, then was the outcome of this increasingly unhappy marriage, with the Scots feeling all the bitterness of consistent neglect, the incorporating *Union of 1707, and not divorce?

The answer lies not in any clear-cut policy, but in circumstance, muddle, and accident. To begin with, absentee kingship which, simply because the king was the crucial figure who personally directed government, looks so deeply problematic, was undoubtedly less problematic in Scotland than elsewhere. For Scotland was a much less centrally governed country than England, partly because the comparative lack of sustained warfare had reduced the need for central government to make

military and financial demands of its subjects, and partly, and of even more relevance, because of the repeated minorities which had beset the house of Stewart since 1406. Thus there was long experience of a high degree of local autonomy even during the reigns of adult kings which contrasts sharply with, say, the sometimes unwilling involvement of the English counties with a government which regularly taxed them and demanded men for its armies, and also a tradition of sustaining government in the absence of an adult king, most recently in the minorities of *Mary, Queen of Scots, and James VI which saw the huge new tensions created by the *Reformation.

It was certainly the case that in James's own personal rule of Scotland there were visible signs of a shift towards a more centralized approach, but the twenty years of that shift before 1603 were hardly enough to dent the old patterns. Thus a kingdom with plenty of practice in doing without kings was in a much stronger position to cope with absentee kingship than one which had not had such experience. James, after 1603, drew on both the old and the new; to the landed aristocracy (see NOBILITY: 3) on whose shoulders the burden of minority government had inevitably fallen were added what might be termed a noblesse de robe, as the king ennobled those of his principal administrative servants, Alexander Seton, Lord Fyvie, and George Home of Spott, for example, who became earls of Dunfermline and Dunbar, and many others, to give them the magnatial status necessary to underpin their authority in the absence of the king.

Moreover, the fact that absentee kingship came into existence because a Scottish king went to London paradoxically lessened the problem. For James was dealing with men who knew him well. In the early years of his rule from London, Dunbar shuttled between his two capitals and that very personal contact was reinforced by the stream of correspondence between the king and his Scottish council, facilitated by his new and admirably efficient postal system. And there was the added bonus that, with the exception of Dunbar who died in 1611, all those who had served him in the 1590s lived on until the end of his reign. Absentee kingship did not therefore, in the reign of the first absent king at least, mean the destruction of a personal relationship between the king and his leading Scottish politicians.

The next reign witnessed a quite different kind of paradox. Charles I brought to his Scottish rule the devastating combination of ignorance and interference. Unnecessary tampering with the structure of Scottish government; an Act of Revocation introduced in 1625 which left the landowners, the lawyers (see LAW AND LAWYERS: 1), and indeed the king himself in a state of total confusion about property rights for the next eight years; an offensively Anglicized coronation; and above all a head-on collision with both kirk and political nation with the introduction of the Anglicized Prayer Book in 1637 (see NATIONAL COVENANT, AND SOLEMN LEAGUE AND COVENANT), brought Charles and the Scots to war in 1639 and 1640. The victorious Scots pushed through constitutional reforms which imposed considerable checks on Charles's powers. Their importance went beyond the Scottish border; for in England those who were equally concerned about Charles's arbitrary kingship could make common cause with the Scots. Two peoples forgot the bitterness of long-standing enmity, and came together in opposition to Charles I, first in mutual discussion and then on the battlefield. By the end of the 1640s, friendship had worn thin; and the execution of Charles produced howls of outrage from the Scots about what the English had done to their king, with remarkable indifference to the fact that their opposition to Charles I in the late 1630s and support of his English opponents in the 1640s were hardly insignificant factors in that bloody solution to the problem.

Nevertheless, a monarch who genuinely believed in dual monarchy and a monarch who produced a British crisis had enabled Scotland to regard herself as an equal partner with England. That now changed. Cromwell's military rule and his imposition of an incorporating union whereby Scotland was under-represented in the English parliament began to drive home the reality of James's own fear that Scotland would become as the northern shires, 'seldom seen and saluted by their king'. After 1660, that prophecy came true. No king came north to salute the Scots. The Cromwellian union was broken at the Restoration. But it was rule from London which was imposed, in a way which created only confusion and distrust. Charles II's initial experiment of having a London-based council in which the English outnumbered the Scots was short-lived, but enough to indicate the changed royal approach. And the practice of rule through a commissioner and the secretary who were obliged to negotiate in London the implementation of policies devised in Edinburgh or impose on Edinburgh policies devised in London—which was by no means sensitive to Edinburgh opinion—made Scotland's low priority all too apparent, while giving rise to political infighting between commissioner and secretary, as happened between the first holders of these positions: John, earl of Middleton, and John, earl of Lauderdale. The latter's elevation to a dukedom in 1672 showed who won, but what had really been demonstrated, and would continue to be, was that absentee kings were now clearly

English kings determined to assert their Scottish kingship from afar, and from the viewpoint of London. It was an unpalatable discovery; and the problem was hideously compounded by James VII's advancement of Roman Catholic peers as his agents in Scotland.

James's deposition in 1689 in favour of William of Orange was accompanied by the desecration of the tombs of the Stewart kings in Holyrood. There could scarcely have been a more dramatic symbolic rejection of the royal house of Stewart, in which Scottish pride and identity had for so long been invested. Yet worse was to follow. William saw Scotland as a source of men and money for his wars with Louis XIV. Actually, that in large measure informed his attitude to England also, but understandably the Scots did not draw the parallel. What they saw was an English king whose anti-French foreign policy dragged them in to an involvement in which they had neither interest nor desire. As king of Scots, William's fingers were burned by the horrors of the Massacre of *Glencoe in 1692, but not enough to give him pause. The disaster of the *Darien venture of 1698–1700 was blamed entirely on a king who prevented the originally willing English from aiding the Scots in their attempt to establish a trading colony on the Isthmus of Panama, because good relations with the Spaniards outweighed the interests of his Scottish subjects; there was no need to contemplate the internal deficiencies of the scheme, when it was obvious to all that the legitimate desire of the Scots to free themselves from English economic shackles had been so disastrously frustrated by the king of Scots (see ECONOMY: 3).

That only seven years later, the wholly discredited personal union of the crowns should become the union of the parliaments owed much to sheer accident. The omens had not been good. In 1704, the Scots passed an Act threatening that they would not accept the Hanoverian succession on the death of the childless Anne, and another whereby *parliament asserted its control over the royal prerogative to determine foreign policy. The English response in 1705 was to threaten to prohibit Scottish exports to England. The upshot of both was that commissioners to treat for union now began to negotiate. Corruption, bribery, and a high level of hostility surrounded this great constitutional enterprise. But the pro-Unionists held the trump card: the accident that there was no satisfactory alternative to the Hanoverians. For few wanted the Catholic Stuarts back, and there was no one else. And so a century of absentee kingship, with all its vicissitudes and weaknesses, led to a solution which defied definition: an incorporating union (see UNION OF 1707) in that it produced the parliament of Great Britain, a non-incorporating union in that it left Scots law (see LAW AND LAWYERS: 2), education (see SCHOOLS AND SCHOOLING: 2), and the kirk (see CHURCH INSTITUTIONS: 5) independent of England. That it lasted in its 1707 form for almost three centuries suggests that fudge and muddle had a lot to be said for them.   JW

Knox, John (*c.*1514–72), leading figure in Scotland's Protestant *Reformation of 1560. Born in Haddington and educated at *St Andrews University, Knox was ordained in 1536 and worked as a notary and a private tutor. In 1546, when George Wishart toured through Lothian, Knox became a follower of his heretical Protestant ideas. After Wishart's burning and Cardinal Beaton's murder, Knox and his young pupils went at Easter 1547 to join the killers who were occupying St Andrews castle. Knox was persuaded to accept the call to preach and gave his first sermon in the parish church. During the subsequent debates about ecclesiastical reform he was clearly influenced by John Winram, the sub-prior of St Andrews, later to become a superintendent in the new Protestant church. The castle was recaptured with French help and Knox, along with many of his fellow captives, was sent to the French galleys.

On his release nineteen months later, Knox went to England and served as minister at Berwick and Newcastle where he met the Bowes family and Marjory, his future wife. From 1549 to 1553 he was part of the Edwardian church's radical wing, which sought further Protestant reform. The accession of the Roman Catholic Mary Tudor forced Knox to leave England for the Continent. He travelled with other English Protestants and became successively minister to the exile congregations at Frankfurt and Geneva. During this period, Knox wrote most of his polemical tracts and travelled, establishing contact with Continental Protestant churches. In 1555 he secretly visited northern England and married Marjory Bowes. He then crossed into Scotland and conducted a successful preaching tour among the underground Protestant 'privy kirks' before returning to Geneva in 1556. Elizabeth I's accession as queen in November 1558 made it safe for the English exiles to return to their homeland and Knox would probably have accompanied them and resumed his career in England. However, his pungent criticism of female rule in 1558 in his *First Blast of the Trumpet against the monstrous regiment of women* had aroused the English queen's anger and she refused him entry. Consequently, Knox sailed back to Scotland, arriving on 2 May 1559 at exactly the moment when the tensions between the Protestants and the regent, Mary of Guise, were reaching boiling point.

Knox went to *Perth where, on 11 May, he preached a fiery sermon against idolatry which provoked an iconoclastic riot. It led to direct armed confrontation which developed into the Wars of the *Congregation. Knox acted as one of the ministers and chief propagandists for the Lords of the Congregation who—with English aid—eventually won and established a Protestant regime. He became, and remained until his death, the minister of St Giles, in *Edinburgh. The return of *Mary, Queen of Scots, in 1561 made Knox very fearful for the church's future. He bitterly opposed allowing Mary to hear Mass in her private chapel and broke with many former noble allies over the issue. During the turbulent events of Mary's reign Knox continued to be outspoken, including during his famous three interviews with the queen, but remained on the political sidelines. His first wife had died in 1560, having borne him two sons, and in 1564 Knox married Margaret Stewart, the daughter of Lord Ochiltree, by whom he had three daughters. After Mary's abdication in 1567, Knox preached at the coronation of the infant *James VI and aligned himself with Regent Moray and the king's party during the civil war. By the end of the 1560s Knox's failing health made him less active. The assassination of Moray in January 1570 was a bitter blow to Knox, who preached a moving funeral sermon in St Giles's. He suffered a slight stroke in 1570 and by early summer 1572 was very weak. He died on 24 November and was buried in St Giles's churchyard.

Knox enjoys a reputation, which persists until the present day, as the key figure in Scotland's Reformation, whilst most of his contemporaries have been forgotten. This is partly due to his extensive writings. Among them is his celebrated *History of the Reformation* which gives a vivid account of the crisis of 1559–60 and the first decade of the Protestant church and highlights Knox's own role. This apart, his writings were polemical tracts and letters penned for a particular purpose and full of lively, and sometimes abusive, language. Knox believed himself called by God to be a prophet and bound to deliver the messages entrusted to him. One constant theme was the absolute necessity of avoiding idolatry, which he identified specifically with the Mass. He believed Scotland, like ancient Israel, had entered into a covenant relationship with God and must remain faithful to its promises. Throughout his life Knox also struggled with the problem of obedience to political rulers and came to believe that resistance was justified. In 1558 Knox produced an important series of tracts discussing resistance, including the most notorious, the *First Blast of the Trumpet*.

Knox was neither a systematic theologian nor an original thinker but his ideas have had a long-term influence upon Scottish thought. He had a hand in the compilation of all the key works which helped to establish the new church in 1560: the *Scots Confession*, the *First Book of Discipline*, the *Book of Common Order*, and the Geneva translation of the Bible, but his colleagues should be given more credit than they have received hitherto. Knox was not a good organizer and was too dogmatic to be a successful politician, which limited his influence outside times of crisis. His prophetic voice and inspiring sermons were extremely important, particularly in 1559–60, but the consolidation of the church after 1560 was largely the work of others.

JEAD

Labourism is a catch-all phrase which can be used to describe the working-class political movement which is best represented by the Labour Party. Socialists in Scotland before the First World War were handicapped by a number of factors. First, they were not united into a coherent political organization. The Scottish Labour Party, which was formed in 1888, failed to make any political inroads and soon collapsed. The Social Democratic Federation was active in the 1890s, particularly in the north-east, but refused to cooperate with the ILP in the south. Secondly, in addition to sectarian rivalry, the early socialist movement had little access to the working class. Trade unions remained suspicious of the largely lower middle-class socialists and preferred to retain links with the Liberal Party (see LIBERALISM).

The weakness of the Labour movement in Scotland before the First World War can be demonstrated by looking at its electoral progress. In England, Labour activists had concluded a secret deal with the Liberals in 1903 (the Gladstone-MacDonald Pact) which gave each party a clear run in a number of Conservative-held constituencies. This electoral alliance was concluded at a time of Liberal Party weakness following defeat in the general election of 1900. Yet by the time negotiations turned to Scotland, the divisions within the Conservative Party meant that Liberals felt that their chances were dramatically improved. As a result, no pact was made for Scotland which put Labour at a grave disadvantage. In each of the three seats won by the party before 1914, the candidates did not mention socialism and stressed their Liberal and trade-union credentials. The advent of New Liberalism, which directly appealed to working-class interests, meant that the Liberal Party was able to match any Labour bid for workers' loyalty.

The First World War, however, changed the political landscape of Scotland. Discontent at Liberal government policy radicalized the working class as the former friends of the 'working man' were perceived to defend the interests of the bosses (see SOCIAL CLASS). Industrial action in the Clyde-side munitions factories and the Rent Strike of 1915 demonstrated that independent action by the working class could be successful. The Liberal Party added to its own demise by splitting and a significant section formed a coalition with the Conservative Party, giving lie to their claim that they could keep the Tories out. The Irish Catholic community (see IMMIGRATION, IRISH; ROMAN CATHOLIC COMMUNITY) was appalled at Liberal compliance in the suppression of the Easter Rising in 1916. Finally, the Reform Act of 1918 tripled the size of the Scottish electorate and gave many workers the vote. After modest gains in the general election in 1918, Labour romped home to become the largest party in Scotland in the election of 1922.

Although claims of the revolutionary potential of the Scottish working class have largely been discounted by recent historical research, the main impact of the *'Red Clydeside' was on the imagination of the middle class which took the claims of working-class leaders at face value. In any case, an examination of the beliefs of most Labour leaders in this period reveals a commitment to gradual social change and a rather hazy understanding of what was meant by socialism. Marxist revolutionaries, such as John Maclean, were quickly isolated and Labour politicians such as David Kirkwood, George Buchan, and James Barr equated socialism with the improvement of working-class conditions (see LIVING STANDARDS: 5).

Labour in inter-war Scotland placed a premium on organization and propaganda rather than ideology. Also, the gradualist belief that socialism was inevitable meant that awkward issues of policy could be overcome by putting faith in the future. The limitations of Labour's commitment to ideology were cruelly exposed in the wake of the impact of the Great Depression in the early 1930s. With soaring unemployment and major economic crisis (see ECONOMY: 6), the gradualist position that it was the fault of the international capitalist system did not engender confidence among working-class constituents who were suffering job losses. The refusal by the Labour leadership to abandon economic orthodoxy and the rank and file's refusal to accept social-security cuts split the party, with some members of the cabinet taking the lead in the formation of the 'National' Government in 1931.

The election of 1931 saw Labour reduced to an electoral rump with many of the most talented politicians, such as Thomas *Johnston, losing their seats. The problem was compounded in 1932 when James *Maxton disaffiliated the ILP from the Labour Party. Ideology had to take a back seat as efforts in the 1930s concentrated on rebuilding the party organization and considerable progress was made by the election of 1935, although the first past the post system worked to Labour's disadvantage.

The lessons of 1931 meant that Tom Johnston focused on practical politics and he was greatly influenced by the growing number of independent reports which recommended government intervention as a means to combat economic dislocation and overdependence on a limited number of key but vulnerable industries in the Scottish economy. The Second World War, which witnessed total state intervention, gave Johnston as Secretary of State from 1941 onwards an opportunity to utilize the full resources of the British state for social and economic regeneration.

This policy, and its success during the Second World War, became the template for Labour's ideological position for the next 50 years. Labour's electoral success from the 1960s onwards can be largely attributed to its ability to portray itself as the party of the corporate state. This is especially important as the Scottish economy became increasingly dependent on state intervention and regional policy (see ECONOMIC POLICY: 4) and this is best exemplified in the career of William *Ross who, as Secretary of State, was vociferous in his demands to secure Scotland a disproportionate slice of the British cake. One consequence of placing British state intervention at the heart of Labour philosophy was that there was no place for Scottish Home Rule. Indeed, the marked hostility to a Scottish parliament was based on the belief that this would hinder access to state resources. Labour's espousal of devolution in the late 1980s coincided with a growing conviction in the 'social market' and an acceptance that state intervention on the scale of the post-1945 era was no longer possible.

RJF

land agitation and reform in the Highlands and Islands. There has been an assumption that the great changes which swept Highland society in the 19th century were greeted with a tame response by those affected by them. Closer analysis reveals a more complex picture. Landlord (see LANDOWNERSHIP IN THE HIGHLANDS AND ISLANDS) coercion moved onto a new level in the period after 1815 and produced a more vociferous response from Highlanders and this entry will examine the history of land agitation and land reform since that date. The event which is usually held to mark the beginning of the long cycle of protest against the *Clearances was the attempt in 1792 to repel the advance of sheep farming by the straightforward method of driving the sheep from the northern counties of Ross and Sutherland. The successful use of the military to prevent this was perhaps a decisive event in the prevention of large-scale and widespread resistance to the Clearances. It was also only the first of many instances where the military were used to augment the limited resources of the Highland constabulary.

The deep and widespread economic depression in the aftermath of the Napoleonic Wars had a profound effect on Scotland and the period saw many expressions of political radicalism in Lowland Scotland. Agitation and protest was also evident in the Highlands. Most of the disputes in this period formed a popular response to the massive Sutherland Clearances. Resistance to clearance was also evident at Culrain in Easter Ross in 1820, a fraught period for the authorities who detected a general political conspiracy in the conjunction of protest in the Highlands and Lowlands. The deforcement of sheriff officers was evident in this event and this became a continuum in Highland protest down to the 1880s and beyond. The involvement of *women at the forefront of protest was also evident here and would continue to be evident. This cycle of protest has been characterized as sporadic, apolitical, and lacking in organization but the most important point to note is that it represented an early assertion by Highlanders that the Clearances demonstrated an unwarranted interference in traditional landholding patterns.

The 1840s and 1850s, as clearance began to gather pace, would see a further outbreak of violence. Culrain proved to be a particular site of activity, with further riots in 1840. The most celebrated example of outright resistance to clearance came in 1849 at Sollas in North Uist. A famine-stricken township was offered the choice of eviction or *emigration and responded with riotous objection to both options, neither of them particularly palatable. The protest did not prevent eviction and emigration but the trial of the rioters in Inverness, famously presided over by Lord Cockburn, resulted in lenient sentences of four months' imprisonment being handed down. In this phase of protest, events attracted considerable newspaper publicity, a phenomenon which would become more pronounced in the 1880s. This ensured particular infamy for a number of episodes in this period, such as the Clearances at Borreraig and Suishnish in Skye in 1852 and 1853, which resulted in trials for deforcement; in this particular instance, a not-guilty verdict was returned.

In the period between the famine and the Crofters' War of the 1880s, three key incidents in the history of Highland protest took place. The first occurred at Coigach in Wester Ross, with a well-documented series of deforcements of sheriff officers' parties in 1852 and 1853. This episode not only had familiar characteristics, the involvement of women for example, but also extreme elements, such as the humiliation of the sheriff officers by the forcible removal of their clothes. This episode of protest was also notable for the fact that the attempt to clear the area was abandoned in the face of the concerted opposition of the people involved. A further feature of this case was the realization by the landowners that the police forces in the Highlands were insufficient in number to deal with such protest. The interest of the media, and the inevitable polemical debate which surrounded such events, was a final element of this episode worthy of comment.

The second key event in this transitional period was the so-called Bernera riot of 1874. This event demonstrated several elements of the insecurity of the crofting community. The factor for Sir James Matheson of Lewis, Donald Munro, sought to deprive the crofters of Bernera of rights to grazing land on the island of Lewis itself. The Bernera crofters had constructed a dyke at their own expense to delineate the march with a neighbouring deer forest. Thus, the eviction not only involved the deprivation of grazing land but also the loss of a permanent improvement without any compensation. The displeasure expressed by the Bernera crofters resulted in the serving of summonses of eviction. The trouble which ensued resulted in three Bernera men being charged and acquitted after a trial which focused to a greater extent on the conduct of Munro than on the alleged crimes of the accused.

The third event involved protest at a different level. The attempt by an absentee estate owner at Leckmelm in Wester Ross to transform his crofters into estate employees in 1879–80 resulted in a public campaign to prevent what became known as the Leckmelm evictions. This campaign was largely conducted in newspaper columns with the Leckmelm crofters being ably represented by a vociferous Free Church minister. This event was indicative of the growing assertiveness of the crofting community and the growing interest in their plight in urban areas where Gaels were becoming more organized.

Prior to the 1880s, it can be argued that land agitation in the Highlands was made up of a series of apolitical and largely unconnected incidents. During the 1880s both features would be dramatically altered. From the late 1870s, land reform was one of the key issues on the British political agenda. This was largely driven by events in *Ireland, especially after the 'New Departure' of 1879, which saw the land and nation questions combined in a powerful challenge to the status quo. In a Highland context, the events in Ireland were one of a combination of factors which transformed the nature of the agitation. The decade began with a series of catastrophic storms, which wrecked both fishing gear and crops in many parts of the western seaboard and the Hebrides and led to a return of social and economic conditions the like of which had not been seen since the 1840s (see ECONOMY OF THE HIGHLANDS AND ISLANDS: 3). The continuing tradition of landlord coercion in many parts of this western area, combined with the dramatic return of bad times and the growing politicization of the urban Gael, resulted in a new dimension of protest. Rent strikes on the Kilmuir estate of Colonel William Fraser, one of the most coercive of landowners, were the first hint of this but the most significant event in this new cycle of protest was the series of events in April 1882 which came to be known as the battle of the Braes. This was an assertive attempt by a number of crofting townships to recover control of grazing lands which they had lost over the previous generation. Repeated deforcements led to the augmentation of the local police force in a determined attempt to arrest those involved. This was resisted strongly by the crofters but the arrests were carried out.

There were a number of traditional elements to this protest—the involvement of women, the tactic of deforcement, and the weakness of local police resources—but there were also some new elements, most obviously the level of publicity in the national press which was accorded to events at the Braes. Further protest was evident in Glendale in the west of Skye in late 1882 and 1883. Escalating protest and the growing organization of the crofters, with the formation of the Highland Land Law Reform Association, elicited the attention of the government. A Royal Commission was established under the chairmanship of Lord Napier in 1883. This inquiry into the conditions of the crofting community produced a remarkable response from that community. Although they were encouraged to respond to the Commission by journalists such as John Murdoch and Alexander MacKenzie, there can be no doubt as to the significance of the rhetoric produced in evidence to the Commission. The proposals contained in the report were of far less lasting significance than the evidence of the crofters.

Napier's recommendations were rather idealistic and were rejected as such by the government. The appointment and work of the Commission had induced a lull in the agitation but the disappointment engendered by the report and the subsequent rejection by the government produced a revival in the campaign of the crofters' movement. The movement became more proactive and developed a political programme at conferences at Dingwall in 1884 and Portree in 1885. A further dimension of protest in this period was the growing use of the ballot box to elect crofter candidates to parliament. This became possible with the extension of the franchise in 1885 and the elections of 1885 and 1886 saw the election of a group of Crofter MPs for Highland seats. After the rejection of Napier's proposals, the government turned to the Irish Land Act of 1881 as a model for Highland land reform. This Act had afforded the rights of fixity (or security) of tenure, fair rent, and free sale to Irish tenants. It was adopted by the government in a Highland context in 1885 and 1886 and passed into law as the Crofters Holdings (Scotland) Act of 1886. This granted security of tenure and the right to appeal to a newly constituted crofters' commission for a fair rent to all crofters resident in crofting parishes in the seven crofting counties of Shetland, Orkney, Caithness, Sutherland, Ross, Inverness, and Argyll. Crofting parishes were defined as those where the existence of the common use of land could be demonstrated in the 80 years prior to the passage of the Act, and 151 out of a possible 163 parishes were so defined.

The passage of the Act in June 1886 did not immediately lead to a cessation of the agitation. This was due to the fact that the Act did not address the central concern of the crofters' agitation, the urgent requirement of the crofting community for more land. More agitation occurred on the islands of Tiree and Skye, but most extensively on the island of Lewis. If Skye had been the focus of agitation in the years from 1881 to 1886, Lewis, with its large numbers of cottars excluded from the benefits of the 1886 Act, became the focus of agitation in the years 1886–7. There was a particular concentration of protest in late 1887 and early 1888, with a large-scale organized invasion of the Park deer forest in November 1887 and, encouraged by the acquittal of the raiders, violent incidents at Aignish and Galson in January 1888. Stiff sentences handed down to the latter protesters helped to conclude this agitation in Lewis. Throughout the 1890s, protest continued but at a much lower intensity; the large-scale confrontations with authority which had characterized the 1880s were replaced with minor damage to property and symbolic acts of protest. The period prior to the First World War saw the next cycle of agitation, most of it concentrated on the estate of Lady Gordon Cathcart in Vatersay, and on Barra, South Uist, and Benbecula.

During the First World War, incidents of protest were less numerous although they did occur and a recent author has noted the refusal to hand back land temporarily awarded to crofters under the Defence of the Realm Act. The years from 1918 to the mid-1920s saw the greatest concentration of protest incidents since the 1880s. The principal feature of this cycle of agitation was the land raid, or threatened land raid, which was used in an attempt to apply pressure to the government to grant more land to the crofting community.

The period since 1886 had seen further land reform activity which helped to produce the peak of protest in the 1920s. The Conservative government of the late 1890s had attempted to interest crofters in the idea of land purchase which was proving so popular in Ireland. This did not prove a success in Scotland and the Liberals, on their return to power in 1905, reverted to the principles of 1886 in their attempts to legislate on the land issue. The fact that the Liberal measure did not reach the statute book until 1911, partly due to the opposition of the House of Lords, and its obvious inadequacies once in operation, had helped to stimulate the protests of the 1906–14 period. The post-war coalition government had promised a major measure of land reform and produced the Land Settlement (Scotland) Act in 1919. This did much to increase expectations which could not be fulfilled due to the weight of applications for land. This, and the widespread perception that those who had enlisted had been promised land on their return, stimulated the Hebridean land raids of the 1920s.

Land agitation in the Highlands returned to a lower level of intensity after the 1920s. The Highland land issue had not gone away but the grievances which it had generated tended to be expressed through non-violent political campaigns. Over the long period from 1815 down to the mid-1920s there was a continuity of land agitation in the Scottish Highlands. There had of course been different phases within that period. The years from 1815 to 1870 saw sporadic protest. The growing politicization of Highland issues in the 1870s created the possibility for wider prominence for incidents of protest and this helped to move land agitation onto a new level in the 1880s. The 1890s and early 1900s were quiet decades by comparison but protest flared up once again in the 1920s.

There have also been thematic continuities, the most important being the fact that the principal objective of protest was initially to oppose acts of clearance and then, in the post-1850s period, to try to recover lands which had been lost to the crofting community through clearance. In the later period, this operated as a limiting factor on the objectives of protesters as the incidents of agitation did not broaden to become an assault on the landholding structure of the region. In the wider context of peasant protest, the experience of the Scottish Highlands has not been anachronistic in terms of its nature or intensity. Land reform in the Highlands, although arguably required on a comprehensive scale, has, since the 1919 Act, been limited to reforms of the crofting system.   EAC

landownership in the Highlands and Islands has been a major influence in the social, economic, and political development of the region, with the changing nature and pattern of ownership in the 18th and 19th centuries having a lasting impact on how land is regarded in Highland culture and society (see HIGHLANDS AND ISLANDS: COMMUNITY LIFE).

As the feudal system of political authority spread throughout Scotland in the 12th century, chiefs of *clans of the Highlands and Islands were noticeably slower to submit to the authority of the Scottish crown than their Lowland counterparts. Whilst Lowland Scotland was under the full control of the crown by the end of the 13th century, it took until the end of the 15th century for most Highland chiefs to obtain crown charters to their lands.

By the end of the 16th century, following a 1598 Act requiring all owners in the Highlands to produce their title deeds, few landowners could ignore the political wisdom of obtaining a feudal charter. In a region of contested loyalties and often violent territorial conflict, a crown charter could provide a useful safeguard against the unwelcome claims of neighbours. Contrary to some popular views, clan chiefs were now, in legal terms, landowners as were their contemporaries in Lowland Scotland. There was a distinction, however, between feudalism in the Highlands and Islands and elsewhere in Scotland during this period. Highland landowners generally respected the older Gaelic tradition of landholding known as *duthchas* based on kinship ties; a feudal charter, whilst useful politically, did not imply the loyalty to the crown shown by Lowland landowners. Crown authority in the Highlands remained weak (see HIGHLANDS AND ISLANDS AND CENTRAL GOVERNMENT: 2) and this left landownership in the region as a hybrid of two very different sets of assumptions.

As the native aristocracy sought to improve upon their social and economic position in wider British society in the 17th and 18th centuries, they sought to maximize rents to support such aspirations. This decisive change in the motivation of the Highland landowners, allied with wider economic factors, led to the introduction of large-scale sheep farming in the early 19th century and to a period of voluntary and forcible eviction (see

CLEARANCES IN THE HIGHLANDS AND ISLANDS) from the interior to the coast or overseas to North America (see CANADA; USA). Highland society's faith in the endurance of older understandings of land tenure was shattered as clan chiefs exercised their feudal authority and sold land to people with very different ideas about community relations, some of whom subsequently authorized the Clearances, which to this day endure as a manifestation of the despotism of much Highland landlordism at this time.

Landowning power in the Highlands and Islands was consolidated in the 19th century and a final round of clearance and *emigration in the early years of the century left Highland landowners in a position of unrivalled power. Furthermore, such power was invariably exercised not by the landowner but by the factor, or manager, whose influence on local affairs was in many cases greater than that of the owner. At this point, with the sheep economy in decline, deerstalking and other sporting pastimes became popular. Deer forests were established and developed rapidly from 1850 onwards, supported by the surplus wealth created by the southern industrial economy. Wealthy individuals purchased estates and spent vast sums on roads and hunting lodges. Game laws were introduced to protect hunting rights and the interior of the region became one huge playground consisting of large private estates extending to tens of thousands of acres.

The pattern of landownership in the 19th century became more concentrated as the new Highland elite extended their holdings. By 1870, for example, Sir James Matheson, who had amassed a vast fortune from trade in China, owned 424,560 acres (171,947 hectares) of land, including the entire island of Harris and Lewis. Sutherland Estates comprised over 1.2 million acres (486,000 hectares), almost the entire county of Sutherland. Throughout the 19th century, 90 per cent of Scotland was owned in never fewer than 1,500 estates. By 1900, over half the land area of the Highlands and Islands was held by just fifteen landowners.

Meanwhile, in the coastal fringes and islands, crofters and cottars enjoyed no legal rights to the land they occupied. Civil unrest and the report of the Napier Commission, however, culminated in the 1886 Crofters' Act, which gave them statutory rights for the first time. It applied only to the western counties of the Highlands and Islands; Perthshire and the north-east counties of Aberdeenshire, Morayshire, and Banffshire were all excluded from its scope.

The settling of the most obvious source of crofting unrest in the late 19th century did not satisfy continuing demands for land, and the state promoted land settlement in the years from 1890 to 1930 by purchasing land to create new croft holdings. Agricultural depression and depopulation (see POPULATION PATTERNS: 2) from the 1920s effectively ended land settlement, but the state expanded its role as a landowner in the form of the Forestry Commission, which bought extensive areas of land for afforestation following its establishment in 1919.

The 20th century also witnessed the fragmentation of the largest Highland estates, a process which accelerated after the First World War. Estates continued to fragment and new types of owners have emerged. In the 1970s and 1980s these have included conservation charities, overseas nationals, and private forestry investors, many of whom are gradually building up large landholdings. The pattern of landownership is still dominated by a few large holdings. In 1996, fewer than 100 owners still owned over half of the Highlands and Islands. Contemporary debate on the question of landownership in the region was significantly boosted in the 1990s by the purchase of land in Assynt and on the Isle of Eigg by community-based organizations. Such developments represent modern responses to a long-standing problem which has received further attention from the Scottish *parliament. Land reform, it is now argued, would benefit the whole of Scotland, but it has been in the Highlands and Islands that the case for reform has been most frequently demonstrated and articulated.   AWi

languages of Scotland, pre-1100. Throughout the first millennium AD the majority of the population spoke one or other of the Celtic languages: Pictish, British, or *Gaelic. At certain periods, sizeable regional minorities spoke Germanic languages: Anglian or a form of Norse (see SCANDINAVIA: 1). Latin, in both spoken and written forms, was the common language of the church. The linguistic situation in early medieval Scotland was complex and multi-layered. Bilingualism, even multilingualism, was the norm for many as languages coexisted or eventually succeeded one another. The introduction and spread of languages, language change, and language death all come about, not for linguistic reasons, but because of social, political, and cultural upheaval. Thus, language provides historical evidence not merely as a medium, but by its very nature.

Evidence for the languages spoken in early medieval Scotland is often meagre and difficult to interpret. Very few contemporary texts have survived, although a few are known from later manuscript copies, preserved mostly outside Scotland. The only extended prose is in Latin, but small quantities of poetry have survived in all but one

(Pictish) of the early medieval languages of Scotland. The entire poetic corpus, mostly formal panegyric, eulogy, or religious verse, in complex metres, appears in translation in *The Triumph Tree: Scotland's Earliest Poetry*, ed. T. O. Clancy (1998). The earliest continuous Gaelic prose is the 12th-century property records written in the Book of Deer.

An important body of linguistic evidence is provided by the names of Scottish people, places, and tribes embedded in contemporary or near contemporary texts written outside Scotland. These include early classical sources, such as Ptolemy of Alexandria's *Geography*; later Irish, Welsh, and English literature and chronicles; and Norse sagas. A small number of inscriptions, in the roman, ogham, and runic alphabets, provide at least some evidence for all the languages spoken in early medieval Scotland. These epigraphic texts are of particular importance because they have not been modified by later copying. Perhaps the most valuable evidence of all, though far from the most straightforward, is that provided by *place names. Also useful are the occasional statements about language made by contemporary commentators, for example, the early 8th-century Northumbrian historian Bede's listing of British and Pictish as separate languages, or St *Adomnán's 7th-century evidence for the mutual unintelligibility of Pictish and Gaelic in his depiction of the Gaelic-speaking St *Columba needing an interpreter to converse with *Picts.

Scant traces of the pre-Celtic (and possibly pre-Indo-European) languages of Scotland are reflected in a handful of extremely archaic river and island names but they had already died out as spoken languages by the time of the earliest written evidence in the first and second centuries AD. This early material, which derives from Roman military sources (see NORTHERN ENGLAND AND SOUTHERN SCOTLAND: ROMAN OCCUPATION), reveals a Celtic language or languages being spoken throughout the whole of the area of modern Scotland; from Kintyre, the territory of the Epidii ('people of the horse (god/ess)') to Orkney, the Orcades ('islands of the "young boars" '). The earliest named Scots, Calgacus ('swordsman') and Argentocoxos ('silver leg'), have names that are linguistically Celtic. Scholars divide the Celtic languages of the British Isles into two groups: Goidelic (i.e. Gaelic) and Brythonic (i.e. British). In reference to the differing treatment of the 'kw' sound inherited from an earlier 'Common Celtic' stage of the language, the Goidelic family (which initially retained the sound) is also known as 'Q-Celtic', and the Brythonic family (in which the sound developed into a 'p') is also known as 'P-Celtic'.

The origin of the Goidelic/Q-Celtic language spoken in Scotland is disputed. At first Gaelic was spoken only in *Dál Riata. Traditionally it was thought to have been brought there by immigrants from *Ireland in the 5th century AD. More recently it has been argued that Gaelic, in fact, developed *in situ*. Proponents of this controversial theory point out that Argyll is united to the north of Ireland by water, and divided from the rest of Scotland by harsh mountain ranges (see GEOLOGY AND LANDSCAPE). The ease of communication across water, they argue, meant that as Goidelic and Brythonic diverged during the later Iron Age the linguistic divide fell not on the Antrim coast but at the Highland massif. From the outset there would have been dialectal differences between the Gaelic spoken in Scotland and in the different parts of Ireland. These intensified over the centuries but Gaels were always mutually intelligible to one another. Gaelic-speakers would not, however, have been able to understand spoken Pictish or British (Cumbric).

Whether indigenous or imported, Gaelic spread beyond its initial 6th-century limits until, by 1100, it was spoken throughout virtually the whole of Scotland (with the exception of the Northern Isles). This remarkable growth was due in part to eastward migration by Gaels, but probably had more to do with the prestige of Gaelic as the language of the Columban church (see CHURCH INSTITUTIONS: 1), and, above all, its use by the dynasties who ruled the eastern kingdoms of the Picts from the mid-9th century. The process which led to the creation of the new kingdom of 'Alba' (see KINGSHIP: 1–2; NATIONAL IDENTITY: 1) led, in turn, to the death of the Pictish language in the generations after 900.

From the evidence of place names alone the differences between Pictish and British appear no more than dialectal, but it is clear that contemporaries viewed them as separate languages. In the medieval period, however, as in the modern, the distinction between a dialect and a language was primarily political. Although Pictish apparently began to diverge from the rest of the P-Celtic continuum during the Roman period, its separate identity is probably primarily the result of the 7th-century Anglian settlement of Lothian, which drove a wedge between Pictish-speakers to the north and British-speakers to the south and west. Another wedge was driven, this time between the Britons of southern Scotland and their linguistic cousins in Wales, by the English assumption of overlordship of Lancashire and Cumbria. The language of these northern Britons, also known as Cumbric, is reflected in a remarkable body of formal elegiac and praise poetry. This corpus, which includes the famous *Goddodin* poems, was preserved in Wales because it was regarded as the foundation of later Welsh poetry. After 900, British expanded back into areas of south-west Scotland formerly lost to Anglian speech. The language was still widely spoken there into the 11th century, although it was by then rapidly losing ground to Gaelic and probably did not survive much beyond 1100. The adoption of Gaelic by tens of thousands of Pictish- and British-speakers resulted in discernible P-Celtic influence on the language, reflected both in loan-words and, more significantly, in syntax. The study of this Brythonic influence on Gaelic has only just begun.

Germanic languages were brought by immigrants to various regions of Scotland in the latter half of the first millennium AD. Anglian, a northern dialect of Old English and ancestor of Scots, was introduced to Lothian in the 6th century. Place names show that at its fullest pre-1100 extent it was also spoken throughout the *Borders and in Dumfriesshire and *Galloway. The number of speakers dwindled at times, however, and in the 11th century Anglian was losing ground to Gaelic. Only in the 12th century, with the creation of the first towns (see URBAN SETTLEMENT: 1), did the English language begin its rise to dominance. The sole survival of Anglian literature, ironically the longest surviving Anglo-Saxon inscription, is a version of the Old English poem 'The Dream of the Rood' carved *c.*700 on the spectacular Ruthwell Cross, Dumfriesshire.

The most recent linguistic introduction to early medieval Scotland was Norse, also known as Old Scandinavian (divided into two dialects: 'East', from Denmark, and 'West', from Norway). In the years following *c.*800, the language was brought by Norse settlers to the Northern and Western Isles and adjacent mainlands, where it was also adopted by the formerly Pictish- and Gaelic-speaking native population. Place names form the bulk of the evidence for Norse but there are also a few fragments of Norse poetry written in Scotland in the 10th century. Although most of the extant Norse literature of Scotland dates to the 12th century and later, when the *earldom of Orkney and Caithness was an important centre of Norse culture. Norse died out in the Western Isles in the period after 1100, though not without leaving its mark on Gaelic vocabulary and phonology. In Orkney and Shetland, however, Norn, a language derived from Norse, survived as a spoken language until the 18th century.   KF

Latin America. Long before the *Union of the Crowns (1603), individual Scottish sailors and adventurers travelled with the Spanish and

Portuguese navigators (and others) in their forays to the New World in the wake of Columbus's momentous discovery of 1492. According to early reports, Scottish sailors went with Magellan (1519) and Sebastian Cabot (1527) on their voyages of exploration. Pedro de Mendoza, the first discoverer of Buenos Aires, had several English and Scots sailors on board his ship. Sir Francis Drake, who went to South America in 1566, visited the River Plate region several times before the second and definitive foundation of Buenos Aires by Juan de Garay in 1580. Although others from the British Isles, including Scottish mercenaries and businessmen, not to mention explorers, smugglers, and pirates, displayed more than a passing interest in the reputedly rich Iberian colonies of the Caribbean and South American continent in the 16th and 17th centuries, there was no attempt at a permanent settlement till the 1690s—and not in the larger regions of what are now present-day Mexico, Peru, or the River Plate regions of Argentina—whose name, ironically, belies the lack of the coveted gold and silver described by all the explorers and chroniclers, like Columbus, Cortés, Bernal Díaz del Castillo, and Pizarro. When the first official Scottish settlement was realized, it was in a region situated strategically between the two American continents, and based on a concept that was supposed to show the business acumen and the adventurous spirit of the canny Scot.

By the end of the turbulent century that began with the Union of the Crowns, and saw much disorder, revolution, covenanting, and restoration, not to mention a short-lived colonial Scottish settlement in *Canada in 1629 surrendered by Charles I to the French in 1632, some enterprising Scots chose their first site in the geographical centre of the Americas. By the last decade of the century, relations between King William and the Scottish parliament were not always happy, and matters came to a head with the failure of the aforementioned *Darien Scheme. The 1693 Act of Parliament authorized the establishment of a 'Company trading to Africa and the Indies', an idea that appealed both to the trading instincts of many Scots and the colonial desires of some disgruntled nationalists. It did, however, also receive support from several English opportunist merchants with a hidden agenda: the undermining of the EIC. Under the guidance of the Scot William Paterson, the founder of the Bank of England (1694), and with £300,000 of Scottish capital, the plan was to establish a storehouse/commercial centre for imports and exports on the Isthmus of Darien, through which the trade of both the Atlantic and the Pacific would be funnelled. Despite royal opposition and the withdrawal of support by the English directors, three Scottish ships

and two tenders sailed from Leith in July 1698, and founded the township of New Edinburgh. Within the year, due to dissension, bad climate, ill-health, and English opposition, the settlers abandoned the site. After retaking the settlement in 1699, they were finally defeated in March 1700 by the Spaniards who claimed the land for their monarch. The Darien fiasco cost the Scots about £300,000 and 2,000 men, greatly inflamed the bitter feelings against England, contributed to the Act of Settlement, which was imposed without reference to Scotland, and prepared the way for the parliamentary *Union of 1707.

With the Union now a historical and political fact, any further ventures would be subject to the approval and the support of the Westminster parliament. Henceforth any relations between Scotland and Latin America would perforce have to be achieved through the efforts of individual Scots or small pioneering groups. Also, events in the New World colonies would be dictated by shifting dynasties and dynamics in the Old World, and especially in France, Spain, Portugal, and Britain. By the 18th century the setting up of the South Sea Company (1711) was a concrete manifestation of the British government's aims, both political and commercial. The Treaty of Utrecht (1713), which ended the War of the Spanish Succession, helped to establish trade links with Latin America, including an infamous slave trade agreement in the River Plate region. British interest in gaining a foothold in Latin America as a source of trade and commerce was always strong, especially after the loss of the northern colonies in 1776. By the end of the 18th century, with the ideological and political influence of the American War of Independence and the French Revolution, events in the Spanish colonies were coming to a climax. The Creoles, long shut out of the business of government, were already dealing in contraband goods, and the smuggling of materials and ideas (free trade, laissez-faire, not to mention dangerous revolutionary concepts of liberty, equality, and fraternity) was rampant.

If the first two decades of the 19th century were to represent the period of revolution, emancipation, and independence in the New World, the Scots had a hand in it. Many soldiers and sailors, mercenaries, conscripts, and enlisted men, participated in the various wars of independence in the old viceroyalties—what are now Argentina, Chile, Venezuela, Colombia, Peru, and the like—fighting for ideas, ideals, not to mention money and adventure, in the armies of the great liberators Bolívar, San Martín, José Antonio Páez, and Bernardo O'Higgins (an Irish manifestation of the same phenomenon). None was more famous than the ubiquitous, skilful, but thrawn Scottish Admiral Cochrane. Described by the historian Hubert Herring as a 'queer combination of crusader for liberty and frank freebooter', Lord Cochrane had been dismissed from the British Navy under doubtful circumstances. When he arrived in the New World in 1818, the vain, overbearing Scot worked for Chilean independence under O'Higgins, a kindred spirit, and then less happily under San Martín in what was then Upper Peru. Ever the opportunist, the ambitious Cochrane also appeared on the Brazilian scene with a squadron of foreign mercenaries (including Scottish sailors) to expel the Portuguese from Brazil and so secure independence for the Emperor Pedro in 1823. He was not, however, to gain the financial and material rewards which he had been promised. With their military duties over, many of his crew jumped ship, married local women, sometimes Castilianized their names, sometimes became Catholics, and often became the founding fathers of families who were to play an important role in the development of the independent nations over the next two centuries. In fact, even earlier, after the failed British invasion of the River Plate region in 1806 and 1807, several Scottish soldiers refused repatriation, thus sowing the seeds of a future strong community. The treatment by the Creoles of the captured British officers has been well documented by Major Alexander Gillespie, the son of the principal of St Andrews University, in his *Gleanings and Remarks* (1818).

When the Argentine people did finally achieve independence from the mother country, and regularized diplomatic relations with other countries, Britain, the old ambivalent ally, was one of the first to take advantage of the commercial and political benefits that previous travel writers had praised in their reports, letters, and chronicles (such as those of Gillespie). With the opening up of the colony in the 1820s under President Bernardino Rivadavia and his European-orientated government, British immigrants started to move to Argentina. In the vanguard was a 220-strong group of Scots who sailed from Leith in the *Symmetry*, to found the Monte Grande settlement in 1825, masterminded by the Scottish brothers John and William Parish Robertson. By dint of hard work, they improved the land, prospered, and by 1828 had already built a church. Unfortunately the pioneers became the victims of the numerous civil wars that plagued post-independent Latin America. Caught between the marauding armies of the federalist Caudillo Rosas and his rival the unitarian Lavalle, the Scots abandoned their settlement and fled in 1832, mostly to Buenos Aires, leaving the Robertsons bankrupt, with but three settlers remaining. The resilient entrepreneurs became involved in trade and commerce at all levels throughout the Plate region, including a rough stint in Paraguay where they ran foul of the xenophobic dictator Doctor Francia. Monte Grande failed, but the seeds were sown yet again.

The history of 19th-century Argentina cannot be told without mentioning the contribution of the Scots. They worked the land from the Buenos Aires province of Patagonia and extended their influence even to the ill-fated Falklands. Wherever they went, they built their churches and their schools, generally taking an interest in commerce, education, transportation and sport, but rarely becoming overtly involved in local or national politics, which they considered infra dig. Robert Bontine Cunninghame Graham, who first visited the New World as a youth in 1870 and died in Buenos Aires in 1936, was the most gifted of the travellers (missionaries, engineers, miners, businessmen) who have recorded their stories of the achievements of the Scots. Graham's motives were vaguely commercial and personal (adventure). Although his ranching and sales enterprises failed, the future writer-politician gained valuable experience and much material for his later writings. Of the 40 books of sketches, biographies, and histories published between 1896 and 1936, most are devoted to Latin America, which he was to visit several times before his final pilgrimage in 1936.

When the British invaded in 1806–7, three Scots were recorded in the statistics list. By 1885, the Mulhall brothers estimated 2,000 Scots in Argentina, with their own churches—even a rancho kirk—high schools, and societies. The St Andrew's Scots School, started in 1838, has a worldwide reputation, whilst the St Andrew's Society of the River Plate still organizes Caledonian balls, the Gathering of the Clans, Burns nights, the annual 'Trip Doon the Watter' (River Tigre), and other manifestations of tartanry and Balmorality. Although the Scottish influence, like that of all the British, has waned somewhat in the 20th century (see NATIONAL IDENTITY: 6), two world wars, two Peronista governments, several military dictatorships, the 'Dirty War', and the Falklands fiasco have not eradicated the Scottish spirit introduced by the early pioneers.

At about the same time as the Robertson brothers were welcoming the Monte Grande settlers in Argentina, a group of some 200 Highlanders from the north-east of Scotland made their way to La Guaira district near Caracas in Venezuela. The Topo estate had been founded by two young Scotsmen, Beaton and Faulkner, and, with the help of Sir James Mackintosh of Inverness, the exiles left Cromarty Bay on 10 October 1825 in good spirits. By January 1826, however, the pioneers were disgruntled due to the lack of land and the conditions of the soil, which was unsuited to agriculture, whilst the snobbish British consul, Sir Robert Ker Parker, deemed the motley crew of Highlanders drunken and idle. The 1812 earthquake, the political unrest in Venezuela within Bolívar's Confederation of Gran Columbia, the poor leadership of Revd John Ross, the anti-Protestant hostility of the Creoles, and dissension within the Colombian Agricultural Association, all contributed to bankruptcy and the dispersal of the settlers, some of them to the *USA. Despite the intervention of the educator Joseph Lancaster, a friend and supporter of Bolívar, and the political involvement of Canning, the enterprise, like Bolívar's Confederation, collapsed. Unlike the Scots in Argentina, the Guairans preferred to leave as a group, fortuitously profiting from a timely commission organized to settle Scottish workers in *Canada. Through the auspices of another Scot, John Galt, a group of 135 destitute Scottish settlers arrived in Guelph (Ontario) in 1827—another chapter in Scottish pioneering which is not, however, part of this story. Obviously there are faults on both sides in the Venezuela fiasco, with the settlers and the association both having some just cause. As in Darien, the climate and the land were wrong; as in Argentina, the political and religious situation militated against the settlers. Charges of indolence and insobriety were met with accusations of fraud and exploitation. The character and the types of settlers were also a factor.

Although all three Scottish ventures in Latin America failed, the quality of the individual components of the groups had a lasting effect. The Monte Grande band of some tradesmen and some professionals spread out over Argentina, despite the adversities of 19th-century civil wars, to become the rock of the British community; their descendants were to become the 20th-century cattle barons and transport magnates. The La Guaira settlers, more at home with British North American culture, language, customs, and religion, worked the land in more modest terms, less ambitious, with fewer bureaucratic problems and more attuned to the social, economic, and political conditions in which they thrived. Many of their descendants still occupy the same land worked by their 1827 forefathers.

Darien, La Guaira, and Monte Grande are only exemplary manifestations of the Scottish need and desire to emigrate and carve a place for themselves, even if it is only what the Scottish-Canadian novelist Frederick Niven called a 'kingdom of the mind'. Chile and Uruguay, for example, are also full of smaller cases of individual and group initiatives, if not national projects, despite the unlikeliness of such enterprises after 1603, and certainly after 1707.

The 'lad o' pairts' often travelled further than London. As Cunninghame Graham illustrates in his many sketches, without the Scots there would have been no *British Empire, and certainly not in those unofficial little corners of the empire in Latin America. Despite the individual and sporadic failures like Darien, the overall long-term effect of the Scots in Latin America has been positive and beneficial.   JWa

law and institutions, Gaelic. One of the most striking features of Scots law is the continuity of its development, unbroken by conquest or lasting revolution over many hundreds of years. Although surviving sources are scanty, it is evident that this continuity stretches back, before the advent of Norman and feudal influence, to the early medieval period when four peoples inhabited what was later to become Scotland: the *Picts, the Scots, the Britons of Strathclyde, and the Anglo-Saxons of Northumbria (see BRITONS AND ANGLES). Of these, the Scots and the Britons were Celtic, and the Picts at least partly so.

Little is known of the law of the Picts or the Britons. It has been claimed that a law of matrilineal succession (presumably non-Celtic) operated in the Pictish royal line (see KINGSHIP: 1), but this is disputed. The law of the Britons is likely to have resembled that of their compatriots in Wales, later referred to as 'the Law of Hywel Dda'. It was, however, the Gaelic-speaking Scots and their dynasty who helped to forge first the kingdom of Alba, and then the later Scottish kingdom. Indeed the most obvious institutional link between this early period and the present day, and the best example of continuity, is the monarchy: the queen rules in Scotland by virtue of her descent through *James VI, *Robert I, and Malcolm III 'Canmore' (Mael Coluim mac Donnchada), from *Kenneth mac Alpin (842–58) and Fergus mac Erc, the traditional founder of the dynasty in *Dál Riata c.500 AD.

The Early Irish Law Tracts, already in writing by 800, provide the best clue as to the law of the early Scots (see IRELAND: 1). They disclose a society which was kin-based and status-conscious, in which blood feuds were common, and which was much concerned with notions of honour or 'face'. Areas regulated by law include suretyship—of key importance where there is no central law-enforcing mechanism—marriage, and aristocratic fosterage. The law of marriage, in origin pre-Christian, and sometimes termed 'Celtic Secular Marriage', allowed at first for many types of union, including concubinage and polygamy, and for divorce. One remarkable early document to survive which includes both Picts and Scots in its ambit is Adomnán's Law (697 AD), the Law of the Innocents (Lex

Innocentium), which lays down rules of war designed to protect women and non-combatants, and was brokered by St *Adomnán, abbot of *Iona, and guaranteed by rulers and churchmen in Ireland and in Scotland. Another source which provides a tantalizing glimpse of the ordering of pre-feudal society in Scotland are the Gaelic Notes (or *notitiae*) added to a Gospel book of the monastery of Deer in Buchan (the Book of Deer), which record grants of land given to that monastery. The Notes disclose the king of Scots at the apex of society, beneath him the mormaer of a province, such as *Moray or Buchan, and below that again the *toiseach*, sometimes described as leader of a kindred or clan.

As the Scottish common law took shape from the 13th century onwards, such Celtic law elements as remained—and there were many—were gradually assimilated until eventually they became virtually unrecognizable. The old dynastic line of kings continued, the mormaers became earls, and the *toiseachs* became barons and chiefs of *clans. The pattern of Celtic landholding (see RURAL SETTLE-MENT: 1; RURAL SOCIETY: 1) appears to have adapted fairly readily to accommodate feudal structures. One office holder under Celtic law, the *breitheamh* or judge (Latinized *iudex*), can be traced down the centuries gradually losing status, until he became the 'doomster', or speaker of the sentence or 'doom' of the court, finally disappearing from the High Court of Justiciary in the late 18th century. The office of *magnus iudex*, or chief *breitheamh*, of Scotia is mentioned about 1128. Arguably this office merged into that of justiciar, and survives to this day in that of Lord Justice General, Scotland's highest criminal judge. The render of *cain*, exigible under Celtic law from land in token of a lord's authority, can be traced comfortably through to the 19th century, and perhaps beyond. One remarkable case decided by the House of Lords in 1971 (*McKendrick* v. *Sinclair*) dramatically illustrates the continuity of Scots law since Celtic times. Because of deficiencies in the modern law of delict recourse was had to the medieval action of assythment, raised in respect of death criminally caused, and originally designed to regulate the blood feud, by which compensation or 'assythment' was sought by the kin of the victim from those responsible. The action was held to be still competent although inapplicable to the facts of the case. In their judgements the Lords referred to technical terms of Anglo-Saxon law, and also to 'Letters of Slains' by which the kin of the victim acknowledged that assythment had been made, and sought a royal indemnity for the guilty party. 'Slains' incorporates a technical term of Celtic law (although the judges did not realize this): the word *slan*, meaning indemnification or immunity.

Although much Celtic law and custom was absorbed into the continuing mainstream of later Scots law, in some parts of the country elements of Celtic law continued a separate existence throughout the Middle Ages and beyond. This was particularly true of those parts of the Highlands and Islands (see HIGHLANDS AND ISLANDS AND CENTRAL GOVERNMENT: 1) which fell under the rule of the MacDonald lords of the *Isles. Thus the *breitheamh* (or *iudex*) continued to exercise his judicial functions until the fall of the lordship. Some of these judges are still remembered in oral tradition in Lewis, where their house at Habost, Ness, used to be pointed out, and also in Skye and Islay. In a lordship charter of about 1485, William *archiudex* of the Isles acts as a witness. Traces of marriage customs related to Celtic law survived in the Isles until the 17th century, while the aristocratic institution of fosterage continued for a further century.   WDHS

law and lawyers: 1. to Stair; 2. Stair and after.

1. to Stair

Although elements of an earlier order long survived, the mainstream history of Scots law begins in the 12th century. Two major influences shaped the legal system. First was the emergence under the authority of the kings of Scots (see KINGSHIP: 3) of a customary system of law and courts, which, despite its essentially decentralized or localized administration in sheriff, burgh, and justiciary courts, was sufficiently mature by the 13th century to have both internal and external recognition as a system of law common to the whole kingdom. Although contemporaries clearly distinguished their law from that of other countries and in particular England, a leading characteristic of this development was selective and critical borrowing, mainly occurring before 1300, from the burgeoning English common law. This had its main substantive impact in the feudal land law, still the root of modern Scots landholding (see RURAL SETTLEMENT: 2), and in certain aspects of civil procedure such as the use of initiating writs (brieves) issued by the king's chapel, and the deployment of the assize (or jury) to decide cases. Although an important part of the medieval law was thus built around forms of action recognizably English in origin, only a chosen few, such as the brieves of right, mortancestry, and novel dissasine—all actions for the recovery of land—came north, and they were never quite the same as their English counterparts. Nor was there the vast elaboration of writs found in England: there were only a half-dozen or so forms of 'pleadable brieve' for contentious litigation, plus a few others of a more administrative nature, to be categorized as 're-tourable' and 'non-retourable' depending upon whether or not the verdict of the assize had to be returned to the king's chapel for further action. Institutionally, the offices of sheriff and justiciar were also transplanted to Scotland from England, and the courts which they held remain today in the form of the sheriff court and the High Court of Justiciary. Scotland also developed its own *parliament which legislated actively and some of whose medieval statutes still form part of Scots law.

The second major aspect of law in medieval Scotland arose from its full and generally loyal membership of the medieval church (see RELIGIOUS LIFE: 2). In consequence, many areas of social life were subject to the canon law and ecclesiastical jurisdiction, to the exclusion of secular authority. The interaction between the secular and ecclesiastical in legal matters was complex. A degree of integration existed: for example, the secular rules on succession to land were dependent upon the laws of marriage and legitimacy, which were the province of the church, while ecclesiastical sanctuary, often territorially supplemented by royal grants of 'girth', afforded protection from unlawful harm to those accused of certain secular crimes. Thus the secular distinction between homicide by 'forethocht felony' (premeditation) and by 'suddenty', with only the latter entitling the perpetrator to sanctuary, sprang ultimately from the law of the church. There were more subtle influences: for example, Scots land law seems to have kept sharp a distinction between ownership and possession despite the analytical problems posed by the dependent nature of feudal tenure in which A held land of B as a return for some service to him rather than outright; this must have been influenced by the law of the church. Pleading in the secular courts was also much influenced by the canonical model, and direct reference by pleaders to the canon law and to its near relation (in medieval terms), the Roman or civil law, was certainly not uncommon. If there can be said to have been a legal profession in Scotland before 1450, its ranks were almost entirely formed by the clergy. Indeed, in the 15th century the belief that more knowledge of and skill in the civil law would be of benefit to the kingdom and its people in the administration of lay justice in part underlay the foundation of *universities at St Andrews (1411), Glasgow (1451), and Aberdeen (1495). No doubt that belief also encouraged the steady flow of Scots churchmen to the great universities of continental Europe (notably Paris and Orléans) to study canon and civil law. Finally, parliament relied on the civil law for models in the drafting of legislation; for example, in statutes on prescription and tutory.

The principal text of medieval Scots law is known from its opening words as *Regiam Majestatem*. It was composed in the 14th century, begins as a heavily edited version of the English treatise *Glanvill*, has an extensive Romano-canonical section on pacts and arbitration, continues as a lightly edited *Glanvill* (the editing being mostly by omission), and concludes with a miscellany of purely native laws from the 12th and 13th centuries. At some stage it was divided into four books, apparently on the model of Justinian's *Institutes*; from whence also, via *Glanvill*, its proemium and the title of the work. Something of the overall nature of medieval Scots law may be seen in the mixed characteristics of this work.

The 16th and 17th centuries form an age of change in the law, but change of a developmental rather than a revolutionary character. The secular court system became more centralized with the establishment in Edinburgh of the Court of *Session as the principal judicial body, the outcome of a slow process of regularization of the long-established judicial function of the king's council rather than of any sudden decision to set up a new court and system. Part of the same process was the emergence around the court, not only of the group of professional lay pleaders who well before the end of the 16th century had established their corporate identity as what was to become the Faculty of Advocates, but also of those who produced the documentation needed for litigation, the Writers to the Signet. The Faculty of Advocates developed an examination in civil law for entrants which became a keystone in the civilian arch in Scots law. The origin of the Court of Session in the king's council was to give its decisions, or 'practicks', an especial authority; judges and advocates such as John Sinclair (d. 1566) and Sir Thomas Hope (c.1580–1646) collected them; and Scots law became to a degree a system based on precedents. But at the same time many judges and advocates had been students of the canon and civil law, and extensive reference to the learned laws was a characteristic of pleading in their court.

A second crucial change was the Protestant *Reformation of 1560, which abrogated the direct authority of the canon law and the Roman Catholic church in Scotland. Although politically and institutionally this was a revolution, its impact on law was perhaps not so severe. While the canon law became open to challenge on the grounds of inconsistency with the true reformed religion, so long as it was theologically neutral or consistent with Protestant doctrine, it remained the law in force except that henceforth it would increasingly be seen simply as part of general Scots law, as in the case of court procedure rules, or the doctrine of marriage by cohabitation with habit and repute, or was available as at least a persuasive source. The real change therefore lay in the subsequent gradual secularization of matters hitherto subject only to ecclesiastical jurisdiction. This may have had an important effect with regard to such areas of law as obligations (in particular contract) and movable property.

The reformers looked upon the civil law with favour, perhaps encouraging the increasing resort to it in the courts. Hence also there was no interruption in the flow of Scots to European universities to study the learned laws, although certainly later in the 17th century students were looking to the universities of the Protestant Netherlands (see LOW COUNTRIES) rather than Catholic *France for their legal education. However, apart from a late 16th-century flowering at St Andrews under William Skene (c.1520–82) and William Welwood (c.1550–c.1630; author of *The Sea-Law of Scotland* (1590) as well as other works published at Leiden which attracted the critical attention of the great Dutch jurist Grotius), legal studies largely withered in the Scottish universities after 1560, and failed to become established at the Town's College founded in *Edinburgh in 1583.

A third important aspect of the early modern period is the conscious pursuit of system in the presentation and analysis of the law. From the 15th century on there was a clear concern about determining what Scots law was or might be—the problems of transmission and gaps in a system which depended upon individually (rather than officially) compiled manuscripts and upon oral tradition for its continuity. Parliament set various 'codification' projects in train, with at best limited success; but it is of interest to note that in 1567 the systematics of the civil law were seen by parliament as the best model for the task. Pursuit of this objective may have underlain the compendious but still unsystematic practicks attributed to Sir James Balfour of Pittendreich (c.1525–83), compiled around 1579 but not published until 1753. The first publication of the statutes from 1424 took place in 1566 under the editorship of the humanist Edward Henryson (1510–90), who had previously taught law at Bourges. Henryson acknowledged the help of Balfour in his task. Another edition of the post-1424 statutes was produced in 1597 by Balfour's former assistant, Sir John Skene (c.1543–1617, brother of William), who also appended a commentary on the terminology of the medieval law entitled *De Verborum Significatione*. In 1609 Skene, an advocate and royal official who had studied law at Wittenberg, published his Latin and Scots editions of *Regiam* and other medieval treatises and sources. But the greatest success in stating Scots law upon a systematic basis came in the writing of Thomas Craig (1538–1608), graduate of Paris, legal humanist and advocate, who took the learned feudal law as the basis for his *Jus Feudale* (completed around 1606, first published 1655). This work gained a European reputation and was republished at Leipzig in 1716.

Craig and Skene both worked against the background of the *Union of the Crowns in 1603, which prompted moves, ultimately abortive, towards unification of Scots and English law. The period also saw the rediscovery of the link between *Regiam* and *Glanvill*. Craig was led to denounce *Regiam* as a forgery, while others, mainly in England, saw it as indicative of the ancient, and therefore renewable, unity of Scots and English law. The debate which ensued over the next two centuries was to draw a veil over the contribution of the Middle Ages to the development of Scots law.   HLM

2. Stair and after

Scots law retains its identity today as a separate legal system partly because the *Union of 1707 provided safeguards for its continuing independence, but partly also because of a succession of able writers who systematized and expounded the law. The greatest of these writers is James Dalrymple, viscount of Stair (1619–95), whose *Institutions of the Law of Scotland* first appeared in 1681.

Stair's *Institutions* have long been recognized as a work of genius. Although he modestly claimed that he had only brought together and expounded the decisions of the Court of *Session, Stair systematized and rationalized the whole of Scottish private law, and placed it within a wider European context. Stair's vision was a broad one. His early training had been in philosophy (see CULTURE: 5, 11), and he was strongly influenced by the natural law school exemplified by the Dutchman Grotius (Hugo de Groot 1583–1645), and by ideas of equity and natural justice. 'Equity is the body of the law', said Stair, 'and the statutes of men are but as ornaments and vestiture thereof.' When Scots lawyers followed Roman (or civil) law, it was because of the equity of its solutions, rather than on account of any inherent authority. Stair's *Institutions* has gone through many editions, the last published in 1981, and is still cited in the courts today. Unlike his famous predecessor Thomas Craig (1538–1608), who wrote his *Jus Feudale* in Latin, Stair wrote in elegant, well-balanced English. As a result, Stair's work is still readily accessible and, with the spread of the English language, has come to be appreciated and admired in the late 20th century by a wider international audience than ever before.

Stair's contemporary Sir George MacKenzie (1636–91) also wrote an *Institutions of the Law of Scotland* (1684), smaller in scale than Stair's, which was long used as an elementary textbook; while his *Laws and Customs of Scotland in Matters Criminal* (1678) was the first treatise on Scottish criminal law. Stair's work was continued and consolidated by

Andrew McDouall, Lord Bankton (1685–1760), John Erskine of Carnock (1695–1768), and George Joseph Bell (1770–1843). These writers, together with Baron David Hume (1756–1838) who wrote on the criminal law, are known as 'Institutional Writers'—writers whose works are treated with particular respect by the courts.

Despite the Union, the 18th century saw no dramatic change in the course of Scots law. Indeed, this period has been described as the 'classical age' of the Scottish common law, brought to fruition by the Institutional Writers. Civilian influence on Scots law continued strongly until well into the century, and many aspiring advocates, such as James Boswell, studied law at the Dutch (see LOW COUNTRIES) universities. There was little active legislation, one notable exception being the Criminal Procedure Act of 1701, which laid down important safeguards against detention without trial. There were, however, significant changes in the administration of justice. One immediate consequence of the Forty-Five rebellion (see JACOBITISM) was the effective ending of the many heritable jurisdictions which had existed since the Middle Ages, and their incorporation into the regular system of courts: regality jurisdiction was abolished entirely, and barony jurisdiction severely curtailed. Hereditary sheriffdoms came to an end, and the sheriff became, by stages, the legally qualified professional judge familiar today. Between 1808 and 1830 the Court of Session itself was reorganized and its procedure reformed.

From the 19th century onwards, the English common law came to influence Scots law more than at any time since the 13th century. This was partly because legislation was now passed by a parliament based in London, partly because the House of Lords in its judicial capacity had become the supreme court of appeal in civil matters for Scotland by virtue of the Union, and partly for reasons commercial. Lord Cooper of Culross, Lord President of the Court of Session in the 1950s, although a committed political unionist, believed that much of the growing English influence on Scots law was malign, and stultified the natural development of Scots law. He wrote of English influence coming 'unsought and indirect', and of 'the haphazard inoculation of one system of law [Scotland] with ideas taken from another'. Although there is some truth in these observations, it is also arguable that many of the changes which brought Scots law closer to English were willingly made, and represented a natural convergence at the heart of a great commercial and imperial power. Unlike the 18th century, the 19th was a period of active statutory law reform in both Scotland and England. Whatever the analysis, there can be no doubt that by the end of the 19th century Scots law was in danger of losing touch with its civilian roots, and was well on the way to being regarded as an honorary member of the Anglo-American legal tradition. Scotland's gradual separation from the mainstream European tradition was further emphasized by the adoption of codes of law on the Continent, notably the Code Napoléon of 1804 and the German Bürgerliches Gesetzbuch of 1900.

A measure of the increasingly close correspondence between Scots law and English law is the fact that the most celebrated case in the law of torts in the Anglo-American legal world, *Donoghue* v. *Stevenson* (decided by the House of Lords in 1932, and sometimes referred to as 'the case of the snail in the bottle'), is a case on the Scots law of delict. Contract, like delict, is a branch of the law of obligations, and here again Scots law and English law have moved very close, although Scots law has never adopted the English doctrine of consideration. In the third branch of obligations, however, the law of unjustified enrichment (which corresponds to the law of 'restitution' in England) Scots and English law have remained quite distinct.

Scots *family law, land law (see RURAL SETTLEMENT: 4), and criminal law have also remained, on the whole, distinct from English law. They have not, however, remained unchanged. On the contrary, the 20th century has been a period of sweeping legal change which has affected every area of the law, public and private. Arguably, there have been greater changes in the last 35 years of the century than in any comparable period for upwards of 700 years. Some reforms have been technical and narrowly legal, but others have reflected deepseated changes in society as, for example, the altered perception of the role and rights of *women, and the recognition of the rights of the child (see CHILDREN). This rapid translation of social change into law is by no means a purely Scottish phenomenon, but has been characteristic of Western society generally.

On the public front, too, there have been great changes. Britain joined the European Union in 1972, since when an ever-increasing flow of directives and regulations has reached every corner of national law, justiciable ultimately in Luxemburg. Britain has also been a member of the Council of Europe since its inception in 1949. One consequence of this has been the acceptance of the European Convention on Human Rights, and with it the jurisdiction of the European Court of Human Rights at Strasbourg. The Human Rights Act of 1998 makes the Convention justiciable for the first time in the ordinary courts of the land. At the other end of the spectrum, but by no means incompatible with European integration, the principle of a devolved Scottish parliament was accepted by referendum in 1997. Although the Scottish parliament has extensive legislative powers under the Scotland Act 1998 (see PARLIAMENT: 4), many matters have been reserved to Westminster, and questions as to the competence of proposed or actual legislation are bound to arise. In the last resort, such questions will be settled by the Judicial Committee of the Privy Council, which will, in this respect, take on the mantle of a constitutional court. Indeed, the combined effect of the Human Rights Act and the Scotland Act will greatly increase the role of judges, as against parliament, in the interpretation of basic constitutional provisions and human rights. Again on the public front, the expansion of the remedy of judicial review has led to increased judicial control over administrative action in both Scotland and England.

This entry began by praising Stair. It is only right to end with the names of two other Scotsmen who have helped to ensure the continuing survival of Scots law in good heart into the 21st century: Lord Cooper of Culross (1896–1955) and Sir Thomas Smith (1921–92). When Scots law seemed most under threat as a separate and coherent system of law Lord President Cooper and Sir Thomas Smith worked tirelessly to safeguard the integrity of the Scottish legal system. The *Stair Memorial Encyclopedia of the Laws of Scotland* (25 volumes, 1987–96), of which Sir Thomas was the true begetter, provides an authoritative restatement of the law of Scotland at the close of the 20th century.   WDHS

Liberalism was the dominant political doctrine in 19th-century Scotland, shown by the Liberal ascendancy in elections between 1832 and 1914. The Scottish Liberals were the party of democracy. They had campaigned for the First Reform Act, and its impact in Scotland had been disproportionately greater than in England. The credit for removing the unrepresentative and corrupt *ancien régime* was continually stressed subsequently. The introduction of municipal franchise reform immediately after 1832 reinforced the credentials of Liberalism. Liberals subsequently firmly supported further franchise extension, notably leading the agitation in and out of parliament for the 1868 and 1884 Reform Acts. The beneficiaries of both these Acts—the urban and rural working classes (see SOCIAL CLASS)—were generally absorbed quite painlessly into the Liberal camp. Female suffrage (see WOMEN: 3) was also strongly endorsed by most Scottish Liberals, and it caused less internal dissension between 1906 and 1914 than in England.

The demand for land law reform and an assault on landownership had a particular appeal in Scotland. The identification of many great landowners with the abuses of the unreformed system was a long-standing issue. This was sustained by the efforts by landowners after 1832 to manipulate loopholes in the new Act to continue manufacturing faggot county voters. Much play was made with this, even as late as 1880.

In the 1840s, the land question remained prominent because of the refusal by some proprietors—frequently those tainted with support for the pre-1832 political order—to permit the Free Church (see DISRUPTION) to erect places of worship on sites owned by the lairds. The Whigs and Liberals used parliamentary committees to publicize this grievance. A vigorous protest movement in the 1860s and 1870s by tenant farmers against what they regarded as the harsh enforcement of game and hypothec laws by landowners guaranteed the continuing saliency of land in Scottish politics.

The crofters' resistance in the 1880s (see LAND AGITATION AND REFORM IN THE HIGHLANDS AND ISLANDS) to landowner pressure generated a further bout of commitment to land reform. The claims of the Highlanders were enthusiastically championed by Lowland urban Liberals, notably Duncan MacLaren and Charles Cameron. The Scottish Liberals became strong advocates of the single (i.e. land) tax policy from the 1880s, and Lloyd George's attack on landownership in the 1909 Budget and his subsequent Land Campaign on the eve of the war produced an overwhelmingly positive response in Scotland. A Labour Party (see LABOURISM) committee sent from London in 1911 to ascertain why the party was making only limited headway in Scotland pinpointed the land question as the main reason why the Liberals remained more buoyant in Scotland than in England.

Free trade evoked intense loyalty in Scotland. This was not just because the concept was advocated by Adam Smith (see ECONOMIC POLICY: 2). The economic interests of the country were firmly wedded to the pursuit of non-protectionist policies. The breaking of the EIC's monopoly (see INDIAN SUBCONTINENT) had been spearheaded by Scottish merchants in the early 19th century. The demand for the abolition of the Corn Laws was enthusiastically taken up by a broad spectrum of Scottish society. There was only limited opposition to the agitation, since Scottish farmers were far less dependent on grain-growing than their English counterparts.

Scottish business was firmly in favour of free trade, even when tariff reform began to make inroads into the industrial and commercial interests in England. When the Conservatives (see UNIONISM) moved to espouse tariff reform after 1903, the opposition among the Scottish business community was particularly strong. The primary reason was that the great preponderance of Scottish industry was geared to the international economy (see ECONOMY: 5), with relatively little being for the domestic market. Hence any restrictions on world trade would adversely affect the staple industries like shipbuilding, textiles, heavy engineering, steel, and coal.

Liberalism drew greatly on the strength of religious dissent in Scotland. After 1843, the non-established Presbyterian churches outnumbered the Church of Scotland for most of the period to 1914, so their political clout was numerically greater than English dissent. The Voluntaries were identified with Liberalism before 1832, as the Whigs had regularly championed their civil and religious rights. Although many of those who formed the Free Church had been sympathetic to the Tories before the Disruption—most notably Thomas *Chalmers himself—this changed after 1843. Peel's Conservative government was blamed for failing to avert the secession, and the ham-fisted bid by Disraeli's administration in 1874 to woo the Free Church by abolishing patronage backfired. Both the Voluntaries, from the 1830s, and the Free Church, from the 1870s, advocated disestablishment of the state church in Scotland. This, of course, tied them ever more firmly to the Liberals, who were seen as the only party likely to deliver this demand.

Liberalism was also identified with championing the rights of Scotland, and by extension, with Scottish nationalist sentiment (see NATIONAL IDENTITY: 5; NATIONALISM). After 1886, Scottish Home Rule was a pillar in the party's programme, although it was anticipated that this would follow Irish self-government. Nevertheless, the SHRA was a Liberal-dominated organization, at least until 1914, and the Young Scots, a Liberal ginger group, espoused Home Rule enthusiastically in the pre-war decade.

While the 19th-century Liberals had little to offer in the field of social reform beyond a string support for *temperance, the party did move significantly towards collectivist approach from the 1900s. Inspired by the radical Young Scots, the party embraced the New Liberalism, often adding a Scottish accent. Issues such as the minimum wage and social insurance were taken up by the post-1906 intake of MPs. Afforestation and rural regeneration had a marked appeal in Scotland, and by 1914 the party was even starting to tackle the hydra of the housing crisis (see LIVING STANDARDS: 5).

Yet after 1918, Scottish Liberalism lost its forward-looking element. It remained absorbed in land reform policies between the wars, while free trade, still resonant in the 1920s, had little appeal in the next decade. There was little in 20th-century

Liberalism to appeal to the urban working class, while *Unionism/Conservatism spoke more powerfully to the business and propertied classes. The rise of the SNP eclipsed the appeal of the Liberals' Scottish Home Rule policy. It is no accident that most of the surviving loci of Liberal electoral support after 1945 have been in highly rural areas, where modernization is least advanced.   IGCH

libraries. In Scotland the collecting of books began well before the advent of printing (see PRINTING AND PUBLISHING). Details of medieval private collections are scarce but there is evidence of manuscript accumulations in abbeys, priories, and monasteries. The monastic and merely lending catalogue *Registrum Liborum Angliae* (c.1280) indicates seven Scottish monasteries with an average of 60 books, the largest being Melrose with 93, and that Scottish monasteries were as well stocked as most English counterparts. *The Catalogus Scriptorum Ecclesiae* (1440) reveals a subsequent 50 per cent reduction in Scottish abbey stock, no doubt due to the Wars of *Independence. But the 15th-century foundation of *universities at St Andrews, Glasgow, and Aberdeen, as well as the cathedral libraries of Aberdeen, Brechin, Elgin, and Glasgow, provided new magnets for further book accumulation and a recovery in library collecting had occurred by the early 16th century. The collection built up by Thomas Chrystall and Robert Reid, later bishop of Orkney, at the Cistercian monastery of Kinloss was one particular highlight. Individuals also gathered printed and manuscript volumes including Archbishop William Schevez (d. 1496) and Henry Sinclair (1508–65)—the latter's collection, the largest surviving pre-Reformation group, mostly passed to the advocate Clement Little (d. 1580). Little left his entire collection to the town and ministers of Edinburgh and it became the foundation of the Edinburgh University Library, established in 1583–4.

After the *Reformation many books vanished and some clergy, such as James Beaton, archbishop of Glasgow, fled overseas with their libraries. It is customary to see the Reformation fathers as destroyers of books although destruction has been confused with dispersal. At least royal libraries and those of enthusiastic nobles continued, including that of the regent, James Stewart, earl of Moray. The earliest royal libraries for which we have catalogues were those of *Mary, Queen of Scots, and *James VI but the royal library never became the depository of the nation as in England. Yet within the British Isles Scotland could boast the earliest post-Reformation libraries under municipal control. In addition to Little's Edinburgh library endowed in 1580, St Mary's Church Library in

Dundee, latterly the town library, was endowed in 1599 and in 1585 the 'Common Library of New Aberdeen' was founded by burgesses, lawyers, and ministers and housed in St Nicholas church. It passed in 1632 to the newly established Marischal College Library.

The creation of the Advocates' Library in Edinburgh in 1682 was the highlight of the 17th century. Lord Advocate, Sir George MacKenzie of Rosehaugh, took a leading part in the foundation of this general rather than purely legal library and his inaugural speech of 1689 is sometimes taken as the foundation date, although James Naismith was appointed first librarian in 1684 (see LAW AND LAWYERS: 2). Such was the Advocates' standing that along with the universities it became a deposit library under the British Copyright Act of 1710. The universities lost this right in 1836 but not the Advocates' Library and eventually in 1925 it transformed into the NLS, which today is also home to numerous manuscript collections including the large Wodrow Collection.

In general the 17th century was one of endowments and legacies. Edinburgh University Library was gifted hundreds of books by William Drummond of Hawthorden in the 1620s and 1630s and a large collection by a former librarian James Nairne in 1678, while the library of Aberdeen academic William Guild was gifted to St Andrews in 1657 and those of James Boyd, bishop of Glasgow, and Zachary Boyd, academic and poet, passed to Glasgow University in 1627 and 1651 respectively. While Scotland's cathedral libraries were not of great significance after the Reformation, a glorious exception is Leighton Library at Dunblane, founded in 1688 under the will of Bishop Robert Leighton who bequeathed his personal library. The most remarkable endowed library from a secular bequest is Innerpeffray Library, near Crieff, Perthshire, founded in 1694 under a bequest from David Drummond, third Lord Madertie, and housed in a special building from the 1740s at which time it became a lending library to a wide social mix. Both the Leighton and Innerpeffray libraries remain intact.

Wider access and the notion of public libraries became the new philosophy of the 18th and 19th centuries. At the turn of the 18th century, the minister James Kirkwood (d. 1708) produced his schemes for a library in every parish paid for by heritors and, while his 1699 proposals were seen by the General Assembly as impractical, his more modest plans of 1702, for a free library in each Highland parish, were adopted. Over the next twenty years, with support from the SSPCK and its English equivalent, nearly 80 such libraries were established in the Highlands. The proliferation of types of library also increased markedly. In 1722 the fine

Signet Library was founded in Edinburgh by the Society of Writers to HM Signet. In 1725 the poet and bookseller Allan Ramsay opened in the capital the first circulating library in Britain and John Smith of Glasgow followed suit in 1753. Working men's reading society libraries spread, such as the Leadhills Reading Society library formed in 1741 by Lanarkshire lead miners. Public subscription libraries appeared from the middle of the century, such as that established in Kelso in 1751. Libraries attached to mechanics institutes providing technical education were a facet of the next hundred years and by 1850 some 55 of these institutes existed with many thousands of books. At last in 1854 the Public Libraries (Scotland) Act enabled the first rate-supported public libraries and by the 1880s many Scottish burghs had established town libraries. The responsibility of all local authorities for library provision was now firmly established by law and yet in the early 20th century the library movement as a whole was still indebted to private initiative, and grants from Andrew Carnegie trusts financed buildings and the spread of county libraries. The continuing advantages and difficulties of municipal control can be seen in Glasgow's Mitchell Library: founded in 1877 through a bequest by the tobacconist Stephen Mitchell (d. 1874), it still provides unequalled public access but also a financial headache for the city.   AMa

Lindisfarne is a tidal island off the coast of Northumberland which became the centre for the 7th-century Columban mission to Northumbria. It was celebrated as the home of St Cuthbert, prior and bishop (d. 687), and the alternative name Holy Island was given by Durham monks who founded a Benedictine priory after 1122. This, and the chapel on the nearby Inner Farne, were fortified against Scottish seaborne attacks in the 14th century.

The island measures 3 miles (5 km) in length and is low-lying with extensive sand dunes, although whin dykes to the south form two rocky crags: the Heugh overlooking the harbour and priory and Biblaw at the south-east corner. Both were defended by 16th-century fortifications against Scottish and French naval activity, and may have been occupied earlier. Lindisfarne is identified with Metcaut, where an Anglian force was besieged by the Britons in the late 6th century.

The island was granted c.635 by Oswald, king of Northumbria (d. 642), to the Iona monk Aidan (d. 651) as his monastic and episcopal seat. It was in sight of the royal stronghold of Bamburgh and conveniently situated for sea-travel to daughter houses such as St Abbs near Coldingham (Berwickshire) and Old Melrose on the Tweed. The historian Bede admired the piety of the Columban monks and the simplicity of their buildings. Even the larger church erected by Aidan's successor Finan (d. 661) was of oak timbers and reed thatch, 'in the manner of the Irish'. Little archaeological evidence of the early monastery has been identified, although traces of buildings on the Heugh may be of this period. Many carved stones of the 7th to 10th centuries have been found in the area of the priory, on the raised beach above the harbour. The axial alignment of the 12th-century priory and 13th-century parish church may preserve an early arrangement. It is possible that an enclosure comparable with that at *Iona included this area and is perpetuated in the layout of the village. A chapel of St *Columba, documented in 1395, may also have been of early origin.

Following the royal decision in 664 to adopt Roman usages, Bishop Colman with most of the Irish and some Anglo-Saxon monks departed to Iona and thence to western *Ireland. However, Cuthbert, who came to Lindisfarne from Old Melrose in 664, was an ascetic in the Columban tradition. He regularly withdrew to the small tidal island, a few metres from the shore, that bears his name, and spent most of his latter years as a hermit on the Inner Farne, which had been a retreat of Aidan. Bede's description of the circular stone enclosure with its oratory, cross-slab, burial place, living-cell, and latrine, can be closely matched in surviving sites in the Hebrides and western Ireland. Cuthbert's body, translated in 698 to a wooden coffin-reliquary in the church of Lindisfarne, became the focus of a major cult. An early manifestation was the writing and decoration by Eadfrith (d. 721) of the Lindisfarne Gospels, one of the most magnificent of insular manuscripts. A savage attack on the island in 793, lamented by the great scholar Alcuin, was the first recorded Viking raid on a British monastery. The saint's relics accompanied the 'community of St Cuthbert' in their repeated wanderings following later attacks until they settled at Chester-le-Street (Co. Durham) in 883 and Durham in 995. A notable relic of Aidan, his original timber church, was also removed to Norham (Northumberland) in the 840s.

The sculpture of the island is remarkable for the absence of any simple cross-marked stones of Iona type, although one is known from the daughter house on Coquet Island (Northumberland). Small 'name-stones' bearing outline crosses and Anglian personal names in runes and capitals date from the late 7th and early 8th centuries. Most of the other carvings are shafts or fragments of free-standing crosses dating from the 9th and 10th centuries (see MONUMENTS: 1). The later ones must represent continuing secular patronage of a venerated burial ground.   IF

Lipton, Thomas (1850–1931), founder of a goods retail chain which by the 1890s was the largest in the world. Born in Glasgow, his first job was as an errand boy for his parents who, having migrated from Ireland, had set up as small grocers. This filial duty was combined with several casual tasks until he sailed for America in 1865, where he appears to have been similarly aimless until he gained employment with a prosperous grocer in New York. Returning to Glasgow in 1869 with $500 in savings and a clear appreciation of American retailing methods, Lipton established his first 'Irish Market' at Stobcross, specializing in imported ham, butter, and eggs. By 1878 he had opened three more such shops in Glasgow. The pace then quickened: stores elsewhere in Scotland were followed by others in the English provinces and in London. Selling an ever-widening range of food products (see DIET) at prices lower than the traditional 'family provision merchant', in carefully located, well-appointed shops, staffed by smartly dressed assistants, the growth of Lipton's—which ultimately depended upon aggressive advertising and publicity stunts—was phenomenal. Working tirelessly and retaining his profits within the business, Lipton kept costs down by backward integration, acquiring farms and tea plantations, curing capacity, jam-making, bottling, and meat-packing plants.

With his annual turnover exceeding £1 million, Lipton floated his company on the stock exchange in the late 1890s but, by retaining one-third of the shares, he retained ultimate control. Only then did he relax. Charitable donations, which brought him a knighthood in 1898, and an unsuccessful pursuit of the America's Cup with a series of yachts named the *Shamrock*, increasingly absorbed his energies. The firm he had created continued to grow, though not so rapidly nor as profitably until, burdened with debt, it passed into the hands of Van den Burghs in 1927. Four years later, Lipton died. He left his estate to various charities, but perhaps his greatest legacy was to have demonstrated the profitability of bringing inexpensive, fresh, and wholesome food to the general public.   PLP

literary rhetoric. Until Latin-based education declined in the 19th century, Scottish *historians learned how to write through the study of Graeco-Roman rhetoric, which normally followed grammar in the curricula of school (see SCHOOLS AND SCHOOLING: 1–3) and *university. Originally teaching the art of public speaking (Greek *rhetor* = orator), rhetoric had from Roman times been adapted to literary forms such as history, which came to be regarded as its province.

Thus early Scottish histories reflect uncertainty among rhetoricians over which of the traditional divisions of oratory history belonged to. Barbour and Boece seem to see it as panegyric—the praise of a man or a nation—while in Buchanan, *Knox, and Lesley panegyric, though present, is subsumed into forensic rhetoric—history arguing a case. Both types of rhetoric put pressure on history's invariable claim to truth-telling. Persuasive rhetoric emphasized contact between writer and reader. Like the orator, the historian must study his public, anticipate its responses, and mould them to his point of view.

Style, however, was where rhetorical skill could best be displayed and, although a plain style was generally required for narrative, there were occasions when history could be more ambitious: most obviously in fictitious speeches and debates but also in battle scenes and character descriptions. Scottish historians, especially those writing in Latin, competed in the production of such set pieces, commonly prescribed as classroom rhetorical exercises. Buchanan's rhetorical skill was evident in his dazzling mastery of Latin prose styles, which possibly did more than his doctrine to assure the international fame of his *History*. But overlong reliance on Latin contributed to the relative failure of Scots to develop their own language as a medium for historical prose in the 16th century. Here Knox was the exception. His *History of the Reformation* is vigorously rhetorical in its arguing of a case, but its heated, often pungently colloquial style showed the pulpit rhetoric of Protestant reformers losing patience with the rhetoric of the schools.

Knoxian rhetoric dominated Scottish historical writing in the following century; only Spottiswoode and Drummond, both Episcopalians, pallidly reflected the classical tradition. Associated with either contentious pamphleteering or scholastic pedantry, rhetoric had become discredited in polite Scottish circles by the mid-18th century, when Adam Smith's influential lectures refocused the subject in a way that would support the 'philosophical' history of Hume and Robertson. Still teaching mainly through classical examples, Smith resolved the conflict between persuasion and the new cult of impartiality by dissociating rhetoric from polemical argument. Persuasiveness became a matter of intelligent readability, of engaging the interests and sympathies of readers in a professedly dispassionate enquiry after truth (see CULTURE: 11).

The writings of Hugh Blair (Smith's pupil) and George Campbell kept classical rhetoric alive, in Scotland and abroad, until well into the 19th century. Many issues that it raised, particularly with regard to objectivity and interpretation, remain pertinent to later historical theory.   DD

Lithgow, Sir James (first Baron Ormsary) (1883–1952), leading Scottish industrialist who started his career in the family firm of Lithgows Ltd and quickly excelled to become president of the Clyde Shipbuilders in 1908 (see ECONOMY, SECONDARY SECTOR: 2). He left business to serve in Europe during the First World War, where he was wounded and mentioned in dispatches. He returned to Britain in 1917 and was seconded to the Admiralty as director of shipbuilding production where he was able to use his expertise to help maximize the production of ships which were taking a heavy toll from the U-Boat campaign. Lithgow emerged as a major figure in the Scottish business community in the inter-war years and was prominent in encouraging the 'National' Government to pay subsidies to keep the shipbuilding industry afloat during the early 1930s, a notable example being the *Queen Mary* which was launched in Glasgow (see ECONOMY: 6; ECONOMIC POLICY: 4). Lithgow was typical of the hard-headed businessmen who advocated cuts in public expenditure in the period of the Great Depression and believed that market forces would eventually bring things right. He was a trenchant opponent of trade unions which, he argued, were reducing economic competitiveness by demanding high wages which priced industry out of the market. Lithgow's conventional approach to the problems of the Scottish economy won him critics and supporters in equal measure and he was appointed president of the Federation of British Industries where his anti-Union and anti-public spending view made him popular with fellow employers. Although Lithgow's politics went out of fashion during the Second World War, his business expertise was such that he was made a member of the Board of Admiralty and given the responsibility for overseeing the repairs and building of the merchant fleet. He retired from the Board of Admiralty in 1946.   RJF

living standards: 1. to 1700; 2. 1700–1800; 3. 1800 onwards; 4. the old and new Poor Laws; 5. housing: 1770s onwards.

1. to 1700

Survival for pre-industrial folk depended on food, shelter, and security. Their *diet had to maintain health and ability to labour. Their clothing (see DRESS), *housing, and fuel had to protect them against the weather. And security meant having these things all the time: even in old age, and even in years of poor harvest, which could otherwise lead to starvation.

These things had to be provided by a largely subsistence economy (see ECONOMIC POLICY, PRIMARY SECTOR). Much trade was in luxury goods, irrelevant to the peasant majority. Most of the rest was a one-way outflow from the peasant economy: agricultural surpluses, grain and cattle, extracted from them as rent. The market provided few of the people's necessities. The most basic necessity was food. Late medieval peasants (see RURAL SOCIETY: 1) had a prosperous and varied diet: oatmeal, meat (mutton or beef), dairy products, sometimes fish, and ale (brewed from barley). Their prosperity followed the Black Death (1349–50) (see HEALTH, FAMINE, AND DISEASE: 1), which reduced the population (see POPULATION PATTERNS: 1) by about a third. Land became abundant and rents fell. Less is known of earlier times. The land was less fully cultivated (see RURAL SETTLEMENT: 2), and more peasants were pioneers, requiring diversion of resources from current consumption. So their diet was probably poorer and perhaps more grain-based.

Better documented is the 16th-century collapse in living standards. As population pressure on the land increased, so rents rose once more, and the people's diet declined in value. Meat was largely eliminated, dairy products were reduced, and oatmeal came to dominate the daily diet. Cattle were now exported, with the proceeds from their sale going as rent. The new diet was about as nutritious as the old, but less prestigious, or indeed palatable. Moreover, in hard times people could no longer shift down to a cheaper form of calories; oatmeal was already the cheapest.

Seventeenth-century houses were mainly of turf, framed by timber 'crucks', which became valuable possessions in the Lowlands as timber scarcity spread. Whether better houses were constructed in the prosperous late Middle Ages is unknown but perhaps doubtful. Warmth was a growing problem. Firewood and coal were reserved for the elite; the standard fuel, labour-intensive to cut and prepare, was peat. Poorer peasants sometimes had to burn turf or dried animal manure, which would otherwise have fertilized the fields. Clothing was important, but little is known of trends in its availability or quality. There was some trade in coarse woollen cloth for peasants' clothing, but much clothing was probably produced within the community (not necessarily within individual families).

Peasants (see RURAL SOCIETY: 3) did not usually live at the very brink of subsistence. Ale-brewing shows that; so does periodic feasting—harvests, weddings, funerals. But insecurity was never far away. There was life-cycle insecurity, with those unable to work, mainly older people, depending on charity—mainly an undocumented affair within families and communities. From the late 16th century there might also be poor relief (see LIVING STANDARDS: 4) from kirk session (see CHURCH INSTITUTIONS: 3), or burgh council (see URBAN SOCIETY: 2).

All charitable efforts could be overwhelmed by a serious harvest failure, and starvation would ensue. Peasants tried to prevent harvest failure by playing safe—avoiding risky innovations, and concentrating on low-yielding but reliable crops like oats. But with the weather's vagaries (see CLIMATE), the threat of famine was ever present. It could strike even in the prosperous 15th century, as it did in 1439.

Famines (see HEALTH, FAMINE, AND DISEASE: 2) were commonest in about 1550–1650, because population growth outstripped food production and led to cultivation of marginal land where grain-growing was more risky. Deterioration in the *climate (the 'Little Ice Age' of 1550–1850) made things worse. The mid-1580s, the late 1590s, and above all the early 1620s, saw widespread starvation. In a final national disaster in the 1690s, perhaps 13 per cent of the people starved to death. Famines caused vagrancy, with uprooted country folk swarming as beggars into towns. Wage labourers may have increased in number. The early 17th century saw a mass exodus (see EMIGRATION: 1) to join Continental armies—one in five of all young men in Scotland (see MERCENARIES IN EUROPE). Few returned. Without substantial transfers from the elite, little could be done to alleviate famine; grain was imported, but only those with money benefited. The slowly increasing monetarization of the 17th-century economy may have helped here. After 1650, population pressure eased, but living standards stagnated for another century.

Living standards were not wholly material; status and leisure mattered too. Peasants, or at least male peasants, did not routinely work hard; they had bursts of intense effort, and longer periods with much less to do. They could take increases in prosperity in the form of leisure rather than material goods. As for status, the 14th century did not just see material prosperity grow; it also saw the freeing of the serfs. Peasants may well have valued their leisure time, and their freedom from masters, as much as their material conditions; but here too their position was eroding in the 17th century.   JG

2. 1700–1800

Our information on standards of living in this period is drawn from a wide range of contemporary sources, none of which can be said to be scientific in its measurements. At the start of the century the Scottish *diet was monotonous but fairly healthy. Porridge and green vegetables were staples, which were supplemented by small amounts of meat and fish from time to time. Dairy products such as milk, butter, and cheese were the main sources of protein. Beer (see ROUGH CULTURE) was also a significant source of calories, although it was more prevalent in the towns and cities. The fact that Scottish soldiers were on average an inch (2.5 cm) taller than their English counterparts in the 18th century may be explained by a better diet in childhood. By 1800, the normal Scottish diet consisted of two-thirds bread and oatmeal, with less than a fifth of meat, with cheese, butter, and eggs as an added luxury. Also, by the end of the century, the consumption of alcohol had risen as whisky became more popular than ale as a result of the Malt Tax in 1725. The average Scottish working male, it is reckoned, consumed about a pint of whisky per week.

*Housing was primitive and cramped. In the countryside, shelter from the elements was the most important feature in house construction (see RURAL SETTLEMENT: 3–4). Made from local materials, houses were built with thick walls made from piled stones, while the roofs were constructed out of thatched bracken or straw resting on a timber frame. The walls were usually not much taller than 5 feet (1.5 m) and the floor was made from compressed earth. A fire would be in the centre of the building underneath a hole in the ceiling to allow ventilation. The beds were either wooden boxes filled with straw or straw on its own. A table and some primitive eating utensils made from horn were the most common pieces of furniture. In the towns, housing was better constructed (see BUILDING MATERIALS AND TECHNIQUES). The hierarchy of *urban society was reflected within the tenement structure with the lower orders confined to the bottom and the higher ranks ascending to the top (see URBAN SETTLEMENT: 2). Sanitation was crude, with chamber pots being emptied into open sewers or discarded from windows, There were surprisingly few epidemics in this period. After c.1760, the emergent middle classes moved away from traditional urban settlements into exclusive areas such as the New Town in *Edinburgh or Hutcheston and the Gorbals in *Glasgow.

As the pace of economic change began to increase after 1760 (see ECONOMY: 4), it is safe to say that on average most Scots experienced a rise in the standard of living at least until 1790. The impact of agricultural improvement (see ECONOMY, PRIMARY SECTOR: 2) and the subsequent demand for increased labour meant that living standards in rural Scotland increased between 30 and 50 per cent in this period. Increased agricultural productivity helped to stabilize food prices, removing one of the most acute causes of price inflation. Urban expansion also contributed to a rise in urban workers' wages with most tradesmen experiencing significant improvements in levels of pay and some managing up to a 50 per cent improvement. Also, the differential between unskilled and skilled workers

was narrowing in this period which tends to suggest a general improvement and the gap between Scottish and English wages was declining. The increasing opportunities opened up by trade with the *British Empire, improved agricultural productivity, and the beginnings of industrialization contributed to growing middle-class incomes and the demand for more luxury goods. Further evidence of a general improvement in the standards of living can be gleaned from an examination of the statistics on mortality rates. The fact that the death rate was declining in the latter part of the 18th century can be attributed to better health as a result of improved feeding and diet; however, it is worth emphasizing that infant mortality was still very high with one out of six children not making it to their first birthday (see POPULATION PATTERNS).

The impact of the French Revolutionary and Napoleonic Wars (1793–1815) put the brake on Improvement. Price inflation ate away the benefits of increasing wages, trade disruption contributed to unemployment, and rising taxes reduced consumption, all of which helped to stagnate the standard of living. By the end of the century, it is safe to say that the average Scot was working much harder than a century earlier. In 1700, most Scots rose and retired with the sun and their main priority was to grow enough food to feed themselves and their family. By 1800, that world had gone and was replaced with one which was regimented and ordered around the clock. Although there were material improvements, arguably the key factor in this was the fact that the average working day now consisted of fourteen hours.   RJF

3. 1800 onwards

It is notoriously difficult to measure the standard of living in Scotland after 1800. Certainly the gap between Scotland and England narrowed and the period is one in which more Scots enjoyed an increase in prosperity. Yet, the fact remains that Scotland has been a low wage economy with rates of pay lagging significantly behind England and other industrial countries and this can be seen in the extraordinary rate of *emigration as nearly two million Scots left the nation in order to improve their social and economic well-being.

Estimates show that in the 1860s Scotland on a per capita basis earned about 75 per cent of English income; this narrowed to about 90 per cent before the First World War, where it remained with minor fluctuations until the gap closed in the 1980s. In a British context, however, these figures do not do justice to the true extent of the differential between Scotland and England because prices in Scotland remained consistently higher. Not only was Scotland paid less than England, it also was more uneven in its distribution of national income. Using estimates of Scottish national income in 1867, 70 per cent of Scots were in the lowest economic bracket of unskilled and lower skilled where wages were under £50 per annum. The higher skilled workers who earned over £50 per annum were just less than 10 per cent. 'Lower small' incomes which earned up to £100 per annum made up 11 per cent of the total, while 'middling and upper small' incomes which earned £100 to £1,000 made up just under 8 per cent of the total. Finally, there were the very wealthy who earned over £1,000 and made up 0.33 per cent of the total. Statistically, this reveals that the society of Victorian Scotland consisted of a large group of unskilled and semi-skilled workers who formed the vast bulk of the population. There was a significant number of skilled workers and lower middle class who made up about a fifth of the population and a small middle class of less than 10 per cent.

One effect of having such a small middle class and a rather large group which occupied the economic borderland of working class and middle class was that the resultant spin-off in the retail and services industries were conspicuously lacking in Scottish society. This reinforced reliance on the traditional heavy industries (SEE ECONOMY, SECONDARY SECTOR: 2) and held back economic diversification. Although Scotland had one of the highest incomes per capita in the world in the 19th century and exported more capital per head of population than England, the distribution of income reveals a very divided society. The bottom 70 per cent of the population earned a third of the total income, while the top 8 per cent earned 46 per cent of the nation's wealth. Just under 5,000 individuals actually earned over a quarter of national income. These bald statistics, however, fail to do justice to the harsh realities of life for most Scots in this period. The reliance of Scottish industry on export markets meant that the economy was prone to cyclical fluctuations. This meant that short-term unemployment was a reality for most working-class families. Rates of emigration and prostitution rose during these downturns which illustrates the quite significant social effects they had on Scottish society.

One consequence of precarious employment was a tendency to use the cheapest *housing which would minimize the weekly outlay on rent. Housing was a major blight. In 1861, 34 per cent of all Scottish houses had only one room and 37 per cent had two rooms. In Glasgow, the situation was especially bad with a third of all families living in one room. As late as 1914, 75 per cent of all new houses constructed in this city consisted of only one or two rooms, while half the Scottish population was still living in these cramped conditions. Although the situation improved in the inter-war period, largely through the Wheatley Housing Act of 1924, it was not nearly enough to make good the deficit recognized by the royal commission of 1917. The impact of economic depression and government cuts in grants to local authorities meant that overcrowding in Scotland was six times greater than England and Wales in the period between the wars. In 1951, 15.5 per cent of Scots were still living in overcrowded conditions and this was rectified only by the Conservative government's housing expansion (at any cost, but usually the cheapest) which resulted in tower blocks and bleak council estates which brought more social problems in their wake. Notions that life was healthier in the countryside were invalid with poor and damp housing as standard. Indeed, the Depression of the inter-war years meant that many statutory regulations on housing were not applied and conditions were worse than in the towns.

Related to problems of housing were problems of health. Desperate overcrowding was a major factor in promoting alcoholic escapism in the 19th century (SEE ROUGH CULTURE). The number of gallons of spirits drunk every year per head of population in Scotland was 2.38 (10.8 litres) in the 1840s, 1.93 (8.8 litres) in the 1870s, and 1.6 (7.3 litres) in the 1910s. Taxation during and after the First World War was a major factor in quenching Scottish thirst and thereafter consumption declined. Overcrowding also promoted disease (SEE HEALTH, FAMINE, AND DISEASE: 3) with Glasgow and Dundee cited for special condemnation in the 1842 report on sanitary conditions. Tenements promoted the rapid spread of typhus and cholera. Infant mortality rates in Scotland rose in the period from 1860 to 1900 and was still very high at 122 per 1,000 births on the eve of the First World War. In spite of improvements during the war, the figures for both infant and maternal mortality in the 1920s and 1930s remained stubbornly higher than the rest of the UK.

Scotland retained most of its pre-war social problems after 1918 and received an additional new one: mass, long-term unemployment. As a result of structural imbalance in the economy and efficiency savings during the war, the traditional industries shed labour at an alarming rate (SEE ECONOMY: 6). The onset of the Great Depression in 1929 reinforced and exacerbated this trend and, even with rearmament in the late 1930s, Scotland suffered a much higher proportion of unemployment than the rest of the UK. The rate of unemployment for the insured workforce never dropped below 10 per cent in the 1920s and rose to over 27 per cent at the height of the Great Depression in 1932. Given the large amount of casual labour in the Scottish economy which would not pay insurance, these figures tend to underestimate the impact of unemployment. Also, they do not take into consideration the substantial numbers of lower middle-class shopkeepers and tradesmen who would have been the victims of the knock-on effect of industrial closures. According to some contemporary accounts, one in three Scots were affected by unemployment. Comparisons of unemployment with the rest of the UK underestimate the extent of Scottish suffering because not only are the figures for Scotland included in the British total, it is also artificially swollen with the north-east of England and Wales, which glosses over the devastating regional impact of the depression.

Yet, for the vast majority of the British people, including Scots, the 1930s were a time of unprecedented increasing prosperity, although a substantial minority experienced unprecedented hardship. The reality of unemployment was that it was to be found in large pockets which could affect up to 60 per cent of a local community. Few Scottish towns experienced the 'average' rate of unemployment. Communities in the western industrial belt such as Motherwell, Airdrie, and Coatbridge were devastated, while Edinburgh and its satellites were relatively unscathed.

The impact of unemployment on physical well-being can be demonstrated by an examination of the statistics which reveal that average height and life expectancy were reduced and the comparatively greater incidence of unemployment on Scottish society in the 1930s helped to pull these average figures for the nation behind the rest of the UK. Although impossible to quantify empirically, working-class mothers were probably the greatest victims of unemployment. Although much of the industrial structure had collapsed, the patriarchal values which imbued it did not. *Women were forced out of necessity to take on part-time menial work which many skilled workers would have thought degrading for themselves. But women were still expected to do the household chores, look after the children, and make 'sacrifices' for the family.

The advent of the Welfare State and the corporate economy did much to improve the standard of living for most Scots. Although wages lagged behind the rest of the UK, full employment, municipal housing, and greater income distribution based on need assessment did much to improve the quality of life for most Scots. Like most of the rest of the industrial west, people in Scotland were able to take advantage of developments in new technology which improved life and formed part of the consumer revolution. Testament to the success of the post-war era is to be found in the fact that, by the late 1980s, although containing significant pockets of deprivation and a poor health record, Scotland is the second most prosperous region of the UK and attains the European Union average on a wide range of socio-economic indicators. RJF

4. the old and new Poor Laws

In 1846, following the introduction of the Poor Law (Scotland) Amendment Act, the newly created Board of Supervision for the Relief of the Poor gave the first formal estimate of the minimum income required to maintain a pauper in Scotland. The Board had received a number of complaints that parochial authorities had failed to increase allowances in line with what many paupers had expected as a result of the Act. In the south of Scotland, the Board reckoned that the minimum income required for a single pauper was about 2s. 3d. per week (£6 per annum), whilst in the Highlands, where the general standard of living was considered less and paupers usually lived rent-free, an allowance of 1s. 3d. was thought adequate. Such an amount was felt sufficient to buy 'essential' foodstuffs (see DIET), such as potatoes (17.5 lb (7.9 kg) per week), oatmeal (3.5 lb (1.6 kg) per week), and occasionally some fish (totally 1s. 3d. per week for food); rent (6d. per week) (see LIVING STANDARDS: 5); fuel (3d. per week); clothing; and a few other items. Taking into account additional allowances for a married couple with children, a family of four could expect to receive about double that amount.

Throughout the 19th century the Board never again reviewed the adequacy of its estimate of what was termed 'needful sustentation' and assumed that it provided a pauper with a standard of living that prevented either starvation or 'absolute want' (see LIVING STANDARDS: 3). At the same time, the Board's pronouncement ensured that living standards for the pauper remained below that of the new industrial and other classes who maintained themselves in employment. The wage of a day labourer in 1846 was reckoned to be about 7s. per week (and that of a weaver not much more), which meant that if he was in regular work, his family's standard of living was about 50 per cent higher than that of the pauper. By contrast, a ploughman earned about £24 a year in wages (see RURAL SOCIETY: 4), whilst skilled workers in industrial towns (such as masons and wrights) could earn twice that amount (see URBAN SOCIETY: 4). An income sufficient to maintain a family at a standard of living four times that of a pauper indicated the distance, in social as well as pecuniary terms, that existed between those who had prospered from Scotland's growing industrial economy (see ECONOMY: 4–5) and those who had not.

As intended by the proposers of the Poor Law (Scotland) Amendment Act, the period immediately after 1845 led to a general increase in allowances to the poor and, in many respects, represented a revolution in attitude towards their maintenance. By the 1860s virtually every parish in Scotland had introduced a poor rate on its inhabitants and a local bureaucracy, headed by an 'inspector of poor', emerged to assess an applicant's condition and award relief. Poorhouses were opened for the care of the sick and the elderly and the Board insisted that every parish contribute to a 'combination', if they were not large and wealthy enough to afford their own. (The Board had the power to issue a 'minute' on complaint by a pauper of inadequate assistance, which enabled the pauper to petition the Court of *Session to amend the parochial authority's decision.) Such a system of a centrally managed redistribution of wealth between the ratepayer and those less fortunate stood in contrast to that which had existed before 1845. Although the concept of 'needful sustentation' existed in law, in practice this was largely determined by historical custom of what that meant within the particular locality. Thus in the south-east by the late 1700s, the majority of parishes had introduced a 'legal' poor rate and provided regular allowances at rates not dissimilar to those paid in England. The agricultural wealth of the area, which had undergone considerable transformation during the 18th century (see ECONOMY, PRIMARY SECTOR: 1–2), could support a more formal system of assistance. The same applied to the majority of the larger towns, where, in any case, large congregations of poor without visible means of support threatened civil order. In other areas in central and southern Scotland, parishes sometimes urged their inhabitants to establish a voluntary fund for the poor without recourse to a legal rate.

The 1844 Royal Commission on the Scottish Poor Laws indicated that such provisions rarely met all the need within a parish and only occasionally provided allowances at a level comparable with those in the south-east. Elsewhere, particularly in the far south-west and the Highlands (see ECONOMY OF THE HIGHLANDS AND ISLANDS: 2–3), parishes invoked a system of 'licensed begging', which with a badge enabled approved paupers to seek eleemosynary aid from their neighbours and other travellers. Inevitably, the vicarious nature of the giving did little to ensure that the poor could rely on a steady income to maintain themselves. The alternative in these areas was *emigration, which was sometimes supported by a voluntary fund, but as often as not by the deliberate activities of the landowner (see LANDOWNERSHIP IN THE HIGHLANDS AND ISLANDS) and other heritors.

That by the 1830s Scotland had undergone a considerable transformation from the largely subsistence agricultural society of the mid-18th century into one based on the twin pillars of industrial expansion and market-oriented farming was not lost on many contemporary commentators. Equally, it was evident that a system of collective support for the maintenance of the poor could not survive the arrival of the industrial worker and the vagaries of the economic trade cycle. The Amendment of the English Poor Law in 1834 (which established a central Poor Law Board), a Church of Scotland inquiry in 1839, and the subsequent publication of numerous pamphlets on the condition of the working classes—interestingly mainly from Scottish Tories—led to the establishment of the 1844 Royal Commission. Its exhaustive parish survey outlined both how far Scotland had advanced into an industrial age and how far the operation of its civil institutions could no longer match the aspirations of the new working class for a nationally determined minimum standard of support below which no family should fall. The Board's definition of that standard and the conditions under which relief could be supplied, perhaps better than any other civil reform of the period, demarcated the boundary between the ways of an older kind of Scotland and one much more certain of its place amongst other 'self-improving' nations (see ECONOMIC POLICY: 2–3). The living standard of the pauper could improve only if real wages rose, but not at the expense of the differential established by the Board, or if it threatened the willingness of the poor to work hard and endeavour to support themselves.

IL

5. housing, 1770s onwards

The architectural hallmark of Scotland was the tenement (see HOUSING: 3–5). In the 18th and 19th centuries, Scottish housing diverged so much from two-storey, self-contained English terraced cottages that different standards of overcrowding were adopted to obscure the deficient living standards north of the Border. British statutes concerning housing and slum clearance proved unworkable in Scotland because of the tenement style of living. The tenement tradition was the product of weak purchasing power for urban (see URBAN SOCIETY: 5) Scots and explanations based on *climate, fortified towns, the availability of stone, and cultural preferences for high-rise housing can be discounted since such conditions applied equally to the north of England. According to a government inquiry (1905) Scots paid 25–30 per cent more in rent than in any other part of the UK except central London; for a standard basket of foodstuffs, prices paid by Scots were even higher than in central London and about

10 per cent more than in the cheapest English regions. Even for fuel Scots paid more of their weekly income than elsewhere. Overall, urban Scots' real wages were 10–15 per cent below those of English boroughs and about 10 per cent lower than in Irish towns.

The impact on living conditions was considerable. Had the English standard of overcrowding (more than two persons per room) been applied in Scotland, then the inhabitants of most Lanarkshire, Renfrewshire, and Stirlingshire burghs were ten times more overcrowded than the inhabitants of Liverpool or the locus of Robert Roberts's *Classic Slum*, Salford. Since 47 per cent of Scots in 1911 lived in one- and two-roomed houses (seven times more than in English boroughs), the impact on daily life and family routines was considerable. Tenement rooms were multifunctional and privacy limited; additional tasks were created by rolling away beds each morning and night; internal plumbing was not standard until the 1870s; water had to be carted up several flights of stairs; shared toilets, kitchen sinks, common stairs, wash-houses, and drying greens involved rotas and friction, as well as negotiating skills, gossip, and a culture of mutuality rather than the self-contained independence of terraced cottages.

With congestion, shared amenities, and overcrowding, the tenement was also associated with dark, ill-ventilated, and insanitary courts. Quantification associated with the introduction of a Registrar for Births, Deaths and Marriages after 1855 drew attention to the variability of mortality rates (see POPULATION PATTERNS: 2) and legitimated the appointment of Medical Officers of Health. From the 1860s, when municipal regulation and slum clearances were introduced, some environmental improvements were achieved and urban mortality rates stabilized before beginning a slow decline. Forty years later, however, in Edwardian studies involving over 100,000 schoolchildren (see CHILDREN) in the Scottish cities, the continuing impact of adverse living conditions showed a very high correlation between the number of rooms in a tenement flat and the heights, weights, skeletal, dental, and psychological condition at all ages under 14. When the boys in these studies became wartime army recruits, it was evident that those from the Scottish industrial heartland were 2–3 per cent shorter than those north of the Highland line or from the Border counties.

Living conditions in Scotland were partly determined by feuing—a system of tenure in which the superior relinquished future development interest in the land for an annual payment or feu duty. Sub-infeudation—the creation of further tiers of feu duty—could be created by vassals, so long as they covered their obligation to their immediate superior, and produced cumulative charges on building land, so increasing building costs. Since the feu duty was fixed in perpetuity, there was an inclination on the part of the superior both to hoard land for development and to release it for as high a price (feu duty) as possible. Alternatively, the superior could sell his interest in all future feu-duty income for a lump sum, a practice which also imposed substantial financial strains on builders. Land costs were higher in Scotland than in the remainder of the UK and builders attempted to spread these costs by more intensive development of the plots. Tenements were the result of legal forces, characteristics of the building industry, and weak purchasing power.

The *Edinburgh New Town, the Blythswood estate in *Glasgow, and *Aberdeen's Bon-Accord district were late 18th- and early 19th-century examples of areas created principally for those comfortably-off members of urban society able to buy their way out of the hostile living conditions associated with industrialization (see ECONOMY: 4) and rapid urbanization (see URBAN SETTLEMENT: 2; URBAN SOCIETY: 5). By the 1870s, rising real incomes for those regularly in work and declining family size affected elements of Scottish urban society who were increasingly able to move to areas purpose-built for their income bracket. From the second half of the 19th century, therefore, the pre-modern residential pattern in which residents were segregated vertically within tenements had given way to socially segregated working-class and middle-class suburbs. Increasingly from the 1860s, socially homogeneous areas were created within Scottish burghs.

The process of social segregation was accelerated by trends in housing policy and Treasury finance after 1919. It was a measure of weak purchasing power and the shortcomings of pre-1914 Scottish housing stocks that in the inter-war years four out of five houses built were in the public sector and that rent controls on private landlords were more durable than anywhere in the UK outside London. Undoubtedly, the imposition of Ministry housing standards—two- or three-bedroomed flats with kitchens, internal WCs, and running water—improved living conditions, though the scale of building programmes produced visual monotony on peripheral housing estates with only the most basic infrastructural provisions. By contrast, private-sector bungalow building in the 1930s reinforced social segregation begun in the First World War, though in a physical form more distinctive than in pre-1914 middle-class tenements. The social polarization of living conditions was repeated from the 1950s when, for a twenty-year period, public-sector housing was heavily concentrated in multi-storey tower blocks compared to self-contained bungalow and villa building in the private sector.

Nationwide reactions against living conditions in tower blocks and an awareness of the intrinsic quality of Victorian tenements produced an end to inner-city demolition and an embrace of rehabilitation and refurbishment in the 19th-century housing stock. By contrast, the invasion of national construction firms such as Wimpey and Barratt has produced another element of homogeneity in the built environment of Scottish towns by cloning designs for detached villas which were initially targeted at an English market more familiar with this form of accommodation. If a measure of visual variation has been introduced in paint colours and door and window designs since 1980 by tenants' 'right to buy' their previously public-sector rented houses, probably more significant has been the demolition of tower blocks, a cessation to invasive transport routes, and the adoption of 'greening' measures to improve parks and playgrounds. In treating the environment of the home in a holistic way, Scottish councils have made important contributions in the 1980s and 1990s to living standards.

RR

local government to 1707. Medieval government meant lordship (see NOBILITY: 2), and lordship meant courts. The king had a court, his barons had courts, bishops and abbots had courts, and burghs and sheriffs had courts. These courts are discussed here as institutions, but the pattern of lordship in which they were enmeshed should always be kept in mind.

The earliest recognizable units of local government were thanages. In these pre-feudal districts of Scotia (Scotland north of the Forth), a thane collected royal tribute and held a court. Two thanages, Clackmannan and Kinross, survived as miniature sheriffdoms. The others were subsumed in the two dozen larger sheriffdoms, mostly created between 1124 and 1293, which continued as governmental units until 1975. The 12th century, the century of feudalization, also saw the creation of burghs (see URBAN SETTLEMENT: 1) and parishes: there was now much more government.

The broad principle of feudal courts (see LAW AND LAWYERS: 1) was that the lord held a court for his vassals, in which the vassals served as 'suitors': witnesses and jurymen. The court dealt with disputes among vassals (both civil and criminal), between lord and vassals; it supervised land transfers and inheritance. Its officers arrested malefactors and enforced its decrees. The most characteristic medieval courts were baron courts, held by

all important landlords, ecclesiastical and lay, for the tenants of their lands. Originally they could punish serious crime, but this was curtailed by the 14th century; they mainly judged assault, petty debt, and unpaid rents. They supervised economic life (see ECONOMY: 2; RURAL SOCIETY: 1) and enforced lords' rights.

Above baron courts were the crucial sheriff courts. Their chief tasks were adjudicating on disputed land titles, entering heirs to their lands, and judging crime—particularly slaughter and spuilyie (spoliation of goods). They held wapinshawings (military musters), and enforced hornings (outlawries for failure to obey legal decrees). Royal burghs (see URBAN SOCIETY: 1) had courts similar to sheriff courts, which also adjudicated on commercial disputes. Merchant and craft guilds regulated their members' activities; a loose parallel may be drawn between the private guild within the burgh and the private barony within the sheriffdom. Burghs also hosted royal officials, the customers, collecting customs dues.

Royal travelling courts (see KINGSHIP), justice ayres, visited each sheriffdom biannually between the 13th and 15th centuries to try the 'four pleas of the crown' (the most serious crimes: theft, murder, rape, and fire-raising). They were then partly superseded by commissions of justiciary, authorizing a local individual to convene a court to try a specific case. These led to abuses, so during the 17th century more criminal cases were heard in Edinburgh. In 1672 the High Court of Justiciary (which itself went on circuit) was established.

There existed a more powerful version of the barony known as a regality. This was also possessed heritably by the landlord, and usually possessed an exclusive right to try all crimes by the tenants. Baronies were usually small (there were at least 986 before 1560), but the 54 regalities covered half the country.

In the Highlands, central government had little authority (see HIGHLANDS AND ISLANDS AND CENTRAL GOVERNMENT: 1). Chiefs (see CLANS OF THE HIGHLANDS AND ISLANDS) had courts, and the *breitheamh* or brieve was a hereditary judge adjudicating on land titles—a system that antedated feudalism. *Breitheamhan* also existed in the Celtic Lowlands north of the Forth, but feudalization reduced them to ceremonial 'dempsters', pronouncing the feudal courts' decrees (see LAW AND INSTITUTIONS, GAELIC).

Sheriffships too became hereditary in the 14th and 15th centuries in local magnate families, recognizing the magnates' vital role. The crown recovered numerous heritable sheriffships in the early 17th century; they were abolished in 1748, along with regalities (whose practical powers had long been declining) and baronies (the bare title remained). All justice thereafter fell under direct government control.

The 16th-century expansion of professional civil justice in Edinburgh, especially the Court of *Session, undermined the jurisdiction of all local courts. In the 1530s the Court of Session took over the sheriffs' central power, adjudicating on disputed land titles. However, the late 16th-century expansion of statute law (see JAMES VI; PARLIAMENT: 2) heaped administrative responsibilities on sheriffs: enforcing economic regulations and, above all, collecting parliamentary taxation.

From then on, institutions proliferated. Church courts are dealt with elsewhere (see CHURCH INSTITUTIONS: 2–3), but the commissary courts established in 1564, adjudicating on marital and testamentary cases, were secular. Notaries flourished from the 14th century, legally trained registrars of contracts and land transactions. They were partly superseded in 1617 by the register of sasines, a network of public land registration offices. Justices of the peace were introduced in 1609, gradually finding a role in regulating the rural economy (see ECONOMY, PRIMARY SECTOR: 1). The 1640s introduced commissioners of supply: tax gatherers who also became administrators of the funds they collected.

Most of these institutions concerned themselves largely with disputes about property or among propertied people. There were also neighbourhood courts for lesser folk. Small towns—burghs of barony—had courts regulating economic life and settling minor disputes. Rural areas had similar courts, known as birlaw courts. Few of their records survive, and nobody was much concerned with them, except the common people.   JG

Low Countries, the region of the European mainland which lies closest to most of Scotland. While the sea, with its obvious dangers, is a factor of division between countries, it is easy to underestimate its role in facilitating links between peoples. For Scottish mariners it was but one step from home to the Low Countries, France, northern Europe, and the Baltic; the sea journey from, say, Leith to Riga was at almost all seasons of the year easier and less dangerous than the (equally long) overland journey to, say, Bosnia. As far as relations between Scotland and the Low Countries are concerned, the North Sea has always been of great importance, and contacts were as close as the distance was short.

The links were of many kinds. The organization of the medieval church necessitated frequent travel to Rome, and the route was often via the Low Countries; medieval Scottish sovereigns, churchmen, and merchants regularly commissioned products in the markets of Flanders; the *staple

port for Scottish trade was strategically located at the mouth of the Scheldt; Scottish students were a familiar sight at Leuven (Louvain) and at universities founded in the northern Netherlands after the break with Spain (see NORTHERN EUROPE: MONKS AND SCHOLARS; UNIVERSITIES: 1); between the 16th and 18th centuries Scottish mercenary soldiers (see MERCENARIES IN EUROPE) were in constant demand in the Low Countries, where, in the cockpit of Europe, the Spanish, French, English, Germans, and Netherlanders fought out a series of wars. More peaceful contacts led to Low Countries' influence upon Scottish architecture (see ARCHITECTURAL STYLES AND FEATURES) and church music, while the many Dutch loanwords in Lowland Scots (see LANGUAGES OF SCOTLAND, PRE-1100) are another testimony to this influence.

Scottish contacts with the Low Countries were at their most intense and varied during the period of the later Middle Ages and the Renaissance; after the *Union of the Crowns, relations between Scotland and the Low Countries gradually lost their particular character. The *Reformation saw the establishment of Calvinist churches in both Scotland and in the northern Low Countries; both countries shared an enthusiasm for Protestant theology and neo-Latin culture (see RELIGIOUS LIFE: 3). The narrowing of the relations became yet more apparent in the 19th century, when the abandonment of Latin as the language of university instruction caused a decline in the enrolment of Scottish students in Dutch universities. Paradoxically, however, the years of the First World War were one of the greatest single periods of contact, at least as far as this concerns sheer numerical presence of Scots in the Low Countries (specifically Belgium). In more recent times, contacts have been mostly in the sphere of business.

The territorial integrity of Scotland during the medieval period was relatively clear and stable; by contrast, the Low Countries, being a congeries of duchies, counties, free cities, and ecclesiastical territories, is harder to grasp. Much of the Low Countries belonged to the Holy Roman Empire, while in the South other parts owed allegiance to the king of France. Even during the 15th century, when the dukes of Burgundy were at their apogee, and as semi-independent princes had consolidated their control of most of the Low Countries, this remained the case. While the 'Auld Alliance' with *France is an *idée fixe* in Scottish historiography, it has proved a matter altogether more elusive to do justice to the extent and nature of Scottish relations with the Low Countries, a region at once so complex and variable. Language use can also be confusing, and it has sometimes been too readily assumed that everything written in French must necessarily be connected with France rather than with the francophone Burgundian Low Countries. The poet William Dunbar, for example, is often said to be indebted to the 'Grands Rhétoriqueurs', a group of poets who figure in all the literary histories of France. Several of the most prominent members of this group of poets, however, in fact hailed from the Low Countries (For example, Georges Chastellain, Olivier de la Marche, Jean Molinet, Jean Lemaire des Belges). Even the chronicler Froissart, who visited Scotland in 1365, is usually thought of simply as a Frenchman.

In the disputed Scottish succession after the death of Alexander III (1286), one of the claimants was Florence (Floris) V, count of Holland (see GREAT CAUSE). This was by virtue of his descent from Ada, sister of King William I 'the Lion' (d. 1214). Interestingly, the count of Holland shared with the Scottish king at least one thing: the heraldic lion rampant. Among the more notable events of the 15th century are the visit to Scotland of the Burgundian knight Jacques de Lalaing (1448) and the marriage of James II to Mary of Gueldres (Gelderland) in 1449. This marriage to the niece of Philip 'the Good' considerably stimulated Scottish interest in the affairs of the Low Countries. In 1457 Philip 'the Good' sent the huge cannon, known (from its place of manufacture, in 1449) as Mons Meg and now in *Edinburgh castle, with an escort of 50 men-at-arms, as a present to his Scottish nephew. After the death of James II (1460), his widow founded the Trinity College church in Edinburgh, and an altarpiece was commissioned from Hugo van der Goes (of which only the side-panels survive). Nor is this the only work of art in medieval Scotland to betray Flemish influences, a good example being the Last Judgement painting in Fowlis Easter church (see CULTURE: 3). In the early 1470s James III seems to have entertained thoughts of claiming his mother's duchy, and it has been suggested that he may even have dreamt of proposing himself as candidate for the Empire. Charles 'the Bold', however, put paid to these ambitions by his incorporation of Gelderland into his own territories but it remained a point of diplomatic concern for *James IV.

After the downfall of the Boyd family (1469), Mary Stewart, elder sister of James III, together with her husband Thomas Boyd, earl of Arran, sought refuge in Bruges, and lived at the house of Anselmo Adorno, a distinguished Flemish merchant of an originally Italian family. Adorno visited Scotland on several occasions, and was made commissioner at Bruges for Scottish trade for all Burgundy. In 1470–1 he went on a journey to the Holy Land and dedicated his *Itinerary* to the Scottish king, who in 1470 had created him a knight of the new chivalric Order of St Andrew (later known as the Order of the Thistle). James III granted Adorno the lands of Cortachy (in Angus), a place which, interestingly enough, had forest and had been awarded as security for her dower to Mary of Gueldres. The new knight, who was killed in 1483 in rather obscure circumstances, may have influenced the king in his construction of the chapel royal at Restalrig, which has been said to resemble architecture which Adorno would have seen in Rhodes.

At this period Bruges and Ghent were famous as centres for the production of *illuminated manuscripts, and several of these made their way to Scotland. A fine prayerbook, for example, was ordered by Dean Brown of Aberdeen cathedral as he passed through Flanders en route to Rome in 1498, and was collected by him on his return journey in the following year. At this period the Conservator of the Privileges of the Scottish Nation in the Netherlands, Andrew Halyburton, was related by marriage to the celebrated Bening family of miniaturists. The most lavish manuscript to be imported into Scotland was the Book of Hours made for *James IV and Margaret Tudor (now in Vienna). The *Treasurer's Accounts* reveal that Flanders was the principal source of all sorts of objets d'art purchased by Scottish kings and ecclesiastics.

One important result of James II's marriage was Mary's importation into Scotland of Observant Franciscanism. These friars were initially under the leadership of Fr. Cornelius of Zierikzee, and the province of their order was centred in Cologne. Observant Franciscans made an important contribution to reforming religious life in late medieval Scotland, and between 1469 and 1494 they founded nine houses. James IV's confessor was Patrick Ranny, warden of the Stirling house; he it was who advised the king to wear an iron belt as penance for involvement in the rebellion against his father, James III. Another strong religious influence from the Low Countries was that of the *devotio moderna*. This movement had its origins in the towns along the river Yssel, whence it spread to centres of education in the rest of the Low Countries, to neighbouring parts of northern Germany, and to Paris. The University of Leuven and the Collège de Montaigu at Paris under Jan Standonck were places where Scottish students came under this particular influence, which had a quickening effect on the spiritual and devotional life, and which also overlapped with the northern humanism characteristic of the Low Countries. Awareness of the *devotio moderna* is reflected in the lists of books surviving from medieval Scottish *libraries (see RELIGIOUS LIFE: 2).

After the death of Mary of Burgundy (1482), the Low Countries passed into the control of the

Habsburgs. Mary's husband, the later Emperor Maximilian I, ruled in the name of their infant son, Philip 'the Fair', who predeceased (1506) his father. Interestingly, in 1495 a Scottish delegation, led by Bishop William Elphinstone, travelled to Worms to attempt *inter alia* to negotiate a marriage between James IV and the daughter of the emperor. On Maximilian's death (1519), his grandson, Charles V, inherited the Low Countries together with huge possessions in the Old and New Worlds. During this period Brussels became the principal imperial residence, while Charles's aunt, Margaret of Austria (d. 1530), regent of the Low Countries, had her court at nearby Mechelen (Malines). Between the years 1528 and 1532 there was much talk of a marriage between *James V and Mary of Hungary, daughter of Ferdinand I, younger brother of the emperor; in 1530 Charles appointed Mary regent of the Netherlands. Sir David Lindsay's seven-week visit to Brussels in 1531 was in connection with this projected alliance. In 1532, however, the Scots refocused their main attentions on the French court, and the period of close political engagement of Scotland with the Burgundian Netherlands (Valois and Habsburg) was at an end.

The Low Countries were important to Scotland as a source of paper and printed books. Bound up with the Chepman and Myllar prints (the earliest products of the Scottish press, 1508) is the *Gest of Robyn Hode* (in English), probably printed by Jan van Doesborch at Antwerp (1510–15). In the important collection of Catholic devotional literature now in the British Library, London (Arundel MS 285, *c*.1550), woodcuts found in books printed in the Low Countries early in the century are pasted in at places where one might have hoped for illuminations. The Reformation also impacted on the book trade with Scotland. John Gau's translation from Christian Pedersen, *The Richt vay til the Kingdome of Heuine* (1533), was a product of the Antwerp printer Johan Hochstraten, with a Malmö imprint. On the other hand, the Scottish translation of the *Commonitorium* of Vincentius Lirinensis by the Counter-Reformation controversialist Ninian Winzet (one of the earliest vernacular renderings of this important work) was printed at Antwerp, by Aegidius Diest, in 1563 (see PRINTING AND PUBLISHING).

After the Reformation in the southern Netherlands was suppressed, the Low Countries divided into the Catholic Spanish Netherlands and the Protestant United Provinces, and Scottish contacts thereafter are seldom free of a specific religious dimension. Thus, Ninian Winzet spent several years at Leuven, Paris, and Douai before his appointment (1577) as abbot of St James's monastery at Regensburg (Ratisbon) (see SCHOTTENKLÖSTER). For his part, the Protestant William MacDowell

(1590–1660) gravitated to the northern city of Groningen, where he became the first professor of philosophy at the new university (founded 1614), and later the commander of the city militia. Inevitably, however, it was the northern Netherlands which came to dominate Scottish attention. The United Provinces were represented at ceremonial events at Edinburgh during the reign of *James VI. The universities of Leiden (founded 1575), Franeker (1585), Groningen, and Utrecht (1636) became popular with Scottish Protestants, and remained so into the 18th century. One of the most colourful Scottish students was James Boswell, who enrolled at Utrecht, partly to annoy his father, who himself had studied at Leiden (see UNIVERSITIES: 1–2).

In certain Dutch towns there grew up sizeable Scottish communities, with their own churches: for example, at the ports of Rotterdam, Amsterdam, Middelburg, and Veere (see STAPLE PORTS), and the garrison towns of Breda and 's Hertogenbosch (Bois-le-Duc). Quite a few works by Scottish authors were published in the Netherlands: from Middelburg there issued Calvinistic works and books of Psalms, while the soldier-poet George Lauder published collections of verse at Breda and The Hague. In the 17th and 18th centuries printers in the Low Countries were active in publishing influential works of Scottish Latin culture (for example, *De Animi Tranquillitate* (Leiden, 1637; The Hague, 1642)) of Florence Wilson (Florentius Volsenus), originally published at Lyons in 1543; numerous editions of the works of George Buchanan; and the poetry anthology *Delitiae Poetarum Scotorum* (Amsterdam, 1637). Throughout this period the international scholarly language of Latin guaranteed large sales. Dutch printers were also keen to export to Scotland, a pattern of trade which lasted well into the age of the Enlightenment. Deserving of special note here is the export trade in salted herring from the waters round Orkney and Shetland (see REGIONAL IDENTITIES: 4); for a long time this trade was almost entirely in Dutch hands.

During the Cromwellian Commonwealth, the court of Charles II was based at The Hague. Members of the Scottish nobility who passed through the Low Countries on the Grand Tour absorbed the current fashions, and collected paintings (including such Dutch specialities as townscapes and sea-scenes) and other works of art, which they took back home to decorate their country houses.

The 19th and 20th centuries saw an appreciable decline in Scottish connections with the Low Countries. After the defeat of Napoleon, Scottish soldiers were much less in demand on the European mainland, and were rather employed in winning colonies overseas. At the same time, numbers of Scottish students in Dutch universities also fell off, and Scottish theology students were henceforth more likely to proceed to Germany. The industrial revolution in Britain meant that there was much less need to import books from abroad, and the Scots took control of the fishing round their own coasts. Previous patterns of trade were transformed and globalized, and the direct traffic between Scotland and the Low Countries was of greatly reduced significance.

The two world wars of the 20th century brought about short periods of intense involvement in the Low Countries; it is questionable, however, to what extent in this context one can speak of relations between two peoples. Otherwise, contacts in modern times have largely been commercial in nature: for example, one Anglo-Dutch firm has been much involved in exploiting the oil resources of the North Sea and around the Scottish coasts.　　　AAMacD

Macbeth (Mac Bethad mac Findláig) (b. before 1020, r. 1040–57) (Shakespeare's Macbeth) was recognized as king of Alba following his slaying of his predecessor, Duncan (Donnchad ua Maíl Choluim) (1034–40), in battle at Forres. As early as 1031, however, he appears to have held some sort of kingship as he is listed in the *Anglo-Saxon Chronicle* as one of the three northern kings who met Cnut in or shortly before that year. The others were Malcolm II (Mael Coluim mac Cinaeda) (king of Alba, 1005–34) and Echmarchach (d. 1065, one of the competitors for the Uí Ímair sea-kingdom which included Dublin, *Man, the Isles (see ISLES, KINGDOM OF THE), and *Galloway). The explanation for this seems to be that Malcolm's kingship of Alba had been contested by members of Macbeth's family, based in *Moray, since his succession. Cnut doubtless preferred to have Scotland split into as many units as possible and may have been playing the broker on this occasion. Duncan's ill-fated attack on Macbeth in his Moray heartland followed a disastrous attack on Northumbria and he may well have felt that a victory was needed to maintain his credibility amongst the Albanian nobility. Macbeth's great achievement was in realizing the claims to the kingship his kindred had put forward for nearly half a century. In 1045 he faced a challenge from Duncan's father, Crinán, abbot of Dunkeld, but this seems to have been dealt with without too much trouble. By 1050 Macbeth was secure enough in his rule to travel to Rome on pilgrimage—possibly attending a major church council whilst he was there.

It is in Macbeth's reign that we first begin to get information about Scottish kings that goes beyond simple obituary and battle notices in the chronicles and the reign-lengths in the king-lists (see KINGSHIP: 2). His wife was called Gruoch and was the daughter of Boite (probably the son of Cinaed mac Duib, king of Alba 997–1005). She is associated with him in an early charter granting land to the *céli Dé* community of Loch Leven. In 1052 some of the Norman friends of Edward 'the Confessor' (king of the English, 1042–66) who had been expelled in order to placate English resentment were taken into service by Macbeth. In 1054 Macbeth suffered a setback when Earl Siward of Northumbria invaded the southern portion of his realm and installed a certain Mael Coluim in the kingship of Strathclyde. This may have been Mael Coluim mac Donnchada (Malcolm III 'Canmore', king of Alba, 1058–93), as later medieval chroniclers claimed, but as this king did not count his reign as beginning until 1058 and accepted the legitimacy of the reign of Macbeth's stepson Lulach (1057–8) this seems unlikely. For the most part Macbeth seems to have maintained peaceful relations with his southern neighbours but was engaged in serious warfare on his northern frontier against the powerful Earl Thorfinn of *Orkney (c.1030–60).

In 1057 Mael Coluim mac Donnchada did make an attempt at regaining his father's kingdom but was defeated at Lumphanan in Mar. Macbeth, however, was mortally wounded in this battle and died a few days later (15 August) in *Scone. Gruoch's son Lulach mac Gilla Comgáin succeeded to the kingship and held on to it until 17 March the following year when Mael Coluim defeated and slew him at Essie in Strathbogie. Contrary to the image presented by Renaissance writers, notably Shakespeare, there is little evidence that Macbeth was any more tyrannical than the run of early medieval kings and his claim to the kingship was probably as good as that of his predecessor the young, rather than aged, Duncan. He may even have begun some of the transformation of the kingdom usually credited to Malcolm III. AW

McIntyre, Robert. Robert Douglas McIntyre (1913–98) was a leading figure in the SNP. After a short spell in the Labour Party, McIntyre became disillusioned with the lack of commitment to Scottish Home Rule and joined the SNP, becoming membership secretary in 1940. He sided with the radicals in the split of 1942 and at the Motherwell by-election in April 1945, McIntyre became the SNP's first MP. He was party chairman from 1948 to 1956 and worked hard to give the SNP a separate political identity from the other main British parties. By choosing a broadly social democrat basis for nationalist policies, it was hoped that the SNP would be able to distinguish itself from the

Labour (see LABOURISM) and the Conservative (see UNIONISM) parties. Although making little headway in the 1950s and early 1960s, McIntyre worked hard to keep the SNP to its principles of contesting elections as a separate and distinctive political party in order to secure an electoral mandate for independence. He insisted on discipline in the party and recognized that there would be no quick fix for the attainment of independence. Consequently, much time was spent in the 1950s and early 1960s on organizational matters, building up an electoral machinery and recruiting new members.

McIntyre was keen to present the SNP as a moderate and reasonable party and was largely responsible for expelling those who promoted anti-English sentiment and violent or illegal tactics. These efforts paid dividends in the mid-1960s when an influx of new members were able to meld into a mature party organization which took advantage of growing dissatisfaction with the Labour government to secure a by-election win in Hamilton in 1967 and sweeping gains in local government in 1969. The period from 1974 to 1979 was a tumultuous one in Scottish politics and McIntyre, as SNP president (1958–80), worked hard to steer the party through many difficult obstacles. Ever the pragmatist, he tried to ensure the SNP would stick to its key objective. He was suspicious of attempts to move the party to the left and turned his face against endeavours by militants to take direct action following the defeat of the 1979 referendum on devolution. Again he was proactive in expelling militants who, he argued, were diverting the party from its key objectives. More than anybody, he is credited as the father of modern Scottish *nationalism (see also NATIONAL IDENTITY: 6).   RJF

Mackintosh, J. P. John Mackintosh (1929–78) combined the academic study of politics with its practice, being more successful in the former than the latter. He was educated at Melville College, Edinburgh, and at Edinburgh, Oxford, and Princeton universities. As an academic political scientist, he was a prolific author and wrote a number of significant works. The *British Cabinet*, first published in 1962, was seminal and contributed to debates on the position of the cabinet and prime minister in British politics. He held chairs in politics in Strathclyde University (1965–6) and Edinburgh University (1977–8), the latter while serving as an MP before he died. He was Labour MP for Berwick and East Lothian (1966–February 1944 and again from October 1974 until his death in 1978), but never made ministerial rank due to his independence or, as his critics suggest, recklessness. He was, as he told friends, the 'Enoch Powell of the Left'. He was a staunch advocate of Scottish Home Rule and

membership of the European Communities before these became fashionable inside the Labour Party (see LABOURISM) and was firmly on the right of the party. In the late 1970s, he rebelled against his party by opposing the nationalization of shipbuilding. He was often involved in intrigues and plots against Harold Wilson and was described by Ben Pimlott, Wilson's biographer, as one of the 'Wilson-hating desperadoes'. There was little surprise that Wilson refused to consider him for ministerial office. Controversy continued to surround Mackintosh even after his untimely death in 1978. When the Social Democrats were established in the 1980s, it was claimed by members of that party that he would have joined had he lived while Labour loyalists dismissed the suggestion, arguing that he would have remained within the party despite its shortcomings. Blair's New Labour would have been a party in which he would have found a home though he might have found the internal discipline difficult to stomach.   JM

MacLaren, Duncan (1800–86), MP for Edinburgh 1865–81, the foremost exemplar of middle-class Victorian radicalism (see EQUIPOISE, AGE OF). He was described at the time as 'the member for Scotland'.

Of Highland parentage, MacLaren became a successful draper in Edinburgh. As a dissenting Presbyterian, he was excluded alike by religion, occupation, background, and education from the charmed circle of Church of Scotland lawyers and lairds who controlled Edinburgh's political and social life (see DISRUPTION). For two decades he led the ultimately successful dissenters' campaign against Edinburgh's iniquitous Annuity Tax. He became burgh treasurer after municipal reform in 1833, rescuing Edinburgh's finances from the insolvency bequeathed by the unreformed council. He was Lord Provost from 1851 to 1854.

An inveterate political manoeuvrer, MacLaren created the Voluntary churches' highly influential political lobby, the Scottish Board of Dissenters, in 1834. In 1847 he was instrumental in engineering a Free Church–Voluntary alliance which defeated the Whig T. B. Macaulay in the Edinburgh election. MacLaren, himself defeated in the 1852 election, had to wait until 1865 to enter parliament as Liberal member for Edinburgh. He held the seat until he retired in 1881.

MacLaren was closely identified with numerous reform causes. He was perhaps the most prominent member of the Scottish Anti-Corn Law campaign. In the 1830s he advocated the introduction of the ballot, and was an early champion of female suffrage (see WOMEN: 3). In the 1860s he agitated for the extension of the franchise to the urban working class. He also spearheaded the revived demand for disestablishment in the 1870s, and supported the crofters' cause in the 1880s (see LAND AGITATION AND REFORM IN THE HIGHLANDS AND ISLANDS). Beginning with the Scottish Rights movement of the 1850s, he argued for Scottish *nationalism from a radical standpoint. Nevertheless, he left the Liberals in 1886 over *Irish Home Rule. There were, clear limits to his radicalism, and he fell out with his erstwhile supporters, the local trade unions, when he refused to support legislation to protect unions because of his laissez-faire principles (see ECONOMIC POLICY: 3).   IGCH

MacLeod, George (1895–1991), Lord MacLeod of Fuinary, church leader, and founder of the *Iona Community. Born in Glasgow, the son of a Conservative MP, he belonged to a Highland ecclesiastical dynasty which has given many prominent ministers to the church. He was educated at Winchester, Oxford, and Edinburgh, and received the degree of DD from the University of Glasgow in 1937. He served as minister of the Church of Scotland at St Cuthbert's in Edinburgh, 1926–30, and then at Govan Old, 1930–8. During the Depression years on Clydeside he decided that the church would have to undertake a radical experiment in order to minister more effectively to working-class communities. His adventurous founding of the Iona Community in 1938 was the result. MacLeod wished to provide a training ground and support group for ministers to work in industrial areas. In the early years, ministers and craftsmen worked together to rebuild the ruins of the living quarters of the abbey at Iona, which became the base for the Community's service in the world. Inspired by MacLeod's radical vision and energetic leadership, the Community has become internationally known for its commitment to renewal in worship and to social justice. Although criticized initially for being halfway towards Rome and halfway towards Moscow, it now consists of over 200 members both ordained and lay, who belong to different Christian traditions. MacLeod was elected as moderator of the General Assembly of the church in 1957 and, on resigning as leader of the Iona Community in 1967, was elevated to the House of Lords. He became president of the International Fellowship of Reconciliation and continued to be an outspoken and controversial figure in the church and beyond. It was appropriate that a new international youth and reconciliation centre on Iona, opened in 1988, was named in his honour.   DMM

Maitland family. The Maitland family's origins date from the Anglo-Norman era of settlement in Scotland; the name is typically Norman and translates as evil genius. Their distinguished antecedents

included Sir Richard Maitland whose exploits in the Wars of *Independence earned him a place in Gavin Douglas's *The Palis of Honour*. It was in the 16th century that the Maitland family began to take centre stage in Scottish political life through their nepotistic dominance of the Scottish secretariat, a practice not uncommon in Spain, France, or England at this time.

The most politically significant members of the family were two sons of the blind lawyer, poet, and judge, Sir Richard Maitland of Lethington (1486–1586). William Maitland of Lethington (c.1526–73) was secretary of state to *Mary, Queen of Scots, and universally recognized as pivotal to Scotland's fortunes from 1558 to 1573. His younger brother John, lord of Thirlestane (c.1545–95), became chancellor to *James VI in 1586.

Sir Richard's reputation as a poet has in recent times received critical acclaim and illustrates strong Scottish patriotism and an Erastian approach to the religious disputes of his lifetime. William Maitland has, by contrast, not enjoyed a favourable historical reputation. He was Scotland's Machiavelli and Buchanan's chameleon, so called because of the only colours chameleons cannot assume: red and white, symbols of bravery and loyalty. Yet the powerful opprobrium poured on Maitland by his enemies testified greatly to his vast skill and ability. It was precisely because his enemies in the civil war of 1567–73 had benefited so much from his brilliance in masterminding the Congregation's (see CONGREGATION, WARS OF THE) victory in 1560 and Mary's deposition in 1567 that such a vitriolic propaganda campaign was sustained.

Like so many Scots in the 16th century, Maitland was very well educated, following in 1540 the well-worn route from St Leonard's College to Paris. His correspondence displayed a fluency in six languages. He was very well equipped theologically, conversant with the opinions of Calvin, Luther, Bucer, and Melancthon. He embraced what was termed the new learning of humanism and Elizabeth I regarded him as 'the flower of the wits of Scotland'.

The successful personal reign of Mary saw Maitland at the heart of her government. As secretary, he developed an intriguing relationship with William Cecil, his English counterpart, as he relentlessly pursued the amity. However, following the Darnley marriage, Maitland had a heavy hand in the controversies that were to lead to her fall in 1567. He openly confessed this in 1570, when he returned to Mary's allegiance as head of the queen's party after his split with the regent, Moray. Despite his skilful leadership the destiny of the civil war lay, as with so much else in Scotland from 1558 to 1573, in English hands. It was far safer for Elizabeth to keep Mary incarcerated in England than to support her restoration. After the fall of *Edinburgh castle in 1573 Maitland died in mysterious circumstances, cheating the hangman (see ANGLO-SCOTTISH RELATIONS: 3).

John Maitland shared the literary and intellectual gifts of his family and followed his brother in the civil war. His successful political rehabilitation was completed following the fall of Morton with his appointment as secretary in 1584 and later as chancellor. Jealousy and faction were endemic in the Jacobean *royal court and Maitland fell victim on more than one occasion, most crucially in the fallout created by the death of the 'bonnie' earl of Moray. It has been suggested that Maitland's subsequent crucial support of the establishment of the church on a strictly Presbyterian basis in 1592 was politically inspired to hit back at his enemies at court. He died in 1595, having enjoyed victory against his rival Bothwell but never quite regaining the pre-eminence he once enjoyed.   MLo

Man, kingdom of. Man with its anomalous international position, outside the European Union but owing allegiance to the crown, is the last vestige of the kingdom or lordship of the *Isles which, at times, included the Hebrides, from Lewis to Islay. This kingdom from the 10th to the mid-13th century, with its wealth of Viking ships and armed men, played a central role in the politics of the Irish Sea region. Culturally it was a mixture of Norse and Gaelic elements, although the exact nature and proportion of each is still subject for debate. Man has a plethora of Norse inscriptions, but when island forces overran Anglesey in 1193 they were described as Gaels. The Tynwald (Manx parliament) is living example of this mixed milieu, being a Norse administration structure which proclaims its laws in Manx Gaelic.

Its origins lie deep in the 9th century when a Scandinavian (see SCANDINAVIA: 1) presence made itself felt in the west with extensive settlement in the Hebrides, Man, and the north of England, and the establishment of Scandinavian towns like Dublin in *Ireland. It was, however, not until the 970s and 980s that kings based in the Isles asserted their identity in the annals. During these two decades the brothers Maccus and Godred Haraldsson, probably of the royal kindred of Dublin, the Uí Ímair (descendants of Ivar), were involved in Irish affairs and in the politics of North Wales, raiding Anglesey in 971, 980, 982, and 987. Their power clearly extended throughout the Isles: Maccus was described as *plurimarum rex insularum* on his meeting with King Edgar at Chester in 973, while Godred's obit in the *Annals of Ulster* describes him as *Rí Innse Gall* (King of the Hebrides or 'Foreigners

Isles'). It was not until the appearance of Godred Crovan, who usurped power in 1079, that the kingdom enjoyed a period of renewed vigour. Although his origins are obscure, Godred was probably also of the royal kindred of Dublin. He was certainly interested in the city, adding it to his kingdom in 1091–4, before being driven out to die of plague in Islay in 1095. His greatest success was the establishment of a tenacious dynasty which ruled the kingdom until the death of King Magnus in 1265.

This dynasty ruled a viable medieval kingdom with its own bishopric, Sodor, founded during the reign of King Olaf Godredsson in c.1135. The kings were providers or leaders of war fleets for their neighbours, for example, to Dublin in 1091, 1155, and 1171 and Caithness in 1199—both King John and Henry III of England engaged fleets of 50 ships to 'guard the coasts'. The kingdom, however, was not without internal and external problems. There was a struggle with rivals from the coastline of Argyll, the kindred of Somerled, which ultimately left the kingdom divided. In 1156, Somerled defeated King Godred Olafsson, and in 1158, with 53 ships, he drove Godred out altogether. Godred returned, but Somerled's sons continued to rule the more southerly isles and from Glenelg to Mull of Kintyre, leaving only Lewis and Skye with Man. This division lasted until the end of the kingdom.

In 1098, Magnus III Olafsson 'Bare-Legs', king of Norway, conquered the Isles, ushering in over 160 years of Norwegian overlordship. The relationship with Norway was loose and did not dramatically infringe the freedom of action of the insular kings; indeed it was not until c.1154 that they officially became vassals, when Godred Olafsson, due to internal threats to his kingdom, swore allegiance to King Inge of Norway, and Sodor passed from York to the new Norwegian archbishopric of Nidaros. Norwegian overlordship was not uncontested: during the 13th century the expansion of Scottish royal power saw the struggle for control of the Isles culminate in the Treaty of Perth in 1266, when Magnus VI Haakonsson of Norway handed the kingdom over to Alexander III, for the sum of 4,000 merks and an annuity of 100 merks in perpetuity.
            APJ

maps and map-making. Scotland's rich cartographic heritage derives from several distinct phases of map-making over five centuries. Because map-makers select only certain features and then portray them as they wish them to be seen, the content and form of the extant maps of Scotland's past reflects the social and political circumstances of their compilation.

There is little evidence of demand for maps, or of indigenous map-making in Scotland, prior to the late 16th century. The earliest maps of Scotland were compiled in Italy, Germany, and Holland. The coastline was mainly derived from maritime sources, in particular, the 'rutter' compiled for the circumnavigation of Scotland by *James V in 1540 (*The Booke of the Sea Corte called the Rutter*). The landward content was obtained in part from Scots exiles, such as John Elder and George Lily. The earliest known printed map of Scotland alone was engraved in Italy in the 1560s. That depiction was much improved by Ortelius in his *Scotiae tabula* of 1573, but in the absence of new data, engravers thereafter could do little more than copy the work of their predecessors. There is great similarity in the maps of Scotland by Mercator (1595), Camden (1607), Speed (1610), Blaeu (1635), Janssonius (1636), and Hondius (1636).

In 1654, Scotland became one of the best mapped countries in Europe, with the publication of volume 5 of Blaeu's *Atlas Novus*, containing 47 regional maps of Scotland, plus a new map of the whole country. This was the outcome of events in the late 16th century, when church and state sought to extend their authority throughout Scotland. Maps were potential tools of authority. Robert Pont, the prominent reforming cleric and lawyer, obtained ecclesiastical support for his son Timothy, who seems to have spent the years between 1583 and 1596, or possibly longer, travelling through most of Scotland, compiling a record in notes and maps of many aspects of local geography, history, economy, and genealogy. Pont's work was not published in his lifetime, despite the support of *James VI, but his manuscript maps were to be the sources of most of Blaeu's engravings, which record some 20,000 contemporary Scottish *place names. Remarkably, 38 of his manuscripts containing 78 maps are extant in the NLS. Because these are unaltered by the processes of engraving, they are primary sources of detailed information on *rural settlement distribution, large houses, townscapes (see URBAN SETTLEMENT: 1), churches, bridges, mills, woodland, and other features. They are not consistently objective in their portrayal of visible features in the landscape, however. Pont was not a topographic surveyor. He was a chorographer, concerned with *regional identities, ecclesiastical authority, and individual status and he would have selected his subject matter accordingly.

Pont's achievement was not an isolated incident. His work inspired Robert Gordon of Straloch to try to utilize and build on it. He involved his son, James Gordon, parson of Rothiemay, who compiled new maps of Fife and Aberdeenshire, as well as plans of Edinburgh and Aberdeen. James was asked to compile new maps of other counties, which suggests demand for maps by the mid-17th century. The entire collection of the manuscripts of Pont and the Gordons was acquired in 1682 by Sir Robert Sibbald who was given royal authority to prepare a new geographical description of Scotland. Sibbald appointed John Adair to prepare new regional maps, using more sophisticated techniques than those of Pont. Sibbald and Adair proved to be professionally incompatible and the work was not brought to fruition, but some of Adair's manuscript maps are extant.

The mapping of Scotland went into abeyance at the end of the 17th century. New maps were published but with little original content. For example, what Herman Moll entitled in 1725 'A set of 36 new and correct maps of Scotland . . .' are mostly small-scale reproductions of Blaeu's maps of 1654.

In the mid-18th century, Scotland once again became one of the best-mapped countries in Europe, although this time the work was not entirely initiated internally. The original protraction of the military survey of Scotland was supervised by William Roy, with the second and best-known manuscript edition, the fair copy, draughted by Paul Sandby. The Highlands (see HIGHLANDS AND ISLANDS: GENERAL) were observed between 1747 and 1752, with the south of Scotland covered in the three years thereafter. The survey was conducted by field parties using rudimentary traversing techniques which gave rise to gaps and inconsistencies. The scale of approximately 1,000 yards to the inch potentially allowed much detail to be recorded, but the map is not comprehensive in the depiction of its subject matter. It is often assumed that the map was compiled for purposes of military logistics. This is open to question, on grounds of content, subsequent provenance, and the absence of documentary evidence of its purpose. Alternatively, it has been suggested that the survey was a demonstration of Hanoverian authority throughout Scotland, that there was no longer anywhere to hide.

The improving movement (see ECONOMY: 3; ECONOMY, PRIMARY SECTOR: 1–2) of the 18th and 19th centuries gave rise to a great many large-scale surveys before and after the reformulation of the rural landscape (see RURAL SOCIETY: 4–5). Many of the earlier manuscript documents are still in Highland and Lowland estate muniments. Many more have been transferred to public collections. Most of these maps were the work of professional engineer/surveyors and are of a high standard of accuracy. Their content is summarized at smaller scales in John Thomson's single-volume *Atlas of Scotland* (1832). A remarkable contemporaneous publication, John Wood's *Town Atlas of Scotland* (1828), contains 48 original urban plans. Road maps, geological maps, agricultural maps, historical maps, and railway and canal plans (see TRANSPORT AND

COMMUNICATIONS: 2) were increasingly published in the 19th century.

The Ordnance Survey (OS) commenced work in Wigtownshire in 1843 but progressed slowly at first because of national controversy over scales. Publication at the 1 inch (2.5 cm) scale was completed in 1887, with successive series culminating in the Seventh Series completed in 1961. The frequency of new 1 inch series suggests a useful record of landscape change, but comparisons through time are hindered by changing subject matter. The first edition of the OS 6 inch (15.2 cm) series, surveyed from 1846 to 1878, is possibly the most useful historical source.   JCS

Margaret, St, queen of Malcolm III 'Canmore' (Mael Coluim mac Donnchada) (c.1046–93). Malcolm III's marriage to Margaret, the daughter of the royal English prince Edward and Agatha, daughter of King Stephen of Hungary, may be said to be the first step in the 'Europeanization' of Scotland, joining as it did the house of Alba to two other important European royalties. Most important here is the English connection. Although her early years were spent in Hungary, Margaret returned with her father during the reign of Edward 'the Confessor', but was forced to flee to Scotland with her brother, Edgar Atheling, in 1068, after the Norman conquest of the English throne. Malcolm, the king of Alba, made her his second wife in 1072, a pointed gesture in the new political climate. Much (such as French ways and language) has been attributed to Margaret which can certainly not have been her doing, but her presence certainly brought an English air into the Gaelic-speaking Scottish court. Her sons, Edward, Edmund, Ethelred, Edgar, Alexander, and *David I, certainly introduced a new nomenclature into the royal house, and English Benedictine monks were brought to Dunfermline, possibly to provide an English-speaking royal church for the queen's retinue (see CHURCH INSTITUTIONS: 2). Certainly it was ultimately her sons and their descendants, rather than those of Malcolm's first wife Ingibjorg of Orkney, who formed Scotland's medieval dynasty, and it was through these sons, raised as many were as hostages in the court of William and his successors, which brought Norman influence proper into the elite circles in Scotland (see ANGLO-SCOTTISH RELATIONS: 1; KINGSHIP: 2).

We are fortunate to possess a Life of Margaret, written by Turgot, royal confessor and later bishop of St Andrews. It makes sweeping claims for Margaret's influence over her 'savage' husband, her introduction of European clothes and fashions into the court, and especially her influence on the church. Turgot gives an account of Margaret con-

vening an ecclesiastical synod, using her husband as interpreter, with items of aberrant Scottish practice on the agenda. That Margaret's concerns in this synod match Turgot's own as bishop so closely cannot be a coincidence; nonetheless we cannot exclude a certain amount of the new European ecclesiastical thinking coming into Scotland with Margaret, raised as she partly was in a newly converted nation. Certainly we know Margaret, with her husband, also patronized long-standing foundations, such as the *céli Dé* of Loch Leven. Margaret became an important figure within the royal Scottish dynasty, and she was canonized as a saint in 1249 by Pope Innocent IV. After the Reformation, her relics seem to have gone first to the Low Countries, and ultimately to Madrid, where they appear to have been lost (see RELIGIOUS LIFE: 2).   TC

Mary, Queen of Scots (1542–87). The reign of Mary remains one of the most contentious in Scottish history, and probably for the wrong reasons. The quatercentenary of her death in 1987 saw another flood of Mariana, which has shown few signs of decreasing since. She remains both a tragic enigma and one of the chief assets of the Scottish tourist trade, which has an interest in keeping the romance and half-truths alive and well.

Understanding of the reign, however, has greatly advanced in recent years. Gordon Donaldson's dictum that most who had power or influence were more motivated by kinship, self-interest, or a conservative attitude to sovereignty than by religion is now generally accepted, although it has a potentially explosive impact which has not always been thought through on relations between Mary and John *Knox and the effect a Catholic queen had on the fledgling *Reformation. A counter-argument that Mary was a failure, personally incompetent, obsessed with the English succession, and a Catholic monarch who neglected her duty, has not found general acceptance, not least because it fell foul of the classic difficulty of proving a negative. Yet there remain uncertain or unresolved a series of questions, mostly about her personal reign (1561–7).

By contrast, Mary's minority spent in Scotland up until the age of 6 (1542–8), and her period in *France (1548–61) (see also FRANCO-SCOTTISH RELATIONS: 2) have not provoked new disagreements, although much new work has been done on both periods. The *Rough Wooing did not create a significant pro-English party in Scotland and, as yet, there was no automatic link between support for England and Protestant sympathies (see ANGLO-SCOTTISH RELATIONS: 3). She was brought up in a happy family atmosphere at the court of Henri II, with her eventual husband, the Dauphin François, one of her childhood friends. The long-term ambitions of Henri for his daughter-in-law, who married François in 1558, were evident as early as 1550: Scotland was treated, at least in French propaganda, as part of its empire.

Equally, the period of captivity in England (1568–87) has a generally agreed agenda. Few historians now believe, or even wish to consider, the Casket Letters, which formed the substance of the charges against her at her first 'trial', at York in 1568. Most also suspect that the eventual plot which brought about her execution in 1587, organized by an obscure English Catholic Anthony Babington, was a put-up job, orchestrated and certainly monitored by Francis Walsingham's agents. Differences arise as to when the English authorities decided that Queen Elizabeth's cousin could not be returned to Scotland and when they, in effect, accepted that the drastic solution, sooner or later, was their best option. For some, it was 1569 and her marginal involvement in the Norfolk conspiracy and the accompanying revolt of the Catholic earls. For others, it was the Ridolfi plot of 1571. But by 1572, the English Commons was baying for her blood and the obituary notices, on all sides, were already beginning to be composed.

Within two weeks of her return to Scotland, on 19 August 1561, Mary was caught up in a dramatic confrontation with John Knox and radical Protestantism. It was a classic demonstration of the conflict of faith, loyalty to the crown, and personal interests which lasted for most of her personal reign. Mary and the Protestant regime which had pushed through the Reformation in her absence and without her permission had already agreed that she would be allowed the Catholic Mass in her own private chapel despite the fact that the 'Reformation' Parliament twelve months before had declared it illegal. On the first Sunday after her return, Knox and a band of Protestant demonstrators tried to break into her chapel at Holyrood. Their way was barred by Lord James, Mary's half-brother and leader of the Protestant revolt in 1559–60. For Knox, it was the ultimate betrayal. The next day, the privy council, acting in the queen's name, imposed a religious standstill. And the next Sunday, Knox, undeterred, preached an inflammatory sermon in St Giles's, claiming that one Mass was more dangerous than an invasion of 10,000 armed enemies. In a sense, he was right. Mary's Mass would spread, as she toured the country on progresses over the next few years. And, in her absence, her Holyrood chapel would become a haven for *Edinburgh's Catholics.

Just two days later, more surprises were in store for the young queen when she made her formal entry into her capital. An entry was usually a glittering occasion, signifying a kind of marriage between monarch and capital. When Mary was handed the keys of the burgh, she was also given a Protestant bible and psalm book. To add insult to injury, they were English. But worse was to come. One of the set-piece pageants depicted the fate of the three Israelites who had defied Moses; the earth opened up and they were consumed by fire as the price of their idolatry. This was the most pointed clash between a Catholic monarch and militant Protestants in the 16th century. It must have come as a shock to a princess brought up in the French court of a king as powerful as Henri II: not only was her religion challenged but her authority was called into question. It is not surprising that, two days later, in the first of her notorious interviews with Knox, she demanded to know why he commanded her subjects to obey him rather than their queen. But this first fortnight had also shown that most of Mary's nobles (see NOBILITY: 3), Protestant as well as Catholic, were more inclined to support their monarch than Knox.

What were Mary's motives? In 1562, she staged the downfall of the most powerful Catholic magnate in Scotland, the earl of Huntly (see GORDON FAMILY), when he threatened the 1561 agreement by an open invitation to her to attend the Mass in his own castle at Strathbogie. For some, it has raised the question of how genuine Mary's own Catholic convictions were. Yet there can be little doubt that she had a simple but fairly strong faith. Her family, on her mother's side, were resolute Catholics. Her grandmother had ended her days in a convent and her mother never wavered. Mary herself, on what she believed to be her deathbed, when she fell ill at Jedburgh, in October 1566, claimed that she 'died of the faith Catholic'. It is not always acknowledged that, in 1561, it was difficult to know what stance a Catholic monarch should take. The Council of Trent did not decide on its hard-line Counter-Reformation stance until 1563. In France, her Guise uncles were in 1561 still trying to reach agreement with the Lutherans and so exclude the hard-line pro-Geneva Calvinists. Mary, on instructions, was almost certainly trying to do the same in Scotland.

By 1565, however, when Mary married her cousin Darnley, the shutters were beginning to come down over Europe. France had been enmeshed in a bitter religious civil war in 1562–4. Protestants feared an international Catholic crusade against them. Mary's mother-in-law, Catherine de Medici, advised her to assassinate Protestant leaders—advice which Mary ignored. Elizabeth I's advisers thought in terms of a beleaguered Protestant isle. Caught between an aggressive Catholic international and a Protestant militant, Mary tried to follow a middle course.

In 1565, she shrugged off a revolt led by her half-brother, Lord James (now earl of Moray). The issue was not so much religion as the influence over her of Darnley and his family, the Lennox Stewarts. Yet there was no dash by Mary for a pro-Catholic policy and no systematic purge of Protestants from her government. Against a background of increasing fears of the General Assembly about the spread of the 'pollution of the Mass', she held to the compromise reached in 1561.

The dramatic murder of Mary's Savoyard servant David Rizzio, in her own privy chamber at Holyrood in March 1566, was a Protestant demonstration against what the conspirators saw as a drift towards Catholicism at court. It may also have been an attempt on her life for she was six months' pregnant at the time. The plot posed two problems for Mary. One, which she solved, was how to isolate the extremists. The next nine months, climaxing in the elaborate baptism staged for her son at *Stirling castle in December 1566, were an orchestrated political recovery. The other problem was more difficult. Darnley had been part of the murder gang. This impetuous adolescent, still only 19, was a dangerous vehicle for others' ambitions. Too young to be given the crown matrimonial, he came from a mixed family, with a devout Catholic for a mother and a convinced Protestant for his father. He played at both roles. At Candlemas 1566, five weeks before joining the Protestant assassins, he had publicly boasted that he would return Scotland to the Mass.

Despite the concerted attempts of many historians, there is no convincing evidence to suggest that Mary was involved in a plot to rid herself of the embarrassment of her husband. Yet the assassination of Darnley, who was recuperating, probably from syphilis, in the Kirk o' Field just outside Edinburgh, caused an explosion which rocked Mary's government to its foundations. In life, Darnley had swung both ways in religion. In death, his publicity-conscious family turned him into a Protestant martyr. Between 1562 and 1566, Mary had survived one Catholic rising, two failed Protestant coups, and the mysterious illness which struck her down at Jedburgh. She had recovered from each of these trials and there is some reason for thinking, at the end of 1566, that she and her dynasty were secure. She was still only 23 and she had a son and heir. Compromise and conciliation had generally worked. The radicals in the kirk, including Knox, were on the retreat.

It took a family dispute to undermine her. This was not the first time the chief threat to a Stewart monarch had come from the ranks of the Stewarts themselves. But a dead Darnley proved even more awkward than a live one. Her marriage to the earl

of Bothwell, whom many suspected of the murder, was a serious miscalculation. Bothwell also had many enemies. The ceremony, carried out by Protestant rites, probably alienated some of Mary's Catholic supporters. The fact that he was married, and a Catholic annulment quickly arranged, added the whiff of scandal. The charisma of Mary, Queen of Scots, surrounded by a glittering, Renaissance *royal court (see CULTURE: 4), was suddenly dented. Rumours of a rape, a pregnancy, and even the still-birth of twins swirled about the courts of Europe. Even the pope condemned her. Yet the precise circumstances of Mary's fall and the emergence of a coalition of Catholic and Protestant nobles against her, which confronted Mary and Bothwell at Carberry, near Musselburgh, in June 1567, still defy a satisfactory explanation. Even now, the die was not cast for most nobles wanted only to be rid of Bothwell. It took a coup within a coup to hand power to the radicals. Mary was imprisoned on Lochleven, and literally forced to sign a deed of deposition in favour of her infant son.

Yet when Mary escaped from her island prison in May 1568, less than eleven months later, she was able to raise an army of over 6,000 men within eleven days. It took the incompetence of the *Hamiltons to lose at Langside against an inferior force led by her half-brother Moray. It is, however, generally agreed that it was at this point that Mary made her most serious error, when she fled to England, to seek the help of her cousin Elizabeth. This, however, was not quite the last act of the tragedy. The English regime, still insecure, was in a real dilemma. Mary in exile gave them an opportunity to make sure of a pro-English regime in Scotland. But Mary in England was a likely focal point for a Catholic rising or plots against Elizabeth. That dilemma was not quickly resolved. And in Scotland, a decisive drift away from Mary's party in the ensuing civil war did not take place until 1571.

The real difficulty that confronts the historian of Mary's reign is hindsight. The slippery slope to her fall is too easy to construct too early. And there is hardly another reign where historians have been more tempted to put their subject on the psychiatrist's couch. Historians, however, do not make good psychiatrists. Viewed more clinically, the short personal reign could have gone either way. From mid-1565, when the first Protestant plot, the so-called Chaseabout raid, failed, radical Protestantism felt itself on the retreat. Most Protestant nobles, however, including most of those involved in one or other of the plots of 1565 and 1566, showed themselves willing to accept Mary's patronage or her attempts at reconciliation. That remained the case into 1567. It even seemed so for a time after her husband's murder. Four of the five reigns which preceded that of Mary had seen conspiracies against the monarch; two—against James I and III—had succeeded, and both of them were, in part, family conspiracies (see KINGSHIP: 5). Mary's reign did have new and extraordinary dimensions to it, including the religious issue and the fact that she was a female ruler, although elaborate detective work on her character and its flaws is not necessary. Her actual fall need not be seen as out of the ordinary for Stewart monarchs, yet its effects certainly were seismic: in a very real sense, it made secure both the Scottish and British Reformations.

Her execution, which took place in February 1587, almost exactly twenty years to the day after the mysterious death of Darnley, followed a brief show trial at her last prison of Fotheringhay castle. It was the first test of the formal league with England, concluded just seven months before. *James VI, already a pensioner of the English crown, muttered about taking some form of revenge but kept any grief he felt for the mother he had not seen since he was an infant to himself. But in a flamboyant gesture in 1612, following his accession to the throne of England, he arranged for the transfer of the corpse of his 'dearest mother' from Peterborough cathedral to Westminster abbey. The queen of Scots brought up in France, who wanted to be buried beside her Guise relations at Rheims, was the first of the Stewart dynasty to be buried amongst the kings and queens of England. ML

Maxton, James (1885–1946), politician who might be regarded as the socialist icon of 20th-century Scotland. His bohemian appearance and his stirring oratory made him the personification of the *'Red Clydeside' legend.

Maxton was born in Pollokshaws, near Glasgow, the son of schoolteachers. He too, followed this calling and it was his experience of the poverty of the pupils in a Glasgow school which moulded his social radicalism. He became a member of the ILP (see LABOURISM). During the Great War he was sent to prison for sedition and his reputation as a rabble-rouser was born. In 1922 he was returned as Labour MP to Westminster for the Glasgow constituency of Bridgeton, which he was to represent until his death in 1946.

In 1923 he provoked outrage by labelling as 'murderers' Conservatives who supported a government motion to cut health grants to local authorities. This led to his suspension from the House of Commons. Later in the 1920s he and his Glasgow colleague and mentor John *Wheatley attempted unsuccessfully to lead the Labour Party in a more left-wing direction, a campaign organized around the ILP programme 'Socialism in Our Time'. Maxton was at the time chairman of the ILP, which he

viewed as the conscience of the Labour movement. During the 1929–31 Labour government, Maxton was a relentless critic and the ILP's relations with the Labour Party deteriorated beyond repair. In 1932 Maxton and the ILP chose to disaffiliate and thus inherit a position on the political margins from which they never recovered the influence of earlier years. Maxton's political reputation was also decisively shaped by his pacifism, especially during the 1930s. He opposed the war resolutely when it came in 1939. His health was generally poor in his later years, a sign perhaps of burn-out after the passion spent in his prime. Notwithstanding the image portrayed of him as a wild man, he had friends across the political spectrum and among his greatest admirers was Winston Churchill. GW

medicine and the origins of the medical profession were inextricably bound up with the evolution of Scottish society itself. Scottish medicine led the world in the 18th century—many individual Scots were pioneers in a number of medical fields—and so an account of medicine and medical practitioners is vital to the understanding of Scotland as a whole.

Little evidence remains from earliest times, although it is clear that the Romans practised some sort of formal medicine during their sojourn in Scotland. Native Scottish peoples had for centuries treated themselves and their families with a combination of herbs (see TRADITIONAL HEALING), superstition, religion, and astrology. The western humoral medical tradition, as derived from Hippocrates and Galen, was the basis of most practice, whether or not the practitioners knew this. Humoral medicine stemmed from the assumption that diseases were caused by an imbalance in the bodily humours, and in order to cure the ailment, evil humours had to be eliminated before the balance could be restored. With the advance of the Christian church throughout Scotland, ancient beliefs and practices became Christianized. Pagan holy places, such as healing wells, now became linked with saints. The well of St Triduana in Edinburgh was one such site, reputed to be beneficial in the treatment of eye diseases.

Medieval Scotland was, as was most of the Christian world, dominated by the church (see CHURCH INSTITUTIONS: 2). Churchmen treated the sick, and the progress of medical knowledge was severely hampered since the notion that people were sick because they were sinners was preached widely. Religious communities had a monopoly on official medicine and treatment. They were often the only literate individuals in a community; they also acted as lawyers and teachers, and so had many influences on the bodies and souls of the people. Religious institutions provided the only hospitals to be found in medieval Scotland. These hospitals offered hospitality in its widest sense, often being situated near major overland routes and caring for travellers and pilgrims as well as the sick. Long-term excavations at Soutra, on a major Scotland–England route, are revealing much about these institutions, and also demonstrating the wide variety of plants and other substances used to treat diseases. In medieval Scotland body and soul were very much united in terms of medical knowledge and treatment. In the Highlands, geographically and culturally isolated, a different, kin-based, medical tradition developed in the so-called learned orders, though one based also on humoral medicine. Surviving Gaelic medical manuscripts reveal a detailed knowledge of Greek, Roman, and Arabic medicine—knowledge of which was passed down from father to son. Folk medicine was practised everywhere, superstitions and customs being modified according to particular local beliefs. In rural areas there was little access to medical help, and a complex set of beliefs characterized healing methods and practices.

The secularization of medicine and parting of the ways between medicine and surgery may be dated from a papal edict of 1163, which forbade clerics from letting blood, and is also associated with the flourishing of European universities. After this, surgery was performed by barbers who had been employed to maintain clerical tonsures. Surgeons were trained by apprenticeship, and physicians took the high academic route to European universities such as Padua and Salerno. This was the origin, and at the same time the source of conflict, between the two major branches of the future medical profession. Although some medical teaching became available at Scottish *universities—a mediciner was in post at Aberdeen from its foundation in 1495—this was intermittent and inadequate, so that in the early modern period, medical students continued to make the journey to Europe, increasingly to the university of Leiden (see LOW COUNTRIES), which would have great influence on the foundation of the first medical school in Scotland, at *Edinburgh, in 1726.

Early modern Scotland saw the development of the burgh network (see URBAN SOCIETY: 2), with Edinburgh at the centre, dominant in terms of size and its many political, social, and economic functions. Not surprisingly, it was in Edinburgh that the earliest evidence of institutional or professional medical progress appears. The surgeons and barbers of Edinburgh became incorporated in 1505, at a time when groups of craftsmen were forming similar protective organizations. Thereafter they began to acquire the attributes of a modern profession, including self-regulation, formal examinations, discipline, the promotion of anatomical study (which had received a significant boost by the publication, in 1543, of Vesalius's *de Fabrica Corpori Humanis*) and, importantly, trying to prevent non-members carrying out operations. The strictly applied requirement for literacy in Latin ensured that apprentices could read textbooks. The small group of surgeons and physicians in Glasgow, uniquely, formed a joint organization in 1599 and were influenced greatly by Peter Lowe, a Scotsman who had served the French monarch and army. A separate incorporation of surgeons was established in Glasgow in the mid-17th century. Other Scottish towns were too small to sustain groups of practitioners large enough to form an organization. The Edinburgh surgeons built a dissection theatre in 1697, and in 1699 opened their library and museum, which housed many curiosities including 'six German lancets' and 'an Italian padlock for women'. No matter how well trained these surgeons were, though, the surgery which they could perform was limited severely by the lack of anaesthetics and the means to control infection, and in rural Scotland there was little access to trained surgeons. The day-to-day work of Scottish surgeons was mostly concerned with the treatment of wounds, fractures, dislocations, infections, cataracts, and hernias. The recurrent conflicts of the times, from the Wars of *Independence to the Bishops' Wars and the *Jacobite interludes, meant that surgeons became as expert as it was possible to be in military surgery. They also served successive royal houses with distinction. In 1567, *Mary, Queen of Scots, granted the surgeons permanent exemption from bearing arms, provided that they offered impartial treatment to the wounded of all sides. The high status and good reputation of Scottish surgeons placed them above their rather less well-regarded English counterparts.

Scottish physicians had no organization until the last quarter of the 17th century when, after repeated attempts, and helped by the patronage of the duke of York, who would become—briefly—James VII and II, the Edinburgh physicians finally gained a royal charter in 1681, establishing the Royal College of Physicians. Once founded, this organization also developed professional characteristics. The publication in 1699 of the first edition of the *Pharmacopoeia Edinburgensis* was a milestone in the classification and regulation of drugs, and the physicians set entry standards, acquired suitable buildings, and treated the poor gratis. Notable individuals such as Sir Robert Sibbald and Archibald Pitcairne were instrumental in the formation of the College. Again, though, what the physicians could do was limited. They continued to use the humoral approach and prescribed increasingly complex remedies, containing as many as 80 ingredients, from gold leaf to crushed beetles, in order to treat fever, scurvy, and other diseases. Qualified physicians were to be found mostly in Lowland, urban areas, and patients in rural parts had to obtain the best advice they could, often from their minister or teacher. Professionals and amateurs alike could do little to combat plague, leprosy, syphilis, or the many fevers which afflicted the people.

A crucial development in Scottish medicine was the medical school established at Edinburgh University in 1726. This was the culmination of a process which had started in the 1680s, with the appointment of three physicians, including Sir Robert Sibbald (who was also the Geographer Royal), as professors of medicine by the town council, which, unlike other Scottish universities, was a municipal institution. Helped by the visionary schemes of George Drummond, the grandee of Edinburgh politics, by 1726 four professors of medicine were in post, together with Alexander Monro primus, the first of an anatomical dynasty. Comprehensive medical teaching was at last available in Scotland. The school was organized very much along the lines of the Leiden medical school, which had been attended by a number of the most prominent physicians. In 1729 the first infirmary was established with only six beds, but none the less crucial for medicine and medical education. Clinical teaching became an important part of the medical curriculum, allowing close observation of patients as well as instruction of students. Once the second, larger infirmary opened its doors in 1741, clinical teaching on a much larger scale was organized, initially by John Rutherford, though the infirmary was disrupted during the 1745 Jacobite uprising, when it was used as a military hospital. A chair of medicine was established in St Andrews in 1722, and notable men such as William Cullen and Joseph Black taught in Glasgow University in the 1750s. However, friction between the University and the Faculty of Physicians and Surgeons hampered institutional progress in Glasgow, as was the case in Aberdeen, where the conflict was between the King's and Marischal Colleges.

It was well into the 18th century before the structure and functions of the body began to be understood better, but the foundations laid in the early modern period helped Scottish medical men to become world leaders. The medical profession needed these tentative roots in order to flourish. (See also CULTURE: 16, 19, 23).   HMD

Mediterranean lands in the Middle Ages.
Medieval Scots were well aware of the apparent re-

moteness of their land. The barons who sealed the Declaration of Arbroath sent to the pope in 1320 referred to 'this poor little Scotland, beyond which there is no dwelling-place at all'. In these geographical circumstances, early links with southern Europe might be expected to be tenuous in many respects. The distances involved seem formidable. From Edinburgh Jerusalem was approximately 2,400 miles (3,862 km) distant; Rome, some 1,200 miles (1,931 km); and even the notable shrine of St James at Santiago di Compostella in northern Spain was about 950 miles (1,529 km) away. But medieval people were not all as static as may be imagined and mobility was in fact endemic throughout Christendom. Where motivation was strong enough, some Scots did choose to venture from their often chilly home to the sunny lands of the Mediterranean. Indeed a Scottish propensity for travel abroad was notable enough to produce a late medieval French proverb proclaiming that rats, lice, and Scotsmen are found the whole world over.

It is no surprise that Scotland's most essential links to medieval Christendom centred on religion itself. Two principal manifestations of this were crusading and pilgrimage, both of which took Scots to the Mediterranean. Some Scots were present on the First Crusade in 1096 and were noted for their outlandish dress. Their names are entirely unknown to us, but it is striking that the papal call to arms to rescue the Holy Land had produced a response among ordinary folk. Those at higher levels, however, were also conscious of the appeal and the recorded wish of King *David I (1124–53) to go on crusade looks entirely authentic; but he never went (see CRUSADES, THE).

From the later 12th and 13th centuries we do have occasional names of barons who departed on crusade: Bruces, *Balliols, and Setons among others. As the *Chronicle of Melrose* reveals, crusading became a prominent topic and began to draw aristocrats to these distant fields of action. A papal legate preached the crusade in a church council at Perth in 1201 and raising funds for expeditions was a frequent concern. Various Scottish magnates died on crusade, frequently as a result of illness rather than fighting in battle. Those who succumbed to disease included Saher de Quincy, earl of Winchester and possessor of major Scottish estates (d. Damietta, 1219); Patrick, earl of Dunbar, on crusade with King Louis IX of France (d. Marseilles, 1248); and David de Strathbogie, earl of Athol (d. 1270, perhaps at Carthage). From the 1240s to the 1270s crusading was a particularly active business and Scots were certainly participants.

After the fall of Acre in 1291 the Christian kingdom of Jerusalem collapsed and crusades of the traditional kind became a thing of the past. But the crusading ideal remained alive and one of the most remarkable of all Scottish crusaders was King *Robert I, who died in 1329. He made a deathbed plan that his heart should go on crusade in his stead, and in 1330 his close friend Sir James Douglas died fighting Muslims at Teba, in Spain, the heart of his deceased monarch in a silver casket around his neck.

A significant by-product of the crusading movement was the establishment in the 12th century of two major military orders: the Knights of the Temple at Jerusalem and those of the Hospital of St John at Jerusalem. The Templars had only one house in Scotland, at Balantrodoch or Temple, Midlothian. They were suppressed in 1309 and their properties passed to the Hospitallers, whose only major house was at Torphichen, West Lothian. The landed possessions which they held were very widespread, but mainly in small units: proof of a fairly common desire to support the crusading enterprise. The Wars of *Independence had negative effects on the Hospitallers and English interference in their affairs and finances became common. But linkages to the headquarters of the Order, latterly at Rhodes, then Malta, continued to function. Some Scots, both Hospitallers and laymen, spent time on Rhodes and a few actually took part in the mid- and later 15th-century warfare against the Turks. King *James IV became imbued with ideals of a great anti-Turkish crusade and even tried in 1510 to have himself appointed captain of the Venetian fleet. But these schemes were politically ill-founded and came to nothing. By the 16th century Scottish Hospitaller relations with Rhodes had become largely formal and financial. Long before the Reformation, Hospitaller functioning in Scotland was essentially secularized.

Pilgrimage to the remoter shrines of Christendom lacked the drama of crusading, but might still spell danger for participants passing along difficult roads and inconstant seaways. Three destinations dominated the thinking of Scots who went on pilgrimage to the Mediterranean area: the Holy Land, Rome, and Compostella. Most other shrines had little attraction. A Scots visitor to that of St Giles, in Provence, did bring back in 1455 an arm-bone of that saint to his church in Edinburgh. But even the tomb of St Andrew at Amalfi failed to draw many Scots: they presumably preferred his home-grown shrine, on the Fife coast.

The Holy Land, although so distant, was the goal for many pilgrims. From the 12th to the 16th century a quite steady flow of Scots, from the great to the insignificant, took this perilous route. As early as 1122 John, bishop of Glasgow, went to Jerusalem and Rome. Only one Scottish monarch made the journey: King James I, in the form of his em-

balmed heart, which was taken there in 1444–5, then returned via Rhodes for burial with his body at Perth. Perhaps stirred by the crusading fervour at the court of James IV, in 1508 Robert Blacader, archbishop of Glasgow, with a party of 36 set off for the Holy Places. He travelled by Venice, where he was noted by one Marino Sanudo as a 'rich Scottish bishop' and given much hospitality. But this journey ended in tragedy, for plague struck the ship on its way to Jaffa and nearly all the pilgrims, including Blacader, died. At almost the same time as the archbishop began his travels, a much more modest Scottish figure, Patrick Gillies, bailie of Peebles, got licence for his Jerusalem journey. Whether he went with Blacader, and whether he survived, remains unknown. Such 'Jerusalem-farers' certainly travelled far and hard to obtain the religious credit which they sought, in the form of ample remissions for sins. Enhanced social status must have resulted too, along with endless tales of adventures to entertain their friends.

As the headquarters of the universal church, and a city full of highly prestigious saints and shrines, Rome was the most accessible religious magnet in all Christendom. Its appeal as a pilgrimage centre was widely felt from the Dark Ages to the Reformation. The earliest—and probably the only—Scottish monarch who visited was *Macbeth. A contemporary Continental chronicler, Marianus Scotus, records his presence in 1050 and notes that 'he scattered money like seed to the poor'. The papacy encouraged the pilgrim traffic more specifically in the later Middle Ages by declaring, at more or less regular intervals, years of Jubilee, during which special indulgences were granted. In that of 1450 Scottish visitors of note included James Kennedy, bishop of St Andrews, and William, earl of *Douglas, each of course with a retinue. A pilgrimage to Rome must often have been combined with the ever-present matters of church administration, law, and patronage; and it is not surprising to find the establishment of a hospice for Scots travellers at the church of S. Andrea delle Frate, probably about 1500.

The shrine of St James the Greater at Compostella could be reached either by a direct voyage across the Bay of Biscay or by land along the well-known pilgrim routes from south-western France through northern Spain. Evidence of named Scots who made the journey seems rather scanty, but indications exist that Scots did go. The scallop shell which was the symbol of the shrine occurs on a few pilgrim badges from Scottish excavations and on occasional seals. In 1457 Thomas Dysart, a Scot living in France, repaired and endowed a pilgrim hospital at Dax, near Bayonne, and presumably intended his fellow countrymen on the pilgrimage road to use it. But one aristocratic Scottish family reveals an early and distinct devotion to this saint. About 1169 Walter the royal steward had founded at Paisley a Cluniac priory dedicated in the name of St James. Walter's great-grandson Alexander made arrangements in 1252 to depart to Compostella; and in almost every generation of Stewarts from the mid-13th to the later 14th century the name James occurs. The family acquired the crown in 1371 and from the accession of James I in 1406 until 1688 (see KINGSHIP: 5–7) all male monarchs of Scotland, except two, had that name. Compostella's effect on the naming of Scottish royalty was distant but long-lasting.

The less spiritual but still vital processes of church business and administration drew many people, both clerics and laymen, to the top of the hierarchy, usually at Rome, but for a spell at Avignon (see CHURCH INSTITUTIONS: 2). The reasons for their travels were many: financial procedures, legal cases, the need to influence officials, the desire to speed the system onwards through personal attendance. As the papacy spectacularly developed the system of supplications, especially from the 14th century, more and more made the journey. An Argyll cleric attended the Curia in person in 1425 to press his case for grant of the rectory of Kilmore in Upper Lorn. In February 1495 Bishop William Elphinstone of Aberdeen appeared before Pope Alexander VI in support of his petition for establishment of a university in his diocese. Since 1192 the church in Scotland had been a 'special daughter' of the Holy See and lacked archbishops till the late 15th century. This element of the structure encouraged Scottish contact with the Curia and led many Scots to visit it. In the later Middle Ages a small body of specialist procurators handling Scottish cases can be identified in the Roman courts and they did not lack for business.

The need for discussion of church policy at the highest levels led to the summoning of general councils. In the 13th century these were particularly prominent and Scots played their parts. Scottish bishops attended councils in Rome, but also at Lyons in both 1245 and 1274. Each bishop, of course, would be accompanied by servants and members of his household. Great councils of the church became even more significant in the period of papal schism and met in various places in southern Europe between 1409 and 1449. Scots were quite frequently involved in the attempts to resolve ructions at the topmost level of the church. More than 60 of them either attended or were closely involved in the sessions of the Second Council of Basle in Switzerland, between 1431 and 1449. Through both attenders and concerned intellectuals, the conciliar movement had a distinct influence on Scottish political and constitutional thought. It has been successfully argued that ideas evolved in the First Council of Basle (1414–18) can be traced through the works of John Mair (see HISTORIANS: 2) and George Buchanan to the 'Glorious' Revolution of 1688.

Especially by the later Middle Ages, many of those active in the highest affairs of the church were university graduates (see UNIVERSITIES: 1). Before the foundation of a university at St Andrews in 1410, and afterwards as well, the majority of Scots who sought higher education on the Continent went to institutions in *northern Europe, notably Paris, Orléans, and Cologne. But a few reached famous schools in Italy. By the later 13th century the university of Bologna was attracting some Scots, notably on account of its law school. Its best-known Scottish graduate of that era was Baldred Bissset, MA, DCL, who may latterly have taught there, but who is particularly remembered for his exposition of the Scottish patriotic case pleaded against Edward I at the papal curia in 1301. Occasional Scots can be observed at Bologna in the 15th century and a few also emerge then at the universities of Pavia, Ferrara, Padua, Perugia, and Rome. Of uncertain university, and only probably a Scot, the famous intellectual Mr Michael Scot had been active in Spain and Italy as early as the 1220s and 1230s, as astrologer, magician, alchemist, medical writer, and translator, notably at the court of the Emperor Frederick II. But Michael was distinctly *sui generis* and represents no trend of exporting Scottish brains to southern Europe.

The diplomacy of medieval Scotland was often in the hands of those who were senior churchmen or graduates, or both. Much of this activity, especially from the later 13th century onwards, was closely connected with, and at times even dominated by, the concerns of *France. Diplomatic links to secular powers in the Mediterranean region were usually, therefore, infrequent. That position changed for a time during the reign of James IV (1488–1513), whose ambitions and idealism led him into attempts to cut a figure on the European stage and to take a major share in a projected anti-Turkish crusade. In an attempt also to arrange a Scottish royal marriage alliance beyond the traditional northern European area, his government entered negotiations with Ferdinand of Aragon and Isabella of Castile. The effort to fix on a Spanish bride for the young king produced various embassies, in both directions, on a rather on-and-off basis, between 1489 and 1498. But nothing resulted in the end and the principal legacy to history from these involvements was a lively and perceptive account of Scotland and its king, written for the Spanish monarchs in 1498 by their personable ambassador, Don Pedro de Ayala.

King James's desire to join, or even to lead, a European crusade took him into negotiations with an intensely political and self-interested pope, Julius II. He was anxious to counter the power of France, as well as to extend the papacy's secular possessions in Italy. He created an alliance named the Holy League, directed against Louis XII of France, and was keen to draw James within it. This created a dilemma for the Scots, since France was the 'auld ally'. James's efforts to mediate among squabbling European powers and to stimulate much-needed action again Turkish expansion have been condemned as futile and unrealistic. His involvement in southern European politics may have been sincerely intentioned, but it produced in the end no actual results, except for some further steps along the path which led to his own death at Flodden.

Two further elements of Scotland's concern with the south look decidedly contrasting in nature: warfare and commerce. Scots in warfare (see WARFARE, WEAPONS, AND FORTIFICATIONS: I) in the Mediterranean area were never a result of Scottish government expeditions. As already indicated, crusading took some Scottish soldiers there, even as late as 15th-century battles against Turks. But as a by-product of Scottish military concerns in Anglo-French warfare, Scottish mercenaries (see MERCENARIES IN EUROPE) did sometimes penetrate to the far south. One 'Hagre l'Escot', who was possibly the earl of Angus, was part of the Black Prince's expedition to Castile in 1366. Two members of the Leslie family were present in 1364 at an agreement between Sir John Hawkwood's infamous band, the 'White Company', and the commune of Florence, but it is not known whether the Scots fought alongside that group or not. As a result of the establishment of the French monarchy's Garde Écossaise (Scots Guard) in the early 15th century, Scots were certainly drawn into French military aggression in Italy in the years around 1500, and were combatants in at least half-a-dozen battles between Seminara (1495) and Pavia (1525). The foremost military leader of the French in this era was a significant Franco-Scot: Bernard Stuart of Aubigny, whose family were also the Stewarts of Darnley, in Renfrewshire. He led his troops to many victories, especially in Italy, and was at various times appointed by the French government to be governor of Calabria, viceroy of Naples, and ruler of Milan. He maintained his contacts with Scotland and certainly had many Scots among the troops he led (see FRANCO-SCOTTISH RELATIONS: I).

Scotland's overseas trade in the Middle Ages was essentially a northern European business, with Flanders (see LOW COUNTRIES) in general, and Bruges (see STAPLE PORTS) in particular, as hub points in the operation. Trade with the Mediterranean was therefore on the periphery of Scottish commerce, but at times it did occur. Imports are probably more visible than exports, and consisted frequently of manufactured and luxury goods. Silk, spices, and exotic fruits may have originated from as far away as the Middle East. Wine from southern France and later also from Spain was in demand by the wealthy classes. By the later Middle Ages Spanish iron, timber, cloaks, and gloves are on record as imports. But direct Scoto-Spanish trade may have been limited and some Spanish goods may have reached Scotland through the great entrepôt of Bruges. About a dozen pieces of late medieval Spanish lustreware pottery have emerged from excavations, ranging in location from Elgin to Melrose. No evidence of trade with Portugal seems to survive until a Portuguese wine merchant is recorded at Dumbarton in 1498, but the activities off the Iberian coast and elsewhere of the two privateering brothers Robert and Andrew Barton are a reminder of enforced Portuguese imports in the times of James IV and *James V. Piracy proves that warfare and commerce may indeed be interlinked.

Along with fish and hides, wool was a principal export from medieval Scotland. There is record evidence that in the later 13th and early 14th centuries it sometimes reached Italy, travelling by way of Bruges. As early in 1255 Coldingham priory did business with merchants of Siena in London, probably wool purchasing. The same priory sold wool to Florentine merchants in 1286. This trade was not merely occasional. The trading handbook of an Italian merchant, datable to about 1300–20, states expected prices in Flanders of wool from numerous monasteries. This list includes fifteen Scottish houses, mainly Cistercian. Not all of them would have exported as far as Italy every year; but the products of Scottish sheep might sometimes end as costuming for an Italian *contessa*.

Merchants were often bankers as well and a few financial transactions with Italians are visible. At some point before 1240, for example, the dean and chapter of Glasgow cathedral contracted a debt to merchants of Florence. Somewhat surprisingly, the dean at Glasgow from 1318 to about 1335 was Robert de Bardi, whose family were prominent bankers in Florence; and at times he was actually in residence at his benefice. The wealth levels and the politics of 14th-century Scotland were not likely to attract hordes of Italian bankers. But the country's reputation as being distant, ancient, and perhaps mysterious produced a sideline in the existence of a merchant banking family named the Scotti of Piacenza, near Milan. They claimed to have arrived in Italy from Scotland in the time of Charlemagne and eventually took the name Douglas Scotti. They had transactions with Edward I in the 1270s; and spread to other cities in Italy, including Siena. Their story of Scottish origins looks like a myth, but this distinctive tale about their alleged background was presumably a useful status-building operation.

Scots went to the Mediterrean lands, but there was clearly also some traffic in the opposite direction. The church was responsible for quite a few visitors from Italy to Scotland, particularly in the 12th and 13th centuries. Papal legates, nuncios, and judges-delegate arrived fairly frequently. The papal tax collector Mr Baiamundus de Vitia, canon of Asti, laboured with much difficulty between 1275 and 1290 to collect a crusading tax. His record of the valuation of Scottish church benefices became known under the vernacular title of Bagimond's Roll. As late as 1507 Pope Julius II, already mentioned, sent messengers carrying the papally blessed Sword and Hat to James IV. These two distinguished Italian emissaries presented the gifts to the king in Holyrood abbey on Easter Day. They were Antonio Inviziati, a knight of Alessandria, in north Italy, and 'captain of justice' of Bologna, and Fra Daniele Filago, a professor of sacred theology. Festivities followed the occasion and Italian minstrels were among those who contributed to the merriment.

Others also came from the south as individuals and not for official purposes. We have to notice here a definite trend for highly qualified professional men to travel to Scotland for longer or shorter periods of residence. Foreign physicians employed by the wealthier classes provide an example. In the last few years of his life King *Robert I was attended by an Italian doctor, Mr Maninius de Maneriis of Milan, who lived in a house in Perth at the king's expense. Between 1455 and 1460 James II had an Italian doctor named Serapion, who came from Venice but who, from his name, presumably had a Greek background. A century later Archbishop John Hamilton of St Andrews had two foreign doctors. From 1548 William Cassanate, a Spaniard, was his personal doctor and in 1552 a notable Italian physician, Girolamo Cardano of Milan, attended the archbishop for a short time as a consultant and astrologer. Even foreign financial experts sometimes became resident: two Neapolitan bankers, the Evangelist Passers, father and son, were active in the reigns of James IV and James V.

The profession of notary (see LAW AND LAWYERS: 1) reached Scotland at the end of the 13th century and in the reign of Robert I very few of them were in practice. During the important procedures leading to the conclusion of the Treaty of Edinburgh-Northampton (1328) the king employed in Edinburgh an Italian notary: Rayner, son of James

of Poggibonsi, near Florence. He is also on record as a procurator for the king at the Roman court. Once again, sparsely available professional expertise was being imported from abroad, to assist in the diplomacy of 1327.

At a less exalted level, skilled craftsmen from overseas are sometimes visible. In the service of the Scottish royal mint (see COINAGE) from 1364 to at least 1393 was Mr Bonagio, an Italian moneyer and eventually Master of the Mint. In 1434 a noted Tuscan master in stained glass, Francesco di Domenico Livi de Gambassi, worked in Scotland, but then returned home to a post at the new cathedral in Florence. Later a few Portuguese shipwrights had a small part in James IV's great push to create a Scottish navy.

Why did these experts from the south, though few in number, still find it worth while to come so far north? Perhaps it is not too harsh to suggest that Scotland's relative lack of wealth and somewhat underdeveloped economy created openings in which those who had scarce professional services to offer could find opportunity? More research on these specialist visitors is needed.

Certainly by the era of James IV and James V those of Mediterranean origin were a tiny but distinct part of the Scottish social mix, particularly in the circles of the *royal court, the aristocracy, and the major towns. A small group of black African servants, including 'Peter the Moorish drummer', occur among the court staff of James IV. In 1520 a pardoner monk from the monastery of St Catherine at Mount Sinai, in the Levant, visited *Edinburgh. Such may seem very exotic figures to modern eyes, but were perhaps less so to their acquaintances and neighbours. One Greek-speaking arrival deserves note, since his career was carefully disentangled by Monsignor David McRoberts. This was George de Brana, originally a citizen of Athens, a somewhat wandering cleric who was used at various times for stray ecclesiastical tasks in Rome, Scotland, and the dioceses of London and Worcester. He was provided in 1483 to the impoverished see of Dromore in Ireland; and was translated in 1499 to the no less minor Irish diocese of Elphin. It may be doubted if he spent much, if any, time at those places. By the 1520s, an elderly man, he had settled in Edinburgh and was known as 'the Bishop of Gres'. He purchased a house, with a chapel, at the top of the Royal Mile, on the Castlehill; and it was probably there that he died, in 1529. David McRoberts remarks that George de Brana should not be seen as an extraordinary figure, amazingly coming to rest in a remote backwater of Christendom. The town of Edinburgh, though small by European standards, was by the later Middle Ages a decidedly cosmopolitan place. A Greek bishop, a papal sword, a Spanish lustreware jug: all were ready reminders that southern Europe existed.

By way of a brief postscript, it is vital to move from investigating people to looking at cultural influences, which are in some ways more difficult to pin down. The intellectual and artistic movement which we label 'the Renaissance' certainly started in the south and undoubtedly influenced Scotland (see CULTURE: 4). On a European timescale the Renaissance came relatively late to Scotland, but in some respects the renewed classical models of Greece and Rome had rather specific effects here. A few early humanists are visible, such as Archibald Whitelaw, archdeacon of Lothian, who was King's Secretary from 1462 to 1493. He had an excellent knowledge of classical Latin and collected manuscripts relating to classical history. But most elements of the Renaissance in Scotland do not emerge until after about 1500. Knowledge of Greek, for example, seems to have been very limited until the 1520s and after. Humanistic script, evolved in Italy in the early 15th century, was seemingly not used by any Scot until after 1500. Even in the 1520s it was rare and the royal secretariat made no use of it until it was applied to certain documents sent abroad, from about 1537. In relation to architecture, there is controversy as to whether some buildings are proto-Renaissance or late revival Romanesque. But traditionalist building styles remained obstinately visible well after 1500. In King's College chapel, Aberdeen (erected 1500–9), for example, no Renaissance stylistic features are visible in the construction. Yet Bishop James Stewart's pulpit (datable to the late 1530s), made for St Machar's cathedral in Old Aberdeen, but now in the chapel, has panels of strongly classical busts surrounded by typically Renaissance wreaths. In royal building works late in the reign of James V (d. 1542), classical revival style, mainly French-inspired, becomes very evident. The inner courtyard façade at Falkland palace, for example, has been described by John G. Dunbar in *Scottish Royal Palaces* as one of the 'earliest examples of coherent Renaissance design in Britain' (see ARCHITECTS, ARTISTS, AND CRAFTSMEN). As the Middle Ages were themselves waning, revived influences from the ancient Mediterrean world were having an effect, although sometimes patchily and indirectly.

A final question must concern the thoughts which the remote Mediterranean inspired among those Scots who had some form of contact with it. In respect of most of them we do not have an answer. But a remarkable literary survival takes us into the mind of a Gaelic poet, writing in the 1220s. Muiredhach Albanach O' Dalaigh was Irish by birth, but largely Scots by residence. He and several companions went on crusade between about 1218 and 1224, and made poems about their adventures. Anchored in the Adriatic, they think longingly of home:

> Help from Cruachan is far off
> across the wave-bordered Mediterranean.

Reaching mid-Argyll after a wearisome journey back, via Rome, he exclaims:

> As I sit upon the hillock of tears,
> without skin on either toe or sole;
> O King!—Peter and Paul!
> far is Rome from Lochlong.   GGS

Melville, Andrew (1545–1622), academic, Latin poet, and churchman. After receiving his early education at Montrose, where he acquired some knowledge of Greek, he matriculated at the University of St Andrews in 1559, graduating with an MA (1563). In 1564, he left to study on the Continent, being taught at Paris by Pierre de la Ramée (Peter Ramus) and going on to study law at Poitiers. In 1568, he went to Geneva where he was welcomed by Theodore Beza and took up a post at the city's college. After a number of requests to return to Scotland, he did so in 1574.

On his return, he declined George Buchanan's recommendation that he should take a post with the regent, the earl of Morton, and became principal of the University of Glasgow. He reformed the curriculum (see UNIVERSITIES: 1) by introducing theology and downgrading philosophy, and adopted specialist teaching in place of regenting, where one master took a class through the whole course. He obtained a new foundation for the University and increased its revenue by appropriation of the revenues of the parish of Govan. He also had a hand in reform at Aberdeen and at St Andrews, to which he moved in 1580 to become principal of St Mary's College, making it a specialized theological college.

Although not the successor of John *Knox as 'leader' of the church, he took a prominent role, attending General Assemblies from 1574 and being elected moderator four times. He served on committees for various matters, including those which drew up the *Second Book of Discipline*, although he did not write it. In the factionalism which dominated Scottish politics between 1578 and 1585, he clashed with the crown on a number of occasions, most notably in 1584 when he fled to England, after conviction for sedition. In 1585 he returned and was soon restored to his university post, becoming rector in 1590 and, in the same year, he delighted *James VI with Latin verses written for the coronation of Queen Anne. He famously confronted the king at Falkland in 1596, standing up for ecclesiastical independence and proclaiming that James was a member of the church, not its head, and that he was but 'God's sillie [weak] vassal'. In the following year he was excluded from ecclesiastical courts and deposed as rector of St Andrews. Five years later, he was confined to St Mary's College for criticizing the pro-episcopal drift of royal policy, although in 1603 he attempted rehabilitation by writing verses to celebrate the regal union.

In 1606, Melville was summoned to court in London along with seven ministers. He incurred the king's anger in written criticism of the English liturgy for which he was called before the English privy council and, in 1607, confined to the Tower. In the following year, he wrote a letter of apology to the privy council and some conciliatory verses and eventually, in 1611, he was allowed to leave Britain for France where he became professor of biblical theology at Sedan. He died there in 1622.

ARM

mercenaries in Europe. Since the 15th century the Garde Écossaise had served as the personal bodyguard of the king of France, although their number seldom exceeded 100 men. Elsewhere, numbers were higher. Between 1573 and 1579, 3,100 Scots were levied for service in the Low Countries to assist in the fight against Catholic Spain. Shortly after, a permanent Anglo-Scottish Dutch brigade was formed. Contemporaneously, Scots also became a regular component of Scandinavian armies. In the 1570s, Archibald Ruthven received a royal licence to levy 1,600 Scots for Sweden and limited enlistment continued thereafter, particularly during the Thirty Years War (1618–48).

When Elector Frederick of the Palatinate accepted the throne of Bohemia in defiance of the soon-to-be Habsburg emperor, Ferdinand II, war flared. Frederick's marriage to Elizabeth Stewart, daughter of James VI, led many Scots to enlist in the conflict. Some 40,000 Scots eventually volunteered for the war to reinstate Elizabeth and her family to their electoral and regal titles. First to the standard was the Catholic Sir Andrew Gray, who recruited 1,500 Scots in 1620 to fight in Bohemia alongside 1,000 fellow countrymen in Colonel James Seaton's regiment. The Bohemian army collapsed under the imperial offensive. Nonetheless, Seaton held the Bohemian town of Trebon until 1622, nearly a year and a half after the rest of the army had disintegrated. Gray recruited in Scotland again in 1624 and eventually led 4,000 Scots in an army of 12,000 Britons to serve with Count Mansfeld. Over 6,000 of these men died of disease en route to the war. After the destruction of Mansfeld's forces in 1626, some survivors joined the Scandinavian armies.

By March 1627, patents were issued to raise 9,000 Scots for Danish-Norwegian service. These were

to be in three regiments of 3,000 men under colonels Alexander Lindsay Lord Spynie, James Sinclair Baron Murckle, and Robert Maxwell, earl of Nithsdale. They joined 2,000 Scots already in Danish service under Donald Mackay. Perhaps more important than the numerical contribution was input into the military command. Between 1625 and 1629, 303 Scottish officers joined the army of Christian IV, outnumbering indigenous officers by three to one. Twenty-five of them held the rank of major or above while two became generals: Robert Scott and Nithsdale. The efforts of the Danish army against Ferdinand came to naught and Christian IV retired from the war in 1629 through the Treaty of Lübeck.

This treaty paved the way for Swedish intervention. Sweden already had 12,000 Scots in service in 1630. By the war's end in 1648, some 30,000 had fought for Sweden in Germany. Of the 3,262 officers at the disposal of Gustavus Adolphus in 1632, over 410 were Scots, making up 13 per cent of Sweden's officer elite. Between 1624 and 1660 the Scots produced 8 field marshals and generals, 69 colonels, 49 lieutenant colonels, and 57 majors, providing a military pedigree the Swedes themselves found hard to match. These men were joined in Germany by Scots in French service. In 1632, the marquis of Huntly raised a regiment of Scottish troops for France. Another regiment entered French service in 1634 under Sir James Hepburn, with reinforcements still arriving in 1637. The following year Lord Gray's regiment joined the other two. All three were led by Catholics who opposed Habsburg hegemony in Europe. Recruiting for Sweden continued throughout the period and many reinforcements arrived from Scotland throughout the decade, the last group in 1638 as the Covenanters began to build their own army.

The Treaty of London in August 1641 formally concluded hostilities between the Covenanters and Charles I. Thereafter, James Campbell, earl of Irvine, established a regiment of 4,500 men for the king of France. The regiment of Lord James Douglas, formerly Hepburn's, received new recruits in 1642, as did that commanded by Colonel James Fullerton. Indeed, by 1648, warrants for 10,320 soldiers for French service had been issued. Soon after the war, all surviving Scottish units were merged and served on as the Régiment de Douglas.

Another Scandinavian enlistment occurred in 1655–6, when Lord Cranstoun and William Vavasour led regiments of 2,000 Scots each to Sweden. These were the remnants of unsuccessful Royalist risings against Cromwell in Scotland. General Monck had agreed that Royalist officers could take their troops to any country not hostile to the Cromwellian regime. Unlike previous professional soldiers, these men were not ideologues, but military refugees. For the remainder of the century such exiled Scots continued to serve in foreign armies. High-profile individuals like General Patrick Gordon in Russia became famous for their foreign service. However, the age of the mass enlistment previously witnessed by Denmark, Norway, Sweden, and France had temporarily ceased (see FRANCE: THE 'AULD ALLIANCE'; GERMANY, POLAND, AND THE BALTIC: 2; LOW COUNTRIES; RUSSIA; SCANDINAVIA: 2–3). SM

mercenaries in Ireland. The movement of large numbers of men from the Hebrides and western Scotland to fight in *Ireland was a notable feature of the links between the two areas during the medieval and early modern period. The earliest form of military contact between the two regions was mutual maritime raiding, but in the later Middle Ages Hebridean lords and families were increasingly to be found fighting in the service of Irish lords in Ireland. Accounts of Scottish forces in Ireland usually concentrate on two distinct periods in which the influx of Scottish soldiery is said to have been particularly intense and influential.

The first phase encompasses the century from about 1250, when the involvement of Hebridean leaders in military engagements inside Ireland began to be recorded on a regular basis. Aside from Hebridean participation in short-lived and specific campaigns, the period also saw branches of a number of prominent Hebridean families migrate permanently to Ireland where they formed a hereditary military caste acting as armed bands available for hire for short periods or, as was increasingly the case, holding land in heritage from powerful Irish lords in return for the provision of military services. The name given to these men was *gallóglaigh* (gallowglass), 'young foreign [i.e. Hebridean] warriors'. The *gallóglaigh* retained their own kinship structures and fought under their own hereditary leaders who were referred to as 'captains' or 'constables of gallowglass'. The most famous of these *gallóglach* families, such as the MacDomhnaills (MacDonalds) and MacSuibhnes (MacSweens), became integrated into the social structure of a number of Irish lordships as a professional military cadre, with cadet branches spreading into new areas as new employers and patrons sought their expertise. The key feature of the *gallóglaigh* migration to Ireland was its permanence. A number of factors in the late 13th and early 14th century encouraged this development. The *gallóglaigh* were often men displaced from their ancestral lordships in the Hebrides, Argyll, or other areas of the Scottish west coast. Some families, such as the MacDubhgaills, were refugees from the civil wars

associated with *Robert I's seizure of the Scottish throne in 1306. Others, like the descendants of Alastair Óg MacDomhnaill, represented a lineage which had been excluded after losing out in the internal struggle to control the MacDomhnaill lordship in the southern Hebrides. Another famous *gallóglach* family, the MacSuibhnes, were ousted from Kintyre and Knapdale by the expansion of the Stewart lords of Bute and Cowal during the 13th century. At the same time conditions in Ireland were encouraging the recruitment of larger military retinues, providing more opportunities for men to become soldiers on a permanent basis. *The gallóglaigh* were thus a part of the militarization of Irish society which also produced permanent retinues of native Irish soldiery, the so-called kerne.

After two or three generations resident in Ireland, the identification of most *gallóglaigh* with the Hebrides and the Scottish west coast must have been tenuous, and the description originally restricted to Hebridean warriors may have come to designate simply a soldier armed and fighting in the 'gallóglaigh manner'. The *gallóglaigh* certainly introduced a new element into the military equation in the lordship of Ireland where they formed an elite heavy infantry. The individual *gallóglach* fought on foot, wore a mail shirt, and wielded the distinctive *gallóglach* weapon, the long-shafted battleaxe. The advent of increased numbers of these warriors is said to have enabled native Irish lords to pursue their quarrels with each other and the Anglo-Irish with greater efficiency and ferocity. The arrival of the *gallóglaigh* has thus been seen as one of the factors feeding in to the so-called 'Gaelic resurgence' in 13th- and 14th-century Ireland, in that it helped native leaders match the military potential of the Anglo-Irish.

Aside from the hereditary *gallóglaigh*, the temporary recruitment of Hebridean forces by Irish lords for short-term political/military objectives on an ad hoc basis continued throughout the later Middle Ages, particularly in Ulster. Here the situation was complicated by the establishment of a cadet branch of Clann Domhnaill as major lords in Antrim through marriage to an heiress in the 14th century. A considerable part of the manpower of the MacDomhnaill lordship of the *Isles could thus be deployed for short periods in the north of Ireland in defence of the independent interests of the family in the region.

The second major phase of Hebridean and Scottish involvement in Ireland occurred in the 16th century, when the temporary and/or seasonal recruitment of large-scale forces became much more intense (or at least better recorded). These movements, unlike those of the 13th and 14th centuries, did not lead to any permanent settlement in

Ireland. The troops who passed back and forward across the north channel were called 'redshanks' by English-speakers to denote their seasonal migratory habits, but to the Gaelic Irish they were simply 'Albanaigh' (Scotsmen). Typically, these troops would be available for summer campaigns in Ireland, between the sowing and harvesting of crops in their home areas. It is argued that the export of Hebridean manpower in this period was encouraged by the break-up of the MacDomhnaill lordship of the Isles in the wake of the forfeiture of the last lord in 1493. The poor conditions and restricted economic opportunities in the Hebrides are also seen to provide a general explanation for the continued vitality of the trade in warriors. The trade was also dictated, however, by the political strategies of the dominant lords in the west of Scotland. Irish chiefs accessed the military resources of the Hebrides and Argyll by concluding marriage alliances and political deals with prominent Mac-Domhnaill lords and/or the *Campbell earls of Argyll. The redshanks, like the earlier *gallóglaigh*, played an important role in Irish warfare and allowed Irish lords to maintain a military capability which made them, from the viewpoint of the representatives of the English crown, difficult to coerce. The large-scale movement of military personnel from the Hebrides to Ireland remained a significant feature of the Gaelic world until the conquest and plantation of Ulster in the early 17th century undercut the structures of lordship in the north of Ireland that drove and sustained the traffic. SB

metalwork, gold and silver. Gold and silver are precious metals which have been used in Scotland since prehistoric times (see CULTURE: 1) to make vessels, jewellery, and ornaments. The craftsmen who worked these metals referred to themselves as goldsmiths, although the majority of their wares were made of silver. There are specific references to goldsmiths in Scotland from at least the 13th century, when they were concentrated in the growing burghs (see URBAN SETTLEMENT: 1). From the earliest days *Edinburgh was the main centre for the trade, but other towns also played an important part. It is not until the mid-16th century, however, that we can begin to tie individual makers to surviving examples of their work by means of the marks they stamped on their wares.

Pure gold and silver are too soft for practical use. They have to be alloyed with cheaper metals, such as copper, to make them more durable. This process was open to fraud, as a great deal of the cheaper alloy can be added to the precious metal before it can be detected by appearance alone. Many laws were passed to try to prevent fraud. From 1457,

Scottish goldsmiths had to identify their wares by stamping them with a personal mark and have the quality of the metal tested, or 'E assayed', by the deacon of the craft, who would then also stamp his mark. From 1485 a mark signifying the town where it had been made was also to be added. Town marks were usually based on the arms of the burgh, Edinburgh being a three-towered castle, Glasgow a tree with fish and bell, and Inverness a camel. These were the original hallmarks, so called because the testing and marking were originally carried out in the goldsmiths' meeting place or hall. This is one of the earliest forms of consumer protection which continues to the present day. It also allows us to identify and accurately date pieces made by individual craftsmen, particularly after legislation introduced variable annual date letters in 1681.

As Scotland's most important burgh, Edinburgh had enough goldsmiths by 1492 to have established an independent incorporation. In other burghs goldsmiths tended to belong to the Incorporation of Hammermen. These bodies controlled most aspects of their members' working lives, particularly the right of membership, for no one could set up as a craftsman on his own account in a burgh unless he was a member, or freeman. Before becoming a freeman of the Edinburgh goldsmiths, each craftsman had to serve a seven-year apprenticeship with an established master, make a competent test piece or essay, serve several years as a journeyman, pay a large entrance fee to the Incorporation, and finally be 'of guide lyfe and conversatioun'!

Scottish goldsmiths made a wide range of items, determined by the wealth and desires of their clients. Their form and function changed with time, and goldsmiths used different constructional and decorative techniques, often to create distinctively Scottish forms. Perhaps the most famous example of a goldsmith's work is the Scottish crown (see KINGSHIP: 5; ROYAL COURT: 1) commissioned by *James V which was extensively remodelled in 1539 by John Mossman of Edinburgh, using gold mined at Crawford Muir.

The small group of 16th-century Scottish standing mazers show considerable skill and craftsmanship, particularly the magnificent Galloway Mazer, made by James Gray of the Canongate in 1569. In the 17th century the large surviving corpus of church silver for the sacraments of communion and baptism (see RELIGIOUS LIFE: 3) is one of the glories of the period. By the 18th century Scottish goldsmiths were well aware of the prevailing fashionable tastes. These could reflect the simple elegance of the Queen Anne period, such as the beautiful ewer, basin, and box from a toilet set made for Charles, first earl of Hopetoun, by Thomas Ker of

Edinburgh in 1705. Scottish goldsmiths were also capable of making more richly ornamented items, such as the travelling canteen of Prince Charles Edward Stuart, made in 1740–1 by the *Jacobite goldsmith Ebenezer Oliphant.

Over the period from the 16th to the early 19th century goldsmiths in the other burghs also grew in numbers and produced many fine wares. *Glasgow especially had numerous excellent craftsmen. Trade there prospered to such an extent that in 1819 an Assay Office was opened to cater for the city and the surrounding area. Firms such as Milne and Campbell, Robert Gray & Sons, and R. & W. Sorley made a huge range of very high-quality items, from teapots to race cups, to supply their burgeoning market.

At around the same time, however, the death knell was being sounded for many of the makers in the smaller centres. In 1784 an Act was passed which required every maker in Scotland to send his wares to Edinburgh for marking. This was not, however, rigorously enforced, and with the exception of most of the Glasgow silversmiths and a few others in Perth, Aberdeen, and Dundee, most of the smaller makers continued to use their local marks. In 1836 the Act was repeated and this time stringently policed. The centralizing tendencies of government made all locally struck marks illegal, and gradually those makers for whom it was not economically viable to send their work to Edinburgh or Glasgow went out of business, taking with them a fascinating heritage of Scottish provincial silver.

GRD

migration is movement within a country, and although a region, a parish, or even a street may experience population decline, the migrant is still within the country of birth: it is not a national loss. Early records of migration usually chronicle only something exceptional, such as the scheme of *James VI to settle Lowlanders in Kintyre and Lewis, and migrations were generally very localized until the mid-18th century. The overall impression is of an increasingly mobile population (see POPULATION PATTERNS), so that by the mid-20th century almost everybody had migrated at least a short distance by the age of 25.

By the 16th century, Scottish rural society was beginning to change, the increasing commercialization of farming forcing some to become migrants. There were clearances in both the Lowlands and the Highlands and many tenants and subtenants experienced dispossession (see ECONOMY: 3). In the *Borders people were being cleared for sheep farming, and already some areas had been depopulated. In the 17th century multiple tenancy was replaced by single tenant farms and in Angus 37

per cent of tenants disappeared from the rentals within five years. For many, migration was localized and over three-quarters of those moving to another farm travelled less than 3 miles (5 km). Subdivision of farms between children was severely controlled, so in every generation siblings had to find work elsewhere. Farm servants were employed on short-term contracts, and rarely stayed more than a year, leading to considerable local mobility. Work, however, remained labour-intensive and there is no evidence that less workers were required. At busy seasons such as harvest, farmers relied on temporary migrants from the Lowlands and Highlands. Unmarried farm servants lived on the farm, and there was a particular shortage of provision for married people, so marriage often forced migration. In addition farms employed only relatively few married men, and marriage itself usually caused localized migration of one partner.

Planned villages were often built when estates were reorganized to absorb surplus farm labour and tradesmen, thus encouraging local migration. Only the merchants and manufacturers were outsiders and long-distance migrants. Industrial expansion (see ECONOMY: 4) initially needed water power, and so was rural-based, thus movement to the nearest industrial centre was usually local. Migrants could then learn industrial skills which made subsequent transition to an urban environment less traumatic. By the mid-19th century a rural lifestyle could no longer compete with the attractions of the city and female workers (see WOMEN AND SOCIETY: 3) in particular were in short supply.

In the Highlands the deliberate dismantling of the old martial system, the break-up of joint tenancies, and the introduction of the crofting system meant loss of land and status, thus encouraging out-migration. Some *clearances began in the 1760s, and there were several processes at work, each forcing at least localized migration. However, in the late 18th century large-scale commercial sheep farming began moving rapidly north and west, requiring the peasants' land for wintering. At first, it resulted in resettlement of the coast or marginal land, although some preferred to leave and localized migration was common. Compulsory removals were mid-19th-century phenomena. The Highland famine of 1846–55 prompted the last major Highland migration. In the face of destitution many were convinced of the need to seek work outside their homeland. Highland migration to major Lowland towns had a pronounced regional dimension, each urban centre having its own catchment area, such as Greenock from Argyll, but migration became more distant over time. Migrants did not necessarily travel directly to their final destination, 334 Highland migrants taking an average of twelve years to reach *Glasgow.

Detailed consideration of rural–urban migration shows urban growth beginning slowly but then steadily increasing in speed. Greatest growth was in the west, especially Glasgow, Greenock, and Paisley. Large towns were notoriously unhealthy places (see HEALTH, FAMINE, AND DISEASE: 2), and it was only through constant in-migration that their populations continued to increase (see URBAN SETTLEMENT: 2). This enabled *Edinburgh to double its population in the first half of the 17th century. Thus rural–urban migration performed two functions: first, it enabled the rural areas to shed surplus population and secondly it permitted the growth of towns. Moreover, in periods of hardship or famine towns provided refuge for the destitute, especially in the 1690s when privation forced many to migrate in search of food. Migration to Edinburgh in the late 17th century showed gender bias, there being 100 women for every 76 men, probably because domestic service was numerically the most important job. Nearly all these females were 15 to 25 years old. Many remained within the city, but others would have taken their experiences of city life back to their rural roots, providing a source of information for future potential migrants (see WOMEN AND SOCIETY: 1).

In 1639 Scotland was the eleventh most urban country in Europe, yet by 1900 she was second only to England. Migration permitted a major redistribution of the population in the 19th century, Scotland becoming an urban society concentrated in the central Lowlands. Migrants remained an important component of urban growth; in 1851 44 per cent of the inhabitants of Glasgow were born there, and 35 per cent came from other parts of Scotland. Even in 1911 over a quarter of the inhabitants of Glasgow, although Scots, were not natives (see IMMIGRATION, IRISH). It was not just the Highlands that provided the migrants, 21 per cent of the migrants to Lanarkshire in 1891 being born in south-west Scotland. By the 1860s the vast majority of Scots lived in an urban environment and the greatest volume of movement was inter-urban (see URBAN SOCIETY: 5).

Many Highlanders first experienced Lowland life through seasonal migration. By the late 18th century temporary migration was already giving the Highlands an important cash injection, maintaining existing lifestyles, especially after 1815 when other bi-employments failed and it was the young and single of both sexes that left (see LIVING STANDARDS: 3). Initially, temporary migration was mainly for agricultural work, but also for military employment and in urban centres. By the 1870s the east coast herring fishery was the single most

important employer (see ECONOMY, PRIMARY SECTOR: 4).

Scots also went to England as seasonal migrants in Cumberland as early as the 15th century, this continuing into the early 19th century. Temporary migrants benefited from seasonal demands for labour and took advantage of the spectacular growth in the herring fishing industry at Great Yarmouth, which in the year of 1913 employed about 38,000 Scots. The long journey was justified by potential earnings of £25, after expenses, for female gutters from Helmsdale, this being more than the value of fish landed at Helmsdale in the year. Other industries probably also attracted temporary migrants.

England also attracted both professional and unskilled Scots, there being about 10,000 Scots south of the Border as early as 1440. Migrants were mainly from eastern Scotland and settled in eastern England. The unskilled were predominantly in the north-east, and professionals in the south-east, particularly London. After 1660 the wage rates diverged, making England increasingly attractive, and the *Union of 1707 probably created new opportunities for Scots. Thereafter England was an attractive alternative to emigration overseas. Since the 1920s there has been a huge increase in Scottish migration to England, because the Scottish economy has been relatively depressed and overseas *emigration has become more difficult.

JB

missions at home. Home missions were organized efforts to spread the Gospel and meet human need. In the 18th century their chief target was the Highlands (see CHURCH INSTITUTIONS: 6), where Protestants discerned a blend of ignorance, popery, and political disaffection. From 1725 a Royal Bounty was provided for the Church of Scotland to maintain itinerant catechists and missionary ministers in remote and usually Catholic areas. The state, however, was soon superseded by voluntary societies as the main backer of missions. The Edinburgh-based SSPCK, founded as early as 1709, operated charity *schools in the Highlands, 229 of them by 1795. Gaelic School Societies eventually followed—beginning with Edinburgh in 1811—in order to support travelling schools, mostly in the northern and western Highlands. In 1798 the undenominational Society for Propagating the Gospel at Home was launched by James Haldane. Its lay preachers were responsible for establishing a string of Independent churches in the Highlands, and after the acceptance of believer's baptism by James Haldane and his brother Robert in 1808 many of them spawned Baptist causes (see RELIGIOUS LIFE: 8). Although the Society collapsed in that year, the Congregational

Union of Scotland was formed four years later to promote home mission and in 1827 the Baptists consolidated their efforts in the Baptist Home Missionary Society. The state briefly ventured back into the cause in 1824 with a grant that enabled the Church of Scotland to build 32 churches and 41 manses in the Highlands (see CHURCHES: 2). The great transformation in the religious provision in the region, however, came in the wake of the *Disruption, chiefly as a result of the achievements of the new Free Church: in the decade after 1841 church sittings in the Highlands increased from 240 to 474 per 1,000 in the population.

The industrial cities presented the churches with a new challenge in the 19th century. Thomas *Chalmers provided the blueprint for much subsequent enterprise in his *Christian and Civic Economy of Large Towns* (1821–6), commending the example of the system of lay visitation he had pioneered in the inner-city parish of St John's in Glasgow. Territorial missions on Chalmers's model were created by the Free Church after the Disruption, and from the 1870s the Established Church under the leadership of A. H. Charteris took up the same pattern. The aim was to turn ventures of missionary outreach into regular parochial charges. The intensive visitation of homes in working-class districts must be one of the primary explanations of the high urban church attendance in Scotland in later years. Mission stations, usually run by probationer ministers, were set up in rural districts as well. The Highlands and Islands were not forgotten, over 40 mission stations there being maintained by the Free Church in 1882. The Church of Scotland concentrated more on church building and helping weak congregations than on initial evangelism.

Much outreach, however, was interdenominational. The city missions, the first of which was begun in Glasgow by David Nasmith in 1826, drew support from all Protestant denominations. Missions to seamen and fishermen, starting with the Seamen's Friend Societies (1820–2), likewise represented a 'united front'. The evangelistic tour by the American revivalists Dwight L. Moody and Ira D. Sankey in 1874–5 gave a fresh impetus to sustained co-operative missionary work. The Glasgow United Evangelistic Association was its immediate fruit, the Tent Hall for gospel and relief work following in 1876 and the Bible Training Institute for lay evangelists in 1892.

Women played an increasing part in home mission, Biblewomen, for example, being employed to read the Scriptures to the poor. The Woman's Guild of the Church of Scotland was originally founded in 1887 for those engaged in 'practical Christian work'. Women were the mainstay of the Sunday schools which, at their peak in 1891, enrolled fully 60 per cent of the 5- to 15-year-olds in Glasgow (see SCHOOLS AND SCHOOLING: 4). The Boys' Brigade, launched in 1883, was a uniformed organization for older children that gained a substantial following. The Episcopalians (see EPISCOPALIAN COMMUNITY), who organized their own mission halls, and the Roman Catholics (see ROMAN CATHOLIC COMMUNITY), who developed specialist agencies such as the Apostleship of the Sea for mariners (from 1920), stood apart from the interdenominational agencies. These bodies were essentially an expression of Evangelical solidarity.

Early in the 20th century home mission in the Presbyterian churches broadened. The Church of Scotland set up a Social Work Committee under David Watson in 1904. Eight years later, the United Free Church equivalent reported that the church should be engaging with employment, industrial legislation, housing, poor relief (see LIVING STANDARDS: 4–5), charity organization, and the moralization of trade. The churches entered the field of organized social work, the Church of Scotland becoming particularly noted for its network of old people's homes. The reunion of the main Presbyterian churches in 1929 spurred a renewed interest in church extension, the chief result being the erection of many new parish churches during the 1930s. Meanwhile smaller bodies were pursuing more traditional Evangelistic work, though sometimes with fresh methods. The Faith Mission, founded in 1886, sponsored 'pilgrims' who conducted missions wherever they were invited; in the universities the Student Christian Movement, so named from 1909, and the more theologically conservative Inter-Varsity Fellowship (1928) ran student missions; and in 1930 there was a rousing visit to Edinburgh by the Oxford Group under the direction of the American Frank Buchman. There was a post-war resurgence of pan-Protestant enthusiasm for spreading the Gospel embodied in the Tell Scotland campaign, led by the minister Tom Allan, that in 1955 sponsored the Glasgow crusade of the American Evangelist Billy Graham. At the same time the Roman Catholic Church was organizing parish missions, usually led by preachers from the regular orders. The collapse of Protestant church attendance figures from the 1960s, however, was accompanied by an apparent loss of nerve that led to a decay of home missionary activity. Perhaps the most successful continuing venture was the Scripture Union that published Bible reading notes and organized meetings for children inside and outside schools. Mission was increasingly seen as a congregational responsibility, but its impact on late 20th-century Scotland was only a shadow of what had been achieved a century before.   DWB

missions overseas. Scottish missionaries enjoyed considerable status at home. The nation took great pride in the many men and women who left the home shores to go out and preach the Word all over the globe. Although Scotland was comparatively slow in sending out missionaries compared to other nations—David Livingstone, for example, was sent to *Africa by the London Missionary Society—the Scottish churches soon made amends and from the mid-Victorian period onwards, there was a considerable outpouring of missionary endeavour.

Part of the explanation as to why the Scots should be so preoccupied with spreading the Word overseas can be found in the competition that existed between the three Presbyterian churches which followed the *Disruption in 1843. The Church of Scotland's mission to Nyasaland (present-day Malawi) at Blantyre was followed up by a Free Church mission in Livingstonia. Both churches were eager to capture the Livingstone inheritance as can be seen from the names of their stations. Also, overseas conversions were able to be presented as more glamorous than endeavours at home. The persistence of the godless multitudes in the inner cities was a constant source of strain to the churches and the fact that the number of conversions overseas could be tallied up at a spectacular rate may have been important in diverting attention away from problems at home (see MISSIONS AT HOME; ROUGH CULTURE).

The cult of Livingstone was very important in fuelling Scottish missionary endeavour. He was seen to embody the very characteristics which most Scots could identify with. Livingstone was a lad of parts. He was from a humble background but, through hard work and diligent effort, he had educated himself and gone on to become famous for his exploration of the African continent. He was lionized in a whole range of publications, many written for children, and Mary Slessor, a missionary in Nigeria, described how she was inspired by the story of Livingstone's life. The churches paid particular attention to the efforts of missionaries and accounts of the sterling efforts were given out regularly in the various journals. Missionaries and missionary activity was popularized in children's books, and publishers such as John Ritchie of Kilmarnock produced a whole range of literature which was designed to inspire and enthuse youngsters. Often such books were used as Sunday school prizes. The work of missionaries was brought home to Scots by means of the Magic Lantern Show. Audiences in church halls throughout the country were treated to images of the strange and the exotic and this novelty appeal was important in raising funds. Literature produced by and about missionaries emphasized the importance of their work. Lurid stories of cannibalism, infanticide, human sacrifice, polygamy, slavery, and every other conceivable and inconceivable vice were reported in all their gory details to demonstrate the importance of missionary endeavour as critical to the extension of civilization.

Such activity was important in providing a moral imperative for British imperial expansion in the era of the 'new' imperialism, but it should be emphasized that Scottish missionaries played an important part in promoting the notion that Scotland was an active partner in the *British Empire. After all, Presbyterianism was the national religion of Scotland. Missionary endeavour was often portrayed as part of the Scottish religious tradition (see NATIONAL IDENTITY: 5). Many were inspired by the *Covenanters and their tales of suffering and hardship chimed in with the notion of persecution for the faith. The hardship of disease and the danger of attack from hostile natives or wild animals were presented as a continuation of the struggles of the 17th century. Those who died were described as martyrs and brought within the Covenanting tradition. In the late 1880s funds were raised in Scotland to mount a limited war against Arab slavers in Nyasaland. Missionaries also played an important role in linking Scottish local communities with the British imperial mission. Most churches had their own missionary who would write back home describing their endeavours. Often these letters would be read out in church or at the Sunday school and the local congregation would pray for their own missionary's safety. Money raised in the community would go to that individual's station. This was important in that it established a highly personal link with missionary activity.

The strength of feeling surrounding missionary activity was demonstrated in the late 1880s and early 1890s when the United, Free, and Established churches petitioned the prime minister, Lord Salisbury, not to cede Nyasaland to the Portuguese. It was an effective protest and a protectorate was established; it was perhaps the one instance in the 19th century when Scottish national sentiment influenced British foreign policy. The importance of missionary activity at home can also be seen in the controversy which surrounded the church in Blantyre. It was condemned by many as being too ornate and a betrayal of Presbyterian simplicity. Arguments that decorations were needed to appeal to the African mind cut little ice with many back home.

Missionaries were also important in expanding scientific, linguistic, and anthropological study in Scotland. A heavy emphasis was placed by missionary societies on the acquisition of practical skills.

Doctors, engineers, and scientists were dispatched overseas and brought back considerable knowledge about new environments. Henry Drummond, for example, was important in stimulating scientific interest through his publication *Tropical Africa*. Donald Fraser made an anthropological study of the Ngoni tribe in southern Africa and was vociferous in promoting the rights of natives. The fact that there was such extensive contact with different races and peoples did impact on thought back home. The moderator of the Free Church, the Revd John Cairns, for example, claimed that missionary activity was important in the demise of hard-line predestination Calvinism in Scotland. At the unification of the Free and Established churches in 1929 (see UNION OF 1929), special attention was conferred on Revd Law and Heatherwick for their work in Africa. Although missionary activity declined after the First World War, the Church of Scotland still continued to attach importance to its missionary endeavours. By the 1950s much of the imperial ethos of Scottish missionary endeavour had gone as can be seen by the prominence given to humanitarian efforts in Africa.   RJF

Mod, Royal National (Am Mòd Nàiseanta Rìoghail). The term *mòd*, which originally meant a court or assembly (from Old Norse, *mót*), nowadays usually denotes the annual competitive festival of An Comann Gàidhealach (The Gaelic or 'Highland Association') founded in 1891. The first National Mod, held in Oban in 1892, was modelled on the Welsh Eisteddfod, and the format then adopted has remained, though with significant modifications and developments, essentially the same throughout. Although both junior (5–18 years) and senior competitions (now organized to run consecutively) cover literature, music, and storytelling, in common assessment the main emphasis is on song (see SONG, TRADITIONAL AND FOLK: 2). The objects of the Mod are basically those of An Comann, namely 'to promote the cultivation of Gaelic literature and music and home industries in the Highlands, to encourage the teaching of Gaelic in Highland schools; to hold an Annual Gathering at which competitions shall take place and prizes be awarded; to publish at intervals a volume of such prize compositions'.

The Mod was thus designed from the start to encourage an interest in Gaelic (see GAELIC LANGUAGE; GAELIC LITERATURE), to provide a platform for aspiring singers, writers, and musicians; but it was also intended to bring as many aspects of Gaelic culture as possible to the attention of a wider audience, both within Scotland and further afield. To achieve these aims, and in order to canvass the widest support, the association decided on a strictly non-political agenda, with the primary focus on the arts rather than economics. In the political and cultural circumstances of the time, it is clear that consensus was otherwise impossible.

In those circumstances also, it was predictable that the Mod would encourage certain developments that were innovative for Gaeldom. This was particularly so in the field of song and music. Choral singing, for instance, was introduced and became a prominent feature of the competitions. Professionally trained singers were the most highly esteemed. But overall, the ideal was to remain faithful to Gaelic roots while moving away from whatever external critics could brand as 'primitive' or 'unrefined'. These Gaelic arts would then find acceptance in the metropolitan world of music and the conservatories of western Europe. Unfortunately, in the process, the sophisticated craft of the best traditional singers (with subtleties of rhythm and ornamentation) was actively discouraged. The vision of the founding mothers and fathers was limited, their ideas were not properly thought through, but their motives are understandable. The problems involved remain to the present without much productive analysis or debate.

Rules for literary competitions were less stringent. Indeed, experimental writing was probably not envisaged. If not actually frowned upon, its appearance would no doubt have baffled the literary adjudicators of the past. At all events, the literary renaissance of literature in the 20th century developed outside the ambit of the Mod (see CULTURE: 21).

Although the Mod reflects only a part of An Comann's activities, it is popularly regarded as the culmination of the year's events. Local mods throughout Scotland act as feeders and fund-raising events, organized over a wide area of the country by voluntary workers. This selfless devotion, entailing a vast expenditure of time and energy, has naturally attracted much praise and not a little censure, since, it is argued, the Mod has done nothing to reverse the decline of Gaelic as a spoken language. In other words, effort and money alike have been misdirected. The essential thrust of this argument is that An Comann Gàidhealach failed to act as a realistic cultural and political pressure group.

More incisive criticisms have been voiced by linguists and musicologists. English, not Gaelic, is the working language of the Mod. Singers often learnt their texts parrot fashion and there are still winners of gold medals whose conversational ability in Gaelic is elementary. Music adjudicators, who are rarely if ever speakers of Gaelic, have imposed extrinsic standards. Language adjudicators tend to favour an affected, 'elocutionary' style of articulation.

The validity of certain of these arguments has been acknowledged, sometimes with reservations. Independent observers have pointed out that an 'artificial' style of delivery is only a concomitant of standardization. Competitors now undergo a language competence test. In choral singing, for instance, despite some bizarre arrangements, the Mod has produced performances whose subtlety is little short of miraculous. Traditional singing was never completely excluded; from the mid-1960s official competitions for traditional song were established, with Gaelic as the language of adjudication. From the same period, folk groups were invited to compete. An *Iomall* ('fringe') of entertainment rather than competition was introduced. In 1975 drama began to feature on the official syllabus.

The Mod, which on its centenary in 1992 became the Royal National Mod (Mòd Nàiseanta Rìoghail), has an important role in a community of few major social institutions. As an annual festive holiday, it has long enjoyed immense popularity. Winners of gold medals in singing are the star performers of the Gaelic world. Many aspects of the Mod are supported by public demand and adulation from Gaels, from people of Gaelic ancestry, and from numerous other adherents who now regard it as an event of cultural significance to the whole of Scotland.   JMacI

monuments: 1. early Christian; 2. modern.

1. early Christian

The sculptured stones of early medieval Scotland are among the country's most notable artistic achievements. They are national treasures which stand witness to the faith of the earliest generations of Scottish Christians. Inscriptions are few and in almost every case refer to people who are not otherwise known. The historical value of these monuments lies, instead, in what they reveal about the social and religious organization of early medieval Scotland and the country's intellectual and artistic contacts and cultural values (see also CULTURE: 2).

Over 1,500 stone sculptures have survived from the period before 1100, although in various states of preservation. Further examples continue to be discovered every year. The tall, upright cross-slabs are perhaps the best known, but the corpus includes a wide range of different types of monument, some known elsewhere in the British Isles, others unique to Scotland. In most cases the sculptures are datable solely on stylistic grounds and often no more precisely than to the nearest half-century. The earliest, which date to the 5th, 6th, and 7th centuries, are natural pillars, unshaped upright slabs of local stone, carved with simple designs or short texts.

The technique used was an incised line which was first pecked then smoothed. This early group includes the famous 'symbol stones' of the *Picts (nearly 200 examples) and the dozen or so inscribed memorial stones of the British. Stones such as these are often associated with burials and were typically placed in open landscape settings rather than at ecclesiastical sites.

Technical innovations in the dressing and working of stone were made in the early 8th century, traditionally following the introduction of Northumbrian stonemasons by *Nechtan, son of Derile, king of Picts, in 710. New techniques of relief carving, allied to indigenous expertise in the composition of complex geometric designs, led to the creation of far more ambitious monuments in the 8th and 9th centuries. Considerable resources were directed at stone-carving in this artistically dynamic period during which many of the finest works were produced. Social and cultural changes in the 10th century led, however, to a decline in technical excellence and from the 11th century surviving sculptures are rare, as patronage was channelled in other directions, including towards church buildings (see CHURCH INSTITUTIONS: 1).

Most of the monuments belonging to the period after the 7th century were erected at ecclesiastical sites where they performed a variety of functions. Some marked burials; many did not. The dominant motif was, of course, the Christian cross: not the crucifix of the later Middle Ages but the empty cross, symbol of the risen Christ. Large, freestanding crosses are known among the Picts (for example, the Dupplin Cross) but are more characteristic of the Gaelic west (for example, crosses on *Iona and at Kildalton, Islay) and, in the south, of British (Barrochan) and of Anglian territory (Ruthwell, Thornhill). The upright cross-slab is typical of Pictland, where there are over 200 examples. These are rectangular dressed slabs, carved with the outline of a cross, the body of which is profusely decorated with geometric ornament. The background to the cross and the reverse of the slab provide further fields for ornament or figural scenes. Fine examples are known from throughout mainland Pictland but a remarkable concentration of exceptional quality is found on the *Tarbat peninsula in Ross-shire, at Shandwick, Nigg, Cadboll, and Portmahomack.

The crosses and cross-slabs of early medieval Scotland are decorated in the so-called Insular style which grew out of the dynamic fusion of aspects of Celtic (see IRELAND: 1), Germanic, and Mediterranean art in the British Isles in the mid-7th century. Characteristic features of this style, which is also found on metalwork and manuscripts, include complex ribbon and zoomorphic interlace, rectilinear 'key' or 'fret' patterns, grouped spirals, and lively animal ornament. The style varies little between Gaelic, Pictish, British, and Anglian regions of the British Isles, but the forms to which it is applied are often regionally distinctive. Pictish carvers had a particular flair for interlace: intricate interlace patterns are found in greater variety in Pictland than anywhere else in the British Isles. The Picts also had a taste for fantastical beasts. Horrific, self-devouring monsters which gnaw on human limbs are depicted on Pictish sculpture: grotesque embodiments of evil and reminders of the horrors of hell. The earnest hope of salvation is reflected in the choice of Old Testament iconography which includes Daniel in the Lion's Den and Jonah and the Whale.

One feature which sets Pictish sculpture apart is the extent to which its imagery reflects the preoccupations of the secular elite. The *nobility are depicted in their finery, on horseback, at the hunt, or at war (as on the Aberlemno battle-stone and on Sueno's stone, Forres, which at over 19 feet (6 m) tall, is the largest early medieval sculpture in Scotland). The depictions of non-biblical women, though few, are also highly exceptional for the period. One is shown hunting side-saddle, another sits by her loom. The secular elite appear because they were the endowers and patrons of the churches and monasteries at which these stones stood. The crosses and cross-slabs were major art works erected to the glory of God and of the patron saints of the locality, and also to honour the magnates who sponsored their erection. These are public monuments which assert status and identity as well as belief. They are as much political as they are religious (see RELIGIOUS LIFE: 1). The developing ideology of *kingship, for instance, is reflected in the use of David iconography, most famously in the late 8th-century St Andrews sarcophagus, one of the most accomplished of all the early Christian monuments of Scotland.

In addition to the upright slabs and crosses, there are several types of recumbent monuments, mostly grave-covers. These include the simple monastic gravestones of Irish type seen at Iona, the profusely decorated thick slabs of southern Pictland, and the distinctive shrine-shaped 'hogbacks', a form derived ultimately from Norse (see SCANDINAVIA: 1) communities in northern England. For the translated bones of saints and favoured kings there were reliquary shrines, either a hollowed-out sarcophagus, as at Govan, or, more commonly, a large slab-built box. The latter form was popular in Shetland and elsewhere in Pictland but a particularly fine example is also seen at Jedburgh. A hint at the grandeur of the church buildings which housed such shrines is provided by the rare survivals of architectural features, including decorative panels, altar-frontals, and, uniquely, an arch from *Forteviot.

At first, crosses and slabs were erected singly or in small groups at even fairly minor churches, but later monuments tend to be concentrated at a smaller number of more wealthy foundations. Large collections of sculptured stones have been preserved at some of the major monasteries, especially those which enjoyed royal patronage; for instance, Iona, *St Andrews, *Govan, Portmahomack, Meigle, St Vigeans, Kinnedar, and *Whithorn. Not all the surviving monuments, however, are on such a grand scale. The numerous simple, cross-marked stones evoke the spread of Christianity on a more humble, local level.

In the 10th and 11th centuries Norse-speakers, newly converted to Christianity, carved runestones, often adopting local monument forms. Inscriptions were also carved at various times in Latin, British, Pictish, and Gaelic using the roman alphabet, and in Gaelic and Pictish using the ogham alphabet (see LANGUAGES OF SCOTLAND, PRE–1100). Inscriptions, however, are rare and most monuments were not inscribed. Perhaps the most remarkable aspect of early medieval epigraphy in Scotland is the use by the Picts of an utterly unique set of symbols. Combinations of these symbols, which appear to have functioned as a limited kind of writing system, were inscribed on early unshaped pillars (Class I) and, accompanying other carvings, on cross-slabs (Class II). Despite considerable scholarly endeavour and ingenuity, the meaning of the Pictish symbols remains unknown.

KF

2. modern

Built memorials, usually civic statuary or symbolic architecture, are designed to commemorate an event or person and to symbolize national or local identity (see NATIONAL IDENTITY). Public monuments have been used in this way largely since the early 19th century. Research on monuments, commemoration, and national identity has discussed the built form of cities as expressive of 'the spirit of the age'. It is possible to consider, too, for Scotland as elsewhere, that the landscape itself is an enduring monument to the people who have made it (see GEOLOGY AND LANDSCAPE; RURAL SETTLEMENT). More generally, studies have concentrated upon monuments as a means to explore issues of *nationalism, local or *regional identities, and the memory of war. The use of monuments in such ways is often related to a collective public memory and statues are often gendered either through the allegorical use of the female form as the representation of Liberty or Motherland, for example, or simply because most figures commemorated are male. War memorials as monuments of commemoration have been the focus of historians interested in the politics of remembrance. If, then, monuments are figurative representations of national sentiments and of myths 'cast in stone' as part of the ways in which national 'imagined communities' are structured, they may also subvert authority's claims and become the focus not of collective memory but of disputed renditions of the past.

Many of these themes are apparent in Scotland's modern monuments. In Scotland, the Royal Commission on Ancient and Historical Monuments formally distinguishes between public commemorative monuments and free-standing sculpture. A National Monument for Scotland was first proposed by the Highland and Agricultural Society of Scotland in 1816, as a memorial to the Scots dead of the Napoleonic Wars. Minute books of the National Monument Committee show that the memorial, initially either a pillar or a triumphal arch, was intended 'so that Scotchmen may be grateful with the contemplation of some striking emblem of their country's prowess and glory'. But the same sources reveal a fascinating story of failure to embody national feeling in monumental form. In 1818, the Committee had plans for 'a monumental church of ornamental architecture'. By 1819 the plan centred upon a monument modelled on the Pantheon in Rome, to be sited on the Mound in Edinburgh. By 1821, such intentions were replaced by plans to use the Parthenon in Athens as the adopted design, a choice driven by 'the near resemblance of Edinburgh to the most celebrated city of antiquity'. By 1822, the chosen site had moved to Calton Hill, and the ceremony for the laying of the foundation stone was held there on 27 August 1822. Even then, however, the proposal for a National Monument was in difficulty. Astronomers using the nearby observatory complained; rows continued over the design; some people objected to the fact that it was housed in Edinburgh and was, therefore, a matter of particular civic pride and not national identity. Most importantly, funds were insufficient. Work began in 1825 but ceased almost immediately. By 1846, the Committee spoke of 'the stigma resting on the country, consequent on the unfinished state of the National Monument' and, in 1859, noted 'a great indifference with regard to the National Monument'. The story of the National Monument is more a story of contested local politics than of shared identity with a national past.

To some degree, the same is true of the Scott Monument in Edinburgh. The architect was one George Meikle Kemp, the son of a Borders' shepherd and carpenter to trade, who did not win the competition but who was given the brief following

argument among the judges. Begun in 1840 and finished in 1846, it is as much a monument to the Gothic style as it is to Scott himself. The Wallace Monument (see STIRLING/STIRLING CASTLE; WALLACE, WILLIAM) on the Abbey Craig overlooking the site of the battle of Stirling Bridge is situated so as to ensure memory of a major historical figure. Despite the fact that it commemorates someone famous for opposing English rule, the Wallace Monument, erected by public subscription and built 1861–9, was designed to memorialize the qualities that Scotland brought to the *Union of 1707.

Most modern monuments in Scotland were erected well after the events they commemorate, a fact which raises questions about the processes by which a national public memory is created. In most cases, such a memory seems to stem initially from individuals proposing civic commemoration rather than from widespread public sentiment. The Glenfinnan Monument, for example, was erected in 1815 by Alexander MacDonald of Glenaladale to commemorate the *Jacobite rising 70 years before. Similarly, most of the monuments on Drummossie Moor, the site of the battle of Culloden, were erected in the later 19th century.

As attempts in 1994–5 to remove the statue to the first duke of Sutherland atop Ben Bhraggie in Sutherland suggest, however, and as the recent erection in the Outer Isles of monuments to the Highland Land Wars also shows, the same view of Scottish, particularly Highland, history is not shared by all (see CLEARANCES OF HIGHLANDS AND ISLANDS). Monuments may, then, be used to reject as well as to confirm a nation's sense of itself and to give meaning to 'subaltern' views. In such ways, from the scale of domestic ornamentation to the largest commemorative building, the study of monuments in terms of their being 'the objects of a people's national pilgrimage' offers considerable potential for further research.   CWJW

Moray: 1. to 1130; 2. 1130–1500.

1. to 1130

In the century or two before 1130 the name Moray described a polity, far larger than the later county or district of the name, which may have extended at its greatest from Drumochter in the south to the Scandinavian-held lands (see SCANDINAVIA: 1) of Caithness and Sutherland in the north, and from Buchan in the east to the Atlantic. Moray was ruled by a Gaelic-speaking dynasty (see GAELIC LANGUAGE), the best-known member of which was the celebrated *Macbeth, also king of Scots from 1040 to 1057. These rulers are sometimes styled rí (king) in contemporary annals, and sometimes mormaer, (great steward). With the exception of Macbeth, however, reliable records are few.

Irish annals record the killing of Findlaech, son of Ruaidrí, 'mormaer of Moray', in 1020 by the sons of his brother Mael Brigte. The death of Mael Coluim, son of Mael Brigte, is recorded in 1029 and, in 1032 that of his brother Gilla Comgain, burned to death with 50 of his men. Both Findlaech and Mael Coluim are styled 'king of Alba', rather than 'of Moray', in one of their obits, but this may be an error or an exaggeration. Gilla Comgain's successor—probably also his killer—was his cousin Macbeth (Mac Bethad mac Findláig). Macbeth married Gilla Comgain's widow Gruoch, a princess of the mac Alpin dynasty (see KENNETH MAC ALPIN), and became king of Scots in 1040, after defeating and killing Duncan I (Donnchad ua Maíl Choluim) in battle. Later sources suggest that Macbeth had a claim to the Scottish throne through his mother, but his Gaelic pedigree, on record only two generations after his death, traces his descent through his father Findlaech, and grandfather Ruaidrí, from the Dalriadic kings (see DÁL RIATA) of the house of Loarn.

After the defeat and death of Macbeth in turn in 1057, his stepson Lulach, son of Gilla Comgain, and presumably also of Gruoch, claimed the Scottish throne briefly before being himself slain in 1058. Lulach's son, Mael Snechtai, died in 1085 as 'king of Moray'. An earl named Aed (or 'Heth') who witnesses royal charters early in the 12th century may have been based in Moray. The last ruling member of the dynasty, styled 'king' or 'earl' (that is mormaer) of Moray, was Angus 'son of the daughter of Lulach', who challenged *David I (1124–53) in battle, but was defeated and killed at Stracathro in Angus in 1130. His death was followed by the rapid feudalization of Moray under the Fleming Freskin and his descendants (see LOW COUNTRIES) who soon adopted the significant designation 'de Moravia' ('of Moray'). Malcolm MacHeth, who rebelled against David I, but was later made earl of Ross, may have been related to the old rulers of Moray, as may also have been the mysterious Wimund. Later MacHeth claimants to Moray made common cause with MacWilliam claimants to the Scottish throne, but to no avail.

Macbeth's pedigree offers a clue as to the origins of his dynasty in Moray. Despite some evidence of manipulation, the general claim to descend from the house of Loarn may be accurate, and reflect a movement of Gaelic aristocrats from the territory of Loarn in *Dál Riata to northern Pictland (see PICTS) by way of the Great Glen or Loch Laggan in the 9th or 10th centuries, parallel to the movement of the dynasty of Kenneth mac Alpin further south. It has been suggested that Moray may have been for a time a separate kingdom, independent of the dynasty of Kenneth mac Alpin. However, it seems more likely that the rulers of Moray were subject, albeit loosely, to the kings of Alba. Whatever the case, Moray acted as a significant buffer against further Scandinavian penetration from the north, and its rulers were remembered with respect in Scandinavian sources such as *Orkneyinga Saga*. The Gaelic notes in the Book of Deer, dating from the mid-12th century, offer a tantalizing glimpse of the holding of land and the ordering of society in Moray (as also in Buchan) about the time of the last mormaers.

WDHS

2. 1130–1500

*David I's suppression of the earldom of Moray in 1130 did not mark the end of the province's significance or of the problems its management caused to Scottish kings. Despite the expulsion of its line of rulers, Moray continued to be referred to in the early 13th century as a land separate to Scotia. Even once the realm of Scotland was acknowledged as stretching as far as Caithness, Moray was still recognized as one of the chief northern provinces.

The actions of the royal government during the century after 1130 seemed to create or widen differences between the upland regions of the province and the coastal districts, the Laich of Moray, between the Spey and Inverness. The crown's existing estates were concentrated in these coastal regions and between 1130 and 1230 the kings established sheriffdoms centred on Inverness, Nairn, Forres, and Elgin, providing a framework for royal authority in the province. The extension of royal government was accompanied by the settlement of immigrants in the Laich. Lands were given to the crown's supporters, the most important of whom was the Fleming Freskin, founder of the Moray family. The foundation of a string of burghs between Inverness and Banff operated as centres of economic and social influence on the surrounding populations (see URBAN SETTLEMENT: 1). The final area of change was religion. Though there was probably a bishop in Moray before 1130, a diocese with an established centre and cathedral at Elgin and with a parochial structure was achieved only during the 13th century, while reformed religious houses were founded at Beauly, Pluscarden, and Kinloss (see CHURCH INSTITUTIONS: 2).

However, while these changes in the Laich secured the authority of the crown, the interior of the province from Lochalsh to Strathbogie remained a source of difficulty and threat. Attempts to revive the old earldom of Moray or challenge the kings' officials seem to have found support in these areas. Leaders such as Wimund, son of Earl Angus, and the MacWilliam family were able to raise allies from the Gaelic kindreds of upland Moray leading to warfare in the region from the 1140s to the 1220s.

From 1200 kings left the defeat of these enemies to their aristocratic vassals. They rewarded success with grants of lordships to a group of men from outside Moray. The interior of the province from the Great Glen to Strathbogie was divided between six or more families, the greatest of which were the *Comyn lords of Badenoch and Lochaber.

Moray's importance in the kingdom was demonstrated during the years of major warfare between 1296 and 1340. The province was relatively untouched by direct fighting. Royal-led English armies penetrated into Moray on only three occasions during the Wars of *Independence, in 1296, 1303, and 1335, and significant English occupation occurred only in 1296–7. This security meant that it was a vital refuge and recruiting ground for the Scottish guardians between 1297 and 1303 and provided *Robert I with a base and allies during his northern campaign against the Comyns and their allies in 1307–8. In particular, the role of the Moray family in providing leadership against the English and their allies determined local loyalties. When the province was forced to submit, as it was by Edward I in 1303, the future of Scottish resistance as a whole was thrown into jeopardy. Robert I clearly recognized the significance of Moray for the security of his realm. In 1312 he re-established the earldom of Moray for his nephew, Thomas Randolph. The new earldom included all the old province and represented the surrender of the crown's lands in the Laich.

The activities of Thomas Randolph and his son, John, in defence of the Bruce cause meant that they had little time to run their earldom in person. When John was killed in 1346, Moray was left without an accepted heir. The failure of the Randolph line, combined with the disappearance of the Comyns, Strathbogies, and Morays between 1300 and 1350 deprived the province of leaders. The instability of Moray was increased by other factors. The worsening of the *climate in this period restricted the areas of cereal production to the Lowlands. The men of upland Moray probably reverted to a pastoral, semi-nomadic economy (see ECONOMY: 2), which was accompanied by a revival of *Gaelic language and custom. In the absence of noble leadership, power devolved to lesser figures who functioned in kin-based groupings like Clan Donnachaidh of Atholl and the federation of Clan Chattan which centred on Badenoch.

The failure of Moray's leading families also drew in lords and their men from outside the province. From further south the Dunbars and Stewarts staked claims to act as leaders in the province and in 1372 the earldom was divided between them with John Dunbar receiving the coastal districts and Alexander Stewart, favourite son of King Robert II,

being made lord of Badenoch in the Uplands. This division was a recipe for local conflict which was exacerbated by the activities of local kindreds and the eastward spread of the Gaelic superpower, the lordship of the *Isles. By the later 14th century the lords were extending their influence up the Great Glen from Lochaber. The activities of the Islesmen and of kindreds in the service of Alexander Stewart made Moray the area of greatest conflict between the revived power of Gaelic Scotland and the structures of Anglicized society established during the previous centuries. As part of this Anglicized settlement, churchmen and burgesses made repeated complaints about the attacks of raiding caterans, the most spectacular of which saw Alexander Stewart, 'Wolf of Badenoch', burn Elgin cathedral in a dispute with the bishop of Moray (see HIGHLANDS AND ISLANDS AND CENTRAL GOVERNMENT: 1).

Scotland's rulers were slow to react to the problems of Moray. When they did so, their response was largely indirect. Though the governor, Robert, duke of Albany, campaigned in the region in 1405 and 1411 and James I followed suit in 1428 and 1429, they preferred to rely on a lieutenant, Alexander, earl of Mar, son of the 'Wolf of Badenoch', to govern in their name. The dangers of this approach became clear on Mar's death in 1435 when a new power vacuum allowed the lords of the Isles to dominate Moray between the 1430s and 1450s. The earldom, restricted to coastal Moray, was held by lords whose main resources lay elsewhere (see NOBILITY: 2). When the last of these, the *Douglases, were forfeited in 1455, a new power emerged in the province. The *Gordons, earls of Huntly and lords of Strathbogie, had secured Badenoch in 1452 and, three years later, occupied Moray. The crown refused to allow the Gordons the provincial dominance of the Randolphs. The Gordons would be the chief lords in the area from the 15th century onwards, but Moray itself would remain in the possession of the royal line.   MBr

Muir, Thomas (1765–99), prominent radical during the political agitation inspired by the *French Revolution. Born and educated in Glasgow, he completed his studies in Edinburgh and was called to the Bar in 1787. Energetic and earnest, he became active in the restricted reforming circles of the time. When the Friends of the People, a movement originating in London, extended into Scotland, Muir helped to found its branch in Glasgow in 1792 and was chosen a delegate to its Scottish convention. He emerged as leader of its smaller, less moderate faction. He was also in touch with the United Irishmen and he read out to the convention an address from them. It called for a joint campaign in favour of reform by Scotsmen and Irishmen and expressed nationalistic sentiments which Muir endorsed. As a result he was arrested for sedition early in 1793. He compounded his offence by going to Paris while on bail to witness the Revolution at first hand. France meanwhile declared war on Britain and he had great difficulty in getting back. At his trial in August he faced a hostile jury and the implacable Lord Braxfield, determined to make an example of him. Muir got fourteen years' transportation, a sentence regarded on every hand as inhumanely harsh. Yet it was allowed to stand and he arrived at Botany Bay in 1795 (see AUSTRALIA). He stayed only a few months before he managed to escape on a merchant's ship. He sailed to North America, then made his way through Mexico and Cuba to Spain. The vessel on which he entered Cadiz was attacked by ships of the British blockade and Muir suffered severe wounds. He went to Paris to be greeted as a revolutionary hero, but his efforts to encourage the French to invade Scotland came to nothing, and he died in drunken obscurity.

MRGF

music, ecclesiastical. The specifics of Scottish history—invasions, the radical change of aesthetics and cultural practice wrought by the *Reformation, and even the *climate—have had an extremely destructive impact on ecclesiastical music. The exiguous surviving monuments of pre-Reformation church music are entirely random survivals of what must have been a vast repertory, while after the Reformation, the role of composers and trained musicians in worship was curtailed to the point of silence. Nothing can be said with certainty about the music of the pre-Roman Celtic liturgy (see RELIGIOUS LIFE: 1), and indeed there are no surviving manuscripts earlier than the 13th century. The musicologist John Purser has convincingly argued that some of the music we possess for the services of St Kentigern and St *Columba, in the Sprouston Breviary and the Inchcolm fragments respectively, must have its roots in this lost repertory of liturgical chant. The bulk of surviving Scottish chant, however, faithfully reflects the prevalence of the English 'Use of Sarum', the music and ritual developed at Salisbury cathedral, closely related to the Roman use, but considerably more elaborate and with many insular idiosyncrasies. The Sarum rite continued to be used in Scotland right up to the Reformation. When *James IV spoke of 'our awin Scottis use' he was referring, as far as all the surviving evidence shows, not to a different type of chant, but to the specifically Scottish calendar of saints and all that this implied in terms of the feasts and commemorations of the church year (see RELIGIOUS LIFE: 2; CALENDAR AND SEASONAL CUSTOMS).

Medieval European liturgical life was rich and complex, at least in places where there was sufficient money for the upkeep of choirs. Plainchant would have constituted the staple ingredient of all divine offices (vespers, compline, matins, lauds, the Mass, and the canonical hours). This would have been enlivened with polyphony (music deploying two or more independent voice parts) at given points, the blaze of harmony and interweaving lines creating an effect analogous to stained glass. Hearing such music outwith its plainsong liturgical context gives no impression of its true impact. In ordinary Scottish country parishes, poor as they were, it is unlikely that much music was heard, and certainly not the dazzling and virtuosic polyphony found in the great St Andrews Music Book ('W1' to musicologists) now in Wolfenbüttel. Copied c.1230–50, it alone of all such early medieval Scottish choir books survived the Reformation because it was filched from the cathedral priory of *St Andrews by Marcus Wagner in the 1550s. A huge collection of pieces, it contains much music from Notre-Dame in Paris, for whose famous repertory the manuscript is a major source. There are also strikingly inventive works by unknown Scottish composers. The book's Scottish provenance is generally ignored in international writing, but its existence demonstrates that Scotland's geographical remoteness did not mean cultural impoverishment.

In the later Middle Ages, 'fine music' would have been sung not only in cathedrals and wealthy monasteries, but also in the wave of new collegiate churches endowed by wealthy patrons for the specific purpose of supporting a college of singing priests devoted to praying for the founders and their families, living and dead. Sadly, no requiem music from Scottish sources is extant. The patrons ranged from the *nobility or the new class of rising Lords of Parliament to town councils (see URBAN LIFE: 1). Burgh churches such as St Nicholas in *Aberdeen, one of the largest in the country, supported sizeable choirs, and a network of song schools (see SCHOOLS AND SCHOOLING: 1) existed to train singers and composers. Occasionally, town council records provide tantalizing glimpses of what kind of works patrons expected to be sung in polyphony, as at Crail. Even in remote Inverness, on the very eve of the Reformation, the council planned to rebuild the choir of the parish church. The chance survival in a bookbinding of some sheets of music which appear to have come from the Inverness song school provides some idea of the sort of thing the boys were expected to be expert in, and corroborates the contents of a teaching text now in the British Museum, 'The Art of Music collectit out of all ancient doctouris of music'.

Dated to c.1580, and *James VI's 'tymeous remeid' re-establishing burgh song schools, this work is clearly based on pre-Reformation teaching material. It contains much on the technique of faburden, exemplified in the Inverness Fragments: plainsong melodies, normally in the tenor voice, were harmonized according to fixed rules, to produce simple choral music of great beauty which did not require rehearsal.

As for highly wrought polyphony from the later Middle Ages and early Renaissance, a mere three Scottish sources are extant, while some music by Scottish composers survives in English manuscripts. The indications are that Scotland was, in music (see CULTURE: 10) as in literature (see CULTURE: 7), open to both English and mainland European influences, and that Scottish church music may have been rather more European than its southern counterpart. Under Henry VII, England developed a highly individual musical language, 'English Decorated', best documented in the Eton Choirbook. Eton choirbook works and others in that idiom are to be found in the Scottish 'Carver Choirbook', while aspects of this insular style are echoed in the highly personal and often spectacular work of Robert Carver (1485–c.1567), alongside various mainland features. The work of later Scots composers, however, shows little or no trace of the Eton idiom.

The sheer scantiness of the surviving evidence makes generalization difficult, though the complexity and splendour of what does survive indicates that the wealthier foundations continued to prize quality and that musicians capable of providing it were not lacking. This applies above all to the nation's premier collegiate foundation, the Chapel Royal founded within *Stirling castle in 1501. Yet it is a useful rule of thumb, in the history of Scotland's culture in both the medieval and Renaissance periods, that developments often took place a reign in advance of what textbooks suggest. The reign of James III, which has significantly less documentary record than that of his son, may well be a case in point. The myth of James III's favourites hanged at Lauder Bridge indicates how much that monarch appreciated music, and it would seem that his foundation of a new Chapel Royal, dedicated to St Andrew and located at Restalrig, near Holyrood, in a specially designed hexagonal chapel, suggests a significant establishment of choristers. Yet we have concrete details only of James IV's foundation at Stirling castle, a lavishly equipped establishment with a large choir, clearly meant to emulate St George's at Windsor. There is no extant music, however, which can be unequivocally identified as emanating from this institution, although it has been shown to have acted as a focal point for various other kinds of artistic and intellectual activity.

In the Middle Ages and Renaissance, monarchs often used the music of their chapels to impress messages on visiting dignitaries, and the existence of a Mass based on the Burgundian song 'L'Homme armé' from the pen of Robert Carver may well indicate that his music was in the Chapel Royal's repertory, and served as part of James IV's ambitious schemes for a pan-European crusade against the Turks. Survivals of individual works from c.1530, and c.1555 from St Andrews and St Giles's, Edinburgh, indicate the very high standards cultivated at those centres, and post-Reformation music from the abbeys of Dunfermline and Holyrood, and St Andrews priory, by composers trained before the Reformation, corroborate the claims of an English visitor who professed to admire nothing the Scots did, except their making music.

In the immediate aftermath of the Reformation, the imposition of a Genevan liturgy involving no choral singing at all put an abrupt stop to the ambitious musical training provided by the song schools. Without the career structure of cathedral and collegiate choirs (see CHURCH INSTITUTIONS: 2) to provide both employment and a context in which large-scale musical composition could develop, church music withered and died. Former vicars choral became readers and ministers in the new Protestant church (see CHURCH INSTITUTIONS: 3), but musical life was restricted to harmonized versions of the many (and very fine) tunes of the 1564 metrical psalter, with the congregation singing the melody and the trained musicians available adding two or three other parts. In the early 1560s, at the instigation of the future regent, Moray, work began in St Andrews on producing a complete harmonized version of the 105 'proper tunes' of the metrical psalms. The selfless diligence of Thomas Wode, a former monk of Lindores turned Reformed clergyman, brought this to completion. Wode gathered and preserved the results in the precious partbooks which now bear his name. He also saved several works of Scottish polyphony from oblivion. The 1564 psalter, inspired by the French Genevan psalter, contained a vast variety of metres, and consequently tunes, as well as a restricted number of canticles. Though much of the verse is doggerel, of no poetical merit whatever, the melodies are excellent, and composers did what they could, even developing a kind of primitive fugal technique in the 'psalms in reports'.

By the time of the *National Covenant of 1638, however, choral singing itself was seen by the Presbyterian party as an idol to be torn down (see RELIGIOUS LIFE: 4; DEATH AND BURIAL), and their victory meant the issue of a new, standardized metrical psalter in common metre in 1650. The first printing contained no music at all, but the idea was that all the psalms could now be sung to one of the twelve 'common' tunes. The distance from the sumptuous liturgical life of a century earlier could not have been greater, and this situation was to prevail for some 150 years. It goes a long way towards explaining both the loss of any material that might have survived the initial *iconoclasm of the Reformation and the general indifference to the art of (composed) music which remains characteristic of Scotland right up to the present day.   JRB

music hall began in public houses around the mid-1800s where there would be a stage for performers, with the audience eating and drinking. Most of the performers would be amateurs. The 1843 Theatre Act removed the monopoly of the patent theatres, namely Covent Garden and the Theatre Royal, Drury Lane, London, for the performance of drama and created a split between dramatic performances and the selling of liquor. If licensed by the Lord Chamberlain, legitimate theatres were not allowed to sell alcohol in the auditorium, whereas concert rooms were licensed to sell drink, but not to perform stage plays. Establishments had to decide whether they wanted to present drama, or sell alcohol and provide some other style of entertainment. This encouraged the development of music halls selling alcohol, providing entertainment, and charging an entry fee, thereby creating commercial establishments, run for profit.

It is suggested that it was mostly the working class, and usually men, who attended music hall, which offered some consolation and escape from their poor housing conditions (see ROUGH CULTURE). Most in-depth studies on music hall in Scotland centre round Glasgow. However, there were also music halls in other Scottish towns and cities, for example, Edinburgh, Dundee, Aberdeen, and Paisley.

The registration of music halls increased after the 1843 Act. The 'free and easy', in the 1860s and 1870s, was described as a room in a public house, with a platform and a piano at one end of the room. The chairman would be in charge of proceedings and was expected to introduce the acts and control the audience participation. When the licence to sell drink in the auditorium was withdrawn, the loss in revenue had to be compensated for. From the 1880s more luxurious halls were being built, with the audience now separated from the performers—who were now professional—and seated in fixed seats. The chairman was no longer required. The intention was to attract larger, more respectable, family audiences, thereby generating more income. For example, in 1892, Edward Moss opened

the Empire Palace Theatre in Edinburgh, the first theatre in the Moss Empire circuit, which seated 3,000 people. It presented 'High Class Music and Varieties'.

In Glasgow, in the 1890s, the Good Templars Harmonic Association, part of the *temperance movement in Scotland, offered their non-alcoholic alternative to music hall. These were known as 'the bursts'. On paying their entry charge, the audience members were given a mug and a bag of buns. Tea was served at the interval. When the bags were empty, they were blown up and burst as a sign of appreciation for the performer, hence the name 'the bursts'. W. F. Frame and Harry Lauder appeared in these concerts.

Music hall entertainers could also be found performing in the 'penny geggies' which toured the country. These were travelling wood and canvas booth-like structures, and provided a stage for performers in both town and country. A penny was the admission charge. Will Fyffe, a great music hall star, began his career in his father's penny geggy.

The 1890s are believed to have been the golden age of music hall. By 1906 the term 'variety' was in more common use. Variety shows employed acts such as jugglers, acrobats, animal acts, singers, and dancers. However, it was always the comic who topped the bill. By 1912 the halls were facing financial difficulties. The new theatres were expensive to maintain. This led to twice-nightly shows to try to recoup the costs in ticket money. After the First World War, cinema (see FILM, SCOTLAND ON) and broadcasting (see RADIO AND TELEVISION) were gaining in popularity, as were jazz and ragtime. However, touring variety shows continued in Scotland in the 1920s and 1930s, with such performers as Harry Gordon, Tommy Lorne, Tommy Morgan, and Alec Finlay.

During the Second World War the troops were entertained by ENSA and many artistes became known over a wider area. Post-war the increasing popularity of television (see RADIO AND TELEVISION), providing visual home entertainment, competed with both theatre and cinema, leading to many closures. A demographic shift from city-centre tenements to peripheral housing schemes ended the practice of attending the local theatre once or twice a week. Variety was in decline.

Popular holiday resorts still provided shows for the summer season, particularly in the heyday of the Clyde resorts. Many performers, such as Jack Milroy and Johnny Beattie, worked here. That heyday is now past, but variety continues with touring shows, for example, Johnny Beattie with *Pride of the Clyde*; variety theatre, such as *The Gaiety Whirl* in the Gaiety Theatre, Ayr; and Jimmy Logan with his biographical show *Lauder*.   MM

music, Highland. Defining what is actually meant by 'Highland music' is a difficult task. Although we are dealing with musical instruments that are associated with the Highlands, they were certainly not exclusive to Highland society. Moreover, on what basis do we define the Highlands? Much of the rich musical tradition of the region occurred in the cultural interface between Highland and Lowland society: between Gaelic (see GAELIC LANGUAGE; GAELIC LITERATURE), Scots (see SCOTS LANGUAGE), and English culture. If we take the Northern Isles into consideration, the strong Norse influence would add another facet to the definition of Highland music. Paradoxically, this very hybridity, this rich and varied fusion of different cultures has produced music that is recognized today as Highland.

The earliest historical records of instrumental music in the Highlands and Islands, as depicted on stone crosses and slabs, relate to the harp. Although other instruments are sometimes portrayed on these artefacts and the music of the harp or its variants was heard in other parts of the country, it did play a key role in Gaelic society. Harpists formed part of the elite within Gaeldom and their music formed the background for bardic performances and the recital of genealogy. Some of the more adept harpists within Gaeldom were visitors from *Ireland but there were also dynasties of harp players within Scotland. Though we are reliant on oral records for the majority of the information, we know that the Galbraith family, and more importantly the MacShannons, served the lord of the *Isles from a base in and around Kintyre. Though soon to be superseded by the bagpipes, harpists were sometimes retained by the clan chief into the 17th century and even the early part of the next century. The life story of Roderick Morison known as *An Clarsair Dall* (the Blind Harper), and arguably the most famous harper of his time, illustrates the passing of harp music from Highland society. Trained in Ireland before enjoying the patronage of John MacLeod of Dunvegan, he ended his days as a travelling bard, singer, and musician disillusioned with the 'alien' forces disrupting what he and others regarded as the natural order of Gaelic society.

The great Highland bagpipe was subject to the same complex web of pressures but because of its adoption by the military and its subsequent iconic status to the nation it survived, albeit in a different form. Probing into the historical record to discover the origins of the distinctive Highland bagpipe presents problems caused by the lack of corroborating evidence and the different interpretations that are drawn from the extant source material. Though there is evidence to suggest that the bagpipe was played at the battle of Bannockburn (1314), the instrument in its recognizable modern form only appeared during the 16th century. Moreover, because it predominated in the Gaelic-speaking areas of Scotland, scholars are heavily reliant on the *oral tradition for their analysis of the development of the music and the function of the bagpiper in clan society.

This material demonstrates that pipers were also part of the upper echelons of the Gaelic social order, a key component of the clan chief's retinue. Under the tutelage of certain schools of piping, there developed an intricate and powerful form of music: *Ceol Mor* (pibroch). The MacCrimmon College of Piping in Skye was the first piping dynasty and under their influence others such as the MacKays of Gairloch, the MacKays of Raasay, and the MacArthurs of Ulva composed and taught the art of *piobaireachd* (pibroch) through a syllabic language called *canntaireachd*. Recent scholarship has helped to deconstruct some of the myths surrounding the lineage of this musical tradition and the relationship with Gaelic song (see SONG, TRADITIONAL AND FOLK: 2).

But whatever the process by which the tunes were composed, their titles reflect the varied nature of Gaelic society. The position of the chief as the embodiment of the *clan was eulogized in tunes such as 'The Earl of Seaforth's Salute' or 'MacLeod of MacLeod's Lament'. Other tunes were devoted to specific individuals, clans, or incidents within Gaeldom. As in the bardic tradition, battles and campaigns were commemorated, indeed valorized, in powerful compositions like 'The Battle of Auldearn' or 'My Prince has landed in Moidart' (see JACOBITISM). These tunes reflect the importance accorded to the martial tradition within the Gaelic social formation but they also highlight the way in which the Highlands were being absorbed into the wider machinations of the state (see HIGHLANDS AND ISLANDS AND CENTRAL GOVERNMENT: 3). After the Forty-Five, the Highlands were pacified, the Gaels were rehabilitated, and certain features of Highland culture were appropriated through a process of invention and re-presentation as Scottish and indeed British society attempted to project a distinctive *national identity. The way in which bagpipe music developed exemplifies these changes with *ceol beag* (light music) gaining in popularity as Highland dance became more of a feature and marches were composed to celebrate the military prowess of the Highland regiments (see ARMY: 3–4) in imperial campaigns.

This is also the historical backdrop for the development of the Scottish fiddle, an instrument which because of its central role in the music of Scottish country dancing also claimed a strong association with the Highlands despite the fact that it was played throughout the nation. The origins and development of the fiddle in Scotland are subject to a certain degree of conjecture due to the paucity of historical records. Early stringed instruments that were played in Scotland include the *fedyle* (fiddle), the *rybid* (rebec), and the *croud*, though only the last is thought to be a native Celtic instrument. These different stringed instruments, along with the viol, were superseded in the 17th century after the introduction of the Italian violin. Traditional fiddlers in Scotland quickly recognized its musical qualities and its widespread adoption was facilitated by the establishment of Scottish fiddle makers devoted to adapting the Italian model for national consumption (see CULTURE: 15).

Aristocratic patronage was important for sustaining this particular musical tradition and indeed it facilitated a 'Golden Age' of fiddle music centred in Perthshire and associated with the famous player and composer Niel Gow. Born in Inver, near Dunkeld in 1727, Gow's distinctive style of playing was popularized through a variety of musical channels, including his talented son Nathaniel. Permanent records of fiddle tunes become more common as the 18th century progressed and arguably the most famous, the Drummond Castle MSS of 1734, was transcribed for the Duke of Perth. It contains the earliest written records of popular tunes such as 'Tulloch gorum' and 'Caber Feidh'. The titles are indicative of the close relationship with Highland, and indeed Gaelic, society. Moreover, scholars have highlighted the existence of a distinctive west Highland style of playing where the influence of the bagpipe was clearly apparent. As with the Shetland idiom, the local character stamped its own imprint on the fiddle playing, but whereas the former continued to develop, the latter tradition proved to be largely ephemeral, though echoes of it could be found in Cape Breton (see CANADA)—an area where the Gaelic diaspora settled in significant numbers.

By the 19th century, the focal point for fiddle music shifted to the north-east (see REGIONAL IDEN-TITIES: 2) of Scotland where in James Scott Skinner—the 'Strathspey King'—fiddlers had an expert exponent of the art. Skinner played in a variety of arenas from Balmoral to concerts in the urban centres of the south down to the local functions in his native Banchory. When Skinner died in 1927 the Royal Scottish Country Dance Society had just been founded with the accordion now a central instrument in the type of music being played at Highland balls for the 'country set' or in townships throughout the north of Scotland. The advent of radio (see RADIO AND TELEVISION: 1) helped to bring the music to an urban and middle-class audience but though the listeners may have increased in the early part of the 20th century, changes to the rural way of life and other cultural influences reduced the number of actual musicians.

In recent decades, people have reacted against some of these forces and the folk revival of the late 1950s and 1960s has helped to reinvigorate Highland music. Old instruments in this broadly (and perhaps inappropriately) defined field have been reintroduced—the *clàrsach*, the 'jaws' ('Jews') harp' or *tromb*, the whistle, and the bellows pipe—whilst the number of other musicians has increased greatly in recent years.

The emergence of 'world music' has added another dimension with the fusion of traditional material with other musical forms presented in a contemporary manner. This willingness to experiment with hitherto conventional forms has led to a further resurgence in Highland music in the 1990s. Piping, formerly one of the most conservative of musical traditions, has witnessed exciting new developments through talented artists like Gordon Duncan and Fred Morrison. Some players have reservations about what they regard as a dilution of the traditional but it is precisely this willingness to embrace other influences which lies at the heart of Highland music. Providing the foundations of the traditional music are solid, these new artists can only advance the music which is associated with the Highlands.   JAB

National Covenant and Solemn League and Covenant.

The National Covenant (1638) and the Solemn League and Covenant (1643) were the defining documents of two distinct phases of the mid-17th-century Covenanting Revolution. The more famous of them, the National Covenant, was drawn up by the Edinburgh lawyer Archibald Johnston of Wariston and the minister of Leuchars in Fife, Alexander Henderson, both deeply committed to the Presbyterian cause. First signed on 28 February 1638 in Edinburgh's Greyfriars church, copies were rapidly circulated around the country, attracting widespread support from all levels of Scottish society.

The extraordinary popularity of the National Covenant is a measure of the depth of resentment felt throughout Scotland at the policies pursued by Charles I, not least the introduction of the new Prayer Book the previous year. In stark contrast to the religious fervour it sought to harness, however, the National Covenant is a dull and drily legalistic document. It begins by repeating the so-called Negative or King's Confession of 1581—a condemnation of all things Roman Catholic drafted by an earlier generation of Scottish Protestants for the benefit of King *James VI—before citing a lengthy catalogue of parliamentary statutes construed as defining the polity and liturgy of the reformed church in Scotland. Rhetorically uninspiring, the National Covenant was nonetheless a masterpiece of studied ambiguity. For just as it implicitly underwrote Presbyterianism without ever explicitly condemning episcopacy, so it implicitly condemned the recent innovations in worship without ever explicitly saying what those innovations were or what true worship might be. Moreover, it succeeded in combining what amounted to a direct defiance of the will of the king with a reaffirmation of its signatories' allegiance to both Charles I and the ancient laws and liberties of his native kingdom.

The appearance of working within a framework of established constitutional precedent was as crucial as its vagueness in enabling the National Covenant to appeal to all sections of Scottish society. Charles I's remote and unresponsive government of Scotland had not only generated massive religious dissent but also a range of other grievances widely perceived as stemming from Scotland's provincialization within an essentially English imperial system. The constitutionalism of the National Covenant thus tapped a deep reservoir of patriotic outrage at the iniquities of a governmental system which was seen to subordinate Scotland's interests to those of England. At the same time, however, as a covenant, its religious form and content drew on a deep-rooted tradition of biblical literalism which read the Old Testament as a source book of legal precedent of universal validity. As a covenanted nation, Scotland was no less bound than biblical Israel to fulfil the law of God; likewise, she was no more exempt from God's plagues and punishments for breaking the terms of that covenant. It was fear of God's wrath as much as the assurance of God's favour that animated the Covenanters, and that lent the identification of Scotland as a latter-day Israel its revolutionary dynamism (see NATIONAL IDENTITY: 3).

While the idea of the covenant might underwrite the Scots' sense of themselves as God's chosen people, it also set such claims to national 'election' within the universal framework of a cosmic struggle between the forces of Christ and Antichrist. This sense of participating in an apocalyptic battle between God and the Devil in the latter days of the world lay in part behind the second defining document of the Covenanting movement, the Solemn League and Covenant. Drawn up in August 1643, with Henderson and Johnston of Wariston again to the fore, this was a treaty between the Scots and Charles I's parliamentary opponents in England, designed to protect the religious and constitutional revolution already accomplished in Scotland, while affording the English parliament the Scottish military muscle necessary to defeat the forces of Royalism. The outbreak of civil war in England in 1642 allowed the Scots to redefine from a position of strength the nature of the British union from which the 'troubles' had largely stemmed, but to which they remained wholeheartedly committed. Yet it also allowed them to project onto a wider stage their sense of participating in an apocalyptic drama whose denouement would transcend not just national frontiers but human history itself.

British Protestant solidarity, however, rapidly fell foul of wide differences of opinion over church government and worship. While the Scots were utterly committed to exporting Presbyterianism to England, the English parliamentarians would not countenance religious uniformity on the Scottish model. The Solemn League and Covenant committed them only to reforming their church 'according to the word of God', a formula which each side interpreted to its own satisfaction. While Presbyterian Scots might remain covenanted to England as well as their God, divisions within their own ranks, and the rise of Cromwell's New Model Army, put paid to any notion of pan-British solidarity (see also CHURCH INSTITUTIONS: 3; COVENANT, WARS OF THE; COVENANTERS; PARLIAMENT: 2; RELIGIOUS LIFE: 3; UNION OF THE CROWNS). RAM

national identity: 1. early medieval and the formation of Alba; 2. from the Wars of Independence to John Mair; 3. 1500–1750; 4. the age of Enlightenment; 5. the Victorian and Edwardian era; 6. modern.

1. early medieval and the formation of Alba

It is anachronistic to talk of national identities in the early Middle Ages. National identities, however, are often reformulations of older identities, so it is appropriate to ask when and how Scottish identity first came into being, long before this became anything which may be recognized as a national identity.

Who were the first to think they lived in 'Scotland'? To answer this question we need to remember that Alba is the Gaelic word for Scotland, and that from at least the 10th century Gaelic was the first language (see GAELIC LANGUAGE) of most people living in what is now Scotland. Alba first appears as the kingdom's name in the year 900. The fact that in contemporary record 'Alba' and 'Albanaig' ('people of Alba') replaced 'Pictland' and *'Picts' suggests that Alba was, in this context, another word for Pictland. This change from Pictland to Alba has, in the past, been explained as the result of a 'union' of *Dál Riata and Pictland initiated by *Kenneth mac Alpin. The only evidence for this is a politically charged statement, written a century after Kenneth's death, which was intended to justify the monopoly on the *kingship in the 10th century exercised by his descendants. There is evidence, moreover, that Alba did not include Dál Riata, or the west Highlands and Isles at all, but was thought of as, at most, stretching from Caithness in the north to Fife in the south, an area corresponding to mainland Pictland. But the kings of Alba can never have ruled all this territory, which in the north was firmly under Norse control (see SCANDINAVIA: 1).

In this period kingdoms did not have fixed bounds. Instead there was a core, where the king's authority was regularly acknowledged and directly exercised, surrounded by regions or other kingdoms which only occasionally recognized the king of Alba as overlord and rarely, if ever, experienced direct rule. In this situation Alba could not refer simply to the kingdom's territory, but could mean different things depending on the context. At one extreme it might denote Pictland, or (by the 12th century) all Scotland north of the Forth and Clyde. At the other extreme it might mean the kingdom's core in the east between Stirling and Aberdeen (especially after *Moray had ceased to be within the core area by the end of the 11th century). 'Scotland' in this period was partly an ideal harking back to a historic sense of Pictish territory and partly a reflection of political reality. There was no doubt, however, that the Forth marked the southern limit of 'Scotland'. The persistence of this boundary long after Falkirk and Lothian were securely within the kingdom's core shows that 'Scotland' was determined by a mix of historic ideal and political reality, not just the latter on its own. This boundary also coincided with a major topographical divide. Those of social standing who considered themselves as Scots in this period were people whose sense of community was determined by their experience of royal authority, their sense of history, and the constraints of geography. Beyond the area of the east between Stirling and Aberdeen—Scotland proper in this period—the mix of politics, history and geography produced different communities, some with their own kings, such as *Galloway, Argyll, the Isles (see ISLES, KINGDOM OF THE), and (by 1085) Moray. The idea that 'Scotland' meant all the territory of the king's realm, encompassing the mainland down to the border with the kingdom of England, is not stated unambiguously in Scottish sources until the 13th century, by which time the nature of social and political relationships had been transformed.

Alba, 'Scotland', may have had Pictish roots, but it was also conceived as a Gaelic kingdom. Its first appearance in 900 marked the beginning of the reign of *Constantine II, the probable architect of the power-sharing arrangement which allowed the two branches of Kenneth mac Alpin's descendants to work together rather than fight each other. The objective was to monopolize the kingship, a feat never before achieved by a ruling family for more than two generations. The *kingship had thus taken a new form which hinged on descent from Kenneth mac Alpin. As a result there was a fundamental change in the ancient roots which the

437

kingship claimed in order to acquire prestige and to justify its political pre-eminence. They now focused on Kenneth's male ancestry from kings of Dál Riata and legendary Irish kings, instead of the long succession of ancient Pictish kings which had been promoted (and largely invented) in the reign of Kenneth's son, *Constantine I (862–76). Kenneth's male-line descent from Gaelic kings became of paramount importance in defining political power, so that any family with high social and political pretensions needed to sport a Gaelic pedigree. Gaelic ancestors were no doubt invented in the same way as Norman ancestry was concocted for leading families in the late Middle Ages (see CAMPBELL FAMILY). In this way the kingship's Pictish identity was superseded by Irish identity. A specifically and distinctly Scottish identity for the kingship is not found until the end of the 13th century.

Irish identity (see IRELAND: 1) was also sustained by Gaelic language and culture. Social status was underpinned by a literate elite whose authority was based on a mastery of Gaelic history, law, and literature, which was acquired to the highest degree at centres of learning in Ireland (notably Armagh).   DB

2. from the Wars of Independence to John Mair

John Mair's Latin chronicle, *The History of Greater Britain as well England as Scotland*, first published at Paris in 1521, has the distinction of being the first history of Scotland ever to appear in print. Its author was one of the most distinguished intellectuals of his age, a theologian who had spent 25 years in Paris before returning to Scotland in 1518 to teach initially at Glasgow University and subsequently at St Andrews. It was on his return to Scotland that Mair turned his attention to the writing of history, approaching it from the perspective of a medieval scholastic, and developing a deeply unflattering picture of a Scotland dominated by over-mighty feudal barons all too eager to challenge the authority of the Scottish monarchy (see NOBILITY: 2). It was this bleak analysis of Scottish political culture that led Mair to advocate a union of the Scottish and English crowns and the creation of a British kingship capable of controlling the nobility's pursuit of their own self-interested ends. Significantly, however, Mair's pioneering advocacy of Anglo-Scottish union was predicated on the belief that Scotland was and always had been an independent kingdom. Mair would have no truck with English claims to feudal superiority over Scotland, arguing rather for a union in which the ancient Scottish kingdom was accorded parity of status and esteem with that of England.

In elaborating this case, Mair drew heavily on the highly patriotic Scottish chronicle tradition

that had developed in the later Middle Ages. Although dismissive of the ancient Celtic origins' legend that traced the Scots' descent from the eponymous Scota, daughter of the biblical pharaoh of Egypt, Mair did insist that the Scottish kingdom was first founded by the equally legendary Fergus I in the 4th century BC and that it had had an independent existence under a continuous line of kings ever since that date. Likewise, he clearly saw the wars of the late 13th and early 14th centuries as a triumphant vindication of Scottish right over English might. This was a view of the Scottish past that was itself largely a product of the Wars of *Independence. While elements of both the descent myth and the foundation legend long pre-dated 1296, it was Edward I's attempt to provide clear historical proof of England's claim to suzerainty over Scotland that crystallized a coherent account of the Scottish past deliberately designed to bear out the antiquity and continuous independence of the northern kingdom. Such a usable Scottish past is evident both in the opening paragraphs of the celebrated Declaration of Arbroath of 1320 and in greater detail in the various versions of the case for Scottish autonomy put to the papal curia by Baldred Bisset and his associates in 1301. It was not, however, until the 1380s that the shadowy figure of John of Fordun, a cleric from the diocese of Aberdeen, systematized the available material in the form of a lengthy Latin *Chronicle of the Scottish People*.

Fordun's chronicle established the chronological framework and intensely patriotic bias that was to dominate the Scots' understanding of their history for the next two centuries and more. The availability of a coherent account of their past, and the shared myths and memories that it embodied, was crucial to sustaining and developing the Scots' sense of who and what they were. Perhaps inevitably, Scottish identity was based to a large extent on not being English. Reflecting on a visit to the court of James I in the 1430s, Aenius Sylvius Piccolomini (later Pope Pius II) commented that 'nothing pleases the Scots more than abuse of the English'. It was an observation reiterated almost a century later by Mair who recalled from his youth in the 1470s the visceral Anglophobia generated by the first appearance of Blind Harry's vernacular verse epic *The Wallace* (see ANGLO-SCOTTISH RELATIONS: 2).

Yet the Scots' sense of themselves was not always or exclusively articulated in such negative terms. Fordun's chronicle is not only anti-English, but is also a positive celebration of the shared martial heritage that had enabled the Scots to defend their freedom throughout their long and glorious history. Both the value of freedom and freedom as a value, notably celebrated in the vernacular verse of John Barbour's *The Brus* (c.1375), are integral to

Fordun's Latin chronicle. When in the mid-1440s Walter Bower, abbot of Inchcolm, incorporated Fordun's work into the larger format of his highly influential *Scotichronicon*, he ended his work with the resounding valediction, 'Christ! He is not a Scot who is not pleased with this book.' Smug and self-serving this may be, but it is also indicative of how a shared history—a common store of myths and memories—served to reinforce the Scots' sense of themselves as a single people under a sovereign king (see HISTORIANS: 1).

Such collective self-awareness, however, is not necessarily the same as national consciousness and identity. In so far as the latter presupposes, not just a shared sense of the past, but also a community of language, culture, custom, and law, late medieval Scotland was only just beginning to acquire the defining characteristics of nationhood. The Wars of Independence had done much to mobilize the Scottish kingdom's ethnically diverse and polyglot peoples in a common cause. Their aftermath, however, witnessed the entrenchment of regional power—and with it cultural and linguistic diversity—at the expense of national solidarity and identity. In particular, the establishment of a quasi-autonomous Lordship of the *Isles provided a cultural as well as political focus for Scotland's Gaelic-speaking population, while the emergence of vernacular Scots as the language of government and the *royal court accentuated the deep cleavage between the two distinct linguistic and cultural communities that now comprised the Scottish kingdom (see LANGUAGES OF SCOTLAND, PRE-1100; GAELIC LANGUAGE; GAELIC LITERATURE; SCOTS LANGUAGE). There is no small irony in the fact that the chronicle tradition of Fordun and Bower, drawing heavily on Scotland's Celtic past in order to demonstrate the kingdom's independence in the present, was appropriated so thoroughly by Lowland Scots who were becoming notably hostile to their Gaelic countrymen. What was for Fordun and Bower a neutral distinction between inhabitants of the same kingdom became for Mair the difference between Lowland 'civility' and Highland 'barbarism'.

Crucial in reinforcing this distinction was the consolidation and extension of royal authority under the 15th-century Stewart kings. An increasingly powerful royal dynasty, keen to impose its will on the outlying regions of the kingdom, provided the framework within which the language, law, and culture of the Lowlands became the basis of a redefined national community (see KINGSHIP: 5). By the end of the 15th century, the aspirations of the Stewart monarchy had come to be expressed in the iconography of the arched 'imperial' crown, a visual expression of the civil law doctrine that the king was emperor in his own kingdom. Symbolic

of both the territorial integrity of the realm and the crown's complete jurisdictional supremacy within it, the arched imperial crown served to define Scottishness more clearly than ever before in terms not only of obedience to the king and a common body of law, but also of conformity to the language and culture of Lowland society. When, in 1493, Gaeldom lost its most dynamic political focus with the suppression of the lordship of the Isles, the foundations were laid for a process that would render the language and culture of the Gaels not so much marginal to a Lowland-based Scottish identity as wholly inimical to it.

Neither Scotland's Renaissance monarchy, however, nor its Scots-speaking subjects were able to abandon their Celtic heritage altogether. It was, after all, only through grafting themselves onto the continuities of an ancient Celtic past that Lowlanders could properly root themselves in Scottish soil. Hence when Bishop William Elphinstone sought to create a national liturgy for Scotland, his research into the lives of Scottish saints drew him to *Iona and the Western Isles. The result was the publication in 1509–10 of the *Aberdeen Breviary*, replete with the lives of some 80 Scottish saints, most of Celtic origin and many appropriated from Irish tradition (see RELIGIOUS LIFE: 1). Such liturgical nationalism was matched—and surpassed—by Hector Boece's ebullient reworking of the patriotic chronicle tradition of Fordun and Bower. A protégé of Elphinstone's, who was appointed principal of Aberdeen University in 1505, Boece approached the Scottish past as an exercise in patriotic humanist rhetoric. Published at Paris in 1527, his *Scotorum Historia* exploited sources of dubious provenance to provide a remarkably detailed account of Scotland's remote Celtic past which, echoing Livy's evocation of the early history of Rome, used the pristine virtue of the early Scots as a benchmark against which generations of their descendants were made to measure their accomplishments. The result is a compelling narrative that, in contrast to John Mair's bleak picture of Scottish political culture, presents the Scots as animated by a colourful blend of civic and chivalric idealism that draws its inspiration from the Celtic past. Significantly, unlike Mair's work, Boece's chronicle was almost immediately translated into Scots by John Bellenden and printed at Edinburgh in the mid-1530s. The publication of the first full-length vernacular chronicle of Scotland was undoubtedly a key moment in the formation of Scottish national consciousness and identity (see HISTORIANS: 2).   RAM

3. 1500–1750

The compelling, aggressive identity which had emerged during and after the Wars of *Independence was consolidated in the reigns of *James IV (1488–1513) and *James V (1513–42). An imperial crown had first appeared on James III's coinage. By 1539, an actual closed, imperial crown, now part of the 'Honours of Scotland', had been made. The cult of St Andrew, reflected in the chivalric order founded by James III, appeared in its mature form in the new royal armorial, complete with Andrew, a thistle as a badge of Scottishness, a redesigned lion rampant, and a blue saltire, designed by Sir David Lindsay, royal poet and herald. James V commissioned the translation by John Bellenden from Latin into Scots of the last of the medieval chronicles of Scotland by Hector Boece. It had, in effect, become an official history of the nation (see HISTORIANS: 2), just as the *Scots language had increasingly been acknowledged, from the 15th century onwards, as the official language of government. Despite his marriage to the daughter of Henry VII of England, which brought the promise of a 'perpetual peace', James IV cultivated an image of himself as a warlord—against England. The building of new palace complexes at *Stirling, Holyrood, Linlithgow, and within *Edinburgh castle, gave three-dimensional expression to a cult of honour in which new metaphors were found to express a national identity rooted within the Stewart dynasty. The lion had long been a symbol of Scottish kingship; but James V went one step further, with a real lion kept within Stirling castle (see CULTURE: 4; ROYAL COURT: 1; STEWART DYNASTY, KINGSHIP: 5).

The *Reformation of 1560 brought an end to the so-called 'Auld Alliance' with France (see FRANCO-SCOTTISH RELATIONS: 2) and opened up an alternative, new 'amity' with England (see ANGLO-SCOTTISH RELATIONS: 3). It also demanded a reworking of Scottish identity. The two centuries between it and Culloden saw the emergence of different versions of the Scottish past as well as alternative versions of the future. A new national church, a body of codified law, and the emergence of a historiographical tradition were the main ingredients of what has been termed a new 'imagining' of Scotland. And Scots law, culminating in Stair's *Institutions of the Law of Scotland* (see LAW AND LAWYERS: 2), was, like history, drawn together by an overarching moral purpose. History as a morality play linked the work of John Mair and his circle in the 1520s; George Buchanan, apologist for the revolutionary regime which deposed a Catholic queen; and the Enlightenment philosophical historians (see CULTURE: 11).

The process began with the Reformation of 1560 and culminated in a second reformation in the 1630s and 1640s, when Scots rediscovered themselves as the true heirs of the nation of Israel. The church,

described by radicals such as Samuel Rutherford as the suffering bride of Christ, by then had become the guarantor of the liberties of the nation, supplanting an absentee monarchy. The 'commonweal' of the 1530s had, a century later, turned into the covenant. The Covenanters (see COVENANT, WARS OF THE) in the 1640s fought under the national flag of the saltire rather than the lion rampant and proclaimed their cause in slogans such as 'For Religion, Country, Crown and Covenant'. Scotland was a nation born again—covenanted under a demanding Lord.

These were all centripetal forces, forging a new, very Protestant identity. But many of these images were exclusivist rather than inclusive; they reflected the internal frontiers which had descended on Scottish society during the same century. There is an alternative explanation of this period: other, centrifugal forces were at work, involving locality, creed, religious faction, or kinship. The century after 1560 brought a new questioning of the single, all-embracing national identity which had been the product of the Wars of Independence. It produced clashes between Catholics and Protestants, Presbyterians and Episcopalians, Highlanders and Lowlanders, and Scots and Britons (see CHURCH INSTITUTIONS: 3; REGIONAL IDENTITIES). The bitter civil war of 1568–73 which followed Queen Mary's fall, the campaign waged by the new Scottish state from the 1590s onwards against what was seen as an alien and semi-barbarous *Gaidhealtachd* (see HIGHLANDS AND ISLANDS AND CENTRAL GOVERNMENT: 2), the Bishops' Wars of the late 1630s, and the religious wars of the 1640s were part of a pattern of internal conflicts and recurrent civil war which lasted until 1746. In the process, what has been called a conservative north-east confronted the power of the Covenanting state and, after 1660, a radical south-west defied the Restoration regime. Scotland was divided in a way it had not been since the 10th or 11th centuries.

The 'amity' produced an Anglo-Scottish Protestant culture (see RELIGIOUS LIFE: 3), for much of the new weaponry of the Protestant church, in catechisms, prayer books, and bibles, was in English. Yet it did not produce an overnight Anglicization of Scottish culture for the same period saw a renewed popularity of the classic texts of the long 'cold war' between Scots and English: the first extant printed editions of Barbour's *The Brus* and Blind Harry's *The Wallace* belong to 1570–1 and successive reprints established them as best-sellers. The work of Henryson and Sir David Lindsay, in unapologetic Middle *Scots, was available to a far wider reading public in the late 16th and early 17th centuries than when their authors were alive. The clash of rival cultures, Scots and English, continued throughout the 17th century and the last-ditch struggle, of Ruddiman and the 'patriotic publishers', came only in the 1710s.

The two strains of Calvinism, representing presbytery and bishop, squabbled over squatters' rights to St *Columba and the culdees, supposedly Protestants before their time. Calderwood and Archbishop Spottiswoode in their rival histories hailed Columba as a presbyter or Protestant bishop ten centuries before the Reformation. Each was laying claim to the roots of their version of a new, Protestant nation. In much the same way, rival chronicle traditions battled for the moral high ground: Boece celebrated the long line of mythical kings of Scots stretching back into pre-history and Buchanan used the same mythology to forge a revolutionary tradition (see KINGSHIP). Despite a Buchanan industry amongst present-day historians, it was probably the Boece tradition which had a wider audience, at least until the end of the reign of James VI.

*James VI's reign (1567–1625) sought to establish a pan-British identity, based on what he himself called a 'perfect union'. There were some dedicated unionists: David Hume of Godscroft, historian, neo-Latin, poet and the most important lay figure in Scottish Calvinism in the age of Andrew *Melville, thought of himself as 'Scoto-Brittanus'. It was members of the *Campbell family and Scottish settlers in Ulster (see IRELAND: 2) who first thought of themselves as 'North Britons'. But the first generation of convinced British unionists who belonged to the reign of James VI and I, who insisted on describing his kingdom as 'Great Britain', barely survived his death.

The common Protestantism of Scots and English had by the second half of the 17th century become an obstacle rather than an asset. A common religion and law were both off the agenda at the time of the *Union of 1707. 'Great Britain' was reborn, but without the benefit of a shared identity or even a feeling that it was a precondition of union. Scots and English shared a monarch but little else before 1707. After 1707, they had unequal shares in a combined parliament and an economic union. Convincing themselves that they were Britons, of a sort, took the Scots some time. 'North Britain' as an alternative identity did not reappear until the 1740s.

ML

4. the age of Enlightenment

National identity is a concept which belongs in the political historian's vocabulary. For whatever ideas of ethnicity, culture, class, and religion a people may share, what gives its members a distinctively national identity is their ability to imagine themselves as part of a community which once enjoyed a past and can imagine a future as citizens of a sov-

ereign, independent political entity. Moreover, it is from this shared sense of a political past and a political future that the nationally conscious citizen will derive his or her sense of how to think and act as a modern patriot.

The Act of *Union of 1707 necessarily brought about a revolution in Scottish thinking about national identity. Hitherto it had been possible to think of Scotland as a state with a distinct, if compromised, sovereignty. Henceforth Scots—and particularly those who belonged to the political and professional elite—were obliged to think of themselves as North Britons, a people with their own distinctive civil and ecclesiastical society and their own economy and culture, a people who had surrendered their political independence to the crown and parliament of one of the enormous monarchies which had come into existence in the modern age.

The origins of this line of thinking are to be found in the long and often sophisticated debate about the need for a new union with England which was precipitated by the failure of the *Darien Scheme in 1698, intensified by the passing of the Act of Security in 1703, and brought to a conclusion by the passing of the Act of Union in 1707. It was in the course of this debate that those who supported and opposed an incorporating union with England developed a shared portrait of Scotland as a failing nation whose political integrity had been compromised since the *Union of the Crowns by the absence of her kings, the venality of the great *nobility, and the jealousy—particularly the commercial jealousy—of the English. It was here that Scots of all parties and political persuasions articulated their fear that without a vigorous commerce the Scottish *economy would fail, rich and poor alike would emigrate, and the fabric of civil society would disintegrate. It was here that many (but not all) Scots came to believe that in the modern world small countries could survive only under the patronage of great states and would do so only if they had patriots enough to safeguard their liberties. It was here, too that it was generally recognized that the only way in which all this could be accomplished was by means of a new union with England.

The hopes and fears generated by the prospect of an incorporating union were to penetrate every level of political discussion throughout the 18th and early 19th centuries. It was hoped that such a union would break the political and economic power of the nobility and put an end to faction. It was hoped that it would stimulate economic growth and release the patriotism of the Scottish elite. It was even possible to hope that such a union would strengthen Scottish independence and lead to a more perfect, more friendly union between the two countries. These hopes were counterbalanced by the equally pervasive fear that an incorporating union would compromise Scottish independence still further, eroding the integrity of the church (see CHURCH INSTITUTIONS: 5), the legal system (see LAW AND LAWYERS: 2), the economy, and the culture of north Britain, turning a once-independent country into what Sir Walter Scott memorably called 'an inferior species of Northumberland'.

The peculiar sense of national identity that developed in this period and survived into our own age was distilled out of these two governing sets of hopes and fears. At one level, it gave rise to a preoccupation with the 'improvement' (see RURAL SOCIETY: 4)—or what we should call the modernization—of Scotland's economy and its civil and ecclesiastical society, something that meant drawing a backward country into a cosmopolitan world of commerce and politeness. At another, it gave rise to a pervasive fear that the progress of commerce and politeness was turning Scotland into an Anglicized province and this in turn made Scots sensitive to supposed political and cultural insults on the part of the English—particularly London. The campaign for the right to raise a militia during the Seven Years War and Scott's extraordinary Swiftian crusade against a clumsy attempt to impose English currency regulations on Scottish banks (see ECONOMY, TERTIARY SECTOR: 2) in 1826 are classic examples of a Scottish ability to view English policy shortcomings as national insults to be noisily avenged.

At the same time, the Scottish intelligentsia, led by the great historian William Robertson (see HISTORIANS: 3), embarked on an extraordinarily sophisticated and culturally successful attempt to rewrite Scottish history and to reconstruct the historical foundations on which the Scottish sense of national identity rested. Robertson showed that Scotland's ancient constitution had become archaic and redundant with the progress of civilization and that it had only sentimental and antiquarian relevance for the present. It was on such historiographical foundations that one of the central images of national identity that is characteristic of the 18th and early 19th centuries was constructed, the image of the bard who amuses his listeners by celebrating the glories of an heroic age, but warns them of the need to live in the present. This image was most famously enshrined in the figure of Ossian and adopted most memorably by Scott. It generated a popular historical literature which deeply penetrated the culture of the civilized world at a time when its fabric was being transformed by revolution, war, and the massive expansion of commerce. It was a literature which showed how a nation

could learn to celebrate its past without allowing this past to damage the prudential concerns of the present. It was a legacy which gave a once-failing nation a cultural reputation it could not have possibly enjoyed without losing its old political identity.   NP

5. the Victorian and Edwardian era

In this period national identity was an expression of loyalty, affection, and identification with the nation, however it was governed. Usually the wish is for the nation to be a nation state, a political ideal known as *nationalism, but this is not always the case. It has been argued in an influential book by Linda Colley, *Britons: Forging the Nation, 1707–1837* (1992), that British national identity had come to dominate by the beginning of Victoria's long reign in 1837. Yet in the Victorian and Edwardian eras in Scotland, loyalty to the state (British patriotism) coexisted along with national identity. Undoubtedly, a sense of British patriotism had fully matured in the years following the Great Reform Act of 1832, but a strong sense of national identity continued to exist within Scotland.

There had been a number of recent examples of radicalism, republicanism, and romanticism in Scottish national identity prior to Victoria's accession. In 1814, the republican-supporting David Steuart Erskine, eleventh Earl of Buchan, had constructed an imposing monument of Sir William *Wallace at Dryburgh. The bloodthirsty rallying cry to the memory of Wallace—'Scots Wha Hae', written by Robert Burns—was used to inspire throughout the unrest of the 1817–19 period and during the Radical War of 1820. In 1821 and 1822 George IV became the first Hanoverian monarch to set foot in Ireland and Scotland. The visit to Scotland was organized by Sir Walter Scott and instigated the laying of the foundation stone to the National Monument in Scotland commemorating the British dead in the Napoleonic Wars. It also led to the formation of Clan MacGregor for the first time for nearly a century who, along with the Celtic Society, were invited to guard the Scottish Regalia. The Welsh *Eisteddfodau* were patronized and Anglicized by the British gentry with the duke of Sussex (George IV's brother) in 1828 and the young Princess Victoria in 1832 attending. Victoria's interest in her Celtic domains was to be highly significant throughout her reign.

These events and processes contributed to the marriage of British patriotism with Scottish national identity. Victoria acquired the Highland estate of Balmoral in 1848, cementing the love affair of the gentry and elites with sport, leisure, and society in the Scottish Highlands. Victoria displayed great affection for the Highlanders in her employ at

Balmoral, commissioning watercolours of each (1865) and retaining a special regard for her personal servant John Brown. Her interest in Scotland did much to romanticize the Highland image and to make it the sign of Scotland, despite the experience for most Scots being an industrial and urban one. Mid-century Scottish nationalists also exploited this image and that of Scotland's heraldic honours when campaigning against the dangers of centralized government for Scotland's localities and its total share from the Treasury. The NAVSR (1852–6) feared that the centralization of government would lead to revolution in Britain as, they argued, it had done in Europe. Their nationalism supported the Union settlement only if it were enacted fairly and they expressed their national identity within a sense of loyalty to the Hanoverian monarchy and to what were essentially English constitutional traditions.

The balance of state and nation had been critical to the lead-up to the *Disruption in 1843 when the Free Church was created from those who seceded from the Church of Scotland. Historians have found it difficult to prove a direct link between the events of 1843 and explicit nationalist statements. Yet the events fractured the leading Scottish institution to survive the *Union of 1707 with England, and, in those terms, the Disruption impacted immensely on Scottish life and society, and therefore upon its national identity.

More explicit statements of Scottish national identity were made throughout the period. *Monuments were proposed or built to commemorate Sir William Wallace at regular intervals: Lanark (1820), Ayr (1837), Stirling (1838, 1846), Edinburgh (1859, 1929), and Aberdeen (1888) are some of the more notable examples. The National Wallace Monument Movement had been founded in Glasgow in 1856 from the surviving activists of the NAVSR. When the foundation stone to its Wallace Monument at Abbey Craig in Stirlingshire was laid in 1861, it was claimed that 50,000 attended; it was completed in 1869. Nor were other heroes neglected. The Scott Monument in Edinburgh was opened in 1846; the centenary of Burns's birth (1859) was celebrated by many events and by all classes; the 1846 centenary of Charles Edward Stuart's defeat at Culloden was commemorated only superficially (a stone monument was finally put in place in 1881). The 1880s witnessed a resurgence in *clan societies of a type different from those of the 1830s and 1840s. The new versions were strongly antiquarian in outlook, keen to place the *clan name at the centre of Scotland's historical past. They were helped by political change which pushed the issue of Home Rule (c.1880–c.1920) firmly on the agenda of all the major parties.

Yet Scotland's literary output in the years c.1880–c.1914 has been regarded as weak and immature (see CULTURE: 20). Referred to as Kailyard literature (cabbage patch or backyard literature), the product of émigrés, and consumed by the middle classes, it has been castigated as parochial, small-town-biased, backward-looking, and therefore symptomatic of a weakness in Scottish national identity. A counter-reaction took place in the 1920s with the publication of less celebratory, more urban- and industrial-based literature. Yet neither genre can be taken solely to represent Scotland's national identity. The number of reprints of Blind Harry's (see HISTORIANS: 1) 15th-century epic *The Wallace* had declined in the 19th century to be replaced by a surge in cheap and popular pamphlet and poetic tributes. Scotland's regional *newspapers kept up the use of Scots as a means of discussing contemporary concerns without this romantic downside.

Scottish national identity in the Victorian and Edwardian period was sustained in many different areas of society, some explicitly nationalist, some less so, and it coexisted with a strong sense of loyalty to the British monarchy, *British Empire, and British constitution.   GM

6. modern

National identity was thrown into turmoil following the end of the First World War. Many of the basic assumptions which had governed Scottish self-perception before 1914 were swept away. The carnage of the Western Front had dented pride in Scottish militarism. The gradual drifting apart of the *British Empire undermined notions of the Scottish imperial mission as the 'Workshop of the Empire' lay in ruins as a result of post-war economic dislocation. *Emigration which had been a source of pride in the pre-war era was now recognized as an escape from poor social and economic opportunities at home. The political landscape had also changed. The rise of Labour (see LABOURISM) demonstrated that the Scottish working class were more interested in bread and butter issues than grandiose middle-class notions that the Scots had special qualities as a race of empire builders.

It was in this changed environment that contemporaries debated the state of Scottish national identity. The impact of economic dislocation dealt a severe blow to Scottish national self-esteem. In addition to the social effects of mass long-term unemployment, Scotland ceased to be a major manufacturing centre as demand slumped for the products of the traditional Scottish heavy industries (see ECONOMY: 6). Scottish companies were prone to takeover, closure, and the 'southward drift' as industries relocated near the more prosperous markets of Middle England. Scottish industrial production in 1931 was less than it had been in 1913. For many at the time, it seemed that the Scottish nation was locked into a spiral of decline. As George Malcolm Thomson wrote in *Scotland: That Distressed Area* (1927): 'The first thing about the Scot is he is a man eclipsed . . . the Scots are a dying race.'

The social effects of economic dislocation made grim reading and were exacerbated by the impact of the Great Depression in 1929. In terms of health (see HEALTH, FAMINE, AND DISEASE: 3), *housing, overcrowding, and a whole range of social indicators (see LIVING STANDARDS: 3–5), Scotland was performing abysmally against the rest of the UK. Given the prevailing political orthodoxy of limited government intervention (see ECONOMIC POLICY: 4), it was believed that little could be done to solve the overwhelming social and economic problems which blighted inter-war Scotland. It was against this background that many voices were raised in protest at what was seen to be unfair treatment.

Whereas nationalism in the 1920s was associated with the left, from the 1930s many middle-class Scots began to join the chorus of disapproval which bemoaned the decline of Scotland. Although there were manifestations of *nationalism, the National Party of Scotland and its successor the SNP failed to mobilize this discontent into a significant political force. Yet, the leaders of the 'National' Government (1931–45) harboured fears that nationalism could emerge as a significant threat. It was in response to both the fear of nationalism and the general disquiet which surrounded the nation's perceived treatment at the hand of government that the decision was taken to move the *Scottish Office to Edinburgh in 1937. It was argued that this would bring the government of Scotland closer to the people and that it would act as an important focal point for Scottish national sentiment. In spite of this, the Scottish Secretary of State, Walter *Elliot, acknowledged that, until the social and economic problems were removed, nationalism would remain a potential threat.

The Second World War and massive state intervention provided Scottish politicians with the solution to the problem of how to make the Union work for the benefit of Scotland again. The war initiated an ideological revolution which held that it was the responsibility of the state to secure the economic and social well-being of its citizens. This idea was especially attractive to Scottish politicians because there was much for the state to do in Scotland. Ambitious reconstruction plans were drawn up in which the state would regulate the economy to provide full employment and provide welfare benefits for all Scots. Culturally, the war engendered a greater sense of Britishness through the use of state propaganda and the widely accepted notion of the 'island race' in a shared struggle against Nazi tyranny.

The period from 1945 to the late 1960s might be characterized as a 'New Britain'. Full employment, the Welfare State, and social reconstruction made it sensible for Scots to think of themselves as British and demonstrated that the Union could be made to work to their benefit (see CORPORATE STATE AND SCOTTISH POLITICS). Nationalism could offer little against the material improvements of the Union in this period, although the National Covenant in the late 1940s and the furore over the coronation in 1953 demonstrated that it was not entirely dead. When nationalism did come to the fore in the late 1960s and mid-1970s it was driven by economic discontent. Voting for the SNP was an ideal way to make British politicians sit up and take notice of Scottish concerns. Evidence for this can be taken from opinion poll surveys which showed that, even although the SNP was winning about 30 per cent of the vote, only 12 per cent believed in the flagship policy of independence. Further insights into the true state of political nationalism in the late 1970s can be gleaned from an examination of the devolution referendum which showed that the nation was divided on the issue of whether or not to have an assembly. In reality, most Scots wanted London government to deliver on the post-war deal which guaranteed state intervention to ensure social and economic well-being.

The advent of 'Thatcherism' in the 1980s initiated a major reassessment of both Scottish and British identities in Scotland. The attack on state intervention in the fields of social and economic policy, the so-called 'nanny state', meant that a core pillar of British identity in Scotland came under threat. From the 1980s onwards, Scottish and British electoral behaviour diverged with the Scots repeatedly rejecting the Conservative Party (see UNIONISM) at the polls. This was in spite of the fact that the socio-economic profile of Scotland moved closer to England, which in turn suggests that electoral behaviour north of the Border was being influenced by cultural notions of what Scottish voters believed to be acceptable political values. Increasingly defence of the Welfare State was portrayed as a Scottish value. For many, the solution to the problem of divergent Scottish and British or English political behaviour was the creation of a parliament in Edinburgh which would enable Scottish values to be expressed without being swamped by the Westminster system. An all-party Scottish Constitutional Convention was formed to press for this in 1988 and it was endorsed by the Labour government in 1998 with the passing of the Scotland Act. A Scottish *parliament opened in 1999.　RJF

nationalism is the outcome of the political mobilization of *national identity. Its clearest expression is as a parliamentary political movement which has the aim of obtaining or sustaining a state for a delimited geographical territory. The clearest definition has come from Ernest Gellner in *Nations and Nationalism* (1983): 'Nationalism is a theory of political legitimacy which requires that ethnic boundaries should not cut across political ones, and, in particular, that ethnic boundaries within a given state . . . should not separate the power holders from the rest.' The creation of the nation state is the end point for nationalist movements. This can take the form either of 'the struggle for independent nation-statehood', the project of the SNP in the 20th century, or the maintenance and stability of an already existing nation state, such as the oft-trumpeted constitutional coherence of the British state and its four nations of union.

Nationalism is attractive to many people for many different reasons. It is probably the most influential political ideology of the 19th and 20th centuries. Nationalists usually appeal to ethnic or monarchical purity throughout a historical past. Myth-histories (see HISTORIANS: 4) and the emphasis on what are commonly perceived to be decisive events in a community's formation are celebrated. Nationalists offer a dialogue between what is remembered and what is forgotten from a nation's history. We remember and celebrate our victories; we forget, or at most eulogize, our defeats. Once the nation is justified, self-determination is claimed on the grounds that in ancient times a particular people lived on a particular land, and this people were genetically, culturally, and religiously homogeneous. The appeal of nationalism is therefore an appeal to our human emotions—playing on what is vaguely described as natural, or moral, or of a lost golden age. It is about a homeland that is theirs or ours, one that is handed down from generation to generation. It is often expressed in terms of the *patria*, the national family (whether expressed as motherland or fatherland), which links the generations.

On balance, the weight of theoretical opinion supports the view that nationalism is a political doctrine which dates from the late 18th century. The *French Revolution is often acknowledged as a central touchstone linking the nation and the people through ideals of participatory democracy. Despite this view of the modernists, as its supporters are called, there is powerful evidence to sustain the view that national identity pre-dates the 18th century. It is counter-argued that nations and nation identity (meaning loyalty and attachment to the nation) are very old and indeed filter back to the earliest times. Recent opinion amongst this group,

the ethno-symbolists, tends to accepts the timing offered by the modernists, but maintains that nationalism cannot be formed independently of older ethnic ties and identities.

Whichever theoretical framework is used, all commentators on nationalism are referring to the transformation from personal, local, and *regional identities to national identity and to nationalism. This not only results in loyalty to the nation state, but it signifies wider social behaviour. An influential phrase of Benedict Anderson in his book *Imagined Communities: Reflections on the Origin and Spread of Nationalism* (1983) captures this process: it is the 'imagined community'. To say that the national community is an imagined one is not to say it is unreal, but is to explain how a group of people, of many millions, who will never meet each other, are able to identify with one another. Developments in communications, particularly the written word via the printing press, are important for beginning the process of diminishing concern with solely local affairs, promoting common national experiences in their stead.

Nationalism in Scotland gained its own political organizational identity with the formation of the SHRA in 1918, the National Party of Scotland in 1928, and the SNP in 1934. The SNP made its major political breakthrough in a by-election victory in 1967, but there had been signs of the nationalists doing well since the 1950s. By the October 1974 election the SNP took 30 per cent of the vote—their highest share at a general election to date. Although they claimed to be poised to gain as much or more of the vote at the elections for a new Scottish *parliament in 1999, they came a distant second, with 35 seats to Labour's 56.

The SNP has always done proportionately well among all social classes, but particularly amongst those who are socially and geographically mobile members of the lower middle and working classes (see SOCIAL CLASS). Yet at no time has there been a straightforward correspondence between support for the policy of Scottish independence and support for the SNP. In Scotland, outright hostility to the *Union of 1707 with England has always co-existed with significant support for that Union, and for Britain, although it remains contingent on Scotland's governance being prioritized or treated equally with that of England. This is a result of the terms of that 1707 settlement. Scotland was not conquered but instead gave up its parliament, as did England, to form a new parliament of Great Britain. This settlement also guaranteed the maintenance of Scotland's Presbyterian (see CHURCH INSTITUTIONS: 5) form of Protestantism as the established religion, its legal system (see LAW AND LAWYERS: 2), and its broad-based educational structure (see SCHOOLS AND SCHOOLING: 2; UNIVERSITIES: 2). These three institutions, so important to the governing and the ethos of Scottish life in the period from the Union until (at least) the establishment of the *Scottish Office in 1885, structured civil society in Scotland.

Civil society consists of these institutions which are not part of the state, but are more formal and impersonal than family or household associations. Because Scotland was a parliament-less nation from 1707 until 1999, civil society sustained Scottish nationalism until, and in part beyond, the formation of dedicated political nationalist parties. Within civil society, Scotland's nationalism has been institutionally based, rather than culturally rich. Because of the Union settlement, civil society has both carried a sense of difference within Scotland and, at the same time, deflected demands for political independence.   GM

natural history. Today's tourists may be impressed by the extent of Scotland's sparsely inhabited 'wilderness' areas, but they should not assume they are seeing 'natural' landscapes, free of the influence of people. Even the earliest human colonists of landscapes scrubbed clear by glaciation may have been changing the developing natural ecology, not only as other species do as incidental effects of their gathering and hunting, but also by deliberate modification of their environment. For example, not all the evidence of early conflagrations in Scotland's increasing forest cover may be due to strikes of lightning. Views differ, but ethnographic parallels suggest that non-agricultural communities find it profitable to torch woodland to create clearings where animals will come to graze on the new growth of shoots. There may thus have been a very early start to the modification of Scotland away from being a country which could support a dramatically greater amount of natural forest cover than we see today.

The growing populations of prehistoric and historic times of course made deliberate clearances for agriculture, house- and ship-building timber, and fuel. But sometimes their impact on the natural ecology was unintended or indeed not even realized. Much woodland disappeared, not because of felling, but because natural regeneration was prevented by domesticated animals eating up the seedlings. The complexity of some of the processes affecting Scotland's natural history is only now being understood. Thus, to show their zeal to protect grouse chicks on sporting estates, gamekeepers shot raptors. Without these natural predators, vole populations soared and prevented regeneration of woodlands by their extra consumption of seeds. With the loss of binding tree roots, serious soil erosion then occurred where slopes were steep.

The vulnerability of Scotland's environment to change has varied through time, partly reflecting climatic variations (see CLIMATE). For example, during cold wet phases, if established forest cover was disturbed, it might not recover if new growth could not survive without the sheltering microclimate lost with the mature trees.

Paradoxically, it is above the natural tree line that some of the longest surviving elements in Scotland's natural history may be observed. Until recently, the summit plateaux of the Cairngorms and Grampians saw little human activity. They have thus remained the home of flora and fauna, such as ptarmigan, which characterized Scotland when the latest phase of the Ice Age ended. There were reindeer, too, in Scotland then. These disappeared, presumably eliminated by human action since they have proved viable when reintroduced to the Cairngorm environment.

Scotland's commonest deer species is the red deer. Many are now stocked at unnaturally high densities in tree-less 'deer forests'. When restored to their natural habitat of woodland, they increase significantly in body weight. It has been suggested that wolves, which lasted in Scotland until the 18th century, might be reintroduced as a natural control on deer numbers but, unsurprisingly, sheep farmers do not favour this.

Sheep have undoubtedly been a major factor in the modification of Scotland's natural history, their selective grazing affecting the flora with complex ramifications for many classes of fauna. Popular perceptions of their impact are dominated by the *Clearances of the Highlands and Islands of the 19th century, still an emotive political issue, but the effect of managed flocks started in the neolithic and attained major dimensions in medieval times, not least through the internationally organized monastic order of Cistercians (see CHURCH INSTITUTIONS: 2).

Many of the deer now live on heather moorlands. Heather can be functional as well as being an emblem of historic Highland Scotland in tourist eyes. Managing grouse moors by burning produces habitats for rich ranges of insects and microorganisms, with different combinations inhabiting regularly burnt, infrequently burnt, and mature unburnt moors. Much of the heather moorland is in the eastern Highlands, and wet sedge-grass moors are more characteristic of western Scotland, high and low. The altitudinal limit between the zones with potential for tree growth and those permitting only montane types of vegetation declines markedly towards the north-west of Scotland. The effect of increasing oceanicity is exacerbated by both the latitudinal decline in temperature and exposure to very high windspeeds. Parts of the Outer Hebrides near sea level thus have 'montane' vegetation similar to that of the Grampian tops.

Wetlands and peatbogs of many different kinds used to be much more common, and this should be kept in mind in considering many aspects of Scottish history. The relative recency and severity of glaciation compared to further south in Britain had left a legacy of disrupted drainage, both by eroding rock basins and by leaving hollows in glacial and fluvioglacial deposits. The landscape was strewn with ponds and boggy patches which fostered a wide range of wildlife. Furthermore, when Scotland's isostatic recovery from the loading caused by the departed ice cover finally lifted Holocene estuarine clays above sea level, thick peats developed on their ill-drained and very extensive low-gradient surfaces. This, for example, made it problematic to cross north or south anywhere between Stirling and Lake of Menteith (see TRANSPORT AND COMMUNICATIONS: 1). Though peat was cut for fuel from prehistoric times onwards, in many parts of Scotland it was not until the 18th and 19th centuries that land clearance and drainage schemes made really major impacts on the landscape. These facilitated travel and agriculture (see RURAL SETTLEMENT: 3; RURAL SOCIETY: 4), but made radical changes in the natural history of many areas.

Peat cover on surrounding landscapes affects the ecology of many freshwater lochs. Their waters are often dyed deep brown by the run-off. Even on a sunny day, just 16.4 feet (5 m) below the surface darkness may be complete. Many lochs occupy steep-sided glacially eroded troughs, without shallow shelves which light could reach. With photosynthesis inhibited, the development of food chains is limited and the biological productivity is low, with few fish or eels to be caught.

The Powan is unique: a freshwater herring. At the end of glaciation, ocean water flooded into what is now Loch Lomond. Then isostatic recovery lifted the mouth clear of the sea, trapping shoals of herring. The dilution of the enclosed seawater by rainwater inflow was gradual enough for the herring to adapt. Sadly, they are now under threat of extinction by competition from escaped foreign species, live bait of anglers. One denizen of lakes and rivers which did become extinct in Scotland was the European beaver. Confirmed from prehistoric finds and documentary evidence until the 16th century, it might be reintroduced.

*Place names and documents show salmon were a valued feature of Scotland's economy for centuries; indeed there were complaints that they were too frequent an item of diet. They were caught at sea and in estuaries as well as rivers, and Scotland's estuaries offered a wide range of natural resources (see ECONOMY, PRIMARY SECTOR: 4), throughout the millennia before modern pollution: from shellfish to overwintering geese; from many species of fish to whales.

The prehistoric Forth was a veritable whale trap. Over twenty skeletons have been recorded from west of Falkirk, many indeed in the carse clay inland of Stirling, including several almost 98 feet (30 m) long. They were probably trapped naturally by fell, though artefacts and marks on bones show mesolithic people exploited the carcasses. It is not clear when actual pursuit of whales started in Scottish waters but, like seal hunting, it continued into the 20th century in the Northern and Western Isles.

Both prehistoric and historic evidence emphasizes the enduring human importance of the natural resources in the seas around Scotland. Besides being affected by different levels of exploitation at different periods, their availability has reflected variations in climatic and oceanographic factors. Thus cod require a particular band of water temperatures, and the variable behaviour of herring shoals made reliance upon them problematic long before the present era of overfishing; this helps explain why herring shoals disappeared from western seas between the 13th and 16th centuries.

For some communities, coastal birds rated highly amongst their resources. On St Kilda, the productivity of the bird cliffs was such that the islanders specialized in harvesting gannets, auks, puffins, and eggs, doing relatively little fishing even though the grounds there attracted fishermen from as far as Ireland and eastern Scotland.

The flightless great auk is known from Scottish sites. It eventually became entirely extinct, but some birds temporarily lost to Scotland have been reintroduced. These include such contrasting species as osprey, capercaillie, and white-tailed sea eagle. Others, such as the crane, have not been reestablished though recorded by archaeology and literary sources. Cranes are listed in a particularly vivid evocation of medieval ornithology, the scurrilous account by William Dunbar, James IV's court poet, of how all the birds of Scotland mobbed Damian, the Fenyeit Friar of Tungland, when he had the temerity to try to fly from Stirling castle in a feather suit. Sometimes human history can be illuminated by recourse to natural history. It is pleasant that the reverse can sometimes also be the case.

IM

Nechtan (Neiton), **son of Derile** (king of *Picts, c.710–29, d. 732). This king had a Pictish mother and a Gaelic father, Dairgart mac Finnguine, probably a member of the Cenél Comgaill of Cowal. He succeeded his brother Bridei, son of Derile, some-time after 706. The year 711 saw conflict between Northumbrians and Picts over the plain of Manaw, now the region around Falkirk; in 713 Ciniod, a brother of Nechtan's, was killed, and it is not until after this date that we can be sure that Nechtan was in control of the Pictish kingship. He faced growing challenges to his rule in the 720s, and entered a monastery in 724, resigning the kingship to Drust, but must have emerged from the monastery not long after, for Drust was obliged to imprison him in 726. Then began a fourfold struggle for the kingship, in which Nechtan continued to play his part, regaining the kingship briefly in 728, only to lose it to *Ungus (Onuist), son of Uurgust (729–61), nine months later. He died in 732.

Nechtan's reign is famous primarily for events relating to ecclesiastical politics. Bede records for us the details of correspondence between Nechtan and abbot Ceolfrith of Monkwearmouth-Jarrow concerning the dating of Easter. This correspondence gives us the impression of a well-educated king: Bede tells us in his near-contemporary *Ecclesiastical History* that Nechtan had been 'convinced by his assiduous study of ecclesiastical writings' that his kingdom should change their practice to the Catholic ('Roman') system of dating Easter, but wished further written details to help him refute opponents, and also asked for architects to build a church in stone. Ceolfrith complied with these requests, and Bede tells us that he enforced reform of Easter and also the tonsure throughout his kingdom, in all churches and monasteries, and dedicated his kingdom to St Peter, building a church to him.

This important testimony suggests strongly that the Pictish church was, at this stage, fairly fully developed, but also that the king (see KINGSHIP: 1) had strong authority over it. This correspondence began the close relationship between Pictland and Northumbria to which the art styles of the 8th century bear witness, especially on the 'Class II' Pictish cross-slabs, usually with hunting or battle scenes or genealogical details on one side of the stone and the Christian image of the cross on the other, such as Hilton of Cadboll or among the collection of Pictish stories held at St Vigeans Museum in Angus (see CULTURE: 2; MONUMENTS: 1). It is certainly these events which lie behind the 'expulsion of the family of Iona across Druimalban by Nechtan' recorded in 717. Significantly, this was after *Iona submitted to the new dating of Easter, but before it had changed its tonsure. Although it would appear that 717 represents hostility between the Picts and Iona, there are other interpretations. One is that this merely represents the exclusion of the authority of Iona over Pictish churches, a sign that the Pictish church

had 'grown up'. Another would see contemporary factions in Iona working alongside Nechtan in his reform of Pictland, and see his expulsion of the Iona *familia* in 717 as an attempt to pressurize them into full reform. If the latter is the case, it would appear to have worked.

Recent research has tended to see many of the ecclesiastical *place names in and around eastern Scotland as dating to the reigns of Bridei and Nechtan, the sons of Derile. Clusters of names containing the element *cill*- may be found in Easter Ross, Atholl, and east Fife, and these have links to individuals known to have been active in the decades on either side of 700, while the *both*- place names of west Fife and further west seem to tie in to the activities of St Serf of Culross, who is traditionally linked with Bridei, son of Derile. Furthermore, the dedications of some of the place names in *eccles*- to apostles such as John and especially Peter (d. Egglespether) suggests that these too may date from the opening decades of the 8th century. Place names would thus seem to confirm Nechtan's reign as one in which the pastoral infrastructure of the church had become increasingly secure. It has been suggested that Nechtan is the subject of the St Andrews sarcophagus. TC

Neill, A. S. (1883–1973), radical teacher. Born in 1883 in Forfar of schoolteacher parents, he left school at 14 having been judged by his father not to be academically capable of attending university. He occupied several posts as a pupil teacher while preparing to take the entrance examination of Edinburgh University, from which he graduated in 1912. He worked for a while in journalism in London, and then returned to Scotland as head of Gretna School in 1914. After a brief spell in the army in 1917–18, he was influenced by the ideas of what later came to be known as child-centred education (see CHILDREN). These fitted well with the hostility to didactic teaching which he had acquired as a pupil and a teacher in Scotland. Neill resolved to found a school modelled on child-centred ideas and, after several attempts, achieved this at Summerhill, first in Lyme Regis and then (from 1927) at Leiston in Suffolk. Summerhill not only sought to enable children to be autonomous learners, growing at their own rates rather than under the tutelage of adults; it also gave them and the teachers (although not the ancillary staff) a democratic role in the running of the school. Neill remained at Summerhill until his death; the school survives until the present day.

Neill's significance lies in his philosophy and his model of practice. Although he remained an outsider, he acknowledged the influence which some of his disciples had within the public system. He wrote in 1972 to the most noted of them, R. F. Mackenzie in Aberdeen: 'You must feel lonely amongst the local teachers who are so anti-life. I admire your sticking to the state system . . . I ran away from it' (see SCHOOLS AND SCHOOLING: 4).   LP

Neilson, James Beaumont (1792–1865), inventor of the 'hot blast' which revolutionized the production of iron in Scotland (see ECONOMY, SECONDARY SECTOR: 2). After a basic education, Neilson went to work in the Glasgow Gas Works where he became manager and head engineer. It was during this time that he became interested in the scientific application and manufacture of gas. In addition to his own observations in the Gas Works, Neilson attended courses at the Anderson University in Glasgow which augmented his scientific skill. His invention of the hot blast contravened accepted wisdom in the smelting of iron ore. It was believed that cold air assisted the process, based on the observation that smelting performed better in winter than summer. Neilson contended that the reason for this was that there was less moisture in the air in winter and that during the summer it was this dampness which held back the process. Neilson tested his theory by piping hot air, rather than cold, at the Clyde Iron Works in 1828. The result was a startling success. The greater efficiency of the hot blast meant that the abundant supplies of indigenous coal and blackband ironstone could be freely used in the production of iron. Neilson's invention removed the bottleneck which had held back the expansion of the Scottish iron industry and this is reflected in its spectacular growth from 5 per cent of British production in the early 19th century to 25 per cent in 1850. Unfortunately, Neilson did not benefit much from his invention. The idea was copied and attempts to use the legal machinery to acknowledge his patent proved fruitless. Also, many companies, such as *Bairds of Gartsherrie, took out licences but did not pay.   RJF

New Zealand. About 21 per cent of New Zealand's 19th-century immigrants came from Scotland. Over 90 per cent were Lowlanders. This statistic is a little misleading in that many immigrants' names suggest earlier Highland origins, but it is quite clear that Lowlanders, particularly from around the industrial centres of Edinburgh and Glasgow, dominated Scottish migration to New Zealand (see EMIGRATION: 4).

A few ventured to Wellington and Auckland in the 1840s, but most Scots came in three major waves: the 1850s to the Otago settlement; the 1860s to the Otago goldrushes (many via Victoria in *Australia); and the 1870s to Otago and Canterbury. The first wave were almost exclusively Lowlanders. It was only during the assisted migration of

the 1870s that Highlanders constituted more than 10 per cent of migrants. During these hungry years in the Highlands when migration to North America proved difficult, some individuals and nuclear families moved to New Zealand but whole clans never shifted to the deep south as they did to *Canada. Norman MacLeod's odyssey in which he led a large group from Scotland via Nova Scotia to Waipu was untypical. Smaller waves of immigration in the 1900s, 1920s, and 1950s reinforced 19th-century patterns.

Whether Highlander or Lowlander, very few of Scottish migrants wanted to return to any kind of feudal order, romantic or otherwise. Although generally people of only modest means (farm and general labourers, domestics, and artisans), few came from the lowest levels of Scottish society. Most held a little capital and were literate and respectable. These origins and attributes meant that nearly all were committed to modernity and capitalism. Consequently, Presbyterianism (see RELIGIOUS LIFE: 6) and Puritanism became very important components of New Zealand history. Equally important was the very tangible contribution which Scots made to the development of commerce, farming, and manufacturing. Even more important was the notion of rough equality brought in the cultural baggage of the majority of Scottish migrants. This desire for greater equality and democracy is readily observed in the emphasis placed upon educational reform, efforts made to secure greater gender equality, and in the careers and actions of a group of radical politicians largely of Highland background.

The disproportionate economic contribution is most easily demonstrated. Scots brought in capital in rough proportion to their numbers but were over-represented amongst entrepreneurs and bankers. This was especially so in the 19th century, when Dunedin served along with Auckland and Wellington as one of three dynamos within the New Zealand economy. John MacFarlane Ritchie, manager of the big Anglo finance company the National Mortgage Agency and solicitor for the Glasgow-backed New Zealand and Australian Land Company, was the most important of this group within the south. John Logan Campbell proved equally influential in the development of Auckland. William Soltau Davison, manager of the Glasgow-owned New Zealand and Australian Land Company, also deserves special mention for the key role he played in the development of the frozen meat trade. Ironically, the most remembered banker of Scottish origin, William Larnach, who built a large folly on the Otago peninsula misleadingly called a castle, was amongst the least successful of the Scottish entrepreneurs.

Scots were also over-represented amongst manufacturers, especially in the specialist field of woollen milling. In the case of John Roberts, money came directly from his father's mills in Selkirk. Others, such as the canny Caithness men John Ross and Robert Glendinning, were self-made. After establishing the successful Roslyn Woollen mills, they expanded their interests into runholding and coal mining.

Scottish engineers were over-represented within this profession in New Zealand. They built roads, bridges, railways, agricultural machinery, and goldmining dredges. Some such as A. and T. Burt and Kincaid and McQueen went on to establish heavy engineering works, especially in Dunedin and Christchurch. Reid and Grey of Oamaru were particularly successful manufacturers of farm machinery for the grain-growing estates of North Otago.

Scots were significantly over-represented amongst big 19th-century landowners, making up 40 per cent of persons owning estates of over 10,000 acres (4,050 hectares) in 1892. The majority came from relatively humble or middling origins. Watson Sheenan, for example, owner of the very profitable Conical Hills estate, bought himself a coat of arms even though he began life as an agricultural labourer. More typical were businessmen such as the Deans brothers of Canterbury and John Douglas of Mount Royal near Palmerston in North Otago. Those who made money in Australian sheep farming prospered most in New Zealand. One of the few vaguely aristocratic Scottish landowners, Robert Campbell of the Otekaike estate, fitted into this category. So too did the Maclean brothers, sons of an impecunious tenant farmer on Coll. They ran the largest of the runs (large sheep farms held on leasehold from the crown) in New Zealand of about 1,000,000 acres (405,000 hectares). Later, John went on to own the 20,000 acre (8,100 hectare) Redcastle estate at Oamaru and Allan bought the 48,000 acre (19,440 hectare) Waikakahi estate. Allan soon rose to become the second wealthiest man in New Zealand, leaving an estate in 1907 valued at over £600,000. Others such as George Rutherford and Donald Reid came straight from a farming background in Perthshire. Rutherford soon owned a large estate in the Amuri district of North Canterbury and Reid a large property on the Taieri plain near Dunedin. Reid also profited from the goldrushes by establishing a successful stock and station agency. Another group made sufficient money from army service in India to own large estates in New Zealand.

Scots were much more heavily over-represented amongst farmers who operated on a more modest scale owning about half of the farms of over 100

acres (40.5 hectares) in 1882. Overall, Margaret Galt's unpublished doctoral research on wills and estates confirms that by the First World War Scots had accumulated a share of the nation's wealth out of proportion to their numbers.

The other area of significant over-representation occurred in both local and central government. Scots became involved from the beginnings of settlement and succeeded in tempering English domination of the political system even though the legal system had always been essentially English. The democratic ethos at the heart of Presbyterianism inspired several leading radicals, while even more conservatively inclined politicians of Scottish origin supported educational reform and the promotion of greater opportunities for girls. A dialectic emerged in Otago between the conservative utopianism of Captain William Cargill and the more democratic notions of Revd Thomas Burns, nephew of Robert. Cargill's thesis persists in subtle ways, but Burn's antithesis won out during the 19th and early 20th centuries.

Burns promoted the notion of a fair day's pay for a fair day's work from the beginnings of the Otago settlement in 1848 and Donald Reid subsequently advocated closer settlement of the land. The Shetland-born politician Sir Robert Stout built on these initiatives, even if he produced more radical rhetoric than action. He abandoned Presbyterianism to become New Zealand's (and one of the world's) first 'freethinking' prime ministers and, in conjunction with his remarkable wife Anna (New Zealand born but of Scottish descent), and another radical of Highland extraction, Robert McNab, succeeded in passing some of the most progressive legislation anywhere on women's rights to inherit property and to receive more equitable divorce settlements. He and Anna also brought control of the practice of incest out from the confines of canon law into the civil code as early as 1900.

Even though few migrants came from areas of the Highlands cleared for sheep and deer, John MacKenzie, the land reformer from Easter Ross, set out to break up the great estates and so avoid repetition of the Highland *Clearances. He had some success and certainly assisted New Zealand farming to restructure and modernize its practices with a minimum of social dislocation. Although a social conservative, he supported promotion of girls' secondary education in Oamaru. The Aberdonian James MacAndrew had earlier played a vital role in opening Otago Girls High School in 1871. This was one of the first state secondary schools for girls in the world. The University of Otago also admitted women from its establishment in 1869.

The problem with radicals such as MacKenzie, Stout, and the fiery rhetorician Alexander Hogg, however, was their blindness to Maori aspirations to develop their own land by themselves. These 19th-century Scots radicals, along with the great majority of British settlers, viewed Maoris as a bar to progress and judged them incapable of becoming capitalist farmers, despite earlier Maori success in commercial farming. They helped dispossess Maoris of their land almost as effectively as the English and Lowland Scots dispossessed the Highlanders, a paradox unnoticed by MacKenzie and most other Highland settlers.

The most important Scottish radical in the 20th century, the Labour leader Peter Fraser, fared rather better in this respect. As a Highlander born only a few miles away from the place of MacKenzie's upbringing, he identified with the plight of Maoris and did his best to help them reassert their rights and regain control of their destiny. Fraser also worked with a young educationalist, Clarence Beeby, to overhaul New Zealand's education system in the late 1930s so that it operated for the public good rather than private gain and made secondary and tertiary education accessible to all New Zealanders at extremely low cost.

Since Fraser's death in 1950 the Scottish connection has weakened considerably, although Scots would probably be sensitive to the irony that the man who attempted to overturn all the reforms of both the Liberal and Labour governments and head back to Adam Smith's vision of a world controlled by market forces, is named Roger Douglas.

The other side of Scottish radicalism was puritanism, which inflicted rigid moral codes on sexual behaviour and subjected New Zealand to uncivilized drinking patterns. This repressive code, however, did stimulate the emergence of a distinctive New Zealand literature in rebellion against its rigidity and provided some women with a clear sense of psychological satisfaction by establishing prescribed gender roles. Ironically, the education received by daughters of Scottish immigrants subverted these codes and Presbyterian women seem to have been the first systematically to control their fertility.

Scottish conservatives seemed much less distinctive. Some, such as the founding father of the Otago settlement Captain William Cargill, were doggedly pugnacious, but most differed little from their English-born equivalents. Sir James Wilson, foundation president of the New Zealand Farmers' Union, promoted afforestation and Sir Thomas MacKenzie, prime minister for a few brief months in 1912, helped found the Forest and Bird Protection Society.

Outside the arena of entrepreneurship, farming, religion, education, and politics, distinctive Scottish influences are harder to discern, partly because

the demise of the *Gaelic language by the 1930s removed the most obvious cultural marker. Nevertheless, the Scottish influence is identifiable in naming of both places and individuals, in architecture and modification of landscape, and in music and literature. Place-naming in New Zealand seems rather random but concentrations of obviously Scottish names can be found in areas where Scots migrants dominated. Dunedin (the Anglicized Gaelic name for Edinburgh) shares many of the same street names as Edinburgh and Scottish names abound throughout Otago and Southland. Sometimes they are a little contrived, as in the case of Invercargill, and upon occasion they are melded with a Maori name as in the case of Ben Ohau. Nearly a fifth of southern high country 'runs' have Gaelic names, reflecting the crucial role played by Highlanders as shepherds and managers in these areas.

Scottish personal names seem about equal to the percentage of migrants within the overall population, although the high degree of intermarriage between Scots and Maori means they are nearly as common within the Maori as the Pakeha (white settler) world. Christian names come and go with fashion but Robert, Andrew, and Graham remain firm favourites amongst boys, while Margaret and Fiona are still popular amongst girls.

Queen Anne towers as well as more typically Balmoral types of architecture are easily spotted in Dunedin. Presbyterian churches (SEE CHURCHES: 3) are not unlike their Scottish equivalents and First Church in Dunedin is said to be similar to St Giles's in Edinburgh, despite its own colonial peculiarities. Masons from Caithness or Orkney built the drystone walls above Dunedin and stone cottages in treeless Central Otago. Even so, wooden villas and bungalows originating from Melbourne, California, and India are the predominant form of domestic architecture.

The Edinburgh influence can also be seen in Dunedin where the founders left an area known as the 'green belt' to act as a kind of cleansing lung for the city. Similarly, the urban improvement movement which grew out of Edinburgh and Glasgow had an impact from the late 1880s, when concerned citizens established an Amenities Society and set about beautifying the city and removing slums.

The practicality of Scots is also reflected in their distinctive patterns of acclimatization. They introduced trout and salmon into Otago whereas the English leaders of Canterbury concentrated on game birds such as partridge and quail. It was not mere coincidence that a Highlander in the person of John MacKenzie made certain that the game laws of Britain were not duplicated in New Zealand, nor that he ensured everyone had access to hunting and fishing opportunities in his Land Act of 1892.

Highland bagpipes were brought by solo pipers, especially in the 1860s and 1870s, when most Highlanders migrated to New Zealand. These players assumed a high profile at annual Caledonian sports gatherings (see CALEDONIAN SOCIETIES) and from 1896 began to form themselves into regimental-style pipe bands (see MUSIC, HIGHLAND). Both solo pipers and bands still perform on ceremonial occasions; over a century of development certain kiwi inflections have emerged.

Jessie MacKay tried valiantly at the turn of the century to combine Maori and Gaelic mythology in verse. The efforts of this early feminist and Scottish nationalist were popular at the time but changing stylistic preferences mean that she is little appreciated today. Amongst New Zealand's leading literary figures, obvious Scottish influences can be readily discerned only in the work of poet James K. Baxter. He generated much of his energy by attacking the narrow puritanism of Free Church Dunedin. His whisky-distilling and bagpipe-playing McColl and Baxter ancestors represent life-affirming character in his mythic world. New Zealanders of Scottish extraction clung to the literary works of Robbie Burns, Sir Walter Scott, and Robert Louis Stevenson until the resurgence of New Zealand writing in the 1960s.

Overall the Scots ensured that New Zealand became a different kind of country from Australia, at least before the Second World War. Their influence on the economic, social, political, and cultural life of the new country was subtle yet discernible. What could be more Scottish? TB

newspapers: 1. to 1900; 2. since 1900.

1. to 1900

Dating from the mid-17th century, the Scottish newspaper press developed rapidly following the removal of the 'Taxes on Knowledge' in the mid-19th century. The first Scottish newspaper, dating from 1642, was the *Diurnal Occurances* (Edinburgh)—a reprint of London reports on parliamentary activities. Thereafter, following some short-lived Edinburgh publications between 1640 and 1660, the Scottish press developed apace in the early 18th century, with the foundation of the bi-weekly *Edinburgh Courant* (1705); Glasgow's first newspaper, the tri-weekly *Glasgow Courant* (1715); the *Caledonian Mercury* (1720); and the *Glasgow Journal* (1729). Scotland's most famous dailies, however, date from the mid-late 18th and early 19th centuries, with the *Aberdeen Journal* (1747); the *Glasgow Herald* (originally the *Glasgow Advertiser*), dating from 1783; and the *Scotsman* (Edinburgh), established in 1817. By 1855, the circulation of the

Glasgow Herald approached 561,000 per annum, and outwith the central urban centres, significant growth was also apparent. By 1860, around 50 titles were produced in Scotland. Growth continued in the late 19th century, encouraged by the development of the railway infrastructure (see TRANSPORT AND COMMUNICATIONS: 2), the exploitation of telegraphic technology, increased capital investment in the industry, the improvement of Scottish education (see SCHOOLS AND SCHOOLING: 4), and the adoption of high-speed presses. By 1875, the *People's Journal* (established 1858) alone could boast sales of around 130,000 a week—an impressive circulation which would soon be eclipsed by the *Daily Record*, established in Glasgow in 1895—the first ½ d. morning paper in Great Britain.

Local loyalties, the development of foreign correspondence in the Scottish dailies, the relative lack of Scottish news in the London press, and earlier distribution problems faced by the metropolitan titles in the north of the country, guaranteed a healthy future for the native press in Scotland into the early 20th century. However, by the inter-war years, amalgamations, closures, and the encroachment of English interests in the north were becoming more apparent. By the late 20th century, the number of separate Scottish titles had declined to around 160, and despite the success of Scottish-owned titles like the *Sunday Post* (proprietor D. C. Thomson, Dundee) with weekly sales of over one million, many Scottish newspapers were reliant on external ownership and investment. Still, even in the early years of the 21st century, newspapers produced in Scotland dominated sales in the north, played a significant role in shaping public opinion, and—in association with other popular media—did much to assert the peculiarities of Scottish *national identity. CMMM

2. since 1900

At the turn of the 20th century the principal form of communication within Scotland about current affairs, social events, sport, and other leisure activities was through either the newspaper or other weekly printed journals. The predominance of the printed form of communication in conveying such information remained virtually unchallenged by the arrival of the radio (see RADIO AND TELEVISION: 1) in the early 1920s. Although radio did devote time within its schedules to 'news bulletins', restrictions operated as the result of an agreement with newspaper proprietors and prevented a serious challenge to their hold over the dissemination of information. The BBC radio during the Second World War did attain a degree of authority in its bulletins and other current affairs programmes which began to rival the newspapers' position (the shortage of newsprint reduced their size), but it was not until the late 1950s, with the arrival of independent television (see RADIO AND TELEVISION: 2) to complement BBC television programmes, that newspapers found a serious rival in mass communication which affected circulation. The arrival of colour television and a second BBC channel in the 1960s, together with television's increased technical ability to display global images almost as they happened, further reduced the hold of printed communication. Scottish newspapers, like those elsewhere in the western world, found the public's appetite for information changing and both the format and style of papers that remained in circulation altered, with generally less attention given to the detail of events and more attention given to the style of presentation (headlines), photographs (now in colour), and commentary. Nevertheless, newspapers in the first two-thirds of the 20th century form a major and unparalleled source (see HISTORICAL SOURCES: 3) of information on events (whether political, economic, or social), on those in the news, and on the general milieu of the period.

Although 'morning' UK papers such as The Times and the Daily Telegraph were available to Scottish readers (brought north by the overnight train service) and did have a substantial readership, their coverage of Scottish events was relatively sparse. The leader columns of The Times, however, remain a useful source information on 'semi-official opinion' on the state of Scottish society and politics and its published index on its contents is an invaluable guide in itself. On one occasion in 1953, the day before the Permanent Secretary of the Treasury gave evidence to the Royal Commission on Scottish Affairs in camera on the disadvantages of political devolution, the paper published a leader almost paraphrasing the Permanent Secretary's views. A number of UK papers, such as the Daily Express and the Daily Mail, published Scottish editions for most of the period, combining Scottish with UK and overseas news, and these provide a useful source of information on coverage of events by the more popular press. The same is true of purely Scottish popular papers such as the Daily Record. In general, from the 1920s, the popular press, whether the left-leaning Daily Record or the right-wing Scottish Daily Express, attained a considerable mass circulation by the skilful use of storyline, often aimed at social rather than political events, the more widespread use of photographs, and a substantial amount of space devoted to sport.

Quality morning Scottish newspapers had been in circulation since the early 1800s, but by 1900 there were only four of any note in terms of circulation, each based in one of the four major cities and their hinterland. The Glasgow Herald held the

largest circulation and was generally regarded as Scotland's foremost newspaper in terms of its coverage of events and its ability through its leader columns to represent Scottish industrial and business opinion. Indeed the *Scottish Office always looked to the paper first if it required information on Scottish events and on the opinion of the Scottish business community. Thus during the Scottish Covenant movement of the late 1940s (see NATIONALISM), Scottish Office memoranda to the cabinet borrowed heavily the tone, if not the words, of the anti-devolution stance of the paper. (The paper's sub-editor, Alastair Hetherington, was, in fact, the brother of the official who first drafted the cabinet papers.) It also heavily promoted the post-war plan (see ECONOMIC POLICY: 4; SCOTTISH COUNCIL (INDUSTRY AND DEVELOPMENT)) to rejuvenate the Clydeside economy by a planned programme of new towns and overspill settlements (see URBAN SETTLEMENT: 4). The Glasgow Herald's index of contents (1906–68) provides a useful and unique guide to virtually any contemporary subject of interest and can complement other indexes of the period, such as the parliamentary Hansard.

The Edinburgh-published Scotsman was less well regarded, partly because its leaders in the inter-war and immediate post-war period were more stridently anti-labour and in favour of strict financial orthodoxy than Scottish policy seemed to demand, but also because its news-gathering within Scotland tended to be more restrictive. However, a change of editorial policy in the late 1950s (after the paper had been bought by the Thompson international publishing firm), which saw it seeking a wider Scottish readership and adopting state-interventionism as a response to Scotland's economic problems, resulted in the paper being more seriously read by Scottish Office ministers and officials.

The 'quality' newspapers generally devote more space to current affairs than the popular press and usually give almost verbatim accounts of the public and other meetings in Scotland that its journalists attend. Such, together with the local weekly papers, give an invaluable source of information of the activities and views of a wide range of people, whether national or local politicians, trade union and business leaders, local officials such as medical officers of health, those involved in sport, and others who hold prominent positions within Scottish society. It is the general policy of these newspapers to provide reasonable space for the comment of individuals in news items, irrespective of their opinion, even if it differs from that held by the paper's editorial policy. In that respect, the papers represent the rawness of contemporary opinion better than perhaps any other source, whether from their reporting of the unemployment riots of the early 1920s to the crisis in Scottish football after the infamous 1960 Hampden European Cup match between Real Madrid and Eintracht Frankfurt. Finally, these papers also chart out, through their advertisements, the various changes in contemporary habits and purchasing preferences, from the arrival of labour-saving household goods to Mediterranean holiday destinations (at the expense of those in Scotland) and the appearance of the bungalow (see HOUSING: 3) as the ultimate status symbol of the Scottish middle class (see SOCIAL CLASS).

IL

nobility: 1. early medieval; 2. medieval; 3. 1500–1700; 4. post-1707.

1. early medieval

In the early Middle Ages, throughout Britain, the key to nobility was the possession of landed wealth. Since all the peoples of Scotland practised the equal division of inheritance between brothers it was very difficult for households to maintain a pre-eminent position in their districts over several generations. There were two mechanisms open to rich men to ensure that their wealth continued to grow rather than diminish. On a local level, the wealthy could encourage their poorer neighbours to mortgage their own farms to them in return for loans of livestock, seed-corn, or other necessities, in the hope that a significant number would fail to meet their repayments and be forced to forfeit their land (see ECONOMY: 1). At a wider level the powerful attempted to win the favour of the king and get a share of the property which came his way through judicial forfeiture and conquest. This latter policy encouraged the concept of a nobility of service. Young men of good families would be sent to serve in the retinue of the king or queen and would hope to be endowed, after five or ten years' service, with an estate of their own. The belief that the king, as an effective judge and war leader, would provide plenty of land to share out amongst his leading followers was the main motivation for powerful men to support the institution of *kingship. It also governed their preference for one candidate for the kingship over others.

By the end of the 8th century the kings of the Northumbrians and the *Picts (the latter probably following the former) seem to have developed this system of patronage in such a way that no longer required them to constantly alienate their own lands. When kingdoms had been small-scale affairs the size of Fife or Lothian (in the 6th and early 7th century) much of the kings' sustenance had come from tribute in foodstuffs delivered by the freemen of the kingdom to the nearest royal villa or estate centre. The king would then travel round with a

small retinue eating each villa's pantry empty in turn. By AD 750 the Pictish kingdom and Northumbria were both vast agglomerations of half a dozen or so of the earlier small kingdoms. The kings could no longer visit every royal villa in a given year or season. Instead the institution of 'thanages' was set up, whereby a young nobleman awaiting his family inheritance would take up residence temporarily at a royal villa and, maintaining himself and his staff on the royal revenues of food renders from the surrounding district, would also administer royal justice in that district. The district dependent upon a royal villa was known by the Northumbrian word *scir* (modern 'shire'). In contrast to the traditional system, which still continued to some extent, a king's thane would be expected to vacate the royal villas when, upon his father's death, he came into his own inheritance. His tenure as thane, however, allowed him to start his own family earlier than might previously have been possible and to make important connections with influential men in both the royal service and in the district where he had held his thanage.

Another Northumbrian innovation which seems to have been adopted by the Picts was that of the 'Great Steward'. The provinces which had formerly been independent kingdoms within both Northumbria and Pictavia maintained their own discrete identities and characters. An intermediate level of administration was introduced between the king and the local nobility in the form of the 'Great Steward' (Northumbrian *heah-gerefa*, Pictish *mármaer*, Gaelic mormaer). We know nothing of the family origins of these men so it is hard to tell if they were the descendants of the former royal houses of these provinces, cadet members of the new royal families, or nobility of service—perhaps this varied from province to province.

Thanes, shires, and mormaers survived the transition from Pictavia to Albania, c.900, and from Albania to Scotia, c.1100, and formed the backbone of the medieval Scottish kingdom. AW

2. medieval

Historians have not been kind to the medieval nobility, at least from the 15th century onwards. Writers have depicted them as a disruptive and negative force in Scotland's development, residing in massive strongholds, defying the crown, and committing violent and lawless acts at the head of private retinues. More recently, however, more rounded accounts have stressed the importance of the nobility in the management of a decentralized and diverse society like medieval Scotland. Rather than being seen as violent and reactionary, the ability of the noble estate to act responsibly and conservatively and to regulate local society has been stressed. An accurate assessment needs to consider both the positive and negative elements of the nobility's reputation.

As with many other facets of medieval Scotland, the aristocracy, its composition and values, were fundamentally altered during the 12th century. In a process which was largely sponsored by King *David I and his grandsons Malcolm IV and William I 'the Lion', lords from the French-speaking nobilities of England, Normandy, and Flanders were encouraged to settle in Scotland and given extensive estates in many parts of the kingdom. Families like the Bruces, Stewarts, *Comyns, and *Douglases arrived in Scotland as part of this process and great lords brought lesser men in their wake, rewarding them with land in turn. The arrival and promotion of such men changed Scotland. Structures of law, language and landholding, warfare and settlement were all shaped by the importation of a relatively small number of men and their aristocratic values (see FRANCO-SCOTTISH RELATIONS: 1).

Similar changes took place in many parts of Europe between the 11th and 13th centuries but in Scotland, unlike the rest of the British Isles, they occurred, not in the form of external conquests, but by influence. Much of the personnel of the Scottish nobility remained in place and retained their importance in the kingdom and in their respective provinces. Though the kings did break up the great province of *Moray and grant it to outsiders to the region, all the other earls, from Lennox and Fife to Buchan, and the provincial rulers of *Galloway responded to change by adaptation. Like the kings, they encouraged settlement by Anglo-French outsiders, while maintaining their place at the head of provincial Gaelic-speaking societies (see ISLES, LORDSHIP OF THE). Even in the far west and the Hebrides, where royal authority was at its weakest, the symbol of aristocratic power was the mounted knight, indicating the influence of the new aristocratic culture (see ARMY: 1; WARFARE, WEAPONS, AND FORTIFICATIONS: 1).

In most of Scotland, by the mid-13th century distinctions between native and newcomer were being eroded by time and intermarriage and instead of racial origin, what defined this nobility was their ties of allegiance to the king of Scots. However, while these ties formed the framework of aristocratic politics, they were not the only factor. The Comyns, Stewarts, and earls of Ross pursued lands and lordship in the west on their own behalf as much as the king's, while the lords of Galloway remained independent figures in the west until the end of the native dynasty in 1234. As the minority of Alexander III showed, once the bond of personal royal lordship was removed, the ties of family allegiance, inherited rights, and personal ambition determined aristocratic behaviour. Furthermore, this nobility was not purely Scottish in outlook or interest. Almost all the principal vassals of the Scottish king held some lands in England, while many English magnates had Scottish estates. Families like the Bruces and *Balliols had strong interests in both kingdoms by the 1280s and owed obligations to two royal lords (see ANGLO-SCOTTISH RELATIONS: 2).

In the peaceful 13th century this caused few problems. However, the problems of dual allegiance in the years of crisis for Scotland after 1286 have led to a traditional view of the Scots nobility as lukewarm or duplicitous in their defence of the Scottish kingdom (see INDEPENDENCE, WARS OF). Events like the capitulation of Bruce and Stewart to the English in 1297, the desertion of the Scots cavalry before Wallace's defeat at Falkirk in 1298, and the catalogue of aristocratic submissions to England encourage such perceptions. Instead it has been suggested that the true upholders of Scottish resistance were lesser men, the 'middle folk', squires or freeholders, the level of society which produced William *Wallace. Such a picture is misleading. Aside from Wallace's brief period of leadership, the Scottish cause was directed by great magnates. To these men, Robert Bruce, John Comyn, and others, this cause was about the defence, not of abstract national sentiments, but of the laws and rights, lands and followers which gave them their status in Scotland. Rather than being purely self-seeking, in the 1300s such attitudes were seen as the maintenance of the structures which defined the Scottish realm.

Aristocratic loyalties were further complicated by the dispute over the throne between Bruces and Balliols which threatened to erupt into civil war from 1286 and finally did so in 1306 and again in 1332. *Kingship, the force which had created the medieval nobility, became a source of rivalry and division, increasing the uncertainties of aristocratic life. In these conditions, the price of miscalculation could be disastrous. Even the greatest family of the 13th century, the Comyns, paid for their hostility to the Bruce dynasty with loss of lands and expulsion from the kingdom. In their place *Robert I raised his own men, promoting squires and knights, barons and earls who had backed his cause. At the top the main beneficiaries were the king's allies, Walter Stewart, Thomas Randolph, and James Douglas. The value of aristocratic support was shown after Bruce's death when it was the families of Stewart, Randolph, and Douglas which upheld the Bruce family's claim to the throne.

The hundred years from Robert I's death in 1329 were the century of the great magnate. In the absence of effective royal authority for much of the period, families like the Douglases, the MacDonald lords of the Isles, and the Stewarts were able to accumulate lands and influence allowing them to dominate various regions of the kingdom. The Douglases, for example, developed their role as defenders of the *Borders from English attack, using their military exploits to claim a special place in the kingdom and to establish rights to command extensive armies of retainers from southern Scotland. When Robert Stewart ascended the throne in 1371 after a long career as a magnate, it marked the merging of aristocratic values with royal government. By his death he had distributed lands and power amongst his sons and forged marriage alliances with most of the leading noble dynasties, transforming the Scottish polity into an extended family.

This concentration of aristocratic power into the hands of a very small elite perhaps inevitably created pressures. Lesser noblemen were dependent on the goodwill of one great magnate, while ambitious barons may have resented the dominance of one or two families. Most importantly, the hereditary possession of royal rights and offices by men like the earls of Douglas and dukes of Albany placed extreme limits on the crown's authority. The advent of kings who appreciated this difficulty from 1424 caused three decades of tension and conflict between the crown and its greatest noble subjects which brought about the greatest change in the structure of the nobility since the 1300s. In the course of this both the Black Douglas earls and the Albany Stewart family were eliminated, while a total of eleven earldoms had passed, temporarily or permanently, to the crown. The beneficiaries of this upheaval were not just the crown but also a group of baronial families. Families like the *Gordons, *Hamiltons, *Campbells, Scotts, and Grahams were ancient members of the nobility, but had always been of the second rank. The removal of the greatest magnates by royal action altered this. Instead of half a dozen great magnates, the nobility was headed by 30 to 40 lesser lords. While the collective resources of the nobility were not much altered by this change, it widened the gap between the crown and individual nobles in terms of resources, and between the crown and nobility as a class (see KINGSHIP: 5).

The history of the medieval nobility is, though, not simply confined to the rise and fall of its greatest members. As a class, the nobility included families of vastly differing incomes and importance from royal princes and rulers of provinces to the owners of a single, small estate. Unlike other realms, the issue of noble status and the qualification for that rank was never a major source of dispute or litigation in medieval Scotland. The lack of any clear definition of nobility is also suggested by the absence of a division between lords and commons in *parliament, where those present who were neither clergy nor burgesses sat as a single estate. The poorest of those claiming nobility would probably fit into the group labelled 'middle folk', indistinguishable from other freeholders and rooted in the local communities to which they belonged.

Perhaps the key to noble status lay in the connections possessed by even minor landowners. Someone like Thomas Dicson, a tenant of the Douglases, was rewarded for his support of James Douglas in 1307 with new lands at Symington and his family became the hereditary keepers of Douglas castle. Though they remained a family of minor and local importance, Thomas's descendants were unmistakably noble, their status proved by the office they held, the small estate they had been given, and above all by their connection with the house of Douglas. Great magnates, like the Douglases, had vast estates and large revenues. They were, however, not simply plutocrats. Throughout the Middle Ages, the importance and power of a noble family was measured less in financial terms than as lords of men. The number and type of men who served a lord was the measure of his strength. Obligation to serve a lord could be based on a grant of an estate to a lesser man. This might specify that the new tenant owed military service to his lord but, even when it did not, such a gift formed a bond of service between the granter and the recipient. Less formal connections also existed. Cash fees or gifts of food were frequently dispersed by lords to their retainers, whilst links of kinship were continually seen as a crucial element in alliances between greater men and their less fortunate relations. By the 15th century, written agreements of lordship and obligation, called bonds of manrent, had begun to appear, formalizing some relationships between lord and man.

The functions of these relationships were manifold. The lord sought to build and maintain his affinity, the men he could call upon. Tenants, kinsmen, and allies would provide the basis of the retinue he led to war, either in the host or in his own interest. They also backed him in political and judicial affairs and provided him with servants to run his estates, keep his castles, and serve in his household. The possession of a large following was the chief measure of rank and an instrument of power. The efforts by kings to limit the size of such households was a mark of the threat they posed. In return, lesser men gained protection and support. The backing of a great lord like Douglas or Albany would guarantee success in local disputes, while his hostility created problems.

The household was not simply a political or military body, but served as the framework of aristocratic society. Its head was by no means always male. Great noblewomen possessed separate establishments from their husbands, while widows, like Devorguilla, lady of Galloway, in the 13th century or Isabella, duchess of Albany, in the 15th, ruled their own provinces and participated fully in the politics of the kingdom. The household also served as a place of entertainment. Works like Barbour's *The Brus*, Richard Holland's *Buke of the Howlat*, and Gilbert Hay's *Boke of Knighthood* were designed to appeal to noble audiences, encouraging pride in martial and dynastic achievements and the values of aristocratic society (see CULTURE: 3; ROYAL COURT: 1). As patrons of literature, supporters of the church, and the focus of local society in medieval Scotland, the nobility was a determining force in the development of a distinctive Scottish state and society.   MBr

3. 1500–1700

The most powerful social group in early modern Scotland was the nobility. In a society imbued with the values of tradition, its traditions were among the most prestigious, notably the chivalric virtues of loyalty, honour, and martial valour, and the kin-based reverence for ancient lineage. In a predominantly *rural society, when economic power rested on income from rent-paying peasants, the nobility had the lion's share of the rental income. And in a society with no state monopoly of political violence, it was the nobility who organized themselves and their followers for warfare, both public and private. The early modern period saw one of the biggest-ever shifts in the nature of the nobility, as private warfare was eliminated and the nobles learned that their martial role would be exercised only at the behest of the state.

The nobility was hard to define. Contemporaries usually thought of it as the titled peerage, which had established itself as the pre-eminent aristocratic group in the mid-15th century. This consisted mainly of lords and earls; gradually viscounts (1606 onwards), marquises (1599 onwards), and dukes (1581 onwards, but rarely) were added. There were 49 peers in 1500. In the 16th century, ennoblements only just exceeded natural wastage. The number had reached 57 by 1599, of whom only 6 were new or promoted; but in that year a flood of ennoblements began. When the flood slackened, in 1633, Scotland had 102 peers of whom 43 were new or promoted. Slow growth continued, and by 1700 there were 136 peers of whom 21 were new or promoted.

Below the peers were an increasing number of lairds who are also integral to any understanding of the nobility. Their economic power came from the same source as the peers (landed rents), they possessed similar jurisdictions (often baron courts) along with their lands (see LOCAL GOVERNMENT, TO 1707), and their royal charters often proclaimed them, like the peers, to be feudal tenants-in-chief of the crown. Lairds, or at least larger lairds, were 'lords', and in many ways were themselves nobles. But great lords had clients who were themselves smaller lords. The most significant political division within the landlord class was not between peers and non-peers as such, but between greater lords who had clients and lesser lords who were clients. Nevertheless, most greater lords were peers, while most lesser lords were not. Peers were not exempt from direct taxation, unlike in many Continental countries, but they did have special privileges: formally, in personal membership of *parliament and increasingly lucrative customs exemptions, and informally, in ease of access to the monarch. Nobles did not have to be peers, but it helped.

In the 16th century, nobles' client networks were military alliances aiming to defend their lands and to wrest more from neighbours. Disputes about landed property often became matters of honour, so that neither side could back down and violence would break out. Killings called for vengeance, and blood feuds persisted for years and even generations. Blood feuds were settled through negotiation and compensation based on a code of honour; royal justice, if involved at all, usually did no more than ratify the outcome. Fighting was normal when the nobility perceived itself as a warrior elite.

Nobles could also fight in royal service, which helped to legitimize their military role. The 16th-century crown (see KINGSHIP: 5–6) had no *army of its own; royal armies consisted of nobles and their armed followings, unpaid. Nobles regarded their lands and honours as rightful rewards for this service. In their localities, they governed. A nobleman protected his clients, took counsel from them, and settled their disputes, just as the monarch protected the realm and took counsel from his nobles. For much of the 16th century, royal minorities meant that Scotland was run by regents who were neither willing nor able to disrupt noble self-government. The one regent who was, Mary of Guise, was overthrown in 1560 by an aristocratic coalition that ushered in the *Reformation. Many nobles initially supported the Reformation, but the Protestant church's criticisms of noble violence, and hostility to nobles' possession of former church property, discouraged nobles from becoming 'godly magistrates' (see RELIGIOUS LIFE: 3).

The nobles remained social and political leaders, but the growth of a more integrated state in the late 16th and early 17th century forced them to abandon their autonomous military role. Law courts (see LAW AND LAWYERS: 1), notably the Court of *Session, offered an attractive and peaceful (if costly) dispute-settlement service that eventually made aristocratic armed followings redundant. *James VI and the church (see CHURCH INSTITUTIONS: 3) both attacked the blood feud as barbarous. After a crucial law of 1598 calling for feuds to be submitted to royal justice, nobles were actually executed for vengeance killings. By 1625, feuding had largely been stamped out, at least in the Lowlands where it mattered to the state. Nobles' armed retinues withered, and their castles became comfortable houses with largely symbolic fortifications.

Despite his curbing of the nobles' autonomous military power, James VI was not hostile to the nobility as such. He and Charles I cultivated a special partnership with the nobility, whose client networks they relied on for royal service; this is one reason for the flood of peers they created. After the *Union of the Crowns in 1603, nobles could still obtain direct access to the *royal court, whereas others had to go through the privy council in Edinburgh. Yet despite the union, Scottish nobles remained a homogeneous social group. Few married English heiresses or became Anglicized. Nor did they marry Highlanders until the late 17th century, by which time Highland chiefs (see CLANS OF THE HIGHLANDS AND ISLANDS: 2) had lost their autonomy and were trying to enter the Lowland nobles' world. On the other hand, the aristocratic elite was always international, and Scottish nobles served many foreign crowns including Denmark and Sweden (see SCANDINAVIA: 3), England, *France, the Dutch Republic (see LOW COUNTRIES), and Spain (see also MERCENARIES IN EUROPE).

The Covenanting revolution of 1638, like the Reformation, initially attracted many nobles, but the revolution they wanted was a distinctly moderate one. Their ties to the crown kept them more royalist than other sections of society (foreshadowing the widespread aristocratic *Jacobitism of the 18th century). In the Wars of the *Covenant, nobles commanded regiments, reviving a version of their military role, but the Covenanters' supreme commanders were professional soldiers rather than traditional aristocrats. The nobility found its composition further modified as such men gained peerages. After 1638 a standing army came into being. Now that it monopolized fighting and paid its officers, traditional aristocrats discovered the attractions of the military career, anticipating the post-1707 rush into the army. Some of the nobility was still a warrior elite, but warfare was now a specialized branch of state service.

The nobility's political role also became specialized. Many nobles were politicians, many were army officers, but few were both. When politics focused on parliament rather than the crown—in the Covenanting period 1638–51, and again after the 'Glorious' Revolution of 1688–9—nobles formed political alliances and marshalled their clients into parliamentary groupings aiming to win votes. While peers found personal membership of parliament convenient, the leading politicians' main characteristic was not that they were nobles but that, in an age when government was the preserve of the rich, they were the rich.

As landed estates ceased to function as sources of fighting men for their lords, there was increased concern that they should provide cash. Greater nobles probably benefited less than lairds from the mid-16th-century feuing movement that transferred church lands to the laity. By the end of the century the nobles faced financial crisis. After the cost of the royal court was removed from the Scottish treasury in 1603, the crown could come to their aid, and it did, pouring out royal revenues in a spate of pensions and gifts to leading nobles. Yet conspicuous consumption, particularly necessary at the court in England, meant that the nobles were never free of financial worries even before 1638; and heavy taxation and forfeitures during the 1640s ruined many. In the late 17th century there was some recovery, and the balance of economic advantage tilted back towards larger estates. Some nobles supplemented their rents by rural enterprise: grain and cattle exports, and also coal mining, iron smelting, and salt manufacture (see ECONOMY: 3; ECONOMY, PRIMARY SECTOR: 1). This indicates the scale of the transformation that had occurred: such estate management would have been unthinkable in 1500. While the nobles were the keenest supporters of the parliamentary *Union of 1707, many were hoping that union would benefit their business activities.   JG

4. post-1707

The Union roll of the Scottish peerage was 154 in 1707. By Article XXII of the Act of *Union of 1707, sixteen members of this nobility were to sit in the House of Lords in the new parliament of Great Britain at Westminster as 'Representative Peers of Scotland'. The decision to make representation of the nobility at Westminster elective was an extraordinary one. A hereditary peerage embracing the principle of elective representation was quite novel in early modern Europe, and the Scottish peerage elections were unique in British constitutional practice until the union with *Ireland in 1801. The nobility continued to lead the landowning class which dominated Scottish society and politics until the middle of the 18th century, although the wealth and influence of individual members varied widely. This was a period punctuated by two Jacobite rebellions after which 26 peerages were forfeited for treason. A substantial number of these titles were later restored as *Jacobitism became romantic history rather than an absolutist rebel threat, but the forfeitures reduced the role of the nobility in the north-east of the country and in the central Highlands, allowing the emergence of local leadership in public affairs and in agrarian improvements from non-noble landowners.

Many members of the Scottish nobility, of course, were obscure even in 1707. The British Treasury Secret Service Accounts from 1754 to 1762 recorded annual payments of £150–£250 to 'Lord Morton's Lords'—Lord Rutherford, Lord Kirkcudbright, and Lord Borthwick—described by Lewis Namier 'as noblemen on the dole or on old age pensions' (*The Structure of Politics at the Accession of George III*, 1957 edn.). The political leadership of the country, however, was in noble hands after 1707 as Whig magnates such as the *Campbell dukes of Argyll, *Hamilton, Montrose, and Roxburghe vied for influence while the earl of Mar, the earl of Panmure, and the various lesser nobility ended up flirting with Jacobitism. The second duke of Argyll, a soldier, defeated the Jacobites at Sheriffmuir in 1715, and eventually he and his brother came to exert a degree of influence in Scotland that marked a quite extraordinary status in the public life of the country until 1761 (see GOVERNMENT AFTER THE UNION, 1707–c.1750).

The Hamilton affair of 1712 in which the House of Lords at Westminster refused to allow Hamilton to sit within it by virtue of his British peerage became a defining moment in the post-Union history of the Scottish nobility, condemning them for ever to secondary status to the English peerage. In fact the Hamilton decision was doubly insulting. Not only was Hamilton refused entry to the House of Lords by virtue of his British peerage, but his British peerage was held to disqualify him from the right to vote in Scottish peerage elections. At the same time, English nobility who held a Scottish title were entitled to vote by proxy in Scottish peerage elections, an issue which led to opposition to the government by a group of 'independent' Scottish peers such as the duke of Buccleuch from 1768 to 1780. The removal of this restriction in 1782 marked the beginning of full assimilation for the Scottish nobility as potential equals to the nobility of England in British terms.

After 1782 the Scottish nobility, in many ways led now by the third duke of Buccleuch and the fifth duke of Argyll, represented more thoroughly than perhaps any other group in Scottish society the aspiration of British assimilation, allied with the secure sense of place and status within Scotland that

came with the hereditary ownership of land. By the end of the 18th century the Scottish nobility were less directly involved in politics and to a great extent more involved with estate management, as typified by the third duke of Buccleuch's career as paternalistic landowner and military leader of volunteer and militia regiments recruited from his estates for home defence (and possible use against domestic radicals) during the Napoleonic Wars.

Political change during the 19th century brought some diminution of status for the Scottish nobility, but the *Disruption of the Church of Scotland began the acceleration of the detachment of the nobility from a leading role in Scotland (see ELITES IN MODERN SCOTLAND). In religion, more and more members of the Scottish nobility became Episcopalian (see EPISCOPALIAN COMMUNITY) or Roman Catholic (see ROMAN CATHOLIC COMMUNITY) rather than Presbyterian. Unlike their 18th-century predecessors, more and more of them became absentee landowners, or even sold their estates. There were always exceptions, but by the end of the 19th century landowning in Scotland was no longer closely identified with the Scottish nobility either in regions like the Highlands suffering acute dislocation or in areas such as the Midlothian coal field, where paternalistic management by factors employed by aristocrats gave way to joint-stock control to maximize profit for the commercial investor. Some members of the nobility continued to play a part in public life in Scotland during the 20th century, and some families such as those of Argyll and Buccleuch continued to hold substantial estates, but as a national group the nobility were very much part of a British peerage by the end of the 20th century, by which time they all could sit in the House of Lords at Westminster, joined by an increasing number of Scottish life peers recruited to that house from the ranks of politicians, professionals, and public servants.   AJM

northern England and southern Scotland: Roman occupation.

The Roman occupation of Scotland and England north of the Tyne-Solway isthmus extended over some 150 years, but was both chronologically intermittent and geographically variable. Occupation of any substantial part of the area was limited to some 40 years spread over three separate episodes, with the primary focus lying to the south of the River Tay.

Credit for the conquest of Scotland and northern England is usually assigned to Julius Agricola, the action occurring over five years of his governorship between AD 79/80 and 83/4. A good deal is known of his activities because of the survival of a brief eulogistic biography by his father-in-law, the historian Tacitus. This account, which inevitably stresses Agricola's role, has greatly influenced modern interpretations. Preliminary campaigning in the area, however, probably occurred in the governorship of one of his predecessors, Petillius Cerialis, early in the 70s. Thereafter the conquest seems to have been something of a stop-go affair as emperors and policy changed. Agricola's campaigns culminated in 83/4 in the battle of Mons Graupius, somewhere in north-east Scotland, at which the final resistance of the Caledonians was crushed. This was followed by a circumnavigation of the island by the Roman fleet.

Consolidation of the conquest, involving the building of forts and roads, seems to have followed immediately after each year's campaign. In 80/1 a relatively short-lived frontier was established across the Forth-Clyde isthmus, probably extending northwards along the Roman road up to the crossing of the River Tay, before advance was resumed. The most northerly forts subsequently founded skirted the southern edge of the Highland massif and included the legionary base at Inchtuthil in Perthshire. Yet by 87 Roman occupation had been withdrawn to the southern Uplands, the northern forts had been abandoned, and the legionary fortress dismantled even before its construction had been completed. By shortly after the turn of the first century Roman occupation did not extend north of the Tyne-Solway isthmus.

The establishment of Hadrian's Wall, begun in the early 120s, also saw outpost forts located on the fringes of the Lowlands, but the Romans did not return to occupy Scotland until the reign of Antoninus Pius. Reconquest began probably in 139, shortly after the accession of the new emperor, but with a more limited objective. The reoccupation of the Lowlands seems to have been completed by 142, culminating in the construction of a linear barrier, the Antonine Wall, across the Forth-Clyde isthmus, with outpost forts extending northwards as far as the River Tay. With some minor fluctuations, the details of which are still a matter of debate, this occupation continued until the late 150s or mid-160s.

The third and final Roman occupation of Scotland was even more short-lived. Between 208 and 210 the Emperor Septimius Severus conducted campaigns in Scotland either personally or through his elder son Caracalla. Only two garrison posts are known to have been occupied at this time, at Cramond on the Forth and Carpow on the Tay, but neither seems to have continued in use for more than a year or two after Severus' death in 211. Thereafter the Roman frontier reverted to Hadrian's Wall and its outposts in northern England, though some would still argue that Rome maintained political control through the supervision of tribal meeting places within the Scottish Lowlands. Subsequent campaigns into Scotland were solely punitive exercises and did not result in any further attempt to occupy territory.

Roman contact with the indigenous population, however, was not restricted to the battlefield, nor should relations be regarded as uniform. The recovery of Roman artefacts from native sites attests to more peaceful interaction, either in the form of trade or diplomatic exchanges, though such contacts seem to have been restricted to the periods of direct occupation and to the elite members of native society. Indeed, there are hints that some tribal groups, notably the Votadini and Venicones, may have been less overtly hostile to the Roman presence than others. The coins which attest to contacts outside the periods of Roman occupation relate either to the payment of subsidies to certain tribes, such as the Caledonians and Maeatae, to maintain the peace, or to the acquisition of booty from raiding.

The influence of geography and topography on the conquest and occupation of Scotland is becoming increasingly apparent. Though Roman armies traversed north-east Scotland as far as Moray, perhaps marching back through the Highlands, no Roman forts are known to have been constructed north of the Highland boundary fault. Such a disposition is the minimum necessary to ensure the inclusion of virtually all agricultural land considered to be of first-class quality. The attraction of the Forth-Clyde and Tyne-Solway isthmuses as transverse lines of demarcation and communication is unsurprising. Less obvious are the geographical factors which influenced other strategic dispositions. Outpost forts were located beyond the Forth-Clyde frontier along a road which follows a natural routeway north through the Stirling gap and then eastwards to the Tay, a pattern of dispositions which occurs in both the 1st- and 2nd-century occupations.

Though the location of forts must have been linked to political geography, to facilitate the control of recently conquered tribal groups, it does not seem to have been dictated primarily by population density. Lowland areas of Scotland, such as Fife and East Lothian, which show the greatest density of native occupation, do not appear to have been provided with Roman garrisons. There are, on the other hand, remote military posts where location seems to bear little relationship to the local population. The overriding criterion evident in the location of Roman installations seems to be the control of movement. Forts were invariably disposed at regular intervals along natural lines of communication, usually following river valleys. They were often positioned at river crossings, confluences, or other key topographical positions, such as at the mouths of glens (see GEOLOGY AND LANDSCAPE).

Clearly the Roman presence in Scotland was primarily military in nature. The only non-military personnel would have been those resident in settlements immediately outside the forts. Though the existence of such settlements (*vici*) is generally assumed to have been the norm, they appear at Scottish sites infrequently, particularly in the 1st century, and have rarely been examined archaeologically.

The impact of the Roman presence continues to be debated, but the general picture remains one of broad continuity. Extensive deforestation and substantive changes in the settlement pattern can no longer be attributed to Rome, while extensive depopulation cannot be substantiated. The impact of the military demand for foodstuffs and other resources remains difficult to calculate. These could have had either a stimulatory or depressing effect depending upon the potential for increasing local productivity, but the periods of Roman occupation are now considered too short-lived to have brought about major change. However, the amalgamation of a tribal-based social structure into larger political units during the later 3rd and 4th centuries may have been an indirect result of interaction with Rome. Our understanding of the Roman occupation of Scotland is heavily reliant on archaeological evidence. As such, it is open to sometimes widely variant interpretations, not only of its nature and effects, but even of its fundamental chronology. Indeed, the latter has seen quite dramatic changes in the last 30 years and continues to undergo intermittent adjustment. It is one of the inherent characteristics of archaeology that a single new discovery can result in quite fundamental reassessment.   WSH

northern Europe: monks and scholars. Apart from trade, the most active and consistent channel of communication between Scotland and northern Europe was provided by the clergy (see CHURCH INSTITUTIONS: 2; RELIGIOUS LIFE: 2). The new reformed religious orders of the 12th century—Augustinians, Cistercians, and Premonstratensians—were all French in origin. They brought to Scotland and after the reign of *David I (1124–53) successive waves of foreign monks, such as the austere Tironensians whose headquarters was at Tiron near Chartres. With other orders, however, including the Cistercians whose mother house was at Cîteaux in Burgundy, most of the first monks came from houses already established in Norman England (see ANGLO-SCOTTISH RELATIONS: 2). There is thus only partial truth in the saying that every Scottish monastery was 'a little bit of France'. Yet the impact was greater than merely that of clerics for alongside the monks came lay brothers and masons. And the link between mother and daughter houses was real: Cistercian abbots attended regular meetings at Cîteaux and it was the duty of the abbot of the mother house to visit each part of his monastic empire every year. By the reign of Alexander III (1249–88), however, most of the clergy, both religious and secular, were native Scots. The 15th century saw a new wave of incomers with the founding by James I of Scotland's one and only Carthusian monastery, the great charterhouse at Perth, and the establishment of a dozen friaries of the new, stricter order of Observant Franciscans, founded in the *Low Countries in the 1440s. Again, the patronage was royal: in this case, James II's Burgundian princess, Mary of Gueldres (or Gelderland). Clerics in this period were amongst the most important patrons of art and architecture (see CULTURE: 8) as well as conspicuous consumers: the elaborate Beaton Panels and the Fetternear Banner, commissioned respectively by Cardinal Beaton and by Gavin Douglas while dean of St Giles's in Edinburgh, both now housed in the *Royal Museum of Scotland, are testimony to the diversity of their taste. And it was no surprise that it was the higher clergy, with their established contacts in the Low Countries and *France, who during the minority of James II acted as brokers in the process of putting the young king's tribe of sisters on the European marriage market.

Traffic in the other direction was regular. Before Scotland had its own *universities, Scots attended universities in Italy (see MEDITERRANEAN LANDS IN THE MIDDLE AGES) and England especially. By the 15th century, many gravitated towards the new and more conveniently situated universities of Louvain and Cologne, situated close to well-established trade routes (see STAPLE PORTS; GERMANY, THE BALTIC AND POLAND: 1). In the third quarter of the 15th century, the Scots, while making up only a fraction of the student population, were probably prominent out of all proportion to their numbers; they made up a majority of the *pauperes*, clamouring for bursaries. Even after the founding of three universities in 15th-century Scotland, training in civil and canon law remained prerequisites for the career of ambitious churchmen and this could be obtained only abroad. By the early 16th century, more and more Scots were going to the University of Paris. Two of the most notable were John Mair and Hector Boece (see CULTURE: 4). Mair's career took him to Cambridge, Paris, Glasgow, St Andrews, and then again to Paris. Boece, logician and philosopher as well as historian, left Paris in 1497 to return as principal of the new university of Aberdeen.

461

These wandering scholars brought back to Scotland the culture, taste, and fashions of their alma mater. The fierce debates between nominalists and anti-nominalists at Paris and Louvain were reproduced at St Andrews in the half-century after 1475. Similarly, the heresy trial at St Andrews in 1528 of Scotland's first Protestant martyr, the precocious scholar Patrick Hamilton, could have come as no surprise to John Mair, who had seen similar devil's advocates overstep the mark in theological debates at the University of Paris. If it was clerics with European contacts who were amongst the first to spread Protestant ideas, it is equally unsurprising that a virtual generation of various kinds of clerics and schoolmen with Protestant sympathies fled abroad in the later 1530s and 1540s. Very few returned; John *Knox, in this as in so many other things, was the exception. Most, like John Macalpine (Maccabeus) or Alexander Alane (Alesius), remained in exile, making significant contributions to reformations in northern Europe, especially in Scandinavia and Germany. If scholars' networks in the trade routes brought Protestant ideas, they also provided the route for early attempts at a Counter-Reformation by orthodox Catholic reformers: Archbishop Hermann von Wied's reforms in Cologne provided the touchpaper for the attempts by the provincial council of the Scottish church in the 1540s and 1550s to recover ground lost to heresy on the eve of the *Reformation.

The traffic in scholars and clergy did not end with the Reformation of 1560. Andrew *Melville went to Paris in the early 1560s and ended up in Calvin's Geneva, under the tutelage of Theodore Beza. Many more went to the Huguenot *académies* such as Montauban and Saumur, as well as Heidelberg, after the Palatinate went Calvinist in 1583. But by the 17th century, most Scots, now budding lawyers and doctors as well as clerics, went to the Netherlands. It was only with the gradual elimination of Latin as the medium of instruction in Dutch universities in the course of the second half of the 17th century, which produced a novel Balkanization of scholarship, that the phenomenon of the Scots academic who found better paid and more prestigious employment in foreign universities began to disappear. Scholastics stayed at home, thereby helping provide George Bernard Shaw with ammunition for his dictum: 'For brains and religion, you need'st go to Scotland; that is why it is the most damnable place on earth'.

ML

Onuist. See UNGUS.

oral history. The term 'oral history' gained wide currency in the 1960s and in the decades following for the use of personal experience and inherited information, orally transmitted and recorded on tape, as a source of evidence in studying the past, with associated techniques of collection, documentation, analysis, and presentation drawn from a variety of disciplines in the arts, humanities, and social sciences (see ORAL TRADITION).

In Scotland, however, and particularly but by no means exclusively in the Gaelic-speaking Highlands and Islands (see HIGHLANDS AND ISLANDS: GENERAL), the centrality of the oral tradition for knowledge and understanding of family and community history has long been attested and can be said to have a pedigree extending back to the medieval period. Among the learned orders of medieval Gaelic Scotland were historians and genealogists whose role in the household of chief, noble, or gentry was to act as a repository of data relating to family descent and exploit. The *seanchaidh* who is said to have recited the king's pedigree in Gaelic at the inauguration of Alexander III in 1249 provides a dramatic instance of such activity, an image echoed in Richard Holland's *Buke of the Howlat* two centuries later. Poets too, were provided with patronage for composing *bardachd* in praise of the living and the dead and song became and has remained a vital source of contemporary witness and attitude.

With the restructuring of Gaelic society in the 18th and 19th centuries, the patrons of the historian and the bard came to be their peers in the crofting townships which replaced the farms held by joint tenants or by sub-tenants of a resident or non-resident tacksman. The individual skilled in the knowledge of genealogy (see HISTORICAL SOURCES: 4) and family and township history continued to play a valued role. For example, as long as the tradition of the funeral invitation persisted, with its strict protocol invoking connections past and present, it was important to have guidance on matters of *càirdeas is comain is eòlas* (relationship, obligation and acquaintanceship) relating to the deceased and his or her predecessors (see CALENDAR AND SEA-

SONAL CUSTOMS). The township bards found subjects in contemporary individuals and events. Their satire and their praise continued to be a potent reflection of their own society's values and an essential source for historians on topics such as the land agitations or emigration.

In Scotland as a whole, the parish ministers who contributed to Sir John Sinclair's systematic, country-wide survey of life in the 1790s, the OSA, and those which followed, might well be described as oral historians. As requested, they not only gathered current data but provided comparative material from 50 years earlier, though the digests of their findings contain little in the way of direct quotation. The Revd Mr Lachlan MacKenzie's 'Statistical Verses' in his account of the parish of Lochcarron in volume 13 may reflect something of the human interaction in that information-gathering process.

Collectors such as John Francis Campbell of Islay (1821–85) and those who assisted them often were at pains to take down by hand verbatim the tales and other oral traditions, along with contextual information relating to society and culture, supplied by their interviewees. But it was the advent of the recording device, particularly as it became more and more portable, which marked the commencement of oral history work in Scotland as it is known today. The acknowledged pioneer in mechanical recording of this kind was John Lorne Campbell of Canna (1906–96) who, with his wife Margaret Fay Shaw, undertook from the 1930s extensive collecting work among tradition-bearers in the Outer Hebrides and elsewhere, including autobiographical accounts, most notably that of Angus MacLellan (Aonghus Beag) of South Uist.

The School of Scottish Studies, founded in 1951 at the University of Edinburgh, also began from the outset to record contextual data referring to material and oral culture, songs, tales, music-making, custom and belief, and *place names, while the collections of the Linguistic Surveys of Scotland (Gaelic and Scots), initiated slightly earlier, also include information which may be termed oral history. The School's commitment to developing the use of oral evidence for community studies was reinforced by the appointment to its staff in 1966 of

Eric R. Cregeen (1921–83). He had been responsible for a systematic folk-life survey of the Isle of Man, following principles established by the Irish Folklore Commission. Subsequently, while resident tutor in Argyll for Glasgow University's Extra-Mural Department, he had begun to investigate the rich vein of oral history and tradition in the area, most notably on the island of Tiree, in combination with written sources such as the Argyll Estate papers.

In 1978, with colleagues in the SRO (now the NAS) and elsewhere, he was instrumental in founding the Scottish Oral History Group (SOHG), some years after the creation of the Oral History Society by Paul Thompson (University of Essex) and others. The SOHG continues to encourage oral history work and promote good practice through its conferences, workshops, and publications. The Scottish Labour History Society also aimed from the start to make oral history a priority and the pioneering work of Ian Macdougall merits special mention.

Milestones in the expansion of oral history activities in Scotland include the schemes funded by the Manpower Services Commission and the BBC Radio Scotland series *Odyssey: Voices from Scotland's Recent Past* produced by Billy Kay and published first in two volumes (1980 and 1982) and subsequently in a combined volume (1996). Projects have been—and continue to be—carried out by individuals and a wide range of groups and local and national institutions in all parts of the country, including the Workers' Educational Association, the Scottish Working People's History Trust, unions, museums, libraries, archives, local history societies, schools, community education and development auspices, hospitals, professional bodies, and the European Ethnological Research Centre (National Museums of Scotland). Universities have embraced this important resource for exploring their own histories in undergraduate curricula, postgraduate research, and projects and centres, including the Scottish Oral History Centre at Strathclyde University. Publications with oral history content proliferate and the millennium has provided an incentive for BBC projects as well as local, regional, and national initiatives.

Oral sources give a voice in Scottish historical studies to people, groups, and subjects absent from or inadequately represented in documents or other forms of evidence. As with these, appropriate methods of use and analysis are essential and Eric Cregeen's words from the *Scottish Oral History Group Newsletter* of October 1979 remain valid: 'They demand from those who use them not only enthusiasm and wide sympathy for the human condition but an alert and critical judgement and sufficient detachment to weigh the recorded testimony.' MAM

oral tradition: 1. general; 2. collectors.

1. general
Oral tradition in Scotland in its broadest definition covers all the forms of narrative, song, belief, and practice, including the present wide range of community languages, that are passed down verbally. The current practice in Scottish ethnology, however, is to interpret the term as 'verbal art' (folk tales, legends, songs, oral poetry, proverbs, riddles) through the living indigenous languages, together with custom and belief (see CALENDAR AND SEASONAL CUSTOMS), and *place names. There has been a developing interest in the areas of performance and performance occasions, verbal/visual memory techniques, and the 'economy of language', but the emphasis in publications has continued to be on synchronic and diachronic views of the *song and oral narrative traditions associated with the Scots and Gaelic speech communities.

From a 20th-century perspective, both the indigenous languages of Scotland possess storytelling traditions that are remarkable in western Europe for their variety and the degree to which they have survived alongside modern institutions. Folk tales in Scots cover the area from the *Borders to Shetland, with a wide variety of legends concerning witchcraft, fairies, seal-people (seals who join human society for a time, only to assume their former appearance and return to the sea), ghosts, Burkers (accounts of body-snatchers based on the notorious activities of William Burke and William Hare in the early 19th century), origins, and historical events being well represented. Examples of the more widely known international tale types are also present: animal tales, wonder tales (*märchen*), and tales of cleverness and stupidity, particularly the travellers' popular Jack-tales. The first mention of storytelling in Scots is in *The Complaynt of Scotland* (Paris, 1550), which names tales that appeared in print for the first time in Robert Chambers's *Popular Rhymes of Scotland* (1826). Also from the early 19th century are Walter Gregor's descriptions of storytelling events on a working farm in Banffshire (*An Echo of the Olden Time from the North of Scotland*, 1874), where the fare was mainly legends. Hamish Henderson's discovery in the 1950s of folk tales among the marginalized travelling people, notably Jeannie Robertson (1908–75) and the Stewarts of Blairgowrie, added greatly to the 30 Scots versions of wonder tales known previously, yielding such important examples as 'The Green Man of Knowledge', a Scots variant of 'The Magic Flight'. Traveller storytellers, among them Willie MacPhee, Stanley Robertson, and Duncan Williamson, continue to recite their tales to a high standard and are much in demand by audiences and researchers.

Gaelic storytelling in Scotland is closely linked to that of Ireland, deriving to some degree from a tradition of professional storytellers belonging to the medieval Gaelic learned orders. The Common Gaelic aristocratic tradition was not entirely an oral one, but is better understood as the product of a complex interaction between oral and written modes of transmission. Toward the end of the 17th century with the demise of the Gaelic nobility in Scotland (see CLANS OF THE HIGHLANDS AND ISLANDS: 2) and the consequent collapse of the patronage system, a repertoire of elaborate tales survived in oral versions among the population and continued to be recited by a few storytellers until well into the present century. Among the materials retained were complete versions or parts of heroic tales, for example, the epic *Táin Bó Cualnge* ('The Cattle Raid of Cooley') and the story of Deirdre from the early medieval Ulster Cycle; stories from the Finn cycle; and the (late medieval) romantic hero tales *Conall Gulbann*, An Ceatharnach Caol Riabhach ('The Lean, Grizzled Ceatharnach'), *Fear na h-Eabaide* ('The Man in the Cassock'), and *Leigheas Coise Céin* ('The Healing of Cian's Leg'). Not all of these prestigious tales, which are unique to Gaeldom and often incorporate motifs or storylines borrowed from international tales, can be traced to manuscript originals, but their characteristics—for example, the frequent use of 'runs' (passages of elaborate, largely alliterative, archaic-sounding language)—often indicate they were once literary romances. Also prominent in reciters' repertoires is a large variety of international tales, often with close counterparts in Ireland, which can reach a considerable length. Animal tales such as 'The Theft of the Butter (Honey) by Playing Godfather', together with formula tales along the lines of *Biorachan Beag agus Biorachan Mór*', were generally intended for children, unlike the ordinary folk tales which were recited in a *céilidh* setting to a mixed audience. These occasions routinely featured tales of magic (wonder tales), 'The Dragon Slayer' being a prime example; religious tales, of which some like 'The Sinful Priest' derive from medieval exempla; versions of romantic tales (novellas) such as 'The King and the Abbot' or 'The Old Robber Relates Three Adventures to Free His Sons' which can originate from literary as well as oral sources; jokes and anecdotes, generally considered of lesser consequence by reciters but comprising numerous evolved and full-length tales, for example, 'The Rich and the Poor Peasant' and 'Whittington's Cat'.

The clan sagas, a variety of historical legend, serve to distinguish the repertoire of Gaelic Scotland from that of Ireland. They recount episodes from the period of feuding and political anarchy in the Highlands in the 16th and early 17th centuries known as 'The Age of Forays' (Gaelic, *Linn nan Creach*) which followed the collapse of the lordship of the *Isles. Their outlook is that of a heroic age with its warrior aristocracy, presented in an economical style recalling their counterparts in medieval Iceland. Legends of this type can involve historical families or personages: a famous archer, Gille-Pàdruig Dubh and the Clanranald family of South Uist appear in a local variant of the William Tell legend (see ORAL HISTORY). The supernatural element is often prominent in heroic legends: the piper Ranald MacDonald ('Raghnall mac Ailein Òig') of Morar, also a historical character, is the subject of a series of accounts which describe his defeating of natural and supernatural adversaries by his exceptional strength. Also associated with localities, place names, or families in Gaelic Scotland is a wealth of supernatural legends. These commonly concern supernatural beings such as witches, ghosts, fairies, the devil, the *each uisge* (water horse); or the extraordinary powers of families of bards or physicians. Migratory legends, exemplified by 'The Robbers and the Captive Girl', or a piper disappearing into a cave, can occur across cultures and over a wide geographical area. Among the outstanding Gaelic reciters of such narrative genres recorded this century are Duncan MacDonald and Donald Alasdair Johnson of South Uist, Angus MacMillan of Benbecula and the traveller Alexander 'Ailidh Dall' Stewart of Sutherland.

The Scots ballads (see SONG, TRADITIONAL AND FOLK) are the most widely known of the varieties of folksong in either language. Although the genre occurs elsewhere in Britain, the greatest concentration (numbering in the thousands) has been recorded in Scotland's north-east, and to a lesser extent in the Borders, but ballads are encountered throughout the Lowlands as well and even in parts of the still Gaelic-speaking Highlands. In addition to the great collections published in the 19th century an important living ballad tradition was brought to light in the 1950s among families of travellers in Aberdeenshire. As a result of encouragement and exposure to larger audiences a number of these modern tradition bearers, most notably the late Jeannie Robertson, became the leading ballad exponents and internationally regarded folk performers. Like their Continental counterparts, the ballads are narrative song-poems and are considered to belong to the upper stratum of folk song as evidenced by the term 'the muckle sangs'. They are anonymous and approach the crucial situations described in the narrative with objectivity, through a distinctive 'ballad-Scots'. The usual ballad metre, originating with medieval models, consists of four-line stanzas, with refrains allowing for audience participation. Many have been contributed by un-lettered singers, but in the presence of numerous and widely available broadsides the genre must be regarded as the product of combined oral and liter-ary elements. Most ballads cannot be shown, pre-sumably for lack of records, to go back beyond the 18th century (the earliest text is from the late 16th century), but some contain references (for ex-ample, Thomas of Erceldoune in 'Thomas the Rhymer' and the 'Maid of Norway' in 'Sir Patrick Spens') to historical figures and events from three centuries earlier. Many were shown over a century ago to have international affiliations: both the well-known 'Lord Randal' and 'Clark Colven' have counterparts distributed between northern Eur-ope and the Mediterranean. The supernatural is a favourite theme, appearing in the form of the Devil in 'The Fause Knicht', or in contact between mor-tals and fairies in 'Tam Lin'.

Gaelic folk song embraces an unusually wide spectrum and includes types familiar in neighbour-ing European traditions. The strong current of popular song still extant in communities incorpor-ates songs concerning love in its various aspects (trysting, matchmaking, rejection, night-visiting) (see COURTSHIP AND MARRIAGE); panegyrics (eulo-gies, laments); religion; drinking; satire; politics; ballads (heroic, sailors', and soldiers' songs); the supernatural (fairies); labour songs (waulking, spinning, milking); lullabies and pibroch songs. *Canntaireachd* and mouth-music (*puirt-a-beul*), both forms of verbal music, are closely allied to instru-mental music. Narratives are likewise frequently associated with songs, and anonymity is by no means the rule. The oldest datable song in living tradition, a pibroch song, refers to events in the early 15th century; others are linked with the late 16th and early 17th centuries. The heroic ballads (Gaelic, *duain*), among them the Ossianic ballads from the Finn cycle which remained in the reper-toires of a few singers in the Outer Hebrides until the 1970s, are a unique continuation of a heritage shared with Ireland, based on a classical form of the language and associated with a manuscript litera-ture extending back at least as far as late medieval times. From its earliest appearance, Gaelic folk song has contained a strong element of women's compositions, exemplified by the distinctive waulking songs: communal work songs for shrink-ing the wool tweed and performed in Scotland by women only. Earlier these choral songs were dis-tributed over the west of Scotland; they are now re-stricted to the north-west. Their subject matter, with its frequent changes in topic, reflects the world of the 16th and 17th centuries with its aristo-cratic values. From the late 18th century with the publication of song collections printed texts be-came a factor in transmission. Thus an Ossianic ballad based on a Perthshire version published in 1786 was recorded as part of the oral song reper-toire in South Uist in the 1950s. During this and the previous century local bards have figured promin-ently in song composition, producing a number of songs that have gained wide popularity.   JS

2. collectors

Collectors of oral tradition in late 17th-century Scotland were concerned primarily with folk cus-tom and belief. A letter in 1692 from the English antiquarian John Aubrey (1626–97) seeking infor-mation on 'Highland customs, the bards, second sight and other matters' led Professor James Gar-den of King's College, Old Aberdeen, to collect and forward folklore materials from as far afield as Strathspey. Revd Robert Kirk of Aberfoyle pub-lished *The Secret Commonwealth of Elves, Fauns and Fairies* (1691), and Martin Martin of Skye c.1695 compiled his *Description of the Western Islands of Scotland* incorporating similar materials. The Welsh polymath Edward Lhuyd in the course of his enquiries c.1699 obtained and copied a manu-script, *A Collection of Highland Rites and Customes*, belonging to Revd James Kirkwood. The following year Lhuyd took down valuable Gaelic traditions from Revd John Beaton of Mull.

Eighteenth-century collectors in the Highlands were drawn toward oral texts, producing collec-tions of heroic verse by ministers such as Revd Alexander Pope of Reay (c.1739) and Revd Donald MacNicol of Lismore. The publication of James Macpherson's *Fragments* and subsequent 'epics' of *Ossian* (1760–3)—and the ensuing controversy—provided a stimulus to collectors of Gaelic heroic verse and folk-song, among them John Gillies of Perth (1786), which continued into the early 19th century. In the meantime collectors of Scots trad-itions emerged: Robert Chambers's works on folk-tales and urban folklore from the 1820s; Sir Walter Scott on Borders' traditions and Peter Buchan of Aberdeenshire whose pre-1829 collection of tales first appeared in 1908. Beginning in 1859 John Fran-cis Campbell of Islay (1822–85), the most important Scottish folk-tale collector in his time, introduced new methodologies to fieldwork. His *Popular Tales of the West Highlands* (4 vols., 1860–2) remains the standard work in the field. Campbell's colleague Alexander Carmichael amassed and published *Carmina Gadelica* (6 vols, 1900–71), an important collection of prayers and other lore, in the course of his career as a civil servant in the Highlands. Also in the west from c.1860 Frances Tolmie gathered folk-songs in Skye and Revd John Gregorson Campbell, minister of Tiree, Fr. Allan MacDonald of Eriskay, and other clergymen-scholars were active in the final decades of the 1800s. Marjorie Kennedy-Fraser noted down folk songs in the Western Isles from 1905 which appeared as art songs in *Songs of the Hebrides* (1909), and later made phonograph recordings of Barra singers; concurrently the north-east through the efforts of Gavin Greig and Revd James Duncan yielded one of the world's major folk-song collections.

Modern fieldwork began with J. L. Campbell's (1906–96) pioneering recordings in Barra and Uist in the 1930s. Calum Maclean's extensive fieldwork throughout the Highlands was complemented by Hamish Henderson's discoveries in the 1950s of living ballad and folk-tale traditions among the Scots-speaking travellers and his recordings of the Gaelic-speaking Sutherland Stewarts. Since the founding of the School of Scottish Studies in 1951 the gathering of many kinds of oral material, including modern traditions, has been carried out by its students and staff throughout the country.   JS

Orkney and Caithness, earldom of. The earldom of Orkney was a Norwegian dignity which had its origins in the Viking period and which was passed down through the same family line throughout the Middle Ages. It survived until the pledging of Orkney to the Scottish crown in 1468 and the title was resigned to James III by Earl William Sinclair in 1470. It was thereafter revived for the illegitimate son of James V, but its tenure by Robert Stewart and his son Patrick marked an inglorious tailpiece to the remarkable 600 years of its existence as a Norse earldom. For most of its existence it was held conjointly with Caithness, a Scottish earldom covering the north-east corner of the Scottish mainland and the two earldoms were thus united by the Pentland Firth, a notoriously dangerous waterway. While this unusual situation suited the political circumstances of the early centuries of Norse domination (see SCANDINAVIA: 1) around the northern and western coasts of Scotland, it became much more difficult to sustain once the Scottish kings extended their authority northwards.

In the 9th century, the Orkney Islands and Caithness were far removed from the activities of the Scoto-Pictish kings who had their own problem Vikings to face in the central Lowlands. Norwegian Vikings had swarmed into the Northern Isles from the beginning of that century, if not before, probably overrunning the native Pictish population, although the extent of domination or of collaboration is very much debated. The establishment of an earldom dynasty in the islands is recorded in Icelandic tradition as having taken place *c*.870, and we have the story of how this happened in the earls'

own saga, *Orkneyinga Saga*, a compilation of skaldic verse and prose elaboration written down by an anonymous Icelander *c*.1200. A remarkable source of information though the saga is (a unique account of the deeds of the earls from the late 9th to the early 13th centuries), it cannot be relied upon fully for the early centuries of the earldom. The account of how Rognvald of Møre was given Orkney and Shetland in grant from Harald I Halfdanarson 'Fine-Hair', king of Norway, as compensation for the death of his son Ivar during the king's war expedition to the British Isles, involves royal participation because this was considered automatic by the later saga-writer. Another medieval Norwegian account, the *Historia Norwegiae*, makes no mention of any royal grant but says that the islands were conquered by Earl Rognvald entirely on his own authority. The reality of the situation was probably that this powerful dynasty of Viking 'jarls' (earls) from western Norway seized control of Orkney as part of a programme of expansion to the islands off the coasts of north Britain, and that they carried the title of 'jarl' with them, as pertaining to their family. The unifying Vestfold dynasty, of which Harald 'Fine-Hair' was the most powerful member, had not yet succeeded in dominating Møre, and was even less likely to have any authority in the islands 'west-over-sea'. The concept of a royal grant was elaborated later, in a more royalist political climate.

The underlying tension between kings and earls is a constant theme throughout the history of the Norse earldom, and is reflected in the story of Torf-Einar, the youngest son of Rognvald of Møre, killing the son of Harald 'Fine-Hair' in Orkney and establishing full power throughout the islands in the face of attempts to depose him. Torf-Einar was a famous skald and many of his verses are incorporated into the saga text, giving some reliable basis to the record of his deeds and of his ritual killing of the king's son. He had to compensate Harald for this deed by a payment of 60 gold marks, and this was later remembered as the occasion when the earl lost his family's udal right over the earldom and had to recognize that he held it in fee from the king. Struggle for acknowledgement of royal authority was clearly taking place, even though the king could not dislodge the family from their position of power in the islands.

From their power base in Orkney the earls rapidly expanded onto the Scottish mainland in a phase when maritime power gave them the ability to dominate the coastal territories of northern and eastern Caithness, as far south as the River Oykell. Indeed the *Orkneyinga saga* says that Sigurd 'the Mighty' (*c*.870–90) overran 'the whole of Caithness and a large part of Argyll, Moray, and Ross', although raiding alone would not give lasting authority in areas where Norse settlement petered out (as recognized from the evidence of *place names). The saga stories make it clear that the earls were faced by stiff opposition from Celtic chieftains, the most powerful of whom were the rulers of *Moray. It was as a result of an encounter with an 'Earl Maelbrikte' that Sigurd met his death, not in battle (he had defeated Maelbrikte), but ignominiously as a result of an infected scratch from the dead Scot's tooth projecting from his severed head which was being carried back in triumph by Sigurd. This story is an interesting example of the incorporation of a Celtic literary motif into the saga account, that of the 'avenging head'. More reliable is the account of Sigurd's burial in a mound on the banks of the Oykell, probably near the place known today as 'Cyderhall' (Sigurd's 'howe').

The authority of the kings of Scots (see KINGSHIP: 2) over the northern part of the mainland was slow to be established or even asserted. Although there is reference to some of the 10th-century earls receiving grants of Caithness from the Scottish king, the reality of the situation was otherwise while the Scottish kings were involved in establishing their power on the southern frontier. Not until the marriage alliance at the beginning of the 11th century, when Sigurd II 'the Stout' is said in the *Orkneyinga saga* to have married a daughter of Malcolm, king of Scots, was the earldom dynasty brought into close contact with the kings. This alliance was probably forged with the powerful and ambitious Malcolm II (Mael Coluim mac Cinaeda) (1005–34) as a useful counterbalance to the power of the province of Moray, which lay between Orkney and the southern Scottish kingdom. The offspring of this alliance, Thorfinn 'the Mighty', was brought up at the court of his Scottish grandfather after the death of his father at the battle of Clontarf (1014), and then given Caithness and Sutherland to rule, with Scottish advisers. But it was not until the end of the 11th century that Caithness and Sutherland, along with the west coast, was formally recognized as Scottish territory by the Norwegian king, Magnus III Olafsson 'Bare-Legs', even though it continued to be ruled by Norwegian earls. The process of incorporating the area within the Scottish kingdom was slow and painful, and the church bore much of the brunt of the earls' resentment at the encroaching authority of the Scots through the second half of the 12th century and early 13th century.

The conversion of the earls was initially carried out under the auspices of the Norwegian kings, and the story of Earl Sigurd 'the Stout' receiving enforced baptism from Olaf Triggvason (who had sailed into the bay of Osmundwall while returning to Norway from a raiding expedition in England)

was such a well-established tradition that it cannot be doubted that some form of coercion took place. Indeed, the Scottish king would have been very unlikely to have entered into a marriage alliance with Earl Sigurd unless his Christianity was secure. Thorfinn Sigurdsson is the earl who can be credited with the real establishment of Christianity in his earldom, which required the appointment of bishop and clergy for the baptism and preaching which was a necessary basis for the imposition of a new raft of beliefs and rituals (see RELIGIOUS LIFE: 1). Where the earl led the way the population of the earldom would follow and the building of churches on the earl's estates would be copied by his close friends and kindred building chapels on their own lands. Above all, Earl Thorfinn established a bishop at *Birsay and built a 'fine minster' for him, dedicated to Christ, which he copied from other episcopal mother churches which he would know and had probably visited himself, such as Christ Church cathedral, Canterbury, and Christ Church cathedral, Dublin. The desire to emulate and enter the ranks of the European princely elite was part of the process by which the earldom became part of Christendom, and Thorfinn emulated the most notable emulator of all when he walked in the steps of the great Cnut and visited the Pope at Rome.

The Norse earldom of Orkney was at the forefront of cultural development in the north, uniting as it did the world of Scandinavia and the north Atlantic with the ancient kingdoms and bishoprics of Scotland, Ireland, and England. This position was fuelled by its own wealth gained from the fertile grainlands of Orkney and Caithness and the trade which the earls controlled from their well-placed island empire. Their place in 12th-century Europe is exemplified by the cult of the saint-earl, Magnus Erlendsson (d. c.1117), and the building of the great Romanesque cathedral at Kirkwall dedicated to his memory by his nephew and successor, Rognvald Kali Kolsson. The growth of the cult of St Magnus, who was executed by his cousin Haakon Paulsson (both grandsons of Thorfinn 'the Mighty') in a struggle over earldom lands and rights, is a phenomenon of the newly converted Scandinavian kingdoms: the cults of national saints who were kings of the developing national entities of Norway, Denmark, and Sweden. Religious and national fervour came together in these northern areas, and the earldom of Orkney was a political unit with the same sense of identity (see REGIONAL IDENTITIES: 4) where religious fervour was similarly embodied in a member of the ruling family who met a violent death—no matter what the cause. In the case of Earl Magnus, we have a hagiographical account of his violent end—which has the same sort of problems which all such accounts entail. But we also have the sober and realistic story of how his nephew Rognvald set out to win his uncle's half of the earldom and based his campaign on the growing belief in Magnus's holiness. This includes an account of the founding (in 1137) and building of the cathedral dedicated to Magnus, and the transfer of the corporeal relics to Kirkwall from Birsay, the seat of the rival earldom line. This is a very rare source of information about the reasons for the construction of one of our medieval architectural treasures.

This great political and cultural achievement, and the rule of Earl Rognvald who was also revered (after he met a violent end, while pursuing an outlaw in Caithness), marks the pinnacle of the medieval earldom. The late 12th century brought a big change in the earls' fortunes, dramatically recorded in the saga accounts of Harald Maddadson's struggles to maintain his independent existence against the encroaching authority of both his overlords, King William I 'the Lion' of Scotland and King Sverrir Sigurdsson of Norway. Retaliatory action was taken by his Scottish overlord when the earl became implicated in disturbances in Ross and Moray in the 1190s: he also quarrelled with the Scottish bishop in Caithness, which foolishly led him to attack and maim Bishop John, thus providing King William with ample justification for sending an army right to the very north of Caithness and attacking the earl's stronghold in Thurso. Heavy fines, loss of lands, and humiliating submission followed. Likewise, in his Scandinavian earldom, he antagonized his royal overlord by supporting a rebellion against Sverrir, which failed, and the earl forfeited Shetland, as well as having to hand over half of his judicial incomes from Orkney. The king's main card was the power to appoint earls from rival branches of the earldom family, as well as the installation of royal officials, who survived so long as the king himself was in a strong position. Such administrative officials were henceforth the main means of assertion of royal authority in the earldoms.

The 13th century saw the apogee of royal power, when the tentacles of kingship reached out furthest and the earls became formalized members of the feudal aristocracy in both Scotland and Norway. This position could be exceedingly dangerous if their royal overlords came to blows, as indeed they did in the 1260s. By this date, the balance of identity in the earldom family had decisively moved towards the Scottish element, mainly because the direct inheritance failed after a tragic shipwreck of earldom family and friends in the 1220s, and the title passed to Scottish cousins. At just the same time we enter into a period when the saga of the earls dries up and historical information is exceed-

ingly sparse; little more is known of events in Orkney than the bare succession of the earldom from father to son. It is likely that the earls' links with Norway became merely formal, and that their marital and family connections were all with the south-east of Scotland. So when King Haakon IV Haakonsson led the last royal expedition to the Norwegian colonies in the west, in order to reassert his authority over the Western Isles, Earl Magnus of Orkney was in attendance while his king remained in Orkney, but failed to follow the royal fleet westwards, aware of the impending conflict with his Scottish overlord. He maintained his position with regard to both kings, but had to compensate with the loss of more lands and rights.

During the next century direct inheritance failed again and the earldom came to Malise, earl of Strathearn, who had only daughters, so that for 30 years from his death c.1350 both earldoms were fought over by his daughters' husbands and sons. This period of lawlessness ended with the earldom of Caithness being acquired by the crown in 1376, and with Henry Sinclair being awarded rights in Orkney and the title of earl in 1379: rights and title were kept separate by the kings of Norway. So the Sinclair dynasty moved into Orkney and Caithness and managed to assert authority in the north even though they maintained their southern power base at Roslin in Midlothian. From this period we have the installation documents stating the restrictions under which the first and third Sinclair earls were appointed. The problem, as always, was how to ensure the obedience of the earls, particularly when as Scottish magnates they played important roles in the Scottish kingdom.

The position of the earls, vassals of two kings, became increasingly anomalous in the 15th century when *national identity equated with territorial unity, which included offshore islands. The Stewart kings cast covetous eyes on the islands of Orkney and Shetland and pursued direct tactics in order to acquire them. This involved ignoring obligations to pay the annual sum of money promised when the Western Isles were handed over to them, and utilizing negotiations over a marriage alliance for the young James III to demand the cession of the Northern Isles as part of the 1468 marriage contract. The last Sinclair earl was put into an extremely difficult situation, in which his earldom was also an object of royal ambition, but he managed to negotiate quite a favourable package when exchanging his earldom rights for the castle of Ravenscraig in 1470. He had also reacquired the title to Caithness, although probably not much land with it in 1455, when James II felt obliged to reward him for his support in the action against the *Douglas threat. So the Sinclair family maintained some influence in both Caithness and Orkney although the substance of their authority was but a pale reflection of what their ancestors had exercised throughout the preceding 600 years.   BEC

Owen, Robert (1771–1858), businessman, social reformer, and pioneer socialist. He and his partners early in 1799 bought the New Lanark Mill which Richard Arkwright and David Dale had established fifteen years previously. The mill already had a reputation as a humane place of work, but Owen, now married to Caroline Dale, extended paternalistic control. In 1813 he published *A New View of Society* in which he argued that character was formed by 'circumstances', the environment in which an individual was educated and raised, and consequently could be shaped. He began putting these ideas into practice with the establishment of a pioneering infant school and the opening of the Institution for the Formation of Character in 1816.

Owen believed initially that the moral transformation of human society could be achieved from above. He campaigned for legislation to shorten working hours in factories to provide the necessary space for education. In his *Report to the County of Lanark*, in 1820, he also argued that the problem of unemployment should be tackled by means of self-supporting communities of unemployed workers.

Owen's ideas of moral regeneration through community were taken up by various groups and a community was set up at Orbiston near Motherwell. Owen meanwhile had moved to America and, between 1824 and 1827, created the community of New Harmony. On his return he sold his share in New Lanark and became a full-time campaigner. His main constituency was now largely among trade unionists, attracted by co-operative production as an alternative to capitalism. But Owen always had difficulty in dealing with the working classes other than in autocratic terms.

From 1834 his ideas were kept alive by the weekly *New Moral World*, by regular lecture tours, and by bodies such as the Association of All Classes and All Nations and the Universal Community of Rational Religionists. Branches existed in all the main cities, but were particularly strong in Glasgow and Paisley. A belief in community remained important, but the Queenwood Community in Hampshire in the 1840s broke up in acrimony. He continued to produce ideas which enraged the clergy, by denouncing the family as a barrier to the new moral world and advocating easier divorce and marital unions based on mutual affection. Despite a deluge of ridicule, Owen remained utterly convinced of his rightness until his death in 1858.

WHF

P

parliament: 1. medieval; 2. 1513–1707; 3. 1707–1999;
4. 1999–.

1. medieval

Parliament was first so called in July 1290, when the
term was used to describe an assembly of Scottish
magnates at Birgham-on-Tweed. Its function on
that occasion was the vital one of negotiating an
Anglo-Scottish treaty which would preserve the
independence of the Scottish kingdom from a predatory Edward I (see ANGLO-SCOTTISH RELATIONS: 2;
GREAT CAUSE). The business to be discussed—
matters of high policy—and the composition of the
parliament—clergy, earls, and barons—alike reflect parliament's 13th-century origins as a colloquium, a formal assembly of the king's counsellors.
The shift in terminology from 'colloquium' to 'parliament' did not immediately produce a change in
function; parliaments, like colloquia, remained
gatherings of important men summoned on 40
days' notice, advising the ruler on affairs of state,
applying the law, enacting new laws, and—on
occasion—levying taxation.

During the reign of *Robert I (1306–29), the
king's wars with England and his search for security
at home provided parliament with various roles: to
legitimize the king's usurpation (*St Andrews,
1309), to condemn his Scottish enemies (Cambuskenneth, 1314, and *Scone, 1320), and to vote
taxation to him in recognition of his services to his
country (Cambuskenneth again, 1326) (see INDE-
PENDENCE, WARS OF). On these occasions we see
parliament dutifully complying with the king's
wishes, though there is a hint of things to come in
1326, when royal burghs were first consulted over
the matter of taxation, anticipating the regular appearance of a third estate in parliament (see ROYAL
BURGHS, CONVENTION OF; URBAN SOCIETY: 1).

Robert I's death in 1329 was swiftly followed by a
succession crisis and a bitter renewal of the Wars of
Independence. From 1346 to 1357 the second Bruce
king, David II, was a prisoner in England, returning
home pledged to pay an enormous ransom which
had to be found through taxation. The burden fell
not only on parliaments, but also on general councils, bodies which could be summoned at shorter

notice and had equal competence in all parliamentary matters except judicial business. The third
estate, consisting solely of representatives of the
royal burghs, began to appear on a regular basis
from the late 1350s, and soon joined the first and
second estates (clergy and nobility respectively) in
deliberating and deciding on matters fiscal and
diplomatic. More significantly for the future, as
early as 1366 all three estates of parliament sought
not only to criticize, but also to restrict, certain unpopular crown actions, above all royal requisition
of victuals as 'prises' without prompt—or any—
payment (see KINGSHIP: 4).

Until recently, the late medieval Scottish
parliament was discounted as an inferior, single-
chamber, version of its English counterpart, lacking the power to resist royal demands, famously
put down by Sir Robert Rait in the 1920s as little
more than a rubber stamp for crown policies. Not
so; evidence abounds for the Scottish estates,
whether meeting in parliament or general council,
adopting policies quite different from, or even directly opposed to, those of the crown.

This is especially the case after the advent of the
Stewart dynasty in 1371 (see KINGSHIP: 5). In the ensuing 130 years, the crown's functions were exercised
by a lieutenant or governor for almost half that
time; rapid alternations of minorities, governorships, and periods of adult rule produced a situation
in which the three estates, though an occasional
body meeting for no more than three weeks at a sitting and frequently much less than that, developed
as a volatile political forum which on different occasions supported and opposed crown policies.
The estates' ability to do this may have been based
on a requirement laid on successive rulers to call
parliament or general council at least once in the
year. The origins of this practice, which produced
annual parliaments between 1424 and 1496, may
perhaps be traced back to 1388, when King Robert
II, in an effort to place checks on the power of the
new guardian, the earl of Fife, commanded that
meetings of parliament or general council should
take place before the end of each year.

In 1424, James I, returning to Scotland after
eighteen years' captivity in England, attempted to

reform the Scottish parliament along English lines, above all by introducing shire commissioners, but the scheme failed; and though Abbot Walter Bower (see HISTORIANS: 1) described James as 'our lawgiver king', James's laws were for the most part little more than re-enactments of earlier statutes. Some parliamentary innovations, however, were introduced in the first half of the 15th century. The Lords of the Articles, a committee made up of elected members of the estates to draft legislation, is first recorded in James I's reign; and early in his son's reign we find the term 'Lords of Parliament' used to describe nobles below the rank of earl whose enhanced status cost the crown nothing beyond sending the new peerage individual summonses to attend parliament.

These devices may have been intended as a means of binding the estates closer to the crown, of securing support and loyalty; but if so, they failed to do so. Certainly on some occasions—for example during the crises of 1452 and 1483—it was possible for the crown to pack parliaments and get its own way. But not all parliamentary legislation emanated from the crown, and the Lords of the Articles, far from being a royal board of control as was once thought, was an elected body which could on occasions contain the king's opponents— as it did, with decisive effect, in the spring of 1482.

Essentially the estates looked for the king to 'live of his own'; that is, from his own resources. Trouble arose when rulers attempted to impose regular taxation. There was an abortive effort to arrest James I for this reason in the 'Hallowe'en' Parliament of 1436; the Act of Annexation of 1455 was intended to provide James II with sufficient resources to avoid resorting to taxation; James III was repeatedly criticized for levying assessments, and roundly told in 1473 that he could not travel abroad because parliament would not provide him with his expenses. Small wonder that *James IV, the most successful Stewart king, followed European fashion by raising money in other ways, allowing him to dispense with regular parliaments after 1496 (see LAW AND LAWYERS: 1; NOBILITY: 2).   NATM

2. 1513–1707

In this period, parliament's functions were transformed. From being an occasional assembly consulted by the government, it became the senior partner in the government. But the transformation had its vicissitudes, and there were times when parliament might have ceased to exist. Indeed the Scottish parliament did cease to exist in 1707—but the principle of parliamentary government was vindicated in the process.

Who comprised the Scottish parliament? In the early 16th century it consisted of the traditional three estates: prelates, nobles (see NOBILITY: 3), and commissioners from the royal burghs (see URBAN SOCIETY: 2). In 1531 there were ten bishops, ten heads of monasteries, eight earls, thirteen lords, and commissioners from eight burghs. Numbers had fallen since the 15th century, indicating parliament's declining importance. Membership was modernized in 1560 when the 'Reformation' Parliament was successfully gatecrashed by 95 Protestant lairds. In 1587 (see JAMES VI) a formal system of shire representation was devised. The lairds had become a fourth estate, alongside the burgh commissioners (chosen by burgh councils). Meanwhile the noble and clerical estates were entangled by the secularization of the monasteries (see CHURCH INSTITUTIONS: 2–3): most holders of monasteries received secular peerages. Schemes for Protestant ministers' representation came to nothing, so the only real churchmen remaining were the bishops, who were almost eclipsed in the 1580s and 1590s, revived after 1600, abolished in 1638, restored in 1661, and finally abolished in 1689. In 1681, attendance had grown to 12 bishops, 61 nobles, 57 shire commissioners, and 60 burgh commissioners.

As well as parliaments, Scotland had conventions of estates, broadly the same in membership and functions. They could include non-noble privy councillors, and were more flexible for political consultation. In general, parliament's evolving and expanding membership helped it to maintain its position as a legitimate representation of the body politic. The ceremonial opening and closing procession, the 'riding' (see ROYAL COURT: 2) of parliament, affirmed this publicly.

However, parliament was mainly important for what it did, rather than for who comprised it. Traditionally, it was a forum in which the government—formally the king (see KINGSHIP: 5–7) alone—consulted the political nation on major decisions. The king took the advice of his councillors on small everyday matters, and the advice of his parliament on big decisions. Parliament's members thus negotiated with the government. Important legislation had sometimes been enacted and taxes imposed, but not often. Parliament was also a court of law (see LAW AND LAWYERS: 1), but it heard hardly any cases after the foundation of the Court of *Session in 1532. Late medieval parliaments had met more or less annually, but James *IV had ceased to summon parliament regularly—an indication that it might well be surplus to requirements.

The enactment of the *Reformation by parliamentary authority in 1560—a tremendous event in every way—galvanized parliament at a crucial time, ensuring the institution's survival by demonstrating the power that statutes could wield. The publication (see PRINTING AND PUBLISHING) of the parliamentary statutes in 1566 also enhanced their influence. From the 1580s, a flood of important Acts transformed Scots law, while parliamentary taxation became heavy, regular, and controversial. Taxation was apportioned among the estates—half paid by the benefice-holders (not necessarily clergymen after the Reformation), one-third by lay landlords, and one-sixth by the royal burghs—by an ancient system that was modernized in the 1640s.

What lay behind this was the gradual development of legislative sovereignty. The making of law became important to the business of government, and law could be made only by the crown in parliament. Parliamentary taxation, too, became an ever more essential component of government revenue. Conventions of estates could not pass permanent legislation, but made temporary acts, often lasting until the next parliament. Because they could impose taxation, some governments preferred them to parliaments for this purpose. Legislative sovereignty opened up the possibility that parliament, instead of negotiating with the government, could become the government.

But it was more natural to see the crown in this position; James VI indeed claimed to possess power to legislate alone. There was a trend towards Continental-style absolute monarchy in the early 17th century. The royal prerogative took over numerous areas of parliamentary business, notably the customs and foreign policy; the flood of legislation receded, though taxation remained important. James also influenced parliament through its steering committee, the Lords of the Articles. 'Articles' were legislative proposals, which had to go through this committee. It was elected with the bishops choosing the nobles' representatives and the nobles those of the bishops; these then chose the burghs' and shires' representatives. Since the bishops of James VI and I were all royal nominees, this allowed him in effect to nominate the entire committee. However, its draft legislation still had to be approved by the full parliament. Here, there was frequent dissent, and government proposals often had to be withdrawn. The Lords of the Articles could smother unwelcome proposals; they could not positively make parliament do the government's bidding.

Parliamentary sessions usually lasted two or three weeks. The initial meeting simply elected the Lords of the Articles. While the latter were drafting legislative proposals, the individual estates met separately to discuss them—until 1621, when this was banned in an attempt to stifle opposition. Parliament reassembled on the final day, the Lords of the Articles submitted their report, and voting took place with no debate. Regular voting replaced consensus-seeking at this time, dividing parliament visibly into opposed groups. Intervals between parliaments lengthened as taxation was voted for longer periods. Parliament's existence was again in jeopardy.

The Covenanting revolution (see NATIONAL COVENANT, AND SOLEMN LEAGUE AND COVENANT) of 1638 transformed the Scottish constitution. The crown's authority was nullified, debate was freed, and parliament took over the executive government through a permanent 'committee of estates'. Parliaments had sometimes appointed executive commissions before, but only on specific and limited matters. There were huge numbers of commissions during the 1640s, and would be again after 1689, when parliament supervised the executive actively.

The *Restoration restored royal government, but not the restrictions on parliamentary debate, and the government still needed parliaments—mainly for taxation. Bitter controversy ensued. In the 1660s, Sir George MacKenzie of Rosehaugh opposed governmental measures in eloquent parliamentary speeches. In 1684, now an officer of state, he insultingly called parliament 'the king's baron-court'. In 1686, parliament sternly rejected a government proposal for religious toleration for Catholics.

Parliament scored a decisive victory over the crown in 1689, when the revolutionary convention of estates dismissed James VII from the throne and appointed William and Mary. It was now clear where ultimate power lay. There were usually annual parliamentary sessions thereafter (though there was only one more 'general election', in 1702). Politics became a matter of securing a numerical parliamentary majority. The estates' separate identities were gradually blurred. How members arrived in parliament remained constitutionally significant, but once in the *Parliament House, Edinburgh, all were politicians together. Alliances were formed, and marshalled their votes as embryonic political parties.

Seventeenth-century Scotland and England were both unusual in defeating moves towards absolute monarchy, and in placing parliaments in control of government. In schemes for Anglo-Scottish union (see UNION OF THE CROWNS), the initial emphasis was on union of laws and churches, but after 1640, 'union' meant parliamentary union. This briefly happened in the 1650s, during the English occupation. The *Union of 1707 is discussed elsewhere, but it should be noted that the end of the Scottish parliament was also a vindication of its career. The principle that government should be carried on by representatives of the political nation—an unusual one in Europe at the time—was the basis of the Union. JG

3. 1707–1999

After the Union of 1707 Scotland had no separate parliament but sent MPs to the House of Commons and a select number of peers to the House of Lords at Westminster.

4. 1999–

On 1 July 1999, the new Scottish parliament was formally opened by Queen Elizabeth II. The ceremony, carefully constructed to encompass differing interpretations of the event, passed off to general acclaim. The queen was pointedly greeted by the Presiding Officer, Sir David Steel, as 'Queen of Scots'. There was no formal riding of parliament. Rather, the new MSPs strolled through cheering crowds from Old Parliament Hall, where the pre-1707 parliament had met, to its temporary new home, the meeting place of the General Assembly on the Mound. Royal protocol, bowing, and scraping was kept to a minimum. Only the crown from the Honours of Scotland, carried gingerly by Scotland's senior peer, the duke of Hamilton, figured in the proceedings, together with a token presence of heralds. Yet the queen's gift to the new parliament of a mace, even if it was one fashioned by a Scottish craftsman out of Scots silver, underlined the potential tensions. The pre-1707 parliament had no mace. Only the Honours of Scotland—crown, sword, and sceptre—were needed to fence it. The mace seemed to belong to a different parliamentary tradition of Westminster, which in its proceedings the new assembly had in many ways determined to eschew. Did the mace convey the message of the autonomy of the new parliament and the 'marriage of parliament, land and people' which formed the focal point of the speech made by the new First Minister, Donald *Dewar? Or, was there a camouflaged message that power had really been granted by Westminster, a parliament for which the mace is a central symbol of authority?

The new parliament was the product of the 35th Home Rule Bill to be put before the Westminster parliament in a little over 100 years. All previous 34 had failed or foundered, the last of them following the ill-starred referendum of 1979, in which 51.6 per cent of those who had taken part (32.5 per cent of the Scottish electorate as a whole) had voted 'yes'. The results of the referendum of 1997 were much more clear-cut: 74.3 per cent voted 'yes' to the principle of a parliament; and even 63.5 per cent agreed to the proposition that it should have limited powers to vary taxation. The shift of opinion was striking, although some of it might be down to the fact that in 1979 a messy pot-pourri of a bill was at

issue, whereas in 1997 the government was astute enough to restrict the referendum to two simple propositions. And even the most curmudgeonly of Scottish Conservative opponents made little of the fact that only some 46 per cent of the electorate as a whole voted 'yes'. Perhaps it would have been too much of a reminder that, in 1979, both the dead and the disenfranchised voted 'no', on the notorious 40 per cent rule. At that time, it was doubted whether any referendum could produce a result of over 40 per cent. The fact that it was comfortably met in 1997 was a measure of the discontent felt in Scotland during the long reign of Margaret Thatcher. It also seemed to make the new parliament's position all the more secure.

The weight of expectations thrust upon the new parliament inevitably brought early disappointments, although some were orchestrated by tabloid newspapers with little better to do in a long summer. The complicated, severely modified form of proportional representation devised for the parliament failed to produce the Labour majority it was designed to, though only just. The new administration, a coalition of Labour which won 56 of the 129 seats and Liberal Democrats who won 12, had to find its feet quickly and frequently stumbled, because of both the novelty of coalition politics and the inexperience of its talented but precocious ministerial team. Also, a series of unexpected issues, including student finance and the site of its own future home at Holyrood (see ROYAL HIGH SCHOOL, EDINBURGH), became booby traps. Yet such is the inbuilt inertia of Scottish politics that the new parliament's future seems secure. What remains deeply unclear, however, is not the role of Holyrood but of Westminster. In a thoughtful editorial on the day after the Scottish parliament opened, *The Times* argued that devolution was not merely the 'settled will of the Scottish people', in John Smith's celebrated phrase; 'the real business for the United Kingdom', it predicted, 'had only just started'. The dynamics of the Union itself, now almost 300 years old, and the nature of Britishness, a favourite theme of the administration of Tony Blair, are both at stake and in question.

ML

Parliament House, Edinburgh. The Parliament House of Scotland lies, masked by ponderous classical clothing, on an urban platform immediately to the south of St Giles's church, High Street, Edinburgh. Its construction had been ordered by Charles 1 who wished to remodel St Giles as a cathedral, which required the eviction of both Court of *Session and the parliament from the nave. The cost was to be a burden upon the city (see EDINBURGH: 1).

In 1632, Sir James Murray of Kilbaberton, the King's Master of Works, and court architect, provided the necessary drawing, and construction proceeded over the next seven years. The building was constructed on the site of the St Giles's manses and the sloping St Giles graveyard, requiring storey-height underbuilding and cellars (for the town's gallows) at the southern end. The building was L-plan, comprising the Great or Outer Hall, 122 feet by 49 feet (37.2 m by 14.9 m), with an almost square eastern wing containing the Court of Session, with the Court of Exchequer above. The Outer House was split into a large antechamber to the north and the main House in which the three estates of Scotland sat in U-formation facing the king or chancellor. Beneath the Outer House was the arcaded Laigh Hall, later the repository for Scottish Records, and location of the Advocates' Library from 1701.

Architecturally, the Parliament House resembled other Murray buildings in the court-style—most notably the palace block in *Edinburgh castle. The two principal façades facing St Giles' were of excellent ashlar (the other two harled), the composition focused upon the enormous, floridly mannerist principal entrance; the round and square ogee-capped turrets on each corner; the corner staircase; the visually flat roof; buckle quoins; the strapwork parapet; and the ornately carved aedicular windows. The glory of the interior remains the magnificently encrusted oak roof by John Scott, rising from vigorously carved corbels.

After the parliamentary *Union of 1707, the Parliament House became the preserve of the Scots law (see LAW AND LAWYERS: 2). The antechamber of the Outer House was given over to booksellers', hardware and coffee stalls, and a small sheriff court; and the principal chamber to a place of congregation for lawyers and writers prior to being called into the courts—which remained in the building to the east.

With pressure on the courts growing, the Inner House was reconstructed by Robert Reid, 1804, and new courts added, together with a Library for the Writers to the Signet to the north-west, 1809. The overall exterior was designed by Reid, who—to the outrage of many—recased the Parliament House, in ponderous sub-Robert Adam classical, a heavy Ionic arcade at first-floor level, lusty sphinxes on the skyline. (From certain corners, surviving roof parapets and ogee turrets can be glimpsed.) Lord Cockburn, in *Memorials of his Time*, lamented the change: 'no-one who remembers the old exterior can see the new one without sorrow and indignation'. The interior of the Signet Library—one of Edinburgh's finest neoclassical spaces—was designed by William Stark, 1813. The saucer dome,

two-third-way down this classical cathedral with its Corinthian-columned nave and aisles, was painted in 1821 by Thomas Stothard with suitably elevated antique scenes.

The complex continued to grow: courtrooms to the south were added by William Nixon in 1844; in 1888, the 1824 Bank of Sir William Forbes of Pitsligo on the east side of Parliament Square was pressed into service as another court, reached by a bridge; and in 1892 the Solicitors' Library and Building, soaring up from the Cowgate in florid red sandstone Scots Renaissance, was added by J. B. Dunn.

Parliament House is still used for clients and lawyers meeting counsel (wonderfully described in the early 19th century by Thomas Carlyle), and is occasionally open to the public. The windows, stained glass, and decoration are largely 1868, glass by James Ballantyne & Son. Of particular note are the statues of Duncan Forbes of Culloden, 1752, by Roubiliac; to Robert Dundas, 1824, by Chantrey; and to Cockburn by Brodie. The two giant statues of Justice and Mercy, 1637, which flanked the main entrance of Parliament House by Alexander Mylne, lie just inside the south doorway. CAMcK

Perth. The earliest settlement in Perth predates its formal foundation as a royal burgh in 1124 × 1127 by almost 150 years (see URBAN SETTLEMENTS: 1). It is not surprising that a town should be situated at what was the first fording point on the dangerous, tidal waters of the River Tay, still one of the most volatile rivers in Britain, or that its first buildings would be located at the riverside, in what was called the Watergate. By the reign of Alexander I (1107–24), Perth was a thriving port and market centre. It thrived as a wool and cloth town in the 12th and 13th centuries, when it, along with *Berwick and *Aberdeen, were probably Scotland's leading burghs. Despite the extravagant promotion of modern tourist outlets, Perth was never the 'ancient capital' of Scotland.

Perth has a better claim. It is the most excavated town in Scotland and, as a result, more is known of its settlement patterns than any other burgh of any size. More than 60,000 animal bones have been dug up, underlining the early importance of streets such as Skinnergate and Candlemaker Close. A tantalizing reference of 1178 × 1195, referring to William I 'the Lion''s 'new burgh' of Perth, suggests that new plots and streets were laid out away from the river for properties close to the bank were prone to flooding. Even the royal castle, a motte and bailey structure on what is now the North Inch, was swept away in a storm in 1209. By the later 15th century, Perth had developed suburbs to the west of the town, the first major Scottish burgh to do so. And it was here that James I (1406–37) established the great charterhouse, the only Carthusian establishment in Scotland (see CHURCH INSTITUTIONS: 2). Ironically, it was here, too, that he is buried following his assassination within its walls in 1437.

Perth's economy was governed by its location. It was an inland town dominated by its manufacturing trades. The early prosperity based on its export trade in wool and cloth faded in the general trade slump which followed the Wars of *Independence (see ECONOMY: 2). Just as important a factor, however, was the gradual silting up of the River Tay, which increasingly made it, as its craftsmen gleefully claimed in the 1550s, 'a dry town far from the sea', losing out to *Dundee, its rival nearer the river mouth. In the mid-14th century, Perth was recognized by the *staple port of Bruges as one of the 'four great towns of Scotland', along with *Edinburgh, Aberdeen, and Dundee. By the 16th century, it was a craft town, its merchants largely made up of chapmen and hucksters rather than overseas traders (see URBAN SOCIETY: 2). One result was that there were sharper social tensions in Perth than in any other sizeable burgh.

It was these internal frictions that John *Knox exploited when he singled out the parish church of St John in Perth for the first inflammatory sermon which he made on his return from Calvin's Geneva in May 1559. The 'rascal multitude' (though he called them his 'brethren' at the time) ransacked and razed to the ground the charterhouse and the towns' two friaries in the space of two days. The only surviving vestige of the Catholic cult was the banner of St Bartholomew, patron saint of the glovers, which was at the menders at the time of the riot (see RELIGIOUS LIFE: 3). Yet Perth's reputation of being a largely Protestant town before the *Reformation may be misleading. When kirk session records become available, in the late 1570s, they are full of references to 'superstitious' practices, especially amongst certain crafts such as the bakers. What is clear from the Chronicle of Perth, a journal drawn up by the depute town clerk, is the continuing nervousness of the burgh authorities about riot and disorder, especially at harvest time when it is likely that the town's population of some 4,000 may almost have doubled.

The 17th century brought a steady decline in Perth's fortunes and perhaps also in its population (see POPULATION PATTERNS: 1). One reason for this was undoubtedly the vulnerability of its vital 14th-century bridge across the Tay; it was three times partly washed away in the 16th century and a new, ten-arch structure built in 1615 lasted a mere five years. It was not replaced until 1766 (see TRANSPORT AND COMMUNICATIONS: 1. pre-1770). In the 1690s, the burgh complained bitterly about the proliferation of small market centres around it which threatened its economy, now largely based on linen rather than cloth. And an annuity tax of 1712 recorded only about 440 households within the town.

Textiles, principally cotton, and associated trades such as dyeing and haberdashery remained the mainstay of its economy throughout the 19th century. The 20th century has largely seen the addition of service industries, such as insurance. Yet Perth remains a curious enigma: one of Scotland's most historic towns but with little above ground to show for it of a date earlier than the later 18th century and seemingly oblivious to much of its real, as distinct from its invented, past. It is particularly ironic that it, the town in which Highlanders were as late as the 18th century obliged to customize their alien 'mac' names, now prides itself on being the 'gateway to the Highlands'. ML

photography. There is a good case to be made for the proposition that the greatest contribution that Scotland has made to the visual arts, possibly to the arts as a whole, is in the art of photography. The key to the claim is the work of David Octavius Hill (1802–70) and Robert Adamson (1821–48). Their output of about 3,000 images in four years is acknowledged as the first, and some would say finest, use of the medium of photography for artistic purposes. The proof of that status is not hard to find. A glance at any international history of photography, wherever it is written and in whatever language, will probably find the Rock House partnership in chapter 1, and frequently on page 1.

Hill and Adamson came together in the extraordinary circumstances of the *Disruption of the Church of Scotland in Edinburgh in May 1843. The connection was made by Sir David Brewster (1781–1868) who with Adamson's brother John (1809–70) and others in St Andrews had succeeded with the Calotype system of paper negatives and positives very recently invented by the Englishman William Henry Fox Talbot (1800–77) and which was not covered by patent north of the Border. Hill had undertaken to record the 500 'Fathers and Brethren' present at the Disruption in a huge painting (see CULTURE: 18) and Brewster persuaded him to team up with Robert to use photography as a means of capturing images to use as sketches of the people.

Hill and Adamson quickly realized that the method had the potential to provide much more than convenient portraits of the members of the new Free Church and they began to turn to other subjects including the great, the good, the famous and infamous, landscape, the fisherfolk of the Firth of Forth, the military at *Edinburgh castle, the building of the Scott Monument, and much else.

They had plans to publish and maybe to work in London and elsewhere but Adamson's health was very poor and he died when the partnership had been in existence for less than five years.

Most of their work is now held in the *Scottish National Portrait Gallery (SNPG) but there are significant collections elsewhere in Scotland, including Glasgow University Library, the RSA (of which Hill was the first secretary), the NLS, and internationally in Texas, New York, California, Germany, London, France, and Japan.

There is much more to Scottish photography, however, than Hill and Adamson. The nation produced many world-class pioneers and exponents, such as Thomas Keith (1827–95); George Washington Wilson (1823–93) who has a claim for the invention of 'instant' photography; James Valentine (1815–80); Thomas Annan (1829–87) whose 'Old Closes and Streets of Glasgow' is the classic account of the urban poor (see GLASGOW: 3) and, at the other end of the social spectrum, Clementina Hawarden (1822–65). The physicist James Clerk-Maxwell (1831–79) (see CULTURE: 19) pioneered colour photography as early as 1861.

The Scots whose reputations were made abroad, frequently being the first to exploit the medium in another land, include William Carrick (1827–78) in Russia; William Notman (1826–91) and Alexander Henderson (1831–1913) in Canada; James Robertson (1813–88) in Turkey; James MacDonald (dates unknown) in Israel; John Thomson (1852–90) in Asia and, latterly, London; Robert MacPherson (1811–72) in Italy; Alexander Gardner (1821–82) in the USA; and George Valentine (1852–90) in New Zealand.

The international influence of Scottish photography is clearly traceable. James Craig Annan (1864–1946), himself one of the greatest Scottish photographers, introduced the work of Hill and Adamson to the American photosecessionists at the beginning of the 20th century and their admiration for 'the Great Scotch Master'—as Stieglitz, Steichen, and their colleagues called Hill (knowing little of Adamson)—extended not only to including the Calotypes in 'Camera Work' and exhibitions but to the style of the Hill and Adamson images being absorbed into the mainstream of American photography, where (it can be argued) it remains to be seen today.

Naturally, Scotland has been attractive to photographers from other places, beginning with Fox Talbot himself. The list of distinguished names would be far too long for this entry but two Americans, both declared admirers of Scottish photography, deserve special recognition. The atmospheric illustrations of Robert Louis Stevenson's 'Edinburgh' by Alvin Langdon Coburn (1882–1966) and the Hebridean photographs of Paul Strand (1890–1976) are among the most important and beautiful works made in this country.

It is true that for some decades of the 20th century the level of attainment of indigenous Scottish photographers was not high. Perhaps the legacy of pictorialism from the late 19th century was not entirely healthy and a brake on innovation and experiment. There was nonetheless some notable work such as the Gorbals photographs by Bert Hardy (1913–95), Joseph MacKenzie (b. 1929), and Oscar Marzaroli (1933–88) but it was in the 1970s that Scottish photography began once more to re-establish itself in the forefront of the medium and to regain international standing.

The reasons for this renaissance are various but among them it is certainly the case that the establishing of Stills Gallery in 1977 by Richard Hough (1945–85) and the emergence or arrival of important practitioners and influential figures, including Murray Johnston (1949–90) and the American Thomas Joshua Cooper (b. 1946), had much to do with it. The range of contemporary talent was demonstrated in the key exhibition 'Light from the Dark Room' in 1995. Once more, there are many names to celebrate, including those of Calum Colvin, Robin Gillanders, Owen Logan, Patricia Macdonald, Pradip Malde, Gunnie Moberg, Ron O'Donnell, Maud Sulter, Andy Wiener, and David Williams.

Although Scotland is badly lacking a national museum of photography and the stimulus such a centre would provide, it is reasonably well served by degree courses on photography, including those at Edinburgh College of Art, Napier University, Glasgow School of Art, and at Duncan of Jordanstone Faculty in the University of Dundee, where there is special emphasis on leading-edge technology. There are also numerous courses at further education colleges throughout the country. The history of photography is also taught, usually in the wider context of art history in general, at, for example, St Andrews University. There are galleries solely devoted to photography 'Stills' and 'Portfolio' Galleries, as well as dedicated space at the SNPG in Edinburgh and 'Streetlevel' in Glasgow, and to an increasing extent traditional art galleries and centres are accepting photographic exhibitions.

As yet, no full-scale history of Scottish photography has been written, although many excellent publications on individual artists (often in the form of exhibition catalogues) exist. The Scottish Society for the History of Photography actively promotes the medium through its 'Studies in Photography' and in a high-profile annual celebrity lecture.

DBr

Pics

Picts, the inhabitants of Scotland north of the Forth (excluding Argyll) from the end of the Roman period until c.900. The first reference to the Picts comes in a panegyric to the emperor, written c.297 by the Roman poet Eumenius. The term he uses, *Picti*, has been taken to be a derogatory Latin nickname, 'the painted ones', but a Celtic origin cannot be ruled out (recalling the Pictones tribe of the Loire Valley). Medieval Latin writers adopted the classical term *Picti*, and from them it was borrowed into Old English as *Pehtas*, hence Scots *Pechts*. The Gaels called the Picts *Cruithne* and to the British they were *Prydyn*. Both these words go back to the same common Celtic root: *Priteni* or *Pritani*, meaning perhaps 'people of the designs'. This word also lies behind *Britanni* (Britons) (see BRITONS AND ANGLES). The Picts were clearly recognized by their contemporary neighbours as some kind of Britons, even though their lack of Romanization made them appear increasingly different from their Romano-British cousins to the south (see NORTHERN ENGLAND AND SOUTHERN ENGLAND: ROMAN OCCUPATION). A slightly archaic form of the old common name of Britons was therefore applied in a more restricted sense only to them (as in the modern distinction between 'Britons' and 'Bretons'). This view of the Picts as an early offshoot from the ancient British continuum is supported by linguistic evidence which indicates that Pictish began to diverge from the other Brythonic (or 'P-Celtic' languages) during the Roman period (see LANGUAGES OF SCOTLAND, PRE-1100).

No Pictish texts have survived, although some historical scraps of Pictish origin have been preserved in a later Gaelic 'king list'. The history of the Picts must instead by pieced together from scattered references in Irish, Welsh, and English sources. It is impossible to construct a narrative history: the scant historical record presents little more than a disjointed succession of battles. Pictland (which, in addition to the mainland territory, included the Hebrides north of Ardnamurchan, Orkney, and probably Shetland) was comprised of a number of regional kingdoms. Particularly successful kings were able to impose overlordship over subordinate kings, but this was a personal rule which could be contested on the accession of a new king (see KINGSHIP: 1). Such jockeying for power might entail an opportunistic alliance with neighbouring Gaels, Britons, or Angles against a Pictish rival. At the level of the elite, such ethnic labels may, in any case, have been irrelevant: the dynasties which ruled the various peoples of northern Britain were closely interconnected through marriage. The 7th-century king of Picts, Bridei, son of Bile, was brother to the king of British *Dumbarton. The Northumbrian army he defeated in 685 at the crucial battle of Nechtansmere, near Forfar, was led by his maternal cousin, King Ecgfrith.

Bridei's stunning victory allowed the Picts to reverse Northumbrian expansion. Within a century, it was Pictish hegemony which was expanding, as one of the greatest of all kings of the Picts, *Ungus (Onuist), son of Uurgust, imposed his rule on *Dál Riata. Ungus appears to have founded a dynasty which, in succeeding generations, was able to consolidate control of a unified kingdom of southern Pictland. By the death of *Caustantin son of Fergus (Uurgust) in 820, this was the strongest and most stable kingdom in northern Britain.

The Picts were the most numerous of the peoples of early medieval northern Britain, and occupied the best land. It seems remarkable, then, that less than a century after the death of Caustantin they should have entirely disappeared from the historical map. The processes by which this happened are not yet fully understood, but in the middle decades of the 9th century Pictland was subjected to a series of devastating attacks by Viking armies (see SCANDINAVIA: 1). A particularly disastrous defeat in 839 appears to have destabilized, or even destroyed, the old ruling elite, enabling *Kenneth mac Alpin to seize the kingship of southern Pictland. As his successors in the following generations tightened their grip on the old eastern kingdoms, it was to the Gaelic west that the dynasty continued to look. The new kingdom of Alba (see NATIONAL IDENTITY: 1) which had emerged out of the disruptions of the 9th century was thoroughly Gaelic in language and culture (see GAELIC LANGUAGE). The inhabitants of Alba turned their back on their Pictish heritage, or at least ceased to think of it as 'Pictish'. The mysterious disappearance of the Picts is thus more apparent than real, for the roots of the medieval kingdom of Scotland go deep into old Pictish soil.

Pictland became Christian in the 7th century, although there had been communities of Christians, especially in the south, as early as the 5th or 6th centuries (see CHRISTIANITY, CONVERSION TO). The southern and eastern distribution of the earliest Christian cemeteries in Pictland reflects an early strand of British influence, but there was continuing close contact with the church in Northumbria, most famously during the reign of *Nechtan, son of Derile. The strongest and most enduring links, however, were with the Gaelic church of the west (see IONA), especially, though not exclusively, the successors of St *Columba and St *Adomnán.

Although historical sources are limited, archaeology provides a wealth of information about Pictish society and culture. Everyday life revolved around agriculture, both stock and arable (see ECONOMY: 1; RURAL SOCIETY: 1), and the exploitation of marine and woodland resources. The elite ruled from major power centres such as the hill fort of *Dundurn, the promontory fort of *Burghead, and the royal palace at *Forteviot. The high level of Pictish artistic accomplishment (see CULTURE: 2) is reflected in surviving metalwork and, above all, in the extraordinary legacy of sculptured stone (see MONUMENTS: 1). On their stones and elsewhere, the Picts used a unique and mysterious system of abstract geometric and animal symbols which remains to be deciphered. In other respects, however, the Picts may be regarded as very similar to their neighbours.   KF

place names: 1. linguistic areas; 2. languages of Scotland.

1. linguistic areas
The history of the place names of Scotland reflects the country's complex linguistic and political history. It is convenient to divide Scotland up into nine different linguistic areas. Each area is distinctive both in the languages which have been spoken there over the last 1,500 years and in the sequence of these languages. Both these aspects strongly influence the toponymy of any given area. It must be stressed that the boundaries of these areas, as shown on the Map, are far from clear-cut, and that the toponymy of these boundary areas can show an even more complex pattern of linguistic interaction.

Area 1
The Northern Isles (Orkney and Shetland) and north-east Caithness. Although very little toponymic trace remains of the pre-Norse language of this area, there is no good reason to doubt that it was Pictish. The first element of 'Orkney', which first appears in Diodorus (Greek, fl. c.25 BC), drawing on 4th-century sources, is Celtic. It was almost completely overlaid by Norse W, introduced by settlers from Norway (see SCANDINAVIA: 1), who were well established in this area by the early 9th century (see ORKNEY AND CAITHNESS, EARLDOM OF), and this language accounts for the bulk of the place names, such as the two island capitals Kirkwall (*kirkju vágr*, 'church-bay') and Lerwick (*leirvík*, 'mud-bay') (see REGIONAL IDENTITIES: 4). The direct descendant of this language, Norn, was in everyday use in many of the islands as late as the 18th century. The north-east corner of the Scottish mainland (now north-east Caithness) also became extensively settled by the Norse, as its overwhelmingly Norse toponymy clearly shows. That the *Picts occupied this area when Orkney first became Scandinavianized (see SCANDINAVIA: 1) is illustrated by the name the Norse gave to the stretch of water which separates Orkney from Caithness: the Pentland Firth, meaning 'Pictland Firth'. Scots was introduced by settlers chiefly from eastern Lowland Scotland in the later medieval and early modern period, and accounts for many minor names such as Boardhouse (Orkney).

Areas 2 and 3
The west of Scotland, including the islands, from Cape Wrath in the north to Mull of Kintyre in the south (see HIGHLANDS AND ISLANDS: GENERAL). These two areas are most conveniently taken together. Their chief characteristic is defined by the presence of extensive Norse W toponymy, overlaid by Gaelic. In Area 2, especially the Outer Hebrides, it is unclear whether there were Gaelic speakers there before the Norse settlement of AD c.800, or whether, as in Area 1, Norse directly ousted Pictish. A clue to the presence of Gaelic-speakers as opposed to Pictish-speakers in Skye at the time of the Norse settlement of the Outer Hebrides might be provided by the Norse designation of the Minch as *Skotlandfjörðr* ('Scotland Firth'). Historical sources testify to Pictish settlement in the 6th and 7th centuries, and this Pictish presence is confirmed by place names such as Applecross, Wester Ross, and Òb Apoldoire, Skye, both of which contain the Pictish *abor 'river- or burn-mouth'.

In most of Area 3, especially south of Mull, the heartland of the Antrim-derived (see IRELAND: 1) *Dál Riata, Gaelic was well established by the 5th century at the latest, and in the following two centuries spread northwards and westwards with Dál Riata power to include Ardnamurchan on the mainland and the islands of Mull, Coll, and Tiree. The name Argyll (Gaelic *Earra-Ghàidheal* from earlier *Airir Gáidel*), 'coastland of the Gael', well describes this area from the very earliest historic period, and at its greatest extent denoted the whole littoral from the Mull of Kintyre in the south to Loch Broom (Ullapool) in the north.

It was probably not until the late 8th or early 9th century that Norse place names began to be coined in Area 3. Recent toponymic research suggests that down the western seaboard two cultural provinces can be identified within the Norse period: a western one (2a and 3a), consisting of northern Skye, Coll, Tiree, the Outer Hebrides, and western Islay, and an eastern one (2b and 3b) consisting of the western littoral and the remainder of the Inner Hebrides, including southern Skye, Arran, and Bute. Provinces 2a and 3a show a much more thoroughgoing Scandinavian toponymy than 2b and 3b. Throughout the whole of Areas 2 and 3 Gaelic overlaid Scandinavian, giving rise to its characteristic Gaelicized Norse toponymy, such as Stornoway, Lewis (Gaelic *Steòrnabhadh*), from Norse W

Stjórnarvágr ('steerage bay'). It has been estimated that in Lewis 79 per cent of village names are of Norse origin. Other names are entirely Gaelic, such as the various places called Tarbert ('place of portage'), and in Area 3 many of these names were coined before the Norse period. Tarbert Loch Fyne, for example, is first mentioned in 712. Although many Hebridean island names are Norse (Raasay, Eriskay, Barra, Jura), others have also survived from the pre-Norse period, such as Iona, Coll, Skye, Mull, and Lismore. Norse topographic terms were borrowed into Gaelic as appellatives (common nouns), and have themselves generated place names, such as Gaelic *òb* from Norse *hóp* (sheltered bay), giving Oban, with Gaelic diminutive ending *-an* (Gaelic *An t-Òban Latharnach*, 'the little bay of Lorne').

Except in the Clyde islands of Bute and Arran (3c), Scots has scarcely contributed to the toponymy of this area, since by the time Gaelic started to wane, from the 19th century onwards, the language of the Scottish ruling classes was Scottish Standard English. This has given rise to such names as Leverburgh, Harris. The mixed linguistic situation has spawned such anomalies as Broadford, Skye. Originally Norse meaning 'broad firth', it was assimilated to Scottish Standard English 'broad ford', then translated literally into Gaelic as *An t-Àth Leathann*.

Area 4

Easter Ross, eastern Sutherland, and most of Caithness. In this area, as in Areas 2 and 3, it is equally unclear how far Gaelic had ousted Pictish before the introduction of Norse. Also as in those areas, the Norse stratum is of variable density, with fewer Norse names towards the south, and none south of the Beauly valley. The spread of Norse names in this area is closely linked with the power of the earls of Orkney (see ORKNEY AND CAITHNESS, EARLDOM OF), which was at its height in the 11th century: the place name Dingwall ('field of the legal assembly') probably dates from this period. Unlike Areas 2 and 3 (apart from 3c), we have a strong additional stratum of Scots place names, with affixes such as *meikle* ('great') appearing in charters from the later 15th century in names near the east coast.

Area 5

This covers much of the historical kingdom of Strathclyde (see BRITONS AND ANGLES), and shows the sequence Cumbric, Gaelic, Scots, Scottish Standard English. Many of Strathclyde's most important settlements in this area are of Cumbric origin, such as Glasgow ('green hollow') and Lanark ('clearing in wood'), while the capital of the kingdom was Al Clud, Cumbric 'rock of the Clyde', renamed by the Gaels *Dumbarton ('fortress of the Britons'). Gaelic will have penetrated this area at very different rates. The last king of Strathclyde (see KINGSHIP: 2) died in 1018, although Gaelic from Alba may well have been used to name places in Strathclyde as early as the 10th century. Cumbric names were also (partly) Gaelicized: *Caerpentaloch*, recorded in the 10th century with Cumbric *pen ('head, end'), is *Kirkentulach* by c.1200 (with the Gaelic equivalent *ceann*). By this later date the first Scots (see SCOTS LANGUAGE) names are appearing, such as Rogerton, East Kilbride LAN, whose formation with the Scots generic *toun* ('farm, estate'), can be dated, like several other *toun*-names in Areas 5–9, to the last few decades of the 12th century through the probable identity of the eponym—in this case Roger de Valognes (fl. 1185). Such names can be formed with Continental and Scriptural names as well as names of insular origin (Anglo-Scandinavian, Celtic).

Area 6

This includes the pre-1975 counties of Dumfriesshire, Kirkcudbrightshire and Wigtonshire, southwest Scotland, the latter two comprising the region known as *Galloway. The place names reflect a complex sequence of languages, some of which must have coexisted for a considerable time. The strata, not necessarily in chronological order, consist of Cumbric, Anglian, Gaelic, Norse, Scots, and Scottish Standard English. Cumbric is represented by such names as Leswalt 'grass enclosure' WIG and Penpont (parish) 'bridge-end' DMF. Anglian names, which must date from the period when much of this area was annexed to the kingdom of Northumbria in the 7th century, include the important early church centres of *Whithorn WIG ('white house') and Hoddom DMF ('Hodda's elm'?). Norse names are to be found along the coastal strip from the Whithorn peninsula WIG to Annandale DMF, and must have been the result of Norse settlement from the 9th century onwards. Within this area two distinct colonizing movements have been recognized: one moving northwest by land from around Carlisle; the other moving east and south by sea from Ireland, Man, and the Hebrides (see ISLES, KINGDOM OF THE). The last two will have consisted of the mixed Gaelic-Norse population known as the *Gall Ghàidhil*, literally 'foreign Gael', from which is derived the territorial name 'Galloway'. The Dumfriesshire parish name Pennersaughs is Cumbric, 'end of Saxon territory', and gives a good indication of the limit of Anglian expansion. Scots was already penetrating this area by the early 13th century: the minor Gaelic place name Tibereba (*tiobar na bà*), which appears in a charter of Holyrood abbey c.1230 (near Urr KCB), is given also in its Scots form

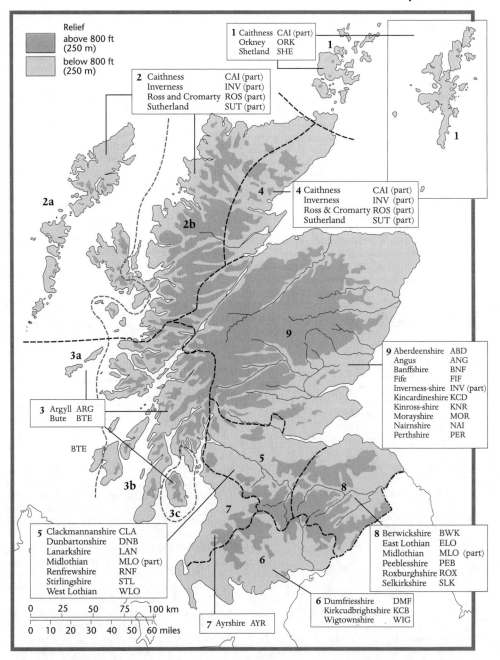

Relief
above 800 ft
(250 m)
below 800 ft
(250 m)

1 Caithness CAI (part)
Orkney ORK
Shetland SHE

2 Caithness CAI (part)
Inverness INV (part)
Ross and Cromarty ROS (part)
Sutherland SUT (part)

4 Caithness CAI (part)
Inverness INV (part)
Ross & Cromarty ROS (part)
Sutherland SUT (part)

9 Aberdeenshire ABD
Angus ANG
Banffshire BNF
Fife FIF
Inverness-shire INV (part)
Kincardineshire KCD
Kinross-shire KNR
Morayshire MOR
Nairnshire NAI
Perthshire PER

3 Argyll ARG
Bute BTE

5 Clackmannanshire CLA
Dunbartonshire DNB
Lanarkshire LAN
Midlothian MLO (part)
Renfrewshire RNF
Stirlingshire STL
West Lothian WLO

8 Berwickshire BWK
East Lothian ELO
Midlothian MLO (part)
Peeblesshire PEB
Roxburghshire ROX
Selkirkshire SLK

6 Dumfriesshire DMF
Kirkcudbrightshire KCB
Wigtownshire WIG

0 25 50 75 100 km
0 10 20 30 40 50 60 miles

7 Ayrshire AYR

This map of Scotland shows the different linguistic areas with approximate boundaries. Each area is described in terms of the pre-1975 counties, although these only give a rough indication of the areas involved. The three-letter county boundaries are those used in the text.

481

Cuwelle ('cow well'), showing both languages already coexisting, and interacting, here at this time.

Area 7

Ayrshire: similar to Area 6 but with a far less significant Norse stratum. There are several Anglian place names which have been incorporated into Gaelic names, clearly showing the sequence Anglian, then Gaelic; for example Dalmellington (Gaelic, *dail* 'haugh' + *Mellintun) and Tarbolton (Gaelic *tòrr* '(conical) hill' + *Botheltun). This early Anglian stratum would appear to date from the Anglian occupation of parts of Ayrshire in the mid-8th century. There is a significant number of shared church dedications, expressed in place names, between this area and Kintyre ARG, suggesting that there were strong cultural and linguistic links between the two, probably dating from the Scottish expansion in the later 9th and 10th century. This Gaelic influence remained strong until it was gradually superseded by Scots, with the first Scots place names appearing in documents of the early 13th century.

Area 8

Lothian: Cumbric, Anglian, Gaelic, Scots. Anglian settlement in this area can be dated from historical souces to the early 7th century, and Anglian place names which show early features, such as Tynninghame, 'settlement of the Tyne-dwellers' (referring to the river Tyne in East Lothian), must belong to this first period of settlement. However, many Cumbric settlement-names survived, such as Pencaitland ELO 'enclosure (or church) at wood-end' or possibly 'orchard-end' (Welsh *coedlan*); or Pentland MLO ('end-enclosure or end-church'), both medieval parishes. Gaelic place names, such as Ballencrieff WLO, ELO (*baile na craoibhe*, 'farm of the tree'), which must have been introduced with the southwards expansion of Scottish power in the 10th century, become markedly fewer towards the eastern part of this area (see ANGLO-SCOTTISH RELATIONS: 1).

Area 9

Geographically the largest of all the areas, stretching from the Firth of Forth to the Beauly Firth, it comprises the bulk of the kingdom of the Picts. Many important settlements still bear Pictish names, such as *Aberdeen, *Perth, Abernethy, and Arbroath. Many more contain elements which were borrowed from Pictish by the language which succeeded it, Gaelic. Some of these elements are still widely used as part of the Gaelic lexicon, such as *dail* ('water-meadow, haugh'), *monadh* ('hill'), and *preas* ('bush'), and can therefore still be productive in the onomasticon. Others have become obsolete in the Gaelic lexicon, but were clearly once part of it since they often appear in place-names in combination with Gaelic elements. One such is the common place name element *Pit-*, from *pett* ('estate, land-holding'), which was also exported, presumably in a Gaelic-speaking environment from the 10th century onwards, south of the Forth. Another category of Pictish-influenced place names contains Gaelic elements which have a markedly different usage from that which the same Gaelic element has in Ireland. In such cases, it is simplest to assume a Pictish substrate influence. Examples of this would be *blàr* ('field, muir'), which occurs in scores of Scottish place names in most areas where Scottish Gaelic was later spoken. Although occurring in the Irish Gaelic lexicon, with the meaning 'battlefield', it is not found in Irish place names. We can therefore assume that there was a Pictish cognate which affected the usage of this word in Scottish Gaelic, and furthermore that this was already being used in Pictish to form place names. Another important place-name element which shows Pictish substrate influence is *Fetter-*, found throughout Area 9, but unknown in Areas 1, 3, 5, 6, 7, 8, and in Ireland. It occurs in important early names, such as Dunottar KCD, Fettercairn KCD, and Forteviot PER, and probably derives from a Pictish word for some kind of territorial/administrative unit, which is similar to the meaning 'region, district' ascribed to its Welsh cognate *godir*.

In this area, Scots place names are first evidenced in the later part of the 12th century, and the settlement element *toun*, equivalent to Gaelic *baile*, first appears in Fife around this time (see Area 5 for more details).

General Patterns

Throughout Areas 5, 7, 8, 9 there is a scattering of Norse names, including *c.*30 names ending in *bý* (farm); Fiddra, an island in the Firth of Forth; and Kirkness KNR, an important estate on Loch Leven recorded in the 11th century. They most likely date from the 10th century.

Underlying all the above-mentioned toponymic strata is one which goes back to a period before the early medieval polities such as Dál Riata and Pictland had emerged (*c.*6th century AD), thus pre-dating, possibly by many hundreds of years, the earliest strata shown on the map. The names which preserve this earliest stratum, mainly river names (hydronyms), such as the Ayr (whence the settlement name, formerly Gaelic *Inbhir-àir*, 'Ayrmouth'), the Farrar (INV), and the Tay, are generally ascribed to an Indo-European linguistic stratum which pre-dates the arrival of Celts (very approximately put, for the British Isles, at sometime between 700 and 500 BC).

The history of Scottish place-name studies is almost as fragmented and varied as the history of the place names themselves. There is no convenient all-Scotland reference work (see Guide to Further Reading, below: Section 11). There has never been the systematic approach to the subject which has been seen in England, where since 1923 the English Place-Name Society has been publishing detailed place-name analyses of high academic standard county by county. Only a handful of Scottish counties have been subjected to comparable treatment, and the toponymy of some, such as Angus, Argyll, Ayrshire, East Lothian, and Kincardineshire, has never been subjected to rigorous academic attention. The Scottish Place-Name Survey at the School of Scottish Studies, University of Edinburgh, has had general responsibility for place-name studies in Scotland since its inception in the 1950s. This has never been a large unit, but it has brought together a wide range of toponymic material, including a rich oral collection (see ORAL TRADITION), especially from the *Gàidhealtachd*. The Scottish Place-Name Society, founded in 1996, is helping raise the profile of Scottish toponymics, and together they are working towards the setting up of a Scottish Place-Name Database, as well as the production of a Scottish County series.

ST

2. languages of Scotland

The place names of Scotland directly reflect the different *languages of Scotland (see also GAELIC LANGUAGE; SCOTS LANGUAGE). The following list, or-ganized aphabetically, gives examples of common place-name elements of each.

Anglian
This is a northern dialect of Anglo-Saxon or Old English, introduced into what is now southern Scotland in the 7th century: *hām* ('settlement'), for example Whittingeham ELO; *tūn* ('farm'), for example Haddington ELO.

Cumbric
This is a P-Celtic, Brythonic language closely related to Welsh: *tref* ('homestead, farm'), for example Tranent ELO, Traquair PEB; Terreagles DMF, *pen* (end; hill; lit. 'head'), for example Pencaitland ELO, Pennersaughs DMF.

Gaelic
This is a Q-Celtic language very closely related to Old Irish; it was spoken in Argyll (*Dál Riata) from the 5th century AD at the latest. Probably first introduced into Pictland by the church (see ADOMNÁN, ST; COLUMBA, ST; IONA; RELIGIOUS LIFE: 1) from the late 6th century onwards, it became the language of the ruling class of Alba by the early 10th century at the latest, and reached its zenith in the 11th, when it was spoken throughout most of mainland Scotland. Only Area 1 (see PLACE NAMES: 1) shows no

toponymic trace of Gaelic. Since it was the chief language during the crucial formation-period of the Scottish kingdom (see KINGSHIP: 1; NATIONAL IDENTITY: 1), it became the language in which the bulk of settlement names (see RURAL SETTLEMENT: 1–2) were coined. Its interaction with different language substrata and superstrata across Scotland has given a variety of different textures to the Scottish Gaelic toponymy. Typical Gaelic place-name elements are: *baile* ('farm'), as in Balcanquhal FIF ('of the sons of Anacol'); Balnagown ROS (*gobha*, 'smith'); Balnamoon BNF (*mòine*, 'moss, (peat-) bog'); *achadh* ('field; (secondary) farm'), as in Auchenleck ABD, AYR (*leac*, 'flagstone'); *druim* 'ridge', as in Drumdil ROS and Drumdreel FIF (both containing *daol*, 'beetle', i.e. 'dark'); also several important elements borrowed from Pictish: *pett* ('farm'), as in Pittencleroch PER (*cléireach*, 'cleric'); *monadh* ('hill, muir, upland grazing area') as in Kinninmonth FIF, ABD ('end of the white hill'); *dail* ('water-meadow, haugh') as in Dail Mhàrtuinn ROS ('Martin's haugh'), Dallas MOR ('place of the haugh(s)'); Dollar CLK ('place of the haugh(s)') and Dull PER are probably closer to the original Pictish (cf. the Welsh cognate *dôl*).

Norse
This is used here to designate both Old West Scandinavian (from Norway) and Old East Scandinavian (from Denmark). Where there is certainty as to which grouping Norse belongs, it is followed by W[est] or E[ast]: *bólstaðr* ('(secondary) settlement') as in Isbister ORK 'east settlement'; *bý* ('farm') as in Humbie ELO, FIF, WLO (? 'farm of the dogs') (see SCANDINAVIA: 1).

Pictish
This is a P-Celtic language, closely related to Cumbric, spoken throughout the territories of the historical *Picts. The place-name evidence is crucial to any construction of a Pictish lexicon, since Pictish has otherwise left behind very few traces. Place names probably coined in the Pictish period (before AD c.900)—as opposed to place names which contain Pictish loan-words into Gaelic (see Gaelic, above)—contain such elements as *abor* 'river- or burn-mouth', as in Aberdeen ABD, Arbroath ANG ('mouth of the Brothock Water'), Aberdour ABD, FIF ('mouth of the Dour (Burn)'); *pert* ('grove') as in Perth PER, Logie-Pert ANG; *pren* ('tree') as in Prinlaws FIF ('green tree') (see CULTURE: 2).

Scots
This is a development both of the Anglian of Lothian, and of northern Middle English, which itself had been exposed to strong Norse E influence. Introduced into Scotland north of the Forth in the late 12th century, it was well established as the language of the Scottish *royal court and *parliament

by the 14th: *toun* ('farm', 'estate') as in Otterston FIF ('Ottar's *toun*': Ottar lived in later 12th century); *feild* ('field') as in Stewartfield ABD; *muir* ('rough-grazing') as in Pilmuir (most Lowland counties).

Scottish Standard English

This is standard modern English as spoken in Scotland: Leverburgh, Harris INV (founded 1923). ST

political system: 1. 1707–1832; 2. 1832–1918; 3. post-1918.

1. 1707–1832

The Scottish political system after the *Union of 1707 became subject to notorious electoral abuses which led one Victorian reader of the papers of Viscount Sidmouth, briefly prime minister as Henry Addington just after the turn of the 19th century, to write 'Scotch Jobbery' over any letter in the collection which had been addressed to Addington from Scotland! It is important to remember that these abuses were not the product of the system so much as the effect of its divorce from access to direct parliamentary control, as the British Westminster parliament had little knowledge of Scottish electoral matters nor inclination to discuss them. Yet soon after the Union the appellate status of the Court of *Session was usurped by the House of Lords at Westminster, which invariably followed the advice of a series of Scottish members of that house who had some legal training, first the last Scottish Lord Chancellor, the earl of Seafield, and through the dukes of Argyll, the earl of Marchmont, and Lord Mansfield—the last of whom, although not trained in Scots law, spoke for Scottish legal matters in the Lords by virtue of his birth there! Of course there had been some electoral manipulation by ambitious politicians trying to influence elections before 1707 (see PARLIAMENT: 2), but the removal of a distinctive Scottish forum for political debate, allied with retention of Scots electoral law as a condition of the Union, led to increasing corruption over the course of the 18th century.

Government influence in Scotland from 1707 to 1832 was increased by the use of patronage, the distribution of government offices and pensions to those who in return committed themselves to its support on the basis of obligation rather than ideological commitment. As Scotland was a poor country, offices of quite small value could become objects of political attention and influence in the system of customs and excise collection, or even in the network of linen stamp offices established to guarantee the quality of Scottish textile production from 1727. Initially this system very much reflected the social structure of a society in which kinship loyalties were every bit as important as party politics, and in which the most significant ideological

differences in that society, between Hanoverian unionism and *Jacobite separatism, were blurred by the treasonable status assigned to an opposition which thus was never able to express its opposition openly (see GOVERNMENT AFTER THE UNION). Yet there were differences in ideology between the Whig court party increasingly dominated by the duke of Argyll and the *Campbells, but the so-called 'Squadrone' Whigs of Lowland Scotland, more and more confined to the Lothians and Borders, became committed to their programme of assimilation to England less by conviction than in the hope of possibly regaining office.

The patronage system undoubtedly was expanded after 1725 as the duke of Argyll and his 'Argathelian' followers sought to extend their influence and that of the state into banking (see ECONOMY, TERTIARY SECTOR: 1), law (see LAW AND LAWYERS: 2), the church (see RELIGIOUS LIFE: 5), the universities, and local government. This certainly exalted 'Campbell power', but it also promoted a coherent programme of secular economic and cultural improvement on a national basis. It led to the creation of a national block of MPs at Westminster that were put at the service of the government in most votes, in return for parliamentary time for legislation on Scottish issues relating to economic development in particular. Pessimists point to the paucity of this legislation in quantitative terms, but in an age in which government activity in any area other than war was minimal, the record of government legislation for Scotland under a system of purportedly corrupt patronage had much to recommend its consideration in a more favourable light. Indeed, after the Jacobite rebellions in both 1715 and 1745, excessive state reprisal in Scotland was prevented by the bartering of Scottish votes at Westminster in return for ministerial restraint.

By the election of 1768, however, the need for electoral reform was obvious, since in the absence of a Scottish 'manager' local contests across Scotland, but particularly that in Forfarshire, degenerated to the basest level of bribery and deceit. The 'fictitious vote' was presented as a threat to the traditional Scottish constitution based on votes in the counties that represented ownership of land, but by 1768 lawyers had adapted the lack of precision in existing legislation to the boundless complexity of Scots feudal law and established ways in which the feudal superiority of land could be detached from physical possession in a manner which allowed the holder of the superiority the right to vote under the landowner's patronage. Such a development of course maximized the influence of the larger landowner, often a nobleman (see NOBILITY: 4), who could split superiorities to increase his influence and thus overcome independent landowners of more modest means. On the other hand these developments, subject to control to prevent gross bribery, were favoured by politicians such as Henry *Dundas for retaining the constitutional influence of the larger landowners, and by judges such as Lord Mansfield, who viewed an increase in the number of voters as a positive development in an electoral system hitherto restricted to the very smallest minority of the population when compared to the electoral systems of England and Wales, or by the 1790s with that of Ireland.

The outbreak of the long wars against republican and Napoleonic France (see FRENCH REVOLUTION, AGE OF THE), however, made it impossible to debate reform, at least for those who felt their position in society to be fundamentally challenged. Thereafter, even after peace in 1815, any change to the existing system was viewed by the majority of the small number of voters as leading inevitably to revolutionary excess. Voters became detached from the rest of a Scottish society that was changing very rapidly. The issue in the political system after 1815 between Tories and Whigs, both from similar groups in society, was whether to reform the political system or not, and whether full civil rights for the *Roman Catholic community for what after 1801 was the United Kingdom of Great Britain and Ireland was a necessary prerequisite for such reform. The Scottish aspect of this British debate was obscured by the British context of the constitutional issues, and this contributed to a general feeling that the Scottish political system would pass away with the end of its *ancien régime*. Such was not to be the case. AJM

2. 1832–1918

Two characteristics of the 19th-century electoral system merit attention: the franchise and the constituencies. The First Reform Act of 1832 heralded a much greater breakthrough than in England. Until the Act, the Scottish electorate was extraordinarily restricted, with a grand total of perhaps 4,500 voters for the whole country. So after 1832, the share of adult males with the vote rose from a ratio of substantially worse than 1 : 100 to 1 : 8. In burghs, the new electorate consisted mainly of £10 householders, and in counties, mostly, £10 property owners and, £50 long lease tenants. The Act's drafting was not watertight. In county seats, it was possible to create fictitious votes by exploiting gaps, such as joint leaseholds, and this was practised in a number of seats, although mainly only up to the mid-1840s.

The voters qualified under the 1832 Act were quite different from those previously enfranchised. In burghs, the voters were overwhelmingly drawn from the middle class, including professional men, large merchants and manufacturers, and the petty bourgeoisie—small shopkeepers, self-employed tradesmen, and the like. Only a very small number of working-class males entered the registers at this stage. In the shires, the new voters were mostly landowners hitherto excluded because they did not hold feudal superiorities, and tenant farmers of substance, along with rural businessmen, traders, and so forth.

The Second Reform Act of 1868 admitted a large swathe of urban working-class men on to the registers. The vote was bestowed on male rate-paying householders and £10 lodgers in burghs. The result of the measure was to increase the electorate to just under one-quarter of a million, approximately one-third of the adult male population. This brought the Scottish enfranchisement level closer to England. In the more industrialized places such as *Glasgow, the working men constituted a clear majority of the new electorate.

The Third Reform Act of 1884/5 extended the franchise to the rural counterpart of the urban working class. The main qualification stipulated in the legislation was, again, the rate-paying householder. The number of voters was increased to some 560,000, or 60 per cent of adult males. This was somewhat below the English proportion of 67 per cent. The new categories of voters included crofters, whose enfranchisement coincided with their politicization, so leading to the electoral breakthrough achieved by the Crofters' party in the 1885 general election. Elsewhere, agricultural workers and miners were the main beneficiaries of the Act.

Yet the level of enfranchisement, as noted above, did not attain the English proportion even after the Third Act. Scottish burghs had only about 57 per cent of adult males on the registers, with even lower figures for industrial centres like *Dundee and the east end of Glasgow. The reasons for this difference are a mix of legal and socioeconomic factors. To qualify under Scottish law, a person had to have resided twelve months at the address. Yet in many urban areas, large sections of the population moved house annually. In Glasgow, for example, the burgh surveyor estimated that around one-third of the city's people changed accommodation every year (see HOUSING: 3). This reflected the fluctuating nature of activity in the heavy industries (see ECONOMY, SECONDARY SECTOR: 2) which dominated Scotland: these were subject to unpredictable cyclical movements and made a settled residential arrangement virtually impossible to achieve. Moreover, the requirement that the prospective elector should have personally all local rates due ran counter to a practice common in Scotland, by which the landlord paid the rates on cheaper houses (usually those under £4.00 p.a.), recouping the cost from the tenant by an addition to the weekly or monthly rental charge. As a result, many were disqualified in the poorer parts of urban centres.

The distribution of seats did not follow the changing balance of voters, so that wide anomalies existed in the ratio of voters to MPs. Essentially, burghs and industrial areas were under-represented at Westminster. After 1832, an additional eight seats were given to Scotland, taking the total number of MPs to 53. Most of these new seats were given to larger cities: Glasgow got two, while Aberdeen, Dundee, Perth, Greenock, Leith, and Paisley each gained a member to themselves, no longer being grouped with three or four other burghs, as under the old dispensation. Edinburgh was granted one extra member, bringing it up to two. Yet small county electorates, such as Sutherland, with 84 voters, sat beside Glasgow, with 3,495 voters for each MP.

The redistributions accompanying the succeeding franchise extension measures produced a somewhat less distorted allocation of MPs. This was mainly achieved by the addition of new seats: by 1914, Scotland returned 72 members to Westminster (including two Scottish universities' seats, elected by graduates). But inequalities remained. The Wick Burghs seat in 1910 had 3,037 voters, whereas Lanarkshire Partick, with 24,617, was eight times bigger. The counties of Inverness, Ross, Sutherland, Caithness, Orkney, and Shetland between them in 1910 returned seven MPs, while Renfrewshire had 25 MPs—yet the latter's population, at around 314,000, was some 15 per cent larger than the combined six northern counties. The sweeping redistribution which came with the Fourth Reform Act in 1918 did a great deal to promote the rise of Labour (see LABOURISM) and the eclipse of the Liberals (see LIBERALISM) by requiring all constituencies to be of nearly equal size.

Before 1832, Scottish politics were notorious for corruption, bribery, and intimidation. Perhaps because of the distaste felt at these practices by the new electors, corrupt electoral practices after 1832 were almost non-existent. This contrasts most favourably with the situation in the rest of the British Isles. Ireland seemed hopelessly sunk in bribery and corruption, and the widespread persistence long after 1832 of similar influences in England has been fully documented. Candidates who fought contests in both Scotland and England were fulsome in their praise for the cleanness and integrity of elections north of the Border. There were barely any instances of a Scottish constituency being investigated by the House of Commons Committee on Electoral Malpractice. Intimidation by landowners and employers was rarely reported

in Scotland: the removal of the famous progressive tenant farmer George Hope of Fenton Barns was an isolated episode.   IGCH

3. post-1918

There are two features to the Scottish political system which give rise to its distinctiveness within the UK: Scottish political culture and Scottish political institutions. Significantly, the values, myths, habits, and behaviour making up Scotland's political system which are relevant in the period after 1918 are those of the public at large and not just the political classes. Mass democracy and a widened franchise have been the hallmark of the period and this has had a considerable impact on the political system. There are many political cultures in Scotland but the strength and nature of these differ compared with other parts of the UK. Similarly, some political institutions are common to Scotland and the rest of the UK while others are specific to Scotland or have a distinctly Scottish dimension. It was and is the interaction of the political institutions and the political culture of Scotland which constituted the Scottish political system.

Scottish political culture in the 20th century can be understood by considering each of the four key cleavages found in western European states: *national identity, religion, *social class, and the urban–rural divide (see URBAN SOCIETY: 4; RURAL SOCIETY: 5). The 'Scottishness' of Scottish politics is the most obvious distinguishing feature of the Scottish political system. Throughout the period of mass democracy, it has been necessary for politicians and political parties to stress their Scottishness alongside their Britishness. The relative weight of each has changed, with the Scottish dimension becoming increasingly important and increasingly politicized. At no stage since the *Union of 1707 has an exclusive Scottish or British national identity predominated but some mixture of the two has existed. Religion has been important and at times has been closely aligned with national identity. Scottish Presbyterianism has been important, not only as a distinguishing feature of Scottish national distinctiveness but also in its contribution to notions of democracy and social ethics. The religious divide in Scotland was once a potent feature of the system with Protestants and Roman Catholics (see ROMAN CATHOLIC COMMUNITY), the latter mainly immigrants from Ireland (see IMMIGRATION, IRISH), divided politically and socially. The tendency for Protestants, including working-class Protestants, to vote *Unionist (Conservative) while Catholics voted Labour was a feature of the system which has been receding in recent elections.

Parts of urban Scotland have a tradition of radical working-class politics (see LABOURISM) in sharp contrast to the conservatism and deference which was to be found in parts of rural Scotland, though radicalism in the Highlands and Islands (see LAND AGITATION AND REFORM) of Scotland has been a recurring feature. In the 20th century there have been few occasions when an obvious party-political divide on an urban–rural basis has existed or when industries commonly associated with either area, notably agriculture (see ECONOMY PRIMARY SECTOR: 2) in rural areas and heavy industry (see ECONOMY, SECONDARY SECTOR: 2) in urban areas, have caused serious tensions. The rise of suburbia, modern communications, and technology has altered and weakened any divide which might have existed between the town and countryside. As elsewhere, class has been the key cleavage in Scottish politics in the age of mass democracy. The rise of working-class politics was most evident in the rise of the Labour Party.

Scholars have noted the rise of 'new social movements' and 'new political cleavages' in different parts of the world. Scotland has been relatively unaffected by these. It has been suggested that in relatively wealthy societies, of which Scotland is undoubtedly one, people will tend to have 'post-material' concerns: about the environment, equal rights for women, and matters which are unrelated to the cleavages of the past. While an active environmentalist movement has emerged in Scotland, it has been small relative to that found elsewhere in Europe and gender equality was relatively late coming onto the political agenda, succeeding largely by attachment to debates on constitutional change. To a significant extent, 'new politics' were beginning to reach Scotland only by the end of the 20th century and are distinguished from their reception elsewhere in Europe by the relative weight or manifestation they took and the relationship between each. For much of the 20th century the class and national identity cleavages cut across each other and were in conflict. Working-class solidarity across Britain as a whole, combined with a strong sense of Scottish cultural identity, permeated the labour movement in Scotland, the trade unions, and the Labour Party. From the 1970s onwards, however, these two cleavages came to reinforce each other, with working-class and Scottish national identities tending to coexist and share aims and aspirations.

Scottish political culture and the cleavages in Scottish politics are manifested and mediated in and through various institutions. The most notable of these are the political parties. The SNP (see NATIONALISM) is the most distinctly Scottish party but each of the other main parties has some peculiarly Scottish features. Labour, the Conservatives, and Liberal Democrats each are British parties but have a Scottish organization and some degree of autonomy. The establishment of a Scottish *parliament in 1999 is expected to result in greater autonomy for each of these parties and enhance the distinctiveness of the Scottish political system. Pressure groups active in Scotland are similar to the parties, with some being branches of British groups with some degree of autonomy while others are entirely Scottish.

Also important is the media. The Scottish print media (see NEWSPAPERS: 2) has had a popular following in 20th-century Scotland and London-based papers have fared less well, though in recent years technology has allowed London papers to produce Scottish editions with some pages devoted exclusively to Scottish matters. Scotland also has a very lively local press. The broadcast media (see RADIO AND TELEVISION) has developed in a similar way. Television and radio stations catering for Scotland or regions within Scotland have developed since the 1950s. Contrary to the expectations of many scholars immediately after the war, mass communications have encouraged a sense of distinctiveness in places like Scotland rather than leading to assimilation and homogeneity. Formal political institutions have also developed in the 20th century to maintain or enhance the distinctiveness of Scottish politics. The *Scottish Office, Scottish local government, and numerous official and semi-official bodies exist. This 'institutional thickness' has given Scottish politics an official status. The key to understanding the distinctiveness of Scottish politics is that it has rarely been undermined by political change. Indeed, the dynamics of politics affecting Scotland has, if anything, served to augment the Scottishness of the political system.   JM

population patterns: 1. to 1770; 2. since 1770.

1. to 1770

The population of Scotland in 1755, according to the Revd Alexander Webster's private census, was 1,265,380 or a fifth that of England. How many people lived in Scotland before that date is largely a matter for speculation. Rising land values and the encroachment of arable farming on marginal upland areas (see ECONOMY: 2), however, suggest that population growth was rapid in the 12th and 13th centuries. This phase, which may have seen a doubling of population to over one million, came to an end with the famine of 1315–18 and above all the Black Death (see HEALTH, FAMINE, AND DISEASE: 1) of 1349. It is possible that this combination of bubonic and pneumonic plague reduced the population by 25–30 per cent and subsequent epidemics of plague and other diseases brought about a further fall in this 'golden age of bacteria'. Scotland with its more dispersed population may have been less hard hit than some other countries and recovered sooner but it would be surprising if more than 700,000 people lived there in 1500. There then followed another period of rapid growth which began to slow down towards the end of the 16th century and came to a halt in the 1640s. The famine of 1695–9 reduced the population from a size only a little lower than that of Webster's census, to just under 1.1 million, about the same as before the Black Death. Growth resumed again in 1700 but it was slow and uneven until at least the 1770s, if a contemporary estimate of 1.4 million in 1775 is to be believed.

Webster's census shows a geographical distribution of population that was probably typical of earlier centuries. Compared with today, it was much more evenly spread out, with over half of all Scots to be found north of the Tay. About a third of the population lived in the eastern Lowlands between Angus and the Lothians. Despite the rise of *Glasgow from the early 17th century onwards, the western Lowlands had a smaller population than either the north-east and the *Highlands and Islands and not many more inhabitants than the *Borders. The most striking change over time was in the level of urbanization (see URBAN SETTLEMENT: 1). In 1560 only 2.5 per cent of Scots lived in towns with more than 2,500 inhabitants, one of the lowest rates in Europe. Despite stagnation or even decline in the second half of the 17th century, this had risen to 17.3 per cent by 1750, a figure exceeded only by England, the Low Countries, and Italy. It is possible that the number of people living in the countryside at the latter date was no greater than before the Black Death and may even have been smaller.

In explaining these changes over time, most emphasis has been placed on the role played by mortality crises: short-lived but violent increases in the death rate as a result of war, famine, and disease (see HEALTH, FAMINE, AND DISEASE: 2). The demographic impact of war (see WARFARE, WEAPONS, AND FORTIFICATIONS), has largely been ignored though c.100,000 soldiers and civilians may have perished as a result of its consequences—mainly disease—between 1639 and 1651. As regards famines, bad harvests were frequent but the major subsistence crises such as those of 1315–18, 1585–7, 1594–8, 1621–3, and 1695–9 occurred when crops failed three or more years running. That of 1695–9 may have reduced the population through a combination of high mortality, reduced fertility, and massive emigration to Ulster (see IRELAND: 3), by as much as 13 per cent. It was particularly severe in the north-east where there was also a slump in cloth exports which provided essential part-time employment for many small tenants and subtenants. Although the last nationwide famine, it was not necessarily

the worst. However, disease was more important than either war or famine.

Until its disappearance in 1650, bubonic plague was the most feared disease but although it had a case fatality rate of 60–70 per cent, by the 16th century it was confined mainly to the towns. Thus although the last epidemic of 1644–9 reduced the population of the towns by about a fifth, this was the equivalent of only 2 per cent of the national total. Other diseases, many simply described as fevers, did more harm, especially smallpox. Highly contagious and airborne, smallpox was found in both the countryside and the towns and was eventually responsible for one in ten of all deaths (see URBAN SOCIETY: 2). Mortality was particularly high among infants and young children but in the countryside, where epidemics took place at longer intervals than in the towns but were more lethal, large numbers of adults also died of the disease. Although mortality crises declined markedly in importance after 1700, there was no decline in the crude death rate since 'normal' or non-crisis mortality increased, particularly among infants, as many diseases became endemic (see CHILDBIRTH AND INFANCY).

Population trends were also controlled by fertility which was determined largely by nuptiality. In Lowland Scotland the west European marriage pattern prevailed, whereby couples married only when and if they were able to establish their own households (see COURTSHIP AND MARRIAGE). This meant that in the late 17th and 18th centuries Lowland *women married on average for the first time at 26–7 years and 20–5 per cent remained celibate. This was a powerful brake on fertility, particularly when combined with a long period of breastfeeding (which meant that the interval between births was 24–30 months). In the Highlands and Islands, however, cultural, economic, and social factors resulted in a mean age of marriage for females of only 22–3 years and only c.10 per cent never married.

Although mortality crises were probably more severe than in England and celibacy by the 18th century much lower, at least in the Lowlands, what particularly distinguishes Scotland from many other countries, including England, is the scale of its *emigration. From the late Middle Ages large numbers of Scots left for the Continent, particularly Denmark, Sweden (see SCANDINAVIA: 2–3), Prussia, and above all Poland (see GERMANY, THE BALTIC, AND POLAND). Many were soldiers (see MERCENARIES IN EUROPE) but even more were pedlars, merchants, and craftsmen. This peaked between 1580 and 1640, when pressure of population and resources was severe, but throughout the 17th century there was heavy emigration to *Ireland. During that century c.200,000 Scots emigrated, the equivalent of 40 per cent of the natural increase. Although there was then a slackening off, another 80,000 left between 1700 and 1775, now mainly to North America (see CANADA; USA).

Scottish population before 1770, therefore, was subject to a variety of forces which combined to prevent sustained, long-term growth. This was achieved only after 1770, when a new demographic regime began. RET

2. since 1770

At its 1971 peak of 5.23 million, Scotland's population was more than four times its 1755 level. Growth was fastest in the 19th century, averaging more than 1 per cent per annum; after the First World War it slowed markedly, and numbers actually declined in the 1920s and again after 1971. By 1991, as Table 1 shows, the figure had fallen below five million. Between 1971 and 1991, Scotland's population was more depressed than that of any national state in the European Union; in every decade since the 1770s, it grew more slowly than that of England.

Regionally, there were marked differences in Scotland's pattern of growth. Consistent comparisons are difficult over long periods of time; Tables 1 and 2 use 1975–96 regions, but with Argyll and Bute in Highland rather than Strathclyde. They show rapid expansion in *Glasgow and its region up to 1951, and its subsequent decline. Grampian's

share fell markedly up to 1841, but stabilized thereafter. After 1841, the dominant features were rapid proportionate reductions in both the *Highlands and Islands and the *Borders (especially in the south-west). The shares of Lothian, Tayside, Fife, and Central were initially stable, but rose significantly after 1841.

Proportions can be misleading. Every region except the north-east saw marked population growth between 1755 and 1801, and all did so between 1801 and 1841. In the north-west between 1755 and 1841, numbers rose especially fast in the Inner and Outer Hebrides and in some parts of the adjacent mainland, but were more controlled in many other mainland areas in the north and north-west. This contrasted with the south-west, where the population of Wigtownshire grew almost 2.4 times between 1755 and 1821. From the 1830s, however, numbers fell back in several rural counties, and after 1861 rural decline became almost universal. Between 1861 and 1951, the largest proportionate falls (more than a third) were in Caithness, Sutherland, and the Northern Isles, but population declined by more than a fifth in Ross and Cromarty and Argyll, and also in Berwick and Wigtown. Within counties, depopulation was very uneven, especially rapid in some of the islands (except Lewis where population rose until 1911, and in areas distant from commercial, industrial, or transport development. Everywhere, people increasingly

Table 1. Population of Scotland (000s, of total population), by region, 1755–1991

	1755	1801	1841	1911	1951	1991
Highland and Islands (including Argyll and Bute)	266	318	420	369	309	347
Grampian	211	212	312	455	451	494
Tayside, Fife, and Central	322	386	554	871	936	994
Lothian	132	164	282	615	691	724
Strathclyde (less Argyll and Bute)	183	341	799	2,190	2,452	2,152
Dumfries, Galloway, Borders	151	187	253	261	257	251
TOTAL	1,265	1,608	2,620	4,761	5,096	4,962

Table 2. Population of Scotland (% age of total population) by region, 1755–1991

	1755	1801	1841	1911	1951	1991
Highland and Islands (including Argyll and Bute)	21.0	19.8	16.0	7.8	6.1	7.0
Grampian	16.7	13.2	11.9	9.6	8.9	10.0
Tayside, Fife, and Central	25.5	24.0	21.1	18.3	18.4	20.0
Lothian	10.4	10.2	10.8	12.9	13.6	14.6
Strathclyde (less Argyll and Bute)	14.5	21.2	30.5	46.0	48.1	43.4
Dumfries, Galloway, Borders	11.9	11.6	9.7	5.5	5.0	5.1
TOTAL	100.0	100.0	100.0	100.0	100.0	100.0

concentrated into towns (see URBAN SETTLEMENT: 2–4; URBAN SOCIETY: 3–5). By 1891, half of Scotland's population lived in towns of more than 10,000 people. Glasgow, *Edinburgh, Leith, *Aberdeen, *Dundee, Greenock, and Paisley contained well over one-third of Scotland's population in 1911, but less than a third in 1991, mainly as a result of commuter sprawl. From the 1970s, oil development, tourism, and hostility to urban living encouraged some population recovery in many rural areas in the north-west, and, especially in the 1970s, in Shetland.

Population change results from the difference between numbers of births and of deaths, and from the balance between in- and out-migration (see EMIGRATION: 3–4; IMMIGRATION, IRISH; MIGRATION). Through most of the period since 1770, the Scottish national death rate was roughly similar to that of England. By contrast, compared with similar groups of the population both there and in much of continental western Europe, Scots tended to marry later and less frequently, had higher fertility within and outwith marriage, and were much more likely to migrate long distances internally within Scotland, elsewhere in the British Isles, and overseas.

Recent estimates of mortality suggest a Scottish death rate of over 30 per 1,000 population in 1755, 24 in the 1790s, and 22 in the early 1860s. Urban death rates much higher than rural; when first measured in 1860–2, they were 28.1 in the four cities, but 17.9 in rural areas. Mortality probably peaked in Glasgow in the 1840s, when rapid urban growth outran sanitary provision, and large inflows from Ireland and the Highlands combined with serious trade depression. The result was devastating outbreaks of epidemic disease (see HEALTH, FAMINE, AND DISEASE: 3). From the early 1870s, the national death rate turned down, with especially rapid reductions in the cities, as environmental conditions improved. In 1930–2, the crude death rate in the four cities was 14.1; in rural areas it was 12.8; the Scottish average was 13.4. Thereafter, as older people made up a growing share of the population, the national death rate fell only slowly, to around 12 per thousand in the early 1990s.

Mortality began among younger adults, and children over the age of 1. Between the 1860s and the 1930s, mortality fell by more than three-quarters at ages 1–14, and by about two-thirds at ages 15–34. However, infant mortality peaked in the 1890s at 135 per thousand live births (the English and Welsh rate was 153) and was still 82 per thousand in the 1930s, significantly above the English/Welsh rate of 60 (see CHILDBIRTH AND INFANCY; CHILDREN). In some urban areas, infant mortality stayed much higher. In 1911–13, when the national infant mortality rate was 109, Dundee's rate was 160; the rate was also high in some smaller towns (for example, 148 in Dumfries). By contrast, rural rates were often much lower: 58, for example, in Skye. After 1945, as deaths from infectious diseases became rare, young adult, child, and infant death rates fell rapidly (infant deaths to below 6 per thousand live births for the first time in the summer of 1992). But improvement remained slow for older people, especially men. Expectation of life at birth for all males was 40 in the 1860s, 50 in 1910–12, 64 in 1950–52, and 71.4 in 1991. But for a man aged 65, it was 10.8 in the 1860s and only 13.3 in 1991; the figures for women were 11.6 and 16.8.

The Scottish birth rate was probably around 35 per thousand population between the later 18th and the mid-19th centuries, similar to English levels. As in England and Wales, it turned down sharply in the mid-1870s, falling to 26 before the First World War, and to 18 in the 1930s. It peaked again in 1946 at 22, fell back to 18 in the early 1950s, rose to over 20 in the early 1960s, then declined steadily to below 12 by the mid-1990s, slightly below the English level.

The number of births results from the number of children born outside marriage, the number of *women who are married, and the fertility of married women. On all these dimensions throughout the period, Scotland differed markedly from England. Births to unmarried mothers were probably below the English level in the later 18th century, but, by the early 1860s, unmarried women bore nearly 10 per cent of all children in Scotland (more than 15 per cent in Banffshire, Aberdeenshire, and Wigtownshire), but only 6 per cent in England and Wales. In the early 1930s, births out of wedlock were 7 per cent in Scotland (but 19 per cent in Banffshire and 17 per cent in Wigtownshire). The figure for England and Wales was 4.3 per cent. From a low point of 4.2 per cent in 1957–9, the Scottish national ratio passed 10 per cent in 1979, and, as increasing numbers of children were born to cohabiting couples, exceeded one-third of all births in 1995.

Within marriage, Scottish women seem to have had higher fertility than women elsewhere in Great Britain even in the 18th century. From the 1860s until the late 1970s, this was certainly the case. In 1859–63, the number of legitimate births per thousand married women aged 15–44 was about 15 per cent higher in Scotland than in England and Wales; it was 16 per cent higher in 1900, and over 35 per cent higher in the 1930s. The gap only fell below 10 per cent in the late 1960s. Within Scotland, for most of the period after 1870, age-standardized marital fertility was highest in the crofting counties of the north-west and in the mining and heavy industry areas of the central belt (see ECONOMY: PRIMARY SECTOR: 3), and was low in the east and especially in the eastern Borders. However, almost every county had figures above the English average.

Nevertheless, Scottish overall fertility was very similar to that for England and Wales. This was because Scotland had among the highest rates of celibacy and highest marriage ages in western Europe, a pattern already present in the 18th century (see COURTSHIP AND MARRIAGE). In 1851, 21 per cent of Scots women aged 45–54 were unmarried, compared with 12 per cent of English women; comparable figures for 1951 were 20 per cent and 15 per cent. Similar though smaller differences were also found for men. Within Scotland, differences were even greater. In 1911, 36 per cent of women in Shetland had never married by age 45–9, and more than 28 per cent in all the crofting and island counties, in Nairn and Perth, and throughout most of the Borders. By contrast, less than 20 per cent were never married in all the counties of the central belt except Clackmannan. The median age at first marriage for women was 28.7 in Sutherland, and 23.5 in West Lothian.

Restricted marriage meant that, throughout the period, overall fertility and natural increase (the difference between births and deaths) were extremely low in many parts of Scotland. In the early 1860s, though its marital fertility was well above the European average, Sutherland had the lowest age-standardized overall fertility of any similar administrative unit in Europe outside France. By 1901–11, Sutherland's natural increase was below 3 per cent; nowhere in the north and north-west or in the Borders had natural increase above 10 per cent.

Where, as in much of the Highlands and Islands after 1850, marriage was highly restricted and fertility consequently low, even modest rates of out-migration produced actual population decline. In the 1860s, net out-migration from Sutherland was 10.5 per cent of the 1861 population, but natural increase of only 6.8 per cent produced a fall in population of nearly four per cent. By contrast, net out-migration was 17.4 per cent in West Lothian, but the population rose significantly because high levels of marriage produced natural increase of 23.4 per cent. Overall, for the period 1861–1900, the highest proportional population losses through migration were (in order) in Wigtown, Berwick, Banff, Caithness, Roxburgh, Kirkcudbright, East Lothian, and Moray. Ross and Cromarty was twelfth, Sutherland sixteenth, Argyll nineteenth, and Inverness twenty-second. Between 1901 and 1951, the largest proportional losses were from Banff, Caithness, West Lothian, and Wigtown. Inverness was twentieth and Argyll twenty-sixth.

Overall, Scotland has been characterized by the persistence and pervasiveness of population loss through out-migration, not just from rural areas but even from towns and cities. Nationally, a net figure of nearly one million people left Scotland between 1861 and 1911 (including those going to other parts of the UK); as a proportion of the population, this was more than three times the loss from England and Wales. For 1911–91, net emigration from Scotland exceeded 1.7 million, equivalent to more than one-third of Scotland's 1911 population. Losses were, moreover, geographically widespread. In the 1880s, Dunbarton and Bute were the only Scottish counties without net out-migration. Between 1901 and 1911, only three counties had net gain and all four cities lost population. High emigration, and highly restricted marriage, both clear signs of restricted opportunities at home, thus dominated Scotland's population history over the past 250 years.   MA

printing and publishing. Printing arrived in Scotland in 1507–8 when the merchant Walter Chepman (*c*.1473–*c*.1528) and bookseller Andrew Myllar (fl. 1503–8) established their press in the Southgait (now the Cowgate) in Edinburgh. *James IV issued them a patent in September 1507 for the printing of 'bukis of our Lawis, actis of parliament, croniclis, mess bukis, and portuus efter the use of our Realme'. These printers were also licensed to produce Bishop William Elphinstone's *Aberdeen Breviary* (1509–10), the most significant of their surviving works, along with fragments of the poetry of William Dunbar, Robert Henryson, and Blind Harry's *The Wallace*. The Southgait press was short-lived, nothing surviving after 1510, and no other major printers are known to be active before Thomas Davidson (fl. 1532–42), the first to be designated King's Printer, who produced a fine edition of Hector Boece's *The Hystory and Croniklis of Scotland* (1542), translated from Latin to Scots by John Bellenden.

From the *Reformation there was an almost continuous line of royal printers but the development of printing was slowed by civil war, poor economic conditions, and competition from England and mainland Europe, the latter the main source of Latin books until the 18th century. During the Marian civil war the presses of the royal printer Robert Lekpreuik (fl. 1561–82) and the bookseller Thomas Bassandyne (fl. 1568–77) fought a propaganda war representing the young King *James VI and his mother *Mary, Queen of Scots, respectively. After the English and former 'Martin Marprelate' printer Robert Waldegrave (fl. 1590–1603) was appointed royal printer in 1590, greater political stability allowed him to increase press output and to introduce Anglicization in both language and manners, such as dedications and patronage over specific editions. Waldegrave printed James VI's own writings including *Basilikon Doron* (1599, reprinted 1603). Nonetheless, vernacular Scots remained important and Scotland's greatest printer-publisher of the 16th century, Henry Charteris (*c*.1561–99), published and reprinted much vernacular poetry from his own and other presses including the first extant edition of *The Works of Sir David Lindsay* (1568). Charteris was also publisher for George Buchanan and commissioned the first edition of Buchanan's controversial *De Jure Regni* (1579) (see BOOKSELLING).

Domestic printing expanded during the 17th century though the rate of growth was irregular. Edward Raban (fl. 1620–50) began Aberdeen's first press in 1622 and George Anderson (fl. 1637–47) set up in Glasgow in 1638 where he famously printed *The Protestation of the General Assembly of the Church of Scotland* (1638) against the Prayer Book of 1637, but printing failed to establish itself in other centres until the 18th century, in spite of brief appearances in St Andrews and Stirling. However, after the economic stagnation of the 1650s the *Edinburgh press expanded swiftly, the late 1670s being a boom period by which time dozens of printers, journeymen, booksellers, and bookbinders were active, almanacs being the most profitable printings (see EDINBURGH: 2). The greatest publisher of this century was the Edinburgh bookseller Andro Hart (fl. 1589–1621), who began printing himself in 1608. Hart continued the vernacular tradition and also produced a fine Geneva bible (1610) so accurately that it was widely used as copy by Dutch printers. Hart also published John Napier's *Mirifici logarithorum canonis constructio* (1619) and the poetry of William Drummond of Hawthornden. At the end of the century the main figure of the book trade was Agnes Campbell, royal printer 1676–1712 and widow of the printer Andrew Anderson (fl. 1653–76), who became the most litigious and wealthy Scottish book trader of the early modern period.

At the turn of the 18th century the general spread of literacy (see SCHOOLS AND SCHOOLING: 2) supported an expanding press output in popular ephemera, ballads, and chapbooks. The demand for news also grew. After several false starts in the 1640s and 1660s the first true Scottish newspaper, the *Edinburgh Gazette*, appeared in 1699 from the press of James Watson, the younger (fl. 1695–1722). Watson also became famous for publishing the anthology *Choice Collection of Comic and Serious Scots Poems* (1706–11) and his contemporary Thomas Ruddiman (1674–1757), with various partners including his brother Walter, edited, published, and printed new editions of Gavin Douglas and George Buchanan and the poetry of Allan Ramsay.

As literary and popular output developed simultaneously, so did the spread of printing to numerous 'provincial' centres. The 18th century saw the growth of the Glasgow press supplying the Americas and Ireland. The *Glasgow press of Robert and Andrew Foulis (fl. 1746–76) became famous throughout Europe for quality editions of Latin and Greek classics. The Edinburgh publisher William Smellie's (1740–95) first edition of the *Encyclopaedia Britannica* (1768) was another Enlightenment highlight. However, much of the Scottish trade depended on reprints that infringed the copyright of English copyholders and a deluge of legal disputes was not resolved until the 1770s. Only by then had the invention of stereoplates, made by the Edinburgh goldsmith William Ged (1690–1749) in the 1730s, overcome the restrictive practices of the English press. Stereoplates along with Stanhope's iron press delivered the technical means for further Scottish expansion in the following century.

Both periodical and book publishing activity were essential elements of the Enlightenment (see CULTURE: 11) and at the turn of the 19th century a group of Edinburgh publishers became the focus for a golden age of the Scottish book trade. Archibald Constable (1774–1827) began the Whig *Edinburgh Review* in 1802, published Sir Walter Scott from 1803 (including 'the *Waverley* novels' from 1814) and the prose of James Hogg from 1807, and also acquired the *Encyclopaedia Britannica* in 1812. Unfortunately, the failure of Constable's London agents in 1826 led to the collapse of Constable & Co., accompanied by the bankruptcy of Scott's printer James Ballantyne (1772–1833) and Scott himself. The Edinburgh bookseller William Blackwood (1776–1834) was a contemporary who began publishing in 1804 and soon gained a reputation as a major force in British literary publishing, starting the Tory *Blackwood's Edinburgh Magazine* in 1817; issuing the works of Susan Ferrier, John Galt, and James Hogg; and, as John Murray's Edinburgh agent, co-publishing Byron, Shelley, and Hazlitt. Also William (1800–83) and Robert (1802–71) Chambers began from the 1830s to publish a range of popular reference, encyclopaedic, and natural history works. Meanwhile in Glasgow John Blackie & Co., founded in 1809, had became important education publishers and William Collins (1789–1853), starting in partnership with Charles, brother of the clergyman Thomas *Chalmers, rose from the 1820s to be one of the greatest religious and Bible printer/publishers of the modern period.

By the late 19th century the golden age of Scottish publishing had passed but significant developments continued to appear including the printer/publisher Thomas Nelson (1822–92), who specialized in children's books and technological innovation, inventing the first rotary press, and John Bartholomew & Co, the Edinburgh cartographer and map printers (see MAPS AND MAP-MAKING) who went into partnership with Nelson. By the turn of the century the introduction of Monotype and Linotype typesetting brought mechanical compositors to the Edinburgh printing trade, many of whom were women, and printing continued to flourish. The Linotype machines in particular facilitated the expansion in local and national newspapers before the Second World War and were the foundation of newspaper and periodical empires such as D. C. Thomson & Co. of Dundee formed in 1906.

Since the Second World War Scottish book publishing has struggled in the face of predatory multinationals and the harsh realities of the market. Only Edinburgh University Press survives of the university presses and a number of publishing and printing firms are no more, with even the likes of William Collins now part of the Harper/Collins multinational under Rupert Murdoch. The 1970s, however, were fruitful, seeing the literary output of Canongate Press, including authors like Alasdair Gray and the emergence of the Mainstream Press, which remains independent. Despite pressure and competition, Scottish book publishing continues in modest scale. AMa

printmaking, etching, and engraving. The first great printmaking project in Scotland was John Slezer's *Theatrum Scotiae*, a collection of engravings of the towns and great houses of Scotland published in 1693, but though all the drawings were prepared by Slezer in Scotland the prints were produced in London and Holland. It was only when Richard Cooper (fl. 1720–64) settled in Scotland in 1720 that quality engraving was established in the country for the first time. Cooper was a versatile printmaker whose work ranged from music publishing to engraving medical illustrations which he did in collaboration with Alexander Munro Primus. Richard Cooper's pupils included Andrew Bell (1726–1810), a successful engraver and sometime proprietor of the *Encyclopaedia Britannica*, and (Sir) Robert Strange who went on to become one of the most distinguished engravers of the later part of the century. He collaborated with William Hunter and in the hands of such artists engraved medical illustration became very important in the evolution and dissemination of Enlightenment medicine (see CULTURE: 16). It was not only artists who were involved. Munro himself understood the importance of drawing and engraving for medicine and following his example the brothers John and Charles Bell actually learnt to draw and indeed to etch in order to illustrate and publish their own surgical investigations. One result of this expertise, Charles Bell's *Anatomy of Expression* (1806), was widely influential among artists quite independently of the success of Bell's surgical publications.

In the first half of the 19th century, in harness with the boom in publishing, engraving flourished and *Edinburgh became a world centre. William Lizars (1788–1859) especially produced work of the highest quality. Audubon, for instance, originally intended his *Birds of America* to be engraved by Lizars, but in the end this project was abandoned and Audubon went elsewhere because Lizars had a dispute with his colourists. Like Strange, Lizars was also outstanding as a medical engraver and his prints remained current throughout much of the century. Topographical prints of Scotland were also very popular. They were produced by a number of different engravers and were often published as books. A number of artists tried the new form of lithography in the 1820s and in 1840 Frederick Schenk established the first commercial lithographic workshop in Edinburgh to provide for the market in topographical views.

Richard Cooper also established a tradition of artist-printmakers. He taught the Runciman brothers who produced some remarkable etchings. David Allan also etched and his illustrations to *The Gentle Shepherd* are particularly important in his pioneering use of aquatint. There were also important amateur etchers such as John Clerk of Eldin. He specialized in the historic landscapes (see GEOLOGY AND LANDSCAPE) of Scotland, but also collaborated with James Hutton in his geological enquiries. John Kay (1742–1826), a barber by profession, was also an amateur etcher and his *Edinburgh Portraits* (1837) are an invaluable record of the characters of the time. David Deuchar was another amateur who, as an interpreter of the Dutch tradition, was an influence on both Raeburn and Wilkie.

The production of artists' prints was continued by Wilkie who made very fine etchings, Andrew Geddes (1783–1844), Hugh William Williams (1773–1829), Walter Geikie (1783–1837), and David Scott (1796–1849) and his brother William Bell Scott (1811–90). Geikie's etchings of Edinburgh characters are a unique record of the ordinary street life of the period. Wilkie also understood the importance of having his work circulated in engraving. His friend and contemporary John Burnet (1784–1868) engraved *The Blind Fiddler* and thereafter virtually all Wilkie's major compositions were engraved, giving his art enormous circulation throughout Europe. Reproductive engraving of artists' work continued to be a very important part of the art economy for much of the 19th century through the publications of the (Royal) Association for the Promotion of the Fine Arts, for instance, which commissioned and published by subscription works by leading painters.

Protestant sects and disestablishment

At the end of the 19th century, following Whistler's lead, there was a dramatic revival in etching. William Strang (1859–1921), (Sir) D. Y. Cameron (1865–1945), (Sir) Muirhead Bone (1876–1953), James McBey (1883–1959), and a number of others brought the art to a new level of achievement and enjoyed wide success. Strang's etched portraits and Bone's powerful images such as *The Great Gantry, Charing Cross* (1906) are outstanding in the period. Bone, the first official war artist, also published suites of lithographs from his war drawings. The market for prints crashed with the slump in the late 1920s, but the example of the printmakers of Muirhead Bone's generation was nevertheless transmitted through E. S. Lumsden (1883–1948) and others to younger artists like Ian Fleming (1906–96) and William Wilson (1905–72) who were themselves the outstanding printmakers of the thirties. The 1920s saw also a revival of woodblock printing, notably in the work of Agnes Miller Parker (1895–1980) and Iain McNab (1890–1967). For a brief period in the late 1950s Harley Brothers in Edinburgh, an old-established lithographic workshop, provided an opportunity for a number of artists to work in lithography, while outside Scotland, Eduardo Paolozzi (b. 1924) was one of the pioneers of screen printing as an artist's medium during the 1960s. Through these and other examples, the tradition of printmaking was carried on into the movement to found printmaking workshops in Edinburgh, Glasgow, and Aberdeen during the seventies, and using these facilities several leading artists, notably John Bellany (b. 1944) working with Edinburgh Printmakers, Will Maclean (b. 1941) with Peacock Printmakers in Aberdeen, and Elizabeth Blackadder (b. 1931) in the Glasgow Print Studio, developed into outstanding printmakers. DM

Protestant sects and disestablishment. Outside the Church of Scotland, and after 1843 the Free Church of Scotland, there flourished a large number of other Protestant bodies, some of which formed the backbone of the disestablishment movement that tried to sever church from state. One of the most significant strands began with the secession from the Church of Scotland in 1733 of Ebenezer Erskine, a minister of Stirling, in disgust at patronage and the decay of doctrine and discipline in the church. Only two years later the Secession Church split in two, the so-called Burghers and Anti-Burghers (officially the Associate and General Associate Synods), the dividing issue being whether or not it was legitimate for members of the church to take the burgess oath to uphold the religion 'authorized by the laws'. The apparently recondite nature of the issue illustrates the proclivity of the Seceders for an old-fashioned punctilious

rectitude in matters of religion. A second strand of Presbyterian Dissent, the Relief Church, was altogether more forward-looking, a product of the Evangelical Revival. It began in 1761 under the leadership of Thomas Gillespie, a Fife minister who had been deposed by the General Assembly for refusing to acquiesce in the enforcement of patronage. Gradually other congregations affiliated as they were forced out of the established church for unwillingness to accept ministers whom they judged not to be preachers of the Gospel. A similar warm evangelistic spirit gained ground in the Secession Churches, leading to debates over 'New Light', the fresh insights of the 18th-century revival movement, against 'Old Light', insistence on the terms of the Westminster Confession from the 17th century. In 1799 the Burghers, and in 1806 the Anti-Burghers, split into New Lichts (New Lights), who no longer believed the civil magistrate must regulate ecclesiastical affairs, and the Auld Lichts (Old Lights), who clung to the traditional conviction that he must. Both parties of New Lights grew, especially in the rising urban areas, as a result of vigorous evangelism, and in 1820 they merged as the United Secession Church.

Other dissenting groups multiplied. The other strand of Presbyterianism was the most extreme, the inheritors of the Cameronian tradition (see COVENANTERS). In 1761 the scattered adherents of this Reformed Presbyterian Church maintaining the continuing obligation of the Covenants were first divided into pastoral charges. They were strong enough to form a synod in 1811, and were to remain independent until the majority joined the Free Church in 1876.

Other bodies rejected Presbyterianism altogether. The followers of John Glas, deposed from the ministry in 1730, formed independent churches that held communion weekly and claimed that faith was a matter of intellectual assent rather than personal trust. The Old Scots Independents, beginning in 1768, and the Scotch Baptists (1765), with their able theologian Archibald Maclean, were almost identical in organization, insisting on a plurality of elders rather than a regular ministry. Like the Baptists of 'English' order, which appointed ministers, the Scotch Baptists practised the baptism of believers only. Both the Independents and the Baptists drew strength from the Evangelistic work of James and Robert Haldane during the earlier 19th century. The Independents organized themselves into a Congregational Union in 1812, the Baptists not managing to create a permanent equivalent until 1869. Another small group, the Bereans, followers of John Barclay, another deposed minister (1773), virtually died out by the 1840s. There were a number of Universalist churches in the late 18th century, and they merged into the Unitarian tradition. Quakers were also to be found, affiliated to the Meeting for Sufferings in London. Methodism sprang from the preaching of John Wesley, and, although its anti-Calvinist theology made it suspect in many quarters, it put down roots in Scotland, especially in Shetland. By 1851, 9 per cent of churchgoers were non-Presbyterians, whether Roman Catholic or Protestant dissenters.

From 1829 the United Secession Church spearheaded a militant campaign under the banner of 'Voluntaryism' to separate church and state entirely (see DISRUPTION). That became the watchword of the United Presbyterian Church that resulted from the merger in 1847 of the United Secession and Relief churches. From 1874 to 1895 the disestablishment crusade achieved a central place in Scottish politics, inducing Gladstone to declare it in 1889 the policy of the Liberal Party. The United Presbyterians owed much to prosperous Liberal entrepreneurs such as the Cox family, jute manufacturers of Lochee. It was the first Presbyterian body to allow organs (1872) and to relax its adhesion to the Westminster Confession (1879). The Evangelical Union had been formed by James Morison in 1843, based on the revivalist methods and the non-Calvinist views of the American Charles Finney. Its merger with the Congregational Union in 1896 is a sign of the broader weakening of Calvinism. Revivalism was also largely responsible for the rise of the Brethren, keen Evangelists under entirely lay leadership, and the Salvation Army (1879).

The union of the United Presbyterian Church and the Free Church in 1900 left a minority of the former Free Church, the so-called Wee Frees, in defiant mood as the champions of a firm Calvinism and traditional mores. Like the Free Presbyterians, who had seceded from the Free Church in 1893 at the prospect of reunion, the continuing Free Church was largely confined to the Highlands (see CHURCH INSTITUTIONS: 6). The consolidation of most Presbyterianism in 1929 left another continuing body, the United Free Church, led by the doughty minister and Labour MP James Barr. Wesleyan theology inspired a Holiness denomination from 1909 that from six years later was part of the American Church of the Nazarene. Pentecostalism, marked by speaking in tongues, appeared in Scotland in 1908, and emerged in the 1920s in three main streams: Elim, the Assemblies of God, and the Apostolic Church. Although the main trend of the 20th century was towards greater church unity, splits continued: the Free Presbyterians lost a third of their number to the Associated Presbyterian Churches in 1989 when the main body condemned the Lord Chancellor, one of its members, for attending a Roman Catholic funeral; and charismatic renewal, generating excited worship (see RELIGIOUS LIFE: 8), has also created a number of separate and vigorous congregations from the 1980s. It is clear that Scotland has been fertile ground for smaller Protestant bodies (see RELIGIOUS LIFE: 8).   DWB

public utilities, business enterprises or organizations dedicated to the provision of essential services to the public. Examples include gas, water, and electricity supplies, as well as connections to sewerage, hydraulic power, and postal and telecommunications systems. In Scotland, as elsewhere in the UK, the impetus behind the evolution of public utilities was rapid urbanization (see URBAN SETTLEMENT: 3–5) in the 18th and 19th centuries. The resulting urban masses first required clean and reliable water supplies, and later became dependent upon gas, electricity, and other public services, as did rapidly growing numbers of industrial and commercial consumers.

Of all the public utilities, water supply is perhaps the most fundamental. The earliest co-ordinated Scottish water-supply schemes were those in Edinburgh (1674), Stirling (1774), Greenock (1796), and Glasgow (1807). Some, such as Robert Thom's Shaw's Water Works at Greenock, were particularly significant, and provided water both for domestic and industrial use. However, in general, inadequate volume and quality of water, rapidly increasing demand, and sequences of cholera and typhoid epidemics, prompted most cities to incorporate water supply into municipal control, beginning with *Glasgow (1855). In Glasgow, the newly incorporated water supplies required urgent attention, and the city embarked upon a huge project involving the damming of Loch Katrine, and the construction of 34 miles (54.8 km) of aqueduct to the city, the scheme being completed in 1860. The success of the project heralded the beginning of a new era of capital investment by the public sector in water supplies throughout Scotland, and attracted interest from all over the world.

The earliest supplies to cities had been achieved by laying comparatively small-bore wood and lead pipes, and although initially effective, these were soon to become inadequate. One of the greatest factors behind the improvement of water supplies was the development of high-pressure cast-iron mains, water pressure being vital for efficient distribution. During the early 19th century, Scotland had become one of the world's most important centres for the manufacture of pig-iron (see ECONOMY, SECONDARY SECTOR: 2). The expertise extended to include specialist pipe castings, and companies such as Thomas Edington of Glasgow grew to prominence. Scotland's growing engineering industries also contributed to the development of public water supplies, a fine example being the hydraulic engineers Glenfield Kennedy of Kilmarnock.

Having achieved great advances in water supply, the next major challenge was posed by growing quantities of both solid and liquid waste. In Glasgow, for example, drainage of streets by covered sewers had existed only since 1790 and by 1818 only 5 miles (8 km) of sewers had been laid. Pressure for sanitary reform grew from 1840, particularly with the proliferation of water closets in private dwellings. The issue of hygiene, however, was compromised by the commercial value of horse and human manure, which had various industrial and horticultural uses, and which prolonged the use of ash closets in working-class dwellings, and the routine collection of nightsoil.

From the 1840s, legislation encouraged improvements in sanitation, but it was not until the 1880s that major new sewers were constructed in cities such as Glasgow, where a major new sewer diverting the system to a new purification plant at Dalmarnock was completed in 1894, with further treatment works and pumping stations being added in subsequent years. Similar, though smaller, schemes were introduced in other Scottish cities, particularly between 1900 and 1910. Having addressed the disposal of sewage, the problem of solid waste remained. Prior to the introduction of systematic collection from the 1850s onwards, refuse was often left in the streets to rot, encouraging pests and disease. Thereafter, many cities established Cleansing Departments to deal with the waste. Some became sophisticated operations, as was the case in Glasgow where by the 1880s refuse was collected, sorted, and riddled, organic waste being sent to farms and market gardens, the remainder being cremated in refused destructors.

Gas supply, which has its origins in the pioneering work of the Scot William Murdoch (1754–1839), first appeared in Scottish cities in the early 19th century, the earliest companies being established in *Edinburgh (1811) and Glasgow (1817). It was used initially for street lighting, later being applied to interior lighting in domestic as well as commercial and industrial buildings. Wider use both in the home and by industry was not significant until after 1870. As was the case with water, the inadequacy and variable quality of supply, combined with attendant safety issues, encouraged the city councils to incorporate gas manufacture and supply into municipal control from the late 1860s. By 1947, 83 per cent of the output of Scotland's 195 gasworks was in municipal control.

Electricity was first exploited commercially in Scotland in the 1870s, but it was not until the mid-1880s that cities such as Glasgow established their first public supplies. By the 1890s, many had incorporated electricity into municipal control, usually with the aim of securing and developing a supply for growing electric tramway networks (see TRANSPORT AND COMMUNICATIONS: 2). These reached their peak between 1900 and 1907, later being replaced by diesel-powered buses, Britain's last tram service ceasing in Glasgow in 1962. Demand for electricity, meanwhile, had grown swiftly, driven primarily by rapid growth in industry, but also by increasing domestic use. Unlike gas, electricity was not so geographically restricted to towns and cities, and electrification programmes eventually also connected consumers throughout rural areas.

The importance of public utilities has tended to ensure a degree of public-sector control because of health and safety issues, the need for standardization, and because most have become consolidated into natural monopolies with immense potential commercial power. The first phase of intervention occurred between 1855 and 1900, and involved local authorities taking control of water, gas, and electricity. A second phase was at a national level, and commenced with the takeover of telephone services in 1912 by the General Post Office. This was followed in the 1920s and 1930s by state support for the development of the National Grid, the aim of which was to standardize and expand electricity generation, and to guarantee supply.

After the Labour Party's victory in the 1945 general election, the state was expanded to embrace public utilities at a national level. Both gas and electricity were nationalized by Acts of Parliament in 1947. In the case of gas, twelve area boards were formed, the largest of which was the Scottish Gas Board. Town gasworks were gradually phased out after the introduction of natural gas from the North Sea, the first town to convert being Kelso in June 1970. Gas was subsequently distributed through a 'Supergrid', previously established in the 1950s, and based at Westfield in Fife. The last town gasworks at Millport (Great Cumbrae) closed in 1981.

Electricity was also transformed after entering the state sector, eventually being divided into two autonomous groups, the North of Scotland Hydro-Board and the South of Scotland Electricity Board. Huge increases in demand resulted in large capital investment programmes, especially in the 1950s and 1960s. In the Highlands (see ECONOMY OF THE HIGHLANDS AND ISLANDS: 3), new hydroelectric schemes were begun, building on the substantial investments of the 1930s. Similarly in the Lowlands, large centralized generating capacity was established through the construction of coal-fired stations such as Cockenzie and Longannet, which were briefly augmented by oil-fired capacity at

Inverkip. In addition, nuclear stations were added at Hunterston and Torness.

In 1979, a new phase of government by the Conservative Party heralded a major change in policy towards public utilities, which, with the exception of the Post Office, were privatized and deregulated during the 1980s and 1990s, the state retaining some control through regulatory bodies. In Scotland, the gas industry was taken over by British Gas PLC, and electricity in the south by Scottish Power PLC and in the north by Scottish Hydro PLC. In England and Wales, water and sewerage services were also taken into the private sector, but in Scotland, political pressure prevented privatization. Instead, responsibility for water was taken from local authorities and vested with three new water authorities: Northern, Eastern, and Western Scottish Water.   MKO

radio and television: 1. BBC; 2. independent broadcasting.

1. BBC

Broadcasting in Scotland began on 6 March 1923 with the opening of a BBC main station (call sign 5SC) at Glasgow, four months after the start of broadcasting from London. In October 1923 a second main station was opened, at Aberdeen, followed by the opening of two relay stations at Edinburgh (May 1924) and Dundee (November 1924). Post Office communication links enabled programmes to be relayed simultaneously from London to all stations. The station director for each local station supervised organizational and programming matters, subject to general control from London. A diverse range of programmes was broadcast, not necessarily on Scottish topics. These consisted of local news, weather forecasts, talks, plays, music concerts, comedy, a children's hour, and appeals for good causes. National news was taken on a simultaneous broadcast (SB) from London. Local programmes could also be offered for SB to London or to other stations. There was rivalry between the local stations. For example, Edinburgh and Dundee preferred to take their programmes from London rather than Glasgow; and Aberdeen broadcast its own programmes rather than take them from Glasgow or on SB from London.

The novelty of radio, together with lack of experience, talent, and resources, led to the production of some poor quality programmes. This factor, along with the desire to extend broadcasting beyond the main cities, persuaded the BBC in 1926 to adopt a policy of centralization and plan the introduction of a Regional Scheme. The location of any production was now expected to be governed by where programmes could be produced economically and to the highest standards; that location invariably turned out to be London. Under the Regional Scheme, the four local stations were replaced in 1932 by two high-power transmitters at Westerglen. This improved and extended programme reception and also provided listeners with a choice of programme: the National Programme

from London and the Scottish Regional Programme. The Scottish service focused on items of local interest, supplemented by programmes taken from London and other BBC Regions.

During the 1930s, radio increasingly filled the leisure hours of many people. Broadcasting created radio personalities and widened cultural horizons. It also exposed listeners to metropolitan culture (see CULTURE: 21). Programmes broadcast at regular times provided a structure to daily life, but there was also standardization of news, accent, values, and culture. This reflected the views of John Reith, the first director-general, that radio should operate as a public service with uniformly high standards, and with a duty to inform, educate, and entertain the audience. Unfortunately, centralization resulted in a diminution of Scottish and other Regional programme activities. It also relegated the BBC in Scotland to the status of a National Region, representing only one part of a unitary BBC. Moreover, with the outbreak of war in 1939, the Scottish Regional Programme was merged into a single Home Service which was planned in London. Many Scottish staff left to join the forces and there was a reduction in the number of Scottish items broadcast. Nevertheless, radio was popular during the war years because it was an important source of news and entertainment. The BBC's reputation was enhanced because of its role in boosting morale and its refusal to use radio as an instrument of propaganda.

After the war, a Scottish Home Service was introduced on 29 July 1945. In 1947 a Scottish Advisory Council was formed, to be succeeded in 1953 by a Broadcasting Council for Scotland with control over the policy and content of radio (and from 1962, television) programmes produced within and for Scotland. The period from 1947 to 1955 has been regarded as the golden years of Scottish radio because of the wide range and quality of programmes and the absence of competition from television, for the audience and for resources. Television arrived in Scotland on 14 March 1952 with the opening of the Kirk o' Shotts transmitter. Programmes consisted primarily of outside broadcasts until studio equipment was provided. But within a few years, television began to eclipse radio. BBC2 was extended to Scotland in 1966, and colour television in 1967. BBC radio in Scotland was restricted to an opt-out service from Radio 4. Unlike England, Scotland was not provided with BBC local radio. The revitalization of radio in Scotland did not occur until the late 1970s when Radio Highland (the first of several community radio stations) was opened in 1976 and Radio Scotland was transformed in 1978 into a self-contained national programme service. Devolution also became an important issue, within and outwith BBC Scotland.

A more competitive era has prevailed since the 1980s with the advent of new radio stations and the proliferation of new television channels via cable and satellite. With a dwindling share of the audience, the BBC in Scotland argued that its ability to reach a larger audience geographically was what legitimized the retention of the licence fee. But there was now a greater recognition within the corporation of the need to make more large-budget Scottish programmes for the network, use the public-service remit to introduce greater experimentation in programme formats, and capitalize on the digital revolution to offer a wider choice of programmes. With the approach of a new millennium, the BBC began to reassess its role and think about transforming the identity of the BBC in Scotland into that of a Scottish BBC. It also had to meet the programming challenges posed by the advent of a Scottish parliament, not least the need to keep the UK fully informed about Scottish political, social, and economic developments.   WMcD

2. independent broadcasting

Independent television began in London on 22 September 1955. Two months later, the Independent Television Authority (ITA) invited applications for the central Scotland franchise. But the financial problems experienced by the four ITV companies in England discouraged businessmen in Scotland from applying. However, a Canadian, Roy Thomson (owner of the *Scotsman* newspaper) was more optimistic about the prospects for commercial television. His application to the ITA was successful and on 30 May 1956 Scottish Television (STV) was appointed programme contractor. The Theatre Royal in Glasgow was later converted into studios, and STV affiliated with Lew Grade's ATV to obtain access to ITV network programmes, and did so on very favourable terms. STV began broadcasting on 31 August 1957 from the Blackhill transmitter.

STV became a prosperous company because of its monopoly and the popularity of the network programmes it transmitted. The latter provided the main competition for BBC Scotland and the main source of revenue for STV. Reductions in staff costs and low investment in programmes increased profits. The former led to union militancy, the latter resulted in poor-quality programmes. STV's prosperity was reflected in Roy Thomson's famous phrase, spoken to a journalist in Canada in 1959, that operating the franchise was 'a licence to print money'. From 1964 the government began to impose a levy on ITV profits.

STV appeared more attuned than the BBC to popular taste in Scotland. It broadcast a popular lunchtime variety programme, pioneered the first news magazine, and produce the renowned film documentaries of John Grierson. In 1960, two additional companies were selected as programme contractors: Border Television and Grampian Television both opened in September 1961. Border served a population on both sides of the Scottish–English border, whereas Grampian broadcast to geographically scattered communities. STV was fortunate to have its franchise renewed in 1964 and 1968. The company also experienced financial difficulties, poor industrial relations, and a fire at the Theatre Royal. The financial problems were so acute that from 1969 the company was forced to arrange overdraft facilities and to defer rental payments to the ITA until 1971. STV opened a new studio complex at Cowcaddens in 1974, and began to invest more resources in programme-making. Its franchise was renewed in 1980 and 1992, the latter with a token £2,000 bid under the new competitive tendering procedures.

The demand for commercial radio was created by pirate radio in the 1960s. Legal commercial radio did not arrive until the 1970s with the introduction of independent local radio. The first ILR station in Scotland, Radio Clyde, opened in December 1973. This station attracted a larger share of the audience in the west of Scotland than BBC Radio Scotland or other radio networks. Radio Clyde's popularity was partly attributed to its attempt to study the character and needs of its listeners, and partly to the novelty of commercial radio, particularly in the absence of BBC local radio. Music and local news represented important ingredients in programme output. A second ILR station, Radio Forth, opened in Edinburgh in January 1975. In the early 1980s, further stations were opened: Radio Tay (Dundee and Perth), NorthSound Radio (Aberdeen), West Sound Radio (Ayr), and Moray Firth Radio (Inverness). In the early 1990s, a few smaller 'incremental' community ILR stations were also opened in Scotland.   WMcD

'Red Clydeside'. The term 'Red Clydeside' is more than a generally accepted description of some important events; it is a concept over which commentators on 20th-century Scotland still divide, on politically revealing grounds as well as those of historical interpretation. Social scientists of the new (1990s) Scottish school pay little attention to it—perhaps because they think the new (devolved) Scotland is more in need of a 'usable history' organized around the unifying theme of 'civic nationalism' (see NATIONALISM; NATIONAL IDENTITY: 6) than of an analysis haunted by the spectre of class struggle (see SOCIAL CLASS). Nevertheless debates about 'Red Clydeside' remain central to contemporary Scottish history.

In August 1914, the Glasgow schoolteacher and Marxist propagandist John Maclean (1879–1923), whose parents were refugees from the Highland Clearances, launched a militant agitation against the war along the lines of the German Social Democrat Karl Liebknecht's slogan: 'The chief enemy is at home.' There was also a broader, pacifist movement led by the ILP (see LABOURISM). And the demands of the wartime economy created conditions which, in 1915 (contrary to a national trade-union pledge to suspend industrial action), led to strikes by Clydeside engineering workers. The dilution of skilled labour by the employment of low-paid, less skilled, workers resulted in more general action organized by the first shop stewards' movement and in the state deportations (from *Glasgow) of leading stewards in March 1916. The threat posed from the area seemed all the greater because of the late 1915 rent strikes against profiteering landlords—involving communities and led by women—which forced the government to introduce a historic Rent Restrictions Act.

In 1918 John Maclean—appointed a consul for Russia's Bolshevik government—received the longest of his several prison sentences for seditious activities. But five years became little more than six months when the end of the war, fears for Maclean's health, and working-class pressure, led to his release. Early in 1919 the west of Scotland was at the centre of the post-war labour unrest. The 40 hours' strike resulted in a riot which the Scottish Secretary told the cabinet was a 'Bolshevist rising' and in a low-level military occupation of central Glasgow. Historians eager to discount the threat posed by militant labour in Britain tend to ignore the international context in which all this happened, and to underestimate the intensity of the manoeuvrings of the Lloyd George government against the 'threat of revolution' at home and abroad.

The immediate post-Russian Revolution situation over, Red Clydeside secured its place in the history books with the dramatic breakthrough in Glasgow at the 1922 general election by the Labour Party, and particularly its left-wing affiliate, the ILP. Ten out of fifteen seats were won (compared to one in 1918); and the Clydesiders were seen off to

Westminster by jubilant masses, singing psalms and socialist songs. John *Wheatley (1869–1930) and James *Maxton (1885–1946) promised socialism soon. The best they achieved was the housing reforms piloted by Wheatley as a minister in Ramsay MacDonald's first Labour government (1924).

Although the history of the Communist Party of Great Britain is mostly a sorry tale, its significance has been underestimated by most historians. Its origins (in 1920–1) owed much to the events of Red Clydeside; and the area supplied the Party (it lasted until 1991) with leading personnel, notably the former shop steward William *Gallacher (1881–1965); and (until he resigned over political principles in the early 1950s) the former John Maclean supporter Harry McShane (1891–1988)—the 'last of the Red Clydesiders', as obituarists called him. Maclean, who latterly supported the idea of a Scottish workers' republic, was also a political inspiration, from the 1930s on, for Scotland's most significant 20th-century cultural figure, the poet C. M. Grieve or Hugh MacDiarmid (1892–1978) (see CULTURE: 24). Future studies of Red Clydeside will have to take more systematic account of gendered, cultural, and other recently developed approaches to history, as well as of new, post-Cold War thinking about Marxism. TBr

Reformation. For generations of Scots, 1560 was the most important year in Scottish history. It has a sense of inevitability about it—the overthrow of an ailing, corrupt institution, the pre-Reformation church, which was rejected quickly and decisively (see CHURCH INSTITUTIONS: 2). And for some, there was also a whiff of destiny. As late as 1960, the quatercentenary of the Scottish Reformation, the professor of church history at Glasgow University, J. M. Reid, claimed that the church was a 'national symbol' and that 'one may doubt whether there could be a Scotland without it'.

History helps explain to us where we are. For many Scots living in present-day Scotland, however, two of the key elements of Scottish identity—a Protestant church for a Protestant people—no longer seem such an automatic alliance. Only 17 per cent of Scotland's adult population are now members of the Church of Scotland. The Reformation is no longer a usable past. Contemporary politicians, of all parties, with one eye on the troubles in Ulster, prefer to avoid the arcane, inflammatory religious struggles of the Reformation. Just as Protestant historians of the 19th century preferred to leapfrog the Middle Ages to find Protestants before their time, and discovered the culdees or St *Columba, so now many late 20th-century Scots, looking for moral certainties to help reconstruct a new national identity, pass over the confusions of the

Reformation period, preferring William *Wallace and the Wars of *Independence.

Aficionados of John *Knox tend to be *historians of ideas, ecclesiastical historians, or his occasional biographers. Much the same is true of the Reformation itself. Many who study it are those for whom it still has real meaning; it is, in essence, their past. Some use arguments such as the power of the 'simple faith of the Gospel'. Where else in Scottish history is such crude ideological determinism allowed to operate? Yet, in course of time, Protestantism came to embrace some 90 per cent of the Scottish people. More than that, it gave Scotland a new identity (see NATIONAL IDENTITY: 3) and distinctive human characteristics—of entrepreneurship, thrift, and education. The growth of a Protestant nation deserves a more convincing explanation.

A Rapid Reformation from Below?
The Scottish Reformation came late, over 40 years after Martin Luther's first protest in Wittenburg. After its slow start, Protestantism had, from the viewpoint of the authorities, spread at an alarming rate from the mid-1550s onwards. In 1552, after the confused years of the *Rough Wooing, the execution of George Wishart, the murder of Cardinal Beaton and the seizure of his castle in St Andrews, and the expulsion of the Castilians, including John Knox, into French prisons, the provincial council of the church was congratulating itself on the fact that the 'fiery flame of heresy' had gone out. By 1555 the authorities were worried by a fresh upsurge of heretical literature. 'Privy kirks' sprang up in *Edinburgh, Angus, and *Dundee at about the time Knox visited Scotland in the winter of 1555-6. The First Bond of the Congregation (see CONGREGATION, WARS OF THE), which suggested a new level of organization, was drawn up in December 1557. In September 1558, a Protestant demonstration broke up the annual St Giles's Day procession through the streets of Edinburgh, seized the saint's statue, and ritually drowned it in the nearby Nor' Loch. The revolt of 1559-60 began eight months later with a popular riot in *Perth, after an inflammatory sermon by Knox. Over the next seven weeks, the Congregation systematically toured central Scotland, stripping out 'idolatry' as they went. They reached *St Andrews on the night of 10 June, when the inhabitants went to bed as Catholics. They woke up as Protestants. Overnight, the walls of the parish church were whitewashed, the high altar pulled down, communion rails, reredos, choir stalls, organs, statues, and side altars all removed. In their place was installed a simple pulpit where they heard John Knox preach on the expelling of the moneylenders from the Temple (see RELIGIOUS LIFE: 3).

The Scottish Reformation was carried out in the name of the 'commonweal'. Matthew Parker, archbishop of Canterbury and no friend of Knox, compared events in England, where things had been done with order and decorum, with the extraordinary happenings in Scotland, where, as he saw it, 'the people are the orderers of things'. Parker saw not only a rapid reformation but also one from below.

Despite a series of temporary setbacks in the autumn and winter of 1559, the Reformation in Scotland was complete by August 1560. The French troops who had backed the regent, Mary of Guise, had been withdrawn; the regent herself was dead. A *parliament, acting in the name of the 'commonalty of Scotland', with an unprecedented 100 lairds drawn from most quarters of Scotland, proscribed the Catholic Mass, banned the jurisdiction of the pope, and gave authority to a Protestant Confession of Faith, largely drawn up by Knox. A sea change in worship followed quickly.

The Reformation encountered unexpected difficulties after *Mary, Queen of Scots, came back to Scotland in August 1561 after the death of her husband, François II. On her return, a band of Protestant demonstrators tried to break into the queen's private chapel at Holyrood to stop the Catholic Mass. They were held back but, just eight days later, her official entry into her capital was turned into an extraordinary demonstration of Protestant triumphalism: the queen was presented by a boy descending from the clouds with the keys to the burgh and also an English Protestant bible and psalm book. She was treated to a series of demonstrations of Protestant militancy; one piece of street theatre told the story of the defiance of Moses by three heretical Israelites who were consumed by fire. The message could hardly have been more uncompromising. This spectacle was the bluntest confrontation anywhere in 16th-century Europe of Catholic monarchy by a no-surrender radical Protestantism. It took place just two days before the first of Mary's infamous interviews with Knox. It was small wonder that Mary asked Knox why he obliged her subjects to obey him rather than her. Protestant expectations were held in check until Mary was deposed in 1567. At that point, at an excited meeting of the General Assembly, there was talk of a second Reformation. After 1567, the prospects of a Catholic revival ebbed quickly away. The new church steadily consolidated its position. By the time John Knox died, in November 1572, the Reformation was utterly secure.

A Rapid Reformation from Above?
There is truth but also a good deal of half-truth in such an analysis for the Reformation was also

inextricably linked to the power of the nobles and a vacuum in the power of the state. The play *Ane Satire of the Three Estates*, written by Sir David Lindsay of the Mount (see CULTURE: 7), is often taken as a paradigm of the Reformation period. This rollicking farce was also a bitter satire on the corruption and ineptitude of the hierarchy of the church and a blunt warning to incompetent kings; King Humanity spends much of the play in a drunken slumber. Its hero, in most modern productions, is the figure of John the Commonweill and the comic high point is when he seizes the chance as the king finally falls drunkenly off his throne to jump into it. It is little wonder that this play became one of the best sellers in print of post-Reformation Scotland. But the *Satire* was primarily written as a court entertainment, written by a royal herald. Played before a court (see ROYAL COURT: 2) audience, it was a warning, on the eve of the Reformation, of the awful prospects that might follow from a reformation of the 'rascal multitude'. John was not the hero but the anti-hero, representing the threat of what the people, the many-headed monster Hydra, might do if kings or bishops fell down on the job.

The Scottish Reformation came late. There is a rough but accurate rule of thumb for reformations in Europe, whether urban or territorial. The later they came, the more rapid and authoritarian they were. In Scotland, a magistrates' reformation took charge, with little or no role for the people. The Congregation which had pushed through the revolt which had stopped short of being a revolution were the Lords of the Congregation; the initial five signatories of the First Bond were all from the landed classes. One result was that in Scotland, a revolution took place in which virtually no one lost their jobs, in government, the law courts, or town councils.

The 'Reformation' Parliament, despite the 100 lairds from various parts of Scotland who attended it, was orchestrated by leading nobles. It was their kinsmen or dependants who filled it to overflowing. There was no sudden power grab by a new elite of smaller men. Control of politics rested, as before, with the nobles. Lairds would not attend another parliament in such numbers for another 50 years. The leading nobles commissioned Knox to draw up a Book of Reformation to present to the parliament. But they were dissatisfied with it, and especially with the section on their own role, as godly magistrates. They told Knox to redraft it, and added five other advisers to help him. The odd result was that what we now know as the *First Book of Discipline* missed the 'Reformation' Parliament and was never fully adopted.

What is clear about the events of 1559–60 is that the nobles (see NOBILITY: 3) were firmly in control.

The radicals had key demands: they included an Act of Uniformity on all clergy and a Test Act, obliging all office holders in both church and state, ranging from law lords to school masters, to subscribe the new Protestant Confession of Faith; and they wanted the wholesale transfer of the lands of the old church to the new. But they achieved none of these things. A Test Act did not come until 1573, an Act of Uniformity not until the 1580s, and the wholesale inheritance of the lands and wealth of the old church never happened. On each of these points the elites had vital interests. They did not want a wholesale reformation in which brother, spouse, kinsman, or neighbour would be excommunicated. Society as they knew it would have collapsed if Knox or John the Commonweill had been given their head. The nobles opted instead for a drip-feed reformation—with high ideals but only moral persuasion to back it.

Both Protestant and Catholic landowners already enjoyed possession of much church land through feuing. That process began in the 1530s and reached a climax ten years either side of the Reformation of 1560. In towns, the town council, usually dominated by wealthy merchants, remained in control (see URBAN SOCIETY: 2). Above all else, they saw retaining control as more important than religion. And they succeeded: except for Perth, there is little evidence of popular unrest, still less of significant popular Protestantism.

The result was not so much a reformation from below—although its organizers would use the rhetoric of popular protest as propaganda, such as the 'Beggars Summons' of 1559—as a reformation pushed through and carefully controlled from above, against a backcloth of nervousness about popular discontent and riot. The Reformation began with a noble revolt in 1559–60. It was consolidated by a second revolt, in 1567, when Mary, Queen of Scots, was unexpectedly deposed by a coup within a coup. It is easier to argue that the real hero of the Scottish Reformation, defined in these terms, was not Knox but Lord James Stewart, earl of Moray, half-brother of Queen Mary.

A Slow Reformation from Above?

History is a two-speed process. Taking the fast train allows a glimpse of events. It is often wiser to take the slow train to see what is really going on. What were the underlying processes which made the Reformation possible and, through consolidation, gave it deep roots?

The Reformation, above all else, needed manpower. The evidence for the growth of a parish ministry, sometimes described as the most reliable indicator of the spread of the Reformation, is highly problematic in its interpretation. By the end of 1561, Scotland had more than 240 of a new Protestant ministry installed; by 1567 the figure was about 750; and by 1574 about 1,000 of the country's 1,100 parishes had a Protestant clergyman in place. Translated into more realistic terms, which take account of the fact that until the 1590s three out of four of the new ministry were only readers, unable to preach or to administer communion, the Reformation progressed patchily for at least the first two generations after 1560. In many rural parishes (see RURAL SOCIETY: 3), a sermon would have been heard only once a month and communion was available only once a year—little different from the situation before 1560. The new church might have achieved a basic level of conformity relatively early but genuine conversion needed dedicated, trained missionaries and a campaign spread over decades. Those ministers also needed to be paid. The new church, although the fact was unpalatable to many clergy, progressed only at the pace allowed by the state, which financed it.

In a few places, such as the hothouse of St Andrews, there was a 'big bang' reformation. In many others, there was a slow-burning fuse. *Aberdeen seems to have had the ingredients of a fast reformation from above: the town council joined the revolt of the Lords of the Congregation late, in the spring of 1560; they sent representatives to the 'Reformation' Parliament and, while there, appointed a new Protestant minister and purchased a Geneva gown for him. Yet Aberdeen had no kirk session until the queen and her Protestant privy council visited the town in the autumn of 1562. The new session was the town council at prayer, but most of them were Catholics. The story of the Protestant Reformation in Aberdeen, as a top-down phenomenon, is not complete until after the ruling Menzies faction lost control, at the end of the 1580s. In effect, it took 30 years.

In the late 1580s, the General Assembly commissioned surveys of the religious affiliations of the Scottish nobility. The results were not comforting. About a third were reported to be papists. These reports probably reveal as much about the fears of the church as they do about the persistence of Catholicism (see ROMAN CATHOLIC COMMUNITY). But they do also suggest that conversion to Protestantism was not a once-for-all process. Do they also indicate that we need to begin to think of the Reformation century in much the same terms as most other centuries in Scottish history—as one in which the forces of continuity are likely to have outweighed the pressures making for change? Is it the case that, even with the Reformation, the more things changed, the more they remained the same? Or, did the reformation of religion also bring about

what a social historian might call a reformation of manners?

The nobles were repeatedly appealed to by the church to act as godly magistrates. Usually, they fell somewhere short of that ideal. The Reformation in Scotland coincided with the rise of new landed classes and new groups in urban society. It took place against a background of a steep price rise, an active market in land, rack-renting, and a sharply increasing divide between rich and poor (see ECONOMY: 3). The groups that benefited—newly ennobled peers, lairds who profited from the sale of church lands, wealthy merchants, and lawyers (see LAW AND LAWYERS: 1)—were all anxious to find new emblems of their status. But there were also new, extra instruments of power available: the new power of the state was seen in the new prominence of the privy council and the central law courts; the rising influence of new groups in local society was reflected in the baron court and kirk session, dominated by merchants and lawyers in the towns, and by lairds and greater tenants in the countryside. It was little wonder that the session became an instrument of social control, with no less than 60 per cent of its business taken up with sex.

A Slow Reformation from Below?

This leaves a vital question, and especially for those who think of the Reformation as a liberating force. How long was it until the Reformation had a real impact on the way ordinary people thought? It is known that in 1638 Jenny Geddes threw a stool at the pulpit of St Giles in protest against the new Prayer Book, provoking not only a riot but a revolution against Charles I. Or is it? For Jenny Geddes, symbol of the religion of the people, was an invention of the 19th century, when a variety of different Protestant churches were each trying to lay claim to be the authentic inheritor of Scotland's Protestant past. The riot of 1638 was almost certainly orchestrated by leading figures within the capital. The *National Covenant itself, signed by every sector of Scottish society ranging from nobleman to humble cottar, at the time was called the Nobleman's Covenant. The godly magistrate was still in control, though perhaps the grip was beginning to slip.

What is the first evidence that is available to prove what has been called a 'new enthusiasm for worship'? It comes fully twenty years after the Reformation. In 1582, one of Edinburgh's ministers, John Durie, made a spectacular entry into the capital after a period of enforced exile, greeted, one account claims, by a crowd of 2,000 who broke out into Psalm 124, 'Now Israel may say', the battle hymn of Calvinism, in unrehearsed four-part harmony. But why should it all have taken so long?

The 'simple truth of the Gospel', argue some historians, was enough. But what Gospel? The only bible available in the vernacular was in English, an alien tongue, and cheap bibles did not materialize before the 1630s. Instead, the Psalms, sung to familiar, common tunes, were the most potent communicator of Protestant ideas. But necessarily, this was a fairly basic message.

It is easy to fall into a trap of expecting that something as seismic as the Reformation would have a profound and immediate effect on the lives of ordinary people caught up in it. The real irony of the Reformation is that it was impossible overnight for the aspiration of the few to become the conviction of the many. Instead, it probably took three or four generations. On a range of issues—attendance, irreverent popular attitudes to communion and church services, ineffective preaching, and catechizing the young—it is not difficult to find parallels which show that the problems of the Protestant Church in 1600 were not greatly different from those of the Roman Catholic Church in 1550.

Successes and Failures of the Reformation?
These are different kinds of reformation, with differing agendas, assumptions, and expectations. Each needs to be thought of in terms of both success and failure. One fairly plausible benchmark is as follows: the Reformation succeeded most where it changed things least. This was only natural in a society which was conservative, suspicious of change, and especially fearful of social unrest. Where the Reformation reinforced existing habits and institutions, it succeeded most readily. The kirk session was the partner of the new central law courts and the local baron court. But where it did make decisive and violent changes, the Reformation usually failed, at least to begin with.

Did the Reformation bring a new freedom to the Scottish people—of thought and independent-mindedness? Eventually it did, but not for a century or more after 1560. The heirs of John the Commonweill were the radical *Covenanters of the 1670s and 1680s. In the meantime, the Reformation brought a new freedom only to the people who mattered: those who had power and status or were already in process of acquiring them. The symbol of this version of the Reformation was not so much the Bible, which remained the preserve of the moneyed few until the 1630s, but the communion token and catechism: one was used to monitor the behaviour of congregations, and the other was relied upon by successive generations of schoolmasters, ministers, and kirk elders to thump the basic tenets of the faith into the ungodly.

The accompaniment to the Reformation was both a state church and a new kind of state, more interfering, intrusive, and authoritarian than before. Claims about the separation of the 'two kingdoms' advanced by radical Presbyterian ministers such as Andrew *Melville have obscured that simple fact. The task for Scottish Protestants throughout the 17th century and beyond was twofold: how to throw off that part of the legacy of the Reformation and how to preserve intact their faith in doing so. The battle between the people above and the people below was one of the most important products of the Reformation. The script for much of the internal dissent, schism, and reunions (see CHURCH INSTITUTIONS: 4) which so marked the history of Scottish Protestantism was already written in outline.   ML

regional identities: 1. general; 2. the north-east; 3. the Borders (including the Common Ridings); 4. Orkney and Shetland.

1. general
Regional identity is one of culture and sense of place. It is often said that persons from any of the towns in the Scottish *Borders (see also REGIONAL IDENTITIES: 3) are conscious of having three identities and indeed pride themselves on this fact. At one and the same time they claim citizenship of their particular town, for example, Hawick, Galashiels, or Melrose, but will call themselves a Borderer as well as a Scot. These different identities blend into one another and become fused during local festivals and international rugby matches when players from the various Border teams frequently make up the bulk of the Scottish national team. The Borders' regional identity is expressed through a number of occasions and festivities. The March and the Common Ridings are the most common. Hawick's centrepiece celebration marks the routing of English 'plunders' in 1514. The gathering of the Galashiels Braw Lads is a challenge to the English raiders of 1337. Jedburgh celebrates the town's role in the defeat of the English in 1575. Duns commemorates the opposition raised to Charles I crossing the Tweed, and the Peebles Beltane alludes to a period of imperialism depicting the symbols of the *British Empire with Peebles at the core.

Regional identity is an affirmation of where we are from. Its frame of reference is our locality rather than our nation. Clearly, too, some localities have a stronger sense of place than others. The Borders' regional identity is a close and coherent one. It is the border where England and Scotland meet and it is an area of Scotland relatively isolated from the rest of the country, poorly served by road, and no longer linked by rail to Edinburgh and Glasgow. Here an intricate and sustained regional identity is constructed out of an undisturbed sense of place, particularly when a community is culturally bounded and relatively isolated from other regions and influences. It is also sustained by cultural tradition, especially when mobilized in counter-reaction to wider socio-economic change. The Ettrick Shepherd James Hogg founded the St Ronan's Border Games in 1827 as a reaction to the demoralization of Border life in the face of such change.

Regional identities, like other forms of identity (see NATIONAL IDENTITY; SOCIAL CLASS), are both something we are born with and something we can choose (or not choose) to acquire. There is also a sense in which they can be called up, for example, during moments of crisis, and dismissed when we wish to emphasize other features. We can select from the range of identities provided by our family, our religion, our ethnicity, our region, our nation, or our state, amongst many others. Regional identity in Scotland remains divided between north and south, and east and west. The former is more clearly demarcated between Highland and Lowland. Each has seen the other as different, be they Sassenach or teuchter (see REGIONAL IDENTITIES: 2). Each has its own internal regional divisions too, as we shall see. Yet it is the Highland (see HIGHLANDS AND ISLANDS: GENERAL) region which provides the dominant symbols of Scotland's national identity: the *clans and their tartans, kilt and bagpipes in a scenic world of heather and the land of mountain and flood; the *Clearances of the Highlands and Islands, the *Gaelic language, Balmoral, and the symbolism of Bonnie Prince Charlie. The particularities of the Highland region have dominated the Scottish identity.

This social construction ignores historical reality as much as regional subdivision, yet its resonance is strong. The north-west has been the stronghold of Gaelic, the north-east has preserved the Doric language (see SCOTS LANGUAGE). Nor should the island identities of Orkney and Shetland (see REGIONAL IDENTITIES: 4) be ignored for their own regionalisms are strong. Recent years have seen the development of a carefully constructed Orkney Islands' identity. Renewed interest in the 'Uppies' and the 'Doonies' battling for the Kirkwall 'Ba' on Christmas and New Year's Day is distinctive, but Orkney Island regionalism is a well-rounded one. From agricultural and cheese production, the Highland Park distillery to tourism, there continues a sense of unity. Diversity has still been stressed, the local nature reserve of Mull Head, the ornithological sanctuaries of Brodgar and Eynhallow, the 12th-century old town structure of Kirkwall, the Churchill barriers, and the military history of Scapa Flow. But it is a diversity which has enhanced rather than fragmented the sense of place in and of the Orkney Islands.

It is also the case in the Lowlands that differences are great, certainly symbolically if not in reality. The urban–rural contrast is important, but regional identities often combine a mixture of both: it is the cultural identification which is crucial. The Edinburgh 'people' and Glasgow 'folk' can make a distance of 40 miles (64.4 km) seem culturally unbridgeable. Each of these two cities has developed along divergent but often complementary lines. *Glasgow has historically sustained a strong mercantile and industrial economy, particularly in the towns which surround it and comprise Strathclyde region; *Edinburgh has promoted its financial and legal services, having maintained printing, publishing, and brewing as part of its mixed industrial base. The often hostile civic divide which exists between Scotland's two largest cities exacerbates differences and ignores similarities. In the tourist literature, each city will promote itself on the back of what is perceived to be its essentialisms. Similarly, the rather blandly named 'Central Region' has recently made much of *Stirling's association with Sir William *Wallace to promote itself as 'Braveheart Country'. The new district of East Ayrshire, doggedly trying to convince itself that its Elderslie (and not that in Renfrewshire) is the true birthplace of Wallace, has yet to capitalize on the same legacy. Regionalism, like nationalism, is something to be promoted or denied as appropriate.

It seems plain, then, that despite the rise of the nation state and supranational organizations (such as the European Community and NATO) the region retains its role as a persistent pull in the construction of identity. For Scotland, too, it is the Highland region which, like the Borders' identity, is strong in itself, but is one which furnishes the dominant symbols of a wider identity, that of the Scottish nation. GM

2. the north-east

The north-east of Scotland has been seen either as a geographically isolated, reserved, and insular region or as a European bridgehead retaining strong historical, trading, and cultural links with *Scandinavia, the *Low Countries, *Russia, and the Baltic states (see GERMANY, THE BALTIC, AND POLAND), and Catholic Europe. Both are true.

The region is bounded to the west by the Grampian Mountains, which also extend along the southern border as the Mounth; both these ranges have many passes. There is a plain of varying width to the east and north with a coastline which is largely inhospitable, although there are river estuaries, bays, and natural harbours offering degrees of shelter and access. The rivers are largely shallow, fast-flowing, and not navigable to any great distance inland. Thus even from earliest times *migration, traffic, and trade has tended to be mainly coastal or across the North Sea, and less with the neighbouring Highlands (see HIGHLANDS AND ISLANDS: GENERAL) and Lowlands.

For 10,000 years there have been immigrations from Europe. Hunter-gatherers around 8000 BC were followed 4,000 years later by farmers, with their stone barrows and henges. From 2000 BC Beaker People from the Rhine erected unique stone circles beside their prolific farms. The Celts who arrived after 1000 BC (and were defeated by the Romans at Mons Graupius in AD 83/4) were from the 3rd century AD apparently superseded by—or merged with, perhaps?—the enigmatic *Picts who erected symbol stones throughout the region, and held the Vikings at bay. The Celts returned via Ireland when Scotland was united under *Kenneth mac Alpin in AD 843 and Gaelic predominated until the advent of the feudal Anglo-Norman families and their followers around 1125 to maintain King *David I's peace—spending ensuing centuries in internecine warfare.

Converted via Ireland from the late 9th century, Celtic monasticism (see RELIGIOUS LIFE: 1) gave way three centuries later to Romanized Christianity; even after the Protestant *Reformation of 1560 much of the region remained strongly Catholic and later, Episcopalian (see EPISCOPALIAN COMMUNITY), with significant links to Europe. The earl of Buchan, for example, provided Joan of Arc with her Scottish troops; Catholic earls lent support to the Spanish Armada. This culminated in ruinous support for the *Jacobites. In 1715 the Old Pretender raised his banner on the Braes of Mar; his failed venture also sent his Keith supporters, the Earls Marischal of Scotland, into exile for ever. In 1746 north-east Jacobites failed to stop the duke of Cumberland occupying Aberdeen. He there trained his army in techniques which helped win the battle of Culloden, where the north-east men were defeated and their leaders exiled. Pacification was followed by active participation in the *British Empire, both in colonial trade and service; the duke of Gordon raised his Highlanders (see ARMY: 3) in 1794, heroes of Waterloo and many other battles. Although the region enjoyed prosperity, especially from its central role in the North Sea oil industry, in the post-imperial world it has gradually moved from a political conservation to favouring Scottish *nationalism—within a European Community context.

During the Wars of *Independence, the north-east with its unblockaded ports was to prove strategically important. but by supporting the *Comyn cause suffered *Robert I's savage retaliation in 1308. Donald, lord of the *Isles, invaded in 1411 in support of his sound claim for the earldom of Ross

whose exclaves extended to Aberdeenshire, but was defeated at great cost at Harlaw by forces in forward defence under the ruthless earl of Mar. The Highland/Gaelic influence declined rapidly in the region thereafter, though lingering to the 20th century.

Much of the area remained trackless moor and bog until the advent of good roads and railways (see TRANSPORT AND COMMUNICATIONS: 2) in the 19th century, accompanying an agricultural revolution from the 1790s (see RURAL SOCIETY: 4) which did away with simple husbandry, arable farming, and the runrig system, and reclaimed and engrossed the land into larger farms ('farmtouns') run as family units with occasional hired labour (see ECONOMY, PRIMARY SECTOR: 2). Occupying a relatively narrow coastal strip, long-standing, religious, insular fishing communities flourished, especially during the herring and whaling booms of the 19th century. They had more affinity with similar communities around the British Isles from Lewis to Ireland than their farming neighbours but their centuries-old trade with northern Europe was shattered by the Great War. For centuries the region as a whole, especially via Aberdeen, has traded with Europe (and later with America (see USA) and the colonies) in a wide variety of commodities: wool, linen, fish, hides, grain, whisky, granite, paper, oil.

Education has been prized from the establishment of two *Universities (King's College, Old Aberdeen, in 1495 and Marischal College in New Aberdeen in 1593, amalgamated in 1860) with strong Continental links to the establishment of a parochial system of education staffed largely by university graduates, enabling 'lads o' pairts' to gain generous university bursaries (see SCHOOLS AND SCHOOLING). Continental and other outside influences, together with relative geographical isolation, have combined to produce and sustain a remarkable cultural richness and diversity, strongly flavoured by the neighbouring Highlands. A vital Lowland Scots ('the Doric') (see SCOTS LANGUAGE) is still written and spoken, and in music and song (see SONG, TRADITIONAL AND FOLK: 1) especially, the region has been acknowledged for centuries as one of the culturally richest in Europe, with which it shares a famous great balladry.   IAO

3. the Borders (including the Common Ridings)

Enclosed by a horseshoe of high ground broken only to the east, the Scottish Borders are, in many respects, a land of contrasts. There are some of the finest stately homes (see ARCHITECTURAL STYLES AND FEATURES) in Scotland, such as Bowhill, Traquair House, and Abbotsford, as well as peaceful salmon fishing on the River Tweed and ancient ruined abbeys and castles. The Borders also has bustling industrial towns, which, although small, are famous for the production of high-quality knit-wear and tweeds. An intense local patriotism flour-ishes in the Borders and civic loyalties can be summarized in the saying: 'I would rather be a lamp-post in Hawick than provost of Galashiels.' Border towns are close, homogeneous commu-nities where non-natives are sometimes treated with suspicion. Local identities are enhanced by an active, occasionally xenophobic, local press and by distinct accents and dialects.

The principal expression of civic loyalties can be found in an annual series of festivals known as the 'Common Ridings'. These are derived from the old burgh custom (see URBAN SOCIETY: 1) of a ceremon-ial procession around the boundaries or 'marches' of the burgh common in order to delineate the area and check encroachment upon it by neighbouring landowners. Several of the ridings also commem-orate events from the Anglo-Scottish wars, in par-ticular the battle of Flodden (1513), whilst some of the customs and ceremonies suggest that the rid-ings were associated with pagan summer festivals (see WORK AND LEISURE, TO 1770S). There are four genuine or 'real' Common Ridings in the Borders: Selkirk Common Riding, with its 'Casting the Col-ours' ceremony, dates from the early 16th century; Hawick Common Riding was first recorded in 1640; Langholm Common Riding, which Hugh Mac-Diarmid loved to attend, dates from 1816, although the Langholm marches were perambulated before then; finally, Lauder Common Riding, like many other traditional customs, lapsed in the 19th cen-tury but was revived in 1911 to commemorate the coronation of George V. There are also a series of modern or 'invented' ridings, which are based on the tradition of the town 'riding out'. Peebles 'Bel-tane Festival' (1897) features a colourful parade of schoolchildren and the crowning of the Beltane (or Summer) Queen, whilst Galashiels 'Braw Lads Gathering' (1930) focuses on, amongst other things, the granting of the town charter. Large concourses of riders take part in these events, testifying to the Borderer's close affinity with the horse—some-thing which was commented on in the 16th cen-tury.

The ridings have many individual features, but their general outline can be briefly summarized. Several weeks before the riding, a young native bachelor is chosen to be the symbolic leader of the year's event and to carry the burgh flag on the day itself. The correct nomenclature for this rider is very important and is strictly observed: Hawick, Langholm, Lauder, and Peebles appoint a Cornet; Selkirk, the Royal Burgh Standard Bearer; Gala-shiels, the Braw Lad (and Braw Lass); Kelso Laddie; Duns Reiver; the Melrosian; the Coldstreamer; and

so on. Preliminary events include practice rides or 'ride-outs' concerts of local songs, school and hos-pital visits, and a civic reception for local emigrants who have returned to the town for the riding. The riding itself begins with the formal presentation of the burgh flag to the principal, who then leads his mounted supporters on the day's ride. In the older ridings, riders make a symbolic inspection of the burgh lands, which may include a ceremonial turf-cutting to mark the site of a boundary. Participants in the new ridings visit historic local sites. Most ridings are accompanied by a programme of horse races—the Borders is the centre of British 'flapping' or unlicensed racing—and there are also athletic events and a travelling funfair. The riding ends with the return of the burgh flag, followed by dinner and a grand ball. Local people are very proud of their riding, and these events arouse strong emotions. In 1996, a bitter dispute occurred over the participa-tion of *women riders in Hawick Common Riding, which many locals—both men and women—saw as a dangerous break with tradition. The depth of feeling aroused by the dispute highlighted the trad-itional maleness and conservatism of the ridings, and indeed of much of Borders' culture.

Inter-town rivalries are also expressed through *rugby, which, unlike the rest of Scotland, attracts broad popular support in the Borders. Ball games are an ancient feature of Border life, and street *football survives in some Border communities, notably in Jedburgh. The rugby union code was introduced in the 1870s, and possibly took root in the Borders because, in the words of the *Hawick Ex-press* in November 1873, it was 'manlier and more congenial to the Border nature than the tamer Association game'. The intensity of local rivalries led to the formation of a Border League in 1901, whilst Border teams, notably Hawick and Melrose, have dominated national competitions. In 1883, Melrose staged the world's first seven-a-side tour-nament and the annual Border sevens (or 'sports') remain important social gatherings.   KRB

4. Orkney and Shetland

Orkney and Shetland have shared administrations from time to time, but rarely their social histories. The two groups of islands are geologically and geographically distinct. Shetland (540 square miles (1,400 square km)) is 50 miles (80 km) north-east of Orkney (359 square miles (930 square km)), and far less well favoured from an agricultural point of view. Orkney has less access to good fishing grounds.

Already in prehistory the cultural histories of the islands diverged. Orkney's neolithic monuments are large and impressive in their flat, green land-scape. They are also world-famous: Skara Brae, the

Stones of Stenness, the Ring of Brodgar. They betoken religious practices and class structures which we can only guess about. Shetland's chambered cairns, on the other hand, are small and clumsy, and her tiny neolithic houses—many hundreds survive—point to a more egalitarian society. During the Iron Age brochs appeared in both archipelagos, in large numbers; but the Orcadian examples often seem to be the centre of flourishing villages, a kind of settlement virtually unknown in Shetland.

Around AD 800 immigrants from Norway arrived in both groups of islands. The fact that the aboriginal language and *place names disappeared suggests strongly that the immigration involved violence; however, some archaeologists argue wistfully for integration (without describing the modalities of it). There are few signs of Viking settlement in either Orkney or Shetland, presumably because the settlers and their successors continued to live in the best-favoured sites. There is, however, a well-preserved sequence of houses from this period at Jarlshof in Shetland, dug out of sand in the 20th century; but its chronology is still controversial.

During subsequent centuries powerful earls in Orkney ruled both groups of islands, and smaller or larger parts of the Scottish mainland. The *Orkneyinga Saga* presents tales of the earls' achievements, and, used cautiously, can throw light on the islands' social history. Shetland features far less in the saga: there is evidence, if we probe, that the northern group of islands was a staging-post where claimants to the earldom—Rognvald Brusason, Magnus Erlendson, Rognvald Kali Kolsson—solicited support for ultimately successful campaigns. The 12th century was a peak of achievement for the earls: the period when the cathedral of St Magnus was built in Kirkwall in Orkney.

From the 1190s onwards the histories of Orkney and Shetland diverged even more sharply. King Sverrir Sigurdsson of Norway confiscated Shetland from the earls of Orkney, following an unsuccessful rebellion. During the late Middle Ages Shetland's institutions became increasingly Norwegian in character, and Shetlanders traded with fish-merchants in Bergen. The Black Death (see HEALTH, FAMINE, AND DISEASE: 1) afflicted both groups of islands, and the subsequent depressions had a particularly unfortunate effect on Orkney's grain-growing economy. Shetland, meanwhile, was buoyed up by enterprising merchants from North Germany, who from about 1400 onwards began to sail directly to the islands to bargain with the Shetlanders for fish.

In 1468–9 the king of Denmark mortgaged his royal rights in Orkney and Shetland to the king of Scotland. During subsequent centuries lessees and donatories of the king's revenues and rents made their presence felt in the islands to a greater or lesser extent. None of them did so more dramatically than Earl Robert and Earl Patrick Stewart, who administered justice from the 1560s until 1611. Both indulged in expensive building campaigns in Orkney and Shetland, and Patrick in particular infuriated the islands' home-grown landowners. After Patrick's execution, in 1615, for treason, the local landowners played an increasingly active part in the politics of both groups of islands. However, the economies of Orkney and Shetland now began to diverge spectacularly.

Orkney continued to be a successful grain-growing society, afflicted by depression from time to time. In Shetland, on the other hand, there was major crisis at the turn of the 18th century, when the German merchants ceased to come to the islands. A new class of merchant-lairds filled the vacuum, by inaugurating major fishing enterprises. Whereas in Orkney landowners had a fairly traditional relationship with their tenants and other estate-workers, in Shetland fishing became a condition of tenure. As the 18th century progressed Orkney landowners became interested in the kelp business, and employed Orcadians to work in it. In Shetland fishing tenants were remunerated by goods at the merchants' truck shops (see ECONOMY, PRIMARY SECTOR: 4).

There were differences, too, in the spiritual development of the archipelagos. Again Orkney took a rather traditional road, by Scottish standards; in the early 19th century Congregationalists, Baptists, and especially Methodists, flourished in Shetland. As a result, the Free Church in due course found less to do in Shetland than in Orkney. The Methodists had mopped up most of the dissent in Shetland by the 1840s.

The Crofters Act of 1886 was an important event in the history of the islands, but in Shetland it was truly an act of emancipation: there were more applications for fair rents in Shetland than anywhere else in Scotland. During the 1860s and 1870s, when steamers were able to carry animals out of the islands in bulk for the first time, merchants and landlords had cleared Shetlanders from their crofts in some areas and confiscated common grazing. Security of tenure thus became essential for Shetlanders. In Orkney the most exciting events were confined to a single island, Rousay, where Colonel Burroughs had held sway (see MIGRATION).

The Crofters Act gave Shetlanders and Orcadians security of tenure. Many Shetlanders went to work in the Scottish herring industry which, fortuitously, had arrived in the islands at exactly the right moment. Orcadians continued to work in agriculture. During the 20th century, with myriad nuances, Orcadians and Shetlanders have continued to work in these very different spheres. Perhaps as a result the atmosphere of Orkney is relatively bucolic and conservative. Orcadians and Shetlanders have usually voted Liberal and Liberal Democrat since the Crofters Act, but there are more Tories in Orkney and more socialists in Shetland.

It has been argued, perhaps improbably, that Orkney's rustic character has nurtured greater literary achievement: there is no Shetland author to compare in achievement with George Mackay Brown, Eric Linklater, or Edwin Muir. Perhaps, however, Shetland has preserved her distinctive folk culture and dialect more effectively (see also ORKNEY AND CAITHNESS, EARLDOM OF; GERMANY, THE BALTIC, AND POLAND; SCANDINAVIA).   BS

religious life: 1. early medieval; 2. medieval; 3. 1560–1650; 4. 1650–1750; 5. Moderatism; 6. Evangelicalism; 7. secularization; 8. Highlands since the Reformation.

1. early medieval
The written sources which shed light on the life of the church in this period are mostly of monastic origin, for monks were the literati of the early Middle Ages. Naturally the monastic writers' viewpoint influenced what they wrote about and how they wrote about it, and this may result in a certain monastic bias in our perception of the life of Christians of the period.

We have a relatively clear picture of the monastic life: the cycle of daily prayers; the celebration of the Mass; the work of agriculture, fishing, and sealhunting; the relationship of abbot to monks and laity; and so on. From monastic writings we can also build up a picture of their literary culture: the role of reading in the contemplative life, the constant work of copying books, and the importance of the community's library. In the 8th century, the known contents of the *Iona library show that monks were immersed in the mainstream of European Christian thought—though few Scottish monasteries would have had the wealth to build up such a library.

But monasteries represent only one form of Christian life. In spite of a long-standing conventional wisdom that the 'Celtic' church was monastic in character, recent studies of canonical and legal texts have stressed the importance of bishops and their clergy in nourishing Christian life. In the early 8th century, an Iona monk helped to compile the *Collectio Canonum Hibernensis* with its descriptions of, and prescriptions for, Christian life. Its vision of church order is primarily episcopal. The roughly contemporary 'Rule of Patrick' probably reflects Christian life in much of Scotland, insisting

on the key role of the bishop and on his ministry to the *túath* (the 'tribe' or 'kingdom'): 'A chief bishop for every *túath*, for ordaining their clergy, for consecrating their churches and for soul-friendship with princes and with chiefs, and for sanctifying and blessing their children after baptism.' The bishop must also ensure that his clergy are capable of baptizing properly. In the *Collectio* the bishop must care for the poor, feed the hungry, clothe the naked, redeem captives, support widows and orphans, and so on.

Some texts describe a contractual relationship between church and *túath*: the *túath* gives tithes, burial dues, and such like offerings. In return the Church provides a priest in every church to baptize, to offer Mass, and to pray for the dead, together with 'the recital of the word of God to those who listen to it and keep it' (*Córus Béscnai*). The clergy offered other ministries as well: anointing the sick with oil, and bringing *viaticum* or communion to the dying—there is an *Ordo* for this in the Book of Deer. Clergy also administered penance, the means by which sinners were reconciled with the church and returned to share communion.

The large number of existing *place names containing elements such as *cill, both, eccles,* and *annat* (all meaning 'church') suggests that the church's ministry was exercised very locally. In many of these sites only the name indicates its early Christian use, as nothing remains of the wooden churches that once stood there. Many other sites, however, contain stone-carved crosses, Christian burials, or other material evidence of worship. The name *annat* also reveals something of the organization of pastoral care, referring as it does to 'mother churches' (rather like English minsters) which served a local congregation but also had lesser churches within their jurisdiction. A similar system of mother churches probably existed in non-Gaelic areas, where the term *annat* was not used. In the south they may have been in such places as Hoddom, Melrose, Stobo, Jedburgh, and Kirkcudbright.

Strictly speaking, monks as such had no pastoral role. Monasteries, however, did include ordained clergy—bishops, priests, and deacons—who ministered not only to their own monks but also to the laity further afield in churches subject to their religious houses.

Secular rulers also founded churches and recruited clergy to serve people in their own household or territory. This, of course, presented a challenge to bishops who sought to maintain some control over the churches in their jurisdiction and over what went on in them. Though there was no clear unified structure of pastoral care, these different classes of church—episcopal, monastic, and secular—existing side by side, always had to maintain some fundamental connection to the bishops, for without bishops to consecrate churches and ordain clergy no sacramental ministry would have been possible.

For the laity, a wide range of non-sacramental rites nourished belief. Elements of pre-Christian culture could always be incorporated into Christian life. As lawyers and canonists agreed, any judgements of the pre-Christian Gaelic lawyers which were in accordance with natural goodness and did not contradict God's word, still had legal force. This applied particularly to laws, but also held true in more general ways. Wells and springs had always been centres of religious activity, and many of them became places of Christian prayer. The Christian inauguration of kings welded together pre-Christian rites, biblical anointing, and clerical supervision (see KINGSHIP: 1; SCONE).

The cult of saints was centrally important. The cosmic triumph of Christ over sin and death was a vast overarching fact, but it was in the lives of one's holy neighbours and kin-folk that this fact became tangible, intelligible, and local. Saints made Christ's power manifest. Early medieval saints were not moral examples whose holy lives were offered for imitation, but rather patrons, protectors, and advocates whose prayers could protect folk in this life and save their souls from damnation. Just as there was a contract between church and *túath*, there was a contract between saintly patron and believing client: in exchange for honouring the saint in prayer and offerings made to his church, the saint would beg God to show the client mercy.

Lives of the saints should therefore never be treated as a simple quarry of biographical facts. They express the relationship between a saint and his protégés at the time when they were written. Powerful families and monasteries had their own patron saints, and when they moved they took their saints with them. This explains the removal of St *Columba's relics from Iona to Dunkeld in 849, when *Kenneth mac Alpin established his power centre there, and it explains the appearance of dedications to Cenél Loairn saints in the north-east, as the rulers of Lorn took power in Moray.

In addition to prayer, the church promoted almsgiving and hospitality as moral dimensions of Christian life. Other regulations governed marriage and inheritance, fasting and Sunday observance. Christian faith also shaped people's lives in ways which were manifestly not 'moral', but reflected a sense, often biblical, of taboo or ritual purity. So the consumption of horse-flesh was sometimes discouraged in Gaelic texts, as was eating animals which had not been properly slaughtered. Some rules forbade priests to attend the

dying, for fear of contracting pollution, following the old law of Leviticus 21. Where the modern mind might be tempted to distinguish theology, moral demands, administrative arrangements, and rules of ritual purity, Christian life in the early medieval church involved all these, woven together into a more or less seamless garment (see CHRISTIANITY, CONVERSION TO; CHURCH INSTITUTIONS: 1; CALENDAR AND SEASONAL CUSTOMS; MONUMENTS: 1).   GMa

2. medieval

The history of the medieval church in Scotland is of necessity the history of bishops and kings. Yet, there is more known about the religious life of ordinary clerics and lay people than might at first be supposed. The settled and unchanging features of the period were the supremacy of St Andrew and of the town of his name on the east of Fife. Centre of the great pilgrimage route through Fife, *St Andrews grew in stature throughout the Middle Ages, finally procuring primacy and an archbishopric in 1472. The diocese of St Andrews was not the largest in Scotland but in terms of soil fertility, population density, and urban trade it was undoubtedly the richest. Pilgrims made their way to other sites, to see the relics of St Kentigern at *Glasgow, for example, or the shrine of St *Margaret in Dunfermline.

Pilgrimage brought with it money and in the early medieval period the attractiveness of money as a means of exchange was beginning to be felt. As rents previously paid in cattle or cheese began to be changed to heritable tenancies giving a fixed cash return, the church began to lose money through inflation. The relationship between religious and lay became one of landlord and tenant (see ECONOMY: 2). If one's overlord was a distant and large monastery this would have a lesser effect than if it was in an urban setting. In the towns, the Dominicans and conventual Franciscans feued their lands and became both pastors and rent collectors. The use of feu-ferme by mendicants is peculiar to Scotland and demonstrates just how deeply the feu had been accepted by Scottish society.

The celebrant before the altar was representative of Christ to the people. This representational relationship could vary from the simple parish priest, indistinguishable from his flock, to the cathedral priest with university degree, to a bishop in all his finery. In rural areas, the priest would farm a glebe and have a semi-subsistence lifestyle. The taxes raised from rural parishes were often appropriated to other institutions, such as monasteries, cathedrals, or universities. This had two effects: to enhance the splendour of the big institutions of Scottish religious life and also to drain the parishes of resources which had been canonically intended to sustain the parish priest. The main problem with appropriation was that it escalated over the years. By 1300, about 50 per cent of Scotland's parishes were affected. By 1560, that figure had risen to some 85 per cent. However, appropriation was not the only source of funds for the church. Grants of lands and revenues from kings and nobles provided for the foundations of most monasteries, and later in the period, collegiate churches.

During the Middle Ages the worshipping habits of the nobility began to change. Where they had, at first, held special seats or places within the parish churches, they began later to prefer private chaplains. This meant either having a chapel with consecrated altar in their great houses or having a priest with a consecrated portable altar travelling in their retinue. The nobility would therefore worship within their own households.

It is important to remember that the vast majority of the church's wealth was for worship. The laity of medieval Scotland valued prayer and were prepared to pay for it. The monasteries provided communities dedicated to prayer and frugal living which were worshipping in the Christian tradition on behalf of all. This inclusive view of the life of prayer is most clearly seen in the foundations for prayers for the dead. From the late 14th century onwards foundations were made by royalty and nobility to pray for the souls of deceased relatives. Separation in life by rank and status was mirrored at death. Founding collegiate churches was a way not only of demonstrating wealth and power but also of procuring the best for one's nearest and dearest in the life to come. Within these services a bier and pall would be placed to represent the coffin and the funeral rites would be rehearsed, with varying splendour depending on the foundation (see DEATH AND BURIAL). The liturgy was not as elitist as the display of wealth and power which accompanied these early foundations might suggest as in most there were to be prayers said for 'all the faithful dead'. In later years burgesses and other comfortably-off, but not wealthy, people were able to set up similar prayers, or at least commission part of the services, within the friars' churches and parish churches. Also, craftsmen used their professional guilds to provide for themselves collectively services, palls, and biers, which individually they would not have been able to afford.

Festivals emphasized the worshipping community's responsibilities to each other (see CALENDAR AND SEASONAL CUSTOMS). At Whitsun and Martinmas fairs were held and people commonly got married, moved house, and conducted other public business. In midwinter the festivities of Yule were celebrated from house to house during a fortnight

of revels. Even the clergy would join in, there being a note in the account book of the Dominicans of Perth for costumes for the 'Yule folly'. Corpus Christi became a more and more central festival: held in June, it celebrated the body of Christ, both as the bread and wine of communion, and as the worshipping community.

Easter was the main festival of the Christian year. It was on Easter Sunday that the majority of the Scottish laity would take their annual eucharist, receiving consecrated bread from the priest who would come to the nave side of the choir screen to serve his people. Through the 40 days of Lent preceding, the populace fasted and prepared themselves for communion. Sermons would be preached on the need for honest confession, and confessions heard, usually in the aisles of the churches by priests and friars. The fasts of Lent as set out by the church in Rome excluded butter, preferring the use of olive oil, but oil was so prohibitively expensive that *James V obtained from the pope permission to use butter instead. In this way the church of Europe allowed regional differences to flourish, in sympathy for local peculiarities, while maintaining a unity of vision, worship, and theology across the Continent.

Another way of ensuring the unity of the universal church was through the education of the clergy. Scotland was not alone in sending men abroad to study and the travelling of student priests and noble sons kept the Scots at home in touch with the latest developments abroad. This can be seen not only in architecture, such as the Renaissance sculpture in *Stirling castle, but also in the traditions of the church. John Mair was one of the most famous Scottish scholars to study and then teach abroad, in Paris, before returning to write his *History of Greater Britain* (1521). The history of Scotland had been for the medieval period very much in the hands of its clerics: in the 14th century John Barbour and John of Fordun were both priests in Aberdeen diocese, in the 15th century Andrew Wyntoun and Walter Bower were both in religious orders, the former being prior of Lochleven and the latter abbot of Inchcolm (see HISTORIANS: I).

As well as providing the intellectual elite of the land the Scots clergy had one more link with the Continental church, through the courts of Rome. The absence of an archbishop before 1472 has usually been cited as the reason for the particularly high number of Scottish cases settled in Rome, although this does not explain why the figure continued to rise after that date. It is clear that the contacts with Rome, the Scottish presence at the church councils of the 15th century, and the studies of Scots abroad made Scotland an intellectually richer country.

The religious life of the medieval Scot was varied and colourful. Much has been lost but that which does survive suggests a community which unquestionably placed the Christian faith at the centre of its business; its birthing, marrying, and dying; and its hopes in the life to come. The towns and countryside may have been a world away from the glories of court but it was the same universal faith which ministered to all.   JF

3. 1560–1650

The 'Book of Reformation', compiled in 1560 by the reformers of the new Protestant church, set out their ideal of a new, godly society. The marks of the new church—true preaching of the Word, right administration of the sacraments, and godly discipline—were contrasted with the idolatry from which Scotland had escaped. By 1564, when John *Knox composed Book 4 of his *History of the Reformation in Scotland*, he claimed that no church anywhere had them 'in the like purity'. And in the same year, the kirk session of *St Andrews hailed the 'perfyt reformed kirk' set up in the city since 1559.

The contrast in worship was stark. The *Reformation had seen the abolition of auricular confession, the unleavened wafer in communion, and Latin in services, along with prayers to Mary and the saints, the doctrine of purgatory, and the idea of the Mass as a 'work'. In churches, the high altar, altar rails, rood-screen, choir stalls, statues, and pictures of the saints had all disappeared, along with side altars (St Giles's in *Edinburgh had as many as 45) in a fit of 'cleansing' of the temple. In their place were most often bare walls, whitewashed to obscure old murals, a pulpit and lectern, with an ordinary table for the Lord's Supper and some pews. The rich frenzy of colours in the pre-Reformation church was replaced by a black and white frieze, the new as dramatically different from the old as the print and negative of a colour photograph (see CHURCHES: 2).

The new church tried to recast in a new image the local community which it served. Before 1560, the *corpus christianum* of worshippers had a double identity. In towns, they represented the congregation as a whole but also, in one or other of the side altars, crafts such as the hammermen or skinners would worship before an altarpiece dedicated to their own saint with the Mass said by their own chaplain (see URBAN SOCIETY: 1). After 1560, all acts of worship, including the rites of passage of baptism, marriage, and burial, were carried out in front of the whole congregation. And at communion, rather than kneeling at the altar rails, people would sit around domestic tables, passing ordinary bread and wine from one to another. The centrepiece of

the new religion was now the *sermon, delivered from a centrally placed, simple pulpit, often extempore, as the Spirit moved the minister, for anything up to three hours, if some of the few printed sermons, such as those of the Edinburgh minister Robert Bruce, are typical.

Such was the ideal of the new reformed worship, and in St Andrews and in Knox's parish church of St Giles it was undoubtedly achieved almost overnight in 1559 or 1560. Elsewhere, matters were slower and often more ambiguous. *Aberdeen acquired a new minister in August 1560, bought him a Geneva gown, and installed him in the parish church of St Nicholas. But no kirk session materialized until late 1562, on the eve of a visit to the town by the privy council and even then it was largely made up of Catholics. As late as 1574, when Regent Morton visited the burgh, St Nicholas, to all appearances, still looked like a Catholic church, with its rood screen, reredos, and choir stalls intact—all, it was pleaded, to keep out Aberdeen's chill draughts. St Andrews, with its overnight reformation in June 1559, and Aberdeen, which acquired an unambiguously Protestant religious culture only in the 1590s, provide sharply contrasting pictures of Scotland's *Reformation. For most Scots, the changes in religious life fell somewhere in between these two experiences.

The new church felt obliged to reject many of the instruments for inculcation of the faith used for centuries. The penitential exercise of the rosary or pilgrimage were not easily replaced by printed works of spiritual devotion, especially in a society where only one in four (or perhaps one in three in towns) could read. The main aid to evangelization was not the Bible, for the age of cheap bibles did not come before the 1630s, but the blunt instrument of the catechism and the more congenial one of the Psalms, sung to familiar common tunes (see MUSIC, ECCLESIASTICAL). Most of the printed works, such as the Genevan *Book of Common Order*, adopted by the General Assembly in 1562, Calvin's *Catechism*, or the Bible itself, in the translation of William Tyndale, were in English, a largely alien tongue. For the *Gaidhealtachd*, John Carswell, bishop of the Isles, produced a translation of the *Book of Common Order* in 1568, but this was in the Gaelic of the learned orders to which he belonged and could have made only an indirect impact on ordinary Gaels. It was also the only printed book in Gaelic until the 1630s (see CULTURE: 4; GAELIC LANGUAGE; SCHOOLS AND SCHOOLING: 1).

Optimists are content to write of the steady progress of the Reformation after 1560, measuring it by the spread of a parish ministry. Pessimists, with a more jaundiced view of human nature, prefer to distinguish between mere conformity to the new religion and genuine conversion, which could often take three or four generations to effect. Until the 1590s, many if not most parishes were served, not by ministers, but by readers, who could not preach or administer the sacraments. A rural congregation might hear a sermon once a month. The Lord's Supper would take place once a year, not unlike Catholic communion, also generally taken once a year, at Easter, by their forebears. The General Assembly fretted regularly, as had its per-Reformation counterpart, the provincial council of the Scottish church, about poor attendance, neglect of the young, and irreverent behaviour, especially at communion (see CHURCH INSTITUTIONS: 3).

These perennial concerns are not always to be taken at face value, for the church was in the business of dreaming the impossible dream, in constructing a truly godly society. By the 1620s, ministers and intellectuals, despairing of converting the ignorant multitude, began to take refuge in a pilgrimage of the mind, turning to spiritual autobiographies, like that of Archibald Johnston of Wariston, and penitential works, such as those of the English Puritan William Perkins. Yet the church also recognized, as the prominent Edinburgh minister Robert Bruce put it, that God 'selects a certain number out of this rotten race' for salvation. For the chosen, the elaborate funerary monuments, to be seen in many post-Reformation graveyards and even within some churches, such as the elaborate marble, quasi-baroque tomb erected by the Cunningham family in the Skelmorlie Aisle at Largs, testified to their place both in this world and the next. The Covenants of the 1630s and 1640s, which was when the Scots discovered that they were the true people of Israel and that God was Scottish, provided a promise of better things to come.   ML

4. 1650–1750

Although religious life remained for the most part centred on the worship and discipline of the parish church, there were some exceptions to this pattern as when the *Covenanters held conventicles, particularly in the south-west. Informal Praying Societies were also formed which continued to exist well into the 18th century, when in some cases they joined the growing movement of Presbyterian dissent (see PROTESTANT SECTS AND DISESTABLISHMENT). The Toleration Act of 1712 allowed Episcopalians (see EPISCOPALIAN COMMUNITY) loyal to the crown to worship using the English Prayer Book. The nonjuring Episcopalians continued to survive in the north-east and used the Scottish Liturgy, although they suffered for their support of the *Jacobite cause. There were also relatively few Roman Catholics (see ROMAN CATHOLIC COMMUNITY) living mainly in the Highlands and Western Isles.

Within the Church of Scotland there was a growing number of Evangelical ministers who wished to offer the Gospel freely to all, but a more legalistic interpretation of the doctrine of election in the Westminster Confession was upheld by the General Assembly in 1720 when it condemned the teaching of the book *The Marrow of Modern Divinity*. The dominant influence in the church in the 18th century, however, was to become that of the Moderates (see RELIGIOUS LIFE: 5) who stressed the place of reason and morality in religion, and wished to relate the Christian faith to contemporary culture. They did not find the Calvinism of the Confession congenial, but could not admit so openly because of its legal position. Those who cast doubt on traditional orthodoxy, such as Professor John Simson of Glasgow, were treated leniently by the General Assembly.

In the mid-17th century Presbyterian worship took the form which it would have until the liturgical revival of the 19th century. After the adoption of the Westminster Directory in 1645, services were influenced by the English Puritan opposition to set forms and there was a rejection of the earlier reformed practice of saying the Creed, the Lord's Prayer, and the Ten Commandments, and of singing the Doxology. The lecture, a lengthy exposition of the Scripture reading, also became more common. Since the *sermon was seen as the most important part of worship, services had a wordy and heavily didactic character. The only participation by the congregation was in singing the metrical psalms without accompaniment. There was a brief interlude during the *Restoration and the second period of Episcopacy, 1662–90, when the Directory was rejected and there was officially a return to the earlier practices, but this meant that the use of such set forms as the Creed and the Lord's Prayer came to be associated in the popular mind with rule by bishops.

Communion throughout this period was celebrated infrequently, at most once a year. Communicants had to be examined by the minister and elders with regard to their way of life and knowledge of the Shorter Catechism. Only those considered worthy would receive communion tokens and thus be able to take their place at the long tables which were set up in the middle of the church for the sacrament. A minister might not consider his people to be ready to receive the sacrament or, at the other extreme, he might be too lazy to carry out the examination. In either case the celebration of communion was postponed. This infrequency was overcome to a certain extent by the holding of joint communions when parishioners would gather from the surrounding area. Such celebrations were discouraged by the General

Assembly which passed several acts during the early 18th century in favour of more frequent communion. These mass communions attracted large crowds who were interested in activities of a less spiritual nature and they were justly exposed to the satire of Robert Burns in *The Holy Fair*. But such celebrations could also be the occasion of Evangelical revival, as at Cambuslang in 1742.

Kirk session discipline in moral matters continued to be strictly applied. The authority of kirk sessions (see CHURCH INSTITUTIONS: 3) was backed up by the civil power, and both parish education (see SCHOOLS AND SCHOOLING: 2) and poor relief were the responsibility of the ministers and elders. The punishment meted out to offenders included the public humiliation of sitting on the stool of repentance in church on Sundays. There was, too, a concentration upon sexual misconduct, especially fornication and adultery. Just as it is easy to exaggerate the level of church attendance and the extent of sabbath observance in this period, so too it would be wrong to think of such discipline as being uniformly carried out. Its operation was affected by the upheavals of both the Restoration in 1660 and the Revolution of 1688–9. In addition, the impact of the church in the more remote parts of the Highlands (see RELIGIOUS LIFE: 8; CHURCH INSTITUTIONS: 6) was limited and in the Episcopalian north-east discipline seems to have been less effective. As with other aspects of religious life in this period, there was great variation in practice.   DMM

5. Moderatism

Moderatism, a term never used during the 18th century, captures the dominant mood in the Scottish church between the 1750s and the 1830s, when the Moderate party, though never comprising a numerical majority, held sway in the church by virtue of the political skills and intellectual calibre of its leadership. Unfortunately, historical understanding of Moderatism has been hampered by the enduring caricatures of lukewarm Erastian compromise handed down to posterity by its opponents, from John Witherspoon's satirical *Ecclesiastical Characteristics* (1753) to the denunciations which came from the Evangelicals during the Ten Years Conflict (1834–43) (see DISRUPTION). Since the early 1960s historians, however, have begun to recover the theological orthodoxy and principled views of ecclesiastical polity hidden beneath the traditional picture. In addition, the phenomenon of Moderatism is now generally disaggregated into a series of sharply contrasting phases. While it is not unfair to describe post-1780 Moderates as the clerical branch of the Henry *Dundas machine, the original Moderate party, which was led by William Robertson between 1762 and 1780, upheld the

church's autonomy within its own sphere, and succeeded in liberating churchmanship, for a while, from an earlier dependence upon state factions.

Before the formation of the Moderate party proper, there had been expressions of moderation within the church. From the Revolution of 1689 onwards several influential figures in the church perceived the strategic necessity of watering down the high ecclesiology of 17th-century Covenanting (see COVENANTERS) in the interests of winning support from Williamite and Hanoverian regimes suspicious not only of nonjuring *Jacobites but also of the Presbyterian extremes of Whiggery. During the second quarter of the 18th century, lay politicians came to exert considerable influence within the church through the clerical agents of the leading Whig factions, Robert Wallace acting for the Squadrone and Patrick Cuming for the Argathelians. The Moderate party opposed this creeping Erastianism, even as it enjoined upon the church the necessity of respecting the civil law on matters of patronage.

The main feature of first-generation Moderatism, which emerged in reaction to the insubordination of the lower courts during patronage disputes, was a concern to defend the established hierarchy of church courts (see CHURCH INSTITUTIONS: 3), from kirk session up to General Assembly, which counterbalanced the democratic parity of ministers. The drive for autonomy from lay politicians came to fruition during the early 1760s, when the demise of the early Hanoverian party system and the death of the third duke of Argyll created a vacuum in the arrangements for Scottish management which remained unfilled until the rise of Henry Dundas. Throughout the Robertsonian ascendancy, the General Assembly continued to issue its annual plea for the repeal of the Patronage Act, which was dropped only in 1784 with the emergence of a more pliant strain of Moderate leadership. Nevertheless, such assertions of ecclesiastical independence were predicated upon a close practical relationship with lay elites, whose exercise of patronage, although repugnant in theory as an intrusion into the spiritual sphere, helped to further the Moderate goal of a learned and unfanatical ministry.

Although Moderate preachers reneged upon the traditional preoccupations of Scottish Presbyterian divines with predestination, shifting the emphases of their *sermons instead towards issues of practical morality, they do not seem to have abandoned Calvinism. While some liberal Moderates contextualized the Westminster Confession of Faith as the product of a less enlightened age, they continued to subscribe to its tenets. Only in the 19th century would confessional subscription become a major issue in Scottish ecclesiastical affairs. On the other hand, the optimistic view of human benevolence which characterizes Moderate moral philosophy sits uneasily with the Calvinist vision of human depravity. Although current interpretations downplay the notion that Moderatism provided a screen for closet heterodoxy of an Arminian or Socinian cast, the sermons and treatises of the Moderate ministers themselves gingerly sidestepped the doctrinal orthodoxies which carried their nominal endorsement. In 1755-6, moreover, the Moderates organized effectively to frustrate the formal censuring of impieties in the works of David Hume (see CULTURE: 11) and of necessitarian errors detected in a treatise by Lord Kames. Moderatism did not comprise a coherent body of doctrine, but is most accurately described as a distinctive style of churchmanship.

Recent scholarship suggests that, far from there being an enormous intellectual gulf between the Moderate supporters of Enlightenment and the theological diehards of the church's Popular wing (see RELIGIOUS LIFE: 6), the latter body was also receptive to the mainstream of the Scottish Enlightenment. Although the Popular party proved more sympathetic to the cause of American independence and the Moderates to Roman Catholic relief, both parties espoused Whiggish political values of a broadly similar stamp. Despite differences in other spheres, it was the issue of lay patronage which, above all others, determined factional alignments within the church.

Later Moderatism inherited some of the characteristic features of its earlier incarnation, but was a very different phenomenon, not least because of the external pressures under which it operated. The church did not escape the reinvigoration of political management, the Moderate grouping providing a convenient tool for the ambitions of Dundas. This trend was exacerbated by the French Revolution in whose aftermath the Moderates shed intellectual openness for conventionality. Defeat in 1805 at the hands of the Evangelical supporters of John Leslie, the successful candidate for the Edinburgh chair of mathematics whose orthodoxy was suspect because of his support for Hume's theory of causation, signalled the decline and timid political correctness of the new Moderatism.

George Hill (1750–1819), the leader of the Moderates from 1780, owed less to Robertson, whose carefully crafted anti-Erastian position he discarded, than to his sponsor Dundas, from whose techniques of management the nepotistic ways of the clerical-academic Hill dynasty derived. George Cook (1772–1845), the Moderate leader during the Ten Years Crisis, for example, was a nephew of Hill's, though also a distinguished ecclesiastical

historian in his own right. Although the Moderate opponents of Chalmers appeared to hold fast to the constitutional shibboleths of their party's founders, an arid and reactionary legalism had now replaced the vigorous championship of Presbyterian polity found during the Robertson era.   CCK

6. Evangelicalism

The term 'Evangelicalism' refers to the movement embracing those Christians who have placed particular emphasis on the Bible, the doctrine of the atonement, the need for conversion, and the responsibility to be active in practising and spreading the faith. Dwelling on the Bible as the source of sound teaching as well as spiritual nourishment, its adherents have normally insisted on the maintenance of orthodoxy. Evangelicals have particularly stressed the cross of Christ as the means of salvation from sin. They have, nevertheless, been divided between those who have held, in the Calvinist or reformed tradition, that the atoning work of Christ was limited to those predestined to salvation and those who, with John Wesley and the Arminian tradition, have believed that the atonement was available for any who chose to believe. Evangelicals have contended that atonement as conversion to the Christian life through the kindling of saving faith is essential. Yet they have maintained a variety of views about whether conversion is a gradual, protracted process or a sudden and self-conscious crisis. They have, however, been consistent in an activism that seeks to bring about conversions through evangelism. Commonly, though not uniformly, they have also expressed their zeal in a commitment to schemes for social welfare. They have formed the predominant form of Protestantism in the modern world.

The movement arose roughly simultaneously in America, Wales, and England as well as in Scotland during the second quarter of the 18th century. Its earliest Scottish proponents were the ministers who saw in the Cambuslang revival of 1742 a sign that the Almighty was stirring his people to fresh Gospel efforts. The movement was essentially forward-looking and pragmatic, and so was distinguished from traditionalists such as the Seceders who demanded punctilious conformity to church order and inherited doctrine. It was epitomized in its leader John Erskine, a minister of Old Greyfriars, Edinburgh, from 1767 to 1803, who, though firmly orthodox, promoted changes of ecclesiastical practice, sympathized with the Enlightenment, and (according to his biographer T. Davidson) did not uphold 'the vulgar Calvinism, which, exhausts itself on intricate and mysterious doctrines' (*A sketch of the Character of John Erskine* (1803)). Erskine corresponded with church leaders abroad including the New England theologian Jonathan Edwards, whose teaching did much to mould the ideas of the movement. Concern that ministers should be committed preachers of the Gospel led Evangelicals to oppose the principle of patronage, which allowed landowners to impose nominees of their own choosing, who were often Moderates (see RELIGIOUS LIFE: 5), on unwilling parishes. Although there were others who adopted this defining conviction of the 'Popular party' in the Church of Scotland, it was a hallmark of Evangelicals to resist what was called 'Intrusion'.

The rising tide of Evangelicalism within the Church of Scotland was seconded by those who came to adopt similar views in the Secession Churches and by those who deserted the established church over patronage disputes to become the Relief Church. From about the beginning of the 19th century these Presbyterian denominations were joined by the smaller bodies of Independents, Baptists, and Methodists (see CHURCH INSTITUTIONS: 6), all of them vigorously Evangelical (see PROTESTANT SECTS AND DISESTABLISHMENT). The initial strength of Evangelicalism in the central belt was complemented by its rapid expansion in the Highlands (see RELIGIOUS LIFE: 8) during the early 19th century. By 1834 the Evangelicals led by Thomas *Chalmers gained for the first time a majority in the General Assembly of the Church of Scotland, so precipitating the conflicts with the courts and the state over patronage that led to the *Disruption. In the same year, 1843, there were also secessions by Evangelicals from the Scottish Episcopal Church (see EPISCOPALIAN COMMUNITY). It was hard for existing institutions to contain the dynamic of the growing movement.

Progress was primarily achieved by means of regular preaching (see SERMONS), but there were also local revivals, such as that at Kilsyth in 1839, in which whole communities were seized with concern for the welfare of their souls. Tracts, such as those issued by Peter Drummond at Stirling from 1848 onwards, helped promote the movement, as did the circulation of bibles. In 1859–60 parts of the country, especially where fishermen lived, were gripped by revival, and during the following decade popular Evangelicalism put down fresh roots, as among the miners of Lanarkshire. The visiting American Evangelist Dwight L. Moody and his singing colleague Ira D. Sankey stirred Edinburgh and Glasgow in 1873–4, attracting huge crowds. Philanthropic efforts burgeoned, as when the Tent Hall erected on Glasgow Green in 1876 gave 1,000 free breakfasts a week. Victorian Evangelicals typically put energy into the causes of *missions overseas, sabbath defence, anti-Catholicism, and, in many cases, *temperance. Calvinism was gradu-

ally eroded and biblical criticism caused unease from the controversy over the views of the Free Church professor William Robertson Smith in the 1870s, but evolution was more easily accommodated, as by the scientist-evangelist Henry Drummond. The Free Church in particular produced an able group of theologians, among whom James Orr was probably the most distinguished.

By the opening of the 20th century Evangelicalism had permeated Scottish life, as the 'Kailyard' school of literature illustrated (see CULTURE: 20). The movement extended far beyond the middle classes to mould the spirituality of working people too; and there is evidence that its appeal was almost equal to men and women (see RESPECTABLE CULTURE). There were still spontaneous revivals, notably that among north-eastern fishermen led by Jock Troup in 1921. The denominations officially sponsored Evangelistic efforts in the inter-war years and there continued to be extensive support for the Tell Scotland campaign that brought Billy Graham to preach in Glasgow's Kelvin Hall in 1955. Yet sections of the movement had moved in different directions, the more liberal welcoming modern knowledge and the more conservative endorsing more rigid views of the Bible. Although there was never a Fundamentalist controversy in Scottish Presbyterianism, there was a division between the Student Christian Movement and the (more theologically conservative) Inter-Varsity Fellowship that divided undergraduate Evangelicals. The more liberal gradually shed the label 'Evangelical', but from 1970 many of the conservatives gathered in the Crieff Fraternal around the venerable Aberdeen minister William Still. In 1994 some 23 per cent of adult churchgoers attending places of worship claimed to be Evangelical.   DWB

7. secularization

It has generally been accepted that the power of religion in Scottish society rapidly declined after the First World War. Certainly, the statistics of religious adherence fell more rapidly than at other time in the modern era. The rise of powerful nation states in the late 19th and 20th centuries in Europe increased the power of secular authority in the running of most peoples' lives and pushed back the influence of religion. On the surface, it would appear that Scotland did not escape from this process. After all, the *Disruption of 1843 had split the national church, the late 19th century had witnessed the rise of alternative ideas and ideologies such as socialism and scientific rationalism which challenged the primacy of religious belief, and the state had increasingly limited the role of the churches in the provision of education and poor relief. Yet, although there was a decline in religious adherence and the authority of the churches did diminish in Scottish society after 1914, this process was not straightforward. Religion could and did play a significant role in Scottish society and although decline is the dominant theme of religion in this period, it was subject to peaks and troughs and demonstrated a quite remarkable degree of resilience in the face of secularizing tendencies.

The figures for religious attendance indicate that Scotland was a more religious society in the 1950s than it was in the 1840s. Adherence figures show that just under 50 per cent of the population had some form of relationship with a Christian church in the 1920s. This level was maintained throughout the Depression in the 1930s and dipped to just over the 40 per cent mark only in the period of the Second World War. Religiosity increased in the mid-1950s, largely as a result of revivalist preaching campaigns and in particular the 1955 tour by Billy Graham, and recovered most of the lost ground of the war years. Thereafter, there was a steady decline which gathered momentum in the 1960s, and by the mid-1980s, just over 30 per cent of the population had some form of connection with the churches. This pattern of decline was not even and the Catholic Church (see ROMAN CATHOLIC COMMUNITY) has been better able than the Protestant churches to maintain membership. Also, in terms of the social composition of religious attendance in the 20th century, it has been the Protestant middle class which has proved most susceptible to secularizing influences. The collapse of traditional heavy industry and the demise of the culture of the skilled working-class Protestant may be a factor in the dramatic haemorrhage of membership from the Church of Scotland after the 1960s (see RESPECTABLE CULTURE).

Although the formal influence of the churches may have decreased as a result of the extension of the power of government in the period after 1914, religion remained a major social, cultural, and political force. The inter-war years were marred by sectarian tensions. Ethnic and ingrained tribal hostility, exacerbated by the impact of economic depression, was an obvious factor in promoting religious rivalry between Protestants and Catholics in this period. Yet, altogether more sinister, were the activities of the leaders of the Free Church of Scotland and the Church of Scotland (the two united in 1929), who orchestrated a racist campaign against the 'Irish' Catholics in Scotland. Accusations that Irish *immigration was a major 'threat to the Scottish race', made up with bogus figures, helped to create a climate of intolerance. Demands that Catholics should be turned away from jobs so that they could be preserved for the Scots were a prominent feature of many newspaper and journal

letter columns. Writers such as George Malcolm Thomson and Andrew Dewar Gibb made frequent denunciations of the supposedly inferior racial qualities of the 'Irish' Catholics. Although this hysteria was effectively disproved by official Scottish Office figures in the early 1930s, the climate of anti-Catholic intolerance carried on for several years. The political complexion of the Presbyterian churches in the inter-war period was bitterly anti-socialist. The General Strike of 1926 was denounced and the Church of Scotland made little concessions to issues of social policy in the thirties.

As with other major institutions in Britain after 1945, the church began to moderate its views and became more liberal, although the possibility of a merger with the Church of England in the 1950s produced a popular Presbyterian backlash. The Church of Scotland increasingly devoted more time to issues of decolonization, social policy, and inequity within Scottish society. Paradoxically, the period of liberalization coincided with decline in membership. The Catholic Church, on the other hand, did not liberalize, and this may be a factor in maintaining comparatively higher rates of attendance. Also, the hostility of Protestant Scotland and institutionalized sectarianism meant that Catholicism had a more important cultural dimension than Protestantism. Catholic social mobility was promoted after 1945 as the traditional industries which had fostered sectarian work practices declined and were increasingly replaced by international concerns with little understanding or appreciation of Scottish bigotry. Also, improved access to higher education (see UNIVERSITIES: 3) led to an increase in the Scottish Catholic middle class which helped to bolster and reinforce the community's identity. Finally, by the 1980s, the Catholic Church was successful in reinventing itself as a Scottish institution and casting off its Irish garb.

RJF

8. Highlands since the Reformation

The churches have had a powerful influence on Highland society since the 17th century, through their political alliances, their regulation of morals through the kirk session, and through social welfare, education, and mission (see CHURCH INSTITUTIONS: 6). The Protestant church in the Highlands originally had a civilizing role. It was not a direct arm of the government, but it was nevertheless seen as an important means of achieving the overall goals of Lowland Scottish, and later British, government in the region. The maintenance of the Protestant church in the Highlands was one of the obligations which were placed on Highland chiefs by the Statutes of Iona in 1609 (see HIGHLANDS AND ISLANDS AND CENTRAL GOVERNMENT: 2). A century later, the SSPCK was established. Operating through schools and schoolmasters (see SCHOOLS AND SCHOOLING: 2), it supplemented the parochial work of the established church, and was formally committed to the 'wearing out' of Gaelic and popery. There was therefore a political dimension to the role of the church in the Highlands. The civilizing of the Highlands included, in theory and as far as possible in practice, the eradication of the *Gaelic language, which was seen as one of the causes of barbarism in the region. The Protestant church and the SSPCK may have subscribed to the theory, but the practice was much more difficult, and more pragmatic policies were created as required, particularly after the mid-18th century.

The Protestant church also promoted a programme of moral improvement. The eradication of habits which were deemed unhelpful to ordinary living was high on its list of priorities. Christians were to be different from the world, and the world itself required to be cleansed of its evil. Thus the church waged a campaign against excessive consumption of alcohol (see TEMPERANCE), and immorality. In effect, the church was a moral policeman, and inculcated its programme through the kirk session. Parishioners who had transgressed were summoned before the kirk session, made to sit on *stòl an aithreachais* (the stool of repentance), and fined. The church also tried to separate people from 'bad' practices, such as superstitious customs and revelries of various kinds (see CALENDAR AND SEASONAL CUSTOMS) which it considered might be harmful to life. It has to be said, however, that during the course of the 18th century, the established church was rather lax in the preservation of these aims in the southern and western Highlands, where the relative dominance of Moderate (see RELIGIOUS LIFE: 5), non-Evangelical ministers led to what Evangelicals regarded as nominalism and barrenness. In the northern Highlands, chiefly in Ross-shire and Sutherland, a strong vein of Evangelicalism (see RELIGIOUS LIFE: 6), linked to a deep loyalty to the Covenant, had taken root by the mid-17th century, and the 'Fathers of Ross-shire' were long regarded as the true spiritual patriarchs of the North.

The balance elsewhere was redressed firmly when a fresh wave of Evangelicalism began to enter the Highlands, from Perthshire to the Hebrides, by the end of the 18th century. This wave was spearheaded by Congregational and Baptist itinerant preachers. In some significant cases, their fervour and devotion helped to convert formerly Moderate ministers of the Church of Scotland into firebrand Evangelicals. The latter strengthened the ranks of earlier Evangelical ministers, such as Lachlan MacKenzie of Lochcarron (1754–1819), who had

been active chiefly in northern mainland. What was in effect a second Evangelical movement, leading ultimately to the *Disruption of 1843, was created within the church. As a consequence, admission to the sacraments became much stricter than in earlier days. The increasingly Evangelical complexion of the church meant that great stress was laid on separating genuine Christians from the evils of the world; the lines of demarcation between the church and the world were firmly drawn. Sabbath-keeping was given a high priority.

The life of the churches in the Highlands and Islands stemmed from, and naturally embraced, missionary activity. The churches' concern with mission increased during the 18th century, and was intensified by the missionary drive which was inherent in post-1800 Evangelicalism. At the end of the 18th century, the Highlands had the status of a foreign mission field in the eyes of the various voluntary bodies which were set up to engage in *missions at home. In the national context, the distinctive nature of the Highlands as a mission field came to be acknowledged by the creation of special sections of the wider denominational structure. These were given a particular remit to look after the Highlands. For example, the Glasgow and West Coast Mission, which operated from 1856 to 1949, maintained up to 30 mission stations in the Outer and Inner Hebrides as well as the Highland mainland. In 1949, four of its five remaining mission stations were assigned to the Church of Scotland Home Board, and one to the Free Church.

Well into the 20th century, all the Protestant churches tended to regard the Highlands and Islands as an area in particular need of spiritual attention, compared with other parts of Scotland. Indeed, the Church of Scotland maintained lay missionaries in the islands until the 1960s. Such an approach had a somewhat patronizing ring to it, but it helped to preserve Gaelic commitment. Most Church of Scotland missionaries were Gaelic-speaking men. However, as the Highlands and Islands became more evidently bilingual and were penetrated increasingly by Lowland culture, the need to create and maintain special arrangements for the Highlands became less pressing, and specific Highland agencies were absorbed into the larger structures of the denominations. 'Home mission' was assumed to be a normal part of the churches' work, rather than a distinctive aspect in need of promotion by special structures. Thus the Baptist Home Missionary Society of Scotland, once an independent body established in the 1820s 'chiefly for the Highlands and Islands', became part of the Baptist Union of Scotland in 1931, and Highland missionaries (in effect, the pastors of the Baptist churches in the area) were supervised thereafter by the Home Mission Committee. In 1971 the Committee itself was abolished, and its work was absorbed within the wider Church Extension programme. At the beginning of the 21st century, it is debatable how far the churches are able to maintain a strong missionary role, except in the broadest terms. As financial support declines, often as a result of secessions or internal conflict, or simply through loss of members, survival rather than mission is becoming the chief concern of most churches. Concern for the Highlands is, nevertheless, still evident, and Baptists have recently created a Highlands and Islands Strategy Group, with its own co-ordinator, whose remit extends from Islay to Orkney and Shetland, and includes the Highland mainland.

The consequence of the various missionary thrusts into the Highlands was the creation of a deeply serious commitment to the Christian faith on the part of its 'professors'. An underlying concern about spiritual matters (cùram anama, 'concern of soul', in Gaelic, sometimes flippantly caricatured as 'the cùram') became part of the Highland psyche, and this concern was often heightened through significant teaching, preaching, and social gatherings. A broad knowledge of the faith was instilled at the individual level by regular catechizing, using Gaelic and English versions of the Shorter Catechism. Knowledge of the catechism, which provided a systematic, question-and-answer vademecum of the faith, helped to furnish a sense of liturgy within Highland Protestantism generally. Rote-learning ensured that 'the chief end of man' was a concept acknowledged on the tongue, if not always in the heart. For deeper theological learning, Highlanders were given regular diets of preaching (see SERMONS) at their local churches, and Presbyterians enjoyed the edification and celebration offered by the usually twice-yearly communion season.

Communions, which were in effect 'holy fairs' in the late 18th and early 19th century, were transformed by Evangelicals into sacred occasions, where preaching by popular ministers and the sharing of spiritual experience became the keynotes. The communion season extended from Thursday to Monday, with preaching and testimony. Highlanders travelled great distances to attend communion services, and lodged in the homes of friends and relations during the 'season'. Bonding by spiritual kinship was of great significance to the Gaelic people, and was encouraged in different ways during the communions. The sharing of experience was vital at all levels, and was particularly evident at the Friday meeting, Là na ceist ('The question day'), when the 'Men'—the spiritual leaders of the parishes—shared their interpre-

tation of a verse of Scripture chosen by the minister. The communion festival found its climax in the sabbath-day celebration of the Lord's Supper, often out of doors, in natural amphitheatres, such as the Burn at Ferintosh, where the greatest of all Gaelic Evangelical preachers, Dr John MacDonald (1779–1849), held sway in the first half of the 19th century. MacDonald, 'the Apostle of the North', a tireless itinerant preacher, was seldom in his own pulpit; he travelled as far as St Kilda, where his preaching caused deep soul-searching and implanted the impulses of spiritual revival. Nowadays, the communions are held in churches, and only occasionally is there an attempt to replicate the earlier practice of open-air preaching.

Communions were closely linked with spiritual renewal and revival within the Presbyterian bodies. Nevertheless, they were probably no more than triggers in stimulating corporate manifestations of cùram anama; the assembling of a couple of thousand people to the communion no doubt reinforced, in itself, a sense of spiritual kinship, and it certainly encouraged older Gaelic social customs of hospitality and mutual support (see HIGHLANDS AND ISLANDS: COMMUNITY LIFE). Spiritual revival, when whole townships and communities were gripped by a desire to have a deeper knowledge of God and mass conversions resulted, was associated with all the Protestant bodies, and could take root beyond the communion services. Throughout much of the 19th century, Baptists and Independents, who did not have a communion season, experienced revival movements within their congregations, and their itinerant preachers helped to spread the message to out-of-the-way parts of the Highlands and Islands.

The revival movements of the Highlands and Islands had probably reached their peak by the middle of the 19th century. In the 1830s and 1840s they were stimulated by the Ten Years Conflict prior to the emergence of the Free Church, and it seems likely that tensions within the communities, as population (see POPULATION PATTERNS: 2) grew and resources diminished, played their part. Waves of spiritual revival tended to peak immediately prior to periods of more intense emigration. The movements of the 1840s, which outlasted the Disruption, were halted by the potato famine of 1846 and the emigration which it induced. Revival returned in the late 1850s, and again in the 1880s, and intermittently in the 20th century. The Lewis revival of 1949–53, initiated by the preaching of the Revd Duncan Campbell (1898–1972), a Faith Mission Evangelist, was followed by smaller movements in Tiree in 1955 and in North Uist in 1958. Despite the Highlands' reputation for 'quiet' revivals, these movements almost all had an emotional side, and were sometimes accompanied by phenomena such as prostration, crying, and shouting. These phenomena stood in contrast to the doctrinal rectitude of Westminster Calvinism, and doubtless offered an outlet for repressed expression of spiritual elation, for the faithful as well as for those still seeking a living faith.

*Migration and *emigration took people away from the Highlands, and away from the churches, especially during the 19th century. Social change, of which the notorious *Clearances form an emotive part, transformed the demographic and spiritual landscapes. The smaller churches, notably those of Baptists and Independents, were seriously damaged by chain migration. Highlanders who migrated to the Lowlands established Gaelic chapels in *Edinburgh, *Glasgow, and *Aberdeen and in places like Cromarty. This pattern was replicated in North America (see CANADA; USA). Wherever Highlanders settled, they re-established their forms of worship, and sought Gaelic preachers to maintain their services. As in the Highlands, the festival of the communion service was the focal point of the godly community, and descriptions of communions identical with those of the Gaelic-speaking Highlands can be found as widely scattered as North Carolina, Nova Scotia, and *Australia. Revival movements also occurred regularly within the emigrant communities, sometimes at the same time as movements in the Highlands.

Emigration allowed Highlanders to replicate the religious experiences of their homelands, but it also gave them the opportunity to find new ways of communicating the faith. It is particularly noteworthy that the printing of Gaelic sermons first appeared in North Carolina in 1791, when two orations by Dugal Crawford, preached at the Raft Swamp in 1790, were printed at Fayetteville. Similarly, Gaelic sermons found their way into print in the cities of the Scottish Lowlands in the later 1790s, and a regular stream of printed Gaelic prose, including many translations of Puritan works, was established during the 19th century (see GAELIC LITERATURE). In this way, the faith was wedded to a desire for education (see SCHOOLS AND SCHOOLING: 3) and literacy in Gaelic as well as English. It was also taken into less austere contexts. In the cities of Lowland Scotland, para-church bodies, such as the Glasgow Highland Mission, led by Duncan MacColl (1846–1930), provided an Evangelistic and social programme which, to some extent, was a sacred counterbalance to the secular *céilidh* circuit frequented by émigré Highlanders. The Glasgow Highland Mission produced its own 'little red book' of Gaelic hymns, which drew on the hymnology of poets such as the 19th-century Baptist composer Peter Grant (1783–1867), but it also gave

a place to contemporary revivalist songs, as well as translations of English hymns associated with the Moody and Sankey campaigns of 1874–5. In this way, Moody and Sankey, whose theology of revival was contested in 1874 by the influential Free Church minister of Dingwall Dr John Kennedy, exerted some degree of influence on the Gaelic spirituality of the Highlands, though it must be noted that it was only in the southern Hebrides, in the context of the Church of Scotland, the Baptists, and the Congregationalists, that these 'light' Gaelic hymns of spiritual experience found any significant place in regular worship. In the north, they were accommodated usually in informal gatherings beyond the churches, and did not displace the Metrical Psalter as the sole source of acceptable praise.

Although the main churches in the Highlands and Islands entered the region from outside, they were influenced strongly by the Gaelic culture of the area. While some churches may appear to have worked against the culture, the fact is that they have been able to absorb parts of it, and to work with it, almost without knowing it. All came into existence at a time when Gaelic culture was strong in the region. Gaelic culture imparted to them a particular flavour, making them culturally different from the corresponding wings of the same churches in the Lowlands. It could indeed be argued that churches within churches were formed, because of the distinctiveness of the Highland dimension.

The Protestant church originally had a strong interest in education in the Highlands and Islands. This followed from the commitment of the Scottish reformers to the provision of schooling (see SCHOOLS AND SCHOOLING: 1) in the parishes. In theory, the church had to acquiesce in the wider aims of government, and it subscribed to the overall design to eradicate Gaelic. But in practice it had to use Gaelic as a means of communication. Scholars like Donald Withrington have argued that the provision of parish schools, with some Gaelic commitment, in the Highlands was probably more extensive than has been allowed by writers such as Victor Durkacz and Charles Withers. By the early 18th century, the educational role of the church was being supplemented by ancillary agencies like the SSPCK. The latter's teachers included the celebrated Gaelic religious poet Dugald Buchanan (1716–68), stationed at Kinloch Rannoch, Perthshire, who saw the Gaelic New Testament through the press in Edinburgh in 1766–7 (see PRINTERS AND PUBLISHERS).

The Protestant church was committed to the production of books of basic instruction for the Highlands. It produced the first printed Gaelic book, a Gaelic version of John *Knox's *Book of*

Common Order, translated by John Carswell and published in Edinburgh in 1567. Translations of catechisms followed from c.1631, and the Synod of Argyll attempted unsuccessfully to translate the Bible into Gaelic in the 1650s. The Gaelic New Testament was eventually published by the SSPCK in 1767 and the Old Testament was completed in 1801—a remarkable change of direction in terms of SSPCK policy. In the 19th century, the Highland educational programme, so to speak, was intensified by the arrival (from 1811) of the Gaelic Schools Societies, which aimed to make the people sufficiently literate in Gaelic to be able to read the Gaelic Bible, which became the main textbook of the Gaelic schools. Both the Church of Scotland and (after 1843) the Free Church established their own schools, with a strongly Gaelic element in their teaching.

As part of its educational role, the established church produced books for the benefit of those who became literate in the Gaelic schools, and it was able to implant political, social, and moral perspectives through literature. In the first half of the 19th century these were uniformly pro-establishment. The Disruption of the Church of Scotland in 1843 tended to divide the resources and the readerships, however, and important journals were unable to find sufficient subscribers. In 1872, when the Education Act nationalized education, the role of the churches was severely curtailed. Gaelic scholarship, too, gradually lost ecclesiastical support. Ministers of all the major denominations had made significant contributions to collecting, editing, and writing Gaelic folklore (see ORAL HISTORY; ORAL TRADITION) from at least the middle of the 18th century, but by the early 20th century ministerial devotion to Gaelic studies had diminished considerably, and was the exception rather than the rule by 2000.

In assessing the ways in which the churches approach Gaelic in the present day, we need to bear in mind that Gaelic culture, including language, has given a distinctive shape to the Highland sectors of these churches. This means that the churches must strive to meet a range of culturally conditioned expectations, which can create tensions when they cannot be readily fulfilled. The churches have to acknowledge the simple fact that Gaelic preaching is still preferred in many parts of the islands, though less so on the mainland. Worship, to be meaningful to a considerable proportion of people in Lewis, for instance, has to be Gaelic worship. Yet the numbers of Gaelic preachers are gradually declining in all the churches and, in the case of the Free Presbyterians, have dried up for the time being. This is not necessarily because the Almighty has turned his back on Gaelic, as an occasional Free Presbyterian minister

might claim. Rather, the problem results partly from the churches' chronic failure to develop adequate strategies for the training and placement of Gaelic ministers.

The Gaelic cultural context in which the older churches operate has been, and continues to be, a conservative one. This has helped the churches to maintain a conservative view of theology, worship, and culture, though they are now inclined to reject Gaelic as a medium of communication. Beyond the language, however, it is evident that styles of preaching, praying, and singing (see MUSIC, HIGHLAND) have been influenced by Gaelic tradition. Even in areas where Gaelic has ceased to be used, it is often possible to recognize a Gaelic or Highland tone to the worship of the more conservative churches. This distinctive tone is preserved in the cadences of preaching, as the preacher warms to his theme and heightens his pitch, and in unaccompanied psalm-singing, in which a precentor 'lines out' the psalm. This was not a peculiarly Highland phenomenon originally; it was found throughout Scotland until the arrival of organs and music in the churches in the later 19th century, but it has survived longest in the Highlands, and has become indigenous in terms of style.

Each of the Highland churches has had to devise its own response to the culture and the challenges which confront it. This is equally evident beyond the Presbyterian bodies. It is noteworthy that the Roman Catholic Church (see ROMAN CATHOLIC COMMUNITY) has been able to maintain a supply of Gaelic-speaking priests fairly successfully, at least for its island charges within the diocese of Argyll and the Isles. This may have something to do with the close sense of Gaelic identity within the diocese; but it also has to do with the way in which Roman Catholics view culture. At parish level, Catholics do not maintain the dividing line which so clearly separates sacred from secular in the Evangelical wings of the Protestant churches. Even so, the Roman Catholic Church has not been without its difficulties in preserving its Gaelic commitments, particularly within the episcopacy. In 1996, Roderick Wright, bishop of Argyll and the Isles and a Gaelic speaker, abandoned his diocese, and took up house with his future wife. The diocese remained vacant until 1999, when Bishop Ian Murray was appointed. Although he supports Gaelic initiatives strongly, Bishop Murray does not speak Gaelic, and a well-maintained tradition of providing a Gaelic-speaking bishop for this strategic western diocese has thus been broken, at least temporarily.

The Highlands and Islands of Scotland have been deeply influenced by religious experience, and the churches have helped to shape the intellectual, social, and moral perspectives of the region. It is, however, hard to know how long the Highland churches will be able to maintain their influence in the fields which are still within their grasp, or how long they will maintain a serious commitment to Gaelic. Until the mid-20th century, the main Highland churches were closely contextualized in Gaelic culture, and breathed a Gaelic ethos. Since 1950 or so, Highland culture has changed with increasing rapidity, and has been infiltrated steadily by the English-language mass media (see RADIO AND TELEVISION) and the mores of greater Britain. Highland patterns of worship are thus under pressure to conform to wider conventions.

As we enter the 21st century, the older churches are devoting much of their energy to maintaining the status quo in the face of diminishing (and increasingly divided) resources, rather than promoting any new approach to evangelism and social action. For old bodies, as for new, survival is the first priority. The maintenance of the status quo is becoming harder, not only because congregations are dwindling, but also because the more conservative Presbyterian churches have an inbuilt, and at times self-defeating, tendency to secession or fragmentation over theological matters. In the current climate, moral and social issues may also become bones of contention. In the meantime, there is a distinct possibility, indeed a probability, that the new charismatic fellowships, already established in small towns from Kyle of Lochalsh to Tain, will occupy an increasingly significant place in Highland church life as disenchantment with existing structures grows.   DEM

respectable culture might be defined as the value system which was used by members of the Scottish working class to differentiate themselves from those who were deemed 'unrespectable' or 'rough' (see ROUGH CULTURE). By conforming to accepted forms of behaviour which revolved around sobriety, *temperance, thrift, hard work, religiosity, and self-improvement, members of the respectable working class sought to create a stable social environment for themselves and their families. The best exposition of these values can be found in Samuel Smiles's *Self Help* (1853) which encouraged members of the working class to look to their own endeavours as a means of improving their conditions.

It was conventional wisdom in the mid-Victorian period that material improvement was dependent on moral improvement and that efforts to improve working-class conditions which were imposed by the state would not bear fruit as individuals had to accept responsibility for their own actions (see ECONOMIC POLICY: 3). Unless workers could improve themselves, they would become de-

pendent on the actions of others and thus incapable of doing things for themselves. The creation of dependence on charity was regarded as a greater sin than doing nothing. Many Victorian social investigators analysed the symptoms of poverty as the causes of poverty (see URBAN SOCIETY: 4). Poor conditions in working-class areas (see LIVING STANDARDS: 3) were blamed on a predilection for drink, gambling, prostitution, and a feckless approach to finance. It was argued that things would improve only when members of the working class learned to cultivate sober and hard-working habits and spend their money wisely. Consequently, middle-class moral reformers devoted much effort into inculcating those values of independence and respectability among the working class. For some historians, the imposition of Victorian values on Scottish society was a means of social control as workers would become sober, hard-working, and deferential. In other words, the promotion of respectable culture was bound up with middle-class demands for a pliable and docile workforce.

Yet, the widespread adoption of such values in Scottish society was also dictated by the needs of the working class. The absence of social safety nets meant that members of the working class had no option other than self-improvement as a means to provide security for themselves and their families. The middle class may have been prominent in the denouncement of drink, but from the perspective of the working class, alcoholism was a major social blight. The testimony of numerous labour leaders eloquently bears witness to the terrible damage drink had on family life in Victorian Scotland and the passion with which former victims condemned it. In an economy which was vulnerable to cyclical downturns, the careful saving of money was a practical necessity. Self-education was a tool to be used for greater security and prosperity. Cleanliness and respectability were life choices taken by many working class families which had more to do with human dignity than bourgeois ideology. In any case, the respectable working class did not have far to look to see the consequences of alcoholism and a lack of care with money. The proximity of neighbourhoods in which social relationships had all but broken down was more of an effective deterrence to feckless ways than middle-class preaching. The cult of working-class respectability was not simply an aping of middle-class values as greater emphasis was placed on notions of community and communal self-help. Also, it has to be remembered that perhaps the greatest propagators of these values were members of the labour movement and trade unionists who sought working-class social and economic advancement against middle-class employers.

'Rational recreation' was a major feature of respectable culture. It was stipulated that pastimes and hobbies had to serve a function which was more than simple enjoyment. Leisure was to be used constructively and this can be seen in the many activities pursued by the working class. Brass bands and the playing of music were a means of inculcating discipline and elevating the spirit. The growing of flowers and prize vegetables was a way to demonstrate expertise, as were numerous other hobbies such as pigeon racing and model making. Education and the accumulation of knowledge were ways to improve the intellect. Such activities were important in promoting both individual and communal pride and respect. The promotion of domestic ideology which curtailed the activities of *women was an inherent part of respectable culture. Women were meant to perform activities restricted to the management of the home and family. Mothers were judged on the cleanliness of their homes and children and their ability to look after their husbands. With some exceptions, men who allowed their wife to work were indicted. Yet, while respectable culture confined the opportunities for women, it has to be borne in mind that women were often the greatest propagators of these values. Women were active in the temperance movement, no doubt because they were the main victims of alcoholic husbands and fathers. Also, while life for women in the scheme of respectable culture may have been very limited, the acceptance of its values and standards was essential to attract a husband. In a society where there was a relative shortage of marriageable males and a social stigma was attached to spinsterhood, women were encouraged to develop the skills of domesticity as a necessary device for marriage. Failure to marry would lead to a life of dependency on male relatives and failure to attract a good husband could lead to degeneracy into rough culture and all the horrors that this entailed.

These notions of respectability and independence entailed a hostility among many members of the working class towards state interference. Attempts by politicians to introduce social legislation were not always greeted with widespread enthusiasm and the labour exchanges which were set up in 1911 were regarded with suspicion. The arrival of the teetotal, earnest, and dour Clydesiders (see LABOURISM; 'RED CLYDESIDE') in Parliament in 1922 illustrated how deeply entrenched these values were in Scottish society. The impact of the economic downturn in the inter-war years consolidated and reinforced working-class notions of independence and respectability. Indeed, those hardest hit by unemployment were the skilled workers and contemporary accounts reveal the psychological trauma of forced idleness on proud and independent men. With the impact of greater state intervention and the decline of community entertainment in the post-war era, these values began to disappear.   RJF

Restoration. The Restoration took place in 1660 with the return of King Charles II to his British kingdoms after political exile in Holland during the Cromwellian ascendancy and military occupation of Scotland. As a political event the 'Restoration Settlement' in Scotland was enacted in the Scottish parliament between 1 January and 12 July 1661. Despite the fact that Charles II had been crowned as king of Great Britain, France, and Ireland at *Scone in Perthshire on 1 January 1651, the Restoration in a British context was primarily an English political event. The emphasis was on England, with Scotland accorded a subordinate and marginal role. Prior to the meeting of the Scottish parliament on 1 January 1661, the government and administration of Scotland was devolved by the king to a committee of estates. This committee of estates operated as a provisional government before parliament convened and was based on the precedent of previous committees of estates which had been established by the Covenanters (see COVENANT, WARS OF THE) between 1640 and 1651. The last committee of estates established in 1651 before the Cromwellian conquest of Scotland was recalled as a provisional government in 1660.

The mood of the Scottish political nation was strongly Royalist in 1660–1. The elections of shire and burgh members to the 1661 Scottish parliament were held throughout November and December 1660 and were managed in the king's interest. Enthusiasm for the king's cause was reflected in the attendance levels of the 1661 parliament which were higher than any of the Covenanting parliamentary sessions between 1639 and 1651 and amounted to 195 members: 75 nobles, 59 shire members, and 61 burgh members. A clear Royalist political agenda had been articulated before it met and it sought to firmly reassert and reimpose the royal prerogative in Scotland.

A sweeping legislative programme was enacted which restored the traditional powers of the crown. The monarch was given sole power in the appointment of privy councillors, officers of state, and ordinary and extraordinary Lords of Session. Parliaments and conventions of estates could be called and dissolved with the approval of the king alone, whilst the conduct and execution of foreign policy was likewise recognized to lie solely with him. Personal loyalty to the crown by office-holders was demanded by national subscription of the Oath of Allegiance of 27 February 1661.

Subscription was extended to ministers of the church in June 1661. Retrospective recognition of Royalist support was evident in the restoration of estates of Royalists who had been forfeited by the Covenanters. Charles II was also generously rewarded with an annuity of £480,000 per annum for life, a sum to be raised primarily from excise duties. The Act Recissory of 28 March 1661 annulled the parliaments of 1640 to 1648 and separate legislation dealt specifically with the 1643 Convention of Estates and the radical parliament of 1649. An Act of Indemnity was passed on 9 September 1662, although a total of 896 individuals was exempted from it. Payment of varying levels of fines was required before a full pardon and indemnity could be applied. The reaction against the Covenanting movement was symbolized in the execution of prominent Covenanters, most notably Archibald Campbell, eighth earl and first marquis of Argyll, and James Guthrie, the infamous Protestor minister. Sir Archibald Johnston of Wariston, one of the key architects of the *National Covenant and a central figure in the Covenanting politics of church and state, was later executed in 1663 after being captured in France.

Matters of religious controversy were not clarified until 1662 with the formal reintroduction of episcopacy as the appropriate government of the Church of Scotland. Factionalism within the Church of Scotland had focused on the clash between Resolutioners and Protesters. The reassertion of royal control over religious issues was initiated by the Act concerning religion and church government of 28 March 1661 which stated that the settlement of the church was to be that which was most agreeable and suitable to monarchy. Bishops were restored to parliament and the ancient government of the church by archbishops and bishops was effected by two separate Acts of May 1662. In addition, the 1663 parliamentary session reintroduced the Lords of the Articles on 18 June according to the traditional model of 1633. Bishops and archbishops were therefore accorded their traditional place on the Lords of the Articles and the Articles as a parliamentary committee resumed a dominant role in the parliaments of the Restoration era. (See also COVENANTERS; CHURCH INSTITUTIONS: 4; PARLIAMENT: 2).   JY

Robert I, king of Scots (1306–29), one of Scotland's greatest historical figures, fought a long, but ultimately successful, war to have his kingship, and Scotland's independence, recognized by England. He was born Robert Bruce in 1272 into a powerful south-western family which had held the lordship of Annandale since the time of *David I (1124–53), in addition to lands in England. The earldom of Car-

rick had also recently been acquired through his father's marriage to the heiress Marjorie. As a young man, Bruce was married to Isobel, daughter of Donald, earl of Mar, a family ally.

On the death of Alexander III without a direct male heir, the Bruces fervently believed in their right to inherit the Scottish throne through their descent from the second daughter of David, earl of Huntingdon, being fewer generations removed than the descendant of the first daughter, John Balliol. However, Robert's grandfather, Robert Bruce 'the Competitor', lost out to Balliol when Edward I adjudicated on the issue between 1290 and 1291. A few days before the contest was settled on 17 November 1292, Bruce received the earldom of Carrick from his father (also Robert); the latter had recently been invested with the Bruce claim to the throne by 'the Competitor', who retained Annandale. The middle Bruce would thus not have to swear homage and fealty to Balliol for lands in Scotland, leaving him free to pursue the family's regal ambitions (see BALLIOL FAMILY).

When war (see INDEPENDENCE, WARS OF) appeared imminent in 1295, the Bruces threw away their nominal allegiance to Balliol and joined openly with King Edward. The young earl of Carrick was therefore present in the English army that invaded Scotland in March 1296. A year later, he seems to have changed his allegiance, joining Robert Wishart, bishop of Glasgow, and James the Steward, a close ally of the Bruces, in rebellion, ostensibly over expected demands for military service on Edward's overseas campaigns against *France. When that rebellion was settled by negotiation at Irvine on 7 July 1297, Bruce was supposed to hand over a hostage, probably his daughter, Marjorie; he failed to do so and the English authorities remained unconvinced of his allegiance, despite his father's adherence to Edward I. It is therefore highly unlikely that he fought on the English side against the Scots led by William *Wallace at the battle of Falkirk on 22 July 1298, though others in the family may have done. Certainly the next reference to him places him on the Scottish side, burning Ayr castle as Edward's army proceeded west after Falkirk.

Defeat at Falkirk terminated Wallace's stint as guardian and by the end of 1298 Scotland's leaders were Carrick and the pro-Balliol John Comyn, younger of Badenoch (see COMYN FAMILY). These two represented quite different power factions and in August 1299 the bishop of St Andrews was made guardian to mediate between them. By May 1300, however, the Comyn power block was able to remove Bruce from the guardianship and by mid-February 1302, when it seemed likely that King John would return to Scotland, Carrick returned to

Edward I's peace. His reward was marriage with Elizabeth de Burgh, daughter of Edward's friend, the earl of Ulster.

By the end of 1303 the English king was on the point of subduing Scotland again. However, as early as June 1304, Bruce had begun to canvas support for himself as king. There are also some hints that Edward was not treating him very favourably. Bruce's meeting with Comyn in Dumfries in February 1306 was surely about a potential bid for Balliol's throne, probably once Edward was dead, but their differences resulted in murder. Bruce, perhaps prompted by Wishart, had little choice but to take the throne, though with little real support. His enemies were everywhere and he was soon in exile, perhaps in Ireland, his supporters facing execution if captured. However, a series of surprise attacks on the west coast resulted in some success, compounded by Edward's death on 7 July 1307.

With England occupied domestically, Bruce turned on his Comyn enemies and defeated them in their heartland of the north-east, while his lieutenants made inroads in the south-west. By 16 March 1309, King Robert was strong enough to hold his first parliament and garrisons continued to fall, despite an English invasion in 1310. By 1313, he demanded that Scottish noblemen choose to support him or be forfeited within a year, a demand made more effective by his success against a full-blown English army at Bannockburn on 23–4 June 1314. His control of Scotland now secure, Bruce began the systematic plundering of the vulnerable north of England. The only false step seemed to be the abortive conquest of Ireland from 1315, led by his brother, Edward, resulting in the latter's death on 14 October 1318 (see IRELAND: 2). By 2 April 1318 even *Berwick had fallen, albeit at the price of excommunication for continuing the war against the pope's wishes. The Scottish response—the Declaration of Arbroath—had some effect in eliciting papal sympathy, but it should not be forgotten that in the same year (1320) Bruce foiled a plot against his life by Balliol sympathizers, Bruce was determined to gain recognition of his kingship, and Scotland's independence, from Edward II (1307–27), but nothing worked, even as England degenerated into civil war. Eventually, the English king's overthrow on 20 January 1327 provided the key: the regency government for Edward III, facing mounting internal opposition, came to a deal with the Scots and the Treaty of Edinburgh on 17 March 1328 finally brought Bruce his retirement. He died a year later on 7 June 1329 and was succeeded by his 6-year-old son, David (1329–71).

Bruce dominated Britain militarily in the years after Bannockburn and there is no doubt that he alone proved capable of liberating Scotland of an English presence, temporarily at least. Capable of great ruthlessness tempered with an ability to compromise when necessary, he will always be a great figure in Scottish history. That Bruce's priorities on occasions deviated from what others might deem a strictly Scottish agenda was a necessary part of his boundless determination to succeed. The mighty propaganda machine that backed him from his early years has proved able, until very recently, to rewrite history in his image. (See also ANGLO-SCOTTISH RELATIONS: 2; GREAT CAUSE; KINGSHIP: 4; NATIONAL IDENTITY: 2.) FW

Roman Catholic community. Catholicism in Scotland in the 19th century underwent four revolutions; geographic, numerical, organizational, and spiritual. It changed out of all recognition in becoming a major urban presence from a remote rural institution, in numerical strength, organizational structure, and spiritual style. It achieved status and credibility. In politics it shifted. Tory sympathies around the French Revolution shifted to popular support for Catholic Emancipation and Home Rule, to demands for domestic and international social justice. Adjustment to 20th-century social transformation has proved awkward and at times divisive. With the erosion of old Irish and Ultramontane identities in recent times, the need for more substantial philosophical underpinning has become obvious. Immigrants (see IMMIGRATION, IRISH) and migrants (see MIGRATION) provided an expanding Catholic base. Thousands of Irish, not all of them Catholic, continuously arrived in Scotland over several decades. Other ethnic groups—Italians, Germans, Poles, and Lithuanians—made smaller but significant contributions while handfuls of Spaniards and Portuguese arrived in the later 19th century. Groups of Poles and Ukrainians came after the Second World War. The old dominant church of the Highlands and Islands (see CHURCH INSTITUTIONS: 6) was submerged. Catholic strength increasingly lay in the urban industrial south-west.

From the late 18th century numbers of faithful grew in an unparalleled way. Following the 1798 rebellion, many Irish entered Scotland. By 1808 the vicars-apostolic were unable to provide adequate pastoral care to some 500 Catholics in Paisley and Greenock. More followed in the course of the Napoleonic Wars and the industrial revolution. Many settled in the *Glasgow area: in the year 1829 there were 1,188 baptisms in the city and eleven Sunday schools with some 3,000 children and young adults.

The Evangelical revival and the arrival of the Orange Lodge from Ireland in 1798 served to differentiate differences. By 1840 an estimated 120,000 Catholics were in Scotland. The massive influx of

Roman Catholic community

Famine immigrants after 1846 changed irreversibly the religious map (see IRELAND: 3). Further large groups came after the second Irish famine in the late 1870s. Many settled permanently but to many others Scotland was but a transit lounge en route to North America or south of the Border.

Agrarian areas previously conspicuous for the absence of Catholics also showed remarkable growth. Seven new churches opened in Ayrshire, Dumfries, and Wigtonshire before 1840, the highest increase in Scotland. Wigtonshire had the largest number of Irish. One priest, Revd Richard Sinnott, ministered through 1,000 square miles (3,590 square km). Seasonal agricultural labourers from Ireland have persisted until modern times. Ironstone and coal mines (see ECONOMY, PRIMARY SECTOR: 3) offered long-term opportunities while the quarries and small textile mills generally proved short-lived. Poor Irish, often handloom weavers, settled in west-central Scotland: in the 1840s around 40 per cent of Dumfries handloom weavers were Irish. They were downwardly mobile.

After the famine of 1846, Lanarkshire was the preferred Irish destination. Catholic presence in churches, schools, and other institutions massively expanded: in five years (1846–51) seven chapels were opened in the Glasgow area. Poverty, competition for jobs, labour militancy and strike-breaking, and increasing Evangelical-Ultramontane confrontation heightened tensions. The *Disruption contributed to Protestant fears of a united Catholicism. In the wake of the failed revolutions of 1848, the Irish were scapegoats: populist bigot and liberal intelligentsia alike despised them. Protestant platforms welcomed Kossuth, Gavazzi, 'Angel Gabriel' Orr, and real and alleged former priests and nuns in their attacks on the 'alien' undemocratic character of Catholicism. Such feelings were reinforced by popular pamphlets and papers like the *Bulwark*. Later papal infallibility, the Irish question, the liturgical revival in Protestantism (see RELIGIOUS LIFE: 6), and the populist anti-popery of Revd Jacob Primmer and Alfred Long further exacerbated relations.

If tensions with the host Protestant community were often severe, relations within the Catholic community between Highlander and Irish were strained. Sharing some of the misgivings of the host group, Scottish Catholic clergy hoped the Irish were but a passing interruption to their quieter tradition. They suspected the quality and commitment of Irish priests to Scotland, seeing them as ebullient, demonstrative, and wedded to an alien Irish culture. Irish priests in turn felt ill-served in promotions, esteem, and workloads. Irish laity, sometimes more politically active, felt betrayed by Scottish—or more accurately Banffshire—indifference and inadequate pastoral care and concern. Wrangles and jealousies around the *Glasgow Free Press* culminated in the period 1861–7. Bishop John Gray, the vicar-apostolic of the Western District, was seriously ill. His closest advisers were Highlanders who to Irish minds manipulated him to their advantage. The Irish demanded an Irish bishop from Rome. But the appointment of Bishop John Lynch of the Irish College, Paris, as coadjutor merely exacerbated the situation. The intervention of Archbishop Henry Manning of Westminster as apostolic visitor led to the removal of both bishops and the succession of the Englishman Mgr. Charles Eyre as bishop and subsequently as archbishop of Glasgow.

In his first act of his pontificate, Leo XIII restored the Scottish hierarchy in 1878. It meant the introduction of Tridentine discipline: six new dioceses, two archdiocesan seminaries, regular synods, and canon law. Effective quality control, uniformity and cohesion were firmly established. Romanita prevailed. From the re-establishment of the *Scots college in Rome after 1815, the Roman character of the church grew. The pressing need for priests meant clergy were recruited not merely from Ireland but also from the Low Countries, Germany, and Italy. Some Lithuanian and Polish priests also served. Although some early Irish recruits, especially from All Hallows' College, proved awkward to Bishops Scott and Murdoch in the Western District, the vast majority proved zealous, dedicated, and long serving. Even so, the Irish element should not be exaggerated. Even in 1867 only 20 of the 106 clergy in the Western District were Irish. Priests trained increasingly in Rome and Roman-dominated seminaries developed a sense of camaraderie and cohesion reinforced by close supervision: they set the tone for the laity within the church, who were also to be disciplined and controlled in the most rigorous way.

The quantitative resurgence of Catholicism was assisted by old elite families like the Lovats and Constable-Maxwells and by high-quality converts. The friend of Tennyson, Newman, and Ignatius Spencer, Robert Monteith, son of an immensely wealthy Glasgow entrepreneur; Archibald Gerard of Rochsoles, whose Jesuit son edited the *Month*; A. Campbell of Skerrington; W. D. B. Turnbull, historian; James A. Stothert, poet, antiquarian, and priest; V. Allen of Inchmartine; David Hunter-Blair, later abbot of Fort Augustus as well as several Episcopalian priests, gave substance and status. Even more impressive was a succession of aristocratic converts from mid-century: the Lothians, the duchess of Buccleuch, and, above all, the marquess of Bute. The duchesses of Leeds and Hamilton further generously aided their faith. Social standing and influence contributed to make Catholicism more conservative, more British, and more credible. The Catholic literary contribution has similarly grown from James Grant, Patrick Macgill, Compton Mackenzie, Fionn MacColla, and George Mackay Brown among others. But intellectual achievements have been few beyond the *Mercat Cross* and *Innes Review*.

Numerical growth demanded a more effective administrative framework, which was reflected in the expansion in 1827 from the two Northern and Lowland vicariates to three vicariates: Northern, Western, and Eastern. Popular outbursts against the restoration of the English Catholic episcopacy (1850) and later British government pressure on the Vatican delayed the restoration of the Scottish hierarchy until 1878. Internecine strife and financial chaos accelerated that decision. The sheer size of Glasgow meant the archdiocese dominated: with some 80 per cent of the total Catholic population it was at once an oak and a upas tree. Lesser dioceses like Galloway and still more, Dunkeld or Argyll and the Isles, were hard pressed to sustain themselves. After the Second World War, the dioceses of Paisley and Motherwell were carved out of Glasgow while ten parishes were handed to Galloway. Scotland was one of the most clericalized daughters of the church (see TABLES).

Formal structures were reinforced in several ways. Education was vital for the poor masses. Initially the migrants had little English: most, Irish or Scottish, were Gaelic speakers (see GAELIC LANGUAGE). By the later 19th century, almost all were English speakers as education spread into the remotest areas of Britain. From 1815 Catholic education had been developed, initially by some significant Protestant patrons including Revd Dr Thomas *Chalmers. The demands of a more complex society and threats of Protestant proselytism accelerated that commitment. A basic system was up and running. But sheer numbers and lack of qualified laity in a very poor community meant the introduction of and dependency on several religious orders of women from the 1840s and subsequently of men: the Marists (1858), Jesuits (1859), and Benedictines (1876). Marists provided advanced practical schooling and supervised several schools in Glasgow. Jesuits aimed at a small aspiring middle-class market. Most religious were either elite converts, drawn from the traditional northern heartland of English recusant tradition, Irish trained in France, or French themselves. Equally, pupil-teachers who wished to go on to professional teacher training had until 1894 to go to England; men to Strawberry Hill, London, or women to Liverpool or the short-lived college at St Leonard's. Only in 1895 did Notre Dame College Glasgow begin Catholic teacher training in Scotland. In schools, the preferred textbooks were English rather than of the Christian Brothers. Education was primarily to inculcate a moral code, secondly a sense of respectable behaviour, and finally high literary and scientific awareness. In a poor community, marked by early deaths, incredible hardships, and disappointments, such priorities were understandable: they, however, differed little from those inculcated by Dr Arnold at Rugby. In short, education proved unifying within a British and Ultramontane mindset (see SCHOOLS AND SCHOOLING: 2).

If after 1847 religious garb was legal in public, some Scottish vicars-apostolic still feared popular resentment. Religious orders of men brought Catholic revivalism with them. Priestly, parochial missions and retreats had begun in the 1830s and 1840s. Rosminians conducted missions in Glasgow in 1850-1. Jesuits, Redemptorists, and Franciscans soon followed through the length and breadth of Scotland: even secular priests were drawn into citywide missions, as in Glasgow during the 1880s. Whatever the effectiveness of these initiatives, missions heightened religious identities and loyalties. They also inculcated clerical leadership, respectability, and restraint.

The proliferation of religious orders in Scotland in the second half of the 19th century reinforced Romanitas. The First Vatican Council, stiffening

Table 3. Roman Catholic community, 1818–1994: priests, churches and laity

	Priests	Missions	Churches	Chapels and stations	Ratio of clergy to laity
1878	262	251	—	300,000	1:1,145
1902	476	220	351	546,000	1:1,147
1920	600	257	428	548,000	1: 913
1939	805	279	472	614,000	1: 762
1951	1,024		506	785,000	1: 766
1970	1,290*			808,000	1: 626
1984	1,224		476	814,000	1: 655
1994	992		462	744,600	1: 750

* in senior seminaries only

Roman Catholic community

Table 4. Candidates for the Roman Catholic priesthood in Scotland and colleges abroad

	No. of candidates
1875	85
1900	162
1920	200
1950	313
1960	330[a]
1970	281
1980	251*
1994	84*

* in senior seminaries only
[a] peak figure

opposition to papal infallibility, Orange and Conservative resistance to *Irish Home Rule, and fears for Catholic rights as the parliamentary franchise extended to the Protestant masses pushed Catholics back up on themselves.

The community around 1880 was poor and youthful as the famine generation of 1846 became parents. Endogamy became increasingly pronounced. Choice of partners within the Catholic community expanded as clergy zealously encouraged Catholic marriages; mixed marriages declined, a point reinforced by the papal decree Ne Temere (1908). Unity was reinforced in other ways. The laity were mobilized in numerous voluntary organizations. The most prominent was the St Vincent de Paul (SVP) Society. Established in Scotland in Edinburgh in 1846, the body spread slowly through the main urban industrial centres. Its aim was to succour the poor in spiritual and material ways. At that time abject poverty did not mean outdoor relief but often (illegal) deportation back to Ireland even if resident in Scotland for ten or more years or entry into the workhouse, orphanage, or farming out. In each case proselytism was rampant as Catholics sought to establish their civic rights. Even after 1862 these were often overridden. The SVP paid school fees, provided books, shoes, treats, and even prizes for the pupils: it activated the faithful and prevented leakage.

The Catholic Young Men's Society was introduced into Scotland in 1853. Its objectives were to safeguard and uplift the cultural and spiritual life of young Catholic males through reading rooms, sober recreation, and lectures. A Catholic Temperance Society had flourished in the 1830s. Individual priests, especially some Irish clergy, fostered a continuing commitment to *temperance through the introduction of the League of the Cross in 1870s: many parishes had invariably organized sober New Year entertainment for the faithful. Archbishop Eyre spread the organization to every parish in his archdiocese: by 1900 there were thousands of members.

Other organizations, such as the Holy Family, the Rosary Association, the Confraternity of Christian Doctrine, the Confraternity of the Sacred Heart, Bona Mors Society, the Children of Mary, Guild of Angels, and others fostered a shared experience at every stage and need of life. Monthly communions in organizational garb, parochial trips to Carstairs House, the Borders, or the seaside were significant group events: thousands attended. They improved their public image by impeccable sober behaviour. In a few parishes, savings schemes and, at St Mary's Glasgow, even house-building were undertaken. Regular choir competitions and outings, soirées, festivals, and concerts were other methods. *Football and cricket (see SPORT, COMMERCIAL) were useful in solidifying community. Not surprisingly, Celtic FC and Hibernian FC came out of this background as a service to the unfortunate: recreation had moral overtones. Outreach, if understandably low key in a poor body, did exist. Stella Maris, the Catholic organization concerned for seafarers, and the Catholic Women's League came out of Glasgow.

Increased male enfranchisement from 1832 to 1918, the decline of the Irish issue by 1921, and upward mobility (see SOCIAL CLASS) altered the cohesive community. Clergy and Irish laity occasionally clashed over the playing of the British national anthem in the late 19th century. Earlier strains between the haves and have-nots from the days of Catholic Emancipation, the First Reform Act (see POLITICAL SYSTEM: 2) and the *Chartists, resurfaced with renewed vigour from the 1880s. They coincided with the slow emergence of experienced Catholic office holders in school board elections, the first Catholic councillors in Edinburgh and Glasgow. The influential Henry George, Michael Davitt, and the Irish Land League and the eroding position of significant Catholic gentry in a clerical-dominated church made for a new agenda. A former Irish MP, D. H. MacFarlane, a convert, was elected for Argyllshire on a Land League or Crofting platform as the first Scottish Catholic MP. More critical notions were gaining ground among the faithful. Rerum Novarum (1891) condemned socialism and endorsed social justice. Using the encyclical to further their arguments, John Wheatley and his kind were restless at any attempt to dampen down effective social criticism. As newly enfranchised Catholics deserted the Liberals (see LIBERALISM) who had been largely responsible for the 1918 Education Act and found class more significant than nationalism after 1921, so they moved onto Labour (see LABOURISM). Soon they would play a prominent role in the Labour Party and the election of the first Labour government in which Wheatley would be a cabinet minister.

The first Catholic professor in Scotland since the Reformation, J. F. S. Phillimore, Humanity, Glasgow, a convert friend of Belloc and Chesterton, was symptomatic of larger social changes. He welcomed the drive of another distinguished convert, Revd Eric Hanson SJ, headmaster of St Aloysius's Glasgow, to push pupils on to higher education. One of his pupils, James Donald Scanlan, became by turns an army officer, a barrister, and later archbishop of Glasgow. Sir Denis Brogan, son of a founder of the Gaelic League in Glasgow and distinguished scholar on all things American and French, came from the same stable. A Catholic middle class was emerging (see RESPECTABLE CULTURE). The spread of Revd Dominic Plater's social discussions, especially in the west of Scotland, showed the strains and concerns for the masses. They wanted a world safe from proselytism and atheistic socialism, and for their own pupils.

While vocations to the priesthood remained high—recruitment to the priesthood peaked as late as 1960, when 330 candidates were admitted—a quiet lay revolution was also under way. Better educated, professional, and more independent-minded, they deepened their faith through pilgrimages, the booming retreat movement, old boys' associations, and the Catenians. In a way, the 400-plus priests who emerged from St Aloysius's School over its first 50 years were also 'new' professionals. Popular faith was aided by the Scottish Catholic Truth Society, the shrine at Carfin, and parochial social activities. Although many emigrated following the First World War, a cultural network sustained cohesion amid the worst of the Depression.

The warfare and post-war welfare states transformed the community. Improved opportunities, better education (see SCHOOLS AND SCHOOLING: 4), health, and *housing disproportionately benefited poorer sections of Scottish society. In the wake of expanding secondary education, the Catholic body became more differentiated in class and status, if not in political loyalties. A final lingering sense of Irishness persisted in the Anti-Partition campaign in Lanarkshire in 1948–50 but the Scottish nature of Catholicism was well established. A slow decline of old industries, coal, steel, and shipbuilding, made Scotland less attractive to Irish migrants. By 1970, Irish-born presence was insignificant. The end of recruitment of Irish priests for Scotland reinforced that point.

The Second Vatican Council, the election of Kennedy as president of the USA in 1960, and the improved Catholic status made for a more confident approach. Four Scottish cardinals have followed in the last 40 years (see GRAY, CARDINAL GORDON). Lay activism coincided with a slow decline in vocations to the priesthood and the religious life. Rethinking the nature of the church, sacraments, devotion, and the role of laity have continued. Anti-Communist campaigns in trade unions and political life, particularly during and after the Second World War, had hidden the cracks in the monolithic church. Affluence, a reinterpretation of vocation, and the sexual revolution were undermining older communal expectations and mores. Suburbanization, commuter dormitory areas, and a revolution in the work ethic made the parish pastoral role far more complex and in some cases dispiriting: television, divergent lifestyles, and parochial fragmentation made many older organizations moribund. The liberation of women made the Catholic male but particularly the celibate priest somewhat less certain in his role. The idea of the church as the whole community of faithful rather than a subservient body further eroded his previously largely unchallenged role. The debate over the papal encyclical *Humanae Vitae* (1968) provoked internal dissension and the departure of laity and some priests. It gave rise to the Scottish Catholic Renewal Movement (1968–73), a group of lay professionals, who in their enthusiasm demanded a warmer welcome for the reforms of Vatican II. More conservative views found expression with Hamish Fraser and his *Searchlight*, Colum Brogan, and Latin Mass Societies. In the whirlwind, Catholic schools, challenged by television, popular press, a freewheeling ethos, and increasing numbers of broken Catholic families, struggled to maintain a Catholic ethos. Ethnic and class solidarity were collapsing: a sense of religious renewal proved hard to achieve. The Scottish church was ill prepared for Vatican II. Routine spiritual mechanisms had left comparatively little room for creative growth. Confusion amid adjustment was common. It was difficult to link the old and new spirituality, the older and younger generations of Catholic. Old hymns, music, and choirs disintegrated. Authenticity, relevance, and personal fulfilment were inadequately articulated: new liturgical celebrations proved as disappointing as poorly performed Masses of an earlier day. Only slowly did a new musical tradition form around James Macmillan and some notable parish choirs. Even the graduate Newman Association ran into severe difficulties. Pentecostalism, ecumenism, and restless self-examination were further attempts to hold the line.

Catholics increasingly shared social, political, and cultural values of other Scots. Although from a largely Labour community, three Catholics have served recently as Tory MPs. The symptomatic Association for Separated and Divorced Catholics finally received official blessing in the 1980s. As numbers of pupils in general declined and local government struggled to find adequate resources, even the role of Catholic schools came under scrutiny: the debate centred on continuance of the 1918-style settlement, new ecumenical religious schools or integrated secular schools with optional religious education. Many professional Catholics patronized fee-paying Catholic or notable private schools. Middle-class religion as lifestyle flourished but the traditional working-class loyalty to the church was fast disappearing.

In 1982 the largest crowd ever assembled in Scotland welcomed Pope John Paul II to Glasgow: it was the last cry of triumphalism. A point had been made. Now it was time to come to terms with revolutions around and within Catholicism. It has proved an exhausting if debilitating exercise. A variety of Catholic attitudes, styles, and incomes stretched from extreme wealth to abject poverty as never before. Varied approaches to the post-industrial order were apparent. Increased leisure time, whether from choice or unemployment, more consumer choices, and greater diversity of available identities made old cohesion, even if desirable, impossible. Attendance at Sunday Mass plummeted to around 30 to 40 per cent but in some parishes levels of 80 per cent were common. Even so, in the 1990s, around a quarter of a million Scottish Catholics attended each Sunday, more than double the attendance at all four senior divisions of Scottish football. In a multicultural society, spiritual hunger and angst continue amid affluence, poverty, and loneliness. Eternal questions persist. The church still tries to respond to the mainstream and the marginalized, to the other Christian churches and other faiths, and less effectively to the lapsed or unchurched. A new identity is in formation.   BA

Rosebery, Archibald Primrose, fifth earl of
(1847–1929), the most influential Scottish politician in the late 19th century. Hailed 'the uncrowned king of Scotland', 'the man of the future', and the 'first citizen of the Empire', Rosebery is remembered as an unsuccessful prime minister, a Foreign Secretary without any memorable feat of diplomacy, a devotee of the turf with three Derby victories, an unrivalled orator, and a popular historian.

Rosebery rose to the peerage in 1868. In 1878, he married the heiress Hannah de Rothschild (1851–90), making him one of the realm's richest peers. They had four children before a happy marriage was shattered when Hannah died of typhoid. Rosebery won the rectorial elections at the Universities of Aberdeen (1878) and Edinburgh (1880), making him the coming man to a rising generation of Scots. He masterfully orchestrated the Midlothian Campaigns (1879, 1880) which restored Gladstone to the

premiership. Rosebery served as under-secretary at the Home Office with responsibility for Scottish affairs (1881–3). He resigned in frustration because Scotland was low on the government's agenda. Nonetheless, his lobbying secured the resuscitation of the *Scottish Secretary (1885). After an extended tour of the Empire (1883–4), Rosebery served as Lord Privy Seal (1885) and Foreign Secretary (1886, 1892–4).

Rosebery encouraged Scottish authors, founded the Scottish History Society (1886) (see HISTORICAL CLUBS AND SOCIETIES), and was instrumental in establishing the NLS. He wrote several biographies including *Pitt* (1891) and *Lord Randolph Churchill* (1906).

In 1894, Gladstone resigned and the queen summoned Rosebery. He inherited a fragile majority in the Commons, insurmountable opposition in the Lords, and a divided cabinet; his ministry lasted fifteen months. To his credit, he established the Scottish Grand Committee (1894). Following Gladstone's Armenian Speeches, Rosebery resigned the leadership of the Liberal Party (1896). Returning to prominence after his Chesterfield Address (1901), Rosebery tried to rally the nation under the banner of Liberal Imperialism and National Efficiency. After he broke with Campbell-Bannerman over *Irish Home Rule (1905), he drifted into the sea of political irrelevancy.   RJA

Ross, William (1911–88), the longest-serving Labour Secretary of State for Scotland. He held this office throughout the years when Harold Wilson was prime minister (1964–70; 1974–6). Ross was born in Ayrshire in 1911, educated at Ayr Academy and Glasgow University, and was a schoolteacher before entering parliament at a by-election in 1946 representing Kilmarnock. Unlike many who held the office of Secretary of State for Scotland, Ross was a formidable politician. His career straddled the period before and after devolution came onto the political agenda. He was fiercely Scottish. Before their return to power in 1964, he led Labour attacks (see LABOURISM) on the Conservatives (see UNIONISM) for abandoning Scotland and was a strong advocate of economic planning on a Scottish basis. In 1965, he protested when a House of Commons Christmas card carried a scene from Simon de Montfort's English parliament in 1278. During his period as Scottish Secretary, Scotland's share of public expenditure increased and this was at least partly due to his persistent and determined advocacy of Scottish interests. Richard Crossman, his cabinet colleague, remarked in his Diaries that Ross and his friends 'accuse the Scot. Nats. (see NATIONALISM) of separatism but what Willie Ross himself actually likes is to keep Scottish business absolutely privy from English business'. His style at the *Scottish Office has often been compared with that of the schoolmaster: benign but rather dictatorial. One apocryphal tale captures this. On accepting a junior ministerial position at the Scottish Office, an MP asked Ross 'what shall I do?', to which Ross replied, 'Ye'll dae as yer telt'. The rise of the SNP forced Labour to accept devolution. Ross was never a true convert but he was loyal to the party and to Wilson and Labour's conversion to devolution in 1974, which in time became genuine, owed much to Ross. He was replaced as Scottish Secretary when Wilson unexpectedly resigned in 1976. He maintained that 'for the Scot it is the top job; any other job would be dull indeed after the hectic, crisis-ridden life as Scotland's Secretary of State'. Ross was one of the few to have held the office who probably genuinely felt this way. 　JM

rough culture. The term is used in a number of different ways: to describe aspects of popular, pre-industrial lifestyles under challenge from the more capitalist-oriented cultures which were being created in the 18th and early 19th centuries; to describe those aspects of popular culture which were generally contrasted with the 'improving', rational recreation of the 19th century; and finally to describe a popular culture which rejected the notion of, and the usually middle-class control implied in, 'respectability'. It could take many different forms (SEE RESPECTABLE CULTURE).

Industrialization (see ECONOMY: 4) required a much clearer division between work time and non-work time and the increased regulation of work patterns. The 18th century brought new time discipline into the lives of most workers and criticism of those older patterns which hindered the imposition of such discipline. But, it took time for the older patterns to disappear. Any reader of Burns is soon aware of the central position which whisky played in popular culture by the end of the 18th century. Public festivals were all associated with bacchanalian consumption. There was and remained a popular admiration of the ability to consume excessive quantities of spirits and a tolerance of drunkenness. All social activities—funerals, weddings, christenings, holidays, excursions, fairs, *rites de passage*, pay days—were occasions for, especially, male drinking.

The public house was a central institution of male popular culture. As that became licensed and regulated in the 19th century and as the *temperance movement gained ground, so this aspect of popular culture became 'rough culture'. To a much greater extent than in England, public houses were by the 1840s losing their role as meeting and eating places and becoming instead 'plain pubs'. There

was immense pressure on the 'free and easies', where singing and dancing accompanied the drinking; and by the 1870s *women had largely been driven from the public house. Drinking was pushed firmly into the rough end of culture with illicit shebeens to provide after-hours drink and an open flaunting of the Sunday drinking laws by means of the bona fide traveller rule. The powerful temperance pressures ensured that most Scottish bars, well into the second half of the 20th century, remained relatively bare and bleak places—barmaids, partitions, games were all banned at various times—where men could engage in serious, perpendicular drinking, with 'manliness' displayed through the quantity of consumption and the generosity of 'standin' the hand'. The 1960s brought an increasing number of 'lounge bars' alongside 'public bars' to try to attract the 'respectable', but it was not until after the Clayson Report of 1973 that public drinking moved out of the rough shadows.

A feature of many popular celebrations was that of a 'world turned upside down', where it was possible with impunity to play pranks on elders and social superiors. This was long a feature of the king's birthday celebrations. Some of it was little more than youthful exuberance, with beaver hats flicked from the heads of respectable passers-by, but they were also frequently an occasion for drunken ribaldry, which could occasionally degenerate into riot, against some individual or symbol of authority. The 1792 and 1796 riots in Edinburgh are well known, but there were many other serious incidents: in Glasgow in 1819 and again in 1821. As late as 1836, an attempt by the police in Aberdeen to stop the traditional boat burning and the firing of brass cannon on William IV's birthday led to the jostling of the provost and the smashing of the Town House windows. Trysts, feeing markets, and local festivals, such as the riding of the marches in the Borders (see REGIONAL IDENTITIES: 3), were all occasions when custom and Dutch courage allowed the defiance of authority. The expressions of disapproval of such activities in the early 19th century are legion and, by the mid-century, there were few such incidents as activities became policed, formalized, and gentrified, with 'roughness' pushed to the margins of the event.

Yet another feature of unregulated popular culture was its violence. The combination of crowds and drink could often lead to fights which were also encouraged by a culture of manliness. 'Fechtin fairs' between men from different trades or firms were common. The primitive ball games in various places, such as Jedburgh's 'uppies and dounies' or Kirkwall's Ba' game, where there were only a few customary rules, were all occasion for considerable brutality. Fairs and sideshow booths almost always

had a boxing ring and, despite moral and legal disapproval, bare-knuckle fighting continued to be a
feature of mining communities. Even as spectator
sports became more organized at the end of the
19th century, there were concerns about rowdiness
and a lack of decorum.

Most popular sports were almost always associated with gambling, another key feature of rough
culture. Despite its illegality from 1874, gambling
was a feature wherever there were large working-
class audiences and participants, too, expected
to have the opportunity to make some money
whether it was running, fighting, cycling, or pigeon racing. Early in the 19th century boxing and
cockfighting were the most popular areas for gambling, with the added frisson of being disapproved
of. As late as 1835 a new cockpit was built in Glasgow and, although it was banned in 1850, even in
the 20th century incidents of cockfighting were reported in mining communities. By the 1850s, dog
racing, short-distance pigeon racing, and men
racing—or pedestrianism—were gaining in popularity. From the 1870s, cycling and *football were
another popular area for betting and there were
constant complaints that 'the baleful influence' of
the bookmaker was 'lowering the tone of athletic
meetings'. The law banning off-course betting was
regularly flouted and, in the 20th century, gambling continued to spread, with slot machines and
football pools being added to street betting. Concern about anything which might make public
houses attractive led to a specifically Scottish Act in
1917 against automatic gaming machines. But by
the 1930s gambling in Scotland was largely out of
control. The courts bowed to massive popular
defiance of the law in 1930 by recognizing the legality of football pools and, although it was not until
1961 that off-course betting was legalized, legal actions were rare long before then.

It was the attempts at control, regulation, and
banning and the determined resistance to these
which created a division between 'respectable'
popular culture and 'rough' culture. As urbanization (see URBAN SOCIETY: 5) generated fears of popular gatherings so restrictions were increasingly
brought in to curb potentially rowdy behaviour.
Early in the 19th century, games had been largely
driven off Glasgow Green. Under various local
acts, the police tightened control over street behaviour and were still protecting property against
the occasional football through the window by
prosecuting the offenders as late as the 1950s. Prize-
fighting and cockfighting were driven underground. Trysts and feeing markets, riding of the
marches and horse fairs, rumbustious 'fechtin'
fairs', all the subject of increasing middle-class disapproval in the first half of the 19th century, gave

way in the second half to middle-class organized
agricultural shows, race meetings, innocuous local
galas, formalized common ridings, or Up Helly
Aa's full of invented traditions. By the mid-19th
century, popular sports were getting rule books,
uniforms, and proper grounds and a clear division
between spectators and players.

The pressure towards rational recreation was relentless, but the persistence of older patterns was
equally powerful. The convivial, drunken 'brake'
clubs which followed their football teams in the
late 19th century had their successors in the convivial supporters' coach in the 20th century. The
aficionados of the 'fechtin' fair' had their parallels
in the football hooligan or the neighbourhood
gang. The largely class battle between professionalism and amateurism, which went on for nearly a
century in most sports, reflected the resistance to
the pressures of respectability. There were particular spectator sports, such as greyhound racing from
the late 1920s or speedway, which never achieved
total respectability because of their class identification and their association with gambling.

The wilder elements of popular culture were
usually the domain of youth and the 20th century,
in particular, brought the identification of a youth
culture and therefore a youth 'problem' which
regularly caused moral panics. These led to demands for ever more control and regulation,
whether of billiard halls and ice cream parlours at
the beginning of the century or of drugs and 'raves'
at the end of it. The search for respectable alternatives in the youth club and sports centre has intensified in the last 30 years, but with little evidence
that the 'rough' alternatives have lost their appeal.
On the other hand, the pressures towards a more
homogeneous popular culture, shaped first by cinema and then by television (see RADIO AND TELE-
VISION), have largely made the division between
'respectable' and 'rough' one decided by the nature
of the venue—which bar, which dance hall, which
sport, which football stadium, which holiday resort (see ECONOMY, TERTIARY SECTOR: 3)—rather
than by the nature of the actual activity.   WHF

Rough Wooing. The name 'Rough Wooing' derives from the famous quip made by the earl of
Huntly after the battle of Pinkie, fought on 10 September 1547 near Musselburgh. At it, more than
10,000 Scots were killed, though most of them fell
in the murderous carnage that followed rather
than on the battlefield itself. Huntly, who had been
in the front line, made the point to an English agent
that he had supported England's aims of uniting
the two realms by the marriage of his queen,
*Mary, Queen of Scots, to England's Edward VI
(1547–53), 'but I like not this wooing'. Since the

Wars of *Independence, war or a bitter cold war had been an almost daily fact of life for many, especially on the *Border. The Rough Wooing of the 1540s, however, produced a huge escalation in both violence and military investment by the English crown in trying to solve what it convinced itself was the 'British problem'. It resulted in what was, in effect, the last major Anglo-Scottish war. Pinkie was the one major pitched battle in it, but *Edinburgh was sacked, following a daring amphibious raid on its port of Leith in 1544; *Dundee was reduced to a virtual pile of rubble in 1547; the Border zone was repeatedly savaged, and tens of thousands were killed, many homes burned and razed to the ground, and possessions and livestock stolen.

Many Scots think that the country's wars with England (see ANGLO-SCOTTISH RELATIONS: 3) stretch from Falkirk (1297) to Culloden (1746). Actually, they go back much further, but they did end, in a real sense, in 1560 (see REFORMATION). When Cromwell appeared at Dunbar in September 1650, he did so to keep united the conglomerate of three kingdoms that were the inheritance of James VI and I. When 'Butcher' Cumberland annihilated the ragtag army of Bonnie Prince Charlie near Inverness in 1746, his regiments had more 'Scots' in them than Charlie's, which was in any case almost half-Irish. They were fighting not over Scotland, but the Hanoverian succession to the crown of Great Britain and Ireland (see JACOBITISM).

Pinkie thus stands as the last (and arguably the largest) Anglo-Scottish battle in history. The Scots lost, but it actually was a very close run thing. And in the end, as always happened, the Scots won the war. Actually one should say wars, for the Rough Wooing was in reality a series of interlocking periods of military belligerencies: 1542 (if only briefly), 1543–6, 1547–50, or 1551. The scene was set by a brief, almost token exchange of hostilities in the summer and autumn of 1542, between Henry VIII and Mary's father, *James V. The root cause had been the English king's determination to shine on Europe's battlefield stage of glory in France. Although James's minor campaign had seen some success, his defiance of his uncle ended with the debacle at Solway Moss (24 November). It figures in all the textbooks, but was little more than a brawl: only seven Scots died in the engagement. Yet it was part of the war in which Mary, Queen of Scots, found herself when she became queen on 14 December 1542, as an infant barely a week old.

Her birth in a sense rescued the country, for the regency government of the next man in line to the throne, the earl of Arran, was able, in the months between January and July 1543, to dangle the prospect of her marriage to Henry's son Edward so as to bring that conflict to an end. The Treaties of Greenwich (ratified by the Scottish government and nobility at Holyrood in August) also contracted that Mary should at the age of 10 be married to Edward Tudor. Henry's vision was that the two kingdoms would thus be united through this 'golden and godly marriage' into one with the accession to both monarchies by the heir of Mary and Edward's consummated and fruitful marriage. But it was not just any imperial vision of Henry which motivated him: Mary Stewart had a powerful claim through her grandmother, Margaret Tudor (Henry's sister and bride of *James IV), to the English inheritance should the Tudors die out. This, of course, they were to do in 1603, making the Tudors something of a failure: one of the shortest-lived dynasties in European history. The last child born into that family was Edward, in October 1537. It was to head off the Stewart threat to his family line that Henry was so ardent for his boy to marry Scotland's queen.

Once the campaigning season of 1543 passed, Arran promptly renounced the whole scheme and by December had revived Scotland's adherence to France, and indeed to Rome. Working with Scotland's most redoubtable politician, David Beaton, and then with Mary's mother, Mary of Guise, after 1545, Arran resisted Henry VIII's war of revenge for over two years. English main field armies invaded the realm in 1544 (Edinburgh) and 1545 (the Borders), 'Donald Dhu', the Pretender lord of the *Isles, was used to attack Scotland's soft underbelly in the west (1544), the Borders were raided almost nightly, and even the Emperor Charles V was induced to declare war against Scotland: all to no avail (and indeed the Scots utterly defeated Charles V and made massive profits from their war with him). By the time Henry finally died in January 1547, the fruits of his massive expenditure of treasure (some £350,000 sterling) was Langholm, a feeble tower house on the West Marches.

Henry did bequeath to his son's guardian and effective ruler of England, Edward Seymour, self-promoted to be duke of Somerset, a working relationship with the murder gang who had assassinated Beaton in May 1546 and still held St Andrews castle. Although Arran had effected numerous minor military triumphs during this period (Ancrum Moor in February 1545 and the recapture of Dumbarton in July 1546), St Andrews for a number of reasons was too hard a nut for Scottish military capability to crack. Also, his own son was inside it, a prisoner. Arran thus called in the experts and a French rapid deployment force appeared off the Fife coast in July 1547 and by ingenious engineering (hoisting cannon onto the steeple of St Salvator's College) reduced the 'Castilians' in a week.

This was how John *Knox found himself chained to the oars, as a prisoner of war in a French galley.

Henry's 'Wooing' had been a total failure. His main goals had always lain in France where he captured Boulogne in September 1544—a victory which, in retrospect, sowed seeds of destruction for England's Continental ambitions. But his war had been an enormously productive learning experience for Somerset who, once in power, resolved to tackle Scotland with much more resolution, and intelligence, than his former master had done. His stunning victory at Pinkie was important, for it destroyed Scotland's only army, but was not an end in itself. It created the conditions whereby he could plant fortified garrisons of English troops in and about the kingdom. This would, in turn, facilitate year-round warfare rather than a succession of 30-day campaigns and, by process of attrition, wear down Arran's supporters so that finally they would accede to the marriage.

Somerset's strategy was highly focused, coherent, and enormously expensive—costing over £600,000. He employed the most modern technology available (see WARFARE, WEAPONS, AND FORTIFICATIONS: 2): potent artillery housed in an utterly new form of fortification, the *traice italienne* (see BUILDINGS: 4), which provided secure protection to soldiers who could then issue forth and terrorize the Scottish countryside, as happened around Kelso and Roxburgh. Dumfries was taken, as was Dundee. English naval vessels, harboured at Inchcolm in the Forth estuary, harried the Fife coast. The Tweed valley became an English pale. It was total war: as one commander mused, 'this winter war much grieves the hearts of the Scots'.

The brilliance of Somerset's tactics can be especially seen as he responded to setbacks: the southwest was lost in February 1548 to a Scottish counter-attack and Inchcolm had to be abandoned so fierce was Scottish resistance. By June 1548, he had also to deal with the prospect of massive intervention in the war by one of the most professional armies in Europe: that of France. Instead of withdrawing, he raised the stakes and constructed almost overnight one of the largest Italianate fortifications in Europe, at Haddington. Near Dundee, he similarly protected his Tayside hold of Broughty by forts on the hill there. Lauder also had a brand new and highly intricate fortification quickly erected.

When the French then settled down to besiege Haddington, they were staggered at what confronted them and defeated by it, at least in the summer of 1548. The war thus became one for the county seat of East Lothian, which was just 18 miles (30 km) from Edinburgh: William, Lord Grey of Wilton, declared, 'Keeping Haddington, you win

Scotland'. But Somerset had made a massive miscalculation. He thought that the French would either be engaged in Italy or simply could not sustain a war so far to the north of their shores. And indeed the French did have their problems and had to send relief armies in 1549. These forces gradually wore the English down. Hume was retaken and Haddington had to be abandoned because of its isolation and an outbreak of the plague in September. Broughty fell in February 1550, after a siege.

The war broke not the French, but the English regime. During the summer of 1549, some of the most serious domestic rebellions in the whole of the century (the Western Rising in Devon and Cornwall, followed by Kett's in East Anglia) shattered the Somerset protectorate. In August, a massive French army laid siege to Boulogne. The earl of Warwick, less of a soldier but a more astute politician and soon to become duke of Northumberland, took charge. He quickly extricated England from its disastrous adventures. The Rough Wooing juddered to a close on 24 March 1550. Peace was finally settled with Charles V in January and then, in a separate treaty, along the Borders in 1551.

The critical triumph of Henri II of France was to gain the actual person of the child Mary into his hands. By August 1548, she was in *France, living in his growing family and beloved by all at court as 'the most perfect child'. Both Catherine de Medici and the king's mistress, Diane de Poitiers, had a hand in her upbringing. Henry even called her his very own daughter. By 1558, she became, through her marriage to his eldest son, his daughter-in-law. And that husband thereby became François, king of Scotland (see FRANCO-SCOTTISH RELATIONS: 2).

The 'Rough Wooing' had provoked a profound backlash. England, by trying to conquer Scotland yet again, found itself in a much worse position: first subservient to France (1550–3) and then under Habsburg influence, following Mary Tudor's marriage to Philip of Spain, who became king of England in 1554, until Mary's death. In November 1558, Elizabeth Tudor became queen of England by Act of Parliament. In many people's eyes, she was no such thing: the bastard offspring of an illegal sexual union between her father and his whore, Ann Boleyn. When Mary Stuart (as her name was now spelt) became queen of France in July 1559 on the death of Henri II, she thus in Catholic eyes stood as queen four times: Scotland, France, England, and Ireland. Thus, it might be argued: in her beginning was her end. But what a beginning it was!   MM

Royal Burghs, Convention of. A court of the four burghs, originally comprising Roxburgh, *Berwick (from 1368 Linlithgow and Lanark), *Edinburgh, and *Stirling, is known to have existed in the 13th century. It drew up the Laws of the Four Burghs, which applied to all royal or king's burghs throughout the realm (see URBAN SETTLEMENT: 1). By the 1550s, when its formal records first begin, a Convention had materialized, representing all the royal burghs as well as abbots' and bishops' burghs such as Arbroath and *St Andrews; it had extensive powers, including the assessment of individual burghs for taxation, carrying out negotiations relating to foreign trade, and lobbying monarch or parliament. The effect of the Convention, which met annually from 1578 onwards, was to make the burgesses the most organized of all the estates represented in *parliament. Another result was that urban government was much more uniform in Scotland than in England, producing, as the commissioners' inquiry into the Municipal Corporations of Scotland discovered in 1833–5, considerable corruption amongst self-electing, clone-like burgh establishments. Like the present-day SFA, minnows such as Anstruther or Cullen had equal voting rights with big fish such as *Glasgow and the main concern of the Convention from the 1790s on was the blocking of reform. The Municipal Reform Act of 1834 sharply reduced its influence and its abolition was considered for a time. The admission to it of parliamentary burghs in 1879 and police burghs in 1895 gave it an added lease of life though probably little extra influence. Following local government reorganization in 1975, it was succeeded by the Convention of Scottish Local Authorities. The Convention can probably lay claim to being one of the wordiest of Scottish institutions, if measured by the voluminous nature of its records. But its importance was relatively slight (see LOCAL GOVERNMENT, TO 1707). ML

royal court: 1. to 1542; 2. 1542–1603.

1. to 1542

Cultural centre, symbol of the ruling dynasty and even of the kingdom itself, the court was always much more than a functional body servicing royal needs. The heterogeneity of court culture—which once discouraged serious study—has created new interest in the subject as well as the recognition that such cultural diversity represented an important strength. The courts of medieval Scottish monarchs certainly responded to changing circumstances but at the same time each bequeathed a powerful cultural legacy of which their successors could not be unaware. Thus, it is possible to speak of a recognizable Scottish court culture which, while it developed considerably over a 450-year period, can be characterized by several distinctive themes and motifs.

Ethnically, linguistically, and culturally, Scotland has always been a hybrid society. Nowhere is this more clearly seen than at the royal court where the waves of Anglo-Norman immigration which occurred in the course of the 12th and 13th centuries exercised a profound and lasting impact. The details of life at court may be somewhat hazy but the crown's introduction of new household officials and the installation of arriviste knights signalled a determination to take up the style and practices of European monarchy. Indeed, according to the English Barnwell chronicler, so completely did Malcolm IV and William I identify with such an ethos that they professed themselves to be French 'both in race and in manners, language and culture'. Yet simply acknowledging the enormous debt owed to the Anglo-Norman tradition both overstates and oversimplifies the matter. Just as assimilation and adaptation characterize the changes wrought in Scottish society as a whole, so at court new practices and ideas rested against old. The most well-known example of this is the appearance of 'a wild Highlander' at the inauguration of Alexander III in 1249 who, in time-honoured fashion, recited the new king's genealogy tracing his descent from the eponymous Scota. Although this custom had probably died out by the 14th century, it is still possible to envisage the fusion of cultures at a more mundane level with the king calling for a lyric of courtly love followed by a rousing Gaelic praise poem. Despite a growing hostility towards Gaelic tradition, this was to remain a striking feature of Scottish court life throughout the Middle Ages. *James IV can credibly be acclaimed a Renaissance monarch but he still spoke Gaelic, employed Highland bards and musicians, and presumably enjoyed their art (see HIGHLANDS AND ISLANDS: GENERAL; MUSIC, HIGHLAND).

The existence of a vibrant native tradition was one of the reasons why the Scottish court never became a simple reflection of its southern neighbour. The other was, of course, generations of war fought against England. The Wars of *Independence seriously disrupted court life and, with its kings in exile or fighting for survival, Scotland was frequently without a recognizable court at all. Nevertheless, the conflict possessed significant cultural implications. The aggressively Anglophile policies of David II, for example, were reflected in a court which reverberated to the same type of chivalric ideals cultivated by Edward III. Significantly, beyond the kings' immediate circle, both were unpopular. Partly as a result of the continuing struggle in the defence of Scottish independence, the dual concepts of king and kingdom became increasingly central to Scottish attitudes both political and cultural, and the ideological fusion of dynasty and nation initially personified by *Robert I was gradually embodied by his Stewart successors.

Robert II is not noted for his pursuit of the courtly arts but—perhaps more importantly—he assiduously fostered this aspect of his royal image, thus paving the way for future Stewart self-confidence. As patron of John Barbour, archdeacon of Aberdeen, Robert may even have commissioned *The Brus* which, as well as offering a stirring account of the Scottish struggle, represents arguably the finest example of Scottish medieval verse.

During the reign of James I, the idea of the royal family as a caste apart was to become firmly established. A potent and very visible weapon in his campaign to assert political authority over the nobility, James's lavish spending on luxurious clothing, fine foods, and innovative architecture also set the pattern for an increasingly self-confident dynasty. The desire to cut a dash on a European stage can be seen in events such as the great tournament presided over by James II at *Stirling castle when the celebrated Burgundian adventurer Jaques de Lalain fought in the lists against the flower of Scottish chivalry (see LOW COUNTRIES). Sixty years later, the dazzling tourneys staged by James IV again underlined the king's enthusiasm for the cult of chivalry and his determination that Scotland play a part in this most cosmopolitan of activities. Here, as in so many areas, the eagerness with which the Scottish court looked beyond its own frontiers signified not a sense of inferiority but one of strength and, probably as a result of this, Scottish court culture remained distinctly 'Scottish'. The tournaments of 1449, 1507, and 1508 could not have taken place in any other country.

The growing political and cultural poise of the monarch was strikingly enunciated in the buildings which he inhabited. While the itinerant Robert II preferred the thrill of the hunt and the companionship of his Gaelic aristocracy to the cultivation of courtly ceremonial, James I spent vast sums (in some years approaching a tenth of his income) on the construction of royal residences at Edinburgh (see EDINBURGH CASTLE), Leith, and above all Linlithgow. Partially modelled on French and English examples, Linlithgow was striking for its virtual lack of fortification. As was recognized at the time, this was truly a palace rather than a castle. James IV and *James V also spent prodigiously on architecture and building works at Stirling and Falkland in particular testify to the fact that while the Scottish court remained a peripatetic one throughout this period, it kept pace with the latest trends in Renaissance design.

The eagerness with which the Scottish court looked beyond its frontiers can be seen in any number of activities. Not only were great works of art imported from abroad but the surviving accounts for the period are littered with references to foreign craftsmen and artists. In addition to employing a recognizable 'King's Painter' (a title first used in 1434), James IV also made payments to the Frenchman Piers the painter and the Englishman John Maynard. A similar picture emerges with regard to music for as well as patronizing various visiting musicians, such as Thomas de Avarencia whose services James V begged of the duke of Milan, the crown maintained its own liveried players. Music of all sorts played an enormously important role both in secular entertainment and Christian worship. James I, James II, James IV, and James V all sang or played themselves and in the case of James IV a keen personal interest was translated into the endowment of the Chapel Royal at Stirling as well as the patronage of Robert Carver, Scotland's greatest composer (see CULTURE: 10).

The haunting beauty of Carver's polyphonic settings must have contrasted strikingly with some of the more traditional songs and ballads also performed at court. As this suggests, it is a mistake to deem the culture of the medieval court exclusively 'high' culture. Literacy was by no means universal and to judge by the payments made to humble songsters and players, songs and verses passed down through generations loomed large in everyday entertainment. The catholicism of courtly taste is further illustrated by the literary sources and the contrast between the scatological invective of a verse such as William Dunbar's *The Flyting of Dunbar and Kennedie* and the staggering achievement of Gavin Douglas's *Eneados*, the first vernacular translation of Virgil and a work of great poetic merit in its own right. Admittedly this was composed for a member of the nobility rather than the king, but as the bishop of Dunkeld and a member of one of Scotland's most powerful magnate families, Douglas was very much a member of the establishment.

The presence of clerics whether in a spiritual or an administrative capacity ensured that court culture was not all chivalry and spectacle. The renowned theologian John Ireland, for example, acted as confessor to James III and made his own contribution to the literature of the court with the *Meroure of Wyssdome*, a work dedicated to the young James IV. By the end of this period, however, there were hints of a significant shift in cultural life as growing numbers of laymen not only occupied royal office but also helped define the courtly ethos. Such was Sir David Lindsay of the Mount, servant to the young James V, herald and poet. One of the many factors underpinning increased lay participation in public life was the influence of humanist thinking and, with Scotland firmly plugged into the mainstream of European learning, it is not surprising that such ideas found a receptive audience at court. But it was not only amongst scholars that these took hold. The imagery of Renaissance monarchy was enthusiastically adopted by artists and presumably by the crown itself. The coinage of James III, the triumphal arch built at Stirling by James IV, and the imperial crown worn by James V all convey a view of the elevated nature of Scottish kingship. The court during this period may have been frequently rocked by political and financial crises, but such notions ensured ideological continuity and encouraged Stewart aspirations. When these were met, they were met with assurance and aplomb (see also KINGSHIP: 5; NOBILITY: 2–3; CULTURE: 4–10).　　CE

2. 1542–1603

There was during the reigns of *Mary, Queen of Scots, (1542–67), and *James VI (1567–1625) no building programme of the intensity seen in the reigns of *James IV and *James V. Minor works were undertaken at *Edinburgh castle after the siege of 1573, at *Stirling in the early 1580s, when a viewing platform was built to survey the Scottish historical landscape surrounding the castle, and in the north wing of Linlithgow palace in the 1610s. Otherwise, the two reigns were when these new assets, three-dimensional displays in stone of the majesty and divinity of the Stewart monarchy, were exploited in propaganda and festival, with the court a political theatre.

The two 'bodies' of Queen Mary—her household and privy council—were very different: one was French in influence (see FRANCE), Catholic in tone, and populated by lesser men; her council was largely Protestant and made up of powerful magnates. It was at the court that Mary tried to square this circle. At Candlemas, in February 1566, she tried to induce Catholic nobles to return to the Mass amidst the celebrations surrounding the investiture of her husband, Darnley, with the French order of St Michel. It failed and helped provoke the murder of her servant Rizzio. In December 1566, however, Mary staged an extravagant three-day Renaissance festival at Stirling to mark the baptism of her son and heir, the future James VI. The event was important enough for her to risk the only national tax levied during her personal reign. It was the culmination of an attempt to regain control after two attempted Protestant coups in 1565–6. The three-day spectacular copied some of the festival held at Bayonne in the summer of 1565 by her cousin, Charles IX of France. It included the ritual assault on a fort built outside the castle by forces representing the enemies of the state, including fake wild 'Highland men'. All were repulsed since the message was that the Stewart dynasty (see KINGSHIP: 6), represented by Mary and her son, were the only guarantors of peace and stability.

The court was again used as political theatre when the young James VI emerged from his schoolroom prison in Stirling castle in 1579. An elaborate royal entry into Edinburgh camouflaged the meeting of a parliament called to eclipse *Hamilton power. It established many of the metaphors for James and his court for the rest of the reign. It was here that the biblical King David and King Solomon made their first appearance: the young godly prince was hailed as both. With the court established at Holyrood, where it was centred far more than in any previous reign, James held court in the 1580s as Apollo, patron of the arts, at the centre of the glittering 'Castalian band' of poets, including Alexander Montgomerie and William Fowler (see CULTURE: 9).

Despite the lack of capital building projects, the court proved to be outrageously expensive. That may have been one of the motives in the protest coup known as the Ruthven raid staged in 1582. Access to the king and rivalry between the king's household and council produced envy and factionalism, which often turned to violence. After James's marriage to Anne of Denmark in 1589–90, spending on the court spiralled out of control. A group of courtiers attached to the queen's household, called the Octavians, tried to take control of her finances in 1593. When they extended their activities to the king's spending in 1596, they incurred the wrath of a phalanx of disgruntled nobles (see NOBILITY: 3) who saw the court as their personal gravy train. They were dismissed in 1598.

In the 1590s, the court saw a greater stress on protocol and ceremony, though that also provoked frequent and sometimes lethal disputes, especially over precedence. An inflation of honours gathered pace, especially after 1598. Renaissance kingship and the aristocracy were increasingly being put on pedestals, and nowhere was that more obvious than in the elaborate three-day festival staged by James to celebrate the baptism of his first son, Prince Henry, at Stirling in 1594. The baptism itself was held in a rebuilt Chapel Royal, built to scale as a miniature version of Solomon's Temple.

Court culture also spilled out into aristocratic society. Nobles were distancing themselves from their kin and tenants in elaborate tower houses, built for show. In them, formal galleries were built, as at Holyrood, to display family memorabilia; mock battlements and crenellations were constructed, as at Stirling castle, not for defence but as viewing terraces over their landed possessions (see ARCHITECTS, ARTISTS, AND CRAFTSMEN; ARCHITECTURAL STYLES AND FEATURES). In the process, a country-house culture, which emulated the royal court, was forming. It provides one answer to the question of what happened when James VI and his household left for London in 1603. A court party remained in power and the cult of honour, which had lain at the root of court culture of James VI's reign, flourished in his absence—for probably the better part of a generation after 1603. ML

Royal High School, Edinburgh. The precise origins of the High School are obscure. Attached to the Augustinian abbey of Holyrood, itself founded in 1128, the school moved in 1577 to a vacant site adjacent to the old Dominican friary, at the southern edge of the burgh, in present-day Infirmary Street. What is now called the old Royal High School, a significant icon of the Scottish Greek revival, was built in a dramatic setting on the southern side of the Calton Hill above Regent Road in 1825–9. Vacated in 1969 by its pupils, who decamped to the leafy suburb of Barnton, the 'A' listed building, based on the Temple of Theseus and facing St Andrew's House, built to house the *Scottish Office in the 1930s, became an Edinburgh icon without a role. In 1979, it acquired a new role, as the debating chamber for the proposed Scottish Assembly, which failed to materialize despite the slender majority achieved in the referendum staged by the Labour Callaghan government. In limbo during the long reign of Mrs Thatcher, who turned her face decisively against devolution, the school became the focus of political discontent after the unexpected victory of Mr Major's government in 1992. A day and night vigil was staged outside it for 1,979 days and nights—an ironic number in itself—until the successful referendum of 1998, which produced a majority of almost three to one in favour of a Scottish *parliament. The new Labour government, however, aware of the status which the school had acquired both within the SNP and the wider nationalist movement which had emerged in the 1980s and 1990s, decided on a somewhat bizarre competition amongst rival sites, which ranged from a shopping centre complex at the western edge of Edinburgh to Leith Docks and a brownfield site near Haymarket railway station. The victor was a site close to Holyrood, remote from public services, transport, and even pubs. The High School remains, as a result, the parliament building which Scotland never had. ML

Royal Museum of Scotland, a stretched Venetian *palazzo* facing Chambers Street as if onto a canal in Edinburgh's Old Town. Behind the now grey exterior the main hall (262.5 feet (80 m) long, 70.5 feet (21.5 m) wide, 82 feet (25 m) high) and galleries feature slender iron pillars supporting two floors of balconies around open central wells. This monument to mid-Victorian Crystal Palace-style architecture houses extensive international and Scottish collections of geology, natural history, science and technology, archaeology and ethnography, and decorative arts. The building links to the Museum of Scotland, opened in 1998, where the Scottish collections are displayed.

The museum was founded in 1854 when parliament voted £7,000 for acquisition of a small plot of land and buildings next to the University and agreed for the transfer of the University's natural history collection to the new museum. Acts of Parliament in 1855 and 1860 established the 'National Museum of Industry for Scotland' to be managed by the Department of Science & Art in London. Dr George Wilson was appointed director early in 1855 and sought to establish 'a Museum of the Industry of the world in special relation to Scotland'. He collected technological, scientific, and industrial material, established a laboratory for examining industrial materials, a library to include industrial art, and as professor of technology gave regular lectures.

Plans were commissioned from Francis Fowke, a captain in the Royal Engineers, contracted as Architect and Engineer to the Department of Science & Art. Fowke produced drawings in 1857 and a more detailed series with many features of the final design by early 1859. The senior architect of the Office of Works in Scotland, Robert Matheson, meanwhile produced an alternative 'Elizabethan' scheme. Fowke's greater display space was preferred and both men were instructed to collaborate in designs for an enlarged site.

Various schemes for the façade followed with Fowke's ideas triumphing. He included front corridors with glass set directly into stone pillars to give the impression of open arcades, decorated with encaustic floor tiles as examples of industrial art. The narrow streets in front of the building were replaced by the City Council's formation of Chambers Street in the 1870s.

Wilson died before building work started and before Prince Albert laid the foundation stone on 23 October 1861. Funding, acquisition of land, and building progress were slow, seen from the Scottish end as a result of the inefficiencies of management through London. On 19 May 1866 the first phase was opened by the prince of Wales as the 'Edinburgh Museum of Science and Art', a name change agreed in 1864.

The 1866 museum was just the eastern part of the main hall and east pavilion with galleries 8 and 11, linked by the bridge to the University and ending with a blank gable wall at the west. Gaslights allowed evening opening to visitors. Completed under Robert Matheson, the main hall and gallery 18 were formally opened in 1875. The west pavilion and wing completed Fowke's building when opened in 1889, although without the planned west entrance. The southern boundary of the museum was the Flodden wall, still traceable on the present floor plan. A licensed refreshment room, criticized for making under-age drinking too easy, was abolished in 1893 and converted to administrative offices.

Responsibility for the museum moved from London to Scotland in 1901 and in 1904 it was renamed the 'Royal Scottish Museum' and roof glazing, heating, and ventilation were improved. Risk of fire from adjacent bonded warehouses and spirit stores caused much concern until plans by the Principal Architect of the HM Office of Works in Scotland, W. T. Oldrieve, were approved in 1910. Structural work on new galleries crossing the Flodden wall started before the 1914–18 war, but only administration offices were completed. Post-war progress was slow: gallery 13 opened in 1927, galleries 2 and 9 in 1929, and the north part of gallery 10 in 1930.

In 1932 the South staircase opened followed by work on gallery 22, opening as the Shipping Hall in 1938. During the war the collections were evacuated, one of the cellars strengthened for an air-raid shelter, and galleries used for hospital stores and administration. Subsequent re-establishment was chronically slow. The blacked-out roof glazing was replaced and lighting and electrical supplies gradually upgraded. Floor loading worries closed both front pavilions, only reopening in 1971 and 1975 after cast-iron pillars were replaced with concrete, while 1954 saw the bottom sections of many of the iron pillars in the main hall replaced with steel.

A lecture theatre was started in 1959 designed by Stewart Sim, again of the Office of Works, taking up earlier schemes to expand southwards. It opened in 1961 and soon included the library. A Tree of Life, man's progress culminating in Sputnik and atom bomb, remains carved on one of the external doors.

Cleared of Victorian plaster casts the empty main hall was landscaped with two ponds in 1964, polished travertine slabs replacing the floor tiles in 1970/1. A first floor inserted in gallery 2 gave more display space in 1966 followed by a second floor completed in 1972. In the late 1980s the roof glass in the main galleries was replaced with various levels of solar control. In galleries 11, 12, and 18 daylight was completely excluded to allow better preservation of the collections under artificial light. Rooftop offices were constructed on the Lecture theatre block in the early 1990s.

Amalgamated with the National Museum of Antiquities in 1985 into the National Museums of Scotland the building was renamed the 'Royal Museum of Scotland'. Construction of the Museum of Scotland started in 1992 immediately to the west and links between the two buildings caused some alterations to the west wall and new openings at each level. The architects, Benson & Forsyth, redesigned the gallery 20 block, which was demolished internally and rebuilt with additional administrative offices behind a new south elevation over Brighton Street. JT

rugby. Anyone who believes in the exclusively English antecedents of rugby union has reckoned without a long footballing tradition north of the Border. The game, according to its hagiographers, goes back far beyond a famous incident at Rugby school when William Webb Ellis picked the ball up and ran. According to this Scottish school of thought, rugby has its origins in the Romans' *harpastum*, a game in which two teams ran, passed, and threw a ball with the aim of crossing the opponents' line at the far end of a rectangular field. This ancient game is thought by some to be the precursor of the Ba' games in the Borders (see REGIONAL IDENTITIES: 3).

While such versions of football might be found in many parts of Europe, there is certainly evidence of rugby in Scotland well before Webb Ellis had his day. A game in which kicking and handling the ball was allowed was being played by the middle of the 19th century by public schools and universities. Codified in 1846, the sport achieved a certain consistency, although there were many changes before it began to wear the look of modern rugby union.

The first international match was mooted in 1870 when the captains of five Scottish teams challenged English clubs to a representative match. The Scotland–England game was played at Raeburn Place in Edinburgh on 27 March 1871, and Scotland won by one goal (a converted try) and one try to England's one try. The Scottish Football Union (SFU) was formed in 1873, though internationals were played at different venues in Glasgow and Edinburgh before the SFU finally found a home of its own. Inverleith in Edinburgh hosted its first international, against Ireland, in 1899. By this time, a Scot had invented Sevens rugby. Ned Haig suggested a seven-a-side tournament to raise money for his club, Melrose. Thus, on 25 April 1883, the first tournament took place at the Greenyards. The home team Melrose won, beating rivals Gala in the final.

After the First World War, rugby continued to grow in popularity and huge crowds flocked to see the great players of the era, such as the famous national captain G. P. S. Macpherson and the flying wing Eric Liddell. In 1922 the SFU bought 19 acres (7.7 hectares) of land at Murrayfield, which had been home to the Edinburgh Polo Club. Murray-field Stadium (now the property of the newly formed Scottish Rugby Union) was officially opened with another international fixture against England. The 70,000 spectators watched an excit-ing game in which the lead changed hands several times before Scotland won 14–11, to take their first Grand Slam. Scotland achieved a consistent series of results in the years which followed, finally win-ning the Triple Crown (seeing victories over Eng-land, Ireland, and Wales) in 1933. Five years later Scotland won the Triple Crown at Twickenham, beating the English 21–16, and by five tries to one. Two of these were scored by Wilson Shaw, who was carried from the field in triumph. After the Sec-ond World War, however, the game went into a gradual decline. The Fourth Springboks beat Scot-land at Murrayfield 44–0, inaugurating a run of eighteen successive defeats, ending only in 1955 with a win against Wales at Murrayfield.

As more people tuned into televised sport, a gradual Scottish revival through the 1960s and 1970s saw the emergence of some fine players, whose skills received testimony by their selection for the British Lions. The Lions tours of 1971 and 1974 featured Ian McLauchlan, Gordon Brown, Sandy Carmichael, Billy Steele, Ian McGeechan, and Andy Irvine, rare talents who helped spread the popularity of the game. This was also the time of the great Welsh side and when Wales came north in 1975 a world-record crowd of 104,000 wit-nessed Scotland win 12–10.

The greatest international phase began in the 1980s. With Jim Telfer as coach, the team in 1984 in-cluded a great back-row of Iain Paxton, Jim Calder, and David Leslie and an exciting half-back pairing of Roy Laidlaw and John Rutherford. Scotland beat Wales at Cardiff, England at Murrayfield, Ireland in Dublin, and finally defeated France 21–12 at home, after Jim Calder's late try, to win the first Grand Slam since 1925. Former internationalists Ian Mc-Geechan and Jim Telfer coached Scotland in their memorable 1990 season. With wins over Wales, Ireland, and France, this time it was England which had to be beaten to gain the Grand Slam, the Triple Crown, and the Calcutta Cup. England came up to Murrayfield favourites to win all three themselves, having also won all their previous games. In the event Tony Stanger scored a famous try just after half-time, and Scotland held on to win 13–7. Scot-land reached the semi-final of the Rugby World Cup in 1991, and this time met England at Murray-field for a place in the final. A Rob Andrew drop goal with only a few minutes remaining left the Scots in a third-place play-off, this time against New Zealand, a game which they lost 13–6 in Car-diff.

The transformation of Murrayfield into a 67,500 capacity stadium began in 1992, when safety re-quirements dictated the demolition of the old terracing. The entire project cost more than £50 million—funded mainly by debentures, as the ori-ginal stadium had been in 1925—and was com-pleted for the visit of the South Africans in 1994, when the patron of the SRU, HRH the Princess Royal, opened the stadium.

A game which had remained amateur through-out more than a century of its formal existence adopted professionalism in 1995, when only months before the SRU had rejected a change from amateur status. Top club sides combined with four larger regional teams to pay the game's best play-ers. Within a couple of years, de facto amateur status had been re-established at club level and the regions were reduced to two district sides.

There have been some significant recent suc-cesses on the field, most notably Scotland's victory in 1999 in the last Five Nations Championship. But while club and international rugby has established itself on a firm footing in England and Wales, the uncertain structure of the game in Scotland, and falling crowds at some clubs, causes concern for the future of the game.   MW

rural settlement: 1. medieval; 2. 1500–1770; 3. 1770–1914; 4. Highlands.

1. medieval

The rural settlement of this period is not well rep-resented in the Scottish archaeological record. Des-pite this, some idea of the nature of settlement can be adduced from a combined study of the results of field survey and documentary sources, in addition to the small number of excavated sites.

At the start of this period, there were no burghs and, at best, only proto-urban settlements; by far the greater part of the population lived in the coun-tryside in dispersed settlements and were occupied in subsistence agriculture (see ECONOMY, PRIMARY SECTOR: 1). What little we know of the period indi-cates that the 12th century was a time of consider-able change. The foundation of numerous castles and burghs (see URBAN SETTLEMENT: 1) by *David I (1124–53) and his Anglo-Norman followers, com-bined with the establishment of the reformed monasteries (see CHURCH INSTITUTIONS: 2), saw the introduction of many agricultural ideas that were current in England and France, and the growth of trade in surplus agricultural goods via the new burghs. King David also established hunting re-serves or forests, mainly in southern and eastern Scotland, which involved a change in the trad-itional rights of Scots to the game on their land, re-serving it to the crown or the landowner who was granted a licence to establish a private hunting reserve.

These changes led to a number of developments in rural settlement. The reformed monasteries, such as Kelso abbey, built granges in moated or ditched rectilinear enclosures, such as that of Colpenhope in the Halterburn Valley of the Cheviots. These formed the centre of new agricultural enterprises that were outwith the communal agriculture practised elsewhere. In Lowland areas, by the end of the 13th century, when evidence is more plentiful, many unfree bondmen (see RURAL SOCIETY: 1) lived in row settlements or villages, with tofts or farmsteads adjacent to one another. Certainly small semi-rural burghs, like that excavated at Rattray in Buchan, appear to have been laid out as row settlements in the same way as those in the Border counties, such as that at Springwood Park, near Kelso, where settlement of the 12th to 14th centuries has been excavated. Outside the Lowland areas, no such order to settlement is evident. In the Highlands (see RURAL SETTLEMENT: 4), settlement emerges as dispersed in the post-medieval period. In Perthshire, at the beginning of this period, dispersed farmsteads, based upon the longhouse, as excavated at Pitcarmick, are to be found.

The broad, high-backed, cultivation ridges that may be observed throughout eastern Scotland from Roxburghshire to Sutherland were produced by strip cultivation, probably with a heavy mouldboard plough, such as the 'Old Scotch Plough'. It is possible that this practice was the result of tenurial changes introduced by the Anglo-Normans, and involved the communal organization of agriculture for all landholders (runrig), who had shares in the township. However, in the north and west of Scotland, there are other forms of rig, often spade-dug lazy-beds, or narrow, low plough ridges.

In the hunting forests of southern Scotland, a particular form of settlement developed in response to the limitations of forest law. This development also gives an indication of the expansion of settlement from the 12th to the early 14th centuries. Here we find that assarts were carved out of some of the forests, examples of which can still be seen in Southdean in the royal forest of Jedburgh and in the private forests of Liddesdale and Annandale. As in the Highlands, settlement in these upland dales was dispersed, based upon what are termed forest steads, comprising the individual holdings that were assarted from the forest. These assarts, as required by the administration of the forest, were enclosed by a bank and a ditch, or deer-dyke, where the ditch was external and served to prevent the ingress of deer, but not their egress. The resultant landscape is extant only in those areas of southern Scotland where the late or post-medieval changes

saw these steads abandoned, such as Liddesdale or Southdean, but it is not typical of those areas which underwent an expansion of settlement in the late or post-medieval periods, such as the royal forests of Alyth and Clunie in Perthshire or the forest of Mar in Aberdeenshire. It may well be that the creation of parks, which became popular in the late medieval period, and acted as reserves within the overall hunting reserve, allowed the restrictions on the establishment of permanent settlement in a hunting forest to be relaxed (see NATURAL HISTORY).

The hunting park has traditionally been viewed as an enclosure, defined by a park pale, comprising an internal ditch and a bank topped by a fence, to prevent the escape of deer. Many of the great royal castles such as *Stirling, Kincardine, or Jedburgh had parks from the 13th century, providing a handy source of hunting close to the castle, but the archaeology of parks has been little studied. At Hermitage castle in Liddesdale, a partial enclosure around a natural gully to the west of the castle provides a killing-ground for the huntsman, whereby the deer were driven off the hill into the gully by the lord's tenants.

In addition to this landscape of permanent settlement many Highland and Lowland settlements were possessed of shieling-grounds. There is *place-name evidence from southern Scotland which suggests that shieling was a practice that was already superseded by permanent settlement during this period, or possibly that the growth of permanent settlement pushed the practice of shieling to the extreme margins, with Lowlanders travelling long distances to their shielings, whilst for the Highlanders the shieling-grounds often lay on nearby pasture. Numerous shielings have been identified by fieldwork throughout Scotland; many are based on stone-footings, and there is evidence for turf walls or turf-on-stone walls, as well as post-medieval evidence for estates requiring tenants to use materials other than timber for their construction as timber became exhausted. Examples of medieval shielings, dated by pottery, have been recovered from excavations on Ben Lawers, in Highland Perthshire, and from huts at Muirkirk, formerly in the forest of Mauchline in Ayrshire.

The building that typifies the farms of this period is the longhouse (see also HOUSING: 1). Longhouses or buildings which housed both peasants and farm animals have been interpreted from excavations at Springwood Park, near Kelso. These buildings date to the 13th and 14th centuries and are rectangular cruck-framed houses, with stands for domestic animals at one end, a mid-building hearth, and what is presumably a retiring area at the other end. The walls of these houses did not need to be weight-bearing, since the cruck-frame supported the weight of the roof; instead, they were based on foundations of stone, but may have had a super-structure of clay or turf.

The economy of Springwood Park was based on cereal production, including wheat, barley, oats, and rye, with cattle, sheep, pigs, and horses present—the last animals, in particular, being evident both from bone fragments and from the many horseshoes and nails found on the site. Grain was milled at the laird's mill; broken millstone fragments indicate that this is unlikely to have been far away, and it may have been stored in bundles, un-thrashed. Domestic spinning and weaving were practised, and most tools were in iron. The richness of the site is revealed by the recovery of several silver coins. The need for security is indicated by the presence of both casket keys and barrel locks for doors.   PJD

2. 1500–1770

Post-medieval Scottish rural settlements was characteristically dispersed in hamlet clusters, known as farmtouns in the Lowlands and *clachans* in the Highlands. The origins of these have been viewed as being prehistoric. Recent excavation and survey work, however, suggests that they may have been associated with the spread of feudalism from the 10th century and may have reached some areas, like the Outer Hebrides, quite late in medieval or even post-medieval times. These clusters were often occupied by a number of tenants holding shares in a farm, along with dependent subtenants or cottars (see RURAL SOCIETY: 2). In other cases, farmtouns consisted of a single large farm worked by one tenant with the aid of cottars. Larger settlements developed around nuclei such as parish churches (kirktouns), castles (castletouns), and mills (miltouns). In the south-east, a number of nucleated villages, possibly originating with the Anglo-Norman settlement, also existed. Small burghs (see URBAN SETTLEMENT: 1), village-sized rather than urban, formed another element in the settlement hierarchy. Excavation at the site of the deserted 16th-century burgh at Rattray in Aberdeenshire has provided interesting insights into the socio-economic background of the settlement. Single small farms and cottages also existed, giving many areas a mixed settlement pattern.

From the 14th century, the *climate became wetter and colder, reaching a low point at the end of the 17th century. Cultivation limits and settlement retreated downhill, probably encouraging the abandonment of high-lying communities in areas like the Lammermuirs and Cheviots. During the same period the opening-up of hunting reserves such as Ettrick Forest allowed some expansion of settlement. Renewed population (see

POPULATION PATTERNS: 1) growth in the 16th and 17th centuries was often linked, in the Lowlands, to an expansion of settlement into less favourable valley-floor and moorland areas. Such settlements often have names incorporating indicative elements such as bog, moss, or muir.

In the Lowlands baronial castles and fortified tower houses (see ARCHITECTURAL STYLES AND FEATURES), occupied by smaller estate owners, remained in widespread use well into the 17th century. Excavations at sites like Smailholm (Borders) have shown that tower houses did not stand alone and isolated in the landscape but were often associated with halls and other outbuildings. At Lour, near Peebles, and at other sites in the Tweed valley, the foundations of small tower houses are surrounded by farmtouns which were occupied into the late 17th or early 18th century. Recent excavations in Upper Clydesdale have revealed that a number of deserted farmtouns there were associated with a smaller kind of fortified house, similar in layout to the castle houses of northern England. They were solidly built of mortared stone, with a first-floor hall over a stone vault. Many of these would have been occupied by prosperous tenant farmers rather than landowners.

The increasing commercialization of livestock farming in the southern Uplands during the 18th century led to a reduction in the labour force and the amalgamation of farms (see ECONOMY, PRIMARY SECTOR: 1). These trends may be linked to the abandonment of many farmsteads and farmtouns, only a limited number of which have been surveyed in detail or excavated. Recent landcape surveys by the Royal Commission on the Ancient and Historical Monuments of Scotland in locations ranging from Dumfriesshire to Sutherland have revealed richly varied pre-Improvement landscapes of settlements, field boundaries, and associated structures surviving in semi-marginal areas. There has been considerable progress in the identification and recording of such landscapes, and growing concern to ensure the preservation of the best examples. In core Lowland areas, by contrast, known deserted settlement sites are far fewer and most of the evidence has been ploughed out by later farming. While processes of settlement change—such as township splitting, expansion, and abandonment—are well recorded on many sites, continuity from medieval to recent times is likely to have occurred so that many early sites may underlie and have been obliterated by modern buildings. A perennial problem with the study of pre-Improvement Scottish rural settlement is the poor quality of documentary and cartographic sources before the 18th century which makes it difficult to tie field remains into securely dated contexts without excavation.

But excavations of post-medieval sites have been relatively few and have often been done on a rescue basis at sites threatened by destruction due to development rather than on ones carefully chosen for their potential interest.

In the Highlands, prehistoric settlement forms like the crannog and possibly circular huts continued into post-medieval times. The excavation of sites, such as Lix in Perthshire and Rosal in Sutherland by Horace Fairhurst, and more recent research by archaeologists have provided a picture of the last phase of rural settlement before the clearance (see CLEARANCES OF THE HIGHLANDS AND ISLANDS) of population for sheep farming. Detailed survey of sites in areas like the Strath of Kildonan is starting to identify traces on the ground of earlier medieval and post-medieval settlement layers but much more excavation is needed to establish clear chronologies of settlement development and to identify regional variations.

In terms of building construction (see BUILDING MATERIALS AND TECHNIQUES), the use of rectangular longhouse layouts, where people and animals were accommodated under the same roof, was universal in the Lowlands and widespread in the Highlands in post-medieval times. The walls of such houses were often of drystone, or alternate layers of turf and stone, sometimes with clay mortar. Walls of solid clay were also used in many parts of the Lowlands, including the Carse of Gowrie and Ayrshire. Roofs were usually supported by cruck frames (see HOUSING: 1, 5). The timber crucks were often the most valuable part of a house, especially in the Lowlands where construction timber was in short supply. Such a house can be seen as a major feature of the first floor of the new *Royal Museum of Scotland. Excavations at sites like the Udal in North Uist have shown that the Hebridean black house, in its familiar late 19th and early 20th-century form, was not of ancient origin as was once thought, but developed from more simple pre-19th century types.

The use of shielings had virtually died out in the Lowlands by 1500 but continued throughout the Highlands until the end of the 18th century or later. On islands like Rhum, which were almost depopulated in the early 19th century, shieling remains can be clearly related to their environmental setting. Pressure of population in the Highlands from the later 17th century led to the temporary cultivation of land around some shielings and even the conversion of some sites to permanently occupied steadings, often in association with the opening-up of former hunting forests, as in Atholl and Mar. By the later 18th century, the reduction in the numbers of tenants on many Lowland estates and the amalgamation of holdings was leading to the re-placement of farmtouns by larger single farmsteads with better-quality houses for the farmers.

IDW

3. 1770–1914

Scotland's perennial drive for improvement traceable from at least the time of *David I moved onto a new plane in the 18th century, especially in its closing decades. But now, Improvement was promoted not by kings or ecclesiastics, but by landowners, and as part of a national programme grounded essentially in ideas of progress and a culture of social, cultural, and fiscal advancement. The driving forces for change varied from one locality to another, depending on the specific agenda of individual landowners. This was so especially in the Highlands, where from the 1730s, the concept of *duthchas* (hereditary right of tenure) was substituted by *oighreach* (hereditary right of possession), which could be embraced by the legal system, and provided landowners with colossal powers (see LANDOWNERSHIP IN THE HIGHLANDS AND ISLANDS). It was said by James Hogg of MacKenzie of Dundonnell in 1803: 'He is even more so in his domains than Bonaparte is in France.'

This period witnessed a dramatic reconstruction of Scotland's landscape (see GEOLOGY AND LANDSCAPE), as part of an integrated programme of Improvement which embraced twin strands. The combined effects of agricultural advances (see ECONOMY, PRIMARY SECTOR: 1) and mass industrialization (see URBAN SETTLEMENT: 2), which both created new towns and (more usually) transformed and hugely extended towns and cities (especially *Glasgow) had, by the middle decades of the 19th century, more or less transformed the landscape into that which we have today.

These structural changes to the landscape had ready precedent: on Lockhart of Carnwath's estates, for instance, agricultural improvements were in hand by c.1702, while the sixth earl of Mar had, well before his involvement in the Jacobite rising of 1715, illustrated the concept of integrated investment, utilizing the outflow from Gartmorn Dam as both a landscape feature associated with his private estate and a utilitarian power source for new industry in nearby Alloa. Such agricultural developments were grounded in experiment and scientific and economic processes, as illustrated at Experiment Farm, created c.1796 (rebuilt 1860–2, and renamed Barsliosnach), part of the programme of improvements and drainage at Crinan Moss.

The pre-Improvement, traditional multiple- or joint-tenancy farm was substituted by single tenancies. In the Highlands, the role of the tacksman (holder and sub-lessee of a lease) ended, after the new ideas were introduced on the Argyll estates, where bidding for leases was introduced in the 1730s. There was a logical economic process, necessitating maximizing of rentals and, consequently, wealth-generation from the land. Improvement implied investment, and where—as at Auchindrain—investment seemed unlikely to repay itself, the improvers passed by.

Improvement of estates was typically linked to updating or replacement of landowners' houses (see HOUSING: 4), a process which first took on a new vigour in the *Restoration period, as fashions in aristocratic manners changed and prestigious architects (see ARCHITECTS, ARTISTS, AND CRAFTSMEN) were employed. Townships (notably at Inveraray although there were earlier examples at Kinneil and Hamilton) close to rich houses were erased or relocated to create extended policies, typically wooded, with stone-walled perimeters and lodges, and a diversity of estate architecture in characteristic—and so, readily identifiable—style (for instance on the Atholl estates). The Entail Act papers in the NAS illustrate this integrated approach to Improvement, for instance at Over Rankeillor in Fife, in the decades around 1800.

The physical and visual changes to the landscape comprised eradication of the traditionalist rural system and its near-subsistence-level economy, and its replacement with the most up-to-date system which could be devised. Such wholesale changes had obvious consequences for the population, much of which became surplus in both rural Lowlands and Highlands. The process became more dramatic in the Highlands, where military subjugation of *Jacobite sympathizers at and after Culloden (1746) was an opening for accelerated change, and where *Clearances were usually more sudden and concentrated than in the Lowlands, where by contrast displaced people appear more readily to have been accommodated. Clearances were carried out in most populated areas until the Crofters' Holdings Act in 1886 provided security of tenure. Ironically, this process has bequeathed a rich archaeological legacy of pre-Improvement settlement systems: for, throughout the Highlands, the stone-built shells of innumerable cleared townships exist, sometimes—as at Kilmory on Rum—with their ruined medieval churches alongside.

Interventions can be divided into landscape and buildings (see BUILDINGS: 3). The landscape was transformed by unifying arable land into appropriate units, clearing or blasting away rocks (used to build dykes), and typically creating rectilinear and much larger fields than before. In marginal west Highland areas sheep-walks (for instance, at Glencalvie) rather than arable fields were created, and in especially the west, far north, and in the Northern

Isles, crofts were laid out on a likewise linear plan (for instance, Sollas, in North Uist). Previously unusable areas were brought under cultivation through modern drainage methods, either below ground, where tile drains became commonly used—often still visible as parallel lines of lusher growth in low-lying fields—or more ambitious engineering interventions. The latter included canalization (as on the River Eden, in Fife) or even draining vast lochs, as at the Loch of Spynie in the Laigh of Moray—originally 3 miles (4.8 km) long by ¾ mile (1.2 km) broad, it was reclaimed as arable land between 1779 and 1860. Water levels on Lochleven were managed to power a linear industrial estate through Leven and Markinch to Methil.

The chief architectural interventions at farms comprised a house and steading, either integral or, at usually grander or later instances, alongside. The house would have a walled garden, and often matched in grandeur a parish manse or even a pre-Improvement small lairds' house, illustrating farmers' heightening social status. This was paralleled, of course, by a knock-on rescaling of landowners' houses. A sizeable steading might comprise a formal courtyard, buildings both single-storey (for instance, for byres) and two-storey (perhaps stables with hayloft above for some lofts were a full storey high), and might additionally contain a tall barn and sheds for coach or coaches as well as implements. Especially in the Lothians, Fife, and wider environs, pre-existing buildings were often incorporated, indicative of a greater scale or wealth of pre-Improvement farming in these areas.

Particularly after the invention of the threshing machine by Andrew Meikle, patented in England in 1788, power sources were required, and these might help dictate where farms should be built; for instance, where a dam and water course could be created to turn a waterwheel. Other power sources comprised horse-mills or horse-gangs, steam engines (in coal-rich areas) or windmills, and sometimes—as at Shortrigg, Dumfriesshire—power sources in combination. Pendicles might include a grieve's house and workers' cottages, the latter often grouped or in a row, while sheep farms might have upland fanks. Almost without exception, these buildings were stone-walled and slate-roofed, houses with sash and case windows, and each building individually tailored in correspondence with the expectations from each farm. Typically, new farm layouts involved surveyors, and buildings were often architect-designed, perhaps ambitiously so. One example of this was on the Drumlanrig estates where, in the 1820s, William Burn, one of the most prestigious architects of his time in Britain, worked with the local architect Walter Newall. Massive investment was being made; it would not be done other than to best possible standards. As also happened elsewhere, the smaller of these same Drumlanrig farms were enlarged by addition of wings containing bigger rooms (in the latter case, during the 1860s by the estate's architect, Charles Howitt).

A legion of new towns was built throughout the entire land and existing ones extended. All, typically, were on a predetermined and often architect-designed linear, gridded, or geometric plan (such as at Fochabers, from 1776, designed by John Baxter, or Ardrossan, by Peter Nicholson, c.1806). These were commercial and administrative centres, often housing industry. Sometimes, a pre-existing name was used or translated from Gaelic to English, but the landowner could name a new settlement as he pleased, perhaps after himself or family members. New Leeds, on the other hand (established in 1798, though the venture failed), conveyed a specific reference to the prodigious flax-spinning industry of that town.

Fishing (see ECONOMY, PRIMARY SECTOR: 4)—an industry Stewart kings had sought to develop—at last reached industrial scale. After the Annexed Estates were wound up in 1784, the British Fisheries Society, established in 1788, became the most interventionist body in the Highlands. It began an ambitious programme of development, building Pulteneytown (a new town at Wick), Tobermory, and Ullapool (though Lochbay (Stein) in Skye, never came near to fulfilling hopes). Other industries necessitated intervention on the landscape: the most obvious example was New Lanark, where massive new mills and tenement blocks were built and the famous Falls of Clyde part-diverted as a power source for spinning machinery.

New roads and bridges (see TRANSPORT AND COMMUNICATIONS: 3) were first built in the Highlands as an anti-Jacobite measure, but a new grant-giving government programme (the Commissioners for Highland Roads and Bridges) headed by Thomas Telford was underway in the early 19th century. It reached towards the Inner Isles and included harbour provision: for instance, on Jura, a road linked Lagg and Feolin, with harbours built both there and on the corresponding ferry terminals opposite. In the Lowlands, the Commissioners of Supply had greatest impact in this area, their bridge-building activities well documented in, say, Dumfriesshire, where Auldgirth Bridge (designed by David Henderson, 1789) is an exemplar, though Alexander Stevens, both father and son, were also employed there and elsewhere. Canals were also built, notably the Caledonian Canal, again by Telford (following a survey of 1785 by James Watt), and the Forth and Clyde and Union canals linking Glasgow and Edinburgh. From the mid-19th century, railways made dramatic impact, their lines extending to Berwickshire, Stranraer, Kyle, and Thurso. Both the Forth Railway Bridge (designed by Sir John Fowler and Benjamin Baker) and Glenfinnan Viaduct are famous exemplars, while Ballochmyle Viaduct was claimed to incorporate the world's widest single-span stone arch. Other large-scale engineering works included piped water supplies, notably from Loch Katrine, where the loch was dammed, vast tunnels were made through rock, and pipes laid all the way to Glasgow.

Parish *churches and manses were rebuilt, usually on a larger scale than before, sometimes (for instance, Closeburn) with the old church left as a shell alongside. From the late 18th century to about 1850, new manses were typically flat-fronted, centre-doored, and two-storeyed, and remain with us still. Secessionist congregations strove to match their Church of Scotland counterparts, their churches often visually plainer, though the Free Church, established as a result of the *Disruption of 1843, often built grand manses. Parliamentary churches were provided for highly populated poorer areas following an Act in 1823; sometimes, ironically—as at Croick—shortly prior to clearances, while by the late 19th century, poorer areas sometimes acquired prefabricated corrugated-iron churches and schools.

The unprecedented, vast building programme demanded materials: limekilns were built and quarries abounded (see ECONOMY, PRIMARY SECTOR: 3). Their products were exported; for instance, at Ballachulish (providing slate), Peterhead (granite), and Caithness (flagstones). Likewise, there were sawmills and brick and tileworks. Local materials helped create a local character (see BUILDING MATERIALS AND TECHNIQUES), as in Fife, where many farmhouses and steadings were built of dressed black whinstone with contrasting light-coloured stone highlights.

Heightened maritime activity, related in part to the expanding markets of the *British Empire and the increased demands of tourism (see ECONOMY, TERTIARY SECTOR: 3) and commuting, also impacted on the landscape. Lighthouses were built around the coastline, mostly by the Stevenson family, while the phenomenal and essentially urban development of shipbuilding on Clydeside (see ECONOMY, SECONDARY SECTOR: 2) nonetheless impacted more widely, for instance with navigational markers at the Tail o' the Bank and measured mile markers at Skelmorlie in Ayrshire.

Consequences of all this rural change to the pre-existing archaeological landscape are difficult to quantify, though an incalculable amount of pre-Improvement architecture was swept away. Sometimes, ancient monuments were carefully retained and skirted round or, as at Dryburgh, taken into private care. At Rodel, in Harris, the ancient church was reroofed in the 1780s to serve a newly built fishing town of which it was to be a part. At other times, the monuments were removed: most famously, Arthur's O'on, near Falkirk, one of Scotland's most significant surviving best preserved Roman buildings, was made a quarry for an improver's mill-dam.

The scale of rural transformation was almost absolute. But besides economically driven change, there was room for the (supposedly) ornamental: the improver of the Sutherland Estates, for instance, was commemorated by a vast monument on a mountain (Beinn a' Bhragaidh), while other *monuments commemorated lineal or British military triumphs. The earl of Hopetoun, for instance, was commemorated in the 1820s by two giant columns, visible from across the Forth. Other sympathies caused creation of a sequence of monuments to William *Wallace, the greatest of all being at Stirling, designed by J. T. Rochead and opened in 1868, likewise visible for miles.

The situation was exemplified in microcosm by Islay, where a succession of *Campbell landowners transformed the island. New farms were made throughout the island with a new home farm, mills, distilleries, a tile-drain manufactory, roads, harbours, and bridges (including Scotland's earliest documented iron bridge to have been built), while lead mining was developed and slate quarries exploited. New towns (beginning with Bowmore, 1767) included one named after Walter Frederick Campbell's mother (Charlotte), and two after his wife: Port Wemyss—latched onto rock on the Atlantic fringe—and Port Ellen. Port Charlotte, Port Wemyss, and Keills were non-agricultural in conception (being based on distilling, fishing, and weaving respectively). Crofts were provided, though on a small scale, and Kilchiaran was cleared and a new model farm built c.1826.

Well before the turn of the 20th century, the rural transformation was effectively complete, though other interventions continued. These included distilleries (such as at Bunnahabhain, 1881), and aluminium smelters at Foyers (1896) and Kinlochleven (1908). The next phase of dramatic physical change to the landscape lay with the unwonted pressures of a world war: the creation of wartime installations, military new towns (for instance, Gretna), and airfields (such as Montrose) were obvious novelties but as significant were Forestry Commission plantations and agricultural intensification. Scotland's rural landscapes were—sometimes radically, but always intentionally—shaped in this period to become those familiar to us today.

AMacKe

4. Highlands

The archaeological study of the settlements that housed the rural population of the Scottish Highlands in the past few centuries is a comparatively new field of research with a history of barely 40 years. For a level of society barely mentioned in contemporary writings, the application of archaeological techniques in the investigation of these sites is as necessary as in the study of prehistoric societies. The process involves the discovery, recording, and analysis (often, but not always, including excavation) of the remains on the ground and the examination of relevant documentary materials.

In general terms, the main unit of settlement was the farm township, also referred to as the town, toun, or farm, and within this the settlement form was usually a non-village cluster of buildings, referred to by some writers as a *clachan*; its main function was to shelter the tenants, subtenants, crofters, or cottars with their animals and farming tools. One or more of these clusters were scattered across a township. The remains of these settlements are located at heights ranging from a few metres above sea level on the west coast to more than 400 metres (984 feet) in much less hospitable regions such as northern Perthshire.

Field remains, where they survive, consist of the drystone ruins, often only the turf-covered foundations, of the houses of the joint tenants, crofters, cottars, and farm servants plus the byres, barns, and sheds for ploughs and tools. There were stock-, stack-, or kail-yards within the settlement cluster and the remains of corn-drying kilns (occasionally built into the end of a barn or kiln-house) associated with one or more clusters and, less frequently, traces of lime-burning kilns (see HOUSING: 5).

Apart from the buildings, traces often survive of the plough rigs or lazy beds in the former arable land; of drystone or turf-built dykes and other enclosures; and of the all-important head dyke that separated arable, meadow, and woodland from common grazings, moor, and mountain. There are also vestiges of that more detached component of the Highland farming economy, the grazings or hill pastures of the shieling system, with remains of the small round, oval, or subrectangular bothies constructed of dry stone and turf, often strung along the banks of a burn.

The documentary sources can be subdivided into published material available in books and journals such as the OSA and NSA; original manuscript sources and collections of estate papers; and plans and early maps such as the Military Survey of Scotland usually referred to as Roy's Map, of 1747–55. The earliest editions of the Ordnance Survey's 1 : 10,560 maps have also been used. The most important materials of all are the collections of estate papers and plans, many now held in the NAS, some in the NLS, and some still in the possession of estate owners or their factors. Many of these estate documents contain surveys commissioned by the landowner and undertaken by land surveyors in the 18th century, before any major changes, improvements, or clearances, and they can be invaluable in attempting to reconstruct some of the elements of the post-medieval rural landscape.

There is also a necessity, by whatever means possible, to take account of the beliefs, customs, and traditions (including elements of story, song, and poetry that have survived in *oral tradition) of the people who inhabited the sites, since these were closely linked with their material culture and economic and social practices.

The available evidence must be treated with care for various reasons. There are differences and inconsistencies in available documents and estate plans and in their chronological range; many 18th- and 19th-century land surveyors showed only some of the existing buildings on their estate plans and this serves to confuse the fieldworker. We do not know, in many cases, what the remit of these surveyors might have been and their recorded information varies widely in consistency and quality.

There is also great variety and discontinuity, as well as widely differing levels of survival of material remains in the field, often due to the ephemeral nature of building materials at quite late dates in some regions. Within the general area of the Highlands there are many local physical environments, and this will have had a bearing on the raw materials available for building as well as exerting some control over shape of building and settlement form. Finally, there are socio-economic factors such as the decisions of chiefs, lairds, or landowners; systems of tenure; methods of working the land; and the great influence of tradition.

Excavation has so far revealed little that could be dated to before the middle of the 18th century, but occasionally wall remains and foundation trenches unrelated to, and orientated quite differently from those of, existing buildings have been uncovered, indicating that the later 18th- or earlier 19th-century layout was not necessarily the original layout. Patches of ash and charcoal and sherds of pottery in the floor of a barn can indicate that it may at one time have been a dwelling. Older pottery from pits may indicate an earlier, perhaps pre-18th-century, occupation. Excavation has also yielded greater detail of the dimensions, functions, and reuse of various structures than could be derived from field survey alone. J. Henderson, in his *General View of the Agriculture of the County of Sutherland* (1815), described contemporary houses in the

area: 'In some cases the walls are built with a tier of stone betwixt each tier of feal [turf], and in some the first three feet high of the walls and gables are built with stone, and the remainder with feal and sods.' This seems to be a quite accurate description of the houses at Rosal in Strathnaver, Sutherland, which was cleared in the second decade of the 19th century. Excavations at this site showed insufficient tumbled material to indicate any great height for the drystone walls, and they may have been stone-built for only 2 to 3 feet (0.6 to 0.9 m) as a base for turf walls.

Excavation has also shown something of the complexity of the changes brought about by Improvement and reorganization of settlement clusters in the later 18th and earlier 19th century; one such case is East Lix, in Glendochart, where investigations showed clustering, dispersal, and reclustering between 1755 and 1822. Small unpublished excavations in the floors of upstanding and ruined buildings in the settlement that is now the Auchindrain Museum of Country Life have revealed traces of earlier floors under the present ones and slight but obvious changes in alignment and internal subdivision. Above all, the evidence reveals just how completely mid-18th-century structures—most of which had no subterranean foundations, and with drystone building and reuse of materials—could be obliterated when this was part of deliberate policy. Sufficient documentary evidence exists to show that the names of many of these sites, if not the contemporary remains, have survived through centuries.

It would be wrong to give the impression that there was some kind of general settlement plan, township form, or system of agriculture common to the whole of the Highlands. Surveys have already shown differences of layout, building shape, and building materials over space and time, and the idea that all these necessarily represent long-term survivals of 'Celtic' traditions is being modified by recent research which shows, for example, that many west Highland and Hebridean townships have evidence of a pre-runrig system of enclosure of land in historic times.

Research is now concentrating on detailed studies of small regions, different types of evidence (from fieldwork, excavation, and documentary research), or single elements (field systems, transhumance systems, agricultural techniques, vernacular buildings, material culture, demographic studies (see POPULATION PATTERNS), and fluctuations in *climate) within or affecting the rural settlement complex. New techniques of site prospection are being attempted, including the intensive investigation of small areas with geophysical and soil (for example, pH and phosphate) analysis techniques, as well as different approaches to the cartographic presentation of settlement data.

Some of the settlement remains in the Highlands represent the final vestiges of evolution over a long period, but ending at different points on a timescale of about 1750–1850 because of a number of negative and positive changes including 'improvements', rationalization of holdings, and clearances for sheep. Many seem to offer evidence of only the last phase of occupation before abandonment; other sites may have remains of more than one period, which are difficult to recognize without excavation and other more intensive field methods. The socio-economic systems which produced the physical remains must have altered greatly through time and the picture is further blurred by the late adoption and retention of ideas and techniques of farming and building which had already disappeared from other regions of the British Isles and by the necessity for adjustment to what was in many areas a difficult environment.

These former township remains have been recognized as an important cultural resource and the question of their protection and conservation has become important enough for Historic Scotland to set up a Medieval or Later Rural Settlement Advisory Group, consisting of historians, geographers, and archaeologists.

One highly important point about Highland rural settlements is the fact that many sites have traces of much earlier, particularly prehistoric, occupation close by. The apparently missing material remains of sites of the medieval period, the names of which occurred in medieval documents, may have to be sought by the more intensive survey and excavation techniques already mentioned, and particularly in those areas that have traces of very early and much later periods of settlement in close proximity. It can thus be appreciated that the archaeological study of these sites will in many instances lead to the unravelling of a much longer history of occupation of the surrounding landscape.   AM

rural society: 1. medieval; 2. 1500–1700; 3. 1700–1770s; 4. 1770s onwards.

1. medieval

There is neither a national blueprint nor a single model for medieval Scottish rural society. The complex underlying cultural mix of Scottish society, together with topographical and climatic determinants, produced a wide variety of responses at local and regional level (see REGIONAL IDENTITIES). It is overly simplistic to divide Scotland between largely arable lowland and pastoral upland cultures, for neither were mutually exclusive and the patterns of regional specialism that character-

ize the modern Scottish agriculture regime were established only after the Improvement era of the later 18th and 19th centuries (see ECONOMY: 4). Where variations can be detected, however, it is primarily in the technical systems of measurement, or the units of fiscal assessment, rather than in the underlying economic units upon which rural society was built.

Throughout much of Scotland, the basic element of rural organization was the toun or, in the Gaelic-speaking areas, *baile*. This was a peasant community, holding the land for rent and service from a superior lord. Archaeological and documentary evidence suggests that the average toun comprised the households of some four to eight husbandmen, the most substantial class amongst the peasantry, who collectively would provide the oxen and equipment for the heavy mouldboard plough with which the surrounding fields were cultivated. Alongside them were men of lower grade, such as the cottars, who had their house, toft, grazing rights, and a few acres of arable, and who supported themselves through craftwork or through selling their labour. Beneath them were the grassmen, who had only rights in the common grazing, and landless labourers, who were employed by the substantial husbandmen. In parts of the north, west, and south-west, alongside these nucleated communities, there is also evidence for a more dispersed settlement structure with single households lying in isolation. Wherever possible, however, small areas around these houses were cultivated with spades or light ploughs.

Around most touns were zones of intensive plough cultivation, shaped characteristically by the plough into long, sinuous strips or rigs. Following the pattern common across much of northern and western Europe, these were open fields broken up into blocks and strips, with the individual holdings of the cultivators tending to be scattered rather than forming discrete blocks, thus ensuring shares in good and poor land. The demesne of the landlord was likewise scattered. Each peasant holding was subject to reallocation on a regular basis, either by drawing of lots or the award of rigs on a rolling sequence. There is no clear record of the arable regime(s) practised, with conflicting evidence for both a two- or three-course rotation following the English Midlands system and a model based on the continuous cropping of a regularly manured 'infield' and the rotated cropping of a poorer and infrequently manured 'outfield'. Crops were almost exclusively cereals, chiefly oats and barley (see DIET) but with wheat grown in some areas, especially in Lothian and the Merse where a strong market for grain had developed in the burghs (see URBAN SOCIETY: 1; URBAN SETTLEMENT: 1) by the early

13th century. Cultivation of peas and beans appears to have become more common after *c*.1300.

Whilst charter sources tend to stress the arable element in the touns' make-up, each toun held extensive grazing rights in the area beyond the limit of cultivation and animal husbandry was, throughout the Middle Ages, the key element of the rural economy. Twelfth-century evidence suggests a preponderance of cattle and pigs, particularly in the west and south-west, with dairying the dominant regime. In most of the upland zone extending from *Galloway into the Highlands and Islands (see HIGHLANDS AND ISLANDS: GENERAL), a localized transhumance system operated, with flocks and herds being moved to outlying shielings for summer pasture, where cheese would be produced. From the mid-12th century, there was a growing emphasis on sheep and cattle as European demand for wool and hides increased. The role of the monasteries (see CHURCH INSTITUTIONS: 2) as large-scale sheep farmers and cattle ranchers is well known, but it has been estimated that in excess of 50 per cent of the national flock and herd was owned by the peasantry by the later 14th century.

Profits from the sale of wool and hides may have aided the development of a rural elite in the 14th century, but changes in the basic structure of rural society are evident from the 1200s. In the 12th and earlier 13th centuries, in common with much of Europe, there was a clear divide between free and unfree classes. In Scotland the division was between freemen and *neyfs* (serfs). *Neyfs* were part of the property of a lordly estate, were tied to its land, and were obliged to perform a range of labour services on their lord's demesne. In the 13th century, as the population (see POPULATION PATTERNS: 1) expanded and produced a substantial surplus pool of cheap, employable labour, and direct cultivation of lordly demesne diminished, rigorous enforcement of seigneurial rights over *neyfs* declined and by the later 14th century this servile class had effectively disappeared from the social landscape. Certain jurisdictional aspects of serfdom remained, however, particularly thirlage, by which the peasants were obliged to have their grain milled at the seignurial mill—and pay for the privilege—a system of short leases whereby landlords could maximize their rents through the insecurity of annual renewals, and the non-heritable nature of peasant holdings.

With the disappearance of serfdom, there emerged a greater stratification in peasant society, with a growing divide in terms of wealth and status between the husbandmen and the rest. Through the 13th century, population expansion ensured that individual peasant holdings remained small, and, although some of the pressure may have been offset through the taking in of assarts from the

waste, lords had no difficulty in obtaining tenants for their touns. Surviving areas of rig and furrow cultivation in marginal zones, such as the Lammermuirs, probably reflect this pre-1300 peak of agricultural expansion. The wars (see INDEPENDENCE, WARS OF) and plagues (see HEALTH, FAMINE, AND DISEASE: 1) of the 14th century, however, threw this process into reverse and potential tenants became more difficult to obtain, which in turn saw a decline in rents, an increase in the size of peasant holdings, and a reduction in landlord incomes. Larger peasant holdings produced a rise in income, fuelled by the rapid expansion of the wool and leather trade in the later 14th century. Surplus income permitted some individuals to take increased shares or the lease of entire touns, the evidence of the 1376–7 rental for the estates of the Douglases of Dalkeith showing some husbandmen holding shares in several touns and holding up to three others in their entirety. They were also able to secure longer leases, often for up to three years. Such men represented a peasant aristocracy, who directly cultivated only a portion of their expanded holdings for themselves, while they sublet the remainder to poorer husbandmen. This cleavage within peasant society was accentuated in the later 15th century with a growing trend towards longer leases, which permitted the peasant elites to consolidate their position to some extent. Nevertheless, insecurity of tenure produced by the old short-leasing tradition, but particularly the non-heritability of peasant holdings, remained inherent weaknesses in Scottish rural society and checks on the social and economic development of this class until the introduction of feuing in the 16th century turned these former substantial tenants into a new class of hereditary landowners. RO

2. 1500–1700

Most Scottish people lived on the land, as peasants: small family farmers who subsisted largely from the produce of their own holdings. That produce maintained not only the peasants themselves, but also—through the rents they paid—most of the elite. Peasant farming had endured for centuries, but by 1700 it was deeply troubled.

Peasants rented 'holdings' of land from a landlord and farmed them with their family's labour. They lived in farmtouns: settlements with perhaps a dozen households (see RURAL SETTLEMENT: 2). The farmtoun's fields were divided into individual strips, while the community controlled the crop rotations, and animals were herded communally. In upland areas, even the holdings could be rented jointly by two or more households.

As well as peasants with a full holding (typically 26 Scots acres, 133 hectares), there were cottars with only a house, an acre or two, and animals on the common lands. They worked part-time on the larger holdings, on which they were often sub-tenants. Rural artisans (carpenters, blacksmiths, leatherworkers) would also be cottars. The cottar class was about half the population.

There were also some landless wage labourers. Young people often spent their teens working in another peasant household, before taking up hold-ings of their own (often on marriage). This was in-tegral to peasant agriculture. A few, however, continued as farm servants all their lives. They thus resembled cottars, who partly lived by working for others, but many farm servants were boarded in the farmer's household and had less autonomy. They presaged the way in which peasants them-selves, in the course of the 18th century, would be superseded by larger farms worked by hired labour (see ECONOMY: 3; ECONOMY, PRIMARY SECTOR: 1).

How did an increased population (see POPULA-TION PATTERNS: 1) (perhaps doubling between 1530 and 1660) adjust to the structure of peasant hold-ings? In France, holdings were reduced in size, but not in Scotland. A few extra holdings may have been carved out as marginal land was ploughed up. But some holdings also became much larger—100 acres (51 hectares) or more. So the proportion of cottars and wage labourers must have increased.

Rents were heavy. Usually paid in grain, they came to about a third of the crop. Another third would be reserved for seed corn, giving rise to the proverb 'Ane to saw [sow], ane to gnaw, ane to pay the laird witha [also]'. Peasants were also liable to teinds (tithes), a notional tenth of their gross pro-duce, to the church. Teinds were gradually secular-ized during the 16th century, often standardized at one-quarter of the rent; the teind 'tacksman' (lease-holder) was rather like a second landlord. Then the lord's mill usually had a legal monopoly, its dues often being a twentieth of the gross crop (adding about 13 per cent to rents). Finally, lords demanded unpaid seasonal labour services. That peasants could never hope to prosper in the long term is in-dicated by persistent rent arrears, with which the landlord could cream off any surplus that arose. In return, lords usually furnished building timber but little else. Landlords' main utility to peasant com-munities was in protecting them from attacks by other landlords.

There were four different kinds of Lowland landlord in 1500: crown, church (bishops and mon-asteries) (see CHURCH INSTITUTIONS: 2), *nobility, and lesser laymen (lairds). In the Highlands, the landlord was not so much an individual as a ruling family—the *clan. Peasants answered to a junior member of the clan, the tacksman, who collected rents and answered in turn to the chief.

During the 16th century, crown and church lands disappeared. Their lands were largely 'feued'—granted out to feuars who became the heritable proprietors. Feuars had to pay annual feu duties, usually equivalent to the original rent, but fixed in perpetuity and diminishing through infla-tion. The former landlords remained the nominal superiors of the feuars, but had little control over them; feuars could bequeath or sell their lands freely. About a third of church estates (and prob-ably crown estates) were feued to the peasant ten-ants, the rest going to outsiders (members of the existing lay landlord class). Peasants who obtained feus of their holdings enhanced their legal security and status—though the initial outlay was high, and those who contracted debts might discover eco-nomic insecurity. More saw their lands feued over their heads, and thus acquired a new landlord seek-ing a return on his initial outlay.

The movement of rent is not entirely clear, partly because of inflation, but real rents may have risen (as they did in England). There is a good deal of literary comment to this effect. Most rents were paid in grain, so at least inflation did not diminish them. The more pastoral south-west and High-lands paid in cash (obtained by the sale of cattle and cattle products). Here, real rents declined until the early 17th century, which saw dramatic increases.

Traditional peasants had 'customary' tenures—'custom' being a local tradition recognized in the lord's baron court. They often had some control over their holdings (unlike the downtrodden cot-tars), and could exchange or even sell them. The ideal was for one's son to inherit the holding. 'Kindly tenants' ('kindly' meant to do with kinship) were heritable by custom. Landlords in 1500 re-spected peasants' inheritance customs because ten-ants were in short supply. The peasant who sold his rights saved the lord the trouble of finding a re-placement tenant.

But custom required landlords' concurrence, and with competition for holdings from the late 16th century, this was less readily forthcoming. Local custom was increasingly circumscribed by the central courts. Lay landlords began issuing written leases in the 1620s: nineteen-year leases be-came normal. They increasingly specified crop rotations or other practices, asserting more con-trol over tenants. Life tenure, at fixed rent, and normally renewed to the heir, was a thing of the past.

Many peasant feuars sold up in the 17th century, partly through low grain prices. Large estates in-creasingly dominated the landscape. Gradually, holdings became larger and more oriented to the market. By the 1690s, 40 per cent of adult men in Lothian and Berwickshire were farm servants, and tenants were an entrepreneurial elite. In this advanced farming region, at least, peasant agriculture was already on its way out.   JG

3. 1700–1770s

In the period before the onset of agricultural Improvement, about nine out of ten Scots lived in the countryside with the vast majority eking out an existence from subsistence farming (see ECONOMY, PRIMARY SECTOR: 1). The verdict of historians on the state of Scottish agriculture before the age of Improvement is mixed. Farming was based on the farmtoun, a *rural settlement of no more than twenty families. Land was divided into two areas: the outfield, which was used for grazing, and the infield, which was used for crops. The infield and outfield were sometimes changed periodically to deal with soil exhaustion caused by intensive cultivation but, by and large, the infield was the area closest to the settlement. The infield was divided into strips of land (rigs) separated by waste ground (baulks) with tenants responsible for the cultivation of individual strips. These strips of land were changed around periodically to ensure that everyone was able to cultivate at some time all the available land. Animal and human dung, rotted turf, and household waste served as fertilizer. The crops grown were oats and barley, with small patches of land used for the cultivation of kail, a form of cabbage. Yields were low and the return was between 2 : 1 and 4 : 1. Sowing was done by hand and crops were harvested with a sickle. The cultivation of the rigs resembled gardening more than modern-day agriculture.

The orthodoxy, which was originally promoted by Enlightenment improvers (see CULTURE: 11), castigated the backward nature of Scottish farming in the first half of the 18th century. The separation of land into strips was wasteful and the periodic rotation of land ensured that there were no incentives to make improvements. The scientific breeding of livestock was unknown, modern fertilizers were not used, and the entrepreneurial horizon of the Scottish peasant was limited to subsistence. This view was modified by historians in the 1980s when it was shown that Scottish agriculture made slow if unspectacular gains through the latter part of the 17th and most of the 18th century by modifications within the old system (see HISTORIANS: 5). There is evidence that lime was increasingly used to reduce acidity in the soil and that the principles of commercialism were making an impact. Certainly the major test of agricultural efficiency at this time was the ability to feed the population which it was able to do without too many problems. The only significant shortages occurred between 1739 and 1741.

The countryside was dominated by the landowners and although there is evidence of increasing land consolidation and the use of commercial leases in the first part of the 18th century, the real explosion of agricultural Improvement did not take place until the 1760s. Most landowners had little to do with the day-to-day running of their estates, the only exception being the small gentry or 'bonnet lairds' who were owner-occupiers. The peasant economy was dominated by the 'gudeman', a tenant farmer who had about 100 acres (40.5 hectares) of land, and evidence of the embryonic development of commercialism can be seen in the fact that the number of leases to single tenants (as opposed to multiple tenants) was increasing throughout the 18th century.

Tenant farmers were dependent on cottars for labour and services, which were given in return for land which the farmer would plough for them as part of the contract. Cottars formed the bulk of the rural population and their lives were geared around the production of food for subsistence, although any surplus could form part of the rent. Allocated no more than about 5 acres (2 hectares) of land, cottars formed a large reserve of labour which could be used at busy times such as ploughing in the spring or bringing in the harvest in late summer. Cottars had usually one, possibly two, cows which were permitted to graze in the outfield, although the number of animals was regulated to prevent overgrazing. Beneath the cottars in the social hierarchy were the landless or, more accurately, near landless servants who may have had a small patch of land, but existed almost entirely on selling their labour to survive. Unlike the cottars, servants were paid in kind. Although tenant farmers were able to sell surplus crops at market for cash, by and large, the rural economy existed without money. Tailors, cobblers, weavers, and other artisans who made their living in the rural community were paid in foodstuffs or with services.

Rural society had little contact with the outside world and the Scottish peasantry's mental horizon was limited to the immediate locality. The church was the main agent of officialdom in the local community and was responsible for education, poor relief, and moral discipline (see RELIGIOUS LIFE: 4). Figures for religious attendance in the early 18th century show that Scottish society was not as 'godly' as was often claimed, although the church was able to make its presence felt in a number of areas of social life. The Scottish peasantry was comparatively well educated, a fact noted by many travellers, and most could read (see SCHOOLS AND SCHOOLING: 2). Although illegitimacy was common, the Church was able to coerce the majority of 'fornicators' into accepting paternity. The provision of poor relief for the destitute was subject to rigorous examination and was designed to help those deemed deserving, rather than the able-bodied who had fallen on hard times (see LIVING STANDARDS: 2).

The idea of an 'uninflammable people' has been questioned recently by historians who have shown that, although Scottish rural society was remarkably peaceful during this period, the peasantry would rise against things which were believed to contravene the accepted moral order. The Levellers' riots in Galloway in the 1720s, sabotage of improvements, and disputes over the imposition of an unpopular minister on the local church reveal that the Scottish peasantry could have its hackles raised by authority. Little is known of the mindset of the Scottish peasant at this time, although it is recorded that superstition and folk belief (see CALENDAR AND SEASONAL CUSTOMS) survived to a large extent.   RJF

4. 1770s onwards

In the 1770s, Scotland was still a rural country, in which the land was the main source of living for the many, and marked the power and social standing of the few. The Lowlands was also a land of small towns, many of which were little more than villages, concentrations of craftsmen and tradesmen that mostly served the surrounding countryside (see URBAN SETTLEMENT: 2). Although the Carron Iron Works (1759) had been joined by a growing band of similar concerns, the increasingly common riverside spinning mills and the coal heuchs (see ECONOMY, PRIMARY SECTOR: 3) across central Scotland were still part of the country scene. Urban industry on the scale that would follow was scarcely a hand on the horizon. A century later and half the population were urban (see ECONOMY: 4; URBAN SOCIETY: 5). Two centuries later, farming people would constitute barely 4 per cent of the population, and were becoming a minority even in the countryside.

Drastic though this change was, industrialization meant much more than just urbanization. The agricultural revolution was both the destroyer of a peasant society that consumed most of what it produced and the creator of a distinctly rural form of industrial society. The various subtenants who worked to the tenants for their little plots and payment in kind all went. Many would have become labourers on the new enlarged farms. Others would have become labourers to tradesmen, or expanded the ranks of the many new jobs requiring skill but which were not counted as trades, from dyking and draining to mole-catching and gamekeeping. In the higher parishes of the Lowlands, there was often a wholesale amalgamation of ten-

ancies to make what would become the recognizably modern hill farm, and the previous tenants had to find new tenancies or jobs. What remained of the old joint tenancy system in the Lowlands also went.

Whether they remained in the area or moved, most farming people faced being rehoused. The old pre-Improvement houses were built of fieldstone, turf, and thatch, some of which would be recycled with fuel ash and soot and animal muck onto the land. Their replacements were usually differently sited and built with stone, lime mortar, and sawn timber (see HOUSING: 1). The new habitations were not necessarily a great advance on the old which, although clarty and smoky, were also built by the inhabitants' hands to suit their needs. The damp and draughty tied cottar houses that accommodated generations of farm servants from the late 18th century were a major source of complaint until their widespread improvement following the Second World War.

New farm buildings were just one product of a new race of country tradesmen. By 1800 the developed areas often show the tradesmen, service trades, and their adherents equalling those cultivating the soil. The tradesmen were integral to the technology that caught up with the changes in land use occasioned by the agricultural revolution. Who was to shoe the horses that went on the new roads, furnish the metalwork on the new box carts, or repair the iron parts of the new swing ploughs? Who would make the leather harness for the new-bred Clydesdale horses that replaced the old home-made graith? Who would maintain the new generation of larger corn mills made possible by the strong and cheap iron-bound gearing available in the late 18th century, or erect the new threshing mills for which there was such a brisk demand from 1788?

The farm workers were feed or hired for a six- or twelve-month, with distinct regional patterns of differing character throughout the Lowlands. The tradesmen formed the most settled part of the population, thus getting the benefits of education and a stable place in local society. The tenant farmers ranged from small family concerns employing little labour to men of substantial capital renting over 600 acres (243 hectares). A small professional class separated them from the laird and his lady in their seat. There were very few owner-occupier farmers, and not many small lairds. This distinct rural industrial society dominated the 19th century, with the addition of considerable numbers of public service workers as railways, post, police, and state education became established. Depression from the 1870s fossilized it and after the Great War the estate system began to break up. The triumph of the combine harvester and the Ferguson System tractor from 1950 demolished the traditional roles of horseman and many country trades.

Drastic though the initial upheaval was, there is no widespread tale of social anguish at the creation of industrial farming in the Lowlands. There were jobs, opportunities, and money in it. Robert Burns was involved in the change during his short life (1759–96). Any criticism was directed at the greed of lairds expecting fat rents from half-improved lands, not the new system as such. Yet Burns's *Address of Beelzebub* expressed outrage at MacDonald of Glengary's treating his Highland tenants as if they were his property to dispose of or keep. For much of the Highlands and Islands (see HIGHLANDS AND ISLANDS: GENERAL), the attempt to modernize the old system was a social disaster. In order to create large new sheep farms and have a labour force to gather and burn seaweed to produce industrial alkali, whole populations were shifted to new crofts or smallholdings on the coasts. When the kelp failed in the 1820s and the potato famines overwhelmed the north-west from 1845, secondary evictions drove people to the Lowland towns and abroad (see MIGRATION). Mainly in the Western Isles, a partly landless population hung grimly on. Paradoxically, there the severe social disruption produced a still-expanding population (see POPULATION PATTERNS: 2) until near the end of the 19th century. Popular opinion in the Lowlands and the fear of Irish-style politics spreading to the Highlands first halted the evictions and led to the Napier Commission and the Crofters Act of 1886. The result was reduced rents and security of tenure. It did little for the already dispossessed, some of whom only reoccupied their grandparents' holdings in the Hebrides after the Great War. The present-day crofting community is a much-altered but direct descendant of old Europe's pre-industrial farmers.

GS

Russia. There has been considerable speculation about the origins of the significant relationship between Russia and Scotland. No less a document than the Declaration of Arbroath states that the Scots first lived in the land of the Scythians by the Black Sea where the early Russians would have been near neighbours. Some archaeologists have suggested similarities between the animistic beliefs of the people of Novgorod and other north-western localities on the one hand and those of Scottish Celts on the other. Possibly, there were early contacts between Scotland and Kievan Rus. Most of the medieval meetings, however, were probably on the battlefield during the Northern *Crusade of the Teutonic Knights. The first Scottish individual known certainly to have visited Muscovite Russia was 'Petrus Davidis de Scotia

Aberdonensis' or Peter Davidson, sent by King Christian I of Denmark as ambassador to Tsar Ivan III 'the Great' in or around the year 1495. In 1556, the first Russian ambassador to England, from Ivan IV 'the Terrible', was shipwrecked near Fraserburgh.

From such diplomatic beginnings, indirect and accidental, the relationship between Scotland and Russia was to evolve for nearly two centuries in a mostly military manner (see MERCENARIES IN EUROPE). Scottish prisoners seized by Ivan 'the Terrible' during the Livonian War for a foothold on the Baltic Sea were employed by this tsar in campaigns against the Crimean Tatars. In the War for Smolensk of 1632–4 Alexander Leslie of Auchintoul led a Scottish mercenary force some hundreds strong on behalf of the first Romanov, Michael. While relations developed at the highest level between Romanovs and Stewarts, other Scottish officers, including Thomas Dalyell of the Binns and most notably Patrick Gordon of Auchleuchries, plied their trade in later phases of the 17th century. The polymath Gordon was in the early entourage of Peter I 'the Great', which also came to include the brothers James and Robert Bruce, savants as well as soldiers; Dr Robert Erskine, the tsar's physician; and Henry Farquharson of Marischal College, an outstanding teacher. Peter adopted the saltire as the flag of his navy (albeit blue on a white ground) and instituted the Order of St Andrew, thus in all probability reinforcing an affinity which he himself felt.

After the death of Peter 'the Great' in 1725, the number of Scots in the tsarist armed forces declined, partly because of the eclipse of the Stewarts but also because of increasing opportunities for adventure and advancement in the nascent *British Empire. Certainly, there were more outstanding fighting men such as James Keith who later served as field marshal for Frederick 'the Great', but medical men (see MEDICINE AND THE ORIGINS OF THE MEDICAL PROFESSION), professional people, and teachers now became more common, and women began to appear in their own right. Twelve doctors, of whom nine were trained at the University of Edinburgh, helped modernize the healing profession in the wake of Erskine through the 18th and early 19th centuries. Catherine 'the Great''s reign (1762–96) was an especially significant period, the versatility of some of the individuals involved being perhaps best exemplified by Matthew Guthrie, who wrote and published on subjects widely ranging beyond his professional expertise such as music and the arts, antiquities, and minerals. The last in the line, Sir James Wylie, was chief medical inspector of the Russian army from 1806 to 1854, and carried out many good works beyond the strict call of duty.

Russia

The entrepreneurs included Charles Gascoigne of the Carron ironworks, manufacturing cannon for the Russian navy at the invitation of Admiral Samuel Greig and emigrating to Petrozavodsk in 1786. Among his employees was Charles Baird, who struck out on his own to produce the first Russian steamship in 1815 as well as all kinds of ironwork for St Isaac's cathedral and other projects. There were merchants too, including Andrew Muir and Archibald Mirrielees, who set up a department store in Moscow in the late 1880s (still in existence as the Central Universal Store), while herring fishermen from Aberdeen to Wick expanded trade with Russia in the late 19th century. Charles Cameron was outstanding among architects and craftsmen, receiving important commissions from Catherine 'the Great' and her son Paul. There were all kinds of teachers, including governesses, one of whom, Catriona MacKinnon from Mull, was said to have taught Alexander II some Gaelic phrases and songs, and missionaries, such as Henry Brunton from Selkirk, one of the founders in the early 19th century of the settlement in the Northern Caucasus which became known as 'Shotlandka' or Little Scotland. William Carrick, whose grandfather and father were merchants in St Petersburg, established himself as a successful photographer, while Christina Robertson painted portraits for high Russian society.

Literary interaction was stimulated in spectacular fashion from the end of the 18th century into the early 19th century by the impact James MacPherson's *Ossian* made on the works of many Russian writers including the great Pushkin, but most appropriately in the case of Lermontov. Descended from George Learmonth, an early 17th-century mercenary, Lermontov wrote in 1830 and 1831 nostalgic poems including 'The Grave of Ossian', with such lines as 'In the mountains of my Scotland', and 'The Wish', lamenting his separation from his ancestral land. By this time, the reputation of Sir Walter Scott was catching on in Russia, and probably exceeded that of any other foreign author in the 19th century. Again, Pushkin and Lermontov were affected, but so were Turgenev and Tolstoy and a host of lesser literary figures. Burns would make his greatest impact later, in the Soviet period, especially through the translations of Samuil Marshak.

The First World War and the Revolution of 1917 inaugurated a new era typified by the appointment as first Soviet consul in Great Britain of John Maclean. Strong links were developed by the Communist Party in Glasgow, Fife, and elsewhere in Scotland with headquarters in Moscow. If prerevolutionary literary influences had been mostly from Scotland, the direction was now largely reversed. Examples may be found in the works of those sometime collaborators Lewis Grassic Gibbon and Hugh MacDiarmid. Gibbon claimed to have set up a soviet in Aberdeen soon after the Russian Revolution, and injected some revolutionary fervour into the third part of his trilogy *A Scots Quair*. MacDiarmid drew inspiration not only from the ideas of Lenin but also from the *zaumny* (transsense) language of Velimir Khlebnikov. Older and newer Scotland–Russia ties were officially celebrated during the Second World War, but the ensuing Cold War left their continuance to a handful of enthusiasts. From 1985 onwards, however, the relationship has blossomed anew, from business associations, oil and gas especially, to collaborative cultural ventures. A *Caledonian Society was formed in Moscow in 1995, and quickly developed links with counterparts in the major Scottish cities and their hinterlands. The first-ever Scottish *Highland games in Russia were held in Moscow in 1997, following a joint folk festival.

Such events, often fortified by comparisons of national drinks and dishes, may sometimes lead to overimaginative celebrations of affinities between Scotland and Russia, and on occasion to neglect of those between Scotland and other Slavic countries, where Celtic and other ancient roots may also be found for present friendships (see CENTRAL EUROPE). The broader context for the relationship, both present and past, throughout Europe and beyond, must be given its full due. Moreover, contacts have been more west–east than east–west, from Scotland to Russia rather than vice versa. Nevertheless, the weight of the evidence, military and civil, economic and cultural, provides a solid enough basis for the assertion that this relationship does indeed possess a special quality.　　PD

St Andrews: 1. before 1100; 2. since 1100.

1. before 1100

The site now occupied by the town we know as St Andrews has a long and interesting past. Excavations at Hallowhill and Kirkhill, both within the confines of the modern town, revealed cist burials dating from prehistoric times, probably the Iron Age. It is not surprising to find such early settlement, whether permanent or transient, since the location offered many of the essentials for human survival: a site on a rocky headland that could be readily protected from both human and animal predators; an excellent water supply in the Kinness Burn and the River Eden; and food, in the form of fish and shellfish immediately at hand, as well as hunting grounds inland.

The first firm evidence of permanent occupation of the site comes in AD 747, in the *Annals of Tigernach*, written in Ireland. In this early documentary source, the death of Tuathal, abbot of Cennrighmonaid (Kilrimund or Kinrimund), is recorded. The *place name means either 'head of the king's mount' or 'church on the head of the king's mount'; and is the headland above the present harbour of St Andrews, now called Kirkhill. The existence of a religious settlement here is confirmed by the finds of early Christian sculpted stones and two important burial *monuments. Skeletal remains have also been discovered; radiocarbon dating suggests the burials range from the 5th to the 11th century.

The foundation legend argues that there was a monastery here, delineated by free-standing crosses and enclosing seven churches within its precincts. All this suggests that on the site of St Andrews there once stood a Christian establishment, perhaps organized on Irish lines; and this was an establishment that was a major religious centre.

Often, such centres had attached secular settlements. This seems to have been the case in Kinrimund. Twelfth-century documentation indicates a small hamlet close by the religious settlement. It was this small lay settlement that would form the nucleus of the 12th-century burgh.   EPD

2. since 1100

The burgh of St Andrews was founded close by,

and with strong links to, the religious settlement of Kinrimund in the 12th century. Bishop Robert of St Andrews' charter of 1144 × 1153 announced the foundation of the burgh and granted to Mainard the Fleming, the first *praefectus* and official responsible for the formal layout of the burgh, three tofts, or burgage plots, on South Street. Significantly, however, this same charter indicates that it was *David I (1124–53) who had given permission for the founding of a burgh and granted to the bishop the existing vill.

It is probably fair to assume that this vill was a small lay community attached to the religious settlement. A charter of Bishop Richard (1163–78) suggests that this early urban nucleus ran down the street now called North Castle Street and possibly into a section of the current North Street; and a charter of Roger, bishop-elect of St Andrews (1189–98), permitting the transference of the market cross from 'where the clochin used to be', also implies a movement of settlement away from the early vill. Certainly the two wide streets leading up to the ecclesiastical precinct, with burgage plots of equal width—twelve paces—were established by the mid-12th century: South Street (*vicus burgensium*) by 1144 × 1153 and North Street (*vicus aquilonalis*) by 1163 × 1178.

Over succeeding centuries, town expansion continued westwards; and by the late 15th century, and possibly as late as 1518, the properties of the Greyfriars (Franciscans) and Blackfriars (Dominicans) probably denote the west limit of the town—a mere 656 yards (600 m) or so from the cathedral. To the north of North Street, however, Swallowgate, once probably a significant street, leading as it did to the Bishop's castle, founded c.1200, did not expand westwards, the port or town gate that enclosed it being set considerably further east than the other town gates, on the plan depicted by John Geddy c.1580. One major additional transformation of the townscape, however, was the insertion of Market Street between North and South Street; it became an important medieval thoroughfare (see URBAN SETTLEMENT: 1).

In spite of the elevated position of the town as the seat of bishops and from 1472 of archbishops and primates of Scotland, with the associated wealth and importance of their buildings, St Andrews was not a prosperous medieval town in relation to the larger east coast burghs. A stent of 1483 for burghs north of the Forth, for example, assessed St Andrews at £10, compared with *Dundee and *Aberdeen at over £26 and *Perth at £22. Cupar and Crail, however, were assessed at merely 10 merks and £2 respectively. The burgh's prestige received a further fillip when, in 1413, it received a bull of foundation for the first of Scotland's *universities. St John's College was formally established in 1419, to be followed by St Salvator's in 1450; and in the early 16th century by two further colleges—St Leonard's and St Mary's.

The 16th century, however, was not to be one of general progress for St Andrews. The *Rough Wooing of Henry VIII and Edward VI of England in the 1540s brought disruption, followed by the murder of the Francophile Archbishop Beaton, the holding of the castle by the pro-English party, and its consequent attack by the forces of the French-born noblewoman, Mary of Guise. The *Reformation crisis was to bring *iconoclasm and more destruction to the cathedral, priory, churches, chapels, hospitals, and houses of the religious orders in the town.

For many, the very *raison d'être* of the town had disappeared. Indeed, even the university considered transferring to Perth in 1696. Visitors in the 17th and 18th centuries unanimously commented on the past glory of the town, still evidenced in spires and ruins, but, also, on the air of neglect and 'dreary solitude'. Dr Johnson, on his famous perambulation, visited St Andrews in 1773 and dismissed the town as one 'which only history shows to have flourished'. Within twenty years, however, improvements to the harbour and the efforts of the town's craftsmen were to begin to reap rewards; by the 19th century the townscape would see vast renovations. And, already in existence, a portent for the future: the main industry of the town was leather-coated golf balls. The St Andrews *golf club had been formed in 1754; and 80 years later was to receive the honour of being called 'Royal and Ancient'. The historic burgh was entering a new and significant phase of its long history.   EPD

Scandinavia: 1. to 1312; 2. 1312–1600; 3. since 1600.

1. to 1312

The countries of Scandinavia, Norway especially, are Scotland's nearest neighbours across the North Sea. The Scottish mainland lies in the same latitudes as Denmark and southern Norway. South-eastern Scotland and Denmark are comparable in that both have stretches of good arable land suitable for the creation of wealth and to form a basis

for political unification. North-western Scotland has some close similarities with Norway's west coast, consisting of strings of islands and a deeply indented coastline making it a home from home for Vikings from western Norway. For it is the sea which dominates the history of Scotland and Scandinavia and which has always provided links between them. These were links which could be exploited once man had the technical expertise to traverse the North Sea regularly.

The development of superb sailing vessels was the stimulating factor behind the Viking Age, and although there may have been contact across the North Sea prior to the year 800, it was about then that the written sources record the start of regular visitations of Norwegian raiders around the eastern and western coasts of north Britain. The *Annals of Ulster* for 794 speaks of the 'Devastation of all the islands of Britain by the gentiles', and many other records tell us how these attacks were directed initially against the unprotected monasteries of Scotland, Ireland, and north England, centres of wealth in the form of ecclesiastical vessels and adornments, and repositories of secular treasure. The raids must have had a dire impact on secular society also, as the sea pirates overran the islands and peninsulas of Shetland, Orkney, and the Hebrides, establishing control over the seaways and transport routes around north Britain and in the Irish Sea. It was not long before the raiders accessed southern Scotland by the main routes and riverways, and conflict is recorded in the central Pictish province in 839 and 866, when hostages were taken and tribute imposed (see PICTS). Their astonishing mobility and co-ordination with Danish raiders in eastern England resulted in a combined attack on the stronghold of the Strathclyde Britons in 870, after which *Dumbarton Rock became a Viking control point on the River Clyde.

From this activity it would appear that the priority of the Vikings in central Scotland was to exercise control over the important routes, and in the process bring the Pictish kings into a tributary relationship. We know very little about these policies and ambitions, although we know a great deal more about their permanent success in colonizing north and west Scotland. The evidence here derives from archaeology, from *place names, and from the saga account of the establishing of the earldom of *Orkney and Caithness at the end of the 9th century. Finds of pagan graves and of Norse homesteads throughout the Northern and Western Isles, along with a remarkable implanting of Norse farm and topographical names, give us a rich source of evidence for the nature, the extent, and the density of settlement by Norwegians in the 9th and 10th centuries. The family of earls from Møre in west Norway who established themselves in the Orkney islands also extended their authority on to the north mainland of Scotland and the toponymic evidence shows that they created the right circumstances for Norse settlers as far south as the Firthlands of Ross and Cromarty. North Scotland became thus a part of the Scandinavian world while the Northern and Western Isles were eventually drawn into the Norwegian kingdom for several centuries.

This did not of course happen in the central Lowlands where the Picto-Scottish kingdom maintained its freedom from Viking control and emerged as a strong political entity by 900. The dynasty possibly came to terms with Norse or Danish elements, which mingled with the native societies, leaving only faint traces of any Scandinavian influence. The kingdom of Alba, by extending its power southwards over the former Bernician territories, established a frontier with the province of Northumbria. This brought it close to the Anglo-Danish empire of Cnut and his sons (1016–42), who used Norwegian and Danish earls to rule Northumbria for them. The Scottish kings (see KINGSHIP: 2) also had a powerful Scandinavian warlord on their northern frontier at the same time and established close relationships with the Orkney earls who dominated Caithness and Sutherland.

From the 11th century onwards the national kings of the post-Viking world sought to extend political control to their territorial boundaries; in the case of Norway this included those settlements west-over-sea which were the permanent result of Viking activity. While they had sufficient naval power this was possible: kings like Magnus III Olafsson 'Bare-Legs' could be remarkably successful in establishing authority over all the settlements around the northern and western coasts of Scotland, and could even attempt to exert some influence in Ireland. Magnus is said in his saga to have come to an agreement with the king of Scots in 1098 whereby the boundary between their respective dominions was to be the sea along which King Magnus could sail. This meant that those parts of the mainland territories which had been under the influence of Norse settlers in the Isles (see HIGH-LANDS AND ISLANDS AND CENTRAL GOVERNMENT: 1) were to come under the authority of the king of Scots. A coastal boundary is not always the most suitable dividing line and tradition preserved the memory of Magnus being dragged in his boat, with rudder set, across the isthmus at Tarbert in Argyll in order to claim the Kintyre peninsula as Norwegian territory. Permanent control was another matter and the attempt to put his son in charge of the Northern and Western Isles lasted only as long as Magnus himself was alive. After his death in Ul-

ster in 1103 one of his three sons, Sigurd, went back home to claim his share of the kingdom. Thereafter Orkney reverted to the earls: *Man and the Western Isles were under the authority of a dynasty, which called themselves kings, and which acknowledged Norway's overlordship. They had to pay a tributary render to each new king of Norway, although they seem to have had few other obligations. This situation was to last only another century and a half. The earls of Orkney were more tightly controlled, especially after Earl Harald Maddadson made the mistake of supporting a rising against King Sverrir Sigurdsson at the end of the 11th century, losing fiscal rights in Orkney and the whole of his authority over Shetland as a result.

In the 13th century, the kings of Scots started to look to their northern and western fringes as part of their rightful dominion, providing useful opportunities for land and sea to be won and brought under their authority. This of course resulted in the development of tense relationships with the king of Norway and the kings of Man and lords of the *Isles who held sway over the Hebrides. The political situation in the Isles had been complex ever since the sons of Somerled established themselves in the southern Hebrides in the mid-12th century, leaving the kings of Man with only half their former island dominions: the outer isles of Lewis, Harris, the Uists, and Barra. The ambitions of the Scottish kings seem to have brought the kings of Man closer to their Norwegian overlord, and members of the dynasty sought support from Haakon IV Haakonsson (who ruled from 1217 to 1263), one of them, Harald Olafsson, even being favoured enough to receive the hand of Haakon's daughter in marriage. The problem of the Manx kings' political circumstances, caught between the competing ambitions of national dynasties—and with the kings of England also sometimes involved—is not always appreciated by historical commentators.

We are fortunate to have, in the saga of Haakon Haakonsson, an account written at his court towards the end of his reign, which gives full details of the negotiations which led up to his expedition of 1263, and a remarkable description of that campaign. Alexander II—'a great prince, and very greedy of this world's honour' as the saga-writer says—sent embassies to Haakon in the 1240s to persuade him to give up the Southern Isles (Suðreyar = Western Isles), claiming that King Magnus 'Bare-Legs' had won them unfairly from Malcolm in the 1090s. The Norwegian king replied that he knew well that there had been an agreement between the two kings, and anyway King Malcolm had had no power in the islands when Magnus conquered them; moreover Magnus claimed them as inheritance won by his own predecessors (a very interesting insight into the Norwegian interpretation of what the situation had been *c*.1100). Alexander's death in 1249 allowed the situation to lapse, but it blew up again when his son reached maturity, and aggressive actions by the Scots instigated the launching of a naval expedition by the Norwegians in the summer of 1263. This force of 40 ships—augmented to perhaps twice that number with levied forces from the Isles—was said in the usually laconic Icelandic Annals to have been a greater force than men ever knew to have gone to sea from Norway. It was nonetheless 'more fitted to demonstrate power than actually assert it' and was something of an anachronistic expression of northern imperialism. It failed to achieve anything, except decide the political situation in the Hebrides, which the Scottish victory at the so-called battle of Largs set the cap on. The death of King Haakon at Kirkwall during his sojourn there over the following winter was a poignant symbol of the demise of Norway's power and influence in the west. It is even doubtful whether the earl of Orkney would have been in attendance for the obsequies of his Norwegian overlord, for he had failed to follow the Norwegian fleet south from Orkney the previous summer.

Magnus VI Haakonsson the 'Law-Mender', Haakon's successor, faced the reality of the situation and came to terms with Scotland in 1266 when the Treaty of Perth was drawn up to establish the basis of the transfer of sovereignty over Man and the Isles from Norway to Scotland. The terms of the settlement, by which Scotland paid a sum of 4,000 marks 'for the sake of peace', and committed the kingdom to the payment of 100 marks per annum to Norway 'in perpetuity', was not the best basis for future good relations between the two countries. The reason lying behind this annual payment has never been fully understood, but it is unlikely to have any sort of feudal implication. The continued position of Orkney and Shetland as part of the kingdom of Norway was explicitly agreed, and this treaty formed the basis of closer relations than had hitherto existed, for a century and a half. These involved two royal marriages during the remaining part of the 13th century, the first of which resulted in the inheritance of the Scottish throne passing to the young granddaughter of Alexander III, Margaret the 'Maid of Norway', in 1284. After her tragic death, again in Orkney, in 1290, her father Erik II Magnusson of Norway felt compelled to put forward a claim to the throne of Scotland in 1292 (see GREAT CAUSE).

So long as Norway remained an independent nation and its kings free of external control then relations with the nearest great power 'west-over-sea' would naturally be of some significance. But the

14th century saw changes within Scandinavia, and the increasing economic control of the Hanseatic League meant that political relations with the south and east were going to have greater priority. This probably led to commercial tensions in the North Sea, for there is evidence that both English and Scottish merchants were implicated in violent actions involving Norway. The earliest source of evidence to have survived about trading relations between Scotland and Norway is a memorandum of 1312 attached to a renewal of the 1266 treaty drawn up at Inverness. This very formal renewal probably related to the requirements for establishing of political relations with the newly established king in Scotland, *Robert I; it also suggests that the terms of the 1266 treaty, regarding payments from Scotland, had not been fulfilled. But above all it provides an interesting insight into the fraught and turbulent situation in North Sea trading relations which particularly involve activities in Orkney and Shetland. This is a pointer to the next big issue which would create hostility between Scotland and its Scandinavian neighbours.　　　　BEC

2. 1312–1600

For most of the 14th and 15th centuries Scotland and Scandinavia moved in different commercial and political constellations. Scotland's trade was focused above all on the *Low Countries. That of Scandinavia—especially Norway—fell increasingly under the influence of the Hanseatic League. Scottish diplomacy was primarily concerned with the complicated interrelationship between England (see ANGLO-SCOTTISH RELATIONS: 2), *France (see also FRANCO-SCOTTISH RELATIONS: 1), and latterly Burgundy. Meanwhile, the political agenda of the Scandinavian kingdoms was governed chiefly by relations with the Hanse and the attempts to forge unity between the three Scandinavian kingdoms. The latter was established by the union of Kalmar in 1387, but attempts to make or break the fragile authority of the Copenhagen-based royal house continued to preoccupy Scandinavian politics.

As a consequence of these developments, the intimacy of earlier relations between Scotland and Norway was not resumed following the Treaty of Inverness (1312). The primary purpose of this agreement had been to confirm the commitment of the Scottish government to the annual delivery of 100 marks, in return for the acquisition of the Western Isles in 1266 (See ISLES, KINGDOM OF THE; MAN, KINGDOM OF). Whether payments continued after 1312 remains uncertain, but, if so, they probably ceased during James I's captivity in England. His release in 1424, and the impecunious straits of the Scandinavian monarch Eric of Pommerania, prompted a second confirmation of the Scottish government's financial obligations regarding the Western Isles, agreed at Bergen in 1426 (see HIGHLANDS AND ISLANDS AND CENTRAL GOVERNMENT: 1). There is, however, little evidence that payments were resumed.

While Scandinavian kings sought in vain to re-establish their rights to 'the annual', the interest of Scottish monarchs turned increasingly towards the acquisition of Orkney and Shetland (see ORKNEY AND CAITHNESS, EARLDOM OF), which had remained part of the Norwegian kingdom in 1266. The Northern Isles were eventually ceded to the Scottish crown in 1468–9, though in somewhat ambiguous terms. The Treaty of Copenhagen provided for the marriage of James III to Christian I's daughter, Margaret, who was to be accompanied by a dowry of 60,000 Rhenish florins. Unable or unwilling to pay this sum in full, Christian instead pledged his rights in Orkney, assessed at 50,000 florins. Similar rights in Shetland, valued at 8,000 florins, were conveyed in 1469. The imprecise nature of these rights and the means of their transfer left open the possibility that the Scandinavian crown might seek to reacquire the islands. Indeed, while Scandinavian monarchs continued to exercise ecclesiastical patronage (see CHURCH INSTITUTIONS: 2) and commercial jurisdiction in the Isles after 1468, the commitment of later Scottish governments towards retention of the Isles occasionally wavered. In 1524, for instance, an offer was made to return Orkney in return for 6,000 paid soldiers.

That the Scandinavian crown never repossessed the Northern Isles was partly due to its ongoing financial problems. Moreover, the Scandinavian crown was probably reluctant to press the issue of the Isles in the later 15th and early 16th centuries, since it sought Scottish assistance against the Swedes. The Treaty of Copenhagen constituted a full military alliance between the two kingdoms, though in the event James III did not involve himself too closely in Christian's wars with his rebellious subjects. The alliance was, however, confirmed in the 1490s by their respective sons, *James IV and Hans; and in 1502 James dispatched a Scottish army to Scandinavia to assist in the suppression of revolt. It met with at most limited success, and thereafter, despite repeated pleas for aid from his cousin, James adopted a more cautious approach. His diplomats were active in brokering the Peace of Nyköping (1507) between Hans and his Swedish enemies and their Hanseatic allies. Although this failed in the longer term to deliver peace to the Baltic, James avoided further military entanglements in the region, though he permitted Scottish sea captains, such as Andrew Barton, to enlist in Danish service. Similar unofficial aid was extended

to the deposed Christian II in the 1520s, though this, together with the ongoing disagreement over the status of the Northern Isles, did little to strengthen ties with Christian's rival, Frederick II. Indeed, Scotland's official relations with both the kings of Denmark-Norway and newly independent Sweden remained formal rather than close for the remainder of the 16th century, until *James VI married the Danish princess Anne in 1589.

By contrast, commercial relations between Scotland and Scandinavia blossomed from the later 15th century. Scottish vessels heading for the Baltic (see GERMANY, THE BALTIC, AND POLAND: 1) were obliged to pay a toll at Elsinore, upon entering or leaving the Øresund. Although many of these vessels headed for the more significant markets of Gdansk and Stralsund, some Scottish merchants also traded in the Sound towns, including Copenhagen, where they sold salt, coal, and cloth. In the later 14th century some Scots had purchased herring at the Scanian fairs, but by the 16th century Scottish merchants sought timber rather than fish in Scandinavia. Timber was also the mainstay of the revival of trade with Norway and, by 1546, with the Swedish port of Lödöse, though as yet Scottish vessels rarely reached the eastern Swedish or Finnish ports. Some indication of the importance of the timber trade is indicated by the arrival, at *Dundee alone, of at least eleven Scandinavian vessels in 1551, ten of them laden with timber.

This burgeoning trade—developed following the introduction of saw milling techniques to Scandinavia in the later 15th century—encouraged *emigration to the Scandinavian lands. Small Scottish communities of up to several hundred inhabitants were established in the major ports of the Sound region and at the Norwegian port of Bergen from the later 15th and early 16th centuries. Those at Elsinore and Copenhagen were large enough by the early 16th century to establish their own altars, dedicated to St Ninian, in local churches. Emigration was not, however, confined to merchants. Craftsmen, many of them involved in branches of the textile industry, also migrated, as did a substantial number of small-time pedlars, who traded in the rural areas of Denmark and Scania in particular. In addition there were students (see NORTHERN EUROPE: MONKS AND SCHOLARS; UNIVERSITIES: 1) and, in the early 16th century, Protestant exiles (see REFORMATION, THE), though both were vastly outnumbered by the pedlars and by the mercenaries (see MERCENARIES IN EUROPE) who were recruited by the Danish army in the 16th century. By the later 16th century other soldiers were to be found in Swedish service. Indeed, despite the frequent lack of close diplomatic relations between Scotland and Scandinavia, many thousands of Scots became familiar with Scandinavia in the later medieval and early modern periods through their own commercial enterprise or in mercenary service.   DDi

3. since 1600

Already by the late 16th century, Norwegian timber proved an enticing commodity to the Scottish trader. The mercantile association led many Scots to cross the North Sea, first to trade and then to settle. Trading links, based on the geographical proximity of Scotland and Norway, were bolstered through diplomatic ties in 1589 when Anne of Denmark, daughter of Frederik II, married *James VI of Scotland. Equal status for Scottish and Danish-Norwegian citizens in each other's kingdoms followed the marriage, fostering improved trading relations. In the century that followed, Scottish communities flourished throughout the Danish-Norwegian realm, particularly in Norway. So great did their presence and influence become that the 17th century is referred to in Norway as *Skottetide* (the Scottish period) while the trade in timber is called *Skottehandelen* (the Scottish trade).

Bergen, the most important trading centre in Denmark-Norway, hosted some 200 Scottish burgesses throughout the century, mostly from Orkney, the north-east, and Fife. As with any city, burgesses constitute only a fraction of the overall Scottish community. The numbers are extremely high, however, with few other cities anywhere in the North Sea and Baltic boasting over 30. Bergen can, therefore, clearly be seen as one of the most significant Scandinavian towns to Scotland in terms of trade and settlement. Nonetheless, elsewhere in Denmark-Norway, Scottish communities burgeoned, particularly around Stavanger, Trondheim, and Finnmark. This last, the most northerly part of Norway, was governed by John Cunningham from Fife between 1619 and 1651. He had a monopoly over all fishing in the region and encouraged the settlement of family and friends as part of his stabilization policy for the region. Cunningham was only one of several important Scots whose personal presence encouraged Scottish-Norwegian trade and settlement. By the 1630s Axel Mowatt, son of the Scottish admiral Andrew Mowatt, traded more timber to Scotland than any other individual and is reputed to have been the richest man in the kingdom. Scottish communities also grew around the towns flanking the Danish Sound, particularly in Malmø and Elsinore where the Leyell family proved particularly influential as tax collectors.

The influx of some 30,000 Scots into the Swedish army in the first half of the 17th century attracted many other Scots to Sweden (see MERCENARIES IN EUROPE). Soldiers often brought their families with

them and records of their kith and kin networks are abundant in Swedish archives. Individual Scots were often rewarded for their military service by land grants and ennoblement. Since much of this land had been newly conquered, this often placed the Scots on the frontiers of the Swedish empire, particularly along the Finnish border with *Russia and on the southern Baltic coast in Swedish Pommerania. However, the largest concentrations of Scots outside the army were found in the major cities of Stockholm, Gothenburg, and Åbo. Some 30 Scots received citizenship in the Swedish capital during the century. The majority of these men settled during the reign of Gustavus Adolphus and the regency of Axel Oxenstierna, a lifelong patron of the Scottish nation. Other Scots arrived in Stockholm during the Cromwellian occupation of Scotland after being invited there by their well-heeled countrymen.

It is said, with some justification, that Gothenburg was built by Scots. From the outset, Scotsmen formed part of the Council of Commerce in the city. Over 20 Scotsmen and one woman, Anna Cummings, became burgesses of the town after its foundation in 1619. The majority of these gained citizenship in the 1620s although their legacy spanned the century. John Spalding proved to be one of the most influential of these, serving as a councillor after 1640 and president of the Council of Commerce in 1658. He famously ejected the only English burgess of the city, Anthony Knipe, in 1643 although the reason for their dispute is unclear. John's son Andrew became governor of the city in 1697. The richest person in Sweden was also a Gothenburg burgess, John Maclean (Macklier) from Mull, the son of Hector Maclean, fifth baron of Duart. A Swedish parliamentarian and town councillor, his sons effectively controlled the town until the close of the century. Baron David Maclean became governor over the city and region of Gothenburg; Hans became president of the Court of Justice between 1676 and 1696; and Gustaf Maclean acted as commandant of the city garrison. John Maclean himself was so well established that he provided military support for the Covenanters in 1639 (see COVENANT, WARS OF THE) and privately funded the marquis of Montrose's expedition in 1649–50.

The causes of Scottish *emigration were different in the two Scandinavian kingdoms. In Denmark-Norway, the regal alliance between the Scottish and Danish-Norwegian courts sparked a new wave of mercantile migration after 1589. In Sweden, Scottish communities came largely as a spin-off from the massive military engagement of Scots in Sweden throughout the 17th century. In both instances the Scottish community made a significant impact on both their native and adopted homelands. SM

schools and schooling: 1. to 1696; 2. 1696–1872; 3. Highlands; 4. mass education, 1872–present.

1. to 1696

The records we can draw on for medieval Scottish education are scarce compared with those available for the later 16th and the 17th centuries: mostly, they consist of a few surviving burgh records and monastic and episcopal registers. For the early medieval period and for Celtic schools, record is even more meagre. In the 11th century, Sulein, later a Welsh bishop, studied the seven liberal arts at an unknown Scottish site. The Celtic *ferleyn* might be a teacher of theology as well as arts. The so-called *rex scolarum* (chief of the schools) had a lesser status. Tenants of school lands (*scolocs*) left traces of education in the Highlands in *place names, but further details are hard to come by.

The reorganization of the church in and after the reign of *David I (1124–53) resulted in new-style foundations. Seats of sheriffdoms, like Perth, often had schools, usually under monastic patrons. The new diocesan chancellors might have authority not just over cathedral schools, but also over diocesan schoolmasters elsewhere. Some Benedictine and Augustinian houses might have almonry schools. Paisley abbey's problem was solved by employing secular chaplains as schoolmasters. At *St Andrews, seat of the bishop as well as the site of a major Augustinian foundation, the grammar school was under the archdeacon and the music school under the priory. Visitors spoke highly of Scottish musicianship. Perhaps the most celebrated polyphonic composer was Robert Carver, a canon of the Augustinian abbey at Scone (see MUSIC, ECCLESIASTICAL). The place of other religious orders has been undervalued in the past. At Kinross, Cistercian monks were taught by an Italian humanist in the 15th century. At religious houses from Beauly in the north to Sweetheart in the south-west, gentlemen's sons received a training. And daughters of good family were taught in nunneries such as Elcho, Aberdour, and Haddington. Dominican friars, themselves usually the product of the *urban society in which their houses were located, often taught grammar, as at Glasgow and Ayr.

The century after 1450 saw the foundation of over fifty collegiate churches of secular priests. Such churches required the education of boy choristers, who sometimes, as at Lochwinnoch, were trained in grammar as well as music. Most schooling was, as late as 1500, run by one of the branches of the church. But lay interest and control was growing. The result was sometimes conflict, as between the town and the cathedral chancellor when the burgh of *Aberdeen appointed a lay graduate, Hugh Munro, to its grammar school in 1538, or when Andrew Simson, a married man, was appointed to a similar post in Perth. In the countryside, 'household schools', based in the houses of lairds, are the most enigmatic of medieval foundations but where they can be proved to have existed, as at Huntly, they provided for sons of kin or farming neighbours as well as the sons of the house itself. Boys could board with kinsfolk as the Homes of Wedderburn did at Elphinstone. Distance was not a problem: a young Waus from Wigtownshire was educated over 100 miles (161 km) away in Musselburgh. Although lay control was increasing, the main educators were chaplains supported by minor benefices or by stents on parish ploughgates. They were, as a result, often poorly paid.

The notion that it was the *Reformation which brought about a school in every parish is misconceived. Documentation exists for about 100 schools before that. Yet the need for a national programme for education of the young was by the 16th century part of a broad, agreed humanist agenda. It featured in the first Council of Trent, which adjourned in 1547, and the provincial council of the Scottish church (see CHURCH INSTITUTIONS: 2) which met in 1549 issued a stern reminder of the need for a school in every parish. Education is rather better documented after the Reformation, but this documentation has been neglected in favour of speculation: over 300 massive volumes of the Registers of Deeds starting from 1554 supply names of schools and masters and help confirm not only teaching but continuity of schooling before and after 1560. The *First Book of Discipline*, compiled by a team of the 'six Johns', Protestant reformers who included *John Knox, was specific about its aim of a parish school in every parish and for urban centres they specified 'schools of full exercise' on the French and Genevan model. Yet, a substantial part of the *Book of Discipline*'s long section on education was modelled on, and even copied from, Trent. The Reformation marked not the beginning of a parish school network but its refoundation on a different and more secure basis. The initial problem for the Protestant reformers was that many church and chapel schools were rootless or in the control of 'sacrilegious' lairds. And Catholic schoolmasters, who had contracts of employment, were less easy to dislodge than Catholic priests. William Roberton, Catholic master of Edinburgh's grammar school, successfully resisted his dismissal by taking his Protestant employers to the Court of *Session; he was not pensioned off until 1584.

The reduction of ecclesiastical music to four-part tunes (see CULTURE: 10) is reflected in an apparent lack of interest in musical education until *James VI's decision to revive the song schools. Meantime, collegiate churches were no more, cathedral vicars choral were disbanded, and the Chapel Royal at Stirling, founded by *James IV, neglected. The new song schools could take scholars only so far. A few were much better than the others: those at *Aberdeen and *Glasgow, where Duncan Burnett was the teacher in the 1620s, were familiar with European music, but it was hard to train composers with no prospects of advancement beyond the song-school stage. Aristocratic households were often music centres, however, so somehow the musical tradition survived. Instrumental, rather than advanced choral work, was developed (see CULTURE: 15).

The scarcity of trained men in the early years after the Reformation put the Protestant ministry and schooling into competition with each other. Parish ministers were paid more than schoolmasters, though as yet neither as much as envisioned in the *First Book of Discipline* because of the failure of the new church to inherit the whole income of the old. Even so, the General Assembly in 1580 considered reducing the number of parishes listed (over 900) to 600, due to a continuing scarcity of candidates for the ministry. Parish schoolmasters must have been in a still worse plight: they were paid from parish dues, teinds, or annual rents for taking on extra duties as readers, session clerks, or precentors (takers-up of psalms). They were, in a sense, the equivalent of the pre-Reformation chaplain, underpaid and underqualified. They were skilled only in the vernacular, not Latin, and as a result could teach only in the vernacular or 'Inglis' schools, which taught children up to the age of about 7, and not the grammar schools, which gave boys a much more specific education up to the age of 12 or so. Often, lay lairds were forced to make good the deficiency, preferably on sites that suited themselves. In time, however, a new breed of university-trained masters would fill the gap. These learned schoolmasters produced new Renaissance-style grammar and conduct books; they would come much closer to fulfilling the aim of education in a godly society, which was, the *Book of Discipline* insisted, training in religion and virtue.

The reformers' plans were ambitious. How great an impact they had, in the first generation after 1560, on parishioners who were already adults is a matter of conjecture. For a considerable time after 1560, the device was hit upon of using the young to educate the old or the recalcitrant. Parents as well as servants and apprentices from the 'rascal multitude' were forced to learn their catechism, by rote, in Aberdeen by repeating passages read out to them by two boys from the grammar school. At a higher level, it is doubtful if any town but Edinburgh could aspire to the 'full exercise' status envisaged in 1560. Latin schools varied in their aims: some were full-course grammar schools, giving a training for *university to follow; some were shorter course schools; and some provided only elementary competence in Latin. Greek is occasionally to be found in a few of these schools but, like Hebrew, it was essentially a university subject, though the alphabets could be attempted.

As late as the first two decades of the 17th century, the General Assembly was worried about school numbers, though the fact of increased numbers at universities suggests that there must have been more schools and a higher school population. But the Assembly may have been more concerned about control of education. It regularly fretted about girls' and other unregulated, private schools, which it saw as potential seedbeds of papistry. An act of the privy council of 1616 encouraged parish schools where convenient for heritors (a new term of the 17th century for landed proprietors), though many of them were only emerging from debt and reluctant to fund large-scale enterprises. Of the c.800 schools recorded between 1560 and 1633, somewhat more than a half were sited in or next to the parish church. But over 300 were not, and were thus less under church supervision. The government, convinced of its mission to reduce the influence of the *Gaelic language, promoted Lowland-type schools in the Highlands: Lochhead (Campbeltown), for example, was founded in 1622. The 17th century saw steady advance, even in the furthest margins of the country. A school was founded at Scalloway in Shetland in 1612 and Orkney had no fewer than seven schools by 1633.

Bibles were expensive and little used in schools before the 1630s. The Arbuthnot bible, printed in Edinburgh in 1579 and authorized by the General Assembly for use in parish churches, cost almost £5, the equivalent of a craftsman's wage for about six weeks. The main religious texts used in schools were Calvin's catechism, usually in rudimentary question-and-answer format and costing a few pence, and the psalmbook; psalms sung to a handful of well-known common tunes provided some of the sugar to make the medicine go down more readily. It was only at about the middle of the 17th century that New Testaments, often in an abridged format for children and produced in large print runs, were becoming available at an affordable cost. Other kinds of schools were by then proliferating. Writing schools opened, as did fencing schools. By 1663 Glasgow had no fewer than seventeen authorized teachers, including Huguenots hired by the city to teach French. Dutch was available in Edinburgh. High standards prevailed everywhere in Latin verse and prose. And basic schooling, by the time of the Education Act of 1696, was widely established, in what already amounted to a national network of parish schools.   JD

2. 1696–1872

The *Book of Discipline* of 1560 remained as a widely agreed point of reference well into the 19th century for both church and state in framing their educational policies: first, the provision of publicly funded 'community' schooling—especially in reading—for all, girls as well as boys; secondly, the ensuring of free or assisted schooling for the poor, and support for the able poor (boys) in gaining instruction in the higher subjects and then in their university courses; thirdly, not only an assurance of meritocratic advance for the able poor, but also a commitment from all that their sons would not be withdrawn from training for public and professional service in 'the commonwealth'. Despite the political and religious tumults of the 17th century, there was clear progress in implementing the programme: the state in 1633, 1646, and 1696 gave parliamentary backing for the funding of a parochial school system and the church acted as managers for the whole enterprise, locally and nationally.

By the 1690s, such was its success that—in the Lowlands, and in the southern and eastern Highlands at least—some 90 per cent of parishes were certainly provided with public schooling, perhaps supplemented in larger parishes by an extra community-funded school and/or small private schools. A very high proportion of the 'official' parochial schoolmasters were able to teach Latin and so prepare their charges for university studies. The 1696 Act was thus not, as often claimed, a beginning to national schooling in Scotland but, rather, a government reminder of the educational duties laid on hard-pressed localities in a decade of widespread famine (see HEALTH, FAMINE AND DISEASE) and of economic and social distress. Scotland was already before 1696, and remained thereafter, remarkably well supplied with schools.

Certainly, when in 1700 the synod of Glasgow and Ayr—comprising presbyteries across westcentral Scotland—set up an enquiry into schooling within its bounds, the replies from presbyteries showed not the least concern about any lack of provision of schools but concentrated entirely on the curriculum that was being taught and on the effectiveness of its teaching: they wanted to make early instruction more enjoyable for the youngest children, and hence more productive; and then to offer, at the higher stages, alternatives or additions to Latin, with more practical mathematics, modern languages, geography, and commercial history for those whose careers did not depend on their

going to university. And this, it should be noted, was before the parliamentary *union of 1707 with England. This interest in Scotland in expanding the curriculum and providing 'modern' subjects of instruction—the better to serve a commercial nation—would continue throughout the century.

And so too, where still needed, did efforts to ensure easily accessible schooling to all, especially where the sheer physical extent of the parishes (particularly the very unwieldy parishes of the Highlands, rent apart by rivers and lochs and mountain ranges) made it impossible to serve the entire population by one well-placed parish school. By the end of the 18th century only the smallest of Lowland parishes—and few of them—had only one school; local effort supplemented public provision, including sharing schools with neighbouring parishes, to serve outlying or detached districts (see RURAL SOCIETY: 5). Where evidence is available to us, we find, very generally in the Highlands and Islands, valiant efforts being made to extend school provision, publicly and privately. There was also some help from the work of the SSPCK; its charity schools were intended to supplement local efforts in public school provision but its insensitive regulations sometimes badly hindered local initiatives (see SCHOOLS AND SCHOOLING: 3).

In both Lowlands and Highlands, deficiencies in the extent of public schooling were often supplied, privately, by local parental effort: initial teaching of reading was very frequently given in the home, with further instruction being provided (in districts far from a parochial school) by crofters and tenants engaging 'a young man' to board with them in the winter months and teach the three Rs. In the Lowlands especially, when parents were dissatisfied with the condition and efficiency of the local public school, they might gather subscriptions to provide a good salary to another teacher, who was able to instruct well in whatever subjects they demanded (including Latin and Greek if these were not otherwise available).

The results of all this activity are well shown in Sir John Sinclair's very remarkable parish-by-parish OSA in the 1790s. Throughout over 900 returns there was matter-of-fact expectation that the local population—certainly all but the oldest inhabitants—should read with some ease, and that many (but fewer girls) would also be able to write as well as 'compt'. Scotland may be said to have achieved—more likely, to have continued to achieve—the goal of a very substantially literate population. The OSA was in general little concerned with the extent of available schooling, much more with publicizing the poor state into which the legal provision had sometimes fallen, because able teachers could not be attracted to parish schools which too often offered only very low levels of stipend (fixed in 1696, and since seriously eroded by inflation) and low returns from the stated fees allowed by kirk sessions. In many districts, effective teaching in the higher subjects could be had only from private and subscription teachers. These revelations forced government to act in 1803 to amend the earlier legislation: salaries were significantly upgraded and conditions improved, while additional (side) schools could be funded from increased local taxation. The parochial school system was clearly revitalized as a result. And, yet, in the 1820s and 1830s it was still responsible for schooling only about half of the nation's children.

The 18th century had seen an explosion in the teaching of modern subjects, partly through the development of the so-called Academy movement. As we have seen, this was heralded in 1700 in the suggestions sent in to the synod of Glasgow and Ayr; in 1723 the burgh school of Dumfries had added a range of 'commercial' subjects to its classical teaching, while by the 1740s the burgh school of Ayr was reconstructing itself as three schools in one, in a pattern that would later be widely followed—an English school, a mathematical school, and a classical school—it being open to parents to send their children to any one or two or even to all three. By the 1760s when the Perth Academy, the first so named, was opened, there were already schools (including a number of parochial schools) where the masters had taken on the teaching of modern subjects—including practical mathematics, land mensuration, and bookkeeping, as well as geography and French or Italian. The larger and more innovative academies founded on, or as at Perth alongside, burgh grammar schools even ventured to offer an alternative 'modern' university-style course, which was cheaper because it was nearer to home and intended to telescope four annual sessions at college into two very full years of academy instruction. In the burghs and in populous parishes, in the later 18th and earlier 19th centuries, substantial numbers of private schools of all varieties were being set up. They ranged from those teaching the elements (according to whatever was the latest and most novel teaching method, perhaps) to those providing superior instruction in subjects for which parental demand was creating a lively market, whether in classical and modern languages or in general, commercially useful subjects and in career-oriented subjects such as bookkeeping and navigation.

Government was active in the earlier 19th century in making surveys of the extent and effectiveness and, more incidentally, quality of the available schooling. From these surveys we can judge the use that was being made of the schools and also evaluate the likely levels of literacy in the population of Scotland in this period—much more securely than from signatures on marriage registers, for instance. It was then considered, based on Prussian experience, that if a nation had one in eight of its population at school it was likely to be well educated; if it had one in six at school it was making all the provision necessary for a thoroughly educated population. Analysis of the 1834 survey shows that Scotland as a whole had some one in eight at school at the time it was made but, more importantly, that one in five or six were enrolled at school, and were reading or learning to read. The machinery for providing a highly literate population was thus well in place, and by all accounts had been so for some time.

That was to continue in the 19th century, even when particular groups—with particular axes to grind—sought to claim otherwise. Established church Evangelicals, for example, committed to the view that only schooling directly under the management and supervision of the church was truly effective in producing a population morally and religiously as well as secularly instructed, preposterously declared that Scotland in the 1830s was 'a half-educated nation' and gave gullible historians a sharp and wholly misleading phrase to retail later about the state of Scottish schooling. The NSA, again constructed from parish reports in the years 1833–44, confirmed the results of the government surveys and the high literacy levels, even in the industrialized towns (see URBAN SOCIETY: 4).

Successive attempts, after the *Disruption in 1843, made mainly by the now Free Church Evangelicals, to wrest the management of the parochial schools out of the hands of the established church, served in the end only to defeat more balanced proposals to legislate for a new national system of schooling. Meanwhile government became more concerned that its greatly increased expenditure on schools, particularly under the post-1847 privy council grants-in-aid scheme, required much greater and more exacting supervision from the centre. It began, for its own wilful purposes, to proclaim the total inadequacy and unutterable confusion of the existing highly pluralistic provision of schools. By the 1860s it seemed determined to prove that Scottish educational needs in the early 1870s could be met only by an inclusive, nationwide, centrally controlled state system—and that even when its own published researches belied these condemnations. Indeed, its statements flew in the face of the evidence which was to be found tucked away in its own surveys, made by a commission of enquiry in 1864 and then in tables constructed in 1871 as part of that year's census. This evidence showed that—even in the remoter Highlands and in economically deprived urban districts, though there with greater difficulties—enrolments and attendances at school were, especially for those aged 7–12 years, at a very high level: in fact, though this was as yet unknown, at levels which would not be matched in the 1880s and 1890s under the new school-board system with its compulsory attendance regulations. Return after return from parishes in 1864 had commented, 'no additional schools required', and seemed very content with the range and quality of the existing, often highly varied provision of local schooling; but the commission and the government chose to ignore such uncongenial statements. The 1872 Act was to change Scottish school education dramatically, but it was by no means always going to be for the better.   DJW

3. Highlands

Historians have long observed that the Highlands and Islands faced two major hindrances to the provision of schooling after the *Reformation. First, there was the attempt to impose a Lowland-inspired policy to erect parochial schools paid from a local tax based on an alien structure of landholding, as part of 17th-century legislation intended to infiltrate Protestantism and also to extirpate the *Gaelic language and culture. Secondly, such a Lowland-style provision (one public school in a small and compact parish) was entirely inadequate in the vast parishes of the Highlands and Islands, with parish populations scattered and divided off from each other by difficult seas and rivers, by lochs and mountains. Since one public school, wherever placed, was hardly better than none at all, antagonistic and hard-pressed landowners generally provided nothing. Hence, so the presumption continues, the Highlands and Islands were bereft of schools in the 17th and earlier 18th centuries, until outside charitable agencies emerged, ready to supply teachers to the north and west; government and the church combined to spread Presbyterianism and the English language through the SSPCK and, later, Evangelical societies based in the Lowlands began to send out schoolteacher-catechists—a few of them seeking greater success by teaching only in and through Gaelic. And yet, in the 1820s and 1830s, church Evangelicals were still protesting that in much of the Highlands and in the Islands there was widespread moral, religious, and secular ignorance. But what was the true picture? (see RELIGIOUS LIFE: 8).

Church and estate records are less full for the Highlands than for the Lowlands, yet they can still provide good data on educational developments. For instance, we know that in the southern and eastern mainland of the Highlands—Argyll, Perthshire, Easter Ross—there was, in the later 17th century, a provision of schools close to that found in the Lowlands: by the 1690s, nearly 90 per cent of the parishes had schools, including grammar schools, with some parishes able to support additional schools to serve a well-scattered population, either from the legal fund or by subscription. And by the mid 18th century, for all the impact of two *Jacobite rebellions, there was much local innovation in securing schooling to the people. In some parishes, as an SSPCK report showed in 1755, up to five or six schools might be provided out of the legal fund (from two or even three times the obligatory amount). Also, SSPCK teachers were being, happily, pressurized by parents into offering much beyond the three Rs suggested by the Society (including the classics, navigation, bookkeeping); and in remote crofting areas, parents engaged young men in winter to teach those who were not yet old and sturdy enough to walk or ride to a 'proper' school some distance away. In addition, it was not at all uncommon for mothers and aunts to teach the alphabet and to begin reading with *children at home (much noted in Caithness, Orkney, and Shetland).

In the course of the 18th century, parents had made remarkable efforts to secure as good a schooling as possible for their children, and continued to do so in the early 19th century, as we can see from government surveys, covering the whole of Scotland, made in 1818 and 1834. In 1818 the very acceptable proportion of one in nine or ten of the Highland population was at school: over one-third in publicly funded (parochial) schools, less than a quarter in 'outside' charity schools, and over a third in locally funded or private adventure schools. By 1834, when one in eight or nine of the population was actually at school, one in six was recorded as reading or learning to read and one in twelve as writing or learning to write. These were almost exactly the same proportions as were found in the much richer Lowland counties of the central belt, which proudly claimed universal reading literacy.

Evangelical and other (Lowland) churchmen who in the 1830s bitterly complained of the 'educational wastelands' of the Highlands and Islands were either grossly ignorant of the real situation or, much more likely, were—for their own purposes, in their battles with the state—ready to mislead the nation. There were no such educational wastelands, and this was soon to be confirmed in the parish returns made in 1834–44 to the NSA. Indeed, other surveys from the 1820s and 1830s reveal remarkable data about the strength of Highland schooling, for example, in the quality of the teaching force in areas such as Easter Ross, Cromarty, and Caithness. But there is no doubt that such new-found stability in schooling was seriously disrupted by that long period of extraordinary social and economic distress signalled by the widespread famines (see HEALTH, FAMINE, AND DISEASE: 3) of the later 1830s and mid- and later 1840s. Again, however, there was remarkable resilience, for by the 1860s the numbers at school in the Highlands and Islands were at a new high, at one in six or seven of the population, and with rates of attendance which—as in the Lowlands—would not be bettered even after 1872 and the coming of the new state system of schools and compulsory education. No doubt the amount of teaching in, and through, the Gaelic language had reduced in the course of the 19th century, in part again reflecting parental choice; it would be the final decades of that century before it was returned to anything like its former prominence, and achieve formal recognition under the new state regime. DJW

4. mass education, 1872–present

Schooling from 1872 until the present day has aimed to provide a system of mass education for an increasingly broad range of ages and of social groups. Although the development of mass education has been fraught with many difficulties and controversies, these were not nearly so great as in England or in some parts of mainland Europe. Scottish educational culture was quite well disposed towards mass provision because of the legacy of Presbyterian democracy (see SOCIAL CLASS). Indeed, although the 1872 Education (Scotland) Act was formally responsible for establishing the system of mass elementary education (catering for the ages of approximately 6 to 12), in many respects it simply consolidated what had been happening since the 1840s under the auspices of the Presbyterian churches and the various voluntary efforts of secular philanthropists. The change in 1872 was more a matter of governance than of provision: the transfer to secular public authorities, in the form of nearly 1,000 elected school boards, of a very extensive but also fragmented pattern of provision (see GOVERNMENT AND ADMINISTRATION: 2).

A consequence of the fairly uncontroversial nature of the 1872 reform was that attention immediately shifted to the stages of schooling after age 12; until the 1960s, there was little but incremental change to elementary (later called primary) schooling, and there was no systematic structural change to it at any time in the 20th century. In relation to secondary schooling, controversy was fierce, on three main grounds. The first was that the SED—the government department responsible for Scottish schools after 1885—wanted to expand post-elementary provision without, however, creating a system of secondary education for all. Their preferred route for the majority of children was through supplementary courses (later called advanced divisions) in elementary schools, taking them to about age 14 when they would leave to enter work. The curriculum of these advanced divisions was quite narrowly concerned with vocational skills rather than the breadth which characterized the leaving certificate that had been introduced in 1888 as the main route to university. This separation between the advanced divisions and a full secondary education was controversial because it seemed to betray the long-standing Scottish tradition that the parish school could be a route to the university or the professions.

The second source of controversy was that the urban secondary schools which did exist at that time became more selective and therefore more socially exclusive as a result of the SED's preference that elementary schooling should be a stage that would terminate at age 12. Previously, many urban academies had their own primary departments, or—as in the case of the Merchant Company schools in Edinburgh—drew children from local schools across the city. As the urban academies started to define themselves as a clearly distinct secondary stage of schooling, and to charge fees accordingly, the opportunities for working-class advancement were restricted; this selectivity contradicted the belief that opportunities for progress in Scottish education were dependent on merit rather than on wealth or status. Only in rural academies—the 'omnibus schools' of the small burghs—did the tradition of open access to post-elementary schooling survive. There were in total about 60 secondaries—rural or urban—in existence in 1900.

The third source of controversy related to the SED's attempt to respond to some of the concerns about divisive secondary provision by creating about 200 'Higher Grade' schools serving urban areas that were populated mostly by the skilled working class. They were loosely modelled on German vocational schools and offered a vocationally oriented but also liberal secondary education in parallel to the academies. This was controversial because, until the 1920s, the Higher Grade schools were discouraged from presenting their pupils for the main leaving certificate (confusingly also known as the Higher Grade), and because even liberal vocational schools were believed by some to be inimical to the liberal breadth of the traditional Scottish curriculum.

Despite the controversies, however, the debate was resolved in favour of mass secondary education as early as the 1918 Education (Scotland) Act. This established the principle of free and universal secondary schooling, although financial crises and resistance from the SED delayed its full implementation for a couple of decades. The Higher Grade schools joined the old academies as a new senior secondary sector, all permitted to present pupils for the leaving certificate, and now serving a much broader section of the population because of the location of the Higher Grade schools in working-class districts. By the late 1930s, most of the advanced divisions of the elementary schools had been transformed into junior secondaries, from which pupils would leave by age 14. Allocation between senior and junior secondaries was on the basis of a test of general intelligence taken in the last year of primary education, at age 12—the 'qualifying examination' (colloquially known as 'the qualy'). SED officials believed that only a minority of pupils would be intellectually suited to the full five years of secondary education available in the senior secondaries; indeed, Sir Henry *Craik (secretary of the SED between 1885 and 1904) argued that the proportion thus suited would be no more than about 10 per cent.

The same principle of inclusiveness in the 1918 Act also brought into the public system almost all the schools run by the Roman Catholic Church, while retaining a powerful role for the church in relation to the curriculum and to the appointment of senior staff. Most of these schools served areas of great poverty, because most of the Scottish *Roman Catholic community had its origins in Irish *immigrant labour in the mid-19th century. The majority of post-elementary Catholic schools became junior secondaries, but there were also eleven senior secondaries. The 1918 Act also replaced the school boards with 38 specialist education authorities, elected by a form of proportional representation in order to safeguard the interests of the Catholic population and their public schools. These authorities were subsumed into general local government in 1929.

The pattern of provision remained quite stable from the 1930s until the 1960s. The Education (Scotland) Act of 1945 was much more of a consolidating measure than its counterpart in England and Wales in 1944, in the sense that some kind of secondary schooling for all was, by then, more than a decade old. Nevertheless, the political atmosphere of progressive social reform in the post-war period helped to create an expectation that mass schooling was a complement to mass democracy, and from this hope came the next wave of radical ideas. The Labour Secretary of State for Scotland during the wartime coalition government, Thomas *Johnston, had established an Educational Advisory Council to propose ways in which education could respond to the ideals of a common citizen-

ship. The most radical of the Council's reports, in 1947, was on secondary education. It recommended a system of undifferentiated secondary schools, based on what it presented as the traditional Scottish model of the rural omnibus school, and proposed also that external examinations should be ended, replaced by assessment conducted by teachers and moderated by inspectors. The purpose of these and of many other more detailed recommendations was to use schooling as a way of overcoming social divisions, of fostering individual creativity, and of instilling a voluntary acceptance of the value of social cohesion—in the words of the report, 'to fill the years of youth with security, graciousness and ordered freedom'. The proposals, if implemented, would have ended selection for secondary school and would have pre-empted the dominant role which external examinations were later to have in secondary education. That it was not accepted by the Labour government (Tom Johnston having left parliamentary politics) or its Conservative successor did not prevent the report's becoming a point of reference for radical campaigners throughout the 1950s.

Although there was no structural change at that time, the selective system nevertheless did change slowly, aided by the raising of the minimum school leaving age to 15 in 1947. The proportion of children entering the senior secondaries rose from under 30 per cent in the late 1930s to over 40 per cent by the end of the 1950s. There was also an attempt by the SED to develop a coherent and distinctive philosophy of vocational education for the junior secondaries, culminating in a report by the Chief Inspector of Schools, John Brunton, in 1963. But the pressure of academic drift proved irresistible. When the new Ordinary Grade examination was introduced in 1962, it began to be used by many junior secondaries as a way of proving their academic credentials. The sense that academic merit was therefore not confined to the fixed pool which the SED had envisaged in the 1920s was encouraged by research evidence. Gaining access to a senior secondary through the qualifying examination was much more likely for middle-class pupils than for those of the working class, especially among those whose attainment was in the bottom half of the distribution of scores. This was resented not only on the radical grounds that it was unfair and contrary to the Scottish tradition of meritocracy, but also because it was wasteful of talent at a time when national economic success was believed to rest on widespread education.

The Labour government inaugurated the ending of selection in 1965, recommending to the local authorities that they organize just one type of secondary school: non-selective comprehensive schools, taking all the children in a designated neighbourhood, providing all of them with an essentially common education up to the leaving age (which was raised to 16 in 1973), and offering all of them the opportunity to progress beyond that through the Higher Grade examination to higher education. As with the introduction of universal elementary education a century earlier, this reform was less controversial in Scotland than in England, largely because of the experience of omnibus schools which were believed to represent the true national tradition. By the late 1970s, 79 per cent of secondary pupils were in non-selective schools. By the early 1980s, this had risen to 95 per cent, or all pupils in the public sector; the only remaining selective schools were private.

The system rapidly became and remained popular so that, even in the 1990s after a great deal of controversy about comprehensive schooling had spilled over the border from England, surveys showed that three-quarters of Scots opposed a return to selection. One of the reasons for the general acceptance was that Scottish comprehensives turned out to be effective, not only in the sense that they raised attainment for all social groups, but also in that they narrowed the gap in attainment between working-class and middle-class pupils. They had an even more striking impact on differences between boys and girls, so that attainment among girls overtook that of boys by the early 1980s. The capacity of the schools to overcome social inequalities was aided by the 1975 reform of local government, by which education was transferred to nine mainland authorities and three smaller island ones. The large authorities covering urban areas were able to link their educational policies to some limited capacity to redistribute resources from richer districts to poorer ones, and so were able to embed education in a wider programme of social reform.

In helping to overcome the effects of social disadvantage, the comprehensive schools fulfilled some of the hopes of their proponents in the 1950s and the 1947 Advisory Council. They also started to fulfil Tom Johnston's aspirations for a common citizenship. During the 1980s, the curriculum and assessment at ages 14–16 were reformed to cater for the whole ability range, through a new system of Standard Grade courses replacing the Ordinary Grade. This extended worthwhile certification to a much wider population. Thus, in 1965 just 22 per cent of the age group achieved five or more passes in Ordinary Grade; by 1995, the proportion attaining an equivalent level in Standard Grade was 54 per cent. Social class differences in access to the curriculum at these ages declined, and most gender differences vanished. These results at age 16 then

encouraged more pupils to stay on beyond that (up from 22 per cent staying on beyond age 15 in 1967 to 74 per cent staying on beyond 16 in 1994). The 1994 proposals to unify all courses for ages 16–19—known as Higher Still—are likely to have the same effect on that age group as Standard Grade had on the preceding stage. This, in turn, is likely to promote wider access to university; as it was, the effects of comprehensive schooling and the associated curricular changes had increased entry rates to higher education from under 9 per cent in 1962 to 46 per cent in 1996. Staying on, whether beyond 16 or into higher education, was also encouraged by the effects of earlier expansion. The children of better educated parents acquired from them an unprecedented appetite for education beyond the minimum, and so expansion bred further expansion from generation to generation.

The whole style of learning—in primary as well as secondary—became more relaxed. Children began to be treated as individuals, following the SED Memorandum of 1965 on child-centred education in primary schools and the development of the system of child guidance in secondaries from the 1970s onwards. Explicit programmes of promoting equal gender opportunities were introduced in the 1980s, and were joined in the early 1990s by the promotion of equal opportunities for different ethnic groups. Girls certainly responded: their general aspirations for future life had come to resemble boys' by the early 1980s, and their success in examinations translated into success in entering higher education by the 1990s. By that time, too, there was some evidence that Asian ethnic groups were particularly successful in gaining access to post-school courses. Surveys showed, moreover, that pupils of all social types were able to enjoy school, and could develop interests in specific subjects. The changing structure and climate of schools had made that possible even while pupils could also continue to use school as a route to a job or to post-school education.

In many respects, therefore, the system which had been established by the mid-1990s had fulfilled many of the aspirations of the radical campaigners for mass education, and had shown that the doubts from the SED about the possibility of a unified secondary system were misplaced. Nevertheless, the debate had moved on. It had come to be accepted that schooling could not, on its own, overcome social divisions. Thus, by the late 1980s, the principle of the neighbourhood comprehensive had been undermined, partly because the Conservative government after 1979 had allowed parents much greater choice of school for their children, and partly because general social change had widened inequalities between affluent and deprived neighbourhoods. Because of this—and because of declining birth rates (see POPULATION PATTERNS: 2)—some secondary schools in the peripheral *housing schemes of the large cities had become so small as not to be educationally viable, and were, in effect, reinforcing social segregation rather than overcoming it. The Conservative government's reform of local government in 1996 reduced the scope for redistribution in several urban areas, and so eroded local authorities' capacity to plan their schools as a whole. The devolution of managerial responsibilities to headteachers at the same time, although giving schools some flexibility which many professionals welcomed, also constrained the strategic role of local authorities.

The principle of non-selective secondary schooling remained inviolable in Scotland during the Conservative years from 1979 to 1997. So did the principle of public control: despite legislation in 1989 that would permit parents to remove their school from local authority control, only two small schools did so. But there was a sense that more had to be done to ensure that schools offered a broadly similar quality of education. The attention to performance indicators and other ways of measuring the quality of mass schooling was controversial. On the one hand, their proponents argued that they were necessary because a mass system required, in a democracy, some means of accountability. Their opponents argued, in contrast, that they undermined the freedom of individual teachers or schools to respond flexibly to the needs of individual children. Partly because of these disputes about accountability, schooling was politically more controversial at the time that the new Scottish *parliament was set up in 1999 than at any time in the preceding 125 years of striking expansion.   LP

Schottenklöster (monastery of Scots) is the name commonly given to the Irish Benedictine monasteries in south Germany taken over by Scots in the early 16th century. Ten monasteries, founded 1075–1232, were centred on the abbey of St James in Ratisbon (Regensburg) and later, following a decree of the fourth Lateran Council in 1215, were formed into a congregation under the authority of the Ratisbon abbot. In the 15th century, recruitment from Ireland dwindled and four monasteries either passed into German hands or sunk into decay. By 1500 the only community was at Ratisbon.

The Irish monks had continued to style themselves Scoti, the ancient designation of a native of Ireland. Meanwhile the myth had arisen that the monasteries belonged by right to Scots from Scotland, and an influential colony of Scottish traders had settled in Ratisbon. Almost inevitably, after a dispute, judgement was given in 1515 that the monasteries should be handed over to Scottish monks.

Following on the *Reformation in Scotland, Ninian Winzet, John *Knox's chief opponent, at least in priests, became abbot of Ratisbon and built up its community and school. Scots also settled in the Scotic monasteries at Würzburg (Franconia) and Erfurt (Thuringia). For the next two centuries, these three houses were fully integrated into their German setting and also committed to promoting Catholicism in Scotland.

During the Swedish wars Abbot William Ogilvie played a key role during the occupation of Würzburg and Alexander Baillie restored the fortunes of all three abbeys after the devastation of war. The long abbacy of Placid Fleming (1672–1720) raised Ratisbon to a position of prestige which it never lost, while the seminary established by him provided recruits for the monastery and thus a steady trickle of missionary priests in Scotland.

In Erfurt, where the Scots abbey became a priory dependent on Ratisbon, Fleming secured for his monks two permanent university professorships in philosophy. Scots monks made a significant contribution to German academic life, the most celebrated being Andrew Gordon, who died young in 1751. Marianus Brockie contributed notably to monastic historiography, though his Scottish *Monasticon* was less successful. Two monks were prominent in the Academy movement in the later 18th century: Ildephonse Kennedy and Abbot Benedict Arbuthnot.

During the Napoleonic Wars Gallus Robertson completed a highly dangerous mission on behalf of the British government. At this time, in the general secularization of religious houses, Würzburg and Erfurt were wound up. Ratisbon survived and was rehabilitated in 1820 but, despite efforts made by the Scottish bishops to provide recruits, was finally suppressed in 1862. The last monk, Anselm Robertson, helped to found the monastery at Fort Augustus in 1878.   MD

Scone is the traditional inaugural place of the kings of Scots and is the original home of the Stone of Destiny (see SCONE, STONE OF). It is situated in the Gowrie at a natural crossroads on the eastern bank of the Tay opposite *Perth, at the upper tidal limit and the lowest fording place. On the slopes to the north, overlooking Scone, are extensive prehistoric barrows and monuments, which provide an ancient landscape setting. The royal inaugural ceremonies (see KINGSHIP: 2) were held on an artificial flat-topped mound known as the Moot Hill, which stands on a river terrace with wide prospects to the west over the Tay.

The earliest reference to Scone is in AD 906 when *Constantine II and Bishop Cellach of St Andrews proclaimed new ecclesiastical laws from the 'Hill of Belief' (*collis credulitatis*) in the royal town (*civitas*) of Scone. Scone appears to have come to prominence only in the 10th century. There is no evidence for earlier Pictish royal activity there; the site is never mentioned prior to 906, and the name itself is Gaelic. The mound is now within the policies of Scone palace, where Alexander I established an Augustinian monastery c.1120 (see CHURCH INSTITUTIONS: 2). It appears to have succeeded an important early church and in the later Middle Ages became one of the most prosperous of Scotland's monasteries and a popular royal residence. Apart from the Moot Hill, which is a large, low oval mound (c.295 feet by 164 feet (c.90 m by 50 m)) standing 6.5–10 feet (2–3 m) high, there is little evidence of the medieval ceremonial arrangements. The mound is now crowned by a post-medieval church/burial aisle and the position of the monastic buildings is not known with any precision.

Historically, the best-attested inauguration is that of Alexander III in 1249, described in Bower's *Scotichronicon* (see KINGSHIP: 3). The ceremony was orchestrated by the earls of Strathearn and Fife, and involved an enthronement, presumably on the Stone of Destiny, a blessing by the bishop of St Andrews and a reading of the royal genealogy by the royal poet. The concept of a particular stone conferring legitimacy on royal inaugurations is a well-established feature of Irish royal inaugurations, which may have been introduced by the kings of Alba who claimed descent from Irish stock (see IRELAND: 2). In the 14th century the Stone of Destiny was removed to Westminster, where it was incorporated in a throne, which has been used in the coronation of English and subsequently British monarchs to the present day. Following the Wars of *Independence Scone continued to be used for inaugurations and was the site of a royal festival, despite the absence of the Stone.

STD

Scone, Stone of. Sometimes known as the Stone of Destiny, this is a rectangular block of sandstone on which the early kings of Alba, later Scotland, were inaugurated. It is the best known of all man-made symbols of Scottish nationhood. In 1296 it was removed from its site at Scone abbey, near Perth, by King Edward I of England, and placed in Westminster abbey where it became an element in the English and eventually British ritual of coronation. Its removal was the subject of Scottish grievance and of intermittent demands for its return until 1996, when—after 700 years of absence—it was returned to Scotland.

Very little is certain about the Stone's origin and early function. Weighing 335 lb (152 kg), it is a plain, somewhat battered slab of pinkish sandstone which probably comes from the Lower Old Red Sandstone rocks of the Perth region. This suggests (although there is no specific evidence as such) that it may have been an item in royal ceremonies of the Pictish kingdom centred on *Scone, and that it was taken over as a royal inaugural stone when *Kenneth mac Alpin, established his hegemony over the *Picts in AD 843.

The first firmly documented use of the Stone was in the inauguration of the boy-king Alexander III (1249–86) in 1249. But John of Fordun, who described the ceremony in much detail, stated that the seating of a king on the Stone was already an ancient ritual considered indispensable to kingly authority. Possibly Kenneth and all his successors were inaugurated on the Stone. Fordun stated that the Stone was brought out of Scone abbey into the open air; the king was then lifted onto it, apparently by the bishop of *St Andrews and several priests, and the regalia put into his grasp while several powerful earls acted as witnesses. This ritual was not a coronation, the sacramental ceremony involving anointing which spread through western Europe in the early Middle Ages; in the 13th century, this gave the English an excuse to claim that the kings of Scots were not truly sovereign.

The Stone soon became incorporated into Scottish myths of origin. It was said that the eponymous Princess Scota, daughter of a pharaoh, had travelled to Spain and then Ireland and, finding the Stone being used there as a throne, had brought it with her on her final journey to Scotland. By the mid-13th century, the legend was claiming that the Stone had come with Scota from Egypt, where it had been the stone pillow on which Jacob dreamed of the ladder up to Heaven. Modern scholars, however, point out that the use of stone seat-slabs was fairly common in royal rituals of post-Roman Europe, and especially in Ireland. It is thought that they symbolized a sacral relationship between king and land. The Stone of Scone was described by some early chroniclers as a carved marble throne, leading certain historians to think that this undecorated slab is either not the original or was a component of some larger object.

At Westminster abbey in 1296, Edward I offered the Stone to the shrine of Edward 'the Confessor' and a wooden throne—St Edward's Chair—was constructed to contain it, on which the British monarchs are still crowned. It was not clear at this period whether the Stone was royal property or belonged to the abbey. When Edward II prepared to return the Stone to the Scots, after the Treaty of Edinburgh in 1328, the abbot refused to give it up and may have fomented a popular riot at Westminster against its removal.

The emergence of modest, 'heraldic' nationalism (see NATIONAL IDENTITY: 5) in Scotland in the 19th century led to fresh requests for the Stone's return, which grew sharper as *nationalism became more conventionally political. At Christmas in 1950, a group of Nationalist students managed to enter the abbey and remove the Stone, which they brought secretly back to Scotland; it was given up to the authorities and returned to London a few months later. This feat not only inspired many songs and anecdotes but touched the patriotic feelings of many previously indifferent Scots; the Stone now rapidly returned to public awareness as a symbol of national identity.

In July 1996, the British prime minister, John Major, announced that the Stone would be returned to Scotland, although it was to be transported back to Westminster abbey on the occasion of future coronations. This unexpected decision was generally understood to be a political gesture to Scottish national feeling, at a time when support for the Conservative government in Scotland was at a low ebb. In spite of protests from the dean of Westminster, the Stone was extracted from St Edward's Chair and, after conservation work, was ceremonially borne from Holyrood to Edinburgh castle on St Andrew's Day, 30 November 1996. It was placed on permanent display in the Crown Room with the Scottish regalia. No convincing evidence exists for numerous claims that the Stone is a replica, and that the original remains hidden somewhere in Scotland. It is certainly the same object which Edward I took to Westminster in 1296.

CNA

Scots colleges were founded on the Continent, as it was impossible to establish in Scotland the seminaries decreed by the Council of Trent for training priests. The survival of the Roman Catholic Church in Scotland into the 18th century was very largely due to the priests trained in these Continental colleges. Of the four colleges, two were partly survivals of medieval foundations, while two were entirely new. Two were suppressed at the French Revolution and two still exist today (see also SCHOTTENKLÖSTER).

Douai
A college founded in 1580 by *Mary, Queen of Scots, and her ambassador in Paris, Archbishop James Beaton of Glasgow, it moved several times before finally settling at Douai in French Flanders. It was staffed and administered by Jesuits and from 1632 its rector was a Scot. Few if any of the students, however, were ordained priests at Douai; most entered Jesuit noviciates or moved on to the college in Rome. From 1765, after Jesuits were expelled from France, a Scottish Jesuit-run college existed for a short time at Dinant in Belgium, using the old register and thereby concealing the fact that Scots secular priests took over the college at Douai and produced priests for Scotland until it was suppressed by the Revolution in 1793.

Paris
A foundation of bursaries for students from the diocese of Moray had been established at Paris in 1325. In the 16th century it was hardly fulfilling its purpose, but efforts were made to revive it and James Beaton supported Catholic students in Paris. In 1603 he bequeathed a house and endowment for educating Scots priests, together with the archives of the medieval see of Glasgow and his own diplomatic papers. The two foundations were united in 1639–40. The college was staffed by Scots secular priests, with the local Carthusian prior as its superior. It was the only Scots college not conducted by Jesuits, most probably because in 1603 they had been expelled from Paris.

It was never exclusively a seminary for priests and in fact sheltered or educated many notable men. After the flight of King James VII and II to Paris in 1688, and under the leadership of priests of the family of Innes, the college flourished and played an important role in the Jacobite movement (see JACOBITISM). It enjoyed considerable prestige and was the repository of James's royal archives. Less happily, it was also a focus for a Jansenist outlook, which introduced a very divisive factor into Scottish Catholicism (see ROMAN CATHOLIC COMMUNITY) in the first half of the 18th century. In 1793 the college was sequestrated and was never refounded.

Rome
There had been a church and hospice for Scots pilgrims, and what remained of the property was incorporated into a college founded by Pope Clement VIII in 1600. Under Jesuit rectors, at times Italian and at times Scottish, the college suffered from disputes between secular priests and Jesuits, and between Scots and Italians. Nevertheless it provided many priests for Scotland and, together with the Roman Congregation *de Propaganda Fide* in charge of missionary work, was a crucial factor in maintaining the ethos of the Scottish church.

After the suppression of the Jesuits in 1773, the college rectors were Italian secular priests. When French troops occupied Rome in 1798, a Scots priest, Paul MacPherson, single-handedly brought Scottish and English students and Scottish archives from Rome through Italy and France to safety across the Channel, adding students and priceless archives from Paris on the way. Two years later he returned to Rome to be rector of the college. Since then the college has continued to be staffed by Scottish secular priests. In 1964 it moved to a less congested site outside the city.

Spain

The last foundation was in Madrid in 1627, the founder being Colonel William Semple, and the first rector his nephew, the Jesuit Hugh Semple. Administered by Spanish or Scots Jesuits until the Jesuits were expelled from Spain in 1767, it produced very few priests for Scotland and indeed had no students after 1734. The college received the Spanish king's patronage—to this day it bears the title Real Colegio (Royal College)—which gave it status but restricted its liberty. John Geddes, later bishop of Edinburgh, was successful in rescuing the property of the college and refounding it at Valladolid in 1771, since when it has been staffed by Scots secular priests. The college moved to Salamanca in 1988, allowing the students to attend the university there.

To complete the picture, two other colleges should be noted. The seminary at the *Schottenklöster* in Ratisbon contributed priests to the Scottish mission in the 18th and 19th centuries, and a short-lived college conducted by Irish religious at Rockwell, Co. Tipperary, Ireland (1864–74), also helped.

The pressing need for the Scots colleges gradually disappeared. From 1714 small seminaries in the east and west Highlands produced priests, or at least provided the initial education; then, when the French Revolution put an end, temporary or permanent, to the Continental colleges, better equipped seminaries were founded in Scotland. Today most priests are educated in Scotland but the colleges in Rome and Spain introduce an element of broader culture, while bursaries for Scottish priests and clerical students are available in France as compensation for property confiscated at the Revolution.   MD

Scots language is the name now given to the parallel variety of English spoken in Scotland since the first Anglo-Saxon speakers arrived north of the Tweed in the 7th century. It gradually supplanted *Gaelic as the principal spoken, and Latin as the principal written, language. In the 15th century, it was made one of the official languages of public record (see HISTORICAL SOURCES: 1). The name 'Scots' was first used for this language by a Scotsman in 1494; previously it had been called 'Inglis' or English, distinguishing it from Gaelic. During the 16th century it was called either Inglis or Scots. Throughout its history, Scots has developed separately from the southern varieties of English, though it has more in common with northern English, particularly in matters of vocabulary.

There are a series of features of the modern Scots language which distinguish it from modern Standard English.

1. A distinctive sound system. This has developed separately in Scotland since the Anglo-Saxon period. In particular, the long vowels and diphthongs have developed differently, resulting in contrasts such as dead/*deid*; sore/*sair*; cow/*coo*; full/*fou*; one/*ane*; good/*guid*; ball/*ba*; two/*twa, twae*; gold/*gowd*.

2. Vocabulary. Reflecting the different histories of Scotland and England, Scots vocabulary comes in part from different sources from English, though the core of Scots remains Anglo-Saxon:

   Gaelic: *loch, glen, whisky, clan, sporran, brogues, pibroch, ceilidh, ingle*;
   Norse (some shared with northern English): *brae, lass, midden, lug, flit, big* (build);
   Dutch: *golf, scone, croon* (sing gently), *loun* (rogue, lad), *callant* (lad), *bucht* (sheep-pen);
   French: *douce* (decent), *dour* (hard, unyielding), *fash, vennel* (lane), *caddie, hogmanay*.
   northern Anglo-Saxon items retained in Scots: *brig* (bridge), *kirk, greet* (weep), *breeks* (trousers).

   Some Scots vocabulary was later borrowed into Standard English, usually referring to Scottish things (mostly topographic features or cultural items). Some of these borrowings stem from the work of Sir Walter Scott in the early 19th century, which took awareness of things Scottish to a world audience.

3. Word formation. Inflectional: plurals *een* (eyes), *shune* (shoes), *kye* (cows); *thae* (those); verb paradigms, for example *gae* (go), *gaed; lauch* (laugh), *leuch; leap, lap; wirk* (work), *wrocht*.

4. Derivational. Almost entirely as English, but more frequent use of some word-forming elements, such as diminutives in -*ie* (for example, *lassie*); adjectives in -*some* (for example, *eightsome, wearisome*).

5. Syntax. Different rules for pluralizing the present tense of verbs, for example both 'They come here' and 'The boys comes here'; zero plural used for nouns of quantity or measurement with a cardinal number, for example 'twa mile', 'sax pund'.

6. Spelling. This has never been formalized into a standard system in Scots. Nevertheless there have been clearly preferred informal systems of spelling, differing at different periods. So, for example, in early Scots (up to c.1450) the preferred spelling of the Scots equivalent of 'good' was 'gude'; from 1450 on, the spelling 'guid' became more and more common alongside 'gude'; and by the late 17th century 'gude' would almost never be used, but always 'guid'.

Scots is divided into two main periods by linguistic historians: Older Scots (up to c.1700), further subdivided into Early Scots (up to c.1450) and Middle Scots (1450–1700); and Modern Scots (1700 to the present). Each of these periods has been documented in a major period dictionary in the course of the 20th century: for the modern period, SND; and for the Older Scots period, DOST. There is also an abridgement and combination of these into a single volume, with supplementary sources where DOST was still incomplete: CSD, which retains much of their historical detail but has no quotations. Scots is taught in undergraduate courses in some Scottish universities, and is included in postgraduate work worldwide. In addition, there is a considerable body of academic research on the Scots language of all periods, including work informed by modern international linguistic theory.

But how is the Scots language actually used today? Present-day Scottish people mostly speak Scottish Standard English, which combines the vocabulary and syntax of Standard English with the pronunciation system, some vocabulary, and a few grammatical features from Scots. They write in British Standard English. Scots educated in England or in English-style public schools in Scotland, thus including many of the upper middle class as well as the aristocracy (scc SOCIAL CLASS), also speak received pronunciation British Standard English, with perhaps a smattering of more or less self-conscious Scottish vocabulary, but no other features from Scots. Members of the Scottish working class are more likely to speak one of the modern dialects of Scots, and often in addition speak Scottish Standard English in more formal contexts. Indeed, a major feature of both middle- and working-class speech in Scotland is the ability to style-switch, using more or less Scots along an infinitely variable continuum, as the occasion seems to demand.

Scots is currently enjoying a modest revival. Since the 17th century written Scots has been in decline (see CULTURE: 13), with English the favoured language for literature, education, and religion. But the 20th century has seen Scots reintroduced into all these fields (see CULTURE: 24).

In literature, there has been a gradual increase in the use of Scots in all genres throughout this century. There have been two so-called Scottish renaissances (see CULTURE: 21), the first from the 1920s to 1940s, when writers such as Hugh MacDiarmid made the case especially for poetry in Scots; and in the 1970s to 1990s, when demotic speech has become accepted as an increasingly large part of novel-writing (see CULTURE: 25), not just for the dialogue, where it was already used in earlier literature, but also as the voice of the narrator. Scots,

however, has not yet regained much ground within the genre of discursive or narrative prose writing.

In education (see SCHOOLS AND SCHOOLING: 2, 4), there was strong opposition to the use of Scots in both the 19th and first half of the 20th centuries, with pupils traditionally having it beaten out of them if they dared to use a Scots word in class, and never being allowed to write in Scots. The principal permitted use of Scots in schools until perhaps the 1960s was in the reading and reciting of the poetry of Burns. Since then more enlightened regimes in the SED and in individual schools have allowed the use of spoken Scots in class by both pupils and teachers, where they are competent to use it, and actively encourage its use in creative writing in appropriate contexts.

Religion gets much of the blame for the decline in Scots since the *Reformation, largely because of the non-existence of a Scots translation of the Bible (see RELIGIOUS LIFE: 3). The 20th century again has seen a partial restitution in the form of W. L. Lorimer's literary tour de force *The New Testament in Scots* of 1983, a totally new translation into a variety of styles of Scots by an outstanding scholar of both New Testament Greek and Scots. His work has led to much more Scots being heard from the pulpit. However, at a time when organized religion is in decline, fewer people hear it than would have done in the past.

Historically, the Scots language first appears in the record as incidental words, mainly *place names and personal names, in early Latin charters and other legal documents, from the 11th century onwards. Latin remained the language used for official and literary prose until the 15th century, when it was gradually replaced by Scots. The business and record-keeping of the *royal court, the Scottish *parliament, the law (see LAW AND LAWYERS: 1), and the church (see CHURCH INSTITUTIONS: 3), as well as everyday commerce, were mostly conducted in Scots from then on until Scotland's unions with England in 1603 and 1707. The vocabulary of the law and church continued to contain much that was distinctively Scottish after the *Union of 1707, as these institutions were preserved in their distinctively Scottish character by the Act of Union itself.

Written Scots has been most long-lived in the genres of poetry and personal private documents of various kinds, which survive in manuscript or printed versions from the late 14th century onwards. Scots poetry appears in all the contemporary European art forms from the Middle Ages (see CULTURE: 3, 9) to the present, including some works of major importance such as John Barbour's verse-epic romance *The Brus*, composed in the 1370s, which deals with the history of the Scottish Wars of

Scottish Council (Development and Industry)

*Independence in the early 14th century (see HISTORIANS: 1); the wide-ranging poetry of Robert Henryson in the late 15th century; in the early 16th century, the courtly verse of William Dunbar, with its brilliant and lively use of language; and Gavin Douglas's translation of Virgil's *Aeneid*, the first into any variety of English, which served as a model for later southern English writers. This last period of about 40 years is generally agreed to have been the high point for literature in the Scots language, in terms both of the quantity and quality of work produced (see CULTURE: 6, 13).

The influence of southern English, however, became ever more marked, especially in prose writing, from the mid-16th century onwards, accelerating after *James VI became James I of England in 1603, when the royal court moved south. But one of the principal reasons for the written language becoming increasingly more Anglicized was undoubtedly the fact that very little has ever been printed in the Scots language (see PRINTING AND PUBLISHING). There are two principal reasons for this. First, printed work is usually intended for a relatively wide readership, and hence Scottish writers often write in English to achieve this. Written English was always perfectly comprehensible to most Scots, though some of them might have had more difficulty in understanding spoken English. Second, there were very few early printers actually working in Scotland. Such printers would have been the most natural choice to produce work in Scots. Those writers who did write in Scots often had to have their work published in England or on the Continent. Of the medieval and Renaissance authors mentioned above, only Dunbar had work published in Scotland in his lifetime, and that in such a small edition that knowledge of him was lost after his death, or perhaps after antiquarians of the 16th century such as Sir Richard Maitland passed on; his revival did not occur until Allan Ramsay in 1724 published some of Dunbar's poems in his antiquarian collection *Ever Green*, which was based on a surviving manuscript collection rather than the printed text.

Spoken Scots has of course continued to be used, but in an increasingly fragmented way. In the 16th century there was probably a standard form of Scots spoken at the political centre in Edinburgh, in addition to the considerable variety of regional dialects spoken around the country. There was certainly a standard form of written Scots prose used at the court for official documentation. The dialects continued in speech, and enjoyed some currency in written form in 19th-century verse, principally following the success of the poetry of Burns in the late 18th century. There was also some demotic literature in prose in the dialects of north-east Scotland and Shetland (see REGIONAL IDENTITIES: 2, 4) in the late 19th century, and some of the main varieties of urban Scots have featured in mainstream literature in recent decades. But Standard Scots has not existed in spoken form nor in ordinary everyday functional prose writing since the early 17th century.

There is now considerable discussion in academic and other circles about the future of the Scots language in a Scotland poised to take more responsibility for its own affairs. In recent years there has been hotly disputed controversy, which the current political situation has brought more sharply into focus, on a variety of matters. Should there be language planning to reintroduce Scots at the various levels at which it is now lacking? Should a standardized spelling system be created for modern Scots? If so, what should it consist of? If a written and spoken Standard Scots were to be created, how should they relate to the regional dialects? And should Scots be made an official language of Scotland, alongside English and Gaelic?

The next few years, with a new Scots parliament likely to be conscious of the complex issues involved in heritage, identity, language, and literature, could prove very interesting in the history of the Scots language.   HMJR

Scottish Council (Development and Industry) was created by the amalgamation of the Scottish National Development Council and the Scottish Council on Industry. The former was established in May 1931 'to examine and to endeavour to solve the industrial, commercial and economic problems with which the country is faced'. This non-political organization, driven forward by Sir James *Lithgow, set up a series of subcommittees to investigate rating and taxation, exports, agriculture, textiles, electrical appliances and power, the chemical industry, film production, the *economy of the Highlands and Islands, and trade exhibitions. The resulting reports were objective and pragmatic. Had their recommendations been more fully implemented, the Scottish economy might more quickly have diversified, but the very severity of the Depression and the limited ambitions of existing and potential entrepreneurs inhibited change. Greater success attended the efforts of the Economic Committee. Formed by the Council in collaboration with the *Scottish Office to further the new regional policies of the 1930s, it was responsible for the establishment of the industrial estate at Hillington in 1937, the forerunner of several other such estates in Lanarkshire. Another venture by the Council was to help to organize the Empire Exhibition of 1938 in Glasgow.

Although its achievements during the 1930s were but modest, knowledge and experience were gained which promised to be of continuing value. Thomas *Johnston certainly believed this to be so when in 1942 he invited the Development Council to be strongly represented on his Scottish Council on Industry. Since Johnston's Council, initially concerned with maximizing Scotland's contribution to the war effort, inevitably became involved with the long-term future of the Scottish economy, its activities closely mirrored those of the older organization, though it brought greater urgency to improving transport facilities, special attention being paid to the future of Prestwick Airport and the Forth Road Bridge. It made sense, therefore, to merge the two councils, and the Scottish Council (Development and Industry) came into being in June 1946 (see ECONOMIC POLICY: 4). It too depended upon voluntary effort and, once again, there was a proliferation of specialized panels and committees, but the focus was avowedly industrial for it was almost universally believed that the principal need in Scotland was for new industries which would employ men. With considerable prescience, the Council decided that electronics (see ECONOMY, SECONDARY SECTOR: 3) could constitute a vital addition to Scottish economy, and in 1948 it embarked on a pioneering and successful campaign to attract such companies from the USA and to assist in the solution of technical problems encountered by new entrants to the industry. It was the beginning of a process which has seen electronics become the 'crown jewel' of Scottish industry.

In other areas, the Council's initiatives were less successful. Wiggins Teapes's pulp mill at Fort William, the Ravenscraig strip mill, car manufacturing at Linwood, the Invergordon aluminium smelter—each of which was strongly backed by the Council—have come and gone. Nevertheless, for a voluntary body, much was achieved in regenerating Scotland's economy and, in such reports as those of the Toothill Committee (1962), providing blueprints for its future. In a world increasingly dominated by powerful players, it was inevitable that many of the Council's functions should pass into other, government-backed, hands. Thus in 1965 the *Highlands and Islands Development Board assumed many of the Council's responsibilities and, ten years later, the Council's role in encouraging overseas firms to locate in Scotland was transferred to the *Scottish Development Agency. Nevertheless, it continues to play an important part in encouraging international trade by organizing and sponsoring overseas trade missions; in making submissions and representations to government, the Office of Fair Trading, the Monopolies and Mergers Commission, and other organizations; in conducting research into public policy issues; and in fostering links between education and industry. PLP

Scottish Development Agency (SDA). The SDA was created in 1975. For some time there had been growing dissatisfaction in Scotland with the existing arrangements for directing loans and grants to industry under the Local Employment Act. It was believed that a specifically Scottish body would perform this task more sympathetically than an advisory committee in London. The transfer of the administration of selective financial assistance to industry to regional offices of the Department of Trade and Industry (under the Industry Act of 1972) might have been sufficient to meet earlier criticisms had it not been for the rapidity of Scotland's industrial decline and the discovery of North Sea oil. These events fuelled a dramatic rise in support for the SNP, and the new Labour government deemed it politically expedient to create a Scottish development agency. Nothing less, it was believed, would reduce the menace of the SNP (see NATIONALISM) and quell vociferous demands that oil revenues be retained within Scotland.

The SDA was given three functions: investment in industry; the provision of publicly owned factories; and the clearance of derelict land and environmental recovery. To these responsibilities was added (in 1977) the task of co-ordinating efforts to attract foreign investment, a role hitherto performed, most significantly, by the *Scottish Council (Development and Industry).

The expectation that roughly equivalent sums would be expended on its three original functions was unrealized. The provision of capital for industry was inhibited by inexperience, the imposition of the requirement that the SDA achieve an unrealistically high rate of return, and the contemporaneous depressed condition of the Scottish *economy. Not until the early 1980s did the SDA concentrate on investment in high-technology companies (see ECONOMY, SECONDARY SECTOR: 3) or in sectors offering scope for expansion; in its portfolio, lame ducklings were supplanted by vigorous cygnets. Another reason for relatively low industrial investment was the SDA's preoccupation with projects for urban renewal, a bias strengthened when it was given co-ordinating responsibility for the eastern area renewal project in *Glasgow (GEAR). To this task it was to allocate a disproportionate share of its funds.

With the Conservative government in 1979, the direct provision of industrial capital was subordinated to means designed to facilitate access to finance from commercial sources through guarantees and securities underwritten by the SDA. This meshed neatly with both the continuing commitment to the provision of industrial property and a heightened emphasis on the promotion of inward investment from overseas. Although no more than 5 to 10 per cent of the budget was ever spent on Locate (a government initiative and agency) in Scotland, it was remarkably successful, creating perhaps 50,000 new jobs. Nevertheless, the SDA was subjected to constant review by a government anxious to diminish state involvement in economic activity. There was, too, a growing belief in decentralization. This resulted in 1988 in the establishment of seven regional offices intended to perform all the functions of the SDA at the local level, and which culminated in 1991 in the supercession of the SDA itself by Scottish Enterprise, with its Local Enterprise Companies.

Any attempt to assess the achievement of the SDA is made difficult by the short time that has elapsed since its demise, but many believe that it made a significant contribution to the well-being of the Scottish economy. In the words of Professor Neil Hood, 'The SDA did act as a flagship, an advocate, an integrated delivery mechanism [for economic aid] and an agenda setter' ('The Scottish Development Agency in Retrospect', *Royal Bank of Scotland Review*, 171 (1991)). In so doing, perhaps it became too well known and respected, too successful in attracting praise to itself rather than to a jealous government which ultimately funded and directed it (see also ECONOMIC POLICY: 4).   PLP

Scottish links. Situated where the Atlantic and the North Sea meet, Scotland looks in all directions, north, south, east, and west, and its links with places and peoples beyond its borders, near or far, are a central feature of its history. Its geographical positioning, far from being peripheral, has in fact been pivotal when viewed, for example, from the perspective of Norway (see SCANDINAVIA) in a period of westward expansion in the 9th century; or from the ports of the Baltic (see GERMANY, THE BALTIC, AND POLAND) and the *Low Countries when Scotland lay within the natural network of both the import and export trades in the 15th century; or from Poland and Lithuania in times of 19th-century repression and pogrom. Scotland has provided a bridge between the Celtic (see IRELAND) and the Scandinavian worlds, and between them, England, and continental Europe, as well as being a last port of call westward to the Americas.

Home to the ideas of the age of the Enlightenment (see CULTURE: 11) and the products of the agricultural and industrial revolutions (see ECONOMY: 3–4), Scotland's capacity for providing opportunity for its population has nonetheless often been limited by economic, social, political, religious, and resource-based factors, and many have sought

livelihoods, temporary or permanent, in other parts of the world. Scotland itself has become home to people of diverse backgrounds over millennia: *place-name evidence shows a mix of languages and cultures from the earliest periods of written history, while a glance at the telephone directory of any part of the country indicates the multi-ethnic nature of contemporary Scotland. Scots today come from backgrounds which are Chinese, Indian, Irish, Italian, Jewish, Lithuanian, Pakistani, Polish, Ukrainian, and many more. There are few parts of the globe not represented in the Scottish population and as there are more people on the move at present than at any previous time in world history, this diversity is regularly being reinforced. In Scotland's national, university, and local museums, private collections, botanical gardens and arboreta (see GARDENING AND LANDSCAPE) examples abound of Scottish encounters with peoples and habitats worldwide.

In his novel of emigration, *The Flying Years* (1935), Valparaiso-born Scottish-Canadian author Frederick Niven (1878–1944) gives these words to one of his characters: 'We'll take Scotland with us, a kingdom of the mind.' While capable of several interpretations, this phrase serves as a useful reminder of the variety that constitutes Scotland, of the many different Scotlands venturers, emigrants, (see EMIGRATION) or mercenaries (see MERCENARIES IN EUROPE; MERCENARIES IN IRELAND) have taken with them in head, heart, and hand according to their own time and place and social milieu. Against the wide sweep of the Scottish diaspora must be set the components of individual experience, personal or family aspiration, local circumstances, economic necessity, education and opportunity, commitment to ideals, and other factors internal and external which have served as motivation or spur.

The outward movement of the Scots might be said to begin with the Celtic monks (see CHRISTIANITY, CONVERSION TO; IONA) who established island bases in Orkney, Shetland, the Faroes, and Iceland and who ventured as missionaries into continental Europe. Religious activities form a major component in the creation of links between Scotland and other areas from the time when Scotland was part of an undivided Christendom. Scots participated in the *Crusades and in pilgrimages to the holy shrines in Jerusalem, Rome, Santiago da Compostella, and elsewhere (see RELIGIOUS LIFE: 2). In the 12th century, houses of monastic orders were established in Scotland from *France, often via England (see NORTHERN EUROPE: MONKS AND SCHOLARS), and Scots went to learn and to teach at universities on the Continent, some staying and some returning to posts in Scotland.

In the early 16th century, Protestant ideas and those of the early Counter-Reformation were encountered in European institutions, such as Wittenburg, Cologne, and Louvain, and imported into Scotland. Repression of early Protestant ideas in the 1530s and early 1540s forced a virtual generation of scholars and schoolmasters abroad, where they sometimes played a notable role in the *Reformation, especially in Denmark, northern Germany, and France. The establishment of a Protestant reformed church in 1560 gave new points of reference to Protestant Scots in Denmark, Germany, Geneva, and the Low Countries, and new points of reference for Catholic Scots as well. Scots academics taught in universities throughout northern Europe especially. But Scottish *universities also attracted students and scholars from beyond Scotland's borders and religious diversity extended the connections. From the 18th century onwards, *missions overseas took Scots to the *Indian subcontinent, China (see EAST ASIA), and *Africa as well as to North and South America (see LATIN AMERICA), while migration to *Canada, the *USA, *Australia, and *New Zealand saw the creation there of religious and educational institutions which reflected those at home. Incomers to Scotland, in turn, have brought a diversity of religious traditions with them and the major world faiths are represented and practised in the country.

Trade and commerce was another major sphere of activity which brought Scots and others into productive relationships, with Scandinavia, the Baltic, and the Low Countries particularly figuring from the late 13th century onwards. Scots involvement was extensive in the great trading companies established in the 17th century, the EIC bringing tea, spices, silks, and porcelain from India and China, and the Hudson's Bay Company (HBC) supplying furs from North America to the British and European market. The HBC recruited employees in Orkney and Lewis, the latter introducing into Gaelic the term for Canada, *an talamh fuar* (the cold land). The scale of Scottish participation in trading activities is sometimes astounding: it is reckoned, for example, that in the early 17th century there were 30,000 Scottish families in Poland mainly engaged in peddling manufactured goods.

Scottish herring went to *Russia and the Baltic in return for flax and timber. Much of Edinburgh's New Town was built of Scandinavian deals or sawn timber. When trade with North America and the Caribbean brought sugar and tobacco to Scotland for refining, at first illicitly but legalized by the *Union of 1707, manufactured tobacco became a major export to continental Europe, guaranteeing wealth for *Glasgow's tobacco lords. Cotton came to be vital for the textile industry in the west of the country, while *Dundee came to rely on jute from India. Timber and wheat were added to imports from Canada, where Scottish bankers predominated.

The Scots gained a reputation for prowess in military service; Lowlanders were recruited for campaigns in France and Highlanders for campaigns in Ireland in the medieval period. The 16th century saw the creation of the Scots Brigade for service in the Netherlands and Scots were recruited to Sweden for the Russian Wars. Russia itself offered scope for recruitment and it sometimes transpired that Scot was fighting Scot in foreign causes. The scale of mercenary recruitment increased in the 17th century, with many thousands of Scots serving in the Swedish army during the Thirty Years War.

The parliamentary Union of 1707 and the increasing involvement of Scots in British imperial ventures diverted the supply of soldiers into regiments such as the Scottish Highland regiments (see ARMY: 3–4) which fought in North America in the middle of the 18th century and later, although the 19th-century wars of independence in Latin America saw Scots as soldiers and sailors. The accounts of returning soldiers provided information about the New World for would-be emigrants and settlement became an option for the military too, especially after the American War of Independence when there was concern to bolster the British presence on the borders of the USA and British North America. India, too, provided scope for military involvement at all levels, while the Napoleonic and Crimean conflicts and later campaigns through the 19th and 20th centuries have been characterized by heavy Scottish participation in army, navy (including Merchant Navy), and air force in many parts of the world.

Scotland's central place in the philosophical and scientific flowering of the 18th century, in the development of industrial and engineering excellence, and in allied areas such as agricultural improvement meant that Scottish expertise was sought on many topics and its influence in the world of ideas and in practical application widely felt. The landed gentry of Poland and Lithuania sought advice on new agricultural methods and equipment, and recruited farmers to put these into practice. Doctors, architects, craftsmen, engineers, and skilled workers found commissions in many places and railways, canal building, mill construction, and mining enterprises used Scottish experience extensively. A representative and indeed literal icon of these Scottish links can be found in the Chain Bridge constructed in 1849 by Adam Clark to span the Danube linking Buda and Pest in Hungary (see CENTRAL EUROPE). As it began to industrialize, Japan turned to Scotland for guidance in shipbuilding, distillery, and other industries.

All these contacts could, and did, bring Scots to settle in other parts, as the burgess rolls of Bergen, Gothenburg, Stockholm, and Åbo, and parallel sources of evidence elsewhere, reveal. But larger-scale emigration with the purpose of settling has its own dynamics and the migration of Scots to what were to become the USA and Canada, and to Australia and New Zealand, brings another vital dimension to the subject of Scottish links. If the nature of culture transfer and adaptation is to be studied fully, the variety of experience must be acknowledged: an understanding of the time, place, and social milieu which is the context of migration is vital to understanding the complex picture. The Scotland emigrants left could be very different, depending on the period, on personal circumstances, on whether they were Lowlanders, Highlanders, or Western or Northern Islanders, whether they were from an urban or rural background, leaving in a group or singly, under what—if any—emigration scheme, and to what destination, with what expectations.

Micro-studies are providing the basis for in-depth analysis of the emigrant process, in which the Scots were among many participants, and for re-evaluating themes such as the nature of contact of interaction with indigenous peoples and with members of other immigrant groups, and the means by which a sense of belonging was achieved. Such scholarship helps to banish the stereotypes, just as a Gaelic song composed in Manitoba, Canada, on New Year's Day 1880 does. Composed for friends and relations at home on the Isle of Tiree and in a largely Tiree settlement created a generation earlier in Ontario, 'The Tiree Bards' (1932) expresses two sides of the emigrant experience in looking back but also looking forward: *''S nuair gheibh sinn an t-aite gu barr is gu feum, | Cha bhi cuimhn' air na laithean a dh'fhag sinn nar deigh'* ('And when we get the place cultivated and in use, we won't dwell on the days we've left behind us').

These broad categories should not be seen as exclusive, for it is readily apparent that there are connections between and among them. Exploration and mapping, for example, went hand in hand with trade and commerce, with military activity, and—as in Africa—with missionary work. Diplomacy and political relations intersected with all spheres, while colonial administration had its links with trade and with the military, as the Indian experience reveals. The influence of ideas is potent if not always easy to plot and there are many further connections.

In a certain sense, globalization is by no means a new phenomenon for Scotland. A visitor to Shet-land finds a Hanseatic trading booth on the Island of Whalsay; a visitor to Ptuj in Slovenia sees the arms of the Leslie family on the local castle; James Bay Cree fiddlers journey to Orkney to celebrate ancestors recruited there into the Hudson's Bay Company and to share tunes from a common musical heritage with the locals; Gaelic mingles with Spanish on a Patagonian *estancia*; mosque minarets join towers and steeples on the skyline of Glasgow and Edinburgh; a regimental band in Pakistan plays the pipes (see MUSIC, HIGHLAND); a snatch of a Lowland Scots ballad (see SONG, TRADITIONAL AND FOLK: 1) is heard in rural Jamaica. Scottish island children are in e-mail communication with their island counterparts on the other side of the globe and a Scottish parliament and a new voice in Europe and beyond bring the potential for further fruitful Scottish links in the 21st century.   MAM

Scottish National Portrait Gallery. The Scottish National Portrait Gallery (SNPG), Queen Street, Edinburgh, designed in 1885 by Robert Rowand Anderson, the 'premier architect of Scotland', is a significant intruder in both style and colour into the stern, grey, and plain neoclassicism of the first New Town. Money had been gifted by John Ritchie Findlay, philanthropic proprietor of the *Scotsman* newspaper, for a building intended for joint occupation as a portrait gallery (western end) and the Museum of the Society of Antiquaries of Scotland (eastern end). The latter became the National Museum of Antiquities of Scotland (NMAS).

Anderson's inspiration derived principally from the vertically proportioned mediaeval urban houses of southern France, which he had studied and published in the 1860s. He stretched their Gothic verticality into a long horizontal, sculpture-encrusted pavilion capped with a fretted parapet which resembles the Doge's Palace in Venice realized in red Dumfriesshire sandstone. Clasping each corner is a slender, pinnacled *tourelle*, adorned with sculpture of Scots historical figures, most by W. Birnie Rhind (a manuscript detailing all the people represented in the sculptures is in the library of the Royal Incorporation of Architects in Scotland). A typical white brick, black-topped Anderson flue soars from the rear.

The design is based on large, north-lit volumes for galleries and exhibition, flanked to side and rear by pokier administrative departments, library, etc. The celebration lies at the centre, where the influence of Anderson's 1880 design for Lord Bute's seat of Mount Stuart, Bute, is most clearly perceived. The focus is upon a soaring, two-storeyed galleried hall defined by Gothic arcades, its distant, sky-like deep green timber ceiling flecked with gold stars. A vividly painted frieze by William Hole depicting historic Scots sits on the red stone columns, and the first-floor gallery above is walled around by richly glinting mosaics of awesome moments from Scots history, also by Hole. To each side opens out the principal stair—a gracious, shallow ascent in polished red sandstone, echoing the great 1604 Renaissance staircase at Fyvie, Aberdeenshire, a vaulted vestibule at the top. The galleries are now all enclosed, the top ones still roof-lit. The 1996 departure of the NMAS to the *Royal Museum of Scotland in Chambers Street provided the opportunity for the SNPG to expand—much needed in view of its widening remit to add to its excellent portrait collection those of *photography and of topographical paintings. It has an excellent shop and café.   CAMcK

Scottish Office. The founding of the Scottish Office in 1885 began a process of administrative reorganization and consolidation. Prior to that date and for some time thereafter, Scottish central administration was dealt with through a series of appointed boards. Reforms in English central administration in the 19th century aimed at creating a professional bureaucracy appointed by merit rather than through a system of patronage largely passed Scotland by. Boards existed for a range of different functions each dealing with a specific matter—fisheries, poor law (see LIVING STANDARDS: 4), and public health (see FAMINE, HEALTH, AND DISEASE: 3), lunacy and mental deficiency, prisons, education (see SCHOOLS AND SCHOOLING: 4), and agriculture—before the First World War. Each board existed separately and was housed in different parts of Edinburgh. The Scottish Office, under the political leadership of the *Scottish Secretary, was created as a separate body which coexisted, sometimes rather uneasily, with the boards. There was little attempt to co-ordinate the work of the different boards or integrate the central administrative bodies under the Scottish Office until after the First World War.

The pressure for a more co-ordinated and consolidated central administration in Scotland came from two sources. First, the experience elsewhere in Britain where a professional civil service had emerged following the Northcote-Trevelyan report in the 1850s, provided an alternative model to the ad hoc structure based on patronage. Second, the development of the Scottish Office, gaining new responsibilities over time, brought with it new demands and pressures for a more coherent administrative system. The Scottish Office had been given responsibility for education (with the exception of the *universities) when it was created but within two years responsibility for law and order

was transferred from the Home Office. Before the First World War, a Scottish Board of Agriculture under the Scottish Secretary was created and after the war a Scottish Board of Health with responsibility for *housing was added. Further administrative responsibilities were added gradually and unsystematically so that a plethora of bodies and responsibilities were attached in an unsystematic manner to the Scottish Office by the early 1920s.

The Royal Commission on the Civil Service (MacDonnell) which issued a report in 1915 criticized the structure of Scottish central administration and the boards in particular. Three criticisms of the boards were made with adverse comparisons with the Scottish Office: the boards were less effective in securing responsibility for official action and advice than was found in the Scottish Office; boards weakened the distinction between the qualities and the methods of selection suitable for political as distinct from permanent appointments; and the 'higher business of administration' was sometimes performed by men who brought 'no special knowledge of the work' to it. The boards had their defenders in Scotland who saw them as allowing for some measure of 'Scottish control of Scottish affairs' and who viewed a permanent, professional civil service as a process of Anglicization. However, pressure for reform built up and changes were brought about in two reorganizations of the Scottish central administration in 1928 and 1939.

The first reorganization was particularly controversial in parliament. Opponents included *'Red Clydeside' MPs and *Unionists who supported the patronage system. As a consequence of the opposition encountered on that first occasion, the second reorganization was preceded by an inquiry and official report creating a consensus around the changes before legislation was presented to parliament. The reorganization in 1939 coincided with an attempt to rehouse the central administration under one roof. St Andrew's House, on the site of the old Calton prison, was built. The intention had been that all the Scottish central administration would be housed here but, ironically, by the time it opened the staff had grown and not all were based there. The end of the boards in 1939 allowed for a restructuring of the Scottish Office and a semi-federal structure was created. Four departments were created within the Scottish Office: the Department of Agriculture for Scotland; the Scottish Education Department; the Department of Health for Scotland; and the Scottish Home Department. Scotland had its own mini-Whitehall. This remained the model of Scottish central administration until the establishment of the Scottish *parliament in 1999, though the organization and number of departments within the Scottish Office changed.

Scottish Secretary

The Scottish Office continued to gather new functions. A tidying-up exercise followed the report of the Royal Commission on Scottish Affairs (Balfour) in 1954. Various responsibilities, including the appointment of Justices of the Peace, animal health, roads, bridges and ferries, electricity in southern Scotland, and the school milk scheme, were transferred to the Scottish Office. Later, an inquiry into the Scottish economy proposed that a new department should be established to deal with economic development and in 1962 the Scottish Development Department was set up (see ECONOMIC POLICY: 4). In 1973 the Scottish Economic Planning Department was created. Over the half-century after the opening of St Andrew's House, a number of reorganizations and additional responsibilities were added to the Scottish Office. By the early 1980s, one estimate of the Scottish Office's remit suggested that it was the equivalent of approximately ten Whitehall departments (agriculture, education and science, employment, energy, environment, health and social security, home office, industry, trade, and transport). Further changes were made. Even under the Conservatives in the 1980s and 1990s, the Scottish Office added to its list of responsibilities though, of course, there were important changes throughout Whitehall affecting the scope of government and nature of administration. As Sir David Milne (former Permanent Secretary at the Scottish Office) had written in 1957,

Some of the alterations may have been made for political reasons, others out of a desire for administrative tidiness; the river may have flowed erratically, but its main course has been clear. There has been a definite and increasing tendency to assign to a Scottish minister matters in which there is a distinctive Scottish tradition or body of law or where Scottish conditions are notably different from those in England and Wales. The present system of administrative structure is not the result of design, but of constant change and adjustment over a period of 250 years. It is unlikely that it is complete but no one can say what the future changes will be. Time finds its own solutions.

The creation of a Scottish parliament, the most significant change yet, will no doubt bring with it further changes.   JM

Scottish Secretary. The office of Secretary of State dates back to the time of the King's Secretary, both in Scotland and in England, before the *Union of 1707. In modern times, there are many secretaries of state; they are democratically accountable to parliament and each office holder has a specific remit. What makes the Scottish Secretary unusual, though not unique, today is that the tasks allotted to the office are defined territorially rather than

functionally: Scotland is the remit of the Scottish Secretary which includes a wide range of government functions whereas there are or have been secretaries of state with specific responsibility such as for education, health, or social security.

Prior to the Treaty of Union, there were two Scottish Secretaries, the earls of Mar and Loudoun. Though it was not preserved as part of the Union settlement, the office continued in being and until 1746 some member of the Scottish *nobility was appointed as Secretary of State with responsibility for Scottish affairs though there were years during this period when the office did not exist. From then until the end of the 19th century, the office of Scottish Secretary did not exist though Scottish institutions and public officers with considerable power existed.

The office of Scottish Secretary re-emerged in 1885 against a background of discontent at the neglect of Scottish affairs in London. The sense that Scotland was being ignored and that Scottish distinctiveness was insensitively dealt with resulted in a campaign which coalesced around the case for the reinstitution of the office of Secretary of State for Scotland. Scottish grievances were many but the demand was imprecise. While there was remarkable agreement across the political parties, with both the Conservatives (see UNIONISM) and the Liberals (see LIBERALISM) in Scotland accepting the need for a Secretary of State, little attention was paid to the functions which should be attached to it other than the general remit of looking after Scottish interests. Various measures proposing to establish the office were presented before parliament in the early 1880s, each proposing a different range of functions. The Secretary for Scotland Act was passed in 1885 and was unusual in that it had been introduced by the Liberals under Gladstone and finally passed by the Conservatives under Salisbury, a change of government without an election having occurred during its passage.

While the London elite accepted the office it did so without enthusiasm. Prime minister Salisbury was notably doubtful of its value, as was evident in his correspondence inviting the duke of Richmond and Gordon to accept the office. The duke had privately opposed the measure but acceded to Salisbury's invitation in which the premier had argued that someone with status—'two Dukedoms and the best salmon river in Scotland'—was needed as the 'whole object of the move is to redress the wounded dignities of the Scotch people—or a section of them—who think that enough is not made of Scotland'. The office, however, was not accorded the status initially demanded by the parties, local authorities, and others who had campaigned for its reinstitution. It was not until 1926 that the office became the Secretaryship of State for Scotland and not merely the Secretaryship for Scotland, though in practice little actually changed. In theory at least, and relating to the origins of the title, a Secretary of State has direct right of access to the monarch. In practice, the office's position in the pecking order of government is important not only for individual politicians seeking ever-higher status but also in terms of the relative power of the office concerned.

The office's remit increased over time (see SCOTTISH OFFICE) and, from 1892 onwards, the Scottish Secretary always had a seat in the cabinet with the exception of war cabinets during the First and Second World Wars. Until just after the First World War, the Scottish Secretary was commonly a member of the House of Lords, as had always been the case in the 18th century. With the brief exception of the earl of Rosebery in 1945, who served as Scottish Secretary in Churchill's caretaker government at the end of the war, Scottish Secretaries were invariably members of the Commons after 1924. They have also always been MPs with a Scottish constituency. This contrasts with the Welsh and Northern Ireland Secretaries. Welsh Secretaries, after that office was established in 1964, have commonly represented an English constituency in the Commons and Northern Ireland Secretaries have never represented a constituency in Northern Ireland since that office's inception in 1972.

In addition to the widening of the formal responsibilities of the office, a tendency developed for Scots with a grievance to look to the Scottish Secretary for assistance. An enquiry into Scottish central administration in the late 1930s noted that there was 'increasing tendency to appeal to him on all matters which have a Scottish aspect, even if on a strict view they are outside the province of his duties as statutorily defined' (see GOVERNMENT AND ADMINISTRATION: 3; ECONOMIC POLICY: 4). William *Ross, a latter-day Scottish Secretary, was the longest serving Labour Scottish Secretary (1964–70 and 1974–6). Later, he wrote of his experiences under the title *Approaching the Archangelic*, borrowing a phrase from one of Salisbury's letters to Richmond and Gordon: 'as measured by the expectations of the people of Scotland [the Scottish Secretaryship] is approaching the Archangelic'. The consequence of this was that 'power limped lamely behind responsibility' as far as Ross was concerned. Though additional junior ministers were attached to the Scottish Office from 1919 onwards, the Scottish Secretary had a very wide remit and came to be seen as a kind of governor-general of Scotland, especially as the appointment was entirely in the hands of the prime minister and not the Scottish people. This perception became strong in

the 1980s and was important in pressure for the establishment of an elected Scottish parliament (see PARLIAMENT: 4). JM

sermons have been an important part of the worship of the Church in Scotland during much of its history. In the Celtic period sermons would appear to have been simple and biblically based. The amount of preaching by the parish clergy declined considerably during the medieval period. Most sermons were given by the mendicant friars, such as the Dominicans and the Franciscans, and referred to such subjects as devotion to the Virgin Mary, the Passion of Christ, and the Mass. By the mid-16th century many priests were unable to preach and this problem was recognized by the three provincial councils held between 1549 and 1559 (see RELIGIOUS LIFE: 2).

One of the main emphases of the Scottish *Reformation was on the provision of an educated parish ministry. Preaching was regarded as one of the three formal 'marks' of the church, along with the celebration of the sacraments and the exercise of discipline. Due to the continued infrequency of communion, the sermon became the main feature of worship. Passages of Scripture from both the Old and New Testaments were read systematically and sermons were based on one of the lessons. John *Knox set the example of such preaching which sought to apply the biblical message to the spiritual life of the people as well as to the issues of the day.

In the 17th century, sermons came to be given on a single verse or part of a verse and were generally organized into heads of 'doctrine' and 'uses'. Such a structure made sermons easier to remember both for the minister, who preached without the use of a manuscript, and for his hearers. Many sermons, including those given by the fiery field preachers of the Covenanting (see COVENANTERS) period, were biblical expositions and included a direct evangelical appeal to the congregation as well as a condemnation of errors in life and doctrine. Sermons were generally long, lasting up to an hour or more. During the 18th century the Moderates (see RELIGIOUS LIFE: 5) emphasized the need for virtuous living and were more ready to preach on topical issues. The sermons of Hugh Blair in Edinburgh are good examples of the polished literary style which they adopted. Evangelicals (see RELIGIOUS LIFE: 6) tended to concentrate on the doctrine of the atonement, and the need for saving faith and holiness of life. Some preachers wished to offer the gospel freely to all while still holding to the doctrine of election found in the Westminster Confession.

In the 19th century the practice of reading sermons became more common and was adopted by no less a figure than Thomas *Chalmers. Quotations were increasingly made from secular literature and illustrations were drawn from nature and everyday life. Sermons became shorter and the liturgical revival led to the greater observance of the Christian year. The emphasis on the doctrine of the incarnation, and the new developments in biblical criticism, resulted in an increasing focus on the life of Jesus. Social issues, too, came to be examined by ministers. The upheavals of the 20th century, and the impact of 'neo-Orthodoxy', led to a renewed stress on basic doctrines such as God's grace and human sin. In the post-war period there was also a rediscovery of expository preaching by some conservative Evangelical ministers. The days of the city-centre preachers who attracted large crowds had passed, but instead there was an emphasis on faithful preaching ministries in the local church. In the Episcopal Church (see EPISCOPALIAN COMMUNITY), and in the Roman Catholic Church (see ROMAN CATHOLIC COMMUNITY) since Vatican II, an important place is given to both word and sacrament, with the reading of three lessons and a sermon being seen as vital elements in worship.

DMM

Session, Court of. The Court of Session, which sits at *Parliament House, Edinburgh, is today Scotland's principal court in civil matters. Its origins go back to the judicial sessions (sittings) of the king's council which by the later 15th century were becoming increasingly regularized in order to deal with what seems to have been a growing number of complaints and petitions for justice not obtainable before the ordinary courts of the common law (see LAW AND LAWYERS: 1). Regularization came about through the assignment of specialist groups of councillors (the Lords of Session) to deal with the judicial business, and the gradual establishment of timetables for its dispatch. Long before its traditional date of foundation as a College of Justice in 1532, therefore, the court had become an institution. While the College was a royal device to justify papal grants from clerical taxation, the Lords of Session were given more permanent form, and the legislation which established the College and conferred jurisdiction 'in all civil matters' confirmed and sanctioned an already expansionist approach to their powers. The Lords asserted an exclusive right to deal with cases of 'fee and heritage' (landownership), and intruded upon the activities of other courts by means of procedures such as advocation, suspension, and reduction, thereby establishing themselves as the supreme court in civil matters. In the 16th century bodies of professional pleaders—the origin of the Faculty of Advocates—and writers of court documents—the origin of the

Writers to the Signet—grew up around the court, confirming the scope and significance of the business conducted there.

The Lords of Session, headed by the Lord President, were a mixture of clergy and laymen until the 17th century. They sat together, usually in an inner chamber at the Tolbooth of Edinburgh until the *Reformation in 1560, but one or more of their number would be despatched to an outer room to give an initial hearing to complaints and petitions, hear evidence, and determine how cases should proceed. This gave rise to the terms Outer and Inner House. From about 1562 the court sat in premises at the west end of the kirk of St Giles, before in 1639 moving into the new Parliament House just to the south where it remains to this day.

In 1674 controversy erupted over the question of whether an appeal lay from the Lords of Session to *parliament, and the advocates, who supported the right of appeal, withdrew from the court, whose judges did not. The dispute was patched up but not resolved, and the issue was passed over in silence in the parliamentary *Union of 1707; but an appeal to the House of Lords in the new British parliament was established immediately after the Union took effect, and has continued ever since. One other effect of the Union may have been the naming of the court as the 'Court of Session', a title used only very rarely until its appearance in Article 19 of the Treaty, where the existence of the court was guaranteed 'in all time coming'.

A guarantee of existence did not prevent reform, however. The court's cumbersome structures and procedures were much criticized, and early in the 19th century a process of major change began, lasting until 1868, and establishing what is still the basic form of the court. The Outer House became a court of first instance in which a number of single Lords Ordinary sat and determined causes; from their decisions an appeal lay to one of the two Divisions of the Inner House, the First Division headed by the Lord President and the Second by the Lord Justice Clerk. The collegiate nature of the court survived in the possibility, still occasionally used, of the Full Court convening to consider the continuing utility of some established precedent. The 19th century also saw the court subsuming within its jurisdiction the business of the formerly separate Admiralty, Exchequer, and Edinburgh Commissary Courts. In addition, the powers of the Jury Court set up in civil matters in 1815 were transferred to the Court of Session in 1830.

The upshot of all this was that the court acquired a virtually universal civil jurisdiction. The process of reform, mainly designed to accelerate procedure and the dispatch of business, has continued down to the present day. With the establishment in 1999 of a Scottish parliament (see PARLIAMENT: 4) the legislative competence of which is limited by statute, the court appears set to take on something of the character of a constitutional court, the latest stage of a long and varied history.　　　　　HLM

shinty (*iomain* or *camanachd* in Gaelic) is generally believed to have been introduced to Scotland along with Christianity and the *Gaelic language nearly 2,000 years ago by the Irish. Shinty, or some similar version of stick and ball games (for example, *shinham, shinnins, shinnop, shinny*), has been played from windswept St Kilda to the more hospitable and gentler plains of the Scottish Borders, from the Yorkshire moors to Blackheath in London. It is a game of great antiquity, linked (not always with complete accuracy) to *golf and ice hockey, although the exact degree to which shinty influenced the development of stick sports in *Canada is a matter of considerable debate. Shinty is to be found worldwide as a result of the exodus of Gaels from Scotland to the plains of Montevideo (see LATIN AMERICA) in the mid-19th century; to Toronto and Canada's Maritime Provinces; on New Year's Day in *Australia in the 1840s and thereafter; in Cape Town (see AFRICA) and the war-ravaged wastes of Europe through two world wars.

The modern version of the game is played by two teams of twelve on a field not more than 140–70 yards (128–55 m) long and 70–80 yards (64–73 m) wide. The goals consist of two upright posts, 12 feet (3.7 m) apart, with a cross-bar, 10 feet (3 m) from the ground. The ball is spherical, made of cork and worsted inside, the outer cover of leather or some other approved material. Its circumference should be not more than 8 inches (20.3 cm), not less than 7.5 inches (19.1 cm); its weight at the start of the game not be more than 3 ounces (85 gm) nor less than 2.5 ounces (70.9 g). Balls have been made of India rubber, wood, lemons, sheep droppings, and sheep's vertebrae. The head of the *caman* must not be of a size larger than can pass through a ring of diameter of 2.5 inches (6.4 cm) and no plates, screws, or metal in any form may be attached to or form part of the *caman*. Safety helmets are compulsory for some younger players.

Shinty has always been an amateur game. In its organized form it dates from 1893 and the establishment of the game's ruling body, the Camanachd Association. It was usual in the Highlands to have the principal games of shinty at New Year or Old New Year, although other festivals were also marked elsewhere. Contests were often between two districts or parishes, with no limit to the numbers taking part, players arriving and departing at will, often from dawn till dusk.

There was also a very active shinty scene in England in the 1880s and 1890s, with teams such as Birmingham, Manchester Camanachd, Old Trafford, the Highland Camanachd Club of London, Cottonopolis, Bolton, Nottingham Forest, and Stamford Bridge, playing a crucial role in the embryonic structured version of the game. Shinty has approximately 2,000 players with teams playing at various levels from primary school age to senior (adult). In Ireland, the Gaelic Athletic Association (GAA), a multimillion pound business, runs an organization of over 200,000 players—a ratio of 100 hurlers for every shinty player. However, Scotland remains relatively successful in the modern series of shinty/hurling matches played to compromise rules.　　　　　HDMacL

social class. Anyone discussing social class in Scotland will encounter two strong, and in many ways contradictory, perspectives. On the one hand, there is a powerful hypothesis that Scotland's history is one of class conflict and class politics. Even before the industrial revolution had its impact, struggles (see RURAL SOCIETY: 4) between landlord and tenant, landowner and peasant especially but not exclusively in the Highlands (see LAND AGITATION AND REFORM IN THE HIGHLANDS AND ISLANDS), marked out class conflict as endemic to Scotland. The social politics of industrial Scotland were largely constructed around conflicts between capitalists and workers, most obviously in the phenomenon of *'Red Clydeside' in the second decade of the 20th century. For the next fifty years, party politics were surrogates for class struggle, with Labour (see LABOURISM) and Conservatives (see UNIONISM) in a struggle for supremacy. Reinforcing this view of class as the main motor of social conflict in Scotland is the fact that leftist parties such as the Communist Party and the ILP did much better proportionally in Scotland than south of the Border after 1922. Not only was Scotland seen as configured by class conflict, but some even spoke of Scotland as a class in itself. In the 1970s in particular, and under the influence of *nationalism, it was argued by some writers that the country itself was a class or, rather, an ethno-class colony of England.

If one perspective argues that Scotland is indubitably a class society, the other view argues to the contrary. It points to the presence of different cultural traditions which emphasize the openness of Scottish society, the apparent lack of barriers to social mobility in Scotland, summed up by the phrase 'we're a' Jock Tamson's bairns'. Some historians have even argued that social class was an alien intrusion to Scottish society, imported from a much more class-conscious society in England. Thus, the comment from the late Historiographer Royal Gordon Donaldson in his *Scotland: The Shaping of a Nation* (1974): 'It is true to this day that Scotland is a more egalitarian country than England, but as result of class consciousness horizontal divisions into classes have become . . . more important than vertical divisions into nations.'

What Donaldson was touching on is the powerful 'lad o' pairts' myth which has deep roots in Scotland and which argues that social mobility—in common parlance 'getting on'—is significantly more open in Scotland than in England. Scotland is portrayed as a more socially egalitarian country, in which people relate to each other on the basis of merit rather than status. This myth—using the term here to mean a truth held to be self-evident—is similar in content and function to the 'American Dream', the notion that ability and hard work will lead to achievement. In the American context, the Dream is a story, a narrative, which helps to define Americans to themselves, as well as to other people. It is, in other words, an identity-myth, saying who they are and what their defining values are. In like manner, the Scottish myth seeks to define what is distinctive to themselves and to others, carrying the implicit contrast with its large southern neighbour. The Scottish myth is kept alive because there are institutional mechanisms such as the education (see SCHOOLS: 4; UNIVERSITIES: 3) system which are its carriers. In other words, one is dealing here not with some disembodied set of beliefs and values, but with coherent meaning systems which are given institutional expression in Scotland. Ideas about class and social opportunity are firmly embedded in Scottish civil society.

There are, then, two apparently opposed images of Scotland: a society defined and structured by social class, in which class is the engine of social conflict and change; and another Scotland, different from England in being an open and meritocratic society, lacking the class-consciousness of its southern neighbour. Which is correct? To answer that, it is necessary to point to the different dimensions of class which are in operation.

To clarify this, let us sketch out what we mean by social class. First of all, social class is a relationship not a category. Classes exist only in juxtaposition to others. The English historian E. P. Thompson, in his classic book *The Making of the English Working Class* (1963), put it this way: 'class is a relationship and not a thing . . . "It" does not exist, either to have an ideal interest or consciousness, or to lie as a patient on the Adjustor's table.' Secondly, we must disaggregate key dimensions of social class: class structure—how class is 'objectively' constructed and reproduced; consciousness—the level of culture and meaning which surrounds class

and other systems of inequality; and action—how people mobilize, usually but not exclusively in political terms. Thus, 'class' can exist at any or all of these three levels, and the relationship between them is complex.

In terms of class structure, we might adopt Max Weber's definition in his *Economy and Society: An Outline of Interpretative Sociology*: 'We may speak of a "class" when (1) a number of people have in common a specific causal component of their life chances, insofar as (2) this component is represented exclusively by economic interests in the possession of goods and opportunities for income, and (3) is represented under the conditions of the commodity or labour markets.' Social class refers to the structuring of power, mainly but not exclusively economic, which differentiates people in the market place according to the skills and resources they are able to bring to the market and the rewards they derive from it. In very broad terms, all advanced industrial or capitalist societies share similar features. After all, the private ownership of economic resources, coupled with the capacity to transmit such property by sale or by inheritance, structures the broad power structures within them. For most people, their life chances are determined by what they do for a living, what they work at, because that is the source of their income. It characterizes their life security, gives them access to housing, education, social goods, and so on. We might summarize this as follows: there are in modern market societies three main classes—a dominant class based on the ownership of capital; an intermediate class whose power derives from the acquisition of educational or organizational skills; and a subordinate class based on the possession of physical labour.

How does Scotland figure? At the beginning of the 20th century around three-quarters of Scots were working class, our third category, and around 15 per cent in the middle and upper classes (the rest being labelled an 'underclass'). In the course of the 20th century, the manual working class has shrunk in size, mainly in the last 30 years, so that it represents less than half of the working population, and concomitantly the middle or 'service' class has grown to around 40 per cent, with the underclass at 5 per cent. It was from the 1950s that the 'occupational transition' to service occupations developed in Scotland—as elsewhere. The growing share of services, from 19 per cent in 1911 to 43 per cent by 1981 (see ECONOMY, TERTIARY SECTOR: 2–3) has been the major motor of economic and social change (we must recall in passing that this category has changed considerably, from domestic service employment to occupations concerned with functions like education and social services).

The changing occupational structure and concomitant patterns of social mobility, coupled with new opportunities for *women, have ushered in major political and social change. In similar vein, the trend for women to participate in the labour force has been a feature north and south of the Border. In Scotland, however, as far as married women are concerned, the trend has been one of convergence. Until well after 1945, the economic activity rate for married women in Scotland was only two-thirds that of the rest of Britain, and it was not until the late 1970s that Scotland caught up. By 1981, 57 per cent of married women in Scotland under 60 were economically active. The expansion of new occupations for women runs alongside the feminization of certain occupations such as clerical work, in which the percentage of clerks who were female rose from about half in 1961 to three-quarters by 1981. This does not mean that women are more 'middle class' than men, even though around half of men are in manual jobs compared with only one-third of women, because female pay and conditions remain substantially poorer than those of men.

By 1991, the latest available census, the proportions of manual workers had fallen to just over 40 per cent, and while skilled manual workers were still the largest category at 19 per cent, employers and managers were 17 per cent. If we group employers and managers, professionals, own account workers, and farmers, 31 per cent of economically active heads of households were 'middle class'. Manual workers represented 41 per cent, with 24 per cent in the intermediate categories. In other words, 31 per cent of Scots were in the 'service class' (compared with 37 per cent in Britain as a whole), 24 per cent in the on-manual intermediate class (23 per cent in Britain), and 41 per cent in the manual working class (36 per cent in Britain).

What then can we say about social class in Scotland in terms of the broad models we identified at the outset? First, while it is true that Scotland is a marginally more working-class society than England in terms of its occupational structure, something which derives from the broad historical trends in economic activity over the last century, it has moved in line with the trends in all advanced industrial societies to become more middle class in occupational terms, and one in which by the late 1990s women outnumber men in the labour force (albeit that most work part-time). Similarly, the shift across the generations from one class to another—what is called intergenerational social mobility—is broadly in line with Scotland's comparators. While there is considerable upward mobility into the top social classes, there is very little downward mobility into the lowest unskilled

social classes. This lack of reciprocity is due to the fact that while the size of the manual working class has fallen, that of the service class has grown. This allows the offspring of the service class to be retained in the top classes, while there is (or has been in a period of economic growth in the long postwar boom) room for upward movement into top jobs from below. We should bear in mind, however, that social opportunity is by no means equally distributed. The opportunities for sons of fathers in the top social class to 'self-recruit' was over four times greater than we would expect from perfect mobility, while the inflow into the top class from the bottom class was only about half of what might be expected.

Secondly, 'social class' in Scotland cannot be interpreted and explained in the same way as in England, because key institutions, such as law (see LAW AND LAWYERS: 2), education, and religion (see CHURCH INSTITUTIONS: 3), mediate structures and experiences to produce different political and social outcomes. Associated with these institutions are cultures, meaning systems, which frame structure and action. Similarly, class carries its meanings within it, embedded in its culture. Structure alone is not enough to carry it into action. And vitally, historical memory plays a strong part in the story. The narrative of class in Scotland is one in which issues of *national identity play across issues of class. Scotland's relationship with England has taken on 'class' connotations to the extent that class and nationality are often insinuated.

Since the 1950s, electoral patterns in Scotland, and especially the fortunes of the Tory party, have diverged from those in England. Is this because Scotland has more people in the manual working class, more employed in the state sector, more council tenants than England? The short answer is no. It is enough to say that the predicted Conservative vote in Scotland on the basis of the social structure is systematically lower than we would expect. In the 1997 general election, for example, virtually the same proportion (23 per cent) of the Scottish service class voted Conservative as the unskilled working class in England. Being middle class has a different cultural meaning north of the Border. In like manner, middle-class people in Scotland, whether they have fathers who were in middle-class or working-class occupations, have a greater propensity than their English counterparts to describe themselves as working class which suggests that the meaning and culture of social class cannot simply be read off the class structure.

Class relations in Scotland, just as in any other society, take on the substance of social relations generally. They are not expressed in pure form; they are naturalized so that class takes on the shape and form of the society in which it operates. An understanding of social class in Scotland requires not simply an appreciation of how the social structure has altered over the past century, but also how the culture of class relates to social and political action. The sets of meanings and values surrounding social class, that is, the culture of class, are a vital ingredient in a comprehensive understanding. Class relations are frequently encoded and difficult to read, but social class is vitally important as the key motor of life chances at the beginning of the 21st century just as it was at the beginning of the 20th. In Scotland, as elsewhere, class matters.   DMcC

song, traditional and folk: 1. Scots; 2. Gaelic.

1. Scots

Scots traditional song has been an important strand in Scottish culture, both in aesthetic terms and in relation to *national identity (as seen from within the culture) or national image (as seen from elsewhere). It is not always possible or desirable to draw a sharp distinction between anonymous traditional song and the output of named authors since folk songs proved attractive to poets who used them as models and drew on traditional tunes, and conversely the compositions of known poets circulated orally. One illustration of the key place of traditional song in Scottish culture is provided by the case of Robert Burns, who valued folk song so highly that he devoted considerable energy to the collection of the songs he heard sung in informal settings. Performance context is important for the understanding of the way in which folk songs permeated Scottish society (see HIGHLANDS AND ISLANDS: COMMUNITY LIFE). Songs could be sung by people engaged in solitary work with no audience but themselves, but there were focal occasions, such as a meal-and-ale (celebration at the close of harvest) or a rocking (gathering for spinning wool), when songs would be sung by many of those present. The melodic range, as opposed to the instrumental tunes that were also featured at such gatherings, is not extreme, placing them within the reach of most people. Another special occasion for singing was Hogmanay, which was not tied to work patterns from the past, when songs have especially bonded Scots both at home and in emigrant communities. 'Auld Lang Syne', a song with a Burns component on a traditional base, has signalled all over the world both Scotland and associated values of human warmth and companionship.

The 18th century marks the beginning of song-collecting activity in Scotland, as it does in other parts of Europe, and many fine song versions date from this period, either because they were collected then or because they were collected in the early 19th century from people who had been in-

vited to recall the songs known to them in their youth. The collecting was necessary since the songs did not have any easily traced roots in written or printed form and had to be obtained from the singing (or sometimes the dictation) of those who knew them. It is not unlikely that many more of the songs were circulated on broadsides or in chapbooks than we have been able to trace in the surviving examples of these ephemeral publications, but, even when songs were available in print, the song culture was a largely oral one with songs being passed on from one singer to another with the variations and adaptations typical of this type of transmission (see ORAL TRADITION: 1).

Although there are many fine lyric folk songs, including a notable bawdy element, pride of place goes to the narrative ballads, which were first given emphasis in Walter Scott's *Minstrelsy of the Scottish Border* (1802–3). Scott set the ballads in a rich context of Border history and legend whenever possible, although it must be said that many of the ballads he printed (despite his title) had no special link with the *Borders. As regards history, he was able to include, for example, a ballad relating to the battle of Otterburn fought between the Scots and the English on 19 August 1388. As regards ballads on legendary themes, one with a special appeal to Scott which was firmly located in the Borders near Melrose was 'Thomas the Rhymer' which opens with the meeting between Thomas and the queen of Elfland from whom he later receives the gift of truth which turns him into a poet and a prophet. The touches of imagination in the supernatural ballads like this one and 'Tam Lin' (which also concerns dealings with the fairy people) are among the high points of Scottish song, as are also the laconic and moving treatments of tragic themes in such ballads as 'Sir Patrick Spens', 'Mary Hamilton', 'The Douglas Tragedy', 'Clerk Saunders', 'The Dowie Dens o' Yarrow', and 'Clyde's Water'. In a number of cases, the tragedy arises from family opposition to marriage between a young couple who are deeply in love. There are often many versions of ballads since it proved possible to note them down from a number of different singers, and Scotland is indebted to one American scholar, Francis James Child, for bringing together all he knew in his edition of *The English and Scottish Popular Ballads* (1882–98) and to another American scholar, Bertrand H. Bronson, for completing the task by adding the music in *The Traditional Tunes of the Child Ballads* (1959–72).

Scott obtained some of his finest ballad versions from Anna Gordon (the wife of Andrew Brown, minister of Falkland), who is famous in ballad scholarship under the name of Mrs Brown of Falkland. This is an instance of the fact that, whenever we are given the names of the singers from whom the songs were drawn, we find that women feature very prominently. Although the world of ballads and songs was by no means an exclusively female domain, the situation is quite often one of a male collector (see ORAL TRADITION: 2) and a woman who was what could be called his star singer. This was the case in the 1820s when William Motherwell received 22 ballads from Agnes Lyle, Kilbarchan, and Andrew Crawfurd received 47 songs and ballads from Mary Macqueen, Lochwinnoch; still, in the latter part of the 20th century, Hamish Henderson was especially proud to be associated with the fine traveller singer Jeannie Robertson, from whom he recorded many songs.

Motherwell found in the early 19th century that traditional songs were running thin in Renfrewshire and Ayrshire and envied Peter Buchan's luck in being engaged in collecting in the richer field of Aberdeenshire at the same period. Aberdeenshire and the neighbouring counties have remained an especially fruitful source of traditional ballads and songs and in the first half of the 20th century two extensive collections were made there, the first by Gavin Greig and James B. Duncan, principally in the decade 1905–14, and the second by James M. Carpenter, an American scholar who visited the area in the late 1920s and early 1930s. Carpenter's collection is still largely unpublished but the eight-volume edition of *The Greig-Duncan Folk Song Collection* (1981–2000) forms a good basis for surveying the range of traditional song familiar in Scotland. It is observable that songs travelled freely throughout the British Isles, so that a representative collection of what was being sung, like this one, will provide many instances of songs that originated in England or Ireland but found a home in Scotland, such as 'The Sheffield Apprentice' and 'Brannon on the Moor'. Special interest, of course, attaches to locally composed songs which reflect the life of the community, as in the case of the satiric verses, like 'The Barnyards o' Delgaty', sung by farm workers about their working conditions and their employers (see RURAL SOCIETY: 4).

Folk-song study is not simply concerned with the past, however. From the 1950s, recordings of traditional singing have been made for the archive of the School of Scottish Studies at the University of Edinburgh and selections have been released on cassette and CD so making them available to new generations. By contrast with some countries where folk songs were preserved only in print and the continuity of a living tradition was lost, traditional singing has never died out in Scotland but has recently modulated into new forms which still draw on an awareness of specifically Scottish performance styles.

One particularly rich genre that has continued up to the present is that of *children's street or playground songs which has remained oral in the heart of a fully literate culture. Recent debate on questions of literacy and orality in relation to song has been particularly meaningful in Scotland where there has been both a stress on education for literacy and an abundant folk tradition. Conditions seem to have been right for cross-fertilization between two cultural strands that have sometimes proved incompatible. In response to Albert Lord's extremely influential book *The Singer of Tales* (1960), which concerned Serbo-Croatian singers of epics and the light that their performance practice could throw on Homer, David Buchan in *The Ballad and the Folk* (1972) argued that, through some of the ballads received from Mrs Brown of Falkland, we could glimpse an early phase of Scottish tradition when ballad singers held a story in mind and recreated it at each singing—as opposed to what is found at a later period when we can obtain full evidence, where the singer uses memory (rather freely) to retain verbal as well as thematic material. Buchan's main thesis has been rejected by a number of scholars, including Hamish Henderson, but his work drew attention to formal properties of ballads, such as triadic and ring patternings and distributions of character roles, which remain of interest and will undoubtedly be incorporated into future study of oral process as it relates to the field of Scots song. EL

2. Gaelic

There are three types of composition: *Filidh*, *Bard*, and *Clarsair*. *Filidh* produced four-line verse and eight-line verse poems using no regular stress, referred to as syllabic. *Bard* used verses with an unspecified number of lines from 3 to 8, with regular stress, referred to as Bardic. *Clarsair* (harper) used multiples of four lines, with regular stress. The technical name for this metre was Amhrán.

Gaelic song may be divided into two categories as far as performance is concerned: those sung in free rhythm approximating to that of speech and those which have a strong dependence on regularity of rhythm. Some poetry is actually based on the number of syllables in the line, with regularity of rhythm not precluded, but not a prime requirement. Such poetry (see GAELIC LANGUAGE; GAELIC LITERATURE), going back to the early Middle Ages and a common language and culture between Scotland and *Ireland, is hardly sung now, but its rules may have permeated all singing of slow songs in Gaelic. *Cumha Ghriogair Mhic Griogair Ghlinn Streith* and *Oran na Comhachaig* are examples of the four-line variety, from which the oral tradition has effectively selected verses to be sung with a regular stress. The type has disappeared from the sung tradition otherwise, except in a modified form in songs related to the exploits of Finn MacCool and other Scoto-Irish heroes, written between the 12th and 15th centuries. These may be referred to as heroic ballads. The language of the *Filidh* was a classical version which stayed in their poetry while the vernacular was changing. The eight-line variety has continued to be used for serious or mock-serious subjects to the present day, using the vernacular.

The verse typifying the composition of bards had, generally, two stresses per line, with a final line containing one more stress. In verses of three lines, the whole stanza is sometimes repeated. Otherwise, whether the verse is of three lines or longer, the custom is to repeat the longer final line, using it to complete the stanza or as the first line of the next stanza. The great exponents of this type were Mary Macleod and John MacDonald, both of whom lived through the last three-quarters or so of the 17th century. Amhrán has a multiplicity of potential variations, short or long lines, varying rhyming patterns, the presence or not of refrains. It has also been used and is still used for a multiplicity of themes: praise and satire, lament, praise of nature, humour, love, and songs of love of place. A modification of the four-line structure is a five-line refrain, where line 5 is a repetition of line 1. Line 5/1 is then sung after each verse except the last one.

Other forms include stanzas which seem to be of one line, or couplets. These are used for work songs especially, now waulking songs, which were a part of work and social intercourse for women in Scotland—women and men in Cape Breton, Nova Scotia (see CANADA)—until the 1950s. A typical waulking song, used to accompany the beating of home-produced cloth on to a board to clean and shrink it, was sung with lines or half-lines separated by vocable refrains. It is apparent that songs which were not originally meant for this function have been adapted for it by the addition of vocables. There are a few examples of songs which have no recognizable stanza form, which are almost invariably sung with each line repeated, in the progression AB, BC, CD, and so on. They are often similar to the Scots ballad in that they tell a story, but the story is told in the first person, and more details of it are told separately to explain the song. One very popular example, which is also known in Ireland— 'The Jealous Woman/Wife' (*A' Bhean Eudach*)— has been adapted for the waulking song tradition. Some milking songs and songs which are believed to be based on bagpipe melodies contain rhythmically irregular elements but have been adapted for use as lullabies.

Lullabies and *puirt à beul* have a similar structure, that of two lines, the first repeated twice, and a new fourth line AAAB. In each form simplicity is a requirement, and they have probably been composed spontaneously. *Puirt à beul* are sometimes a vehicle for bawdy verse, but they are often, like the simplest lullabies, apparently addressed to a child. The term can be translated 'tune(s) from a mouth', a focus which makes clear that they were first instrumental tunes to which words were added. It is often said that the words do not mean anything, but that takes away from the extremely clever use of vowels and consonants in them.

There is no evidence in literature that Gaelic songs have ever been sung other than in unison. An inkling of how the compositions of the *Filidh* were sung has come down to us in heroic lays, which are sung in a chant-like way, with simple melodies, although there are a few exceptions which have more variety in the melodic line. This is true of both the four-line and the eight-line variety, but the latter is now sung to a variant of the same basic tune. Bardic compositions are in stanzas of unequal length, and so the singer has to know how the fewer or more phrases in each stanza can be accommodated musically. Very few of this type have survived in sung form and we are dependent almost entirely on the work done by the late Revd William Matheson in this regard, whereby he made use of a combination of printed material and oral sources which were still available in his time. He found that changes were accommodated at the beginning or in the middle of stanzas, so that each one ends in the same way, and the whole melodic unit gives out a feeling of fitting well together. The compositions of harpers have a feeling of symmetry in the melodies, giving a variation of an ABBA-type melodic form. This genre accounts for many tunes whose basic melodies are common to songs of other European countries. Favourite tunes which are well known with English or Scots names include 'The Flowers of Edinburgh', '*Woo'd and Married an a*'', and '*When the Kye Come Hame*'. Generally, adherence to major or minor keys is uncommon, and the pentatonic scale and scales on other degrees than the tonic major are the norm.

Rhythm and stress/accent present the most difficulty for singers of Gaelic song not familiar with the rhythms of the language. Syllable verse has had an influence on other songs, in that, ideally, care is taken to give short and long vowel sounds their proper proportional lengths, and the stresses are those of speech. To some extent this is the case whether a song is slow or fast, happy or sad. There are exceptions, however. Not only songs which accompany an activity, like *puirt à beul*, and waulking songs, but any strongly rhythmic song, demand that the stress often lies on unimportant syllables. Ornamentation of the basic melody line varies from place to place, and is something learned from childhood, ideally. The type of ornamentation used in the Hebrides is different from that used in the Connemara districts of Ireland, where it is at its strongest and where it permeates the instrumental music also in the slow air. Unfortunately, our songs have been adopted by Scottish dance bands, without ornamentation, into the strictures of the waltz.

Without a strong oral tradition, much good material would have been lost. Many well-intentioned collectors (see ORAL TRADITION: 2) have published the music of Gaelic songs with accompaniments, with adaptations of the melodies and with vocal harmonies. The *Royal National Mod, begun in 1892 and now established as an annual competitive singing festival, has over 80 set pieces to judge each year for children and adults, males and females, duets, quartets, and choirs. Prescribed music leads to standardization, which was never part of the tradition. Neither was four-part harmony. The title 'traditional' tells its own story of a phenomenon that became untraditional, and a small 'traditional' competition was given higher status in 1971 with the introduction of a new competition in the name of Mary Lamont, the mother of Alistair Maclean, the spy-novel writer. But the singers who are still familiar with the tradition are not the ones who compete, and those who do sometimes have a struggle to find suitable songs. Many do not know what the tradition is.

A craze for 'Celtic' music began in the late 1960s with the popularity of a Breton singer, Alan Stivell. His albums contained songs from all the Celtic countries and he produced a new rock-type sound. This has possibly helped the popularity of the Scottish bands Capercaillie and Runrig who sing traditional and modern songs with a Gaelic feel to them. There is a wish among young singers, however, for authentic traditional songs. There are problems because of the impoverishment of the language, the breakdown of community life, and the power of recorded music. Fame seems to be crucial. To produce an album is crucial for fame. Singers often have to learn a dozen or so songs very quickly, and there is little appreciation of subtleties of rhythm, stress, melody, or text and often texts are truncated almost to the extent of following the fashion for sound bites! Often a singer's only source for songs is other singers' albums, and often mistakes are perpetuated in this way. On the other hand, there have never been such opportunities for learning songs from a variety of areas, with easy access to material through the tape recorder, extended Gaelic radio time, and use of the world wide web. There is even a survival of interest in heroic ballads and in bardic metre songs. The new millennium is a vital time for the *Gaelic language and therefore its songs.   MM

sport, commercial. The Scottish population was too sparsely distributed to provide a viable market for commercial sport on any scale in the 18th century. Sports and recreations requiring capital outlay relied on patronage. Paternalistic landowners provided some, especially at holiday times, as part of their community obligations. Publicans also made provision, arranging and running various aiming, combat, and animal sports in the hope of profiting from increased ale sales and petty gambling. Patronage also stemmed from the gambling activities of the aristocracy and gentry. Generally, they owned the fighting cocks and racehorses and patronized pugilists, pedestrians, and wrestlers, indulging in heavy betting as a form of conspicuous consumption (see ROUGH CULTURE).

Sports events for the masses emerged as a feature during the period c.1800–50 but not on a regular basis. Insufficient non-work time and surplus income prevented the masses from enjoying more than the occasional outing. Rowing matches, race meetings, prize fights, *Highland games, and pedestrian events, although well attended, were arranged spasmodically, invariably associated with local holidays. Evolutionary economic influences during the third quarter of the 19th century led to the development of commercial sport on a regular basis. New technology, improved methods of *transport and communication, rising real wages, and the concentration of free time into Saturday afternoons provided enhanced opportunities for leisure. Economic growth itself and increasing urbanization (see URBAN SOCIETY: 5) created conditions and needs which necessitated that playing and, to a greater extent, watching sport figured extensively in the leisure choices of the masses. Nevertheless, different occupational groups received real wage increases and the Saturday half-holiday at different times and it was 1890 before the economic benefits of industrialization had filtered down to almost all workers and sport became an industry in its own right.

Initially, from the late 1860s, the earliest *rugby, cricket, and *football clubs which owned or leased playing areas, enclosed them to control use and charged gate money to cover costs. Saturday afternoon football emerged as the most popular spectator sport. Enclosed pitches created club identities and football, supported by the traditional ancillary activities of drinking and gambling, emerged as the most popular and exciting spectator sport, providing working men with a keen sense of personal and group identity (see SOCIAL CLASS). Crowds of 10,000 were common at major fixtures in the 1880s.

589

Forcing spectators to pay for their pleasures led to demands for a good view, protection from the weather, regular, exciting events, and winning teams. Clubs responded by purchasing larger grounds, building terraces, erecting stands, employing the best players money could buy, and lobbying to replace friendly games with a more purposeful and competitive national league. The Scottish Football League was established in 1890 and professionalism followed in 1894. At the same time, clubs, following the lead of Celtic in 1897, adopted company status to raise the necessary capital to pay for stadia improvements. Committees of well-intentioned amateurs were replaced by boards of directors, accountable to shareholders. Most directors and shareholders neither expected nor received direct returns on their investments but a minority expected and received indirect returns from winning building, equipment, and refreshment contracts. A remarkable number of shareholders were local publicans, hoping that fans would use their premises both before and after games.

The leading football clubs also constructed cycle and running tracks and promoted competitions in the closed season during the incipient development of professionalism in order to generate additional income to pay for ground improvements and meet the costs of full- and part-time players. Attendances at cycling and athletics events were never as large as those at football matches but nevertheless, the bawbees rolled in. In 1893, crowds of 15,000 were common; five years later, the average gate had risen to 20,000. Income from summer sports, however, never represented more than 11 per cent of the annual income of even the most successful clubs and both clubs and spectators had lost interest in summer sports by 1914: the former were generating sufficient income from football, having completed and paid for major building projects, while the latter had grown tired of predictable running and cycling contests.

A lively and popular sporting press (see NEWSPAPERS), which began in 1882 with the publication of the *Scottish Athletic Journal*, also played its part in fuelling interest in spectating, particularly in football. Crowds of 40,000 in 1900 and 70,000 in 1914 were common at major fixtures. The biennial Scotland v. England fixture in Glasgow drew the largest crowds in Britain while fixtures between Celtic and Rangers attracted the largest domestic crowds as they emerged as contrasting cultural symbols of Irish Catholicism (see IRELAND: 3; ROMAN CATHOLIC COMMUNITY) and Scottish Protestantism respectively. By 1914, Hampden Park, Ibrox, and Celtic Park were the three largest football grounds in the world.

The gate money brought in by the sports industry expanded in response to rising market conditions between the wars. During the slump years of the 1920s and 1930s, there was no relaxation in the commitment to commercial sport. Huge sums of money were invested in sports venues of all descriptions—greyhound stadia, speedway tracks, ice rinks, race courses, and football grounds—and attendances in most sports peaked just before and after the Second World War. Football remained pre-eminent with crowds often determined solely by the capacity of stadia: the 1937 Scotland v. England match was watched by 149,415, a British record.

By the late 1950s, the unprecedented consumption of material hardware, particularly cars and televisions, had diverted interest away from attending live sport. Watching sport on television supplanted attending live events, deepening passive interest in existing gate-money sports such as horse and greyhound racing, speedway, ice hockey, and football and, at the same time, stimulating interest in viewing rugby union, swimming, *golf, *curling, tennis, athletics, and bowls. Television (see RADIO AND TELEVISION) offered unprecedented advertising opportunities and a diverse range of sponsors and sponsorship developed around popular television sports, changing the nature and timing of competitions, the physical appearances of arenas and clothing, and the presentation of media coverage itself. At the same time, all sports, including football, became increasingly reliant on broadcasting and sponsorship fees for survival or profit—a situation exacerbated after 1990 with the arrival of specialist cable and satellite sports channels. PB

staple ports. From at least the 12th century onwards, Scots traders were frequent visitors to the *Low Countries which, along with the Baltic (see GERMANY, THE BALTIC AND POLAND: 1) and northern *France, were Scotland's main trading partners throughout the Middle Ages and beyond. There are many Dutch or Flemish towns which, like Bruges, have streets with names such as *Schottendyk*. The name for cod in 13th-century Flanders was *aberdaan* (see ABERDEEN). Much of Scots exports, typically made up of untreated wool, fells, skins, hides, and fish (see ECONOMY: 2), went to the Netherlands, both before and after the Wars of *Independence. The creation of a formal staple sometime in the first half of the 14th century only legally formalized an arrangement which had already made Bruges and its nearby port of Sluys the main market for Scottish produce. Bruges, by then the most important banking centre north of the Alps and with one of the most important ports in northern Europe, came to dominate Scotland's overseas trade in both directions. A list of ships in the port sometime in 1455 showed that six of the 72 were Scots, including a 500 ton (508 tonne) vessel belonging to Bishop Kennedy of St Andrews. In return, high-quality cloth, mostly made from Scottish wool, was re-exported to Scotland, along with a range of other manufactured or luxury items. Political troubles in Flanders disrupted the arrangement but in 1359 the staple was re-established in what is the first surviving staple agreement.

By the 1410s deteriorating Scottish relations with the Hanseatic League had a knock-on effect on the position of the Scots in Flanders, anxious to preserve its lucrative trade with the Hanse. The Scots moved the staple from Bruges across the Scheldt estuary to Middelburg, situated on the island of Walcheren within the rival province of Zeeland, and over the next five decades the staple shuttled back and forth between the two towns. The marriage in 1444 of a sister of James II to the son of Zeeland's leading nobleman, who was Lord of Veere, opened up a further alternative. As well as diplomatic wranglings, the port of Sluys was steadily silting up and Veere's deep water harbour became an increasingly attractive proposition, not least because, situated at the head of the maze of islands and inlets which led to the rivers Scheldt, Meuse, and Rhine, it offered endless opportunities for smuggling and evading customs duties. In 1508, a decree of *James IV established Veere as the compulsory port of entry in the Netherlands for all Scottish goods, making it the residence of the Conservator of the Privileges of the Scotch Nation in the Netherlands. The ledger of Andrew Halyburton, a *Dundee merchant who was an early Conservator, shows the changing nature of Scottish exports, which increasingly consisted more of cloth, hides, and fish than raw wool. The ledger also lists a wide range of imports including fine spices, beer, wine, altarpieces and pictures, iron, salt, soap, and even feather beds. The staple remained at Veere into the 17th century, although by then it was increasingly being circumvented with specialist cargoes of coal and salt from Forth ports bypassing it in favour of direct trade with Amsterdam and Rotterdam. Today, the tiny port at Veere, with a single quay, belies its importance for Scotland's history.   ML

Stirling/Stirling castle. Stirling is Scotland's most strategic burgh and castle, the 'gateway to the north'. Perched, like Edinburgh, on the remnants of a volcanic plug, the burgh came into formal existence around 1124, in the reign of *David I (1124–53), together with the sheriffdom. However, the strategic importance of the site undoubtedly meant that there had been a settlement there for much longer; the castle site has certainly been occupied

since prehistoric times. Stirling commands the highest crossing point across the treacherous, tidal waters of the River Forth, dominating a landscape of impenetrable ancient mosses surrounded by mountains to the north. From at least the 11th century onwards, representatives of the composite realm of kings of Scots—drawn from Alba to the north and Lothian to the south of what was called by the English chronicler Matthew Paris 'the sea of Scotland'—met annually at Stirling. It was, it has been said by Rosalind Mitchison, the 'brooch' which held the two halves of Scotland together. The bridge and causeway beneath the castle were essential to both north–south and much east–west travel. It is not surprising that so many battles were fought in the vicinity.

The suitability of the castle rock as a defensive site is obvious. The castle is first mentioned during the reign of Alexander I (1107–24), who dedicated a chapel there. Unfortunately, later work has obscured all traces of the buildings in existence before the outbreak of the Wars of *Independence. Stirling was a favoured residence of the kings of Scots in that period, not least because of the good hunting to be had in the area. Alexander III (1249–86) was responsible for the upgrading of hunting facilities with the construction of the new park to the west of the castle. A forester lived on the edge of the park, responsible for maintaining the deer living with it and excluding those living nearby with an interest in venison and timber.

With the outbreak of war with England in 1296, Stirling became the focus of both sides' attention, for obvious strategic reasons. On 8 September 1296, Sir Richard Waldegrave was appointed keeper of the castle and sheriffdom for Edward I. The castle survived the first onslaught of Scottish revolt in 1297 but when the English government finally sent a force against William *Wallace and Andrew Murray, it is no surprise that they met at the crossing on the Forth. The battle of Stirling Bridge of 11 September 1297 saw a Scottish garrison restored to Stirling castle a few weeks later. However, Edward I's victory against Wallace at Falkirk on 22 July 1298 reversed this but by 1300 the castle was restored to Scottish hands, the English proving unable to prevent its isolation and subsequent capture. The end of this phase of the war was marked by another siege at Stirling, between May and July 1304, the garrison, under Sir William Oliphant, having to endure attack by Edward's latest toy, the War Wolf (a massive siege engine).

The next ten years proved comparatively stable in that Stirling remained in English hands as Robert Bruce established himself as king (see ROBERT I) and began to remove his enemies from garrisons in Scotland. As a result, Stirling became increasingly isolated and on 23 June 1313, Sir Philip Moubray, the castle's keeper, made an arrangement with Edward Bruce, the king's brother, that he would surrender if no relieving force arrived. As 1314 approached, a large English army did, unusually, move north. Though the castle was technically saved, Edward II was determined to give battle and the two sides clashed on 24 June in the boggy area south-east of Stirling, at Bannockburn. With Edward II's defeat, Moubray duly handed the castle and town over to Robert Bruce.

The 15th and 16th centuries saw the military stronghold being transformed into a royal residence and symbol of Stewart power. It is for that reason that the castle is virtually unique in Britain, in being a palace within a royal castle (see ARCHITECTS, ARTISTS, AND CRAFTSMEN). A great hall existed in the reign of James I (1406–37), for the king held a parliament and show trial there in 1424, but the present Great Hall, painstakingly restored to its former glory and startlingly conspicuous presence on the landscape in the 1990s, was the work of that most ambitious of Stewart kings, *James IV (1488–1513). It is likely, however, that Stirling had become the centre point of a glittering Renaissance court at least one reign earlier, for it was James III (1460–88) who had constructed what is now called the King's Old Building. The Chapel Royal, an elaborate ecclesiastical foundation and a power house of the arts, was also founded by James IV; Robert Carver, the celebrated musician and composer, although an Augustinian based at Scone, was closely linked to it, as was Alexander Scott, the most prolific poet of the age of *Mary, Queen of Scots (see CULTURE: 9–10). The most elaborate statement of royal power, however, was the palace constructed in the French style of court architecture in the late 1530s for *James V, who was also allegedly in the habit of mingling with his subjects in the town in the disguise of the Guidman of Ballengeich, so named after the steep road which winds down from the castle.

The reigns of Mary, Queen of Scots (1542–67), and *James VI (1567–1625) saw comparatively modest building works but this was the period when the castle was most exploited as a theatre of royal power. In 1566, Mary used it as the backdrop for a three-day Renaissance triumph to mark the baptism of her son by Catholic rites; the celebrations came to a climax with the first fireworks show which Scotland ever had, with a mock fort on the Esplanade, which represented Stewart power and divinity, repulsing the enemies of the realm, including Turks and wild Highlanders (see FRANCE). In 1594, James VI had the old Chapel Royal pulled down and a Protestant replacement built to the dimensions of Solomon's Temple for the baptism of his first-born son, Henry. The climax of those celebrations was a formal banquet, in which a 'ship of state' was hauled into the Great Hall. Ironically, the grandiloquent gesture of getting this 40-foot (12.2 m) high and 8-foot (2.4 m) wide vessel into and out of the hall may have weakened its structure, as was discovered in the modern renovation of the building. But the message conveyed in both the chapel and the hall was unmistakable: kingship was divine and the king's power in the state was unchangeable.

The removal of the monarchy south after 1603 brought to an end the role of the castle as an icon of Stewart power. Its role as a fortress, and subsequently as a military barracks, dominated its later history. A series of new outer defences were begun in 1708 and, after the last *Jacobite invasion in 1745–6, the Great Hall was reconstructed and subdivided to house troops. The legacy of military occupation has proved difficult to erase completely. The castle ceased to function as a regimental depot only in 1964 and there was considerable debate about whether the Great Hall should be restored to its original state or left as it was, a monument to the 18th century rather than the 16th. Stewart iconography, a symbol of Scotland's former glories, won out over Hanoverian occupation. Yet the army clings on: the King's Old Building still houses a regimental museum and the room where, allegedly, James II murdered the earl of Douglas in 1452, has been home to a First World War trench.

The best impression of the castle is probably the first that the visitor has when approaching Stirling, from almost any direction: it sits above and dominates what has been called the Scottish historical landscape—a landscape in which so many key battles in Scottish history have been fought, including Stirling Bridge (1297), Bannockburn (1314), and Sauchieburn (1488). That fact was already well appreciated in the reign of James VI, when a viewing platform was planned for the king and his court to survey the 'brooch' at the centre of his historic kingdom.

The royal burgh, which maintained a port linked to the east coast via the Forth, was in the second rank of Scottish towns by the 15th century, maintaining a reasonable share of the trade in hides. Continued royal patronage must surely have contributed to its prosperity. This largely came to an end in 1603, when James succeeded to the English throne, although further expenditure was incurred in renovating the throne room for Charles I's only trip to Scotland in 1633. British soldiers remained installed in the castle, seeing off the Jacobites, until their withdrawal in 1964.

Stirling has become accustomed to a resourceful existence. A key stronghold in the first three-quarters of the 18th century of a Hanoverian monarchy which after Culloden banned both kilt and bagpipes, it nevertheless groomed itself as a centre for the manufacture of tartans at the end of that century and in the rage of 'Balmorality' which followed the visit of George IV to Scotland in 1822. Otherwise, it prospered modestly as a commercial and agricultural centre, although its old role as a seagoing port on the tidal estuary of the Forth quickly shrank. The building of the Wallace Monument on the Abbey Craig in the 1860s pointed the way towards its future as a major tourist attraction. Yet Stirling remains a mixture of the genuine and the ersatz. The castle, which attracted well over 400,000 visitors in 1999, has as its centrepiece the meticulously restored Great Hall of James IV, ablaze in its original colouring on the landscape above the town. Opposite it, within the Wallace Monument on Abbey Craig, is a 14th-century broadsword claimed to be the authentic weapon of William Wallace and a Mel Gibson lookalike statue adorns its car park. 'Big man, big sword, big fun' was the memorable advertising slogan which marked the town's celebrations of the 700th anniversary of Wallace's victory at Stirling Bridge. And in the old town itself, heritage predominates, with the late 19th-century military prison transformed into the 'old town gaol' and a pedestrianized, tourist-friendly main street which involved the moving of the burgh's historic market cross. It is hard to imagine anywhere else in Scotland where history and heritage come into such stark confrontation. FW/ML

Tarbat, Easter Ross is an archaeological site centred on the church of St Colman at Portmahomack ('Colman's port'), otherwise known as Tarbat Old Church. In the Middle Ages, the parish comprised most of the Tarbat peninsula including the abbey of Fearn from which it was separated only after the Reformation (in 1626). During the 19th century, pieces of carved stone of the early historic period had been found in the graveyard of St Colman's, and one of Pictland's (see PICTS) few Latin inscriptions on stone was recovered from the Manse wall. The inscription, carved in relief, commemorates a person with a name beginning 'REO', and the form of the lettering is comparable with that in insular Gospel books such as Lindisfarne or Kells. Formal investigation of the site began after 1984, when a buried ditch encircling the church was photographed during an aerial survey. The form of the ditch (resembling that at *Iona), and the inscribed stone (which implies knowledge of manuscript production) raised expectations that the site could be an early monastery. A trial excavation in 1991 which showed that the ditch had been backfilled in the 6th century or later was followed by a major campaign of archaeological excavation by the University of York, commencing in 1995.

Results to date show that the Tarbat site was occupied over a long period, beginning in the neolithic, but its main contribution to history lies in the first millennium AD. The excavation of St Colman's church, Portmahomack, which lies at the centre of the archaeological site, was completed in 1997. This produced three main sources of new evidence: a group of medieval burials, a sequence of churches (9th–20th centuries), and finds of early sculpture (8th–9th centuries). About 150 articulated skeletons were recorded, the earliest being long-cist burials and head-support burials, while later interments were laid in wooden coffins. Evidence for an early chapel survives in the east wall of the extant crypt which is skew from the cardinal alignment of subsequent buildings.

The medieval church is founded on a simple building consisting of a rectangular nave with a south door to which had been added a small chancel, incomplete when found but probably square

rather than apsidal; the total length being little more than 49 feet (15 m). This church has been provisionally dated to the 12th century; it seems to post-date burial in long cists, while the head-support burials are contemporary. During the next century, the building was lengthened both westwards and eastwards, giving an overall length of 90.2 feet (27.5 m). The eastern extension included a partially subterranean crypt just under 33 feet (10 m) long, which incorporated the wall of the presumed early chapel, adding a central aumbry. On these walls were found signs of a major conflagration, which might be attributed to a massacre of Sutherland Mackays by Rosses which is recorded to have taken place in the church in 1481.

Major alterations in architecture occurred following the *Reformation: the crypt was converted for burial with a barrel vault and a north aisle was constructed, with a small central burial vault below ground. A flagstone floor was laid in the nave and burial ceased there. The west wall was widened with a relieving arch to provide the seating for a belfry. These modifications probably belong to the early 17th century: the earliest memorials built into the north aisle are those to John Cuthbert and his wife Jean Leslie, and dated 1623, while Sir John MacKenzie, father of the later Viscount Tarbat and first earl of Cromarty, is recorded as rebuilding the church in 1627–34. In the mid-18th century the nave and the north aisle were taken down and rebuilt, the latter extended by 6.6 feet (2 m) northwards and provided with a first floor, fireplace, and separate entrance to give the 'Lairds' Loft'. There was also a Poor Loft with its own entrance at the west end. By the early 19th century, the pulpit was on the south wall facing the Laird's Loft (which presumably reflected the post-Reformation arrangement) and the minister too had his own entrance, with a vestry. At the *Disruption of 1843, the minister and the majority of the congregation removed to a new Free Church a few hundred yards to the north. In St Colman's, the opening to the Laird's Loft was blocked with wooden panelling, box pews were fitted, and the axis of worship was returned to east–west, the minister being provided with a new vestry and pulpit, and a new stepped entrance, at the east end. The new arrangements included an organ. St Colman's church was redundant by 1980 when it was purchased by Tarbat Historic Trust for £1 and developed as a Visitor Centre.

Other excavations, over a T-shaped area adjacent to the church, are ongoing. Settlement of the early Pictish period (2nd to 6th century by radiocarbon dating) includes a bag-shaped building, a souterrain, and the use of rotary querns. At least one residual find can be attributed to the late 7th century—a Frisian 'Porcupine' sceatta—but the main evidence for a Christian Pictish presence consists of finds of sculpture (see MONUMENTS: 1), attributed on stylistic grounds to the 8th or 9th century. From the area adjacent to the church came several fragments, some associated with a layer of burning, while one panel, featuring a bucolic scene of a family of cattle, had been broken up to make a drain. The drain was part of a busy settlement which continued into a time when 13th- to 15th-century pottery was deposited. The people kept cattle, worked iron, and made large heaps of discarded shells. This, the medieval village of Portmahomack, continued in occupation until the site was abandoned and became a ploughed field. The context for this event was probably the need for a glebe field for the minister of the reformed church.

Sculpture recovered from the foundations of the early church brought the total number of pieces from Tarbat to 37 in 1998. It comprised a number of simple grave-markers with crosses, bearing a strong resemblance to those found at Iona, a sarcophagus lid carrying a boar and lion in relief, and at least one, perhaps two, major memorials. One of these carries Pictish symbols (crescent and V-rod, Z-rod and snake) as well as a finely executed plant scroll; another carries a dragon-like Pictish fantasy beast with a biting tail, and four holy men, probably part of a row of thirteen representing Christ and the Apostles. The scheme also includes two lion-like creatures standing over the half-carcass of a deer. The inscribed stone may have originally formed part of this memorial.

At least three other contemporary memorials of similar quality are known, at Nigg, Shandwick, and Hilton of Cadboll, implying that the fertile Tarbat peninsula was shared by a number of equally wealthy estates. Although it remains possible that the Portmahomack site itself had a monastic phase, inspired by Iona, or Northumbria, or both, by the 9th century it was probably one of a number of Pictish secular powers subsumed in Scottish and Norse political structures (see KINGSHIP: 1).   MC

temperance was a great radical popular movement in 19th- and early 20th-century Scotland. It affected the lives of millions who organized themselves outwith the accepted structures of a society cemented by the giving and sharing of drink, played a central part in the development of ideologies of self-improvement and of domestic happiness based on the nuclear family, and was a formative influence on many of those who contributed to the development of socialism and the Labour movement in Britain.

The effects of alcoholic drink were not widely regarded as a social evil until the latter part of the 18th century, when the increased consumption of spirits began to cause concern. The Revd Robert Thomas, of Scone, was one of a number of contributors to the OSA who drew attention to this: 'The public houses, simply as such, would not, it is presumed, have any bad influence on the morals of the people, were it not for the immense quantities of whisky which they retail, in place of well-made ale, which was formerly the only beverage.'

Consumption increased further after spirit duty was reduced from 6s. 2d. to 2s. 3¾ d. per gallon in Scotland in 1823, and it was against this background that news of the formation of a temperance society in Boston in 1826 and Ward Beecher's *Six Sermons on Intemperance* (1827) were brought to Belfast and the Clyde, sparking the formation of temperance societies by the Misses Graham and Allan in Maryhill and by John Dunlop in Greenock in 1829. Dunlop won over William Chambers, who printed half a million temperance tracts in eighteen months, and Henry Forbes, who took the message to England. By 1835 the temperance movement in Britain and Ireland claimed 1.5 million members in 8,000 societies.

Early temperance pledged members to abstain from spirits, while tolerating moderate consumption of wine and beer. This had an uneven social and geographical effect. In spirit-drinking areas it was equivalent to teetotalism for the poor, while leaving the wealthy free to enjoy wine with their dinner; it was of no use to the alcoholic and in beer-drinking areas it had little effect.

The first Total Abstinence Society was founded in Paisley in 1832, but it was Joseph Livesey's Preston-based Total Abstinence Movement, started in 1833, that was to split from and quickly eclipse the original and acceptably reformist societies, patronized by peers, bishops, and from 1837 royalty, to create a radical and largely working-class movement (see CHARTISM) which believed in reclaiming even the hopeless alcoholic.

The vested interests arrayed against temperance were strong. It is estimated in 1840 that drink was sold in 10 per cent of all inhabited houses in Glasgow, and trade directories confirm that there were more drinksellers in most towns than butchers, bakers, fishmongers, greengrocers, cheesemakers, and grocers combined. As John Dunlop recorded in his influential *Artificial Drinking Usages of North Britain* (1836), many workers were paid in pubs; apprentices paid a fine, to be spent on drink when they entered a trade, and another each time they learnt a new skill; miners were given a gallon of whisky when a new seam was discovered; masons received money for drink when a foundation stone was laid, carpenters for laying the first joist, and coachmen when they collected a new carriage. Children at home and in school, patients in hospital, prisoners, soldiers, and sailors were all provided with copious quantities of beer and in many cases spirits as a matter of course (see URBAN SOCI-ETY: 4).

Drink was, in short, the social cement of society, shared at weddings and wakes and at social occasions of every kind; the medium through which bargains were sealed, favours returned, and forfeits paid. Inns and pubs provided lodging for travellers and islands of comfort, warmth, and sociality in what was otherwise, for many, a fairly comfortless existence. Water was, by and large, unsafe to drink; beer was cheaper than tea or coffee and it was almost universally believed that drink was necessary to life and health (see CALENDAR AND SEASONAL CUSTOMS).

Turning your back on alcohol required a rejection of the norms and forms of society; a semi-secularized version of a Pauline conversion. Such conversions were brought about by remarkable temperance preachers. Some like the Milngavie ploughman who had been converted by Beecher's *Six Sermons* were reformed drunkards fired by their own experience. Ministers of many denominations were involved, and others again were professionals like the American J. B. Gough who gave 1,043 addresses and travelled 63,000 miles (101,367 km) during the five years that he spent in the employment of the Scottish Temperance League and the British Temperance Association. The greatest temperance apostle, to the consternation of some, was an Irish Roman Catholic priest, Fr Theobald Mathew. Converted to temperance by a Quaker in 1838, he had inspired a quarter of the population of Ireland to take the pledge by June 1840 and was greeted by huge crowds on his visit to Glasgow in August 1842.

Taking the pledge was, of course, easier than keeping it. To sustain its members in their self-imposed exile from social life, temperance societies provided tea meetings, soirées, fêtes, and outings and encouraged the development of temperance hotels and places of entertainment, famously exemplified by the Glasgow Tearooms. Friendly Societies like the Independent Order of Rechabites, the Sons of Scotland, and the Good Templars pro-vided not only protection against hard times but also a highly structured social life: an opportunity to hold office, acquire important-sounding titles, wear impressive regalia, and take part in street parades.

Children were an important target. John Hope, a wealthy Edinburgh lawyer, organized fêtes for up to 12,000 children and evening classes for 70,000. He founded the British League for Young Teetotallers in 1847—the year in which Ann Jane Carlisle founded the Band of Hope, a hugely successful organization which was able, as late as the 1930s, to persuade a large proportion of Scottish children to take the pledge.

*Children were indeed central to the ideology of temperance which centred on self-help and an ideal of domesticity based on the nuclear family. Like temperance itself the second of these originated in the *USA; indeed its most powerful proponent, Catherine Beecher Stowe, was the daughter of the Revd Ward Beecher. She, like Clara Balfour, whose *Morning Dewdrops* (1853) provided an origin myth for the movement, saw drink as the agent that kept *women in poverty and fear as their husbands spent their wages on alcohol and besot them under its influence.

This analysis is very clear in the Revd John Kennedy's lecture to the Aberdeen Total-Abstinence Society (1841): 'The evils [of alcohol] are not confined to its own. . . . His wife, his children, are robbed of the love and protection and support to which they are entitled. His heart and his home are alike desolated.' The Revd Stewart Bates equally, in a lecture in Glasgow in 1841, talked of 'bringing competence and comfort to thousands of habitations, that are now the seat of extreme destitution. . . . Feeding the hungry, and clothing the naked, and promoting domestic concord and harmony'. Temperance literature, enormous and ephemeral, and visual aids, from the medals of the 1840s to sets of lantern slides used well into this century, envisioned the joys of a family life involving father, mother, and three or four children around a homely hearth. The wider family, indeed the wider community, made no appearance.

Temperance was then profoundly involved with, and influential in shaping, Victorian ideas of self-help and domestic felicity. Yet the radicalism, its ideas, and its example should not be underestimated. As late as 1909 Philip Snowden in *Socialism and Teetotalism* pointed out that the 'ILP . . . Contains among its membership a larger proportion of abstainers than any other political organisation in the country. . . . Every man who has occupied the chair of the TUC in the last six years has been a total abstainer. The majority of Labour MPs are also abstainers' (see LABOURISM).

By the 1950s temperance was in rapid decline, its promised paradise of prohibition a vanishing dream. The rapidity of its eclipse was itself significant. In part it indicated the movement's success in creating a climate in which controls on, and heavy taxation of, drink were accepted; spirit consumption in Scotland had dropped from 2½ gallons (11.4 litres) to ½ gallon (2.3 litres) per head per year. In part, it also reflected a new confidence that the Welfare State had rendered precautionary self-help unnecessary, a greater openness to pleasure, and a declining belief in the ability of individuals to transform their own lives and the lives of those near to them through a continuing act of will (see RESPECTABLE CULTURE; ROUGH CULTURE). MJ

Tennant, Charles (1768–1838), manufacturing chemist and one of the key pioneers in the Scottish industrial revolution (see ECONOMY, SECONDARY SECTOR: 2). After a period of studying bleaching at Wellmeadow, he set up his own bleachfield at Darnly. Techniques for the bleaching of textiles in this period were notoriously primitive and involved the use of the natural properties of the sun or sulphuric acid. With the expansion of the cotton industry in the late 18th century, Tennant was in an ideal position to take advantage of the growing market for bleaching products and in 1798 he took out a patent for the manufacture of a bleaching liquid which was based on chlorine. This innovation was improved upon in the following year and Tennant successfully patented a solid bleaching powder which had considerable advantages over liquid bleach in terms of manufacture, transport, storage, and cost. In 1800 he established a partnership with Charles Mackintosh, William Cowper, and James Know to set up a chemical works in St Rollox, Glasgow. This concern grew to be the most important centre for the manufacture of chemicals in Scotland and was instrumental in providing the necessary dyeing and bleaching materials for the expansion of the Scottish textile industry in the 19th century, although the resultant air pollution did not enhance the local environment which became one of the most polluted sites in Glasgow. 'Sniffer' Tennant's habit of testing his compounds by smelling them left him with a disfigured nose. RJF

traditional healing in Scotland absorbs and reflects a wealth of influences with historical depth and geographical breadth. The remnants of ancient customs rooted in a European and Mediterranean background tell of the movements of peoples and ideas. The use of native plants and other materials, especially in the Highlands and Islands, reveals a strong and discerning empirical tradition. The adoption of obsolete cures from the official medicine of various periods broadens the picture.

Ancient customs, embedded in the incantations, proverbs, and rituals of oral *history and culture, form a blend of superstition and genuine psychological perception. They recognize the importance of human interaction between patient and healer, and the values of drama, music, words, vision, and dance. However fanciful to the rational analyst, they give comfort and hope.

Each community (see HIGHLANDS AND ISLANDS: COMMUNITY LIFE)—agricultural, fishing, urban, mining, industrial—developed distinctive practices as well as continually giving to and taking from other areas, and experimenting with new material. The folk tradition was constantly adapting. For example, potatoes quickly became an 'old' cure for rheumatism; similarly, dynamite was used by miners in Fife and elsewhere for relieving toothache.

Traditional healing is as old as the first unrecorded headache or wart. In Scotland it emerges into the documented past with the arrival of Christian missionaries who would have exchanged their knowledge with that of the *Picts. Centuries later, the clergy were still credited, along with seventh sons or daughters, and blacksmiths, with being able to cure certain ills.

The distinctive form of medicine practised in the *Gaidhealtachd* during the Middle Ages by formally trained doctors, such as the Beaton/Macbeth medical kindreds, blended traditional knowledge with official medicine. Their insistence on maintenance of health, diet, and hygiene, and preventive as well as restorative measures, was in many ways echoed by later folk practitioners. The revered early 19th-century Dotair Bàn (Alexander MacLeod) of North Uist was a late example of a man who combined professional medicine with local cures. Adept healers from far humbler backgrounds commanded equal respect.

Healing materials included a great variety of plant life from trees to mosses, herbs to seaweeds; animal products from deer antlers to goat's blood, mice, and spiders; and minerals from gold to iron and lead. Alcohol, mainly in the form of whisky, was understandably popular. Water cures were numerous and usually combined with rituals. There was usually a sound reason for a practice, healers lacking only the technology and scientific vocabulary to refine and define their methods. Even the swallowing of live spiders has been vindicated by modern science showing that the venom of the common garden spider is highly effective in treating stroke victims.

Modern medicine and a born-again interest in herbalism have 'discovered' the value of St John's Wort. It was well regarded by Scottish healers in the past, although only used externally. Other cures, derived from unsalted oatmeal brose for

insomnia and colds, dulse for rheumatism and ul-
cers, nettle broth for 'clearing the blood', or an
onion in the oxter for bronchitis, have never quite
gone away.

In rural areas the tendency was for herbs to be
treated as 'simples' (one plant at a time as a specific
remedy). Very occasionally two or three herbs
might be combined but rarely more. In towns and
cities, people were more influenced by the touting
of quack remedies and by apothecaries with their
use of up to 40 ingredients in a potion.

In contrast with itinerant peddlers of pink pills,
local healers rarely charged for their services.
While many healers practised in a broad field, specialists abounded. Bonesetters (usually men) and
massagers (usually women) were often highly
skilled, and unofficial surgeons could be remarkably successful with amputations, healing deep
wounds, removing kidney, gall, or bladder stones,
or trephining—cutting a small piece from the skull
to relieve severe pain. Other healers might special-
ize in mental disorders, bloodletting, *childbirth,
or epilepsy. Dentistry, however, remained a crude
trade of rough extractions (often by a blacksmith),
or a variety of desperate but probably not very
effective measures for the relief of pain. There
were numerous cures for cancers, especially for
what appears to have been a prevalence of skin
cancer in Scotland, but diagnoses may not have distinguished between benign and malign and non-
cancerous conditions.

Through necessity rather than whimsy, a strong
tradition of folk healing in Scotland, as much
among the communities of the north-east (see
REGIONAL IDENTITIES: 2) as in the north-west and the
islands, survived in many places well into the first
half of the 20th century and the introduction of the
National Health Service (see also MEDICINE AND THE
ORIGINS OF THE MEDICAL PROFESSION).   MB

transport and communications: 1. pre-1770s;
2. 1770s onwards; 3. Highlands.

1. pre-1770s
Communications in Scotland, especially in the
Highlands (see TRANSPORT AND COMMUNICATIONS:
3), have always been hampered by rugged terrain,
indented rocky coasts, lack of navigable rivers, a
wet climate, and poor drainage. Roman roads in
southern Scotland, particularly Dere Street over
Soutra, were used into post-medieval times. The
main form of investment in overland communications before the 18th century was bridge building.
Early timber bridges at strategic crossings, like the
Forth at *Stirling, were later rebuilt in stone, sometimes financed by burghs or by the church (as with
the Bridge of Dee at *Aberdeen), though fords and
ferries also remained important. From the 17th

century, landowners helped finance bridges which
would serve market centres on their estates or facilitate the export of produce. Before the 18th century, roads were worn rather than made, apart
from occasional causeways through marshy areas
and paved roadways in towns. Nevertheless, studies of the movement of the baggage trains of English armies during the Wars of *Independence
indicate some surprisingly high average speeds. A
statute labour system along English lines was introduced in 1669. Sheriffs and Justices of the Peace,
joined in 1686 by large landowners within each
shire, were constituted as the local road authorities. Special efforts were made to maintain key
roads, such as the one from Edinburgh to Berwick
or the Causey Mounth, the coast road between
Stonehaven and Aberdeen. Surviving traces of hill
roads in areas such as the Lammermuirs and
Tweedsmuir Hills show what such early roads
were like.

Packhorses rather than wheeled vehicles were
the main way of transporting goods overland
before the later 18th century, even bulky commodities like coal and grain, though sleds were used on
steeper slopes for tasks such as transporting peat.
The carts which were in use before the 18th century were mainly bulky and cumbersome. Herds of
cattle were moved on drove roads, which shunned
lower improved land as far as possible and kept to
the ridges.

Problems of overland carriage emphasized the
importance of water transport. Although the lower
parts of rivers like the Forth and Tay were navigable, most larger Scottish rivers like the Spey could
be used only for floating timber down to the Lowlands. Larger lochs, such as Loch Awe and Loch
Ness, provided important means of internal communication. Much coastal trade was undertaken in
small vessels which could use almost any open
beach or small creek. Early harbours were mainly
quays at river mouths, such as at Leith or Aberdeen. From the 16th century burghs began to
finance breakwaters, piers, and other harbour
works. The 18th century, with an increase in internal traffic and trade, brought a significant improvement in road transport and a need for more
bridges. From the 1760s, the pace of bridge building
increased and many multi-arched ones across
major rivers such as the Tay and Tweed were built.

The first turnpike road was authorized in Midlothian in 1713 but it was not until the 1750s that
turnpike trusts began to improve the main roads
leading out of Edinburgh. The construction of
turnpikes in other parts of the central Lowlands
was well advanced by the end of the 1770s. The
most famous road-building programme in 18th-
century Scotland was in the Highlands where

General Wade had over 250 miles (402 km) of military roads built in 1725–36. Wade's most famous achievement was the road over the Corrieyairack Pass, climbing to a height of 2,543 feet (775 m). Another 750 miles (1,207 km) of military roads were added after 1745. These roads were built in a hurry, often in very difficult country, and construction standards were often poor, requiring much later repair. Some of Wade's bridges, however, like the one over the Tay at Aberfeldy, are still in use.

The first colliery tramway was constructed near Tranent in 1722. Others were built to transport coal from mines to the Clyde and Forth in the 1750s and 1760s. The canal era in Scotland began in 1768 with parliamentary approval for a link between the Forth and Clyde estuaries. By 1775, the canal had been completed from the Forth to a point 3 miles (4.8 km) north of *Glasgow but lack of funds delayed final completion until 1790. Work on the Monkland Canal, designed to open up the coalfields of north Lanarkshire, began in 1770, though again lack of finance delayed completion until 1792. Plans for deepening the Clyde, to provide Glasgow with direct access to the sea, were drafted in 1755 by John Smeaton but work did not begin until after 1768. Coastal navigation was aided by the construction of lighthouses. One of the earliest, burning some 400 tons (407 tonnes) of coal a year, was built on the Isle of May in 1636. A more modern example, at Southerness, was built in 1748 by Dumfries burgh council to improve access to the town's port.

IDW

2. 1770s onwards

This is a large subject, about which much has been written. To render it manageable one approach is to look at function, which allows all modes of transport and communications to be dealt with in terms of their reason for being: to move people, goods, and information from one place to another. This implies a starting point, a terminating point, and a way between. Vehicles may be necessary, in which case provision will have to be made for constructing, maintaining, and housing them. Ways may intersect, and means may be required to allow safe and convenient crossing.

Many transport and communications systems are fundamentally linear and the structures required for their use will be strung along the lines of communication. This linearity can in part be compensated for by the creation of networks or webs so that one is then dealing with a matrix of structures. Other modes, notably radio, television, and shipping, are not constrained to single lines but may be affected by geographical features which may require intermediate structures to make communication possible or safer. Each mode of transport

and communication has its own advantages and disadvantages which are in large measure linked to technical possibility and cost in relation to benefit. These general propositions can have significant effects on the structures required. It is important to recognize that transport and communications, though they may appear to be purely economic in their operation, have a strong social and political dimension. The latter may be more evident in communication where radio broadcasting, and more recently, television (see RADIO AND TELEVISION), have clear political and social connotations, but the use, or potential use, of roads, railways, and shipping to move military forces and government administrators are fundamental to any understanding of Scottish history.

The remainder of this entry will look briefly at a number of structure types which can still be seen in significant numbers in Scotland, and whose study illustrates significant features in Scottish economical social and political development. *Buildings will not be discussed, though railway and bus stations, stables and toll-houses, garages and filling stations, vehicle building works, telephone exchanges, and other buildings are clearly essential components of transport and communications systems.

The earliest routes took advantage of natural features, such as well-drained ridges, interconnected valleys, easy gradients, and short crossings of waters, to ensure movement with economy of effort. Where choices are limited, such routes were paralleled by later construction, as in the Upper Clyde valley, where a succession of roads and a railway can still be seen. The earliest routes used the existing terrain, but the passage of pedestrians and animals would consolidate the paths. Late examples of such are the drove roads, sometimes defined by boundary walls, but with no route-forming structures. Wheeled vehicles were not used in Scotland much before the 17th century, and even then their use was largely confined to burghs and their immediate environs. Structures on routes were in the main bridges, such as the surviving medieval and early modern ones in *Aberdeen (Brig o' Balgownie, Bridge of Dee), *Stirling (Old Bridge), Ayr (Auld Brig), Dumfries (Devorgilla's Bridge), and Jedburgh (Canongate Bridge). Seventeenth-century examples include Bridge of Avon (Hamilton), North Water Bridge at Pert (Angus), and the smaller Bridge of Dye (Strachan) and Bishop Brig (Ceres). These are narrow structures, barely suitable for wheeled traffic.

During the 18th century, and particularly after 1750, formal road-making for vehicles developed, with funding by turnpike trusts, by statute labour or its monetary equivalent, and by the government. The military roads built from the 1820s set new standards, with cuttings and embankments, proper drainage, and bridges and culverts. As many of them cut through roadless country and became disused before motor transport, their remains give a good picture of early road building. Military road bridges, such as the White Bridges at Clephanton (Nairn) and near Foyers, Aberfeldy, Gairnshiel, Invercauld, and Grantown-on-Spey, were on the whole solid, well-founded structures, but not sophisticated in engineering terms. The work of the French state engineers on improved bridge design reached Scotland through the work of John Smeaton at Coldstream, Perth, Banff, and Kirkconnel. Alexander Stevens, Thomas Telford, and John Rennie followed. Telford's Highland roads and bridges, built with government assistance, are well known, but Telford also built the Glasgow–Carlisle road, with a cross-route through Lanarkshire, engineered to an even higher standard, as well as some fine isolated bridges such as Glasgow, Dunkeld, and Dean, Edinburgh. Stevens's bridges, such as Bridge of Dun, Teviot, and Drygrange, and Rennie's Kelso, Cree, Ken, and Marykirk are accomplished structures both as engineering and as architecture. Though masonry bridges continued to be built until the first decade of the 20th century (the last major example was probably Kirklee Bridge, Glasgow), new materials and design solutions eventually took over. Suspension bridges were developed by Captain Samuel Brown and others, and were constructed in significant numbers. Good early examples survive near Berwick (Union Bridge) at Kalemouth, in Aberdeen and Glasgow, and at Bridge of Oich, Aberchalder. Cast-iron arch bridges were introduced to Scotland by Thomas Telford, and became fairly popular. Craigellachie, Cambus, and Fochabers are good early examples, the last-built being the Kelvin Bridge on Great Western Road in *Glasgow.

Wrought-iron and steel truss bridges, developed from wooden structures designed in the USA, were first used in Scotland as railway viaducts. From the 1860s, however, they were adopted as road bridges. The first may well have been Durris Bridge over the Dee. The type really became popular when rolled steel sections became generally available in the late 1870s. Steel and wrought iron were also used in arch bridges, such as the North Bridge, *Edinburgh, and the Albert Bridge, Glasgow.

Mass concrete was little used for road bridges, but when new bridges were required for motor traffic in the 1920s reinforced concrete became a preferred material. Most large concrete bridges of the inter-war period were of the open-spandrel arch type, but solid-spandrel arch and various forms of truss and girder bridges were also built. Since the 1950s the large numbers of road bridges constructed have almost all been either concrete or composite concrete and steel. The major exceptions include the Forth Road Bridge (suspension), the steel bowstring bridges at Bonar Bridge and Bonhill, and the steel truss bridge at Ballachulish. Cable-stayed bridges have been used both for road bridges (Erskine, Glenrothes, and Kessock) and as footbridges (Dumfries, Cumbernauld). Road-over-road crossings, rare before 1960, now form a significant proportion of new road bridges.

The way-carrying structures of roads can be paralleled by those of canals and railways. The major differences, until recently, have arisen from the need for canals to be almost level (except at locks), for railways to be easily graded, and for both to have crossings with other modes which interrupt traffic on each as little as possible. For ship canals, which are relatively deep, this means reducing canal-over-road (or river valley) crossings (aqueducts) to a minimum, and having road-over-canal crossings (also reduced to a minimum) movable by lifting or swinging. For barge canals this means many overbridges. For railways underbridges are not a serious problem, so there are many more of these where the terrain demands it, but whereas a canal may reasonably meander along contours, minimizing earthworks (including tunnels), railways for efficient operation should be as nearly as possible straight, thus requiring in many instances major cuttings and embankments, viaducts—some of considerable length—and tunnels.

The fixed overbridges, and to some extent underbridges, on canals and railways are closely comparable to minor road-over-river bridges. Most are and were masonry arch bridges, but cast iron and timber were not uncommon in early railway building, and from the 1860s wrought iron and, later, steel-plate girders were common. Longer single spans, usually skewed ones, were frequently of the steel truss type. Recently, welded steel-plate girder construction has been usual.

The viaducts which are such spectacular features of many railways, and the much smaller number of large canal aqueducts, are linked technically to road viaducts, few of which are visible. In both Edinburgh and Aberdeen the irregularity of the landform close to the city centre led from the mid-18th century to the construction of viaducts, some of which, such as the South and King George IV Bridges in Edinburgh, were not designed to be seen. More obvious ancestors of the railway viaduct are the aqueducts on the Union Canal, on which Telford advised, and that engineer's Dean Bridge, Edinburgh, and Pathhead Bridge, Midlothian.

The great majority of railway viaducts are multi-span structures with relatively short individual spans. The earliest ones were masonry arch, timber arches, or trestles, and cast-iron arches. In the 1850s wrought-iron truss and girder spans of greater length were introduced, and thereafter wrought iron and steel were extensively used. Brick was used where locally available. From the 1880s to the early 1900s mass concrete was used for cheapness on several lines. Exceptionally, two steel cantilever bridges were constructed, over the Forth at Queensferry and over Loch Etive at Connel.

Bridges, viaducts, and aqueducts are the most numerous and spectacular types of structure on transport systems. One should not, however, forget cuttings, such as the Croy and Bishopton rock cuttings on the early railways; embankments, such as the Germiston embankment on the Garnkirk and Glasgow Railway; retaining walls and tunnels, both bored and cut-and-cover. Canals also have locks, of which those on the Forth & Clyde and Caledonian Canals were pathbreaking in size when first built.

Structures for communications include foot-bridges, which are generally slighter versions of road bridges; telegraph and telephone pole routes; visual signalling towers, notably at Hynish and Arbroath; radio and television transmitting stations, microwave and radar stations; and most recently cellphone towers. Hovering on the edge of communications are overhead electricity transmission lines, whose pylons are unquestionably structures, and oil, gas, and water pipelines, which are rarely visible, though a number of pipe bridges of dates from the 1850s can be seen, and the flumes carrying water to hydroelectric power stations can be spectacular. Finally, though not free-standing structures, one should not forget lifts and escalators.   JRH

3. Highlands

Before the 18th century overland movement in the Highlands was, of necessity, by foot or hoof through wild, lawless country and necessitated fording or swimming fast-flowing rivers. The only overland trade of any magnitude was the droving of livestock to the southern markets, notably the 'trysts' of Crieff and Falkirk. Such other goods as it was economic to transport, were carried by pack men or packhorses. Travellers' tales transmitted the news. The sea offered more direct, if intermittent, connections for coastwise and Isles traffic. Short crossings featured open rowed wherries (ferries); longer passages were by sailing vessels.

The *Union of 1707 and the 1715–19 *Jacobite risings generated tensions in the Highlands. In 1724

General George Wade was commissioned to subdue the rebellious clans. Between 1725 and 1736 Wade, using military labour, built some 250 miles (402 km) of road: the Highlands' first strategic network. The stratagem failed to inhibit the early phase of the Forty-Five rising during which Charles Edward Stuart used the new roads to aid his movement south! The military road system was further extended after the Jacobites' defeat in 1746. Long-distance wheeled transport, if yet uncommon and slow, became possible. Pioneering though they were, the military roads were poorly made. By the end of the 18th century they were falling into decay. The Highland people meanwhile suffered demoralization and destitution in the post-Forty-Five economic climate.

Around the turn of the century schemes to address these problems were emerging. Not least of these was the creation, under the auspices of the British Fisheries Society, of fishing stations to exploit the rich west coast herring shoals (see ECONOMY, PRIMARY: 4). The Society's surveyor and engineer was Thomas Telford. In 1801 the Treasury instructed Telford to identify sites for further fishing stations, plan communications, and look at the possibility of a coast-to-coast canal. In the light of Telford's recommendations, two commissions were established in 1803 to construct roads and bridges in the Highlands and to cut the Caledonian Canal between Inverness and Corpach, near Fort William—highly ambitious undertakings, bearing in mind the lack of skills and facilities in the area. Telford was appointed engineer to the commissioners, who set to work immediately. The difficulties were substantial, including bankruptcy of contractors, labour unrest, and innumerable engineering problems. These were ultimately overcome by the thoroughness of Telford and his assistants. Some 2,700 men were employed annually on road and bridge work which continued until 1821. By then 120 contracts had been let, 875 miles (1,408 km) of road constructed, eleven large bridges and several hundred smaller bridges erected. Work on the Caledonian Canal progressed simultaneously. It was opened throughout in 1822. Telford was also involved in a number of other schemes in the Highlands, including the provision of ferry jetties to facilitate better movement across sounds and sea lochs too broad to bridge. Within nineteen years, Highland transport infrastructure was transformed. By 1820 the use of the new roads by drovers had multiplied, seven stagecoaches ran daily to Inverness, other wheeled vehicles became commonplace, and the tourist trade (see ECONOMY, TERTIARY SECTOR: 3) started to develop. It is a testimony to Telford that much of the system he created is still in use today.

During this remarkable period, in 1812, another transport innovation was to have far-reaching effects. Henry Bell, a Helensburgh hotelier, started operating Europe's first commercial steamboat *Comet* on the Clyde. Competitors appeared rapidly on the scene so Bell moved the *Comet*'s sphere of operation to pioneer the west Highland steamboat trade. She thereby became the first steam vessel on the Caledonian Canal.

By mid-century a well-established network of steamer services catered for the carriage of passengers, goods, livestock, and mails on both the west and east coasts. From 1851, most of the year-round services linking Glasgow with the west Highlands and Islands, and with Inverness via the Caledonian Canal, came under the control of David Hutcheson & Co. The Huchesons developed supplementary summer 'swift steamers' to serve the growing tourist trade (see ECONOMY TERTIARY SECTOR: 3). From 1879 this business was carried on by the Hutchesons' nephew, David MacBrayne—a name which was to become synonymous with West Highland shipping for a century to come. The east coast trade between Leith, Aberdeen and Caithness, Orkney and Shetland came to be dominated by the Aberdeen-based North of Scotland Orkney and Shetland Steam Navigation Company. The coastwise shipment of bulk cargoes such as coal and sand remained the province of sail traders—smacks, ketches, and schooners—and later went by steam 'puffers'—typically owned by local families.

Scotland's steam navigation was soon paralleled by the introduction of steam locomotion on the developing railways. By 1848 the Lowland lines were linked with each other and with the English system, so creating a national network. The Highlands, however, had not been penetrated. Rival schemes were proposed for extension to Inverness via Aberdeen, or direct to Inverness from Perth over the mountains. The Aberdeen scheme—the Great North of Scotland Railway—won the parliamentary battle but financial difficulties inhibited rapid progress with the line. The route via Aberdeen, when eventually completed in 1858, proved inconvenient and pressure was renewed for a more direct link with the south. The new main line of what became the Highland Railway from Stanley, just north of Perth, via the formidable summit of Druimuachdar (Drumochter) to Forres and thence to Inverness, was opened throughout in 1863. Over the next few decades lines were extended north to Caithness and west by stages to Kyle of Lochalsh. By 1899 the company's lines, including branches, extended over 500 route miles (805 km). Other railway promoters focused on the west Highlands. The Callandar & Oban Railway reached Oban in 1880. In 1894, the West Highland Railway opened

to Fort William and its extension to Mallaig in 1901 completed the Highland and the British railway system.

By the end of the 19th century steam power had integrated the economy of the *Highlands with that of the rest of Britain and the *British Empire. This was aided by the national postal service which reached the remotest communities and by the development of *newspapers and, telegraph and telephone communications. Manufactured goods and tourists came northwards by sea and rail. Highland products such as livestock, fish, and whisky were sent south by the same means. Roads served as local distributors on which horse-drawn traffic linked with railway stations or sea ports.

Twentieth-century Highland transport echoed world trends. The internal combustion engine revolutionized road transport. Motor vehicles become the dominant transport mode for people and freight. Asphalt surfacing enabled existing roads to handle motor traffic. As the century progressed, growth in the numbers and size of vehicles necessitated new road and bridge schemes. These ranged from widening and improving alignments of single track roads to major strategic schemes. Of these, the construction in the 1970s of a wholly new high specification 'A9' trunk road from Perth to Inverness and beyond was the most ambitious. This project involved several major bridge works, including spanning the Inverness and Cromarty Firths.

The railway network was a casualty of road transport competition. Branch line closures were followed by proposals in the 1960s to close virtually the entire Highland railway system. Well-orchestrated popular pressure secured the retention of the main lines. Replacement of steam by diesel motive power and other technical advances reduced operating costs on these lightly used lines.

Shipping operators also adopted motor propulsion giving cost savings compared with steam. The dominance of road transport, however, caused a more fundamental reorientation of shipping services. In the 1970s and 1980s new 'roll on roll off' vehicle ferries were introduced to act as floating bridges linking islands with the mainland road system, superseding the pattern of routes which had evolved over the previous century and a half.

Scheduled air services in the Highlands and Islands were developed in the 1930s from Renfrew by John Sword, from Inverness by Ted Fresson, and from Aberdeen by E. L. Gandar-Dower. An early innovation was the air ambulance. By the mid-1930s Inverness, Wick, Campbeltown, the more populous islands of the Inner and Outer Hebrides, Orkney, and Shetland were linked by regular air services. From 1947 the nationalized British European Airways (BEA) supplanted the independent operators on the Highlands and Islands' services. Subsequently privatized, the basic route pattern has remained broadly similar for half a century.

As elsewhere in the 20th century, information and news became increasingly accessible through the development of film, radio, television, digital telecommunications, and most recently the Internet. The Highlands have been no exception. The Highland population (see POPULATION PATTERNS: 2) is growing again after 200 years of out-migration (see MIGRATION). The new sense of confidence is bolstered by a modern, efficient transport and communications system. Concerns about the environment, heritage, and lifestyle have created new transport trends. Freight is moving back to rail, heritage transport caters for the nostalgia market, and growing interest in cycling, sailing, horse riding, and walking bring the experience of Highland travel right back to its origins.   RNP

Ungus (Onuist), son of Uurgust. Known in Gaelic as Onuist or Oengus son of Fergus, Ungus son of Uurgust (king of the Picts *c.*729–61) was one of the most successful and powerful of Pictish kings. He first appears in the historical record in 727 during the fighting that followed the forced tonsuring of *Nechtan, son of Derile (r. 706–24). He was already in middle age, for his son Bredei led military expeditions by 731. At his first appearance he drove out Drest (r. 724–7), Nechtan's successor, and then, in 728, he ousted Elfin, the subsequent king. Up until this point Ungus is not himself called king and it may well be that he was originally a supporter of the ousted king, Nechtan. In 729, however, Ungus defeated Nechtan in battle and took the *kingship himself. All this may imply that Ungus's own claim to the kingship was not good.

Between 734 and 741 Ungus was mainly concerned with the conquest of *Dál Riata, and seems to have effectively destroyed the kingdom. Only rarely from now on did Dál Riatan dynasts play a major role, and then mainly as provincial lords within a Pictish imperium. His forces were also active along the coast of *Ireland and he may have entered into alliance with the parvenu Munster warlord Cathal mac Finguine (721–42), for he seems to have claimed descent from this king's ancestors. Ungus's supremacy in northern Britain began to ebb in 750 when his forces were defeated at Mugdock by Teudebur, king of *Dumbarton (*c.*722–52). Ungus mounted a joint expedition with Eadberht of Northumbria to Dumbarton in 756 which, despite initial success, met with disaster.

Ungus died in 761 and was succeeded by his brother Bredei (761–3). His most enduring achievement was probably the foundation of *St Andrews in Fife (before 747). The St Andrews sarcophagus, the masterpiece of *Pictish art, may even have been constructed to hold his remains.　　　AW

Union of 1707. The Treaty of Union, which abolished the Scottish parliament and transferred political sovereignty to a new British parliament, and which came into effect on 1 May 1707, was greeted with general hostility north of the Border. Historians of the early part of the 20th century, keen to

celebrate the Union and those who brought it into being, tended to dismiss this unpopularity as lack of vision on the part of the population. Loss of sovereignty was the small price which the Scots paid for realizing their historic destiny and reattaching themselves to the forces of movement in European history. At the beginning of the 21st century, views of the Union and its architects tend to be less celebratory, more ambivalent, and, in some cases, downright negative. The Union is no longer seen as inevitable or, in the case of nationalist *historians, desirable. This is not to say, however, that it did not possess a logic. But if this was so, it was (and remains perhaps) an uncomfortable one.

It is easier to say what the Union was than to explain how it came about. The treaty established a single British state: the United Kingdom of Great Britain. Technically, a new British parliament replaced the independent legislatures of England and Scotland; in reality it was an enlarged English parliament. The Scots sent 45 MPs and 16 peers to this parliament, a measure of representation that was generous, if proportioned either to population or taxation, although such proportionality was entirely lacking in the localities of England. The treaty also granted Scotland free trade (see ECONOMIC POLICY: 1) with England, as well as the right to trade freely with the English colonies. In return for financial compensation, Scotland was henceforth to pay taxes and customs at the English rate, although certain important exceptions were given to make the treaty more acceptable to specific economic interests and the *nobility, by far the most important political force in Scotland at this time. The treaty is significant also for what it did not do. Scottish judicial institutions maintained their integrity (see LAW AND LAWYERS: 2). More importantly perhaps, it did not touch upon ecclesiastical questions. Both the Scottish and English parliaments passed Acts preserving the integrity of their churches, and these Acts were appended to the treaty (see CHURCH INSTITUTIONS: 5).

The form which the Union took was a reflection of a fact that might, on the face of it, appear paradoxical. This was that, far from converging, Scotland and England had been, in several important ways, on diverging paths in the later 17th century. This is one of several facts which belies any notion of inevitability about incorporating union. The major, although not only, areas of divergence were legal and religious. A 'national' legal character in Scotland was a product of the later 17th century. While much has been made recently of the shared Protestant identity (see NATIONAL IDENTITY: 3) of the Scots and English as furnishing the basis for the emergence of a sense of Britishness in the years after 1707, the fact is that on matters of doctrine, liturgy, and particularly church government, the Scots and English national churches were, from 1660, profoundly divided. Religious tensions and frictions were to play a major role in souring the atmosphere between the two countries during the negotiations and ratification of the Union.

What convergence there was after 1603 (see UNION OF THE CROWNS) was primarily political, and secondarily cultural and linguistic. Since 1603, there had been a tendency amongst the Scottish political elite to Anglicize as part of a process of coming to terms with a political system in which the principal locus of power and influence was now located at the court in London. English was the commonly understood language outside the Gaelic-speaking (see GAELIC LANGUAGE) parts of Scotland, and even in the Highlands the *clan elites were assimilating increasingly with the south. Yet, even if historians could agree on how far and how fast these assimilationist tendencies were taking hold, or how they should be measured, their significance is not immediately obvious. Scots (see SCOTS LANGUAGE), and not English, for example, remained the usual mode of speech before 1707. More importantly, it simply does not follow that cultural assimilation necessarily promotes political assimilation. In both North America and Ireland in the 18th century, the effect was the opposite. In Scotland, moreover, much more extensive and rapid cultural assimilation with England after 1707 was not incompatible with vigorous assertions of national Scottish identity.

There was also one other area of, if not convergence, growing dependency on the south. This is trade, which some historians have seen as a—perhaps the—key to the passage of the Union. In the decades before the Union, the pattern of Scottish trade was changing in ways which left it increasingly dependent on the English market, especially in the important black cattle and linen trades. Scotland was also, by the 1690s, facing serious economic difficulties. These encompassed famine (see HEALTH, FAMINE AND DISEASE: 2) caused by harvest shortages, and declining exports caused by war and the aggressive mercantilist policies of most European states. Moreover, Scotland appeared to lack the power and capacity to renew

herself economically as an independent state. This was powerfully demonstrated by the fate of the *Darien scheme—Scotland's final and failed attempt to establish an independent overseas empire. If overseas trade was the means to economic growth, as most contemporaries thought, Scotland did not possess the financial, military, and diplomatic muscle to secure her own prosperity. The Scottish state was bankrupt and her navy comprised just two frigates.

From this perspective, union might have seemed the obvious solution, and pro-unionists like Daniel Defoe, dispatched to Edinburgh in 1706 by Robert Harley, then one of the English secretaries of state, to argue in its favour, urged this strongly. Yet, while most thinking Scots could see that the relationship with England needed redefining by the early 18th century, pro-unionists did not have it all their own way on this point. Several anti-unionists, including Andrew *Fletcher of Saltoun, argued that, as the weaker nation, Scotland's economic interests would suffer under the control and direction of a British parliament in London. Wealth would converge on London and Scottish manufactures would be undermined by competition from their southern competitors. Whether, however, these authors were able to offer a viable alternative route to national prosperity and economic renewal is debatable.

Trade was, therefore, one of the strongest cards in the pro-unionists' hand. Yet if it can help to explain why union was accepted, it does not explain its timing. To understand this, we need to turn to political and diplomatic factors. The Union was the product of a crisis (or series of crises) in relations between Scotland and England stemming from the Revolution of 1688–9, the outbreak in 1702 of a European war (the War of the Spanish Succession), and the death in 1700 of the duke of Gloucester, Queen Anne's last remaining heir. Behind these crises was a deeper lying problem facing ministers in London: how to manage a Scotland in which a small number of magnates (see NOBILITY: 3–4)—Hamilton, Queensberry, Atholl, and Argyll—vied for power without any one of them being able to achieve political supremacy. It was this conflict which, alongside the disparate nature of the other major political forces—comprising the *Jacobite Cavaliers, doctrinaire republicans like Fletcher of Saltoun, and the pro-Hanoverian Country party led by the marquess of Tweeddale, which in 1704 became the 'Squadrone Volante'—gives politics in the crucial years of 1701–5 its kaleidoscopic and often tortuous quality. The course of politics was in this period anything but predictable and the route to union full of unforeseen and unforeseeable twists and turns.

The essence of political struggle was that English ministers and their allies north of the Border found it impossible to impose order and control on a Scottish parliament (see PARLIAMENT: 2) which found itself newly powerful after 1689 and the abolition of the Lords of the Articles, a nominated body through which ministers had previously controlled legislative business. The other important elements to the struggle were the economic problems referred to above and the strengthening conviction that the regnal union and English influence were the twin sources of Scotland's difficulties. The stage was set for a revolt against English rule in 1703. The lever Scottish politicians were to use to attempt to prise concessions from the English was the succession.

The parliaments of 1703–4, spurred on by patriots such as Fletcher of Saltoun, laid down a fundamental challenge to the regnal union and England. In 1703, far from declaring for the Hanoverian succession—provided for in England by the Act of Settlement (1701)—the parliament passed a series of Acts directly hostile to English rule. These were first and foremost the Act of Security, which asserted that unless England granted free trade with Scotland, including freedom to trade with her colonies, Scotland reserved the right to settle the crown differently from England after Queen Anne's death, and the Act anent Peace and War, which conferred control of foreign policy on the parliament after the queen's death. The Wine Act allowed import into Scotland of French wine, in defiance of the current war blockade operated south of the Border. These Acts were a self-conscious rebuff to union, for which William III had made overtures in the final two years of his life, and for which Queen Anne had pressed in 1702, although without much support from her subjects in the south. In so far as an alternative to the current regnal union was contemplated in Scotland in 1703–4, it was a federal solution or the imposition of strict limitations on royal rule.

The question is how and why incorporating union came to be accepted in 1706. Part of the answer lies in the response to revolt of the parliaments of 1703–4 amongst English ministers and the changing balance of power south of the Border. Challenge was met by counter-challenge in the form of the Alien Act (1705). This demanded that, unless agreement was reached on the succession by Christmas Day 1705 and progress made on the question of the union, there would be an embargo on the main components of Scots trade with England and all Scots not already domiciled in England would be declared aliens. Given the importance of trade with England, this was a powerful threat indeed. By September 1705, the Scottish parliament had agreed, albeit with some reluctance, to authorize Queen Anne to nominate commissioners to negotiate a union.

The earl of Godolphin, the leading minister in England, and the Whig Junto, whose influence was increasing at this time, were determined to see union achieved and to this end they fixed the composition of the Scots and English commissions accordingly. Ministers in London were also prepared to offer a mixture of inducements, as well as to apply pressure to achieve their goal. The inducements included places, peerages, financial compensation (including about £20,000 in cash for 'expenses' and arrears of payment to office-holders), and concessions on economic and trade matters where important economic interests, and especially those of the nobility, were involved. The scale of these inducements, particularly in the form of money and places, led some contemporaries—notably the Jacobite George Lockhart, himself one of the Scots commissioners—and several subsequent historians to condemn the Union as a flagrant piece of bribery and the Scottish politicians who supported its ratification in 1706 as shamelessly corrupt and self-seeking. The votes of the Squadrone were crucial to the outcome of debates in parliament in 1706, and their support for the union was certainly eased, if nothing more, by promises of influence and compensation from the 'Equivalent', a sum of money offered to the Scots to offset their liability for a share of the English national debt and as compensation for creditors who had suffered in the Darien disaster.

Another absolutely crucial role was that played by the leader of the anti-unionists, the duke of *Hamilton. On several vital occasions, he either switched allegiance or omitted to provide leadership for the opposition. Whatever game he was playing, it was a slippery and complex one; it was also one which is very likely to have been influenced by secret pressures and threats from ministers or their agents. (Hamilton had large debts and estates in Lancashire.) This was an extraordinary situation and, as such, it is hardly surprising that ministers were prepared to go to extraordinary efforts to secure the Union.

Politics in this period always had its sordid side; during the passage of the Union, this was even more than usually the case. Yet it is too easy (and wrong) to regard virtue and principle as being a monopoly of the opposition in the debates about union. The motley collection of anti-unionists included Jacobites, whose real objection was that the Union was designed to secure the Protestant succession in Scotland and England rather than to union per se. Nor were unionists, such as William Seton of Pitmedden and the earl of Cromartie, lacking in substantial and cogent arguments in favour of union; these arguments ranged more widely than simply trade and economic advantages and saw in union greater security for Scottish liberties and property, placing it firmly in the context of contemporary great-power politics and the threat to the European balance of power and English and Scottish interests from the France of Louis XIV. Sir John *Clerk of Penicuik probably summed up the views of many pro-unionists when he argued that Scotland was not giving up sovereignty in the Union, since this sovereignty had for some time been an illusion. Moreover, the pro-unionists were prepared to brave extreme unpopularity and the menace of the anti-union mob in Edinburgh to bring about ratification.

A further crucial consideration was the alternative to union. The consequences of failure to ratify were potentially dire. It cannot be overstressed in this context that the negotiations for union and the ratification took place against the background of the shadow of civil war, and possible invasion and conquest from England. In 1705, there were rumours of a *Jacobite rising supported from France. In 1706, plans were underway for a combined rising of the Highlands, involving Atholl's Highlanders, and the Cameronians (see COVENANTERS) in the south-west. Only Hamilton's cold feet prevented them producing more than a minor rising in the south-west. The realities of power and security were such that England could not countenance further uncertainty about the succession and the menace hanging over it of a Stuart restoration to the Scottish throne.

The Union did not quickly bring about the benefits which pro-unionists, like Defoe, had claimed that it would. Scotland had to pass through two decades of fraught economic (see ECONOMY: 3) and political conditions before entering a period of relative stability and growing prosperity. Before the option of a Stuart restoration to the Scottish and English thrones was crushed militarily and bloodily at Culloden in April 1746, it was armed force which ultimately held together the British state (see GOVERNMENT AFTER THE UNION). Nor did the Union quickly produce an easing of mutual hostility between Scotland and England. Indeed, the circumstances in which it was passed only added to this hostility. Just as achievement of union was not inevitable in 1707, neither was its survival after that date, certainly before the 1730s and perhaps not until 1746 itself.   RH

Union of 1929. The Union of 1929 was the coming together of the two largest Presbyterian churches in Scotland: the Church of Scotland and the United Free Church. They represented the main strands of Scottish Presbyterianism which had arisen from the secessions of the 18th century (see PROTESTANT SECTS AND DISESTABLISHMENT) and the *Disruption of 1843, and the union involved a new settlement of the relationship between church and state.

Previously the Church of Scotland had insisted that any reunion should include an establishment of religion, while the United Free Church had supported the disestablishment campaign. Several factors led the churches to reconsider their positions. The first was the decision of the House of Lords in the Free Church Case, by which a small and mainly Highland (see RELIGIOUS LIFE: 8) minority was awarded the property and assets of the former Free Church following the Union of 1900 with the United Presbyterian Church. The United Free Church, which resulted from that union, became aware that even a 'free' church could be subject to adverse decisions in the civil courts. A union with the Church of Scotland, in which the freedom of the church to change its constitution and unite with other churches would be recognized by parliament, became an attractive possibility. The General Assembly of the United Free Church in 1906 passed an Act anent the Spiritual Independence of the Church, setting out its claims in a clear and uncompromising way. The Church of Scotland, too, came to realize that there were disadvantages in its established status. It could not modify the way in which it adhered to its doctrinal standard, the Westminster Confession of Faith, without recourse to parliament. In addition, the disestablishment campaign began to lose its impetus, and there was growing co-operation between the churches in the field of *missions overseas. Above all, church leaders became aware of the increasing number of people who had no connection with any church, and of the continuing duplication of resources by the two churches at the local level.

Two large committees were set up in 1909 with John *White of the Church of Scotland and Alexander Martin of the United Free Church acting as clerks. They each played a leading role in the discussions and would in due course become the conveners of their respective committees. It became clear that if the union was to take place two obstacles had to be removed: the lack of freedom of the Church of Scotland in relation to the state and in relation to its property and endowments. A key suggestion was made in 1912 by a procurator of the church, Christopher N. Johnston, later Lord Sands, in what came to be known as 'The Memorandum'. Parliament would recognize a new constitutional statement by the church declaring its spiritual freedom, and then it would also bring forward legislation to deal with the endowments. There were thus two distinct stages to the process of reunion. In the first place, two Acts of Parliament would be passed to remove the obstacles, and then the churches would be free to engage in discussions on the act of union itself.

The first stage took much longer to complete. Work was begun on the drafting of a new constitution for the church, but these discussions were interrupted by the outbreak of war in 1914. The statement of the church's freedom, the Articles Declaratory of the Constitution of the Church of Scotland in Matters Spiritual, was finally agreed in 1919. The Articles enshrined the principles of the United Free Act of 1906 and, of fundamental importance, set out the right to change the constitution itself. This right was subject to only one limitation, that any modification had to be in harmony with the provisions of Article 1. This article contained a declaration of catholic doctrine, and was inserted at the insistence of the high churchmen on the committee. In essence, the article declared that the church would lose its identity if it ceased to be Trinitarian and Protestant. The Articles Declaratory also referred to the distinct but complementary roles of the church and the state, and spoke of the Church of Scotland as a national church representative of the Christian faith of the Scottish people. The Articles were recognized by parliament in the Church of Scotland Act of 1921. A further Act in 1925 made over the property and endowments to the church itself so that it was master of its own house in this respect.

The obstacles to union having been removed, new committees were appointed and the Basis and Plan of Union were soon drawn up. The Basis of Union dealt with fundamental matters such as the underlying constitution of the church and its standards relating to doctrine, worship, government, and discipline. The Plan of Union dealt with more practical matters which it was necessary to settle so that the united church could begin its work, and which could be changed later in the light of experience. The plan included issues such as the ordination and training of ministers, the composition of the General Assembly and the other courts of the church, and the amalgamation of the church's central structures and finances. The Basis and Plan of Union were finally approved by both assemblies in May 1929, thus paving the way for the union to take place on 2 October. John White was elected as the first moderator of the General Assembly of the united church. The union, however, was not as complete as the leaders of the movement had wished, and a relatively small number of the United Free Church, who would settle for nothing less than disestablishment and disendowment, stayed out as the United Free Church (Continuing).

It was said that the union resulted in a church which is neither established nor disestablished, but one which is both national and free. It is free in its own sphere and is subject only to the terms of its own Articles, and yet it also has a role as a national church to minister to the people of Scotland (see NATIONAL IDENTITY: 6). DMM

Union of the Crowns (1603). The Scots and the English disliked one another intensely (see NATIONAL IDENTITY: 2–3). Naturally enough; since the late 13th century English kings had sought to assert their overlordship of a vassal kingdom, strenuously under Edward I and III (see INDEPENDENCE, WARS OF; ANGLO-SCOTTISH RELATIONS: 2–3) and much more recently under Henry VIII (see ROUGH WOOING). In 1559–60, the Protestant *Reformation in both countries produced a diplomatic realignment; officially, the Scots moved from their long alliance with the French, established in 1296 (see FRANCO-SCOTTISH RELATIONS), and turned to friendship with England. That was the veneer. Underneath lay continuing hostility. Indeed, if common ground in religious matters brought two former enemies closer together, another new situation created heightened distrust. No longer was it a matter of English claims to royal superiority. Now, as Elizabeth's relentless virginity became an increasingly established political fact, the position was entirely reversed. It would be a Scottish, not an English, ruler who would bring Scotland and England together, for despite threats of English or foreign claimants and Elizabeth's refusal to name her successor, it was impossible to deny that the marriage of *James IV and Margaret Tudor in 1503 made the Scottish monarchs, Mary (see MARY, QUEEN OF SCOTS) and then *James VI, Elizabeth's heirs.

How the English viewed the matter is reflected in the new level of contempt with which Scotland was portrayed by writers like Fynes Morrison and Anthony Weldon; in the past, a country which England thought worth conquering could be given limited praise, but now a country about to destroy the Englishness of the monarchy was to be abhorred. Mary was desperate for, even obsessed by, the English succession; this helped her Scottish Protestant statesmen, because it encouraged this Catholic queen to work with them, for therein lay her best chance of achieving her ambition. But her Catholicism terrified the English, with their obsessive fear of attack by the great Catholic powers, *France and Spain.

After Mary's execution in 1587, the new heir presumptive was much more acceptable: male, Protestant, and, from 1594, a father of a male heir. The prospect of an end to female government and to the grinding uncertainties about the succession had much to commend it. Nevertheless, the 16th century ended on a note of very low morale and fear in England, compared to the cheerful confidence of the Scots and their king. Elizabeth's stubborn determination to stay alive postponed the moment of reckoning; men might hope for the Stewart succession (see KINGSHIP: 6) but until it actually happened could not be sure that her death would lead to foreign invasion—the Spanish infanta was widely, if wrongly, believed to be a candidate—or civil war. Moreover, James behaved with a maddening insouciance, very different from his mother. He rightly saw that Elizabeth could not block his succession, however much she behaved as if she could, and therefore concentrated not on wooing her, to her intense fury, but on offsetting the threat from abroad, admittedly through some shady diplomacy, especially in 1595–6; the king was not above allowing the papacy and Spain to weave dreams of his conversion.

In the event, fears were unrealized. In 1603, Elizabeth finally died. James was immediately recognized as the new king of England, without challenge. His progress south in April–May 1603 was a riotous success, except that the English crowds seem to have regarded him as something akin to a freak, and the joyous king scattered knighthoods with far too lavish a hand. And behind the enthusiasm lay the worry created by his immediate assertion of his authority; this was an experienced king, who did not need to be instructed in his new role by the late Elizabethan leaders of church and state. The English House of Commons reacted with horror to his intention of styling himself 'King of Great Britain'—what would happen to the ancient and famous name of England?—and even more to his plans for an incorporating union; the Scots, responding to English hostility, began to express fears of neglect.

It was as well for the future of the union that its early stages were managed by a man of immensely flexible mind and high political skill. James scaled down his union demands, and began to talk soothingly about England as the greater kingdom. He could afford to do so, because to a greater extent than had seemed possible, he had an Anglo-Scottish court and government; although it was not on the scale initially attempted, the 'English' Bedchamber remained almost exclusively staffed by Scots, and the duke of Lennox was a major figure in English government until his death in 1624. At the same time, no one in Scotland could doubt his continued interest, as he maintained close and constant contact with his Scottish servants. That interest might be unwelcome, as with the Five Articles of Perth (see RELIGIOUS LIFE: 3), but much more important was the reminder that the king the

Scots had given the English remained their king. Given the initial fears and hostility, the fact that by James's death in 1625 union had become acceptable stands as a remarkable testimony to the ability of the first British king. JW

Unionism. In the Scottish context the term 'Unionism' is ambiguous and historically contingent, but signifies—in the broadest sense—a commitment to the terms and spirit of the *Union of 1707. In this regard, Unionism has been expressed paradoxically as both a significant ideology defending Scottish identity (see NATIONAL IDENTITY: 4–6)—most notably in its support for Scotland's distinct legal (see LAW AND LAWYERS: 2), educational (see SCHOOLS AND SCHOOLING), and religious institutions guaranteed by the Treaty of Union—and as the source of Scotland's 'colonial status' within the UK, drawing Scotland into a more dependent relationship with its southern neighbour. Such tensions have underscored the evolution of Unionism in its many manifestations since the 18th century: as a set of popular beliefs, icons, and images reflecting Scotland's place in the UK, as the guiding ethos of administrative devolution; and as a distinguishing feature of Scottish Conservative politics.

The central tenets and icons of British identity rely to a significant extent on the Union of 1707 through which not only a new state but also a new flag and a new free trade empire were created and the Protestant state reaffirmed. Since then, Scottish Unionism has implied and encouraged a commitment to a dual British-Scottish patriotism, the British imperial 'mission', and the Presbyterian faith.

Under the patronage of Henry *Dundas (later Viscount Melville), the Scottish presence in the upper administrative echelons of the *British Empire in the 18th century expanded to significant proportions and was enhanced by subsequent generations through Scottish involvement in the major military campaigns (see ARMY: 3) of the late 18th and early 19th centuries and the Scots' commitment to the missionary impulse (see MISSIONS AT HOME; MISSIONS OVERSEAS) of 19th-century Evangelicalism (see RELIGIOUS LIFE: 6). Through such exploits, Scotland asserted its distinct and successful contribution to the state created in 1707 and earned material rewards in profitable trading relationships with the colonies and cultural dividends in the 'export' of Scottish customs and traditions (see SCOTTISH LINKS). The religious settlement of 1690 (see CHURCH INSTITUTIONS: 5) which the Union confirmed, moreover, was absorbed by Unionism as the spiritual support of the system of government and vision of popular and parliamentary sovereignty it sought to defend. Bereft of a written constitution, the patriotic imperial mission and the doctrines of Presbyterianism served to define Unionism in the public mind until at least the inter-war years of the 20th century.

Despite the continued health of the Scottish *economy in the late 19th century, however, discontent over Scotland's power at Westminster grew in the late 19th century. Neither the Liberal (see LIBERALISM) nor the Conservative parties in Scotland sought to challenge the Union settlement in these years, but both saw the need for administrative reform to appease Scottish sensibilities which had been roused by the influence of the *Irish Home Rule lobby, the Association for the Vindication of Scottish Rights (established 1853), the crofters' cause (see HIGHLANDS AND ISLANDS AND CENTRAL GOVERNMENT: 4), and complaints regarding the time allotted to Scottish Bills in the Commons. In 1885, therefore, legislation encouraged by the Liberal peer Lord *Rosebery, and proposed by the outgoing Liberal government, was passed by Salisbury's Conservative administration, creating a Secretaryship for Scotland. In 1926 the *Scottish Secretary was made a Secretary of State and in 1939 the *Scottish Office moved to Edinburgh. Each of these reforms was enacted by a Unionist government, thus highlighting the duality of Unionist impulses which encouraged reform of the system both as a means of preventing its destruction and as a vehicle for the expression of Scottish distinctiveness within the Union partnership.

A commitment to the Union, however, has not been the sole preserve of Scottish Conservatives. Indeed, Scottish Unionism owes much to the variety of interest groups which have enlivened its discourse both through incorporation and opposition. From the early 19th century the Orange Movement in Scotland proved enthusiastic supporters of the constitutional and religious sentiments inherent in Scottish Unionism and brought the Conservatives significant working-class support in an age of a growing electorate. However, between 1886 and 1965, the legacy of Liberal Unionism proved more significant. The Scottish Liberal Unionists, who abandoned the Liberal Party in 1886 following Gladstone's declaration in favour of *Irish Home Rule, combined with the Scottish Conservative Party in 1912 to become the Scottish Unionist Party—a name which was maintained in Scotland until 1965, when Scottish Tories became the Scottish Conservative and Unionist Party. Significantly, Liberal Unionist influence in Scotland was far more dominant than in the English party and, consequently, Scottish Unionism owed much more to the Scottish Liberal tradition and has proved more supportive of state-sponsored welfare reforms in the 20th century.

From the 1960s, however, the growth of the SNP (see NATIONALISM) challenged the political consensus which, on numerous occasions, had united all the Scottish political parties in defence of the Union. In spite of expressing sympathies with devolution in 1968, the Scottish Unionists opposed devolution in the 1979 Referendum. Such initial support and subsequent rejection of devolution, far from illustrating contradictory tendencies within the party, paradoxically expressed the Scottish Unionists' prioritization of the maintenance of the Union above all other concerns. Tactics rather than goals changed to suit the circumstances. Such flexibility of approach was soon to be abandoned when, in government, the Conservatives under Margaret Thatcher challenged the party's earlier commitment to distinctive Scottish interests promoted by its Scottish MPs. With the steady decline of Scottish industry (see ECONOMY: 6) from the late 1960s, the reduction in welfare spending from the 1980s, the introduction of the 'Community Charge' ('poll tax') in Scotland in 1989, and the threat of privatization to Scotland's water in 1994, the Scottish Conservatives increasingly became identified as an anti-Scottish party and their share of MPs and votes declined until, at the 1997 general election, no Conservative parliamentary candidates were elected in Scotland.

The overwhelming support for a devolved Scottish *parliament which was expressed through the Referendum of 1997, however, did not signal the end of the Scottish Unionist tradition. In opinion polls during the months which followed, few Scots expressed a commitment to Scottish independence and both Labour and Conservative politicians continued to frame their support for the new parliament as a reform of the Union, rather than the herald of its demise.   CMMM

universities: 1. to 1720; 2. 1720–1960s; 3. post-Robbins.

1. to 1720

Before the first Scottish university, Scotsmen went to the Continent for higher education. All three medieval universities were papal foundations: *St Andrews (Benedict XIII, antipope) in 1412, *Glasgow (Nicholas V) in 1451, and *Aberdeen (Alexander VI) in 1495. All were envisaged as university colleges: the College of St John (1419) to Laurence of Lindores as principal arts regent in St Andrews; the Hamilton College (1460) to Duncan Bunch, principal, Glasgow; and King's College (or St Mary's, 1506) to Hector Boece, Aberdeen. Hence the importance of principals in the Scottish universities. To us they seem a plethora of foundations, but regional considerations were paramount then. Two post-Reformation foundations, *Edinburgh

(1583) and Marischal, New Aberdeen (1597), were town-linked, and thus less independent of civil authority. Apart from James I, the medieval universities suffered no state interference.

Regionalization helped to keep down numbers, as also the reluctance of pupils to proceed beyond the grammar school (see SCHOOLS AND SCHOOLING: 1): thus in 1500–59, St Andrews had at least 100 and at most 250 students at any one time. In the first decade after 1560 there were a total of 328 students at St Andrews (figures for Glasgow and Aberdeen are lacking), by the decade beginning 1610 (including Edinburgh and Marischal College) there were 1,749 in all. Before the Wars of the *Covenant Glasgow had about 120 students yearly, by 1696 some 250, and by 1702 400.

The 1429 theological statute of St Andrews shows Paris influence by way of Cologne. Laurence of Lindores regarded nominalism as the best influence against Lollardry (Wyclif was a realist in philosophy), but soon a new realist school of Albertists, based on Albert 'the Great', threatened the nominalist domination. By the time St Salvator's College (1450) and Glasgow were founded, Albertism had taken over in the interpretation of Aristotle, whose works dominated the arts curriculum. Glasgow's Cologne affiliation can be seen in terminology: elsewhere, as in Paris, students finalized their studies by 'inception', in Glasgow (following Cologne) by 'principiation'. Both canon and civil law (both housed in a 'school of decreets') were taught at St Andrews, which hoped in 1432 to attract lay civilists. Glasgow also had a school of canon law where civil law also was lectured on, but only as far as 1472; a chaplainry to support the lecturer in canon law was finally transferred to arts in 1522 (see LAW AND LAWYERS: 1). Theology at Glasgow was taught originally by monks from Melrose, for a period from 1518 by John Mair the historian, and otherwise by Dominicans. William Cadzow, professor in 1507, came from Bologna. The displacement of philosophical theology by philological is reflected at Glasgow by John Davidson's competence in Hebrew (1556) and, about the same time, William Ramsay's in Greek. St Andrews felt the *Reformation crisis most strongly with Patrick Hamilton and Alexander Alesius in the 1520s, but welcomed theological refugees from England in the 1540s.

The Reformation meant the abandonment of Lombard's *Book of the Sentences* for exclusively biblical exegesis, and the Protestant John Winram replaced the Dominican John Grierson as dean of theology at St Andrews. At first no textbooks except the Old and New Testaments were prescribed. At Glasgow, the principal now became a minister and doubtless taught accordingly. At St Andrews the provost was Catholic and left for Paris. King's College remained defiant, having been admirers of Erasmus: George Hay ceremoniously removed the principal with his arts staff, for adhesion to Catholicism and to old-fashioned logic. This heralded many state visitations in post-Reformation Scotland. Glasgow had a new foundation in 1577, with Andrew *Melville's arrival from Geneva. Its absent rector's book (abstracted in 1560 by its then Catholic rector) would have shown that its founder envisaged law teaching which would not be restored till a chair of law was set up in 1714. Meantime King's still had a canonist and civilist as lecturers till a refoundation on Melville lines abolished them briefly. By the end of the 16th century the purely philological approach was being abandoned, fat logic texts were being returned, Aristotle was again the height of fashion, and Franco Burgersdijck of Leiden was adopted as textbook and not abandoned till the 1690s. St Salvator's had fought the Ramists surrounding it, but some dependence on Petrus Ramus was current in all universities.

Apart from Latin, the staple language, Greek was taught, mainly as a first-hand introduction to Aristotle and his late Greek commentators; towards the 17th century's end a separate Greek linguist was desired. Melville's forte was oriental languages, including Hebrew, but we cannot gauge his success as his record-keeping of matriculations and graduations was defective. One 17th-century student's notebook has sketches of King Aristotle and two major Jesuit commentators, Arriaga and Oviedo, but by the 1650s Descartes, 'the noble Descartes', as Thomas Nicolson, a dedicated Aristotelian, calls him, was being championed till the 'Glorious' Revolution of 1688, after which, in the 1690s, he was 'Cartesius and his gang'. The lecturers, especially in Edinburgh, turned to men like Henry More, Robert Boyle the chemist, the Royal Society, and finally, under Gerschom Carmichael, to Isaac Newton. Mathematics, too, needed separate lecturers. Homer Blair was made special lecturer at St Salvator's but the post died with him in 1603. A decade later, however, a permanent chair was founded at Marischal and a university chair at St Andrews in 1668 and in Edinburgh in 1674. At Glasgow, an eccentric polymath, expert on matters from hydrostatics to navigation, held the chair of mathematics in 1691: George Sinclair approved of Galileo. At each governmental change and after the 1715 rebellion (see JACOBITISM) lecturers were deposed and others appointed. A national philosophical course was proposed in 1647 and again in the 1690s, but received without enthusiasm.

The usefulness of history was not altogether disregarded. Andrew Melville taught it from

Melanchthon's edition of John Carion and Sleidan; but this was largely uncritical and based on four ages, the last contemporary. In post-Reformation King's bits of secular history were read at meals. It was sometimes taught with humanity, and in 1692 at Glasgow William Jameson was appointed to a chair of civil history, but his history was universal, mostly church history, though a chair of church history appeared in 1716. Jameson replaced a lecturer in humanity and history. Lecturers in humanity were considered inferior to regents in philosophy (see HISTORIANS: 2).

In the early 17th century Iberian philosophers dominated the teaching scene, as can be illustrated from John Strang at Glasgow and Robert Baron and the 'Aberdeen Doctors'. After 1650 French philosophers took over, though regard was paid to John Locke and, disapprovingly, Thomas Hobbes. Robert Baillie (1599–1662) disliked the resort to 'popish' philosophers, but they continued in use. The traditional offices of rector and chancellor operated, though the rector was often the choice of a small body of masters and the chancellor often a layman. The family of the Glasgow rector who absconded with his records returned the rector's book in 1625 and the mace was reacquired by Principal Sharp (1583–1615). But meantime Glasgow had become a college of theology and arts. *Medicine was apparently taught in St Salvator's College by Provost James Martin but it lapsed, and attempts from time to time were made to revive it along with law, which William Welwood was appointed to teach there too. The philosophers were inhibited for religious reasons for espousing the Copernican heliocentric theory even when they appreciated its use. At Glasgow, when professorships were restored, Carmichael professed ethics and discussed natural law based on Samuel Puffendorf. Even by 1720, a sort of pre-Enlightenment was already germinating (see also FRANCE; GERMANY, THE BALTIC, AND POLAND; LOW COUNTRIES; MEDITERRANEAN LANDS IN THE MIDDLE AGES; CULTURE: 5, 11).

JD

2. 1720–1960

For the first three centuries of their existence, the Scottish universities were small, corporate institutions devoted primarily to training the clergy. In the 18th century, their role expanded, and they assumed a position in the nation's life which they have never since lost, seen both as central to Scotland's cultural identity (see NATIONAL IDENTITY: 5) and as affording uniquely democratic opportunities for individual social mobility (see SOCIAL CLASS). Although the term 'lad o' pairts' dates only from the 1890s, the idea that individuals of modest social origin could fight their way through the university

to become ministers, doctors, or schoolteachers was celebrated long before. How far was it a reality? And did such opportunities increase or decline as industrialization overtook the Scotland of parishes and small towns in which the lad o' pairts had his roots?

Recent historians have seen the 18th-century universities as, above all, the focus of the Scottish Enlightenment (see CULTURE: 11), many of whose leading exponents held professorial chairs and worked out their ideas in university lectures. In this golden age, the Scottish universities were briefly at the forefront of European thought, and flourished educationally when elsewhere universities were stagnant. Their urban location, the replacement of the older 'regenting' system by lectures open to all who paid the fees, and the growth of medical schools (see MEDICINE AND THE ORIGINS OF THE MEDICAL PROFESSION) at *Edinburgh and *Glasgow, were among the reasons for this prosperity. A modernized philosophical and scientific curriculum seemed relevant to contemporary problems of progress and national improvement, and combined liberal and practical education in a way which attracted the growing professional and commercial bourgeoisie as well as the landed class.

Historians' understandable interest in the intellectual history of the 18th-century universities has not been matched by research into their institutional and social history. But it seems clear that, alongside their new appeal to the elite, they continued to be accessible to poorer students. The parish schools (see SCHOOLS AND SCHOOLING: 2), now well established throughout the Lowlands, were linked directly with the universities: the age of university entry was low (15 or less), and little more than rudimentary Latin was needed as preparation, which could be given by parish schoolmasters who were usually university men. Bursaries, endowed over the years to aid recruitment into the church, helped pay university expenses, as did working in the long summer vacation or tutoring richer students. It was at this period, too, that the residential side of the universities withered away. Students lived at home, with relations, or in lodgings, without moral supervision from the university, and attended lectures as they chose; the fixed curriculum decayed, and formal graduation became optional. Scottish university education thus became flexible, cheap, and open, not just for boys from parish schools, but also for adult men drawing on hard-earned savings. These poorer students, it is true, had a limited career choice—the church or schoolteaching—and the extent of egalitarianism should not be exaggerated. Most 'lads o' pairts' were the sons of small farmers, shopkeepers, or artisans rather than the really poor, and much depended on patronage by landowners or other wealthy sponsors, not on merit alone. Nevertheless, the Scottish universities had about 3,000 students in 1800, a high proportion of the population by contemporary standards. And while many small countries managed with a single university, Scotland had five: St Andrews, Glasgow, Edinburgh, and King's and Marischal Colleges at Aberdeen, not united until 1860.

This socio-cultural pattern, the product of a rural society in which education was an adjunct of religion, had parallels in other Protestant countries, especially northern Germany. In most respects, it survived until the middle of the 19th century, and even intensified. In the north-east, competitive bursaries for the Aberdeen colleges and the Dick Bequest (an endowment which from 1833 subsidized classically trained parish schoolmasters) created an archetypal pattern of rural educational opportunity. But as the century advanced there were strong pressures to adapt to new professional and vocational demands, and major university reforms were carried out through Acts of Parliament in 1858 and 1889. Discussion of the issues involved has been dominated by G. E. Davie's *The Democratic Intellect: Scotland and her Universities in the Nineteenth Century* (1961). Davie argued that the 19th-century reforms should be interpreted as a process of Anglicization, in which the broad, philosophical education of the Scottish tradition was replaced by specialization, with a parallel social shift from the egalitarianism of the 'democratic intellect' to a more class-based and socially exclusive pattern. Davie's interpretation has been absorbed into many general books, and helped establish the common view that breadth of curriculum is the main distinguishing feature of Scottish education. But other historians have criticized his arguments, claiming that they simplify a complex story in which Anglicization was only one strand, and exaggerate the extent of specialization. The division between Ordinary and Honours degrees, the compromise arrived at in the 1890s, still allowed a large measure of general education and retained a distinctively Scottish educational ethos.

Most pressures for change arose within Scotland, reflecting the career needs of the growing middle class. Formal qualifications and examinations were replacing patronage and older modes of apprenticeship, as shown in the 1850s by the spread of competitive examinations for the civil service and the reorganization of the medical profession. If Scots were to compete on equal terms for posts in Britain and the *British Empire, the informal curriculum inherited from the 18th century had to be tightened up. Reformers wanted to raise the age of entry to 17 or 18, to introduce a strict examination

at the transition between school and university, and to reintroduce fixed curricula leading to graduation. To make this programme possible, an effective system of secondary schools was needed; following the Education (Scotland) Act of 1872 this developed under the aegis of the state, and a national network was in place by 1900. The introduction of a university entrance examination in 1892, at the same level as the school Leaving Certificate of 1888, taken at the age of 17, marked a crucial stage in these reforms (see SCHOOLS AND SCHOOLING: 2, 4).

University preparation was now the monopoly of secondary schools, themselves more sharply distinguished than before from the elementary sector. Did this close off opportunity? The evidence suggests that, while the mechanisms of social mobility changed, and schoolteaching replaced the pulpit as the classic upwardly mobile career, the overall level of opportunity did not fall. Many secondary schools were free, and there were enough scholarships and bursaries to allow selected individuals to climb the ladder from the local school to the university, aided from 1900 by the Carnegie Trust, which paid their university fees. Analysis of the social origins of students shows, if anything, a broadening of recruitment between the 1860s and the 1900s. Though about half of all students came from professional or business families, 20–5 per cent could be described as working class, even if (as in the past) they were more likely to be the children of artisans, white-collar workers, and small traders rather than miners, factory workers, or labourers. While the traditional system had been most effective in the rural Lowlands, opportunities were now extended to the Highlands (see SCHOOLS AND SCHOOLING: 3) where there had been little advanced education before, and to the cities: the Glasgow matriculation registers show that the children of the skilled workers of Clydeside were staking their claim to a share in the university tradition.

Between 1860 and 1914, the universities enjoyed a period of prosperity and expansion; the growth of the medical schools at Edinburgh, Glasgow, and Aberdeen was especially striking, and a university college was founded at Dundee in 1883. Total student numbers rose from 3,399 in 1861 to 6,254 in 1901, then to 7,776 in 1913. Numbers rose modestly between the wars (to 10,034 in 1938), but it took the Second World War to create a real revolution of expectations. For whatever the degree of social mobility and individual opportunity which existed, it was in a context where university education reached a very restricted proportion of the age group, perhaps 2 per cent before 1914, 3 or 4 per cent in the 1950s.

Of the 7,776 students in 1913, 1,751 (23 per cent) were women. Part-time lecture courses for *women in the university cities had begun in the 1860s, but their full admission as students was delayed until 1892. By then, effective girls' secondary schools were widely available, and women students came from much the same backgrounds as men. Their share in the student body rose to a third in the mid-1920s, but then fell to 25–7 per cent by the late 1930s, mainly because of the reduction of openings in schoolteaching, which was virtually the only outlet for women arts and science graduates. There was a significant number in medicine, but business, law (see LAW AND LAWYERS: 2), and the church were largely closed to women graduates, and the universities themselves hardly set an example, appointing no woman to a chair until after the Second World War. It was only when new occupations opened up after 1945 that a slow move to equality resumed.

The arrival of women was part of a 'corporate' revolution in the social life of students which began in the 1880s. This included student unions, debating societies, student magazines, organized athletics, part-time military activities, and the Students' Representative Councils (SRCs), which began in 1884 and received statutory recognition in 1889. It was now too that rectorial elections became a focus both for student politics (the rectors usually being notable political or literary figures) and for periodic bouts of ritualized rowdyism, lubricated like most student activities by alcohol. Some of this energy was diverted in the 1920s into the annual charity gala or rag, which used street processions, theatrical shows, and bazaars to raise money. Students who had formerly returned after classes to their homes or digs (if not to the bare garrets of literary myth) could now choose from a great range of social activities. The SRC, the Union, the Officers' Training Corps, and the rugby club tended to be strongholds of a male student elite, while women had their own unions and social and athletic clubs. Down to 1914, relations between male and female students remained somewhat formal (see RESPECTABLE CULTURE), but the war permanently relaxed social mores. Dance halls and cinemas, cafés and pubs, provided forms of sociability and contact with youthful urban culture unknown in the 19th century. The Scottish universities did not move beyond this, however, to become residential. There were a few halls and hostels especially for women, but they were not usually run by the university authorities, who were forced to turn their attention to this question only by expansion after 1945.

Some of the classic forms of student life declined after the 1960s. The underlying shift was from seeing the university years as an apprenticeship in the social mores of the comfortable middle classes, to a generational concept of student life as an autonomous interlude free of the pressures of class and status. In retrospect, the period between the 1880s and the 1960s may be seen as an identifiable cultural phase in university life. The familiar parameters were the Leaving Certificate, bursaries and Carnegie grants, the landlady, the student union, the three-year Ordinary degree for the majority, and the four-year Honours degree for the ambitious. As remodelled by the Victorian reforms, the universities succeeded in simultaneously renewing the Scottish professional and business classes, feeding graduates into the British elite and the Scottish imperial diaspora, and keeping open the channels of individual mobility from below. But as in the earlier pre-industrial phase between the mid-18th and 19th centuries, they remained closely related to local schools and to the cities and regions on which they traditionally drew. The progressive decay of these local links was to be a striking feature of the next phase of university development.   RDA

3. post-Robbins

Higher education from the early 1960s until the present day has had to cope with two substantial sources of change. On the one hand, participation has expanded remarkably, from under 9 per cent of the age group in 1962 to 46 per cent in 1996. On the other hand—and partly in response to this democratization of access—the system has faced growing insistence from Scottish civil society that it define itself as Scottish (see NATIONAL IDENTITY: 6); for the older universities, this marked a break with three-quarters of a century in which they had seen themselves as primarily British.

The first phase of the expansion was inaugurated by the report in 1963 of the committee of inquiry chaired by Lord Robbins. Its recommendations applied to the whole of the UK, but their impact on Scotland was distinctive because the legacy was distinctive. The universities were relatively more important in Scotland than in the rest of the UK because they had a long history of providing a broad curriculum that would serve each of the main regions, and because they had a leading role in the preparation of students for the high-status professions of the law (see LAW AND LAWYERS: 2), medicine (see CULTURE: 23), and the church. The SED—the government department responsible for non-university education in Scotland—had built up a system of technological colleges and colleges of education, but these remained complementary to the universities rather than rivals to them until the 1990s.

So the first beneficiaries of expansion were the universities: the ancient institutions of St Andrews, Glasgow, Aberdeen, and Edinburgh, the new

Strathclyde and Heriot-Watt universities upgraded from technological colleges, Dundee University, made independent from St Andrews of which it had been a college, and the one wholly new foundation in Stirling. From the 1970s onwards, governments preferred to encourage expansion in the non-university sector (it being cheaper because less research was carried out there), and so the technological colleges grew to contain about one-half of undergraduate students by the late 1980s. Expansion then became rapid from the early 1990s, and in 1994 the distinction between universities and colleges was finally abolished. By the mid-1990s, a higher proportion of the age group was graduating from university in Scotland than in any other European country.

For most of the period, the expansion benefited all social-class groups equally, but did not mitigate *social class differences, although by the mid-1990s some inroads were being made by means of higher education courses in the socially accessible further education colleges. These provided a much higher proportion of higher education places (27 per cent in 1995) than their counterparts did in the rest of the UK (for example, 12 per cent in England).

The biggest change in patterns of participation was in relation to gender. In 1962, *women made up less than 40 per cent of entrants to higher education, and were under 30 per cent of entrants to the universities. By 1996, women made up one-half of entrants to higher education, and were about 45 per cent of entrants to the universities that dated from the 1960s or earlier. Significant proportions of women also began to take part in the sciences and in the professions of law and medicine, although not in engineering.

The expansion to create a mass system of higher education could be interpreted as fulfilling a putative Scottish tradition of accessible universities—the democratic intellect that was celebrated in George Davie's book of that name in 1961. But, by the middle of the 20th century, the universities were ambivalent about their Scottishness, preferring the apparently higher status and apparent cosmopolitanism of British networks. This British cultural reorientation had been developing since the setting-up of the University Grants Commission (UGC) in 1918, responsible for funding universities throughout the UK. Britishness was consolidated by the 1960s expansion, partly because the universities recruited many staff from outside Scotland and partly because the new common UK entrance system encouraged students to come to Scotland from elsewhere. The universities successfully opposed any Scottish funding body throughout the 1970s and 1980s, and they also were able to prevent the 1970s Labour government from including them within the remit of the proposed Scottish Assembly.

But the universities were also faced with strong pressures to be more Scottish. A Scottish Tertiary Education Advisory Council recommended in 1986 that the universities be removed from the ambit of the UGC and transferred to a Scottish funding agency that would also be responsible for the higher education colleges. This reform was not implemented at the time, but something very similar did come about in 1992, when responsibility for the whole of Scottish higher education was given to a new Scottish Higher Education Funding Council (SHEFC). Although the immediate reason was that the government wanted to bring together universities and polytechnics in England—and could not find a politically acceptable way of transferring the higher education colleges from the SED to any UK-wide body—the ultimate reason was the pressure for a more Scottish system dating from the 1970s. When the Labour government of 1997 proposed to transfer legislative control of the SHEFC to a Scottish *parliament, there was almost no public opposition.

As elsewhere in the UK (and indeed further afield), the advent of a mass system required more stringent attention to measuring the quality of both teaching and research. The 1997 report of the committee of inquiry chaired by Sir Ron Dearing intensified this, as has the subsequent drive for 'quality assurance'. Such pressures, once they are accompanied by a Scottish parliament, will also force the universities to pay more attention to Scottish society and traditions, as was recommended by the Scottish committee parallel to Dearing's that was chaired by Sir Ron Garrick.

So Scottish universities at the beginning of the 21st century were no longer for an elite, no longer mainly British, and no longer essentially autonomous of the state. The transition was painful for the older universities, but political reality and the financial requirement to recruit more students gave them no option but to accept it.   LP

urban settlement: 1. to 1750; 2. 1750–1830; 3. 1830–1920; 4. 1920 onwards.

1. to 1750

There is little evidence of the layout of the first Scottish towns; but, being primarily settlements with a trading focus, it is fair to assume that the earliest urban dwellings clustered near to the nucleus, be it a primitive market space, a natural harbour, the crossing point of trading routes, or a ford. There is no available information to indicate whether there was any formality in the topography of these early towns, but the effect of natural phenomena (see GEOLOGY AND LANDSCAPE) on the unnatural built environment would have been paramount. Early urban settlement, in particular, was determined by such factors. The four basic essentials were security from human and other predators and shelter from the elements; firm, dry ground for building; a local food supply (see DIET); and ready access to drinking water. The last was probably the most important and all first settlement sites would be found by a stream or river, although urban settlement could shift from its early site once wells were dug. In *Dundee, for example, wells, such as the Lady Well and the Cross Well, were sunk at the junction of impermeable igneous rock with the permeable Devonian sedimentary series, the Lower Old Red Sandstone. In Dunfermline, the Causagait or High Street, probably not the original nucleus of the town, was laid out along a spring line; and in *Aberdeen, a probable shift of focal point could be made to the Broadgait/Castlegait area, an open space, ideal economically and physically for a market, where, although ill-endowed with streams, wells might be sunk.

Failure to assess adequately the nature of the terrain could sometimes lead to disaster. The Nethertoun, the first site of Hamilton, or Cadzow as it was originally called, was in an area close by the Clyde and liable to flooding, as it is to this day. If Cadzow was to survive it needed to transfer to higher ground. This had been effected by the mid-14th century. *Perth still suffers from flooding in the 20th century. It lost its royal castle in 1210 to water, and the only area to survive intact in the medieval period was the small ridge that perched above the flood line. And, although without archaeological or documentary evidence it is not certain where precisely urban settlement was originally concentrated at *Glasgow, thanks to the charting of the early medieval flood plain by geographers, the area near the confluence of the Camlachie Burn and the Clyde can be discounted as one of intense, early settlement.

With the granting of burghal status, from the 12th century, there comes evidence of a quite deliberate planning of streets and burgage plots, albeit often respecting natural features such as rivers, marshes, and hills; or pre-existing non-natural nuclei, such as a royal castle or an ecclesiastical establishment. This formal system of territorial planning was reinforced and maintained by the burgh's legal authority. *St Andrews was laid out by Mainard the Fleming and Glasgow by Ranulf of Haddington to precise plans; and both men were specifically invited to perform this role, having earlier laid out *Berwick and Haddington respectively. Early land use has been evidenced by archaeological research and, reinforced with documentary and cartographic information, it may be

concluded that a high degree of precision went into not only the initial dividing up of available street frontage, but also into the subsequent maintenance of these delineations by the appropriate town officers, the liners, appointed by the burgess community. Excavations at Perth have suggested a burgage frontage standard for this town of 20 feet (6.1 m); in Dunfermline there was a variant of 22½ feet (6.9 m), with occasionally 20 feet 9 inches (6.3 m) and 25 feet (7.6 m); and Dundee followed a very similar pattern to that of Dunfermline. Evidence of building regulations and their enforcement in all burghs where medieval records have survived are testimony not only to the continuance of this early insistence on ordered space, but also to the successful control of the townscape by the townspeople.

The typical, although not unique, medieval town plan was one of a single street, with burgage plots, rigs, or tofts, running in herringbone pattern back from the street frontage. To the rear of the burgage plots there were often back lanes, which, in many cases, eventually became thoroughfares in their own right. The focal point of the burgh was the market place, very often a widening of the main street. Here were sited the market cross, the town's tron or weigh beam, and the tolbooth. The tolbooth was the most important secular building, maintained by the townspeople at great expense, whether physical or monetary. It functioned as the meeting place for the burgh court and council and as the town gaol. It was here also that the town weights were kept for security and that the tolls for use of the town market were collected.

Tolls might also be collected at the town ports, or gates. Although a few late medieval or early town ports have survived, for example at *St Andrews and Dundee, these were not typical. Most ports were of the simple barress, or wooden gate, type, and were not intended to be highly defensible. Their function initially was more as psychological than physical barricading and, symbolically, the ports stressed the individuality and independence of the burgh. As well as acting as toll collection points, equally important was the control of undesirable persons likely to be a burden or source of annoyance to the townspeople, particularly during the times of rapid spread of epidemic diseases (see HEALTH, FAMINE, AND DISEASE: I) such as plague. Burgesses also had ready access to and exit from the town through their backlands where their rigs abutted onto the burgh boundary, and many burgage plots had their own small back gates out of the town. This was possible because most Scottish burghs were not walled in the manner of York, Siena, or Carcassone, for example. The traditional Scottish fortification was more like that of Linlithgow: a dyke, and sometimes a ditch, and a wooden palisade that was not always secure enough to withstand strong winds. Although towns such as *Stirling, Peebles, and *Edinburgh had substantial stone defences by the middle of the 15th century, stone walls did not become common until at least the 16th century.

Dominating the townscape of most towns, both architecturally and emotionally, were ecclesiastical buildings (see CHURCHES: 1): cathedrals, abbeys, parish churches, chapels, monasteries, and friaries. The setting of friaries gives an interesting insight into the extent of medieval urban settlement, as they were often deliberately set on the edges of towns, and it becomes very clear how small and closely confined were medieval burghs. Indeed, most towns did not develop suburbs until into the modern period. Most of these ecclesiastical buildings were constructed in stone, in sharp contrast to the majority of domestic dwellings.

The houses of the burgesses were usually set at the frontages of the burgage plots, each toft in the earlier part of the Middle Ages normally housing only a single tenement, with a long garden at the rear. In time, these backlands housed workshops, middens, wells, and outhouses, as well as functioning as gardens and space for animal rearing. Some of the plots on the periphery remained gap sites well into the medieval period—a comment on the small population sizes (see POPULATION PATTERNS: 1). This was not the case in the market centre, where pressure for space encouraged further building at the rear of plots—a process termed repletion. Those who lived to the rear needed free 'ische and entrie' through the foreland; this necessary insistence on access resulted in the central cores of many towns becoming jumbles of closes and tiny vennels. To add to the congestion at the central core, the open market space often became encroached upon or even, as in Montrose and Haddington, the central portion was totally built upon to form an island unit of dwellings. By the end of the Middle Ages some towns, most notably Edinburgh, were responding to urban pressure by building upwards, with multi-storey buildings (see HOUSING: 2).

Such developments in house structure and the constant risk of fire meant that gradually, but only gradually, the traditional form of housebuilding (see BUILDING MATERIALS AND TECHNIQUES) was largely abandoned on street frontages: a substantial timber dwelling, called the 'Woodenland', survived more or less intact in Dundee until 1876. The majority of medieval buildings were of wood, the very earliest urban dwellings being merely basic hut-type houses made of stakes and interwoven wattle with free-standing posts to support the walling and roofs thatched with cut heather or turves of growing plants which offered water re-

sistance. From the late 13th century, there is growing evidence of an increasing sophistication in housebuilding, with stakes set in wooden ground sills, later replaced by stone sills, and exterior walls given extra strength by a reinforcement of heavy clay, dung, mud, or peat cladding. Larger wooden buildings were roofed in colourful pottery tiles and some in slate. Such was the improvement that, when Pedro de Ayala visited Scotland in 1496, he reported that 'the houses are good, all built of hewn stone and provided with excellent doors, glass windows and a great number of chimneys'. This was, undoubtedly, an exaggeration but was at least indicative of changes in the townscape.

The 17th and early 18th centuries brought many advances in the construction of houses, with genuine attempts to remove fire risks by such measures as instructing families to build in stone and removing dangerous industries, such as candlemaking, to the outskirts of towns. Thus, in the larger centres, suburbs gradually grew up around the urban nucleus. The street sights might now include multiple specialized markets and associated buildings, such as slaughterhouses, weigh-houses, and harbour offices. Many grand symbols of corporate pride were also erected: elegant town houses, new or refurbished market crosses, more efficient wells, schools, and mills. Religious and political events would also make statements on the townscape. The *Reformation and subsequent neglect meant the decline of many of Scotland's prestigious town cathedrals and churches. If not totally destroyed, as at St Andrews, many were converted into multiple parish churches, in the larger towns such as Dundee, where St Mary's parish church was divided so as to provide accommodation for four different congregations, or single parish churches, as at Melrose and Old Aberdeen, where the naves of the once-prestigious abbey and cathedral began to function as the new parish churches (see RELIGIOUS LIFE: 3). New parish churches, in styles to suit the changed mode of worship, were also erected in many burghs (see CHURCHES: 2).

The Wars of the *Covenant brought differing problems to Scotland's towns. Some, such as Ayr, New Aberdeen, and Stornoway, were to become dominated by highly fortified Cromwellian forts or citadels, the remnants of some of which remain to this day (see BUILDINGS: 4). Many suffered wholesale destruction, so encouraging the later rebuilding of the institutions of civic pride. Dundee suffered vastly, being treated with unparalleled ruthlessness by Monck's forces in 1651, even though, with its new town walls, it was considered one of the most defensible towns in Scotland. The new building programme necessitated in Linlithgow gives a fair impression of the havoc a visiting army could wreak on a town. The parish church had become incorporated in the defences of the peel; horses were stabled in the nave; and troops occupied the triforium. On the departure of the military, the church heritors estimated that £1,000 was needed to repair the roof and windows alone. Other work had also to be effected. The town was granted a free fair for three days and allowed the burgh to double the custom within the town, according to the *Register of the Privy Council*, 'considering the great loss sustained by the burgh, and the destruction of all their public works by the attack of the usurper, viz. their church, hospital, school, market cross, tolbooth, well, four mills and store houses or granarie at Blackness' (its port, a few miles to the north on the Forth). The defences erected around the palace were all knocked down after the *Restoration. The tolbooth itself was constructed between 1668 and 1670, to a design of John Milne, the king's master mason, with a double staircase giving access to the first floor and a spire added in about 1673. Its original form may be seen prominently on Slezer's engravings of Linlithgow in *Theatrum Scotiae*. This new tolbooth reduced the width of Kirkgate by approximately 8 feet (2.4 m). The records show clearly that, for the town, the 1660s and 1670s were a period of general building activity. Two clocks were made, one for the tolbooth steeple and the other for the church steeple, both in 1670/1. In the same year, it was reported to the council that progress was being made with the building of the grammar school. The Cross Well had also to be reconstructed, as were the flesh and meal markets.

A medieval man visiting at this time would, however, have found little difficulty in finding his way round his home town, whether it was Linlithgow or any other. The street pattern remained almost uniformly that of the Middle Ages, albeit with building encroachment on many medieval streets and additional thoroughfares; the delineation of burgage plots survived, even with subdivisions and assimilation. Indeed, many of these medieval remnants would survive even the vast changes that were to come with industrialization.

Little of this early historic past remains immediately obvious in the 20th century. Virtually intact burghs, such as Kintyre and Culross, are not the norm, and both of these have strong statements to make on the Scottish urban built fabric and form. Remnants of the townscape may remain, however, in less obvious a guise. The sheer size of Montrose's large open market space gives some clue to the once great importance of its medieval market, although encroachment from later buildings has narrowed the open space by several feet on both sides. Inverkeithing's market area, on the other

hand, suffered market repletion, with an infilling of the open area by other urban buildings. This, too, still makes a strong visual impact on the townscape, with its medieval market cross largely intact, standing nearby. The street alignment and lie of burgage plots in such towns as Haddington, Elgin, and St Andrews retain much of their medieval character; pockets of such remnants may be found in many historic towns. Medieval and early modern buildings have not survived prolifically, but those that do may offer considerable information, bearing in mind that numerous alterations and additions have been made over the centuries, including in many cases both horizontal and vertical subdivisions. Provand's Lordship in Glasgow, Mar's Wark in Stirling, and the 'John Knox House' and Gladstone's Land in Edinburgh are well known, but equally significant are Gardyne's House in Dundee and 339–43 High Street, Kirkcaldy, both of which offer an insight into quality merchant housing in east coast burghs. Recent urban archaeological research into historic burghs has also brought to light that even seemingly devastated towns, such as Dumbarton, where the heart of the old burgh has been literally ripped out to make way for modern developments, retain important evidence under the ground. Fossilized in many of our town centres to this day are potent reminders of early town planning.   EPD

2. 1750–1830

Although in some cases, such as *Dundee, circumstances provoked extensive change to the town's buildings and character in the later 17th century, it was generally in the decades after 1750 that much of the modern appearance of Scotland's burghs, great and small, was fixed. In the larger towns, the increases in population (see URBAN SOCIETY: 3; POPULATION PATTERNS: 2) and the acceptance of new ideas in planning and building meant physical expansion beyond the historic limitations.

The most ambitious and influential programme was in *Edinburgh where the published *Proposals* of 1752 envisaged expansion northwards beyond the valley of the Nor' Loch, now Princes Street Gardens. Although there was some residential development to the south—for example, George Square was laid out from 1763—the construction of the North Bridge in 1765 provided greater expansionist opportunities. Two years later, James Craig's winning competition scheme and the laying of the foundation stone of the first house marked the commencement of the New Town. The concept of a northern British capital was made evident by the neologism of the royal and emblematic street names and in the orthogonal plan with the parallel lines of Princes, George, and Queen

Streets terminated by squares dedicated to Queen Charlotte and the country's patron saint: Andrew. With George Street straddling the ridge, Princes Street and Queen Street were each built on one side only thus giving open aspects over gardens, in the manner of the Royal Crescent at Bath. Uniquely in contemporary planning, Thistle and Rose Streets accommodated tradespeople and the servant classes. Craig's model may have been Richelieu in France but without its enclosing wall. Even so, the New Town was finite, a self-contained entity linked to the Old Town by the bridge and by the Mound, made up from spoil from the foundations of the New Town.

Slowly, the new buildings crept westwards from St Andrew's Square, where the houses were set back from the street with a central garden area. The elevations were of random rubble with dressed stone at the margins and openings. In 1781 it was ruled that the building height would be 48 feet (14.6 m) from the basement to the eaves. Ten years later, Robert Adam's design for Charlotte Square set new architectural standards with palace fronts, ashlar faces, and classical ornamentation.

In 1801 the New Town was expanded northwards beyond Queen Street to the designs of Robert Reid and William Sibbald. Though lacking the interspersion of public buildings, such as St George's church which closed the vista westward along George Street, this second New Town had its own interest, as in the closure of the central axis of Great King Street at one end by a hemicycle of houses around a landscaped garden, and at the western termination by W. H. Playfair's circular Royal Circus, a northern echo of its counterpart in Bath. Grander and more imaginative was the development of the Moray estate from 1822 by James Gillespie Graham, whose sense of theatre was expressed in the progression and interlocking of a hemicycle (Randolph Crescent), an ellipse (Ainslie Place), and lastly a dodecagon (Moray Place), where the columned frontages trumpet an architectural finale (see ARCHITECTURAL STYLES).

In the west, mercantilist *Glasgow was expanding westwards along the alluvial plain of the River Clyde. Trongate and its continuation, Argyle Street, were a mix of residential and retail uses. Glasgow's planning innovation was the grid. Being open-ended, it allowed for infinite expansion overlaying without deviation Glasgow's hilly terrain. From Argyle Street, new streets were driven at right angles northwards, often cutting through earlier suburban developments of mansions environed by large gardens. In Miller Street, the pedimented villa of the wright John Craig of 1775 still stands but now aligned with the pavement. To the west, Glasgow's second New Town, composed of uniform terrace frontages, was built over the Blythswood estate. At its heart on the highest hill, a square on the Edinburgh model, dated 1823 onwards, has the unadorned elevations characteristic of neoclassicism.

The same effect occurs in *Aberdeen in part because of the prevailing style and because the local granite does not allow for indulgent ornamentation. In 1794, a perceived need for better communications with the south led to the creation of Union Street which involved levelling the summit of a hill and bridging the Denburn with a single span in 1805, thus opening a direct route to the 16th-century Bridge of Dee and the south. It would be long, however, before the lands beyond were built over so that Archibald Simpson's Bon-Accord Square and Crescent—the latter possibly imitating Edinburgh's Abercromby Place—remained for many years as detached enclaves. Houses were to line Union Street but from an early date shops began to appear, as happened in Edinburgh's Princes Street.

With a landholding society it is not surprising that in the countryside also there were instances of formal planning. The third duke of Argyll removed the old town of Inveraray from its proximity to his new Gothic castle, begun in 1745, to a spit of land by the shore of Loch Fyne, where first John Adam and later Robert Mylne successively built the Great Inn, the chamberlain's house, and manse, all connected by screen walls and bisected by a main street which opens at the top with a church in the centre. James Gillespie Graham's courthouse and gaol are on one side and a school on the other. With white harled walls and blue slate roofs, Inveraray gleams over the foreground of water and the backdrop of wooded hills.

Another ducal village is Fochabers, Morayshire, which was relocated beyond the gates of Gordon castle in 1775. With three streets and lanes, the plan is akin to Craig's but with the church, by John Baxter, placed to one side of the central square. More than a dozen planned villages proliferated in the north-east, where the grid-iron plan was popular as at Keith, Banffshire, in 1750 and the new burgh of Laurencekirk, Kincardineshire, laid out in 1770. Tomintoul, often dubbed the highest settlement in Britain, unusually, is a linear plan. Many were intended to provide employment in the production of textiles. Perhaps the prettiest village is Eaglesham, Renfrewshire, founded by Lord Eglinton in 1796 with streets flanking a triangular green.

The application of technology enabling the mass production of textiles and the need for waterpower meant the establishment of mills in the countryside which in turn necessitated workers' housing as at Stanley, Perthshire, in 1785. The largest cotton-spinning establishment was New Lanark, Lanarkshire, which was laid out by the Glasgow cotton entrepreneur David Dale and sold in 1799 to his son-in-law Robert Owen. The mill buildings bordering the Clyde, now a World Heritage site, are overlooked by three-storey tenements. On the coasts at Ullapool, Ross-shire, in 1788 and at Pultneytown, Wick, Caithness, in 1803 fishing villages were created. Another at Helmsdale, Sutherland, was laid out by the first duke of Sutherland in 1814 to give sustenance to his tenants forced (see CLEARANCES OF THE HIGHLANDS AND ISLANDS) from their inland holdings. JMac

3. 1830–1920

From 1800 onwards, the nature of urban settlement was fundamentally shaped by the pace of population growth. Driven by economies of scale and the advantages of an urban location, industrialization (see ECONOMY: 4) assumed a sufficient momentum in the early 19th century to attract large numbers of migrants (see MIGRATION) from Highland and Lowland Scotland, as well as from Ulster and southern Ireland (see IMMIGRATION, IRISH). The population of *Glasgow quadrupled and that of Paisley doubled between 1801 and 1841; in *Edinburgh and Leith, the increased population (see POPULATION PATTERNS: 2) in these four decades was itself greater than the accumulated population of previous centuries. By 1851, one in five Scots lived in the four cities (see URBAN SOCIETY: 4)—Glasgow, Edinburgh, *Dundee, and *Aberdeen—and by 1911 the ratio was one in three. Together, natural increase and migration produced a 48 per cent increase in the population of burghs with over 5,000 people between 1831 and 1861 and a further 113 per cent increase between 1861 and 1901. With 50 per cent of the population living in towns of 20,000 or more, Scots were a more urbanized nation than any other in the world, except for the English.

To house such a rapid expansion put immense strain on existing accommodation (see HOUSING: 3; LIVING STANDARDS: 5). Flats were 'made-down' or subdivided, floor space was shared, and common lodging houses originally intended as short-stay accommodation for single persons new to the city became long-term accommodation, often for families. For an emerging urban industrial working class (see URBAN SOCIETY: 5) with low and irregular wages, new housing was both scarce and unaffordable; builders and developers, given the substantial capital and time required to build tenements, were unable to respond in the short term, even if they judged it profitable. Consequently, in the first half of the 19th century, the initial phase of urban expansion was met by a more intensive use of properties and plots within the ancient burghs.

As the quality of dwellings was progressively downgraded by overcrowding, disrepair, and sanitary arrangements shared by an increasing number of occupants, inevitably the physical degradation of the housing stock was progressive. Proximity amongst tenement dwellers particularly exposed the Scottish urban population to epidemic disease (see HEALTH, FAMINE, AND DISEASE: 3), and consequently to high urban mortality rates. Cholera epidemics in 1832, 1848–9, and 1853–4 drew attention to the public health risks associated with the intensive tenement developments of Scottish towns and cities.

By national and international standards Scottish cities stood indicted. In 1836 Frederick Engels commented that the 'brilliant aristocratic quarter [of Edinburgh's New Town] . . . contrast[ed] strongly with the foul wretchedness of the poor of the Old Town', and Edwin Chadwick's best-selling Report (1842) stated that the most wretched living conditions in the country were to be found in the wynds of Edinburgh, though those in Glasgow were criticized severely, too. In relation to Edinburgh, William Chambers, publisher (1840), concluded that 'the construction of the town is radically unfavourable to health' and the absence of water closets either within tenements or in back courts means that the 'excrementitious matter of some forty or fifty thousand individuals is daily thrown into the gutters, at certain hours appointed by the police, or poured into carts which are sent about the principal streets'.

The residential responses to the escalating dirt, disease, and depravity of urban life were varied. Though the Edinburgh New Town was the best-known and most extensive example, the flight to the new town suburbs of Glasgow (Blythswood), Aberdeen (Bon-Accord), and Leith's Charlotte Street and Hermitage developments across the Links were typical responses for an emerging social and professional elite in Scottish burghs determined to put space and clean air between them and the contamination of the inner cities. In the second half of the 19th century, suburban villas increasingly replaced neoclassical Georgian terraces as the cities extended their boundaries to take account of middle-class housing preferences. If the process was more extensive in the cities, discrete suburban settlements also developed in smaller towns associated with their social networks and middle-class values.

By the 1860s and 1870s, the vertically segregated residential pattern of pre-modern urban Scotland in which different social classes occupied the various storeys of the same tenement had been replaced by a horizontally segregated residential pattern. The inner city was abandoned to the poor;

specific industrial districts developed, often with their skilled working-class quarters, carved out between the spaghetti of railway lines which developed in the 1840s and 1850s (see TRANSPORT AND COMMUNICATIONS: 2); and suburbs inoculated the middle class against both.

Qualitative improvements in housing were achievable by the middle class (see SOCIAL CLASS) through market mechanisms. It was they who had the resources to buy outright or to obtain mortgages to finance the purchase of flats and villas and, in the last third of the 19th century, innumerable groups of individuals clubbed together rather like terminating building societies to finance a few tenements within a street. For the skilled working class, builders modified tenement design so as to be affordable to them, and occasionally, as with the Edinburgh Co-operative Building Company's construction of over 2,000 houses between 1862 and 1914, workers' self-help initiatives improved the supply of accommodation (see RESPECTABLE CULTURE). Philanthropic efforts and company housing, as in Clydebank and in mining communities, increased the supply of housing for manual workers, though often at the expense of visual monotony in the landscape and a high degree of compliance on the workers' part with the company's priorities. Though hostels and lodging houses continued to be of importance to the poorest elements in Scottish urban society, the construction of very modest one- and two-roomed flats in four-storey tenement blocks with communal entrances, stairs, washhouses, water closets, and drying greens enabled significant numbers to move a short distance from the most congested inner districts.

In the larger Scottish burghs, municipal slum clearance developed in the 1860s in response to the seemingly intractable public health problems identified by prominent Medical Officers such as Henry Littlejohn, J. B. Russell, and later A. K. Chalmers, which were associated with deficient housing. This municipal intervention altered the townscape, even if the impact on health and housing varied from place to place. City Improvement Trusts in Glasgow (1866), Edinburgh (1867), Dundee (1871), Leith (1877), Greenock (1877), and Aberdeen (1884) demolished insanitary and overcrowded central sites, displacing large numbers of their occupants as a result. While Glasgow City Council did little to build on cleared sites, Edinburgh City Council encouraged developers and stipulated designs and housing densities. The Scots baronial style of St Mary's, Blackfriars, and numerous other thoroughfares adjacent to the High Street was the result, and as elsewhere, the council followed this up with a limited number of council housebuilding ventures of their own from the 1890s. By 1913, coun-

cil housing in urban Scotland averaged only 1 per cent of the total housing stock with Greenock and Glasgow amongst the highest with just 1.4 per cent.

Despite intervention from public and philanthropic organizations and overlooking the hyperbole of contemporary reports, the Royal Commission in 1917 commented on 'the clotted masses of slums' and expressed 'amazement' at the streets of 'new tenements developed with the minimum regard for amenity' and the 'gigantic' proportions of the housing deficiency in Scotland. In 1911, one in twelve Scots lived in single-roomed houses; two in five lived in two-roomed houses. Every other Scot lived in a one- or two-roomed house; in England the figure was less than one in fourteen. More than two-thirds of residents in Wishaw, Coatbridge, Kilsyth, Clydebank, Cowdenbeath, Airdrie, Govan, Hamilton, Motherwell, Barrhead, Johnstone, Port Glasgow, and Renfrew lived at a standard considered overcrowded by the Registrar-General. Forty-five per cent of Scots were overcrowded in 1911 compared to 9 per cent in England. This was the housing legacy which faced Scots after a century of industrialization and rapid urbanization (see URBAN SOCIETY: 5).   RR

4. 1920 onwards

Two fundamental changes, public-sector council housebuilding and private enterprise bungalow building (see LIVING STANDARDS: 5), altered the residential landscape of urban Scotland in the interwar years. These were the joint instruments of a spatial and social segregation which reinforced processes initiated by suburbanization in the late 19th century.

The spur to change was the conclusion of the Royal Commission on Housing in Scotland in 1917 which 'was driven to the conclusion', presumably reluctantly, 'that the sources and forces . . . available for the provision of working class houses had failed to provide anything like a sufficiency of houses . . . of a reasonable standard of accommodation and habitability'. With an abrupt decline in housebuilding in the decade before 1914, residential construction during wartime limited to strategic centres such as Rosyth, Gretna, and Greenock, restrictions on rent increases after 1915 acting as a disincentive to private landlords, together with increases in the number of families, the housing shortage in 1917 was estimated at 236,000. The Royal Commission concluded that 'most of the [housing] troubles we have been investigating are due to the failure of private enterprise to provide and maintain the necessary houses sufficient in quantity and quality'.

Armed with these conclusions and against the background of political instability associated with

*'Red Clydeside', Bolshevik Moscow, and de-mobilization, the government paid an 'insurance premium': subsidies to build houses in order to secure popular support when faced with labour unrest from policemen and miners. Once the immediate crisis had passed, the subsidies were withdrawn in 1921. Reinstated in 1923 and 1924 when successive Conservative and Labour administrations recognized the continuing shortfall in accommodation, subsidies were also available to private enterprise. It was the decline of interest rates after 1932, however, from 5 per cent to 2 per cent which stimulated a private housing boom as mortgage costs fell appreciably. Bungalow building was the result (see HOUSING: 3).

Local authorities built 70 per cent and private enterprise 30 per cent of all new dwellings in the years 1919–41—an exact reversal of the percentages in England. The significance was much wider than simply the substitution of a public for a private landlord. Though graceful curves and garden suburb principles informed the layout of both public and private housing, differences in tenure stigmatized estates, as did housing designs. Single-storey owner-occupied bungalows set in generous plots could hardly be more distinct than the three- or even four-storey public-sector flats accessed from a common doorway. Since entire council estates were built within a short space of time, they acquired a high degree of visual uniformity which was reinforced by the scrutiny imposed by the Ministry of Health, and its administrative appendage in Scotland, the Local Government Board. The rapid construction of bungalows by relatively few large building contractors and according to a limited number of designs introduced another element of drab uniformity in the Scottish townscape.

Regional planning emerged before the Second World War in such agencies as the SSHA (1937) but it was boosted by a wartime commitment to macroeconomic planning and the triumph of Keynesianism. The Clyde Valley Plan (1946) encapsulated many of the post-war principles—decongestion and overspill policies, the development of New Towns and quangos—and a friction between the Scottish Office and the local authorities, specifically *Glasgow, as the local tax base was undermined by decanting the poorly housed to locations beyond the city's boundaries.

In opposition to regional policy, the Scottish cities in the 1950s and 1960s sought to defend their interests by demolitions and intensive rehousing within their boundaries and were encouraged in this between 1956 and 1965 by graduated Treasury subsidies which were 230 per cent greater for twenty-storey blocks than for four-storey ones. Over 33,000 flats in multi-storey tower blocks were built in Glasgow between 1956 and 1972—more than in any other city in the country. Concrete shuttering and reinforced steel-frame construction were the preserve of quoted companies, often with headquarters outside Scotland; accountability for housing was ceded by council chambers to boardrooms as system building marginalized the small builder and altered the Scottish urban skyline.

High-rise dwelling became virtually synonymous with council housing and was quickly stigmatized as such. The indicators of social deprivation—unemployment, infant mortality, educational attainment levels, shared amenities, nutritional standards, violence, and drug and alcohol abuse—indicated that Scotland remained 'Two Nations'. In the second half of the 20th century the peripheral housing estates and tower blocks were just as much no-go areas for the middle-classes as Victorian slums had been (see ROUGH CULTURE). Housing allocation policies assigned accommodation on the basis of need as determined by levels of social deprivation, and this both implicitly and explicitly perpetuated divisions in society. The detrimental effect of high-rise housing on the social life of inner city areas is difficult to overestimate and was one of the most unacceptable outcomes of the 1950s and 1960s phase of public housing. As design standards declined, so litter, graffiti, vandalism, and urine in the towers each became more common; inevitably there were adverse effects on the social behaviour of residents.

Not surprisingly, a reaction against the dehumanizing nature of multi-storey living increasingly discredited the planning process in the 1970s. This took several forms. The emphasis switched to qualitative housing improvement with projects such as Glasgow Eastern Area Renewal (GEAR) in 1976, SSHA housing for the elderly and infirm, and in more limited efforts by Saltire Society and Civic Trust to retain and restore individual properties and ensembles of historical interest. 'Green' and heritage issues gradually informed the re-creation of Scottish towns and cities, and parks and plantings became part of an integrated strategy to provide diversity and visual interest in the townscape.

Crucially, another reaction to the brutalism of planning and public housing brought a virtual cessation to council housebuilding which was already in decline by the mid-1970s but which fell sharply with the election of the Conservatives in 1979. By 1986, public housing was only one-sixth that of ten years earlier and only one-tenth that of the peak years of council housebuilding in the 1950s. Instead, the vacuum was filled by the private sector building of 'low, brick terraces which began to spring up' and which increasingly resembled 'Salford or Oldham bodily transplanted to Scotland'.

Simultaneously, the Tenants' Rights, etc. (Scotland) Act 1980 laid down a tenants' entitlement to purchase their public-sector house. The SSHA shed more than 10 per cent of its 100,000 housing stock around Scotland in the first five years following the Act as the Conservative government embarked on strict cash limits in an undisguised assault upon local government and civic services.

The landscape of council housing changed with the changes in tenure: stone-cladding, and neo-Georgian front doors marked out the erstwhile tenant as a new owner-occupier. However, large elements of the public housing stock remained so deeply unattractive as to be unsaleable, however heavily discounted, and the demolition of many high-rise flats and inter-war council estates was probably more influential in countering residential segregation than the 'right to buy' policy itself.

RR

urban society: 1. medieval; 2. 1500–1700; 3. 1700–1830; 4. 1830 onwards; 5. urbanization, 1800 onwards.

1. medieval

The first documentary evidence of urban society comes as late as the 12th century, with the founding of burghs, although societies that had the characteristics of an urban or proto-urban nature existed before this. The people who populated the first burghs were a mixed group. Some were of local origin, recognizable by their locality names; others came from further afield attracted by the incentive of 'kirseth' (a period of time when an immigrant was permitted to build his burgage plot without payment of burgh dues); and yet other incomers came from abroad, from Flanders (see LOW COUNTRIES), the Rhineland, England, and *France, encouraged by the crown for the skills they could offer. It is unlikely that all the local people were granted the status of burgess. They may merely have been assimilated into the new burgh as an 'unfree', indwelling workforce, technically not part of the burgess 'community'. How far, in reality, such a disparate group of burgesses could act as a community, however, is unclear. Likewise, the roles performed by these early burgesses were intermingled. Although burghs were essentially trading centres, the early town dwellers who were merchants were also probably often craftsmen and farmers (see RURAL SOCIETY: 1).

Although all early town dwellers were very much 'of the country', this division in burghal society, albeit perhaps more apparent than real, set one group apart from another. Burgh status assured fundamental rights for the burgesses: the privileged inhabitants. Most striking in a feudal society was the relative freedom that was granted: while

recognizing the authority of the burgh and its superior, other feudal ties were severed; and allied to this personal freedom went a right to hold burgage tenure, protected originally by the king's peace and later by burgh law. Major legislative policy decisions, as well as some judicial, were taken at the head courts, held usually three times a year at Michaelmas, Christmas/Epiphany, and Easter, normally under the leadership of the chief officer of the burgh, the alderman or *praepositus* (later called the provost). All burgesses of the burgh were obliged to attend. Allied to this were the burgh courts (see LAW AND LAWYERS: 1), meeting usually fortnightly as the *curiae legales*, and the more frequent meetings of the courts or assizes to deal with more minor matters were manned by burgesses under their burgh officers, the bailies. A further legislative and advisory body developed, possibly out of an informal grouping of burgesses: the burgh council. The members of this council were also burgesses. Through their own council, with their own officers, the alderman, bailies, and lesser officials such as liners, dempsters, sergeands, wine and ale tasters, meat and bread pricers, all aspects of town life were monitored. And it was not merely the lives of the burgesses that were thus controlled, but also those of all indwellers within the burgh's bounds.

In time, an even more specific delineation would develop; and, in many burghs, the merchants of the community began to adopt a greater role than others in burghal administrative affairs. They were often the more substantial members of the townspeople and, if they possessed a formal guild merchant, the most vocal and able. In many burghs, as a result, the merchants, and their guild, as the most fit burgesses, not as merchants per se, increasingly gained control of the municipal organization. Early guilds merchant, however, were not exclusively of an overseas merchant membership: tavernkeepers, cordiners, weavers, masons, skinners, and plumbers—all craftsmen—were potential members of the guild. Once craft guilds began to adopt a formalized existence in the larger burghs in the last quarter of the 15th century, and in the smaller a little later, they, through collective interest, mutual aid, and fraternity, polarized into exclusive sects within the burgh community; as did the guild merchant.

From the 13th century, the term the 'community of the burgh' held a recognized place in legal parlance. Given the apparent divisions already in urban society, it is unclear how far this concept was all-embracing. But there is much in medieval burgh life to suggest that 'the community' could include, through common interests, the greater grouping of all townspeople. Townspeople, both free and unfree, were psychologically set apart from their rural neighbours by ports, or gates, ditches, and wooden palisading; all in the town lived in close proximity in a confined urban space (see URBAN SETTLEMENT: 1); and the common seal of the burgh might have signified a commonality of thinking and action. This sense of oneness was reinforced by the notion of a single parish; worshipping as a single spiritual community, the town became synonymous with a *corpus christianum* (see RELIGIOUS LIFE: 2). The dual wholeness of the spiritual and secular urban community perhaps reached its apotheosis in the annual Corpus Christi procession. Underlying this urban spectacular was a pervading theme: the image of the body, oneness and wholeness. The significant element in the procession was the body of Christ in the form of the host, supported by clerics, accompanied by the magistracy, the guild merchant, and the crafts of the burgh in order of precedence, all of which was witnessed by the passive participants, the ordinary townspeople. The body politic was thus portrayed as a structured and stratified whole community.

But it is this very display of the element of structured stratification that epitomizes the true nature of medieval urban society: its inequality. Just as the Corpus Christi procession may be viewed as the expression of urban unity and wholeness, it is equally valid to see in it a vivid enactment not of oneness but of exclusion. There were many who were distanced: *women played no role in the burghal hierarchy; the poor received only minimal support; prostitutes were isolated to the edges of towns; lepers, the plague-ridden (see HEALTH, FAMINE, AND DISEASE: 1), and those with syphilis were expelled from the town—all perhaps prudent measures to modern eyes, but an indication that within the medieval burgh community there were those who were acceptable and those who were not. Even on the most egalitarian of occasions, when the social order was officially turned upside down, as at the May Games or during the Robin Hood or Abbot of Unreason revelries, a close monitoring by the burgh authorities ensured no undue excessive freedom of expression by the common people.

There was otherwise, perhaps inevitably, an element of elitism in burghal affairs. Apart from the town clerk and the notary, even into the 15th and 16th centuries, burgh government was basically conducted by amateurs, who had to forgo working for their livelihood while on burgh business, with only occasional expenses being reimbursed. Some deliberately avoided office; but disenchantment with the right to hold burghal power went deeper. Public apathy could be such that the compulsory attendance at the head courts was not always obeyed. The net result was that urban government

became largely plutocratic or 'aristocratic' in the Aristotelian sense—the best and the wisest, that is the wealthiest, should rule for the good and benefit of all. There was a sense of hierarchical order within the community: each man, woman, and child had a specific role within a stratified society. All were not equal, whether socially, politically, or culturally. Social tensions did exist; but, as far as we know, social unrest was never of such a nature or magnitude as to seriously threaten the working of the medieval town; and this is significant. EPD

2. 1500–1700

The nature of urban society was undergoing a quiet and often camouflaged transformation in the 15th and early 16th centuries as the long slump in the wool trade intensified and towns sought to diversify their economies into other areas, such as the leather trade and fish. Much of overseas trade came to be increasingly concentrated in a few larger towns and this had various consequences: many small and middling towns must have experienced decay in the parts of their economy geared to the export trade and increasingly relied on inland and regional trade; and in larger towns the share of a contracting cake went to an elite of overseas merchants and an emerging craft aristocracy, made up of skinners, metalworkers, tailors, and bakers (see ECONOMY: 2). These were the crafts which were usually the first to be given incorporated status as guilds and granted the most prestigious positions in the new civic ceremony which emerged in this period, in processions such as Corpus Christi. In it, closest to the Holy Blood, which usually was commandeered by the merchant guild, were the banners of St Eloi of the hammermen, St Crispin of the skinners, and St Obert of the bakers (see RELIGIOUS LIFE: 2).

By 1530, the dual process of incorporation of craft guilds and the development of civic ceremony was all but complete, at least in larger towns. This was part of a broader pattern which saw the consolidation and narrowing of the burgh establishment at a time when the population was beginning to expand. The 'long 16th century', between 1500 and c.1650, saw a doubling of the population (see POPULATION PATTERNS: 1) of most towns. Larger burghs, however, probably experienced greater population increase than that. The proportion of the townspeople granted burgess-ship, however, such as booth owners, peddlers, and ordinary master craftsmen, was falling. Power was increasingly concentrated on those who held the full rights of burgess and guild, such as overseas traders and craftsmen employers who did not soil their hands in their trade. Both trade and industry was becoming concentrated in fewer hands: in *Edinburgh, the number of merchants exporting overseas was about 100, less than a quarter of those who nominally enjoyed the name; and craft employers, such as in the baker trade, were flagrantly ignoring the old Statutes of the Guild which limited them to four employees. Head courts of the burgh persisted, but such was the rate of absenteeism that, as in the Canongate, names were taken, not of those who attended but of those who did not. The old notion of the burgh community became more and more exposed as a fiction. As towns grew, the gap which had always existed between rich and poor widened.

Craft saints and most of civic ritual disappeared with the *Reformation. The apparatus of craft altars, with their own dedicated chaplains, was dismantled after 1560. The new Protestant worship, which removed the barriers within the church between clergy and congregation, should have placed a renewed emphasis on the community as a *corpus christianum*. In practice, it gave an extra dimension of discipline to those in power, now kirk session elders as well as town councillors or deacons of their crafts (see CHURCH INSTITUTIONS: 3). With civic processions and the careful layout of urban hierarchy within the burgh church now removed, crafts, anxious to preserve their rights and status, became litigious; some even hired lawyers to take their own town council to court. In time, this tension took on religious overtones. In the Edinburgh session in 1618, bitter disputes between the establishment and 'mean men' culminated in a skinner throwing a Geneva bible at a former provost of the burgh.

The 16th century saw an increasing presence of landed families in towns (see NOBILITY: 3). In *Aberdeen, the Menzies, a family of rural lairds, took over the office of provost in the 1480s and held it for a century. In *Stirling, the Erskine family, hereditary keepers of the castle, built a town house called 'Mar's Wark' in the 1540s, complete with gun loops, which dominated the market street of the burgh. One result was that violence was never far away. The chancellor of the realm was shot in a brawl in Stirling's main street in 1578. In the same year, two *Glasgow University students, both sons of powerful noble families, who had been disciplined by their tutor attacked him in the street; it led to a full-scale confrontation between the university authorities and their kindred who were branded as 'bangsters'. Yet the economic fortunes of both *universities and towns were increasingly dependent on landed families who brought conspicuous consumption as well as violence.

The growth of the professions—lawyers (see LAW AND LAWYERS: 1), ministers, schoolmasters (see SCHOOLS AND SCHOOLING: 1), surgeons and physicians (see MEDICINE AND THE ORIGINS OF THE MEDICAL PROFESSION)—indelibly marked out a new era for urban society. There was a paradox here. These were groups which were quintessentially urban yet did not belong to the historic burgh community. Lawyers, in particular, thronged towns as far apart in size as Elgin and Edinburgh. Like ministers, they were developing the characteristics of a professional caste. Son followed father into both the law and the manse. Neither lawyers nor ministers paid burgh taxation and both tended to have large amounts of disposable cash, which they often lent, at interest, to their clients and congregation respectively.

It is only in this period that *women, a hidden majority in the records, begin to emerge. A surprising proportion, however, were either single or widowed. They comprised 18.7 per cent of households in Stirling in 1550. Female domestic servants were also much more prominent than before, though rarely in such proportions as in 17th-century Edinburgh, where they made up over 20 per cent of the population. In such circumstances, it is not surprising that both the burgh authorities and the kirk session in Stirling turned their attention to 'common scolds'—women with attitude who were ritually carted through the town and their tongue silenced by the metal device of the 'branks'. More girls (see CHILDREN) were being given at least a rudimentary education by the 17th century; private sewing and writing schools for girls attracted the suspicion of the authorities.

Literacy in general probably saw a decisive upswing in 17th-century towns. In larger towns, probably about one in three amongst males were literate in 1550. The godly society outlined by the Protestant church in 1560 was interested in the ability to read rather than to write and most indexes refer to 'sign literacy', the ability to sign one's name. In the 17th century, arithmetic and other practical schools were set up alongside the standard provision of the vernacular or 'Inglis' school, which taught boys up to the age of 8 and the grammar school, with its Latin curriculum, which catered for boys of the elite up to the age of 12. But universal literacy, even in the largest towns, was still an aspiration, even in 1700.   ML

3. 1700–1830

Significant growth in the urban population (see POPULATION PATTERNS) and the development of new types of *urban settlement, notably the overseas trading towns of the Clyde and industrial towns such as Paisley, wrought massive changes in the character of urban society over the 18th century. In 1700 Scotland was a country of many small burghs and even the largest places were 'walking' cities where it was possible to travel on foot from one side to the other in less than half an hour. Urban communities were intimate, many aspects of social life were conducted out-of-doors, and there was little social differentiation between different areas of the town. Wealthy and powerful burgesses mostly lived in the urban centres, close to the market place and town house or tolbooth, where the burgh council held its meetings and local justice was dispensed. But the poor were always nearby and face-to-face social relationships were normal.

Though the majority of towns remained small and familiar, by 1830 rapid population growth in the bigger cities had resulted in significant physical expansion, with new exclusive suburbs for the rich at a growing distance from city centres, which were increasingly given over to commercial or professional facilities and *housing for the poor. As elite housing evolved in size and comfort and as indoor social facilities such as assembly rooms were built in most towns from the 1760s, the leisure of the rich tended to move indoors and assume a more genteel and fashionable character. The annual *calendar of fairs, markets, and holidays was more likely to be observed by labourers than by the wealthier classes and was gradually dismantled after 1800 by town council interventions in the interest of public order. The result was the gradual erosion of face-to-face relationships, the reduction in cultural uniformity among urban peoples, and the undermining of a strong sense of communal identity, particularly in the large industrial cities and in *Edinburgh. Rising tensions between the rich and poor, fuelled by new political aspirations from the later 18th century and by fears of falling *living standards as free-market policies were introduced, often spilled over into protest and rioting.

The middle layers of society, comprising merchants, skilled craftsmen, and professionals, dominated towns throughout the period, having privileges that were enshrined in the charters of the royal burghs and that secured the rights of election and office holding in town government in the hands of a powerful few. But in the first half of the century the landed elites maintained town houses in the towns close to their estates and through patronage and market influence were able to exercise considerable control over urban affairs. Later the landed distanced themselves from such local affiliations and, with improved *transport communications, were able to spend more time in Edinburgh, often acquiring modern houses there, where urban politics, residential developments, leisure, and the creation of fashionable social institutions were shaped by the needs of this elite.

The mass of the urban population were labourers engaged in trade, transport, and building, with large and growing numbers of workers involved in the rising consumer industry of textile manufacture. Apprenticeship-trained craft workers were an important group, but their abilities to withstand the impact of skills-dilution and such changes as the erosion of wage-setting, were often limited. Standards of living were considerably higher than among rural workers, but the very poor were always a striking feature of urban society, often attracted from the countryside by the welfare and charitable institutions that proliferated in Scottish towns (see LIVING STANDARDS: 4). Strategies to cope with the growing presence of poverty and pauperism, which was fuelled by industrial unemployment and displacement from the land in the early 19th century, became a major preoccupation of urban government and the middle layers of society in general as the period advanced.

*Women were a strong and increasing presence in urban society. Gentry women, particularly those who were single, were more likely to be found in towns than countryside because of easier access to housing and opportunities to engage in appropriate work, leisure, or consumption. The rising demand for domestic servants, which went hand-in-hand with improvements in housing, ensured that a large element of any urban population comprised young single women living in the houses of their employers. Developments in urban industry (see ECONOMY: 3–4), with a massive demand for unskilled labour in textile manufacture, also generated a strong female presence. Cities as different in character as Edinburgh and *Dundee in the early 19th century had a predominantly female population.

Significant changes in the physical appearance of Scottish towns (see URBAN SETTLEMENT: 1–2), including the building of 'new town' areas comprising symmetrically laid-out streets and modern town houses for the rich, along with new types of urban institution built in the neoclassical style, such as hospitals, lunatic asylums, and prisons, were influenced by Enlightenment notions of rationality and by the rising need to try to exercise order and control over the rapidly expanding and changing character of urban society. A strong belief in improvement and reform was communicated in measures to incarcerate and cure those who were insane, criminal, or sick. The increased incidence of diseases (see HEALTH, FAMINE, AND DISEASE: 2–3) of overcrowding, culminating in the cholera crises of the early 1830s, suggests the extent to which urban society existed under a state of anxiety and threat. The Enlightenment (see CULTURE: 11) had spawned new ideas about the nature of desirable social interactions within cities, giving rise to many debating clubs and societies. But contemporary awareness of the instability of urban life was acute by the early 19th century, particularly within the Church of Scotland, which had greatly declined as an institution for social cohesion in bigger towns since the beginning of the 18th century. The Evangelical movement (see RELIGIOUS LIFE: 6), which flourished among the middle classes, was devoted to the recreation of a moral community in towns and cities.

Though a minority of the population lived permanently in towns at this time, many who lived in the countryside spent some part of their life in a town or a city. This was especially true of the young, who migrated for apprenticeships and employment in such areas as domestic service. Contact with towns increased among rural inhabitants with the growth of market exchanges in Scotland, encouraging the trend towards permanent *migration in search of better-paid work and higher *living standards. By the early 19th century, the majority of the urban population, especially in the fast-growing industrial cities, was rural-born. *Newspapers, which were published in all the large cities by the mid-18th century and had a wide circulation in the countryside, generated an impression of the wealth and opportunities that towns offered. The reality for many poor migrants was often very different.   SN

4. 1830 onwards

Perceptions of change in Scottish urban society became particularly acute during the 1830s, because of the reality of political reform after years of pressure to alter the electoral system. The base of democracy was still exceptionally narrow under the provisions of the 1832 and 1833 legislation, which enfranchised the middle classes on a £10 property basis. However, the point of principle overrode disappointment about the cautious nature of constitutional change, and there was initially a passionate belief that further progress could be made to open out the power base.

Hope for the future meant that during the 19th century there was often millenarian zeal about tackling the complex range of problems associated with Scotland's unprecedented urban growth. Political radicals were particularly vocal about the need to forge a new order, and repudiate the apparent excess and indulgence that had become indelibly connected with the ruling elite during the pre-reform era. They especially stressed self-improvement (see RESPECTABLE CULTURE) as a means of demonstrating that the working classes had as much moral fibre as anyone, hence the popular support throughout Scotland's towns and

cities for the *temperance movement from the 1830s. Scottish *Chartism, which briefly flourished from 1838, similarly shared the emphasis on working-class advancement through self-help and exemplary rectitude. In this context, the focus was on creating an integrated society, where character rather than wealth would determine status.

Power, however, rested emphatically with the middle classes, who assertively projected their own moral agenda in an attempt to maintain their post-reform legitimacy. *Liberalism came to be the reflection of middle-class political values, focusing above all on free trade as the potent symbol of personal liberty and economic prosperity. That urban growth was the product of commercial and manufacturing enterprise reinforced Liberal individualism as the motivating impulse behind the positive changes in society (see POLITICAL SYSTEM: 1). Yet there was also an inherent conundrum, as Scotland's industrial success could not prevent the rapid deterioration of the urban fabric or stem the intrusion of deprivation and disease. The burgeoning number of slums, of which particularly gross examples were Blackfriars Wynd in *Edinburgh and the Old Wynd in *Glasgow, became disturbing symbols of the dislocated nature of urban life in Scotland (see HOUSING: 3; URBAN SETTLEMENT: 3).

From the 1830s there was a growing tendency for urban communities to develop along separate residential spheres, with the middle classes settling as far from the tainted heartland as the *transport system would allow. This became especially marked during mid-century, as a building boom allowed for the construction of villas and terraces on the pastoral fringes of towns and cities. Yet this was realized to be no solution to the pervasive problem of urban blight. More effective control of the environment was thus deemed essential to retain the integrity of communities and offset dangerous tendencies towards social fragmentation. From 1850, the Burgh Police Acts made it easier in Scotland's populous districts for local authorities to initiate improvement policies, and in the larger towns and cities existing powers were consolidated and extended by town councils. Such autonomy in urban affairs characterized Scotland into the 20th century, building upon the long-standing tradition of the 'common good', but also reflecting Liberal individualism at the local level.

Liberalism also came to be closely associated with the missionary commitment of Presbyterian Evangelicalism (see RELIGIOUS LIFE: 6), creating a dualistic ideology that blended moral redemption with material improvement. It had the advantage of giving spiritual credibility to policies that might otherwise be deemed unacceptable by cost-conscious taxpayers, especially some of the grander *public utilities that were acquired by municipalities from mid-century. Not surprisingly, it also made for heady rhetoric, notably in journalism, a profession that thrived as urban communities became more populous. Scotland's first daily newspaper, the Glasgow-based *North British Daily Mail*, exemplified this ideological stance throughout its existence between 1847 and 1900. The church was thus important as tangible testimony to faith in the city and as a monument to the controlling influence of elites. Moreover, ideology and culture were combined, notably in the flourishing social activities of the churches, which afforded the urban dweller a variety of inducements to refrain from less decorous pursuits, and steer clear of public houses (see RESPECTABLE CULTURE).

The focus on 'rational recreation' intensified as the century progressed, bequests from philanthropists and municipal provision ensuring that communities benefited from such elevating influences as libraries, parks, and art galleries. The encouragement of competitive sport also indicated that there was concern to channel energies constructively. Association *football clubs, which became inextricably bound up with Scottish urban culture in the 20th century, were often founded with a character-forming aim in view, the Young Men's Christian Association the force behind Glasgow's pioneering Queen's Park club in 1867. Yet increasingly commercialism became a directing influence in urban society, especially after Scotland's railway network was established. Conspicuous consumption had long been a symbol of middle-class gentility, with Edinburgh's Princes Street an early example of a specialist shopping thoroughfare. Increased purchasing power also opened out choices for the wider community, not only in the availability of goods but also in services and entertainment. The theatre and *music hall may have been regarded as morally dubious by strict Evangelicals, but their reputation altered from the late 19th century as a plethora of prestigious new playhouses emerged in Scotland's cities, featuring companies and performers of international standing.

Indeed, cosmopolitanism in the urban context was a marked feature of the 20th century, as communications—cinema, *radio and television—made global culture more readily accessible. Overseas connections were nothing new, given Scotland's deep-rooted trading links and the tradition of emigration. Moreover, incomers (see MIGRATION) from a variety of ethnic origins had come to settle in Scotland's urban centres, notably the Irish (see IMMIGRATION, IRISH). However, the First World War had the effect of calling into question the moral values which had maintained the relative cohesion of urban society, and precipitated the drastic decline of Liberal hegemony. A more secular and less hierarchical society emerged, especially after universal suffrage was eventually achieved in 1928. Yet old influences died hard, Scotland's stringent, Evangelically inspired liquor laws of the 1850s surviving as late as 1976. This significant social change coincided with the beginnings of de-industrialization (see ECONOMY: 6), a phenomenon that devastated many communities, notably in central Scotland. Ironically, the vestiges of control that had been such a feature of urban society in the post-1830 period were removed as the traditional economic base was virtually obliterated.   IMa

5. urbanization, 1800 onwards

In the 19th century Scotland became a highly urbanized country, second only to England in the proportion of its population who lived in urban areas. At the start of the period, one in five of the population lived in towns of more than 5,000 inhabitants; by the 1861 census this had nearly doubled to 39.4 per cent of the population (see POPULATION PATTERNS: 2). It was in the 1880s that urban dwellers surpassed the numbers living in the countryside. By 1901, 57.6 per cent were in towns of over 5,000 inhabitants, 74.3 per cent in towns of over 1,000; by 1951, the proportions were 69.9 per cent and 83 per cent. Much of the growth was due to natural increase as well as to immigration from the countryside (see RURAL SOCIETY: 4). It was an urban population which became especially concentrated in the great conurbation of *Glasgow and west-central Scotland and in three other large cities. In 1851, 22 per cent of Scots lived in the four main cities of Glasgow, *Edinburgh, *Dundee, and *Aberdeen; by 1951 this had reached 37.6 per cent of the population. In recent decades, there has been a downturn in the proportion in the four cities to 28 per cent, although the proportion of population living in towns has continued to rise.

In 1801 Edinburgh was the largest city (83,000) but Glasgow (77,000) was catching up rapidly. The next three, Aberdeen (27,000), Dundee (26,000), and Paisley (25,000), were beginning to grow slowly, together with Greenock (17,000). By the 1850s, Edinburgh had grown by 133 per cent to 194,000, with its peak growth of 3.4 per cent per annum having come between 1811 and 1821; but it was now clearly surpassed by Glasgow, whose population had grown by 348 per cent in half a century to 345,000, with astonishing peaks of 4.6 per cent per annum between 1811 and 1821 and around 3.6 per cent per annum over the next two decades, faster than almost anywhere else in Europe. Not until the 1870s did Glasgow's annual rate of growth fall below 2 per cent per annum. Dundee's growth rate peaked in the 1820s and 1830s when it was over 4 per cent per annum and again in the 1860s when it was 3.2 per cent per annum.

None of the other Scottish large towns reached such high levels of growth. Aberdeen's population rose to 72,000 in 1851 with an average 2.7 per cent growth rate between 1811 and 1831. Only in Glasgow and Dundee did the Irish (see IMMIGRATION, IRISH) influx of the 1840s make a noticeable difference, with Dundee surpassing Aberdeen in size in the 1851 census, and growing by 32 per cent in the 1860s, as the jute industry grew. For Paisley, the 1840s was a desperate decade in which the population did not grow at all and Paisley actually lost population in the next decade. Not until the late 1870s and 1880s are there signs of substantial numbers being attracted to the thread and engineering industries (see ECONOMY, SECONDARY SECTOR: 2). After the setbacks of a collapsing textile industry in the 1850s, Aberdeen also began to show signs of a new attractiveness in the 1870s, 1880s, and 1890s, no doubt helped by problems in farming. Greenock, having grown to 37,000 by 1851, with the expansion of sugar and shipping in the 1860s, went through a period of rapid growth, but it was not sustained and the 1880s saw Greenock's population fall by some 6 per cent.

In the 40 years before 1914, Scotland became the second most urbanized country in Europe with 42.4 per cent of its population living in towns of over 20,000 inhabitants. By 1912, Glasgow's population had crossed the million mark with the incorporation of Govan and Partick into the city. Edinburgh's had reached 400,000. But urbanization in Scotland did not only mean the development of a number of large cities. By 1901 there were nine burghs with a population of between 20,000 and 40,000, some of which had grown very rapidly in the previous twenty years: Inverness by 22 per cent, Ayr and Dunfermline by around 30 per cent, Kilmarnock by 37 per cent, Falkirk by 56 per cent, Kirkcaldy by 68 per cent, and Hamilton by a spectacular 134 per cent. In 1901 there were 75 burghs with over 5,000 inhabitants and even in the Highlands (see HIGHLANDS AND ISLANDS: GENERAL) one in ten lived in a town, while in the *Borders region the urban population had increased from 10 per cent to 23 per cent.

In the first half of the 20th century Aberdeen, of the larger towns, showed the most consistent population rise, eventually in 1951 surpassing Dundee as the third city. Greenock was badly hit by the inter-war depression and lost population, while both Glasgow and Dundee in the same period had slow growth rates. Since 1951, with the development of the new towns of East Kilbride, Irvine, and Cumbernauld, together with the spread of suburbs beyond the city boundaries, Glasgow's population has fallen by some 30 per cent. A lesser fall occurred in other cities, with the exception of Aberdeen where the impact of the oil-related developments brought a slight rise in the last three decades.

Whereas in the 19th century most urban growth was the product of a search for work, in recent decades at least some of it has been a search for an improved environment. Much of the largest urban expansion has been in suburbs and in small towns near the cities, which, thanks to improved road networks, have attracted middle-class commuters keen to escape rising city taxes, city schools, and city problems. Hence the significant expansion of places like Dunblane, Helensburgh, Linlithgow, South Queensferry, Penicuik, and Banchory. The new towns have continued to attract industry and population with Glenrothes (37,850 in 1991), Livingston (41,065), Cumbernauld (47,700), and East Kilbride (69,376) among Scotland's urban centres.

WHF

USA. Scotland's involvement with the USA began with the origins of that country. A number of scholars have (with limited success) attempted to communicate to an American audience the idea that much of what the colonists of what was then British North America drew on to create the USA came from the civic tradition of the Scottish Enlightenment (see CULTURE: 11) as much if not more than from sources identified in more traditional American accounts emphasizing the importance of the ideas of the Englishman John Locke and the Frenchman Charles Montesquieu. Americans like Thomas Jefferson had, through Scottish teachers like Jefferson's William Small of Aberdeen (who taught at the College of William and Mary in Virginia), become acquainted with some of these ideas, just as James Madison did after John Witherspoon of East Lothian and Paisley became president of Princeton College in New Jersey in 1768. As Andrew Hook has so succinctly put it in *Scotland and America, 1750–1835* (1975), Scottish ships brought tobacco back from America to help create commercial wealth in the central belt of Scotland, wealth which played a key role in the rapid modernization and industrialization Scotland experienced by the end of the 18th century, but these same ships brought people to America from Scotland who took with them ideas that helped create the USA (see EMIGRATION: 3–4).

The ideas the Scots brought to America were not native to Scotland but derived from their reading of Locke and Montesquieu and their adaptation of these sources in a Scottish context. Although the great thinkers of the Scottish Enlightenment, above all Hume and Smith, are part of the intellectual inheritance of the modern mind, much of their intellectual energy came from their reaction to European ideas, above all those of Locke and Montesquieu, as they observed their own country modernize in the middle of the 18th century. Scots knew that their ancient independence based on the military ability to defend the kingdom had ended in the 17th century with the conquest and occupation of their country by English armies led by Oliver Cromwell. They knew that their country had always been poor and that in a larger state they could never aspire to metropolitan status. Montesquieu had written as a judge in a provincial French *parlement*. The Scots adopted both his and Locke's ideas in a Scottish setting which, with the creation of a British state in the 18th century, was by definition provincial. Scotland was a medieval kingdom transformed into a British province in its search for modernity. The English colonies in North America became British as a result of that Scottish decision, and by the end of the third quarter of the 18th century had become English-speaking societies that were more provincial than colonial. The Scottish provincial experience within Britain became a model for what Americans might aspire to, although by the end of the century the result was that as the Americans left Britain the Scots became more central to its future development, and the origins of modern *Canada reflected that process as a new kind of British North America post-1783 (see NATIONAL IDENTITY: 4).

How did this transference of ideas to what became the USA come about? Most Americans today would be reluctant to acknowledge that it occurred, reflecting the sense of exceptionalism at the centre of American national identity as it was created in the 19th century. Scotland's first contacts with the North American continent occurred in the years after *James VI became James I of England, first with his grant of lands in Nova Scotia to Sir William Stirling, then with the transportation of indentured servants who were Scots to the West Indies and Virginia, including some taken prisoner by Cromwellian armies during the conquest of Scotland in 1651–2.

During the absolutist Restoration regime of the 1670s and 1680s, Presbyterian dissenters sought lands in America in South Carolina and New Jersey, although as Scottish subjects they were emigrating to what were still legally English colonies. They were refugees from the Scottish royalist regime directed by the privy council in Edinburgh rather than the Stuart monarchs as such. The same privy council which allowed emigrants to go to English colonies in America welcomed the importation of American goods back to Scotland,

even if such trade was legally in breach of the English parliament's Navigation Acts. Scotland was still an independent kingdom with its own *parliament under the *Union of the Crowns, and the Scottish privy council representing the king in Scotland did not see its role as encompassing enforcement of English restrictions on colonial trade in what remained a separate kingdom with its own laws.

The first indications of Scottish trade with English colonies in the West Indies and Virginia date from the 1670s, when sugar refineries were set up in *Glasgow with the encouragement of the Scottish privy council and some references to importation of tobacco can be found in contemporary records. We know that John Campbell of Shawfield, involved in the American trade in the early 18th century, spent time in America before the Union made such trade legal, and the practice of Glasgow firms sending young men to Boston and Virginia as part of their mercantile training definitely began around this time. Obviously, however, it was neither in the Scottish privy council's nor the Glasgow mercantile community's interests to draw attention to this trade if this might arouse attacks on it in the English parliament and its early history is poorly documented.

With a change of regime in 1689 Dutch influence in Scotland increased, emphasizing by example the possibilities of a small country acquiring wealth through colonial trade. The new principal of Glasgow College, William Dunlop, had been a member of the Presbyterian colony in South Carolina and had acted as an emissary for it with the Spanish at St Augustine in Florida before their attacks forced the Scots back to Charleston, there to return to Scotland or remain as part of the pluralistic community of Europeans and West Indians in that city. Increased knowledge of the western hemisphere and the Dutch example, allied to the obvious shortcomings of the domestic Scottish economy (see ECONOMY: 3), led to support for proposals to establish a company in Scotland to engage in foreign trade, the Company of Scotland Trading to Africa and the Indies, whose single and first attempt at overseas colonization on the Isthmus of Panama at the Bay of *Darien was a turning point in the history of Scottish modernization. On the one hand it was a failure, with two expeditions failing to establish a permanent colony; on the other hand, it brought surviving colonists into contact with settlements that were still English colonies across the West Indies and North America from Jamaica to Charleston to New York to Boston. Scotland's failure as a colonial nation marked the beginning of the development of a network of Scots resident throughout the English-speaking colonies of the western hemisphere. From this network Scottish trading connections with America continued to grow, partly founded on the favourable geography which gave Glasgow privileged access to the Atlantic trade, and partly because the merchants of Glasgow shared economic problems and dissenting religion with the growing centre of American commerce at Boston, from which trading links extended to Virginia, Charleston, and the West Indies.

By the third quarter of the 18th century the American colonies equalled Scotland in population, albeit spread over a much greater area with urban centres emerging not just at Boston and Charleston but also at New York and Philadelphia in the so-called 'middle' colonies as well. There were small groups of Scots settled as urban professionals and artisans in all the American towns, and small settlements of Scots in New Jersey and Carolina that retained a demonstrably Scottish culture in rural American frontier society. The so-called 'French and Indian' War in America in 1754–63 brought the first Scottish Highland regiments (see ARMY: 3) to America: the Black Watch, Montgomery's, and Fraser's (the last two named after their colonels). Highlanders were likened to American colonial soldiers in their ability to fight in a dispersed manner; they were good Indian fighters, and they saw for themselves good land available for farming just at a time when rents were rising in Scotland as commercial agriculture began to develop (see ECONOMY, PRIMARY SECTOR: 1).

The post-war period brought large-scale emigration from the Scottish Highlands all up and down the western seaboard, from Argyll in the south to Sutherland in the north. There was also substantial emigration from the western Lowlands around the Clyde, without the dramatic social effects it had on Highland estates where landowners' agents came to fear that the entire population might emigrate in reaction to changes in Highland society. Hector St John De Crevecoeur, in his *Letters from an American Farmer*, published in London in 1782, facetiously argued that the British government should cease sending convicts to America as punishment, but instead allow the entire population of the Scottish Islands to emigrate to America, where they would have access to better land, leaving the inhospitable climate of their homeland for residual use as a penal colony!

Paradoxically, the sturdy Scottish Highlander who became central to American ideas of the frontier between 1750 and 1775 as Indian-fighting soldier or settler at the outermost bounds of civilization became equally a symbol of perfidious British brutality during the American War of Independence, as colonies of Highlanders in upstate New York and the Cape Fear Valley of North Carolina became notorious centres of British loyalism and the disproportionate number of Highland regiments in the British armies sent to enforce imperial authority in America identified Scotland with Tory monarchism. In fact, as with other groups of colonists, Scots divided on the question of loyalty with John Witherspoon of New Jersey and James Wilson of Pennsylvania emerging as patriot leaders of Lowland Scottish birth and Lachlan Macintosh of Georgia as perhaps the best-known Highland-born American patriot. Isolated communities of Scottish Highlanders on the frontier were more readily identified as alien to the American cause, subject like the French in Canada to medieval ideas of pre-Enlightenment absolutism, their frontier lifestyle encouraging them to adapt the savage ways of their Indian neighbours. After the war, many Scottish loyalists moved to *Canada, and those Scots who remained were more anxious to adapt to American ways than emphasize their European origins.

But what was an American? This is where Andrew Hook's book *Scotland and America, 1750–1835* (1975) opened up underexplored aspects of the extent to which later Enlightenment Scotland acted as a cultural model for an American republic which had achieved political independence in defence of what were perceived as traditional English liberties and then had to come to terms with the fact that time and geography had conspired to deny Americans Englishness. Paradoxically, the Scots, having sacrificed political independence for what many perceived as economic and cultural development, formed a role model for American aspirations to establish what might be called their cultural independence while retaining the English language in an appropriately modified form. Thus the colossal impact of the works of Scott (see CULTURE: 11, 14) on American culture in the early 19th century, as first in poetry and then in prose he demonstrated the romance of provincial history and landscape in a manner that soon called forth American imitation in the works of James Fenimore Cooper. Even before this literary impact, the American college curriculum had been moulded by Scottish example in pursuit of cheap, practical, and moral instruction in the medium of English using textbooks which poured off the presses of Edinburgh and Glasgow in their hundreds of thousands, published by Constable, Chambers, Collins, and many others, cheerfully pirated by American publishers and booksellers beyond the reach of British copyright law! (see SCHOOLS AND SCHOOLING: 2).

Why was this seminal Scottish influence on the developing culture of the early American republic forgotten by later generations in America? In part it was because the Scots were not just speaking to the Americans, but also provided a model for aspiring urban middle-class professionals all over Europe and the European colonial world. Scottish Common-Sense Philosophy provided simplistic, comfortable responses for many of the troubling issues consequent upon modernization, popularized by intellectuals like Thomas Carlyle. Scott's romantic Scottish history was presented as part of a vanished or vanishing world accessible to the modern mind only on a sentimental level.

Yet by the mid-19th century this cultural eminence had passed away as Scottish *universities, publishers, writers, and professionals failed to sustain the achievements of the previous century. The USA, having become a continental power, confronted the issue of whether it would be a nation tolerating slavery or not. Moral interest in this issue in the USA was intense in Scotland, but Scottish influence on American debate was slight. Scots were involved on both sides in the American Civil War, there were even regiments raised in 1861 which adopted Highland *dress, but the slavery question as a defining issue in American history never directly involved Scotland. The interest in the war in Scotland, however, and the effect of its outcome on world history, marked a watershed in the history of the cultural relationship of the USA and Scotland, from the earlier cultural impact of the older nation upon the younger, to the influence of a vast emerging world power upon the economic fortunes and social development of a small part of the *British Empire, marked by the arrival of American entrepreneurs in Scotland to undertake manufacturing through firms like the North British Rubber Works in Edinburgh and the Singer Sewing Machine Company in Clydebank.

The emergence of the USA, like Germany, as a major industrial centre in the second half of the 19th century had an important impact on the Scottish economy, reducing the profitability and scale of the textile, iron, and coal industries that had supported its early industrialization. The emergent Scottish shipbuilding industry that sustained continued industrial expansion in Scotland into the 20th century helped underpin a revolution in transatlantic communications that brought the west of Scotland in particular into daily contact with the USA, as ships arrived bearing tourists, Evangelical missionaries like Moody and Sankey, cheap food, and new manufactures, and departed with emigrants who might one day return, like Andrew Carnegie, or those who did not, like the American environmentalist John Muir. After 1860 it was American economic and cultural influence on Scotland that significantly altered modern Scottish history, rather than the many Scots who emigrated to America who altered the USA.

In the American South the influence of Scott was said to linger as post-Civil War recovery created a significant regional subculture within the USA significantly at variance with the dominant characteristics of industrialization and urbanization in the American Midwest and North. The use of the cross of St Andrew for the Confederate flag during the Civil War and the emergence of the Ku Klux Klan with its Celtic imagery as a vehicle for white southern identity after the war has drawn increasing comment in the USA at the end of the 20th century, as America developed into more of a multi-ethnic society. Yet this appeal to a Scottish heritage has often been based on little more than surname identification and the modern tartan kitsch that has emerged as the tawdry detritus of much of Scottish popular culture in the 20th century (see HIGHLAND GAMES). Scottish Americans like Paul Green of North Carolina are remembered in their home states for acts of filiopiety such as Green's outdoor pageant based on Flora MacDonald's brief residence in North Carolina, The Highland Call (1939). Note of this work seldom identifies Green as the collaborator of the great American black writer Richard Wright in adapting his novel Native Son for the stage in New York. Green's ancestors had altered their, to English-language ears, unpronounceable Gaelic surname to a simple English colour word when they arrived in North Carolina at the end of the 18th century, but although Green took pride in that Scottish Highland ancestry, he knew as an American white southerner that there were other parts of his native culture that had as much to do with Africa as Scotland.

At the end of the 20th century many in the USA with Scottish surnames (see HISTORICAL SOURCES: 4) or ancestry look to Scotland as part of their heritage; many others, perhaps more, look to Scotland out of regard for the great ideas of the Scottish Enlightenment, although significantly they often do so in widely varying ideological contexts. Still others are interested in Scotland because of the seminal influence of the country on European Romanticism through the works not just of Scott but also of now largely forgotten literary phenomena such as the Ossianic poetry rendered from the Gaelic tradition (see ORAL TRADITION) into English by James MacPherson in the 18th century. They encounter an urban Scotland which, like much of the rest of Europe, has been profoundly influenced by American consumerist material culture and its dominant role in the second half of the century in culture and communication through cinema, television, and the internet. Scots are as likely to admire the music of Elvis Presley (who bore a Scottish surname) or Nashville country music drawing on the rural traditions of the American South as the authentic songs (see SONG, TRADITIONAL AND FOLK: I) of Robert Burns or the strathspeys and reels (see MUSIC, HIGHLAND) of Scottish country dancing. They illustrate the symbiotic cultural and historical traditions of two countries whose histories in modern times have had a significant impact on one another, reflecting the still greater import of the broader hemispheric exchanges between Europe, America, and Africa in modern times.

AJM

Wallace, William (*c*.1270–1305). The reputation of Wallace, the otherwise obscure younger son of a Clydesdale laird, in Scottish history is formidable. The patriot and warlord who defied Edward I, 'hammer of the Scots', became a potent symbol in later centuries of the defence of Scotland's independence against English aggression. His brief career began in May 1297, when he emerged as one of the two public leaders of a seemingly spontaneous yet widespread revolt, stretching from Galloway to Aberdeenshire, against the occupying army of Edward I of England. The most sensational episode was the killing by Wallace of the English sheriff of Lanark, which was the trigger for a rising of the men of Clydesdale. Linking up with Andrew Murray, who had led the rising in the north-east and was closely connected to the *Comyn family, the two orchestrated the sensational victory over a superior English force led by the earl of Surrey at Stirling Bridge on 11 September. Victory by unconventional military tactics in 1297, however, was followed by defeat at the hands of Edward I in a pitched battle at Falkirk in July 1298, when the traditional device of the schiltrom, a hedgehog-like formation of spearmen (see ARMY: 1), devised for defence against armoured knights, fell victim to the deadly accuracy of English archers. Although there was undoubtedly an element of popular protest about the rising of 1297 (see INDEPENDENCE, WARS OF), for resistance percolated through the ranks of Scottish society, most historians prefer to emphasize Wallace's connections with the traditional leaders of society rather than to enhance his role as the 'people's champion'. His father was a minor landowner, who owed allegiance to James the Stewart. Wallace himself had links with Robert Wishart, bishop of Glasgow, as well as with the Stewart. His acceptance as guardian of the kingdom in March 1298 would have been unthinkable if he had not had the confidence of men such as these. His collaboration with Murray, son of a well-connected knight who had served as justiciar of Scotia, further suggests a man drawn from the 'middle folk' rather than a man of the people. His knighthood, conferred when he was appointed guardian, suggested his acceptance by the nobility.

The details of Wallace's activities after Falkirk are sketchy. Both for him and for the Scots, the battle marked a turning point. Defeat had the effect of strengthening the resistance movement and provoked leading nobles into open revolt. Wallace resigned the guardianship, in favour of a collective, if somewhat uneasy, leadership by representatives of the two leading families of Bruce and Comyn, who were later joined by Bishop William Lamberton. By the time he left for the Continent in 1299, however, Wallace had pointed the way to the future with three key developments. His repeated raids into Northumbria in 1297–8 were the harbinger of 30 years of harrying of the English north, latterly by *Robert I. His engineering of the appointment of Lamberton as bishop of St Andrews in November 1297 ensured the commitment of the Scottish church (see CHURCH INSTITUTIONS: 2) to the struggle. And the Guardianship had been restored, in the collective identity of the 'community of the realm'.

Wallace had certainly returned to Scotland by 1303 and, characteristically, was associated with the last remnants of active resistance to Edward I's blitzkrieg of 1304, which culminated in the siege of *Stirling castle. It is possible, and it would not be surprising in the desperate circumstances of 1304, that Wallace, along with the other resistance leaders, considered submission. But Edward I's terms for a man who had in English propaganda become the devil incarnate were so uncompromising as to offer Wallace little choice but to remain a fugitive. After his capture in September 1304, the subsequent show trial in Westminster Hall, ritual humiliation, and execution at Smithfield in August 1305 smacked of a deep personal animus felt by the 'hammer of the Scots' against the man who, for him, symbolized the stubborn, grim resistance of the Scottish nation.

The *bête noire* of contemporary English propaganda, not unsurprisingly, became the subsequent icon of Scottish patriotism and resistance, long after the Wars of Independence. Yet the facts of Wallace's brief career, scanty as they are, need to be separated from the cult which has grown up around him, and has been regularly embellished since the largely fictitious account, *The Wallace*, written by the poet Blind Harry (from which many of the inaccuracies of the film *Braveheart* were derived) as a protest against the pro-English drift of foreign policy by James III. It was printed as part of the propaganda campaign waged by the pro-English king's party during the civil war following the deposing of *Mary, Queen of Scots, in order to demonstrate their patriotic credentials. In the 19th century, Wallace was celebrated as a freedom fighter by various national movements, including that of Garibaldi in Italy. By then, rival Bruce and Wallace cults had grown up, with Wallace (like Robert Burns) being hailed as a 'people's hero'. Even so, the revival of the cult in the wake of the Hollywood epic *Braveheart* showed new levels of excess. One 'quality' Sunday newspaper, in a fit of near hysteria endorsed by the leader of the SNP, urged the repatriation from Germany of the 'most important document in Scottish history', the letter of October 1297 sent by Wallace and Murray as 'leaders of the army of the kingdom of Scotland and the community of the same' to Lubeck to restore trading links after the battle of Stirling Bridge, so as to make good the fact that the new *Royal Museum of Scotland had no artefact devoted to Wallace. Unlike William Tell, Wallace did exist, but so little has survived of him that myth is relatively easy to construct. A telling example came with the commission offered by the district council of East Ayrshire to university history departments to prove the unprovable, that *its* Elderslie, and *not* the traditional Elderslie in Renfrewshire, was the true home of Scotland's hero (see REGIONAL IDENTITIES). More understandably, if less than tastefully, the burgh of Stirling exploited the 700th anniversary of the battle of Stirling Bridge and the 'big man, big sword'. And the 19th-century Wallace Monument atop Abbey Craig, above the battle scene, had a late 20th-century adornment added to its car park, a Mel Gibson lookalike statue. Like medieval saints, national heroes need to be repackaged in successive ages to satisfy their adoring public. With Wallace, it needs real effort to remember that, behind the myth making, there is a truly remarkable story.

ML

warfare, weapons, and fortifications: 1. to 1450; 2. 1450–1600; 3. 1600–1750.

1. to 1450

The way a people waged war was regarded as one of their principal distinguishing features in the Middle Ages. Between the 7th and 15th centuries the Scots' style of fighting, their military equipment and use of fortifications, did indeed develop in ways which paralleled the development of other political and social structures in Scotland. Traditional native practices were influenced, but never entirely replaced, by technological advances and cultural change, primarily from England and continental Europe.

Throughout the Middle Ages the Scots were predominantly a people who fought on foot. Accounts of the Scots fighting the southern English in the 10th century describe them forming in dense shield walls like their Scandinavian allies. Such dense bodies of footmen also formed the bulk of *David I's army at the battle of the Standard in 1138, of those of William *Wallace and *Robert I at Falkirk (1298), Loudon Hill (1307), and Bannockburn (1314), and of later medieval kings and nobles at battles like Neville's Cross (1346) and Homildon (1402). Such masses were composed of men armed with small shields and long thrusting spears, weaponry which appears in carvings from the 8th century of *Pictish origin and which remained the customary equipment of levies raised from Lowland Scotland until the 17th century. Most of these spearmen would have been lightly armoured and in numerous encounters, from the battle of the Standard onwards, fell victim to massed English archery. It was as an attempt to guard against this that Robert I passed legislation in 1318 which specified that, while the poorest troops were required to have just a spear or bow, all men with £10 or more of goods should wear a helm and either a quilted or chain mail coat. A century later James I would attempt an even more radical change. To answer the English longbowmen, in 1429 James ordered Scots to arm themselves with bows rather than spears, but his effort was unpopular and was abandoned after his death.

As the authority of the kings of Scots (see KINGSHIP: 3–4) grew in the 12th and 13th centuries, men from different military traditions appeared in Scottish *armies. Contingents of knights fighting as armoured horsemen became a prestigious, if not always effective, component of the king's armies provided by his new Anglo-French vassals or by Scots lords who were obliged to furnish knights in return for their lands. Regions of western upland, like *Galloway, Ross, and *Moray, also provided contingents as they came under closer royal control. Lightly armed raiders and skirmishers from these provinces allowed royal forces to penetrate the moors and hills of north and west in pursuit of native Scots enemies. The establishment of royal lordship over the Hebrides gave access to a highly militarized world and armoured axemen from the Isles were used to good effect by Robert I. During the following century, though, the combination of light raiders and heavily armed axemen led by the lords of the *Isles, proved a major threat to the crown at battles like Harlaw in 1411 and Inverlochy in 1431.

The Gaelic character of the Scottish kings' armies, and especially the Gallovidians, made a deep impression on English writers. Between the 1070s and the 1290s descriptions of Scottish invasions of northern England included graphic accounts of barbaric practices inflicted on the local populace. While many of these descriptions were hostile propaganda, practices like the taking of enemy heads had been traditional in Scottish warfare of the early medieval period, remaining in vogue until at least the beginning of the 13th century. By massacring or enslaving non-combatants in the 12th century, Scots were identifying themselves as waging war by different rules to the Anglo-Normans who regarded such practices as barbaric.

Fortification in medieval Scotland was revolutionized by the arrival of Anglo-French settlers and styles in the 12th century. Early defensive structures like brochs, crannogs, and hill and promontory forts (see BURGHEAD) were probably quite widespread and often served as political centres as well as simple refuges. However, from the 1120s fortified structures in Scotland were modelled on examples from abroad. In almost all cases this meant the castle. Though some of these occupied the sites of earlier forts, as at *Edinburgh, the number and form of these signalled a break with the past. Before 1200 most castles centred on earthworks, usually in the form of a mound or motte. Over 300 mottes have been identified in Scotland, most of them constructed by the nobility, both native and settler. During the 13th century a far smaller number of castles were constructed in stone. A significant proportion of these were built in the north and west where they occupied sites of strategic importance, for example at Inverlochy near Fort William. However, the expensive and impressive castles built at Kildrummy and Caerlaverock were not simply military installations but demonstrations of power and status. Similarly, during the largely peaceful 13th century royal castles functioned much more as administrative centres of sheriffdoms and royal residences than fortresses. During the same period, the new burghs remained unfortified. Only rare examples, like *Berwick and *Perth, possessed even defences of earth and timber (see URBAN SETTLEMENT: 1).

Perhaps not surprisingly, in Edward I's invasion of 1296, Berwick was stormed with ease and the rest of Scotland's castles were rapidly surrendered. Though during the subsequent decade Scottish garrisons steadfastly defended *Stirling, Kildrummy, and other castles, it became accepted practice under Robert I to demolish castles to prevent them acting as English bases. Though there were exceptions to this policy, it was largely the

English who rebuilt castles and fortified burghs in the early 14th century. Castle-building only resumed after 1350, when, with the English threat reduced, great magnates like the earls of *Douglas built new strongholds, initially to secure their local authority, but later as palatial residences, many of them massive stone towers, like Threave in Galloway. The development of effective artillery in the 15th century initiated a divergence between fortification and the residences built by the crown (see KINGSHIP: 5) and *nobility.   MBr

2. 1450–1600

The fact that the course of the 16th century was punctuated by a string of humiliating and occasionally catastrophic Scottish defeats at the hands of England leaves the distinct impression that Scotland as a nation was singularly lacking in combat effectiveness. The battles of Flodden (1513) and Pinkie (1547) saw numerically superior Scots forces in the field utterly devastated on a scale perhaps not seen elsewhere in Europe except at Pavia (1525) or Mohács (1526). *Edinburgh was sacked with ease (although not the castle) in 1544, the *Borders in 1545, *St Andrews held out for over a year (1546–7) and English garrisons were planted over eastern Scotland (at Eyemouth, Roxburgh, Inchcolm, and Broughty) in 1547 and then enhanced in 1548 (at Haddington, Lauder, Broughty Fort, and Dunglass). On the other hand, in the years after Flodden, Scots armies floundered in a series of inept or abortive invasions of England: in 1522, 1523, 1542, 1545, and 1557 (see FRANCO-SCOTTISH RELATIONS: 2).

Failure, however, is relative. Defeat at Pavia saw the king of France ignobly carted from northern Italy to incarceration at Madrid, one of the most squalid of Habsburg castles; his young sons, who were exchanged for him, had to live off gruel for four years. Mohács saw Hungary virtually erased from the map of European nations until 1699. Yet Scotland, by contrast, emerged from her humiliations intact and still a threat to England. Nowhere can this be better seen than at *Berwick where in 1514, 1523, and 1550–2 major strengthenings to the fortifications were seen as vital by London. In 1558, Mary Tudor authorized what became the largest single construction exercise in the second half of the Tudor century: by 1570, its costs had accumulated to over £128,000.

The Scottish wars cost England dear: almost £1,000,000 was spent during 1542–50, destroying Somerset's protectorship (1547–9), bankrupting the regime, and putting a strain on English finances for a generation (see ANGLO-SCOTTISH RELATIONS: 2). While English adventures in France were more costly, the Scottish distraction played no small part in French victories: the reconquest of Boulogne in

1549–50 being a classic example. During 1557, almost 10,000 English troops were seen as necessary for the defence of an utterly inadequate Berwick; these were men who should have guarded Calais, which fell in 1558. Moreover, no Scottish territory was lost, despite English attempts to wrest Berwickshire away in 1549 so as to create a buffer guarding the garrison town of Berwick. They did not even gain extended fishing rights in the Tweed.

What needs to be appreciated is Scottish resilience. Mauled they may have been, but this 'feudal' military policy was always able to re-form and fight back. In the first place, English tactics almost invariably (1547–8 being a major exception) allowed them to do so. Given the weather, its lateness in the campaigning season, and the disorganization of their victory on 9 September 1513, no post-Flodden invasion occurred. Again, because of the lateness of the season and the truly awful winter, Solway Moss (24 November 1542) had no military consequences. When the earl of Hertford staged an ambitious, amphibious landing of a main field army onto the shore of Leith in May 1544 and sacked the burgh of Edinburgh, within three weeks it had to bustle back to Dover to invade France. In September 1545, his army hugged the Tweed Valley and nipped home as quickly as it could, doubtless because of the large Franco-Scottish force which shadowed it. Only Pinkie (10 September 1547) had long-term fallout: the establishment of a range of permanent garrisons in the East March, at Castlemilk and Dumfries in the west, at Roxburgh and in the Forth estuary, and on the shore of the Tay. These forts created a springboard for expansion in 1548 (most notably at Haddington in April–June) before the French arrived in June. But that 'long term' lasted only until April 1550, at the end of which England was left dangerously exposed: first almost a French conglomerate in 1551–3 and then into a Habsburg one in 1553–8 (see FRANCE: THE 'AULD ALLIANCE'; GERMANY, THE BALTIC AND POLAND: 1).

What gave Scotland its extraordinary staying power? 'Feudal' armies (see ARMY: 1) may well have been unprofessional, poorly trained, and primitive, especially in comparison with England's, but they were incredibly cheap and were fighting for their home lands, and not involved in foreign conquests. The Scots could and did put very large forces into the field in 1513, 1514, and 1547. And never should it be forgotten that both Flodden and Pinkie were, by all accurate English accounts, very close-run things. Moreover, Scottish governments learnt as they went along. Caught napping in 1544, Arran ensured that his spy network gave him plenty of warning in 1547: his pioneers entrenched the Scottish camp at Musselburgh with diligence and high intelligence, with a stout earth wall facing the sea,

and his army was richly supplied with ordnance. That army was remarkably large for such a small country: no less than 25,000, thanks to his early warning alerts sent to every shire, a remarkable beacon system, and, of course, the Fiery Cross.

Next, it should be appreciated that while major battle victories eluded Scottish commanders, minor ones abounded, and many of these represented turning points which, in retrospect, were vital to the winning of the war. The classic victory on the rebound was Ancrum Moor in February 1545, which was trumpeted by the French all over Europe. Haddon Rigg in 1542 was only a fraction less notable. But the Scots were also adept at preventive defence. In May 1544, for example, Hertford attempted to besiege *Edinburgh castle, something the English did quite successfully in 1573. But so heavily armed had Arran made it and so stoutly was its artillery employed that the one English mobile siege machine (what we might now call a 'tank') to be manhandled up the High Street was sundered and had to be abandoned, spiked. The next time the English were near Edinburgh, which was in 1547, they did not even try.

Another piece of preventive fortification concerned Dunbar, which Arran rearmed and made impregnable during the summer of 1547. That was a critical success, forcing Somerset to place his forward garrison at Haddington, a disastrous decision which critically damaged English hopes of a speedy conclusion to the war. Even that erection had to take place entirely too late. Somerset had intended to subdue East Lothian in February 1548 and indeed the army which first settled at Haddington made numerous conquests: at Saltoun, Hailes, and Yester. Yet the earl of Angus slipped a large cavalry force over the formidable Cheviots and fell decisively upon a large English force which had invaded as far north as Drumlanrig. In the panic which followed that debacle, the whole of the south-west was lost and Somerset withdrew his East Lothian prong and returned only two months later, just before a French expeditionary army arrived to bolster the Scots. Haddington was supposed to be a major attack point; instead, the English found themselves entombed in it. They abandoned it in September 1549.

There were many such English miscalculations and minor Scottish triumphs. An English garrison and maritime force was stationed on the island of Inchcolm, in the Forth, after Pinkie. It was an utter failure, unable to block trade into Leith and constantly hounded by what was left of the Scots navy. Raiding parties into Fife were repeatedly rebuffed and, by March 1548, the position was renounced. In June 1549, the island fortification of Inchkeith was taken; it fell to the French in under a month.

warfare, weapons, and fortifications

The primitiveness of the Scottish main field army was a drawback, but it had its advantages, not least that being lightly armed and a citizens' army, it could be quickly called up. Virtually every able-bodied man had at least a pike, leather jerkin, and helmet at home, especially in the *Border zone where normal 'domestic' survival required the bearing and use of arms. But more sophisticated weapons began to be normal, such as handguns. Most tower houses (see ARCHITECTS, ARTISTS, AND CRAFTSMEN) now incorporated gunloops for their use. At Ancrum, every commentator remarked upon the vast clouds of black gunpowder smoke which enveloped the field from the Scots. Disasters such as Flodden and Pinkie meant not just the loss of men, but also of weapons, particularly the well-made and highly prized Scottish artillery. Such losses could be grievous, but foreign replacements could be and were made. Within Edinburgh castle there evolved Scotland's first major industrial factory: a cannon foundry. The French expeditionary armies of 1522, 1523, 1545, and 1547 brought munitions, as did the major armies of 1548 and 1549. When Albany had Dunbar rebuilt (c.1520) not only was its garrison French, but so too its armament. François I made the artillery in it a wedding present to *James V in 1537.

The pressure of the wars of the 1540s also saw the Scottish government increasingly resort to taxation so as to field permanent, paid horsemen in Teviotdale and the Merse in 1545 and bands of 'wageouris' were soon maintained by many nobles, not to mention by John Hamilton, archbishop of St Andrews. Much of the money (to Angus, Glencairn, Cassillis, Arran) came from France with the betrothal of Mary to the Dauphin François and this continued after 1550 through the purses of Mary of Guise and Henry Cleutin, the French ambassador. Mary became princess of Orange in the 1550s, the revenues from which sustained soldiers as well as her household and pensioners.

The French did not just expel the English by 1550. They cast their professional expertise wide and far so as to make Scotland, in their eyes at least, both secure and offensive. Scotland under *Robert I had been remarkably offensive: looking towards and threatening northern England, the Isle of *Man, and *Ireland. But thereafter, except for David II's disastrous excursion, they clung to the Border-line, witness all of James IV's incursions. Moreover, they allowed geography to do their defensive work for them, as Bruce had also done. Thus there were no major fortresses in the Borders. Only Dunbar, Edinburgh, and *Stirling were deemed necessary and they did their tasks admirably. The French found such a strategy anathema. Immediately after the end of the *Rough Wooing, in 1551–2, they set about establishing a defined border, the straight-line frontier known as Scots Dike. During 1548 Edinburgh, Stirling, and Dunbar were all massively modernized by the erection of huge Italianate single bastions in front of each of them. A massive citadel was staked out about Leith in 1548 and completed by 1558; Inchkeith was crowned with a *trace italienne* stronghold. Langholm, too, had a large fortress in earth erected. Plans were made for Kelso and some work done at Jedburgh. But their most aggressive move was to build a massive artillery park at Eyemouth which also was recast to the most modern design idiom of the age. It conspicuously threatened the frontier garrison at Berwick, a mere 6 miles (9.7 km) away (see BUILDINGS: 4).

The Scots were never so inert or ineffective as some would have us believe. Certainly Elizabeth I did not think them thus, hence her actually spending massive sums of money, the one thing she detested doing most of all, at Berwick. Charles I certainly would find them a redoubtable military foe, but that is entirely a different story.   MM

3. 1600–1750

Scotland experienced a remarkable transformation in military affairs between 1600 and 1750. In the 1500s state-funded military activity had become the defining mark of many European states. Instead of developing a standing royal army, however, Scotland still relied on medieval terms of 40 days' service or raised ad hoc forces. Likewise, its style of fortifications remained underdeveloped compared with states that adopted Italian artillery bastion system. By 1750, the Scottish military was transformed through its integration into a British force using the most modern European methods.

*James VI's military resources were minuscule. Manpower under direct royal control was limited to the garrisons such as those of *Edinburgh, Dumbarton, and *Stirling castles. The retention of the militaristic tower houses of the landholders had more to do with making a socio-economic statement (see ARCHITECTS, ARTISTS AND CRAFTSMEN) than one of military efficacy. For military expeditions the crown called upon the feudal host led by magnates, and local leaders. The disorderly Borderers justified their depredations as providing necessary military training for operations against England. Most Lowland infantry carried pikes, while some had muskets or arquebusques. Highlanders tended to have swords, Lochaber axes, and bows. With the exception of the *Gordons, the Highlanders lacked cavalry. Due to a shortage of suitable mounts, Scots horsemen were predominantly light (hobliars) or medium. Scottish involvement in the military revolution of the 16th century was limited to service in Continental units, such as regiments in the pay of the United Provinces (see LOW COUNTRIES). The *Union of the Crowns, by ensuring peace with England, instituted further demilitarization. The king took advantage of the situation to bring order to the *Borders and recruited a body of horse to enforce it. To establish royal control of the Highlands and Islands (see HIGHLANDS AND ISLANDS AND CENTRAL GOVERNMENT: 2–3), the privy council authorized expeditions of fire and sword involving *clan and kin groups, forces led by local notables, and burgh militia and shipping. James's pacific foreign policy removed external pressure for military innovation. Thousands of Scots, however, became skilled in the new ways of war developed by the Dutch and refined by the Swedes through service in the Continental wars (see MERCENARIES IN EUROPE). Between 1624 and 1637 the crown allowed recruiters to enlist over 40,000 Scots for the Dutch, Danish, Swedish (see SCANDINAVIA: 3), French, and Russian armies.

A temporary burst of activity altered the situation in Scotland in 1625–30 when royal foreign policy led to simultaneous wars with Spain and France. The privy council sponsored a meagre naval effort, ordered the training of shire and burgh militia, and tried to improve burgh fortifications. An attempt to establish a national militia under the command of Alexander Lindsay, second Lord Spynie, disintegrated upon arguments from the burghs about cost. Despite a survey of the eastern coastal burghs for the creation of new fortifications, only tiny Anstruther actually built any. In 1629 Scots, unaware of a truce in the war with France, captured Quebec—the sole victory of the two wars, and Scotland's only colonial military enterprise outside the *Darien expeditions in the 1690s.

From the late spring of 1638 Scots at home became thoroughly indoctrinated in developments of the military revolution. The Tables brought home hundreds of commissioned and non-commissioned officers from regiments serving on the Continent (including Alexander and David Leslie, William Baillie, and Alexander Hamilton). They trained the new levies (see ARMY: 2) of the Covenanters in the pike and musket developed by the Swedish army (see COVENANT, WARS OF THE). The musket began to predominate as the chief infantry weapon, with more than 60 per cent of the foot carrying firearms (chiefly matchlocks). The Covenanters also developed dragoons (mounted infantry) and medium horse (troopers protected by helmets, breast and back plates, and buff coats, and armed with swords and pistols, but lacking the powerful horses of their English counterparts). Returning mercenaries also introduced bastioned artillery fortifications to their homeland. The Covenanters quickly implemented them at Leith,

Burntisland, and Greenock. The new-style fortifications spread throughout the country, and played a major role in the defence of Edinburgh in 1650. Covenanting armies campaigned in Scotland, northern *Ireland, and England from 1639 to 1651. Initially, successful against English royal armies in the Bishop's Wars and containing the Irish rebellion of 1641, they also contributed to the defeat of the English Royalists at Marston Moor and the sieges of Newcastle, Carlisle, and Newark.

The alliance of Irish troops, led by the Scot Alasdair MacColla MacDonald, and Royalist Highlanders in forces under James Graham, first marquis of Montrose, posed a far more serious threat to the Covenanter regime than other Royalist forces of the period. Despite victories at Tippermuir, Aberdeen, Inverlochy, Auldearn, Alford, and Kilsyth, and gaining draws at Fyvie and Dundee, Montrose's force succumbed to an overwhelming force of cavalry at Philiphaugh. Involvement as allies of the English Royalists in 1648 brought defeat to the conservative and moderate Covenanters, and their replacement by the radical Kirk Party. Although successful against internal foes, the Kirk Party suffered a military debacle in 1650 at Dunbar after the end of an otherwise successful campaign. A conservative reaction created a truly national army (with Highlanders composing at least a fifth of the men). However, it failed to withstand the invincible English New Model Army either at home or in England. By autumn 1651 Scottish military fortunes had declined to the extent that an English conquest was merely a matter of time. With the surrender of Dunottar castle, the last bastion of regime, in May 1652, government-sponsored military activity had ceased.

The English occupation, however, did not bring a close to military operations in Scotland. Between 1651 and 1660 modern fortifications continued to be built (at Ayr, Leith, Kirkwall, Inverness, Perth, and Inverlochy), although by the conquering English New Model Army. Within weeks of Dunottar's surrender Royalist leaders relying on family loyalties or local power rebelled against the invaders. The conflict, known as Glencairn's rising (1653–4), spread throughout the country, but was quickly contained in the Highlands. Rapid English reaction (for the only time in the history of the Royalist rebellions, a large force of veterans was on hand) was blessed with success, including a victory in rough terrain at Dalnaspidal in Glengarry. Peace came and with it the extinction of Scottish military activity except on the Continent.

The *Restoration brought a return to the Scottish military operations at home. The privy council established a standing army of several horse troops and infantry regiments, armed as during the

Covenanter wars. While the crown abandoned the English-built fortresses, it regarrisoned Edinburgh, Stirling, Dumbarton, and Blackness castles. Meanwhile efforts were undertaken to create a national militia based in the shires. Both the standing army and militia found employment in suppressing the extreme *Covenanters, crushing their rebellions in 1666 and 1679, and the ninth earl of Argyll's in 1685, and occupying the south-west Lowlands in the 1670s and 1680s. From 1679 to 1688 the most militant Covenanters maintained a guerrilla struggle against the royal forces. Scottish mercenary involvement on the Continent continued, but at a much-reduced scale primarily in France, the Netherlands, and *Russia. State-sponsored naval activity was nil.

The revolution of 1689 ushered in several long-term trends. Due to William II's Continental and Irish military campaigns permanent Scottish regiments started integrating into a truly British army—an evolution completed by the *Union of 1707. The invention of the plug bayonet and its development into the ring and socket versions led to elimination of regimental pikemen. A further change in infantry weapons was the replacement of the matchlock musket by the firelock or flintlock, which was completed by 1702. Scottish regiments served in the Wars of the Spanish Succession (1702–13), Quadruple Alliance (1718–20), against Spain (1727–9 and 1738–48), and the Austrian Succession (1740–8). Loyalty to James VII and his heirs fostered a series of rebellions (1689–91, 1715–16, 1719—instigated by Spain, 1745–6) that rocked the period (see JACOBITISM). Some Jacobite infantry copied the government troops by arming themselves with flintlocks. In response, the government continued to man the principal castles, improved their fortifications, and created new fortresses at Fort William, Fort Augustus, Fort George (first in Inverness, then at the mouth of the Moray Firth), Corgraff, and Ruthven. In addition, the government armed some Highlanders to maintain order, including the Black Watch (see ARMY: 3). The privy council sponsored naval activity in 1689–97, then the Union brought Scottish integration into a truly national fleet: the Royal Navy.   EMF

weights and measures. One of the provisions of the Act of *Union of 1707 of the parliaments of Scotland and England was that Scotland's independent system of weights and measures was to be replaced by English units. As well as forming the basis of trade of all sorts in Scottish towns and markets (see URBAN SOCIETY: 2), specifically Scottish units had been used for centuries in land contracts, as the basis for taxation, and in rental and tenancy agreements, and were involved with the process of

assessment and in the payment of dues in kind. Such practices could not be swept aside overnight, and Scottish weights and measures continued in widespread use well into the 19th century, indeed some traditional unit names (such as the forpit and lippie, which were used particularly in the sale of root vegetables and oatmeal) are still recalled.

The first quasi-official account of the Scottish system was Alexander Huntar's *Treatise of Weights, Metts and Measures of Scotland, with their Quantities and True Foundation*, published in 1624, six years after the last major overhaul of the weights and measures in a parliamentary 'assize' of 1618. A recognition that the courts required the legal basis of the old units to be maintained led to historical enquiries in the second half of the 18th century, and the first historical survey of the intractable legal record was published by the advocate John Swinton in 1779.

In common with other mercantile nations, Scotland had well-defined systems of weights and measures for external and internal trade, and the legal and administrative structures for enforcing their use. Our first view of this—a stricture not to use one size of measure to buy goods and another for selling them—comes in the laws framed for the earliest royal burghs, the *Leges Burgorum*. As might be expected, Scotland's weights and measures evolved over time and were influenced by the metrologies of her principal trading partners, notably England (see ANGLO-SCOTTISH RELATIONS), Flanders (see LOW COUNTRIES), and *France. The Scottish system may well have been imported from England by *David I (1124–53) and his predominantly Anglo-Norman followers in the 12th century: there are good reasons to suggest a common origin for the medieval metrologies of England and Scotland. Certainly, the first administrative document which describes the weights and measures of Scotland—an assize which derives its authority from a traditional attribution to David I, but which survives in a form which is of a later date—is closely related to an equivalent English document of the mid-13th century.

Only the slightest traces survive of the earlier Celtic units, although one well-known example is a late 11th-century charter which described the ancient 'cain' (or land revenue) granted to a culdee religious community at Loch Leven, of various goods including 30 chudremes of cheese. There has been some success in relating this to a weight term derived from a Gaelic source, and this places it in a different context to the Scots-speaking royal burghs with their foreign trading privileges to which the David I assize was addressed.

As in England, linear measure was based on an inch (indeed on the same inch), and the larger linear units used, for example, in survey work and the laying out of plots of land in burghs (see URBAN SETTLEMENT: I), were the ell of 37 inches (94 cm) (used, however, in fractions of a sixteenth) and the fall of 6 ells. This ell, also employed in England at this time (although soon supplanted by another ell, the Saxon 36 inch yard (91.4 cm)), was found across north *Germany and later known as the rath of three Rhineland feet. Weights were specified in ounces, pounds, and stones and, as in England, they were initially based on the same Cologne bullion ounce and used the same multiples. But some bullion weighing (including metrological definition) was conducted with the numerically related ounce of the mark of Troyes—the centre of the great fairs in the Champagne region—also adopted in Paris: the earliest English and Scottish gallons are explicable in terms of definition in pounds of this French ounce.

Liquid was measured by the pint and gallon, with smaller units known as the chopin and mutchkin, and dry goods were measured in large coopered vessels by the firlot and boll (the approximate analogues of the English bushel (36.4 litres) and quarter (291 litres)) which in turn were defined by their dimensions and their capacities in pints. The apparent simplicity of this, however, disguises the fact that there were several separate variants of each unit (different pounds were appropriate for weighing different goods, ale gallons differed from wine gallons, etc.), and measuring practice (and therefore the quantities measured) depended on the circumstances and whether, for example, allowances or 'charities' were to be applied.

The diversity of units also extended to the use of dominant units of foreign markets. The Scottish wool trade was conducted almost exclusively through Bruges (see STAPLE PORTS), and was as important a generator of royal revenue through customs duty as was the English wool trade. Wool was bundled in sarplars which were reckoned in terms of an internationally recognized woolsack (initially with a Florentine definition), and the quoted Scottish size for the sack enables us to recognize that Flemish commercial weight was also in use in Scotland. Another example of external commercial influence affecting unit sizes was the import of wine, in French standard-sized 'tun' vessels: early 15th-century figures show that the sizes of English, Flemish, and Scottish wine gallons used in this trade were simple multiples of each other and not independent volumes.

The first detailed information about Scottish weights and measures in the legislative record is an important assize of 1426, when the influence of James I's (1406–37) English advisers can perhaps be seen in changes made to mirror aspects of the evolving metrology of England, including definitions couched in the comparatively new English troy ounce (apparently based on the ounce of the Bruges silver mark). By 1500, however, the Scottish system was realigned to a basis in the Paris ounce, although much of the mercantile trade was clearly conducted in the marginally larger variant weight units of the Burgundian Netherlands.

A succession of assizes in the 16th century, culminating in the final assize in 1618, give the impression of disruptive change of the type that the market would be unlikely to absorb. In reality, however, continuity was preserved in most trading, with the exception that the large dry capacity measures (the firlot and boll) were progressively increased in size at each major assize. This was done by engrossing traditional heaping allowances or charities, and then failing to prevent further allowances being taken on the enlarged measures. Although it was always claimed that contracts in force would be recalculated using the new sizes, in practice there must have been abuses, and the crown's underlying motive may perhaps have been the raising of additional revenue from royal estates. The winners were the landed interests and the major merchants who controlled the burghs, and the losers were undoubtedly the small producers and the tenant farmers.

There are several difficulties in interpreting assize literature, which is often tantalizingly incomplete and imprecise and has in some instances been subject to alteration. First, traditional practices such as the taking of heaping allowances and other charities form part of the tacit knowledge of the market and are almost never explicitly mentioned. The largest allowances were used at ports for dry goods (where the so-called 'water measure', as opposed to 'land measure', was used) and in many such circumstances it may not be possible to establish the quantities actually traded.

Secondly, assize legislation is selective in scope and it normally provides information only on some aspects relevant to merchant activity: it is not intended to illuminate other issues such as the nature of the units of internal market trade (see ECONOMY: 3). Thus trone weight, described to officials in 1613 as 'the ordinair and proper weght of the kingdome', does not figure in assizes at all, except in 1618 when the administration made an unsuccessful attempt to suppress it: only by inference can its mass be established at a constant one and a quarter times that of the merchant weight series. Finally, certain units appear to be redefined from time to time, but this seems principally to have involved applying the name to an existing and larger multiple in the course of establishing the relationship with another unit. Thus, for example, the pint was increased in volume in 1426 and c.1500 (the parliamentary record of the latter assize is lost). But in terms of the chopin or measuring jug of the pre-1426 pint, the 'pint' is merely redefined as two, three, and then four chopins: although the name of the unit may have changed, continuity in practice was preserved.

Each burgh was required to hold physical standards of the measurement units so that the weights and measures used in trade, and in particular in markets, could be checked by burgh officials and destroyed if found to be inaccurate. A number of early burgh standards exist in museum collections and elsewhere, and perhaps the best known is the ell of 1706 mounted in the square in Dunkeld, Perthshire, a centre for the linen industry. The standards themselves were checked against national standards by the Chamberlain in the course of his ayre, or progress round the royal burghs. Cases of using false weights and measures were tried in the burgh courts but appealed in the Chamberlain's Court of the Four Burghs (or subsequently heard at the Convention of *Royal Burghs). The construction of national standards (none of which is now known to survive) is associated with specialist workers at the mint and at the royal artillery workshops, and at the time of major assizes authenticated copies were issued to a limited number of principal burghs. In due course *Edinburgh, *Stirling, Linlithgow, and Lanark (the four burghs of the Chamberlain's former court) were given the right to issue copies of their retained standards of the ell, pint, firlot, and stone respectively. Their rights were revived in 1707 for the marketing and distribution to the other burghs of the new English measurement standards required for compliance with the terms of the Act of Union.   ASi

Weir, William. William Douglas Weir (first viscount) (1887–1959) was a leading industrialist. As president and director of the family firm G. and J. Weir Ltd, Glasgow, he was appointed as Scottish Director of Munitions between 1916 and 1917. This was a tricky task as the Clyde was experiencing a wave of industrial protest and wildcat strikes over pay and conditions (see 'RED CLYDESIDE'). Weir's approach was uncompromising and he had strike leaders arrested which tended to inflame the situation, although at the same time he was forced to offer concessions. Weir was instrumental in bringing new working practices to the munitions industry which helped to improve productivity and increase output. Such changes, however, were not popular with the workers who believed that this was the introduction of 'Taylorism' from America which would see jobs deskilled and working con-

ditions eroded. In 1917 he was appointed as Controller of Aeronautical Supplies and was a member of the Air Board which helped to bring the Royal Army Flying Corps (the future Royal Air Force) into existence. Weir was soon in charge as Director-General of Aircraft Production which helped to establish the modern aircraft industry in Britain with engines being built at Beardmores (see BEARDMORE, WILLIAM, & CO.) in Glasgow. After the war, Weir continued to maintain his interest in aircraft by taking an active role in the development of civil aviation. Weir built a reputation for himself as a hard headed, practical man of business during the war and, in spite of favourable recognition from the Conservative Party (see UNIONISM), did not maintain an active role in politics during the inter-war period. Even his activities in the business community during this period were fairly low key. Weir's services were called upon again during the Second World War where his expertise was put to use as the Director-General of Explosives at the Ministry of Supply. His knowledge of industrial machine production led to his appointment on the Tank Board in 1942.   RJF

Wheatley, John, (1869–1930), one of the most influential figures in the early Scottish Labour movement (see LABOURISM). Wheatley was a member of the Edwardian Scottish ILP and in 1906 he founded the Catholic Socialist Society which sought to demonstrate that socialism was not antithetical to the interests of the Catholic Church (see ROMAN CATHOLIC COMMUNITY). Although this organization was important in the long term in reducing clerical hostility to socialism, Wheatley had to endure considerable opposition from the church for his political activities. He was closely involved in the political turmoil which characterized much of the *'Red Clydeside' during the First World War and emerged as one of the 'Clydesiders' after the 1922 general election when he won the Glasgow seat of Shettleston. Wheatley was the foremost intellectual in Scottish Labour's ranks in the 1920s and played a considerable role in directing election strategy. His talents were put to good use by the first (minority) Labour government in 1924 when as a health minister he pushed through a major piece of *housing legislation which enabled more central government funds to be used by local authorities for the building of municipal housing (see URBAN SETTLEMENT: 4). Many have hailed this legislation as the most significant achievement of the first Labour government. Wheatley was an original thinker and was one of the few Labour politicians to address the issue of how socialism could be attained within a capitalist world economic system. His solution was for greater centralization and control of British and imperial resources which would be utilized in a managed economy. Consequently, Wheatley believed that Home Rule would be an ineffective way of restructuring Scottish society and economy damaged by post-war dislocation. This could be done, he argued, only by using the greater resources of the British state. His death in 1930 robbed the Scottish Labour Party of one of its most gifted thinkers.   RJF

White, John (1867–1951), Church of Scotland minister and ecclesiastical politician. He was born in Glasgow and educated at Glasgow University, where he was a protégé of the philosopher, Edward Caird, later Master of Balliol College, Oxford. White was ordained Church of Scotland minister of Shettleston in 1893, and was translated to South Leith in 1904 and to the Barony parish in Glasgow in 1911. A dedicated pastor and a patriotic Scot, he embraced the social gospel ethos of the 1890s and was committed to restoring the social influence of Church of Scotland. During the First World War, he served as a chaplain with the Cameronians on the Western Front and took a leading role on the General Assembly's Commission on the War.

White's major achievement was in the area of church union. In 1909, the two largest Presbyterian denominations in Scotland, the Church of Scotland and the United Free Church, began negotiations for union. White was appointed secretary of the Church of Scotland negotiating committee, and soon emerged as the dominant figure in the union movement. The negotiations proved long and arduous. Not until 1929, was the church union finally completed (see UNION OF 1929). Recognized as the main architect of the union, White was elected the first moderator of the General Assembly of the united church. In 1931, he led the Forward Movement, a national crusade which aimed to revive the social authority of the united Church of Scotland; two years later, he launched a church extension campaign, which erected churches and church halls in the new housing areas. There was, however, also a darker side to White's social activism. He embraced a racial nationalism, organizing a Scottish churches' campaign between 1923 and 1938 to persuade the state to halt Irish *immigration into Scotland and to deport many Irish-born residents (see IRELAND: 3). One purpose of a national church, he argued, should be to protect the racial purity of the nation (see NATIONAL IDENTITY: 6).
                                                                SJB

Whithorn is identified in popular culture as the 'cradle of Scottish Christianity'. This claim relies upon a brief account in Bede's *Ecclesiastical History*, 8th- and 12th-century lives of St Ninian, and an anachronistic view of the antiquity of Scotland. These sources tell of a British bishop, Nynia, who had converted the southern Picts, and built a stone church (Candida Casa) at Whithorn, dedicated to St Martin. Ninian's tomb in this church had become the focus of a healing cult by the 8th century, and Whithorn was a major centre of pilgrimage in the later Middle Ages (see RELIGIOUS LIFE: 2). There is insufficient evidence to date St Ninian with any confidence, but there is reliable evidence of an 8th–9th century Northumbrian bishopric. There are no further references to Whithorn until the appointment of a new bishop c.1128.

This sparse, sometimes controversial, picture has been greatly supplemented by recent excavations by the Whithorn Trust. These have revealed continuous settlement from AD c.500 with traces of earlier occupation and evolving urban qualities from an early date. The settlement is characterized by its organization with an inner ritual precinct and an outer residential zone, emulating a supposed Irish monastic model, though evident centuries earlier than known Irish examples. It is also characterized by its enduring prosperity revealed by Mediterranean and Gaulish imports in the 6th and 7th centuries, by Northumbrian coins in the 8th and 9th, and by *Scandinavian and Hiberno-Norse objects dating from the 9th to 13th centuries. Manufacture and industry are also evident from the earlier 6th century, peaking in the 12th and 13th centuries, though virtually absent in the 8th and 9th. The abundant economic evidence does not establish the ecclesiastical status of the settlement. It could have been a monastery, but there are no secure records, and it is likely to have been ruled by a bishop throughout this period (see CHURCH INSTITUTIONS: 1).

The earliest record is an enigmatic, though precise, Christian inscription—the Latinus stone—probably dating to the mid-5th century. Early structures including a road and a boundary ditch could have been of similar date, and there are hints of Romano-British activity. The earliest well-preserved settlement originated AD c.500, and comprised regular rows of small sub-rectangular buildings lying beyond an inner enclosure. The settlement expanded c.550, and by then had an inner precinct containing graves and shrines, and an outer residential zone including workshop areas. This settlement continued to develop for some 180 years, possibly undergoing major cultural change in the early 7th century. A lost life of St Ninian, used by later authors, probably dates to this time, suggesting that Whithorn was already a cult centre.

The settlement seems to have come under Northumbrian control in the late 7th century. An

Anglian bishop—Pechthelm—was appointed shortly before AD 731, and the settlement was re-designed on a rectilinear grid at about this time. It soon included a large timber church, a clay-walled mortuary chapel, halls, and smaller wattle buildings. The halls have been identified as part of the guest quarters, and an 8th-century verse life of St Ninian promotes Whithorn as a centre of healing. This settlement survived till about AD 845, when a brief period of decay was followed by the burning of the two principal ecclesiastical buildings. These were rebuilt shortly afterwards, but the character of the settlement had changed, and artefacts reveal new contacts with Viking—and subsequently Hiberno-Norse—markets. A distinctive group of disc-headed cross-slabs shows that Whithorn remained the focus of a small ecclesiastical territory in the Machars of Wigtownshire during the 10th and 11th centuries.

The appointment of a new bishop—Gilla Aldan—by 1128 and the construction of a new Romanesque cathedral (see CHURCHES: 1) in the mid-12th century had no visible impact upon the prosperous and populous settlement surrounding the earlier church, and the new burgh of Whithorn (see URBAN SETTLEMENT: 1) does not seem to have been established until the early 14th century. A new life of St Ninian, ascribed to Aelred of Rievaulx, recast him as a pillar of orthodoxy, and helped to assure the status of Whithorn as a major pilgrimage centre in the later Middle Ages.   PH

witch-hunts took place in Scotland between about 1550 and 1700, during the general European persecution of witches of that era. People had believed in witches long before then. Magic and the supernatural were part of everyday peasant life; some people had supernatural powers, for good or ill. Those who were thought to cast malicious spells on their neighbours were shunned or conciliated, or counter-magic was employed against their sorcery. No more was needed or expected. Witchcraft occasionally became criminal when high politics was involved. The earliest known executions of Scottish witches took place in 1479 when John, earl of Mar, was accused of employing their sorcery against his brother, King James III (1460–88); this was an isolated incident.

The peasants did not ask where witches' powers came from. But when late medieval Continental theologians started to ponder the links between village sorcery and Christian heresy, this was the first question they asked. Their answer—that witches' powers came from the Devil—led to the spread of elaborate demonological scholarship. King *James VI (1567–1625) made a notable Scottish contribution to it with his book *Daemonologie* (1597).

This new intellectual model saw village witchcraft as heretical and diabolical, rather than (as earlier medieval scholars had believed) superstitious and ignorant. Witches were now seen as an underground sect of Devil-worshippers, the mirror image of Christians worshipping God. They sold their souls to the Devil in a rite known as the demonic pact—the equivalent of baptism—and worshipped him in witches' sabbaths—the equivalent of church services. Sixteenth-century demonologists elaborated these ideas with material from witches' confessions, and circulated them throughout Europe. Scots ascribed particular importance to the 'Devil's mark' on the witch's body, which James VI argued was essential to the demonic pact. The courts had suspects' bodies pricked with pins until an insensitive spot was found. Female witches were also assumed to have sex with the Devil, and fears of witchcraft were linked to fears of deviant female sexuality.

While peasants thought only of individual witches who harmed their neighbours, the elite thought of a conspiracy against God and society. It was those who feared this conspiracy who led witch-hunts. Scottish witch-hunters were mainly local lairds and kirk sessions: leaders of local society and local representatives of the godly state. There was most witch-hunting in the core areas of the state, like Fife and Lothian; hardly any in the Highlands, where there were hardly any state institutions.

Witchcraft became a statutory crime in 1563, in a Protestant package of measures against biblical offences. Witch-hunting should be seen in the context of godly discipline by kirk sessions (see CHURCH INSTITUTIONS: 3). It was often a kirk session that first discovered and interrogated a witch, turning the case over to the criminal courts once sufficient evidence had been gathered. The best evidence was the witch's confession, usually obtained not by physical torture (with a few headline-hitting exceptions, mostly in 1590–1) but by 'waking' the witch. Sleep deprivation for about three days leads to hallucinations; some confessions included exotic detail.

There were between 1,000 and 1,500 executions for witchcraft, plus another 2,000 or so formal accusations which did not end in execution. This was fairly typical for Europe as a whole, where there were between 50,000 and 100,000 executions. Unusually, however, more than half of all Scottish witch-hunting took place in brief periods of national panic: 1590–1, 1597, 1628–30, 1649, and 1661–2. Other years saw a trickle of individual cases; the panics produced a flood. In panic periods, 82 per cent of the cases where the outcome is known ended with executions; in non-panic periods, it was only 50 per cent. The supply of witches was readily increased by asking the initial suspects (those denounced by their neighbours) to name their accomplices. When the authorities were most frightened by witchcraft, they were most willing to see it as a conspiracy. About half of all Scottish witches had a neighbourhood reputation for witchcraft before their arrest; the remainder seem to have been blameless until they were named by a witch under interrogation, and then hauled in and interrogated until they in turn confessed.

The witches themselves were mostly women (85 per cent). Most were older women, while some younger women were accused because their mothers were witches. Male witches were mostly husbands of witches, or were folk healers (see TRADITIONAL HEALING). Folk healers as such were not targeted (it is untrue that witch-hunting was prompted by a jealous medical profession) (see MEDICINE AND THE ORIGINS OF THE MEDICAL PROFESSION), but might be denounced if they were thought to have misused their powers. Witches were mostly settled members of their communities, not vagrants or beggars; it took years to build up a reputation for witchcraft among one's neighbours. A few poorer women even sought respect by encouraging this process, cursing anyone who crossed them. Malevolent curses, followed by misfortune to the victim, provided regular confirmation of peasant witch-beliefs. It was once argued that witches were a pagan cult surviving from pre-Christian times, but this theory has been wholly discredited. It was neighbourhood quarrels that initially prompted and validated witch-hunting, while the state's determination to enforce godliness on the peasants directed the process.

In the late 17th century, witch-hunting declined all over Europe. Belief in witchcraft largely continued, but it ceased to be central to the belief-system of the elite. The Scottish godly state declined as religious pluralism arose. Adopting a new rationalist empiricism, courts hesitated to accept evidence of witchcraft. Witch-pricking largely ceased after 1662, when some prickers were exposed as frauds; this removed an important source of evidence. Sceptical lawyers carefully agreed (at least publicly) that witchcraft could exist in theory; they simply could not accept the evidence for it in particular cases. Traditional witch-hunters found this frustratingly hard to argue against. Witchcraft prosecutions now tended to end in acquittal, so there was little point in continuing with them. There were no mass panics after 1662, and hardly any cases at all after 1700. The last execution was in 1727. The 1563 witchcraft statute was repealed in 1736. Witch-hunting faded quietly away (see also CALENDAR AND SEASONAL CUSTOMS; WOMEN: 1).   JG

women: 1. to 1700; 2. 1700–1770s; 3. 1770s onwards.

1. to 1700

Legally, women played a subservient role to their fathers, husbands, and sons; and this was considered a natural and just position in a hierarchical society that had no modern concept of women's liberation. As early as the 12th century, in the *Leges Burgorum*, it was laid down that a man had the right to speak for his wife in a court of law (see LAW AND LAWYERS: 1); and, once married and away from the control of her father, a woman had no legal persona. Her movable property, including rentals of heritable property, annuities, and interest on loans of money, passed to her husband. She retained merely her *paraphernalia*—that is dress, personal ornaments, jewellery, and repository in which to keep them—and *peculium*—a gown or gift to the wife if the husband sold lands in which she had interest as a tercer. The post-Reformation marriage service of the 1560s reinforced this position with the words that a wife 'is in subjection and under governance of her husband, so long as they both continue alive'. This is also reflected outwith the marriage partnership. Within *rural society and *urban society rarely are women found functioning in the administrative hierarchy, although there are several examples of medieval women becoming burgesses and a few of guild sisters. Even festivities (see WORK AND LEISURE, TO 1770s), such as the lay celebrations of Robin Hood or the Abbot of Unreason, or the religious processions such as that of Corpus Christi (see RELIGIOUS LIFE: 2), were all male affairs; women might merely spectate.

In practice, however, women are often evidenced as determined and dominant in roles that were different from those of men, but nevertheless offered them a largely free hand. Within her own household, particularly if she had a number of servants, a woman had considerable control. The bearing and rearing of *children was a female occupation, as were all the domestic chores within the home. But outwith the home there is ample evidence of wives and widows substituting for their husbands, in such positions as factors, shipowners, and customs tax collectors, in spite of the cultural norms which set demarcations between typically male and female work. And, unusually in medieval western Europe, women occasionally acted as procurators for other litigants in Scottish courts.

Certain occupations were largely the remit of women. The brewing and selling of ale and the food retail trade were dominated by females, although not exclusively their preserve. Women worked alongside men as shore porters in Aberdeen and, interestingly, it seems, received the same wage. A few women were also to be found as bearers in coal mines and at salt pans in the 17th century. Both demanded excessive physical effort, with little financial reward: by 1700 a woman coal-bearer would bring home only fourpence per day, but if her husband worked in the mine she was expected to assist. Seamstresses and female bonnet-makers plied their trade in the burghs throughout this period. Domestic service, clothes washing, wet-nursing, foster mothering, and prostitution offered employment to many; and for a very few others a nunnery, in pre-Reformation times, was the solution.

By the end of the Middle Ages, girls were being accepted into some *schools, and were taught by women, the song schools and grammar schools having previously been geared almost entirely towards male education and the training of boys for the church. Literacy was not high, even the ability to write a signature being beyond the majority of men. Some fortunate girls may have received a modicum of education at home. Katherine Bra, sister of the common clerk of Dunfermline, added her signature to the Dunfermline Burgh Court Book in 1493. Although perhaps the earliest extant example of a middle-class (as opposed to well-born and privileged) woman placing a signature, it suggests, however, that female literacy was not as rare as once believed. Many more would probably have been able to read. By the 17th century, sewing schools and female schools theoretically widened the potential for more girls of the non-privileged classes to receive a minimum of education. In practice, however, few girls attended, probably because they were of great assistance to their mothers in the home and, in rural areas, also in seasonal work on the land; and the subjects taught tended to be vocational, rather than academic, while the schoolmistresses were often of a poor educational standard themselves.

Widows might hold a dominant position within society, although those who lived alone might at times find themselves under suspicion, and single women, in particular, suffered in the *witch-hunts of the later 16th and 17th centuries. Particularly if she was wealthy, however, a widow was in a position to negotiate a suitable further marriage. If she did not have a son and her deceased husband had been a member of the guild merchant, she had the right to hand on this privilege to her new husband. She might also repossess any of her own properties alienated by her deceased husband if her permission had not been given for such a transaction. Widows were also numerically a strong group within burghal society: in *Stirling, in c.1550 it has been estimated that 18.7 per cent of householders were women. If she could survive the childbearing

years—in Aberdeen, one survey of skeletal remains suggested that only one-third of medieval women achieved this—she might outlive most men of her age. Indeed, it was not unusual to find women marrying three or four times.   EPD

2. 1700–1770s

According to religious and Enlightenment (see CULTURE: 11) thinking, the ideal woman of the period was practical, sensible, industrious, and godly. Obedience to men and to church defined female existence among rich and poor alike. Most adult women were married, but in an age of restricted income-generating opportunities for families and increasing overseas *emigration by young men, large numbers—possibly as many as 25 per cent in the first half of the 18th century—remained spinsters throughout life. Spinsterhood was especially high among the landed gentry.

Few women provide accounts of their life and times. Literacy was not as high as among men and although Calvinism (see RELIGIOUS LIFE: 4) encouraged self-reflection and the writing of diaries was in vogue, this was not a common cultural practice among Scottish women as in other countries. The few personal accounts that do exist are mostly those of wealthy women and are dominated by their concern with the practical affairs of family and household, in a context where most people lived in the countryside and most houses maintained vegetable plots and domestic animals. Even the privileged, such as Dame Grizel Baillie (1665–1746), who kept remarkable records of her domestic life, were active in the kitchen garden and dairy. Women of this type spun yarn and made clothing, concocted medicines (see TRADITIONAL HEALING) for the household, and concerned themselves with the affairs of servants and children. Women were particularly close to their female kin and lived in a relatively semi-detached way from their menfolk. Love between spouses did exist but was rarely the main reason for marriage. Love between mother and *children and in particular between mothers and daughters, was a stronger bond. In widowhood and old age, married daughters often took their mothers into their own houses.

Entry to the first phase of womanhood was marked at about the age of 14 when a girl left the household of her parents to enter another as farm worker or domestic servant, where she laboured for her upkeep and a modest wage under the watchful eye and discipline of the 'gudewife' (see RURAL SOCIETY: 3). Girls were trained in useful skills, including cash-earning skills in developing rural industries such as linen spinning, that would fit them for their future as wives, mothers, and domestic managers; if they were lucky, they picked up a husband along the way. Those that did not marry remained servants throughout their lives, or returned to their own homes to care for a widowed father or bachelor brother. Some girls were sent to cities, in particular to *Edinburgh, where there was a rising demand for domestic servants. Or, if their family could afford it, they went to learn a trade through a formal apprenticeship in an area such as dressmaking or millinery. The consumer revolution provided much employment for young women. Those that did not marry and possessed a modest sum to invest in a business, found that various areas of retail offered them opportunities for a reasonably secure independence. Prostitution also flourished in big towns, providing employment of a sort for many in less fortunate circumstances.

Among the gentry, girls at this age often went to nearby towns—such as *Stirling or *Perth, which were popular among the Highland gentry—to get the smatterings of a genteel education and enjoy a season or two of urban leisure before returning to their home country to marry within their kinship circle. Wealthier families sent their girls to Edinburgh and to one of the growing numbers of schools to be found there. They usually lodged with relatives, engaged in conspicuous consumption befitting their status, were introduced to potential marriage partners acceptable to their father, married young, and were then dispatched back to the country to bear children and manage their husband's household. Only the daughters of aristocratic families went to London. But even for privileged women, marriage normally entailed a narrowing of experience. Contacts with a wider circle were maintained by letter and occasional visiting, yet opportunities for the broadening of horizons were improving through the revolution in print (see PRINTING AND PUBLISHING) and though there were few Scottish publications with a female audience in mind before the late 18th century, English books and magazines were available and increasingly in evidence, even in remote country houses.

Many women died in *childbirth within a few years of marriage. Those that survived the childbearing years often lived with broken health, the consequence of frequent pregnancy, poor nutrition (see DIET), and hard labouring. Older women were respected for their practical skills and experience and among the Highland peasantry were the valued guardians of the stories and genealogy of the *clan, a knowledge that was passed from mother to daughter and celebrated within a distinct female oral culture. Yet in middle and old age, often widowed and infirm, most ordinary women experienced poverty. The poor rolls were dominated by such women. Their place as worthy objects

of charity within the rural parish defined the Calvinist ideal of the 'moral community'. SN

3. 1770s onwards

Scottish women's history has until recent times been very much neglected. Whilst mention has been made of Scottish women's past by a number of (eminent) mainstream historians, it has tended to be in their capacity as wives or mothers, not as women in their own right. This is a situation which is slowly being rectified, with much more research being conducted and published on the important subject of Scottish women's past.

During the period 1750–1950 Scottish women's experiences of both marriage and *family witnessed many changes. However, it was not until the second half of the 19th century that legislation gave important rights to married women, such as the Conjugal Rights (Scotland) Act (1861) and the Married Women's Property (Scotland) Act (1877). In the earlier period, most Scottish women, regardless of class, were expected to marry and bear *children who, in turn, would contribute to the overall family economy. Whilst the average age at which Scottish women married altered very slightly, from 25 in the early 19th century to 26 in 1911, the number of those never marrying rose at a relatively steady rate, particularly amongst women of the middle classes (see COURTSHIP AND MARRIAGE). More significantly, the number of children conceived fell quite dramatically. In the second half of the 19th century the percentage of women having seven children or more was 43 per cent falling to only 2 per cent by 1925, with the crude birth rate falling from 35 : 1,000 in 1850 to 25 : 1,000 by 1911 (see CHILDBIRTH AND INFANCY). This gradual decline in family size occurred first in middle-class families and then in many working-class families (see SOCIAL CLASS), largely as a result of the wider access and availability of family planning advice and contraception in the post-1918 period. Due to changes in the educational system (see SCHOOLS AND SCHOOLING: 4), children ceased to be a financial asset and became instead an economic burden upon many families. Throughout this period, illegitimacy rates also declined in Scotland from 9.79 per cent in 1861–5 to 6.78 per cent in 1921– 5. There were notable regional and class variations to this trend, with the north-east and south-west of Scotland sustaining significantly higher numbers of illegitimate births than the national average.

Whilst marital status and class clearly had an impact upon family life so too they largely dictated the working experiences of Scottish women throughout this period. Even prior to the agricultural and industrial revolutions of the 18th century most working-class women worked in the formal economy combining their productive roles with their reproductive and domestic duties. However, as the 18th century progressed, the nature and form of their labour altered with the gradual separation of the home and workplace into separate spheres, and paid work increasingly took place largely outwith the family home. However, the number of women engaged in agriculture rose between 1830 and 1880, largely due to changing work practices and movement of males from the rural to urban (see RURAL SOCIETY: 4; URBAN SOCIETY: 4) areas in search of higher paid employment in the heavy industries (see ECONOMY, SECONDARY SECTOR: 2). In 1871, 26 per cent of the Scottish agrarian workforce was female compared with only 5.8 per cent in England and Wales, although rapid decline was recorded thereafter. There were also some regional disparities, for example, in *Dundee (dominated by female labour in the jute industry) many married women continued to work in the textile factories. The vast majority of married women, however, were gradually pushed out of the formal economy but, for the most part, they nonetheless continued to work in the informal economy: childminding, taking in washing and sewing, sweated work, and 'helping out' in family farms and shops. For the most part, however, they were not permitted to work freely in the formal economy on the same basis as their male counterparts. For example, informal and formal marriage bars continued to operate in many occupations beyond the post-1945 period. The number of married women entering paid work in the public sphere, however, did rise quite dramatically in the first half of the 20th century, from only 5.3 per cent of the female labour force in 1911 to 23.4 per cent in 1951. For the most part, this was associated with a growth in part-time employment following the Second World War. Indeed, between 1931 and 1951 the rise in part-time female employment in Scotland was of the order of 185 per cent; moreover of those employed on a part-time basis in 1951, 93 per cent were women.

Yet the largest group of women enumerated as employed throughout the period of industrialization were younger single women who continued to enter the formal economy en masse. For many paid employment, however, was merely a transitional period between school and marriage, as the Victorian ideal of a 'woman's place' crossed class boundaries. Until the outbreak of the First World War women were concentrated in only a few occupations, with the single largest employer of female labour in Scotland being domestic service. 'Service' employed RURAL 129,550 women in 1871, rising to 143,699 in 1901. The second biggest employers of female labour were the textile industries, which employed

120,709 women in 1871. During the inter-war period there were some limited alterations to the working practices of Scottish women, particularly those from the middle classes, but for working-class women, the reality of the inter-war years was generally either unemployment or a return to domestic service or the textile industries, which in 1931 employed 138,679 and 100,633 respectively. Whilst the 20th century witnessed the virtual extinction of the domestic servant, who made up 24 per cent of female employees in 1901 and only 11 per cent in 1951, the nature and form of service merely altered to accommodate changing classifications in the public sphere. The growth in demand for institutional public cleaners, cooks, and carers created many low-paid, low-skilled, low-status 'opportunities' for many working-class women. The 1951 Census showed that 145,796 Scottish women were employed in 'personal services'.

For most Scottish working-class women throughout this period, employment clearly tended to be concentrated in a few sectors of the economy, with the only changes being where their actual labour took place. For most of the 19th century, middle-class women generally did not enter paid employment, with the exception, perhaps, of shopkeepers; landed aristocratic women were often left to tend to estates in their husbands' absence. For the most part, Scottish middle-class women occupied themselves with philanthropic work, often as a means of entry into the public sphere, given the restrictions placed upon them by Victorian society. However, after the Sex Discrimination (Removal) Act (1919) many professions such as *law were opened up to some of these women with Margaret Henderson becoming the first Scottish female advocate in 1926. Just as the first half of the 20th century saw a decline in working-class women being employed as domestic servants, it also witnessed a rise in the number of middle-class women entering a variety of professions previously closed to them. For example, the number of Scottish women employed in the teaching profession rose from 6,059 in 1871 to 25,546 in 1951. However, for the most part, both horizontal and vertical segregation prevailed in the teaching profession. Very few women were engaged as headteachers in Scottish schools and female teachers tended to be concentrated in a narrow range of subject areas both in primary and secondary educational establishments.

Despite the introduction of compulsory elementary education for all children aged 5–13 in 1872, opportunities for many female pupils were limited, with most education merely preparing them for their future roles in industry, service, or the home (see SCHOOLS AND SCHOOLING: 3). This was partly reinforced in 1873 when the Edinburgh School of Domestic Economy was established, followed by the Glasgow School of Cookery two years later. Just as elementary education was limited in scope, so too was higher education for Scottish women (see UNIVERSITIES: 2). In 1865 Sarah Siddons founded the Edinburgh Essay Society and in 1867 Mary Maclean established the Edinburgh Ladies Educational Association (ELEA) which held classes conducted by a number of lecturers from Edinburgh University. In 1876 the first Association to Promote the Higher Education of Women was formed in St Andrews, where women were permitted to attend certain classes to diploma level. In the same year, the Russell Gurney Enabling Act was passed which permitted universities to confer degrees on women and allowed for women to be examined in medicine and thus placed on the Medical Register. In 1892 Queen Margaret College, Glasgow, was established and Aberdeen University formally decided to admit women and permitted them to graduate in all its faculties. Marion Gilchrist and Lily Cumming were the first female medical graduates in Scotland (Glasgow University 1894), and thus became fully recognized as equal recipients of the rights and privileges accorded by universities. In 1889 the Universities (Scotland) Act empowered each of the Scottish universities to admit women on equal terms with their male counterparts and to graduate with degrees (including medicine). In the same year Elsie Inglis graduated as a surgeon (Edinburgh) and established a female surgical hospital (1901) staffed entirely by women. Inglis later founded the Scottish Women's Hospital Unit for Foreign Service (SFWSS) in 1914. However, not all women were so successful, nor granted this equal status within higher education. For example, Glasgow University's medical faculty denied women professorial teaching and clinical instruction and Edinburgh female medical students were permitted to become full members of the University only in 1916. However, whilst women were permitted to graduate in medicine from the latter part of the 19th century, with the exception of a few hospitals dealing directly with women or children's health, very few institutions admitted women doctors prior to 1943 when the demands of war made it necessary.

State legislation and trade unions both, to a large extent, supported the ideology of separate spheres and were instrumental in maintaining occupational segregation and exclusion. Throughout the 19th century there were a number of acts of parliament passed concerned with restricting the employment of women. The first important act was the Mines Regulation Act of 1842 which forbade women (and certain children) to work under-

ground (see ECONOMY, PRIMARY SECTOR: 3). What this Act failed to take into account, however, was the importance of women's earnings to the family economy and the lack of alternative employment opportunities (see LIVING STANDARDS: 3). For example, 2,500 women in the east of Scotland became unemployed as a direct result of this legislation. There were also numerous Factory Acts which placed restrictions upon the employment of women. Much of this legislation was instigated and supported by the trade union movement which, at this time, was attempting to secure a family wage for their predominantly male membership.

In the period down to 1914, the majority of Scottish women were not members of official trade unions. Yet this did not render them passive in the workplace, and many women formed their own associations in attempts to secure better pay and working conditions. The first recorded dispute was in 1768 and, in the period 1850–1914, 300 strikes involving Scottish women were reported. In the closing decades of the 19th century there was an array of activities in the official trade union movement to attract female members, not least due to the fact that Scottish women were earning only around 43 per cent of the male rate of pay. In 1887 the Scottish Women's Trade Council (SWTC) was formed from which emerged the Women's Protective and Provident League (WPPL) and the Glasgow Council for Women's Trades (GCWT). In 1893, the National Federal Council of Scotland for Women's Trades (NFCSWT) was established, followed by the Scottish Council for Women's Trades (SCWT) in 1900 (formerly the GCWT). All of these bodies worked closely together and by 1895, the NFCSWT alone had an affiliated membership of sixteen trade councils and 25 trade unions, representing a membership of 100,000. Two prominent women in the trade union movement during this period were Margaret Irwin and Mary MacArthur, both of whom made long-lasting contributions to women's activity within this realm. Irwin was the full-time organizer of the WPPL from 1891–5, secretary of the SCWT throughout its 44-year existence, and the first elected secretary to the Scottish Trade Union Congress (STUC) in 1897. MacArthur was secretary of the Women's Trade Union League (WTUL) 1903–21 and secretary of the National Federation of Women Workers (NFWW) 1906–21, which alone had a membership in Scotland of 2,000 women prior to the Great War.

The 20th century continued to witness a numerical rise in women's participation in the official trade union movement. In 1923–4, 78,470 (24.2 per cent) of the STUC's membership was female, rising to 140,189 (18.8 per cent) in 1951. Again, much of this rise was directly related to the numbers of Scottish women engaged in the public sector in the post-1945 period. However, women continued to be under-represented in any positions of power within the STUC. Apart from Irwin, the only other women elected to the STUC Parliamentary and General Councils throughout this period were Isabella Blacklock (1898), Kate Maclean (1911–13), Grace Mewhort (1921), Agnes Gilroy (1932–4), Bell Jobson (1933–42), and Isobel Barrie (1940–2). Whilst the Second World War perhaps heightened many Scottish women's awareness of trade unions, this under-representation continued to be the status quo in the post-war period.

If by the latter part of the 19th century Scottish women were becoming more visible in the official labour movement, what of political representation? Following the 1867 Reform Act, Scottish women could vote in local town councils and poor law boards, in 1871 female property owners and married women were allowed to vote in local elections, and in 1881 this was extended to cover all women, regardless of marital status. In 1888 women were permitted to stand for election to parish and county councils, and in 1873 to school boards: the first woman in Scotland to be returned was Jane Arthur (Paisley Board 1873). In 1907, women could stand as candidates in town councils and the first female town councillor was Lavina Laing Malcolm (Dollar 1907) who, in 1913, also became the first woman provost in Scotland. However, the right to vote in parliamentary elections eluded all women. Women's fight for the right to vote had a long legacy in Scotland, given their very active and visible role in the Chartist campaigns of the 1830s and 1840s, but it was not until the disappointment of the Second Reform Act (1867) that a highly visible campaign for votes for women was embarked upon. On 6 November 1867 a new Scottish Women's Suffrage Society (SWSS) met in Edinburgh, and by the beginning of the 20th century the Scottish Federation of Women's Suffrage Societies (SFWSS) included 26 organizations. In 1902, the Glasgow and West of Scotland Association for Women's Suffrage (GWSAWS) and the Scottish Universities Women's Suffrage Union (SUWSU) were formed. A Scottish Branch of the Women's Social and Political Union (WSPU) opened in Glasgow in January 1908 and the Women's Freedom League (WFL) likewise opened a Scottish interest in 1909. There were numerous leaders and activists involved in these various organizations, such as Eunice Murray, Priscilla McLaren, Helen Fraser, Lily Bell, Flora 'Bluebell' Drummond, Mary Philips, Kate Evans, Anna Munro, Maggie Moffat, Helen Crawfurd, Ethel Moorhead, and Elizabeth Dorothea Chalmers Smith (some of whom were arrested and tortured

under the Liberal government's 'Cat and Mouse' Act). In 1918 the vote was finally granted to certain women over the age of 30 and in 1928 extended to cover all women over 21, on a par with men. In November 1918, the Eligibility of Women Act was passed which allowed women (ironically aged 21 and over) to stand as MPs and Eunice Murray became the first Scottish woman to stand as a parliamentary candidate in 1919. The first Scottish women to be returned to parliament were Katherine Marjory, duchess of Atholl (ironically a leading anti-suffragist) in 1923 (Conservative and Unionist—Perth and Kinross), followed by Jennie Lee (aged only 24) in 1929 (Labour—North Lanark), Florence Horsbrugh in 1931 (Conservative and Unionist—Dundee), Helen Shaw in 1931 (Conservative and Unionist—Bothwell), and Agnes Hardie in 1937 (Labour—Springburn). In 1945, Clarice McNab Shaw (Labour—Kilmarnock), Jean Mann (Labour—Coatbridge), and Margaret (Peggy) Herbison (Labour—North Lanark) were all returned to the Commons. Women, however, were not permitted into the Lords until 1958.

Clearly, in the late modern period many changes occurred in the social, economic, and political status of Scottish women. Whilst there were some positive changes, predominantly affecting the lives of middle-class women not least in terms of access to careers, education, and politics, for the vast majority of working-class women, change was not always as positive. Many faced exclusion and segregation in the workplace, still earning around only half the average male rate. Moreover, they continued to endure the double burden of work in the private and public spheres, and in the latter were largely under-represented in trade unions and political organizations until well beyond the period of the Second World War.   YB

Woodburn, Arthur (1890–1978), Labour politician, writer, and educationalist. He was born at Polwarth Gardens, Edinburgh, the youngest son of a brass foundry proprietor. After leaving school at 14, he went to work as a clerk for an Edinburgh foundry, completing his education at a Heriot Watt evening class. During the First World War, Woodburn joined the ILP (see LABOURISM) and became a conscientious objector. After speaking at No-Conscription Union meetings, he was arrested in September 1916, court-martialled for failing 'to obey the lawful command of a superior officer', and imprisoned under the authority of the *Scottish Secretary until 1919. He spent much of the time in solitary confinement, refusing to work for the military.

In the 1920s Woodburn began to lecture for the Scottish Labour College and published a number of works, including *An Outline of Finance*, a Marxist attack on capitalism and its inherent contradictions. However, Woodburn rejected calls from the Soviet Union for armed insurrection and by the time he was appointed Scottish secretary of the Labour Party in 1932 was a firm anti-Communist and rewrote much of the Party's Scottish manifesto with an emphasis on state-led economic development. Woodburn also became a firm anti-pacifist, fearing that the growth of fascism in Europe would erode workers' rights. He entered parliament at the Clackmannan and East Stirlingshire by-election in October 1939, winning easily against a pacifist candidate on the ticket of 'no surrender to Hitler's policy of wholesale murder and brutality'.

After Labour's 1945 landslide victory he held a number of junior ministerial posts and became Scottish Secretary in October 1947, appointed by Attlee to deal with a growing post-war demand for Scottish devolution. Against much Whitehall opposition, Wooburn secured an enlargement of the Scottish Grand Committee to take the second reading of Scottish bills, but failed to secure agreement on the establishment of a Scottish production council under his authority to stimulate investment or a public inquiry into Scottish affairs (see GOVERNMENT AND ADMINISTRATION: 3). The cabinet believed that Scottish economic development depended on investment from the nationalized industries and English enterprise (see ECONOMIC POLICY: 4). All Woodburn was offered was the establishment of a non-executive Scottish Economic Conference. However, at the Paisley by-election shortly afterwards, Labour easily retained its seat against a pro-Home Rule candidate and he felt that the matter had been satisfactorily resolved.

The devolution issue re-emerged in 1949 when the Scottish Covenant Movement began a public petition and attracted considerable support. Woodburn responded vigorously and accused its leadership in the Commons of supporting a far-right bombing campaign which would destroy Scotland's attractiveness for foreign investment. The accusation did much to mute Tory and institutional support for the movement, but caused Labour disquiet, especially as the Covenant's leadership contained many respectable and established Scottish figures. Until his outburst Woodburn's ministerial position was considered strong; he had been the first Scottish Secretary to tour Scotland arguing for business to invest in new enterprises and had increased the real level of public-sector investment in Scotland. However, he had also been a strong supporter of the National Health Service and, like Aneuran Bevan, opposed the introduction of charges during the devaluation crisis

of October 1949. After the 1950 general election Attlee offered him another ministerial post, but he refused and was sacked. Attlee wanted to reconstruct his government with more flexible ministers, though in terms of the Covenant little was conceded. Woodburn never held office again and left parliament in 1970.

Woodburn belonged to that very distinct type of early 20th-century Scot, whose loyalty lay primarily with his class (see SOCIAL CLASS). His adherence to Marxist analysis and an intuitive understanding of capitalist finance sustained a particular view of public administration. It was a view he felt the majority of the working class shared; 'scientific socialism' would bring material advance and a more just society. His legacy to Scotland was a political economy heavily based on public sector investment, a free health service, and maintenance of the Union. It was a legacy that structured Scottish debate until new left-wing concerns of participation and lifestyle emerged in the 1980s.   IL

work and leisure, to 1770s. Work predominated over leisure in the medieval period. Indeed, for the majority of people, there was no real concept of holidays or recreation. The working day in towns (see URBAN SOCIETY: 1) began as early as 5 a.m. in summer (although in some towns the 'workman bell' could be heard at 4 a.m.) and 6 a.m. in winter; and, for most, probably did not end until the curfew was called, at darkness. In the countryside (see RURAL SOCIETY: 1), agricultural workers would toil throughout the daylight hours, particularly when seasonal labour, as at harvest time, demanded intensive effort from regulars and temporary hands. Skeletal remains (see HEALTH, FAMINE, AND DISEASE: 1) give clues to the hardship of working life in the Middle Ages. Degenerative change, or wear and tear, often reflects the nature of occupation, particularly if it involved hard manual labour indicated in the condition of the spine, or repetitive work, as in constant bending, chopping, or use of the fingers and wrist, or a habitual position, such as squatting.

Working life began young. Small *children could work in the fields, perform a number of tedious tasks, such as supervising a simple loom or spinning wheel or carting coal or salt, or care for younger siblings and so release the mother for other chores. The involvement of children, as well as wives (see WOMEN: 1), in the family income was facilitated by the fact that most occupations were home-based, either on the fields beside the agricultural cottage or in the backlands of urban burgage plots. Most craftsmen and merchants would ply their trade from their own tenement, with working premises to the rear and a booth, or even merely an open window, to sell on the frontage. 'Family businesses' were precisely businesses run by the family, with or without the assistance of servants or apprentices.

This home-based economy lasted into the late 17th and 18th centuries. But during this period, small manufactories (see ECONOMY, SECONDARY SECTOR: 1) were set up in many of the Scottish burghs. Although the evidence suggests that these employed an extremely slight proportion of the population, they were a portent for a changing workplace, and conditions, in the Scottish economy. By the end of the 17th century, for example, Musselburgh housed a broadcloth factory; Hamilton had a lace manufactory, basically to provide work and care for twelve poor girls, and a wool manufactory by 1705; and by 1760, even little Dunblane had a small factory, supplying linen, thread, and shoes to the Glasgow market. Linen weaving was to become the mainstay of the economy in the 18th century. It was, for example, introduced into Kirkcaldy in the 1670s; and Melrose, as other Border towns, became renowned for its linen and woollen manufacture. But even linen weaving was primarily a domestic, or cottage, industry. As yet, Scotland had no genuinely large manufactories.

In such conditions, leisure time, in the modern sense of the word, was virtually non-existent. But there is evidence, in both the documentary and the archaeological records, of some pastime activities. Drinking, storytelling, and gossiping were welcome diversions. In towns, the 'buttis' could be used for shooting practice; and foot (see FOOTBALL) and hand ball were popular. It is known that hawking (a type of bowls), pennystanes (a type of quoits), and card playing were enjoyed by some sections of society, as was hunting, even though it was normally clandestine for the majority of the people. Bone and slate gaming counters suggest that gambling was a favourite pastime; and skating and sledging provided fun in the relatively cold winters. Small clay animals, found in a few medieval urban settings, also suggest that children had at least a minimum of playthings.

Towards the end of the Middle Ages, there is evidence that the hardship of life was also alleviated by secular festivals and plays, the most noted, perhaps, being the May revels. At this, the 'abbot of unreason' traditionally presided, with the conventional order and rule of society upturned. These celebrations took place in many towns and were, without doubt, an attraction to the nearby country people. There was, for example, an 'abbot' or 'prior of Bonaccord' in *Aberdeen, an 'abbot of unrest' in Peebles, and an 'abbot of narent' and 'lord of inobedience' in *Edinburgh. The cult of Robin Hood was also well known in Scotland from at least the early 15th century and may, in part, have developed out of the 'abbot of unreason'. Both figureheads were found leading the May games.

For medieval men, however, the routine cycle of life revolved around the church (see RELIGIOUS LIFE: 2). Holy days were respected, not merely for their spiritual significance, but also because they were days of rest from work. Processions through the streets on saints' days were not only days to venerate the saints and display the banners of guild merchants and crafts as they progressed in order of importance, but also times to introduce some jollification into life. Strolling companies of players travelled around the country and added to the festivities with jesters, tumblers, minstrels, drummers, and pipers. In the towns (see URBAN SOCIETY: 1) also there were organized entertainments in the form of religious plays—mystery plays, passion plays, and pageants—and these, too, would attract the country people.

Much was to change in the 16th century. Fear of political unrest and disorder meant a tightening of control and, ultimately, banning of Robin Hood and the abbot of unreason. The *Reformation brought to an end the popular spectacles of religious processions and the new church (see CHURCH INSTITUTIONS: 3) attempted to bring in more stringent discipline, by such measures as forbidding church music and not allowing children to carry candles on Candlemas Day. Many of the old traditions survived, however, under very thin guise: Midsummer Eve was celebrated for some time after the Reformation, with the lighting of fires; holy wells, although forbidden to be visited, attracted, rather, those who seemingly wished to 'take the waters'; and Christmas and New Year were still accompanied with dressing up or crossdressing (see CALENDAR AND SEASONAL CUSTOMS).

Secular games remained popular, in spite of a certain official disapproval, and special occasions, such as fairs, took on much of the character of the old Holy Days, but without the religious overtones. These were occasions for drinking—by the end of this period to ale and beer were added neat whisky and cheap West Indies rum—smoking a pipe or chewing of tobacco, and general jollification, while watching such entertainments as football matches (see ROUGH CULTURE) and horse racing, with *curling being introduced from the *Low Countries in the 17th century. A privileged few might even enjoy a game of *golf or enter a shooting competition on the likes of the Links at Musselburgh; and, in Edinburgh, the Enlightenment (see CULTURE: 11) brought intellectual stimulus to the literati. Perambulating of the marches, however, was a significant day in the year for all townspeople. While serving was an official duty, for checking against any encroachment into their territories, it also became an occasion for festivities; and in some towns 'Riding the Marches' (see REGIONAL IDENTITIES: 3) became an important local event in which all could participate, even if, as in the pre-Reformation Corpus Christi procession, participation merely amounted to spectating.

EPD

Young, James 'Paraffin' (1811–83), founder of the Scottish shale oil industry, scientist, and inventor. Born in Glasgow, the son of a self-employed carpenter, Young was educated at Sabbath school, the Mechanics' Institute, and Anderson's University. In 1832 he became assistant to Thomas Graham, professor of Chemistry. When Graham transferred to University College, London, in 1837 he took Young with him. There Young decided to enter industrial management, joining James Muspratt in St Helens before going in 1844 to Tennants of Manchester. One of his friends, Lyon Playfair, drew his attention to an oil spring in a coal mine at Riddings in Derbyshire. Young refined some of this oil and realized that saleable products—naphtha, lubricants, and lamp-oil—could be made from it; he therefore established the first oil refinery in Britain in 1848. Mistakenly thinking that the petroleum had its origins in the coal measures, he began to experiment with the distillation of coals. This error made his fortune for it led him to the Scottish cannel (candle) coals and oil-shales, notably torbanite (a geological freak midway between coal and oil-shale and the richest oilbearing mineral ever discovered). Close to rich deposits of torbanite Young's Bathgate oil-works was established in 1851, using his patent enrolled in 1850. This venture was known to be highly profitable; infringers entered the industry, but Young defended his patent successfully in the courts; yet the technology was applied worldwide. After the expiry of his patent in 1864 a Scottish oil mania developed; 97 firms were founded in Scotland by 1870 but increasingly this industry was faced with American competition. Young turned to philanthropy, scientific experiments, and collecting works on alchemy. He became president and benefactor of Anderson's University and supporter of his friend, David Livingstone, the explorer (see AFRICA). In politics he was active in the Liberal Party (see LIBERALISM).

JBut

Younger, Sir George. A leading Unionist, Sir George Younger, Viscount Younger of Leckie (1851–1929), was described on his death by the *Scotsman*'s political correspondent as one of the 'Few men [who] have exercised a more profound influence on the course of public events without ever having held Ministerial Office'. Younger, the eldest son of James Younger (d. 1868) of the famous brewing company of Alloa, entered politics through local county government when, in 1890, he was elected to the county council of Clackmannan. In the years which followed, he became council convener (1895–1906) and then president of the County Councils' Association of Scotland (1902–4). Younger's early forays into parliamentary politics, however, were less successful and he lost contests in the constituencies of Clackmannan and Kinross in 1895, 1899, and 1900 and Ayr Burghs in 1904. In 1906, however, Younger secured Ayr Burghs for the Unionists and held the seat until 1922. Nevertheless, Younger's most notable political successes were achieved as a party organizer. In 1904 Younger had been president of the National Union of Conservative Associations of Scotland and thereafter, having been appointed Scottish Chief Whip in 1911, he oversaw the merger of the Liberal Unionist and Conservative parties in Scotland in 1912 (see UNIONISM). In 1917 his organizational talents were recognized nationally when Younger became the chairman of the Unionist Party. In the years which followed, tension grew within the Unionist–National Liberal Coalition over the efficacy of the perpetuation of the governmental alliance created during the Great War and in 1922 Younger called for the end of the 'matrimonial alliance' between the parties. Referred to in derisory terms by Lord Birkenhead as 'an ambitious cabin-boy', Younger led the small minority of six Scottish Unionists who supported the end of the coalition at the famous Carlton Club meeting at the end of October which dissolved the alliance. CMMM

Glossary

assarts   land taken into cultivation for the first time

assythement   compensation for loss or injury

ayre   a circuit court

baile, bailtean (pl.)   village, hamlet, small township

bailie   burgh magistrate

baillie   estate officer presiding over a baron court

bardàch, bardàchd (pl.)   bardic compositions

barony   basic unit of local government in rural areas

bawbee   halfpenny

bere (beir)   common, four-rowed variety of barley

birthbrieve   a legal document setting out an individual's descent or status

boll   dry measure, usually of grain

bond   a legal obligation in writing to perform a service or repay money

bond of manrent   a written contract between a superior and vassal, offering protection on the one hand and loyalty on the other as if they were kin

bondager   female field worker

bonnet laird   small proprietor

bothy   rough living quarters for unmarried male farmworkers

branks   iron bridle or gag used for public punishment

burgage   form of feudal tenure in which land in a burgh is held of the king

burgh   chartered town

burgh of barony   burgh under the jurisdiction of a barony

burgh of regality   burgh under the jurisdiction of a lord of regality

burgh, royal   burgh with charter from the crown giving it the rights of a feudal superior

buss   a two- or three-masted vessel, usually of 50–100 tons (51–102 tonnes) in Shetland waters, used in the Dutch herring fishery

cáin   tribute due to a lord or king

caman   stick used in shinty

canntaiceachd   a form of pipe music, in syllables

cas chrom   a kind of spade or foot plough

ceatharnoch   kern

céli Dé   lit. 'servant of God'; monk in early medieval church

céilidh   a social gathering for singing, storytelling, or playing instruments

cess   a land tax

chamberlain   head financial officer on an estate

chanonry   canonry

clare constat, precept of   a legal document by which an heir is recognized by a superior

clavie   a torch carried around fishing boats at Hogmanay to ensure a good season

coal heuch   coal pit

commendator   holder of the 'commend' of an ecclesiastical benefice, especially a religious house

commonty   common pasture land

commonty, division of   the dividing up of a commonty into separate properties

coothy   sociable

co-parcenars   joint owners

cordiner   cordwainer

cottar   the holder of a cotland, but with fewer rights than a husbandman

croft   small piece of land, enclosed for tillage or, more often, pasture

culdee   an Anglicization of *céli Dé*

custom   payments rendered by use and wont

custumar   a collector of customs duties

decreet   the decree of a court or judge

deforcement   violent action impeding a law officer in the execution of his duty

demesne   part of a royal or lord's estate which is held directly and not let out or feued

elder   elected official of a kirk session

fank   sheepfold

farmtoun   small rural settlement

fence   to hold a court of law, forbidding its interruption

ferm(e)   latterly, the part of rent paid in kind, usually grain

feuar   holder of land by feu-ferm tenure

feu duty   annual payment by a feuar to the superior

feu-ferm(e)   system of land tenure where a fixed cash sum is paid in perpetuity as rent

655

Glossary

Fifteen Jacobite rising in 1715

fine kindred

flyting poetic mock combat

Forty-Five Jacobite rising in 1745

freeholder proprietor (latterly laird or heritor)

furth of beyond, outside

Gaidhealtachd the Gaelic-speaking area

gallowglasses lit., in Gaelic, 'foreign youths'; West Highlands mercenaries

gear moveable goods

harling rough-cast rendering

heritor landed proprietor, below the status of a lord or noble

hind a married, skilled farm worker

host knights and retainers owing feudal military service to the crown

howe a low-lying piece of ground

husbandland holding of a husbandman, originally 26 acres (10.5 hectares)

husbandman cultivator of land, more substantial than a cottar

indweller an inhabitant of a burgh without burgess rights or resident of a town which was not a burgh

infield area of farm constantly under crops

justiciar principal administrative officer of the crown, especially in judicial matters

kindly tenant one who has tenancy by virtue of long occupation or heredity rather than specific legal right

kirk session post-Reformation ecclesiastical court

labourer agricultural worker without rights in the land

laird landed proprietor, below the status of a lord or noble

machair low-lying land, usually next to the seashore

mark (merk) two-thirds of a £

manrent see bond of manrent

manse dwelling house provided for parish clergy, both pre- and post-Reformation

mormaer originally literally 'high steward'; ruler under the king of one of the great provinces north of Forth, such as Angus

Mounth the massif now known as the 'Grampians', lying east–west from Stonehaven to Ben Nevis

neighbourhood mutual obligations of members of a community

notary a person licensed to record legal transactions

Ossian, Ossianic relating to the *Poems of Ossian* (London, 1773), published by James MacPherson, and the literary controversy which followed

outfield land periodically allowed to lie fallow

oxgang a division of arable land, nominally the area a plough team could work

pendicle a small piece of land forming part of a larger farm

ploughgate a division of arable land, amounting to eight oxgangs

port, burgh town gate

portioner a small proprietor, sometimes a feuar

provost, burgh alderman or mayor

quaich a drinking cup

quitclaim the formal relinquishing of a feudal obligation

rackrenting the systematic forcing up of rents

redshanks west Highland mercenaries

regality a jurisdiction more extensive than a barony, granted by the crown to an important churchman or lay person

rental a rent roll

rentaller a tenant who held land for lifetime, recognized by inclusion in a rental

runrig division of cultivation rigs amongst tenants in a scattered pattern

sasine the act of formally taking possession of a property

Sassenach an Englishman; it can also mean an English-speaking Lowlander

scallage a farm labourer

sceatta generic term for a small coin of the pre-Viking period

schiltrom hedgehog-like formation of pikemen in battle

seanachaidh see sennachie

sennachie a professional reciter of family history and genealogy

sheriff officer appointed by the crown to be in charge of a shire or sheriffdom

solskifte a system in the Northern Isles of allocating runrig land 'by the sun', i.e. clockwise

Squadrone Volante lit. the 'Flying Squadron', a political faction led by the marquis of Tweeddale at the time of the Union of 1707

steading farm buildings

steelbow a form of customary tenure in which the tenant farmer was given equipment, stock, and seed at the entry to a lease

stent a tax

superior a proprietor who makes a grant of property to another in

	return for an annual payment	thirds	a tax, equivalent to a third of income, paid on benefices after 1562 for the benefit of the crown and reformed ministry
superiority	a fee title held of the crown by a superior		
syboes	spring onions		
Tables	the delegates of the Covenanters representing nobles, lairds, burgesses, and ministers set up in 1637; each sat at a separate table or 'board'	tocher	a bride's dowry
		vassal	in feudal law, one who holds land from a superior
		vennel	narrow alleyway
		vill	small township
tack	lease	wadset	a mortgage; a grant of land as security until repayment of a debt
tacksman	holder of a tack		
tailzie	an entail; the settlement of heritable property	wadsetter	one who holds a wadset of land as security until debt is repaid
teind	tithe		
tenant-in-chief	a vassal holding property directly from the crown		
terce, tercer	right of a woman to one-third of husband's heritable estate	wapinschawing	a muster; lit. a 'weapon showing'
teuchter	a disparaging term, usually for someone from the rural north or north-east	ward	a feudal superior's rights in property during the minority of an heir
		waulking	walking of cloth
thanage	the jurisdiction of a thane	waulking song	Gaelic song by women engaged in walking cloth
thrawn	obstinate, perverse		

Chronology

81	Invasion of Caledonia by Agricola.
83/4	Defeat of Caledonians by Agricola at Mons Graupius.
90	Abandonment of Roman positions north of Forth.
122–36	Building of Hadrian's Wall.
c.143	Building of Antonine Wall.
c.154	Abandonment of Antonine Wall.
160–2	Reoccupation of Antonine frontier.
180–5	Hadrian's Wall overrun.
c.208	Invasion of Caledonia by Septimius Severus.
211	Death of Severus. Roman withdrawal to Hadrian's Wall.
215	Fortress at Carpow abandoned.
367	Picts and Scots overrun Hadrianic frontier.
c.407	Withdrawal of Roman army from Britain.
c.500	fl. St Ninian.
563	Arrival of Columba on Iona.
597	Death of St Columba.
603	Battle of Degsastán: defeat of Aedán mac Gabráin, king of Dál Riata, by Angles, ending his dominance in the east.
634	Oswald returns to Bernicia from exile on Iona and becomes king; reintroduction of Christianity to Northumbria under Iona's auspices, and founding of Lindisfarne.
664	Synod of Whitby.
665	Death of Osuiu, king of Northumbria and overlord of Picts and Dál Riata.
685	Battle of Dunnichen Moss/Nechtansmere: defeat of Ecgfrith, king of Northumbria, by Bridei, son of Bile; Northumbrian overlordship over Picts and Dál Riata broken.
697	The 'Law of the Innocents' (*Lex Innocentium*) promulgated at synod of Birr under direction of (St) Adomnán, abbot of Iona; Adomnán completes his *Life of Columba*.
704	Death of Adomnán.
717	Nechtan, son of Derile, king of Picts, expels Iona clerics from his dominions.
732	Death of Nechtan. Ungus (Onuist), son of Uurgust (Oengus, son of Fergus), wins four-sided war over the Pictish kingship.
741	Ungus (Onuist), son of Uurgust, destroys Dál Riata.
742	Ungus (Onuist), son of Uurgust, joins attack on kingdom of Mercia in the English Midlands; shrine of St Andrew's relics established at St Andrews.
761	Death of Ungus (Onuist), son of Uurgust.
794–5	Viking raids on Western Isles.
802, 806	Attacks on Iona by Vikings.
820	Caustantín son of Fergus (Uurgust), Pictish king, dies; commemorated on the Dupplin Cross.

821	Vikings destroy Pictish dynasty founded (possibly) by Ungus (Onuist) son of Uurgust.
849	Kenneth mac Alpin (Cinaed mac Ailpín), king of Picts, establishes shrine of Columba's relics at Dunkeld.
875–8	Viking devastation of Pictish heartlands.
878	Death of Aed, son of Kenneth mac Alpin, the last to be given the title 'king of Picts' contemporaneously.
900	Death of Donald II (Domnall mac Custantín), the first king given the title 'king of Alba' contemporaneously.
903–4	Viking devastation in east midlands culminating in battle of Strathearn, the first major defeat of Vikings on the Scottish mainland.
906	Promulgation of religious and church laws at Scone by Constantine II (Caustantín mac Aeda), king of Alba and Cellach, the first bishop of Alba.
937	Constantine II allies with Norse against Athelstan, first king of England, and suffers major defeat at battle of Brunnanburh.
952	Death of Constantine II at St Andrews after nearly a decade of retirement from the kingship (he was succeeded in 943 by Malcolm I (Mael Coluim mac Domnaill) (r. 943–54)).
954–62	During reign of Illulb, son of Constantine, Edinburgh falls to the Scots.
970s	Bishop Cellach II of St Andrews, bishop of Alba, possibly went to Rome to gain papal confirmation.
1018	Battle of Carham: Malcolm II (Mael Coluim mac Cinaeda) vindicates Scottish control of the south-east. Loss of control over Moray to Findlaech, who claims kingship of Alba.
1034	Death of Malcolm II, last in the direct male line from Kenneth mac Alpin; Duncan I (Donnchad ua Maíl Choluim), son of Crínán, abbot of Dunkeld, and grandson of King Malcolm II, becomes king.
1040	Macbeth (Mac Bethad mac Findlaíg), ruler of Moray, defeats and kills Duncan I and becomes king of Alba.
1050	Macbeth makes pilgrimage to Rome.
1057	Macbeth killed by Mael Coluim mac Donnchada (see 1058) at Lumphanan; Lulach mac Gilla Comgáin becomes king.
1058	Malcolm III (Mael Coluim mac Donnchada) kills Lulach at Eassie and becomes king.
1072	King Malcolm takes (St) Margaret, sister of the exiled English heir, to the English throne as his second wife; Margaret establishes a Benedictine cell at Dunfermline.
1093	Malcolm III killed in raid on northern England; death of Margaret, and Bishop Fothad II of St Andrews.

658

1097	Donald III (Domnall Bán), Malcolm's brother, deposed by Edgar, son of Malcolm and Margaret, and blinded.
1098	Edgar recognizes king of Norway's overlordship over kingdom of Man and the Isles.
1107	Death of Edgar. Accession of Alexander I.
1124	Death of Alexander I. Accession of David I.
1128	Dunfermline priory raised to an abbey. Foundation of Holyrood abbey.
1138	Battle of the Standard near Northallerton.
1153	Death of David I. Accession of his grandson, Malcolm IV, aged 12.
1157	Border fixed on Solway-Tweed line after loss of four English northernmost counties.
1160–4	Subduing of Galloway and Argyll; death of Somerled, lord of Argyll.
1165	Death of Malcolm IV. Accession of his brother William I 'the Lion'.
1174	Treaty of Falaise.
1187	Defeat of Donald Macwilliam; beginning of subduing of Moray and Ross.
1189	Quitclaim of Canterbury, cancelling Treaty of Falaise.
1192	'Cum universi' bull of Pope Celestine III for Scottish church.
1214	Death of William I. Accession of Alexander II.
1221	Marriage of Alexander II and Joan, sister of Henry III of England.
1230–1	Dominican (Black) and Franciscan (Grey) friars established.
1237	Treaty of York; final settlement of Border line.
1249	Death of Alexander on expedition to Western Isles. Accession of Alexander III, aged 7.
1249–58	Minority of Alexander III.
1251	Canonization of St Margaret (d. 1093). Marriage of Alexander III and Margaret, daughter of Henry III of England.
1263	Expedition of Haakon IV Haakonsson of Norway to Western Isles; battle of Largs (Oct.); death of Haakon (Dec.).
1266	Treaty of Perth between Alexander III and Magnus, king of Norway.
1286	Death of Alexander III. Accession of his granddaughter, Margaret, the 'Maid of Norway'.
1290	Death of Margaret, 'Maid of Norway'. Treaty of Birgham between community of realm of Scotland and Edward I of England.
1291–2	'Great Cause': Edward I adjudicates on Scottish succession.
1292	John Balliol, king of Scots.
1294	War between Edward I and Philippe IV, king of France.
1295	Treaty between John Balliol and Philippe IV: the 'Auld Alliance'.
1296	War between John Balliol and Edward I. Berwick sacked. John defeated and deposed.
1296–1305	First phase of the Wars of Independence.
1297	Risings in north-east and south-west. Battle of Stirling Bridge.
1298	William Wallace appointed guardian. Battle of Falkirk.

1303	Edward I's fourth invasion of Scotland.
1304	Submission of many Scots leaders. Siege of Stirling castle.
1305	Capture, trial, and execution of Wallace.
1306	Killing of Comyn by Robert Bruce. Bruce crowned Robert I. Beginning of second phase of the Wars of Independence.
1314	Battle of Bannockburn.
1315–18	Campaign in Ireland by Edward Bruce.
1318	Capture of Berwick by Scots.
1320	Declaration of Arbroath.
1324	Treaty of Corbeil with France.
1326	Cambuskenneth Parliament.
1328	Treaty of Edinburgh.
1329	Death of Robert I; accession of infant David II.
1332	Coronation of David II.
1333	English siege of Berwick.
1334	David II seeks refuge in France.
1341	Return of David II.
1346	Battle of Neville's Cross; capture of David II,
1346–57	English captivity of David II.
1349	Outbreak of plague.
1357	Treaty of Berwick; ransom and return of David II.
1361–2	Second outbreak of plague.
1371	Death of David II; accession of Robert Stewart as Robert II.
1375	John Barbour's *The Brus*.
1378–1417	Great schism in papacy.
1379	Third outbreak of plague.
c.1385	John of Fordun's *Chronicle*.
1390	Death of Robert II; accession of Robert III.
1406	Prince James captured by English; death of Robert III; accession of James I.
1406–24	English captivity of James I; Albany governor.
1411	Battle of Harlaw.
1412	Foundation of St Andrews University.
1420	Death of Albany; succeeded as governor by son Murdoch.
c.1420	Andrew Wyntoun's *Chronicle*.
1424	Marriage of James I to Joan Beaufort. His ransom and return.
1425	Arrest and execution of Murdoch and others.
1426	Treaty with Denmark.
1429	Rebellion and imprisonment of Alexander, lord of the Isles.
1437	Murder of James I; accession of infant James II.
1437–49	Minority of James II.
c.1445	Walter Bower's *Scotichronicon*.
1449	Marriage of James II to Marie de Gueldres.
1451	Foundation of Glasgow University.
1452	Killing of earl of Douglas by James.
1460	James II killed in siege of Roxburgh; accession of infant James III.
1460–9	Minority of James III.
1468	Marriage of James III and Margaret of Denmark.
1469	Annexation of Orkney and Shetland.
1472	Archbishopric of St Andrews created.
1482	Failure of coup against James III.

Chronology

1487	Papal indult of Innocent VIII.
1488	Death of James III at Sauchieburn; accession of James IV.
1493	Annexation of lordship of the Isles.
1495	Foundation of University of Aberdeen.
1502	'Treaty of Perpetual Peace' between England and Scotland.
1502	Marriage of James IV and Margaret Tudor.
1507	Foundation of first Scottish printing press.
1513	Death of James IV at battle of Flodden; accession of James V.
1513–28	Minority of James V.
1517	Treaty of Rouen with France.
1521	John Mair's *History of Greater Britain.*
1525	First Act of Parliament against heretical literature.
1528	Escape of young James V from Douglases and end of minority.
1532	Establishment of College of Justice.
1535	Further act against heretical literature.
1536–7	Visit of James V to France; marriage to Madeleine, daughter of François I (Jan.); her death (July).
1538	Marriage of James V to Mary of Guise.
1542	Battle of Solway Moss. Death of James V. Accession of infant Mary, Queen of Scots.
1542–61	Minority of Mary.
1543–54	Regency of James Hamilton, earl of Arran, (from 1549) duke of Châtelherault.
1543	Arran's 'godly fit'. Treaty of Greenwich with England (July); revoked (Dec.).
1544–50	'Rough Wooing'.
1546	Burning of George Wishart. Murder of Cardinal Beaton. Seizure of St Andrews castle.
1547	Fall of St Andrews castle. Battle of Pinkie.
1548	Treaty of Haddington with France.
1549	First reforming council of church.
1552	Second reforming council; Archbishop Hamilton's *Catechism.*
1554	Mary of Guise replaces Châtelherault as regent.
1555–6	Visit of John Knox to Scotland.
1557	First Bond of the Lords of the Congregation.
1558	Marriage of Mary to Dauphin François (April). Death of Mary Tudor and accession of Elizabeth I (Nov.).
1559	Last reforming council of church (March). Return of Knox; religious riot in Perth (May). Suspension of Mary of Guise as regent by Congregation (Oct.).
1560	Treaty of Berwick between England and Congregation (Feb.). English siege of Leith (March). Death of Mary of Guise (June). Treaty of Edinburgh between France and England (July). 'Reformation' Parliament (Aug.). Death of Mary's husband, François II (Dec.). *First Book of Discipline* (Dec.).
1561	Return of Mary to Scotland.
1562	Expedition against earl of Huntly.
1565	Chaseabout raid.
1566	Murder of David Rizzio (Mar.). Birth of Prince James (June); his baptism at Stirling (Dec.).

1567	Murder of Darnley (Feb.). Marriage of Mary and Bothwell (May); their defeat at Carberry (June). Mary imprisoned and deposed; James VI crowned (July).
1568	Escape of Mary from Lochleven; defeat at Langside; flight into England.
1568–73	Civil war between queen's men and king's men.
1570	Assassination of Regent Moray.
1572	Death of Knox; Morton becomes regent.
1574	Return of Andrew Melville from Geneva.
1578	*Second Book of Discipline.*
1579	Arrival from France of Esmé Stuart.
1582	Ruthven raid. Publication of George Buchanan's *History.*
1582–3	Foundation of Edinburgh University.
1584	'Black Acts' Parliament.
1585	Outbreak of plague.
1586	League with England.
1589–90	Marriage of James VI to Anne of Denmark.
1591	North Berwick witch trial.
1592	'Golden Acts' Parliament.
1593	Foundation of Marischal College, Aberdeen.
1594	Baptism of Prince Henry at Stirling castle.
1596	Riot in Edinburgh.
1600	Appointment of three 'parliamentary bishops'.
1603	Death of Elizabeth I; accession of James VI as king of England and Ireland.
1606	Andrew Melville imprisoned in Tower of London; later exiled.
1609	Statutes of Iona.
1610	Bishops fully restored.
1617	Visit of James VI & I to Scotland. Five Articles of Perth.
1625	Death of James. Accession of Charles I. Act of Revocation.
1633	Visit of Charles I to Scotland.
1634–5	Trial of Balmerino.
1637	Introduction of new Prayer Book. Riot in St Giles'.
1638	National Covenant (Feb.). Glasgow Assembly (Nov.).
1639	First Bishops' War.
1640	Second Bishops' War.
1641	Second visit of Charles I to Scotland; new constitution accepted.
1642	English Civil War; Scots army sent to Ulster.
1643	Solemn League and Covenant.
1643–4	Westminster Assembly.
1644	Covenanting army enters English Civil War; battle of Marston Moor.
1644–5	Montrose campaigns.
1645	Last serious outbreak of plague.
1646	Surrender of Charles I to Covenanters.
1647	The Engagement.
1648	Defeat of Engagers at Preston. Whiggamore raid.
1649	Execution of Charles I. Act of Classes.
1650–1	Charles II in Scotland.
1650	Covenanters defeated at Dunbar by Cromwell.
1651	Charles II crowned at Scone. Covenanters

defeated at Worcester. Scotland incorporated into English Commonwealth.

1653–4	Glencairn rising in Highlands.
1658	Death of Cromwell.
1660	Restoration of Charles II.
1660–2	Restoration settlement.
1661	Act Rescissory.
1662	Re-establishment of episcopacy.
1666	Pentland rising.
1669	First indulgence.
1672	Second indulgence. Founding of Court of Justiciary.
1679	Murder of Archbishop Sharp; battle of Bothwell Brig.
1679–82	James, duke of York, in Edinburgh.
1682	Founding of Advocates' Library.
1684–8	The 'Killing Times'.
1685	Death of Charles II. Accession of James VII & II.
1688	'Glorious' Revolution in England. Flight of James.
1689–90	Revolution settlement in Scotland.
1689	Claim of Right. Crown offered to William and Mary. Dundee rising; battle of Killiecrankie.
1690	Establishment of Presbyterianism.
1692	Massacre of Glencoe.
1695	Founding of Bank of Scotland. Establishment of Company of Scotland.
1696–1700	Famine years.
1696	Education Act.
1698	Darien expedition.
1702	Accession of Anne.
1702–13	War of the Spanish Succession.
1703	Act anent Peace and War.
1704	Act of Security.
1704–5	Worcester affair.
1705	Alien Act.
1707	Act of Union.
1712	Reintroduction of patronage in church. Act of Toleration.
1714	Accession of George I.
1715	Major Jacobite rising; battle of Sheriffmuir.
1719	Jacobite invasion of Kintail.
1725	Shawfield riots.
1727	Accession of George II. Establishment of Board of Trustees. Founding of Royal Bank of Scotland.
1728	Establishment of Edinburgh Medical School.
1733	Original Secession.
1736	Porteous riots.
1742	Cambuslang revival.
1745–6	Last Jacobite rising.
1746	Defeat of Jacobites at Culloden.
1747	Abolition of heritable jurisdictions. Split of Associate Synods into Burghers and Anti-Burghers.
1755	Dr Alexander Webster's Census.
1756–63	Seven Years War.
1759	Founding of Carron Ironworks near Falkirk.
1760	Accession of George III.
1761	Establishment of Relief Church.
1766–7	James Craig wins competition for design of

	Edinburgh's New Town; building work begun.
1769	James Watt patents improved steam engine.
1772	Failure of Ayr Bank.
1776–83	War of American Independence.
1776	Publication of Adam Smith's *The Wealth of Nations*.
1784	William Pitt prime minister after a general election masterminded by Henry Dundas (later Viscount Melville).
1785	Establishment of New Lanark cotton mills.
1789	Outbreak of French Revolution.
1791	Dundas appointed Home Secretary. Meeting of 'Friends of the People' in Edinburgh. Forth-Clyde Canal opened.
1793–1802	War with France.
1793	Trial of Thomas Muir.
1796	Death of Robert Burns.
1797	United Scotsmen founded. Widespread rioting against Militia Act.
1799	Completion of (*First*) *Statistical Account of Scotland* (OSA) by Sir John Sinclair.
1799–1800	Combination Acts.
1802	*Edinburgh Review* published. Peace of Amiens.
1803–15	Renewed war with France.
1804	Return of Pitt to office; Melville appointed First Lord of Admiralty.
1805	Impeachment and resignation of Melville.
1807–21	Sutherland Clearances.
1812	Weavers' strike in Glasgow and west of Scotland.
1813	Tron riot in Edinburgh.
1813	Kildonan clearance.
1814	Publication of Sir Walter Scott's *Waverley*.
1817	Establishment of *Scotsman*.
1820	'Radical War'. Accession of George IV.
1822	George IV's state visit to Edinburgh.
1824	Repeal of Combination Acts.
1828	Invention of 'hot blast' smelting process by James Beaumont Neilson.
1829	Catholic Emancipation.
1830	Accession of William IV.
1832	Passing of Reform Act (Scotland). Cholera epidemic. Death of Sir Walter Scott.
1833	Passing of Burgh Reform Acts.
1834	Veto Act.
1836	Cotton spinners' strike. Failure of Highland potato crop.
1837–9	Outbreaks of typhus and typhoid.
1837	Accession of Queen Victoria.
1838	Cotton spinners' trial.
1842	Typhoid and typhus outbreaks. Chadwick's *Report on the Sanitary Condition of the Labouring Population of Great Britain*. Royal Commission on Coal Mines. Opening of Edinburgh–Glasgow railway line.
1843	The Disruption. Formation of the Free Church of Scotland.
1844	Royal Commission on Poor Law (Scotland).
1845	Poor Law (Scotland) Amendment Act; Completion of New (*Second*) *Statistical Account of Scotland* (NSA).
1845–50	Railway 'mania'.

Chronology

1846	Potato famine in Highlands. Repeal of Corn Laws.
1847	Formation of United Presbyterian Church by merger of Burgher, Anti-Burgher, and Relief churches.
1848	Last Chartist demonstrations.
1852	Founding of Highland Emigration Society.
1853	Founding of NAVSR.
1854–6	Crimean War.
1858	Universities (Scotland) Act.
1859	Loch Katrine made water reservoir for Glasgow. Opening of National Gallery of Scotland.
1859–69	Building of Wallace Monument at Abbey Craig, near Stirling.
1860	Coal Mines Regulation Act. First Open Championship, at Prestwick.
1861–4	American Civil War.
1862	General Police and Improvement (Scotland) Act.
1865	*Report on the Sanitary Condition of Edinburgh.*
1866	Glasgow Improvement Act.
1867	Founding of Queen's Park FC.
1868	Reform Act (Scotland).
1872	Education (Scotland) Act.
1873	Establishment of SFA and SRU. Founding of Glasgow Rangers FC.
1873–83	Moody and Sankey revivalist campaigns.
1878	Restoration of Roman Catholic hierarchy. Collapse of City of Glasgow Bank.
1879	Gladstone's Midlothian campaign. Collapse of Tay Bridge.
1881	Foundation of University College, Dundee.
1882	Opening of Scottish National Portrait Gallery.
1882	Crofters' War.
1883	Napier Commission on the Highlands. Founding of Highland Land League. Establishment of chair of Celtic at Edinburgh University.
1884	Reform Act.
1885	Re-establishment of office of Scottish Secretary.
1886	Founding of SHRA.
1887	Scottish Office established in Whitehall.
1888	Founding of Scottish Labour Party. Founding of Glasgow Celtic FC.
1888–99	Founding of eighteen clan societies.
1889	Local Government (Scotland) Act. West Highland Railway opened.
1890	Completion of Forth Rail Bridge.
1891	Founding of Highland Association.
1892	First National Mod, Oban. Split of Free Presbyterians from Free Church.
1893	Founding of ILP.
1894	Establishment of Scottish Grand Committee.
1896	Opening of Glasgow Underground.
1897	Founding of STUC.
1899–1902	Boer War.
1900	Merger of Free Church and United Presbyterian Church in United Free Church.
1901	Death of Victoria. Accession of Edward VII. Second Glasgow International Exhibition.

	Establishment of chair of Scottish history at Edinburgh University.
1906	Founding of Labour Party.
1910	Death of Edward VII. Accession of George V.
1911	Third Glasgow International Exhibition.
1912	Establishment of Royal Commission on Scottish Housing. Founding of Board of Agriculture. Merger of Scottish Liberal Unionists and Conservatives as Scottish Unionist Party.
1914–18	First World War.
1915	Unrest on 'Red Clydeside'. Glasgow rent strike.
1917	Report of Royal Commission on Housing.
1918	Education (Scotland) Act.
1919	Demonstration in George Square, Glasgow.
1920	Labour makes gains on Glasgow Corporation.
1922	First broadcast of British Broadcasting Corporation, from Glasgow.
1924	Wheatley Housing Act.
1924–7	Building of Scottish National War Memorial within Edinburgh castle.
1925	Founding of NLS.
1926	General Strike. Scottish Secretary made Secretary of State.
1928	Reorganization of Scottish Office; abolition of Boards. Founding of National Party of Scotland.
1929	Merger of Church of Scotland and United Free Church.
1930	Establishment of Scottish National Development Council.
1931	Founding of National Trust for Scotland.
1933	Labour gain control of Glasgow Corporation.
1934	Founding of SNP. Special Areas Act.
1936	Establishment of Scottish Economic Committee. Opening of St Andrew's House in Edinburgh. Founding of Saltire Society.
1937	Opening of Hillington industrial estate.
1938	Empire Exhibition, Glasgow.
1939	Scottish Office transferred to Edinburgh.
1939–45	Second World War.
1941	Tom Johnston Secretary of State. Establishment of Council of State. Clydebank Blitz.
1942	Formation of Council of Industry. Forming of Scottish Convention by John MacCormick.
1943	Establishment of North of Scotland Hydro-Electric Board.
1947	First Edinburgh International Festival.
1949	Scottish Covenant campaign.
1950	Removal of Stone of Scone from Westminster abbey.
1953	Report of Royal Commission on Scottish Affairs. Accession of Queen Elizabeth II.
1954	Report of Balfour Commission on Scottish Affairs.
1955	Beginning of broadcasting by Scottish Television.
1961	Toothill Report on Scottish economy. Government support for establishment of steel strip mill and motor industry.

1962	Establishment of Scottish Development Department.	1979	Inconclusive referendum on devolution. General election brings Conservative victory. Margaret Thatcher prime minister. Decline of support for SNP. Establishment of Campaign for a Scottish Assembly
1963	Buchanan Report.		
1965	Establishment of Highlands and Islands Development Board.		
1967	SNP win Hamilton by-election. North Sea oil exploration begins.	1983	Conservative victory in general election but reduced to 21 seats in Scotland.
1968	Establishment of Kilbrandon Commission on constitution. Wheatley Report on local government. Declaration of Perth by Conservative leader, Edward Heath.	1987	Conservative victory in general election but reduced to 10 seats in Scotland.
		1988	*A Claim of Right for Scotland*. Founding of Scottish Constitutional Convention.
1971	Upper Clyde Shipbuilders' crisis.	1988–92	Poll tax controversy.
1972	Establishment of Scottish Economic Planning Department. Local Government Act (Scotland) establishes regions and districts.	1992	Conservative victory at general election; 12 seats in Scotland despite predictions of a 'Tory free zone'.
		1992–7	Vigil outside Royal High School, Edinburgh, of pro-devolution supporters.
1973	Kilbrandon Report. SNP victory at Govan by-election.	1993	White Paper, *A Partnership for Good*.
1974	Labour wins two general elections narrowly. SNP gains 11 seats.	1996	Return of Stone of Scone from Westminster abbey to Scotland. Further reorganization of local government.
1975	Establishment of Scottish Development Agency. Foundation of Convention of Scottish Local Authorities. Reorganization of local government boundaries.	1997	Labour victory in general election, Collapse of Conservative vote, with no MPs in Scotland. Referendum on devolution brings large 'yes' vote.
1976	First Devolution Bill.		
1976	Founding of breakaway Scottish Labour Party.	1998	Opening of Royal Museum of Scotland.
		1999	Opening of Scottish parliament. Labour largest party but without an overall majority. Donald Dewar appointed First Minister.
1977	Devolution bill fails.		
1978	Scotland and Wales Act, subject to a referendum.	2000	Death of Donald Dewar (Oct.).

Maps

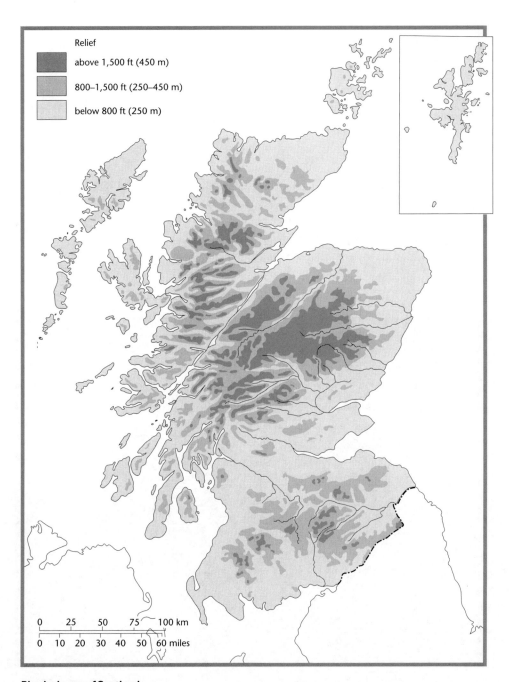

Relief

above 1,500 ft (450 m)

800–1,500 ft (250–450 m)

below 800 ft (250 m)

0   25   50   75   100 km

0   10   20   30   40   50   60 miles

Physical map of Scotland

The administrative boundaries represented reflect the counties as they stood after 1890 until 1975. Although in some cases there was a change of name after 1890, the boundaries generally remained the same.

ORKNEY

SHETLAND

CAITHNESS

SUTHERLAND

ROSS AND CROMARTY

NAIRN   MORAY   BANFF

ABERDEEN

INVERNESS

KINCARDINE

ANGUS

PERTH

ARGYLL

KINROSS
CLACKMANNAN   FIFE

W. DUNBARTON   STIRLING

W. LOTHIAN   E. LOTHIAN
EAST DUNBARTON   MIDLOTHIAN
RENFREW

BERWICK

BUTE

LANARK   PEEBLES

ROXBURGH

AYR   SELKIRK

DUMFRIES

KIRCUDBRIGHT

WIGTOWN

| 0 | 25 | 50 | 75 | 100 km |

| 0 | 10 | 20 | 30 | 40 | 50 | 60 miles |

The administrative regions of Scotland

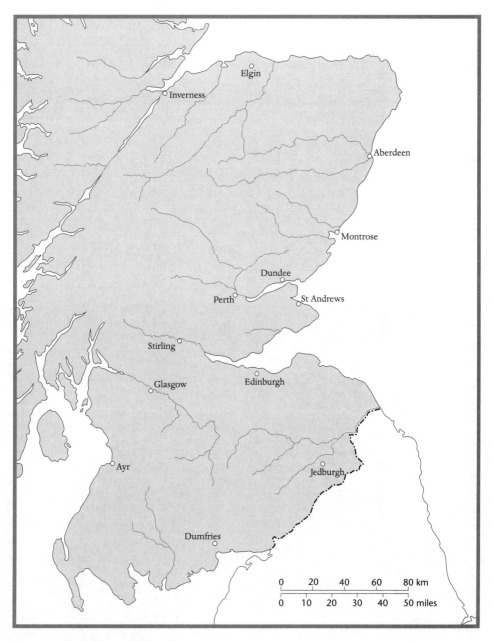

The main towns of Scotland

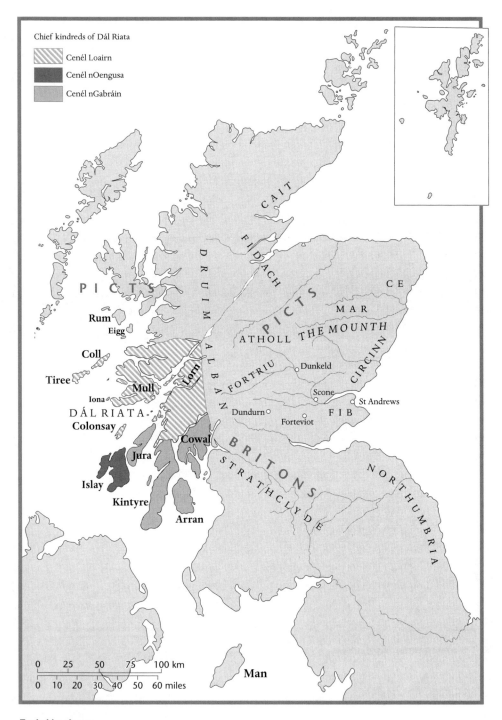

Early kingdoms

Ecclesiastical organization of Scotland

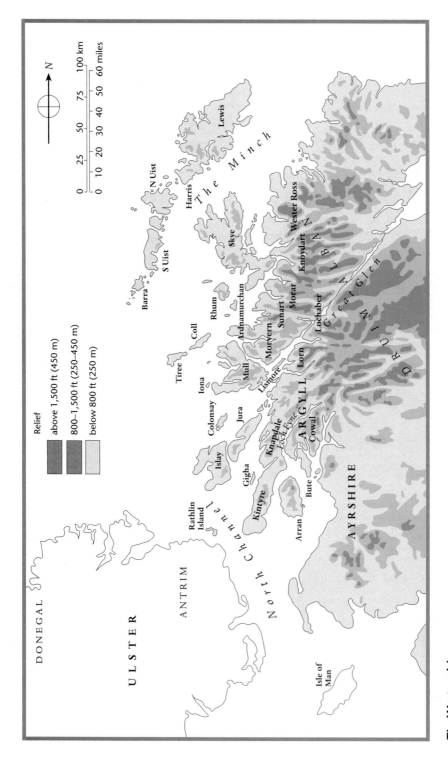

The Western Isles

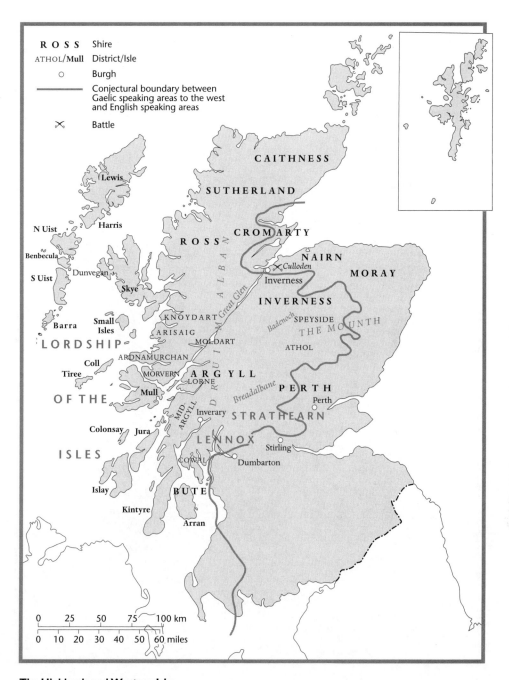

CAITHNESS

SUTHERLAND

Lewis

N Uist

Harris

CROMARTY

Benbecula

ROSS

NAIRN

Dunvegan

×Culloden

Inverness

MORAY

S Uist

Skye

INVERNESS

Badenoch SPEYSIDE
THE MOUNTH

Barra

Small
Isles

KNOYDART

ARISAIG

ARDNAMURCHAN

MORDART

ATHOL

LORDSHIP

Coll

Tiree

MORVERN

ARGYLL

LORNE

PERTH

Mull

Perth

OF THE

Colonsay Jura

Inverary

STRATHEARN

LENNOX

ISLES

Stirling

COWAL

Dumbarton

Islay

BUTE

Kintyre

Arran

ALBAN

Great Glen

DRUIM

MID.
ARGYLL

Breadalbane

| 0 | 25 | 50 | 75 | 100 km |

| 0 | 10 | 20 | 30 | 40 | 50 | 60 miles |

The Highlands and Western Isles

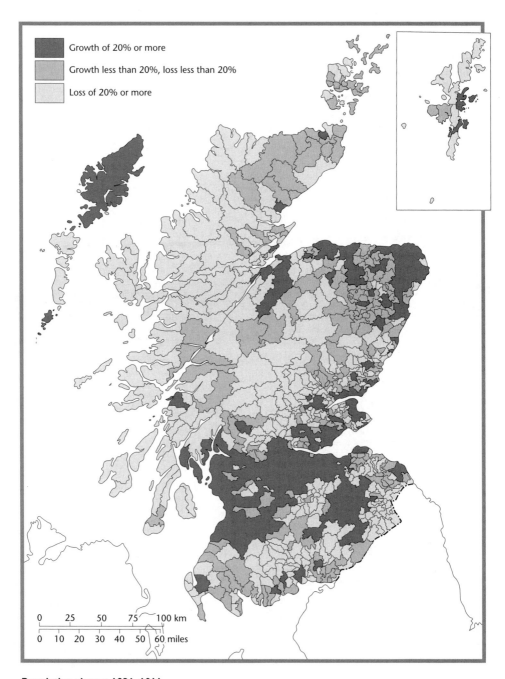

Population change 1831–1911

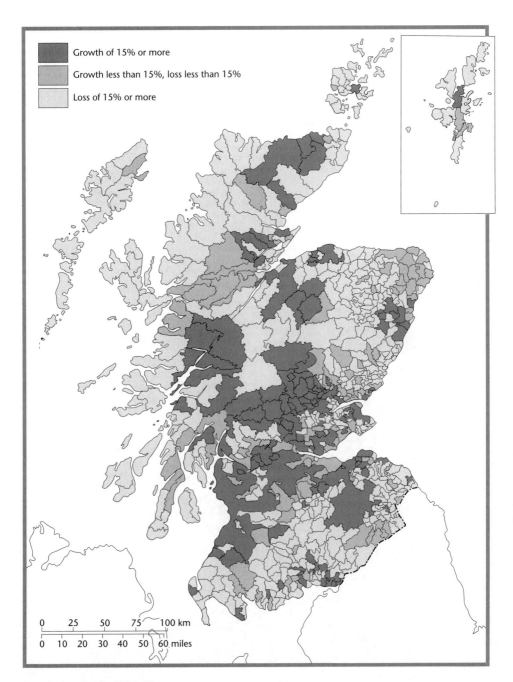

0   25   50   75   100 km

0 10 20 30 40 50 60 miles

Population change 1911–81

Genealogies

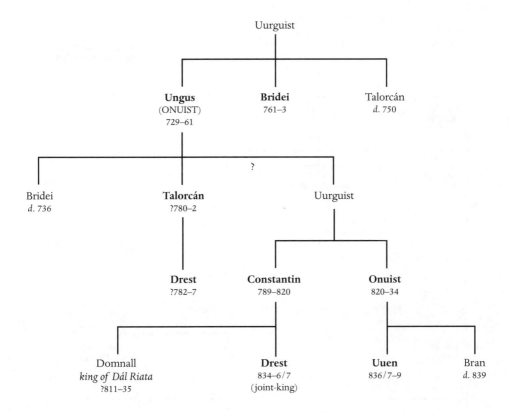

The dynasty of Ungus (Onuist) son of Uurguist (Fergus), king of Fortriu 726–61

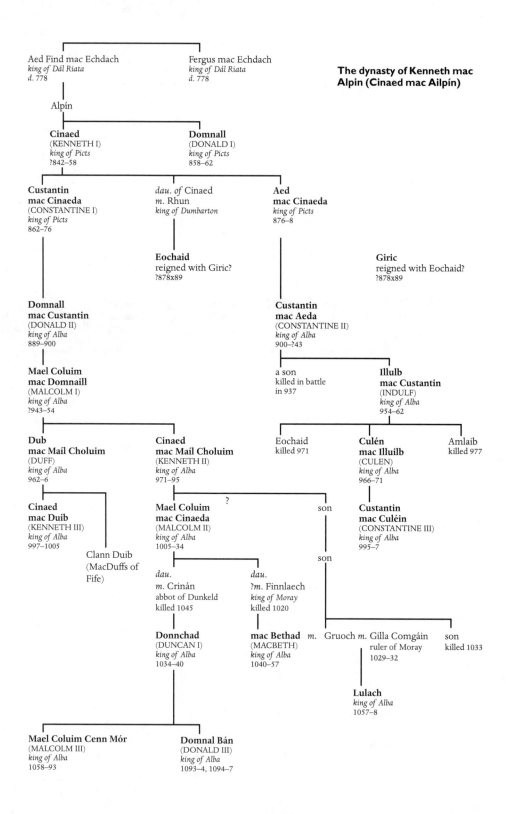

The dynasty of Kenneth mac Alpin (Cinaed mac Ailpín)

Aed Find mac Echdach
king of Dál Riata
d. 778

Fergus mac Echdach
king of Dál Riata
d. 778

Alpín

Cinaed
(KENNETH I)
king of Picts
?842–58

Domnall
(DONALD I)
king of Picts
858–62

**Custantin
mac Cinaeda**
(CONSTANTINE I)
king of Picts
862–76

dau. of Cinaed
m. Rhun
king of Dumbarton

**Aed
mac Cinaeda**
king of Picts
876–8

Eochaid
reigned with Giric?
?878x89

Giric
reigned with Eochaid?
?878x89

**Domnall
mac Custantin**
(DONALD II)
king of Alba
889–900

**Custantin
mac Aeda**
(CONSTANTINE II)
king of Alba
900–?43

**Mael Coluim
mac Domnaill**
(MALCOLM I)
king of Alba
?943–54

a son
killed in battle
in 937

**Illulb
mac Custantin**
(INDULF)
king of Alba
954–62

**Dub
mac Maíl Choluim**
(DUFF)
king of Alba
962–6

**Cinaed
mac Maíl Choluim**
(KENNETH II)
king of Alba
971–95

Eochaid
killed 971

**Culén
mac Illuilb**
(CULEN)
king of Alba
966–71

Amlaib
killed 977

**Cinaed
mac Duib**
(KENNETH III)
king of Alba
997–1005

Clann Duib
(MacDuffs of
Fife)

?

**Mael Coluim
mac Cinaeda**
(MALCOLM II)
king of Alba
1005–34

son

**Custantin
mac Culéin**
(CONSTANTINE III)
king of Alba
995–7

son

dau.
m. Crinán
abbot of Dunkeld
killed 1045

dau.
?*m.* Finnlaech
king of Moray
killed 1020

Donnchad
(DUNCAN I)
king of Alba
1034–40

mac Bethad *m.* Gruoch *m.* Gilla Comgáin
(MACBETH)   ruler of Moray
king of Alba   *1029–32*
1040–57

son
killed 1033

Lulach
king of Alba
1057–8

Mael Coluim Cenn Mór
(MALCOLM III)
king of Alba
1058–93

Domnal Bán
(DONALD III)
king of Alba
1093–4, 1094–7

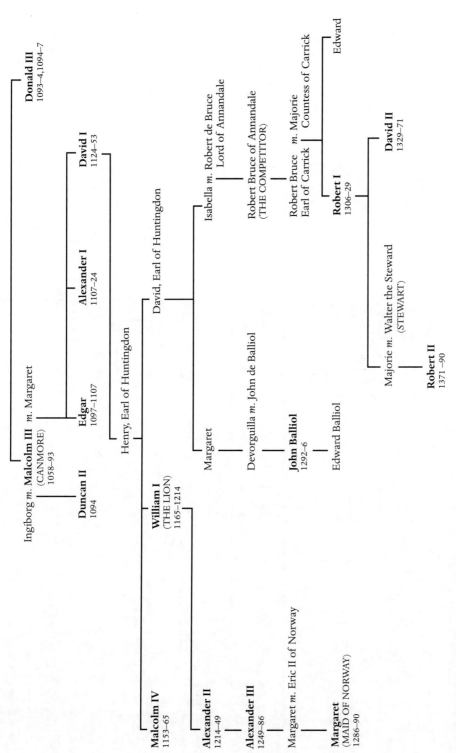

The house of Canmore to the house of Stewart

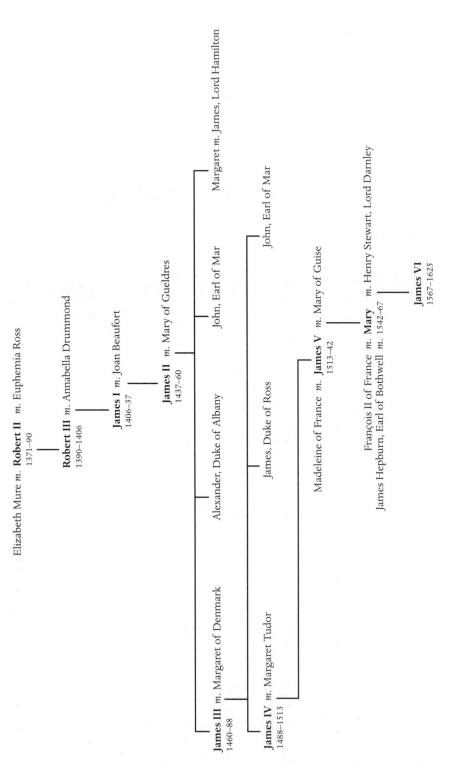

The house of Stewart

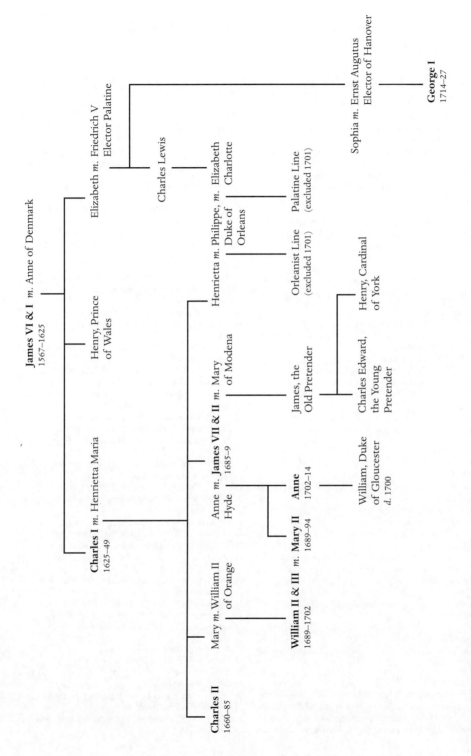

The house of Stewart and the Hanoverian succession

Guide to Further Reading

What follows is intended as a guide to further reading about the institutions, movements, personages, themes, and topics covered in this volume. The Guide is organized on the same basis as the planning for the *Companion*: in seventeen different sections, with subsections. Some works will be found in more than one section, and an attempt has also been made to cross-refer one related subsection to another, such as Urban Society and Urban Settlement. In some areas, where the literature is probably less familiar, such as parts of Section 14, the coverage is fuller than elsewhere. Generally, the underlying principle has been to choose the accessible work rather than the inaccessible and to favour books rather than journal articles, except where it is difficult to suggest a good alternative to the article. In some areas, however, only the out-of-print book or relatively obscure source provides adequate coverage. Some care has been taken to include the most recently published material. Place of publication is given, unless it was Edinburgh.

Abbreviations

EHR	*English Historical Review*
PSAS	*Proceedings of the Society of Antiquaries of Scotland*
RCAHMS	Royal Commission on the Ancient and Historical Monuments of Scotland
ROSC	*Review of Scottish Culture*
SESH	*Scottish Economic and Social History*
SHR	*Scottish Historical Review*
SHS	Scottish History Society
SRS	Scottish Record Society

1. Reference Works

Scotland is well served in certain categories of reference works.

N. M. de S. Cameron, *Dictionary of Scottish Church History and Theology* (1993).

D. Daiches (ed.), *The New Companion to Scottish Culture* (2nd edn., London, 1993).

G. Donaldson and R. S. Morpeth, *A Dictionary of Scottish History* (1977).

—— —— *Who's Who in Scottish History* (Oxford, 1973).

I. Donnachie and G. Hewitt (eds.), *A Companion to Scottish History: From the Reformation to the Present* (London, 1989).

J. and J. Keay (eds.), *Collins Encyclopaedia of Scotland* (London, 1994).

T. Royle (ed.), *The Macmillan Companion to Scottish Literature* (London, 1984).

D. S. Thomson (ed.), *The Companion to Gaelic Scotland* (Oxford, 1983).

2. General Works and Works on Particular Periods

A significant number of general works and textbooks, on all periods of Scottish history, have appeared since publication of the pioneering, four-volume Edinburgh History of Scotland between 1965 and 1974. The assumed periods are the same as in most of the chain entries, such as national identity or rural society, in the *Companion*.

One-Volume Histories

A. Grant and K. J. Stringer (eds.), *Uniting the Kingdom? The Making of British History* (London, 1995).

J. Halliday, *Scotland: a Concise History, BC to 1990* (1990).

H. Kearney, *The British Isles: A History of Four Nations* (Cambridge, 1989).

M. Lynch, *Scotland: A New History* (2nd edn., London, 1992).

S. G. E. Lythe and J. Butt, *An Economic History of Scotland, 1100–1939* (Glasgow, 1975).

R. Mitchison, *A History of Scotland* (London, 1982).

—— (ed.), *Why Scottish History Matters* (2nd edn., 1997).

Medieval (to 1500)

J. Bannerman, *Studies in the History of Dalriada* (1974).

G. W. S. Barrow, *Kingship and Unity: Scotland, 1000–1306* (London, 1981).

—— *The Kingdom of the Scots* (London, 1973).

—— *The Anglo-Norman Era in Scottish History* (Oxford, 1980).

J. M. Brown (ed.), *Scottish Society in the Fifteenth Century* (London, 1977).

B. E. Crawford, *Scandinavian Scotland* (Leicester, 1987).

R. R. Davies, *Domination and Conquest: The Experience of Ireland, Scotland and Wales, 1100–1300* (Cambridge, 1990).

W. C. Dickinson and A. A. M. Duncan, *Scotland from the Earliest Times to 1603* (3rd edn., Oxford, 1977).

A. A. M. Duncan, *Scotland: The Making of the Kingdom* (1975).

R. Frame, *The Political Development of the British Isles, 1100–1400* (Oxford, 1994).

J. Graham-Campbell, *Vikings in Scotland* (1998).

A. Grant, *Independence and Nationhood: Scotland, 1306–1469* (London, 1984).

I. Henderson, *The Picts* (London, 1967).

G. Menzies (ed.), *Who are the Scots?* (London, 1971).

R. Nicholson, *Scotland: the Later Middle Ages* (1974).

G. and A. Ritchie, *Scotland: Archaeology and Early History* (1991).

A. P. Smyth, *Warlords and Holy Men: Scotland, AD 80–1000* (London, 1984).

F. T. Wainwright (ed.), *The Problem of the Picts* (1955).

I. D. Whyte, *Scotland before the Industrial Revolution: An Economic and Social History c.1050–c.1750* (1995).

Early Modern (1500–1770s)

G. Donaldson, *Scotland: James V–James VII* (1965).

W. Ferguson, *Scotland's Relations with England: A Survey to 1707* (1977; repr. 1994).

R. A. Houston and I. D. Whyte (eds.), *Scottish Society, 1500–1800* (Cambridge, 1989).

R. Mitchison, *Lordship to Patronage: Scotland, 1603–1745* (London, 1983).

N. T. Phillipson and R. Mitchison (eds.), *Scotland in the Age of Improvement: Essays in Scottish History in the 18th Century* (2nd edn., 1996).

T. C. Smout, *A History of the Scottish People, 1560–1830* (London, 1969).

I. D. Whyte, *Scotland's Society and Economy in Transition, c.1500–c.1760* (1997).

J. Wormald, *Court, Kirk and Community: Scotland, 1470–1625* (London, 1981).

—— (ed.), *Scotland Revisited* (London, 1991).

Modern Period (1770s–present)

R. H. Campbell, *Scotland since 1707: The Rise of an Industrial Society* (2nd edn., 1985).

O. and S. Checkland, *Industry and Ethos: Scotland, 1832–1914* (2nd edn., London, 1989).

A. Cooke et al. (eds.), *Modern Scottish History, 1707 to the Present*, 5 vols. (East Linton, 1998).

T. M. Devine, *The Scottish Nation 1700–2000* (London, 1999).

—— and R. J. Finlay (eds.), *Scotland in the Twentieth Century* (1996).

—— and R. Mitchison (eds.) *People and Society in Scotland*, i. *1760–1830* (1988).

A. Dickson and J. H. Treble (eds.), *People and Society in Scotland*, iii. *1914–1990* (1992).

W. Ferguson, *Scotland: 1689 to the Present* (2nd edn., 1975).

W. H. Fraser and R. J. Morris (eds.), *People and Society in Scotland*, ii. *1830–1914* (1990).

C. Harvie, *No Gods and Precious Few Heroes: Scotland, 1914–1980* (3rd edn., 1999).

W. W. Knox, *Industrial Nation: Work, Culture and Society in Scotland, 1800–Present* (1999).

B. Lenman, *An Economic History of Modern Scotland* (London, 1977).

—— *Integration, Enlightenment and Industrialization: Scotland, 1746–1832* (London, 1981).

J. McCaffrey, *Scotland in the Nineteenth Century* (London, 1998).

T. C. Smout, *A Century of the Scottish People, 1830–1950* (London, 1986).

Historical Atlases

P. G. B. McNeill and R. Nicholson (eds.), *An Historical Atlas of Scotland c.400 to c.1600* (St Andrews, 1975).

—— and H. L. MacQueen (eds.), *Atlas of Scottish History to 1707* (1996).

Journals and Periodicals

The main journals for the areas covered by the *Companion* are listed below. The *Scottish Historical Review* publishes an annual list of articles and essays on Scottish history and culture; volume 77 (1988) included a comprehensive index of articles and reviews in the journal. Volume 40 (1989) of the *Innes Review* published a similar index, which was updated in volume 50 (1999).

Chapman; Edinburgh Review; Innes Review; Northern Scotland; Records of Scottish Church History Society; Review of Scottish Culture; Scotlands; Scottish Affairs; Scottish Economic and Social History; Scottish Historical Review; Scottish Labour History Journal; Scottish Literary Journal; Scottish Studies; Scottish Tradition; Transactions of the Gaelic Society of Inverness.

3. Power, Politics, Political Movements

This is a large subject and the reading suggested is necessarily designed as introductory.

Medieval

The focus of much recent writing on the medieval period has either been on kingship (covered in Section 4) or the nobility.

G. W. S. Barrow, *The Kingdom of the Scots* (London, 1973).

J. M. Brown (ed.), *Scottish Society in the Fifteenth Century* (London, 1977).

M. Brown, *The Black Douglases: War and Lordship in Late Medieval Scotland, 1300–1455* (East Linton, 1999).

R. Frame, *The Political Development of the British Isles, 1100–1400* (Oxford, 1994).

W. E. Kapelle, *The Norman Conquest of the North, 1000–1135* (London, 1979).

L. J. Macfarlane, *William Elphinstone and the Kingdom of Scotland, 1431–1514* (Aberdeen, 1985).

C. McNamee, *The Wars of the Bruces: Scotland, England and Ireland, 1306–1328* (East Linton, 1997).

N. Reid (ed.), *Scotland in the Reign of Alexander III, 1249–1286* (1990).

K. Stringer (ed.), *Essays on the Nobility of Medieval Scotland* (1985).

A. Young, *Robert the Bruce's Rivals: The Comyns, 1212–1314* (East Linton, 1997).

Early Modern (1500–1770s)

Very few studies bridge the gap between medieval and early modern or between the 16th and 17th centuries. Much, however, has recently been written on the crises of the 16th century, the Wars of the Covenant, Jacobitism, the Union of 1707, and the post-Union political system.

K. M. Brown, *Kingdom or Province: Scotland and the Regal Union, 1603–1715* (London, 1992).

—— *Noble Society in Scotland: Wealth, Family and Culture from the Reformation to the Revolution* (2000).

J. Buckroyd, *Church and State in Scotland, 1660–1681* (1980).

E. Cruickshanks (ed.), *Ideology and Conspiracy: Aspects of Jacobitism, 1689–1759* (1982).

G. Donaldson, *All the Queen's Men: Power and Politics in Mary Stewart's Scotland* (London, 1983).

W. Ferguson, *Scotland's Relations with England: A Survey to 1707* (1977; repr. 1994).

J. Goodare, *State and Society in Early Modern Scotland* (Oxford, 1999).

B. Lenman, *The Jacobite Risings in Britain, 1689–1746* (London, 1980).

—— *The Jacobite Clans of the Great Glen* (London, 1984).

B. P. Levack, *The Formation of the British State: England, Scotland and the Union, 1603–1707* (Oxford, 1987).

M. Lynch (ed.), *Jacobitism and the '45* (1995).

A. Macinnes, *Charles I and the Making of the Covenanting Movement, 1625–1641* (1991).

M. H. Merriman, *The Rough Wooings: Mary Queen of Scots, 1542–1551* (East Linton, 2000).

A. Murdoch, *The People Above: Politics and Administration in Mid-Eighteenth Century Scotland* (1980).

M. Pittock, *The Myth of the Jacobite Clans* (1995).

P. W. J. Riley, *The English Ministers and Scotland, 1707–1727* (1964).

—— *King William and the Scottish Politicians* (1979).

—— *The Union of England and Scotland: A Study in Anglo-*

Scottish Politics in the Eighteenth Century (Manchester, 1978).

J. S. Shaw, *The Management of Scottish Society, 1707–1764* (1983).

—— *A Political History of Eighteenth Century Scotland* (London, 1999).

T. C. Smout, 'The Road to Union', in G. Holmes (ed.), *Britain after the Glorious Revolution* (London, 1969).

D. Stevenson, *The Scottish Revolution, 1637–1644* (Newton Abbot, 1973).

—— *Revolution and Counter-Revolution in Scotland, 1644–1651* (London, 1978).

R. M. Sunter, *Patronage and Politics in Scotland, 1707–1832* (1986).

C. A. Whatley, *'Bought and Sold for English Gold'? Explaining the Union of 1707* (1994).

—— 'Economic Causes and Consequences of the Union of 1707: A Survey', *SHR* 68 (1989).

J. Wormald (ed.), *Scotland Revisited* (London, 1991).

Modern (1770s–1914)

Much of 19th-century politics was tied up with the franchise, ecclesiastical issues (see Section 7), problems of rapid urbanization (see Section 6), or issues of land reform (see Section 12).

D. Brookes, 'Gladstone and Midlothian: The Background to the First Campaign', *SHR* 64 (1985).

M. Dyer, *Men of Property and Intelligence: The Scottish Electoral System prior to 1884* (Aberdeen, 1996).

—— *Capable Citizens and Improvident Democrats: The Scottish Electoral System, 1884–1929* (Aberdeen, 1996).

W. Ferguson, 'The Reform Act (Scotland) of 1832: Intention and Effect', *SHR* 45 (1966).

R. J. Finlay, *A Partnership for Good? Scottish Politics and the Union since 1880* (1997).

H. Furber, *Henry Dundas, 1st Viscount Melville, 1742–1811* (London, 1931).

M. Fry, *The Dundas Despotism* (1992).

—— *Patronage and Principle: A Political History of Modern Scotland* (Aberdeen, 1987).

I. G. C. Hutchison, *A Political History of Scotland, 1832–1924* (1986).

K. J. Logue, *Popular Disturbances in Scotland, 1780–1815* (1979).

C. M. M. Macdonald (ed.), *Unionist Scotland, 1800–1997* (1998).

H. W. Meikle, *Scotland and the French Revolution* (Glasgow, 1912).

G. Morton, *Unionist Nationalism: Governing Urban Scotland, 1830–1860* (East Linton, 1999).

A. Wilson, *The Chartist Movement in Scotland* (Manchester, 1970).

The 20th Century

Until very recently, little had been written on the 20th century. Some work, however, remains a first draft and many issues remain unresolved or under-explored.

V. Bogdanov, *Devolution in the United Kingdom* (Oxford, 1999).

G. Brown, *Maxton* (1986).

I. Donnachie et al. (eds.), *Forward! Labour Politics in Scotland, 1888–1988* (1989).

R. Duncan, *Labour and Class Conflict on the Clyde, 1900–1950* (1992).

R. J. Finlay, *Independent and Free: Scottish Politics and the Origins of the Scottish National Party* (1994).

M. Fry, *Patronage and Principle: A Political History of Modern Scotland* (Aberdeen, 1987).

T. Gallagher (ed.), *Nationalism in the Nineties* (1991).

C. Harvie, *Scotland and Nationalism* (3rd edn., London, 1999).

—— *Fool's Gold: The Story of North Sea Oil* (London, 1994).

J. G. Kellas, *The Scottish Political System* (4th edn., Cambridge, 1989).

W. Kenefick and A. McIvor, *Roots of Red Clydeside, 1910–1914? Labour Unrest and Industrial Relations in West Scotland* (1996).

W. Knox (ed.), *Scottish Labour Leaders, 1918–1939* (1984).

—— *James Maxton* (Manchester, 1987).

R. Levy, *Scottish Nationalism at the Crossroads* (1990).

D. McCrone, *Understanding Scotland: The Sociology of a Stateless Nation* (London, 1992).

C. M. M. MacDonald and E. W. McFarland (eds.), *Scotland and the Great War* (East Linton, 1999).

I. S. McLean, *The Legend of Red Clydeside* (1983).

H. McShane with Joan Smith, *No Mean Fighter* (London, 1978).

A. Marr, *The Battle for Scotland* (London, 1992).

W. Miller, *The End Of British Politics: Scots and English Political Behaviour in the 1970s* (Oxford, 1981).

J. Mitchell, *Conservatives and the Union* (1990).

—— *Strategies for Self-Government: The Campaigns for a Scottish Parliament* (1996).

L. Paterson, *The Autonomy of Modern Scotland* (1994).

—— *A Diverse Assembly: The Debate on a Scottish Parliament* (1998).

B. J. Ripley and J. McHugh, *John Maclean* (Manchester, 1989).

G. Walker, *Thomas Johnston* (Manchester, 1987).

K. Webb, *The Growth of Nationalism in Scotland* (Glasgow, 1977).

I. Wood, *John Wheatley* (Manchester, 1990).

National identity

One of the questions which has attracted much recent attention from both historians and social scientists is identity, in its different aspects. A growing consensus emphasizes that national identity, in particular, was continuously evolving and recycling itself. Nonetheless, national identity, as distinct from nationalism, has been a potent factor in the history of 20th-century Scotland.

D. Broun, R. J. Finlay, and M. Lynch (eds.), *Image and Identity: The Making and Re-Making of Scotland through the Ages* (1998).

L. Colley, *Britons: Forging the Nation, 1707–1837* (London, 1992).

E. J. Cowan, 'Myth and Identity in Early Medieval Scotland', *SHR* 63 (1984).

I. Donnachie and C. Whatley (eds.), *The Manufacture of Scottish History* (1992).

W. Ferguson, *The Identity of the Scottish Nation: An Historic Quest* (1998).

C. Harvie, *Scotland and Nationalism, 1707–1994* (3rd edn., London, 1999).

C. Kidd, *Subverting Scotland's Past: Scottish Whig Historians and the Creation of an Anglo-British Identity, 1689–c.1830* (Cambridge, 1993).

D. McCrone, *The Sociology of Nationalism* (London, 1998).
—— *Understanding Scotland: The Sociology of a Stateless Nation* (London, 1992).
J. Mitchell, *The Strategies for Self-Government: The Campaigns for a Scottish Parliament* (1996).
G. Morton, *Unionist-Nationalism: Governing Urban Scotland, 1830–1860* (East Linton, 1998).
A. Murdoch, *British History, 1660–1832: National Identity and Local Culture* (London, 1998).
M. Pittock, *The Invention of Scotland: Stuart Myth and Scottish Identity, 1638 to the Present* (London, 1991).
B. Webster, *Medieval Scotland: the Making of an Identity* (London, 1997).

Regional and Local Identity
Despite increased social mobility, internal migration, and a series of governmental changes to local authority boundaries in the 20th century, regional or local identity has remained stubbornly intact. Scotland has not had the benefit of an institution such as England's Victoria County History, so coverage of local history is patchy, ranging from the exceptional to the slight. No attempt has been made here at a comprehensive coverage. (For the Highlands and Islands, see Section 12.)

M. Chapman, *The Gaelic Vision of Scottish Culture* (London, 1978).
W. Donaldson, *The Language of the People: Scots Prose from the Victorian Revival* (Aberdeen, 1989).

Borders
I. Brown et al., *Galashiels: A Modern History* (Galashiels, 1983).
J. L. Brown and I. C. Lawson, *History of Peebles 1850–1990* (1990).
G. M. Fraser, *The Steel Bonnets* (London, 1971).
J. M. Gilbert (ed.), *Flower of the Forest: Selkirk, A New History* (Galashiels, 1985).
C. Gulvin, *The Scottish Hosiery and Knitwear Industry 1680–1980* (1984).
—— *The Tweedmakers: A History of the Scottish Fancy Woollen Industry 1600–1914* (Newton Abbot, 1973).
M. Loanhead, *Portrait of the Scott Country* (London, 1976).
C. J. Neville, *Violence, Custom and Law: The Anglo-Scottish Border Lands in the Later Middle Ages* (1998).
G. K. Neville, *The Mother Town* [Selkirk] (New York and Oxford, 1994).
D. Omand (ed.), *The Borders Book* (1995).
T. I. Rae, *The Administration of the Scottish Frontier, 1513–1603* (1966).
S. Smith, 'Bordering on Identity', *Scotlands*, 3 (1996).
Transactions of the Hawick Archaeological Society (annual, 1854–).

Orkney and Shetland
(See also Section 11.)

G. Donaldson, *The Isles of Home* (1983).
A. Fenton, *The Northern Isles: Orkney and Shetland* (East Linton, 1997).
H. D. Smith, *Shetland Life and Trade, 1550–1914* (1984).

4. Government and Administration
This section is a conglomerate, and its different parts have been treated very differently by historians. In the modern period, some of the literature relating to the 'parish state' is to be found in Sections 6 and 7.

Kingship: Medieval
Most Scottish kings from Robert I onwards have received recent authoritative treatment. Coverage of earlier centuries, however, is patchy.

G. W. S. Barrow, *David I (1124–1153): The Balance of New and Old* (Stenton lecture, 1984).
—— *Robert Bruce* (3rd edn., 1988).
S. Boardman, *Robert II and III* (East Linton, 1996).
M. Brown, *James I* (1994).
J. G. Dunbar, *Scottish Royal Palaces: The Architecture of the Royal Residences during the Late Medieval and Early Renaissance Periods* (East Linton, 1999).
A. A. M. Duncan, *James I, King of Scots, 1424–1437* (Glasgow, 1984).
N. Macdougall, *James III* (1982).
—— *James IV* (1989).
L. J. Macfarlane, *William Elphinstone and the Kingdom of Scotland, 1431–1514* (Aberdeen, 1985).
C. McGladdery, *James II* (1990).
R. L. Mackie, *King James IV of Scotland* (1958).
D. D. R. Owen, *William the Lion, 1143–1214: Kingship and Culture* (East Linton, 1997).
N. Reid (ed.), *Scotland in the Reign of Alexander III, 1249–1286* (1990).

Kingship: Early Modern
Recent work has greatly changed understanding of every reign from James V to that of Charles I.

J. Cameron, *James V: The Personal Rule, 1528–1542* (East Linton, 1998).
G. Donaldson, *All the Queen's Men: Power and Politics in Mary Stewart's Scotland* (London, 1983).
C. Edington, *Court and Culture in Renaissance Scotland* (1995).
J. Goodare and M. Lynch (eds.), *The Reign of James VI* (East Linton, 2000).
King James VI & I, *Political Writings*, ed. J. P. Sommerville (Cambridge, 1994).
M. Lee, *Government by Pen: Scotland under James VI & I, 1603–1625* (Chicago, 1980).
—— *The Road to Revolution: Scotland under Charles I, 1625–1637* (Chicago, 1985).
—— *Great Britain's Solomon: James VI & I* (Urbana, Ill., 1990).
M. Lynch (ed.), *Mary Stewart: Queen in Three Kingdoms* (Oxford, 1987).
A. Thomas, *Princelie Majestie: The Court of James V of Scotland, 1528–1542* (East Linton, 2001).
D. H. Willson, *James VI and I* (London, 1956).

Government and Administration
Much more has been written on the mechanics of governing Scotland after 1707 than before. In particular, the pre-1707 parliament has had little study.

W. L. Burns, *The Age of Equipoise: A Study of the Mid-Victorian Generation* (London, 1964).
M. Fry, *Patronage and Principle: A Political History of Modern Scotland* (Aberdeen, 1987).
J. S. Gibson, *The Thistle and the Crown: A History of the Scottish Office* (1986).
I. G. C. Hutchison, *A Political History of Scotland, 1832–1924: Parties, Elections and Issues* (1986).
A. Murdoch, *The People Above: Politics and Administration in Mid-Eighteenth Century Scotland* (1980).

Guide to Further Reading

P. W. J. Riley, *The English Ministers and Scotland, 1707–1727* (1964).

J. S. Shaw, *The Management of Scottish Society 1707–1764* (1983).

Parliament

J. Goodare, 'The Estates in the Scottish Parliament, 1286–1707', *Parliamentary History*, 15 (1996).

A. I. Macinnes, 'The Scottish Constitution, 1638–1651', in J. Morrill (ed.), *The Scottish National Covenant in its British Context* (1990).

R. Nicholson, *Scotland: The Later Middle Ages* (1974).

R. S. Rait, *The Parliaments of Scotland* (Glasgow, 1924).

R. Tanner, *The Late Mediaeval Scottish Parliament: Politics and the Three Estates, 1424–1488* (East Linton, 2001).

J. R. Young, *The Scottish Parliament* (1996).

Local Government

G. C. H. Paton (ed.), *Introduction to Scottish Legal History* (Stair Society, 1958).

M. Lynch et al. (eds.), *The Scottish Medieval Town* (1988).

H. L. MacQueen, *Common Law and Feudal Society in Medieval Scotland* (1993).

G. S. Pryde, *Local Government in Scotland II: The Period of Reform* (Dunfermline, 1935).

—— (ed.), *The Court Book of the Burgh of Kirkintilloch* (SHS, 1963).

A. E. Whetstone, *Scottish County Government in the Eighteenth and Nineteenth Centuries* (1981).

Law

There is a vast, specialist literature on this subject, and the volumes of the Stair Society contain much information, both general and specialist.

G. W. S. Barrow, 'The Justiciar', in *The Kingdom of the Scots* (London, 1973).

J. W. Cairns, 'History of the Faculty of Advocates to 1900', in T. B. Smith and R. Black (eds.), *The Laws of Scotland: Stair Memorial Encyclopaedia*, vol. 13 (1991).

—— et al., 'Legal Humanism and the History of Scots Law', in J. MacQueen (ed.), *Humanism in Renaissance Scotland* (1990).

D. L. Carey Miller and R. Zimmermann (eds.), *The Civilian Tradition and Scots Law: Aberdeen Quincentenary Essays* (Berlin, 1997).

R. Evans-Jones (ed.), *The Civil Law Tradition in Scotland* (1995).

An Introductory Survey of the Sources and Literature of Scots Law (Stair Society, 1936).

K. Jackson, *The Gaelic Notes in the Book of Deer* (Cambridge, 1972).

B. P. Levack, *The Formation of the British State* (Oxford, 1987).

H. L. MacQueen, *Common Law and Feudal Society in Medieval Scotland* (1993).

—— 'Regiam Majestatem, Scots Law and National Identity', *SHR* 74 (1995).

G. C. H. Paton (ed.), *An Introduction to Scottish Legal History* (Stair Society, 1958).

O. F. Robinson et al., *European Legal History* (2nd edn., London, 1994).

W. D. H. Sellar, 'A Historical Perspective', in S. C. Styles (ed.), *The Scottish Legal Tradition* (1991).

—— 'Scots Law and Celtic Law: Continuity and Integration', *Scottish Studies*, 29 (1989).

D. M. Walker (ed.), *Stair Tercentenary Studies* (Stair Society, 1981).

Military: Warfare, Weapons, and Fortifications

Little has been written on the Scottish army before the 17th century and less on the navy. In the later period, most regimental histories are best avoided. Coverage of military fortifications, by contrast, is as good as that of architecture in general.

J. Black, *Culloden and the '45* (Stroud, 1990).

J. Calder, *The Story of the Scottish Soldier, 1600–1914* (1987).

E. J. Cowan, *Montrose: For Covenant and King* (London, 1977).

C. Dalton, *The Scots Army, 1661–1688* (London, 1909).

G. Dickinson, 'Some Notes on the Scottish Army in the First Half of the 16th Century', *SHR* 28 (1949).

J. Fortescue, *A History of the British Army* (London, 1910).

E. M. Furgol, *A Regimental History of the Covenanting Armies, 1639–1651* (1990).

D. M. Henderson, *Highland Soldier: A Social Study of the Highland Regiments, 1820–1920* (1989).

P. Hopkins, *Glencoe and the End of the Highland War* (1986).

R. Monro, *Monro, His Expedition with the Worthy Scots Regiment called Mac-Keys*, ed. W. S. Brockington, Jr. (London, 1999).

S. Reid, *Like Hungry Wolves: Culloden Moor 16 April 1746* (London, 1994).

W. S. Reid, 'Sea-Power in the Anglo-Scottish War, 1296–1328', *Mariner's Mirror*, 46 (1960).

H. C. B. Rogers, *The British Army of the Eighteenth Century* (London, 1977).

C. Sinclair-Stevenson, *Inglorious Rebellion: The Jacobite Risings of 1708, 1715 and 1719* (London, 1971).

D. Stevenson, *Alasdair MacColla and the Highland Problem in the Seventeenth Century* (1980).

—— *Scottish Covenanters and Irish Confederates* (Belfast, 1981).

C. Tabraham, *Fortress Scotland and the Jacobites* (London, 1995).

S. Wood, *The Scottish Soldier* (Manchester, 1987).

Military: Mercenaries and Soldiers Abroad

It has been estimated that as much as a fifth of Scotland's adult male population served in Europe as mercenaries in the period 1570–1640. A separate pattern was the annual exodus of 'gallowglasses' from the Western Isles to Ireland; it lasted until c.1600. (See also Section 14, especially Scandinavia.)

Åberg, A, 'Scottish Soldiers in the Swedish Armies in the Sixteenth and Seventeenth Centuries', in G. D. Dobson (ed.), *Scottish Soldiers in Colonial America* (Baltimore, 1997).

J. Dow, 'Ruthven's Army in Sweden and Esthonia', in *Kungliga Vitterhets historia och antikvitetes akademien: Historiskt Arkiv* (Stockholm, 1965).

J. Ferguson (ed.), *Papers illustrating the History of the Scots Brigade in the Service of the United Netherlands, 1572–1782*, 3 vols. (SHS, 1899–1901).

W. Forbes-Leith, *The Scots Men-at-Arms and Life Guards in France, 1458–1830*, 2 vols. (1882).

J. Grant, *The Scottish Soldiers of Fortune: Their Adventures and Achievements in the Armies of Europe* (1890).

G. A. Hayes-McCoy, *Scots Mercenary Forces in Ireland* (Dublin, 1937).

A. McKerral, 'West Highland Mercenaries in Ireland', *SHR* 30 (1951).

S. Murdoch, 'The House of Stuart and the Scottish Professional Soldier 1618–1640: A Conflict of Nationality and Identities', in B. Taithe and T. Thornton (eds.), *War, Identities in Conflict, 1300–2000* (Gloucestershire, 1998).

—— and A. Grosjean, *Scotland, Scandinavia and Northern Europe 1580–1707* (Aberdeen, 1998; published at <www.abdn.ac.uk/history/datasets/ssne>).

A. K. Murray, *History of the Scottish Regiments in the British Army* (Glasgow, 1862).

Papers relative to the Royal Guard of Scottish Archers in France (Maitland Club, 1835).

G. G. Simpson (ed.), *Scotland and Scandinavia, 800–1800* (1990).

—— *The Scottish Soldier Abroad* (1992).

5. Economic Life

It has been claimed that much of the history of modern Scotland needs to be written in terms of its economy. As a result, there is a vast literature on it.

The Economy: General

A. K. Cairncross (ed.), *The Scottish Economy* (Cambridge, 1954).

R. H. Campbell, *Scotland since 1707: The Rise of an Industrial Society* (2nd edn., 1985).

T. M. Devine, *The Scottish Nation 1700–2000* (London, 1999).

A. A. M. Duncan, *Scotland: The Making of the Kingdom* (1978).

E. Gemmell and N. Mayhew, *Changing Values in Medieval Scotland: A Study of Prices, Money, and Weights and Measures* (Cambridge, 1995).

A. Grant, *Independence and Nationhood: Scotland 1306–1469* (London, 1984).

T. L. Johnston et al., *Structure and Growth of the Scottish Economy* (London, 1971).

W. W. Knox, *Industrial Nation: Work, Culture and Society in Scotland, 1800–Present* (1999).

B. Lenman, *An Economic History of Modern Scotland* (London, 1977).

S. G. E. Lythe and J. Butt, *An Economic History of Scotland, 1100–1939* (Glasgow, 1975).

N. Mayhew, 'A Silver Age?', in N. Reid (ed.), *Scotland in the Reign of Alexander III* (1990).

R. Saville (ed.), *The Economic Development of Modern Scotland, 1950–1980* (1985).

F. A. Shera and G. B. Robertson, 'Structural Change in the Scottish Economy', *Scottish Economic Bulletin*, 43 (1991).

T. C. Smout, 'Where had the Scottish economy got to by the third quarter of the 18th century?', in I. Hont and M. Ignatieff (eds.), *Wealth and Virtue* (Cambridge, 1983).

I. D. Whyte, *Scotland before the Industrial Revolution: An Economic and Social History c.1050–c.1750* (London, 1995).

—— *Scotland's Society and Economy in Transition, c.1500–c.1760* (Basingstoke, 1997).

Economic Sectors: Primary

R. Anthony, *Herds and Hinds: Farm Labour in Lowland Scotland, 1900–1939* (East Linton, 1997).

I. Carter, *Farm Life in North-East Scotland, 1840–1914* (1979).

J. R. Coull, *The Sea Fisheries of Scotland: A Historical Geography* (1996).

T. M. Devine (ed.), *Farm Servants and Labour in Lowland Scotland, 1770–1914* (1984).

—— *The Transformation of Rural Scotland: Social Change and Agrarian Economy, 1660–1815* (1994).

R. A. Dodgshon, *Land and Society in Early Scotland* (Oxford, 1981).

B. F. Duckham, *A History of the Scottish Coal Industry, i. 1700–1815* (Newton Abbot, 1970).

J. Dunlop, *The British Fisheries Society 1786–1893* (1978).

A. Fenton, *Country Life in Scotland* (1987).

M. Gray, *The Fishing Industries of Scotland 1790–1914* (Oxford, 1978).

M. L. Parry and T. R. Slater (eds.), *The Making of the Scottish Countryside* (London, 1980).

T. C. Smout and A. Fenton, 'Scottish Agriculture before the Improvers: An Exploration', *Agricultural History Review*, 13 (1965).

J. A. Symon, *Scottish Farming Past and Present* (1959).

I. D. Whyte, *Agriculture and Society in Seventeenth-Century Scotland* (1979).

Economic Sectors: Secondary

R. H. Campbell, *The Rise and Fall of Scottish Industry, 1707–1939* (1980).

A. J. Durie, *The Scottish Linen Industry in the Eighteenth Century* (1979).

W. W. Knox, *Hanging By a Thread: The Scottish Cotton Industry, 1850–1914* (Preston, 1994).

P. L. Payne, *Colvilles and the Scottish Steel Industry* (Oxford, 1979).

—— *Growth and Contraction: Scottish Industry c.1860–1990* (Glasgow, 1992).

—— 'The End of Steelmaking in Scotland, c.1967–1993', *SESH* 15 (1995).

S. Pollard and P. Robertson, *The British Shipbuilding Industry, 1870–1914* (Cambridge, Mass., 1979).

A. Slaven, *The Development of the West of Scotland, 1750–1960* (London, 1975).

S. Tolliday, *Business, Banking, and Politics: The Case of British Steel, 1918–1939* (Cambridge, Mass., 1987).

C. Whatley, *The Industrial Revolution in Scotland* (Cambridge, 1997).

J. L. Wood, *Scottish Engineering: The Machine Makers* (2000).

Economic Sectors: Tertiary

S. G. Checkland, *Scottish Banking: A History, 1695–1973* (Glasgow, 1975).

T. M. Devine, *The Tobacco Lords* (1975).

A. J. Durie, *The British Linen Company 1745–1775* (SHS, 1996).

—— *Scotland for Holidays* (East Linton, 1999).

J. and M. Gold, *Imagining Scotland* (Aldershot, 1995).

G. P. Insh, *The Company of Scotland trading to Africa and the Indies* (SHS, 1932).

S. G. E. Lythe, *The Economy of Scotland in its European Setting, 1550–1625* (1960).

P. Mathias, *Retailing Revolution* (London, 1967).

M. M. Moss, *Standard Life, 1825–2000* (2000).

C. W. Munn, *Clydesdale Bank: The First One Hundred and Fifty Years* (Glasgow, 1988).

—— *The Scottish Provincial Banking Companies, 1747–1864* (1981).

R. Saville, *The Bank of Scotland: A History, 1695–1995* (1996).

J. Scott and M. Hughes, *The Anatomy of Scottish Capitalism: Scottish Companies and Scottish Capital, 1900–1979* (1980).

A. Slaven and S. Checkland (eds.), *Dictionary of Scottish Business Biography*, 2 vols. (Aberdeen, 1986–90).

T. C. Smout, *Scottish Trade on the Eve of Union, 1660–1707* (1963).

Economic Sectors: New Industry

C. Harvie, *Fool's Gold: The Story of North Sea Oil* (London, 1994).

N. Hood and S. Young, *Multinationals in Retreat: The Scottish Experience* (1982).

J. R. Hume and M. S. Moss, *Beardmore: The History of a Scottish Industrial Giant* (London, 1979).

I. Levitt, *The Scottish Office, 1919–1959* (SHS, 1995).

G. Oliver, *Motor Trials and Tribulations: A History of Scottish Motor Vehicle Manufacture* (1993).

D. Sims and M. Wood, *Car Manufacturing at Linwood: The Regional Policy Issues* (Paisley, 1984).

Transport and Communications

C. L. D. Duckworth and G. E. Langmuir, *West Highland Steamers* (Prescot, 1967).

A. Fenton and G. Stell (eds.), *Loads and Roads in Scotland and Beyond* (1984).

A. R. B. Haldane, *New Ways Through the Glens* (London, 1962).

P. G. Ransom, *Scotland's Inland Waterways: Canals, Rivers and Lochs* (1999).

G. Stell, 'By Land and Sea in Medieval and Early Modern Scotland', *ROSC* 4 (1988).

J. Thomas, *The West Highland Railway* (4th edn., Colonsay, 1998).

A. Valance, *The Highland Railway* (Newton Abbot, 1968).

M. Weir, *Ferries in Scotland* (1988).

J. L. Wood, *Building Railways* (1996).

Economic Policy

N. Hood, 'The Scottish Development Agency in Retrospect', *Royal Bank of Scotland Review*, 171 (Sept. 1991).

C. H. Lee, *Scotland and the United Kingdom: The Economy and the Union in the Twentieth Century* (Manchester, 1995).

C. McGread, *A Brief History of the Scottish Council (Development and Industry)* (Business Archives Council of Scotland, 1993).

A. Midwinter et al., *Politics and Public Policy in Scotland* (1991).

6. Social Life

Rural Society

Enough has been written in recent years to piece together a convincing overview of rural life over ten centuries. Improvement was as much a feature of the 11th and 12th centuries as it was of the 18th. Yet continuity generally more than matched change until the later 18th century. See also Section 5: Economic Sectors: Primary; Section 10: Rural Settlement.

R. Anthony, *Herds and Hinds: Farm Labour in Lowland Scotland, 1900–1939* (East Linton, 1997).

G. W. S. Barrow, *The Anglo-Norman Era in Scottish History* (Oxford, 1980).

T. M. Devine (ed.), *Farm Servants and Labour in Lowland Scotland, 1770–1914* (1984).

—— *The Transformation of Rural Scotland: Social Change and Agrarian Economy, 1660–1815* (1994).

R. A. Dodgshon, *Land and Society in Early Scotland* (Oxford, 1981).

A. Fenton, *Scottish Country Life* (1976; reissued East Linton, 2000).

M. H. B. Sanderson, *Scottish Rural Society in the Sixteenth Century* (1982).

I. D. Whyte, *Scotland before the Industrial Revolution: An Economic and Social History c.1050–c.1750* (London, 1995).

—— *Scotland's Society and Economy in Transition, c.1500–c.1760* (Basingstoke, 1997).

—— *Agriculture and Society in Seventeenth-Century Scotland* (1979).

Urban Society

Until the late 18th century, towns made up a tenth or less of the population. Scotland underwent a process of extremely rapid urbanization after c.1800. Yet urban society in Scotland was distinctively different from that in England in a number of respects, both before and after 1800.

I. H. Adams, *The Making of Urban Scotland* (London, 1978).

A. Briggs, *Victorian Cities* (London, 1963).

E. P. Dennison, *Conservation and Change in Historic Towns* (York, 1999).

T. M. Devine and G. Jackson (eds.), *Glasgow: Beginnings to 1830* (Manchester, 1995).

H. M. Dingwall, *Late Seventeenth Century Edinburgh: A Demographic Study* (Leicester, 1994).

E. Ewan, *Townlife in Fourteenth-Century Scotland* (1990).

W. H. Fraser and C. H. Lee (eds.), *New History of Aberdeen*, vol. 2 (East Linton, 2000).

A. Gibb, *Glasgow: The Making of a City* (London, 1983).

G. Gordon, *Perspectives on the Scottish City* (1985).

—— and B. Dicks (eds.), *Scottish Urban History* (Aberdeen, 1981).

M. Lynch, *Edinburgh and the Reformation* (1981).

—— (ed.), *The Early Modern Town in Scotland* (London, 1987).

—— et al. (eds.), *The Scottish Medieval Town* (1988).

I. Maver, *Glasgow* (East Linton, 2000).

—— and W. H. Fraser, *Glasgow, 2. 1830–1912* (Manchester, 1996).

R. J. Morris and R. Rodger (eds.), *The Victorian City: A Reader in British Urban History, 1820–1914* (London, 1993).

E. P. D. Torrie, *Medieval Dundee* (Dundee, 1990).

—— (latterly Dennison) and R. Coleman, *The Scottish Burgh Survey*, 16 vols. (1995–9; East Linton, 1999–2000).

C. A. Whatley et al., *The Life and Times of Dundee* (1993).

I. D. Whyte, *Scotland Before the Industrial Revolution: An Economic and Social History c.1050–c.1750* (London, 1995).

Diet

The Scottish diet was distinctive and continuously changing before the advent of modern mass consumerism in the late 19th century.

A. Fenton, *Scottish Country Life* (1976; reissued East Linton, 2000).

—— 'Grain Storage in Pits: Experiment and Fact', in A. O'Connor and D. V. Clarke (eds.), *From the Stone Age to the 'Forty-Five* (1981).

—— 'The Greening of the Scottish Countryside in the

Age of Agricultural Improvements', *Acta Ethnographica Hungarica*, 40 (1995).

A. Gibson and T. C. Smout, 'Scottish Food and Scottish History, 1500–1800', in R. A. Houston and I. D. Whyte (eds.), *Scottish Society, 1500–1800* (Cambridge, 1989).

N. Mayhew, 'Medieval Bread in Scotland', *ROSC* 8 (1993).

L. Weatherill, *Consumer Behaviour and Material Culture in Britain, 1660–1760* (London, 1988).

Material Conditions and the Quality of Life
This issue has tended to be dominated by questions relating to the Poor Law. Other aspects of it, particularly in relation to housing, are covered in Section 10.

R. A. Cage, *The Scottish Poor Law, 1745–1845* (1981).

O. Checkland, *Philanthropy in Victorian Scotland* (1980).

E. Gemmill and N. Mayhew, *Changing Values in Medieval Scotland* (Cambridge, 1995).

A. J. S. Gibson and T. C. Smout, *Prices, Food and Wages in Scotland, 1550–1780* (Cambridge, 1994).

I. Levitt, *Poverty and Welfare in Scotland, 1890–1948* (1988).

R. Mitchison, *The Old Poor Law in Scotland, 1574–1845* (2000).

Social Class and Trade Unionism
A vast literature exists for this area, although it has, for some, become an unfashionable topic.

R. P. Arnot, *A History of the Scottish Miners from the Earliest Times* (London, 1955).

A. B. Campbell, *The Lanarkshire Miners* (1979).

R. A. Cage, *The Working Class in Glasgow, 1750–1914* (London, 1987).

T. Dickson (ed.), *Capital and Class in Scotland* (1982).

W. H. Fraser, *Conflict and Class: Scottish Workers, 1700–1838* (1988).

W. Knox (ed.), *Scottish Labour Leaders, 1918–1939: A Biographical Dictionary* (1984).

I. MacDougall (ed.), *Essays in Scottish Labour History* (1978).

A. A. MacLaren, *Religion and Social Class* (London, 1974).

—— *Social Class in Scotland* (1976).

W. H. Marwick, *A Short History of Labour in Scotland* (Manchester, 1967).

J. D. Young, *The Rousing of the Scottish Working Class* (London, 1979).

Medicine and Public Health
The important, related issues of the medical profession, public health, and disease have received relatively little attention. Most of the existing literature relates to the period after 1750.

J. D. Comrie, *History of Scottish Medicine*, 2 vols. (London, 1932).

H. M. Dingwall, *Physicians, Surgeons and Apothecaries: Medical Practice in Seventeenth Century Edinburgh* (1995).

J. Geyer-Kordesch and R. Ferguson, *Blue Stockings, Black Gowns, White Coats: A Brief History of Women entering Higher Education and the Medical Profession in Scotland* (Glasgow, 1995).

D. Hamilton, *The Healers: A History of Medicine in Scotland* (1981).

Famine and Disease
S. Blackden, 'The Board of Supervision and the Scottish Parochial Medical Service, 1845–1895', *Medical History*, 30 (1986).

O. Checkland, *Healthcare as Social History: The Glasgow Case* (Aberdeen, 1982).

G. Rivett, *From Cradle to Grave: Fifty Years of the NHS* (London, 1998).

T. C. Smout, 'Coping with Plague in 16th and 17th Century Scotland', *Scotia*, 2 (1978).

Traditional Healing
M. Beith, *Healing Threads: Traditional Medicines of the Highlands and Islands* (1995).

Caledonian Medical Journal (1883–1968).

D. Buchan (ed.), *Folk Tradition and Folk Medicine in Scotland: The Writings of David Rorie* (1994).

Languages of Scotland
Scotland is well served by its lexicographers. Language, including place names, can be an important tool for the historian.

Gaelic
The extent of the *Gaidhealtachd* has been contracting since the 11th or 12th centuries. Its shifting boundaries have important consequences—economic, social, and political—for the relationship between it and the rest of Scotland as well for questions about identity. As late as 1755, it needs to be remembered, the majority of Scots lived to the north of the Tay. (See also Section 13: Literature, Gaelic.)

M. Chapman, *The Gaelic Vision in Scottish Culture* (London, 1978).

N. C. Dorian, *Language Death* (Philadelpia, 1981).

V. Durcakz, *The Decline of the Celtic Languages* (1983).

S. MacDonald, *Reimagining Culture: Histories, Identities and the Gaelic Renaissance* (Oxford, 1997).

K. Mackinnon, *Gaelic: A Past and Future Prospect* (1991).

C. O'Dochartaigh, *Survey of the Gaelic Dialects of Scotland*, vol. 1 (Dublin, 1997).

D. S. Thomson (ed.), *The Companion to Gaelic Scotland* (Oxford, 1983).

—— *Gaelic and Scots in Harmony* (Glasgow, 1989).

C. Withers, *Gaelic in Scotland, 1698–1981: The Geographical History of a Language* (1984).

Scots
Scots became the official language of government in the 15th century. Its gradual decline, and the consequences of that, are matters as controversial, in theory, as the decline of Gaelic. See also Section 13: Literature.

The Scottish National Dictionary (SND), 10 vols. (1931–76).

A Dictionary of the Older Scottish Tongue (DOST), 12 vols. (1931–).

The Concise Scots Dictionary (CSD), ed. M. Robinson (Aberdeen, 1985).

D. Craig, *Scottish Literature and the Scottish People 1680–1830* (London, 1961).

C. Jones (ed.), *The Edinburgh History of the Scots Language* (1997).

—— *A Language Suppressed: The Pronunciation of the Scots Language in the 18th Century* (1995).

C. Macafee and I. Macleod (eds.), *The Nuttis Schell* (Aberdeen, 1987).

J. D. McLure, *Language, Poetry and Nationhood: Scots as a Poetic Language from 1878 to the Present* (East Linton, 1999).

J. D. McLure, *Scotland and the Lowland Tongue* (Aberdeen, 1983).

—— *Why Scots Matters* (1988).

Schools, Schooling, and Universities

Issues relating to the quality and impact of Scottish schooling are controversial. The extent of literacy, the frequency of the 'lad o'pairts', and the myth or reality of the 'democratic intellect' are all under debate.

R. D. Anderson, *Education and Opportunity in Victorian Scotland* (rev. edn., 1989).

—— *Education and the Scottish People 1750–1918* (Oxford, 1995).

J. Carter and D. J. Withrington (eds.), *Scottish Universities: Distinctiveness and Diversity* (Aberdeen, 1992).

G. E. Davie, *The Democratic Intellect: Scotland and her Universities in the Nineteenth Century* (2nd edn., 1964).

J. Durkan, *Early Schools and Schoolmasters in Scotland 1560–1633* (SRS, 2001).

—— 'Education in the Century of the Reformation', in D. McRoberts (ed.), *Essays on the Scottish Reformation, 1513–1625* (Glasgow, 1962).

R. A. Houston, *Scottish Literacy and the Scottish Identity, 1600–1800* (Cambridge, 1985).

L. Maclean (ed.), *The Highlands in the Seventeenth Century* (Inverness, 1986).

D. E. R. Watt, 'Education in the Highlands in the Middle Ages', in L. MacLean (ed.), *The Middle Ages in the Highlands* (Inverness, 1981).

D. J. Withrington, 'The SSPCK and Highland Schools in the Eighteenth Century', *SHR* 41 (1962).

Leisure and Sport

Surprisingly little has been written on sport, other than 'in-house' works, until recent times. Its importance for identity and class is now increasingly recognized.

Commercial sport

G. Jarvie et al. (eds.), *Scottish Sport in the Making of the Nation* (Leicester, 1994).

—— (ed.), *Sport in the Making of Celtic Cultures* (London, 1999).

M. Polley, *Moving the Goal Posts: A History of Sport and Society since 1945* (London, 1998).

N. Tranter, *Sport, Economy and Society in Britain, 1750–1914* (Cambridge, 1998).

W. Vamplew, *Pay Up and Play the Game: Professional Sport in Britain, 1875–1914* (Cambridge, 1988).

J. Walvin, *Leisure and Society, 1830–1950* (London, 1978).

Curling

J. Kerr, *History of Curling* (1890).

Royal Caledonian Curling Club, *Annals* (1939–).

D. B. Smith, *Curling: An Illustrated History* (1981).

Football

B. Crampsey, *The Scottish Footballer* (1978).

K. McCarra, *Scottish Football* (1984).

B. Murray, *The Old Firm: Sectarianism, Sport and Society in Scotland* (1984).

Golf

R. Browning, *A History of Golf* (London, 1955).

O. Geddes, *A Swing through Time: Golf in Scotland 1457–1743* (1992).

Rugby Football

A. Massie, *A Portrait of Scottish Rugby* (1984).

S. Thorburn, *The History of Scottish Rugby* (1980).

Shinty

H. D. MacLennan, *Shinty: 100 Years of the Camanachd Association* (Nairn, 1993).

Women, Children, the Family, and Society

A great deal has recently been written on both women and the family in the modern period. Before that, however, both subjects remain largely unexplored with a few important exceptions, mostly because of difficulties relating to lack of evidence.

L. Abrams, ' "There was nobody like my daddy": Fathers, the Family and the Marginalisation of Men in Modern Scotland', *SHR* 78 (1999).

E. Breitenbach and E. Gordon, *Out of Bounds: Women and Scottish Society, 1800–1945* (1992).

T. Brotherstone et al., *Gendering Scottish History: An International Approach* (Glasgow, 1999).

M. Craig, *Damn Rebel Bitches: The Women of the '45* (2000).

E. Ewan and M. Meikle (eds.), *Women in Scotland, c.1100–c.1750* (East Linton, 1999).

D. Gifford (ed.), *A History of Scottish Women's Writing* (1997).

E. Gordon, *Women in the Labour Market in Scotland, 1850–1914* (Oxford, 1991).

—— and E. Breitenbach (eds.), *The World is Ill Divided: Women's Work in Scotland in the Nineteenth and Early Twentieth Centuries* (1990).

E. King, *The Hidden History of Glasgow's Women: The Thenew Factor* (1993).

—— *The Scottish Women's Suffrage Movement* (Glasgow, 1978).

L. Leneman, *Alienated Affections: The Scottish Experience of Divorce and Separation, 1684–1830* (1998).

—— *A Guid Cause: The Women's Suffrage Movement in Scotland* (Aberdeen, 1991).

—— *In the Service of Life: The Story of Elsie Inglis and the Scottish Women's Hospitals* (1994).

—— and R. Mitchison, *Sin in the City: Sexuality and Social Control in Urban Scotland 1660–1780* (1998).

—— —— *Girls in Trouble: Sexuality and Social Control in Rural Scotland 1660–1780* (1998).

I. MacDougall, *Hard work, ye ken: Midlothian Women Farmworkers* (1993).

L. Mahood, *The Magdalenes: Prostitution in the Nineteenth Century* (London, 1990).

R. K. Marshall, *Virgins and Viragos: A History of Women in Scotland from 1080 to 1980* (London, 1983).

J. Melling, *Rent Strikes: People's Struggle for Housing in West Scotland, 1890–1916* (1983).

R. Mitchison and L. Leneman, *Sexuality and Social Control: Scotland, 1660–1780* (Oxford, 1989).

F. Paterson and J. Fewell (eds.), *Girls in their Prime: Scottish Education Revisited* (1990).

S. Reynolds, *Britannica's Typesetters: Women Compositors in Edwardian Edinburgh* (1989).

E. Sanderson, *Women and Work in 18th Century Edinburgh* (Basingstoke, 1996).

C. A. Whatley, 'Women and the Economic Transformation of Scotland', *SESH* 14 (1994).

Dress

Much has been written and much has been misunderstood about Highland dress. The subject, however, is a wider one than tartan and plaid.

H. Cheape, *Tartan: The Highland Habit* (1995).

N. Tarrant, *Costume in Scotland through the Ages* (Glasgow, 1986).

J. Telfer-Dunbar, *Costume of Scotland* (London, 1981).

—— *History of Highland Dress* (London, 1962).

7. Religious Life

Much more has been written about ecclesiastical institutions and churchmen than about religious life, piety, or the people in the pews. Surprisingly little has been published on the medieval church in recent times, other than about it on the eve of the Reformation. In the modern period, much has been written on the mainstream Presbyterian churches but comparatively little of substance on Protestant and other sects. Much can be found on the history of the Roman Catholic Church in the journal *Innes Review* and for ecclesiastical history in general in *Records of the Scottish Church History Society*. More recently, since the growth of a skilled working class from the mid-19th century onwards had much to do with the Free Church and other strains of religious dissent, historians' attention has moved to issues such as religious culture, temperance, and sectarianism.

General

C. G. Brown, *Religion and Society in Scotland since 1707* (1997).

J. H. S. Burleigh, *A Church History of Scotland* (1960).

N. M. de S. Cameron, *Dictionary of Scottish Church History and Theology* (1993).

G. Donaldson, *The Faith of the Scots* (London, 1990).

—— *Scottish Church History* (1985).

D. B. Forrester and D. M. Murray (eds.), *Studies in the History of Worship in Scotland* (2nd edn., 1996).

N. Macdougall (ed.), *Church, Politics and Society: Scotland 1408–1929* (1983).

A. Pagan, *God's Scotland? The Story of Scottish Christian Religion* (1988).

Early Medieval

L. Bieler, *The Irish Penitentials* (Dublin, 1975).

J. Blair and R. Sharpe (eds.), *Pastoral Care before the Parish* (Leicester, 1992).

D. Broun and T. O. Clancy (eds.), *Spes Scotorum / Hope of Scots: Saint Columba, Iona and Scotland* (1999).

T. O. Clancy and G. Márkus, *Iona: The Earliest Poetry of a Celtic Monastery* (1995).

Medieval

G. W. S. Barrow, *The Kingdom of the Scots: Government, Church and Society from the Eleventh to the Fourteenth Century* (London, 1973).

I. B. Cowan, *The Medieval Church in Scotland* (1995).

—— et al. (eds.), *The Knights of St John of Jerusalem in Scotland* (SHS, 1983).

M. Dilworth, *Scottish Monasteries in the Late Middle Ages* (1995).

J. Dowden, *The Medieval Church in Scotland: Its Constitution, Organisation and Law* (Glasgow, 1910).

R. Fawcett, *Scottish Medieval Churches* (1985).

N. Macdougall (ed.), *Church, Politics and Society: Scotland, 1408–1929* (1983).

L. J. Macfarlane, *William Elphinstone and the Kingdom of Scotland, 1431–1514* (Aberdeen, 1985).

A. Macquarrie, *The Saints of Scotland: Essays in Scottish Church History, AD 450–1093* (1997).

—— *Scotland and the Crusades, 1095–1560* (1985).

Reformation

F. D. Bardgett, *Scotland Reformed: The Reformation in Angus and the Mearns* (1989).

I. B. Cowan, *The Scottish Reformation* (London, 1982).

G. Donaldson, *The Scottish Reformation* (Cambridge, 1960).

M. Graham, *The Uses of Reform: 'Godly Discipline' and Popular Behavior in Scotland and Beyond* (Leiden, 1996).

J. Kirk, *Patterns of Reform* (1989).

M. Lynch, *Edinburgh and the Reformation* (1981).

D. McRoberts (ed.), *Essays on the Scottish Reformation, 1513–1625* (Glasgow, 1962).

R. A. Mason (ed.), *John Knox and the British Reformations* (Aldershot, 1999).

M. H. B. Sanderson, *Cardinal of Scotland: David Beaton, c.1494–1546* (1986).

—— *Ayrshire and the Reformation* (East Linton, 1997).

Early Modern

J. Buckroyd, *Church and State in Scotland, 1660–1681* (1980).

—— *The Life of James Sharp, Archbishop of St Andrews* (1987).

I. B. Cowan, *The Scottish Covenanters, 1660–1688* (London, 1976).

A. L. Drummond and J. Bulloch, *The Scottish Church, 1688–1843* (1973).

A. I. Dunlop, *William Carstares and the Kirk by Law Established* (1967).

W. R. Foster, *The Church before the Covenants, 1596–1638* (1975).

J. Goodare, 'Women and the Witch-Hunt in Scotland', *Social History*, 24 (1999).

G. D. Henderson, *Religious Life in Seventeenth-Century Scotland* (Cambridge, 1937).

C. Larner, *Enemies of God: The Witch-Hunt in Scotland* (London, 1981).

—— *Witchcraft and Religion* (Oxford, 1984).

W. Makey, *The Church of the Covenant, 1637–1651* (1979).

D. Shaw (ed.), *Reformation and Revolution* (1967).

Age of the Enlightenment

D. W. Bebbington, *Evangelicalism in Modern Britain: A History from the 1730s to the 1980s* (London, 1989).

J. R. McIntosh, *Church and Theology in Enlightenment Scotland: The Popular Party, 1740–1800* (East Linton, 1998).

R. Sher, *Church and University in the Scottish Enlightenment: The Moderate Literati of Edinburgh* (Princeton, 1985).

The Disruption

S. J. Brown, *Thomas Chalmers and the Godly Commonwealth in Scotland* (Oxford, 1982).

—— and M. Fry (eds.), *Scotland in the Age of the Disruption* (1993).

A. C. Cheyne, *The Transforming of the Kirk: Victorian Scotland's Religious Revolution* (1983).

G. D. Henderson, *Heritage: A Study of the Disruption* (1943).

Modern Period

P. Brierley and F. Macdonald, *Prospects for Scotland 2000: Trends and Tables from the 1994 Scottish Church Census* (1995).

Guide to Further Reading

A. L. Drummond and J. Bulloch, *The Church in Victorian Scotland, 1843–1874* (1973).

—— *The Church in Late Victorian Scotland, 1874–1900* (1978).

R. Ferguson, *Chasing the Wild Goose: The Story of the Iona Community* (Glasgow, 1998).

E. McFarland, *Protestants First: Orangeism in Nineteenth-Century Scotland* (1990).

A. A. Maclaren, *Religion and Social Class: The Disruption Years in Aberdeen* (London, 1974).

A. Muir, *John White, CH, DD, LLD* (London, 1958).

B. Murray, *The Old Firm: Sectarianism, Sport and Society in Scotland* (1984).

D. M. Murray, *Rebuilding the Kirk: Presbyterian Reunion in Scotland 1909–1929* (2000).

C. L. Rawlins, *William Barclay* (Exeter, 1984).

G. Walker and T. Gallagher (eds.), *Sermons and Battle Hymns: Protestant Popular Culture in Modern Scotland* (1990).

Episcopalian Community

M. Lochhead, *Episcopal Scotland in the Nineteenth Century* (London, 1966).

R. Strong, *Alexander Forbes of Brechin: The First Tractarian Bishop* (Oxford, 1995).

G. White, *The Scottish Episcopal Church: A New History* (1998).

Protestant Sects

D. W. Bebbington (ed.), *The Baptists in Scotland: A History* (Glasgow, 1988).

H. Escott, *A History of Scottish Congregationalism* (Glasgow, 1960).

J. G. Kellas, 'The Liberal Party and the Scottish Church Disestablishment Crisis', *EHR* 79 (1964).

Roman Catholic Community

(See also Section 9: Immigration.)

P. F. Anson, *The Catholic Church in Modern Scotland, 1560–1937* (London, 1937).

R. Boyle and P. Lynch (eds.), *Out of the Ghetto? The Catholic Community in Modern Scotland* (1998).

S. Bruce, *No Pope of Rome: anti-Catholicism in Modern Scotland* (1985).

T. M. Devine (ed.), *St Mary's Hamilton: a Social History, 1846–1996* (1995).

——*Scotland's Shame: Bigotry and Sectarianism in Modern Scotland* (2000).

T. Gallagher, *Glasgow: The Uneasy Peace. Religious Tension in Modern Scotland* (Manchester, 1987).

C. Johnson, *Developments in the Roman Catholic Church in Scotland, 1789–1829* (1983).

D. McRoberts (ed.), *Modern Scottish Catholicism, 1878–1978* (Glasgow, 1979).

J. Watts, *Scalan: the Forbidden College, 1716–1799* (East Linton, 1999).

Temperance

E. King, *Scotland Sober and Free: The Temperance Movement* (Glasgow, 1979).

M. Lysaght, *Fr Theobald Mathew* (Dublin, 1983).

W. Logan, *The Early Heroes of the Temperance Reformation* (Glasgow, 1873).

N. Longmate, *The Waterdrinkers: A History of Temperance* (London, 1968).

8. Families

No attempt is made here to give a comprehensive guide to family history. It aims to indicate further reading on the important families discussed in the volume. See also Section 3 for works on the nobility and Section 12 for Highland clans.

The Balliol family

W. Greenwell, *A History of the County of Northumberland* (Northumberland County History Committee, vol. 6, 1902).

G. Stell, 'The Balliol Family and the Great Cause of 1291–1292', in K. Stringer (ed.), *Essays on the Nobility of Medieval Scotland* (1985).

The Campbells

S. Boardman, *Clan Campbell* (East Linton, 2001).

A. Campbell, *A History of Clan Campbell*, i. *From Origins to Flodden* (2000).

E. Cregeen, 'The Changing Role of the House of Argyll in the Scottish Highlands', in N. Phillipson and R. Mitchison (eds.), *Scotland in the Age of the Improvement* (1970).

The Comyn family

A. Grant and K. J. Stringer (eds.), *Medieval Scotland: Crown, Lordship and Community* (1993).

A. Young, *Robert the Bruce's Rivals: The Comyns 1212–1314* (East Linton, 1997).

—— *William Cumin: Border Politics and the Bishopric of Durham 1141–1144* (York, 1978).

The Douglases

M. Brown, *The Black Douglases: War and Lordship in Late Medieval Scotland, 1300–1455* (East Linton, 1999).

C. A. McGladdery, *James II* (1990).

The Hamiltons

E. Finnie, 'The House of Hamilton: Patronage, Politics and the Church in the Reformation Period', *Innes Review*, 36 (1985).

G. Hamilton, *A History of the House of Hamilton* (1933).

9. Population Patterns

Scotland's general population patterns were not, in general, dissimilar to those in most of northern Europe for much of known history. The effects of the Black Death in the 14th century are unquantifiable, as are those of most of the epidemics which were a feature of the 16th and early 17th centuries. Scotland nevertheless experienced a general growth in population in what is sometimes called the 'long 16th century', between 1500 and c.1650. This was followed, as elsewhere in northern Europe, by a certain contraction in the second half of the 17th century. A severe crisis hit parts of Scotland in the 1690s; its effects in the north-east lingered for two generations. Much of the 18th century was marked by a slow but steady rise in population. This was followed by a sharp rise in the period after 1810, exaggerated in the cities and industrial areas of the central belt by both immigration and internal migration. From then on, if not before, much of Scotland's history was indelibly marked by the rival patterns of immigration, migration, and emigration. The 1920s, when emigration outpaced other factors, was the first decade in modern times in which Scotland's population fell.

Demography

M. Anderson and D. J. Morse, 'The People', in W. H. Fraser and R. J. Morris (eds.), *People and Society in Scotland*, 2. *1830–1914* (1990).

M. W. Flinn (ed.), *Scottish Population History from the 17th Century to the 1930s* (Cambridge, 1977).

R. A. Houston, *The Population History of Britain and Ireland, 1500–1750* (London, 1992).

R. E. Tyson, 'Contrasting Regimes: Population Growth in Ireland and Scotland in the 18th Century', in S. J. Connolly et al. (eds.), *Conflict, Identity and Economic Development: Ireland and Scotland, 1600–1939* (Preston, 1995).

Emigration: General

(See also Sections 12 and 14.)

R. A. Cage (ed.), *The Scots Abroad: Labour, Capital, Enterprise, 1750–1914* (London, 1985).

T. M. Devine (ed.), *Scottish Emigration and Scottish Society* (1992).

M. Gray, *Scots on the Move: Scots Migrants 1750–1914* (1990).

T. C. Smout et al., 'Scottish Emigration in the 17th and 18th centuries', in N. Canny (ed.), *Europeans on the Move: Studies on European Migration, 1500–1800* (Oxford, 1994).

Emigration to Europe and Ireland

I. G. Anderson, *Scotsmen in the Service of the Czars* (1990).

J. Davidson and A. Gray, *The Scottish Staple at Veere* (London, 1909).

J. Durkan, 'The French Connection in the 16th and early 17th Centuries', in T. C. Smout (ed.), *Scotland and Europe, 1200–1850* (1986).

T. A. Fischer, *The Scots in Germany* (1902).

M. Perceval-Maxwell, *The Scottish Migration to Ulster in the Reign of James I* (London, 1973).

G. G. Simpson (ed.), *Scotland and the Low Countries 1124–1994* (East Linton, 1996).

Migration

J. M. Brock, *The Mobile Scot: A Study of Scottish Emigration and Migration, 1861–1911* (1998).

T. M. Devine, 'Highland Migration to Lowland Scotland', *SHR* 62 (1983).

—— (ed.), *Farm Servants and Labour in Lowland Scotland, 1770–1914* (1984).

R. A. Houston and I. D. Whyte (eds.), *Scottish Society, 1500–1800* (Cambridge, 1989).

D. F. MacDonald, *Scotland's Shifting Population* (Glasgow, 1937).

C. W. J. Withers, *Urban Highlanders: Highland–Lowland Migration and Urban Gaelic Culture, 1700–1900* (East Linton, 1998).

Immigration, Irish

(See also Section 14: Ireland.)

T. M. Devine (ed.), *Irish Immigrants in Scottish Society in the Nineteenth and Twentieth Centuries* (1991).

T. Gallagher, *Glasgow: The Uneasy Peace* (Manchester, 1987).

J. E. Handley, *The Irish In Modern Scotland* (Oxford, 1947).

—— *The Irish in Scotland, 1798–1845* (Cork, 1943).

M. J. Mitchell, *The Irish in the West of Scotland, 1797–1848: Trade Unions, Strikes and Political Movements* (1998).

10. Physical Environment, Settlement, and Material Culture

The importance of climate, geology, natural history, and environment has been recognized by Scottish 'mainstream' historians only comparatively recently. There has been, on the other hand, long been a sustained interest in various aspects of rural and urban settlement.

Physical Structure and Environment

M. L. Anderson, *A History of Scottish Forestry* (1967).

W. J. Baird, *The Scenery of Scotland: The Structure Beneath* (1991).

K. J. Edwards, *Scotland: Environment and Archaeology 8000 BC–AD 1000* (Chichester, 1997).

J. M. Gilbert, *Hunting and Hunting Reserves in Medieval Scotland* (1979).

H. H. Lamb, *Climate Present, Past and Future*, 2 vols. (London, 1977).

J. R. Price, *Scotland's Environment during the last 30,000 Years* (1983).

J. B. Sissons, *The Evolution of Scotland's Scenery* (1967).

—— *The Geomorphology of the British Isles: Scotland* (London, 1976).

T. C. Smout, *Nature Contested: Environmental History in Scotland and Northern Ireland since 1600* (2000).

—— (ed.), *Scotland since Prehistory: Natural Change and Human Impact* (Aberdeen, 1993).

J. B. Whittow, *Geology and Scenery in Scotland* (London, 1977).

I. and K. Whyte, *Exploring Scotland's Historic Landscapes* (1987).

Rural Settlement

(See also Section 6: Rural Society.)

J. A. Atkinson et al. (eds.), *Medieval and Post-Medieval Settlement in Britain* (Oxford, 2000).

R. A. Dodgshon, *Land and Society in Early Scotland* (Oxford, 1981).

J. G. Dunbar, 'The Study of Deserted Medieval Settlements in Scotland (to 1968), ii. The Peasant-House', in M. Beresford and J. G. Hurst (eds.), *Deserted Medieval Villages* (Woking, 1971).

H. Fairhurst, 'The Archaeology of Rural Settlement in Scotland', *Transactions of Glasgow Archaeological Society*, 15 (1967).

C. Sinclair, *The Thatched Houses of the Old Highlands* (1953).

I. D. and K. A. Whyte, *The Changing Scottish Landscape 1500–1800* (Routledge, 1991).

Urban Settlement

(See also Section 6: Urban Life.)

E. P. Dennison, *Conservation and Change in Historic Towns* (York, 1999).

J. G. Dunbar, *The Historic Architecture of Scotland* (London, 1966).

M. Glendinning (ed.), *Rebuilding Scotland: the Postwar Vision, 1945–1975* (East Linton, 1997).

C. McWilliam, *Scottish Townscape* (London, 1975).

D. Mays (ed.), *The Architecture of Scottish Cities* (East Linton, 1997).

P. Reed, *Glasgow: The Forming of the City* (1993).

J. S. Smith (ed.), *New Light on Medieval Aberdeen* (Aberdeen, 1985).

G. Stell, 'Urban Buildings', in M. Lynch et al. (eds.), *The Scottish Medieval Town* (1988).

Guide to Further Reading

A. J. Youngson, *The Making of Classical Edinburgh* (1966).

Housing

Housing in Scotland was distinctive, from the 'black house' in the Highlands to the urban tenement or country seat. In architecture, Scotland typically also adapted various foreign influences into a distinctively 'Scottish' style. The issue of housing figured prominently in Scottish politics from the 1880s onwards. (See also Section 6: Material Conditions and the Quality of Life.)

A. Carruthers (ed.), *The Scottish Home* (1996).

J. T. Coppock, *An Agricultural Atlas of Scotland* (1976).

T. M. Devine, *The Transformation of Rural Scotland: Social Change and the Agrarian Economy, 1660–1815* (1994).

J. G. Dunbar, *The Historic Architecture of Scotland* (London, 1966).

A. Fenton, *The Island Blackhouse* (1978).

—— and B. Walker, *The Rural Architecture of Scotland* (1981).

J. Gifford et al., *The Buildings of Scotland* (1984).

I. Gow and A. Rowan (eds.), *Scottish Country Houses, 1600–1914* (1995).

Report of the Royal Commission on the Housing of the Industrial Population (Ballantyne Commission, 1917).

J. M. Robinson, *The Latest Country Houses* (London, 1984).

Scottish Housing Advisory Committee, *Planning our New Homes* (1944).

Scottish Office, *Scottish Housing: A Consultative Document* (1977).

I. D. Whyte, 'Rural Housing in Lowland Scotland in the Seventeenth Century', *Scottish Studies*, 19 (1975).

Buildings: Churches

(See also Section 7.)

A. L. Drummond, *Church Architecture of Protestantism* (1934).

R. Fawcett, *Scottish Medieval Churches* (1988).

G. Hay, *The Architecture of Scottish Post-Reformation Churches, 1560–1843* (Oxford, 1957).

D. MacGibbon and T. Ross, *The Ecclesiastical Architecture of Scotland*, 3 vols. (1896–7).

Buildings: Civic and Administrative

J. Cameron, *Prisons and Punishment in Scotland* (1983).

C. Cunningham, *Victorian and Edwardian Town Halls* (London, 1981).

RCAHMS, *Tolbooths and Town-Houses: Civic Architecture in Scotland to 1833* (1996).

Buildings: Industrial and Commercial

J. R. Hume, *The Industrial Archaeology of Glasgow* (Glasgow, 1974).

—— *The Industrial Archaeology of Scotland*, 2 vols. (London, 1976–7).

P. L. Payne, *The Hydro: A Study of the Development of the Major Hydro-Electric Schemes undertaken by the North of Scotland Hydro Board* (Aberdeen, 1988).

Buildings: Military and Defensive

N. Ruckley, 'Public Defences of Scotland', in J. Shaw and G. Stell (eds.), *Compendium of Scottish Ethnology: Buildings in Scotland* (2000).

A. Saunders, *Fortress Britain: Artillery Fortification in the British Isles and Ireland* (Beaufort, 1989).

G. Stell, 'Late Medieval Defences in Scotland', in D. Caldwell (ed.), *Scottish Weapons and Fortifications* (1981).

C. Tabraham and D. Grove, *Fortress Scotland and the Jacobites* (London, 1995).

Architecture

J. G. Dunbar, *The Historic Architecture of Scotland* (London, 1966).

R. Fawcett, *Scottish Architecture from the Accession of the Stewarts to the Reformation, 1371–1560* (1994).

J. Gifford, *The Architecture of William Adam* (1989).

M. Glendinning et al., *A History of Scottish Architecture* (1996).

I. Gow, *The Scottish Interior* (1992).

D. Howard, *Scottish Architecture from the Reformation to the Renaissance, 1560–1660* (1994).

D. McGibbon and T. Ross, *The Castellated and Domestic Architecture of Scotland*, 5 vols. (1887–92).

R. Macinnes et al., *Building a Nation: The Story of Scotland's Architecture* (1999).

C. McKean, *Architectural Contributions to Scottish Society, 1840–1990* (1990).

F. Sinclair, *Scotstyle* (1984).

P. Willis, *New Architecture in Scotland* (London, 1977).

Building Materials and Techniques

B. Walker et al., *Thatch and Thatching Techniques: A Guide to Conserving Scottish Thatching Traditions* (Edinburgh 1996).

—— et al., *Earth Structures and Construction in Scotland: A Guide to the Recognition and Conservation of Earth Technology in Scottish Buildings* (1996).

11. Places

No attempt has been made to suggest further reading for a comprehensive list of places or localities. What follows is an indication of some useful works, mostly on some of the places important in Scotland's early history which feature prominently in the volume. For major towns, see Section 6: Urban Society and Section 10: Urban Settlement. See also Section 3: Regional and Local Identity, for the Borders and Orkney and Shetland.

Place-Names

W. F. H. Nicolaisen, *Scottish Place-Names* (2nd edn., London, 1979).

J. Spittall and J. Field, *A Reader's Guide to the Place-Names of the United Kingdom, 1920–1989* (Stamford, 1990).

S. S. Taylor (ed.), *The Uses of Place-Names* (1998).

W. J. Watson, *The History of the Celtic Place-Names of Scotland* (1926).

Birsay

C. L. Curle, *The Pictish and Norse Finds from the Brough of Birsay, 1934–1974* (1982).

J. R. Hunter, *Rescue Excavations on the Brough of Birsay, 1974–82* (1986).

C. D. Morris, 'The Birsay Bay Project: A Resumé', in C. Batey et al. (eds.), *The Viking Age in Caithness, Orkney and the North Atlantic* (1993).

Orkney Heritage, 2 (1983).

C. A. Ralegh Radford, *The Early Christian and Norse Settlements at Birsay* (Official guide, Edinburgh, 1959).

Burghead

K. J. Edwards and I. Ralston, 'New Dating and Environmental Evidence from Burghead', *PSAS* 109 (1977–8).

A. Small, 'Burghead', *Scottish Archaeological Forum*, 1 (1969).

Dunadd
E. Campbell, *Sea-Kings and Saints: The Early Kingdom of the Scots* (1999).
—— and A. Lane, *Excavations at Dunadd: An Early Dalriadic Capital* (Oxford, 2000).

Dundurn
L. Alcock et al., 'Reconnaissance Excavations on Early Historic Fortifications and Other Royal Sites in Scotland, 1974–1984: 3. Excavations at Dundurn, Strathearn, Perthshire, 1976–1977', *PSAS* 119 (1989).

Forteviot/Scone
S. Airlie, 'The View from Maastricht', in B. E. Crawford (ed.), *Scotland in Dark Age Europe* (St Andrews, 1994).
D. Breeze et al. (eds.), *The Stone of Destiny* (2001).

Galloway
R. D. Oram and G. P. Stell (eds.), *Galloway: Land and Lordship* (1991).

Govan
S. Driscoll, 'Church Archaeology in Glasgow and the Kingdom of Strathclyde', *Innes Review*, 49 (1998).
A. Ritchie (ed.), *Govan and its Early Medieval Sculpture* (Stroud, 1994).

Iona
C. Bourke (ed.), *Studies in the Cult of Saint Columba* (Dublin, 1997).
T. Clancy, *Iona: The Earliest Poetry of a Celtic Monastery* (1995).
M. MacArthur, *Columba's Island: Iona from Past to Present* (1995).
RCAHMS, *Argyll: An Inventory of the Monuments, 4. Iona* (1982).
A. Ritchie, *Iona* (London, 1997).

Moray
G. W. S. Barrow, 'Macbeth and Other Mormaers of Moray', in L. MacLean (ed.), *The Hub of the Highlands: the Book of Inverness and District* (Inverness, 1975).
W. D. H. Sellar (ed.), *Moray: Province and People* (1993).

St Andrews
N. P. Brooks and G. Whittington, 'Planning and Growth in the Medieval Scottish Burgh: The Example of St Andrews', *Transactions of the Institute of British Geographers* 34 (1977).
D. McRoberts (ed.), *The Medieval Church of St Andrews* (Glasgow, 1976).

Tarbat
Bulletin of the Tarbat Discovery Programme, 1–3 (University of York, 1995–7).
M. O. H. Carver, 'Conversion and Politics on the Eastern Seaboard of Britain: Some Archaeological Indicators', in B. E. Crawford (ed.), *Conversion in the North Sea Area* (St Andrews, 2000).

Whithorn
D. Brooke, *Wild Men and Holy Places: St Ninian, Whithorn and the Medieval Realm of Galloway* (1994).
P. Hill, *Whithorn and St Ninian* (Stroud, 1997).

Places outside Scotland

Darien
F. Cundall, *The Darien Venture* (New York, 1926).
F. R. Hart, *The Disaster of Darien* (London, 1930).
G. P. Insh (ed.), *Papers relating to the Ships and Voyages of the Company of Scotland trading to Africa and the Indies, 1696–1707* (SHS, 1924).
J. Prebble, *The Darien Disaster* (London, 1968).

Lindisfarne
G. Bonner et al. (eds.), *St Cuthbert, his Cult and his Community to A.D. 1200* (Woodbridge, 1989).
D. O'Sullivan and R. Young, *English Heritage Book of Lindisfarne, Holy Island* (London, 1995).

12. Highlands and Islands

The volume of literature on various aspects of the history of the Highlands and Western Isles is formidable in its volume. In the *Companion*, that history is treated separately only if it is distinctively different from that for the rest of Scotland. That distinction should also be borne in mind in the reading suggested here. (See also Section 6: Languages of Scotland: Gaelic; Dress; Section 8; Section 9: Emigration; Section 13: Gaelic Literature; Section 14: Canada; USA; and Section 15.)

General
W. Donaldson, *The Highland Pipe and Scottish Society, 1750–1950* (East Linton, 1999).
I. F. Grant and H. Cheape, *Periods in Highland History* (London, 1987).
D. M. Henderson, *Highland Soldier: A Social Study of the Highland Regiments, 1820–1920* (1989).
J. Macinnes, *The Evangelical Movement in the Highlands of Scotland, 1688 to 1800* (Aberdeen, 1951).
R. W. Munro, *Highland Clans and Tartans* (London, 1977).
D. S. Thomson (ed.), *The Companion to Gaelic Scotland* (Oxford, 1983).
C. W. J. Withers, *Gaelic in Scotland, 1698–1981: The Geographical History of a Language* (1984).
—— *Gaelic Scotland: The Transformation of a Culture Region* (London, 1988).

Medieval Kingdoms and Lordships
J. Bannerman, 'The Lordship of the Isles', in J. M. Brown (ed.), *Scottish Society in the Fifteenth Century* (London, 1977).
R. A. MacDonald, *The Kingdom of the Isles: Scotland's Western Seaboard in the Central Middle Ages, c.1100–c.1336* (East Linton, 1998).
L. Maclean (ed.), *The Middle Ages in the Highlands* (Inverness, 1981).
J. and R. W. Munro (eds.), *Acts of the Lords of the Isles, 1336–1493* (SHS, 1986).
R. Nicholson, *Scotland: The Later Middle Ages* (1974).

Highlands and Islands and Central Government to 1750
(See also Section 3: Early Modern.)
J. Goodare and M. Lynch (eds.), *The Reign of James VI* (East Linton, 2000).
P. Hopkins, *Glencoe and the End of the Highland War* (1986).
A. I. Macinnes, *Clanship, Commerce and the House of Stuart, 1603–1788* (East Linton, 1996).
L. Maclean (ed.), *The Seventeenth Century in the Highlands* (Inverness, 1986).

Guide to Further Reading

A. Smith, *Jacobite Estates of the Forty-Five* (1982).

D. Stevenson, *Alasdair MacColla and the Highland Problem in the Seventeenth Century* (1980).

Highlands and Islands and Central Government since 1750

E. A. Cameron, *Land for the People? The British Government and the Scottish Highlands, c.1880–1925* (East Linton, 1996).

J. P. Day, *Public Administration in the Highlands and Islands of Scotland* (London, 1918).

T. M. Devine, *The Great Highland Famine: Hunger, Emigration and the Scottish Highlands in the Nineteenth Century* (1988).

L. Leneman, *Land fit for Heroes? Land Settlement in Scotland after World War One* (Aberdeen, 1989).

Economy and Society

R. D. Clyde, *From Rebel to Hero: The Image of the Scottish Highlander 1745–1830* (East Linton, 1995).

T. M. Devine, *From Clanship to Crofters War* (1994).

—— *The Great Highland Famine: Hunger, Emigration and the Scottish Highlands in the Nineteenth Century* (1988).

I. F. Grant, *Highland Folk Ways* (London, 1961).

M. Gray, *The Highland Economy, 1750–1850* (1957).

J. Hunter, *The Making of the Crofting Community* (new edn., 2000).

A. I. Macinnes, *Clanship, Commerce and the House of Stuart, 1603–1788* (East Linton, 1996).

P. L. Payne, *The Hydro* (Aberdeen, 1988).

F. J. Shaw, *The Northern and Western Islands of Scotland: Their Economy and Society in the Seventeenth Century* (1980).

I. D. Whyte, *Scotland before the Industrial Revolution: An Economic and Social History, c.1050–c.1750* (London, 1995).

A. J. Youngson, *After the Forty-Five: The Economic Impact on the Scottish Highlands* (1973).

Land and Landownership

E. A. Cameron, *Land for the People? The British Government and the Scottish Highlands, c.1880–1925* (East Linton, 1996).

J. Hunter, *The Making of the Crofting Community* (new edn., 2000).

—— *The Claim of Crofting: The Scottish Highlands and Islands, 1930–1990* (1991).

I. M. M. MacPhail, *The Crofters War* (Stornoway, 1989).

I. J. M. Robertson, 'Governing the Highlands: The Place of Popular Protest in the Highlands of Scotland after 1918', *Rural History*, 8 (1997).

A. Wightman, *Who Owns Scotland* (1996).

Clearances, Migration, and Emigration

(See also Section 9: Population Patterns; Section 14.)

J. M. Bumsted, *The People's Clearance 1770–1815: Highland Emigration to British North America* (1982).

T. M. Devine, *The Great Highland Famine: Hunger, Emigration and the Scottish Highlands in the Nineteenth Century* (1988).

K. Fenyö, *Contempt, Sympathy and Romance: Lowland Perceptions of the Highlands and the Clearances during the Famine Years, 1845–1855* (East Linton, 1999).

J. Hunter, *A Dance called America: The Scottish Highlands, the United States and Canada* (1994).

—— *The Making of the Crofting Community* (new edn., 2000).

M. MacLean, *The People of Glengarry: Highlanders in Transition, 1745–1820* (Montreal, 1991).

J. Prebble, *The Highland Clearances* (Harmondsworth, 1963).

E. Richards, *A History of the Highland Clearances*, 2 vols. (London, 1982, 1985).

C. W. J. Withers, *Urban Highlanders: Highland Lowland Migration and Urban Gaelic Culture, 1700–1900* (East Linton, 1998).

13. Culture

The guide to reading is organized, as are the Culture entries in the volume, in broad periods. In addition, initial reading in certain cultural areas such as art, literature, music, and song is appended.

General

(See also Section 6: Languages of Scotland, Schools and Schooling, Leisure and Sport; Section 10: Architecture.)

E. J. Cowan (ed.), *The People's Past* (1980).

C. Craig (ed.), *The History of Scottish Literature*, 4 vols. (Aberdeen, 1987–8).

D. Daiches (ed.), *The New Companion to Scottish Culture* (rev. edn., 1993).

P. H. Scott (ed.), *Scotland: A Concise Cultural History* (1994).

D. S. Thomson (ed.), *The Companion to Gaelic Scotland* (Oxford, 1983).

Prehistoric Scotland and Picto-Celtic

K. J. Edwards and I. B. M. Ralston, *Scotland: Environment and Archaeology, 8000 BC–AD 1000* (Chichester, 1997).

S. M. Foster, *Picts, Gaels and Scots* (London, 1996).

I. Henderson, *The Picts* (London, 1967).

E. H. Nicoll, *A Pictish Panorama* (Balgavies, Angus, 1995).

Medieval, Renaissance, and Reformation

(See also Section 4: Kingship.)

A. Broadie, *The Circle of John Mair: Logic and Logicians in Pre-Reformation Scotland* (Oxford, 1985).

—— *The Shadow of Scotus: Philosophy and Faith in Pre-Reformation Scotland* (1995).

—— *The Tradition of Scottish Philosophy* (1990).

A. Cherry, *Princes, Poets and Patrons: The Stuarts and Scotland* (1987).

C. Edington, *Court and Culture in Renaissance Scotland* (1985).

L. O. Fradenburg, *City, Marriage, Tournament: Arts of Rule in Late Medieval Scotland* (Wisconsin, 1991).

R. D. S. Jack (ed.), *The History of Scottish Literature*, i. *Origins to 1660* (Aberdeen, 1988).

G. Kratzmann, *Anglo-Scots Literary Relations, 1430–1550* (Cambridge, 1980).

J. MacQueen (ed.), *Humanism in Renaissance Scotland* (1990).

S. Mapstone and J. Wood (eds.), *The Rose and the Thistle: Essays on the Culture of Late Medieval and Renaissance Scotland* (East Linton, 1998).

R. Mason, *Kingship and Commonweal: Political Thought in Renaissance and Reformation Scotland* (East Linton, 1998).

A. G. Medwin and J. H. Williams (eds.), *A Day Estivall: Essays on the Music, Poetry and History of Scotland and England* (Aberdeen, 1990).

National Museum of Antiquities of Scotland, *Angels,*

Nobles and Unicorns: Art and Patronage in Medieval Scotland (1982).

H. M. Shire, *Song, Dance and Poetry at the Court of Scotland under King James VI* (Cambridge, 1969).

J. H. Williams (ed.), *Stewart Style, 1513–1542: Essays on the Court of James V* (East Linton, 1996).

Enlightenment (1660–1843)

D. Allan, *Virtue, Learning and the Scottish Enlightenment* (1993).

R. H. Campbell and A. S. Skinner (eds.), *The Origins and Nature of the Scottish Enlightenment* (1982).

A. Chitnis, *The Scottish Enlightenment: A Social History* (London, 1976).

D. Craig, *Scottish Literature and the Scottish People, 1680–1830* (London, 1961).

R. Crawford (ed.), *Robert Burns and Cultural Authority* (1997).

D. Daiches, *The Paradox of Scottish Culture: The Eighteenth Century Experience* (Oxford, 1964).

—— *Sir Walter Scott and his World* (London, 1971).

—— et al. (eds.), *A Hotbed of Genius: The Scottish Enlightenment, 1730–1790* (1986).

A. Hook (ed.), *The History of Scottish Literature, 2. 1660–1800* (Aberdeen, 1987).

V. Hope (ed.), *Philosophers of the Scottish Enlightenment* (1984).

R. A. Houston, *Scottish Literacy and the Scottish Identity, 1600–1800* (Cambridge, 1985).

—— *Social Change in the Age of Enlightenment: Edinburgh, 1660–1760* (Oxford, 1994).

C. Kidd, *Subverting Scotland's Past: Scottish Whig Historians and the Creation of an Anglo-British Identity, 1760–1830* (Cambridge, 1993).

G. MacMaster, *Scott and Society* (Cambridge, 1982).

D. Macmillan, *Painting in Scotland: The Golden Age, 1707–1843* (Oxford, 1986).

J. MacQueen, *Progress and Poetry: The Enlightenment and Scottish Literature* (1982).

J. Rendall, *The Origins of the Scottish Enlightenment, 1707–1776* (London, 1978).

K. Simpson, *The Protean Scot: The Crisis of Identity in Eighteenth Century Scottish Literature* (Aberdeen, 1988).

Age of Industry (1843–1914)

R. D. Anderson, *Education and Opportunity in Victorian Scotland* (rev. edn., 1989).

—— *Education and the Scottish People 1750–1918* (Oxford, 1995).

M. Ash, *The Strange Death of Scottish History* (1980).

J. Calder (ed.), *Stevenson and Victorian Scotland* (1980).

I. Campbell, *Kailyard: A New Assessment* (London, 1981).

—— *Nineteenth Century Scottish Fiction* (Manchester, 1979).

A. C. Cheyne, *The Transforming of the Kirk* (1983).

A. G. Clement and R. H. S. Robertson, *Scotland's Scientific Heritage* (1961).

J. G. Crowther, *Scientists of the Industrial Revolution* (London, 1961).

—— *British Scientists of the Nineteenth Century* (London, 1935).

G. E. Davie, *The Democratic Intellect: Scotland and her Universities in the Nineteenth Century* (1961; 2nd edn., 1981).

W. Donaldson, *Popular Literature in Victorian Scotland* (Aberdeen, 1986).

D. Gifford (ed.), *The History of Scottish Literature*, iii. *The Nineteenth Century* (Aberdeen, 1988).

J. D. Hoveler, *James McCosh and the Scottish Intellectual Tradition* (Princeton, 1981).

W. M. Humes and H. M. Paterson (eds.), *Scottish Culture and Scottish Education, 1800–1980* (1983).

H. I. Sharlin, *Lord Kelvin: the Dynamic Victorian* (Penn., 1979).

Modern (1914–1990s)

N. Ascherson, *Games with Shadows* (1988).

C. Beveridge and R. Turnbull, *The Eclipse of Scottish Culture: Inferiorism and the Intellectuals* (1989).

F. Bruce, *Scottish Showbusiness: Music Hall, Variety and Pantomine* (2000).

A. Cameron, *A Study Guide to Twentieth Century Scottish Theatre and Drama* (Glasgow, 1989).

C. Craig (ed.), *The History of Scottish Literature, 4. The Twentieth Century* (Aberdeen, 1990).

—— *The Modern Scottish Novel* (1999).

G. Davie, *The Crisis of the Democratic Intellect: The Problem of Generalisation and Specialisation in Twentieth Century Scotland* (1986).

T. Gallagher (ed.), *Nationalism in the Nineties* (1991).

D. Hutchison, *Modern Scottish Theatre* (Glasgow, 1977).

D. McCrone et al. (eds.), *The Making of Scotland: Nation, Culture and Social Change* (1989).

W. H. McDowell, *The History of BBC Broadcasting in Scotland, 1923–1983* (1992).

E. Muir, *Scottish Journey* (1979).

M. Smith, *Paper Lions* (1994).

R. Stevenson (ed.), *Scottish Theatre since the Seventies* (1996).

G. Walker and T. Gallagher (eds.), *Sermons and Battle Hymns: Protestant Popular Culture in Modern Scotland* (1990).

Art

K. Hartley (ed.), *Scottish Art since 1900* (1991).

D. and F. Irwin, *Scottish Painters at Home and Abroad, 1700–1900* (London, 1975).

G. and C. Larner, *The Glasgow Style* (1979).

M. MacDonald, *Scottish Art* (London, 2000).

D. Macmillan, *Scottish Art, 1460–2000* (1999).

Art and Crafts: General

M. Apted, *The Painted Ceilings of Scotland* (1966).

L. Butler (ed.), *Scotland's Crafts* (2000).

E. Cumming, *Arts and Crafts in Edinburgh* (1985).

I. Finlay, *Scottish Crafts* (London, 1948).

W. Kaplan, *Scotland Creates: 5,000 Years of Art and Design* (Glasgow, 1990).

Metalwork: Gold and Silver

G. Dalgleish and S. Maxwell, *The Loveable Craft: Edinburgh Incorporation of Goldsmiths, 1687–1987* (1987).

I. Finlay, *Scottish Gold and Silver Work* (Stevenage, 1991).

G. P. Moss and A. D. Roe, *Highland Gold and Silversmiths* (1999).

Illuminated Manuscripts

J. J. G. Alexander, *Insular Manuscripts 6th to the 9th Century: A Survey of Manuscripts Illuminated in the British Isles* (London, 1978).

R. Fawcett (ed.), *Medieval Art and Architecture in the Diocese of Glasgow* (Leeds, 1998).

J. Higgitt, *The Murthly Hours: Devotion, Literacy and Luxury in Paris, England and the Gaelic West* (London, 2000).

—— 'Decoration and Illustration', in *Scotichronicon by Walter Bower*, ed. D. E. R. Watt (1998).

D. McRoberts (ed.), *Catalogue of Scottish Medieval Liturgical Books and Fragments* (Glasgow, 1953).

Heraldry

Sir Thomas Innes of Learney, *Scots Heraldry* (2nd edn., 1956).

J. B. Paul, *Heraldry in Relation to Scottish History and Art* (1900).

J. H. Stevenson, *Heraldry in Scotland*, 2 vols. (Glasgow, 1914).

Photography

D. Brittain and S. Stevenson, *New Scottish Photography: A Critical Review of the Work of Seventeen Photographers* (1990).

S. Stevenson, *David Octavius Hill and Robert Adamson* (1981).

—— and A. D. Morrison-Low, *Scottish Photography: A Bibliography, 1839–1989* (1990).

Film

(See also Section 17.)

D. Atwell, *Cathedrals of the Movies* (London, 1980).

D. Bruce, *Scotland the Movie* (1996).

E. Dick (ed.), *From Limelight to Satellite: A Scottish Film Book* (London, 1990).

F. Hardy, *Scotland on Film* (1990).

A. Martin, *Going to the Pictures* (2000).

M. Thomson, *Silver Screen in the Silver City: A History of Cinema in Aberdeen, 1896–1987* (Aberdeen, 1988).

Gardening and Landscape

T. Buxbaum, *Scottish Garden Buildings: From Food to Folly* (1989).

Countryside Commission for Scotland and the Historic Buildings and Monuments Directorate of the Scottish Development Department, *An Inventory of Gardens and Designed Landscapes in Scotland*, 5 vols. (HMSO, 1987).

J. Holloway and L. Erington, *The Discovery of Scotland* (1978).

F. W. Robertson, *Early Scottish Gardeners and their Plants, 1650–1750* (East Linton, 2000).

A. R. Somerville, 'The Ancient Sundials of Scotland', *PSAS* 117 (1987).

A. A. Tait, *The Landscape Garden in Scotland 1735–1835* (1980).

H. I. Triggs, *Formal Gardens in England and Scotland* (London, 1902).

Literature

W. R. Aitken, *Scottish Literature in English and Scots. A Guide to Information Sources* (Detroit, 1982).

C. Craig (ed.), *The History of Scottish Literature*, 4 vols. (Aberdeen, 1987–8).

T. Crawford, *Society and the Lyric* (1979).

D. Daiches, *Literature and Gentility in Scotland* (1982).

D. Gifford, *Scottish Literature: A Study Guide* (2000).

J. MacQueen, *The Rise of the Historical Novel* (1989).

T. Royle (ed.), *The Mainstream Companion to Scottish Literature* (1993).

R. Watson, *The Literature of Scotland* (London, 1984).

—— (ed.), *The Poetry of Scotland: Gaelic, Scots and English, 1380–1980* (1995).

Literature: Gaelic

M. Chapman, *The Gaelic Vision in Scottish Culture* (London, 1978).

W. Gillies (ed.), *Gaelic in Scotland: Alba agus a' Ghàidhlig* (1989).

K. MacKinnon, *Gaelic: a Past and Future Prospect* (1991).

D. S. Thomson, *An Introduction to Gaelic Poetry* (1989).

—— *The New Verse in Scottish Gaelic: A Structural Analysis* (Dublin, 1974).

Libraries, Bookselling, and Printing

W. R. Aitken, *A History of the Public Library Movement in Scotland to 1955* (Glasgow, 1971).

R. Dickson and J. P. Edmond, *Annals of Scottish Printing* (Cambridge, 1890; repr. Amsterdam, 1975).

J. Durkan and A. Ross (eds.), *Early Scottish Libraries* (Glasgow, 1961).

J. Feather, *A History of British Book Publishing* (Kent, 1988).

Imprints in Time: A History of Scottish Publishers Past and Present (1991).

T. Kelly, *Early Public Libraries: A History of Public Libraries in Great Britain before 1850* (1960).

A. J. Mann, *The Scottish Book Trade 1500 to 1720: Print Commerce and Print Control in Early Modern Scotland* (East Linton, 2000).

Music

F. Collinson, *The Traditional and National Music of Scotland* (London, 1966).

W. Donaldson, *The Highland Pipe and Scottish Society, 1750–1950* (East Linton, 1999).

J. Gibson, *Traditional Gaelic Bagpiping from 1745 to 1945* (1998).

D. Johnson, *Music and Society in Lowland Scotland in the Eighteenth Century* (London, 1972).

I. W. Preece 'Our awin Scottis Use': Music in the Scottish Church up to 1603* (Glasgow, 2000).

J. Purser, *Scotland's Music* (1992).

D. J. Ross, *Musick Fyne* (1993).

Song, Traditional and Folk

D. Buchan, *The Ballad and the Folk* (London, 1972).

—— (ed.), *The Scottish Ballad Book* (London, 1973).

J. L. Campbell, *Highland Songs of the Forty-Five* (1933).

—— *Hebridean Folksongs* (Oxford, 1969).

T. Crawford, *Society and the Lyric* (1979).

A. Munro, *The Folk Music Revival in Scotland* (London, 1980).

L. Shepard, *The Broadside Ballad* (London, 1962).

14. Scottish Links

Remarkably little has been written within Scotland itself about the Scots in the Scottish diaspora. Some of the literature on the Scots in various parts of the globe, whether emigrants and settlers, soldiers, entrepreneurs, or travellers, is little known except to specialists.

General

(See also Section 4: Military: Mercenaries and Soldiers Abroad; Section 9: Emigration.)

M. Brander, *The Emigrant Scots* (London, 1982).

J. H. Burton, *The Scot Abroad*, 2 vols. (1864).

R. A. Cage, *The Scots Abroad: Labour, Capital, Enterprise 1750–1914* (London, 1985).

T. M. Devine (ed.), *Scottish Emigration and Scottish Society* (1992).

G. Donaldson, *The Scots Overseas* (1966).

J. Grant, *The Scottish Soldiers of Fortune: Their Adventures and Achievements in the Armies of Europe* (1890).

J. MacKenzie (ed.), *The Scots and Empire* (Manchester, 2000).

T. C. Smout (ed.), *Scotland and Europe, 1200–1850* (1986).

Africa

B. Filling and S. Stuart (eds.), *The End of a Regime: an Anthology of Scottish–South African Writing against Apartheid* (Aberdeen, 1991).

J. D. Hargreaves, *Aberdeenshire to Africa: Northeast Scots and British Overseas Expansion* (Aberdeen, 1991).

National Portrait Gallery, *David Livingstone and the Victorian Encounter with Africa* (London, 1996).

A. C. Ross, 'The Dutch Reformed Church of South Africa: a product of the Disruption?', in S. J. Brown and M. Fry (eds.), *Scotland in the Age of the Disruption* (1997).

—— 'The Kirk and Colonial Policy, 1864–1964,' in J. Kirk (ed.), *The Scottish Churches and the Union Parliament* (2000).

Australia

Australian Dictionary of Biography (Melbourne, 1966–).

K. Cardell and C. Cumming, 'Scotland's Three Tongues in Australia', *Scottish Studies*, 31 (1992–3).

C. Cumming, 'Scots Radicals in Port Phillip 1838–1851', *Australian Journal of Politics and History*, 37 (1991).

—— 'Scottish National Identity in an Australian Colony', *SHR* 72 (1993).

—— 'Scottish Criminals and Transportation to Australia, 1786–1852', *SESH* 4 (1984).

K. S. Inglis, *The Australian Colonists* (Melbourne, 1974).

J. G. Johnston, *The Truth: Letters Received from Emigrants to the Australian Colonies* (1839).

M. Kiddle, *Men of Yesterday: A Social History of the Western District of Victoria 1834–1890* (Melbourne, 1961).

D. S. Macmillan, *Scotland and Australia 1788–1850: Emigration, Commerce, and Investment* (Oxford, 1967).

E. B. Madgwick, *Immigration into Eastern Australia, 1788–1850* (Sydney, 1969).

P. O'Farrell, *The Irish in Australia* (Sydney, 1987).

M. D. Prentis, *The Scots in Australia: A Study of New South Wales, Victoria, and Queensland, 1788–1900* (Sydney, 1983).

E. Richards (ed.), *The Flinders History of South Australia: Social History* (Adelaide, 1986).

—— 'Highland Emigrants to South Australia in the 1850s', *Northern Scotland*, 5 (1982).

—— 'The Highland Scots of South Australia', *Journal of the Historical Society of South Australia*, 4 (1978).

—— 'Varieties of Scottish Emigrations in the 19th Century', *Historical Studies*, 21 (1985).

L. C. Robson, *The Convict Settlers of Australia* (Melbourne, 1976).

G. Serle, *The Golden Age. A History of the Colony of Victoria 1851–1861* (Melbourne, 1968).

G. Sherinton, *Australia's Immigrants* (Sydney, 1980).

D. Watson, *Caledonia Australis: Scottish Highlanders on the Frontier of Australia* (Sydney, 1984).

D. L. Waugh, *Three Years Practical Experience of a Settler in New South Wales* (1838).

Canada

(See also USA, below.)

M. Bennett, *The Last Stronghold: The Scottish Gaelic Traditions of Newfoundland* (1989).

J. M. Bumsted, *The People's Clearance: Highland Emigration to British North America, 1770–1815* (1982).

—— *The Scots in Canada* (Ottawa, 1982).

D. Campbell and R. A. MacLean, *Beyond the Atlantic Roar: A Study of the Nova Scotia Scots* (Ottawa, 1975).

H. I. Cowan, *British Emigration to British North America: The First Hundred Years* (rev. edn., Toronto, 1961).

L. V. Cox, 'Gaelic and the Schools in Cape Breton', *Nova Scotia Historical Review*, 14 (1994).

C. W. Dunn, *Highland Settler: A Portrait of the Scottish Gael in Nova Scotia* (Toronto, 1953).

J. M. Gibson, *The Scots in Canada* (Toronto, 1971).

M. Harper, *Emigration from North-East Scotland*, 2 vols. (Aberdeen, 1988).

D. Hill, *The Scots to Canada* (London, 1972).

N. MacDonald, *Canada: Immigration and Colonisation, 1841–1903* (Aberdeen, 1966).

S. MacDonald, 'Crofter Colonisation in Canada, 1886–1892: The Scottish Political Background', *Northern Scotland*, 8 (1986–7).

M. MacDonell, *The Emigrant Experience: Songs of Highland Emigrants in North America* (Toronto, 1982).

M. Mackay, 'Nineteenth Century Tiree Emigrant Communities in Ontario', *Oral History Journal*, 9 (1981).

M. Maclean, *The People of Glengarry: Highlanders in Transition, 1745–1820* (Montreal, 1991).

D. S. Macmillan, *Canadian Business History* (Toronto, 1972).

W. S. Reid (ed.), *The Scottish Tradition in Canada* (Toronto, 1976).

W. Sheppe, *First Man West: Alexander Mackenzie's Journal of his Voyage to the Pacific Coast of Canada in 1793* (Berkeley, 1962).

H. Smailes, *Scottish Empire* (1981).

J. D. Wood, 'Transatlantic Land Reform: America and the Crofters' Revolt, 1878–1888', *SHR* 63 (1984).

Central Europe

J. M. Bulloch, 'A Scoto-Austrian: John Gordon, the Assassinator of Wallenstein', *Transactions of the Banffshire Field Club* (1916–17).

T. A. Fischer, *The Scots in Germany* (1902).

K. H. Leslie, *Historical Records of the Family of Leslie*, 3 vols. (1869).

J. V. Polišensky, *Britain and Czechoslovakia* (Prague, 1968).

—— *The Thirty Years War* (London, 1971).

H. and C. Seton-Watson, *The Making of a New Europe: R. W. Seton-Watson and the Last Years of Austria-Hungary* (London, 1981).

East Asia

D. Campell, *Records of Clan Campbell in the Military Service of the Honourable East India Company, 1660–1858* (London, 1925).

G. Carnall and C. Nicholson (eds.), *The Impeachment of Warren Hastings* (1989).

P. Hallberg and C. Koninckx (eds.), *A Passage to China: Colin Campbell's Diary of the First Swedish East India Company Expedition to Canton 1732–33* (Gothenberg, 1996).

M. Keswick, *The Thistle and the Jade: A Celebration of 150 years of Jardine, Matheson & Co.* (London, 1882).

S. Leiper, *Precious Cargo: Scots and the China Trade* (1999).

F. Welsh, *A History of Hong Kong* (London, 1997).

P. Woodruff, *The Men who ruled India* (London, 1963).

England to 1603

(See also Section 2; and northern England and southern Scotland below.)

A. O. Anderson (ed.), *Scottish Annals from English Chroniclers 500 to 1286* (London, 1908).

A. D. M. Barrell, *The Papacy, Scotland and Northern England, 1342–1378* (Cambridge, 1995).

G. W. S. Barrow, *The Anglo-Norman Era in Scottish History* (Oxford, 1980).

M. L. Bush, *The Government Policy of Protector Somerset* (London, 1975).

R. R. Davies, *Domination and Conquest: The Experience of Ireland, Scotland and Wales, 1100–1300* (Cambridge, 1990).

W. Ferguson, *Scotland's Relations with England: A Survey to 1707* (1977; repr. 1994).

R. Frame, *The Political Development of the British Isles, 1100–1400* (Oxford, 1994).

B. Galloway, *The Union of England and Scotland, 1603–1608* (1986).

M. Jones and M. Vale (eds.), *England and her Neighbours, 1066–1453* (Hambledon, 1989).

C. MacNamee, *The Wars of the Bruces: Scotland, England and Ireland, 1306–1328* (East Linton, 1997).

R. A. Mason (ed.), *Scotland and England, 1286–1815* (1987).

M. H. Merriman, 'The Assured Scots: Scottish Collaborators with England during the Rough Wooing', *SHR* 47 (1968).

—— *The Rough Wooings: Mary Queen of Scots, 1542–1551* (East Linton, 2000).

M. Moore, *Lands of the Scottish Kings in England* (London, 1915).

R. Nicholson, *Edward III and the Scots* (London, 1965).

M. C. Prestwich, *Edward I* (London, 1988).

C. Read, *Mr Secretary Cecil and Queen Elizabeth* (rev. edn, London, 1965).

—— *Mr Secretary Walsingham and the Policy of Queen Elizabeth*, 3 vols. (Oxford, 1925).

R. L. G. Ritchie, *The Normans in Scotland* (1954).

E. L. G. Stones (ed.), *Anglo-Scottish Relations, 1174–1328: Some Selected Documents* (2nd edn., Oxford, 1970).

K. J. Stringer, *Earl David of Huntingdon 1152–1219: A Study in Anglo-Scottish History* (1985).

F. Watson, *Under the Hammer: Edward I and Scotland, 1286–1307* (East Linton, 1998).

B. Webster, 'Anglo-Scottish Relations, 1296–1389: Some Recent Essays', *SHR* 74 (1995).

France

L. A. Barbé, *Margaret of Scotland and the Dauphin Louis* (London, 1917).

E. Bonner, 'The French Reactions to the Rough Wooings of Mary Queen of Scots', *Journal of the Sydney Society for Scottish History*, 6 (1998).

—— 'The *politique* of Henri II: De facto French rule in Scotland, 1550–1554', *Journal of the Sydney Society for Scottish History*, 7 (1999).

—— 'Scotland's "Auld Alliance" with France, 1295–1560', *History*, 84 (1999).

A. I. Cameron (ed.), *Foreign Correspondence with Marie de Lorraine Queen of Scotland*, 2 vols. (SHS, 1923–5).

B. Chevalier, 'Les Écossais dans les armées de Charles VIII jusqu à la bataille de Verneuil', *Jeanne d'Arc, une époque, un rayonnement, colloque d'histoire médiévale* (Paris 1982).

G. Donaldson, *The Auld Alliance: the Franco-Scottish Connection* (1985).

F. Downie, ' "La Voie quelle menace tenir": Arabella Stewart, Scotland and the European Marriage Market, 1444–1456', *SHR* 79 (2000).

W. Forbes-Leith (ed.), *The Scots Men-at-Arms and Life Guards in France, 1458–1830*, 2 vols. (1882).

J. Laidlaw (ed.), *The Auld Alliance: France and Scotland over 700 Years* (1999).

Y. Lequin (ed.), *La Mosaïque France: Histoire des étrangers et de l'immigration* (Paris, 1988).

M. Lynch (ed.), *Mary Stewart: Queen in Three Kingdoms* (Oxford, 1988).

S. G. E. Lythe, *The Economy of Scotland in its European Setting* (1960).

M. H. Merriman, *The Rough Wooings: Mary Queen of Scots 1542–1551* (East Linton, 2000).

F. Michel, *Les Écossais en France, les Français en Écosse*, 2 vols. (London, 1862).

Royal Scottish Museum, *French Connections: Scotland and the Arts of France* (1985).

G. G. Simpson (ed.), *The Scottish Soldier Abroad, 1247–1967* (1992).

J. A. B. Teulet (ed.), *Relations politiques de la France et de l'Espagne avec l'Écosse au XVIᵉ siècle*, 5 vols. (Paris, 1862).

S. Wood, *The Auld Alliance, Scotland and France: The Military Connection* (1989).

Germany, the Baltic, and Poland

(See also Scandinavia, below.)

A. J. G. Cummings, 'Scotland's Links with Europe, 1600–1800', in J. Wormald (ed.), *Scotland Revisited* (London, 1991).

J. Dilley, 'German Merchants in Scotland, 1297–1327', *SHR* 27 (1948).

M. Dilworth, *The Scots in Franconia* (1974).

D. Ditchburn, 'A Note on Scandinavian Trade with Scotland in the Later Middle Ages', in G. G. Simpson (ed.), *Scotland and Scandinavia, 800–1800* (1990).

T. A. Fischer, *The Scots in Germany* (1902).

—— *The Scots in Eastern and Western Prussia* (1903).

D. G. Kirby, *The Baltic World, 1772–1993: Europe's Northern Periphery in an Age of Change* (London, 1995).

S. G. E. Lythe, *The Economy of Scotland in its European Setting, 1550–1625* (1960).

—— 'Scottish trade with the Baltic, 1550–1650', in J. K. Eastham (ed.), *Essays in Commemoration of the Dundee School of Economics, 1932–55* (Coupar Angus, 1955).

M. K. McLeod, *Agents of Change: The Scots in Poland, 1800–1918* (East Linton, 1999).

P. Panayi, *German Immigrants in Britain during the 19th Century, 1815–1914* (Oxford, 1991).

M. Rodgers, 'The Lanarkshire Lithuanians', in B. Kay (ed.), *Odyssey: Voices from Scotland's Recent Past* (1980).

A. F. Steuart (ed.), *The Scots in Poland, 1576–1793* (1915).

A. M. Stewart, *Scots in the Baltic* (Aberdeen, 1977).

W. Tomaszewski (ed.), *In the Dark Days of 1941: Fifty Years of the Polish School of Medicine, 1941–1991* (1992).

—— (ed.), *The University of Edinburgh and Poland* (1968).

T. Ziarski-Kernberg, 'The Polish Community in Scotland since 1945', in P. Stachura (ed.), *Themes of Modern Polish History* (Glasgow, 1992).

Ireland

(See also Section 4: Military: Mercenaries and Soldiers Abroad; Section 9: Immigration, Irish.)

S. J. Connolly et al. (eds.), *Conflict, Identity and Economic Development: Ireland and Scotland, 1600–1939* (Preston, 1995).

L. M. Cullen and T. C. Smout (eds.), *Comparative Aspects of Scottish and Irish Economic and Social History, 1600–1900* (1977).

—— and —— (eds.), *Scottish and Irish Economic and Social History, 1600–1900* (1977).

R. R. Davies (ed.), *The British Isles, 1100–1500* (1988).

J. E. A. Dawson, 'Two Kingdoms or Three?', in R. A. Mason (ed.), *Scotland and England, 1286–1815* (1987).

T. M. Devine and D. Dickson (eds.), *Ireland and Scotland, 1600–1850: Parallels and Contrasts in Economic and Social Development* (1983).

—— and J. F. McMillan (eds.), *Celebrating Columba: Irish-Scottish Connections, 597–1997* (1997).

S. Duffy, 'The Bruce Brothers and the Celtic Alliance', *Cambridge Medieval Celtic Studies*, 21 (1991).

S. G. Ellis and S. Barber (eds.), *Conquest and Union: Fashioning a British State, 1485–1725* (London, 1995).

R. Frame, 'The Bruces in Ireland', *Irish Historical Studies*, 19 (1974).

C. Kidd, 'Gaelic Antiquity and National Identity in Enlightenment Ireland and Scotland', *EHR* 109 (1994).

J. F. Lydon, 'The Bruce Invasion of Ireland', in G. A. Hayes-McCoy (ed.), *Historical Studies*, I (London, 1963).

—— 'The Scottish Soldier in Medieval Ireland: The Bruce Invasion and the Gallowglass', in G. G. Simpson (ed.), *The Scottish Soldier Abroad, 1247–1967* (1992).

E. W. McFarland, *Ireland and Scotland in the Age of Revolution* (1994).

C. McNamee, *The Wars of the Bruces: Scotland, England and Ireland, 1306–1328* (East Linton, 1997).

M. Perceval Maxwell, *Scottish Migration to Ulster in the Reign of James I* (rev. edn, London, 1990).

R. Mitchison and P. Roebuck (eds.), *Economy and Society in Scotland and Ireland, 1500–1939* (1988).

G. Walker, *Intimate Strangers: Political and Cultural Interaction between Scotland and Ulster in Modern Times* (1995).

Latin America

J. Dodds, *Records of the Scottish Settlers in the River Plate and their Churches* (Buenos Aires, 1897).

A. Graham-Yooll, *The Forgotten Colony: A History of the English-Speaking Communities in Argentina* (London, 1981).

H. Herring, *A History of Latin America from the Beginning to the Present* (2nd edn., New York, 1967).

M. G. and E. T. Mulhall, *Handbook of the River Plate* (1885).

J. Prebble, *The Darien Disaster* (London, 1968).

J. P. Robertson and W. Parish, *Letters on Paraguay* (London, 1838).

—— and —— *Letters on South America* (London, 1843).

I. A. Stewart (ed.), *From Caledonia to the Pampas: Two Accounts by Early Scottish Emigrants to the Argentine* (East Linton, 1999).

D. Thomas, *Cochrane* (London, 1978).

E. Vaughan, *The Guayrians at Guelph in Upper Canada: Scottish Settlers for Canada from Venezuela: A Bureaucratic Problem in 1827* (Guelph, 1979).

J. Walker (ed.) *The South American Sketches of R. B. Cunninghame Graham* (Norman, Okla., 1978).

Low Countries

J. Davidson and A. Gray, *The Scottish Staple at Veere* (London, 1909).

R. Fawcett, 'Late Gothic Architecture in Scotland: Considerations on the Influence of the Low Countries', *PSAS* 112 (1982).

J. Ferguson (ed.), *Papers illustrating the History of The Scots Brigade in the service of the United Netherlands 1572–1782*, 3 vols. (SHS, 1899–1901).

R. Lyall, 'Scottish Students and Masters at the Universities of Cologne and Louvain in the 15th century', *Innes Review*, 36 (1985).

S. G. E. Lythe, *The Economy of Scotland in its European Setting, 1550–1625* (1960).

M. P. Rooseboom, *The Scottish Staple in the Netherlands* (The Hague, 1910).

G. G. Simpson (ed.), *Scotland and the Low Countries, 1124–1994* (East Linton, 1996).

A. Stevenson, 'Trade with the South, 1070–1513', in M. Lynch et al. (eds.), *The Scottish Medieval Town* (1988).

Mediterranean Lands in the Middle Ages

C. Burns, *Golden Rose and Blessed Sword: Papal Gifts to Scottish Monarchs* (Glasgow, 1970).

I. B. Cowan et al. (eds.), *The Knights of St John of Jerusalem in Scotland* (SHS, 1983).

D. Ditchburn, *Scotland and Europe: The Medieval Kingdom and its Contacts with Christendom, 1214–1560* (East Linton, 2001).

A. I. Dunlop, *Scots Abroad in the Fifteenth Century* (London, 1942).

A. Macquarrie, *Scotland and the Crusades, 1095–1560* (rev. edn., 1997).

D. E. R. Watt (ed.), *Biographical Dictionary of Scottish Graduates to A.D. 1410* (Oxford, 1977).

New Zealand

T. Brooking, *And Captain of their Souls: An Interpretative Essay on the Life and Times of Captain William Cargill* (Dunedin, 1984).

—— *Lands for the People? The Highland Clearances and the Colonisation of New Zealand: A Biography of John McKenzie* (Dunedin, 1996).

—— 'Out of Midlothian', in *The Tartan and the Gold* (Dunedin, 1989).

—— 'Tam McCanny and Kittie Clydeside', in R. Cage (ed.), *The Scots Abroad* (London, 1985).

—— and J. Coleman, ' "Piping in a Rough Equality": The Scottish Contribution to the Making of New Zealand Culture', in J. MacKenzie (ed.), *The Scots and Empire* (Manchester, 2000).

E. Olssen, *A History of Otago* (Dunedin, 1984).

G. L. Pearce, *The Scots of New Zealand* (Dundee, 1976).

Northern England and Southern Scotland (the Roman period)

D. J. Breeze, *Roman Scotland* (London, 1996).

W. S. Hanson, *Agricola and the Conquest of the North* (2nd edn., London, 1991).

W. S. Hanson and G. S. Maxwell, *Rome's North-west Frontier: The Antonine Wall* (2nd edn., 1986).

Russia

P. Dukes et al., *The Caledonian Phalanx: Scots in Russia* (1987).

D. Fedosov, *The Caledonian Connection: Scotland-Russia Ties: Middle Ages to the Early Twentieth Century: A Concise Biographical List* (Aberdeen, 1996).

Scandinavia

(See also Germany, the Baltic, and Poland, above; and Section 4: Military: Mercenaries and Soldiers Abroad.)

J. Berg and B. Lagercrantz, *Scots in Sweden* (Stockholm, 1962).

T. L. Christensen, 'Scoto-Danish Relations in the 16th century', *SHR* 48 (1969).

B. E. Crawford, *Scandinavian Scotland* (Leicester, 1987).

—— 'Foreign Relations: Scandinavia', in J. M. Brown (ed.), *Scottish Society in the Fifteenth Century* (London, 1977).

G. Dasent (trans.), *The Saga of Hacon and a Fragment of the Saga of Magnus with Appendices*, in *Icelandic Sagas*, vol. 2 (London, 1894).

D. Ditchburn, 'Trade with northern Europe, 1297–1540', in M. Lynch et al. (eds.), *The Scottish Medieval Town* (1988).

G. Donaldson, *A Northern Commonwealth* (1990).

J. Dow, 'Ruthven's Army in Sweden and Esthonia' in *Kungliga Vitterhets historia och antikvitetes akademien: Historiskt Arkiv* (Stockholm, 1965).

—— 'Scottish Trade with Sweden, 1512–1580', *SHR* 48 (1969).

—— 'Scottish Trade with Sweden, 1580–1622', *SHR* 48 (1969).

T. A. Fischer, *The Scots in Sweden* (1907).

K. Helle, 'Norwegian Consolidation and Expansion during the Reign of King Hakon Hakonsson', *Orkney Miscellany*, 5 (1973).

S. Murdoch and A. Grosjean, *Scotland, Scandinavia and Northern Europe 1580–1707* (Aberdeen, 1998; pub. at <www.abdn.ac.uk/history/datasets/ssne>).

T. Riis, *Should Auld Acquaintance Be Forgot . . . Scottish-Danish Relations c.1450–1707*, 2 vols. (Odense, 1988).

'Scotland and Scandinavia', *SHR* 47 (special issue, 1969).

G. G. Simpson (ed.), *Scotland and Scandinavia, 800–1800* (1990).

J. Yair, *An Account of the Scotch Trade in the Netherlands* (London, 1776).

USA

(See also Canada, above.)

D. Armitage, 'Making the Empire British: Scotland in the Atlantic World, 1542–1707', *Past and Present*, 155 (1977).

B. Aspinwall, *Portable Utopia: Glasgow and the United States 1820–1920* (Aberdeen, 1984).

B. Bailyn, *The Peopling of British North America* (London, 1987).

—— *Voyagers to the West: Emigration from Britain to America on the Eve of the Revolution* (London, 1987).

—— and P. D. Morgan (eds.), *Strangers within the Realm: Cultural Margins of the First British Empire* (Chapel Hill, NC, 1991).

W. R. Brock, *Scotus Americanus* (1982).

T. Bryan, *Twa Tribes: Scots among the Native Americans* (2000).

J. M. Bumsted, *The People's Clearance: Highland Emigration to British North America, 1770–1815* (1982).

D. Dobson, *Directory of Scottish Settlers in North America, 1625–1825* (Baltimore, 1984, 1999).

—— *Original Scots Colonists of Early America, 1612–1783* (Baltimore, 1989, 1998).

—— *Scottish Emigrants to Colonial America, 1607–1785* (Athens, Georgia, 1994).

M. Harper, *Emigration from North-East Scotland*, 2 vols. (Aberdeen, 1988).

C. H. Haws, *Scots in the Old Dominion, 1685–1800* (1980).

J. Hewitson, *Tam Blake & Co: The Story of the Scots in America* (1993).

B. Le Roy, *Lairds, Bards and Mariners: The Scot in Northwest America* (Seattle, 1978).

G. M. Logan, *Scottish Highlanders and the American Revolution* (Halifax, 1976).

D. Meyer, *The Highland Scots of North Carolina, 1732–1776* (Chapel Hill, NC, 1961).

R. B. Sher and J. R. Smitten (eds.), *Scotland and America in the Age of Enlightenment* (1990).

D. Whyte, *A Dictionary of Scottish Emigrants to the U.S.A.* (Baltimore, 1972).

15. Ethnographic

Since the founding in 1951 of the School of Scottish Studies at the University of Edinburgh, which also has its own archive, there has been a growing interest in folk song, customs, and belief.

M. Bennett, *Scottish Customs from the Cradle to the Grave* (1992).

J. L. Campbell, *A Collection of Highland Rites and Customs* (Cambridge, 1975).

A. Carmichael, *Carmina Gadelica*, 6 vols. (1900–71).

I. G. Grant, *Highland Folkways* (London, 1961).

A. Ross, *The Folklore of the Scottish Highlands* (London, 1976).

I. McGregor, *Getting Married in Scotland* (2000).

E. W. Marwick, *The Folklore of Orkney and Shetland* (London, 1975).

Tocher (School of Scottish Studies, Edinburgh, 1971–).

16. Historians, Historical Sources, and Heritage

Many of the sources of Scottish history were made available by the publishing clubs of the 19th century and their successors: the best guide to these are the directories of Matheson, Terry, and the Stevensons, indicated below. The formidable upsurge in writing about the history of Scotland within the past generation has also triggered a fresh concern with historiography. Interest in genealogy has burgeoned enormously, and many of the relevant sources in the National Archives of Scotland are now available on-line. The boundaries between history and quasi-history or heritage are a new concern of some commentators.

Historians

D. Allan, *Virtue, Learning and the Scottish Enlightenment: Ideas of Scholarship in Early Modern History* (1993).

M. Ash, *The Strange Death of Scottish History* (1980).

S. J. Brown (ed.), *William Robertson and the Expansion of Empire* (Cambridge, 1996).

I. Donnachie and C. Whatley (eds.), *The Manufacture of Scottish History* (1992).

C. Kidd, *Subverting Scotland's Past: Scottish Whig Historians and the Creation of an Anglo-British Identity, 1689–c.1830* (Cambridge, 1993).

Scottish Historical Review, 73 (special issue, Apr. 1994): 'Whither Scottish History?'

Scottish Historical Review, 76 (special issue, Apr. 1997): 'Writing Scotland's History'.

Historical Sources and Source Collections

A. O. Anderson (ed.), *Early Sources of Scottish History AD 500 to 1286*, 2 vols. (1922; new edn., 1990).

—— *Scottish Annals from English Chroniclers* (London, 1908).

R. H. Campbell and J. B. Dow (eds.), *Source Book of Scottish Economic and Social History* (Oxford, 1968).

A. A. Cooke et al. (eds.), *Modern Scottish History, 1707 to the Present, 5. Major Documents* (East Linton, 1998).

W. C. Dickinson, G. Donaldson, and I. A. Milne (eds.), *A Source Book of Scottish History*, 3 vols. (1952–8).

G. Donaldson (ed.), *Scottish Historical Documents* (1970).

—— *The Sources of Scottish History* (1976).

J. G. Fyfe (ed.), *Scottish Diaries and Memoirs*, 2 vols. (1928, 1942).

D. Reid (ed.), *The Party-Coloured Mind: Selected Prose relating to the Conflict between Church and State in Seventeenth-Century Scotland* (Edinburgh, 1982).

D. E. R. Watt, *A History Book for Scots: Selections from Scotichronicon by Walter Bower* (1998).

B. Webster, *The Sources of History: Scotland from the Eleventh Century to 1603* (London, 1975).

Historical Sources: Travellers' Accounts

P. Hume Brown (ed.), *Early Travellers in Scotland* (1891).

J. G. Dunbar (ed.), *Sir William Burrell's Northern Tour, 1758* (East Linton, 1997).

Samuel Johnson, *A Journey to the Western Islands of Scotland* (London, 1984).

D. W. Kemp (ed.), *Tours in Scotland . . . by Richard Pococke, Bishop of Meath* (SHS, 1887).

Historical Sources: Genealogical

M. Cox, *Exploring Scottish History: A Directory of Resource Centres for Scottish Local and National History in Scotland* (2nd edn., Hamilton, 1999).

G. Holton and J. Winch, *My Ain Folk: an Easy Guide to Scottish Family History* (East Linton, 1997).

D. Moody, *Scottish Family History* (London, 1988).

C. Sinclair, *Tracing your Scottish Ancestors: A Guide to Ancestry Research in the Scottish Record Office* (rev. edn., 1997).

Maps and Map-Making

J. N. Moore, *The Historical Cartography of Scotland* (Aberdeen, 1991).

Royal Scottish Geographical Society, *The Early Maps of Scotland to 1850*, 2 vols. (3rd edn., 1973).

J. C. Stone, *Illustrated Maps of Scotland from Blaeu's Atlas Novus of the 17th Century* (London, 1991).

—— *The Pont Manuscript Maps of Scotland* (Tring, 1989).

Oral History and Tradition

A. Bruford and D. A. MacDonald, *Scottish Traditional Tales* (1994).

J. L. Campbell, *Hebridean Folksongs*, 3 vols. (Oxford, 1969–81).

R. M. Dorson, *The British Folklorists: A History* (London, 1968).

Monuments

R. Gillis (ed.), *Commemorations: The Politics of National Identity* (Princeton, 1994).

N. Johnson, 'Cast in Stone: Monuments, Geography and Nationalism', *Environment and Planning D: Society and Space*, 13 (1995).

C. W. J. Withers, 'Place, Memory, Monument: Memorializing the Past in Contemporary Highland Scotland', *Ecumene*, 3 (1996).

Heritage

R. Hewison, *The Heritage Industry: Britain in a Climate of Decline* (London, 1987).

D. McCrone et al. (eds.), *Scotland the Brand: The Making of Scottish Heritage* (1995).

G. Rosie, 'Museumry and the Heritage Industry', in I. Donnachie and C. Whatley (eds.), *The Manufacture of Scottish History* (1992).

Heritage Events and Spectacle

E. Donaldson, *The Scottish Highland Games in America* (Gretna, 1986).

G. Jarvie, *Highland Games: The Making of the Myth* (1991).

F. Thompson, *The National Mod* (Stornoway, 1979).

—— *History of An Comann Gaidhealach* (Stornoway, 1992).

Historical Societies and Clubs

M. Ash, *The Strange Death of Scottish History* (1980).

J. A. Mackay, *The Burns Federation 1885–1985* (Kilmarnock, 1985).

C. Matheson, *A Catalogue of the Publications of Scottish Historical and Kindred Clubs and Societies, 1908–1927* (Glasgow, 1928).

R. W. Munro, *Highland Clans and Tartans* (London, 1977).

D. and W. B. Stevenson (eds.), *Scottish Texts and Calendars: an Analytical Guide to Serial Publications* (SHS, 1987).

C. S. Terry, *A Catalogue of the Publications of Scottish Historical and Kindred Clubs and Societies, 1780–1908* (Glasgow, 1910).

Coinage

J. D. Bateson, *Coinage in Scotland* (London, 1997).

R. W. Cochran-Patrick, *Records of the Coinage of Scotland*, 2 vols. (1876).

N. Holmes, *Scottish Coins: A History of Small Change in Scotland* (1998).

D. M. Metcalf (ed.), *Coinage in Medieval Scotland* (Oxford, 1977).

W. W. Scott, 'Sterling and the Usual Money of Scotland', *SESH* 5 (1985).

—— 'The Use of Money in Scotland, 1124–1230', *SHR* 58 (1979).

I. H. Stewart, *The Scottish Coinage* (rev. edn., London, 1967).

Banknotes

S. G. Checkland, *Scottish Banking: A History 1695–1973* (Glasgow, 1975).

J. Douglas, *Scottish Banknotes* (London, 1975).

—— R. W. Pringle et al., *Twentieth Century Scottish Banknotes*, vols. 1–3 (Carlisle, 1984–97).

Guide to Further Reading

Historic Weights and Measures

W. Zupko, 'The Weights and Measures of Scotland before the Union', *SHR* 56 (1977).

17. Media and Communications

Scotland has had its own press, both national and local, since the 1850s. Each, it has been argued, helped preserve national or regional identity, even if most are now owned by conglomerates furth of Scotland. How Scottish the modern broadcasting media are—or are permitted to be—is an issue of current debate. (See also Section 13: Modern Times.)

G. Burnett, *Scotland on Air* (1938).

W. Donaldson, *The Language of the People: Scots Prose from the Victorian Revival* (Aberdeen, 1989).

—— *Popular Literature in Victorian Scotland* (Aberdeen, 1986).

D. Hutchison (ed.), *Headlines: The Media in Scotland* (1978).

C. MacArthur (ed.), *Scotch Reels: Scotland in Cinema and Television* (London, 1982).

W. H. McDowell, *The History of BBC Broadcasting in Scotland, 1923–1983* (1992).

M. Smith, *Paper Lions* (1994).

Index

Index

Index

Index

Index

Index

Index

Index

Index

Index

Index

Index

Index

Index